Ba Carmichael

W9-AYF-749

Leisure Studies

Prospects for the
Twenty-First Century

Leisure Studies

Prospects for the Twenty-First Century

edited by

Edgar L. Jackson and Thomas L. Burton

Venture Publishing, Inc.
State College, Pennsylvania

Copyright © 1999
Venture Publishing, Inc.
1999 Cato Avenue
State College, PA 16801
(814) 234-4561; Fax (814) 234-1651

No part of the material protected by this copyright notice may be reproduced or utilized in any form or by any means, electronic or mechanical, including photocopying, recording, or by any information storage and retrieval system, without written permission from the copyright owner.

Trademarks: All brand names and product names used in this book are trademarks, registered trademarks, or trade names of their respective holders.

Production Manager: Richard Yocum
Design, Layout, and Manuscript Editing: Diane K. Bierly
Additional Editing: Michele L. Barbin and Richard Yocum
Cover Design and Illustration: @ 1999 Sikorski Design

Library of Congress Catalogue Card Number 98-89987
ISBN 1-892132-03-6

For Patrick, Nicholas, and Katherine Jackson
and
Julian Dale-Burton

Contents

SECTION 5

Debating Leisure

Foreword

The year 2000 marks the end of a 200-year cycle of human history which has brought about unimaginable change. The ability of humans to communicate, travel, and live in relative freedom from hunger has increased dramatically. Leaps in understanding of our genetic makeup, the exponential increases in knowledge of information systems, the decline of the nation-state as an overarching governing structure, and a huge increase in the population of emerging nations have produced a world which is vastly more difficult to make sense of even as we possess more knowledge to do so.

In such a world, the importance of understanding what people want to do and will do voluntarily and for pleasure is increasingly important. More people have choice about what to do in the parts and aspects of their lives which aren't ruled by obligation. The portion of life which is devoted to paid work, housework, and childcare is declining. Entry into the labor force generally begins later and ends earlier in relation to life expectancy. Levels of formal education are rising rapidly. All of these trends make recreation and leisure a more central aspect of life. They also make the roles of organizations which provide a myriad of recreation, park, leisure, tourism, therapeutic recreation, cultural, social, and athletic services more central.

The importance of understanding some aspect of life, however, does not automatically mean that intellectual progress will or can be made. Recreation and leisure are reinvented by succeeding cultures and profoundly changed by technology—take television, for example. Recreation and leisure are also used to promote changes in humans—to improve health, stimulate local economies, promote beliefs, and change habits. All of this makes the study of recreation and leisure both difficult and inherently interdisciplinary.

In this edited volume, Edgar L. (Ed) Jackson and Thomas L. (Tim) Burton have attempted no less than an assessment of what is known about recreation and leisure at the beginning of the twenty-first century. In doing this, they have not only drawn on the talents of top scholars in various areas of study but have done so from a carefully conceived vision of what was needed.

Jackson and Burton have also done the reader the great favor of being both aggressive and meticulous editors, a rarity among such edited volumes.

This book, which was many years in the making, represents the only comprehensive statement of what is known about recreation and leisure as the twenty-first century begins, with its heightened potential to create a world in which such knowledge is critical to human well-being.

Geoffrey Godbey
Pennsylvania State University

Preface

Although this book is essentially a new one—28 entirely fresh chapters that have never appeared before, while the remaining ones incorporate substantial revisions—it originates from and builds upon our previous edited collection, *Understanding Leisure and Recreation: Mapping the Past, Charting the Future*. As such, although it was only in the fall of 1994 that we made the commitment to embark on the current compilation, this book has effectively a 15-year history, dating back to when the idea for *Understanding Leisure and Recreation* originated in 1984.

Our previous book came out early in 1990 and was widely adopted as a text and reader across North America and in other parts of the world. Comprising 24 chapters contributed by 24 authors, its intention was to provide a comprehensive review of contemporary leisure studies, from a largely North American perspective. Our goal was to help consolidate and critically assess what leisure scholars had learned to that point, and to set a course for what could and should be accomplished—in substance, in theory, and in methodology—in the ensuing decade.

Much has changed in the 10 years since *Understanding Leisure and Recreation* was published. Certain substantive topics appear to have declined in importance, at least in terms of the attention given to them by researchers and the space they consume in the leading journals. Other topics—ethnicity and leisure, and serious leisure, to name but two—have emerged. Still others have been recast and reconceptualized: *barriers* have become *constraints,* and the then-fledging area of *benefits* has grown into a full-blown theoretical, empirical, and applied body of work under the rubric of the *benefits approach to leisure.* New perspectives have emerged and profoundly shaped the field, not the least being increasing attention to feminism and gender-based frameworks for research and debate. Methodologies have evolved, too, and it is now the norm rather than the exception for the results of qualitative research to appear in the journals and on conference programs.

Little of this would likely have happened in the absence of important changes within the community of scholars who have created the body of knowledge about leisure and recreation and who continue to lead the way in its growth and development. While some prominent researchers have left the field, either by choice or through retirement, many of the most productive senior scholars whose names were familiar to everyone within the community a decade ago have lost none of their spark and enthusiasm, and, indeed, are often at the forefront when it comes to breaking new ground. Equally and perhaps more importantly in the long run, the field continues to be rejuvenated with the emergence of new scholars, whose energy, enthusiasm, and intellectual capacities enrich the field of leisure studies with new ideas. Many of them appear as contributors in this book.

As in many other academic fields and spheres of public life, the approach of the new millennium has spurred both a retrospective glance at what has been achieved in leisure studies in the twentieth century, and in the last couple of decades in particular, as well as a look forward to what might lie ahead: hence this book. We sincerely hope that its appearance will accomplish the goals we had in mind when devising it, and that its contents—both in terms of the individual chapters and the book as a whole—will stimulate thinking among students and established scholars alike.

Like its predecessor, the book is the product of a collective effort, in which the most important participants, and those whom we must thank first, are the 40 authors, who willingly sacrificed their time to write their chapters with the sole reward of knowing that they were unselfishly contributing to this effort to enhance the growth of the leisure studies field. We can-not thank them enough, both for agreeing to write the chapters in the first place, as well as for responding rapidly and with good humor to our critical reviews of early drafts.

At Venture Publishing, Inc., we should like to thank our editors, Richard Yocum and Diane Bierly.

At the University of Alberta, we received support from the Department of Earth and Atmospheric Sciences and the Faculty of Physical Education and Recreation. The figures were drawn by Michael Fisher, Cartographic Technician in the Department of Earth and Atmospheric Sciences.

Finally, we should like to acknowledge the continual support of our wives, Linda Jackson and Lynne Dale, and our children.

We can only conclude by adapting the words we wrote for the Preface of our previous book, since these remarks are even more pertinent today than when we wrote them a decade ago: It has been a privilege to edit this book. We have enjoyed a unique opportunity to be the first to read the most up-to-date thinking of many of the leading authorities in leisure studies around the world, and to gain a sense of what has been achieved, where the field is, and where it should be going. Moreover, we have learned a great deal from each other while cooperating in the editing of the book. While retaining our own disciplinary perspectives (geography and economics/planning), we have constantly endeavored to view leisure studies as a broadly based and vigorous field that will only achieve success if members of the various disciplines cooperate in an open, critically constructive way, characterized by mutual respect. In large part, this is the essential message in what follows.

Edgar L. Jackson and Thomas L. Burton
University of Alberta

Reviewing Leisure Studies:
An Organizing Framework

Thomas L. Burton and Edgar L. Jackson
University of Alberta

It may be argued that the modern era in leisure studies began exactly 100 years ago, with the publication of Thorstein Veblen's volume, *The Theory of the Leisure Class* (Veblen, 1899). In this work, Veblen departed from the longstanding Western tradition, dating back to Classical Greek writers, which emphasized the ideal moral, philosophical, and intellectual state of leisure, its essence as the defining characteristic of the good life, a condition eagerly to be sought. Instead, Veblen subjected the topic to an empirical analysis which stressed the development of theoretical statements about the characteristics and forms of leisure prevalent among the elite industrialists of the capitalist state. While Veblen's methods would be seen by the standards of today's social scientists as flawed, and his observations and data as severely limited, his approach was scientific in kind, based on a process of postulation, observation, and formulation. For leisure studies, Veblen's fundamental contribution was the notion that leisure, like other aspects of individual and social life, could (and should) be subjected to theoretical and empirical analysis and not simply venerated as the ultimate goal of human activity.

For many years Veblen's study stood virtually alone, while the previous tradition continued. Works by Josef Pieper (1952) and Sebastian de Grazia (1964) are only two, albeit significant, writings that, well into the twentieth century, reflected the dominant notion that leisure is *sacred,* in the sense that it constitutes a moral and philosophical condition rather than a topic for scientific inquiry. As the twentieth century progressed, however, the theoretical and empirical examination of leisure and its place in the lives of individuals and social groups gained momentum. A landmark study before the Second World War was Lundberg, Komarovsky, and McInerny's (1934) *Leisure: A Suburban Study,* which examined leisure as an aspect of the social organization of the community. But perhaps the major milestone in this development was the work of the U.S. Outdoor Recreation Resources Review Commission (ORRRC) between 1958 and 1962 (ORRRC, 1962), with its emphasis on explaining recreation behavior by reference to sociodemographic data of numerous kinds. Soon after this monumental 28-volume work was published, leisure studies emerged as a distinct field of study in the scholarly community. The *Journal of Leisure Research* was launched in 1969, followed by *Society and Leisure* (originally in 1969, revived in 1978), *Leisure Sciences* (1977), and *Leisure Studies* (1982). All are dedicated to the dissemination of research ideas and findings about leisure.

Two decades after the appearance of the first edition of the *Journal of Leisure Research,* we published an edited volume, *Understanding Leisure and Recreation: Mapping the Past, Charting the Future,* which sought "to gain a sense of what has been achieved, where the field is, and where it should be going" (Jackson and Burton, 1989, p. xiv). Now, a decade later and on the centennial of the publication of Veblen's classic study, this new volume is offered. Although we have included a few key chapters from our previous book—and these have been extensively updated—for the most part, the current text offers new perspectives on preexisting and emerging themes in leisure studies. Also, while several contributors to the previous volume have written entirely new chapters for this one—thus indicating their own evolving research interests and fresh ideas—many of the contributors have appeared on the scene only in the last decade and a half. Their fresh voices help to ensure that what appears in the next several hundred pages is as up-to-date and as innovative as possible.

Any organization of a text with more than 30 chapters is necessarily judgmental. Topics do not fall conveniently into mutually exclusive sections. Although the chapters here fit well within the sections to which they have been allocated, some could have been located in different sections and many have relevance across several sections. The overall organization of a text such as this is a matter of choice. Many chapters touch on ideas that are dealt with elsewhere in the volume, perhaps in a more central way. The reader is asked to bear this in mind throughout the text.

The first section, "Understanding Leisure," addresses concepts and foundations, the contexts for examining issues. It suggests ways in which to think about leisure and leisure studies. "Exploring Leisure" is concerned with investigations bearing upon concepts—with how to do leisure studies, what has been done, and how leisure scholars have been looking at things in the field. "Experiencing Leisure" focuses upon analyses of leisure experiences from several perspectives, including particular social groups as well as alternative theoretical frameworks. The interest is in how we, as leisure scholars, can understand the leisure experience, given the foundations laid down in the pre-

ceding sections. "Delivering Leisure" then moves on to examine aspects of the management, operations, and delivery systems that make the experience of leisure possible—and, indeed, rewarding—for many people in society. The emphasis is upon approaches to the delivery of leisure opportunities that are innovative, in the sense that they are consistent with, grow out of, and reflect the types of thinking expressed in the earlier sections. Finally, in "Debating Leisure," this book comes full circle; here, the contributors offer reflections, critical perspectives, and evolving ideas about leisure and related social issues.

Understanding Leisure

As noted previously, the chapters in the first section of the book address concepts and foundations in leisure studies. It is our belief that, after 30 years of academic study in its own right, it is no longer necessary to begin a book such as this by attempting to establish the legitimacy of the field of leisure studies. If what Kelly some years ago called "the snickers and smirks" that emerge when one admits to studying leisure are still to be found, this, we suggest, is a problem for those who engage in such behavior. It is emphatically not something that should greatly occupy leisure scholars! Nevertheless, we have chosen to open this section with a chapter by Cooper which does, in fact, set out to justify the study of leisure. We have done so because we believe his arguments in our previous volume were so well-made that they deserve repeating, albeit with modifications.

Following Cooper's excellent rationale for the scholarly study of leisure, Sylvester takes the reader on a journey through Western notions of work and leisure, noting the sterility of much of modern work and drawing attention to the importance of the non-material needs of people in modern society. He concludes that there is insufficient meaningful work in today's economy and society. Both Iso-Ahola and Kelly then pick up the issue of meaning, providing psychological and sociological perspectives. Both refer to leisure's relationship to work and raise ideas about leisure and the quality of life. The former underscores the importance of self-determination in leisure, while the latter traces the evolution of a dialectical sequence in the sociology of leisure which has emphasized successively work and time, family and community, and aging and the life course.

Stebbins then challenges the dominant idea that central life interest and meaning come only from work. While acknowledging the importance of the latter for many people (if not for everyone), he offers an alternative, in the notion of serious leisure, which appears to be central for at least some members of society, and demonstrates its connection to quality of life and self-identity. Rojek follows by taking leisure scholars to task for their indifference to, and neglect of, investigations of deviant leisure. He notes that leisure has been viewed rather uncritically in the past—sometimes as a panacea for social ills, almost always as an exclusively benevolent phenomenon. He demonstrates that leisure has both positive and negative connotations, a theme which is echoed later in the text by both Shaw, and Jackson and Scott, in their observations that leisure is both constraining and constrained. Rojek concludes, first, that the principal context in which deviance emerges in our society is through leisure and, second, that deviant leisure plays a seminal role in social change.

Though we may argue that the study of leisure does not require justification, the same cannot be said for the study of tourism. It seems that those who study tourism still find themselves having to justify what they do. For this reason, and because of its emphasis upon concepts, we have included Butler's chapter on tourism in this section. Butler shows how previous work on tourism has shifted from an excessive emphasis on tourism as a panacea to focus upon the many problems and issues associated with tourism development.

In conclusion, while it is by no means the only theme, the work-leisure relationship pervades this section of the book, but is addressed in innovative and nontraditional ways that leave behind the tired *compensation-spillover* models. Thinking in our field has moved far beyond the explanations of 20 and 30 years ago! Most of the ideas in this section, while outgrowths of previous thinking, simply were not around or were not seen quite as clearly even a decade ago.

Exploring Leisure

The chapters in "Exploring Leisure" address studies that bear upon the concepts and foundations discussed in the previous section. The principal concern is with how leisure scholars conduct their investigations in the context of these concepts and foundations. Samdahl sets the scene by examining the beliefs that have framed much of leisure research: how leisure scholars ask questions dictates how they carry out research which, in turn, profoundly influences the conclusions at which they arrive. She notes, in particular, the tenacious reliance of leisure scholars on positivist approaches to research, notwithstanding growing criticism which holds that the more intriguing aspects of leisure are not amenable to, and may even be obscured by, the tools of positivist science. While this condition is endemic to the field, it is not a problem that lends

itself to easy solution. This is partly because those who have criticized leisure's overly narrow methodological approaches are being heard only by those who are already converted! In the end, solutions will lie in the responses of individual leisure scholars, who must question their underlying ontological and epistemological beliefs as they go about their work.

Kelly then addresses the significance of life course and lifestyle to leisure, while demonstrating that how we do things should flow out of what we want to know rather than the other way around. He proposes that it is time to step back from what has been going on in leisure research, with a view to reconsidering the principal questions: What are the behaviors that leisure scholars call leisure and recreation, and how can they be explained? He shows, too, that understanding will not come from statistics and measurement alone:

> Finality does not wait for that super measure or supreme statistical package, the single model that will answer all questions in some globalizing metaphor. Rather, real contributions to understanding begin with the complex actions that are labeled leisure and recreation.

Mannell and Reid return the discussion to the dominant theme of the previous section, the work-leisure relationship. Their perspective fits nicely into the present section, however, because the topic is examined by reference to empirical studies of relationships between work and leisure in the lives of individuals, and offers insights into the various ways in which leisure scholars have gone about studying this central relationship. Echoing Sylvester, Mannell and Reid suggest that a great deal of modern work is unrewarding. Then, in common with Stebbins, they conclude that satisfactions from other areas of life, particularly leisure, will become increasingly important in the human quest for self-worth and identity.

Henderson and Bialeschki revisit questions about how leisure scholars conduct research into leisure. Specifically, they show how feminist research and perspectives have transformed the ways in which scholars have examined leisure. However, the contributions of the chapter go far beyond feminism and women's leisure, to show how powerful ideas can radically alter scholars' views of what they do and what it is worthwhile to do. As the authors note, there are massive implications in feminist work for other marginalized social groups. However, they add a powerful precautionary note: that, to do so, leisure studies must avoid ghettoizing feminist research and research on women's leisure.

Finally, while the chapters by Smale and Swinnerton are not as obviously linked to particular concepts and foundations discussed in the previous section, they demonstrate clearly that theoretical and conceptual frameworks such as spatial analysis and conservation can enhance the understanding of leisure behavior and generate new insights. They show, too, that there are important applied implications that emerge from leisure studies' frameworks and models.

This entire section offers the opportunity to develop links between study and action by way of policy. The chapters do not emphasize conceptualization as such, but, rather, the exploration of what has been learned (and has not been learned) about relationships between concepts and theories and their attendant social issues, and how we have learned these things. Put simply, these chapters give rise to the thought that if concepts are to have meaning, they must be related to action, a notion that emerges in greater measure in later sections of the book.

Experiencing Leisure

There is a significant volume of leisure research which has addressed how people experience leisure, much of it grounded in the foundations, concepts, and paradigms explored in the two previous sections. This research is not merely descriptive, but shows that leisure studies in general, and the concepts and approaches dealt with in the previous sections in particular, permit leisure scholars to say something of significance about the leisure experience. The chapters in "Experiencing Leisure" are ones in which the authors attempt to respond to the call for linked research and action that emerges from the chapters in section 2. While still theoretical in their attempts to build understanding about each of the diverse areas covered, they focus specifically on issues and topics that have vast policy implications: aging, gender, ethnicity and race, constraints, crowding, and conflict. They also demonstrate that policy will fail—or at best will be irrelevant—without studies that rest upon sound theoretical and empirical bases. Part of this policy orientation is involved not only with barriers to leisure goals, but with ways in which leisure experiences can become part of the quality of life in our society and communities.

The section opens with a chapter by Mannell which examines dominant approaches to explaining the nature of the leisure experience for the individual. The chapter is especially important in identifying and synthesizing the strands that are central to the nature of experience. Mannell recognizes that there is a great deal of interest on the part of policymakers and ser-

vice providers in how leisure experiences are linked to such things as mental health, work, and quality of life. He concludes that attempts to assess the impact of leisure on quality of life depend greatly on the ability to observe and measure the actual amount and quality of leisure experienced rather than the extent of engagement in externally defined leisure activities. This is followed by a series of chapters which address specific, policy-significant issues.

Three of the chapters deal with important socio-demographic groups and processes within North American society that impinge upon the ways in which leisure is experienced. The first of these has to do with aging and the life course. Picking up where Kelly left off in the previous section, Freysinger reminds readers that, while the concept of aging has its roots in biological processes, society has imbued these processes with stereotypical ideas about the ways in which aging affects behavior, lifestyle, ability, and interest. She suggests that leisure studies and programs can serve to reproduce these stereotypical and, often, oppressive notions of age, or they can act to liberate people from the barriers and constraints that such notions imply. In addressing gender issues, Shaw concludes that one of the greatest challenges for leisure scholars is to develop an understanding of cultural and individual diversity, without losing sight of the significance of gender as an organizing principle for study. Most significantly, however, research must address more thoroughly the nature and characteristics of the social construction of gender and its implications for the experience of leisure. Finally, Gramann and Allison, also building on ideas advanced by Kelly in section 2, argue that leisure is often an important social space in which traditional cultural values are tolerated by mainstream society in North America and are expressed and maintained within ethnic subcultures. In short, leisure likely plays a critical role in the preservation of ethnic group identity within a North American society that strongly promotes Anglo-conformity in the workplace, at school, and in other important arenas of life.

The remaining three chapters address issues that do not relate directly to particular social groups, yet have enormous consequences both for society as a whole and for many different groups within it. Jackson and Scott take the reader on a tour of the immense (and immensely complicated) subject of leisure constraints. This is an area of study which began in the 1970s under the rubric of *barriers to recreation participation,* but which had developed by the 1990s into the theme of *constraints to leisure.* As the authors note, this represents much more than a semantic change, reflecting a fundamental shift in focus and conceptualization. The central point, perhaps, is recognition by those working in this area that leisure is both constrained *and* constraining, meaning that while leisure experiences are almost invariably limited by constraints such as a lack of facilities, resources, and partners, they themselves also limit choice. It is this which makes the study of leisure constraints such a complex, yet challenging field. Manning then addresses another important policy topic, the issue of crowding in outdoor recreation. Drawing upon some 40 years of research into the concept of carrying capacity, Manning notes that as the use of parks and related areas has grown over the past half-century or so, perceived crowding and conflict among visitors has also risen. Crowding, whether perceived or measured by some "objective" indicator, seriously affects—and constrains—experience. The significant advance in leisure scholars' understanding of this topic lies in the development and application of normative theory, which has enabled scholars to better understand when and why increasing levels of visitor use cross a threshold into perceived crowding. Finally, Ewert, Dieser, and Voight focus their attention on the relationship between conflict and the recreational experience. While, historically, recreational conflict has been defined as difficulties experienced by different types of users of the same resources (e.g., snowmobilers versus cross-country skiers), its conceptualization has expanded to include cultural and individual dimensions. Traditional research which focused upon activities and their settings has now been joined by studies that seek to measure conflict and to understand associations between different kinds of activities. New models and approaches have been proposed which recognize that people who visit recreation places do so with differing values that lead to differing anticipated experiences.

Delivering Leisure

A great deal of leisure experience is made possible because somebody offers a service that enables participation in an activity. Even watching television and surfing the Internet are possible only because networks, televisions stations, and Internet service providers are available to the potential participant. A recurring theme in leisure studies, then, has been the management of opportunities for people to experience leisure and fulfill goals, dreams, and desires. Facilities, programs, and services are the intermediate goals to opportunities, which lead to the ultimate goal of experience and quality of life—which is precisely the issue that Driver and Bruns take up in the first chapter of "Delivering Leisure." The argument that people seek quality opportunities and experiences rather than activities underpins the benefits approach to leisure. It

is important to note also that, as we move into this section of the book, the policy and applied aspects become more dominant. This is essentially a matter of emphasis, since all that is reported here rests upon a significant base of conceptual development and empirical research and study.

The first two chapters provide a broad base for considering the general subject of delivering public leisure. Driver and Bruns offer the benefits approach as the principal foundation for justifying public leisure services. Though avowedly applied, this approach builds on 20 years of theoretical and conceptual study of benefits, experiences, preferences, motivations, and satisfactions. Driver and Bruns contend that an agency which employs a benefits-based management approach must focus its efforts on the outcomes and impacts of its actions and activities, while articulating to the public and its constituencies how the leisure services that it provides add value to the lives of individuals, communities, and society at large. Burton and Glover look beyond the recent and current turmoil surrounding the privatization of government leisure services to consider historical roles played by governments in ensuring opportunities for quality leisure experiences for residents of urban communities in Canada (and, by extension, the United States). This chapter, too, is based on years of theoretical and empirical research addressing the rationale for, alternative approaches to, and varying methods of, government involvement in the provision of leisure services to the public. The central message is that, while nothing is *entirely* new in the ways in which governments have gone about delivering public leisure services, a great deal is *different* because circumstances and conditions continually change. Thus, there may be cycles in time whereby some approaches enjoy greater popularity than others. Currently, there appears to be a strong preference for government to employ the enabling authority of the state as a means of ensuring that public leisure services are provided by not-for-profit and commercial organizations rather than directly by government agencies themselves.

The remaining five chapters address particular aspects of leisure service delivery that are connected with the ideas expressed in the two preceding contributions. Veal's chapter reflects the long history of research into forecasting and forecasting methods, from simple extrapolation of the numbers of visitors to national parks to complex models that attempt to simulate relationships between a multitude of variables that appear to influence the choice of leisure activity, and from simple number-crunching exercises to sophisticated blends of quantitative and qualitative approaches. The principal message in the chapter is that approaches to forecasting have changed with the changing environments of social development, policy-making, and planning in North America over the past 40 years, and that this change will (and must) continue.

Slack takes up Burton and Glover's theme of evolving governmental involvement in leisure service provision, by considering its implications for the structure and management of leisure organizations in the public, not-for-profit, and private sectors. He cites, in particular, the rise of professionalism in the organizational structure of not-for-profit associations, increased links between the public and private sectors, and the growth of strategic alliances, both within the private sector and across sectors. Slack concludes that one of the most significant effects of these changes is that the lines of demarcation among the three sectors are no longer as clear as they once were. Public sector organizations responsible for delivering public leisure services have forged stronger links with the corporate sector and are relying increasingly on market mechanisms for the provision of services. This notion leads directly to McCarville's consideration of the growing place of marketing in the public sector. He argues that, when viewed as the strategic application of resources to serve clients, marketing processes are perfectly appropriate to all sectors, and not simply to the private sector in which they originated and currently flourish. Marketing consists of a coherent and coordinated effort at influencing behavior and facilitating participation in leisure. McCarville's work builds on Mannell's earlier discussion of the nature of experience, as well as drawing from an immense amount of research on the concepts of plurality and market segmentation. Stankey and his colleagues are also concerned about organizational and institutional challenges for public leisure service delivery—in this case, in the context of the management of natural resources for recreation. They argue that management frameworks such as the Recreation Opportunity Spectrum (ROS) and the Limits of Acceptable Change (LAC) process must be joined with social learning models to enable the development of approaches in which science informs discussion rather than dictates it.

Finally, Dattilo and Williams consider how management and delivery systems have been (and are) changing in response to the idea of inclusion, the notion that leisure services delivery systems should, wherever possible and reasonable, be adapted to include the provision of opportunities for persons with disabilities. This is not simply a matter of furnishing ramps and handrails, but requires fundamental changes in attitudes, sensitivity, and education among managers and those who deliver services. As with each

of the other applied chapters, much of what Dattilo and Williams discuss and advocate rests upon the large volume of theoretical and empirical research discussed earlier—in this case, the work on leisure constraints reviewed by Jackson and Scott.

Debating Leisure

The purpose of this volume is to take stock of accomplishments, identify omissions, and chart directions for leisure study and research. It is emphatically *not* to codify an orthodoxy of leisure scholarship. Much of what has been learned over the past several decades and is reported in the previous sections of the book is the subject of rigorous debate and argument. It is fitting, therefore, to conclude with a section titled "Debating Leisure." The intent here is to offer an open-ended section which will permit reflection and critical thinking about what has been done, what is being done, and what might be done as the next millennium begins. The contributions by Cooper, and Dustin and Goodale, offer ideas about the impacts on leisure of particular societal changes and their implications for leisure research and study. Those by Hemingway and Coalter address changes within the social sciences—in models and methods of analysis and ways of thinking—and the manner in which these have been adopted, or resisted, by scholars within leisure studies. These chapters are all consistent with the model of the evolution of leisure studies that we presented in our earlier volume (Jackson and Burton, 1989, pp. 9–10), where we argued that three sets of factors affect change in leisure studies:

1. the "real world," by way of social trends and changes, and changes specifically within the field of leisure and recreation;
2. developments in the social sciences; and
3. changes in concepts, paradigms, and methodology in leisure studies itself.

As is customary with debates, we do not necessarily agree with all that is said in these chapters. We do agree, however, that an opportunity should be provided for these things to be said. The subjects debated are sufficiently serious to warrant an audience, as well as continued debate beyond the confines of this book—especially in North America where, unlike Western Europe and contrary to what many of the authors in this book say, we tend to be less reflective and critical than we should be about what we do and how we do it.

We have resisted the temptation to offer a final chapter which would somehow serve to bring closure to all that has been presented in the book, because the last thing that we wish to do is to give the impression that everything is cut-and-dried. There is considerable debate in leisure studies and, in their different ways, the authors in this final section capture some of the themes that have been part of this debate, themes that should excite the interest of leisure scholars for some years to come. However, while recognizing that there can be no closure on looking forward, we have been persuaded that there is much to be gained by taking an overall look at where leisure scholars have come from in the field. Thus, we have included a Postscript in which Driver essays an overarching perspective on the evolution of leisure studies during the final 40 years of the twentieth century. This is an unashamedly upbeat view which takes pride in a body of considerable achievement. It seems a fitting way in which to launch ourselves into the third millennium.

References

De Grazia, S. (1964). *Of time, work, and leisure.* New York, NY: Doubleday Anchor Books.

Jackson, E. L., & Burton, T. L. (1989). *Understanding leisure and recreation: Mapping the past, charting the future.* State College, PA: Venture Publishing, Inc.

Lundberg, G., Komarovsky, M., & McInerny, M. (1934). *Leisure: A suburban study.* New York, NY: Columbia University Press.

Outdoor Recreation Resources Review Commission. (1962). *Outdoor recreation for America.* Washington, DC: U.S. Government Printing Office.

Pieper, J. (1952). *Leisure: The basis of culture.* New York, NY: Random House.

Veblen, T. (1899). *The theory of the leisure class.* New York, NY: Macmillan Publishing.

Understanding Leisure

Some Philosophical Aspects
of Leisure Theory

Wes Cooper
University of Alberta

Introduction: Concept
and Conception

Most of us share a concept of leisure as free time, but there is considerable disagreement about which conception of this concept is best suited to guide theory. Does unemployment count as free time, and hence leisure? How constraining can one's choice-situation be? Can one be at leisure while at work? (Some have suggested that this is the peculiarly American way of taking leisure. Is this a debasement of leisure or a way of making it more efficient?) Or is the freedom of leisure the absence of causal determination, as an indeterminist philosopher might suggest? Or is it the freedom to exercise one's faculties as one wants, without care for the instrumental value of doing so (Suits, 1981)? (The deluge of computer games and other cyberspace recreations is perhaps the closest we have come to removal of leisure from real-world instrumentality. Should we praise this detachment from the limi- tations of our bodies and physical environments, or deplore it?) Does our clock-bound modern existence count as free time, or was true leisure available only in a past Golden Age, prior to the Industrial Revolu- tion, when time for us was cyclical rather than linear, thanks to our being closer to the seasons and other aspects of nature (de Grazia, 1964)? Is the freedom of leisure more a reality for men than for women? Is our leisure distorted by class conflict?

These questions are representative of the many theoretical issues that have been posed by people who have thought seriously about leisure. Any adequate ac- count of this subject must address the issues they raise, and the essays in this volume hold out the promise of collectively approaching such an account. A small but important first step towards this goal is realizing that little is to be gained by focusing intently on the con- cept of leisure and related concepts like free time, as though a happy Gestalt switch in one's intellectual per- ception might reveal the true meaning of leisure. Towards taking this first step I shall expand on a distinction between the concept and the conception of a thing.

Briefly, the concept of something—leisure, justice, beauty, and so on—is that which most people would agree upon as what they mean when they talk about that thing, even if they have importantly different beliefs about it. These differing sets of beliefs make up differing conceptions (Dworkin, 1977; Rawls, 1971). For instance, we share a concept of justice as giving to each his due, but we have different conceptions of what is involved in giving to each his due. Are goods distributed justly only when they are distributed equally or according to the market value of a person's skills or according to need or in some other way? Similarly, there are different conceptions of leisure as free time. Is it simply idleness or an opportunity for self-fulfillment or schooling in noble values or a unique mental state of *flow* or *ecstasy* or something else? A conception makes a concept determinate. A theoretically useful conception should make a concept determinate in a way that raises important questions and promises avenues for research. In what follows I shall suggest what I take to be a theoretically useful conception of leisure, which identifies it with doing things for their own sake. I shall try to show how this conception can figure in a systematic theory of leisure, by replying to some objections to the very idea of such a theory. I aim to conclude that leisure theory can be a science in the way that other social sciences are, but that its research should also aim at helping people to live authentic, self-expressive lives.

An observer may be somewhat bemused to learn that social scientists are making a serious study of leisure. Kelly was remarking on this type of reaction, perhaps, when he said that "the smiles and smirks that often follow when people say that they are studying leisure suggest that there is something odd about taking fun and games seriously" (Kelly, 1982). It is tempting to dismiss this attitude, but it is sufficiently prevalent that it warrants a reply. Let it be articulated therefore in the first objection I shall consider.

Objection One: The Oddness Objection

The phrase "the serious study of leisure" is an oxymoron, a contradiction in terms. It is, by definition, fun and games, and consequently the antithesis of serious study. Therefore, the very idea of a serious study of leisure, not to mention a science of leisure, is intellectually suspect. Scholars and scientists should concern themselves with the serious things in life, not its diversions.

Reply to Objection One

There are several confusions in the Oddness Objection. At the risk of belaboring the obvious, I shall emphasize two. First, it commits a logical fallacy in attributing the alleged qualities of a subject matter to the study of the subject matter. This is an instance of what Ryle calls a *category-mistake,* which involves thinking of something that belongs to one logical category as though it belonged to another (Ryle, 1949). Among Ryle's examples are the category-mistakes of supposing that team spirit is an extra player on a team, and of supposing that a university is something different from the buildings, students, and staff that go to make it up, and so on. Some further examples: The particles that physicists study are extremely small, but it does not follow that doing physics is extremely small—whatever that might mean. So, too, a philosopher who studies hedonism is not, ipso facto, reveling in pleasure instead of taking scholarly pains, and a social scientist studying recidivism need not be a convict about to return to prison. In the same way it is a category-mistake to suppose that leisure research is fun and games. To do so is to treat leisure research as leisure, when in fact it is an intellectual activity which takes leisure as its object of study. A leisure theorist need not do his or her research only in his or her free time, and all the more it is not required that he or she be indulging in "fun and games."

Secondly, the Oddness Objection illicitly assumes that leisure must be a mere diversion from serious activity, a matter of fun and games, whereas the only reasonable assumption is that someone's leisure may amount to no more than this. The Oddness Objection takes for granted, in effect, a conception of leisure that is really quite contentious, and which I shall be contending against in this essay. If leisure is intrinsically desired activity, and if, as thus understood, it is crucial to fully expressing oneself, then it seems evident that leisure can be an important matter in a human life. This is what I hope to show. An adequate conception of leisure can only be arrived at by argument and reflection on a variety of considerations, not by appeal to what the word *leisure* means. Anyone who has examined a good dictionary's entry for this word knows that what leisure is "by definition" is a very mixed bag of vague and sometimes conflicting things. Consider an unclothed person, obliged to quake in the cold. Few would view this as leisure activity, yet the *Oxford English Dictionary* (*OED*) cites the following passage from Chaucer as exemplifying a sense of the word leisure (*OED,* 1971, p. 1601):

No more was there
To clothe her with.
Gret leyser had she to quake.

I also assume that a conception of leisure can safely ignore the anthropomorphic projection that is apparent in another *OED* entry, Baxter's sentence "The young blades in the fields have leisure to expand and grow again before the scythe returns to cut them down a second time" (*OED*, 1971, p. 1601). The theoretically central cases of leisure must be activities that people want to do for their own sake. Blades of grass, lacking desires altogether, may be left beyond the pale of leisure theory.

I have suggested that we share a concept of leisure as free time, but this is empty by itself of determinate content. In particular, it is empty of the implication that one's free time is occupied in nonwork. Exploring that implication would at least be a start towards developing a respectable conception of leisure, but to bestow truth upon it by appeal to definition is to enjoy the advantages of theft over honest toil. A specimen of honest toil in exploring the implication that leisure is nonwork is Aristotle's classic statement, which is sufficiently important to warrant being quoted at length (Aristotle, 1953, pp. 303–304):

> Finally, it may well be thought that the activity of contemplation is the only one that is praised on its own account, because nothing comes of it beyond the act of contemplation, whereas from practical activities we count on gaining something more or less over and above the mere action. Again, it is commonly believed that, to have happiness, one must have leisure; we occupy ourselves in order that we may have leisure, just as we make war for the sake of peace. Now the practical virtues find opportunity for their exercise in politics and war, but these are occupations which are supposed to leave no room for leisure. Certainly it is true of the trade of war, for no one deliberately chooses to make war for the sake of making it or tries to bring about a war. A man would be regarded as a bloodthirsty monster if he were to make war on a friendly state just to produce battles and slaughter. . . . Political and military activities, while preeminent among good activities in beauty and grandeur, are incompatible with leisure, and are not chosen for their own sake but with a view to some remoter end, whereas

the activity of the intellect is felt to excel in the serious use of leisure, taking as it does the form of contemplation, and not to aim at any end beyond itself, and to own a pleasure peculiar to itself, thereby enhancing the activity.

Leisure for Aristotle is activity which is, above all, chosen for its own sake. I think Aristotle is right about this, and the point is echoed in the contemporary literature of leisure by such theorists as Iso-Ahola (see chapter 3 in this volume), for whom the core of leisure is intrinsically motivated or self-determined behavior. But Aristotle does not only identify leisure with intrinsically desired activity. He goes on to claim that, ideally, nothing comes of it. This seems to me a very doubtful proposition, but once it is premised, his conclusion that philosophical contemplation excels at the serious use of leisure is quite natural. On the Aristotelian conception of leisure, then, leisure and work (or, more broadly, instrumental activity) are mutually exclusive categories. Suits's Grasshopper presupposes an Aristotelian conception of leisure in this respect, although he thinks that game playing rather than philosophical contemplation is the more plausible candidate for ideal leisure activity (Suits, 1981). Neither proposal is particularly plausible, however. Philosophical contemplation may be an appropriate ideal for a few, but there is no reason to think that only that few are capable of the serious use of leisure. Walzer (1983, p. 186) makes the point nicely:

> That the philosopher's thoughts do not taint the idea of leisure, but the artisan's table or vase or statue do, is a thought likely to appeal only to philosophers. From a moral standpoint, it seems more important that human activity be directed from within than that it have no outside end or material outcome. And if we focus on self-direction, a wide variety of purposive activities can be brought within the compass of a life of leisure.

My own sketch here of a conception of leisure is, in large part, an attempt to focus on self-direction, as Walzer suggests. I hope to explain what might be involved in self-direction and what the implications of that might be for leisure theory.

As for Grasshopper's conception of leisure as game playing, it follows from a premise that he announces as follows: "But the whole burden of my teaching is that you ought to be idle" (Suits, 1981, p. 7). This premise, in turn, follows, in effect, from Grasshopper's assuming the validity of Aristotle's exclusionary principle: leisure and instrumentality are incompatible. So, ideally, he reasons, we would live lives of perfect noninstrumentality. This is his utopia. And in order to have something to do in utopia, so that boredom won't set in, Grasshopper envisages it as a place where mightily complex and unfathomably entertaining games are played.

Whereas Aristotle's conception of leisure restricted it to a philosophical few, Grasshopper's utopia seems to exclude everyone. Although it is hailed as "a dramatization of the ideal of existence" (Suits, 1981, p. 168), it seems not to be my or your or any human being's existence. For any human existence would include instrumental activity, such as breathing and finger movements, which are not typically indulged in for their own sake. So no human being could be a utopian, and, therefore, Grasshopper's utopian conception of leisure, delightful though it may be, is not a conception that could be seriously entertained as a fruitful one for leisure theorists to adopt.

I favor a conception of leisure which does not view it as necessarily devoid of instrumental value. I shall call this a Platonic conception of leisure, because it is suggested by an important distinction which Plato draws in *The Republic*. Glaucon (in italics) is pressing Socrates to explain his theory of goodness (Plato, 1974, p. 30):

> *I want to know how you classify the things we call good. Are there not some which we should wish to have, not for their consequences, but just for their own sake, such as harmless pleasures and enjoyments that have no further result beyond the satisfaction of the moment?*
>
> Yes, I think there are good things of that description.
>
> *And also some that we value both for their own sake and for their consequences— things like knowledge and health and the use of our eyes?*
>
> Yes.
>
> *And a third class which would include physical training, medical treatment, earning one's bread as a doctor or otherwise— useful, but burdensome things, which we want only for the sake of the profit or other benefit they bring?*
>
> Yes, there is that third class. What then?
>
> *In which class do you place justice?*
>
> I should say, in the highest, as a thing which anyone who is to gain happiness

must value both for itself and for its results.

The Platonic conception of leisure supposes that leisure may belong to the "highest class" of things which are of value for themselves and for their results. An implausible form of the Platonic conception would hold that an activity fails to be leisure if it does not belong to this highest class. I hold rather that there is no theoretical ban on leisure having instrumental value, as Aristotle supposed, but, equally, that there is no requirement that it should be instrumental.

If the first main point of the Aristotelian conception of leisure—that leisure and work are mutually exclusive—be rejected, the second main point may be more acceptable. This is the idea that leisure must be valuable. It was not Aristotle's view that any useless activity is leisure, nor is it enough that useless activity should be desired for its own sake. Rather, the activity must be *desirable* for its own sake. Once again it is of secondary importance that he supposed philosophical contemplation to be supremely valuable. This may be denied yet the main point affirmed. So I incorporate in the conception being advanced here an ideal of leisure; that is, a value which renders an intrinsically desired activity desirable for its own sake. Rather than philosophizing or game playing, I propose a more general condition which might be satisfied by a wide variety of activities: what makes an activity desirable and not merely desired is that an individual would want to engage in that activity if he were thinking clearly and were fully informed.

Leisure is ideal when it is motivated by desire which satisfies this condition, but leisure may be less than ideal. Drinking and driving is a form of leisure activity because it is something one may wish to do for its own sake, but it may well be an activity which one would not engage in if one were thinking clearly. Smoking, hunting, and so on are leisure activities which one might avoid if one were vividly aware of the consequences of doing so.[1]

Note that ideal leisure, despite being sharply distinguished from what a person actually wants to do, is

---

[1] The idea here is that full information and vivid awareness might affect one's tendency to engage in these activities. With regard to hunting, vivid awareness of the suffering of hunted animals might do the trick; with regard to smoking, vivid awareness of the cancers that are likely to ensue; with regard to drinking and driving, vivid awareness of the increased probability of causing death and suffering to a pedestrian; and so forth. I do not mean to imply that a diminished probability to engage in such actions is logically guaranteed. But the process of making oneself informed and becoming vividly aware of that information tends to get such results.

tightly connected to desire: it is what a person would want if he were thinking clearly and knew all relevant facts. Brandt calls this process *cognitive psychotherapy,* because a person's desires and actions are altered by a noncoercive confrontation between his beliefs and all relevant available information (Brandt, 1979). He illustrates the idea of cognitive psychotherapy in a simple example:

> Let us suppose small Albert refused to play with the interesting small daughter of a neighbor because she is devoted to a pet rabbit, and he has an intense aversion to rabbits. Let us suppose further that he has an aversion to rabbits because someone once produced a loud noise in his vicinity while he was reaching out to touch a rabbit. Now suppose that Albert would be disabused of his aversion if he repeated to himself, on a number of occasions and with utter conviction, some justified statement as "There is no connection between rabbits and loud noises; rabbits are just friendly little beasts." In this case his aversion would have been removed by cognitive psychotherapy and I shall say his aversion is irrational. (Brandt, 1979, pp. 11–12)

The process is cognitive rather than, say, electro-convulsive or chemical or some other form of therapy, because it is distinguished by the effects of information on belief, desire, and action. It relies simply upon "reflection on available information, without influence by prestige of someone, use of evaluative language, or use of artificially induced feeling-states like relaxation" (Brandt, 1979, p. 113). And the process is a form of psychotherapy because the person who undergoes it is supposed to be more rational as a consequence: "I shall preempt the term 'rational,'" Brandt says, "to refer to actions, desires, or moral systems which survive maximal criticism and correction by facts and logic" (Brandt, 1979, p. 10). I follow Brandt in thinking of the process as "value-free reflection," because it is an entirely open question whether someone who is thinking clearly and who knows all relevant facts will come to want to pursue this or that moral ideal or other value. The ideal is not imposed on desire "from without," so to speak, by reference to some alleged standard of objective value. It is created rather by the uncoerced choice of any rational, fully informed individual. (The conception of leisure I am presenting, consequently, is one which assumes that value is subjective; and so it is skeptical about the existence of things which are valuable quite apart from their being desired.)

Desirability is understood as relative to an individual at a time; so what is desirable for you may not be desirable for me, and what is desirable for a person at one time may not be desirable for him at another time. No one is cut off from leisure because he is indifferent to the allegedly objectively valuable thing. One can be cut off from it only by irrationality or ignorance of fact. Ideal leisure is what this person would want to do for its own sake at this time, if he were properly apprised of all relevant facts.

Consider how this conception of ideal leisure might apply in criticism of Grasshopper's utopia of noninstrumental activity, such as enjoying pleasant sensations or, paramountly, playing wonderful games. Recall that Grasshopper's utopian conception of leisure was rejected because it excluded everybody, since merely instrumental activity, such as breathing and moving limbs, belongs in the life rhythm of everyone. It is an extension of this point to suggest that clear-thinking and well-informed people would want to create worked-at objects in the ideal of their existence, where there is no shortcut such as a magic wand for creating the objects in question. Even if it might be wished that the instrumental aspect of one's activity were quicker or easier, there would be a residue of instrumental activity that would belong to the content of one's intrinsic desires, in the way that a sculptor wants not simply that a sculpture should come into existence, but that it should come into existence as a result of his sculpting.

This is especially clear in connection with instrumental activity that has something important to do with one's conception of oneself, as it might be in the case of the sculptor. For it is, in principle, impossible in this kind of case that there should be a shortcut to the state of affairs desired for its own sake. The relevant kind of case may be described as the kind in which one expresses oneself. I propose to generalize this category in a certain way, following Taylor's lead in developing an "expressivist" view of man, which has its roots in late eighteenth-century Germany, and especially in the Sturm und Drang movement, as a reaction to Enlightenment thought. This expressivist view, according to which, in Taylor's words, "human life unfolded from some central core—a guiding theme or inspiration—or should do so, if it were not so often blocked and distorted," became an important source of what is often called Romanticism (Taylor, 1979, p. 2; see also Cooper, 1985).

I shall put a point on this expressivist notion of the unfolding of a human life, as follows: for each human being there is a life which is molded by what I shall call authentic desires. These are intrinsic desires which one would continue to have, or else acquire, after thinking clearly about all information that was relevant to what one might want to do. Such a life, I shall say, is one in which the subject fully expresses himself. A human life is not necessarily an expressive one. For one's desires may be inauthentic, by virtue of one's not thinking clearly or not being sufficiently informed. This is how I interpret the expressivist idea of a life being blocked or distorted. Self-expression is closely linked to leisure, as it is understood on the conception being advanced here. For self-expression requires living a life in which intrinsic desires are satisfied; to the extent that life is given over to merely instrumental activity, or drudgery, one's life is not expressive. But leisure is intrinsically desired activity, and a pure science of leisure would focus on this category. Furthermore, ideal leisure on the present conception is just authentic intrinsically desired activity; in short, ideal leisure is expressive of the self.

Objection Two: The Arbitrary List Objection

Leisure studies could not have the unity that one expects of a respectable field of intellectual inquiry, because different people and different cultures take their leisure in such different ways. Consider Kelly's sociological survey of what North American respondents took to be the most important leisure activities (Kelly, 1982). The survey's list—call it LL—is a mixed bag, comprising the following: marital affection and intimacy, reading for pleasure, family conversation, activities as a couple, family outings, visiting family and friends, playing with children, watching television, outdoor sports, eating out, religious worship, short auto trips, gardening and yard care, home decoration and shop projects, arts or crafts such as ceramics or painting, entertaining at home, hunting and/or fishing, child-centered events such as school events and sports, conversation with friends and neighbors, walking and/or jogging, hobbies such as collecting, and companionship on the job. LL is an arbitrary list, in just the same way that the following list is arbitrary: paper clips, the Waldstein sonata, landlords, New Orleans, Jack Russell terriers, Dr. Seuss, Jack Bush, dangling participles, and allergic reactions. Call this list Paper Clip. Now if someone were to propose to erect a science of Paper Clip and Paper Clip–type phenomena, or to philosophize about it, then (the objection continues) he should expect some smiles and smirks. Why should the student of LL activities expect anything different? A minimum requirement for a science, surely, is that the objects of its study should have significant similarities with one another, so that lawlike regularities can be discovered

with respect to them. But Paper Clip is an entirely arbitrary list devoid of salient resemblances. And so is LL, according to the Arbitrary List Objection.

Reply to Objection Two

The Arbitrary List Objection fails because there is, indeed, a theoretically interesting unity in a list like LL. It is unified by the fact that the listed activities are done for their own sake, and not just for some instrumental value they might have. According to the conception of leisure that I recommend, this is its central feature. Leisure as that which is done for its own sake, or the intrinsically desired, is the primary subject matter for leisure theory. This is what a science of leisure theory should be about. Amongst the sciences, then, leisure theory is most closely connected to psychology, and in particular to the branches of psychological theory concerned with desire or "valence." Leisure may be studied scientifically by researchers from many disciplines, but the proprietary subject matter for leisure science is intrinsic desire. My claim that LL exhibits a theoretically interesting unity must be qualified. For one thing, any activity on such a list can be done solely for its instrumental value. Someone may jog for his health, for example, even though he hates doing it. So we need a distinction between a type of activity and a token of that type. Some tokens of the type, jogging, may be performed for their own sake, and other tokens of that type may have only instrumental motivation. (Sometimes daydreaming is cited as the quintessential leisure activity, but it too may have a leisure-defeating complexity: I may do it to keep my mind off a vexing problem, for instance.)

Then my claim about LL is that it exhibits a theoretically interesting unity when it is understood to pick out tokens of the types listed in LL, activity tokens which are engaged in for their own sake. I am not saying that the respondents to Kelly's survey were presupposing my conception of leisure. Some of them, for instance, might view instrumentally motivated activity as leisure simply because it occurs during free time, that is, time off from one's paid work and other mundane necessities like doing the dishes, whereas I have argued that leisure, in the most theoretically interesting sense, has a particular motivation. If someone is playing miniature golf at Leisure World Recreation Center simply out of familial duty, he is not at leisure despite the outward appearances. All and only intrinsically desired tokens of LL-type activities exhibit a theoretically significant unity, and they provide leisure science with a distinctive subject matter which can be explored in various ways.

I am not arguing that intrinsic and instrumental motivation are incompatible. As an adherent of the Platonic, nonexclusionary conception of leisure, I believe that one can have both instrumental and intrinsic motivation for leisure. I may golf for the tan as well as for the fun of it, for instance, and this complex motivation is compatible with my golfing at leisure. Leisure science studies intrinsic desire wherever it occurs, and whatever the extent of its contribution to an actor's full motivation. Perhaps only a very small fraction of LL-type activities occurs without some degree of intrinsic motivation, so it would not be misleading in practice to disregard the type-token distinction just introduced. It is also probably true that only a small fraction of LL-type activities occurs without some degree of extrinsic motivation. When I take a novel to the seaside, I read it for pleasure (intrinsic motivation) and also to kill time (extrinsic motivation). Mixed motivation is the rule.

I conclude that the Arbitrary List Objection fails.

Objection Three: The Pseudoscience Objection

Leisure science is no more a science than Christian Science or scientific socialism. Leisure science would be substantially scientific only if it could lay claim to those features of the natural sciences, like physics and chemistry, which make the term *scientific* supremely honorific. At a minimum, one would expect it to discover laws, or at least lawlike generalizations: exceptionless, mathematically precise generalizations about leisure from which accurate predictions can be deduced. But the generalizations of leisure theorists are not in this way scientific. The problem is not simply the one to which Veal has drawn attention—that the methods available to leisure theorists have not been capable of producing accurate results because it is difficult to gather the relevant facts. He observes that the demand for leisure is more difficult to determine than the demand for such services as education or housing (Veal, 1987, pp. 127–128): for a given population of children the demand for school places is known and the consequences of not providing that number of places would be all too apparent. In the case of leisure the situation is different. Demand cannot be so precisely determined—the numbers of people who want to play sport, visit the countryside, or take part in arts activities are not known. The consequence of not providing facilities for these activities is that people do something else with their leisure time, such as watching more television.

The problem to which Veal refers is real enough, but there is a more basic problem for scientific leisure theory than the difficulty of gathering facts. The problem is that leisure is a cultural artifact (like books) rather than a natural kind (like diamonds), and, as such, it requires a different sort of understanding than the sort which is characteristic of the natural sciences. This different understanding has to do with grasping the social rules that govern leisure. Just as it is wrongheaded to try to understand chess by discovering regularities in the behavior of chess players instead of learning the rules of chess that they play by, it is wrongheaded to try to understand leisure by discovering regularities in the behavior of leisure consumers.

Consider a typical example which illustrates the wrongheadedness in principle, not just the difficulty in practice, of seeking scientific laws of leisure: Ewing's paper, "Progress and Problems in the Development of Recreational Trip Generation and Trip Distribution Models," examines the Unconstrained Gravity Model (UGM, as it may be labeled) of recreational trip frequency within a population (Ewing, 1980). The model is expressed in a formula, namely:

$$t(i,j) = \frac{kP(i)A(j)}{C(i,j)}$$

UGM states that the number of trips from an origin i to a destination j—that is, $t(i,j)$—is a certain function (the power function) of the population (P) of i, the attractiveness (A) of j, and the cost (C) of getting from i to j. As Ewing demonstrates, UGM is woefully inadequate, even as a rule of thumb, to be used by leisure managers, such as parks and recreation officials. He makes the point that UGM is insensitive to the number of alternatives available to the population, and he goes on to propose models, different from UGM but motivated by the same aim of uncovering a law of trip distribution, which take into account such points.

If it were legitimate in principle to seek such laws, it should make sense to think of successors to UGM approaching perfect predictive power asymptotically. This is a reasonable hope for the generalizations of the natural sciences, which employ a physico-mathematical vocabulary that is genuinely capable of progressing towards the precision required in a law of nature. But the appearance of precision in UGM-type generalizations is necessarily illusory, since the people who make recreational trips, unlike physical and chemical particles, are following social rules or norms which define, for instance, what counts as an attractive destination in that culture. This makes the variable A in UGM very different from variables, such as length and volume, which occur in natural laws, and for which there is a physicomathematical metric which submits them to increasingly precise measurement. The variable *A* is said to be the "measure of the quality or attractiveness of destination *j, or some surrogate measure, such as size . . .*" (my emphasis) (Ewing, 1980, p. 5). But it is specious to think that size could stand as a surrogate for attractiveness. Tourists can be attracted to small destinations as well as large ones. They might want to visit Europe (a "large" size of destination) or they might want to see a European friend's stamp collection (a "small" destination).

(Other variables in UGM are vulnerable to similar objections. Consider *C*, or cost. A certain formula about cost might capture the outer limits of what most people would want to spend on recreational travel, but if the formula lays down an absolute limit *C*, it may turn out that a particularly wealthy person is not deterred by that limit.)

Of course one might say "UGM, other things being equal," but the immunity from counterexample gained by attaching this "fudge clause" to UGM negates its claim to the status of a scientific generalization. This status, the Pseudoscience Objection runs, requires that a scientific generalization be formulated with mathematical precision in such a way that it can be tested severely, with no possibility of seeking refuge in ad hoc hypotheses about why the generalization did not hold true in a particular instance. Any generalization can be held to be true "other things being equal." One need merely insist, when a counterinstance seems to present itself, that other things aren't equal! The requirements for scientific status, the Pseudoscience Objection implies, are so extremely demanding that only the natural sciences meet them.

Reply to Objection Three

Some of the minor criticisms raised in the Pseudoscience Objection are well-founded cautions to leisure theory, but its force turns primarily on the questionable assumption that the status of a field of research is an all-or-nothing affair. I shall challenge this assumption. Leisure science may be a science to a lesser degree than physics, or display a lesser degree of "scientificity," without losing its claim to be a science. Being a science is a scalar affair. We are indebted to Braybrooke for a "scale of scientificity" which provides a plausible alternative to the all-or-nothing view. The scale involves a list of characteristics, proceeding from the bottom (characteristic 1) to characteristics evermore ambitious. Of any activity or inquiry we may ask (Braybrooke, 1987, pp. 43–44):

1. Is it pursued indefinitely rather than taken up and brought to an end within the confines of one practical crisis?
2. Does it aim to decrease the stock or potential stock of false statements describing the real world and to increase the stock or potential stock of true statements?
3. Does it circumscribe a field of research and aim to fill gaps in the literature identified as pertinent to the field?
4. Does it aim to establish by generalization explicitly related sets of true descriptive statements?
5. Does the activity aim to increase the stock of true causal generalizations? (This implies increasing at the same time the stock or potential stock of true singular causal statements and the number of explanations and predictions that can be argued in some approximation to the covering law form.)
6. Does it distinguish levels of aggregation such that objects on one level in some sense belong to objects on a higher level and supply facts from which facts about the higher level arise?
7. Does it aim to increase the precision of its statements, general and singular, throughout as much of its field as possible?
8. Does the activity aim to bring its chief general statements together in a unified structure expressed or expressible with formal methods as in axiomatic theory?
9. Does it apply statistical analysis in research designs and in interpreting research findings?
10. Does it use, to achieve greater precision or more powerful theories, mathematics beyond arithmetic, elementary algebra, and graphic analysis as found in elementary statistics or economics?

Now the philosophy of science implied by Braybrooke's scale is only one of many, and even if one shares his general outlook one might wish to add or subtract items from his scale. But disagreements of this sort need not interfere with the value of Braybrooke's scale in the present context, which is to call into question the all-or-nothing conception of science.

In applying the scale to leisure theory I shall be concerned with scientific leisure theory in the normal, broad sense, as opposed to the narrow sense I have distinguished. Normal scientific leisure theory is best defined by example, by pointing to leisure research journals in which authors from various disciplines report their attempts to study leisure scientifically. Although leisure research does not score as high on this scale as the natural sciences do, nonetheless it scores well enough to have some standing as a science.

Consider, first, characteristic 1 (Is it pursued indefinitely rather than taken up and brought to an end within the confines of one practical crisis?). Over the past 20 years, leisure theory has been pursued in a regular and systematic manner. There is now a sizable group of inquirers who think of themselves as scientists in this field. They have regular conferences, established periodicals for reporting the results of research, introductory courses and texts, and so forth. Evidently, leisure studies has a high ranking for characteristic 1 of the scale of scientificity.

Consider, next, characteristic 2 (Does it aim to decrease the stock or potential stock of false statements describing the real world and to increase the stock or potential stock of true statements?). Any volume of a major journal of leisure research will exemplify these aims, in attempts to provide informative descriptions and revealing generalizations. Therefore, leisure research does very well on characteristic 2. Volume 5 of *Leisure Studies* may be cited as an example. An article like Heeley's "Leisure and Moral Reform," exemplifying the descriptive aspect of leisure theory, explores the ways in which the Victorian and Edwardian philosophy of rational recreation found expression in a variety of reformist campaigns (Heeley, 1986). As an example of generalization, Jackson's "Outdoor Recreation Participation and Attitudes to the Environment" offers evidence for a strong correlation between participation in appreciative recreational activities and concern for protecting the natural environment (Jackson, 1986). The merit of Braybrooke's scale of scientificity is that it properly relates studies like Jackson's to science rather than pseudoscience, religion, superstition, and other categories in the large area of the "nonscientific."

As for characteristic 3 (Does it circumscribe a field of research and aim to fill gaps in the literature identified as pertinent to the field?), the institutionalization of leisure research attests to its circumscription of a field of research. The creation of university departments of leisure studies, the proliferation of journals and books devoted to leisure research, and the various aspects of a scientific "paradigm" as noted in connection with characteristic 1, all indicate a high ranking for characteristic 3.

With respect to characteristic 4 (Does it aim to establish by generalization explicitly related sets of true descriptive statements?), leisure theory is comparable

to many social sciences, such as sociology. In both areas an enormous literature attempts to establish generalizations, such as Jackson's correlation of recreational activity and concern with the environment, and such as the study of gravitational models of the sort that Ewing discusses.

In my judgment, leisure theory does not rank particularly high on characteristic 5 (Does the activity aim to increase the stock of true causal generalizations?). Many of its characteristic methods—trend extrapolation, respondent assessment, the Delphi technique, scenario writing, cross-sectional analysis—steer clear of claims about causal connections. On the other hand, if my recommendation for a core subject matter for leisure science were acted upon, I think that leisure theory could build upon psychological theory in order to discover significant lawlike generalizations about what people would intrinsically desire under different circumstances of environment and upbringing. For this reason alone I think there is considerable room for growth in this area.

But there is a danger in this area too, a danger which is sometimes called scientism. This involves failing to appreciate the differences between the subject matter of the natural and social sciences, and treating man in society as though he were a molecule or an atom. The critique of scientism has been extended to leisure theory by Rojek, for instance, in his *Capitalism and Leisure Theory* (Rojek, 1985).

Scientism in the social sciences tends to favor the status quo, by treating regularities in social behavior as though they were as inevitable as gravity. Thus it is that the critique of scientism is often undertaken by those who seek large-scale political and social change. A leisure science which limited itself to describing these regular patterns of leisure behavior would be useful to leisure managers in their efforts to deliver leisure products to leisure consumers, and, consequently, it would help to stabilize and reinforce the regularities it describes. This could be viewed as strengthening the socially and politically conservative illusion that patterns of leisure are as immutable as the motions of basic physical particles.

An example may anchor the point: West's "A Nationwide Test of the Status Group Dynamics Approach to Outdoor Recreation Demand" carefully examines and plausibly qualifies Veblen's insight that demand for particular leisure activities tends to diffuse from higher to lower socioeconomic groups (West, 1982). He hopes to predict demand shifts more accurately than Veblen-type models permit, by challenging the assumption that participation rates within subgroups remain stable as diffusion occurs. In particular, he draws attention to *status-based withdrawal,* the phenomenon of a higher status group's withdrawal from a given activity as diffusion occurs. Such studies as West's are legitimate, but it must always be remembered that the regularities they describe are conditional on choices that may change. This complicates things in comparison to the situation for a natural scientist, because molecules and atoms don't make choices. We know that, unlike protons, people can raise normative questions and act on answers to them that lead in directions quite different from the regularities described by West. The classes he describes could be abolished by political activity, for instance, or status-based withdrawal could be eliminated by educational programs. And perhaps such political or educational choices should be made! It bears repeating that this point does not invalidate such studies as West's, but rather emphasizes the peculiarly conditional character of the regularities they describe. And perhaps the point suggests that a purely descriptive leisure theory would be impoverished in a way that a purely descriptive natural science is not, for the descriptive leisure theory would be failing to study the peculiar conditions which make its subject matter uniquely different from the natural sciences: human choice, belief, rationality, and the scope for normative questions created by these conditions.

Leisure theory distinguishes levels of aggregation in the manner typical of the social sciences. It attempts to discover group facts (e.g., patterns of demand for recreation facilities) by deriving them from person facts, such as a person's motivation, his cost of travel, and so on. So with reference to characteristic 6 (Does it distinguish levels of aggregation such that objects on one level in some sense belong to objects on a higher level and supply facts from which facts about the higher level arise?), it shows well—as well as some other social sciences, though not as well as the natural sciences, where there is an elaborately developed body of theory which "reduces" higher level facts to lower level facts, and ultimately to facts described by physics. There is a view according to which the social sciences should look forward to participating in this reductive hierarchy. But one would not expect leisure science—or any other social science, for that matter—to reduce to physics in the way that chemistry does, if it is sound to argue, as I did earlier, that the subject matter of the social sciences is unique by virtue of the fact that people are rational, have beliefs, raise normative questions, and make choices.

Leisure research aims to increase the precision of its statements, as evidenced by tenacious discussion in the journals, in which experimental results are put forward, interpreted, and criticized. Ewing's discussion of the Unconstrained Gravity Model is a case in point.

So, with respect to characteristic 7 (Does it aim to increase the precision of its statements, general and singular, throughout as much of its field as possible?), leisure theory may be judged to show very well. But it will be recalled from the earlier discussion of Ewing and the formula UGM that there is a danger of false formalism in leisure science—of imparting to generalizations about leisure a spurious air of mathematical precision. So precision in leisure theory may take a very different form than the physicomathematical metric of natural laws. In some cases, precision may simply amount to careful and sensitive description of leisure activity, or normatively motivated advocacy of some leisure activity, using the vocabulary of rationality, belief, and choice, which is well-suited to the subject matter of leisure theory, namely people.

With reference to characteristic 8 (Does the activity aim to bring its chief general statements together in a unified structure expressed or expressible with formal methods as in axiomatic theory?), leisure science does not show well. This is so, I suspect, because of the eclectic nature of what I have called hybrid leisure science. That is, it draws scientific conjectures from various disciplines, and though these disciplines may themselves have a unified logical structure, this is lacking in the result of their convergence in hybrid leisure science. But it may be that pure leisure theory, devoted to inquiry into the intrinsically desired, might have a highly unified logical structure. This would be so if, as many psychologists and philosophers believe, there are psychological laws pertaining to desire and intrinsic desire. Pure leisure science would gain a unified logical structure by virtue of its subject matter being derivable from such laws. Employing these laws, and employing, too, a conception of rationality and empirical fact, pure leisure theorists might be able to make significant predictions about leisure behavior, and significant recommendations about what sorts of leisure would help us lead authentic, self-expressive lives.

Statistical analysis is widespread in leisure research, so it shows very well on characteristic 9 (Does it apply statistical analysis in research designs and in interpreting research findings?). This testifies to the effort of leisure theorists to bring scientific objectivity to their studies, by describing regularities in a detached way through statistical analysis. But at this point it is important to take heed of one of the well-founded criticisms in the Pseudoscience Objection, namely the point that leisure is a cultural artifact, and in order to fully understand it one needs to understand the social norms that create and influence leisure activity. And just as understanding the rules of chess is different from knowing statistical regularities pertaining to the movements of pieces, so too understanding leisure activity—indeed, playing chess, for instance—requires the former kind of understanding. This is not to imply that statistical analysis is out of place in leisure studies. It is to say, rather, that objectifying leisure research, such as statistical analysis, should be complemented by norm-sensitive studies, and these call for a more subjective point of view. The researcher will be articulating something like a participant's understanding of the leisure activity he or she is studying, rather than prescinding from such an understanding in order to gain greater objectivity.

Higher mathematics is not extensively used in leisure theory, so it does not show well on characteristic 10 (Does it use, to achieve greater precision or more powerful theories, mathematics beyond arithmetic, elementary algebra, and graphic analysis as found in elementary statistics or economics?). As I have suggested, however, pure leisure theory may be expected to improve in this dimension as its connection with learning theory and other branches of cognitive psychology becomes more fully appreciated. The use of higher mathematics in those areas will be seen to have a direct bearing on questions of leisure theory, as its use will shed light on intrinsic desire and its conditions of formation and satisfaction; and these, of course, are topics of cardinal importance for pure leisure theory. On the other hand, the warning bears repeating that a high ranking on characteristic 10 of the scientificity scale should not be purchased at the cost of false formalism of the sort that was criticized in connection with Ewing's discussion of the Unconstrained Gravity Model of trip distribution.

I am now in a position to reject the Pseudoscience Objection. It is to be rejected because it focuses too narrowly on the absence of true causal generalizations in leisure theory, and on the absence of the precision of higher mathematics in the descriptions and generalizations of leisure theory. But the scale of scientificity broadens the focus in a salutary way. Adopting the perspective of that scale, the Pseudoscience Objection is seen as dwelling arbitrarily on characteristics 5 and 10, to the exclusion of all the rest. Not only is this arbitrary, but also it is dangerous to attempt to make progress in the social sciences by encouraging false formalism and other indicators of scientism. Many social sciences do not show well on characteristics 5 and 10, so if their status as sciences is to be explained, it seems plausible to make reference to the other characteristics on the scale. And with these others in mind, the claim of leisure research to scientific status, or to a social science's degree of scientificity, looks sound enough. It is not at all necessary to show that this claim has the same strength as that of physics. No social

science could show this. So there is no reason here for special skepticism about leisure theory.

The standards of the all-or-nothing conception of science are so high that even the putative laws of physics may not satisfy them. Suppose we knew that events prior to the last Big Bang were not governed by the laws that have governed the universe ever since. Then our physical laws would not be exceptionless, or they would be exceptionless only by virtue of arbitrarily restricting their temporal scope. Should we say that our laws would not be real laws in this case, and that physics is pseudoscience? If not, here is another reason to reject the Pseudoscience Objection's standards for scientific status.

I conclude that the Pseudoscience Objection may be dismissed, finally, as relying on an unacceptable, all-or-nothing, conception of science. This is not to say that the objection cannot be formulated without this conception, in such a way as to pose genuine issues for the methodology of leisure science. I have in mind particularly a formulation which challenges leisure science to acknowledge fully its peculiarities as a social science, specifically its responsibility to acknowledge the rationality of people at leisure, the influence of cultural shared understandings on their behavior, and so forth. Traditionally this acknowledgment has been distorted by a dichotomy between "hard," quantitative, law-seeking leisure science and "soft," qualitative, interpretive leisure science. In my other contribution to this volume I try to explain why this dichotomy is a distortion.

Conclusions

I have advanced a conception of leisure as activity desired for its own sake (intrinsic desire), in the hope that this conception may be suited to guide theorizing about the subject. If it is indeed so suited, leisure researchers may expect to profit by examining the literature of scientific psychology pertaining to desire. Out of this, one might expect to see a major contribution towards what Burton has called "perhaps the most important step in the drive to maturity" for leisure research, "the establishment of a set of unifying concepts and codes for the field" (Burton, 1980, p. 382).

In the spirit of Plato's recognition of the "highest class" of things, and *pace* Aristotle, I understand leisure to permit instrumental as well as intrinsic motivation. And in the spirit of the Romantic movement's faith in the genius of the individual, the core of personality which unfolds in a self-expressive way unless blocked or impeded, I understand ideal leisure to be not just intrinsically motivated, but authentically and therefore self-expressively so. One would not be dissuaded from that activity if one were thinking more clearly or were more well-informed—the desire would survive criticism by logic and scientific fact.

I have proposed that the scientific status of a field of study is best viewed as a scalar matter rather than all-or-nothing. Measured against Braybrooke's scale of scientificity, leisure theorists can legitimately claim that they are participating in a maturing field of social scientific research.

References

Aristotle. (1953). *The ethics of Aristotle.* Translated by J. A. K. Thomson. London, UK: George Allen & Unwin.

Brandt, R. (1979). *A theory of the good and the right.* Oxford, UK: Clarendon Press.

Braybrooke, D. (1987). *Philosophy of social science.* Englewood Cliffs, NJ: Prentice-Hall.

Burton, T. L. (1980). The maturation of leisure research. In T. L. Goodale & P. A. Witt (Eds.), *Recreation and leisure: Issues in an era of change,* (pp. 373–385). State College, PA: Venture Publishing, Inc.

The Compact Edition of the Oxford English Dictionary (Vol. I). (1971). s.v. "leisure." Oxford, UK: Oxford University Press.

Cooper, W. (1985). Is art a form of life? *Dialogue, 24,* 443–453.

De Grazia, S. (1964). *Of time, work, and leisure.* Garden City, NY: Anchor.

Dworkin, R. (1977). *Taking rights seriously.* Cambridge, MA: Harvard University Press.

Ewing, G. (1980). Progress and problems in the development of recreational trip generation and trip distribution models. *Leisure Sciences, 3,* 1–24.

Heeley, J. (1986). Leisure and moral reform. *Leisure Studies, 5,* 57–67.

Jackson, E. L. (1986). Outdoor recreation participation and attitudes to the environment. *Leisure Studies, 5,* 1–23.

Kelly, J. R. (1982). *Leisure.* Englewood Cliffs, NJ: Prentice-Hall.

Plato. (1974). *The republic.* Indianapolis, IN: Hackett.

Rawls, J. (1971). *A theory of justice.* Cambridge, MA: Harvard University Press.

Rojek, C. (1985). *Capitalism and leisure theory.* London, UK: Tavistock.

Ryle, G. (1949). *The concept of mind.* New York, NY: Barnes & Noble.

Suits, B. (1981). *The Grasshopper: Games, life, and utopia.* Toronto, Ontario: University of Toronto Press.

Taylor, C. (1979). *Hegel and modern society.* Cambridge, UK: Cambridge University Press.

Veal, A. J. (1987). *Leisure and the future.* London, UK: George Allen & Unwin.

Walzer, M. (1983). *Spheres of justice.* New York, NY: Basic Books.

West, P. C. (1982). A nationwide test of the status group dynamics approach to outdoor recreation demand. *Leisure Sciences, 5,* 1–18.

The Western Idea of Work and Leisure: Traditions, Transformations, and the Future

Charles Sylvester

Western Washington University

For many people, perhaps most, work is a matter of spiritual life and death. In the words of one unemployed person, "Working is breathing. . . . You just do it and it keeps you alive. When you stop you die" (quoted in Rifkin, 1995, p. 195). Indeed, work is the psychological center of Western society, supplying the main source of personal identity and self-esteem (Pieper, 1952; Rodgers, 1978; Tilgher, 1930; Weber, 1958). Despite the usual exceptions and qualifications, the modern vision of life is guided by the secular scripture of what is good and meaningful—the "gospel of work."

As such, people generally find it hard to imagine that working in an occupation has not always been the cardinal rule of life. Independence from the necessity of being occupied with a job, allowing freedom for "higher" activities, was the dominant cultural ideal for the better part of history (Rodgers, 1978). According to rhetoric that resonated through the centuries, the good life depended on leisure.

Yet, while faint reflections of this attitude can still be detected, an ethic of work persists today, continuing as "a natural necessity that leads to numerous . . . repercussions" (Desan, 1995, p. 15). Not the least of these repercussions are answers to the questions: Who am I? and What difference do I make? Certainly, then, the possibility of the "end of work" would have seismic impact. People might cry, "Impossible!" for work is a "natural necessity," an inescapable and, in the minds of many, a desirable condition of life. True, work must be done to produce life. But not all work must be performed by human hands. Automated technology performs much of the work once done by human beings. Accordingly, several analysts, authors of such ominous titles as *The End of Work* (Rifkin, 1995) and *The Jobless Future* (Aronowitz and DiFazio, 1994), argue that much of the labor currently performed by human beings will be virtually eliminated in the next millennium. While complex and controversial, the issue is bluntly clear. The efficiency of computer technology has made it possible to achieve greater productivity at less cost by minimizing human labor. The result is *restructuring,* whereby thousands of jobs have been eliminated (downsized) in such industries as banking and communications. Previously, jobs lost in the passing of one economy were absorbed by another. Farming was supplanted by manufacturing, and manufacturing in turn has been substantially replaced by a service economy. Some analysts argue that the *information industry* will perform a similar function. Perhaps it will. Yet the logic of technology has always been to reduce human labor, the most costly part of capitalist production. Even where computer technology is producing new jobs, analysts such as Michael Dunkerley (1996) predict that "on balance the future will provide fewer jobs and . . . require fewer jobs to be done" (p. 59). Consequently, more and more people may become unemployed, partially employed, temporarily employed, or multiply employed doing several part-time jobs. Therefore, while computer technology and the Information Age will provide creative and profitable opportunities for an elite group of technicians and professionals, work will never be the same for most of the public. As such, Rifkin (1995) concludes that "a society absent of mass formal employment is likely to be the single most pressing issue of the coming century" (p. xv). The displacement of jobs and the decentering of work as a way of life will raise "crucial questions concerning the purpose of education, the character of economic and social distribution, and, *perhaps more profoundly, what it means to be human*" (emphasis added) (Aronowitz and DiFazio, 1994, p. 33).

Answering questions about justice, education, economics, and the very nature of human existence in a near jobless future implies some degree of control over our destiny, a chance to create our history. Marx asserted, however, that people "do not make [their lives] just as they please . . . but under circumstances directly encountered, given and transmitted from the past" (quoted in McLellan, 1971, p. 137). Understanding how we have acquired our views and attitudes regarding work and leisure, therefore, can help us evaluate how we might change these integral parts of the social structure in preparation for the future. As such, history can reveal what has been both constructive and destructive in our traditions for the purpose of creating a society that enjoys more freedom, justice, and happiness.

A comprehensive history of work and leisure covering its complex social, economic, and political factors is far beyond the scope of this chapter. To cover them all would require several volumes. Therefore, I have concentrated on the main intellectual traditions and transformations that have shaped the dominant ideas of work and leisure in Western civilization. My aim is to introduce nonspecialists to several of the major ideologies as a gateway for further inquiry into the problems, conflicts, complexities, and opportunities of work and leisure. Two streams of thought and their historical confluence have been primarily responsible for dominant beliefs and attitudes regarding work and leisure. One springs out of ancient Greece, particularly the classical city-state of Athens. The other emanates from early Christianity.

Work and Leisure in Classical Greece

The Greeks have been mistakenly treated in leisure studies as sharing a common view on work and leisure. Greek perspectives, however, contain important differences and tensions (see Balme, 1984; Wood, 1988). Nonetheless, a view produced by a small cadre of gentlemen-philosophers who had the leisure and literacy to record their thoughts is preeminent in the Western tradition. Salient in this tradition are the theories of Plato and Aristotle.

Plato on Work and Leisure

In the simplest of terms, Plato believed that the good life consisted of knowing truth and living according to true knowledge. Truth was problematic, however, because Plato posited the existence of two worlds. One was the physical world of sense experience, consisting of what people see, hear, smell, and touch. This was the empirical world of change and impermanence, which most people falsely assumed to be true. The world of true knowledge was eternal and unchanging, existing in a transcendental realm of *ideas* or *forms*. While everything in the physical world was subject to change, decay, and destruction, the transcendental world of ideas was unchanging and eternal. As such, the material world was an imperfect and inferior reflection of the perfect and superior world of ideas.

Besides physical objects, concepts such as love, freedom, and justice also had corresponding forms in a sphere independent of and inaccessible to the senses. Therefore, it was necessary to investigate the transcendental world of pure and true ideas to know how life should be properly lived. Since the error-prone senses were not reliable, the realm of truth could only be discovered through philosophic contemplation. Accordingly, only persons endowed with great intellect and prepared by extensive and rigorous education were capable of attaining true knowledge. These exceptional individuals were the philosophers. Literally *lovers of truth,* they sought to escape the distractions and distortions of the physical world for the bliss of pure thought, the reward of truth, and the distinction of wisdom.

According to Plato, the goal of humanity was to discover truth and to live according to its principles. Truth, however, was only accessible to intellectuals of superior breeding. Possessing genuine knowledge, this select group of philosophers should also govern, organizing society by true moral principles. Labeled *gold* by Plato, *philosopher-kings* constituted the best class of citizens. The remainder of citizens were hierarchically ordered by a division of social labor corresponding to the goodness of their souls (Plato's social and political organization corresponds to his division of the soul into three parts: reason, spirit, and appetite, with reason being the finest [1961a, pp. 4.435–42]). The *auxiliaries* (silver class) assisted and supported the philosopher-kings. The third and lowest class (brass or bronze) consisted of citizens who performed the labor that supplied the goods and services needed by society (Plato, 1961a, p. 3.415a). Plato's ideal state thus operated by an organic structure of specialists performing the function for which they were suited by nature and training. Although all citizens contributed in their special capacity to the welfare and excellence of the state, only philosophers were capable of achieving the virtues of knowledge and civic leadership. As such, in the *Laws* Plato argues that the best citizens must not practice arts or crafts, because:

> A citizen has already a calling which will make full demands on him, in view of the constant practice and wide study it involves, in the preservation and enjoyment of the public social order—a task which permits of no relegation to the second place. (1961b, p. 8.846d)

Leisure was required to respond to this paramount calling, relieving the individual from the necessity to labor for a livelihood. Therefore, common labor had a positive role in Plato's theory, making it possible for a minority of citizens to avoid the necessity of laboring, which in turn permitted them to engage in philosophy and politics. Thus, while Plato valued labor, it was not at all on the same moral plane as the proper activities of leisure.

Moreover, while workers were instrumental in the good life, they could not live it, having neither the capacity nor the leisure required for the morally superior life. In *Theaetetus* Plato writes of two *characters* or types of people. The inferior type is prepared for a life of work. Conversely, the superior type, who are the philosophers, are "nursed in freedom and leisure," allowing them to live "the true life of happiness for gods

and men" (Plato, 1961c, pp. 175.e–176). Plato castigates those who would imagine themselves capable of doing philosophy and achieving the truth, calling them "that multitude of pretenders unfit by nature, whose souls are bowed and mutilated by their vulgar occupations even as their bodies are marred by their arts and crafts" (Plato, 1961a, p. 495.d). Persons who work with their hands are thus incapable of achieving moral excellence because they are naturally inferior to begin with and their work further damages their souls. The difference between leisure and physical work correlates perfectly with Plato's body-soul dichotomy (Solmsen, 1964). With the body representing imperfection and inferiority and the soul symbolizing perfection and superiority, Plato argues:

> So long as we keep to the body and our soul is contaminated with this imperfection, there is no chance of our ever attaining satisfactorily to our object, which we assert to be truth. . . . Worst of all, if we do not obtain any leisure from the body's claim and turn to some line of inquiry, the body intrudes once more into our investigations, interrupting, disturbing, and preventing us from getting a glimpse of truth (Plato, 1961d, pp. 66.b–d).

Thus, manual labor precludes the leisure needed for doing what is best. It also harms the soul, the seat of excellence, which is already naturally weak in workers. Plato directs in the *Laws* that "if a native stray from the pursuit of goodness into some trade or craft, they [the urban commissioners] shall correct him by reproach and degradation until he be brought back into the straight course" (1961b, p. 847.a). Only philosophers can reach the gods, for "no soul which has not practiced philosophy, and is not absolutely pure when it leaves the body, may attain to the divine nature; that is only for the lover of wisdom" (Plato, 1961d, pp. 82.b–c). Leisure, theoretical learning, and political leadership are thus reserved for the best, while the rest—slaves and workers—support their "betters" (cf., De Ste. Croix, 1981, pp. 411–412).

Work is thus honorable because it constructs the road to freedom and excellence. Yet, limited in their ability and spoiled by their labor, workers can only build the road. They cannot reach and enjoy the *summum bonum*. It is reserved for a superior class of citizens, who, instead of working for a living, are destined to spend their leisure working for freedom and excellence.

Aristotle on Work and Leisure

Like Plato, Aristotle's theory also achieves significance in the broader context of his systematic philosophy. In the *Politics* Aristotle makes a critical distinction. He argues that "a state exists for the sake of a good life, and not for the sake of life alone" (1984a, p. 1280a31). Of course, existence is impossible without work. Human beings, like all animals, must expend time and energy to sustain life. Yet there is another kind of life— the moral life—that is reserved for human beings. To understand it, Aristotle's concepts of god and the universe must be traced.

Aristotle's deity was not the Christian God who made the universe out of nothing and then ruled over it. Instead, self-sufficient god was pure reason, consisting of the first and final laws of an eternal and regenerating universe. Everything in the universe depended on god for its existence and purpose, making god the most perfect and finest object in the universe. The sole activity of god consisted of perpetual reflection on the first and final causes of being, which amounted to self-contemplation. Uninterruptedly immersed in reflection on immutable truth, god led the most excellent, independent, and pleasurable existence in the universe.

Aristotle conceived of the universe as a divinely ordered hierarchy that began with god at its pinnacle and descended through all species down to the simplest elements. Everything in the hierarchy was distinguished by a special function or purpose, which by nature it desired to actualize. The function of a species corresponded to its excellence, meaning that which it was best suited to do. Thus the function of a knife is to cut, and how well it cuts determines its excellence. Aristotle uses the example of a lyre-player to illustrate the relation between function and excellence, stating that "the function of a lyre-player is to play the lyre, and that of a good lyre-player is to do so well" (1984b, pp. 1098a11–12).

The place of a species in the hierarchy of being was divinely set by the degree to which it possessed reason and was capable of exercising the supreme contemplative activity that occupied god. Human beings had two unique functions and excellences, moral and intellectual. Moral excellence involved deliberation on how best to live individually and socially. Intellectual excellence involved understanding and delighting in the true principles of the universe. Aristotle contended that "the life according to intellect is best and pleasantest, since intellect more than anything else *is* man [i.e., his function]. This life therefore is also the happiest" (1984b, p. 1178a7). Intellectual excellence was the happiest because it involved "contemplation of god" (Aristotle, 1984c, p. 1249b18). In their capacity for wisdom, human beings were thus capable of participating in a limited way in the unrestricted happiness that god enjoyed in beholding the true nature of the universe (Taylor, 1955). Given that the contemplative being of god was "the best which we enjoy" (Aristotle, 1984d, p. 1072b14), contemplation constituted "the ideal life for man" (Ross, 1963, p. 211). Human beings, therefore, achieved the best life in the pursuit of theoretical wisdom (see Kraut, 1989; Lloyd, 1968; Ross, 1963; Taylor, 1955).

Aristotle recognized, however, that human beings were also social animals who came together to enjoy the good life. As such, "in a secondary degree the life in accordance with the other kind of excellence [moral] is happy; for the activities in accordance with this befit our human estate" (Aristotle, 1984b, p. 1178a8). The exact relation between intellectual and moral excellence has been the subject of extensive discussion and debate (see Ackrill [1974] and Kraut [1989] for different sides of the issue. Also see Hemingway's [1988] discussion on the subject as it relates to leisure). Suffice it to say that Aristotle believed both moral and intellectual excellences were integral parts of the good life. Contemplation was the most perfect and pleasant happiness, giving a divine crown to goodness. All things that were proper to the excellence of human beings, however, including, among other things, speech, music, friendship, gymnastics, and citizenship, were constituents of the good life (Owens, 1981).

The good life made great demands on people's time and energy. First of all was the brute fact of survival. Preoccupation with where the next meal was coming from or rain cascading in from a leaky roof interfered with contemplation. Philosophers were thus faced with a dilemma. Work was necessary to live, which was an obvious prerequisite of contemplation. But work severely encroached upon the good life. Only when people were liberated from having to work for the necessities of life could they turn to the good life. As such, leisure—freedom from the necessity to labor for a living—was a condition of the good life.

Aristotle underscored the moral imperative of leisure in the *Nicomachean Ethics,* declaring "happiness is thought to depend on leisure" (1984b, p. 1177b4). Labor, on the other hand, was inimical to happiness. Aristotle wrote that "no man can practice excellence who is living the life of a mechanic or laborer" (1984a, 1278a20). With its focus on survival and its operation in the hands rather than in the mind, labor precluded the ultimate goal of contemplation. Labor also took time away from participation in the civic and cultural life of the community. Aristotle looked disdainfully upon the common people (the *demos*) who worked with their hands and comprised the majority of Athens' population, contending that "citizens must not lead the life of artisans or tradesmen . . ." because, lacking sufficient leisure, "such a life is ignoble to excellence" (1984a, p. 1328b39). In another passage from the *Politics* Aristotle discusses who should be considered a citizen in the ideal state, asking "is the mechanic to be included?" (1984a, p. 1277b34). He answers:

> The best form of state will not admit them to citizenship; but if they are admitted, then our definition of the excellence of a citizen will not apply to every citizen, nor to every free man as such, *but only to those who are freed from necessary services* [emphasis added]. The necessary people are either slaves who minister to the wants of individuals, or mechanics and laborers who are the servants of the community. (1984a, pp. 1278a7–1278a13)

Aristotle then concludes that:

> the citizens must not lead the life of artisans or tradesmen, for such a life is ignoble and inimical to excellence. Neither must they be farmers, since leisure is necessary for the development of excellence and the performance of political duties. (1984a, pp. 1328b36–1329a1)

Even in the design of the city, Aristotle argues that separate space be set aside in the agora for the working class and the leisure class. He proposes a "freeman's agora," where "all trade should be excluded, and no artisan, farmer, or any such person allowed to enter, unless he be summoned by the magistrates" (1984a, pp. 1331a34–1331a35). There shall be two "agoras," then, a lower one where business and trade are conducted and an upper one devoted "to the life of leisure" (1984a, p. 1331b13). In Aristotle's eyes, then, all morally worthwhile action revolves around leisure.

Led by Plato and Aristotle, Greek philosophy recognizes the necessity of work. Moreover, work is not inherently degrading. What makes work servile is the *dependency* it creates. The condition of leisure cannot be achieved if one must harvest crops or submit to the "beck and call" of an employer. Plato and Aristotle generally speak well of farmers, who were prominent in the tradition of ancient Athens. Nonetheless, Aristotle excludes farmers from citizenship in his ideal state. Furthermore, their highest regard is reserved for *gentle-*

men-farmers, who could put down their tools whenever they wished, having slaves or hired freedmen to perform the farm work. What was demeaning was the *necessity* to labor because it produced dependence, which vitiated the opportunity for leisure and the realization of excellence and happiness in civic and cultural practices. The work of slaves, women, artisans, mechanics, and foreigners was justified by the natural order of the universe, making it possible for the finest human beings to discover truth, govern wisely, and create culture. The often hard, tedious, and painful labor needed to produce the goods and services in a society that lacked efficient technology was rationalized by asserting that workers were morally elevated by a higher culture than they were capable of producing themselves.

According to Austin and Vidal-Naquet (1977), the view of work and leisure espoused by Plato and Aristotle reflected "aristocratic values [that] were by and large not seriously challenged" (p. 17). Yet it is difficult to imagine that the ordinary citizens who performed the labor and comprised the majority of the population would have entirely embraced a cultural ideal that impugned them. More likely they would have taken umbrage with at least those parts that demeaned and attempted to exclude them. Indeed, there was a law in Athens prohibiting slurs based on one's occupation, suggesting an aristocratic prejudice toward labor and a definite reaction to it on the part of citizen-laborers (Ober, 1989). Since they did not systematically record their impressions, however, it is not explicitly known what ordinary Greek citizens thought. What Greek society as a whole thought about labor and leisure has been extrapolated by leisure studies from the writings of a few aristocratic philosophers, the likes of Plato and Aristotle. Nonetheless, there is sufficient evidence to question whether that account is representative.

Another View of Work and Leisure

Social vocabulary suggests that the citizens of the city-state Athens were not of one mind (see Donlan, 1980). In particular, the complex idea of freedom (*eleutheria*) was interpreted differently. For common citizens the idea of freedom included social, political, and economic liberty (Raaflaub, 1983). In her provocative analysis, Wood (1988) argues that common citizens' view of *eleutheria* emerged out of the peasant experience of dependence and independence. Formerly dependent on their aristocratic lords, peasants gained independence through democratic reforms. Central to their sense of liberation was the opportunity to labor for themselves rather than work under an aristocratic yoke. The freedom *to* labor, therefore, was a key component of their understanding of freedom.

Reacting to the new freedom and expanding power of people who were once their subjects, the idea of freedom was reformulated by aristocrats. The terms *eleutherios* (typical for a free man, noble), *eleutherios paideia* (education of a free and noble person), and *eleutheria technai* (free and noble occupations) were aristocratically inspired variations on the general theme of freedom (Raaflaub, 1983). In particular, *eleutherios paideia* was "an aristocratic concept, intimately connected with leisure, dignified and intellectual pursuits, and devotion to friends and public service. It was opposed to 'nonfree' training of the technites and *banausos* [workers] who were neither educated nor capable" (Raaflaub, 1983, p. 530). In opposition to the democratic conception of political freedom, whereby all citizens were free to participate in government, aristocrats stressed the personal qualities of individuals, notably their noble birth and liberal education, which made them, in their eyes, "truly free." By applying higher and more rigorous standards to the concept of freedom, aristocrats were able to underscore their superiority while defining the *demos* as unfree, licentious, and unworthy. Furthermore, aristocrats identified freedom *from* labor, a condition synonymous with leisure, as a vital form of freedom. Of course, this implied that people who found it necessary to work for a living were not free.

Therefore, the idea of leisure (*schole*) was also employed by aristocrats to strengthen their position against the working masses. Hunnicutt (1990) explains that Greeks used the word *schole* in two ways. One was the ordinary sense of having free time. The word was also used "in a comparative or superlative sense as 'freedom from a less important activity for a more (or the most) important activity'" (Hunnicutt, 1990, p. 213). Hunnicutt states that:

> Plato did believe that only a few could handle freedom from necessity [leisure] and that the majority, the uneducated and imprudent, would have to keep working. Because he lived in a relatively poor economy, he had little hope that the majority could be educated or lifted up out of poverty into leisure. (p. 213)

Therefore, only "truly free" aristocrats were prepared for leisure, because they had received *eleutherios paideia,* the education of a free and noble person, qualifying them for civic, cultural, and intellectual pursuits

(Raaflaub, 1983). Conversely, craftsmen were only trained for their narrow, dependent specialty, making them unfit for leisure in the eyes of aristocrats. Observing that "leisure is better than occupation [necessary labor]" (1984a, p. 1337b34), Aristotle recommended "a sort of education in which parents should train their sons, not as being useful or necessary [technical], but because it is liberal or noble" (1984a, p. 1238a31). The aristocratic implications of leisure and liberal education are apparent in Aristotle's discourse on music as a key aspect of liberal education and a noble activity of leisure. He admits that music is salutary for everyone as recreation and relaxation. Its most noble purpose, however, is the influence it has on the character and the soul of free men. Corresponding to his organic distinction between human beings, music performed at the theater should be of two types because:

> the spectators are of two kinds—the one free and educated, while the other a vulgar crowd composed of artisans, laborers, and the like—there ought to be contests and exhibitions instituted for the relaxation of the second class also. And the music will correspond to their minds; for as their minds are perverted from the natural state, so there are perverted modes and highly strung and unnaturally colored melodies. (1984a, p. 1342a18)

The aristocratic appropriation of leisure as a symbol of superiority may also help to explain why the *demos* turned to work as a sign of dignity and respect. Part of the aristocratic ideal of excellence was expressed through competition (*agon*) and heroic accomplishments, demonstrated in war, athletics, and other contests, such as music. The common people were partially or entirely excluded from these practices. Sport, for example, was largely reserved for leisured aristocrats until professionalization in the fourth century B.C. Where they were included, the masses were rarely capable of competing with aristocrats, who were better prepared thanks to their wealth and leisure. Therefore, the masses lacked sufficient access to the traditional stages of socially esteemed expression. Consequently, they may have turned to the virtues of work, emphasizing the freedom of independent labor and the excellence of craftsmanship as a way to show their merit.

Rather than a servile domain, then, independent work was likely a source of respect and dignity for citizens who labored for a living. Unfortunately, the *demos* left little record of their perspectives on work and leisure compared to aristocrats, who had the wealth and leisure to prepare and present their ideas. Nonetheless, a few written sources provide suggestive glimpses.

Some of the more successful craftsmen left evidence of the pride they took in their work, such as the seventh-century sculptor who dedicated a monument to Apollo with the inscription "Euthykartides the Naxian made and dedicated me" (Burford, 1972, p. 11). Competitions were held among craftsmen from the city-states. The epitaph of the fourth-century B.C. potter Bakchios read: "In the competitions which the city staged, of those who combine earth and fire [i.e., make pottery], Greece judged Bakchios the first in both character and in achievement. He took all the crowns" (Burford, 1972, p. 209). Because the practice of preparing epitaphs was rare in ancient Greece, it was remarkable that arts and crafts were mentioned at all, suggesting the standing they had in society (Burford, 1972). A craftsman dedicated his work as a tithe to Athena, the divinity of arts and crafts in Athens, with the inscription: "It is good for the skilled to exercise their skill according to their craft; For he who has a craft has a better life" (quoted in Dillon and Garland, 1994, p. 341).

Tributes to labor and technology grew as trade and craft expanded in Greece. In Sophocles' (1959) *Antigone* the chorus sings praise to the arts and crafts that people use to help themselves, calling "clever beyond all dreams the inventive craft that he has" (p. 171). The crafts are further glorified in Aeschylus' (1959) mid-fifth-century tragedy *Prometheus Bound*. Giving to human beings the fire he stole from Zeus, Prometheus pronounces "from it they shall learn many crafts" (p. 320), thus making it possible for humanity to create civilization. Highly idealized scenes on art work also glorify craft. Both art and literature, therefore, celebrated "the artisan's contributions to society, thereby legitimizing both the profession and its practitioners" (Bryant, 1996, p. 115).

Because leisure studies has mainly relied on the texts of aristocratic philosophers to understand labor, however, it has been commonly believed that the aristocratic disdain of labor was shared by those who had to work for a living. While the popular ideology created by aristocratic literature contained an antilabor ethos, "the masses were . . . willing to regard working for a living—at least by poor citizens—as respectable and proper" (Ober, 1989, p. 276). Similarly, Bryant (1996) concluded that while noblemen would have agreed with Plato and Aristotle regarding the impossibility of true citizenship for craftsmen, artisans themselves did not hold "these stereotypical slurs" (p. 113; also see Raaflaub, 1983, p. 532).

On the other hand, work for the sheer sake of work was not glorified (Wood, 1988). While free labor was probably respected by ordinary citizens, and skill admired and honored, the Greek attitude toward labor should not be confused with a "work ethic" similar to what grew out of Protestant ideology. The center of life for Greek citizens was not work, but rather the *polis,* the civic-cultural community. Moreover, leisure was a vital aspect of Athenian life. Athens provided ample leisure at no cost, including drama, music, dancing, athletic games, and processions (Balme, 1984). Furthermore, the democratic leader Pericles emphasized in his famous "Funeral Oration" that cultivated leisure was part of Athens' greatness (Thucydides, 1900, p. 126). Indicative of their free and equal status, working citizens, even the poorest, had their share of leisure (Finley, 1977), giving them access to the civic and cultural life that represented the best existence possible.

Although work was not despised by most Athenians, leisure was accepted as a cultural standard that stood until the Protestant Reformation. The labor-leisure distinction was likely a divide created by a literate elite to set themselves off from the *hoi polloi,* who were seen as threats to Athens' political and cultural institutions (Glotz, 1926). While the *demos* probably did not glorify work, it was a source of freedom and respect for them. Yet they also enjoyed leisure. Desiring both labor and leisure, however, was not inherently incompatible. Each played an important role in the complex idea of freedom for the common citizen. Leisure was probably preferred, especially by those who were faced with disagreeable labor. Moreover, the *demos* generally subscribed to aristocratic ideals. Nonetheless, a culture oriented to leisure should not be confused for a culture-wide disdain for labor. Neither should respect for labor be confused for its glorification. Both labor and leisure were valued by working citizens as opportunities that made it possible for them to enjoy full and respected lives in their community.

In sum, a monolithic view of work and leisure did not exist in ancient Greece. Greek civilization contained a variety of perspectives. Yet an ethic of leisure formulated by aristocratic philosophers was widely adopted in Greco-Roman times. It was not successfully challenged until the appearance of Christianity and its canon of beliefs.

The Judeo-Christian View

Judeo-Christian ideology represents a sharp departure from the legacy of classical Greece. Although not without its share of ambiguity and contradiction, Judeo-Christian beliefs mainly emphasize the importance of labor. Respect for work was enhanced by elevating it to a means of spiritual development, thus spreading seeds for the modern gospel of work. While work gained greater prominence, leisure assumed a muted role that was revived during the Middle Ages.

According to Richardson (1952), the biblical idea of work is manifested in three principal senses. First is the *work of God's creation.* Allusions depicting God as a creative worker are plentiful. The Old Testament states, "In the beginning God created the heaven and the earth" (Gen. 1:1) and "on the seventh day God ended his work which he had made; and he rested on the seventh day from all his work which he had made" (Gen. 2:2). In I Corinthians, God is described as "a wise master builder" (3:10). Second is *human work,* referring to normal, everyday labor. Created in God's image, human beings are referred to in I Corinthians as "laborers together with God" (3:9). Third, work appears metaphorically in the Bible, as in "working" for the cause of Christ. In Matthew, Jesus tells four fishermen, "Follow me, and I will make you fishers of men" (4:19). They immediately drop their material work to take up the spiritual work of Christ.

God, then, is portrayed as a Divine Worker, and work is part of His plan and ordinance, for the "Lord God took the man and put him in the Garden of Eden to till it and keep it" (Gen. 2:15). Yet a tension surfaces. Work has also been treated as a penalty meted out by God for original sin. Joyous and pleasant in Paradise, work is made painful and exhausting as punishment for Adam's disobedience (Geoghegan, 1945). Human beings must now *toil* to earn a living. Yet work also offers the possibility of redemption in the process of salvation (Ryken, 1995). Work, then, has two sides, one blessed, the other cursed. How work manifests itself depends on the worker's faith in God and attitude toward work.

The once popularly held view that Christianity resulted from class struggle has been refuted (Stark, 1996). Nonetheless, its themes of equality, brotherhood, and respect for work surely appealed to the lower classes. The fact that Christ was a carpenter and the apostles were fishermen, occupations considered servile in the Greek view, further underscores the attraction Christianity probably had for the working class. The appeal of Christianity to burdened workers is pal-pable in Matthew, where Christ says "Come unto me, all *ye* that labor and are heavy laden" (11:28).

Therefore, work was strongly encouraged in early Christianity (Troeltsch, 1931). In II Thessalonians, St. Paul, a tentmaker by trade, commands:

> if any would not work, neither should he eat. For we hear that there are some who walk among you disorderly, working not at all, but are busybodies. Now them that are such we command and exhort by our Lord Jesus Christ, that with quietness they work, and eat their own bread. (3:10–13)

In his monumental *City of God,* St. Augustine (1972) praises the supreme creative power of Almighty God, citing Psalm 46: "Come and see the works of the Lord, the wonders he has placed on the earth" (7:28). Elsewhere he exclaims, "Who can adequately describe, or even imagine, the work of the Almighty?" (22:24). St. Augustine also celebrates the creative capacities of human beings, God's greatest creation. Among other things, he praises agriculture, navigation, pottery, theater, medicine, music, astronomy, and philosophy (22:24).

Besides being necessary for existence, work fostered the important habits of sobriety, discipline, and industry. It also facilitated independence and charity. But work was not an ethical ideal capable of standing on its own, for the ultimate good rested not on earth, but in heaven. Despite all that was performed and produced in the name of work, it was still primarily a means for spiritual development. Work and its products, therefore, were not to be worshipped for their own sake. They were good only insofar as they glorified God and increased the holy fitness of humankind.

As early Christian beliefs elevated the idea of work, the Greek ideal of leisure weakened. The Greek conception of happiness (*eudaimonia*), which consisted of such excellences as philosophy and citizenship, was no longer relevant in a doctrine that was transcendentally fixed on the supernatural. Still, the idea of leisure was not altogether vanquished. While the Old Testament portrays Hebrew leaders working and rabbis engaged in manual labor, "some rabbis argued that the study of the Torah was superior to physical work and that it was impossible to attain wisdom and be engaged in physical work" (Applebaum, 1992, p. 181). The Greek idea of leisure is further evident in Ecclesiasticus, written in Hebrew between 200 and 180 B.C., which reads, "The wisdom of the scribe cometh by opportunity of leisure; and he that hath little business shall become wise" (38:24–39:11; quoted from Barker, 1956, p. 140). The Bible also contains references suggestive of a role for leisure in God's plan. Psalm 46:8 reads, "Come, behold the works of the Lord," followed by "Be still, and know that I *am* God" (46:10), a passage some interpreters have taken as a prescription for leisure (cf., Bregha, 1991, p. 53). Applebaum (1992) refers to the story about Martha and Mary in Luke 10:38–42 as an example of ambivalence toward work and leisure:

> Christ arrives at Martha's house, whereupon Mary, who was helping Martha with the cleaning and the other housework, interrupted her work and went up to Christ to talk to him. When Martha complained to Christ about Mary ceasing to help her, Christ replied that hers [Mary's] was the "better way." This was later interpreted by Christian theologians as indicating that Christ considered the life of contemplation as superior to the life of work. (pp. 207–208)

The Bible contains ample warrant for leisure (Ryken, 1995). Genesis reads:

> And on the seventh day God ended his work which he had made; and he rested on the seventh day from all his work which he had made. And God blessed the seventh day, and sanctified it: because that in it he had rested from all his work which God created and made. (2:2–3)

God's blessing and sanctification of the seventh day is formalized in the Fourth Commandment, where He commands "the seventh day is the Sabbath of the Lord thy God: in it thou shalt not do any work" (Exod. 20:10).

A common interpretation is that God's pattern for life consists of a rhythmic harmony between work and leisure. The Book of Ecclesiastes speaks of a time for everything, "A time to weep, and a time to laugh; a time to mourn, and a time to dance" (3:4). Therefore, a life devoted exclusively either to work or to leisure is incomplete. Moreover, the main purpose of leisure is not just to rehabilitate the worker for another round of work. As Pieper (1952) instructs, the point of leisure is for human beings, made in the image of God, to be free to behold and celebrate the glory and goodness of creation. The principal purpose of leisure, then, lies in worship and celebration. As the Lord worked for six days in creating the heavens, the earth, the seas, and the creatures, He paused to witness the goodness of all that he had made. Similarly, human beings should cease their labors to rejoice in God and His gifts. God

not only made life useful, He also created it as a gift to be lived abundantly and joyously for its own sake (Ryken, 1995).

Despite the dissonance created by the "curse of labor," work was thus a vital source in the development of Christianity. Christian theology, in turn, contributed generously to the ideology of work. Although classical leisure lost much of its authority, it receded rather than disappeared. A legitimate place for leisure was evident in early Christian teachings. Nonetheless, the "gospel of work" was stamped in the Western mind, where it was reinforced by monasticism.

Monasticism and the Middle Ages

Christian monasticism describes the life of Christian devotees who sought religious purity and enlightenment by removing themselves from the worldliness surrounding the Christian Church. Although various monastic figures and movements contributed to enhanced respect for labor, St. Benedict (480–550) and the Benedictines are the most renowned. Benedict gave detailed directions on labor in the *Regula,* a set of rules governing monastic life. In it he ordered that "leisure is the enemy of the soul, and for this reason the brothers must spend a certain amount of time in doing manual work as well as the time spent in divine reading" (quoted in Ovitt, 1986, p. 498). Yet, indicative of the difficulty in identifying a clear distinction between work and leisure in monastic thought, William of St. Thierry distinguished between idleness and the constructive use of leisure, which enhanced the development of the soul (Stock, 1985). Therefore, while monasticism raised the general esteem for labor in the Middle Ages, the Judeo-Christian legacy "was to offer medieval man an ideological arsenal containing weapons for the defense of every position, in favor both of labor and nonlabor" (Le Goff, 1980, p. 77). Applebaum's (1992) description of the disagreement between two monastic orders nicely illustrates the debate:

> The Cistercians accused the Cluniacs of giving up manual labor and setting up a hierarchy of occupations, with prayer and meditation as the higher calling and manual labor as the lower and even despised calling. The Cluniacs argued that it was impossible to engage in prayer and meditation and to also work. They contended that one needed time and release from one activity to devote oneself to the higher callings of the Church. It sounded

much like Aristotle's argument that leisure was the precondition for the life of contemplation. (p. 208)

In general, then, the Middle Ages did not offer a clearly defined theory of work and leisure comparable to the Greco-Roman period (Stock, 1985). Nonetheless, theories of work and leisure were implicitly raised through other conceptual programs. For example, according to the Catholic theologian St. Thomas Aquinas (1225–1274), everything was subordinate to prayer and the contemplation of God. Accordingly, he asserted that whoever could live without working was under no obligation to labor (Tilgher, 1930). Contending that freedom from physical work was required in order to engage in spiritual work, Aquinas explained that:

> the final happiness of man consists in the contemplation of truth. This act alone in man is proper to him, and is in no way shared by any other being in the world. This is sought for its own sake, and is directed to no other end beyond itself. . . . *[I]f we look at things rightly, we may see that all human occupation seem to be ministerial to the service of the contemplators of truth* [emphasis added]. (quoted in Randall, 1926, p. 95)

The classical conception of leisure was thus quietly revived by Aquinas to legitimize the cultural ideal of the contemplative life. What at first appears to be framed as work starts to look more like leisure on closer inspection (Pieper, 1952). Indeed, it was often impossible to distinguish between work and leisure because they were much more interwoven during the Middle Ages compared to today (Stock, 1985).

Attitudes toward work and leisure among the literate in the Middle Ages were often expressed in debates over the *vita activa* and the *vita contemplativa*. The argument focused on whether life should be lived in peaceful solitude or, on the other hand, in an active public life. In the fourteenth century, Petrarch urged retreat into private repose and the pleasures of contemplation (Zeitlin, 1924). Castiglione's (1959) *The Book of the Courtier,* printed in 1528, urges the courtier (court gentleman) to know how to use the blessing of leisure. While the courtier should cultivate both the active and the contemplative spheres, it is maintained that "the end of the active life should be contemplation, as peace is the end of war and repose of toil" (p. 63). Again, however, an explicit theory of work and leisure does not stand out, for the distinction between work and

leisure was not clearly established in an age where the two often blended.

The Renaissance was distinguished by a great burst and flowering of creative energy. Enthusiasm for the arts and crafts burgeoned, boosting the respectability of work. Practiced as an activity of leisure, experimental science also gained credibility, giving further legitimacy to laboring with the materials of nature for the purpose of learning the secrets and benefits of God's creation (Sylvester, 1994).

Despite the enhanced regard for skilled work, however, manual labor continued to receive negative assessments from those who wished to distinguish themselves from manual laborers in order to preserve their power and position. Peacham's (1634) guide for raising gentlemen instructed that "whosoever labor for their livelihood and gain, have no share in Nobility or Gentry" (p. 12). Similarly, Mulcaster (1888) wrote in 1561 that gentlemen had certain things appointed to them by God, including *"great leasure* to use libertie, where the meanest must labor" (p. 193). Therefore, even with religious sanction as an instrument for charity, discipline, and atonement, as well as the respect it gained during the Renaissance, labor was still, in the words of Arendt (1958), "the lowest, most despised condition" (p. 101). A revolution in thinking was in store, however, that would help lift labor "to the highest rank, as the most esteemed of all human activities" (Arendt, 1958, p. 101).

The Great Change

The Protestant Reformation was one of the defining events in the making of the modern identity (Taylor, 1989), producing a "profound spiritual revolution which established work in the modern mind as the base and key of life" (Tilgher, 1930, p. 47). In the process, Aristotle's contention that leisure was the only life fit for a human being was successfully challenged and replaced by Zinzendorf's (1869–1874) maxim that "man works not only to live, but man lives that he may work" (p. 428). This dimension of the Reformation has been thematized as the Protestant work ethic.

The transformation of work and leisure was the product of various social, economic, political, and geographic factors. Nonetheless, the Protestant work ethic was one of the central intellectual developments in changing attitudes toward labor and leisure. Along with Martin Luther's positive evaluation of work, John Calvin's doctrine of callings was among its most paramount features. The idea of a calling included two facets. One was a general calling that consisted of the faithful commitment of all Christians to serve God in every thought and deed. The other was the particular calling God had for each person, which amounted to the job individuals performed. Significantly, all callings or jobs were equal in God's eyes. Puritan literature is replete with references to the value and dignity of all work, "howsoever grosse they appear outwardly" (Perkins, 1616–1618: 391). Joseph Hall preached that "the homeliest service that we doe in an honest calling, though it be but to plowe, or digge, if one in obedience, and conscience of God's Commandment, is crowned with an ample reward" (cited in George and George, 1961, p. 139n). Furthermore, it was expected that one's calling would be conducted with seriousness, industry, diligence, and discipline.

Another critical feature of Protestantism was Luther's concept of predestination. According to this doctrine, human beings were predestined by God to either heaven or hell. Because heaven's elect were known only to God, people sought some evidence they were among the chosen. Laboring continuously at a productive calling was taken as a sign of election, alleviating the pervasive anxiety that accompanied a real fear of hell's eternal flames and torments (Haller, 1939). Consequently, productive labor was increasingly esteemed. On the other hand idleness, condemned as wasteful and depraved, was taken as proof of damnation. Because it was not visibly active and produced nothing useful, the idea of leisure inherited from Aristotle was treated as idle and wasteful (Jones, 1961), leading to its devaluation.

Protestantism also departed from Aristotle on the topic of pleasure. Aristotle praised the pleasure that attended virtuous activity, with contemplative leisure being the best and the most pleasant of all. Pleasure had a restricted place in Protestant life. Because God had created nature, people were not to shun the things of this world. Yet neither were they to become absorbed in them at the neglect of God. Pleasure was condoned in the context of godly living, and there is considerable evidence of Puritans enjoying the pleasures of leisure (see Daniels, 1995). Yet it was more often distrusted as a perilous distraction from the primary duty to glorify God through work and prayer. Puritans inveighed against unholy pleasures and prohibited some. Prynne (1633) wrote that worldly pleasures "are no part, no particle of a Christian's comfort; he can live a most happy joyful life without them; yea he can hardly live happily or safely with them" (p. 966). Therefore, while Puritans were not the killjoys of popular accounts, their ambivalence toward the pleasures of leisure led them to embrace industry and seriousness.

The Protestant work ethic also reinvigorated the debate of the good life. According to the aristocratic philosophers of ancient Greece, the good life centered around the morally superior activities of contempla-

tion and civic participation, which necessitated leisure (Solmsen, 1964). Ordinary life, which consisted of survival and maintenance activities, such as trade, farming, housework, and the mechanical arts, was left to women, slaves, peasants, and foreigners. Passed on through the centuries, this tradition made it possible for the upper class to seek its self-proclaimed excellence at the expense of the laboring masses. Against Greco-Roman elitism, the Protestant Reformation relocated the good life from the so-called higher pursuits of a leisured aristocracy to the wide assortment of virtuous callings found in the ordinary lives of laboring people. This represented a dramatic shift in the hierarchy of social valuation from an aristocratic leisure class to a productive laboring class (Taylor, 1989). With the dignity of all callings celebrated, labor was reshaped into a virtue and the embodiment of the good life. Leisure, on the other hand, took two forms. One was idleness, which for Protestants represented the corruptive breeding ground for ungodly pleasures. The other was recreation, whose derivative value rested in its utility for enhancing the ability of people to perform their callings. Thus, while work was ascending to the core of the good life, leisure was descending from a noble condition divorced as much as possible from work to either the servant of work (recreation) or the accomplice of vice (idleness).

The Protestant Reformation established labor as a virtue, a religious duty, and the embodiment of the good life. St. Paul's admonition to work or starve was raised to the status of a cultural ideal. Furthermore, by rejecting Roman Catholic theology and its intellectual underpinnings steeped in Greek philosophy, the Protestant Reformation devalued classical leisure, characterizing it as idle and useless. As the Protestant work ethic was reshaped by secular forces, however, labor became more an end in itself and less a means of glorifying God. Gradually, labor became an important moral and theoretical category in its own right. Among other secular contributors, the likes of Adam Smith, Jean Jacques Rousseau, and J. S. Mill, two prominent theorists were especially responsible for redefining and consequently redirecting the concept of labor.

Locke's and Marx's Labor Theories of Value

Two more different figures than John Locke (1632–1704) and Karl Marx (1818–1883) are hardly imaginable. Locke was a wealthy landowner who sought to protect property. Marx was sometimes destitute and envisaged the abolition of private property. Locke promoted capitalism, Marx preached its destruction. Locke championed the bourgeois, Marx celebrated the proletarian. Yet they agreed on one thing—labor was the source of value and the essence of humanity.

The task John Locke (1980) set for himself in chapter five of the *Second Treatise on Government* was the justification of property rights. Because human beings were placed on earth by God to "subdue the earth" and "improve it for the benefit of life" (Sect. 32), they had a natural right to appropriate nature as private property. *Labor* was the method Locke designated for appropriating nature and creating useful benefits. Whatever individuals mixed their labor with became their own as long as there was enough property for others and what was appropriated did not spoil. Locke later circumvented these restrictions by means of two principles. First, lack of property available to others was justified if the appropriated land yielded greater productivity and more benefits for all. Second, since money does not spoil, it could be accumulated in unlimited amounts. Consequently, Locke broke through centuries-old religious injunctions against unrestricted wealth by justifying in God's name the endless accumulation of private property in the form of productive capital. In the course of legitimizing the accumulation of private property, Locke provided moral justification for modern capitalism (Macpherson, 1962).

Labor, however, was far more than an instrument of appropriation. It was also the basis of value, "for it is *labor,* indeed that *puts the difference of value* on everything" (Sect. 40). By making productive labor the essence of value and the main expression of personality, Locke secularized the Protestant work ethic, creating the basis for the modern conception of work (Hundert, 1971). Over time, productive labor and profit became concrete reflections of worth, success, rationality, and happiness (see Bernstein, 1997). The creation of wealth, then, became viewed as an economic benefit *and* a moral virtue, which favored the class of bourgeois capitalists seeking sanction for their business practices.

In addition to making productive labor the basis of all that was good and valuable, Locke considered idleness immoral. Idleness was broadly conceived as applying to the nonworking poor as well as to what Locke perceived as the dissipative leisure of the upper class. He recommended industry as a remedy for idleness, which was enforced on the poor and encouraged for the middle and upper classes. Locke was one of the original advocates of what might best be called *industrious recreation.* Dismissing the view of leisure held by his upper class contemporaries as *freedom from labor,* Locke regarded leisure as *freedom for refreshing labor.* Arguing that "[d]elving, planting, inoculating, or any the like profitable employments, would be no less

a diversion, than any of the idle sports in fashion" Locke (1963) cautioned, "Nor let it be thought, that I mistake, when I call . . . exercises of manual arts, diversions or recreations; for recreation is not being idle . . . but easing the wearied part by change of business" (Locke, 1963, Sect. 206). Emphasizing his belief that leisure should be spent in recreative industry, he counseled that "a young man will have time enough, from his serious and main business, to learn almost any trade. It is for want of application, and not of leisure, that men are not skilful in more arts than one" (Locke, 1963, Sect. 208).

By defining the essence of humankind in terms of labor, Locke contributed profoundly to the modern conception of work (Hundert, 1971). Although Protestantism had already lifted work to a virtue, Locke greatly assisted the process of secularization, making labor the essence of value and the main expression of personality. Embodied in capitalism, productive labor became the chief source and symbol of meaning and value. At the same time, Locke reinforced the transformation of leisure, approving of leisure that took the form of rationally recreative labor while dismissing idleness and dissipative pleasure altogether.

Marx represents a striking counterpoint to Locke and one of the pivotal developments in the history of work and leisure. The Athenian ideal viewed reason as the essence of humanity. Hence, leisure was the most desirable condition for the purpose of the good life. Christianity held that all goodness rested in God. Everything else, whether labor or leisure, was a means for achieving that single, superior end. Marx contended, however, that the essence of human beings was found in neither Reason nor God. In Marx's eyes, human beings literally *made* themselves through the various labors they performed. As such, labor defined humanity, making possible self-realization and happiness.

Marx conceived of two spheres of labor in which people realized their powers. One was materially necessary work, the kind required for the survival of individuals and the maintenance of society. The other was creative work, which was needed for achieving higher human capacities, such as art, science, and learning. Thus, the potential of human beings and their social relations—as well as their freedom, fulfillment, and happiness—were realized in both the materially necessary and culturally creative spheres of labor.

Capitalism, however, alienated workers from the life-affirming activity of labor. In order to survive, workers were forced to sell their labor cheaply to the property-owning capitalists. Furthermore, because capitalists controlled the means of production, they were able to dictate the speed, length, and nature of production. Work was experienced as stressful drudgery due to the long hours and rapid pace and as fragmented, monotonous, and meaningless due to the division of labor. Unable to develop and exercise their capacities, dehumanized workers suffered alienation.

Exploited workers could recover their freedom and happiness, however, through a classless society in which the means of production and fruits of labor were shared by everyone. Marx anticipated that in communism individuals would not be constrained by a strict division of specialized labor that stunted their development. Instead, they would assume a variety of activities befitting the multiple capacities of humankind. Marx later realized, however, that such diversely creative occupations were unlikely in an increasingly technological society. Most modern industrial work was simply too dull, fragmented, and repetitive to satisfy human powers. Although technology could produce sufficient material necessities for everyone's welfare, workers continued to suffer degradation and unhappiness due to the conditions of industrial labor. Furthermore, scientific technology was making human labor in the material sphere irrelevant, as workers found themselves simply tending the machines that performed the activity that once affirmed men and women with worth, meaning, and dignity. Marx (1981) proposed to rehabilitate the dignity and well-being of workers in volume three of *Capital,* writing that:

> the realm of freedom actually begins only where labor which is determined by necessity and mundane considerations ceases. . . . Beyond [the realm of necessity] begins that development of human potentiality for its own sake, the true realm of freedom, which however can only flourish upon that realm of necessity as its basis. *The shortening of the working day is its fundamental prerequisite* [emphasis added]. (p. 959)

Machine technology would thus make it possible to reduce to a minimum the time needed to produce the necessities of life, expanding free time or leisure. Leisure, in turn, would consist of free and creative activity, leading to self-realization and happiness. In this respect, Marx and Aristotle are similar. Leisure should not consist of amusements better suited for rest and relaxation. Although they have their place in helping people to recuperate from their labors, they are not the stuff of leisure. In Marx's words, "[Labor] becomes attractive work, the individual's self-realization, which in no way means that it becomes mere fun, mere amusement. . . . Really free working, e.g., composing, is at the same time precisely the most damned seriousness"

(Marx, 1971, p. 611). Thus leisure is spent laboring freely in the production of creative works done for their own sake. In sum, Marx proposes to reduce unfulfilling labor to a minimum so that fulfilling kinds of labor (his examples are drawn from art, learning, and science) may occupy the free time of human beings.

While both Locke and Marx located the essence of human nature and the achievement of self-realization in labor, their theories paved paths that led in different directions. Locke's theory supported a secularized work ethic that prized rationality, industriousness, economic productivity, and the accumulation of wealth. Conversely, Marx sought to unmask the immorality of capitalist labor. Furthermore, Locke saw leisure as a means to strengthen industriousness. Marx, on the other hand, recommended the reduction of necessary labor in order to expand leisure for the purpose of free and creative labor.

Embodied in modern capitalist principles of production, consumption, and accumulation, Locke's theory of labor has prevailed. Indeed, labor and leisure are valued in capitalism insofar as they are economically productive. Yet one of the contradictions of modern capitalism is that work has increasingly been unable to satisfy adequately the moral and spiritual expectations we have learned to ask of it. To quote from Studs Terkel's (1974) *Working,* many modern jobs "are too small for our spirit" (p. xxiv). The stakes are raised further when the failure of jobs to meet our existential needs is compounded by the possibility of fewer jobs in the future.

Conclusion

Many events, developments, and individuals in the rich and complex history of work and leisure have gone unmentioned or have received too few words in this discussion. Social, geographic, economic, and political factors have also been neglected or ignored. Limited space has made it necessary to focus on the main roots and pivotal transformations in the intellectual history of work and leisure. Nonetheless, as a starting point, awareness of the historical theories of work and leisure can open our eyes to the roles they have played, and can be made to play, in our lives. Toward that end, I wish to finish by making a few brief observations.

At the beginning of this chapter, I referred to a group of social theorists who contend that work and leisure are on the verge of a major transformation. They predict that increasing automation aimed at reducing labor costs will dramatically reduce the number of jobs, affecting the nature of work and leisure. Whether or not this occurs remains to be seen. Indeed, the future of work and leisure is a controversial issue. It is easy to find sources that diametrically disagree, one arguing that jobs are disappearing (e.g., Bartlett and Steele, 1996) while another contends that the future of jobs has never been brighter (e.g., Judy and D'Amico, 1997).

The reality is that work and leisure have been steadily undergoing profound changes since the Industrial Revolution. Some of the most significant changes with leisure have occurred as a result of consumption, commodification, commercialization, and professionalization. Automation, deskilling, division of labor, as well as part-time and temporary jobs, have radically transformed work. As a consequence, many modern jobs are unable to deliver on the work ethic's promise of dignity, identity, and self-worth. Furthermore, since capitalism is fundamentally oriented to the needs of consumers rather than those of workers, occupations are, by and large, inadequate for satisfying the creative potential of human beings (Saunders, 1995). Yet leisure is not widely appreciated as an opportunity for unpaid endeavors that meet our creative and spiritual needs. Therefore, even if widespread joblessness does not occur, the question persists of how people will meet their nonmaterial needs in a society that has plenty of jobs, but not enough meaningful work. In short, what will people do without work as the spiritual center of secular life or, on the other hand, with jobs that are despirited? Will free time become a suitable alternative for creative, worthwhile, and meaningful endeavors? Or will leisure continue along a spiritually barren path of enervating entertainment and compulsive consumption?

The respiritualization of work and leisure will require dramatic changes in social, economic, and political landscapes. First of all, however, the capacity to create policies and programs will depend on the understanding and imagination that can be brought to the subject of work and leisure. Structural change, in short, will require a profound change in perspective. Borrowing from Clark and Critcher's (1985) adaptation of a quote by Marx, men and women create work and leisure, but they do not do it just as they please. Their stand in the present and stance toward the future are historically conditioned. Being historically conditioned, however, is not the same as being historically aware, which suggests a conscious hand in creating one's condition. We would benefit, then, from understanding how past ideologies of work and leisure have moved us closer to or farther from more fulfilling lives.

As is often the case, education is our best hope. Yet currently education is mainly structured to prepare individuals for economic roles. A different sort of education is thus demanded that devotes attention to work not only in the form of a job, but as the constructive content of leisure as well. As such, education should prepare people for a variety of creative labors, such as art (including such manual arts as cooking and carpentry), sport, science, technology, languages, the humanities, and civic participation. Different institutions, including leisure services, would assist an eclectically educated public to achieve individual and social goals through autonomous work performed during leisure. Moreover, reformed education should enable people to understand how ideologies of work and leisure have shaped their social circumstances. Historically aware, people might have a greater hand in deciding what in their traditions is worth preserving, what requires adjustment, and what must be discarded. Wishing to emphasize the importance of historical awareness, I would like to conclude with a brief story.

I teach an undergraduate class that surveys the history of work and leisure. I invited the president of my university to join a panel addressing the subject. In the course of a lively discussion, several provocative proposals were suggested, including recognizing the importance of education for leisure as a formal function of the university. (Of course, at one time education for leisure *was* the purpose of a liberal education.) In a subsequent exchange a day or so after the class, the president proffered that perhaps the word *leisure* was problematic, and suggested that a new word should be found that embraced its values without its negative connotations. I used her proposal as a class activity the following day, asking my students if they could recommend an alternative term that conveyed the finest qualities of leisure. After several interesting and a few far-fetched suggestions, a student flung her hand upward in a fit of frustration. She exclaimed, "Why must something new be invented? The answer is behind us if we only bothered to look! Whether it's a job or leisure, people need to work at what they love!" Further provoked, conversation turned to the subject of what deserves our loving care. Drawing from traditions inherited from, among others, Greece, the Bible, and Marx, references were made to friends, family, talents, communities, and higher purposes, both sacred and secular. Thus on this day, as the students critiqued the present, the intellectual past was used as a moral compass, orienting them to their uncertain future.

References

Ackrill, J. (1974). Aristotle on Eudaimonia. *Proceedings of the British Academy, 60,* 339–359.

Aeschylus. (1959). Prometheus bound (D. Grene, Trans.). In D. Grene & R. Lattimore (Eds.), *The complete Greek tragedies* (Vol. 1). Chicago, IL: The University of Chicago Press.

Applebaum, H. (1992). *The concept of work: Ancient, medieval, and modern.* Albany, NY: State University of New York Press.

Arendt, H. (1958). *The human condition.* Chicago, IL: The University of Chicago Press.

Aristotle. (1984a). Politics. In J. Barnes (Ed.), *The complete works of Aristotle* (Rev. ed.). Princeton, NJ: Princeton University Press.

Aristotle. (1984b). Nicomachean ethics. In J. Barnes (Ed.), *The complete works of Aristotle* (Rev. ed.). Princeton, NJ: Princeton University Press.

Aristotle. (1984c). Eudemian ethics. In J. Barnes (Ed.), *The complete works of Aristotle* (Rev. ed.). Princeton, NJ: Princeton University Press.

Aristotle. (1984d). Metaphysics. In J. Barnes (Ed.), *The complete works of Aristotle* (Rev. ed.). Princeton, NJ: Princeton University Press.

Aronowitz, S., & DiFazio, W. (1994). *The jobless future.* Minneapolis, MN: University of Minnesota Press.

Austin, M., & Vidal-Naquet, P. (1977). *Economic and social history of ancient Greece.* Berkeley, CA: University of California Press.

Balme, M. (1984). Attitudes to work and leisure in ancient Greece. *Greece & Rome, 31*(2), 140–152.

Barker, E. (1956). *From Alexander to Constantine: Passages, and documents illustrating the history of social and political ideas, 336 B.C.–A.D. 337.* Oxford, UK: Clarendon Press.

Barlett, D., & Steele, J. (1996). *America: Who stole the dream?* Kansas City, MO: Andrews & McMeel.

Bernstein, P. (1997). *American work values: Their origin and development.* Albany, NY: State University of New York Press.

Bregha, F. (1991). Leisure and free reexamined. In T. Goodale & P. Witt (Eds.), *Recreation and leisure: Issues in an era of change* (pp. 47–54). State College, PA: Venture Publishing, Inc.

Bryant, J. (1996). *Moral codes and social structure in ancient Greece: A sociology of Greek ethics from Homer to the Epicureans and Stoics.* Albany, NY: State University of New York Press.

Burford, D. (1972). *Craftsmen in Greek and Roman society.* Ithaca, NY: Cornell University Press.

Castiglione. (1959). *The book of the courtier* (F. Simpson, Ed. and Trans.). New York, NY: Frederick Ungar.

Clarke, J., & Critcher, C. (1985). *The devil makes work: Leisure in capitalist Britain.* Urbana, IL: University of Illinois Press.

Daniels, B. (1995). *Puritans at play: Leisure and recreation in colonial New England.* New York, NY: St. Martin's Griffin.

Desan, P. (1995). Work in the Renaissance. *Journal of Medieval and Renaissance Studies, 25*(1), 1–15.

De Grazia, S. (1962). *Of time, work, and leisure.* New York, NY: Twentieth Century Fund.

De Ste. Croix, G. E. M. (1981). *The class struggle in the ancient Greek world.* Ithaca, NY: Cornell University Press.

Dillon, M., & Garland, L. (1994). *Ancient Greece: Social and historical documents from archaic times to the death of Socrates.* New York, NY: Routledge.

Donlan, W. (1980). *The aristocratic ideal in ancient Greece.* Lawrence, KS: Coronado Press.

Dunkerley, M. (1996). *The jobless economy? Computer technology in the world of work.* Cambridge, MA: Blackwell.

Finley, M. (1977). *The ancient Greeks.* New York, NY: Penguin Books.

Geoghegan, A. (1945). *The attitude toward labor in early Christianity and ancient culture.* Washington, DC: The Catholic University of America Press.

George, C. H., & George, K. (1961). *The Protestant mind of the English reformation, 1570–1640.* Princeton, NJ: Princeton University Press.

Glotz, G. (1926). *Ancient Greece at work.* New York, NY: Barnes & Noble.

Haller, W. (1939). *The rise of Puritanism.* New York, NY: Harper.

Hemingway, J. (1988). Leisure and civility: Reflections on a Greek ideal. *Leisure Sciences, 10,* 179–191.

Hundert, E. (1971). The making of homo faber: John Locke between ideology and history. *Journal of the History of Ideas, 33,* 3–22.

Hunnicutt, B. (1990). Leisure and play in Plato's teaching and philosophy of learning. *Leisure Sciences, 12,* 211–227.

Jones, R. F. (1961). *Ancients and moderns: A study of the rise of the scientific movement in seventeenth-century England.* New York, NY: Dover Publications.

Judy, R., & D'Amico, C. (1997). *Work force 2020: Work and workers in the twenty-first century.* Indianapolis, IN: Hudson Institute.

Kraut, R. (1989). *Aristotle on the human good.* Princeton, NJ: Princeton University Press.

Le Goff, J. (1980). *Time, work, and culture in the Middle Ages* (A. Goldhammer, Trans.). Chicago, IL: University of Chicago Press.

Lloyd, G. (1968). *Aristotle: The growth and structure of his thought*. London, UK: Cambridge University Press.

Locke, J. (1963). Some thoughts concerning education. In *The works of John Locke* (Vol. 9). Aalen, Germany: Scientia Verlag.

Locke, J. (1980). *Second treatise of government* (C. Macpherson, Ed.). Indianapolis, IN: Hackett.

McLellan, D. (1971). *The thought of Karl Marx*. London, UK: Macmillan Publishing.

Macpherson, C. (1962). *The political theory of possessive individualism*. New York, NY: Oxford University Press.

Marx, K. (1981). *Capital* (Vol. 3). New York, NY: Penguin.

Marx, K. (1971). *The grundrisse*. New York, NY: Harper & Row.

Mulcaster, R. (1888). *Positions*. London, UK: Longmans, Green.

Ober, J. (1989). *Mass and elite in democratic Athens: Rhetoric, ideology, and the power of the people*. Princeton, NJ: Princeton University Press.

Ovitt, G. (1986). Early Christian attitudes toward manual labor. *Technology and Culture, 27*(3), 477–500.

Owens, J. (1981). Aristotle on leisure. *Canadian Journal of Philosophy, 11*, 713–723.

Peacham, H. (1634). *The compleat gentleman*. London, UK: Printed for Francis Constable.

Perkins, W. (1616–1618). *The workes* (Vol. 1). London, UK: I. Legatt Printer.

Pieper, J. (1952). *Leisure, the basis of culture* (A. Dru, Trans.). New York, NY: Pantheon Books.

Plato. (1961a). Republic. In E. Hamilton & H. Cairns (Eds.), *The collected dialogues*. Princeton, NJ: Princeton University Press.

Plato. (1961b). Laws. In E. Hamilton & H. Cairns (Eds.), *The collected dialogues*. Princeton, NJ: Princeton University Press.

Plato. (1961c). Theaetetus. In E. Hamilton & H. Cairns (Eds.), *The collected dialogues*. Princeton, NJ: Princeton University Press.

Plato. (1961d). Phaedo. In E. Hamilton & H. Cairns (Eds.), *The collected dialogues*. Princeton, NJ: Princeton University Press.

Prynne, W. (1633). *Histriomastix*. London, UK: Printed by E. A. and W. I. for Michael Sparke.

Raaflaub, K. (1983). Democracy, oligarchy, and the concept of the free citizen in the late fifth-century Athens. *Political Theory, 11*, 517–544.

Randall, J. (1926). *The making of the modern mind*. New York, NY: Columbia.

Richardson, A. (1952). *The Biblical doctrine of work* (Edumentical Biblical Studies No. 1). London, UK: S.C.M. Press.

Rifkin, J. (1995). *The end of work: The decline of the global labor force and the dawn of the postmarket era*. New York, NY: Putnam's.

Rodgers, D. (1978) *The work ethic in industrial America, 1850–1920*. Chicago, IL: University of Chicago Press.

Ross, W. (1963). *Aristotle: A complete exposition of his works and thought*. New York, NY: Meridian.

Ryken, L. (1995). *Redeeming the time: A Christian approach to work and leisure*. Grand Rapids, MI: Baker Books.

Sanders, P. (1995). *Capitalism*. Minneapolis, MN: University of Minnesota Press.

Solmsen, F. (1964). Leisure and play in Aristotle's ideal state. *Rheinsches Museum for Philologie, 107*, 194–220.

Sophocles. (1959). Antigone (D. Grene, Trans.). In D. Grene & R. Lattimore (Eds.), *The complete Greek tragedies* (Vol. 2). Chicago, IL: The University of Chicago Press.

St. Augustine. (1972). *City of God* (H. Bettenson, Trans.). Baltimore, MD: Penguin Books.

Stark, R. (1996). *The rise of Christianity: A sociologist reconsiders history*. Princeton, NJ: Princeton University Press.

Stock, B. (1985). Activity, contemplation, work, and leisure between the eleventh and the thirteenth centuries. In B. Vickers (Ed.), *Arbeit, musse, meditation: Vita activa–vita contemplativa* (pp. 87–108). Zurich, Switzerland: Verlag der Fachvereine.

Sylvester, C. (1994). Leisure, science, and religion in seventeenth-century England. *Leisure Sciences, 16*, 1–16.

Taylor, A. (1955) *Aristotle*. New York, NY: Dover.

Taylor, C. (1989). *Sources of the self: The making of the modern identity*. Cambridge, MA: Harvard University Press.

Terkel, S. (1974). *Working*. New York, NY: Random House.

Thucydides. (1900). *Funeral speech of Pericles* (B. Jowett, Trans.). Oxford: Clarendon Press.

Tilgher, A. (1930). *Homo faber: Work through the ages*. Chicago, IL: Regnery.

Troeltsch, E. (1931). *The social teaching of the Christian churches* (O. Wyon, Trans.). Chicago, IL: University of Chicago Press.

Weber, M. (1958). *The Protestant ethic and the spirit of capitalism* (T. Parsons, Trans.). New York, NY: Charles Scribner's Sons.

Wood, E. (1988). *Peasant-citizen and slave: The foundations of Athenian democracy*. New York, NY: Verso.

Zeitlin, J. (1924). Introduction. In F. Petrarch, *The life of solitude* (pp. 23–94). Urbana, IL: University of Illinois Press.

Zinzendorf, D. (1869–1874). *Zinzendorf's theologie* (Vol. I; H. Plitt, Ed.). Gotha, Germany: F. A. Perthes.

Motivational Foundations of Leisure

Seppo E. Iso-Ahola
University of Maryland

Introduction

What is leisure? What interests underlie people's participation in various activities? Why do millions of people spend their free time watching television and doing nothing else, while many others are active participants in all kinds of activities from exercise to stamp collecting? Although it is possible to approach these questions from economic and sociological perspectives, such approaches provide superficial explanations at best because of their inherent limitations. If we know that there are differences in leisure patterns between and among various demographic groups, so what? Such findings are only descriptions of large groups' general tendencies and fail to explain the meaning of involvement and thus the fundamental mechanisms and causes of leisure participation. To understand the essence or the true meaning of leisure is to understand why people participate (or fail to participate) and what they strive to get from their involvement. Because an individual is a psychological being, the ultimate explanation of leisure behavior has to be psychological.

This chapter provides a psychological explanation of leisure. It shows that the nature and process of leisure is fundamentally motivational. Human beings are born with basic innate (psychological) needs that are the main energizers of human growth and potential. As will be shown, these basic needs not only define leisure for people but also direct their involvement in activities under various conditions. Thus, it does not matter even if there are hundreds of different types of leisure activities: they all are potentially leisure activities and serve the same psychological functions for their participants. There is no need to explain motives separately for participants in each activity.

The author would like to thank Edward Deci for his helpful comments on a previous version of this chapter.

What Is Leisure?

Based upon de Grazia's (1962) work, Neulinger (1974) theorized that perceived freedom and intrinsic motivation are the central determinants of what people consider to be leisure for them. Subsequently, Iso-Ahola (1979a, 1979b) tested this notion empirically and found strong support for it. Additional empirical work has demonstrated the importance of perceived freedom to the experience of leisure (Csikszentmihalyi and Graef, 1979; Mannell, 1980; Shaw, 1985; Unger and Kernan, 1983), depth of involvement in leisure (Mannell and Bradley, 1986), actual leisure behavior (Thompson and Wankel, 1980), and mental and physical health (Graef, Csikszentmihalyi and Gianinno, 1983; Langer and Rodin, 1976; Rodin and Langer, 1977). Thus, it seems indisputable that a sense of freedom—autonomy—is the central defining characteristic of leisure (Iso-Ahola, 1980; see also Cooper, chapter 1 in this volume).

It is important to note that leisure and free time are not synonymous. In everyday usage of the language, people refer to all nonworking hours as free time. But as we know, only a small portion of this free time may indeed be free, free from obligations and free to do what one wants to do. It is in this latter sense of the word that free time can be equated with leisure because, as noted, people essentially define leisure through perceived freedom and control. Given the fact that most free time is not leisure, the latter can then be considered to represent a small island in the former. On the other hand, the concept of freedom is relative. When people define free time as freedom from work, then any nonwork activities, even the obligatory ones, have elements of freedom in them, and can therefore become closer to the idea of leisure than work. For example, people typically have to do a lot of household activities in nonworking hours, and while such activities are not defined as free-time behaviors per se, these activities contain some degree of freedom because they are free from work. In fact, some men, especially older ones, find such household activities as cooking quite interesting and spend relatively much time in them (Gordon, Gaitz and Scott, 1976). On the basis of the preceding theorizing and findings, it is suggested that the more obligatory people perceive their work, the greater the sense of freedom they find in obligatory nonwork activities.

From Obligatory to Self-Determined

Even small amounts of freedom found in routine, obligatory nonwork activities make these activities psychologically tolerable. The problem of perceived obligation is further alleviated when people begin "identifying" (Vallacher and Wegner, 1987) with extrinsically motivated behaviors. These externally prompted behaviors can become self-determined through the process of identification, or what Deci and Ryan (1991) call "internalization." For example, although it is true that wives still do most of the household activities in dual-career families (Starrels, 1994), an increasing number of husbands are sharing this responsibility with their wives. It is through the process of internalization that these men can turn such initially obligatory "free-time" (extrinsically motivated) activity into a self-determined one—at least partially. Whether it is initially done to save the marriage, to escape stressful work, or for more altruistic reasons to simply help out, does not matter. What matters is that this process of internalization is used in everyday life to turn obligatory free-time activities into leisurelike activities. People grow to perform these activities somewhat willingly and volitionally, thereby personally endorsing the pursuit of extrinsic goals in free-time activities. The longer such activities are performed volitionally, a greater sense of willingness and self-initiation is experienced.

What about women's sense of freedom? Even though women have traditionally done the housework, one cannot assume that they do not hate it. Because the housework in the past has been "assigned" to women, this activity has become totally extrinsically motivated to many of them, similar to men's having to go to work to support the family. Add to this lack of freedom and control the fact that the housework is repetitive, boring and futile, and it is no wonder that women would hate it. When they then have an opportunity to work outside the home, they are likely to find more freedom and self-determination in gainful employment than in the housework—even if their employment is needed for the family's financial survival. The process of internalization helps them turn this "obligatory" employment into one with considerable elements of self-determination in it.

Another process that allows people to engage in obligatory nonwork activity is escape (Iso-Ahola, 1989). Often, overstimulating and overstressful environments encourage people to "escape" through nonworking activities. Although true leisure activities may be more suitable for escaping, obligatory nonwork activities may also be found useful for this purpose. The escaping process in turn is likely to facilitate the identification process discussed previously. Although a person may initially hate household activities that have to be done during his or her free time, he or she may come to realize that it is a good way to escape stress and simultaneously to contribute to the family life. As a result, he or she "identifies" and "internalizes" with the activity and may later perform it willingly.

Nonwork and Free-Time Activity

Figure 3.1 illustrates nonworking activities and their relationship to leisure. At the bottom of the pyramid is participation in obligatory nonwork activities (e.g., household activity). A sense of freedom or autonomy and intrinsic motivation increases as one moves from the bottom to the top of the pyramid. As discussed previously, obligatory nonwork activity participation can be transformed, through the processes of identification-internalization and escape, into leisurelike self-determined activity. This, however, does not occur automatically and necessarily, because many people engage in nonwork obligatory activity grudgingly without any attempt to "identify" with it, and some people refuse to engage in it altogether.

The Case of Television Watching

At the next level, nonwork hours are often spent in free-time activities, such as watching television and physical exercise. Although these kinds of activities can become true leisure for some participants, more frequently they are not. For an example, let's consider television watching. In terms of time spent in it, this activity is clearly the number one nonwork activity in the United States. Yet, it is known that people are dissatisfied with it and are psychologically shortchanged by it. Csikszentmihalyi, Larson and Prescott (1977) reported that all the important indicators of psychological well-being (i.e., mental alertness, sense of control, sense of competence, and sense of challenge) are at their lowest when watching television, while the same indicators are at their highest when playing sports and games.

To be sure, in deciding to watch television people exercise choice and some initiative. In fact, this sense of autonomy, in combination with the process of escape (from daily stress and overstimulation and understimulation), may well explain the widespread use of television in nonworking hours. However limited in their choices, people may be able to feel some autonomy and control when selecting television watching, especially if they feel they are doing other obligatory activities in their free time. Selecting television watching gives them an easy way to feel limited autonomy and control, and this may be psychologically sufficient. The sense of autonomy derived from television watching, however, becomes illusory because it

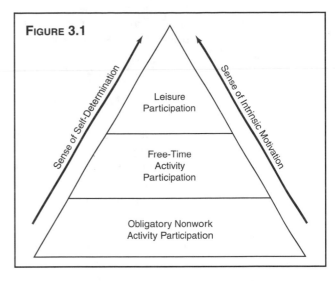

FIGURE 3.1

Sense of Self-Determination

Sense of Intrinsic Motivation

Leisure Participation

Free-Time Activity Participation

Obligatory Nonwork Activity Participation

does not make people feel good about themselves psychologically; at best this activity helps only partially to fulfill their most basic human need: a need for autonomy (Deci and Ryan, 1991). The illusion is furthered by a large number of television channels from which to choose. The bottom line, however, is that television watching is not what many people would really like to do. Thus, the sense of autonomy is far from being fulfilled. Even though the sense of autonomy may be limited because it (television watching) is not what people would really like to do, it nevertheless is powerful; in fact, so powerful that it may mask and hinder people from pursuing the fulfillment of their other innate (psychological) needs, such as needs for personal competence and social interrelationships. If people did not have an option of choosing television for their primary free-time activity, they would more likely choose activities that would promote their sense of competence and social relatedness.

The Case of Exercise

If the choice of television watching is characterized by autonomy by default, then physical exercise may be described by autonomy by "must." Statistically, only 22% of Americans exercise regularly vigorously enough to get the physiological benefits to reduce the risk of various diseases and premature death (Blair, 1993). This leaves 78% of the nation sedentary. Of these 78%, about 54% exercise irregularly and a large percentage of them (and of regular exercisers) exercise because they feel they must do so for their health. Exercise becomes a "should" rather than a "want" for them. Knapp (1988) has shown that when "shoulds" exceed "wants" this "lifestyle imbalance" becomes a major risk factor for relapse into skipping one's exercise routine. When exercise is undertaken for "shoulds" it is not self-determined or intrinsically motivated but rather, internally pressured. The sense of autonomy is then very limited.

It is ironic and paradoxical that people who decide not to exercise may have a greater sense of autonomy than those who exercise because they feel they "should." In essence, they are saying: "I already do what I must and should all day at my work, so I am entitled to do nothing or nothing that I 'should' in my free time." Thus, they have expressed choice and feel autonomous and self-determined, at least to some degree. This feeling is further reinforced when opting to watch television. It is well-established that both exercisers and nonexercisers think that exercise is good for them (Dishman, 1990). Nonexercisers know that it is good for them mentally and physically and that they should do it; yet, they fail to do so. The main reason for this failure may be the masking or hindrance effect of autonomy that occurs when people choose not to exercise. The sense of autonomy and control experienced in that situation masks the beneficial effects of exercise. Given that a need for autonomy is the basic (primary) human need (Deci and Ryan, 1991), this need can be partially fulfilled by choosing to exercise as well as by choosing not to exercise. When one adds to this fact that exercise has a lot of punishing consequences (e.g., fatigue, muscle soreness), is often negatively reinforced (e.g., a nagging spouse), is physically challenging, and is demanding in terms of time and preparation, it should be no wonder that 78% of the population is sedentary.

Those who exercise because they feel they "should," however, have a psychological advantage in the long run. As discussed earlier, they can use the process of identification or internalization to turn this initially extrinsically motivated activity into a self-determined one. Relatively few people find exercise inherently interesting (i.e., true leisure) but instead, do it for instrumental reasons (e.g., to stay healthy). They can, however, learn to value and like it and thus to undertake it willingly with full self-endorsement. The resultant sense of self-determination, though not as full as the one derived from activities done for their pure inherent interest, is sufficient for continued maintenance of exercise in one's behavioral repertoire. This is further enhanced if exercise is used as an avenue to escape from overstimulating and understimulating work settings. As noted earlier, the escape process is likely to facilitate the internalization process.

Unfortunately, however, many people fail to turn exercise into a self-determined activity. Dishman (1988) has reported that 50% of people who start exercise programs quit after six months. This may be due to their failure to use *self-regulation* for their ben-

efit. The self-regulation process (Iso-Ahola, 1992) consists of goal-setting, self-monitoring, self-evaluation, and self-reinforcement. Accordingly, exercise maintenance requires that people personally set specific, hard, and yet attainable goals for their exercise, monitor their exercise behavior, evaluate their progress toward the goals, and reward or punish themselves for reaching or failing to reach the set goals. This self-regulation process is a psychological tool that can be used to "identify" with exercise.

Achievement of goals gives a sense of mastery or competence, which is a main intrinsic reward that people strive for in their leisure activities (Iso-Ahola, 1980, 1984, 1989). Whether it is because of this sense of mastery or some other mechanism, exercise is known to make people feel less tense, anxious, and depressed afterwards (e.g., Byrne and Byrne, 1993; Schlicht, 1994). Such psychological benefits are likely to contribute to people's "identifying" with exercise and their turning it into a self-determined activity. The psychological value of exercise in one's leisure lifestyle can further be advanced by doing exercise in such a way that it becomes a gratifying want. More specifically, the following behavioral strategies can be used (Knapp, 1988):

1. have alternate forms of exercise that are enjoyable and use them especially at times of feeling deprived;
2. plan a special indulgence to follow and reinforce the regular exercise, such as a massage after the workout;
3. build gratifications into your daily life, such as personal time, or pleasure reading.

Unquestionably, these kinds of self-reinforcement strategies help one "identify" with exercise and feel more self-determined about it.

Television watching and exercise cover most of the free time for most of the people for most of the time. These activities are also good examples of the psychological nature of free-time activities in everyday living. There are, of course, other free-time activities, such as things done with either spouse or children. Again, the common denominator for involvement in all of these types of activities is that they are not self-determined initially. As discussed, some people are able to turn them into autonomous participation through the psychological processes. But none of them represents true leisure activities unless people have found them inherently interesting in the first place.

Leisure

Figure 3.1 (page 37) shows that leisure represents the tip of the pyramid or iceberg. It means that there is less of it compared to free-time and nonwork activity in people's lives. It also means that leisure is more difficult to reach and achieve. On the other hand, leisure means full autonomy, freedom, and control. There are no internal or external pressures or coercion to engage in leisure activities. One participates in an activity because he or she finds it intrinsically interesting, for its own sake, out of sheer pleasure and enjoyment. For some people, but not for most, exercise and television watching can be such activities. Any activity can be found inherently interesting. Activities in and of themselves are not intrinsically or extrinsically interesting. It is the individual who through psychological needs and processes finds some activities intrinsically and others extrinsically motivating. In short, autonomy or sense of freedom is the critical regulator of what becomes leisure and what does not. Sense of freedom involves the principle of all-or-nothing, "threshold leisure," after which the effects of other needs and factors can be seen (Iso-Ahola, 1980).

The second dimension that is important for defining leisure is the presence of intrinsic rewards (Iso-Ahola, 1980, 1989). People seek out activities that are likely to provide intrinsic rewards, of which a sense of competence is the most important. This is one of the main reasons why sports and games are popular leisure activities. Psychologically, these activities are well-structured in that participants understand behavior-performance-outcome contingencies, form clear expectations, and receive unambiguous feedback about their performance. Pursuit of the need for competence is by no means limited to sports and games. The need can be fulfilled in any leisure activities. For example, outdoor recreation activities have been reported to be psychologically rewarding because they provide opportunities to master challenging environments and use one's skills. Schreyer, Lime and Williams (1984) reported that experts or "veterans" in river recreation ranked much higher on such motives as "to develop my skills" and "to test my abilities" than novices. This evidence suggests that the more specialized and "serious" (see Stebbins, chapter 5 in this volume) we become about our leisure pursuits, the more important are the intrinsic rewards of involvement, especially the sense of competence. People become serious about leisure because of intrinsic rewards, and achievement of these rewards in turn reinforces continued and deep involvement. Intrinsic rewards provide durable benefits and can be found more readily in serious leisure than in mass or popular free-time activity.

Related to efforts to fulfill one's need for competence in leisure is Csikszentmihalyi's (1990) notion of *flow*. Accordingly, people seek out activities that allow them to match their skills with challenges. Too much or too little challenge leads to anxiety and boredom, respectively. Pursuit of optimal challenges is psychologically beneficial because it maximizes positive states (e.g., perceived competence) and minimizes negative states (e.g., anxiety). This matching of personal skills with challenges is expected to lead to flow experiences in which people function and perform at an unusual ("superhuman") level of consciousness. Flow experiences correlate positively with *activation* (i.e., how active, alert, and strong a person feels), enjoyment (Csikszentmihalyi, 1982), and mental health (Haworth, 1993; Haworth and Evans, 1995). They lead to human growth and development and constitute "the bottom line of existence" (Csikszentmihalyi, 1982). Thus, it is easy to see why leisure activities are pursued in free time: they are vehicles for experiencing optimal challenges and tools for fulfilling one's need for competence.

The final critical dimension of leisure is that it is largely a social experience and phenomenon (Crandall, 1979; Crandall, Nolan and Morgan, 1980; Samdahl, 1992). It involves interrelationships, companionships, friendships, interaction and social support (Coleman and Iso-Ahola, 1993; Iso-Ahola, 1989; Iso-Ahola and Park, 1996). Leisure is also seen as a social context for the development of intimate relationships and for the expression of social identities (Kleiber and Richards, 1985). In exploring common leisure occasions, Samdahl (1992) found that some type of social interaction occurred in 54.4% of the occasions labeled *leisure* by the subjects. Of this number, 44.7% were characterized by informal social interaction, which in turn was positively associated with affective measures (i.e., relaxation and comfortableness) and ratings of true self. Similarly, Argyle (1992) found that social interaction is positively related to mental health and psychological well-being. Crandall (1979) and Larson, Mannell and Zuzanek (1986) also reported that having friends and companions with whom to do enjoyable things together is related to elevated psychological well-being. More recent evidence (Iso-Ahola and Park, 1996; Rook, 1987) indicates that friendship and companionship in shared leisure activities buffer the adverse effects of life stress on human health.

There is evidence, however, that people have to be able to regulate social contacts, interaction, and support. Schulz (1976) demonstrated that it was not social interaction itself that had beneficial effects on nursing home residents' well-being, but rather, whether or not they were able to predict and control social interaction. The idea that social leisure can sometimes have unintended negative effects (Coleman and Iso-Ahola, 1993) is also supported by Caltabiano's (1995) data. She found that engaging in many social activities exacerbated the adverse effects of stressful life events on illness symptoms. Rather than being stress reducing, social leisure can sometimes be stress enhancing, especially if it undermines one's sense of freedom and control (Chick and Roberts, 1989). Regulation of social interaction is "an optimizing process" (Altman, 1975) in which people have to be able to shut themselves off from others at one time and open themselves up to interpersonal contacts at another time. It is not, therefore, surprising that being alone is not an entirely negative experience, especially for the married, as long as disengagement from others is chosen and voluntary (Larson, Zuzanek and Mannell, 1985). In short, social leisure and self-determination are interrelated.

Social interaction is both motivation for and benefit of leisure participation. People interact socially for the sheer socializing with friends and companions, which then becomes motivating and rewarding at the same time. They seek interpersonal rewards, such as "being with my buddies," but they also seek to escape routine social contacts at work and home (Iso-Ahola, 1989). Although the development of friendships is possible through one's work, more often work mates do not become genuine friends. Seeking of interpersonal rewards then becomes important in free time, as reflected in Samdahl's (1992) finding that about half of what people describe as leisure is informal social interaction. The "best" leisure activities are those that involve activity and friends (Crandall, 1979). Such social leisure also enables people to get away from the routine social contacts at work and home. In studying hunters, Copp (1975) reported that being with "buddies" (seeking interpersonal rewards) was as important as getting away from work mates, wife, and children (escaping the daily interpersonal world). Similarly, Larson et al. (1986) found that the greatest amount of time with family members was spent in maintenance and passive leisure activities (e.g., television watching), while active pursuits (e.g., sports and socializing) were much more frequent with friends. It should not then be surprising that the respondents, according to this study, had more positive experiences with friends than with family members. The reported levels of affect and arousal were below the average when with family members and above the average when with friends. Thus, it appears that doing what one wants to do in his or her free time and doing it with whom and when he or she wants to is the essence of leisure.

The power of social interaction, especially if it is wanted and personally controlled, is also evident in turning not-so-likeable activities into likeable ones. For example, it has been shown that finding and meeting friends at fitness clubs, and interacting with them while there and afterwards, increases adherence to exercise (Unger and Johnson, 1995). In this way, social interaction may help in "identifying" and "internalizing" with exercise and thus making it a more self-determined activity. Another but different indicator of the power of social interaction is the finding reported by Chalip, Thomas and Voyle (1992). These authors discovered that those immigrants who became more involved in sports and recreation activities in their new communities developed larger networks of friends, received more social support, and were more likely to socialize with other people than the immigrants who were less involved in sports and recreation. They became more attached to their new communities and were less likely to move out. Although sports and recreation were important, it was the *social contact and support* obtained through these activities that made the difference in their life and community satisfaction. All of this supports the idea that leisure is largely a social phenomenon: either pure social interaction or one's favorite activity done with friends. Social interaction is also a tool that can be used to convert an extrinsically motivated activity into a more leisurelike, self-determined activity.

What Is Motivation?

In general, psychologists agree that a motive is an internal factor that arouses and directs human behavior. People do not simply walk, run, or play games; they strive for some objects and escape from others. Most human actions are directed, and an inner motive (a purpose or a desire) leads to actions that bring people closer to their goals (Gleitman, 1986). The question of where this inner motive comes from is generally answered by saying that internal and external stimuli give rise to human motivation. Internal stimuli refer to such things as memory of a good time in playing sports, whereas external stimuli are likened to factors in the physical and social environments (e.g., a sunny day; a good friend calling and asking to play tennis).

Motivation refers to the psychological mechanisms that govern the direction, intensity, and persistence of behavior (Kanfer, 1994). Thus, behavior is explained by something other than individual differences and overwhelming environmental demands. *Direction* refers to which of the many possible goals a person chooses to pursue, *intensity* to how much effort an individual expends to achieve the set goals, and *persistence* to how long an individual perseveres at goal pursuit. The problem with motivation stems from the fact that it cannot be directly observed; it has to be inferred from self-reports or actual behaviors. The second problem arises from the lack of a unifying theory of motivation. Although approaches to motivation vary from behavioral to cognitive and from achievement motivation to self-efficacy, it is possible to find enough similarities among them to arrive at some key perspectives.

Physiological Needs Versus Psychological Motives

An important question about motivation deals with its physiological foundations. It is well-established that organisms exist in the stable internal equilibrium called homeostasis. Regardless of considerable fluctuations in the external environment, the human body maintains, for example, temperature and water conditions at remarkably constant levels. If, however, certain conditions create homeostatic imbalance, they then lead to motives to restore the internal equilibrium. In this way, some motives grow directly from the organism's regulation of its own internal state. Of these motives, hunger and thirst are most frequently mentioned.

It is important to note, however, that the simple equation of a physiological need or homeostatic imbalance with a psychological motive or drive is not justified (Murray, 1964). While the two are correlated, they are not the same. For instance, feeling hungry may result not only from a physiological need but also from external stimuli, such as smelling a sizzling steak. On the other hand, not all nutritional needs result in hunger. What all of this means is that physiological need is a biological process involving homeostatic imbalance, whereas much more is involved in psychological motives than homeostatic imbalance. While these nonhomeostatic motives can be physiologically influenced, they nevertheless are mainly aroused and shaped by psychological conditions.

Do people have a need for leisure? An answer to this question from the strict physiological standpoint is a categorical no. Leisure is not necessary for our survival in the same sense as food and water are. We cannot survive without food and water, but we can without leisure. On the other hand, human life is not a matter of strict physiological exposition. Over the centuries, human beings have evolved well beyond the stage where gratification of the basic needs is the only or main focus of life. This means that the use of human potential and quality of life become central to the discussion of needs.

People (e.g., the socioeconomically deprived, prisoners, workaholics) are able to survive conditions that are not optimally arousing and that are therefore psychologically and even physiologically damaging to them. Such conditions, however, do not facilitate the use of human potential and capabilities. Consequently, quality of life is significantly reduced for individuals who are underusing (the socioeconomically deprived) and overusing (workaholics) their potential and skills. Although most people fall somewhere in between these extremes, the issue of human potential and growth is central for both individuals and society. To that extent, leisure plays an important role and helps people balance their lives and achieve a better quality of life. On this basis, it could be argued that there is a social need for leisure.

Another point about the existence of leisure needs has to do with the effect of social environments. While people do not need leisure as such, they can grow highly dependent upon it. Social influences can lead to the point where individuals become "serious" about, and even addicted to, their leisure behaviors. But even if people do not go to the extreme of serious leisure or leisure addiction, they can easily become accustomed to being able to engage in certain leisure behaviors on a regular basis. To that extent, they become dependent on leisure, especially if leisure experiences are enjoyable to them, and begin seeing a need for leisure. This, then, means that leisure needs are social motives that can lead even to addictive behaviors, and therefore appear as "desperate needs." But, they are not physiologically determined or based.

Optimum Level of Arousal

Today psychologists generally agree that a search for some optimum level of arousal or general stimulation underlies most psychological motives, but this perspective has not always been accepted. For example, in his famous drive-reduction theory of motivation, Hull (1943) postulated that organisms seek to reduce all stimulation and arousal. The theory, however, was challenged by stimulus or sensory deprivation studies (e.g., Dennis, 1960; Dennis and Najarian, 1957), some of which showed that stimulus deprivation results in retardation in children's locomotor performance. Other studies demonstrated that, if college students were deprived of all visual, auditory, and touch stimulation, they found such nirvana stressful and could tolerate it only for two or three days (Murray, 1964). After that, they experienced periods of confusion, irritability, and stress, and began having visual hallucinations. Students' intense desire for external stimulation was indicated by the fact that they wanted to hear a recording of an old stock market report over and over.

These and other findings (Hunt, 1969) strongly suggest that people seek neither an absence nor an excess of stimulation, but rather an optimal level. Because understimulation and overstimulation is physiologically and psychologically detrimental to humans (Hunt, 1969), the result is a continuous search for an optimal level of stimulation. Of course, there are variations in this basic tendency, so that what constitutes the optimal level varies from person to person and from time to time.

The search for an optimal level of arousal is quite evident in free-time behaviors. People have not only invented many activities that allow them readily to seek and experience stimulation and excitement (e.g., roller coasters, sky diving), but they have also developed many activities which allow for relaxation and passive enjoyment (e.g., meditation, walking for pleasure, picnicking). Further, people have made living arrangements in which leisure is in opposition to work (free time after daily work, weekends after the workweek, and a vacation after a year's work); in this way, leisure provides opportunities to balance understimulating or overstimulating work.

In their search for optimal arousal, people seek stimulus conditions that are appropriately novel. For example, it is well-established that, in their play, children avoid the extremes of total familiarity and total novelty (Fiske and Maddi, 1961; McCall, 1974). If stimuli are optimally novel, they arouse curiosity and a tendency to approach, but *overly* novel stimuli are likely to lead to fear and avoidance. It is also true that all things lose their novelty with repeated exposure. This process of habituation leads people to look for new experiences or activities, or they do familiar activities in a new way. Of course, the more novel or complex the original stimulus, the longer habituation takes (Murray, 1964). It is then reasonable to suggest that free-time activities vary considerably in their ability to resist habituation. Some activities have, by their nature, more elements of novelty and complexity than do others, and therefore provide better opportunities to fulfill one's need for optimal arousal.

Intrinsic Motivation

In their search for optimally arousing experiences, people are motivated by sensory stimulation and novelty and, therefore, are motivated to do and manipulate things. Such activity and manipulatory motivation is especially evident in children. When children discover that they can do something, they repeat it countless times. This interest in an activity for its own sake is also seen among animals. In his classic experiment, Harlow (1950) demonstrated that monkeys learn to disassemble a complex mechanical puzzle without extrinsic rewards. The monkeys worked persistently to learn to open latches that were attached to a wooden board. Because unlocking the latches gave the monkeys no rewards, and yet they continued to do so, the primary motive was presumably to master the manipulatory problem—opening the devices "for the fun of it." Thus, it appears that the intrinsic motives for stimulation and activity are innate, with learning playing only a secondary role (Murray, 1964).

The monkeys in Harlow's experiment acted much like human beings often do: they engaged in the activity for its own sake rather than for any extrinsic rewards. Something interesting, however, happened when some animals were given a food reward for solving the mechanical puzzle. These rewarded monkeys used the problem task only to get food, showing little interest in the activity for its own sake. They came to see the puzzle as a means to get extrinsic rewards (pieces of food). In this way, their original intrinsic motivation for the activity was killed by the introduction of extrinsic rewards.[1]

Children's day-to-day activity is, for the most part, intrinsically motivated. Children do activities for curiosity, sheer manipulation, and such intrinsic rewards as feeling competent in dealing with the environment. They can sustain this activity for long periods of time, interrupted only by intense homeostatic needs like hunger and thirst. But, as they grow older, especially when they reach school age, children seem to lose much of their intrinsic motivation and become more extrinsically motivated. In a similar vein, much of adults' day-to-day activity appears to be extrinsically motivated, leaving leisure time the period when most of the daily intrinsic motivation is aroused and put into action (Graef et al., 1983). This is likely to be especially true if working conditions are not stimulating enough. Butler's (1953) research on monkeys suggested that special deprivation conditions like boredom (e.g., boring work) may account for part of the drive behind intrinsic motivation.

It is clear from the preceding review of research that intrinsic motivation is at the heart of human

---

[1]To avoid confusion, it should be noted that extrinsic rewards undermine intrinsic motivation in the activities that were initially engaged in for intrinsic rewards, such as sheer enjoyment from doing them. A totally different issue arises from initially extrinsically motivated behaviors, such as obligatory housework. These behaviors are maintained as long as rewards or sanctions are in place. But they can also become self-determined behaviors if people learn to perform them willingly and volitionally. In such a case, of course, the activity has elements of both extrinsic and intrinsic motivation.

behavior. This is not to say, however, that all human behavior is intrinsically motivated because such is not possible, if only for practical reasons. Work, for example, is extrinsically motivating for most people (e.g., Shaw, 1985). In addition, much of nonwork time is spent in maintenance and household activities on the one hand and passive free-time activities (e.g., television watching) on the other (e.g., Larson et al., 1986). As discussed earlier, these activities are not intrinsically motivating and enjoyable for most people most of the time, although the sense of self-determination about them can be considerably increased through the process of identification or internalization. But, whenever possible, people prefer intrinsically motivating behaviors. There are four basic reasons for this general tendency toward intrinsically motivated behaviors:

1. they are autonomous and self-determined;
2. they facilitate people's attempts to pursue and achieve optimum levels of sensory stimulation and arousal;
3. they are conducive to feelings of personal competence; and
4. they are inherently enjoyment- and satisfaction-producing.

When an individual is intrinsically motivated, he or she has a full sense of choice and freedom and feels that he or she is doing what he or she wants to do. The activity or behavior chosen is experienced as optimally challenging and is expected to provide a sense of competence and enjoyment. Intrinsic motivation is then "the prototypical form" of self-determination (Deci and Ryan, 1991). Other forms of self-determination consist of extrinsically motivated behaviors. That is, even if people are motivated by extrinsic goals, they can under some circumstances pursue them willingly with full self-endorsement.

Undermining Intrinsic Motivation

Regardless of the overriding tendency toward intrinsically motivated behaviors, people are often hindered from doing self-determined activities, or their initial intrinsic motivation is significantly undermined by certain factors. One such factor is the use of extrinsic rewards. There is an abundance of empirical evidence in the literature to indicate that, in general, rewards undermine intrinsic motivation (Deci and Ryan, 1987). That is, when people are given rewards for doing an activity that they are intrinsically interested in, they

subsequently lose much of their interest and willingness to participate in that activity. This "overjustification" phenomenon (Lepper, Greene and Nisbett, 1973) is most likely to occur when rewards are expected, salient, and contingent on task engagement. As Deci and Ryan (1987) have suggested, people experience such rewards and feedback as controlling, and therefore perceive them as restricting their self-determination. There are, however, sex differences in these perceptions, in that females are more likely than males to perceive any feedback as controlling (Deci and Ryan, 1987). Other factors that undermine intrinsic motivation include the imposition of a deadline for the completion of an interesting activity (Amabile, Dejong and Lepper, 1976; Reader and Dollinger, 1982), the mere presence of a surveillant or evaluator (Lepper and Greene, 1975), the provision of information signaling that one's activity is evaluated, even if the subsequent evaluation is positive (Harackiewicz, Manderlink and Sansone, 1984), and imposed goals (Mossholder, 1980).

A curious, but frequently used, method of controlling children's behavior, and thereby undermining their interest in certain activities, is employed by parents and teachers. *If-then* contingencies such as, "If you do dishes, then you can go out and play with your friends," are common in child rearing, though not by any means limited to children. In an illuminating experiment, Boggiano and Main (1986) showed that when preschoolers were presented with this kind of familiar contingency, their interest in the second activity increased but interest in the first activity decreased appreciably. According to the preceding example, children's interest in washing dishes would have been undermined significantly and their motivation for playing with friends notably enhanced by the use of such a contingency. The problem is that on subsequent occasions when the children are asked to do dishes, they will not be willing to do it without compensation. In this way, intrinsic motivation for the activity is severely undermined. While if-then contingencies may be an effective way of controlling children's behavior, they have definite drawbacks from the standpoint of the development of intrinsic motivation tendencies in children for specific activities.

Sometimes, a reward is given in the form of positive feedback. Does such feedback or reward undermine intrinsic motivation? The answer appears to be no. It has been shown that, if positive feedback affirms or elevates one's sense of competence, it then enhances rather than undermines intrinsic motivation (e.g., Koestner, Zuckerman and Koestner, 1987). According to Deci and Ryan (1991), however, providing competence feedback in controlling situations does not enhance intrinsic motivation, but instead, promotes controlled intentional behavior (e.g., exercise instructors completely controlling their participants' exercise routine, coaches dictating to their athletes what and how to do). On the other hand, if doing well at an activity is important to a person, then *positive competence feedback* is likely to increase intrinsic motivation (Harackiewicz and Manderlink, 1984). In a similar vein, Sansone (1986) made a distinction between competence and task feedback, and found that feeling competent enhanced intrinsic motivation only if attaining competence was a primary goal of the activity. If, on the other hand, doing well is not thought to be central to activity involvement, the competence feedback can undermine intrinsic interest. In that situation, task feedback would be more appropriate and likely to enhance intrinsic motivation for the activity. Task feedback refers to the information that conveys to people how well they are doing various aspects of the activity, or how well they are improving their activity performance, or how well they are doing by certain accepted activity standards. In this way, the individual's performance is not compared to that of others; rather, the focus is on acquisition of the skills needed to master the activity at individually enjoyable levels.

The opportunity to choose what to do enhances intrinsic motivation, while its opposite, lack of opportunity to choose, undermines intrinsic interest. Swann and Pittman (1977) reported experimental findings indicating a significant decline in intrinsic motivation when an adult rather than a child chose the play activity. Similarly, when college students were given the chance to choose which tasks to work on and to decide how much time to spend in their chosen task, their subsequent intrinsic motivation was significantly higher than that of those who were not given the opportunity to choose the activity (Zuckerman, Porac, Lathin, Smith and Deci, 1978).

The importance of choice over rewards was demonstrated in an experiment conducted by Bradley and Mannell (1984). Results indicated that when the subjects were offered the reward prior to the choice to participate in a laboratory game, their intrinsic motivation was significantly less than when the choice was offered first and the reward second. This is consistent with research which has shown that perceived choice or freedom is a critical regulator and determinant of intrinsically motivated leisure experiences (Iso-Ahola, 1979a, 1979b). These studies demonstrated that if subjects did not initially have an opportunity to choose a leisure activity, even the fact that this activity later brought about intrinsic rewards, such as feelings of competence, did not lead to intrinsically motivated leisure experiences. Thus, it appears that freedom of choice is a necessary condition for intrinsic motivation in general and for intrinsically motivated leisure in particular.

External rewards, sanctions, and contingencies not only undermine intrinsic motivation but also have negative effects on creativity, cognitive activity, emotional state, and maintenance of behavior change. Experiments have shown (Deci and Ryan, 1987) that events that are perceived as controlling (e.g., rewards) tend to lower the creativity of children's artistic and writing products, impair cognitive learning among college students, induce negative feelings in general and create less positive views of others, and undercut the persistence of behavior change following the termination of controlling events (e.g., therapeutic treatment). Deci and Ryan (1987) also reviewed empirical evidence indicating that if interpersonal contexts and situations are supportive of self-determination and autonomy, they promote perceived competence and self-esteem and curb aggressiveness in children. A series of field experiments (Langer and Rodin, 1976; Rodin and Langer, 1977; Schulz, 1976; Schulz and Hanusa, 1978) demonstrated that such interpersonal contexts also promote long-term positive effects on physical and mental health in the institutionalized aged.

Intentional-Versus-Automatic Behavior

The concept of motivation seems to revolve around intentions and goals. People are assumed to make intentional choices about goals and how hard and how long to pursue them. The basic premise, then, is that motivation is cognitive activity, based upon conscious mental acts. Deci and Ryan (1987, 1991) argue that both self-determined and controlled behaviors are mediated by intentionality, but only self-determined actions properly characterize the idea of "human agency." Accordingly, intrinsically motivated and self-determined behaviors are intentional actions requiring conscious mental effort. But, is this really true? What about a person who likes to watch news everyday on television after he comes home from his work? Or, a person who reads the daily newspaper after dinner? Are these and similar behaviors comparable to other automated behaviors like brushing one's teeth in the morning or fastening the seat belts before starting to drive?

There are reasons to believe that many human behaviors become automatic when repeated under the same stimulus conditions. Complex behaviors, however, may not be conducive to automaticity because they are not consistently and regularly exposed to the same stimulus. For example, exercising is a complex behavior that requires conscious effort for its execution. On the other hand, for regular exercisers (22% of the population), this activity may be simple and thus automatic because of consistency of situational cues that trigger the behavior. For irregular exercisers (54% of the population), such is not the case. What about other free-time and leisure behaviors? Aside from television watching and exercising for some people, an argument can be made that free-time activities are not done with sufficient consistency and regularity for them to become automatic behaviors. For example, people do not go to movies all the time, nor do they socialize with others on a regular basis, and thus when these activities are undertaken they require conscious planning. *Leisure* behaviors, however, are different because of a full sense of self-determination and intrinsic motivation associated with them, meaning that some of these behaviors are capable of becoming automatic, especially when people become "serious" about them.

What then happens when an individual pursues the same goal over time within a given situation? Bargh and Gollwitzer (1994) argue that "enduring goals or motives are directly activated by situational features." By enduring goals they refer to the goals people are committed to, such as being a good mother or a high achiever. Wanting to be fit and healthy would be an enduring goal. When making this his or her enduring goal a person becomes committed to it and pursues it with regularity and consistency. As a result, Bargh and Gollwitzer posit, automatic links will develop between representations of social situations (e.g., an exercise mate always calling at the same time of the day) and the goal. These representations do not have to be as concrete as a friend calling and asking to go for the exercise; when the mere presence of the triggering situational cues is encountered in the relevant situation, the enduring goal becomes activated automatically. This goal then guides behavior without an individual choosing a particular line of action. The authors postulate that eventually, the choice (to exercise) becomes just another routine of the mental system and is therefore bypassed. The resultant automatic behavior is said to be unintentional at the time when it occurs but intentional in the sense that the choice of the behavior was made in the past.

The preceding idea about motives and goals becoming automatic when a given behavior is repeated frequently and regularly is similar to Iso-Ahola's (1980) suggestion that:

> people do not rationalize to themselves before their leisure participation why they decide to get involved; they do not go

through Tinsley, Barrett and Kass's (1977) list of 45 leisure needs to decide why they should play tennis today. This, of course, does not mean that a person does not have a priori reasons for leisure participation, but that they are concealed in intrinsically motivated leisure, which one does not have to consciously repeat. (p. 247)

Unfortunately, some leisure researchers still continue to repeat Tinsley's original approach and conduct factor analytic studies, in which respondents are given tens of reasons ("leisure needs") and asked to rate the importance of each of them for their participation in a given activity. These efforts (e.g., Clough, Shepherd and Maughan, 1989; Ewert, 1985; Manfredo, Driver and Tarrant, 1996) are futile and add nothing to our understanding of leisure motivation.

Iso-Ahola (1980, p. 247) also argued that "when intrinsic leisure motivation is violated" (i.e., one is hindered from engaging in intrinsically motivated leisure behaviors), people become immediately aware of the a priori reasons for their involvement. When this goal-directed behavior becomes a problem, or is anticipated to become a problem, "implementation goals" (Bargh and Gollwitzer, 1994) are formed to facilitate and promote involvement in the activity. Accordingly, people form intentions on how, when, and where to get the goal-directed behavior started or continued. Empirical evidence indicates that these more specific implementation intentions enhance drastically the chances of getting more general "goal intentions" accomplished (Bargh and Gollwitzer, 1994). But, even these more specific implementation intentions are viewed as simple and crude mental acts that can mimic a central effect of habits. They instigate automatic processes and thus speed up the initiation or continuance of behavior. Whatever the degree of consciousness in implementation intentions, they are used for keeping alive the pursuit of enduring goals.

There is evidence (Vallacher and Wegner, 1987) that people generally prefer high levels of abstraction or identification for their goals and that they move to lower levels of it when they perceive or anticipate barriers to their goal pursuit. Lower levels would mean utilization of implementation intentions. If, for example, a person's enduring goal is to stay fit and healthy (i.e., higher level of abstraction), but on a given day he or she cannot exercise at the regular time during the lunch hour, he or she forms implementation intentions to undertake the exercise routine after dinner (lower levels of identification). Similarly, most people have an enduring goal for their leisure involvement: to participate whenever they can in the activity or activities they love and have "fun" doing. This high level of abstraction for leisure contains the essence of intrinsic motivation: self-determined and optimally challenging and arousing experiences.

When pursuit of this enduring goal for leisure is "violated" or hampered, implementation intentions are invoked and used to minimize the disruption of the process. Implementation intentions are analogous to "negotiation" of leisure constraints (Jackson, Crawford and Godbey, 1993). It appears that constraints to leisure are not overwhelming, because Jackson and colleagues reported that constraints led to nonparticipation only in 11% of the cases in a prior study. This finding indirectly supports Bargh and Gollwitzer's (1994) previously noted contention that implementation intentions "drastically" increase the chances of achieving the general "goal intentions." People may modify their leisure participation (e.g., time and form) but they do not easily give it up. It is then logical to postulate that the negotiation process becomes a highly conscious undertaking only when constraints are severe and overwhelming. Otherwise, for example, changing time for one's exercising becomes a simple and crude mental act requiring little cognitive processing capacity.

Individual Differences

When motivation is being discussed it is important to make a distinction between motivation and motives. Motivation is not a fixed attribute of the individual, but rather an individual state affected by the continuous interplay of personal, social, and cultural factors (Kanfer, 1994). Motives, on the other hand, refer to stable individual differences in dispositional tendencies. So, a person's motivation for specific activities may fluctuate as a function of personal and social factors, while personal predispositions toward certain motivational propensities remain relatively unchanged.

Iso-Ahola and Weissinger (1987) have shown that the more self-motivated people are in general, the less likely they are to experience leisure as boredom. In this study, self-motivation was conceptualized and measured as a personality trait that distinguishes people who are high on the trait from those who are low on it. This predisposition toward intrinsic motivation provides a psychological resource that protects against boredom and suggests that the tendency to experience leisure as intrinsically motivating is as much a matter of individual capacity as it is a matter of social conditions and environment. Although it is important for any human community to provide opportunities for intrinsically motivating experiences, it is also important to recognize that the predisposition toward

intrinsic motivation is an individual capacity. This predisposition appears to be "an inner quality, a psychodynamic dimension that enables the person to discover rewards in mundane events that others find neutral and unrewarding" (Graef et al., 1983, p. 166). In a similar vein, Csikszentmihalyi (1982) concluded that the capacity to experience flow is an important personal skill that cuts across the work-leisure distinction.

The idea that intrinsic motivation is also a rather stable personality predisposition is supported by different lines of research. One of them is Kobasa's (1979, 1982) work on *hardiness*. According to her theory and data, people who stay healthy under stressful conditions differ in a "resistance resource" called *hardiness* or a personality predisposition toward intrinsic motivation. Those who are high in the three components of this trait (i.e., challenge, control, and commitment) are less debilitated by stressful life events than those who are low on the trait. A different approach has been taken by Deci and Ryan (1991). They distinguish three *causality orientations:* autonomy, control, and impersonal. Of these, the autonomy orientation is closely related to intrinsic motivation predisposition. Autonomy orientation refers to people's general tendency toward self-determination. According to Deci and Ryan (1991), this orientation correlates positively with self-esteem, ego development, self-actualization, and the tendency to support others' self-determination.

More recently, Weissinger and Bandalos (1995) have extended and applied Kobasa's and Deci and Ryan's work to leisure behavior. They developed an instrument that measures people's tendency to seek intrinsic rewards in leisure. This 24-item Intrinsic Leisure Motivation Scale was designed to capture four dimensions of intrinsic motivation in leisure: self-determination, competence, commitment, and challenge. The nine studies reported provided strong support for the reliability and validity of the construct. Thus, the instrument appears to be an excellent tool for measuring individual differences in the desire for intrinsic rewards in leisure behavior. People who are high on the trait are predicted to maintain a more active leisure lifestyle than those who are low on it. This is because an active leisure lifestyle is conducive to frequent experiences of self-determination, personal competence, and optimal challenges. Such lifestyle is psychologically rewarding and has positive health consequences (Iso-Ahola, 1997).

If the predisposition toward intrinsic motivation in leisure is beneficial for individuals, a question then is how to acquire this tendency. Are we born with it? Deci and Ryan (1991) argue that infants are born with the "innate" needs for autonomy, competence, and relatedness, but quickly point out that abilities and interests are not predetermined by genetics. Studies comparing biological and adoptive family members (e.g., Grotevant et al., 1977), however, have shown that general patterns of interests (but not interests in specific activities) are significantly influenced by genetic factors but that these general tendencies begin immediately to be shaped by the social environment. Deci and Ryan's point emphasizes this latter finding about the importance of social environment, as they state (pp. 238–239): "From the time of birth, human beings are oriented toward the active exercise of their capacities and interests. They seek out optimal challenges, and they attempt to master and integrate new experiences."

All of this puts onus on the socialization process and suggests that exposure to a wide variety of leisure experiences in early years may be the best strategy. Such experiences would not only help a person acquire many different leisure skills but, more importantly, also would feed and reinforce his or her basic tendency to seek out optimal challenges. Further, by providing enriching and stimulating play and leisure experiences for their children, parents encourage and support, even if inadvertently, their children's desire for self-determination. It is likely that this pattern of child rearing would instill permanent enthusiasm for leisure behaviors and contribute to the formation of predisposition toward intrinsic motivation.

Something, however, must go terribly wrong in this process, because most people end up being sedentary, spending most of their free time in passive pursuits like television watching. How do we, as a society, kill the "innate" predisposition toward intrinsic motivation in most people? The undermining begins when parents stifle their children's self-determination and when they do not provide opportunities for optimal challenges. But it begins in earnest when children enter the school system. There they are stripped of any sense of autonomy and are made dependent on extrinsic rewards and contingencies (e.g., grades). After 12 years of this treatment, a person enters the consumer society in which the work-spend-work-spend mentality (Schor, 1991) is emphasized; a person works hard to be able to buy consumer goods, and the more money he or she spends on them, the harder he or she has to work. This vicious cycle trivializes leisure and discourages the "discovery of leisure" (Iso-Ahola, 1997). Leisure is used for recuperation from and for work. The opposition of leisure to work promotes escapism in leisure, which in turn leads to passive lifestyles.

The problem is compounded if work and family conditions are stressful, especially among dual-career couples. The net result of all this is that people lose their basic drive for self-determination and personal competence, or they adapt to their living conditions by being satisfied with a limited sense of autonomy and competence derived from passive pursuits (e.g., television watching). Ironically, this adaptation is enhanced by escapism in and through leisure. When people use their leisure for recuperating from work in passive free-time activities, they are able to escape from their work and thereby experience some sense of autonomy—no matter how sedentary the chosen activity is.

Summary and Conclusions

This chapter has demonstrated that the nature and process of leisure is fundamentally motivational. From the time of birth, human beings pursue their interests and strive to use their capacities. They seek out optimal challenges in efforts to use and test their skills and to master new experiences. This basic human tendency toward self-determined and competence-elevating experiences constitutes the core of intrinsic leisure motivation. When an individual is intrinsically motivated in leisure, he or she has a full sense of choice and freedom, and feels that he or she is doing what he or she wants to do. The behavior chosen is experienced as optimally challenging and is expected to provide a sense of competence and enjoyment. Intrinsic motivation, however, can be undermined by factors that are experienced as controlling. Controlling factors include extrinsic rewards, sanctions, surveillance, deadlines, external evaluation of one's behavior, and if-then contingencies. On the other hand, positive feedback affirming one's sense of competence appears to enhance intrinsic motivation, especially if doing well at an activity is important to a person.

Although the basic human needs for autonomy and competence drive people toward intrinsically motivated leisure, most nonwork and free-time activities in everyday life are not self-determined. Evidence indicates that most of the nonwork time is spent in maintenance and household activities on the one hand and passive free-time activities (e.g., television watching) on the other, especially with family members. These externally prompted behaviors, however, can become self-determined through the process of identification or internalization. This process of internalization is used in everyday life to turn obligatory free-time activities into more leisurelike activities. People can grow to perform them willingly and volitionally. They are helped in this process by another psychological mechanism, escape. Even if people hate household activities that have to be done during their free time, they may realize that it is a good way to escape from work and stress and simultaneously, to contribute to the family life. As a result, they "identify" with the activity and may later come to perform it willingly.

Television watching and exercise cover most of the free time for most of the people for most of the time. The common denominator for involvement in these types of activities is that they are not self-determined initially. People exercise because they think they "should." The self-regulation process, however, can be used to internalize with exercise and turn it into a more self-determined type of activity. Ironically, those who do not exercise are able to partially fulfill their need for autonomy by choosing not to exercise. Similarly, choosing to watch television gives people an easy way to feel limited autonomy and control, but the evidence indicates that this activity does not make people feel good about themselves psychologically. Nevertheless, the limited sense of autonomy may be powerful enough to mask and hinder people from striving to fulfill their other innate needs (i.e., needs for competence and social relatedness).

Even if people are able to increase their sense of self-determination about their involvement in television watching, exercise, and similar activities, they nevertheless define as leisure only those activities that they find inherently interesting. There is abundant evidence in the literature that leisure experiences have to provide a sense of freedom, optimal challenges (i.e., promoting a sense of competence), and informal social interaction. In other words, doing what one wants to do in his or her free time and doing it with whom and when he or she wants to, is the essence of leisure for individuals. Research has shown, however, that people have to be able to regulate their social contacts, interaction, and support. This further underscores the importance of self-determination in leisure.

Most people's enduring goal for their leisure involvement is to participate whenever they can in the activity or activities they love and have "fun" doing. Evidence suggests that such enduring goals or motives are directly activated by the triggering situational cues, with the choice (to undertake an activity) eventually becoming just another routine of the mental system that is bypassed. The previously mentioned enduring goal, which is the essence of intrinsic leisure motivation, is embedded in the mental system and requires little or no conscious effort for its activation. When this general goal pursuit is hampered and constrained, people become aware of their motives and their importance and begin forming "implementation intentions" to facilitate involvement in the chosen activity.

Although all human beings are born with the needs for self-determination and competence, there are individual differences in this predisposition. These differences can be traced back to early socialization experiences and parental support (or lack of it) for children's drive toward optimal challenges. Some parents stifle their children's self-determination more than others. While the school system in general fails to promote the predisposition toward intrinsic motivation, some schools are worse than others in this respect. The resultant individual differences have a significant influence on how actively individuals strive for fulfillment of their basic psychological needs through leisure. Unfortunately, American society with its emphasis on the Protestant work ethic and conspicuous consumption of consumer goods discourages everybody from using their free time for this purpose. The work-spend-work-spend mentality makes leisure trivial and makes people slaves to work. This promotes escapism in leisure and leads to adoption of passive lifestyles. On the other hand, those who "discover" the motivational nature of leisure have a much better chance of realizing their physical, mental, social, and spiritual potential.

References

Amabile, M., Dejong, W., & Lepper, M. (1976). Effects of externally imposed deadlines on subsequent intrinsic motivation. *Journal of Personality and Social Psychology, 34,* 92–98.

Altman, I. (1975). *The environment and social behavior: Privacy, personal space, territory, crowding.* Monterey, CA: Brooks/Cole.

Argyle, M. (1992). *The social psychology of everyday life.* London, UK: Routledge.

Bargh, J., & Gollwitzer, P. (1994). Environmental control of goal-directed action: Automatic and strategic contingencies between situations and behavior. *Nebraska Symposium on Motivation, 41,* 71–124.

Blair, S. (1993). Physical activity, physical fitness, and health. *Research Quarterly for Exercise and Sport, 64,* 365–376.

Boggiano, A., & Main, D. (1986). Enhancing children's interest in activities used as rewards: The bonus effect. *Journal of Personality and Social Psychology 51,* 1116–1126.

Bradley, W., & Mannell, R. (1984). Sensitivity of intrinsic motivation to reward procedure instructions. *Personality and Social Psychology Bulletin 10,* 426–431.

Butler, R. (1953). Discrimination learning by rhesus monkeys to visual-exploration motivation. *Journal of Comparative and Physiological Psychology 46,* 95–98.

Byrne, A., & Byrne, D. (1993). The effect of exercise on depression, anxiety and other mood states: A review. *Journal of Psychosomatic Research, 37,* 565–574.

Caltabiano, M. (1995). Main and stress-moderating health benefits of leisure. *Loisir et Société/Society and Leisure, 18,* 33–52.

Chalip, L., Thomas, D., & Voyle, J. (1992). Sport, recreation and well-being. In D. Thomas & A. Veno (Eds.), *Psychology and social change* (pp. 132–156). Palmerston North, New Zealand: Dunmore Press.

Chick, G., & Roberts, J. (1989). Leisure and antileisure in game play. *Leisure Sciences, 11,* 73–84.

Clough, P., Shepherd, J., & Maughan, R. (1989). Motives for participation in recreational running. *Journal of Leisure Research, 21,* 297–309.

Coleman, D., & Iso-Ahola, S. (1993). Leisure and health: The role of social support and self-determination. *Journal of Leisure Research, 25,* 111–128.

Copp, J. (1975). Why hunters like to hunt. *Psychology Today, 9 (December),* 60–62, 67.

Crandall, R. (1979). Social interaction, affect and leisure. *Journal of Leisure Research, 11,* 165–181.

Crandall, R., Nolan, M., & Morgan, L. (1980). Leisure and social interaction. In Iso-Ahola (Ed.), *Social-psychological perspectives on leisure and recreation,* Springfield, IL: Charles C. Thomas.

Csikszentmihalyi, M. (1982). Toward a psychology of optimal experience. *Review of Personality and Social Psychology, 3,* 13–36.

Csikszentmihalyi, M. (1990). *Flow: The psychology of optimal experience.* New York, NY: Harper & Row.

Csikszentmihalyi, M., & Graef, R. (1979). Feeling free. *Psychology Today, 13 (December),* 84–90, 98–99.

Csikszentmihalyi, M., Larson, R., & Prescott, S. (1977). The ecology of adolescent activity and experience. *Journal of Youth and Adolescence, 6,* 281–294.

Deci, E., & Ryan, R. (1987). The support of autonomy and the control of behavior. *Journal of Personality and Social Psychology, 53,* 1024–1037.

Deci, E., & Ryan, R. (1991). A motivational approach to self: Integration in personality. *Nebraska Symposium on Motivation, 38,* 237–288.

De Grazia, S. (1962). *Of time, work, and leisure.* New York, NY: Twentieth Century Fund, Inc.

Dennis, W. (1960). Causes of retardation among institutionalized children: Iran. *Journal of Genetic Psychology, 96,* 47–59.

Dennis, W., & Najarian, P. (1957). Infant development under environmental handicap. *Psychological Monograph, 71* (No. 7).

Dishman, R. (Ed.). (1988). *Exercise adherence.* Champaign, IL: Human Kinetics.

Dishman, R. (1990). Determinants of participation in physical activity. In C. Bouchard, R. Shephard, T. Stephens, J. Sutton & B. McPherson (Eds.), *Exercise, fitness, and health* (pp. 75–101). Champaign, IL: Human Kinetics.

Ewert, A. (1985). Why people climb: The relationship of participant motives and experience level to mountaineering. *Journal of Leisure Research, 17,* 241–250.

Fiske, D., & Maddi, S. (1961). *Functions of varied experience.* Homewood, IL: Dorsey.

Gleitman, H. (1986). *Psychology.* New York, NY: W. W. Norton and Company.

Gordon, C., Gaitz, C., & Scott, J. (1976). Leisure and lives: Personal expressivity across the life span. In R. Binstock & E. Shanas (Eds.), *Handbook of aging and the social sciences* (pp. 310–341). New York, NY: Van Nostrand Reinhold Co.

Graef, R., Csikszentmihalyi, M., & Gianinno, S. (1983). Measuring intrinsic motivation in everyday life. *Leisure Studies, 2,* 155–168.

Grotevant, H., Scarr, S., & Weinberg, R. (1977). Patterns of interest similarity in adoptive and biological families. *Journal of Personality and Social Psychology, 35,* 667–676.

Harackiewicz, J., & Manderlink, G. (1984). A process analysis of the effects of performance-contingent rewards on intrinsic motivation. *Journal of Experimental Social Psychology, 20,* 531–551.

Harackiewicz, J., Manderlink, G., & Sansone, C. (1984). Rewarding pinball wizardry: Effects of evaluation and cue value on intrinsic interest. *Journal of Personality and Social Psychology, 47,* 287–300.

Harlow, H. (1950). Learning and satiation of response in intrinsically motivated complex puzzle performance in monkeys. *Journal of Comparative and Physiological Psychology, 43,* 289–294.

Haworth, J. (1993). Skill-challenge relationships and psychological well-being in everyday life. *Loisir et Société/Society and Leisure, 16,* 115–128.

Haworth, J., & Evans, S. (1995). Challenge, skill and positive subjective states in the daily life of a sample of YTS students. *Journal of Occupational and Organizational Psychology, 68,* 109–121.

Hull, C. (1943). *Principles of behavior.* New York, NY: Appleton-Century-Crofts.

Hunt, J. M. (1969). *The challenge of incompetence and poverty.* Urbana, IL: University of Illinois Press.

Iso-Ahola, S. (1979a). Basic dimensions of definitions of leisure. *Journal of Leisure Research, 11,* 28–39.

Iso-Ahola, S. (1979b). Some social-psychological determinants of perceptions of leisure: Preliminary evidence. *Leisure Sciences, 2,* 305–314.

Iso-Ahola, S. (1980). *The social psychology of leisure and recreation.* Dubuque, IA: Wm. C. Brown Publishers.

Iso-Ahola, S. (1984). Social-psychological foundations of leisure and resultant implications for leisure counseling. In E. Dowd (Ed.), *Leisure counseling, concepts and applications* (pp. 97–125), Springfield, IL: Charles C. Thomas.

Iso-Ahola, S. (1989). Motivation for leisure. In T. Burton & E. Jackson (Eds.), *Understanding leisure and recreation: Mapping the past, charting the future* (pp. 247–279). State College, PA: Venture Publishing, Inc.

Iso-Ahola, S. (1992). Mental training. In J. Karvonen, P. Lemon & I. Iliev (Eds.), *Medicine in sports training and coaching* (pp. 215–234). Basel, Switzerland: Karger.

Iso-Ahola, S. (1994). Leisure lifestyle and health. In D. Compton & S. Iso-Ahola (Eds.), *Leisure and mental health* (pp. 42–60). Park City, UT: Family Development Resources.

Iso-Ahola, S. (1997). A psychological analysis of leisure and health. In J. Haworth (Ed.), *Work, leisure and well-being* (pp. 131–144). London, UK: Routledge.

Iso-Ahola, S., & Weissinger, E. (1987). Leisure and boredom. *Journal of Social and Clinical Psychology, 5,* 356–364.

Iso-Ahola, S., & Park, C. (1996). Leisure-related social support and self-determination as buffers of stress-illness relationship. *Journal of Leisure Research, 28,* 169–187.

Jackson, E., Crawford, D., & Godbey, G. (1993). Negotiation of leisure constraints. *Leisure Sciences, 15,* 1–11.

Kanfer, R. (1994). Motivation. In N. Nicholson (Ed.), *The Blackwell dictionary of organizational behavior.* Oxford, UK: Blackwell Publishers.

Kleiber, D., & Richards, W. (1985). Leisure and recreation in adolescence: Limitation and potential. In M. Wade (Ed.), *Constraints on leisure* (pp. 289–317). Springfield, IL: Charles C. Thomas.

Knapp, D. (1988). Behavioral management techniques and exercise promotion. In R. Dishman (Ed.), *Exercise adherence* (pp. 203–235). Champaign, IL: Human Kinetics.

Kobasa, S. (1979). Stressful life events, personality, and health: An inquiry into hardiness. *Journal of Personality and Social Psychology, 37,* 1–11.

Kobasa, S. (1982). Commitment and coping in stress resistance among lawyers. *Journal of Personality and Social Psychology, 42,* 707–717.

Koestner, R., Zuckerman, M., & Koestner J. (1987). Praise, involvement, and intrinsic motivation. *Journal of Personality and Social Psychology, 53,* 383–390.

Langer, E., & Rodin, J. (1976). The effects of choice and enhanced personal responsibility for the aged: A field experiment in an institutional setting. *Journal of Personality and Social Psychology, 34,* 191–198.

Larson, R., Mannell, R., & Zuzanek, J. (1986). Daily well-being of older adults with friends and family. *Journal of Psychology and Aging, 1,* 117–126.

Larson, R., Zuzanek, J., & Mannell, R. (1985). Being alone versus being with people: Disengagement in the daily experience of older adults. *Journal of Gerontology, 40,* 375–381.

Lepper, M., & Greene, D. (1975). Turning play into work: Effects of adult surveillance and extrinsic rewards on children's intrinsic motivation. *Journal of Personality and Social Psychology, 31,* 479–486.

Lepper, M., Greene, D., & Nisbett, R. (1973). Undermining children's intrinsic interest with extrinsic rewards: A test of the overjustification hypothesis. *Journal of Personality and Social Psychology, 28,* 129–137.

Manfredo, M., Driver, B., & Tarrant, M. (1996). Measuring leisure motivation: A meta-analysis of the recreation experience preference scales. *Journal of Leisure Research, 28,* 188–213.

Mannell, R. (1980). Social-psychological techniques and strategies for studying leisure experiences. In S. Iso-Ahola (Ed.), *Social-psychological perspectives on leisure and recreation* (pp. 62–88). Springfield, IL: Charles C. Thomas.

Mannell, R., & Bradley, W. (1986). Does greater freedom always lead to greater leisure? Testing a person x environment model of freedom and leisure. *Journal of Leisure Research, 18,* 215–230.

McCall, R. (1974). Exploratory manipulation and play in the human infant. *Monographs of the Society for Research in Child Development, 39,* No. 155.

Mossholder, K. (1980). Effects of externally mediated goal setting on intrinsic motivation: A laboratory experiment. *Journal of Applied Psychology, 65,* 202–210.

Murray, E. (1964). *Motivation and emotion.* Englewood Cliffs, NJ: Prentice-Hall.

Neulinger, J. (1974). *The psychology of leisure.* Springfield, IL: Charles C. Thomas.

Reader, M., & Dollinger, S. (1982). Deadlines, self-perceptions, and intrinsic motivation. *Personality and Social Psychology Bulletin, 8,* 742–747.

Rodin, J., & Langer, E. (1977). Long-term effects of a control-relevant intervention with the institutionalized aged. *Journal of Personality and Social Psychology, 35,* 897–902.

Rook, S. (1987). Social support versus companionship: Effects on life stress, loneliness, and evaluations by others. *Journal of Personality and Social Psychology, 52,* 1132–1147.

Samdahl, D. (1992). Leisure in our lives: Exploring the common leisure occasion. *Journal of Leisure Research, 24,* 19–32.

Sansone, C. (1986). A question of competence: The effects of competence and task feedback on intrinsic interest. *Journal of Personality and Social Psychology, 51,* 918–931.

Schor, J. (1991). *The overworked American: The unexpected decline of leisure.* New York, NY: Basic Books.

Schreyer, R., Lime, D., & Williams, D. (1984). Characterizing the influence of past experience on recreation behavior. *Journal of Leisure Research, 16,* 34–50.

Schulz, R. (1976). Effects of control and predictability on the physical and psychological well-being of the institutionalized aged. *Journal of Personality and Social Psychology, 33,* 563–573.

Schulz, R., & Hanusa, B. (1978). Long-term effects of control and predictability-enhancing interventions: Findings and ethical issues. *Journal of Personality and Social Psychology, 36,* 1194–1201.

Schlicht, W. (1994). Does physical exercise reduce anxious emotions? A meta-analysis. *Anxiety, Stress, and Coping, 6,* 275–288.

Shaw, S. (1985). The meaning of leisure in everyday life. *Leisure Sciences, 7,* 1–24.

Starrels, M. (1994). Husbands' involvement in female gender-typed household chores. *Sex Roles, 31,* 473–490.

Swann, W., & Pittman, T. (1977). Imitating play activity of children: The moderating influence of verbal cues on intrinsic motivation. *Child Development, 48,* 1128–1132.

Thompson, C., & Wankel, L. (1980). The effects of perceived activity choice upon frequency of exercise behavior. *Journal of Applied Social Psychology, 10,* 436–443.

Tinsley, H., Barrett, T., & Kass, R. (1977). Leisure activities and need satisfaction. *Journal of Leisure Research, 9,* 110–120.

Unger, J., & Johnson, C. (1995). Social relationships and physical activity in health and club members. *American Journal of Health Promotion, 9,* 340–343.

Unger, L., & Kernan, J. (1983). On the meaning of leisure: An investigation of some determinants of the subjective experience. *Journal of Consumer Research, 9,* 381–392.

Vallacher, R., & Wegner, D. (1987). What do people think they're doing? Action identification and human behavior. *Psychological Review, 94,* 3–15.

Weissinger, E., & Bandalos, D. (1995). Development, reliability, and validity of a scale to measure intrinsic motivation in leisure. *Journal of Leisure Research, 27,* 379–400.

Zuckerman, M., Porac, J., Lathin, D., Smith, R., & Deci, E. (1978). On the importance of self-determination for intrinsically motivated behavior. *Personality and Social Psychology Bulletin, 4,* 443–446.

Leisure and Society:
A Dialectical Analysis

John R. Kelly
University of Illinois

Even though sociology was for decades the lead discipline in the study of leisure in North America and Europe, the course of development has not been linear or cumulative. Rather, research agendas, the accepted premises for research and theory, and the "common wisdom" of the field have been challenged and revised more than once. Not only have other disciplines, especially social psychology in North America, directed attention to other issues and assumptions, but also the sociology of leisure has taken a zigzag course from the 1930s to the present. Much that was taken for granted has been subjected to confirming investigation and found to be less than accurate or adequate. Further, critical perspectives have raised new issues as well as recasting old ones.

Change did not come in one great overturning, but in a sequence of revisions. A dialectical model seems to be most appropriate to follow the sequence. Through the 1950s, there was an accepted consensus as to both issues and premises. This common wisdom

(CW1) was eroded as well as challenged by new research, often built on symbolic interactionist approaches (Kelly, 1974) in place of the structure-functional bases of the earlier period. The "revised consensus" (CW2) expanded agendas for both research and theory without completely overturning earlier developments.

The dialectic, however, has not ended with a second common wisdom. Rather, a more critical antithesis has emerged to subject the second consensus to a thoroughgoing revision. The sources of this antithesis (A) have included conflict or neo-Marxist theory, gender-focused critiques, non-Western entry into the field, and various poststructural analytical approaches. Critical perspectives are associated with concepts such as hegemony and power, commodification, gender and patriarchical structures, imperialism, world-views, ideologies, and existential action. Now a central question concerns the kind of synthesis (S) that will be developed in the current dialectic.

The dialectical sequence provides a dynamic framework for a review of central areas in the sociology of leisure. Although many issues and lines of research can be identified, four have consistently been most salient along with others that are emerging to gain greater attention. The subsequent analysis will focus on three dialectical sequences, briefly suggest three others, and close with a fourth central issue. In order, then, and in a highly abbreviated form, we will summarize the dialectics of leisure in relation to;

1. work and time;
2. family and community;
3. age and the life course;
4. the three emerging issues of culture, social development, and political policy; and
5. the conceptualization of leisure.

In each concentration, only main themes can be addressed and references selected. Further, in each area the process continues, as the next synthesis is only beginning to emerge.

Work and Time

CW1—The Work-Determination Model

When sociologists turned their attention to leisure in the 1960s, three perspectives were adopted. The first, based on the earlier community studies of the Lynds and others, approached leisure as a dimension of the social organization of the community (Lundberg, Komarovsky and McInerny, 1934). The second, adopted by David Riesman, viewed leisure as social action that created its own worlds of meaning. The third, the one that came to shape domain assumption and research agendas, emerged from the sociology of work. Its fundamental premise was that economic institutions are central to society and economic roles the primary determinants of other roles. Especially, leisure was assumed to be secondary and derivative. As a consequence, various models of determination by work were proposed that modeled leisure as similar to work ("spillover" or identity), contrasting (compensation), or separate (Parker, 1971; Wilensky, 1960). The bias, however, was clearly toward some kind of determination rather than segmentation.

Some early research seemed to support this model, especially when the focus was on participation in community organizations or other activity that tends to be tied to social status. Further, there was little specification of possible confounding influences such as family background, education, and ethnicity. As research proceeded, however, the "long arm of the job" was found to be both shorter and less powerful than expected when only limited, modest, and sometimes inconsistent relationships were found between leisure styles and occupational level and type (Wilson, 1980).

In a fuller perspective, on the other hand, it was evident that economic roles are determinative of the social context of adult lives—schedules, control of resources, autonomy, and other basic conditions (Blauner, 1964). Leisure is part of the reward structure of a social system with differential access to resources based largely on socioeconomic position. Yet, with activity types as the dependent variable, demographic variables were found to account for as little as 5% and, only with a few costly or exclusive activities, as much as 10% of the variance in participation (Kelly, 1987a, pp. 138–172). It became evident that any connections between work and leisure were far more complex and subtle than any simple work status to leisure activity model could specify. In fact, one possibility proposed was that the differences were to be found in style of engagement rather than in the activities themselves (see Kelly, chapter 9 in this volume.)

The common wisdom toward a second issue also led to a retreat from another early simplistic assumption. The long-term reduction in the average workweek from as high as 80 hours in the early days of the Industrial Revolution to about 40 hours in the post–World War II period, along with the five-day week and paid vacations for many workers, led to an unquestioned assurance that more and more leisure time would be the product of increased economic productivity. Time-diary research was employed to document both trends and intersocietal differences in the availability and allocation of time in everyday life (Szalai, 1974). Leisure was commonly defined as leftover time to be filled with activity other than work and required maintenance (Neumeyer and Neumeyer, 1958). Almost immediately challenges to these truisms emerged. First, the trend toward a reduced average workweek was slowing to a halt. Second, the variety of engagements located in that allegedly vacant time called *leisure* led to a focus on the nature and social meanings of the activity. Time, seldom if ever free of all obligation or ties to the rest of life, came to be seen as an index of opportunity rather than the defining essence of leisure. And, third, variations were found to be more significant than average workweek figures that obscured differences between factory hands and managers or women and men.

CW2—Leisure as a Domain of Social Life

The first challenge to the early common wisdom was a recognition of leisure as a dimension of life with its own meaning and integrity. Leisure is more than left-over and derivative, but has its own place in the rhythm and flow of life. First, leisure came to be defined more as activity than as empty time. In France, Joffre Dumazedier was at the center of what became an international program in sociology to establish the sociology of leisure as an important sociological field. His definition of leisure as "activity—apart from the obligations of work, family and society—to which the individual turns at will for either relaxation, diversion, or broadening his knowledge and spontaneous social participation, the free exercise of his creative capacity" included most of the themes that became central to the field (Dumazedier, 1974). Among them were relative freedom of choice, distinction from the obligations of other roles, and the variety of meanings and aims that might be sought in such activity.

Just as important as the revised definition, however, was the identification of leisure as something more than a derivation of work. At about the same time in the United States, research on the relative salience of life domains found that work was not the "central life interest" of most industrial workers (Dubin, 1963). Rather, life outside of work, including family and leisure, took precedence in their value systems and social ties. Social life could not be divided into a work-versus-leisure dichotomy, but consisted of a multiple set of intersecting roles. Leisure, although having a particular connection with the bonding of family and other immediate communities (Cheek and Burch, 1976), had multiple contexts, connections, and meanings (Kelly, 1978). Dumazedier (1967) was among the first to return to the community study model in which leisure was found to be a significant element of both individual patterns of relationship and meaning as well as of the social interaction related to community institutions.

A—The Challenge of Critical Theory

Although the functional premises of most leisure sociology had been recognized and some critical possibilities suggested (Kelly, 1974), for the most part leisure sociology uncritically accepted the theoretical premises and research agendas of mainstream paradigms, functional in North America and stratification-based in the United Kingdom. The relationship between leisure and work was seldom subjected to the subversion of criticism based on Marxist premises.

East European leisure sociology tended to combine mainstream methods, especially time diaries, with uncritical and cryptofunctional Marxist premises. West European scholars were more eclectic in both methods and theory and more informed from both East and West. North American leisure sociologists have continued, for the most part, to be functional and conventional. It has been in the United Kingdom that the most ferment has stirred. Not only the accepted findings but also their domain assumptions have been challenged by critical analyses with roots in neo-Marxist cultural studies (Clarke and Critcher, 1985), historical study that focuses on power and the struggles of the working class, and social construction approaches that take into account the interpretive activity of social actors (Rojek, 1985, 1995).

The central theme of the critical challenge is social control by ruling elites. Leisure is seen as a critical element in the hegemony of ruling elites in a capitalist society. In order to assure compliance in the workplace, the political arena, and the marketplace, leisure has emerged as central to the capitalist reward and control system. Leisure is, from this critical perspective, a market-mediated instrument that binds workers to the production process and to roles that support the reproduction of the capital-dominated social system. Leisure is defined as a commodity that must be earned and is indissolubly connected to what can be purchased and possessed. Leisure is both time given by the system and a commodity distributed through the market.

Several themes are gathered in this critique. The power to enforce compliance is masked behind an ideology in which "freedom" comes to be defined as purchasing power in the marketplace of leisure. Such "commodity fetishism" (Marx, 1970) of attachment to things defines life and leisure in terms of possessions. Social status is symbolized by leisure display (Veblen, 1899/1953). Work becomes instrumental, a routinized "iron cage" in which the worker is alienated from satisfying engagement with production as well as from other workers (Andrew, 1981). Absorption in mass media legitimates consumption-oriented values and world-views (Habermas, 1975). What appear to be varying styles of leisure reflect the profoundly different conditions of work, family, and leisure assigned by class, gender, and race (Clarke and Critcher, 1985).

In this commodified false consciousness in which both class interests and personal development are misperceived and lost, life is reduced to a single dimension of material possession with the repression of the full creative, sensual, and social elements of life

(Marcuse, 1964). Leisure is neither an integrated function of the social system nor free and developmental action, but is alienated by a preoccupation with possession (Kelly, 1987a, pp. 173–204). This critique of functional approaches to the relation of work and leisure is supported by the rapid growth of market-sector leisure provisions, the time devoted to mass media, and the integration of leisure with retailing in malls, advertising, and the media. Counterevidence based on relative growth rates of cost-intensive and cost-free activities, the centrality of informal home and family activity, and the multidimensionality found in leisure satisfactions does not deter proponents of this critical perspective.

An additional theme of this critique focuses on the differential access to resources by population segments identified by gender, race, and social class. The demands on women in their dual work and family roles are based on male-constructed gender ideologies, enforced by patriarchal power, and intensified by a loss of family stability (Deem, 1986). Women experience acute restrictions on time as well as autonomy. Other scarcities and barriers are based on race and economic position. From this perspective, the alleged freedoms of leisure actually reflect a stratified social system rather than cultural preferences. Freedom may even become a constructed ideology that obscures that leisure is fully located in real social systems and cultures (Rojek, 1995).

S—A Prospective Synthesis

The fundamental presupposition of any sociology of leisure is that leisure is a thoroughly social phenomenon. It is *of* the culture and a product of the social system. Leisure is not separate and secondary, but embedded in the institutional structures, social times, and power allocations of the society. From a functional perspective, leisure is complementary to economic and family roles. In a critical framework, leisure is an instrument of hegemony, caught in a web of false consciousness and commodification. In an interpretive mode, leisure is an arena for the negotiation of self and of community.

Out of the current dialectic between the consensus and the critique, a number of issues call for attention. For all, the fundamental premise is that leisure is neither peripheral and segmented nor determined in a simple economic model. Rather, in a complex social system characterized by interrelated institutions in which both institutional control and individual self-determination differ by gender, race, class, sexual orientation, and other defining factors, leisure is woven into the system. From a social perspective, its resources, opportunities, and orientations are based in the intersecting roles of its interlocked institutions. From the perspective of the social actor, the individual, leisure offers space for action that is at the same time constructed from the symbol and value systems learned and shaped in the particular culture and yet open to redefining interpretation and action.

The first issue to be addressed is to move beyond ideologies to examine the lived conditions of poor, excluded, and disinherited children, women, and men. Their struggles for life in the present and for a future are reflected in what they do to express themselves, create community, fill ordinary hours and days, and seek new possibilities. The issue isn't whether the unemployed have leisure, but how they cope with the everyday conditions of their lives.

The second issue is to move beyond ideology to identify the ways in which economic roles provide contexts, resources, limitations, and orientations for the rest of life—family and community as well as leisure. What are the structural possibilities and limits placed on all the dimensions of life not only by economic roles but also by the nature of the economic system itself? How are the conditions of leisure and all of ordinary life constructed within a socioeconomic context that shapes time, space, and energy as well as market power? The question is not the simple determination of life and leisure by work, but how determinative definitions of both the self and society are learned in a power-differentiated social context.

The third issue is one of meanings. Just purchasing is not commodification and owning is not fetishism. Rather, when actions are dominated by the drive to own and possess rather than to use, experience, relate, and even create, then leisure reflects a more fundamental alienation. Or, is leisure truly a social space for significantly self-determined action? What are the commitments, symbols, meanings, self-definitions, and world-views that are the cognitive context of decisions and actions? What are the meanings and outcomes of leisure-related spending, media use, packaged entertainment, and images of pleasure? Possession may be a way of life or an instrument of activity. Does leisure, in fact, reflect a culture of possession? Or, is there a deep paradox between alienation and creation that permeates the entire society?

The fourth issue revolves around time. Discarding misleading models about average workweeks, what are the actual patterns and varieties of time structure and allocation? How do these patterns and possibilities vary by economic role, gender, life course, family conditions, ethnicity and race, location, and other placement factors? Time remains a basic resource for leisure action, one that not only varies widely but also is one index of the possibility of self-determination.

Finally, as people make their way through the day-to-day routines and rituals of life, does leisure provide only a little social space in which they make their lives, a small world of protection from the larger world of political and social action? Is contemporary leisure privatized and compartmentalized into a domain of family, retail consumption, and attractive trivia? Or, is it also a world of play, segmented just enough so that there is the potential of significant action, the expression of creative concepts, images, and relationships that may even threaten to break out of the private compartments into the given and accepted world? Isn't leisure, after all, the source of the critique?

Family and Community

CW1—Leisure as a Context for Family Bonding

If leisure is not just activity determined by and complementary to work, then is there some other critical relationship to the social system? The evident connection is, of course, to family and other immediate communities (Roberts, 1970). Most leisure takes place in or around the home. The most common leisure companions are family and other close friends and intimates.

The basis of the first common wisdom was the community studies from the 1930s by George Lundberg, Mirra Komarovsky, and colleagues (Lundberg et al., 1934) and the Lynds (Lynd and Lynd, 1956). Leisure was found to be a web of ordinary activity, mostly social interaction and tied to the institutions of the community from the family outward to status-based organizations. Leisure was seen as a domain of life with its own integrity and significance and yet integrated with the roles and resources of the family, home, and community.

From this perspective, the later work of Cheek and Burch (1976) argued that the primary function of leisure is to provide a context for social bonding, especially that of family and ethnic community. Despite differences in taste cultures, leisure serves to integrate immediate communities and to express and develop primary relationships. This positive view of leisure in relation to the family was supported in research that identified a correlation between joint leisure activity and marital satisfaction (Orthner, 1975).

CW2—Role Contexts for Family and Community Leisure

An anomaly in family leisure began a revision to the first consensus. The centrality of the family context was reaffirmed and the centrality of the family to leisure supported (Kelly, 1978). However, despite the traditional focus on freedom as the primary defining theme of leisure, activity with major components of obligation was found to be most important to most adults. Dumazedier (1967) might want to call family activity *semileisure,* but it is consistently most valued by most adults. Initial attempts to distinguish between "relational" leisure chosen because of positive meanings found in the interaction and "role-determined" activity in which the response to expectations was central (Kelly, 1983) were abstracted from the real process of ongoing life.

The major theme was that leisure was closely tied to central roles, not separate from them. In 1975, Rhona and Robert Rapoport added significantly to the perspective with their study of *Leisure and the Family Life Cycle.* This set of case studies demonstrated how leisure reflects the preoccupations, expectations, and opportunities that shift through the life course. Further, leisure is often a central context for working out developmental issues through the life course.

The life course perspective also provides a framework for extending this role-related approach to later life. The Kansas City studies (Havighurst, 1957; Neugarten, 1968; and others) placed leisure squarely in the context of the interests, commitments, identities, and role sets of older adults. The first major life course periods of preparation and establishment are followed by a "Third Age" with its own social contexts and aims (Gordon, Gaitz and Scott, 1976) that are characterized more by continuities of identity and action than by discontinuities (Atchley, 1993).

Leisure, then, is bound to both the roles and the developmental requirements of life. In fact, from this perspective it may be quite central to life, not residual or secondary at all. It is a primary setting for social bonding and expression as well as for human development. The implied issue, on the other hand, is the consequences for the nature of freedom and choice in leisure. No activity embedded in primary role relationships can ever be free of accompanying obligations and responsibilities (Kelly, 1987a, pp. 118–137). Leisure might be more central, but it is also less pure and simple.

A—Power and Self-Determination in Leisure Roles

The most radical response and antithesis begins with the suggestion that leisure, like other areas of life, has roles. That is, the expectations and power differentials that characterize family, work, and community roles are found in leisure as well. Currently, the most salient source of this challenging antithesis is the focus on gender, especially from a feminist perspective (Henderson, Bialeschki, Shaw and Freysinger, 1989). However, there is also the challenge posed by changing family patterns with an unbroken marriage and family through the life course becoming a minority probability.

The critique calls for sociologists to go beneath the leisure rhetoric of freedom and self-expression to the realities of lives without the power of self-determination. From this perspective, the history of the culture is characterized by male domination of women in profound and multifaceted ways that permeate every aspect of life (Deem, 1986). Not only have women been repressed in where they are permitted to go and what they are allowed to do in leisure, but also even in the home women's leisure is fundamentally different from that of men. It is usually women who are expected to do the work that makes "family leisure" possible. It is the "hidden work" of women that offers relative freedom to much of the leisure of men and children. Further, now that most women are in the paid labor force, they are required to continue with a "second shift" (Hochschild, 1989) of unpaid labor to maintain the home and family. Disruptions of the nuclear family only exacerbate such gender differences. Leisure, whatever its satisfactions, may involve considerable obligation in its unpaid labor. Research finding that building and expressing relationships is a major positive value in leisure for both men and women (Kelly, 1978) does not distinguish the sharply different gender contexts.

What, then, is the meaning of freedom and self-determination for any subordinate population segment? What about the poor, the racially and ethnically excluded, those cut off from opportunity in abandoned urban areas, and even many of the old? The resources of time, money, access, and autonomy are evidently unevenly distributed in any society, especially a capitalist one according to critics (Clarke and Critcher, 1986). Repression has shaped attitudes and self-definitions as well as interests and abilities. Even something as basic as the body is defined and directed by sexist criteria that, like most leisure, is based on male power over women. Bodies, even lives, become commodities to be controlled and possessed by those with power.

This direct critique has begun to be placed into contexts of the variety of leisure actions, contexts, meanings, and outcomes. Leisure may never again be uncritically defined as a special state of grace for the elite (de Grazia, 1964). Nevertheless, there is evidence that some may struggle for self-determination even within contexts of unequal power. Women may not only retain some leisure investment significant to their identities (Kelly, 1983), but also may struggle in their leisure to resist the confining definitions of others (Wearing, 1990; see also Shaw, chapter 16 in this volume).

In this antithesis, the connections of leisure to nonwork roles and resources, especially family and community and the positive evaluation of how leisure contributes to development through the life course are brought up against a critical model of society. Leisure may indeed be indissolubly tied to family and community, but in ways that reflect social divisions and dominations as well as expressive action. Leisure, in its centrality and role embeddedness, is subject to the same cultural and structural limitations as the rest of life. As in work, self-determination in leisure may require struggle and resistance.

S—Leisure's Immediate Context: A New Agenda

Leisure takes place in its small worlds, but also in the larger scale of the society. Further, its actualization is in the midst of the lived conditions of real life. Research may be based on premises of systemic integration and the benefits of leisure as well as challenged by critiques reflecting ideologies of subjugation and alienation. A new agenda for research, however informed, should be directed toward the actual lived conditions of decisions and actions, relationships and roles. In such an agenda related to community and family, several themes are highlighted by critiques of the common wisdom.

First, the realities of leisure as struggle for action and self-determination in the midst of acute differences in power and access to resources will receive more attention. Especially gender, race, sexual orientation, and poverty will reconstitute research strategies and frames past the easy assumptions that leisure is equally free and beneficial for all. Further, limits are more than structural. They involve how persons have learned to define themselves, their roles, and their possibilities. Significant dimensions of the struggle are social time and space as well as the immediacy of role expectations.

Second, underlying the new agenda is the theme of differential power, not only power to command resources but also to determine the course of one's life and what is required of others. In the action of leisure, there are both a relative openness for action and modes of repression that stimulate both submission and resistance. Any research that comprehends these dimensions will adopt a dialectical quality that does not presume either easy freedom or total domination.

A third theme is that of the continuities and changes in identities through the life course (Kelly, 1983). How individuals define themselves and are defined by others is central to the aims and outcomes sought in leisure. We are both existential and social beings. In any arena of action there is both freedom and bonding. Leisure is neither one nor the other; rather, it is both in a continually changing process. As such, leisure is more a dimension of life than a domain that can be defined by time and space.

Fourth, the realities of family stability and crisis as well as of community divisions and conflicts will be taken into account as the immediate communities of leisure are reformulated.

Finally, the possibility of leisure becoming increasingly privatized, bound only to immediate communities and the small worlds of personal life construction, is a perspective that runs counter to the functional view of leisure as a context for social bonding. There may be a negative side to a focus on the family basis of leisure activity and meanings. As technologies increasingly make the home a center of varied entertainment, leisure may become more and more cut off from larger communities in the privacy of remote-controlled entertainment and the surfed network. Electronic relationships can be switched off in a nanosecond with no cost or repercussions. Unlike direct and committed primary relationships, there is limited liability rather than intimacy. Again, there may be a dialectic between the spectrum of ethnic and activity-based communities of leisure and its ties to the family and household.

In general, leisure is surely not peripheral to the central concerns and relationships of life. That, however, does not lead simply to bonding without domination, to development without alienation, or to intimacy without conflict.

Aging and the Life Course

CW1—Age as an Independent Variable

The earliest common wisdom was simply that age indexed many kinds of leisure engagement. In a simple mode, age was even referred to as a cause of decreased rates of participation. It was assumed that something decremental happened to people as they aged. The rates of decline varied according to activity: rapid for sports, especially team sports; more gradual for travel and community involvement (Cutler and Hendricks, 1990).

Attention given to those in their later years, generally 60s and 70s but sometimes 50s as well, suggested that such "disengagement" might even be functional. Older people needed to consolidate their activity and recognize their limitations. It was even suggested that retired men no longer had viable social roles, at least ones that were valued. For the most part, however, age was assumed to index a combination of opportunities and abilities. Leaving school, entering the work force, family responsibilities, and retirement were usually "on time" for most adults and could be reliably designated by age.

CW2—Continuity and Change in the Life Course

The revised common wisdom began by recasting age as an index of multiple related changes rather than an independent variable. Further, the revised framework became the life course rather than linear age (Neugarten, 1968). Several themes emerged.

First, in the Kansas City study of adult life, normative disengagement was replaced with activity (Havighurst, 1961). Rather than a necessary or desirable withdrawal from activity, older people were found to revise their patterns and commitments in ways that fit their later life roles and opportunities. Leisure was conceptualized as multidimensional in meaning as well as in forms. Further, those who continued engagement were found to have the most satisfying lives. More recently, this approach has led to a discovery of the "active old," those before and in retirement who adopt lifestyles of engagement in a variety of leisure activities and relationships. Further, such engagement was consistently found to be a major factor in life satisfaction (Cutler and Hendricks, 1990).

As well, the model of inevitable decrement was challenged by research that failed to measure high correlations between age and functional ability. Rather, a model of aging that stressed *continuity* rather than loss and change was applied to leisure as well as other aspects of life (Atchley, 1993). A return to earlier socialization studies provided a base for a model that identified lines of commitment rather than age-graded discontinuity. Especially the "core" of daily accessible activity and interaction remains central to time allocation through the life course (Kelly, 1983).

Finally, the life course also provided a perspective in which intersecting work, leisure, and family roles and opportunities could be related to developmental changes (Rapoport and Rapoport, 1975). Leisure is not a list of activities dwindling with age, but a social environment in which many critical issues of life can be worked out. Developing sexual identity for teens, expressing intimacy for those exploring and consolidating family commitments, reconstituting social contexts after midlife disruptions, and ensuring social integration in later years are all central requirements of the life course that are developed in leisure. Not only interests, but also significant identities are often found in leisure as well as in family and work (Stebbins, 1979).

In the revised consensus, then, the life course with its interwoven work, family, and community roles was accepted as a valuable framework for analyzing both the continuities and changes of leisure. Leisure was seen as tied not only to role sequences, but also to developmental preoccupations. The life course was found to incorporate revisions and reorientations rather than an inevitable downhill slide measured by participation rates in selected recreation pursuits.

A—An Integrated View of Life . . . and Leisure

The fundamental challenge to the life course model has been based on increasing awareness of its presumption of "normality." The life course approach includes both continuities and changes in which all the dimensions of life are interrelated. Work, family, community, and leisure are not segregated domains, but intersecting elements in which change in one impacts the others. Further, individuals seek different "balances" of investment as they move through the shifting contexts of the life course (Kelly, 1987b). The salience of leisure may rise and fall with both role contexts and commitments to those roles (Kelly and Kelly, 1994; Freysinger, 1995.)

The regular and predictable transitions of the life course model, however, seem to gloss over many of the realities of contemporary life. A majority of adults in their middle or later years have experienced at least one disrupting trauma in health, work, or the family that has required a fundamental reconstituting of roles and orientations (Kelly, 1987b). Life courses are smooth and predictable in only a minority of cases. Further, conditions are not the same for all persons in a social system. Race and ethnicity designate different life chances. Gender differentiates opportunities for self-determination, economic and social opportunities, and socialization into roles, values, and self-concepts. Stratified societies offer markedly different opportunities and resources to elites, middle masses, and the excluded.

Nevertheless, all persons have a life course. The framework is challenged by the significant variation in conditions of race, gender, sexual orientation, and class as well as the more specific circumstances of life context. The "on-time" expectations of the traditional life-cycle metaphor are a template against which to measure variation rather than a normative or commonplace pattern.

In this perspective of continuity and change in a metaphor of life as journey, a number of issues call for attention. First, salient differences in life conditions are more than variations in starting points for the journey. Rather, deprivation and denial are cumulative in ways that affect every dimension of life. Second, individuals come to define themselves in the actual circumstances of life, not in an abstracted concept. Identities, the concepts of the self that are central to what we believe is possible and probable in our lives, are developed in the realities of the life course. And, third, the structures of the society, including access to institutional power, provide forceful contexts of opportunity and denial that shape both direction and resources for the journey.

In this revised life course approach, leisure remains as a significant dimension. It is tied to family, work, education, community, and other elements of life. Changes in one may affect all the others. Leisure, then, is distinct from the product orientation of work and the intimate bonding of the family and yet connected to both. It is expressive, focused on the experience rather than the outcome. It is relatively open rather than predetermined. It is relational more than role determined. Yet, it has meanings, resources, and relationships that change through the journey of life.

S—Leisure and the Life Course: New Agendas

From the perspective of the life course, research focusing on leisure now requires several revised issues. The following are among the most significant.

First, leisure is woven through the life course. It is existential in a developmental sense. That is, leisure is action that involves *becoming,* action in which the actor becomes something more than before. At the same time, the life course metaphor provides a dynamic perspective on the social contexts and meanings of leisure. It is social in a dynamic rather than static context. Yet, relatively little is known about just how the dimensions of productivity, bonding, and expression are related in existential action as life course contexts change (Kelly and Kelly, 1994).

Second, the developmental orientation of some leisure is highlighted by this perspective that recognizes lines of action as well as singular events and episodes. What has been termed *serious leisure* by Robert Stebbins (1979; see also chapter 5 in this volume) is activity in which there is considerable personal investment in skills and often in equipment and organization. Such investment places serious leisure in a central position in identity formation and expression. Leisure identities may provide continuity through the transitions and traumas of the life course. Yet, how women and men define themselves and take action toward redefinition has been a subject of speculation more than research.

Third, what is the place of leisure in the schema of life investments and commitments? Further, how do those investments differ according to the life conditions of men and women as they make their way through the shifting expectations and possibilities of the life course? The model does not provide a simple framework when continuities and changes, transitions and traumas, opportunities and deprivation, power and repression are all factored in. Nevertheless, nothing less can comprehend both the existential aims and social contexts of leisure.

Three Important and Undeveloped Themes

Before addressing the final issue of the implications of a new sociology of leisure for understanding the nature of leisure itself, there are three significant but undeveloped areas that should be identified. They revolve around the relationship of leisure to culture, social development, and political policy. Each theme can also be traced in a dialectical pattern.

Leisure and Culture

Culture as learned and transmitted knowledge, norms, symbol systems, world-views, and values, is, of course, the basis of all social behavior. Leisure is always *of the culture;* it is ethnic.

CW1—Leisure as Learned Behavior

Leisure is, from this perspective, a social phenomenon. As such it is learned in specific social and historical times and places. Socialization into leisure is always culture specific. Its forms have their own peculiar histories and development. There may be broad themes of leisure that are cross-cultural, but they are played out in the concrete. Further, the economic resource base of a society sets basic parameters for leisure.

CW2—Symbols and Meanings

An initial addition to the cultural theme was that leisure is more than behavior. Actions are meaningful both to the individual actor and within a sociocultural context. Not only are interests and skills learned, but also the aims and orientations of activity. Leisure is developed within symbolic environments consisting not only of language but also all sorts of signs of identification and meaning. In fact, the life course continuities and developmental directions of leisure can be understood only in the context of cultural values. Further, alienation from dominant cultures is manifested in leisure that may become a focus of social conflict (see Rojek, chapter 6 in this volume). This becomes especially evident when subcultures are identified. For example, age-based youth subcultures may find their primary expression in leisure.

A—The Challenge of the World

Most recently the North American and Western European bias of the field, by both sociologists and historians, has been challenged by a growth in interest and contributions from the East (especially the Pacific Rim and India) and from the South (Latin America and Africa). Even so fundamental an issue as the meaning of leisure comes under radical questioning. Language is only the beginning. More significantly, the meanings of time, health, community, birth and death, and of life itself all impact the meanings of leisure. No longer can Western conceptual frameworks be taken for granted when comparative studies examine what people are doing. Further, from a critical perspective, leisure in all its forms—and, especially, media and tourism—is often a manifestation of imperialism in which dominant developed economies exploit the resources (including the lives and bodies) of those in earlier, or different, periods of economic development. Not only may the resources of economically dominated cultures be exploited, but they may also become markets for the dumping of cultural wastes in media and other products.

S—A World Agenda

A new synthesis can no longer presume the cultural heritage and premises of the West. Rather, a current agenda should adopt a world perspective. The most hallowed premises will be reexamined. Even the fundamental dimension of "freedom" will require a recasting in cultures in which social solidarity takes precedence over individual development. Social action may have quite a different construction in different types of cultures. Conflicts among value systems may be obscured by polite scholarly deference. Cross-cultural studies that remain on the level of forms, implements, and artifacts may reflect an intellectual imperialism no less profound than the exploitation of markets and resources.

Leisure and Social Development

A second theme to be outlined is that of the relationship of leisure to social development.

CW1—The Industrial Base of Modern Leisure

The important conceptual work of Joffre Dumazedier (1967, 1974) was only one development that tied modern leisure to industrialization and urbanization. The presumption was that the segregation of work time and leisure time and the production of an economic surplus were the structural conditions that produced modern leisure. The resources for leisure, including time itself, were the product of the separation of production from the household, the efficiencies of the factory, the divisions of labor, and the segregation of work and nonwork time and the reductions of the former.

CW2—The Loss of Leisure in the Modern World

When leisure is conceptualized as expressive action and bonding rather than as a designation of time, then its existence prior to industrialization becomes quite evident. With this premise, industrialization might be seen to replace indigenous or "folk" culture rather than

create leisure. In the transition to an industrial society, traditional leisure conflicts with the forms that develop in the new cities. Such conflict might result in an anomic loss of traditional norms, values, and customs as well as new opportunities. Further, the inequalities in resources and power created by capitalistic industrialization make leisure a domain of display for the wealthy and of attempts at control over the poor and the dislocated. Leisure as a social space for expression can be a threat to both old forms and norms and to new patterns of social domination. Most recently, leisure in the form of tourism is also defined as an economic asset in developing societies by those who own and control economic resources and who seek outlets for investment.

A—The Transformation of Cultures

An antithesis to a model of the replacement of traditional leisure by modern forms is based on a model of the transformation of culture. Replacement may be benign or even beneficially adaptive. The reality is usually more destructive. There is no place for the traditional, even in adapted form, in the modern context. Rather, workers are wrenched from the village and its culture and placed into a new world in which leisure is a market commodity. As such, it becomes an arena of conflict as well as alienation from former identities and communities. Formerly complementary gender and age-graded roles, often repressive themselves, are lost and replaced by new forms of exploitation based on industrial labor markets. In a capital-based cultural imperialism, the old cultures are destroyed and replaced by cultures of exploitation. Development, then, does not simply produce a new leisure of segregated choice, but transforms an integrated culture into one of division and conflict.

S—Agendas of Survival and Destruction

Research attempting to understand leisure in conditions of economic and social development, then, will have to adopt a dialectical mode. Leisure is not simply a product of new conditions and a social realm of adaptation. It is also a battleground entered by forces of unequal power. The destruction of the traditional is not just a neutral evolutionary process; it may be an orchestrated goal of those who would control a powerless work force. Leisure, then, may be characterized by cultural and personal destruction. Rather than an integrated expressive dimension of a culture, it may be transformed into an expression of repression. And yet, there is the other side of the dialectic. Insofar as leisure also provides even a marginal opportunity for existential action and the development of community, then it may also produce resistance. It may become a standard for the remainder of life, a connection to former meanings when the traditional is not wholly lost in the transformation. The relationship of leisure and development would then be neither just adaptive nor destructive. Analytical approaches would be dialectical rather than either evolutionary or polarized.

Leisure and Policy

The third area to be briefly outlined is that of leisure and policy.

CW1—Public Provisions and Regulations

The conventional wisdom, at least in North America, has been that the public sector led by benevolent social activists responded to the deprivation of residents of the new industrial cities and especially of children by providing parks and recreation programs. New conditions were recognized and social welfare considerations led to a gradual development of provisions. At the same time, various regulations were also put in place by the state to provide some limits to destructive behavior, especially related to alcohol consumption, and to celebrations, organizations, and activities that were believed to threaten the social fabric. Such social control was usually seen as related to the loss of traditional norms in the complexity, crowds, and confusion of the industrial city. However, more critical social historians have also demonstrated that both the provisions and the regulations were a form of social control based on the aim of ensuring a cooperative and productive labor force.

CW2—Indirect and Implicit Policy

An addition to the initial perspective introduced greater complexity to the model, identifying dimensions of more indirect support and regulation. Taxation policies, for example, supported the real estate investments of the affluent while penalizing many common entertainments of the wage workers and the poor. Leisure provision was recognized to be multi-institutional, as schools on all levels as well as churches and voluntary organizations were supported in offering leisure-oriented programs. The "re-creation" of leisure was de-

fined as an economic asset, to be offered but also to be directed and controlled. Further, nation-states with different kinds of polity as well as command-versus-less-directed economies developed different modes of leisure policies and provisions. The special interests of economic, political, and cultural elites were given greater or lesser support in different kinds of social systems with different histories.

A—Leisure and the Market

A major challenge to the social welfare basis of public leisure policies emerged in a retreat from public welfare toward the market sector. Especially in the United States and the United Kingdom, it became policy to depend on the market sector to provide more and more leisure resources and opportunities. Such societies were developing multiple layers of market provisions for leisure. Further, the interdependency of public resources and markets, especially in relation to leisure travel, became a given of the system. Highways, waterways, air travel systems, energy subsidies, and the development of natural resources were combined into gigantic public subsidies of leisure travel. Such implicit policies favored those with the discretionary income and assets to engage in relatively cost-intensive leisure rather than those most cut off from market opportunities. Media licensing and regulation, taxation laws, and exemption from regulation formed policies as a basis for ownership and control of sport franchises, leased uses of public lands, and capital investments of all kinds are protected. Even differing modes of engagement such as venues for drinking and entertainment are differentially taxed, regulated, and supported. Critical analysis demonstrated that what is masked as neutrality or laissez-faire capitalism in leisure is actually policy that discriminates dramatically between those able to enter high-cost venues and those with negligible purchasing power.

S—Leisure and Ideology

There was a time in which leisure was lauded as central to the celebration of cultural consensus (Pieper, 1963). It was seen as being of value in a functioning social system. This ideology seems to be reborn in a climate in which leisure is supported as beneficial to the society as well as to individuals. There is an implicit ideology based on the values of economic productivity, political consensus, and social cooperation. A new agenda for the sociology of leisure can no longer take such an approach for granted. There are too many hidden assumptions in this model. Rather, any study of leisure policy should identify the ideological premises of every argument underlying every policy. There are no neutral policies that merely respond to universal need. Rather, a critical approach to policy will assess costs and benefits, the allocation and protection of resources, with measures of who benefits in multidimensional ways. How is political, economic, and social control maintained or threatened? How are reward systems consolidated or altered? How are the value systems and ideologies underlying the system implicitly affirmed or explicitly challenged? And, perhaps at the most basic level, is the productivity principle on which leisure is justified taken for granted or opened to question?

The Nature of Leisure

As already suggested, perspectives on the nature of leisure have changed in the modern period of scholarly attention from the 1930s to now. The change is not self-contained, but reflects shifts in sociological paradigms as well as drawing from other disciplines, especially social psychology.

CW1—Leisure as Free Time

Despite repeated references to Greek roots, and especially Aristotle, the accepted operational definition of leisure was that of time. This approach reflected the assumption that economic organization set the framework of life in an industrial society and that leisure existed in a time and resource context set by economic roles. The defining characteristics of such time changed, however, from being residual to being "discretionary" (Neumeyer and Neumeyer, 1958). Leisure did not require that all other role obligations be completed, but that the use of the time was more by choice than requirement. How choice was to be measured was seldom addressed.

Concurrently, international *time-budget* research quantified leisure as one type of activity that could be identified by its form (Szalai, 1974). Leisure was assumed to be clearly distinguished from work, required maintenance, and family responsibilities. The implicit operational definition was essentially "activity away from the workplace not required for self or household maintenance." And the measure was duration of time, presented in averages that obscured range and significant variations.

CW2—Meanings of Leisure

The first consensus, although persisting in many research designs, did not endure long without amendment. To begin with, it was obvious that any activity might be required, an extension of work or other roles. Further, even terms as simple as *choice* or *discretionary* implied that the actor's definition of the situation might be crucial. The meaning of the activity to the actor might be more significant than the form or even time and place of the activity. Such meanings were found to be related to roles and identities in the Kansas City adult life research (Havighurst, 1961) and to be multidimensional rather than simple.

In the 1970s the field claimed more attention from psychologists who focused on attitudes rather than activities. Leisure was said to be defined by attitudes or a "state-of-mind" that included elements such as perceived freedom, intrinsic motivation, and a concentration on the experience rather than external ends (Neulinger, 1974). Again, attention was directed toward meanings, but wholly in the actor rather than in definitions of the social context. Such psychological approaches, however, were one salient influence on sociologists who added at least three dimensions to the earlier time and activity common wisdom.

First, it was again the Kansas City research, along with the community studies, that tied leisure to social roles. The psychological approach tended to be asocial, separated from contexts. Sociologists, on the other hand, usually insisted that the meanings and attitudes varied according to social placement that was, in turn, based on gender, economic and family roles, and life course conditions (Gordon et al., 1976; Roberts, 1970; Kelly, 1978, 1983). The satisfactions anticipated in an activity involved meanings and relationships brought to the action context as well as what occurred in the time frame.

Second, the immediate experience might be the critical focus for leisure, but it occurs in particular environments that involve social learning, acquired skills and orientations (Csikszentmihalyi, 1981), and interaction with components imported from other role relationships (Cheek and Burch, 1976). Freedom is perceived or not in actual circumstances. Immersion in an experience is based on prior learning. The outcomes anticipated may extend to personal development far beyond the immediate episode. For example, prior education was found to be central to developing tastes, interests, and skills that shape choices.

Finally, and further, although the dimension of freedom recurs in the literature, studies of actual experiences and activity engagements found that leisure seldom is monodimensional. The meanings, outcomes, motivations, and experiences themselves are multifaceted (Havighurst, 1961; Kelly, 1978). Further, the social context is one important factor in those meanings. Psychological instruments measuring perceived outcomes of activity are actually summations of a process of experience that incorporates complex sequences of emotion, interpretation, engagement, action, and interaction.

Leisure, then, in the revised approaches, is a more complex phenomenon than either the earlier sociologists or psychologists proposed. In fact, the consensus appeared to break down under the weight of multiple approaches that ranged from individualistic psychology to functional sociology, from presumably self-evident quantities of time to interpretive self-definitions and lines of action, and from discrete self-presentations (Goffman, 1967) to actions embedded in life course role sequences (Rapoport and Rapoport, 1975).

A—Revolt Against the Abstract

Antithetical themes came from several directions. The most significant were based on social and sociological theory that calls into question the nature of life in society. The basic issue is whether the critical starting point of analysis is agency or structure, the actor or the society (Giddens, 1971; Rojek, 1985). Other issues include attention to the "real" contexts of leisure, such as poverty and unemployment, gender-determined roles, and a stratified social system; leisure as consumption commodified in a market system of resource allocation; and the self-negating outcomes of accommodation to an alienating system. Perhaps the underlying question is whether that alleged defining dimension of leisure, freedom, has some concrete reality or is a mirage that serves to screen the interests of controlling elites. Is leisure really as beneficent as its promoters assume? Four themes need to be explored.

First, there is agency and structure. Which is fundamental to accounting for life in society, the interpretive acts of the individual or the social context in which the action takes place? Further, since the forms and symbols by which action is directed are learned and reinforced in the society, can action be prior to the context? A number of theoretical frameworks now address this issue by beginning with how action creates and recreates the structure and how the structure both shapes and gives meaning to the action (Giddens, 1971; Rojek, 1995). Such frameworks hold the existential theme, in which action creates meaning, and the social, in which structure informs and resists all action, in a dialectical relationship (Kelly, 1981). Further, leisure itself may better be described as process that holds both agency and structure in a dynamic tension (Rojek, 1989). The nature of leisure, then, is neither a contextual act nor determined social role. Rather, it is actualized in processual action. And this process

has continuities that extend beyond the immediate to personal development and the creation of significant communities.

Second, several critical analysts have raised questions about the positive cast usually given to leisure, especially by those from a "leisure studies" or recreation academic department or agency. Such positive approaches seem to presuppose resources, options, perspectives, and self-determination that are, in fact, unequally distributed in societies (Clarke and Critcher, 1986). Do the unemployed have leisure at all when they are cut off from central productive roles? Do the poor have enough resources for discretion and choice to be meaningful concepts? Do histories of subjugation and life-defining limits for women in male-dominated societies make assumptions of self-determining action a sham? Are contexts of leisure opened and closed by factors of economic and social position? The real contexts of leisure are not voids of time and space, but are extensions of the structures of the society and ideologies of the culture. Leisure does not exist in an ideal world, but in the real and highly differentiated world. Recently postmodern vocabularies and metaphors have been employed to extend the attack on previous simplistic models of leisure as a separate realm of relative freedom (Rojek, 1995).

Third, a related critique is that of commodification. In a market system, leisure opportunities are premised on a consumption model. Leisure is buying, purchasing, renting, or otherwise acquiring marketed resources and opportunities. Although such consumption is not all there is to leisure, it is an element that places biases and limits on action and decision.

Fourth, a consequence of this distorted and constricted context of leisure is alienation. Leisure is not necessarily free, creative, authentic, and community-building activity. It may also be, perhaps at the same time, stultifying and alienating. It may separate rather than unite, narrow rather than expand, and entrap rather than free. It may even be destructive and exploitive. It may, in short, be negative as well as positive. It takes place, or not, in the real lived conditions of people's lives. Sociologically, it is not a rarified ideal or perfect experience. It is real life, often struggle and conflict as well as development and expression.

The dialectic between expression and oppression that characterizes the rest of life in society is the reality of leisure as well. Being role-based in a stratified society means being limited, directed, and excluded. The contexts of any experience, however free and exhilarating, are the real culture and social system. The multiple meanings of leisure include separation as well as community, determination as well as creation, and routine as well as expression. The former simplicity of leisure as essentially a "good thing" becomes alloyed by situating it in the real society with all its forces, pressures, and conflicts.

S—Leisure as a Dimension of Life

The question, then, is what does such extension and critique do to any conceptualization of the nature of leisure? Leisure encompasses both the existential and the social. It has myriad forms, locales, social settings, and outcomes. Leisure is neither separated from social roles nor wholly determined by them. Leisure has developed amid conflict as well as social development, in division as well as integration, with control as well as freedom. It may involve acquiescence as well as resistance, alienation as well as authenticity, and preoccupation with self as well as commitment to community. Leisure, then, is multidimensional and cannot be characterized by any single or simple element.

A further issue is whether leisure is really a domain of life at all in the sense of being defined by boundaries. Is leisure clearly distinguished from work, family, community, church, and school? Or is it a dimension of action and interaction within them all? Several perspectives suggest that leisure is more a dimension than a domain.

In the life course metaphor, leisure is tied to the shifting roles of each major period. In the Preparation Period, for teens leisure is a social space for the exploration and development of sexual identities as well as working out the issues of peer identification and independence from parents and the past. It also stresses the theme of expression that is central to developing a sense of selfhood, of personal identity among emerging social roles. In the Establishment Period, leisure adds the dimension of bonding to intimate others, especially in the formation and consolidation of the family. In the Third Age, leisure has meanings tied to both integration with significant other persons and of maintaining a sense of ability when some work and community roles are diminished in salience. Leisure, then, might be conceptualized as being woven into the intersecting role sequences of the life course rather than being a segregated realm of activity.

Yet, there must also be distinguishing elements of leisure or it disappears into the ongoing round of life. Further, those elements should be significant in relation to central issues of life such as production and work, love and community, sexuality and gender, learning and development, emotion and involvement. It should connect with the lived conditions of ordinary life rather than be an esoteric and precious idea to be actualized only in some rare and elite conditions.

Leisure, then, may be more a dimension than a domain, more a theme than an identifiable realm (Dumazedier, 1967; Kelly, 1987; Kelly and Kelly, 1994). That dimension is characterized by a number of characteristics. First, it is action in the inclusive sense of doing something, of intentioned and deliberate act. Such action is existential in producing an outcome with meaning to the actor. Second, this action is focused on the experience more than the result. It is done primarily because of what occurs in the time-and-space-bound act. And, third, leisure as a dimension of life is characterized by freedom more than necessity. It is not required by any role, coercive power, or repressive ideology. Leisure is not detached from its social and cultural contexts, but is a dimension of relatively self-determined action within the contexts. Its meaning is not in its products as much as in the experience, not in its forms as much as its expression.

The Sociology of Leisure

The sociology of leisure, then, is not a closed book nor a finalized product. Rather, central issues are currently being raised that promise to reform the field in its premises as well as conclusions. No common wisdom will go unchallenged, no consensus remain unchanged, and no theoretical formulation be above conflict. Yet, such a dialectic makes the field exciting. More important, every challenge, every conflict, and every developing synthesis provides a new basis for at least one conclusion: that leisure is a significant dimension of life that calls for both disciplined and innovative attention.

References

Andrew, E. (1981). *Closing the iron cage.* Montreal, Quebec: Black Rose.

Atchley, R. (1993). Continuity theory and the evolution of activity in later adulthood. In J. Kelly (Ed.), *Activity and aging* (pp. 5–16). Thousand Oaks, CA: Sage Publications, Inc.

Blauner, R. (1964). *Alienation and freedom: The factory worker and his industry.* Chicago, IL: University of Chicago Press.

Cheek, N., & Burch, W. (1976). *The social organization of leisure in human society.* New York, NY: Harper & Row.

Clarke, J., & Critcher, C. (1986). *The devil makes work: Leisure in capitalist Britain.* Champaign, IL: University of Illinois Press.

Csikszentmihalyi, M. (1981). Leisure and socialization. *Social Forces, 60,* 332–340.

Cutler, S., & Hendricks, J. (1990). Leisure and time use across the life course. In R. Binstock & E. Shanas (Eds.), *Handbook of aging and the social sciences.* New York, NY: Van Nostrand Reinhold.

Deem, R. (1986). *All work and no play: The sociology of women and leisure.* Milton Keynes, UK: Open University Press.

De Grazia, S. (1964). *Of time, work, and leisure.* Garden City, NY: Doubleday.

Dumazedier, J. (1967). *Toward a society of leisure.* New York, NY: Free Press.

Dumazedier, J. (1974). *Sociology of leisure.* Amsterdam, Netherlands: Elsevier.

Dubin, R. (1963). Industrial workers' worlds: A study of the central life interests of industrial workers. In E. O. Smigel (Ed.), *Work and leisure.* New Haven, CT: College and University Press.

Freysinger, V. J. (1995). The dialectics of leisure and development for women and men in midlife. *Journal of Leisure Research, 27,* 61–84.

Giddens, A. (1971). *Capitalism and modern social theory.* Cambridge, UK: Cambridge University Press.

Goffman, E. (1967). *Interaction ritual.* New York, NY: Anchor Books.

Gordon, C., Gaitz, C., & Scott, J. (1976). Leisure and lives: Personal expressivity across the life span. In R. Binstock & E. Shanas (Eds.), *Handbook of aging and the social sciences.* New York, NY: Van Nostrand Reinhold.

Habermas, J. (1975). *Legitimation crisis.* Boston, MA: Beacon Press.

Havighurst, R. (1957). The leisure activities of the middle aged. *American Journal of Sociology, 63,* 152–162.

Havighurst, R. (1961). The nature and values of meaningful free-time activity. In R. Kleemeier (Ed.), *Aging and leisure.* New York, NY: Oxford University Press.

Henderson, K. A., Bialeschki, M. D., Shaw, S. M., & Freysinger, V. J. (1989). *A leisure of one's own.* State College, PA: Venture Publishing, Inc.

Hochschild, A. (1989). *The second shift.* Berkeley, CA: University of California Press.

Kelly, J. R. (1974). Sociological perspectives and leisure research. *Current Sociology, 22,* 127–158.

Kelly, J. R. (1978). Situational and social factors in leisure decisions. *Pacific Sociological Review, 21,* 313–330.

Kelly, J. R. (1981). Leisure interaction and the social dialectic. *Social Forces, 60,* 304–322.

Kelly, J. R. (1983). *Leisure identities and interactions.* London, UK: Allen & Unwin.

Kelly, J. R. (1987a). *Freedom to be: A new sociology of leisure.* New York, NY: Macmillan Publishing.

Kelly, J. R. (1987b). *Peoria winter: Styles and resources in later life.* Lexington, MA: Lexington Books.

Kelly, J. R., & Kelly, J. R. (1994). Multiple dimensions of meaning in the domains of work, family, and leisure. *Journal of Leisure Research, 26,* 250–274.

Lundberg, G., Komarovsky, M., & McInerny, M. (1934). *Leisure: A suburban study.* New York, NY: Columbia University Press.

Lynd, H., & Lynd, R. (1956). *Middletown.* New York, NY: Harcourt Brace.

Marcuse, H. (1964). *One-dimensional man.* Boston, MA: Beacon Press.

Marx, K. (1970). *The economic and philosophical manuscripts of 1844.* London, UK: Lawrence & Wishart.

Neugarten, B. (1968). *Middle age and aging.* Chicago, IL: University of Chicago Press.

Neulinger, J. (1974). *The psychology of leisure.* Springfield, IL: Charles C. Thomas.

Neumeyer, M., & Neumeyer, E. (1958). *Leisure and recreation.* New York, NY: Ronald Press.

Orthner, D. (1975). Leisure activity patterns and marital satisfaction over the marital career. *Journal of Marriage and the Family, 37,* 91–102.

Parker, S. (1971). *The future of work and leisure.* New York, NY: Praeger.

Pieper, J. (1963). *Leisure: The basis of culture.* New York, NY: Random House.

Rapoport, R., & Rapoport, R. (1975). *Leisure and the family life cycle.* Boston, MA: Routledge & Kegan Paul.

Roberts, K. (1970). *Leisure.* London, UK: Longmans.

Rojek, C. (1985). *Capitalism and leisure theory.* London, UK: Tavistock.

Rojek, C. (1989). Leisure and recreation theory. In E. L. Jackson & T. L. Burton (Eds.), *Understanding leisure and recreation: Mapping the past, charting the future*. State College, PA: Venture Publishing, Inc.

Rojek, C. (1995). *Decentring leisure*. Thousand Oaks, CA: Sage Publications, Inc.

Stebbins, R. (1979). *Amateurs: On the margin between work and leisure*. Beverly Hills, CA: Sage Publications, Inc.

Szalai, A. (1974). *The use of time: Daily activities of urban and suburban populations in twelve countries*. The Hague, Netherlands: Mouton.

Veblen, T. (1899/1953). *The theory of the leisure class*. New York, NY: New American Library.

Wearing, B. (1990). Beyond the ideology of motherhood: Leisure as resistance. *Australia and New Zealand Journal of Sociology, 25*, 36–58.

Wilensky, H. (1960). Work, careers and social integration. *International Social Science Journal, 2*, 543–560.

Wilson, J. (1980). Sociology of leisure. *Annual Review of Sociology, 6*, 21–40.

Serious Leisure

Robert A. Stebbins
University of Calgary

Following on the intellectual foundation laid by Josef Pieper, Sebastian de Grazia, Max Kaplan, and others, the term *serious leisure* made its debut in leisure studies circles in 1982. The initial statement (Stebbins, 1982) and several more recent ones centered on the nature of serious leisure, which is now reasonably well-expressed in what seems to have become the standard abbreviated definition of this type of activity: serious leisure is the systematic pursuit of an amateur, hobbyist, or volunteer activity that participants find so substantial and interesting that, in the typical case, they launch themselves on a career centered on acquiring and expressing its special skills, knowledge, and experience (Stebbins, 1992, p. 3).[1] This is prob-

ably as good a depiction of this form of leisure as can be presented in a one-sentence definition.

Serious leisure is commonly contrasted with *casual* or *unserious* leisure, the immediately intrinsically rewarding, relatively short-lived pleasurable activity requiring little or no special training to enjoy it (Stebbins, 1997). Among its types are play (including dabbling), relaxation (e.g., sitting, napping, strolling), passive entertainment (e.g., television, books, recorded music), active entertainment (e.g., games of chance, party games), sociable conversation, and sensory stimulation (e.g., sex, eating, drinking). Casual leisure is considerably less substantial and offers no career of the sort just described for serious leisure. It can also be defined residually as all leisure not classifiable as amateur, hobbyist, or career volunteering.

The goal of this chapter is twofold: to present an overview of several of the basic components of serious leisure theory and the research supporting them; and to explore the role of serious leisure in the Information Age. Except where noted otherwise, this overview is

---

[1]I use the term *career* broadly in this definition, following Goffman's (1961, pp. 127–128) elaboration of the idea of "moral career." Such careers are available in all substantial, complicated roles, including especially those in work, leisure, deviance, politics, religion, and interpersonal relationships (see also Hewett, 1991, p. 246; Lindesmith, Strauss and Denzin, 1991, p. 277).

based on a 15-year study of eight groups of amateurs (summarized and theoretically elaborated in Stebbins, 1992) and subsequent studies of two hobbyist fields (reported in Stebbins, 1995, 1996a, 1996c) and one volunteer field. The amateur groups were examined sequentially over the 15-year period, starting with groups in classical music and continuing with those in theatre, archaeology, baseball, astronomy, Canadian football, entertainment magic, and stand-up comedy. Upon completing the longitudinal project, I turned to the realm of hobbies where I first studied barbershop singers and then explored the nature of cultural tourism from the serious leisure perspective. More recently, I used the same perspective to examine Francophone volunteers working in two western Canadian cities (Stebbins, 1998b).

The Nature of Serious Leisure

For a more thorough understanding of serious leisure, it is necessary to move beyond the handy but nonetheless limited one-sentence definition to look more closely at its three basic types. Amateurs are found in art, science, sport, and entertainment where they are inevitably linked in a variety of ways with their professional counterparts. For their part, the professionals are identified and defined according to theory developed in the social scientific study of professions, a substantially more exact procedure than one relying on the simplistic and, not infrequently, commercially shaped common-sense images of these workers. In other words, when studying amateurs and professionals it will not suffice to define these two categories descriptively, such as by noting that the activity in question constitutes a livelihood for the second but not the first and that the second works full time at it whereas the first pursues it part time. Rather it must be noted that the two are locked in, and therefore defined by, a system of relations of far greater complexity than this (see Stebbins, 1992).

Hobbyists lack this professional alter ego, even if they sometimes have commercial equivalents and often have small publics who take an interest in what they do. Hobbyists can be classified according to one of five categories: collectors, makers and tinkerers, activity participants (in noncompetitive, rule-based pursuits), players of sports and games (where no professional counterparts exist), and enthusiasts in one of the liberal arts. Fishing (Bryan, 1977), bird-watching (Kellert, 1985), and barbershop singing (Stebbins, 1996a) exemplify the third, whereas field hockey (Bishop and Hoggett, 1986), long-distance running

(Yair, 1990), and competitive swimming (Hastings, Kurth and Meyer, 1989) exemplify the fourth. The liberal arts hobbyists are enamored of the systematic acquisition of knowledge for its own sake. This is typically accomplished by reading voraciously in a field of art, sport, cuisine, language, culture, history, science, philosophy, politics, or literature (Stebbins, 1994).

Volunteers, the third basic type, engage in volunteering, defined and described by Jon Van Til (1988, p. 6) as follows:

> Volunteering may be identified as a helping action of an individual that is valued by him or her, and yet is not aimed directly at material gain or mandated or coerced by others. Thus, in the broadest sense, volunteering is an uncoerced helping activity that is engaged in not primarily for financial gain and not by coercion or mandate. It is thereby different in definition from work, slavery, or conscription.

It should be noted, however, that the field of career volunteering is narrower, even if it does cover considerable ground. The taxonomy prepared by Statistics Canada (1980) lists seven types of organizations, each providing different services with the help of career volunteers: health (physical and nonphysical healthcare for all ages), educational (service inside and outside the formal school system), social and/or welfare (childcare, family counseling, correctional services), leisure (service in athletic and nonathletic associations), religious (service in religious organizations), civic and/or community action (advocacy, service in professional and labor organizations), and political (service in political organizations). Although much of career volunteering appears to be connected in some way with an organization of some sort, the scope of this leisure is possibly even broader, perhaps including the kinds of helping devoted individuals do for social movements or for neighbors and family.[2] Still, the definition of serious leisure restricts attention everywhere to volunteering in which the participant can find a career, in which there is more or less continuous and substantial helping, rather than one-time donations of money, organs, services, and the like (Stebbins, 1996d).

Serious leisure is further defined by six distinctive qualities, which are found among amateurs, hobbyists, and volunteers alike. One is the occasional need to *persevere,* as seen in confronting danger (e.g., in

---

[2] I am indebted to Stanley Parker for calling my attention to this possibility.

eating wild mushrooms; Fine, 1988, p. 181), managing stage fright (e.g., when participating in theater and sport; Stebbins, 1981) or handling embarrassment (e.g., while doing volunteer work; Floro, 1978, p. 198). Yet, it is clear that positive feelings about the activity come, to some extent, from sticking with it through thick and thin, from conquering adversity.

A second quality is, as indicated earlier, that of finding a *career* in the endeavor, shaped as it is by its own special contingencies, turning points and stages of achievement or involvement.

Most, if not all, careers in serious leisure owe their existence to its third quality: serious leisure participants make a significant personal *effort* based on specially acquired *knowledge, training,* or *skill,* and, indeed at times, all three. Examples include such achievements as showmanship, athletic prowess, scientific knowledge, and long experience in a role.

Fourth, a number of *durable benefits* or *rewards* of serious leisure have so far been identified, mostly from research on amateurs and hobbyists. They are self-actualization, self-enrichment, self-expression, regeneration or renewal of self, feelings of accomplishment, enhancement of self-image, social interaction and belongingness, and lasting physical products of the activity (e.g., a painting, scientific paper, piece of furniture). A further benefit—self-gratification, or pure fun, which is by far the most evanescent in this list—plays a minor role in serious leisure, even though it is one of the most appealing benefits of casual leisure.

The fifth quality—participants in serious leisure tend to *identify* strongly with their chosen pursuits—springs from the presence of the other five. In contrast, casual leisure, although hardly humiliating or despicable, is nonetheless too fleeting, mundane, and commonplace for most people to find a distinctive identity there. I imagine that this was the quality Cicero had in mind when he coined his famous slogan: *Otium cum dignitate,* or "leisure with dignity."

The sixth quality of serious leisure is the *unique ethos* that grows up around each expression of it. A central component of this ethos is the special social world that develops when enthusiasts in a particular field pursue their interests in it over many years. Unruh (1979, p. 115) defines the social world as:

> a unit of social organization which is diffuse and amorphous. . . . Generally larger than groups or organizations, social worlds are not necessarily defined by formal boundaries, membership lists, or spatial territory. . . . A social world must be seen as an internally recognizable constellation of actors, organizations, events, and practices which have coalesced into a perceived sphere of interest and involvement for participants. Characteristically, a social world lacks a powerful centralized authority structure and is delimited by . . . effective communication and not territory nor formal group membership.

In a later paper, Unruh (1980) added that social worlds are characterized by voluntary identification, by a freedom to enter into and depart from them. Moreover, because they are so diffuse, it is common for their members to be only partly involved in all the activities they have to offer; after all, a social world may be local, regional, multiregional, national, even international. Third, people in complex societies are often members of several social worlds, only some of which are related to leisure. Finally, social worlds are held together, to an important degree, by semiformal, or "mediated communication." They are rarely heavily bureaucratized, yet because of their diffuseness, they are rarely characterized by intense face-to-face interaction. Rather, communication is typically mediated by newsletters, posted notices, telephone messages, mass mailings, Internet communications, radio and television announcements, and similar means, with the strong possibility that the Internet could become the most popular of these in the future.

Missing from Unruh's conceptualization of the social world, but vitally important for the study of serious leisure, is the proposition that a rich subculture is found there as well, one function of which is to interrelate the "diffuse and amorphous constellations." Consequently, it should be noted that members find associated with each social world a unique set of special norms, values, beliefs, styles, moral principles, performance standards, and similar shared representations. Only by taking these elements into account can we logically speak about, for example, social stratification in social worlds, as Unruh does when distinguishing insiders from regulars, and as I have done in distinguishing devotees from participants in serious leisure (Stebbins, 1992, p. 46).

To the extent that lifestyles form around complicated, absorbing, satisfying activities, as they invariably do in serious leisure, they can also be viewed as behavioral expressions of the participants' central life interests in those activities. Dubin (1992, p. 41) says that such an interest constitutes "that portion of a person's total life in which energies are invested in both physical/intellectual activities and in positive emotional states." Sociologically, a central life interest is often associated with a major role in life. And since they can only emerge from positive emotional states, obsessive and compulsive activities can never become central life interests. Given their substantial appeal and the deep satisfaction they engender, amateur, hobbyist, and career volunteer activities must be regarded as quintessential central life interests, an interpretation validated repeatedly in the various studies in this area.

The Marginality of Serious Leisure

Each of my studies of amateurs, hobbyists, and career volunteers has supported the proposition that they, and in some instances their activities, are socially marginal. This is most evident for the amateurs, who are neither dabblers nor professionals. But it is noted elsewhere (Stebbins, 1998a) that all serious leisure is characterized by a significant level of commitment to a particular pursuit as expressed in processes like regimentation and systematization. This commitment is measured, among other ways, by the sizeable investments of time, energy, and emotion its enthusiasts make in their leisure as a central life interest. These qualities marginalize serious leisure participants in a world dominated by casual leisure, producing a picture that contradicts common sense. For example, participants in serious leisure pursue their activities with such passion and earnestness that Goffman (1963) was led to describe them in his book *Stigma* as "quietly disaffiliated deviants."[3] The views of journalist Charles Gordon (1992) further exemplify the popular attitude:

> In the first place, the reaction of many people to the Age of Leisure is to work longer and harder—in other words to refuse to participate in it. In the second place, others have taken to the Age of Leisure by turning leisure into work.
>
> You have only to set foot—or wheel—upon one of our bicycle paths to appreciate the point. For many people, the bicycle is not a leisure vehicle, used to tootle in a leisurely way through the greenery of the capital. No, it is an instrument of performance—used to create fitness, and to measure it in kilometers per hour, in distance traveled.

> The bicycle is not to be taken lightly. Bicycling is serious business. Do not go slowly in front of a serious cyclist.
>
> Something similar is happening to bird-watching, a pursuit that used to be confined to slightly dotty denizens of the slow lane. There could be no activity less intense than strolling through the woods carrying a book and a set of binoculars.
>
> Now something has happened. In the Age of Leisure, bird-watching is called birding and birding has become competitive. Last month something called the World Series of Birding was in New Jersey. There were 46 teams and heaven knows how many birds.
>
> Which brings us to gardening. . . .

Furthermore, serious leisure tends to be uncontrollable; it kindles in its practitioners a desire to engage in the activity beyond the time and money available for it. Whereas some casual leisure can also be uncontrollable, the marginality proposition implies the presence in serious leisure enthusiasts of a significantly stronger and more enduring tendency in this direction. Finally, the amateurs, who it was just said occupy the status of peripheral members of the profession on which they model their activities, are nevertheless judged in their execution of those activities by the standards of that same profession. It seems that the publics of, for example, a civic orchestra, an industrial league baseball team, or an amateur theater company have the professional counterparts of these groups in mind when measuring the quality of the performances of the amateurs.

The kind of marginality under consideration here differs from the kind afflicting the "marginal man," a concept used for many years by sociologists to explain the lifestyles of immigrants. The latter are marginal because, in the typical case, they are caught between two cultures where marginality becomes a way of life, a condition touching nearly every corner of their existence. Although this ethnic marginality and the leisure marginality on which the present chapter focuses both center on peripheral, ambiguous social statuses, the second kind of marginality is hardly as pervasive as the first. Rather, leisure marginality is a segmented and, hence, limited marginality associated with certain uncommon central life interests.

In leisure marginality, as in ethnic marginality, we find among the marginal people themselves, as well as in the wider community, an *ambiguity*, a lack of clarity, as to who they really are and what they really do. The research on amateurs and hobbyists shows

---

[3]As good a descriptor as "quietly disaffiliated" is, Goffman's decision to classify such people as deviant fails to square with the serious leisure participants' views of themselves and, for that matter, with the canons of deviance theory (e.g. Stebbins, 1996b, pp. 2–7). For a discussion of deviant leisure, see Stebbins (1997) and Rojek (chapter 6 in this volume).

the multifaceted nature of this ambiguity. On the cultural side, ambiguity is manifested narrowly as a conflict of expectations and, broadly, as a conflict of values. On the social side, incongruent status arrangements develop, such as when amateurs in pursuit of their leisure goals help professionals reach their work goals (e.g., amateur astronomers gathering data on variable stars for professional astronomers to analyze, amateur musicians serving as supplementary players in a professional symphony orchestra). On the psychological side, participants may become ambivalent toward their serious leisure as they confront their own marginality during the many and diverse expressions of this ambiguity in everyday life. The following episode taken from the baseball study exemplifies the psychological ambiguity inherent in serious leisure:

> One father arrived at a late Sunday afternoon practice with his two young boys: "My wife had to be away this afternoon," he commented. "She said you watch them or stay home." He had to leave the field several times during the workout to break up a fight between them or soothe a minor injury incurred while scampering around the bleachers or surrounding area. (Stebbins, 1979, p. 220)

In summing up these ideas about ambiguity, it is evident that both the practitioners of a serious leisure activity and the members of the larger community are inclined to see it as marginal to the main problems around which the social institutions of work, family, and leisure have developed and to the principal ways in which members of the society are trying to solve those problems.

My explorations in all three types of serious leisure demonstrate further that family and work and even other leisure activities pull many serious leisure practitioners in two, if not three, directions at once, making time demands that together often exceed the total available hours. Moreover, unlike family and work activities, where institutional supports sustain serious involvement, such support for activities of equivalent substance is absent in leisure. For example, such widely accepted values as providing for one's family, working hard on the job, and being family-centered—all of which help justify our efforts in these spheres—are simply lacking in most serious leisure.[4] In addition,

their very existence in the institutions of family and work threatens amateur involvement elsewhere by minimizing the importance of the latter while inflating that of the former.

Most critical, however, is the observation that serious leisure practitioners are marginal even to the institution of leisure itself. In other words, implicitly or explicitly, they reject a number of the values, attitudes, and patterns of behavior making up the very core of modern leisure, which is constituted mostly of casual activities. For instance, many an interviewee told me about his or her feeble interest in television or in such passive leisure as frivolous conversation and people watching. Like marginal people everywhere, then, those who go in for serious leisure lack key institutional supports for their goals, as well as for their individual and collective ways of reaching them.

Marginal statuses are common in industrial societies where rapid social change frequently gives birth to new forms of work and leisure. Still, as time passes in these societies, certain forms do become less, sometimes even much less, ambiguous and marginal, as seen, for instance, in Rosenthal's (1981) study of chiropractors. In fact, a few forms even become central. Nevertheless, according to the research conducted to this point, such a transformation has so far failed to occur for any of the serious leisure activities. Yet, as I will argue later, the effects of the Information Age and the continued decline in the significance and availability of work could well give this kind of leisure a more prominent place in community life than ever before in modern times. Such a rise in stature is especially likely for volunteering, said in a subsequent section to be poised to take over some of the important personal functions once filled by paid work.

In the meantime, the serious leisure participants with whom I have spoken generally seem quite undisturbed by the marginality of their activities. They see them as harmless social differences of which they are rather proud: indeed, they are committed to a deeply fulfilling serious leisure activity in an era when most people are committed only to the comparatively superficial search for pure fun. A badge of distinction you might say, which they wear with pride, even while most of the other people in their lives have some difficulty understanding the values and motives that explain and justify their love for amateurism, hobbyism, or career volunteering.

---

[4]Some fields of career volunteering, rooted as they are in altruistic ideals, may be shown in future research to be blessed with a higher degree of communitywide support than is given to the typical amateur and hobbyist activities.

Serious Leisure in the Community

Notwithstanding its marginality, serious leisure does make many a significant contribution to the community. One of these comes through the great variety of social worlds it generates, with each one offering a profound sense of belonging and participation for the different types of members found there (see Unruh, 1979, on member types). This sense is evident in nearly every study of serious leisure that has examined this question, including most recently Mittelstaedt's (1995) detailed description of the enthusiasts who populate the bustling social world of American Civil War reenactments. Here the senses of participation and belonging were observed to be linked to their specialized involvements in this social world.

Additionally, serious leisure can stand as evidence for the millions of people who do not pursue it that leisure can be more than pure hedonism and something other than a wretched malady of contemporary Western civilization, Glasser's (1970) bitter indictment set out in *Leisure: Penalty or Prize?* And to the extent it is pursued with other people, serious leisure can contribute significantly to communal and even societal integration. For example, Thompson (1992) found that the members of a women's tennis association in Australia, who met weekly for matches, came from a range of different social classes and age groups. In a similar vein, as part of the observational component of the Francophone volunteer project, I sat on the Board of Directors of a French-language community organization composed of a realtor, teacher, banker, homemaker, data analyst, business executive, high-school student, and myself, a sociologist and university professor. There was also a nearly equal representation of the two sexes who, together, ranged in age from 16 to around 65. Likewise, Olmsted (1988) describes how gun collectors from the city and its hinterland rub elbows periodically at various "gun shows" where they display their collections for, and discuss them with, the general public and no small number of dealers.

Serious leisure also has a far-reaching salutary effect on the general welfare of the community. Put more concisely, it benefits its publics in important ways, as when a community orchestra gives a performance or the local astronomical society hosts a "star night." The latter is open to anyone interested in observing the evening sky through the portable telescopes of the society's amateur members. Finnegan (1989) describes for the English new town of Milton Keynes the complex, positive effect on the different music publics of its entire local amateur-professional-hobbyist music scene.

Given that serious leisure makes many contributions to the community, it is reasonable to interpret participation in such leisure as akin to voluntary simplicity. Elgin (1981, p. 33) writes that, among other things, voluntary simplicity is:

> a way of living that accepts the responsibility for developing our human potentials, as well as for contributing to the well-being of the world of which we are an inseparable part; a paring back of the superficial aspects of our lives so as to allow more time and energy to develop the heartfelt aspects of our lives.

The voluntary simplicity movement, which also goes by the denominations of simple living and creative simplicity, was launched in the mid 1930s with an article written by Richard Gregg.[5] Since its adherents also espouse many other principles, this way of living is by no means identical with serious leisure. Nevertheless, the two share the ideals of encouraging and fostering personal development through realizing individual human potential and contributing to the welfare of the wider community.

The Search for Organizational Roots

Several writers, among them Rifkin (1995), Howard (1995), and Aronowitz and DiFazio (1994), have observed that the number of people with substantial amounts of free time on their hands is growing dramatically, paralleling the rapid spread of electronic technology across all sectors of the economy and the sharp reduction in employment opportunities that nearly always follows in its wake. The Information Age has dawned, and these authors speculate that one possible, far-reaching consequence of this radical transformation of modern life, albeit a consequence these authors only allude to, is that free-time activity of equal substance is now the only substitute people have for the respectable identity and central life interest they once knew in their work.

The work—or more accurately nonwork—situation of many people in the Information Age will consist, in part, of being cast adrift from the key organizational

---

[5]See Elgin (1981, pp. 297–298) for bibliographic information on the several reprinted versions of Gregg's article.

moorings they had when they were employed. More and more these people will find themselves floating without a rudder in an organizationless sea, a result of their unemployment, retirement, or marginal affiliation with a work organization as a temporary consultant or limited-term contractual worker. True, this absence of organizational ties will likely bother some people very little; their family relationships and friendship networks are all they will ever want. Others, however, may well miss the sense of belonging to a collectivity with significantly greater public visibility than that provided by networks and relationships. If this proposition turns out to be true, being cut off from the organizational belongingness they once enjoyed at work will inspire these former employees to search for other organizations capable of replacing this loss.

Although there are forms of serious leisure with little or no organizational structure, most notably the liberal arts hobbies, the vast majority show much the opposite tendency. People seeking new organizational ties can find elaborate social worlds in the latter, consisting of clubs, associations, commercial dealers, useful services, organized routine events, and on and on. Volunteers almost invariably work in or for an organization of some kind. The main exceptions here are the votaries who serve as volunteers in social movements so new that formal organizational structures have yet to evolve.

In addition, although there is no gainsaying that serious leisure and its enthusiasts are marginal in the ways set out earlier, this condition may only enhance their sense of organizational belonging. When the larger community sees them as, say, quaint, eccentric, or merely different, their solidarity is strengthened in significant measure by this public evaluation with which they must all live. In the meantime, the many leisure organizations provide socially visible rallying points for the leisure identities of their members, as well as outlets for the central life interests they share. Furthermore, a club, team, orchestra, or society commonly serves as the hub, or an important hub, of the lifestyle lived by the enthusiasts pursuing the associated serious leisure activity.

These remarks suggest that serious leisure can offer many benefits in the jobless future now faced or soon to be faced by many people in the industrialized world. But, before these benefits can be experienced by the general population, several stubborn obstacles must first be surmounted, possibly one of the most difficult being how to stimulate the popular appetite for leisure.

Conclusion:
Is Leisure Desirable?

For those currently lacking a work-based central life interest, it is unfortunate that, owing to a variety of obstacles at present, a life filled with serious leisure is more a tantalizing vision than an imminent reality. One of these obstacles is personal, whereas the others are social and economic. Space limitations permit discussion only of the first (some of the social and economic obstacles are considered in Stebbins, 1998a).

Reid and Mannell (1994, pp. 252–253) found, in their review of the research bearing on the question of whether leisure is desirable, that many people in the industrialized countries the world over are truly ambivalent toward it.

> A fundamental ideology of industrial society has been the idea of work centrality. . . . Work in the mature capitalist society is comprised mainly of paid employment. In order to maintain an adequate supply of labor, including a sufficient pool of unemployed who are ready to replace those who become too expensive to their employers, workers have been led to believe that paid work is not only noble but the very essence of life. People without paid work come to believe that their lives are incomplete, lacking in self-worth and individual dignity. . . . Traditionally, work is seen as the activity through which an individual's self-identity is created and sustained. The centrality of work is viewed to be the major ingredient for constructing social and psychological as well as economic well-being.

Work has always taken precedence over leisure in modern times, although it appears to dominate more in North America than in Europe. This is true because people generally like work, identify with it, need the money, and hardly know how to use their time after work, or because they are influenced by a combination of these factors and possibly others.

But Reid and Mannell also found research indicating that work has been declining as a central life interest during the last two decades of the twentieth century, with leisure rising in its stead as the more and more attractive alternative. This transformation is still only partial, however. As Aronowitz and DiFazio (1994,

p. 301) put it: "work remains the fulcrum of our cultural aspirations—among them the values of success, well-being, [and] self-worth." The attitude of the unemployed attests to this observation. Unemployment revolves much more around the search for work than around the search for leisure. First of all, unemployment does not automatically result in leisure for its victims; for them it automatically results only in free time, time after obligations are met. Viewed from another angle, unemployment is *forced* free time. As such, it has raised the question in social science circles of whether a person in this situation can find stimulating, or true, leisure of any kind, be it casual or serious.

What evidence exists on the matter suggests that there are many individual differences in the experience of unemployment and in the kinds of activities people turn to when trying to counteract its worst effects (Haworth, 1986). For instance, in comparison with the unemployed in lower level occupations, the unemployed in upper level occupations, including unemployed professionals, are more likely to turn to serious leisure and, in this manner, ride out the dispiriting effects of their economic plight. The former are more often overwhelmed by the act of being thrown out of work, suffering from depression and lethargy to such an extent that pursuing leisure of any kind becomes next to impossible (Kay, 1990). For these people, the feeling of being useless when out of work and the pressure from social convention to continually search for work, help produce a frame of mind that virtually alienates them from true leisure. In short, they are too demoralized to engage in leisure, which is purposive activity designed to achieve a particular end. Meanwhile, languishing in boredom is neither leisure nor work although, according to Isaac Watts's aphorism, "for Satan finds some mischief still for idle hands to do," it could become the impetus for seeking deviant leisure in some circles (Stebbins, 1997).

Moreover, both Reid and Mannell (1994) and Aronowitz and DiFazio (1994) have found that, whereas some workers may aspire to more time after work and more leisure within this period, they nonetheless fail to see leisure as playing a central role in their lives, even in retirement. This outlook on the relationship between work and leisure holds despite the increasingly routine, unattractive character of most work these days. For many people the appeal of modern work is largely extrinsic, emanating primarily from its remuneration and the opportunity it offers for sociality.

Still, ever-growing numbers of workers have no choice in the matter: electronic technology is forcing them out of full-time employment and, increasingly, out of gainful employment of any kind. As a consequence, after-work time is growing at the expense of

in-work time and, whatever the present-day employee's evaluation of work vis-à-vis leisure, he or she will soon likely be in a position to experience much more of the latter and much less of the former. I suggest for all who will face this situation, however, that worthwhile, dignified, serious leisure exists and that, whether this leisure is pursued as a replacement for or a supplement to work, it is capable of serving as a powerful central life interest with an appealing identity and lifestyle of its own. And it does happen on occasion that a participant turns his or her hobbyist, amateur, or volunteer activity into a partial or complete livelihood.

One major legacy passed on to Western civilization by the electronic revolution is the difficult challenge of making the pursuit of serious leisure possible for large segments of the population. A number of thinkers have risen to this challenge proposing a variety of solutions, several of which are reviewed elsewhere (Stebbins, 1998a). This much may be said here: once a person is irrevocably out of work, once he or she is no longer searching for it, the condition of being unemployed becomes much less threatening, and serious leisure can be more favorably regarded as a desirable activity in its own right. Research by Aronowitz and DiFazio (1994, p. 336) attests the validity of this assumption:

> Recipients of guaranteed annual income who are relieved of most obligations to engage in labor do not fall apart. The incidence of alcoholism, divorce, and other social ills associated with conditions of dysfunctionality does not increase among men who are not working. Nor do they tend to experience higher rates of mortality than those of comparable age who are engaged in full-time work. Given the opportunity to engage in *active nonwork* [emphasis added], they choose this option virtually every time.

Assuming that the various serious leisure activities are reasonably well-publicized, people who want to participate in them will somehow find them.

So it seems we are moving into an era where it will be possible for many people to enjoy a serious leisure activity as their central life interest expressed in a rich and satisfying lifestyle enhanced still further by an appealing social-personal identity. Envisaged here is a society where a sizeable segment of the population devotes itself to nonpaid amateur, hobbyist, and career volunteer pursuits in lieu of, or in addition to, working at remunerated jobs. Thus, to the extent that people are willing to regard leisure in a more favorable light, it is possible to argue that the Information Age is on the verge of giving birth to the Leisure Age.

In all this, serious leisure research should be keeping pace with serious leisure demand, which it is not doing. For example, only two qualitative studies have been conducted on career volunteering from this perspective (see Arai, 1995; Stebbins, 1998b), while the research record is even slimmer for the liberal arts hobbies and making and tinkering. And what about children and adolescents in serious leisure? I argued initially (Stebbins, 1979, p. 28) that amateurism was almost exclusively an adult undertaking, but Spector (Corinne Spector, personal communication, October 1997), in the only study on this question, found that all three types of serious leisure occupied a special place in the lives of the Israeli adolescents she interviewed (see also Csikszentmihalyi, Rathunde and Whalen, 1993). There is also a great deal of work to be done with reference to women and serious leisure. Although I approached this subject ethnographically in the studies of theater, magic, stand-up comedy, and barbershop singing (Stebbins, 1979, 1984, 1990, 1996a), no one, to my knowledge, has interviewed women about the diversity of serious leisure they pursue, the meaning it holds for them, the costs and rewards they experience, and so on.

Finally, we have only speculated about the larger public's perception of serious leisure. The participants themselves and many leisure researchers hold that it is highly honorable activity, while some of the latter even hope that serious leisure will eventually "dignify" the broader field of leisure studies. For everywhere in the Western world, and especially in North America, leisure studies has suffered since its inception with the stigma of being the science of the trivial when compared with such "important" disciplines as the study of work or the examination of major social problems. A survey of the general public's estimation of casual and serious leisure could tell us in concrete terms about the dignity of the two forms relative to each other and to work.

References

Arai, S. M. (1995). *Healthy communities and empowerment: A study of process and sustainability.* Unpublished master's thesis, University of Waterloo, Waterloo, Ontario.

Aronowitz, S., & DiFazio, W. (1994). *The jobless future: Sci-tech and the dogma of work.* Minneapolis, MN: University of Minnesota Press.

Bishop, J., & Hoggett, P. (1986). *Organizing around enthusiasms: Mutual aid in leisure.* London, UK: Comedia Publishing Group.

Bryan, H. (1977). Leisure value systems and recreational specialization: The case of trout fishermen. *Journal of Leisure Research, 9,* 174–187.

Csikszentmihalyi, M., Rathunde, K., & Whalen, S. (1993). *Talented teenagers: The roots of success and failure.* New York, NY: Cambridge University Press.

Dubin, R. (1992). *Central life interests: Creative individualism in a complex world.* New Brunswick, NJ: Transaction Publishers.

Elgin, D. (1981). *Voluntary simplicity: Toward a way of life that is outwardly simple, inwardly rich.* New York, NY: William Morrow.

Fine, G. A. (1988). Dying for a laugh. *Western Folklore, 47,* 177–194.

Finnegan, R. (1989). *The hidden musicians: Music-making in an English town.* Cambridge, UK: Cambridge University Press.

Floro, G. K. (1978). What to look for in a study of the volunteer in the work world. In R. P. Wolensky & E. J. Miller (Eds.), *The small city and regional community* (pp. 194–202). Stevens Point, WI: Foundation Press.

Glasser, R. (1970). *Leisure: Penalty or prize?* London, UK: Macmillan Publishing.

Goffman, E. (1961). *Asylums: Essays on the social situation of mental patients and other inmates.* Garden City, NY: Doubleday.

Goffman, E. (1963). *Stigma: Notes on the management of spoiled identity.* Englewood Cliffs, NJ: Prentice-Hall.

Gordon, C. (1992). Another major step forward: Taking the fun out of leisure. *Ottawa Citizen,* June 21, p. 19.

Hastings, D. W., Kurth, S., & Meyer, J. (1989). Competitive swimming careers through the life course. *Sociology of Sport Journal, 6,* 278–284.

Haworth, J. T. (1986). Meaningful activity and psychological models of nonemployed. *Leisure Studies, 5,* 281–297.

Hewitt, J. P. (1991). *Self and society* (5th ed.). Boston, MA: Allyn & Bacon.

Howard, A. (Ed.). (1995). *The changing nature of work.* San Francisco, CA: Jossey-Bass, Inc.

Kay, T. (1990). Active unemployment—A leisure pattern for the future. *Loisir et Société/Society and Leisure, 12,* 413–430.

Kellert, S. R. (1985). Bird-watching in American society. *Leisure Sciences, 7,* 343–60.

Lindesmith, A. R., Strauss, A. L., & Denzin, N. K. (1991). *Social psychology* (7th ed.). Englewood Cliffs, NJ: Prentice-Hall.

Mittelstaedt, R. D. (1995). Reenacting the American Civil War: A unique form of serious leisure for adults. *World Leisure and Recreation, 37*(1), 23–27.

Olmsted, A. D. (1988). Morally controversial leisure: The social world of gun collectors. *Symbolic Interaction, 11,* 277–288.

Reid, D. G., & Mannell, R. C. (1994). The globalization of the economy and potential new roles for work and leisure. *Loisir et Société/Society and Leisure, 17,* 251–266.

Rifkin, J. (1995). *The end of work.* New York, NY: G. P. Putnam's Sons.

Rosenthal, S. F. (1981). Marginal or mainstream: Two studies of contemporary chiropractic. *Sociological Focus, 14,* 271–285.

Statistics Canada. (1980). *An overview of volunteer workers in Canada* (Cat. No. 71–530). Ottawa, Ontario: Minister of Supply and Services.

Stebbins, R. A. (1979). *Amateurs: On the margin between work and leisure.* Beverly Hills, CA: Sage Publications, Inc.

Stebbins, R. A. (1981). Toward a social psychology of stage fright. In M. Hart & S. Birrell (Eds.), *Sport in the sociocultural process* (pp. 156–163). Dubuque, IA: Wm. C. Brown Publishers.

Stebbins, R. A. (1982). Serious leisure: a conceptual statement. *Pacific Sociological Review, 25,* 251–272.

Stebbins, R. A. (1984). *The magician: Career, culture, and social psychology in a variety art.* Toronto, Ontario: Clarke Irwin.

Stebbins, R. A. (1990). *The laugh-makers: Stand-up comedy as art, business, and lifestyle.* Montreal, Quebec: McGill-Queen's University Press.

Stebbins, R. A. (1992). *Amateurs, professionals, and serious leisure.* Montreal, Quebec: McGill-Queen's University Press.

Stebbins, R. A. (1994). The liberal arts hobbies: A neglected subtype of serious leisure. *Loisir et Société/Society and Leisure, 16,* 173–186.

Stebbins, R. A. (1995). *The connoisseur's New Orleans.* Calgary, Alberta: University of Calgary Press.

Stebbins, R. A. (1996a). *The barbershop singer: Inside the social world of a musical hobby.* Toronto, Ontario: University of Toronto Press.

Stebbins, R. A. (1996b). *Tolerable differences: Living with deviance* (2nd ed.). Toronto, Ontario: McGraw-Hill Ryerson.

Stebbins, R. A. (1996c). Cultural tourism as serious leisure. *Annals of Tourism Research, 23,* 948–950.

Stebbins, R. A. (1996d). Volunteering: A serious leisure perspective. *Nonprofit and Voluntary Sector Quarterly, 25,* 211–224.

Stebbins, R. A. (1997). Casual leisure: A conceptual statement. *Leisure Studies, 16,* 17–25.

Stebbins, R. A. (1998a). *After work: The search for an optimal leisure lifestyle.* Calgary, Alberta: Detselig.

Stebbins, R. A. (1998b). *The urban Francophone volunteer: Meaning and community growth in a linguistic minority.* Manuscript for publication.

Thompson, S. (1992). Mum's "tennis day": The gendered definition of older women's leisure. *Loisir et Société/Society and Leisure, 15,* 271–289.

Unruh, D. R. (1979). Characteristics and types of participation in social worlds. *Symbolic Interaction, 2,* 115–130.

Unruh, D. R. (1980). The nature of social worlds. *Pacific Sociological Review, 23,* 271–296.

Van Til, J. (1988). *Mapping the third sector: Voluntarism in a changing political economy.* New York, NY: The Foundation Center.

Yair, G. 1990. The commitment to long-distance running and level of activities. *Journal of Leisure Research, 22,* 213–227.

Deviant Leisure:
The Dark Side of
Free-Time Activity

Chris Rojek
Nottingham Trent University

Academic interest in deviant leisure has been negligible. This is surprising because popular culture in film, television, crime fiction and "real life" documentaries seems to be preoccupied with the question of deviant leisure. See any film by Quentin Tarantino or Oliver Stone; read any novel by Elmore Leonard or John Grisham; follow any "action" television series, such as "LA Law," "Miami Vice" or "The Bill," and you are drawn into an amoral world where casual violence, murder, drug use, destruction of property, double dealing, and theft dominate narrative content. All of this could be explained away as "mere play" or "analytically insignificant" were it not for the fact that millions of us spend our leisure time watching these films and television shows, reading these books and fantasizing and mind voyaging about these worlds where there are no moral limits on free-time behavior. In brief, the consumption of deviant leisure is conventionally enjoyed, albeit vicariously, as a "normal" part of leisure in Western society.

Yet students of leisure have, on the whole, ignored both "real" acts of deviant leisure and the huge culture industries that revolve around packaging deviant leisure to consumers in "entertaining" and "amusing" forms. Instead they have concentrated on the construct of *normal leisure* and treated it methodologically as a universal field (Dumazedier, 1974; Kaplan, 1975; Parker, 1983; Roberts, 1981). Stebbins (1992, see also chapter 5 in this volume) has elaborated some important aspects of the construct with his concept of *serious leisure*. He identifies this with the pursuit of a leisure "career." Six distinctive qualities mark out serious leisure:

1. the need to persevere with some forms of voluntary chosen activity;
2. finding a sense of development and improvement in the activity;
3. expressing personal effort in acquiring knowledge, training, skill;
4. achieving durable benefits;

5. participating in the unique ethos that grows up around an activity; and
6. identifying strongly with the chosen pursuit.

That serious leisure is an aspect of contemporary leisure practice is not in dispute. Stebbins's decision to privilege it over what he calls *casual leisure* is more objectionable. I will return to take up this point in more detail later. At this stage in the discussion it is important to note that what is surprising in Stebbins's account is the absence of a sustainable moral dimension in the sixfold characteristics which he lists as describing serious leisure. Stebbins's model has been approvingly applied by McQuarrie and Jackson (1996) in a study of adult amateur ice-skating, but the characteristics could just as easily describe the free-time activity of drug subcultures, pedophile rings, gang rapists, and serial killers. The amorality of everyday life is a nonissue in Stebbins's discussion. Instead, it is *assumed* that the concept of serious leisure exclusively applies to activity which is personally enriching and socially improving. Deviant leisure is an invisible category in Stebbins's work.

A further difficulty with Stebbins's concentration on serious leisure is that it skates over the sociological significance of casual leisure. The latter refers to the desultory, time-filling, time-killing activities in contemporary leisure practice. Simmel (1971) predicted that this sort of activity would occupy a greater part of everyday leisure in the twentieth century. He maintained that the trend of modern life makes it increasingly difficult to formulate stable, lasting relationships with anything or anyone. He explains the failure of the majority to achieve this end with reference to the increasing velocity, uncertainty and resulting anxiety of urban-industrial life. In a situation where you cannot be sure that you will be able to pay your study fees next semester or be in a job next year or with the same partner next decade or able to pay the cost of the necessary repairs on your property or physically able to think, move and feel for the duration of your natural life, the levels of anxiety and neurosis are bound to get in the way of "seriously" concentrating upon anything. Durkheim (1897) identified broadly similar tendencies in his commentary on *anomie*. He defined *anomie* as a state of normlessness in which the integrative principles that normally hold society together are buckled out of shape and cease to maintain a regulative quality. He regarded this state of affairs to be temporary and he advocated institutional reform as the solution to renew principles of moral integration into social life. Simmel is a much less optimistic thinker. He identifies change and disruption as unavoidable characteristics of modern life. He therefore implies that the conditions associated with anomie will be permanent. Seizing upon this argument, Kracauer (1975), writing in the 1920s and 1930s, argued that the nineteenth-century notion of leisure as a reward for work and an enclave of rest and relaxation in a busy world is already out of date. Taking the case of tourism, he argues that for today's tourist, pleasure does not lie in arriving, but in the constant switch of contrasts and stimuli that accompany tourist movement. Tourism, he submits, will increasingly tend towards a state of "pure mobility" in which constant movement and the search for difference become the dictating ends of travel. Extrapolating from these writers, it is more appropriate to conclude that the general defining quality of leisure relations today approximate to a state of "serious distraction" as opposed to the careerist notion of serious leisure espoused by Stebbins. That is, the discontinuous, fragmented, desultory aspects of leisure are more revealing about the character of modern leisure than the traditional notions of continuity and durability.

To some degree, the emphasis that Simmel and Kracauer place upon velocity, differentiation, fragmentation and hybridity anticipates the central arguments of postmodernism. Although the issues involved in the debate around modernity and postmodernity are well-understood in the social sciences, it is striking and not a little dispiriting that they have been largely overlooked in leisure studies. Publications and conferences involving students of leisure still seem to be preoccupied with critical debates rotating around old-fashioned '70s-style debates on class and sexual politics. Thus, Clarke and Critcher (1985) present a principled and powerful yet bloody-minded defense of the centrality of class in the study of leisure. It is bloody-minded because it never discusses the rather large and growing literature in sociology and cultural studies which questions the use of class as a preeminent concept in social analysis. Instead it dismisses this literature as being irrelevant. Meanwhile, feminist authors like Deem (1986), Bialeschki and Henderson (1986), Wimbush and Talbot (1988), and Scraton (1993), who have done so much to expose the myopia of functionalist thought in the study of leisure, continue to use concepts like the "common world of women" and "patriarchy" as if poststructuralism and postfeminism have simply never happened. The situation is dispiriting because while it is quite common to find that a dominant, hegemonic position in a field of study is out of touch with reality, one looks to the major critical positions in the field to be up-to-date and alive to new ideas. From the foregoing it is apparent that I do not think that this is the case with leisure studies.

So what has caused what I perceive to be a failure to connect with the compelling issues of modern social life and the attempts of contemporary social theory to make sense of them? Four points must be made.

First, leisure studies has defined itself as part of the meliorist, progressive tendency in social development. It is concerned with reinforcing social order and/or improving social and cultural conditions. As a result the positive aspects of leisure practice have been emphasized. Leisure activity which takes the form of antisocial and amoral behavior has been categorized as belonging to criminology and social policy. As with Durkheim's concept of anomie, the antisocial and amoral aspects have been dismissed as intrinsically temporary features of leisure.

Second, leisure activity possesses a positive connotation in Western society. It is seen as the "reward" for labor and the time and space in which we can "be ourselves." There is an important sense in which the culture of leisure is saturated with a heavily progressive ideology which identifies leisure with personal enrichment and social health. Antisocial and amoral behavior is typically associated with pathological behavior per se. This has contributed to medicalization of this behavior in the hands of psychiatrists, psychologists and criminologists. Students of leisure have colluded with this tendency by treating antisocial and amoral forms of free-time behavior as the preserve of the medical and paramedical sciences.

Third, leisure studies has typically regarded the development of leisure practice in strong evolutionist terms. The notion of "breaks" or "ruptures" in practice has been resisted. When new "postmodern" forms of behavior become identified in the social sciences, the "natural" response in leisure studies is to redefine them into the mainstream.

The fourth point is the prosaic observation that the expansion of leisure studies in the university system was concentrated in the late 1970s and 1980s. This was the heyday of the kind of Marxism and feminism espoused by the likes of Clarke and Critcher, Talbot, Scraton, and Bialeschki and Henderson. Their ideas were developed in the context of a powerful establishment consisting of functionalist, male-stream theorists who were typically either bewildered or constitutionally hostile to the new radical ideas being expressed. So it is understandable why neo-Marxist and feminist critics hold fast to their ideas with such a passion. However, the cuts in university funding in the 1980s and 1990s have meant that these critical positions have not been systematically exposed to the new critical positions in poststructuralism and postmodernism. There have been very few full-time academic posts available,

so it has been difficult for people working in these new critical traditions to become established.

Leisure and Productivism

Much of the failure of leisure studies to come to terms with deviant leisure can be explained by the general research and analytical context in which the discipline emerged. Leisure studies took off in social conditions dominated by productivism. Productivism is the philosophy that work is the central life interest. Sayers (1987) argues that productivism expresses our basic "species need" to transform ourselves through labor, and by this means, to transform our world. There is some dispute about the origins of productivism. For example, Applebaum (1992) warns that there are dangers in conflating it with industrialization. Following Weber (1976), he submits that the work ethic has clear preindustrial origins in Christian teachings and particularly in the rise of Protestantism. However, there is no dispute that productivism is the philosophy par excellence of industrial society. The term *industrial society* is used deliberately because both capitalists and socialists have identified work as the cornerstone of personal fulfillment and social well-being. Of course, there are differences in how the two systems identify the meaning of work.[1] But both insist that work is the prerequisite for healthy human existence. The growth of leisure studies in the 1950s and 1960s occurred in a context in which central aspects of productivism were being critically challenged. Before coming to the nature of these challenges it is important to give a description of what was understood by productivism in the period.

In the twentieth century, Fordism is the principal organizational exponent of productivism. Fordism is associated with the management and production techniques associated with Henry Ford.[2] Its essence is that full employment and mass consumption form an integrated circuit of economic and moral regulation. By

---

[1]Briefly, capitalism tended to identify the meaning of work in terms of market value; whereas communism identified work as an element in the construction of a qualitatively better form of society.

[2]Fordism borrowed many practices from Taylorism or "scientific management." The production process was broken down into simple, mechanical tasks in a coordinated system of production. However, Fordism was planned as a system of consumption as well as production. The five-dollar, eight-hour day was a formula used to attract workers (see Gartman, 1994).

introducing large-scale, capital intensive, standardized production systems, Fordism laid the foundations of a job market with a heavy dependence upon the mass employment of semiskilled laborers. The moral aspect was stressed in the requirement of workers to possess the right attitude and show the proper values to remain in paid employment.

Fordism follows the productivist logic of deriving the category of leisure from the category of work. In every essential respect, work is treated as prior and determining. The end of work is held to be income generation rather than job satisfaction. Indeed, Fordism accepts that the work condition of machine-based, assembly line production consists of repetitive, uninteresting, regimented task activity. However, the "reward" for this is an attractive wage scale which is output driven and typically systematized under an incentive scheme; and also the guarantee of full employment. The heavy emphasis on economic return translates into a strong consumerist orientation in leisure. Fully developed Fordism presents the category of leisure as little more than organized consumption activity. The wages generated on the shop floor are devoted to consuming the commodities of mass society. These commodities are portrayed as being open to anyone who is prepared to work. Thus, freedom in leisure is redefined in terms of the ability to realize consumer choice rather than the freedom to drop out of the system or to challenge its moral basis.

A number of additional features follow from the Fordist model of normal work and leisure relations. With regard to relations between the sexes, the most important is the tacit assumption that the male is the breadwinner. Although the strong consumerist orientation of Fordism eventually legitimized the idea of working wives, the philosophy was based in the belief that domestic relations are the preserve of women while it is the duty of the male to achieve and secure gainful employment.

Another assumption is that the Fordist economy ordinarily delivers stable full employment. Workers will typically have a secure work career between the ages of 18 and 65. The promise of this security, together with the commitment to continuous economic growth, legitimizes the system.

A further assumption is that voluntary abstention from labor is the mark of immorality for all save the rich who have sufficient capital wealth to avoid entering the labor market. For voluntary abstention is only possible by accepting the arrangements for subsistence welfare which are the contributions of those in paid employment. To put it bluntly, those who choose not to participate in paid employment can only live by consuming the welfare fund built up by the great mass of workers who voluntarily choose to exchange their time for paid employment.

These features help to remind the reader that Fordism cannot be understood correctly as a mere economic system. The attitude toward women and the voluntary workless points to a system geared to the total social, cultural and moral regulation of subjects. Fordist categories of work and leisure provide the basis for moral judgments concerning the qualities of deviant and abnormal behavior. By the same token they automatically define the criteria for the popular comprehension of order and normality. Fordism must then be understood as an all-encompassing system of economic, cultural, and moral control.

Of course, this power was not without contradictions. Some of the main ones have already been touched upon. For example, the confinement of women to the domestic sphere was at odds with the expansionist logic of mass consumer culture which called upon the consumer to acquire ever-new commodities. The solution was gradually to permit women to enter the work force and to shift from single to dual employment family units. Similarly, the "freedom" promised to the worker via wage labor and the realization of consumer choice was at odds with the dependency of the worker upon the labor market and the limited range of commodities available at any one time in consumer culture. Fordism shackled workers to the labor market and subjected them to what Ferguson (1992) has aptly called "an infinity of wanting" in the market for consumer goods.[3]

Yet with respect to the question of deviant leisure it was perhaps in the matter of unemployment that the contradictions of Fordism were most sharply revealed. As we have seen, Fordism treated full employment as the normal condition in society. The category of leisure is derived from this position. The meaning and legitimation of its consumerist orientation was based in the principle that full employment supplied consumers with the income to enable them to realize consumer choice. Of course, Fordism acknowledged the condition of unemployment. However, it typically operated with a dichotomous model of unemployment. That is, it distinguished between what might be called the transitory and involuntary workless. Briefly, the

---

[3]Ferguson's point is that the individual can never be satisfied under consumer culture. Two processes ensure this. In the first place, the commodities available in any shopping street or metropolis represent a fragment of the whole market of commodities. Secondly, "the constant revolutionizing of the means of production" (Marx and Engels, 1968) is paralleled by the "constant revolutionizing in the means of consumption." Advertising and new inventions mean that consumer wants can never be fulfilled.

salient characteristics of the two types can be enumerated as follows:

1. *The Transitory Workless:* those who have been temporarily laid off or are between jobs. Members of this category have a commitment to work and experience unemployment as a temporary interruption of the condition of wage labor or caring for the family.
2. *The Involuntary Workless:* those who have been without work for more than 12 months. Members of this category may have experienced being in work (e.g., some disabled groups). Or they may be based in regions where traditional local sources of employment have failed (e.g., mining districts, fishing towns, iron and steel communities). This category is committed to work, but unable to achieve the condition of wage labor or family life because of structural or personal reasons.

What is glossed over in this dichotomous model is the strata of social actors who voluntarily choose to be unemployed. The term *strata* is used advisedly because membership of this group is extremely varied. At one end, one finds the aristocracy and super rich who live off investment capital and regard the voluntary abstention from work to be a mark of distinction. Veblen (1899) wrote of "the leisure class" who associate paid employment with a reduced form of life. Although the leisure class is often critical of many aspects of the social order, their lifestyle activities typically function to reinforce the ruling order of things. For the stability of this order is the basis for their investment wealth. The leisure class is basically a conformist stratum that organizes its leisure lifestyle to conserve the social order. For example, Veblen (1899) argues that this class sets standards of etiquette and conspicuous consumption that are emulated by the lower orders. For Veblen the ultimate end of emulation is to engineer voluntary consent to the existing social order. Davidoff's (1973) study of the courtship and recreational rituals of the aristocracy broadly confirms Veblen's argument. At the other end, one finds a motley collection of alternative lifestyle members, such as artists, bohemians, travelers, tramps, thieves, drug addicts, and alcoholics, who have voluntarily chosen not to work. One might refer to this collection as "the alternative leisure class." Three characteristics identify them:

1. they reject wage labor and monogamy as viable lifestyle options;
2. they are often skeptical or hostile to the values of "straight" society, which they regard as being unduly limiting or personally damaging; and
3. they lack private capital, and volunteer to exchange the option of wage labor and/or marriage for a rootless and often nomadic existence.

The members of the alternative leisure class frequently engage in dissent and the dissemination of nonconformist values. They do this by dropping out, producing critical art works, engaging chronically in criminal behavior, protesting, rejecting pecuniary values, and developing a lifestyle ethic that celebrates sharing above personal acquisition, hedonism above instrumentality, and expressiveness above self-discipline. From the standpoint of Fordism, the leisure class and the alternative leisure class are modes of existence which deviate from the standard or "normal" Fordist categories of work and leisure. Fordism explains away their critical, destabilizing activities by redefining them as being located at the margins of society. Fordism disapproves of the profligacy of the leisure class and it denounces the criminal activities of the alternative leisure class. However, because these practices are defined as being situated at the margins of normal life they can safely be left to the moralizing of tabloid newspapers and the policing arrangements of the state.

It is this question of marginality that I wish to take issue with here. The emergence of leisure studies coincided with the development of "the permissive society." A central feature of this configuration was the stereotyping of paid labor as dehumanizing and brutalizing. Marxism was, of course, the crucial source of this outlook. Marx regarded paid labor in capitalist society to be intrinsically exploitative, since the purpose of the labor time is to produce surplus value which is then appropriated by the owner of capital. Advocates of the permissive society stressed that the work relation was the hub of a whole system of exploitative and dehumanizing arrangements in the family, education, urban relations, environmental conditions, and community life. The solution was to practice and promote lifestyle values which were oriented against personal acquisition, domination, and exploitation. These criticisms were articulated at the high point of Fordist domination. In the 1960s the Fordist economy seemed to promise full employment, affluence, and assured continuous growth. A decade later this ceased to be true. Fordism was based in stable supply conditions and predictable market demands. Following the oil crisis of the 1970s, and the onset of unemployment, neither supply nor demand conditions could be guaranteed. Profit margins were maximized by responding to new consumer wants quickly and transferring resources from unprofitable to profitable investment. The economies of scale involved in Fordism militated against flexible accumulation and, since the 1970s, Fordist production systems have been transferred to low-wage economies (Harvey, 1989; Lash and Urry, 1987). The rise of leisure studies reflected the growing criticism of the established mass production system. For example, the notion of "the leisure society" was predicated in the idea that production no longer required a forty-hour, five-day week (Kerr, 1973; Miller and Robinson, 1963). Similarly, *spillover* and *compensatory* models of leisure were constructed on the basis of alienated work experience. These models carried the clear message that dehumanization of labor at work resulted in dehumanized leisure identities, and implicitly they called for the question of dehumanization to be addressed and tackled (Parker, 1983; Wilensky, 1960). An interest in antisocial and amoral leisure was never part of these projects. On the contrary, both carried with them the tacit assumption that redistributive justice would solve most forms of deviant leisure.

The primary contention of this chapter, then, is twofold. First, both leisure studies and Fordism are wrong not to recognize antisocial, amoral and deviant forms of leisure as intrinsic parts of leisure culture. By emphasizing the word *intrinsic,* I wish to make the claim that there is an essential transgressive element in leisure culture per se. Second, economic change has denigrated Fordist categories of work and leisure. Fordism presented lifelong paid labor as the norm and leisure as the reward for the working week. The new technologies and systems of organization in the relations of production mean that more and more people will automatically fall into the "deviant" strata of casualized labor or long-term unemployment. The old rigid, hierarchical divisions within work and between work and leisure have been replaced by more fluid and less stable arrangements. The argument that cultural and moral categories have been dedifferentiated is now commonplace in sociology, cultural studies, and political science (Harvey, 1989; Lash and Urry, 1987, 1994). One result of this is that the marginality that Fordism attributed to the practices of the leisure class and the alternative leisure class is now no longer automatically plausible. I will return to develop this point later. At this stage in the discussion, I want to go deeper into the deviant character of leisure activities in the leisure and alternative leisure classes.

Deviance in the Leisure and Alternative Leisure Class

Veblen's (1899) study remains the best guide to the role of the leisure class in maintaining social order. Interestingly, there have been very few sociological studies of the private practices of the leisure class, although reports of private excess and covert lawbreaking in this stratum continue to feature luridly in the popular press. Not a little of the amazing public interest in the O. J. Simpson trial (1994–95) can be explained by the revelations of the lurid lifestyle of one of the rich and famous. Similarly, the seemingly inexhaustible interest of the British press in the private leisure pursuits of the royal family adds weight to the argument that the practices of the leisure class feature prominently in the organization of popular culture and fantasy. As for the alternative leisure class and its role in promoting change, there is no equivalent to Veblen's monumental study. Yet paradoxically, there is a rich culturalist history and sociology of dissent and unpopular culture (see for example, Hall, Jefferson, Clarke and Roberts, 1978; Hill, 1972; Pearson, 1983; Redhead, 1995; Thompson, 1975, 1993; Yeo and Yeo, 1981). This tradition has cogently articulated the role of deviant cultures in effecting social change. It has been less successful in fully representing the role of leisure as a vital medium through which deviance is practiced and change achieved. Of course, this is not to say that all forms of leisure which conflict with dominant social values contribute positively to social change. Many forms are driven by antisocial values and immediate personal gain. Nonetheless, the culturalist tradition does point to the importance of deviance and dissent in shaping the body politic.

Thompson (1993, p. 10) observes that antinomialism developed from a Greek word which literally meant against the law.[4] It would be rash to regard the various disparate groups that composed this tradition as a uniform social movement dedicated to social transformation. If we confine ourselves merely to the main English dissenting groups of the eighteenth century mentioned by Thompson, namely the Quakers, Muggletonians, Millenaries, Sabbatarians, Thraskites, Seventh Dayists, Adamists (who called their meeting

---

[4]In this respect antinomialism is very similar to leisure. Most academic dictionary definitions note that the term leisure, derives from the Latin term *licere* which means "to be allowed" (see Jary and Jary, 1995, pp. 364–365).

place *Paradise* and whose devotions demanded nudity), Seekers, Brownists, Behemnists, Tyronists, Salomnists, and Heavenly Father Men, it is evident that they adhered to an incongruous and often contradictory set of beliefs and objectives. It is difficult to find a common thread to them, save for a broad and palpable disaffection with the existing order of things. However, what has perhaps not been sufficiently recognized is the place of "free time" and "nonwork space" in the origination and prosecution of these activities. Alehouses frequently operated as meeting places for antinomial groups. More generally art clubs, choir groups, drama groups, Bible and poetry classes, and rambling associations all functioned as conduits for the exchange and development of disaffected and oppositional values (Borzello, 1987; Donnelly, 1986). It is reasonable to propose that leisure is one of the indispensable sites for the emergence and dissemination of antinomial values. Unlike work, leisure takes place in relatively low-surveillance contexts. The culture encourages people to be relaxed, to speak their minds, and be themselves. Of course, the role of transgressive activity in social change has been quite widely explored. For example, Stallybrass and White (1986) argue that poetry, drama, fiction, and comedy all operate as ways of opposing conformity and declaring opposition. But they tend to draw their theoretical inspiration from the paradigm of literary studies. Thus, their analysis is framed in terms of language rather than the concrete, historical origins and modes of transgressive time and space. Textuality is the dominant motif in this analysis. To the extent that leisure figures at all it is presented as the transparent, neutral medium through which radical culture is articulated. What this ignores is that leisure is a cultural activity with a determinate network of rules of relaxation and exchange. The culture of leisure engenders antinomialism because it is practically and symbolically defined in contradistinction to work values.

By making the ethical values associated with work an object, the potential for exposing the tyrannical hold of productivism upon social consciousness is released. The attitude that we must be in paid employment because work activity is the primary human need is opened to criticism. Under Fordism, we are encouraged automatically to view paid employment as our central life interest. It follows that the relationship between leisure and the objectification of social and ethical boundaries is not guaranteed. Leisure may be spent in motor activity, mere distraction, passive consumption and other modes which do not directly lead to objectification or criticism. However, the important point is that the cultural category of leisure releases the potential for objectifying the rules and values of everyday work and morality. Hence the significance of leisure in the antinomial tradition. To take but two examples, leisure played a crucial, largely unacknowledged role in the homosexual reform and Civil Rights movements of the 1950s and 1960s. Bars, private clubs, public meetings, musical events, drama shows, and other leisure institutions acted as the conduits for developing antinomial consciousness. The boundaries of heterosexual and White oppression were objectified in leisure time and space. The boundaries of these hegemonic structures were criticized and the collective political means to remedy them were born. Of course, the equation of antinomialism with criticism and dissent may strike some readers as rather vapid. After all, bending the rules, fare dodging, minor traffic offences, graffiti, trespass, and jaywalking do not necessarily carry over into purposeful transformative action. The same can be said of the incidental criticisms of the government or the temporary frustrations with the banality of routine that express over an informal exchange with friends. Treating these categories in parodic and comedic forms in meetings with friends is part of the small change of general sociability (Simmel, 1971). Accordingly, investing these activities with the import of deviant values and transformation might seem excessive. There is a good deal of published work within the academic study of culture to support this general critical line of thought. For example, in a succession of works, Fiske (1989a, 1989b) has presented consumer culture as an arena of struggle between dominant and subordinate strata. He portrays subordinate cultures as agents of subversion who use the cultural products of the marketplace to oppose and contest the power of dominant strata. Willis (1990) provides a broadly similar account with his somewhat partisan but brilliant discussion of the purposeful and productive character of consumption activity in youth subcultures. He highlights the "symbolic creativity" of subordinate actors in consuming the products of mass consumer culture. Cohen and Taylor (1992) work in rather a different tradition. Their analysis of "escape attempts" in everyday life is an interesting approach to the micropolitics of leisure and its role in both reinforcing and destabilizing the everyday order.

The tendency to translate all forms of deviance into acts of resistance is often a major fault with this type of analysis. Fiske and Willis seem unable to recognize the place of monotony in popular culture or to appreciate the pattern of conformist behavior which it elicits. Cohen and Taylor are more skeptical about the power of escape attempts to break the existing cultural mold. However, a romantic streak runs through their analysis which results in their taking a turn towards the imputation of resistance in their analysis of most forms of deviant leisure. Nonetheless, putting these criticisms to one side, these authors still provide the enormous service of encouraging us to be sensitive to the conditional character of order in everyday life. Indeed, they rather suggest that terms like *ruling order* and *everyday life* are used too casually in social analysis. What passes as the dominant power structure or the normal way of thinking, feeling and acting is meaningful largely at the metaphorical level of social relations. At the level of micropolitics these metaphors are regularly twisted, bent out of shape, and challenged. This may be the result of intentional action which is designed to destabilize the system. However, social rules and laws are inherently ambivalent and deviance is often the unintentional consequence of misinterpretation or misrepresentation. Antinomialism should not, therefore, be read as a critical departure from lawbound behavior, but a corollary of it.

The condition of antinomialism refers to a general critical orientation to the laws of order. As such, it would be wrong to conceptualize it as rooted in one area of life. Work experience provides opportunities for the expression of antinomial values through pilfering, embezzlement, computer fraud, sabotage, and theft. Similarly, our participation in civil society positively abounds with temptations to engage in fiddling, tax dodging, fraud, perjury, and theft. Even so, the culture of leisure shares an elective affinity with antinomialism. This is because the culture provides the individual with the transgressive license to objectify the ethical and routine boundaries of everyday life. The process of objectification often directly leads to activity which breaks the law. Because the alternative leisure class has constructed lifestyle around leisure, their propensity to develop antinomialism exceeds that of other strata. However, the pressure to test rules, to go beyond boundaries, is a constant feature of all forms of leisure culture.

If a propensity exists to encourage the alternative leisure class to participate in antinomial behavior, it follows that it should be possible to construct a typology of the ways in which this social strata engages in antinomialism. Through this one might see more clearly how transformative purposeful action in the antinomial tradition has used leisure to achieve its ends. Of course different social systems produce different regimes of order. To this extent deviance should not be conceptualized in homogeneous terms. However, general patterns in the relation between antinomialism and leisure do occur. The typology below attempts to represent these patterns in diagrammatic form. It presents the relationship between antinomialism and the alternative leisure class in terms of means-ends distinctions. On this basis, four categories are recognized: revolutionaries, political dissenters, retreatist lifestylers, and criminals. These categories are subdivisions within the general alternative leisure class stratum. They differ in respect of their antinomial ends and the means of leisure used to achieve those ends. Let us examine the means-ends characteristics of these categories in more detail.

Revolutionaries

The end of this category of actors is the complete transformation of society. The means they employ is radical political consciousness-raising and militant action. Revolutionaries are prepared to use the ultimate means of violence to achieve their ends. Leisure figures as a key instrument in the spread of revolutionary consciousness. Meetings, processions, rallies, and radical discussion groups are generally programmed to occur in the leisure time of the masses. Revolutionary leaders typically abjure paid labor in order to disseminate their values. Recreational events operate as the platform for distributing propaganda. For example, the Nazis devised the *Kraft dur Freude* (strength through joy) movement of organized recreation to propagate their values. Subsidized day trips and vacations, summer camps, weekend rambles, and sporting events were the transmission belts of Nazi values (Bessel, 1987). Hitler originated the National Socialist Party through a drinking club (Bullock, 1961). Other revolutionary movements such as the Bolsheviks and the Maoists have also used leisure and recreation events to add to their membership and strengthen their power base. The leisure component of these movements is typically represented as apolitical. It is depicted as an occasion for the people to celebrate folk values or engage in healthy physical activity. However, these leisure events always carry the burden of developing ideas and criticisms which destabilize the ruling order. By playing together, revolutionary identity is reinforced throughout the social movement. Revolutionary groups are often heavily policed. Their values and activities may be restricted or outlawed as illegal by the judicial system. However, impeding the public activities of the movement often simply has the effect of intensifying collective revolutionary sentiments. The organized leisure events of revolutionary movements may be driven underground, but their will to engage in purposeful transformative action may be undiminished or even increased.

Political Dissenters

The end of this category of actors is to modify social conditions through criticism, propaganda, agitation, and dissent. Christopher Hill (1972, 1984) describes the history of the various antinomial sects and movements of the 1640s and 1650s. Their pursuit of religious, spiritual, and secular freedoms involved the use of leisure and recreation to heighten critical consciousness. This pursuit was rather more than a segmented or incidental feature of lifestyle. Rather, it operated as the axis of lifestyle planning and development. Moreover, the transformative change that these dissenters accomplished is of seminal importance in world history. For example, it might be argued that America was founded through the activities of political dissenters. Thus, the first Puritan settlers left England to escape the bonds of religious persecution and to pursue utopian ideals of freedom. Similarly, the American rebels in the War of Independence dissented from British rule. In both cases, leisure and recreation settings operated to further the ends of the dissenting actors. Through clandestine discussion groups and rallies, oppositional consciousness was developed and refined. Of course, the use of leisure by political dissenters to engineer transformative purposeful action is not confined to American experience. Many of the most important social and political developments involving political dissenters in Europe owe their origins to leisure. For example, the wealthy middle-class women of the late nineteenth century who founded the suffragette movement used leisure time and space to develop their criticism of patriarchy and recruit new members to the cause (Hayden, 1981). The movement for racial equality also relied heavily on leisure and recreation meetings to raise oppositional consciousness and organize reform. The same is true of contemporary political dissenting groups, such as animal rights campaigners, antinuclear demonstrators, environmental protesters, sexual rights campaigners, preservationist groups, and youth subcultures organized around joyriding, partying, and raving. Some social theorists argue that these groups have attained a point of critical mass in society which compels us to propose a transition from class-gender politics to identity politics (Calhoun, 1994; Giddens, 1990, 1991).

A large and growing literature is devoted to the policing of identity politics (Hall et al., 1978; Cunningham, 1980; Pearson, 1983; Redhead, 1995). Because identity groups typically operate at the margins of established politics, they rely heavily upon leisure and recreation activities to concentrate solidarity. Rock concerts, rallies, pickets, demonstrations, parties, and public discussion groups are typically employed in generating solidarity. For this reason, these activities have also been the focus for moral panics and state intervention. Donnelly (1986) has discussed the running battles between mass trespassers and the police in the development of access rights for the public. Ownership disputes over landmark sites such as Ayer's Rock, Stonehenge, and Alcatraz have also sparked clashes between native peoples and the state (Rojek, 1988, 1993). Political dissent is often channeled through cult leaders. Inevitably, policing extends to the activities of these social actors. Radical thinkers and activists such as Tom Paine, William Blake, Karl Marx, Marie Stopes, Havelock Ellis, the Beat writers, Wilhelm Reich, Timothy Leary, and R. D. Laing were all subject to state surveillance and investigation.

Retreatist Lifestylers

The end of this category of social actors is personal expression. The means employed to achieve this end include dropping out, taking drugs, sexual experimentation, and engaging in practices which are antithetical to conventional life orders. Merton (1968) provides the classical sociological discussion of retreatism. According to him (1968, p. 207) retreatists "have relinquished culturally prescribed goals and their behavior does not accord with institutional norms." As examples, Merton mentions psychotics, pariahs, outcasts, vagrants, vagabonds, chronic alcoholics, and drug addicts. Although Merton's essay did much to awaken sociological interest in retreatism, it no longer offers an adequate approach to the subject. To take the most obvious objection, the paper was originally published in 1949, some time before the advent of the permissive society of the 1960s. Hence, Merton tends wrongly to treat retreatism as a social problem (pariahs, outcasts, vagrants, vagabonds) or clinical condition (psychotics, drunkards, drug addicts). What is absent from his account is any appreciation of social actors who use their own volition to retreat from straight society and construct lifestyle designs built around leisure and personal expression. These actors do not necessarily reject culturally prescribed values and institutional norms. Their relationship with straight society is more complex. It involves limited accommodation and negotiation as opposed to blanket rejection. The relation of retreatist lifestylers to the values of "straight" society is one of calculated disengagement. Retreat is organized on their own terms. If they make the concession of participating in paid labor in "straight" society, it is simply to extract the pecuniary value that enables them to finance the leisure interests that are the basis of their lifestyles. One of the most interesting studies of contemporary retreatist lifestyle is Willis's (1978) account of the hippie and motorbike boy subcultures. He emphasizes the dependence of these subcultures on imagination to mediate with the outside world. Although they experience "straight" society as limiting and inhibiting, they show no interest in initiating political action to change external conditions. Instead, to use Willis's (1978, p. 177) own words, they live "as if the basic (dominant) structures were changed—enjoying that in imagination while making no attempt to bring it about in reality." This mediation with external society is driven by the immediate requirements of sustaining retreatist lifestyle culture. Willis's fieldwork sample felt able to disengage with straight society so long as the essential requirements permitting their lifestyle to continue are fulfilled. However, they also practically engaged with straight society when financial or urgent necessity required. Nonetheless, lifestyle disengagement constituted the basis of existence in these subcultures. This was associated with an introspective attitude which obstructed purposive transformative action. In a telling example, Willis (1978, p. 177) observes that although the leisure time of the motorbike boys revolves around engine technology, they do not make the connections between this technology and the dehumanizing, enslaving machine technologies of external society.

Retreatism typically involves conditions of highly developed, routinized fantasy work which labels external society as a second-order level of existence. The first order of existence is regarded as the lifestyle conditions of the retreatist group. This is where real life happens. Disengagement from the second-order relations of straight society is outwardly demonstrated by dress, linguistic codes, and religious beliefs and practices.

Criminals

A cliché of the American sociology of deviance is that the criminal class uses crime as an illegitimate means to achieve legitimate ends. As Merton (1968) famously argued, one can understand much criminal activity in the United States as an attempt by systematically underprivileged strata to attain the universal American dream of wealth, prestige, and security. Of course, not all crime can be satisfactorily explained in this way. Much criminal activity involves levels of training, discipline, and organization which are akin to work. By the same token, much criminal activity is not oriented to accumulating wealth but to expressing aggression, sexuality, or antisocial values. What interests me here is Merton's evident belief that dreaming about wealth and prestige is a near universal feature of American

life. One might reasonably suggest that America is not alone among the industrial societies in propagating this dream. Indeed, industrial societies feed our appetite for fantasizing about money through countless images of wealth in newspapers, magazines, television shows, and movies. Much of this fantasy-work occurs in leisure. Similarly, the act of breaking the law in order to achieve wealth is also concentrated in leisure. The presentation of images of wealth through advertising and other branches of the mass media does not usually provide us with scripts for achieving these ends through crime. But given the seemingly intransigent inequalities in society, resorting to crime may be regarded by many as a reasonable risk. Thus crime can be interpreted not as a dysfunctional behavioral syndrome, but rather as a form of adaptive living. Leisure may be regarded as the medium through which adaptation evolves.

The links among the alternative leisure class, deviant leisure, and social change have not figured prominently in academic study. As I have noted, the culturalist tradition works with a sophisticated and well-established model of the role of unpopular culture in social transformation. However, it does not recognize the role of leisure in articulating and developing this culture. Before moving on to consider the culture of leisure and its propensities for deviance in greater detail, and also to go more deeply into the question of the effect of post-Fordism upon our understanding of deviant leisure, it is important to acknowledge another major academic resource which is of help in filling in the gaps in our knowledge with regard to deviant leisure: criminology.

Criminology and Deviant Leisure

The study of deviant behavior is usually regarded as the occupation of criminologists. Their work undoubtedly constitutes the prime resource in the study of deviance. What emerges most powerfully from this material is two things. In the first place, the conventional polarization of conformist behavior with deviant behavior is too starkly expressed. The complexities and ambiguities of modern industrial societies mean that everyone is at least occasionally involved in deviant behavior. This is because the rules and laws governing social life are inherently ambiguous and therefore open to different interpretation. To some extent, deviance is nothing but the activity which exploits this ambivalence. By bending rules, finding shortcuts, and telling white lies, cultural life becomes richer and more meaningful. This brings me to the second point.

Becker (1963) argues that the label of deviance is not a quality of the act but a question of the rules and sanctions applied by others. He submits that moral reactions to deviance are value-laden and cannot be couched or legitimated in absolutist terms. Becker shifts the debate on deviance from the moral level of seeing right and wrong or good and bad in social acts to the level of exploring how power shapes our judgments. Later, Michel Foucault (1970, 1975, 1981), working from a very different tradition, also pinpointed power relations as the crux of understanding deviance.

Both general points are relevant for appreciating what criminological work offers for understanding deviant leisure. Thus, only at extremes does it make sense to isolate the category of deviant leisure from the general culture of leisure. There are obvious hazards in presenting deviant leisure and normal leisure as polarized forms of behavior. From relatively minor acts, such as taking soft drugs or breaking the speed limit, deviant leisure activity is something that might be indulged in by anyone participating in ordinary leisure activity. Needless to say one is not consigned into a deviant career by taking these actions. In visualizing the social dynamics of deviant leisure it is helpful to refer to Matza's (1964) concept of drift. Matza is rooted in the relativist tradition of criminology. He aims to reveal the episodic, conditional and, above all, ordinary character of deviant conduct. Matza attempts to explain deviance by making links between the ambivalent character of social rules and the interpretive capacities of social actors. We exploit the ambivalence in rules as and when circumstances dictate. Putting it bluntly, Matza's discussion suggests that only a programmed zombie slavishly obeys all of the rules in social life. Unimaginative obedience is viewed so harshly in this approach that it is tacitly presented as dysfunctional behavior. Matza stops short of advocating breaking the law as a "normal" characteristic of everyday life. At the same time, he insists that a realistic sociology of criminal behavior must acknowledge the interpretive capacity of actors to achieve their ends despite the law. Of course, Matza's concept of drift is not offered as a complete explanation of deviant behavior. It allows that pathological identities and forms of association can develop around deviant behavior. Acts of murder, rape, physical assault, vandalism, and theft belong to a different moral and social universe than breaking the speed limit or taking a shortcut through private property. However, by giving prominence to the concept of drift, Matza redefines deviance as a normal part of everyday life, as opposed to a departure or break from it. Although much of Matza's thinking derives from fieldwork with adolescent boys, he obeys the convention in criminology of treating leisure neutrally. One

would never guess from reading him that deviant conduct is concentrated in leisure or that the culture of leisure has an elective affinity with deviance.

The same is true of Becker's (1963) famous study of marijuana users. The focus of Becker's study is the conflict between dominant social values and the values of deviant subcultures. What the work fails to convey is the crucial role of the culture of leisure in engendering and supporting deviance. The marijuana users in Becker's study do not consciously take the drug to oppose dominant social values. They take it first and foremost for acquisition of pleasure. The setting and ethos of the drug subculture is overwhelmingly recreational. The field of the study is jazz clubs, locker rooms, dens, and drinking clubs. Leisure provides the direct context for the use of the drug. Becker's drug users smoke marijuana as a release from the cares of work, as an accompaniment to playing or listening to jazz, to socialize with friends, or to escape the claustrophobic values of "straight" society. The drug is used as a relaxant and a token of common social values.

The failure of criminology to give the culture of leisure its due in understanding deviance can be illustrated with another example. Suttles's (1968) study of crimogenic territories indicates how youth subcultures control social spaces to permit deviant practices in a relatively unfettered way. According to Suttles (1968, pp. 54–56), settings such as parks, social centers, and playgrounds are "owned" by different ethnic groups. Davis's (1990) thought-provoking study of spatial cultures in south central Los Angeles broadly reinforces this view of gang territories. Ownership is expressed in three ways. First, if the recreation area is situated in the locality of a particular ethnic group it is treated as the possession of this group. Second, if the recreational area is staffed by paid employees, their ethnicity is used to assert territoriality over the formally constituted public space. Third, if a recreational area has a history of use by one ethnic group, that group has a claim upon it. Of course, the assertion of territorial control is the basis for disputes. Gang policing is often interpreted by rival gangs as the incentive for incursions and pitched battles. Gang control renders some sectors of public space as "no go" areas. Drug abuse, physical violence, racketeering, graffiti, prostitution, and other types of illegal activity are often highly visible in these areas. In this sense they are beyond the law. Their existence again illustrates the ambivalence of rules. Suttles's study is usually seen as demonstrating the relationship between crime and inequality in inner city America. However, it can be read with equal insight as an account of how private and public leisure space is constructed in order to fulfill deviant functions. The gangs use their leisure to leave their imprint upon their territories. The culture of leisure has, then, been neglected by criminologists. They have not, of course, ignored the context of deviance. On the contrary, deviant acts are typically analyzed in terms of the opportunities for lawbreaking provided by the social settings of work, business, and family life. But the role of the culture of leisure in forming deviant sensibilities and plans has been ignored. What is it about the culture of leisure that produces an elective affinity with deviance?

Conclusion:
The Culture of Leisure

One of the most important facts about social life is that it is founded upon obligations to others. The first stages in the socialization process of infants teach the lesson that we cannot act as we please. Our self-consciousness of responsibilities to others is consolidated through our involvement in organized education, work, and the other categories of civil society. A prominent theme in sociological literature is the sense of feeling trapped by our obligations and responsibilities. The culture of leisure may be interpreted as providing a sense of balance for lives riveted around the twin demands to take the needs of others into consideration and obeying the normal standards of civilized behavior. It allows for the relaxation of our obligations and responsibilities to others. In the functionalist sociology of leisure, leisure is portrayed as free time for the pursuit of self-determined interests. A considerable critical tradition in leisure studies is devoted to unraveling the notions of identity and freedom upon which the functionalist view is founded.[5] It argues that identity and freedom are socially constructed. For example, under Fordism, identity is related to paid employment and freedom to the power to consume. This might be contrasted with post-Fordist conditions where the prospect of paid employment is no longer guaranteed and freedom is not related to the capacity to buy commodities. Indeed, the social crisis of post-Fordist society derives not only from the collapse of the link between paid full employment and self-esteem, but also from the realization that consumer culture produces deluding values of fulfillment and happiness. However, Fordist and post-Fordist conditions are alike in treating the culture of leisure as the area in social life in which routine obligations and responsibilities can be objectified and transcended. The critique of one-dimensional society (Marcuse, 1964) and the quest for

authenticity in human relations which developed under Fordism was rooted in the culture of leisure. It would be wrong to assume that this critique remains wholly intact under post-Fordist conditions. For one thing post-Fordism queries the validity of authenticity in human relationships by emphasizing the relativized, contingent character of all social values. In addition, the absence of full employment means that the culture of leisure expands to become a prominent element in lifestyle planning and management. Nonetheless, the culture of leisure remains the prime setting for objectifying routine obligations and responsibilities.

The objectification of personal and social conditions through the culture of leisure translates seamlessly into opposition to, or denial of, existing obligations and responsibilities. If we feel trapped in many areas of our lives, it is in our leisure that we confront our chained existence with the greatest candor. Needless to say an inevitable relationship between the culture of leisure and social criticism and acts of transgression does not exist. A cliché of critical traditions in the sociology of leisure is that much leisure time is absorbed with mystification or mere distraction activity.[6] Nonetheless, it is important to insist that the culture of leisure possesses the prime intrinsic potential of social criticism and transcendence. Certainly, the weight of historical and empirical evidence suggests that leisure is the seat of antinomialism. When human beings have freed themselves from the line management of their teachers, their employers, their doctors, and the other controlling actors of mass culture, they have developed initiatives and practices which have challenged the rule of normality.

In putting this case, it bears repeating that two claims for leisure are being made. The first claim is that the stock context in which deviance emerges and develops is leisure. Criminologists have typically treated leisure in neutral terms. This fails to acknowledge the importance of the culture of leisure in producing the general relaxation of social obligations and responsibilities which commonly form the prelude to deviant action. The second claim is that deviant leisure plays a seminal role in social change. To put it concisely, deviant leisure problematizes the coercive structures which regulate our sense of justice, order, and normality. The role of leisure in this regard may be studied historically, through the connections between leisure and the development of the antinomial tradition; but it is also evident concretely, in the role that leisure

---

[5]The feminist, neo-Marxist and postmodernist traditions to leisure have been crucial in this regard.

[6]Simmel's sociology abounds with examples (see Simmel, 1971). Kracauer (1975) also provides a suggestive reading of the place of "distraction factories" in modern life.

settings play in supporting and developing identity politics and critical social movements.

Both claims err on the side of generosity in their assessment of deviant leisure, for they attribute a positive function to deviant leisure. The obvious problem with this is that it is quite easy to think of counter-examples, such as hooliganism, theft, mugging, and chronic drug taking, which appear to support the common-sense view that deviant leisure is dysfunctional. There is no reason to deny that some forms of deviant leisure are pathological. As such, it may be properly inferred that they have no functional contribution to make to society. However, that is no basis for concluding that deviant leisure should be regarded, *sui generis,* as pathological. Indeed, one conclusion of the discussion of the transition from Fordism to post-Fordism is that the central Fordist categories of work, leisure, and morality are not applicable in post-Fordist society. If continuous lifelong paid employment is taken as the bedrock of so-called normal adult existence, and an excess of leisure as proof of deviance, it is plain that many of us now fall into the category of deviant actors. The social and moral categories of work and leisure constructed under Fordism cease to have purchase in post-Fordist conditions. Thus, condemning lifestyles built around leisure and combating the decline in job opportunities with "back to work" campaigns have nothing but rhetorical value in an age where the jobless future has already arrived (Aronowitz and DiFazio, 1994).

One of the challenges facing leisure studies is to incorporate deviant leisure as a central category of theory and research. By this means a direct understanding of the role of the culture of leisure in social change can be accomplished. But although it is necessary and even urgent to face this challenge, a project of greater moment faces students of leisure studies. That is, to come to terms with the disintegration of Fordist categories of work and leisure and the collapse of the ethical codes which were conventionally attached to them. If work is no longer the consistent wellspring of self-esteem in society, it is necessary to consider how social value can be extracted from nonwork categories. In particular, it is important to consider the question of social organization in a context where the culture of leisure, and not work, is the preeminent category of moral consciousness and moral considerations. If this task is not addressed, we will truly succumb to the profane economistic argument that our social and economic problems derive from too many people for too few jobs. It is but a short step from this to the conclusion that some people are expendable and further, that nothing can be done to improve our situation.[7] The institutionalization of a permanent underclass and the retreat into fatalism whereby employment and unemployment are reconceptualized as matters of luck follow from this state of affairs. From this the capacity for human beings to take control of their own means of existence is denied. Our very humanity is impaired. We condemn ourselves to living in a lurching vortex of chance and brutality which no one even aspires to control. Who wants to live in a society like that?

---

[7] Isn't this the practical implication of much current right-wing government policy in the West? The growth of homelessness, low pay and long-term structural unemployment with the acknowledged devastation of regional economies is the tacit assumption behind current economic and social policies in many Western democracies.

References

Applebaum, H. (1992). *The concept of work: Ancient, medieval, and modern.* Albany, NY: State University of New York Press.

Aronowitz, S., & DiFazio, W. (1994). *The jobless future.* Minneapolis, MN: University of Minnesota Press.

Becker, H. (1963). *Outsiders.* New York, NY: Free Press.

Bessel, R. (Ed.). (1987). *Life inside the Third Reich.* Oxford, UK: Oxford University Press.

Bialeschki, D., & Henderson, K. (1986). Leisure in the common world of women. *Leisure Studies, 5*(3), 299–308.

Borzello, F. (1987). *Civilizing Caliban: The misuse of art, 1875–1900.* London, UK: Routledge & Kegan Paul.

Bullock, A. (1961). *Hitler.* Harmondsworth, UK: Penguin.

Calhoun, C. (Ed.). (1994). *Social theory and the politics of identity.* Oxford, UK: Blackwell.

Clarke, J., & Critcher, C. (1985). *The devil makes work: Leisure in capitalist Britain.* London, UK: Macmillan Publishing.

Cohen, S., & Taylor, L. (1992). *Escape attempts.* London, UK: Routledge.

Cunningham, H. (1980). *Leisure in the Industrial Revolution.* London, UK: Croom Helm.

Davidoff, L. (1973). *The best circles.* London, UK: Croom Helm.

Davis, M. (1990). *City of quartz.* London, UK: Verso.

Deem, R. (1986). *All work and no play: The sociology of women in leisure.* Milton Keynes, UK: Open University Press.

Donnelly, P. (1986). The paradox of the parks. *Leisure Studies, 5*(2), 211–32.

Dumazedier, J. (1974). *The sociology of leisure.* Amsterdam, Netherlands: Elsevier.

Durkheim, E. (1897). *Suicide.* London, UK: Routledge & Kegan Paul.

Ferguson, H. (1992). Watching the world go round: Atrium culture and the psychology of shopping. In R. Shields (Ed.), *Lifestyle shopping* (pp. 21–39). London, UK: Routledge.

Fiske, J. (1989a). *Reading the popular.* London, UK: Unwin Hyman.

Fiske, J. (1989b). *Understanding popular culture.* London, UK: Unwin Hyman.

Foucault, M. (1970). *The order of things.* London, UK: Tavistock.

Foucault, M. (1975). *Discipline and punish.* Harmondsworth, UK: Penguin.

Foucault, M. (1981). *The history of sexuality* (Vol. 1). Harmondsworth, UK: Penguin.

Gartman, D. (1994). *Auto-opium.* London, UK: Routledge.

Giddens, A. (1990). *The consequences of modernity.* Cambridge, UK: Polity.

Giddens, A. (1991). *On modernity and self-identity.* Cambridge, UK: Polity.

Hall, S., Jefferson, T., Clarke, J., & Roberts, B. (Eds.). (1978). *Policing the crisis.* London, UK: Hutchinson.

Harvey, D. (1989). *The condition of postmodernity.* Oxford, UK: Blackwell.

Hayden, D. (1981). *The grand domestic revolution.* Cambridge, MA: MIT Press.

Hill, C. (1972). *The world turned upside down.* Harmondsworth, UK: Penguin.

Jary, D., & Jary J. (Eds.). (1995). *Collins dictionary of sociology.* Glasgow, UK: HarperCollins.

Kaplan, M. (1975). *Leisure: Theory and policy.* New York, NY: John Wiley & Sons, Inc.

Kelly, J. (1987). *Freedom to be.* New York, NY: Macmillan Publishing.

Kerr, C., et al. (1973). *Industrialism and industrial man.* Harmondsworth, UK: Penguin.

Kracauer, S. (1975). The mass ornament. *New German Critique, 2,* 67–76.

Lash, S., & Urry, J. (1987). *The end of organized capitalism.* Cambridge, UK: Polity.

Lash, S., & Urry, J. (1994). *Economies of signs and space.* London, UK: Sage Publications, Ltd.

Marcuse, H. (1964). *One-dimensional man.* London, UK: Abacus.

Marx, K., & Engels, F. (1968). *Selected works.* London, UK: Lawrence and Wishart.

Matza, D. (1964). *Delinquency and drift.* New York, NY: John Wiley & Sons, Inc.

McQuarrie, F., & Jackson, E. L. (1996). Connections between negotiation of leisure constraints and serious leisure: An exploratory study of adult amateur ice skaters. *Loisir et Société/Society and Leisure, 19,* 459–483.

Merton, R. (1968). *Social theory and social structure.* New York, NY: Free Press.

Miller, N. P., & Robinson, D. M. (1963). *The leisure age and its challenge to recreation.* Belmont, CA: Wadsworth.

Parker, S. (1983). *Leisure and work.* London, UK: Unwin Hyman.

Pearson, G. (1983). *Hooligan: A history of respectable fears.* London, UK: Macmillan Publishing.

Redhead, S. (1995). *Unpopular cultures.* Manchester, UK: Manchester University Press.

Roberts, K. (1981). *Leisure.* London, UK: Longman.

Rojek, C. (1988). The convoy of pollution. *Leisure Studies, 7*(1), 21–31.

Rojek, C. (1993). *Ways of escape.* London, UK: Macmillan Publishing.

Sayers, S. (1987). The need to work. *Radical Philosophy, 46,* 17–26.

Scraton, S. (1993). *Feminism, postfeminism and leisure.* Mimeo, Leisure Studies Association, Brighton, UK.

Simmel, G. (1971). *On individuality and social forms.* Chicago, IL: Chicago University Press.

Suttles, G. (1968). *The social order of the slum.* Chicago, IL: Chicago University Press.

Stallybrass, P., & White, A. (1986). *The politics and poetics of transgression.* London, UK: Methuen.

Stebbins, R. (1992). *Amateurs, professionals and serious leisure.* Montreal, Quebec: McGill-Queen's University Press.

Thompson, E. P. (1975). *Whigs and hunters.* Harmondsworth, UK: Penguin.

Thompson, E. P. (1993). *Witness against the beast.* Cambridge, UK: Cambridge University Press.

Veblen, T. (1899). *The theory of the leisure class.* London, UK: Allen & Unwin.

Weber, M. (1976). *The Protestant ethic and the spirit of capitalism.* London, UK: Routledge.

Wilensky, H. (1960). Work, careers and social integration. *International Social Science Journal, 4,* 543–60.

Willis, P. (1978). *Profane culture.* London, UK: Routledge & Kegan Paul.

Willis, P. (1990). *Uncommon culture.* Milton Keynes, UK: Open University Press.

Wimbush, E., & Talbot, M. (1988). *Relative freedoms.* Milton Keynes, UK: Open University Press.

Yeo, E., & Yeo, S. (Eds.). (1981). *Popular culture and class conflict, 1590–1914.* Brighton, UK: Harvester Press.

Understanding Tourism

Richard W. Butler
University of Surrey

Introduction

It is, perhaps, even more surprising than was the case in the previous collection edited by Jackson and Burton (1989) that tourism should be treated in this book as a separate aspect of leisure and recreation, because tourism has emerged over the last decade as a major subject of academic interest that is comparable with leisure or recreation in its own right. However, the leisure and recreation literature still makes only limited reference to tourism, and the tourism literature rarely cross-references research in leisure or recreation. Although many of the phenomena studied in these three subjects have remained essentially the same (e.g., motivations, facilities, capacity, forecasts, and impacts), the methodologies used, the examples cited, and the individuals involved in the research remain mostly unrelated. The same set of parent disciplines is involved, however, making the relative lack of cross-fertilization between researchers not only a continuing

disappointment but a significant impediment to the furtherance of research in both areas.

This chapter reviews the development of, and major issues in, tourism and tourism research. It begins with a discussion of definitions and the context in which tourism falls. It then sketches the origins and development of tourism and its major patterns. This is followed by an examination of the dynamics of tourism in society, the way it has changed over the last decade, the nature of tourism as a business, and the positive and negative impacts that result from its development. A short review of the social, cultural, and environmental aspects of tourism leads to a discussion of the problems involved in planning and managing this activity. The chapter concludes with a commentary on future research needs and implications.

Definition and Context

Tourism, like leisure and recreation, suffers from problems of definition. Implicit in most academic studies of tourism is the assumption, if not the requirement, that tourism is something which takes place during leisure time, or when a person is "at leisure." Because tourism also implies travel, and therefore some activity on behalf of the tourist, then it is logically a part of both leisure and recreation. The interrelationships among leisure, recreation, and tourism are strong and interdependent ones. The need to consider these interrelationships was recognized with the publication of a special issue on this topic of the *Annals of Tourism Research*. The editor of that issue commented that the papers raised "more questions than they answered" (Fedler, 1987, p. 311). Since then, there has been little regular attention paid in either the tourism or the leisure and recreation literature to developments in the other fields.

Mieczkowski (1981), in a deceptively simple diagram, illustrated the relative place and relationship of the three elements to each other (Figure 7.1). The relationship implied is that tourism is an aspect of recreation, which in turn is a component of leisure. Leiper (1979) discussed the definitional aspects of tourism, grouping them into economic, technical, and holistic, but found major drawbacks to all of these approaches, suggesting that it could be argued that a definition suitable for general tourism scholarship has not yet emerged. Although his article was written almost two decades ago, there is a great temptation to agree with his statement today. Indeed, the definition he quotes from the *Oxford English Dictionary*—that tourism is

"the theory and practice of touring, travelling for pleasure" (Leiper, 1979, p. 391)—is attractive because of its simplicity, despite its academic inadequacies.

Two major factors account for the definitional problems in tourism studies, although other elements are also involved. First and foremost is the multidisciplinary nature of the topic. Subjects such as tourism and leisure, which attract researchers in as many fields as they do, are bound to face this problem. Those in anthropology, biology, business and management studies, economics, geography, political science, psychology, and sociology take widely differing approaches to research, using very different methodologies and concepts. To produce a definition which is generally acceptable to all researchers in a single discipline is difficult; to find one acceptable to several disciplines is virtually impossible. Cohen (1979) recognized this problem two decades ago, and his conclusion, although specifically focused on the sociology of tourism, still has relevance to the field as a whole:

> The complexity and heterogeneity of the field of tourism suggests that there is no point in searching for *the* theoretical approach to the study of tourism, just as there is no point in searching for *the* conceptualization of the tourist. Rather, a pluralistic and even eclectic research strategy is advocated. The many different empirical problems can only be tackled by utilizing a wide range of concepts and research instruments. . . . The most fruitful work . . . will be accomplished by a skilful blending of different approaches for the elucidation of specific problems. (p. 31)

The second problem which still faces tourism is that, despite a decade of intense academic development and expansion, particularly in the English-speaking world, tourism has yet to be widely accepted as a discipline or field of study in its own right. The relative recency of the academic study of tourism has been noted by several authors, along with the disdain which an apparently "frivolous" subject generates among less enlightened colleagues (e.g., Mathews, 1983; Mitchell, 1979; Wolfe, 1964). Fedler (1987) concludes his introduction to the special issue of the *Annals of Tourism Research* on the interrelationship of leisure, recreation, and tourism by noting:

> the definitional problems of leisure, recreation, and tourism have undoubtedly hindered many attempts at clarifying and specifying any theoretical relationships

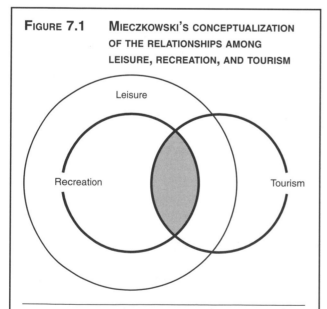

FIGURE 7.1   **MIECZKOWSKI'S CONCEPTUALIZATION OF THE RELATIONSHIPS AMONG LEISURE, RECREATION, AND TOURISM**

Leisure

Recreation   Tourism

SOURCE: "Some Notes on the Geography of Tourism: A Comment," by Z. T. Mieczkowski, 1981, *The Canadian Geographer, 25,* p. 189. Copyright 1981 by Canadian Association of Geographers. Reprinted with permission.

between the three concepts. It may well be that these definitional problems have been grounded by an inadequate understanding of the forms, functions and processes involved with the Leisure-Recreation-Tourism experiences. (p. 313)

Tourism research faces an additional definitional problem compared to leisure and recreation studies. While, as noted earlier, most academic studies of tourism deal with tourism as a form of leisure activity, in reality a significant but generally unknown proportion of what is measured and included in valuations of tourism is non-leisure-related tourism. Most of this is what might be termed business travel, and the great difficulty in separating the economic and supply aspects of business (and related) travel from leisure or vacation travel means that many formal definitions of tourism, such as those by the World Tourism Organization do not attempt to distinguish between these forms of travel. While this is understandable from the supply side, in that much of the infrastructure (such as accommodations, transportation, food services, and even entertainment) is used in both forms of travel, in terms of demand and motivations, as well as other elements of the experience, such as nature of group, purpose of travel, length of trip and expenditure, the two forms are normally radically different. Thus, while most of the academic literature on tourism deals almost exclusively with pleasure or leisure tourism, which is also the focus of this chapter, much of the hospitality literature and studies dealing with the operational aspects of the infrastructure do not differentiate between forms of travel and include both types of tourism. While this problem does not create difficulties with respect to methodologies, it does create considerable confusion and inconsistencies with respect to the economic valuation of tourism and its impacts, and in academic fields such as marketing and motivation studies.

The previous version of this chapter (Butler, 1989) noted the development of journals dealing with tourism and suggested that, despite the still limited period during which tourism has been regarded as an academic subject, considerable progress had been made. The appearance of the two major interdisciplinary refereed journals in tourism in the 1970s, plus a large and increasing number of papers, research reports, and books on the subject have done much to further the quality of the study. Both the *Annals of Tourism Research* and *Tourism Management,* along with the earlier established *Tourist Review* and the *Journal of Travel Research,* are firmly multidisciplinary in orientation. Perhaps more than any single publication, the *Annals* has furthered the dialogue among researchers

in different disciplines by its editorial policy of having associate editors for different disciplines, and by publishing special issues both on thematic topics, e.g., "Evolution of Tourism" (1985), and on disciplinary ones, e.g., "Political Science and Tourism" (1983). In the last decade there has been a virtual explosion of journals dealing exclusively with tourism, reflecting both a rapidly growing academic interest in the subject and increasing specialization within the subject. Those which have appeared or are about to appear include *Journal of Sustainable Tourism, Pacific Tourism Review, Asia Pacific Tourism Journal, Journal of Tourism Studies, Tourism Analysis, Journal of Vacation Marketing, Tourism Economics, Critical Issues in Tourism, Progress in Tourism and Hospitality Research, Tourism Geographies,* and *International Review of Tourism and Hospitality Research.*

Books on tourism have also appeared in much greater numbers in the last decade than ever before. Apart from a few notable exceptions, such as Ogilvie's *The Tourist Movement* (1933), little of real significance appeared before the 1970s. In that decade, however, the first books critical of tourism were published. Those by Bryden (1973), MacCannell (1973), Turner and Ash (1975), and Young (1973) in particular challenged the assumptions of the universal benefits of tourism. Later publications, such as those by Gunn (1979), Mathieson and Wall (1982), Murphy (1985), D. G. Pearce (1981, 1997), and P. L. Pearce (1982), focused attention on such topics as planning, impacts, perceptions, and development issues. In the last decade, as with journals, the book literature has expanded dramatically with the appearance of books on specialized aspects of tourism. These include publications on development (Cooper and Wanhill, 1997; Harrison, 1993), anthropological issues (Nash, 1997; Smith, 1989), native peoples (Butler and Hinch, 1996; Smith, 1989), techniques (Pearce and Butler, 1993; Smith, 1995), alternative forms of tourism (Poon, 1993; Smith and Eadington, 1992), regional studies (Hall, 1994a; Opperman, 1997), island tourism (Conlin and Baum, 1995; Lockhart and Drakakis-Smith, 1997), politics and policies (Hall, 1994b; Hall and Jenkins, 1995), and trends and issues (Butler and Pearce, 1995; Shaw and Williams, 1994), as well as more standard overall discussions (Burns and Holden, 1997; Cooper, Fletcher, Gilbert, Shepherd and Wanhill, 1998). This reflects the increasing fragmentation of tourism, and more than a hundred "types" have been noted in the literature, partly as a result of increasing academic interest and niche marketing approaches.

If there has been one area more than any other which has characterized the growth of literature in tourism in the last decade, it has been that of sustainable development. This topic will be discussed in more detail, but it may be noted here that books on sustainable tourism, and related issues such as ecotourism, have appeared in tremendous numbers (e.g., Bramwell et al., 1996; Nelson, Butler and Wall, 1993; Priestley, Edwards and Coccossis, 1996; Stabler, 1997; Wahab and Pigram, 1997; Weaver, 1998), reflecting the political and public concern over sustainable development generally. The overall trend in the literature has been from mostly descriptive commentaries on tourism to studies that include identification, examination, and proposed amelioration and mitigation of negative effects. The topics examined have both broadened and become more focused, moving from global discussions to the identification of particular problems and remedial actions in specific areas, while recognizing, in the process, the commonality of many of the issues. Thus, the lack of general agreement on methodologies, concepts, and definitions notwithstanding, research on tourism has made considerable progress since its appearance as a topic for serious academic inquiry some 30 or more years ago.

The Origins and Development of Tourism

There is little disagreement that tourism as a term owes its origin to participants in the European Grand Tour of the seventeenth and eighteenth centuries. Although the direct influences of this phenomenon are few in number today, the indirect effects are quite profound, and can be found in much present-day tourist behavior. Considering its importance in influencing twentieth-century tourism, studies of the Grand Tour, its origins, its participants, and its effects have been few and often superficial. One exception is the work of Towner (1985), who analyzed original data from participants on the Tour, reaching some interesting conclusions.

While the first tourists were drawn from a very limited and privileged segment of English society, "mass followed class" and the Tour experienced the democratization process that leisure in general has followed. Travel away from home clearly predates the Grand Tour. The ancient Mesopotamians had summer palaces, Kublai Khan his "pleasure dome," and the Romans their villas on the hills surrounding Rome. The pattern of seasonal migration for comfort (to cooler areas from hotter ones), sport, and social activities is very old, although for most of human history such migration has been confined to the privileged groups in society.

The significance of the Grand Tour as the origin of tourism as we know it today lies in three important areas. The first is in the places made popular by the Tour, which several centuries later are still popular tourist destinations. This is, in part, because of the second factor, the creation of services and facilities to serve the increasing numbers of tourists travelling—in particular, accommodations, transportation facilities, and guide services. The third, and perhaps most revealing, element is in the continuation of the pattern of behavior established by the first tourists, who were advised to remember they had "come abroad to gain knowledge and not enjoy [themselves] in idleness" (Hibbert, 1969, p. 20). Among their instructions were to ascend steeples to view townscapes, collect pictures of places of interest and examples of works of art, and interact with local residents rather than people of their own country.

The comparisons of such behavior with present-day tourist activities are obvious. While contemporary tourists rarely sketch and are unlikely to be able to commission their own works of art, they take photographs and buy postcards, cheap art, and models of significant features on a scale inconceivable even 50 years ago. While the majority of current tourists may not want to learn all the languages and customs of the local population of the place they are visiting, many are at least willing to eat local food and to scale the highest buildings, whether these be church steeples or communication towers.

The principal appeal and purpose of tourism, therefore, appears to have changed relatively little in basic terms: it is to experience something different from the normal pattern of existence. What has changed enormously is the variety of ways in which this experience can be obtained, where it is obtained, and by whom. While still nowhere near as universal as leisure and recreation, tourism is now engaged in by ever-increasing numbers of people, most of whom participate on an annual basis (World Tourism Organization, 1996).

The major growth in numbers participating began in the nineteenth century and continued as a result of improved access to mass transportation, especially in the form of the railway and steamships, increased affluence, the introduction of formal holidays with pay, and entrepreneurship. While tourism could not have grown without facilities and services, the role of entrepreneurs in demonstrating and developing the potential market was crucial. Of major significance is the effort of Thomas Cook, who succeeded in revolutionizing tourism with the introduction of package tours (Swinglehurst, 1982). Working from an idealistic and welfare viewpoint, Cook invented mass tourism as distinct from the individual tourism which had characterized tourism until the middle of the nineteenth century. The story of Cook, his tours and other innovations, which included the creation of the first travel agencies, travelers checks and international rental agencies, warrants much more attention than it has been given.

Cook was a major force in the democratization of tourism (Graburn, 1983), revealing as he did that the attractions of travel and tourism appear to be common to almost all people. The pattern of tourism since the 1850s has witnessed a tremendous expansion in volume and vast technological change, particularly with the appearance of the automobile and the aircraft, but relatively little change in basic purpose and behavior. Perhaps the only real changes in tourism in the last century or so have been the large increase in numbers travelling to warmer climes in the winter, although even that is not entirely new and was well-established at Nice and other Mediterranean resorts by the midnineteenth century (Pearce, 1979), and ever-increasing numbers also travelling in the winter to mountainous areas to engage in winter sports.

Patterns of Tourism

To say that tourism is dynamic is to state a truism of outstanding dimensions. There is no element of tourism which does not change over time—although, paradoxically, there is considerable inertia and stability within the patterns displayed. One of the earliest patterns of tourism to emerge was the movement of people to large bodies of water, most frequently the ocean. Beginning with the stagecoach, followed by the steamship (Wall, 1977), this vacation activity increased dramatically with the advent of the railway. The links between railway companies and resort development are common and well-documented in both Britain and North America (Hart, 1983; Stansfield, 1972). The patterns of tourism which were established by the midnineteenth century are still evident in many parts of Europe and North America today, although the automobile and the jet aircraft have given many tourists wider horizons, as well as the means to reach them.

Of all the patterns that have emerged in the last century, that of sun-seeking hedonistic tourism is the predominant one. The desire to obtain sunshine while on vacation has dominated travel in postwar Europe, and has seen Spain replace France as the dominant summer destination of northern Europeans. The Mediterranean pleasure periphery has expanded, in turn, from France to Italy, to Spain, Greece, Malta, and most recently to Turkey. Expansion into North Africa and the Middle East would almost certainly have occurred on a larger scale by now had not political instability and outbreaks of terrorism deterred it. On a global scale the winter search for the sun has resulted in spectacular growth in tourism in many areas. Heliotropic

tourism has resulted in the increasing popularity of long-haul destinations, including the South Pacific and the Indian Ocean islands (Opperman, 1997). While tourists still travel in increasing numbers to temperate destinations, such as Northern Europe and North America, particularly to visit heritage areas and friends and relatives, to experience new cultures, and for a host of other reasons, "sunlust" travel has become a dominant feature of the pattern of tourism in the last quarter century.

Research on patterns of tourism, particularly those of a spatial nature, has traditionally been the realm of geographers. Early examples include work on the reciprocity of tourism (Williams and Zelinsky, 1970), on patterns of resort development and morphology (Stansfield, 1972), on global patterns (Matley, 1976), and on regional patterns (Christaller, 1963). Geographical research has also been a major component in studies of the process of tourism development, as well as the spatial pattern of that development—for example, in the writings of Murphy (1985) and Pearce (1995). Other researchers have also contributed significantly in these areas in recent years. "The pleasure periphery," as defined by Turner and Ash (1975), has become an established term in the literature, and others (Britton and Clarke, 1987; Harrison, 1993) have focused their attention upon regional development and growth.

Of particular concern to researchers studying the development of destination areas has been the nature and process of such development. In 1963 Christaller wrote of the changes which Mediterranean communities went through once they had become popular with tourists, and, since then, several authors have speculated on and researched the process which tourist destinations appear to pass through. One of the most frequently quoted references on this topic has been my own on the cycle of evolution of tourism destinations (Butler, 1980). Many researchers (Cooper and Jackson, 1989; Debbage, 1990; Hovinen, 1981; Meyer-Arendt, 1985; Strapp, 1988) have since used that model to describe and compare the development of, and changes in, areas studied. Stansfield (1978) applied a similar cycle to Atlantic City, while Wolfe (1982) also suggested a variation on the same theme. Butler's model proposed that tourism destinations are essentially organic, with a definite life cycle, and that their development can be modeled using an S-shaped curve. The consensus to date suggests that there are more examples which approximate the model than not, although suggestions for improvement and modification are still being made (Agarwhal, 1994). In a similar vein, an early article by Plog (1973) gained considerable attention in the literature. Plog suggested that not only was it possible to segment tourists into types by psychographics, but that the types of visitors to destinations change over time, from trend-setting *allocentrics* to more sedentary *psychocentrics*. He concluded with the question as to whether tourist destinations carry with them the inevitable seeds of their own decline. Intuitively this model, again unidirectional, has great appeal, but it, too, has not satisfactorily been tested empirically. To do so for a specific destination would require considerable longitudinal data, which are unlikely to exist.

Whatever the specific merits of the general models discussed earlier, there is little doubt that both destinations and tourists change over time. Resorts rise and fall in popularity and in real and perceived attractivity. Much research remains to be done in this area, which in many respects is at the core of tourism studies, since it deals with the implications facing communities and their populations if they become a part of the global tourist industry. Whether the planning and management of tourism development is possible to the same level that many recreation resources can be planned and managed remains to be seen, but, undoubtedly, if left to its own devices, tourism in many cases seems destined to continually reenact the "tragedy of the commons" (Hardin, 1969), an issue discussed by other authors in the intervening years (Butler, 1991; Healy, 1994).

Tourism and Society

The place of tourism in society has continually evolved and today is clearly very different from that of earlier times. Tourism is now a commonly accepted form of behavior, but has assumed, as with many other commonly held goods such as automobiles, a role as an indicator of status. How the desire and need for tourism fits into the broader hierarchy of needs, such as those defined by Maslow (1954), still remains to be clarified. Dann (1977), along with others (Pearce, 1982, 1993), adopted a more social-psychological view, based upon the examination of the individual needs of tourists in the context of the group of which they are members.

There are, of course, varying views of the roles and purposes of tourism and vacation travel. Krippendorf (1986) argued that society creates the need to travel and that "people leave because they no longer feel at ease where they are, where they work and where they live. They feel an urgent need to rid themselves temporarily of the burdens imposed by the everyday work, home, and leisure scenes, in order to be in a fit state to pick up the burden again" (p. 523). In other words, tourist travel is a form of re-creation. MacCannell (1973), on the other hand, has argued that tourists are not concerned with amusement, but seek authenticity in a manner and with a purpose which makes the tourist essentially a pilgrim, motivated as though on a religious quest. Cohen (1995) has challenged the latter view of tourism as somewhat limited, but shares similar concerns over the authenticity of the phenomena visited by tourists and their effects upon continued authenticity. Between these somewhat extreme views of tourism is the realization that there are, in fact, infinite numbers of reasons for participating in tourism, ranging from combating boredom, through relaxation, to the search for spiritual replenishment. Each type may have a different set of requirements from the host population and environment, impose different impacts upon them, and consist of widely differing individuals. For example, Iso-Ahola (1984) proposed an alternative theoretical framework to explain leisure and tourism motivation, which argued that two forces simultaneously influence leisure behavior—change (or novelty) and escape. Others have discussed the element of role playing in tourism and the ways in which the tourist views the landscapes and settings in which tourism is engaged, epitomized best in Urry's (1990) *The Tourist Gaze.*

A significant emerging trend in tourism is the role of the media in the popularization and development of destinations. The media now have the ability to transform even an event with little sightseeing appeal into a major attraction if it so desires. Such is the power of the media to influence public taste and fashion, both directly and indirectly, that it seems impossible now, for example, to envisage an America's Cup Yachting Competition as anything other than a major tourist attraction, primarily because of media attention. Yet, prior to the successful Australian challenge in 1984, the event had been limited to one location, its attraction was restricted to yacht enthusiasts, and it received minimal media coverage. The hosting of the 1986 challenge in Freemantle, Australia, saw massive investment in tourist-related infrastructure unrelated in any direct way to the racing of several 12-meter yachts. Given the fact that the Freemantle-Perth area (and western Australia generally) was unknown as an international tourist destination, and that the races themselves were all but invisible to the majority of "spectators," the principal explanation for the attendance of several thousand visitors from overseas must be the attention generated by the news media, together with some latent "nautical nationalism" among the visitors. The impacts of such *megaevents* as the Olympics, the World Cup (soccer), and now the America's Cup are such that they are fiercely competed for by potential host cities, even if the real value of hosting such events is uncertain (Syme, Shaw, Fenton and Mueller, 1989).

The media are also having significant impacts upon visitation to other sites, both directly and indirectly. Publicity of almost any event or sight now draws visitors, the most spectacular example in recent times being the patronage of events following and related to the death and funeral of Diana, Princess of Wales, in 1997. This particular phenomenon is likely to continue for the foreseeable future, with all 150,000 tickets for the 1998 visiting season to Althorp, site of the Princess's burial, sold within a week of becoming available in January 1998. At a less spectacular level, but more widespread, is the increasing popularity of sites used or portrayed in film or television, or associated with famous or infamous people. The influence of literature and the lives and homes of famous authors on visitation has long been recognized (Butler, 1990), but the impact of television and movies appears to have become even more significant in recent years (Riley, 1994; Tooke and Baker, 1996). Whether the appeal is vicarious fame, being able to walk down the same street as one's hero, or simply curiosity to see where movies were made is unknown, but as varied sites as the property featured as the home of "Magnum P. I." in Hawaii, the Yorkshire village filling the role of Aidensfield in the British television show "Heartbeat," the cornfield from *Field of Dreams,* the covered bridges in *Bridges of Madison County,* and the Devil's Tower in *Close Encounters of the Third Kind* have all become popular tourist sites. The role of the media in influencing tastes and in creating, perpetuating, and modifying images has not been studied to any great degree (Gartner, 1993).

There are some intriguing research possibilities on related issues, such as the general boredom of affluent sections of the population, the apparent increasing desire of people to be at the scene of happenings, whether they be conventionally leisure related or not, and the unclear (but likely) relationships among tourism, snobbery, and uniqueness. Surrogate and vicarious participation in international events can be claimed by the collection of photographs, souvenirs, and items of clothing emblazoned with information, often false, implying that the wearer was at, or a participant in, some recent event.

As Lew (1987) has commented, research on tourist attractions is limited, despite the importance of such features to the industry. He argued that tourist attractions "consist of all those elements of a 'nonhome' place that draw discretionary travelers away from their homes" (p. 554), but noted that it can be difficult to differentiate between attractions and nonattractions. Perhaps now more than ever, this distinction is even harder to make as the range of attractions varies from authentic native sites available for observation only to an anthropologist, to the Disney Worlds and totally artificial facilities at places such as Las Vegas, and from the deserted spaces of Antarctica to the stores and recreational facilities of West Edmonton Mall in Canada.

While the role and place of tourism in society have changed greatly, so, too, has the society in which tourism occurs. For many centuries, tourism was confined either to areas similar to those from which tourists came (i.e., urban centers), or else to private rural estates, the exceptions being limited to places such as spas, whose special natural attributes eventually gave way to the importance of entrepreneurs, fashion, and specific facilities (Patmore, 1968). Over the last century or so, however, communities have appeared whose primary role or function is to cater to tourists and their needs, of which Las Vegas is perhaps the most spectacular example. The earliest resorts were those associated with the railway and with the seacoast of either the Atlantic or the Mediterranean (Pearce, 1979; Stansfield, 1972), but present-day resorts now have a much wider range of functions and characteristics, including those devoted to health, gambling, sports, adventure, education, and culture as well as relaxation. In many ways the serious leisure that Stebbins (see chapter 5 in this volume) has identified has begun to appear in the guise of intensive and serious tourism, where simple enjoyment is secondary to other motives for participation.

The study of these special tourist places, destinations of many of the world's tourists, and their unique social and physical composition, has remained to a large extent the domain of geographers. Barrett (1958), Brown (1985), and Stansfield (1972, 1978) have all examined the unique and common morphology of traditional resorts and their responses over time to changes in accessibility and markets. While the interest in the communities themselves has not attracted much attention from other disciplines, the study of the perceptions and attitudes of the residents of these communities has attracted much more attention from anthropologists, sociologists, and political scientists as well as geographers.

The often negative attitude toward tourists displayed by locals and by other tourists is one of the other aspects of tourism which appears to have originated with the Grand Tour (Hibbert, 1969), a feature which was heightened by the innovations of Cook (Swinglehurst, 1982), as the increased numbers of mass tourists were not appreciated by the more affluent and class-conscious individual tourists of the time. Few people today describe themselves as tourists while on holiday, preferring terms such as visitor, traveler, or even stranger to being characterized as a tourist, with all which that might imply (Wheeller, 1993). While the impact of the "Golden Hordes" of Turner and Ash (1975) may be as great as that of earlier waves of barbarians, many individuals feel less sure of themselves abroad than the apocryphal El Syd (Coren, 1978), the unworthy descendant of Sir Phillip Sydney, originator of the Grand Tour.

Tourism as a Business

While Sydney, the first "tourist," was on a political mission for Queen Elizabeth I, and earlier seasonal migrants temporarily relocated more for reasons of comfort than anything else, today's tourist is an economic phenomenon. Tourism has assumed such significant economic dimensions in so many parts of the world that it no longer depends upon the whims and preferences of those engaged in pleasure travel. Economies of nation states are now dependent on tourism, with many of these states having little or no control over the industry which is shaping their development, or lack of development (Britton, 1982; de Kadt, 1979). The economic importance of tourism varies widely from region to region across the world. While the dominant countries in absolute figures are the developed countries of Western Europe and North America, in relative terms tourism is more important in other parts of the world, including many "undeveloped" or "less developed" countries (Harrison, 1993).

In several regions of the world the lives of much of the population would be considerably worse without tourism-generated employment and income. This is recognized by politicians, business people, and ordinary citizens alike. What has also become clear, however, is that tourism is increasingly being controlled and manipulated from the center, the regions from which most tourists originate, in which the multinational corporations, which own most of the large-scale tourism infrastructure, are located. Thus, many of the profits eventually return to the center whence they originated. Nash (1977) and others have speculated on "Tourism as a form of imperialism," and Wu (1982) writes of the links between tourism and the political economy of underdevelopment. Nongovernmental organizations such as Tourism Concern have become particularly effective at drawing attention to this and related issues of the real benefits and costs of tourism in such parts of the world.

The identification and determination of the magnitude of economic benefits from tourism depend to a great degree upon who is conducting the research, together with the definitions of who is a tourist and what constitutes tourism. Many agencies involved in tourism development tend to include almost any visitor from out of the country, the area, or the town under discussion. As a result, economic benefits from expenditures by businessmen, students, and even politicians are frequently included in total amounts credited as tourist spending. The media representatives covering events such as the Winter Olympics in Japan and the Summer Olympics in Atlanta were certainly not tourists in the pleasure sense of the word. There is little doubt, however, that their purchases of accommodations, meals, and services will be included in tourist revenues when the final balance sheets for these events are drawn up.

Even within tourism destinations, it is clear that benefits and costs do not accrue evenly, nor are they perceived to do so (Brougham and Butler, 1981). While the private hotel operator and staff may benefit through revenue generation and salaries, another business may suffer because of increased labor costs caused by labor shortages arising from increased employment in tourism-related developments (Mathieson and Wall, 1982). Demand for second homes for tourists may cause inflation in property prices, resulting in increased costs of local houses and land (Cooper et al., 1998). Rapid expansion in tourism-related services and facilities can unbalance the economies of traditional communities, resulting in such negative effects as sizeable increases in local taxes, in land prices, and in labor costs, which can cause severe problems for residents on fixed incomes, who may be unable to benefit from the unanticipated and often uncontrolled rate of growth of tourism and economic activity going on around them (Syme et al., 1989).

A common pattern is that the benefits accrue to those involved in the industry and to some others in a position to sell goods or services required, but the costs are borne by others, principally through opportunity costs and inflation (Britton and Clarke, 1987). The problem is often compounded because the stimulus for, and control of, the development is external to the area experiencing it, particularly as the rate and scale of growth accelerate. Such a situation seems common to areas as different as the Canadian Arctic and the Caribbean or Central Florida and the South Pacific. Even where international corporations are not involved, central or national governments may promote the development and growth of tourism at the expense of regional and local communities, which may have to absorb additional costs, such as local road or harbor improvements or the provision of municipal services on a much larger scale than before.

As more research has been conducted, it has become increasingly clear that the early economic forecasts of the effects of tourism were generally too simplistic, too narrow, and too optimistic. While few reached the level of inaccuracy of the Zinder Report

(Zinder, 1969), most had a single focus—return on investment—which generally typified the early work of economists in tourism. Few economists (Bryden, 1973, and Archer, 1973a, 1973b, being particularly respected exceptions) looked beyond the positive economic implications of the effects of tourism development. The economic and business domination of tourism is clearly illustrated by Richter (1983), who quotes a convention theme of the Pacific Area Travel Association: "The Consumer: The Only One Who Matters."

In recent years, however, the need to take a wider view of the economic benefits and costs of tourism has been widely accepted. Studies have assessed, for example, the difficulties of using multipliers, and have explored alternative ways of maximizing benefits, depending upon the type of economic development and change desired. Publications such as Finney and Watson's *A New Kind of Sugar: Tourism in the South Pacific* (1977), de Kadt's *Tourism—Passport to Development?* (1979), and Harrison's *Tourism in the Less Developed Countries* (1993) have not only queried the true nature of the benefits, but have also inquired into the costs of tourism and tourism-associated development. Other researchers, such as Hovik and Heilberg (1980), have reviewed tourism in the context of center-periphery theory, and few studies of the effects of projected or proposed tourism development now assess only the economic effects of that development (Butler and Pearce, 1995; Cooper and Wanhill, 1997).

The Sociocultural and Environmental Aspects of Tourism

Some of the major and most innovative contributions of social science research to tourism have been through the wide range of studies into the effects of, and interrelationships between, tourists and destination residents and environments. This research began in depth in the early 1970s and has remained a major focus since then. Students of tourism were well-aware of the effects of tourism upon both tourists and the host population of destination areas before this period, but there was little systematic study of this problem in earlier years. What research was done tended to focus on the more positive economic impacts of tourism rather than the rarely documented problems in the social and cultural fields resulting from development.

There are several factors influencing such a state of affairs. In the first place tourism, except where it was seen as a part of development generally, was not seriously studied by academics. Second, research-funding bodies, particularly government agencies, were not (and some are still not) sympathetic to research exposing problems resulting from development. Third, as Wall and Wright (1977) pointed out in the context of the environmental impacts of leisure activities, without longitudinal data and established benchmarks and control sites, it is difficult, if not impossible, to ascribe changes and impacts to one single agent, in this case tourism. Especially with impacts in areas such as language, cultural adaptation, crime, attitudes, indigenous skills, and traditional behavior patterns, it is difficult to measure change, let alone identify beyond doubt the agent of change.

There has, however, been considerable research in anthropology, geography, political science, psychology, and sociology on the effects of tourism on host populations, and on the tourists themselves, including their motivations and desires, their behavior, and their expectations. Two major reports on the effects of tourism (Noronha, 1976; Thurot, 1975) appeared in the mid 1970s, and were followed by several of the monographs discussed previously. The most comprehensive review of the literature on the impacts of tourism is contained in Mathieson and Wall's (1982) *Tourism: Economic, Physical and Social Impacts,* which omits little if anything of significance published in English before that date. This book is still of particular value, not only because of the extent of the material included, but also because of the conceptual framework provided and the analysis and context in which the material is placed, which allow for a rational assessment of the effects of tourism development in a variety of settings. Despite the very large number of case studies and examples of impact research which have appeared in the literature since, the overall conceptualization and conclusions of the book still remain valid.

Despite the additional material which has appeared since 1982, it is fair to say that no really significant new findings or thrusts have manifested themselves. Rather, the more recent work has tended to reinforce and complement the findings from the empirical studies discussed by Mathieson and Wall (1982). Some interesting research has appeared in social psychology (e.g., Furnham, 1984; van Raaij and Francken, 1984), in anthropology (e.g., MacCannell, 1984; Wood, 1984), in recreation (e.g., Perdue, Long and Allen, 1987), and in sociology (e.g., Van den Berghe and Keyes, 1984). The basic issues raised by early writers, such as Butler (1974), Greenwood (1976), and Jafari (1974), still remain as major items of interest, specifically, how tourism affects local populations in such areas as language, traditional patterns of behavior, traditional values, and attitudes toward the visitors. Several authors have focused upon the last point, suggesting that changes in the attitudes of locals toward tourists are indicative of changes in attitudes toward tourism in general. Others, such as Lui, Sheldon, and Var (1987) have examined residents' perceptions of the impacts of tourism, concluding that perception of "the impact of tourism on the environment is shared by all the residents regardless of their geographic locations and maturity levels of tourism" (p. 17).

As may be expected, much of the research by social scientists has focused on the human aspects of tourism. However, some attention has also been paid to the environmental effects of tourism on destination areas. The environmental effects of recreation are little different in nature from the impacts of tourism. Farrell and McLellan (1987), in their paper "Tourism and Physical Environment Research," noted one of the principal problems with environmental impact research:

> A high proportion of well-educated individuals, through possibly ignorance or emotion, attribute an unreasonable amount of responsibility for landscape change and environmental degradation to tourism. For those concerned with tourism, enormous questions are thus raised, and although a number of assertions may seem plausible, they are seldom backed with adequate argument. It is not unusual to hear an otherwise scientifically sound and thoughtful colleague make sweeping allegations concerning the destructiveness of tourism. (p. 2)

Much the same comments could be made about the effects of tourism on the *human* environment. Farrell and McLellan's conclusions bear repeating in the context of research on any impacts of tourism: "It is obvious that research is inadequate; that the area is one of supersensitivity and should be treated as such; and management should, in the interests of all concerned, reflect values that society places on environment" (1987, p. 2).

Sustainable Development and Tourism

It was noted earlier that it is perhaps in the area of sustainable development that there has been the greatest recent development in tourism and tourism research. The concept of sustainable development, promoted most effectively in the report of the Brundtland Commission, *Our Common Future,* was defined in that report as "development that meets the needs of the present without compromising the ability of future generations to meet their own needs" (World Commission on Environment and Development, 1987, p. 4). Few concepts have received the popular and political support which sustainable development has in the decade since it was first put forward, with major policy commitments from world political leaders and a significant shift in public opinion and corporate attitude toward the environment, at least in principle. In tourism the concept has received wide attention and has been seized on as a way of avoiding, if not correcting, the problems and excesses of mass or conventional tourism. It has become a rallying cry for all opposed to the by-now-traditional forms of tourism and their effects. Much hyperbole and beating of breasts has followed, aided by skilled if opportunistic marketing, which has been brilliantly and cuttingly reviewed by Wheeller (1993, 1994).

The desire to reform tourism and to reduce its negative effects, especially on local populations and destination environments, and to increase economic benefits to local residents through sustainable development is entirely praiseworthy, although it is unfortunate that *Our Common Future* does not mention tourism at all. One of the problems is that there is no generally agreed upon definition of sustainable tourism, or tourism developed on sustainable principles (Butler, 1993). There has been a growth industry in reports and publications on sustainable tourism and alternative forms of tourism to conventional mass tourism, such as "new" tourism (Poon, 1993), ecotourism (Boo, 1990; Cater and Lowman, 1995; Weaver, 1998), and nature tourism (Whelan, 1991). Sustainable tourism, in particular, has generated a large number of books (in addition to those noted earlier, the reader is referred to Briguglio, Archer, Jafari and Wall, 1996; Briguglio, Butler, Harrison and Filho, 1996; Hall and Lew, 1998; and Mowforth and Munt, 1998), and even a journal devoted to that specific subject, the *Journal of Sustainable Tourism,* which has published some of the best research studies on this problematic topic.

Whether sustainable development represents anything really different from the concepts of the Club of Rome in the 1960s, expressed in *Limits to Growth* (Meadows, Meadows, Randers and Behrens, 1972) or Gifford Pinchot's ideas of conservation in the first decades of this century (Nelson, 1973) is not really important. What is significant is that for the first time on a large scale there is concern and interest expressed by all elements of tourism—academic, business, political, and consumer—about the effects of tourism, along with thoughts of adjusting development to take into account the limits and capacity of destinations to handle the development which is occurring. This newly resurrected concern over the impact of tourism on the natural environment has also carried over into concern about the effects of tourism upon the human environment of destination areas (Craik, 1995). The social and cultural impacts noted earlier take on added significance with a relatively recent increase in interest in cultural or heritage tourism. Interest in past cultures and their artifacts dates back to the Grand Tour, but in recent years there has been heightened interest in visiting historic heritage destinations, including World Heritage Sites of a cultural nature. The issues raised by this renewed interest are similar to those items of concern with the relationship between tourism and the physical environment, in particular, how much use heritage sites can withstand before the features become damaged, or, in the case of living cultures, before the traditions and attributes become modified to meet the pressures and demands of tourism (Nuryanti, 1996, 1997; Robinson, Evans and Callaghan, 1996).

It is clear that tourists find heritage, both environmental and human, greatly attractive, and visits to heritage sites are increasing dramatically. Attendance figures for popular historic sites and national parks throughout the world bear out this point. Many national park systems in the world owe their establishment and protection to the potential tourist market envisaged by governments (Nelson, 1973), and Inskeep (1987) and Budowski (1976) have both argued that tourism can be a positive force in achieving conservation objectives and maintaining a symbiotic relationship with the environment. Such an objective is hard to attain, however, because in most places the tourism industry is highly fragmented, rarely has agreement among its members, is highly competitive, and appears relatively resistant to external direction and intervention (Butler, 1991). The adoption of sustainable development principles has seen the establishment by public and private sector groupings of Codes of Conduct for tourists and for operators and other sectors in the tourism industry in a number of areas, but the lack of regulation and enforcement means that adherence to such codes is voluntary and often incomplete, and such procedures have yet to be researched as to their effectiveness.

Tourism Planning and Control

The points raised in the preceding discussion highlight a major difficulty with tourism, that of planning and controlling development. The principal efforts of governments and public agencies in many parts of the world have traditionally been aimed at attracting and increasing tourism rather than controlling it (Pigram, 1990). Most tourism-related legislation concerns the establishment of tourism boards (agencies, departments, or ministries), the provision of incentives for development, and the marketing and promotion of the host nation (Pearce, 1992b). Other regulations may deal with hotel and other accommodation registers and grading, employee training, and operator licensing, but rarely does the legislation deal with limiting or controlling development. Where tourism plans have been developed, in few places are they regarded as more than expressions of preference, easily changed to accommodate those willing to develop, but who wish to develop at locations other than those suggested in a plan.

The reason for this situation is that most authorities prefer tourism development of almost any kind to no development at all, because, in general, most governments regard tourism as a clean, nonpolluting, harmless form of development. "Tourists take nothing but photographs and leave nothing but footprints" was the text of an advertisement promoting the tourism industry in Ontario in the 1970s, and this mistaken philosophy still continues in many areas today. The reactions of much-photographed residents suffering from a lack of privacy and the effects of large numbers of footprints in some fragile environments obviously were not considered to be important by the authors of the text.

A related aspect of the problem of numbers is that, while vast efforts are made to attract tourists to a destination, commensurate efforts are not always feasible or contemplated to retain that share of the market. While for a period a destination may succeed in attracting visitors because of its growth and reputation, ultimately it is likely to be eclipsed by newer and more "trendy" competitors, or to outgrow its potential. This state of affairs has been described by Wolfe (1952) as "the divorce from the geographic environment," the reliance upon man-made and social attractions after the natural attractions are degraded or lost. The ongoing appeal of Niagara Falls, for example, probably owes as much or more to the continued addition of artificial creations (wax works, museums, new fantasy or theme worlds) as it does to the natural features which attracted tourists initially, and this is certainly the case for Las Vegas, which continuously adds ever more spectacular developments as it attempts not only to maintain its market share, but also to broaden its appeal to a more family-focused market.

Only a few places manage to retain their initial attractiveness and popularity over the long term. Some are capital cities, such as London, Paris, and Rome, where the major attractions remain, and the appeal of the large urban center is still high, based on being a center of fashion, taste, and power. Some other places remain attractive for different reasons. They manage to retain their appeal, charm, ambience, and atmosphere by exclusiveness and consistency. In so doing, they have eschewed rapid and large-scale expansion, and have maximized revenues by increasing costs to visitors rather than by increasing the numbers of visitors. A higher return per head from each visitor, obtained through high-quality experiences and high prices, has helped to ensure exclusivity and to reduce the demand for change so as to cater to large numbers of less affluent visitors.

To be able to achieve such a position, however, requires an affluent, upmarket clientele at the beginning of development, and a recognition and determination to maintain that clientele (for example, the development of Telluride in Colorado). In turn, this requires specific policies and local control over development, and the ability to limit or prevent it, even where this may be encouraged by other levels of government. Such arrangements are not common, nor is local willingness to set limits to tourism growth, and long-term benefits are frequently sacrificed for short-term gain. Coordination and agreement between different levels in the public sector and with the private sector are also requirements for such sustained success. In the earlier version of this chapter (Butler, 1989), I speculated that it was perhaps too soon to say if examples of mass tourism development, such as the Disney operations in California and Florida, could also survive successfully for many decades. These operations are private concerns which operate as municipalities and, thus, do not need this coordination and agreement, because the private and public sectors are, in effect, combined. As well, in the case of Disney the corporation has total power and almost total freedom to institute whatever changes and innovations it desires in order to maintain attractivity to visitors and offer an atmosphere of continual novelty and freshness. While the Disney Corporation has experienced severe problems with its operation in France and opposition to establishing a new theme park based on the Civil War, the operations in America and in Japan have continued to do well. The opening of the new, if controversial, Animal Kingdom in 1998 suggests that the company is confident of the success of its operations when it has control of the site and the nature and scale of development in an environment with which it is familiar. Together, the two extremes indicate the importance of power and control residing with the planning and management agency in one form, whether this be public or private.

Despite increasing pressure to have such control at least represented at the local level (Boo, 1990; Murphy, 1985), all too often the real power is not vested in the agency responsible for planning, especially at the local level, but resides in boardrooms and legislative corridors far distant from the destination communities—mostly in the countries of origin of the tourists (Britton, 1982). In such cases, local communities, or even small nation-states, can do little but accept the future and the pattern of development as laid down by the elements shaping the market (Harrison, 1993; Weaver, 1998).

One of the major concerns related to sustainable development is that of limits to numbers of tourists. The idea of limiting the number of tourists to destinations has never been particularly attractive to either the public or the private sector for obvious economic reasons. Tourism, much more than outdoor recreation, is driven by the profit motive, and larger numbers normally represent greater income, at least in the short term. Where the destination is an urban resort or a mix of public and private attractions, limiting numbers becomes far more complex than, for example, placing a maximum figure on the number of whitewater canoeists on a river in a national park. The issue of carrying capacity of destinations, in both human and environmental terms, has received little consistent attention in the tourism field. It is, perhaps, ironic that so much excellent research has been conducted on carrying capacity in wilderness areas in which few or no people live, beginning with pioneers in the USDA Forest Service in the 1960s (Lucas, 1964; Stankey, 1982; Wagar, 1964), but that relatively little has been done in popular tourist destinations, where large numbers of permanent residents live and mix with large numbers of tourists.

After an initial early interest in the subject (Bord Fáilte, 1966), little attention was paid to thoughts on limiting numbers of visitors, in part because few areas were experiencing overcrowding except for a few days a year, and because the overriding philosophy was that more tourists meant more income. As the problems of mass tourism and overuse manifested themselves in older tourists destinations in the 1980s, a few studies began to examine the problem of too many visitors (Cheng, 1980; Getz, 1983; O'Reilly, 1986). A major problem in tourist destinations is to satisfy competing and often contradictory demands—by visitors for a quality experience, by local residents for privacy and normalcy, and by business operators and governments for maximum revenue (Kienholz, 1987).

There are some signs that the issue of carrying capacity has returned as a subject of concern and interest in tourism. In recent years, several articles have appeared arguing the need to address the problems of too many tourists and subsequent impacts and problems (Butler, 1996; Johnson and Thomas, 1994; Martin and Uysal, 1990; Saleem, 1994). However, management models or concepts such as the Recreation Opportunity Spectrum (Clark and Stankey, 1979), Limits of Acceptable Change (Stankey, Cole, Lucas, Peterson and Frissell, 1985), or Visitor Impact Management (Kuss, Graefe and Vaske, 1990) have few equivalents in tourism (Butler and Waldbrook, 1991). In the absence of overall management control in most tourism destinations, where problems of excess numbers have arisen, the most frequent response is unilateral imposition of limits by specific operators, and measures such as prebooking for admission to specific attractions. Few countries have imposed national-level limits on development and numbers of tourists, and the levels imposed represent more a desire to contain numbers to present levels than a conceptual or measured response to the pressures experienced. It is ironic that, in tourism, individual operators of facilities have tended to take the initiative in limiting numbers in the absence of information and advice based on research (Butler, 1996).

Conclusions and Implications

In the past decade, research on tourism has been undertaken at a scale not witnessed before, reflecting the much greater interest in the subject among researchers, and recognition within both the public and the private sector that tourism is of major significance, not only in economic terms, but also because of its social, cultural, political, and environmental implications. A good indication of public sector interest has been the rapid adoption of tourism studies at institutions of higher education and the establishment of tourism departments and schools at universities and colleges. Training in hospitality, hotel management, and related areas has long been taught with other technical studies in a number of institutions, and Europe in particular has a long history of applied research as well as education in these areas. The appearance of tourism as a subject at the university level, however, is a relatively recent phenomenon. There are now over 50 higher learning institutions in the United Kingdom offering degrees, certificates, and diplomas in tourism, from the undergraduate to the doctoral level, a figure almost matched in Australasia, and many North American universities have recently added tourism to established programs in recreation, leisure, parks and wildlife, and business studies. In Europe and Australasia, most of the tourism degree programs are in business and management schools, or economics, with relatively few in leisure, geography, or sociology programs, while in North America the subject is more widely distributed and fewer degree programs in tourism exist.

In all continents it is likely that some rationalization of offerings may take place, because expansion through the late 1980s and 1990s was extremely rapid and outgrew the supply of faculty with training or backgrounds in tourism, and the numbers of graduates appear to be exceeding the availability of positions. In many countries in the "pleasure periphery," such education opportunities do not exist and there are considerable numbers of students from these countries obtaining training in tourism in developed countries; indeed the economic well-being of a number of programs depends heavily on this south-north subsidization.

Tourism studies in universities is in an interesting phase in its development, since relatively few of the academic staff have postgraduate degrees in tourism, the great majority having received all or most of their training in "conventional" academic disciplines, especially at the doctoral level. Only recently have graduates with doctorates in tourism been available for employment, and it will be interesting in the decades ahead to see if significant changes occur in either the content of tourism programs or their academic acceptability by other more established disciplines. In this respect tourism is following the path trod by leisure studies two decades ago. Discussions about whether the subject is a discipline and whether there should be a common curriculum are still common and these questions are likely to continue unresolved for some time to come.

As noted earlier, the nature of study and research in tourism has broadened considerably from the early years, when the emphasis was on the economic aspects of tourism, although this focus is still present. As many governments have reduced public investment and made economic development programs more dependent on economic viability, tourism has been seen as a major element in the economic redevelopment of many areas, from marginal rural areas (Butler, Hall and Jenkins, 1998) to derelict inner city neighborhoods (Jansen-Verbeke, 1997), and thus research on the economic gains from tourism through income generation and employment has continued (Wanhill, 1995). As well, international tourism results in an input of foreign currency, as well as a reallocation of internal funds, from generally high-income urban areas to low-income rural areas (Pearce, 1992a). The conclusions of economists, in particular, therefore, have understandably tended to focus upon the material benefits resulting from development and have been positive about tourism. Researchers from other perspectives, such as anthropology, sociology, and geography, and more recently political science, have focused much of their attention on the effects of tourism-related development and have generally been more critical (and in some cases even negative) in their conclusions about the overall effects of tourism upon the destinations and host populations (see, for example, Butler and Hinch, 1996; Smith, 1989).

A significant difficulty for researchers in a field as wide as tourism studies is that of being cognizant of relevant research conducted in disciplines other than their own. Staying abreast of developments in one's own discipline is increasingly difficult given the growth in the number of publications and in the speed of the flow of information. It is a hard, if not almost impossible, task for a researcher in, for example, geography, to know all of the journals in anthropology, economics, political science, psychology, and sociology, in which articles on tourism might appear, let alone keep up-to-date with them. While keyword searches and the electronic storage and retrieval of data make the task more feasible than before, there is no doubt that some (perhaps many) studies are missed by most researchers. In tourism, the appearance of a large number of new journals devoted specifically to the subject has made this task a little easier, along with networks (often discipline-based) and web sites and research listings, but, given the attitudes of assessors of funding agencies and those responsible for evaluating programs and staff, emphasis is still placed on established journals in traditional disciplines. The researcher with an eye to advancement often eschews new journals because their reputation is not established for several years and continues to publish in nontourism journals, continuing the difficulty of staying in touch with advances in research.

There is no easy solution to this problem, which is compounded by the generally unilingual attributes of most researchers, especially those in the English-speaking world, which potentially can result in ignorance of research which may have been published in a language other than their own. Tourism, perhaps more than many academic subjects, is international in scope because of its very nature, and knowledge of the global literature is difficult to acquire. Nevertheless, there is clearly a need for more cross-disciplinary and interdisciplinary research in the field of tourism, if the subject is to be fully understood.

In the areas in which further research is most needed, these comments are particularly true. Research on the motivations of tourists, for example, has been marked by a variety of approaches and conclusions. In his early review article, Gann (1981) noted seven different uses of the expression. He explained the lack of agreement and the divergent views of motivation as being the result of the multidisciplinary nature of the research, as well as a number of differing theoretical perspectives within given disciplines, an argument echoed more than a decade later by Pearce (1993). Similarly, in the research on impacts, while there has been a vast number of individual studies conducted in the last decade, most have been single, one-off case studies, generally of short duration, using a variety of noncomparable methodologies from a multitude of viewpoints, with little coordination or replication of results. Some new thrusts can be noted, such as the attention now paid to residents' adjustments in behavior in response to tourism rather than the simple documentation of attitudes and perceptions (Ap and Crompton, 1990), and attempts to establish common indicators for the monitoring of the impacts of tourism on the environment (Nelson et al., 1993) in a manner similar to those developed for recreation (Marion, 1991). Even in the area of forecasting, while there has been more consistency in approach, there has been little by way of hindsight evaluation or assessment of potential impacts of predictions by those making the forecasts (Witt and Witt, 1992).

The dynamic and responsive nature of tourism makes it difficult to predict and to plan. Wolfe (1966) raised the question, many years ago, of what would happen to travel if the world became homogeneous and the distinction between places disappeared. Krippendorf (1986) raised a similar question when he discussed what might happen to tourism if we made our working and living environments and lifestyles more attractive, and thus reduced the need or desire for change. People may still travel because they believe the places they are going to will offer what they desire but cannot obtain at home, and there is the realization that image has become even more important than ever before. Hunt (1975) noted two decades ago that images may have as much to do with an area's success as its tangible attributes, a point which has been discussed further by Colton (1987) and Gartner (1993). This topic has attracted much more research in recent years, related to the importance of marketing research in tourism, shown by the establishment of journals such as the *Journal of Vacation Marketing*.

Because we are still so unsure about so many aspects of tourism, we face great difficulties in defining it and managing it. It is but one aspect of life, but one which, like leisure and recreation, is assuming an ever-increasing importance in many people's lives. Graburn (1983) noted:

> Tourism is also a barometer of the dynamics of culture change within a society, for it may portend future cultural patterns for the individual . . . and for the society. Furthermore, in patterns of historical trajectory, patterns of tourism may reflect the unfolding of consciousness and interests, e.g., in history, in the environment, and conservation, in health and cures, or in personal awareness. (p. 2)

If that is true, one may ponder the societal implications of recent developments in tourism. These include visits to areas of unrest to experience "challenge and excitement;" the rise in Thanatourism or dark tourism, reflecting an interest in death (Seaton, 1997); sex tourism, which often includes elements of pedophilia; tourism related to rock music and raves; and "virtual" tourism, where the focus is on escaping the real world without real travel. Compared to the above forms of tourism, the conventional family holiday on the beach, despite all the problems of mass tourism, seems positively appropriate, even if a little environmentally and culturally suspect because of the direct impacts related to intensity of use.

References

Agarwal, S. (1994). The resort cycle revisited: Implications for resorts. In C. P. Cooper & A. L. Lockwood (Eds.). *Progress in tourism, recreation and hospitality management* (Vol. 5). Chichester, UK: John Wiley & Sons, Ltd.

Ap, J., & Crompton, J. (1990). Residents' strategies for responding to tourism impacts. *Journal of Travel Research, 29*(2), 47–51.

Archer, B. (1973a). *The impact of domestic tourism* (Bangor Occasional Papers in Economics, No. 2). Cardiff, UK: University of Wales.

Archer, B. (1973b). *The uses and abuses of multipliers* (Tourist Research Paper, TUR 1). Bangor, UK: University College of North Wales.

Barrett, J. A. (1958). *The seaside resort towns of England and Wales.* Unpublished doctoral thesis, University of London, London, UK.

Boo, E. (1990). *Ecotourism: The potentials and pitfalls.* Washington, DC: World Wildlife Fund.

Bord Fáilte. (1966). *Planning for amenity and tourism.* Dublin, UK: An Foras Forbatha.

Bramwell, B., Henry, I., Jackson, G., Prat, A. G., Richards, G., & van der Straaten, J. (1996). *Sustainable tourism management: Principles and practice.* Tilburg, Netherlands: Tilburg University Press.

Briguglio, L., Archer, B., Jafari, J., & Wall, G. (Eds.). (1996). *Sustainable tourism in islands and small states: Issues and policies.* London, UK: Pinter.

Briguglio, L., Butler, R., Harrison, D., & Filho, W. (Eds.). (1996). *Sustainable tourism in islands and small states: Case studies.* London, UK: Pinter.

Britton, S. G. (1982). The political economy of tourism in the third world. *Annals of Tourism Research, 9,* 331–358.

Britton, S. G., & Clarke, W. C. (1987). *Ambiguous alternative tourism in small developing islands.* Suva, Fiji: University of the South Pacific.

Brougham, J. E., & Butler, R. W. (1981). A segmentation analysis of resident attitudes to the social impact of tourism. *Annals of Tourism Research, 13,* 569–590.

Brown, B. J. H. (1985). Personal perception and community speculation: A British resort in the 19th century. *Annals of Tourism Research, 12,* 355–370.

Bryden, J. (1973). *Tourism and development: A case study of the Commonwealth Caribbean.* Cambridge, UK: Cambridge University Press.

Budowski, G. (1976). Tourism and environmental conservation: Conflict, coexistence or symbiosis? *Environmental Conservation, 3*(1), 27–31.

Burns, P. M., & Holden, A. (1997). *Tourism: A new perspective.* London, UK: Prentice-Hall.

Butler, R. W. (1974). The social implications of tourist developments. *Annals of Tourism Research, 2,* 100–111.

Butler, R. W. (1980). The concept of a tourist area cycle of evolution: Implications for management of resources. *The Canadian Geographer, 24,* 5–12.

Butler, R. W. (1989). Tourism and tourism research. In E. L. Jackson & T. L. Burton (Eds.), *Understanding leisure and recreation: Mapping the past, charting the future* (pp. 567–595). State College, PA: Venture Publishing, Inc.

Butler, R. W. (1990). The role of the media in shaping international tourism patterns. *Tourism Recreation Research, XV*(2), 46–53.

Butler, R. W. (1991). Tourism, environment and sustainable development. *Environmental Conservation, 18,* 201–209.

Butler, R. W. (1993). Tourism: An evolutionary approach. In J. G. Nelson, R. W. Butler & G. Wall (Eds.), *Tourism and sustainable development: Monitoring, planning and managing* (pp. 27–43). Waterloo, Ontario: University of Waterloo Press.

Butler, R. W. (1996). The concept of carrying capacity for tourism destinations: Dead or merely buried? *Progress in Tourism and Hospitality, 2,* 283–293.

Butler, R. W., Hall, C. M., & Jenkins J. (1998). *Tourism and recreation in rural areas.* Chichester, UK: John Wiley & Sons, Ltd.

Butler, R. W., & Hinch, T. (Eds.). (1996). *Tourism and indigenous peoples.* London, UK: Routledge.

Butler, R. W., & Pearce, D. G. (Eds.). (1995). *Change in tourism: People, places, processes.* London, UK: Routledge.

Butler, R. W., & Waldbrook, L. A. (1991). A new planning tool: The tourism opportunity spectrum. *Journal of Tourism Studies, 2*(1), 2–14.

Cater, E., & Lowman G. (Eds.). (1995). *Ecotourism: A sustainable option?* Chichester, UK: John Wiley & Sons, Ltd.

Cheng, J. R. (1980). Tourism: How much is too much? Lessons for Canmore from Banff. *The Canadian Geographer, 24,* 72–80.

Christaller, W. (1963). Some considerations of tourism location in Europe—The peripheral regions—Underdeveloped countries—Recreation areas. *Papers of the Regional Science Association, 12,* 95–115.

Clark, R. N., & Stankey, G. H. (1979). *The recreation opportunity spectrum: A framework for planning, management and research* (General Technical Report PNW-98). Portland: USDA Forest Service Pacific Northwest Forest and Range Experimental Station.

Cohen, E. (1979). Rethinking the sociology of tourism. *Annals of Tourism Research, 6*(1), 18–35.

Cohen, E. (1995). Contemporary tourism, trends and challenges: Sustainable authenticity or contrived postmodernity? In R. W. Butler & D. G. Pearce (Eds.), *Change in tourism: People, places, processes* (pp. 12–29). London, UK: Routledge.

Colton, C. W. (1987). Leisure, recreation, tourism: A symbolic interactionism view. *Annals of Tourism Research, 14*(3), 345–360.

Conlin, M. C., & Baum, T. (1995). *Island tourism: Management, principles and practice.* Chichester, UK: John Wiley & Sons, Ltd.

Cooper, C. P., Fletcher, J., Gilbert, D., Shepherd, R., & Wanhill, S. (1998). *Tourism: Principles and practice.* Harlow, UK: Longman.

Cooper, C. P., & Jackson, S. (1989). Destination life cycle: The Isle of Man case study. *Annals of Tourism Research, 16*(1), 377–398.

Cooper, C. P., & Wanhill, S. (Eds.). (1997). *Tourism development: Environmental and community issues.* Chichester, UK: John Wiley & Sons, Ltd.

Coren, A. (1978). *Tissues for men.* Harmondsworth, UK: Penguin.

Craik, J. (1995). Are there cultural limits to tourism? *Journal of Sustainable Tourism, 3*(2), 87–98.

Dann, G. M. S., (1977). Anomie, ego-enhancement and tourism. *Annals of Tourism Research, 4*(4), 184–194.

Debbage, K. G. (1990). Tourism oligopoly is at work. *Annals of Tourism Research, 17*(2), 355–359.

De Kadt, E. (1979). *Tourism—Passport to development: Perspectives on the social and cultural effects of tourism in developing countries.* Oxford, UK: Oxford University Press.

Farrell, B., & McLellan, R. W. (1987). Tourism and physical environment research. *Annals of Tourism Research, 14*(1), 1–14.

Fedler, A. J. (1987). Are leisure, recreation and tourism related? *Annals of Tourism Research, 14*(2), 311–313.

Finney, B. R., & Watson, K. A. (Eds.). (1977). *A new kind of sugar: Tourism in the Pacific.* Santa Cruz, CA: Center for South Pacific Studies, University of California–Santa Cruz.

Furnham, A. (1984). Tourism and culture shock. *Annals of Tourism Research, 11*(1), 41–58.

Gann, G. M. S. (1981). Tourist motivation: An appraisal. *Annals of Tourism Research, 8,* 187–219.

Gartner, W. C. (1993). Image formation process. *Journal of Travel and Tourism Marketing, 2*(2/3), 191–205.

Getz, D. (1983). Capacity to absorb tourism: Concepts and implications for strategic planning. *Annals of Tourism Research, 10,* 239–263.

Graburn, N. H. H. (1983). The anthropology of tourism. *Annals of Tourism Research, 10,* 9–33.

Greenwood, D. (1976). Tourism as an agent of change. *Annals of Tourism Research, 3,* 128–142.

Gunn, C. A. (1979). *Tourism planning.* New York, NY: Crane Russak.

Hall, C. M. (1994a). *Tourism in the Pacific Rim.* Melbourne, Australia: Longman Cheshire.

Hall, C. M. (1994b). *Tourism and politics.* Chichester, UK: John Wiley & Sons, Ltd.

Hall, C. M., & Jenkins, J. J. (1995). *Tourism and public policy.* London, UK: Routledge.

Hall, C. M., & Lew, A. A. (1998). *Sustainable tourism: A geographical perspective.* Harlow, UK: Longman.

Hardin, G. (1969). The tragedy of the commons. *Science, 162,* 1243–1248.

Harrison, D. (Ed.). (1993). *Tourism and the less developed countries.* London, UK: Belhaven Press.

Hart, E. J. (1983). *The selling of Canada.* Banff, Alberta: Altitude Press.

Healy, R. G. (1994). The common pool problem in tourism landscapes. *Annals of Tourism Research, 21*(3), 596–611.

Hibbert, C. (1969). *The grand tour.* London, UK: Putnam.

Hovik, T., & Heiberg, T. (1980). Center-periphery tourism and self-reliance. *International Social Science Journal, 32,* 68–98.

Hovinen, G. (1981). A tourist cycle in Lancaster County, Pennsylvania. *The Canadian Geographer, 25,* 283–285.

Hunt, J. D. (1975). Image as a factor in tourism development. *Journal of Travel Research, 13,* 1–7.

Inskeep, E. (1987). Environmental planning for tourism. *Annals of Tourism Research, 14,* 118–135.

Iso-Ahola, S. E. (1984). Social psychological foundations of leisure and resultant implications for leisure counseling. In E. T. Dowd (Ed.), *Leisure counseling: Concepts and applications.* Springfield, IL: Charles C. Thomas.

Jackson, E. L., & Burton, T. L. (Eds.). (1989). *Understanding leisure: Mapping the past, charting the future.* State College, PA: Venture Publishing, Inc.

Jafari, J. (1974). The socioeconomic costs of tourism to developing countries. *Annals of Tourism Research, 1,* 227–259.

Jansen-Verbeke, M. (1997). Urban tourism: Managing resources and visitors. In S. Wahab & J. J. Pigram (Eds.), *Tourism, development and growth* (pp. 237–256). London, UK: Routledge.

Johnson, P., & Thomas, B. (1994). The notion of capacity in tourism: A review of the issues. In C. P. Cooper & A. L. Lockwood (Eds.), *Progress in tourism,* recreation and hospitality management (Vol. 5). Chichester, UK: John Wiley & Sons, Ltd.

Kienholz, E. (1987). *Tourism and the environment.* Calgary, Alberta: Canadian Society of Environmental Biologists.

Krippendorf, J. (1986). Tourism in the system of industrial society. *Annals of Tourism Research, 13,* 517–532.

Kuss, F. R., Graefe, A. R., & Vaske, J. J. (1990). *Visitor impact management: The planning framework.* Washington, DC: U.S. National Parks Service.

Leiper, N. (1979). The framework of tourism: Towards a definition of tourism, tourist and the tourist industry. *Annals of Tourism Research, 6,* 390–407.

Lew, A. A. (1987). A framework of tourist attraction research. *Annals of Tourism Research, J4,* 553–557.

Lockhart, D. G., & Drakakis-Smith, D. (1997). *Island Tourism: Trends and Prospects.* London, UK: Pinter.

Lucas, R. C. (1964). *The recreational capacity of the Quetico-Superior Area* (Research Paper LS-15). St. Paul, MN: USDA Forest Service.

Lui, J. C., Sheldon, P. J., & Var, T. (1987). Resident perception of the environmental impacts of tourism. *Annals of Tourism Research, 14,* 17–37.

MacCannell, D. (1973). Staged authenticity: Arrangement of social space in tourist settings. *American Journal of Sociology, 79,* 586–603.

MacCannell, D. (1984). Reconstructed ethnicity: Tourism and cultural identity in third world communities. *Annals of Tourism Research, 11,* 375–392.

Marion, J. L. (1991). *Developing a natural resource inventory and monitoring program for visitor impacts on recreation sites: A procedural manual* (Natural Resources Report NPS/NRVT/NRR-91/06). Denver, CO: U.S. Department of the Interior, National Park Service.

Martin, B. S., & Uysal, M. (1990). An examination of the relationship between carrying capacity and the tourism life cycle: Management and policy implications. *Journal of Environmental Management 31,* 327–333.

Maslow, A. (1954). *Motivation and personality.* New York, NY: Harper.

Mathews, H. G. (1983). Editor's page. *Annals of Tourism Research, 10,* 303–305.

Mathieson, A., & Wall, G. (1982). *Tourism: Economic, physical and social impacts.* London, UK: Longman.

Matley, I. M. (1976). *The geography of international tourism.* Washington, DC: Commission on College Geography, Association of American Geographers.

Meadows, D. H., Meadows, D. L., Randers, J., & Behrens, W. W. (1972). *Limits to growth.* New York, NY: Universal Books.

Meyer-Arendt, K. J. (1985). The Grand Isle, Louisiana resort cycle. *Annals of Tourism Research, 12,* 449–466.

Mieczkowski, Z. T. (1981). Some notes on the geography of tourism: A comment. *The Canadian Geographer, 25,* 186–191.

Mitchell, L. S. (1979). The geography of tourism: An introduction. *Annals of Tourism Research, 6,* 235–243.

Mowforth, M., & Munt, I. (1998). *Tourism and sustainability: New tourism in the third world.* London, UK: Routledge.

Murphy, P. E. (1985). *Tourism: A community approach.* London, UK: Methuen.

Nash, D. (1977). Tourism as a form of imperialism. In V. Smith (Ed.), *Hosts and guests: The anthropology of tourism.* Philadelphia, PA: University of Pennsylvania Press.

Nash, D. (1997). *Anthropology of tourism.* New York, NY: Pergamon.

Nelson, J. G. (1973). *Canadian parks in perspective.* Montreal, Quebec: Harvest House.

Nelson, J. G., Butler, R. W., & Wall, G. (Eds.). (1993). *Tourism and sustainable development: Monitoring, planning and managing.* Waterloo, Ontario: University of Waterloo Press.

Noronha, R. (1976). *Review of the sociological literature on tourism.* New York, NY: World Bank.

Nuryanti, W. (Ed.). (1996). *Tourism and culture: Global civilization in change?* Yogyakarta, Indonesia: Gadjah Mada University Press.

Nuryanti, W. (Ed.). (1997). *Tourism and heritage management.* Yogyakarta, Indonesia: Gadjah Mada University Press.

Ogilvie, F. W. (1933). *The tourist movement.* London, UK: P.S. King.

Opperman, M. (1997). *Pacific Rim tourism.* Wallinford, UK: CAB International.

O'Reilly, A. M. (1986). Tourism carrying capacity: Concepts and issues. *Tourism Management, 16*(1), 254–258.

Patmore, J. (1968). The spa towns of Britain. In R. P. Beckinsale & H. M. Houston (Eds.), *Urbanization and its problems.* Oxford, UK: Blackwell.

Pearce, D. G. (1979). Form and function in French resorts. *Annals of Tourism Research, 5,* 142–156.

Pearce, D. G. (1981). *A geography of tourism.* New York, NY: Longman.

Pearce, D. G. (1992a). Tourism and the European regional development fund: The first fourteen years. *Journal of Travel Research, 30*(3), 44–51.

Pearce, D. G. (1992b). *Tourist organizations.* Harlow, UK: Longman.

Pearce, D. G. (1995). *Tourism today: A geographic analysis.* London, UK: Longman.

Pearce, D. G. (1997). *Tourist development.* London, UK: Longman.

Pearce, D. G., & Butler, R. W. (Eds.). (1993). *Tourism research: Critiques and challenges.* London, UK: Routledge.

Pearce, P. L. (1982). *The social psychology of tourist behavior.* Oxford, UK: Pergamon Press.

Pearce, P. L. (1993). Fundamentals of tourism motivation. In D. G. Pearce & R. W. Butler (Eds.), *Tourism research: Critiques and challenges* (pp. 113–134). London, UK: Routledge.

Perdue, R. R., Long, P. T., & Allen, L. (1987). Rural resident tourism perceptions and attitudes. *Annals of Tourism Research, 14.*

Pigram, J. J. (1990). Sustainable tourism: Policy considerations. *Journal of Sustainable Tourism, 1*(2), 2–9.

Plog, S. C. (1973). Why destination areas rise and fall in popularity. *Cornell Hotel and Restaurant Administration Quarterly, November,* 13–16.

Poon, A. (1993). *Tourism, technology and competitive strategies.* Wallingford, UK: CAB International.

Priestley, G. K., Edwards, J. A., & Coccossis, H. (Eds.). (1996). *Sustainable tourism: European experiences.* Wallingford, UK: CAB International.

Richter, L. K. (1983). Tourism and political science: A case of not so benign neglect. *Annals of Tourism Research, 10,* 313–335.

Riley, R. W. (1994). Movie-induced tourism. In A. V. Seaton (Ed.), *Tourism: The state of the art* (pp. 453–458). Chichester, UK: John Wiley & Sons, Ltd.

Robinson, M., Evans, N., & Callaghan, P. (Eds.). (1996). *Tourism and culture: Towards the 21st century* (Vol. 1–4). Sunderland: Business Education Publishers.

Saleem, N. (1994). The destination capacity index: A measure to determine the tourist carrying capacity. In A. V. Seaton (Ed.), *Tourism: State of the art* (pp. 144–151). Chichester, UK: John Wiley & Sons, Ltd.

Seaton, A. V. (1997, February). *War and tourism: enemies or allies?* Paper presented at Progress in Tourism Hospitality Research, Gold Coast, Australia.

Shaw, G., & Williams, A. M. (1994). *Critical issues in tourism: A geographical perspective.* Oxford, UK: Blackwell.

Smith, S. L. J. (1995). *Tourism analysis.* London, UK: Longman.

Smith, V. (Ed.). (1989). *Hosts and guests: The anthropology of tourism.* Philadelphia, PA: University of Pennsylvania Press.

Smith, V., & Eadington, W. R. (Eds.). (1992). *Tourism alternatives.* Philadelphia, PA: University of Pennsylvania Press.

Stabler, M. J. (Ed.). (1997). *Tourism sustainability: Principles to practice.* Wallingford, UK: CAB International.

Stankey, G. H. (1982). Recreational carrying capacity research review. *Ontario Geography, 19,* 57–72.

Stankey, G .H., Cole, D. N., Lucas, R. C., Peterson, M. E., & Frissell, S. S. (1985). *The limits of acceptable change (LAC) systems for wilderness planning.* Ogden, Utah: USDA Forest Service.

Stansfield, C. (1972). The development of modern seaside resorts. *Parks and Recreation 5,* 14–17 & 43–46.

Stansfield, C. (1978). Atlantic City and the resort cycle: Background to the legislation of gambling. *Annals of Tourism Research, 5,* 238–251.

Strapp, J. D. (1988). The resort cycle and second homes. *Annals of Tourism Research, 15*(4), 504–516.

Swinglehurst, E. (1982). *Cook's tours: The story of popular travel.* Poole, UK: Blandford Press.

Syme, G. J., Shaw, B. J, Fenton, D. M., & Mueller, W. S. (Eds.). (1989). *The planning and evaluation of hallmark events.* Aldershot, UK: Avebury Press.

Thurot, J. M. (1975). *Impact of tourism on sociocultural values.* Aix-en-Provence, France: Centre d'études du tourisme.

Tooke, N., & Baker, M. (1996). Seeing is believing: The effect of film on visitor numbers to screened locations. *Tourism Management, 17*(2), 87–94.

Towner, J. (1985). The grand tour: A key phase in the history tourism. *Annals of Tourism Research, 12,* 297–335.

Turner, L., & Ash, J. (1975). *The golden hordes: International tourism and the pleasure periphery.* London, UK: Constable.

Urry, J. (1990). *The tourist gaze: Leisure and travel in contemporary societies.* London, UK: Sage Publications, Ltd.

Van den Berghe, P. L., & Keyes, C. F. (1984). Introduction: Tourism and re-created ethnicity. *Annals of Tourism Research, 11,* 343–352.

Van Raaij, W. F., & Francken, D. A. (1984). Vacation decisions, activities, and satisfaction. *Annals of Tourism Research, 11,* 101–112.

Wagar, J. A. (1964). *The carrying capacity of wildlands for recreation* (Forest Science Monograph No. 7). Washington, DC: Society of American Foresters.

Wahab, S., & Pigram, J. J. (1997). *Tourism, development and growth.* London, UK: Routledge.

Wall, G. (1977). Recreational land use in Muskoka. *Ontario Geography, 11,* 11–28.

Wall, G., & Wright. C. (1977). *The environmental impact of outdoor recreation* (Publication Series No. 11). Waterloo, Ontario: Department of Geography, University of Waterloo.

Wanhill, S. (1995). The economic valuation of publicly assisted tourism projects. In R. W. Butler & D. G. Pearce (Eds.), *Change in tourism: People, places, processes* (pp. 187–207). London, UK: Routledge.

Weaver, D. B. (1998). *Ecotourism in the less developed world*. Wallingford, UK: CAB International.

Wheeller, B. (1993). Sustaining the ego. *Journal of Sustainable Tourism, 1*(2), 121–129.

Wheeller, B. (1994). Ecotourism: A ruse by any other name. In C. P. Cooper & A. L. Lockwood (Eds.), *Progress in Tourism, Recreation and Hospitality Management, 6,* 3–11.

Whelan, T. (1991). *Nature tourism: Managing for the environment*. Washington, DC: The Island Press.

Williams, A. V., & W. Zelinsky. (1970). On some patterns in international flows. *Economic Geography, 46,* 549–567.

Witt, S. F., & Witt, C. A. (1992). *Modeling and forecasting demand in tourism*. New York, NY: Academic Press.

Wolfe, R. I. (1952). Wasaga Beach: The divorce from the geographic environment. *The Canadian Geographer, 2,* 57–66.

Wolfe, R. I. (1964). Perspective on outdoor recreation: A bibliographical survey. *Geographical Review, 54,* 203–238.

Wolfe, R. I. (1966). Recreational travel: The new migration. *The Canadian Geographer, 10,* 1–14.

Wolfe, R. I. (1982). Recreational travel: The new migration revisited. *Ontario Geography, 19,* 103–124.

Wood, R. E. (1984). Ethnic tourism, the state, and cultural change in Southeast Asia. *Annals of Tourism Research, 11,* 363–374.

World Commission on Environment and Development. (1987). *Our common future*. Oxford, UK: Oxford University Press.

World Tourism Organization. (1996). *Tourism statistics*. Madrid, Spain: Author.

Wu, C.-T. (1982). Issues of tourism and socioeconomic development. *Annals of Tourism Research, 9,* 317–330.

Young, G. (1973). *Tourism: Blessing or blight?* Harmondsworth, UK: Penguin.

Zinder, H. (1969). *The future of tourism in the Caribbean*. Washington, DC: Zinder and Associates.

Exploring Leisure

Epistemological and Methodological Issues in Leisure Research

Diane M. Samdahl
University of Georgia

During the reception at a recent leisure research conference, a graduate student made his way across the room. Approaching with an obvious agenda, he barely made introductions before posing the question that he had designated for me. "Tell me," he said in all seriousness, "How should we measure leisure?" I was flattered that he thought I knew, though my answer was sure to disappoint him.

The growth of leisure research during the past 30 years might attest to scholars' success in measuring leisure. At least scholars have measured something that they relate to leisure. However, few scholars would suggest that they have attained effective measurement. In fact, they barely agree on the defining characteristics that would guide them in obtaining those measures! And of greater concern, this entire issue has been complicated by recent debate about whether empirical measurement acts to enhance or confound leisure scholars'

understandings of what leisure is all about. The student's question concerning how to measure leisure was much more complex than he intended it to be.

It is a bit daunting to write a discussion on research methods during this period of great epistemological challenge. The "quantitative-qualitative debate" is forcing leisure scholars to examine their assumptions about knowledge and how it is attained. This debate is evident throughout the social sciences, though in leisure studies it appears more vigorously as a philosophical discussion than as changes to research design. Ten years ago this chapter could have focused solely on research techniques; today leisure scholars believe that the methods they use are invariably intertwined with the questions they ask and the answers they are willing to accept.

This chapter will not answer that student's question about how to measure leisure. He was searching for empirical absolutes, but I am increasingly uncomfortable with them. Instead, I want to reflect on the research questions that guide leisure research and the approaches researchers use when they search for answers. After all, once we as researchers have framed the question and determined how we will go about collecting data, the answer itself has already been defined. Therein lies the power of research methodology.

It would be impossible to write a summative discussion of methodology that encompasses the entire field of leisure studies. This book itself is testimony to the diversity of topics and methods that are subsumed by the field of leisure studies (see also Jackson and Burton, 1989; Kelly, 1991; Stockdale, 1989). Anyone who intends to do research in leisure studies should be well-versed in the methods that have traditionally been used in their specific topical area. However, there are some critical reflections that may be useful for added insight into the strengths, limitations, and assumptions of leisure research methods. A good starting point for this discussion is to examine the research questions that we as leisure researchers choose to pursue.

The Questions We Ask and Those We Do Not

The chapters in this book show how the research focus has changed and evolved over the years for many different areas of leisure research. Not only are there changes in each of these topical areas but also the broad scope of leisure studies has evolved through time as well. The overall pattern of change in North American leisure research has been categorized into several distinct eras based on the topical questions and parent disciplines that have been prominent in leisure studies (see Beckers, 1995; Burdge, 1989; Hemingway and Kelly, 1995).

Initial reflection on the changes evident in leisure studies might suggest a field that has matured through the natural evolution of research (Barnett, 1995). Thus, early studies of leisure patterns gave way to research on motivation and satisfaction, and subsequently to research on social carrying capacity and leisure constraints. This history presumably culminates in the work of contemporary leisure researchers who quite "naturally" ask questions about the benefits of leisure and examine leisure as consumer behavior. Paralleling this increased "sophistication" of research questions, leisure studies moved from simple descriptive statistics to complex multivariate analyses in order to better capture the multitude of interrelationships that influence leisure (Stockdale, 1989; Tinsley, 1984). This cumulative view of leisure studies is sustained by a belief that the most important questions to study are those that refine or build upon previously published research, and a belief that the logical processes of science will result in a cumulative body of objective, tested knowledge.

However, science is not cumulative in this idyllic fashion. Kuhn (1970) suggested that normal science acts to validate and reaffirm a dominant paradigm without mounting a true challenge to the accepted tenets of knowledge. Research questions do not produce an evolution that pushes forward into new frontiers; rather, they refine what is already known while preventing radically new understandings from emerging. In addition, research occurs in a social environment and is influenced by shifting cultural values and concerns. Dominant paradigms and contemporary social beliefs are significant factors that shape the direction of research. Thus, research questions in leisure studies should not be viewed as natural or objective (Dustin, 1992; Goodale, 1991; Hemingway, 1995; Kelly, 1991). Because of this, we as leisure researchers should critically examine those topics that we have chosen to study.

To illustrate this point, note the increasing attention that has been paid to leisure and aging during the past decade. Justification for this research comes from the fact that people are living longer, which raises a real concern about the quality of life throughout their later years. In addition, the population as a whole is aging as the throng of baby boomers begins to approach retirement. The growing interest in "successful aging" and leisure enhancement during retirement reflects a sincere concern about these cohorts. Thus, the growth of research on aging has been premised on the fact that older people represent a large and growing proportion of the population. This presumably neutral demographic fact appears to provide a natural and objective justification for this research.

But to put this in perspective, the U.S. Bureau of Census (1997) reports more people living in poverty (36.4 million) than there are people over the age of 65 (34.1 million). If research on leisure and aging is justified by the large number of older adults, we might expect to find a comparable research agenda on leisure for people in poverty. In fact, if numbers alone were an adequate justification we should expect to see even more research on adults who are functionally illiterate (90.0 million) (Mini-Digest of Education Statistics, 1995). If the *rate* of growth rather than population size explains our interest in aging, we should also be researching Hispanics (33.4 million), whose size and rate of growth exactly matches that of people over the age of 65 (growing to 65.6 million by 2030) (U.S. Bureau of the Census, 1996) or studying people in prison, whose numbers *tripled* during the past 15 years (Bureau of Justice Statistics, 1995). While research on leisure and aging continues to accumulate, leisure studies has given little attention to these other populations.

The explanation that research on leisure and aging is fueled by demographic "facts" is clearly inadequate.

It is apparent from the preceding example that the reasons for studying the topics we choose are much more complex than the simplistic explanations that we often give. In the case of research on leisure and aging, demographic factors are important but are not as influential as those invisible beliefs that make us choose this population over other equally deserving groups in our society. Not insignificantly, baby boomers and Americans over the age of 65 hold considerable monetary and political power in our society, in contrast to the many people who are poor, illiterate, immigrant, or in prison. In addition, many leisure researchers belong to this aging generation of baby boomers. Contemporary interest in people who are old is not a conscious attempt to ignore other important populations in our society, but it certainly is shaped by hidden cultural beliefs and personal values that give status to one group over another.

Feminist researchers were among the first to effectively challenge the assumption that the focus of leisure research is objective and representative. They pointed out how traditional leisure theories and the bulk of leisure research provide little insight into leisure for people who are truly disadvantaged by the hegemonic power systems within our society (see Bella, 1989; Deem, 1988; see also Henderson and Bialeschki, chapter 11, and Shaw, chapter 16 in this volume). While the feminist critique emphasized the invisibility of women's experience in scholars' traditional understandings of leisure, a parallel critique highlighted the absence of ethnic perspectives in leisure research and theory (see Gramann and Allison, chapter 17 in this volume). This work has been very important in challenging assumptions of homogeneity that underlie traditional research on leisure.

Research on women's leisure has become common and research on the leisure of ethnic minorities has been receiving increasing attention. However, the power of hegemonic belief systems makes it difficult to see other factors that shape and limit the scope of leisure studies. Tourism has been promoted for the economic revitalization it can bring to a region but researchers have given little attention to the inequitable ways that this wealth gets distributed among community members, or to which segments of the population are served through the tourism industry. Market-based strategies have been a common response to decreased public funding for recreation but researchers know little about the long-term consequences of this change in administrative style. Therapeutic recreation services exist for many people who are physically or emotionally disadvantaged but researchers

offer little justification for why these disabilities are addressed while homelessness, illiteracy, and other socially stigmatized attributes are not. The point is, leisure research is as telling in the questions it does *not* ask as in the questions that it does. We as leisure researchers must critically reflect on who benefits and who does not from the research that we choose to pursue.

Challenges have also been raised against other assumptions that shape and direct leisure research, most notably against researchers' implicit belief in the goodness of leisure (Curtis, 1988; Jacobson and Samdahl, 1996; Kelly, 1997; Kivel, 1994; see also Rojek, chapter 6 in this volume). The unquestioned belief that leisure is beneficial has made it difficult to see or examine the harm that sometimes occurs in traditional leisure contexts or to acknowledge that leisure is often associated with horrific behaviors (see Rojek, chapter 6 in this volume). Others have challenged the unintended ramifications that result when we define leisure as perceived freedom (Goodale, 1990) and our naive assumption that people will always seek leisure if given the opportunity (Weinblatt and Navon, 1995). By making visible the hidden values and beliefs that shape the way that we think about leisure, these studies potentially open up leisure studies to an expanding set of new research questions.

In a pointed critique of research on the economic value of intangible commodities such as clean air, Dustin (1992) raised other concerns about the questions that guide leisure research. This strategy is used by federal agencies because economic value is more influential than social value for justifying the continued funding of recreation resources. According to Dustin, asking people how much they would be willing to pay for clean air reflects a "degeneration of thought" by implying that clean air is not a right which people should have without purchase. "How is it that we could come to ask such a question?" Dustin asks (p. 325). The peril of such questions, of course, is that they impose artificial and sometimes disturbing assumptions about the world. At a minimum this approach might prevent us from reaching the understandings that we initially sought, but at a more dangerous level it might reinforce the belief that clean air should be bought. Since questions act to reify the results that they produce, we must carefully reflect on the values that are implicit in the questions that guide leisure research.

But we cannot escape our culture entirely. The values and beliefs that drive leisure research are deeply embedded in the broader cultural patterns that surround us (Dustin, 1992; Henderson, 1993; Kelly, 1991). Cultural influences are apparent by examining the differences between North American and British leisure studies (Beckers, 1995; Henderson and Samdahl, 1993; see also Coalter, chapter 31 in this volume). North American leisure researchers typically frame their questions from the perspective of social psychology, examining individuals' attitudes and perceptions that relate to the experience of leisure, while British researchers draw upon conflict theory and cultural studies, examining institutionalized power and inequity that affect people's access to leisure. For example, in the study of women's leisure, North American and British researchers formulate different types of research questions, employ different methods for answering those questions, and ultimately come to very different understandings (Henderson and Samdahl, 1993). On the surface both groups of researchers appear to be studying women's leisure but the differing ideologies (both theoretical and methodological) that prevail in each country lead them to study quite different phenomena.

The way we as leisure researchers state our research questions opens the door for some understandings while simultaneously turning us away from others. As Hemingway (1995, p. 33) stated, "To ask one question entails foregoing the ability to ask another." By its very nature, a research question defines what is important to study. When further shaped into a hypothesis, a research question narrows our focus to the test of a proposed relationship. Traditional processes for data collection and analysis may tell us whether or not a particular relationship exists but they cannot explain why we were interested in that relationship in the first place, or reveal understandings that we had not asked about. In this fashion, traditional research serves primarily to confirm what is already known by the researcher but does not produce radically new insight.

How a research question shapes and limits the ensuing understandings can be seen by examining research on outdoor education for minorities in the 1980s. This work was premised by a growing concern that few minorities were moving into careers in outdoor recreation management. Researchers endeavored to uncover ways to change this pattern, primarily examining whether interventions using outdoor education could influence minority children's attitudes about outdoor resources and associated careers. This body of research was premised on the expectation that minority children would move into those careers in greater numbers if they were given information about and exposure to the outdoors. Because this assumption was uniformly accepted, little attention was devoted to examining the remote, bureaucratic, and sometimes racist atmosphere of land management agencies where many of those jobs would occur (Kivel, Samdahl and Jacobson, 1994), or to examining management philosophies that objectified nature in eco-

nomic or utilitarian terms. It is interesting, though typical of social science research in general, that the assumed solution to this problem was to change the child rather than to change the agency. Because of that starting premise, this research was limited in what it could reveal about minority children and outdoor recreation management.

Traditional scientific endeavors cannot be truly objective because they are influenced by paradigmatic beliefs and filtered through human perception. In the broader social science literature, the argument that research is objective has been soundly refuted (cf., Guba and Lincoln, 1990; Jansen and Peshkin, 1992; Kuhn, 1970; Popper, 1962). The leisure studies literature also contains discussions about the cultural and personal values that shape leisure studies (cf., Dustin, 1992; Goodale, 1990, 1991; Henderson, 1990, 1993; Kelly, 1991, 1997), but much of leisure research proceeds as if it were the natural outcome of an objective scientific process. Values left unquestioned will assert a powerful and sometimes restrictive influence on what leisure research can produce. Without self-reflection, leisure researchers place false hope in the presumed objectivity of research design and measurement.

It is a fallacy to believe that research produces answers; too often, research simply supports the solutions that our questions have already defined. Research questions are not natural nor neutral, nor do they derive solely from existing published research. Our questions reflect hidden values that ignite interest in some topics while preventing us from seeing others. If we are unable to understand how values influence our choice of research questions, our research may do little more than reinforce the status quo. The challenge before us is to examine, as critically as we can, why we are interested in studying those questions that we choose to pursue.

Positivism and North American Leisure Research

Positivism has been the driving force in North American social sciences for the past hundred years (Bernstein, 1983; Guba, 1990; Guba and Lincoln, 1994). Alternately referred to as empiricism or rational science, positivism represents a belief that good science is objective and value-free. Influenced by positivism and modeled after the natural sciences, the social sciences have emphasized the importance of objective empirical measurement and attempted to discover general patterns of conformity and causation.

Positivism is most often associated with quantitative data and traditional research designs such as experiments or structured surveys; emotions and subjective phenomena are not amenable to positivistic research except to the extent that they can be captured through questionnaires or other empirical measures. Given this climate, it may be amazing that North American leisure research—focusing on a subjective phenomenon often portrayed with an emotional component—has flourished as well as it has!

Because of the influence of empiricism, North American leisure researchers have concentrated on clear "objective" constructs that could be easily measured (Hemingway, 1995; Hemingway and Kelly, 1995; Rojek, 1989). Early researchers in this field examined factors associated with recreation participation; in fact, attendance remains an important empirical focus in the political environments of management agencies today. When Neulinger (1974) claimed that the critical dimension of leisure was perceived freedom, leisure studies wholeheartedly embraced attitudinal scales and other psychometric measures from psychology. Some claimed that this development "rendered leisure more and more empirically manageable" (Barnett, 1995, p. viii) and thereby enhanced the scientific respectability of this field (Barnett, 1995; Ellis and Witt, 1991), though others have questioned that outcome.

One goal of research is to refine instruments and improve measurement, at least in the normal scientific traditions described by Kuhn (1970). The journals reporting North American leisure research include an abundance of articles that examine instrumentation and measurement, including scale development, question wording, and sampling techniques. In addition, leisure research frequently employs alternative methods such as single subject design (e.g., Dattilo, 1986), experience sampling (e.g., Samdahl, 1988; Voelkl and Brown, 1989), and user-initiated photography (e.g., Cherem and Driver, 1983; Taylor, Czarnowski, Sexton, and Flick, 1995) in an attempt to address the unique issues faced in the study of leisure. The attention that leisure studies has paid to measurement and methodology is evidence that leisure researchers have been conscientious in their attempt to apply the empirical model.

However, there has been an ongoing critique of the methods used in North American leisure research (cf., Burton, 1996; Dawson, 1984; Harper, 1981; Hemingway, 1990, 1995; Kelly, 1991; Rojek, 1989; Sylvester, 1995; Tinsley, 1984). Much of this critique denounces the overreliance on measurement obtained through questionnaires and survey techniques. Howe

(1985, p. 221) suggested that we have "the methodological cart driving the conceptual horse" in our efforts to polish measurement before developing a critical understanding of what we are trying to measure. Kelly (1991, p. 398) pointed to the "mountains of unused survey data" as evidence that methodology overrides theory in much of leisure research design. In fact, some claim that the emphasis on refining empirical measurement simply disguises the absence of a strong conceptual framework embedded in theory (Hemingway, 1995; Kelly, 1991; Smith and Haley, 1979).

Although accused of being atheoretical, empirical leisure researchers make important theoretical assumptions about the phenomena that they purport to measure. For example, the phrasing of a question on a questionnaire imposes theoretical assumptions about the inherent nature of leisure. When researchers ask participants to assess a situation using a five-point response scale with endpoints labeled "Not at All Leisure" and "Leisure at Its Best," they imply that leisure is something which appears in increments or cumulative units rather than something which is altogether present or absent (Samdahl, 1991). More importantly, they also assume that leisure is a subjective phenomenon characterized by specific contextual conditions—a view that is quite at odds with theories of leisure as a cultural institution. Discussions about theory are sometimes discounted as being too philosophical or esoteric, yet leisure researchers often overlook important theoretical assumptions embedded in every questionnaire that they design.

One danger in positivism is that the assumptions which drive measurement are often so hidden that they become invisible. Positivism is built upon a belief that a true world exists which can be objectively ascertained if scientists adhere to the tenets of careful measurement (Guba, 1990; Guba and Lincoln, 1994). Because they believe that measurement captures facts, positivists view data as objective information about the world. In this manner, measurement itself has become reified and accepted as meaningful without requiring an examination of the values or theoretical assumptions upon which that measurement was based (Rojek, 1989). Hemingway said, "[In empirical analysis] we give up . . . attempting to penetrate beneath the surface. Meaning is reduced . . . to a question of measurement" (1990, p. 306).

Likewise, empirical measurement may wrongly be used to confer legitimacy to ideas that are not truly testable by statistics. This is particularly problematic when research is viewed as confirming a model or interpretation of behavior which inherently is not falsifiable (see Popper, 1962). For example, the concept of constraints was introduced to help researchers understand why people do not participate in desired leisure activities; however, researchers have shown that leisure participation can occur even in the presence of constraints. When this was first noted, researchers might have abandoned the constraints model; instead, they interpreted this finding as evidence of constraint negotiation. At this point it became clear that the constraints model could not be disproven (Samdahl and Jekubovich, 1997): constraints apparently exist whether they prevent behavior or not. The inability to falsify a model or paradigm is not cause for alarm (other models or paradigms that cannot be falsified include Freudian psychology, Maslow's hierarchy of needs, and symbolic interaction), but it forces researchers to admit that the model itself is not being *proven* through the research. Models and paradigms must be judged according to their utility and their ability to provide insight, not through the weight of statistical "evidence."

Another significant assumption in positivism is that events can be broken down into discrete variables that presumably are independent from one another. Positivists measure separate variables in order to isolate their individual effects, often in an attempt to understand causal relationships. The independence of variables is a central tenet of positivism and is a requirement of most statistics, though recent computer programs include complex modeling that supports a greater degree of multicollinearity in the data. Thinking in terms of isolated variables inevitably moves researchers away from contextual environments and interactive relationships which some researchers claim are central to the meaning of leisure (cf., Hemingway, 1990; Jacobson and Samdahl, 1996; Kelly, 1991, 1992; Rojek, 1989). In fact, contextual factors must be "controlled for" in many leisure research designs, and interactions are viewed as confounding effects that remain after individual variables have been analyzed. One important critique of positivism reflects a concern that the study of isolated variables cannot capture the richly complex meanings and interactions that are central to people's lives.

Empiricism has also been accused of promoting a dualistic way of thinking (Burton, 1996; Dervin, 1989; Henderson, 1991). Dichotomies establish categories that are assumed to be mutually exclusive and irreconcilable. In leisure research we establish dichotomies when we compare people with and without a disability, divide market sectors into users and nonusers of public recreation facilities, or examine conflict between hikers and people riding motorized off-road vehicles. Focusing on this one characteristic might be useful for understanding aspects of a narrowly defined situation,

but these labels hide the multitude of ways in which people are simultaneously different from and similar to one another. Because categories are often based on demographic, geographic, or behavioral characteristics they marginalize more important factors, such as how people live, what they think, or their relative access to resources (Dervin, 1989). In this way, categories often serve the needs of the researcher without providing any basis for challenging the status quo or resolving the inequities that create status hierarchy between the people thus categorized.

Empiricism alone is not responsible for the appeal of dichotomies or typologies; they also occur outside of empirical measurement in the social sciences (Max Weber's discussion of "ideal types" is a classic example). However, dichotomies and typologies do tend to oversimplify the world in a way that may inhibit understanding. When matched with the definitive posture of empirical measurement, typologies have an air of formality and finality that can too easily be taken for reality. For example, early researchers essentialized the differences between leisure and work by defining them as polar opposites. Because this categorization was imposed on the methods and measures used in research, the data seemed to corroborate rather than dispute this distinction. This dichotomy prevented researchers from understanding the many situations which have characteristics of both leisure and work (Roadburg, 1983; Stormann, 1989), including experiences of women whose work was not paid employment (Bella, 1989). When this dichotomy was finally challenged researchers were able to see how it had restricted their understanding of leisure.

A highly visible critique has been raised against North American leisure researchers for their tenacious reliance on empirical research methods (Burton, 1996; Hemingway, 1990; Henderson, 1991; Howe, 1985; Kelly, 1991; Rojek, 1989). According to Burton (1996, p. 19), "methods and techniques have hijacked knowledge" and moved researchers away from a fuller understanding of leisure. The field has been called *myopic* (Henderson, 1991, p. 15) for adhering so strongly to traditional positivist traditions and called *orthodox* (Hemingway, 1995, p. 32) for remaining untroubled by the challenges that have been raised against empiricism.

To the extent that researchers remain committed to empirical measurement, leisure studies has forfeited questions that are not easily addressed by empirical design. This includes research on the moral aspects of recreation (McLean, 1995), the study of *process* and *meaning* in leisure or leisure services (Dawson, 1984; Howe, 1985; Karlis and Dawson, 1994), and research on leisure as a *social* rather than an *individualistic* phenomenon (Goodale, 1990; Hemingway, 1990; Kelly, 1992). By enticing researchers to examine individuals rather than more complex social systems, positivism has produced "a misleading view of society" (Rojek, 1989, p. 71) which exaggerates stability while hiding social conflict (see also Howe, 1992; Salomon, 1991).

But there also has been some defense of positivism in leisure research. Sylvester (1990) cautioned against "positivist bashing" that has little constructive purpose. Leisure researchers' goal, he reminds us, must be to seriously grapple with the questions raised by this critique rather than to dictate methodology. Weissinger (1990) suggested that the problems in traditional research arise from an "underreliance on rigorous theory and method" (p. 311) rather than from inherent faults in empirical research design. Weissinger reminded researchers that all science, empirical or not, requires a careful and conscientious application of method and she challenged empirical researchers to respond to this critique by carefully examining the assumptions upon which their research rests. Indeed, many authors who criticize the reliance on positivism propose that researchers retain empirical traditions while concurrently exploring alternative modes of understanding (cf., Burton and Jackson, 1989; Henderson, 1991; McLean, 1996; Weissinger, 1990).

However, the critique about positivism in leisure research will not be resolved by conscientious use of empirical measures or by polite agreement to accept "pluralism" in leisure research designs. The underlying issues are not about methods and measurement but rather about conflicting beliefs on how to approach science. Thus, we must examine what is behind this "quantitative-qualitative debate."

The Quantitative-Qualitative Debate

Let me start by saying that I dislike the terms quantitative and qualitative *methods*, though I sometimes resort to those terms to comply with common practice. My preference is to speak about quantitative and qualitative *data* which represent the different types of information that is collected in the processes of research. Many methods can produce qualitative data, including positivistic research that is not built upon the epistemological premises that define qualitative inquiry. But the quantitative-qualitative debate is not about differences in methods or in data; rather, it is an ideological debate that brings into question fundamental beliefs about knowledge. Unfortunately, both quantitative and qualitative researchers have been labeled by characteristics of their methods and data

which disguises the more significant differences between them.

Guba and Lincoln (1994) discussed the ontological, epistemological, and methodological foundations of different research paradigms. Ontology reflects beliefs about the nature of reality (Is reality an objective phenomenon that holds truth or is reality virtually constructed through social, political, and gendered meanings?); epistemology refers to beliefs about the preferred relationship between the researcher and the researched (Should we remain objective and removed from what we study or should we get immersed in it?); and methodology refers to the techniques we use for collecting information about the world (Should we manipulate and measure variables in order to test hypotheses or should we search for meaning in words and behaviors?). Ontology, epistemology, and methodology are not independent from one another; however, they represent the most significant differences between positivism and other ways of knowing.

The terms quantitative and qualitative *methods* are sometimes used to refer to positivism and other forms of research, even though many methods (e.g., forms of interviewing and observation) can be used by researchers from any paradigm (Denzin and Lincoln, 1994; Henderson, 1991; Schwandt, 1994; Wolcott, 1992). Under the quantitative framework, researchers place much emphasis on defining and adhering to a methodological protocol. Methodological rigor, after all, assures objectivity and reliability in the data. In contrast, qualitative researchers cannot anticipate all the methods they might use in a study; instead, they actively construct their methods as the study progresses. This process has been compared to a loosely choreographed dance (Janesick, 1994) or improvisational jazz (Oldfather and West, 1994). In approaching research in this fashion, qualitative researchers do not forego the importance of methodological rigor, but they define rigor quite differently. While quantitative researchers use methods as a way to remain objective and removed, qualitative researchers use methods as a way to enter the subjective reality of the participant. This clearly is an epistemological distinction even though the methods and data may be different as well. Epistemology, methods, and data are distinct concepts, but association between them is strong enough to explain how the terms quantitative and qualitative methods came to simultaneously refer to differences in epistemology, methodology, and data.

There are many alternatives to positivism (e.g., critical theory, hermeneutics, phenomenology, constructivism, ethnomethodology; see Guba and Lincoln, 1994), each representing a different set of ontological, epistemological, and methodological beliefs.

In the leisure literature it has become common to contrast positivism with *interpretive research* (cf., Hemingway, 1990, 1995; Henderson, 1991), a term that globally encompasses many forms of qualitative inquiry, though some methodologists (e.g., Schwandt, 1994) make careful distinctions between interpretivism, constructivism, and related epistemologies. Interpretive research assumes that reality exists in the thoughts and perceptions of each individual; thus, objectivity is impractical and researchers should try to understand the contextual realities and subjective meanings that shape people's interactions with their world. The interpretive researcher honors the participant's reality by using repeated interviews and asking participants to verify the way that the researcher represents their stories. The participant, not the researcher, is viewed as the authority on the phenomenon under study.

The differences between positivism and interpretive research are depicted in Figure 8.1. As suggested in the figure, positivist researchers are more likely to remain formal or apart from the "subjects" who take part in their studies; they believe that research produces truthful information about an objective world. Positivists commonly employ structured methods such as experiments or surveys that produce quantitative data, but they might use structured interviews or observation to record qualitative data in a systematic fashion. In contrast, interpretive researchers believe in multiple realities rather than a single truth. They will collaborate with participants in an attempt to understand lived experience from the point of view of the participants. Interpretive researchers commonly use repeated or ongoing interviews and field notes that produce qualitative data, though they might use supporting empirical measures or count the frequency of events to supplement their qualitative understandings.

Several important comments must be made about Figure 8.1. First, none of these domains is truly bipolar, as the figure implies, but representing them in this fashion adds emphasis to the nature of their extremes. Second, the labels *quantitative data* and *qualitative data* may be useful for discussion, but this dichotomy should not be essentialized into the belief that all data are easily classified or that these categories are homogeneous. Third, the important step of *analysis* is not reflected in this diagram. Quantitative analysis can vary in terms of complexity; likewise, the casual use of quotes is not the same as phenomenological analysis of interviews and field notes. And last, the variety of research represented in Figure 8.1 is reflective of the ways that social science research is taking place in North America. Methodological approaches used with

critical theory and cultural studies, which are *theoretical* perspectives that guide British leisure research, are not effectively represented in this figure.

Henderson (1991) offered an extended comparison of positivist and interpretive research in leisure studies. Examples of leisure research from the interpretive paradigm include participatory observation of auctions and softball leagues (Glancy, 1986, 1988) and contract bridge (Scott and Godbey, 1994), phenomenological analysis of disability and play (Bullock, 1985), and collaborative interviews with lesbian women (Bialeschki and Pearce, 1997; Jacobson and Samdahl, 1996) and members of Alcoholics Anonymous (McCormick, 1991). In each of these studies the authors established a theoretical justification for their research without making specific predictions about what they would discover, and then used time-consuming techniques to collect and confirm the understandings that emerged from the qualitative data of interviews and observations.

In North American leisure studies, much of the research that we call qualitative does not adhere to the ontological and epistemological beliefs of interpretive research; instead, it is driven by a positivist worldview using qualitative rather than quantitative data. Guba and Lincoln (1994) refer to this as *postpositivist* research, or research that incorporates qualitative data and a belief in the importance of subjective reality without fully abandoning other fundamental tenets of conventional positivism. For example, Samdahl and Jekubovich (1997) used existing transcripts of single interviews with participants from an earlier study to examine a model of leisure constraints. Although the transcripts represented qualitative data, the interviews had been undertaken for another purpose and the researchers had no way to probe or confirm with their study participants any of the post hoc understandings relating to leisure constraints. Labeling this study *qualitative* emphasizes the important ways in which it differs from more traditional research designs; however, this study is significantly different from research driven by the ontological and epistemological premises of interpretivism. Studies using qualitative data are becoming more frequent in leisure literature (cf., Bolla, Dawson, and Karlis, 1991; Cole, 1993; Malloy, Nilson and Yoshioka, 1993). Unfortunately, the label *qualitative research* has been indiscriminately applied, which hides important variations in the epistemological framework behind different research designs.

Leisure scientists have expressed a belief that interpretive research will better reveal the processes and meanings associated with leisure that are difficult to capture in traditional empirical design (Dawson, 1984;

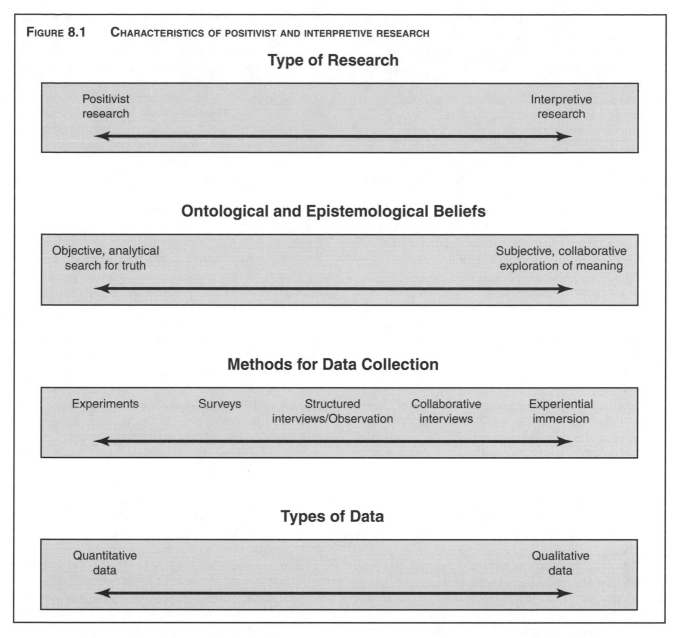

FIGURE 8.1   CHARACTERISTICS OF POSITIVIST AND INTERPRETIVE RESEARCH

Howe, 1985; Kelly, 1991). In addition, interpretive research can positively impact the lives of study participants in ways not possible through traditional inquiry (Pedlar, 1995). In the context of evaluation, interpretive research might produce information about *how* a program works in addition to standard assessments about whether it was effective (Karlis and Dawson, 1994). The hope held out for interpretive research stems from the complex and unexpected understandings that emerge from this type of inquiry.

Interpretive research brings not only new types of methods and data, but it also draws attention to different research questions. For example, when confronted with claims that traditional leisure research ignored the leisure of women and minorities, positivists sought to document the leisure behaviors of those groups in order to compare and contrast them with existing knowledge about leisure patterns. Interpretive researchers, however, became more intrigued with the meaning of leisure for women and minorities and examined how leisure was embedded in broader cultural experiences shaped by gender and race. Survey data might yield information on how often women or minorities go to a park but interpretive research will examine what it *means* to a woman or African American to be at the park. This is not a trivial distinction. Implicit in traditional research that focuses on behavior and ignores meaning is an assumption that behaviors like park attendance have a comparable meaning for everyone. Considering the gendered division of family responsibilities and the prevalence of racism, it is certainly likely that attending a park will result in different experiences for different segments of the North American population.

Interpretive researchers are sensitive to individualized meanings that often get hidden in broader generalizations. In addition, because interpretive researchers believe that distance and objectivity inhibit a fuller understanding of people's lives, they try to set aside attitudes of power and authority that would separate them from the people in their studies. These factors have contributed to the success of interpretive researchers in studying minorities and others who feel devalued by society and dehumanized when they become the "subject" of research. Not coincidentally, interpretive researchers have been successful in studying leisure for women, gays and lesbians, people with disabilities, First Nation residents of Canada, and other groups who have been marginalized in society and ignored by traditional empirical researchers.

The emergence and acceptance of qualitative research has raised troubling questions for those who understand that the central tenets of positivism are being challenged. In an attempt to alleviate this concern, early discussions drew parallels between positivism and other modes of inquiry. For example, Guba (1981) discussed similarities between the concepts of internal validity, reliability, and objectivity in empirical research and the concepts of credibility, dependability, and confirmability in interpretive research. Others have called for tolerance and acceptance of research in its many forms, suggesting that quantitative and qualitative research can coexist in a complementary fashion.

This call for *pluralism* has been prominent in the leisure literature (cf., Burton and Jackson, 1989; Henderson, 1991; McLean, 1996; Weissinger, 1990). Henderson (1991) suggested that qualitative methods will expand leisure studies' repertoire of research techniques and, when used in conjunction with quantitative methods, may provide a richer understanding than either method alone could produce. This has been matched with concern about what would happen if leisure studies were divided along ideological lines as implied in the quantitative-qualitative debate (Henderson, 1993).

In recent years the leisure research journals have published many examples of studies which employed multiple methods (e.g., Reid, 1993; Samdahl and Jekubovich, 1993). These studies effectively illustrate how qualitative data enhance and add richness to the understandings derived from quantitative analysis. Qualitative designs have also been used in pilot tests to uncover issues that became the basis for subsequent empirical study (e.g., Richardson, Long and Perdue, 1988). Without denouncing the value of this research which adds an important new dimension to positivist inquiry, it is necessary to note that mixed methods of this type reflect a postpositivist epistemology (Guba and Lincoln, 1994) which does not fully forego the distant, objective stature of the researcher. That is to say, these studies do not truly mix quantitative and qualitative *epistemology,* even though they employ both quantitative and qualitative data.

When the quantitative-qualitative debate is framed in terms of methods or data, solutions like mixed methods appear feasible. However, if the debate is viewed with full attention to the epistemological differences between positivism and interpretivism, their incompatibility becomes apparent. Positivism and interpretivism are not focused on revealing the same truth; their goals and philosophic premises are quite distinct. The suggestion that positivism and interpretivism are complementary "[leads to] the impression that the two approaches are variations in techniques within the same assumptive framework" and closes off the more important debate about epistemological differences between them (Smith and Heshusius, 1986, p. 6). Guba (1987, p. 31) stated, "one [approach to research] precludes the other just as surely as belief in a round world precludes belief in a flat one." Calling for mixed methods may also divert attention from complex social issues which cannot be represented through positivist forms of inquiry (Salomon, 1991; Smith and Heshusius, 1986). Thus, the call for multiple methods is an unsatisfactory compromise that does not acknowledge the truly radical differences inherent in interpretive inquiry.

Interpretive research is becoming visible in North American leisure research (cf., Bialeschki and Pearce, 1997; Bullock, 1985; Glancy, 1986, 1988; Jacobson and Samdahl, 1996; McCormick, 1991; Scott and Godbey, 1994), though postpositivism (the use of qualitative data) is more prevalent than interpretivism as an alternative to traditional positivist methods. It is important to note that interpretive research is not a panacea for the concerns raised against positivism. The fairly rapid emergence of interpretive research is, in itself, a socially constructed phenomenon embedded in the 1980s and 1990s (McLean, 1996). Attempts to portray interpretivism as having access to "a more profound truth" reflect a reductionist view of scientific inquiry (McLean, 1996, p. 140) which is as narrow as the empiricism that those scholars attempt to denounce.

The quantitative-qualitative debate imposes an unfair dichotomy that does not capture all possible approaches to social inquiry. When this debate is framed as if there were only two alternatives, an unconscious expectation exists that one approach must be inherently superior to the other (Howe, 1992), hiding weaknesses in both forms of inquiry and diverting attention from other forms of research. Howe claimed that "positivism is untenable and interpretivism is incomplete" because it cannot challenge social order or provide insight into structures of conflict within society (1992, p. 243). The quantitative-qualitative debate must be approached not as a question for which there is an absolute answer, but rather as a rhetorical question that raises important issues for reflection.

Leisure Research at the Millennium

Reflections on the nature of leisure research have become commonplace in leisure literature, but there is value in revisiting the messages and concerns that several of those authors have raised. Going back almost two decades, Harper (1981) suggested that the inherent nature of leisure was more amenable to qualitative methods than to empirical measurement. Commenting on researchers' efforts to establish a positivist foundation for leisure studies, Harper wondered if researchers were trying to fit reality to their method rather than fitting their method to reality. His comments stand as an early warning about the limitations of positivist inquiry.

Criticism of leisure researchers' tenacious reliance on positivism has already been reviewed (cf., Burton, 1996; Hemingway, 1995; Hemingway and Kelly, 1995; Henderson, 1991; Kelly, 1991; Rojek, 1989; Sylvester, 1995). Like Harper, these authors argue that the more intriguing aspects of leisure are not responsive to the tools provided by empirical methods. Positivist epistemology has been called "inhospitable" to values (Sylvester, 1995) and inadequate for assessing social and cultural dimensions of people's lives (Burton, 1996; Hemingway, 1990; Kelly, 1991). Added to this is a challenge to keep leisure studies relevant (Dustin, 1992; Godbey, 1991; Goodale, 1991, 1992; Henderson, 1993). Social relevance requires more than examining the research questions that we choose to pursue. Critics claim that positivist forms of inquiry make it impossible to see broader aspects of social order. Traditional positivism reinforces rather than challenges the status quo (Goodale, 1990; Kuhn, 1970) and hides institutionalized power and conflict (Howe, 1992; Kelly, 1992; Rojek, 1989). The most relevant issues in leisure studies may remain invisible until researchers step outside positivism and adopt an epistemological perspective that can reveal these phenomena in all of their complexity.

Pedlar (1995) addressed this point in her discussion of action research, a form of qualitative inquiry in which the study's participants become collaborators in the research process (see also Jacobson, 1996; Reason, 1994). Action research seeks not only to improve understanding for the researcher, but it also strives to "allow research participants to more fully understand and improve their individual or collective situation" (Pedlar, 1995, p. 133). Some types of action research let participants identify which dimensions of the research issue should be explored; thus, even the research questions are not fully determined by the researcher. This form of inquiry places research within a political context with the goal of making a difference in the lives of the study participants. Pedlar argued that this important goal of the leisure research profession should become a goal of leisure research as well.

The ongoing criticism that has been reviewed may make it appear that leisure studies has remained self-reflective. However, it must be noted that these concerns have been raised by a small but vocal group of scholars. Rather than a dialog, which would engage both sides in a constructive examination of the philosophical premises and limitations of research, this criticism appears more like a one-sided commentary. Hemingway (1995) admonished leisure researchers for remaining largely untroubled by these challenges even though their parent disciplines have grown increasingly uncomfortable with positivist inquiry. Kelly (1991) accused leisure researchers of preferring the comfort of tradition over the discomfort of self-reflection, saying, "Leisure research, shaped by public funding and by theoretical timidity, has for the most part adopted familiar methods to examine traditional questions" (p. 398). According to Hemingway and Kelly (1995, p. 25), leisure researchers are "paddl[ing] around in the wading pool practicing the same strokes over and over again," rather than moving toward more exciting scholarly endeavors.

The interesting question, then, is why this field has remained relatively unchanged in light of the increasing challenges to positivist inquiry. The visibility of the critique against positivism makes it clear that leisure researchers are not unaware of these concerns, and the presence of interpretive research in leisure journals is evidence that some members of the leisure studies field are responding. But the continuing prevalence of empirical research and the relative absence of positivists' response to these concerns suggests that a widespread examination of leisure research's epistemological premises has not yet begun to happen.

Many factors contribute to leisure researchers' collective discomfort at this challenge to positivist inquiry.

Kuhn noted that paradigms are resistant to change and that criticism of a dominant paradigm is often diminished and dismissed. The issue is not, as critics may imply, simply selecting the best methodological tools for leisure research. Far from being an issue of technique, the quantitative-qualitative debate is challenging many people's beliefs about the nature of science and the processes of scientific inquiry. Resistance is not a consciously selfish response; it is a consequence of normal science and the processes which create loyalty to the dominant paradigm. "The transfer of allegiance from paradigm to paradigm cannot be forced. . . . [T]hose whose productive careers have committed them to an older tradition . . . may resist indefinitely" (Kuhn, 1970, pp. 151–152).

Added to this is an understanding that the discovery of knowledge is only one of many goals of a scientist. The critique of positivism has devastating ramifications for people whose work and status have been built upon positivist traditions. Leisure researchers are confronted with the demands of tenure, the need for outside funding, and the call to be responsive to practitioners, and they operate in a bureaucratic institution characterized by fragmentation and competition (Goodale, 1991). Booth (1988, p. 52) stated that scholarship "is not free inquiry at all, but one way of preserving power." Indeed, the challenge to positivist inquiry threatens the privileged position of researchers for whom positivism has been a vehicle for success. The unwillingness (or perhaps inability) of many to enter into this debate stems as much from the broader social context of research as it does from epistemological loyalty to positivism.

This discussion also raises questions about the distinction between scholarship and research (Kelly, 1989). In North America, scholarship has been closely linked with the tools of positivist inquiry. Ben-David (1984) suggested that American graduate programs have turned scientific research into a professional career, serving as training grounds to produce effective technicians who lack curiosity and imagination. Few leisure researchers have the skills and resources necessary to undertake scholarship without reliance on positivist methods. What questions would we ask? How would we go about searching for answers? What even is worth knowing? Our entire orientation to scholarship has been shaped by positivist ideology. This critique of positivism raises an intellectual challenge that many leisure researchers are simply not equipped to face.

The purpose of this discussion is not to force one epistemology over another. The most vocal commentators are clear in their preference for interpretive inquiry, but that, too, may be pushed aside by other epistemologies in due time. Rather, this debate will be well-served if it forces every researcher to critically examine the ontological and epistemological beliefs that drive his or her research and to identify the values upon which that research is based. The *field* cannot respond to this criticism; only *individuals* are capable of this type of self-reflection. And though we each should be self-reflective, our strongest hope may lie in the next generation of scholars, for whom qualitative inquiry is already an option at the outset of their careers.

Examining the beliefs that frame leisure research may be the most important issue facing leisure studies today. Every chapter in this book raises questions about the future of leisure studies. Our individual and collective responses to those issues will be shaped, to a large degree, by the ontological and epistemological beliefs that guide our thinking. The twentieth century established a solid foundation for positivist social inquiry, but those traditions are being called into question. Rather than simply moving forward with more of the same, this debate offers the possibility of shaping a new leisure studies for the next millennium which will be relevant, responsive, and perhaps even radical. We must at least try.

References

Barnett, L. A. (1995). *Research about leisure: Past, present, and future* (2nd ed.). Champaign, IL: Sagamore Publishing.

Beckers, T. (1995). Back to basics: International communication in leisure research. *Leisure Sciences, 17,* 327–336.

Bella, L. (1989). Women and leisure: Beyond androcentrism. In E. L. Jackson & T. L. Burton (Eds.), *Understanding leisure and recreation: Mapping the past, charting the future* (pp. 151–179). State College, PA: Venture Publishing, Inc.

Ben-David, J. (1984). *The scientist's role in society: A comparative study.* Chicago, IL: University of Chicago Press.

Bernstein, R. J. (1983). *Beyond objectivism and relativism: Science, hermeneutics and praxis.* Philadelphia, PA: University of Pennsylvania Press.

Bialeschki, M. D., & Pearce, K. D. (1997). "I don't want a lifestyle—I want a life": The effect of role negotiations on the leisure of lesbian mothers. *Journal of Leisure Research, 29,* 113–131.

Bolla, P., Dawson, D., & Karlis, G. (1991). Serving the multicultural community: Directions for leisure service providers. *Journal of Applied Recreation Research, 16,* 116–132.

Booth, W. C. (1988). *The vocation of a teacher.* Chicago, IL: University of Chicago Press.

Bullock, C. C. (1985). *Proving self: The problematic imperative.* Unpublished dissertation, University of Illinois.

Burdge, R. J. (1989). The evolution of leisure and recreation research from multidisciplinary to interdisciplinary. In E. L. Jackson & T. L. Burton (Eds.), *Understanding leisure and recreation: Mapping the past, charting the future* (pp. 29–46). State College, PA: Venture Publishing, Inc.

Bureau of Justice Statistics. (1995). *National prison population growth: A BJS report* [on line]. Available: http://uaa.alaska.edu/just/forum/f124b.html#tab1.

Burton, T. L. (1996). Safety nets and security blankets: False dichotomies in leisure studies. *Leisure Studies, 15,* 17–30.

Burton, T. L., & Jackson, E. L. (1989). Charting the future. In E. L. Jackson & T. L. Burton (Eds.), *Understanding leisure and recreation: Mapping the past, charting the future* (pp. 629–642). State College, PA: Venture Publishing, Inc.

Cherem, G. J., & Driver, B. L. (1983). Visitor employed photography: A technique to measure common perceptions of natural environments. *Journal of Leisure Research, 15,* 65–83.

Cole, D. (1993). Recreation practices in the Stoney of Alberta and Mohawks of the Six Nation Confederacy. *Journal of Applied Recreation Research, 18,* 103–114.

Curtis, J. E. (1988). Purple recreation. *SPRE Annual on Education, 3,* 73–77.

Dattilo, J. (1986). Single subject research in therapeutic recreation: Application to individuals with disabilities. *Therapeutic Recreation Journal, 20,* 76–87.

Dawson, D. (1984). Phenomenological approaches to leisure research. *Recreation Research Review, 11,* 18–23.

Deem, R. (1988). *All work and no play? A study of women and leisure.* Milton Keynes, UK: Open University Press.

Denzin, N. K., & Lincoln, Y. S. (1994). Introduction: Entering the field of qualitative research. In N. K. Denzin & Y. S. Lincoln (Eds.), *Handbook of qualitative research* (pp. 1–17). Thousands Oaks, CA: Sage Publications, Inc.

Dervin, B. (1989). Users as research inventions: How research categories perpetuate inequities. *Journal of Communication, 39,* 216–232.

Dustin, D. L. (1992). The dance of the dispossessed: On patriarchy, feminism and the practice of leisure science. *Journal of Leisure Research, 24,* 324–332.

Ellis, G. D., & Witt, P. A. (1991). Conceptualization and measurement of leisure: Making the abstract concrete. In T. L. Goodale & P. A. Witt (Eds.), *Recreation and leisure: Issues in an era of change* (3rd ed., pp. 377–395). State College, PA: Venture Publishing, Inc.

Glancy, M. (1986). Participant observation in the recreation setting. *Journal of Leisure Research, 18,* 59–80.

Glancy, M. (1988). The play-world setting of the auction. *Journal of Leisure Research, 20,* 135–153.

Godbey, G. (1991). *Recreation and leisure in the 1990s: They are playing our song.* Jay B. Nash Lecture, American Alliance for Health, Physical Education, Recreation and Dance Conference, San Francisco, CA.

Goodale, T. L. (1990). Perceived freedom as leisure's antithesis. *Journal of Leisure Research, 22,* 296–302.

Goodale, T. L. (1991). Spirits sacred and secular: Context as bias in leisure research. In T. L. Goodale & P. A. Witt (Eds.), *Recreation and leisure: Issues in an era of change* (3rd ed., pp. 367–375). State College, PA: Venture Publishing, Inc.

Goodale, T. L. (1992). Educating for social responsibility—Aspirations and obstacles. *Schole: A Journal of Leisure Studies and Recreation Education, 7,* 81–91.

Guba, E. G. (1981). Criteria for assessing the trustworthiness of naturalistic inquiry. *Educational Communication and Technology Journal, 29,* 79–92.

Guba, E. G. (1987). What have we learned about naturalistic evaluation? *Evaluation Practice, 8,* 23–43.

Guba, E. G. (1990). The alternative paradigm dialog. In E. G. Guba (Ed.), *The paradigm dialog* (pp. 17–27). Thousand Oaks, CA: Sage Publications, Inc.

Guba, E. G., & Lincoln, Y. S. (1990). Can there be a human science? Constructivism as an alternative. *Person-Centered Review, 5,* 130–154.

Guba, E. G., & Lincoln, Y. S. (1994). Competing paradigms in qualitative research. In N. K. Denzin & Y. S. Lincoln (Eds.), *Handbook of qualitative research* (pp. 105–117). Thousands Oaks, CA: Sage Publications, Inc.

Harper, W. (1981). The experience of leisure. *Leisure Sciences, 4,* 113–126.

Hemingway, J. L. (1990). Opening windows on an interpretive leisure studies. *Journal of Leisure Research, 22,* 303–308.

Hemingway, J. L. (1995). Leisure studies and interpretive social inquiry. *Leisure Studies, 14,* 32–47.

Hemingway, J. L., & Kelly, J. R. (1995). History and philosophy of leisure: Past, present, and future research. In L. A. Barnett (Ed.), *Research about leisure: Past, present, and future* (2nd ed., pp. 21–42). Champaign, IL: Sagamore Publishing.

Henderson, K. A. (1990). Leisure science, dominant paradigms, and philosophy: An introduction. *Journal of Leisure Research, 22,* 283–289.

Henderson, K. A. (1991). *Dimensions of choice: A qualitative approach to recreation, parks, and leisure research.* State College, PA: Venture Publishing, Inc.

Henderson, K. A. (1993). The changer and the changed: Leisure research in the 1990s. *Journal of Applied Recreation Research, 18,* 3–18.

Henderson, K. A., & Samdahl, D. M. (1993). *Addressing women's leisure: A comparative examination of North American and British research.* Paper presented at the World Leisure and Recreation Association Congress, Jaipur, India.

Howe, C. Z. (1985). Possibilities for using a qualitative research approach in the sociological study of leisure. *Journal of Leisure Research, 17,* 212–224.

Howe, K. R. (1992). Getting over the quantitative-qualitative debate. *American Journal of Education, 20,* 236–256.

Jackson, E. L., & Burton, T. L. (1989). Mapping the past. In E. L. Jackson & T. L. Burton (Eds.), *Understanding leisure and recreation: Mapping the past, charting the future* (pp. 3–28). State College, PA: Venture Publishing, Inc.

Jacobson, S. (1996). *An examination of leisure in the lives of old lesbians from an ecological perspective.* Unpublished dissertation, University of Georgia.

Jacobson, S., & Samdahl, D. M. (1996). *Voices from the fringe: Leisure in the lives of old lesbians.* National Recreation and Park Association Leisure Research Symposium, Kansas City, Kansas, October.

Jansen, G., & Peshkin, A. (1992). Subjectivity in qualitative research. In M. D. LeCompte, W. L. Millroy & J. Preissle (Eds.), *The handbook of qualitative research in education* (pp. 681–725). San Diego, CA: Academic Press.

Janesick, V. J. (1994). The dance of qualitative research design: Metaphor, methodolatry, and meaning. In N. K. Denzin & Y. S. Lincoln (Eds.), *Handbook of qualitative research* (pp. 209–219). Thousands Oaks, CA: Sage Publications, Inc.

Karlis, G., & Dawson, D. (1994). Mental health promotion through recreation: A look at qualitative program evaluation. *Journal of Applied Recreation Research, 19,* 267–280.

Kelly, J. R. (1989). To be a scholar. *Leisure Sciences, 11,* 245–251.

Kelly, J. R. (1991). Leisure and quality: Beyond the quantitative barrier in research. In T. L. Goodale & P. A. Witt (Eds.), *Recreation and leisure: Issues in an era of change* (3rd ed., pp. 397–411). State College, PA: Venture Publishing, Inc.

Kelly, J. R. (1992). Counterpoints in the sociology of leisure. *Leisure Sciences, 14,* 247–253.

Kelly, J. R. (1997). Changing issues in leisure-family research—Again. *Journal of Leisure Research, 29,* 132–134.

Kivel, B. D. (1994). Lesbian and gay youth and leisure: Implications for practitioners and researchers. *Journal of Park and Recreation Administration, 12,* 15–28.

Kivel, B., Samdahl, D. M., & Jacobson, S. (1994). *Ethnic and cultural diversity in park and recreation settings: A review of selected literature.* Report submitted to the USDA Forest Service Southeast Forest Experiment Station.

Kuhn, T. S. (1970). *The structure of scientific revolutions* (2nd ed.). Chicago, IL: University of Chicago Press.

Malloy, D. C., Nilson, R. N., & Yoshioka, C. (1993). The impact of culture upon the administrative process in sport and recreation: A Canadian Indian perspective. *Journal of Applied Recreation Research, 18,* 115–130.

McCormick, B. (1991). Self-experience as leisure constraint: The case of Alcoholics Anonymous. *Journal of Leisure Research, 23,* 345–362.

McLean, D. J. (1995). Applied ethics and recreation practice: An introduction. *Journal of Applied Recreation Research, 20,* 91–94.

McLean, D. J. (1996). Leisure research and methodological pluralism: A response to Hemingway. *Leisure Studies, 15,* 137–141.

Mini-Digest of Education Statistics 1995: Educational Outcomes. (1995). *Educational outcomes: Literacy rates* [on line]. Available: http://www.ed.gov/NCES/pubs/MiniDig95/outcome.html#20.

Neulinger, J. (1974). *The psychology of leisure.* Springfield, IL: Charles C. Thomas.

Oldfather, P., & West, J. (1994). Qualitative research as jazz. *Educational Researcher, 23*(8), 22–26.

Pedlar, A. (1995). Relevance and action research in leisure. *Leisure Sciences, 17,* 133–140.

Popper, K. R. (1962). *Conjectures and refutations: The growth of scientific knowledge.* New York, NY: Basic Books.

Reason, P. (1994). Three approaches to participative inquiry. In N. K. Denzin & Y. S. Lincoln (Eds.), *Handbook of qualitative research* (pp. 324–339). Thousands Oaks, CA: Sage Publications, Inc.

Reid, D. G. (1993). Recreation and social development in Ontario First Nation Communities. *Journal of Applied Recreation Research, 18,* 87–102.

Richardson, S. L., Long, P. T., & Perdue, R. R. (1988). The importance of economic impact to municipal recreation programming. *Journal of Park and Recreation Administration, 6,* 65–78.

Roadburg, A. (1983). Freedom and enjoyment: Disentangling perceived leisure. *Journal of Leisure Research, 15,* 15–26.

Rojek, C. (1989). Leisure and recreation theory. In E. L. Jackson & T. L. Burton (Eds.), *Understanding leisure and recreation: Mapping the past, charting the future* (pp. 69–88). State College, PA: Venture Publishing, Inc.

Salomon, G. (1991). Transcending the qualitative-quantitative debate: The analytic and systemic approaches to educational research. *Educational Researcher, 20*(6), 10–18.

Samdahl, D. M. (1988). A symbolic interactionist model of leisure: Theory and empirical support. *Leisure Sciences, 10,* 27–38.

Samdahl, D. M. (1991). Measuring leisure: Categorical or interval? *Journal of Leisure Research, 23,* 87–93.

Samdahl, D. M., & Jekubovich, N. J. (1993). Patterns and characteristics of adult daily leisure. *Loisir et Societe/Society and Leisure, 16,* 129–149.

Samdahl, D. M., & Jekubovich, N. J. (1997). A critique of leisure constraints: comparative analyses and understandings. *Journal of Leisure Research, 29,* 430–452.

Schwandt, T. S. (1994). Constructivist, interpretivist approaches to human inquiry. In N. K. Denzin & Y. S. Lincoln (Eds.), *Handbook of qualitative research* (pp. 118–137). Thousands Oaks, CA: Sage Publications, Inc.

Scott, D., & Godbey, G. (1994). Recreation specialization in the social world of contract bridge. *Journal of Leisure Research, 26,* 275–295.

Smith, J. K., & Heshusius, L. (1986). Closing down the conversation: The end of the quantitative-qualitative debate among educational inquirers. *Educational Researcher, 15*(January), 4–12.

Smith, S. L. J., & Haley, A. J. (1979). Ratio ex machina: Notes on leisure research. *Journal of Leisure Research, 2,* 139–143.

Stockdale, J. E. (1989). Concepts and measures of leisure participation and preference. In E. L. Jackson & T. L. Burton (Eds.), *Understanding leisure and recreation: Mapping the past, charting the future* (pp. 115–150). State College, PA: Venture Publishing, Inc.

Stormann, W. (1989). Work: True leisure's home? *Leisure Studies, 8,* 25–33.

Sylvester, C. (1990). Overview: Special issue on leisure sciences, dominant paradigms and philosophy. *Journal of Leisure Research, 22,* 281–282.

Sylvester, C. (1995). Relevance and rationality in leisure studies: A plea for good reason. *Leisure Sciences, 17,* 125–131.

Taylor, J. G., Czarnowski, K. J., Sexton, N. R., & Flick, S. (1995). The importance of water to Rocky Mountain National Park visitors: An adaptation of visitor-employed photography to natural resources management. *Journal of Applied Recreation Research, 20,* 61–85.

Tinsley, H. E. A. (1984). Limitations, explorations, aspirations: A confession of fallibility and a promise to strive for perfection. *Journal of Leisure Research, 16,* 93–98.

U.S. Bureau of the Census. (1996). *Resident population of the United States: Middle series projections, 2015–2030, by sex, race, and Hispanic origin, with median age* [on line]. Available: http://www.census.gov/population/projections/nation/nsrh/nprh1530.txt.

U.S. Bureau of the Census. (1997). *Population statistics* [on line]. Available: http://www.census.gov/population.

Voelkl, J., & Brown, B. (1989). Experience sampling method in therapeutic recreation research. *Therapeutic Recreation Journal, 23,* 35–46.

Weinblatt, N., & Navon, L. (1995). Flight from leisure: A neglected phenomenon in leisure studies. *Leisure Sciences, 17,* 309–325.

Weissinger, E. (1990). Of revolutions and resistance: A response to philosophical criticisms of social scientific leisure research. *Journal of Leisure Research, 22,* 309–316.

Wolcott, H. F. (1992). Posturing in qualitative inquiry. In M. D. LeCompte, W. L. Millroy & J. Preissle (Eds.), *The handbook of qualitative research in education* (pp. 3–52). San Diego, CA: Academic Press.

Leisure Behaviors and Styles: Social, Economic, and Cultural Factors

John R. Kelly
University of Illinois

C
H
A
P
T
E
R

9

In architecture, one dictum has been that "form follows function." Translated into research, such a rule would suggest that methods and strategies would be chosen only after questions and types of data are identified. In leisure studies, however, the rule has often been reversed: "design follows methods." Research methods have been assumed rather than selected, standpoints implicit or even hidden (Harding, 1991), and the answers to theoretical questions locked into the kinds of findings amenable to the methods. For example, the fundamental and persistent question of leisure and recreation research has been, Who is doing what? The question is both management and market driven. Agencies managing public resources and those planning investments in recreation businesses want to know the magnitude of their clienteles and the composition of their markets. When they turn to social and behavioral scientists, they receive answers

couched in the terms of the common methods and concepts of their disciplines.

First, sociologists took the stage with their familiar surveys and demographic variables. They answered questions about potential markets with breakdowns of current participation by age, income, occupation, gender, and a few other customary factors. When such simplistic analysis was found to be less than successful, they responded with a new technique. Factor analysis was employed to identify bundles of activities that tended to have common participants. These bundles were labeled *styles,* which were in part an artifact of the analytical method.

Most recently, social psychologists have succeeded in commanding the stage by answering the question of Who is doing what? in individual rather than aggregate terms. With their familiar bag of scales and models, they have turned the answer to one of perceived outcomes from types of recreation experiences. Also using factoring techniques, the question has been changed from behaviors to preferences. Now styles

The author thanks Karla Henderson and Kimberly Shinew for suggestions for improving the first edition of this chapter.

135

are defined in terms of such factors as challenge-seeking, status-symbolizing, and family focus. The nature of the answers is determined by the received methods, in this case those of attitude scales and factor analysis.

Note what has occurred. Sociologists assume that preferences are shaped by socialization, which is indexed by socioeconomic variables such as income, occupation, education, ethnicity, and gender. Further, they have measured what is amenable to their methods—self-reports of participation in designated activities. Social psychologists assume that behaviors are shaped by preferences or relatively stable values. Further, they have measured by their familiar methods—scales of attitudes that are abstracted from presumed experience. Running parallel have been the economists studying "demand" with proxies of cost, such as distance, and of resources, such as income. Several disciplines have also adopted time as both a definition and measure of leisure under the assumption that it is quantifiable across settings and even across cultures. Under the rubric of "leisure time," time duration is presumed to measure action and provide an index of valuation as well as of participation.

I am not suggesting that we have learned nothing of value from such approaches or that there is some magic method waiting in the wings to take center stage and annihilate the naive. It is, however, necessary to step back a little from what has been going on in leisure research to readdress the question. The real question is one of explanation. Whether we focus on activity or participation, on markets and resource commitments, or on leisure as a dimension of life and meaning, research methods should follow the formulation. What are the behaviors we call leisure and recreation? Are such behaviors best understood in patterns we may call styles? Do those styles reflect individual orientations as well as cultural values and access to resources?

The Nature of Leisure: A Nondefinition

It is understandable that we generally define phenomena in terms of our own frameworks. It is also understandable that those frameworks are derived from what we have learned. The "domain assumptions" of the disciplinary and theoretical approaches we have been taught direct us to particular definitions of whatever we are to study as well as to modes of explanation. What is leisure? It is social activity learned in social contexts and employing social resources. It is an individual state of mind of consciousness measured in attitudes and leading to activity and choice. It is economic choice conducted in market or quasi-market conditions and measured by economic exchange. So say the sociologists, psychologists, and economists.

Is it possible to step back enough to examine what each perspective places in its own defining framework? One possibility is that each disciplinary definition presupposes some sort of human action. Whether the focus is on engaging in an activity, making a choice, allocating a resource, or experiencing a state of mind, the individual engages in some sort of action. The action may be physical, intellectual, communicative, contemplative, emotional, or a combination of more than one dimension. Even daydreaming involves action of the imagination. The action may be a context for, as well as content of, the experience. I am aware of no one who is proposing that leisure is or could be a totally self-contained experience apart from what actors do. Even the most narrow "state-of-mind" definition that asserts that it is the nature of the consciousness that defines leisure presupposes that there is an action context. Something happens in directing attention, processing information, defining meaning, and producing the experience.

If action is integral to leisure—or any other meaningful human engagement—then we can begin at a level prior to the consequences of engaging in specified activity, experiencing an identifiable set of attitudes, making a choice, or even completing a period of time. Prior to all measures and methods is human action, doing something in the most inclusive sense. The distinctive element of leisure action is that it is focused on the experience rather than external outcomes. It is engaged in primarily for the experience of the action.

Human action, leisure or any other designated by the convention of a name, always has two dimensions or components. Human action is both existential and social. It involves action with meaning and takes place in a social environment of learned symbols as well as opportunities and constraints. It involves lines of action that are constructed with webs of symbolic meaning for the social actor. Further, the meanings that actors ascribe to actions are learned in social contexts so that the existential and social dimensions of action are interrelated rather than separate. Therefore, leisure acts take on general meanings for the self in lines of action that may be designated as "style."

This is not the place to engage in an extended discussion of the persistent problem of the nature of social action. I have attempted to explore the dialectic of the existential and the social in relation to leisure in *Freedom to Be: A New Sociology of Leisure* (Kelly, 1987a). Here I will only list some dimensions and implications of understanding leisure as human action that is both existential and social.

Leisure is existential as action that produces meaning. Leisure is deciding and doing as well as feeling. The action not only *has* meaning, but also *produces* meaning. Leisure does more than reflect the cultural meanings attached to symbols and settings. Action does more than process information. It creates meaning whenever decision is real and action carried out. Every action is, in at least an infinitesimal way, novel.

Leisure, then, is action that both has and creates meaning. Actors engage in leisure with multiple and complex anticipations. Along with the immediate experience, there is often a dimension of becoming. In the action, the leisure actor anticipates becoming something more or different from the preaction condition. Whether or not there is a long-term strategy of personal development, there is some future orientation. The traditional Aristotelian theme of freedom from necessity implies an openness of the future as well as the possibility of focus on the experience itself.

Leisure is existential in the sense that it is action in which the actor becomes something more, in which the action creates novelty. The relative freedom and openness of leisure may enhance the developmental component of meaning, the becoming in the action context (Csikszentmihalyi, 1981). For example, a sense of competence and self-creation may be central to the meaning of a leisure episode.

At the same time, leisure is social in both its context and orientations. Leisure is learned behavior, thoroughly ethnic in its adoption of the symbols and constructions of a culture. Leisure, even when solitary, incorporates the meaning forms of a culture learned through its social institutions. Further, leisure may be a context for expressing and creating community.

Leisure forms, interpretations, and aims are learned in a particular society. The resources for leisure, including time and skill acquisition, are products of the social system (see Shaw, chapter 16 in this volume). However central the existential elements in leisure, it is also social in its contexts, resources, and learned forms. Leisure always employs the forms of a culture in its symbol systems, institutional role sets, socialization processes, and layers of formal and informal organizations.

This does not mean that leisure is wholly "determined." It is contextual, but may reshape that context. Insofar as the social system is a construction of human action (Berger and Luckman, 1966), leisure is a social domain with the potential for altering that construction. As in the arts we shape resistant materials into something new, so in any social action there is the potential of action upon, as well as in, the society.

Admitting social structure to explanations of leisure is not a denial of its element of openness or freedom. Leisure may exhibit resistance to social forces, coercive roles, and constraints as well as conformity (Wearing, 1990). In fact, recognizing the social embeddedness of leisure admits leisure's openness and historical relativity when social structure is understood as a creation rather than a given.

Leisure, then, is best understood in a dialectical framework as experience-centered action that includes both the existential and the social dimensions. Leisure is situated action. It is contextual but not determined, encultured but not static. It is not existential *nor* social, but both. The relationship is not fixed, but dynamic.

To return to the question of How do we explain what people are doing? we will find that there are a number of approaches and models. Each focuses on one aspect of the existential-social dialectic to the exclusion of all or most of the others. As a consequence, all have been found inadequate, even in their own terms. The sections that follow will summarize and analyze major models of explanation. All will be considered to make contributions to understanding, and none to exclude the actual or potential contributions of the others. Implicit in this approach is the assumption that leisure is changing rather than static. It includes both existential and social dimensions that are integrated into the action scheme of individuals and the social forces of the society. Leisure is not a separate domain of human action, dichotomous with any other domain or segregated from other kinds of action. Leisure is very much a part of life as we know it, on the levels of both the actor and the social system. As such, it is multidimensioned, complex, and always in the process of being created and re-created.

Models of Explanation

One approach to models of explanation is by discipline. There is, however, considerable overlap among, and adoption of similar factors by, different disciplines. Therefore, despite the history of leadership of some modes of analysis by sociologists, psychologists, or economists, the approach here will focus on dimensions of explanation and their employment. Also, what follows is not intended as an encyclopedia of references, but as a critical overview.

Social Determination Models

The terminology may be misleading. Are there *determinants* of leisure behavior in a causal sense, or is the analysis stochastic and statistical? It might be more accurate to refer to *correlates* of behavioral aggregates.

Correlation coefficients between, for example, age and participation in football are high and negative, but between age and golf relatively low. Age is not itself strictly a determinant, but indexes a number of factors that decrease participation in physical contact team sports. Further, the second part of the correlation is measured in aggregate terms: percentages of those in specified age categories. The expectation has been that social aggregates would be found to have distinctive leisure patterns.

The model was simple: a series of socioeconomic variables was correlated to participation rates in one or more activities. Usually data were obtained from samples of populations in communities, states, or nations. For some employing the model, it was atheoretical, just a matter of using a method. For others there was the implicit theory of structure-functional sociology underlying the study. Differential socialization and access to opportunities were assumed to be indexed by variables such as gender, race, occupation, income, education level, and marital status. Age was considered more a measure of interests and abilities, but was entered into most studies.

The disciplinary source was mainstream sociology. In the 1960s most leisure research was being done by sociologists who were focused on such issues as the determination of leisure by work roles, social status and class in the community context, and the unifying power of integrated social institutions. Leisure was usually defined as residual time. Research approaches measured leisure, however, in terms of participation in listed activities. Surveys often asked for some frequency measure, while time-budget methods measured duration. Results were usually analyzed by correlating mean participation rates with the socio-economic and demographic indices. This method was supported by new computer technologies that facilitated dealing with large samples and multiple variables, and by various economists who included the same variables in their demand equations as proxies for resources and tastes.

How well did it work? At first the method seemed reasonably successful, as statistically significant correlations were found in most studies, especially those with large samples. Other studies compared and contrasted occupational groups (Smigel, 1963). Especially when the activities measured were those most differentiated by social status, such as membership in community organizations, the results appeared to validate the assumptions.

The correlations were not large except for a few selected activities, but were almost always significant. Since the likelihood of statistical significance is also correlated to sample size, an N of 1,000 or so seemed to ensure probabilities of 0.01. Time-budget studies indicated small but consistent differences in average times spent in various kinds of activities by much the same aggregates. Moreover, some of the correlations were strong: education level to the arts, age and gender to most sports, social status to community organizations, and rural background to hunting and fishing.

In the 1930s community studies in North America approached leisure in the context of community institutional stratification. In *Middletown*, leisure was viewed as a major social space expressing the value systems of the community (Lynd and Lynd, 1956). In Elmtown, leisure was a significant environment for adolescent development as well as for the reinforcement of social stratification (Hollingshead, 1949). The study of suburban leisure by Lundberg and associates (Lundberg, Komarovsky and McInerny, 1934) analyzed leisure as a derivation of the value scheme of the new upper middle-class setting. In such community studies, leisure was seen as a product of the social context, but not as strictly determined by a single set of institutional relationships.

In the 1970s and 1980s, however, the model has been subjected to considerable attack. One source was methodological. When multivariate analyses that measured the strength of correlations (the proportion of variance accounted for) were employed, the results were surprisingly unimpressive. One analysis of outdoor recreation surveys found that the variance accounted for averaged less than 5% for most activities and approached 10% for only a few special resource activities (Kelly, 1980). The previously found relationships were there, but not with the predictive power presumed.

Altogether almost 20 such surveys were conducted in the 1970s, with numerous analyses of the major national surveys (Snepenger and Crompton, 1985). A second crack in the approach was produced by giving attention to social groups as agents and contexts of decision, rather than to aggregate analysis (Cheek and Burch, 1976; Field and O'Leary, 1973). It was demonstrated that the immediate social contexts of participation, especially family and friendship groups, differentiate participation more than income and occupational indices. Also, the dependent variables in such studies were suspect: frequency of participation in a labeled activity such as "swimming" or "concerts." The variety of meanings and forms subsumed under such a label obscured what may have been real differences in styles, in the hows and even wheres of such activity. For example, the styles of swimming are quite different for indoor lap swimming for health aims and a mother taking children to the beach. As a result of these questions, an important shift in attention began that has now become commonplace in the study of leisure.

A consensus began to emerge that was in direct conflict with the tacit assumptions of the "determination" or functional model:

1. Although there are demographic and socioeconomic variations in leisure and recreation participation, they are only moderately predictive.
2. Much of the variation that is statistically measured can be ascribed to certain constraints (see Jackson and Scott, chapter 18 in this volume):

    - the poor are excluded from many kinds of participation, especially any that require travel or other costly investments;
    - other variations are due to past discrimination in access to opportunities, such as for women in physically demanding sports, or African Americans in travel;
    - regional variations are often due to climate and other resource differences in availability and access;
    - excluding the very wealthy and the poor, commonalities of leisure participation, not style, appear to be far greater than differences. Such commonalities were more likely to be found in time-budget research and in other designs that included the full range of ordinary activities; and
    - period in the life cycle, and especially child rearing, has a considerable impact on leisure and recreation patterns

3. More attention was given to questions of how rather than what. That is, style of engagement rather than just frequency would be found to vary according to socialization factors such as gender, education, and occupational level.

Ordinarily established premises and methods are abandoned slowly and with some conflict. Although surveys continue to be sponsored and completed, the currently expected results are much more limited than a decade ago. Even the most complete surveys with the largest samples must be interpreted carefully to

identify trends and projections (Kelly, 1987b). In the case of the overly simple socioeconomic determination model, its retreat was hastened by more sophisticated statistical techniques that undermined its results, as well as by changes in focus. The computer that made the simple survey possible contained the potential for its own dissolution.

Economic and Opportunity Models

At the same time, another determination model was being explored. The assumption was simple: the economic domain of life determines all others. The framework was usually set as a dichotomy—work and leisure. Underlying the agenda-setting volume edited by Erwin Smigel (1963) was the assumption that the diminution of work would make leisure a problem for the social system. Stanley Parker's influential study, *The Future of Work and Leisure* (1971), was based on a set of models of the relationship. While separation was admitted as one possibility, the bias of the author was that the economic sphere was the major determinant of leisure.

The formulation of the premise was somewhat loose. *Work* was really a tacit way of referring to economic roles, whatever their productive or marginal nature. *Leisure* referred to those activities that occupied time other than that required by the economic roles, self and household maintenance, and domestic tasks. The mixtures of meanings in activity such as child-parent interaction or entertaining at home, for example, were largely ignored, as were gender and life course variations (see Shaw, chapter 16 in this volume).

Economic models tend to assume that both work and leisure are quantifiable as time. The relationship between the two was usually expressed as a trade-off in which remunerated time on the job is chosen or rejected in favor of nonremunerative time called leisure (Kreps, 1968, Linder, 1970, Schor, 1991). Values are indexed by dollars of income or expenditure, or by time as a proxy for economic value.

Parker (1971) proposed a clear-cut model of the relationship of work and leisure. The issues, however, were found to be more complex (Zuzanek and Mannell, 1983). They include the allocation of time between work and leisure, the impacts of work scheduling variations on leisure, relative values placed on the different domains, the relation of work commitment to leisure valuation, and the carry-over of work attitudes and values to leisure. Fundamental, however, has been the attempt to measure direct effects of economic roles on leisure choices and styles.

Some research has found weak spillover effects or multivariate effects that cannot be captured by a single model (Zuzanek and Mannell, 1983). Several studies found little relationship between workplace satisfaction or alienation and leisure (Bacon, 1975). More sophisticated studies have employed complex analysis to identify the carry-over of employment dimensions such as intellectuality and complexity (Kohn, 1990).

A number of factors reinforce this complexity and multidimensionality. On the one hand, individuals with different economic roles have many common histories of socialization, education, and cultural environments. On the other hand, schedules and economic resources are dependent on work roles. Further, there may be reciprocity in learning and expression among such activity elements as skill, sociability, modes of communication, and interaction styles. Negative dimensions of alienation, damage to self-esteem and positive identities, and expression of freedom may have some spillover from work to leisure and family (Torbert, 1973). More profoundly, nonwork spheres of life may come to be defined in terms of market participation, possession, and the purchase of commodified experiences (Clarke and Critcher, 1985; Kelly, 1986).

What seems clear is that the multifaceted and multidimensioned relationship between economic and other roles and relationships cannot be reduced to any simple model of occupational determination of leisure activity choice (Kelly and Kelly, 1994). The same seems to be the case when attention is shifted to economically derived social position. Social class analysis divides the social system into layers measured by "life chances," or the opportunities derived from economic roles. Rather than a direct occupational determination model, social class analysis presupposes that placement in a stratified socioeconomic system determines access to opportunities, as well as the resources the actor brings to those opportunities.

In relation to leisure, there would appear to be some clear ties between social class and leisure. First, the lowest class, the poor and disinherited, are excluded from the opportunities and resources that others take for granted. They have no discretionary income, little likelihood of developing skills and interests in educational settings, and no position that admits them to leisure environments. Their leisure, then, tends to be relatively cost free and without travel and high equipment costs.

Second, the very wealthy are able—through travel and the purchase of access to special resources—to demonstrate leisure styles in which many of the impediments to leisure for others are avoided. They enter a world of private resources that can be purchased at prices that eliminate crowding by more ordinary classes.

Third, one element of class is education. Education not only is an essential credential for economic opportunity, but also is a social space in which tastes and abilities are developed.

Fourth, economic resources to purchase or rent access to leisure opportunities are indexed by social class. With many kinds of leisure offered through the market with prices attached, income is one factor in what can be done and in the style of participation.

Fifth, it is likely that those in the upper investment segments of the economy, as well as many managers and professionals, have more control over their work schedules than those working for hourly wages in the manufacturing or retail sectors of the economy. They are able to integrate work and leisure schedules flexibly, rather than be limited to the time made available by factory or shop schedules. With the majority of employment now in services, irregular schedules and 24-hour requirements in retailing and health services have obliterated former assumptions about weekends, evenings, and coordinated activities.

Perhaps most salient is the fact that those who are marginal economically may be left out by those who supply many leisure markets. Among the costs of stratification in a market economy is that pricing policies offer certain goods and services only to those in the upper strata of the system.

The result is that both resources and opportunities are available, or not, in ways that have economic bases. For this evident reason, it has been assumed that measures of socioeconomic class would be powerfully correlated with the activity patterns of leisure participation. In general, however, the results have been disappointing. When the costly travel of the wealthy and the extreme limitations of the poor are excluded, differences in activity choices by upper middle-, middle-, and working-class people in North America have not been dramatic. When education history is controlled, those differences almost disappear. What seems to be the case is that *styles* vary more than the activities themselves. Rates of camping, listening to music, watching television, or engaging in sports are little different. What may differ is the place and style of participation. Only costly activities such as downhill skiing and golf have substantial class variations measured by frequency alone (Kelly, 1987b). Again, the dependent variable does not adequately measure style.

This tends to shift attention to what has been called *social status*. Class is based on access to and control of economic resources. Status is a matter of style. And it seems to be styles of leisure that vary most. People eat out—some at fast food chains and a few at exclusive clubs. They travel—most by car, staying with friends and at budget motels, and a few by Concorde to pricey resorts. They entertain at home—most with cookouts and potlucks and a few with catered soirees. Even golf may be played on crowded public links or at private clubs so exclusive that even money cannot buy a membership. There are differences in style based on social status, but we have little research on such issues.

Social Factors in Leisure

Styles of leisure participation vary with a number of other factors. Economic resources are only the beginning, and not always the most significant. For example, across a wide spectrum of class or status layers, parents of young children orient much of their leisure toward developmental activity and the expression of family bonds. Social variables such as gender, place in the life course, family status, ethnic background and cultural heritage, age-indexed abilities and expectations, and educational histories are all factors in leisure styles. For example, single mothers have high role demands, low levels of support in those roles, and limited leisure resources.

Two Models

Again, there have been many attempts to identify and measure the "determinants" of leisure. If economic roles alone did not produce clearly differentiated patterns of leisure participation, then the addition of demographic and social factors might complete the task. Two general sets of assumptions were operative. The first was the Opportunity Model and the second the Socialization Model.

The Opportunity Model was derived from the economic approach. The argument was that access to resources and opportunities was the consequence of a combination of economic and social factors. The economic factors alone, at least for those who were not quite wealthy or not quite poor, did not distinguish different participation patterns. If, however, a fuller set of determinants were to be introduced, then the results would be more persuasive. Gender, age, ethnic identification, education level, marital status, urban-rural residence, and other social variables were added to the economic-occupational ones. Each was presumed to measure some differential access to resources or opportunities that would lead to different kinds of activities being chosen. The Socialization Model was somewhat more sociological. The premise was that a number of factors produced different life histories. As a consequence, different interests and values were learned in a lifelong process. Gender and educational history, especially, were presumed to index different socialization patterns.

The results were generally significant but not spectacular. Again, differences in both opportunity and socialization produced considerable male predominance in such activities as team sports, hunting, bar visiting, and some individual and pair sports. Females, on the other hand, were disproportionately represented in the fine arts and in some domestic activities. Those with higher education experiences made up almost all the participants in most fine arts engagement, both creation and appreciation. Even when controlling for economic resources, socialization factors were found to be significant. Further, little attention was given to the fact that females and males, for example, might engage in the same activity in different ways, especially with different companions.

The results, however, continued to obscure differences due to the focus on frequency of participation in designated activities. Styles of engagement were ignored, as were locales. Swimming was undifferentiated by locales that impacted styles—in public pools versus private and club pools, at exclusive resort beaches versus public urban beaches, or in social-versus-competitive settings. A trip was a trip, a party a party, and reading anything from the sports page of the newspaper to Thomas Hardy was just reading.

Styles tend to vary more than can be demonstrated by time diaries and activity lists. The styles of behavior learned as appropriate are age-based, gender-differentiated, and culture-varied. Socialization into leisure is a lifelong process in which taking up and discarding activities is only one dimension. Going to concerts, one category in the national recreation surveys, is not much alike for the teen rock crowd and the adult symphony audience. There is a variety of leisure styles within social categories as well as similarities across social strata. The institutional context of participation and socialization incorporates factors of contexts, opportunities, resources, orientations, values, and cohort, as well as personal histories.

The Life Course Approach

One response to this complexity is to employ the computer to sort out everything imaginable that can be put into a research design. Inclusive designs, although they tend to account for somewhat more variance than simpler ones, are plagued by two problems. The first is methodological: the more variables that are included, the more they are likely to overlap. As a consequence, the explanatory power added by the twentieth or even the tenth factor is quite small. A second limitation is that such designs contribute little to explanatory theory.

Additions of 0.02 to variance accounted for are of little help in developing models of explanation. This is especially true when single measures are purported to represent complex socialization processes.

When it is admitted that no model seems to include all factors or to order them into a single all-encompassing explanatory model, then the strategies of explanation are somewhat more modest. Perspectives are chosen that do not pretend to do it all. Rather, any metaphor of explanation (Kelly, 1987a) focuses on some aspects of the totality to the exclusion of others. The issue becomes one of choosing metaphors that are most closely aligned with explanatory models that fit what is known of the phenomenon under investigation.

For leisure, a new focus was gaining support. It replaced statistical aggregates with groups, categories with communities. Further, the Socialization Model was given substance in the content of its framework. Moving from family studies (Rapoport and Rapoport, 1975), attention to social bonds (Cheek and Burch, 1976), and discovery of immediate communities of family and friends as the primary school context of leisure (Burch, 1965; Field and O'Leary, 1973), the metaphor of the life course was given increased attention (see Freysinger, chapter 15 in this volume).

The dialectic of leisure behavior is demonstrated in this perspective. On the one hand, leisure is viewed as profoundly social, embedded in the roles and relationships that change through the life course. On the other hand, it is seen as purposive action with intentions that include both the immediate experience and longer term outcomes of personal development. Leisure is one dimension of life in which action is oriented towards "becoming," as well as towards the present.

One aspect of the dual perspective is that of socialization. Leisure is learned behavior, attitudes, and meanings. We are socialized into leisure through our histories of experiences and choices. Leisure socialization is learning how to be leisure actors. There is, however, also socialization in leisure. In leisure events and episodes we are in the process of becoming. We are learning and developing. This learning is both positive and negative, as the self develops strength or fears, competence or inhibitions.

In general, the life course in contemporary societies consists of three biosocial periods: preparation, establishment, and culmination (Kelly, 1983a, 1987a). In the preparation period, learning and growing are the central tasks as the young person is getting ready for adult or productive life. The central social institutions are the school and the family of socialization. In establishment, the themes are productive activity and securing a place in the social system. The family of procreation and the economy are salient social institutions. In the final or culmination period, the end point of death is anticipated in ways that make meaning and the passing on of life's outcomes significant. Life is seen as a journey in which the human actor seeks to have some continuity of meaning and identity, rather than just a series of experiences.

From this developmental perspective, leisure is found to be an integral dimension of the entire process, not "time-out" from its meaning. Activities are more than time fillers or discrete forms of action and interaction. Leisure takes place in contexts that change through the life course. These contexts include institutional roles with opportunities and expectations that change through life's journey. For example, teens create their own social worlds made up of immediate experiences incorporating the highly marketed products of the mass media. Then, all the organized and informal possibilities for sport, the arts, entertainment, and interaction that are associated with the school are left behind in the transition to the establishment period. As a consequence, participation in many kinds of leisure declines suddenly and may be replaced with activity more related to the home and community.

Opportunity structures change through the life course, as do role expectations and self-definitions. In early establishment years, leisure has been found to be altered by the assumption of the roles of spouse and parent as well as full-time worker (Shaw, 1994). Through the changing social expectation and opportunity contexts reflecting the gendered division of labor in the home as well as the workplace, the value systems and world-views of individuals may be altered as they move through their life spans. The kinds of travel, parties, sports, and cultural engagements sought by students may be avoided by the same persons five years later as they seek to find accepted places in the adult world. Again, the changes may be more a matter of styles than of activity designations. Locales, attire, companions, and modes of interaction considered appropriate at one age may be seen as damaging to social identity at a later period.

Socialization into leisure is a dialectical process that continues through the life course. As we learn leisure interests and skills, we also learn something about ourselves. We make decisions both in the context of perceived opportunities and expectations and of how we perceive ourselves. We learn in leisure engagement to define and redefine our aims and our selves. We are always in the process of becoming, selecting life investments in changing situations.

Csikszentmihalyi (1981) has argued that it is in leisure experiences that we are most likely to develop criteria for the rest of life. Expressive activities may be those in which experiences of the highest quality become the standard by which other experiences—as in work or education—are judged. We may become dissatisfied with events and circumstances that are largely instrumental and devoid of their own meaning. That is, we come to expect some expressive and developmental dimensions in most social spaces.

One aspect of much leisure is that its relative openness allows for more immediate and direct feedback than in many routinized contexts in which the outcomes are predetermined. In the leisure of games, there are discrete and measured outcomes. In social situations, we may choose companions whose feedback is most salient to us. We try new and different initiatives, portrayals, and ventures, knowing that the outcomes are significant for us but not fateful for our major social roles. As a consequence, we may be most likely to learn and develop in such times of relative openness.

There are a number of models of the life course. Each emphasizes one or more dimensions of the life journey. The *family life cycle* stresses the predictable sequences of gendered family roles and contexts. The *life span* model points to age-related changes in the individual and often combines biological with psychological factors in explanation. The *life course* approach defines continuities and transitions in multiple roles that intersect in a variety of ways in each life period. The *crisis* model suggests that there are traumatic upheavals at crucial points in the life journey, such as midlife economic blockages or divorce, that realign self-definitions as well as role commitments. The *developmental* perspective proposes certain sequential stages of development that build on previous ones and require some completion in order. Each approach stresses dimensions that have relevance for understanding shifts in leisure activities, social contexts, meanings, and styles through the life course (Kelly, 1987a, pp. 66–68).

It is clear that both continuity and change characterize the individual actor as well as social roles and contexts (Kelly, 1983a; see also Freysinger, chapter 15 in this volume). Leisure is not a separate domain of life, but is woven through all sorts of roles and relationships (Rapoport and Rapoport, 1975). As the transitions and traumas of life develop and have their impacts on everything—resources, opportunities, values, self-images, and aims—so leisure takes on different meanings and functions (Kelly, 1987c). Further, such changes are different for men and women, those with economic security and the poor, those with intact families and those without, and others with significant differences.

Core Plus Balance

Continuity and change in leisure through the life course can be approached in terms of changes in the individual, in contexts and opportunities, and in expectations and aims (Freysinger, 1995). Another approach focuses principally on the kinds of activities pursued. The *core plus balance* model proposes that one element in the failure to find dramatic differences in activities across population categories, or even through the life course, is the persistent core of activities that occupy most adults most of their lives. This core consists of engagements that are relatively accessible and low cost. Watching television, interacting informally with other household members, conversing in a variety of settings, and engaging in sexual activity are common to adults through most of the life span. Other such activity includes reading, walking, shopping, residential enhancement such as lawn and garden activity, and meeting with kin and friends. This core occupies the greatest amount of time, especially in those periods between scheduled events. Further, such core activities often express and develop those primary relationships that are highly valued by most adults. They are woven into the household roles and investments that are the core of values as well as of activity patterns.

The balance, on the other hand, suggests variety. It also offers one way of answering the old questions about whether leisure is a compensation for work requirements or a spillover from its content (Wilensky, 1963). Is leisure escape or intense engagement, relaxation or focus, solitary or social, restful or demanding, physical or mental, and so on? The balance approach suggests that the usual answer for an individual is "both/and" rather than "either/or." In patterns that change through the life course, we usually seek both engagement and separation—in different activities and settings and at different times. Leisure is multidimensional, not monothematic. Further, the balance shifts as we and our lives change and with life conditions that are becoming more common such as singleness, living alone, and a variety of transitions. Most people do not seek just one kind of activity to the exclusion of all others, but do a variety of things in a variety of ways. In the balance metaphor, a leisure style is the composite of the balance, its integration of differing elements.

Social factors, then, reflect both external factors such as resources and opportunities as well as different sets of relationships and roles. They may be indexed by demographic categories that give some measure of differences in socialization as well as of life circumstances. These factors may be analyzed from a number of perspectives, of which that of the life course is one of the most inclusive and useful.

Lifestyles: The Ethnicity of Leisure

When we focus on styles of leisure, how people act and interact rather than which activities they undertake, it becomes apparent that there is little research on the issue. William Burch (1965) offered an analysis of styles of camping that was based on observation rather than surveys. More recently, a wider spectrum of camping styles has been described from a combination of survey and observational analysis (Kelly, 1987d). Several studies of travel styles have been done for marketing purposes. This range of variability in how leisure is done is based only on one activity. More recently, Shamir (1992) has analyzed styles based on values as well as life conditions.

Much more fundamental is the evidence that the entire mix of cultural elements shapes every aspect of leisure. Studies of the social interaction patterns of poor White urban dwellers, urban Italian families, Hispanic families, and others demonstrates how all the learned and transmitted values, modes of communication, interaction expectations, and cultural heritages make a difference in how people gather and form social events (Kelly, 1996). Not only are there differences among national, regional, and religious cultures, but also among subcultures within geographical areas. Leisure, like all domains of life, is thoroughly ethnic, in and of particular cultures.

The concept of style incorporates both what people do and how they do it. The evident diversity in environments, activities, aims, and outcomes is only the beginning. Take as simple an event as a family dinner. How many are invited, who does the work, the frequency and timing of the event, the foods prepared, how the eating is sequenced, where people gather in subgroups differentiated by gender, age, marital status, and position in the family, affective behaviors and expressions of emotion and affection, topics of conversation, language conventions, and many other elements differ from one ethnic group to another. And those differences have meaning beyond the single event, as identities are presented, tested, evaluated, and reinforced or rejected.

Stereotypes and Specialists

One danger is that leisure becomes stereotyped. Stereotypes are a form of convenient classification, labels usually based on a single identifying factor. Lei-

sure stereotypes presuppose that individuals are essentially monothematic in their leisure. The stereotype of the passive blue-collar worker, employed mother, the aesthetic professor, the "jock," or the artist, suggests that they devote most or all of their leisure to one kind of pursuit. It is true that there are those who are quite single-minded in their leisure engagement. They hone the skills of an activity, fashion their social relationships around its groupings, and define themselves in terms of that leisure identification (see Stebbins, chapter 5 in this volume). Such "amateurs," however, are exceptions to the majority core-plus-balance patterns. Their focused commitment is remarkable, partly because it is extraordinary. It is no surprise to find that research on such devotees begins with the special group rather than with population samples (Stebbins, 1979). In much the same way, stereotypes based on consumption of leisure commodities presume that purchases alone define the actor whose leisure styles in reality may be quite diverse and complex. More likely is that complex and multidimensional identities may be expressed through the choices of sets of activities (Haggard and Williams, 1992).

One particular research methodology for a time threatened to produce an artifactual analysis. Factor analysis that grouped recreation participants according to the sets of activities that differentiated them was employed to delineate varieties of leisure styles. Factors were based on commonalities in participation beyond those that were common to most of a sample. Early results seemed to indicate that "status-based," "sports," "water-based," "backwoods," and even "fast living" might characterize the leisure of identifiable aggregates of people.

A number of assumptions, however, were being overlooked. Different samples produced different factors (Schmitz-Scherzer, Rudinger, Angleitner and Bierhoff-Alfermann, 1974). Heterogeneous lists of activities did not produce the same neat categories as more limited sets (Kelly, 1983b). In fact, often the same activities were found in different factors from one sample to another. There were several reasons for these discrepancies. First, individuals have leisure patterns that involve engagement across factors. Stereotyping individuals according to a single factor is misleading. Second, many activities that rank highest on frequency and duration of time do not enter the factors at all. These informal and accessible activities, the "core" already discussed, do not differentiate sets of participants just because they are most common. Yet, to ignore television, reading, shopping, and informal socializing when typologies are formulated requires fixing on the occasional at the expense of the ordinary.

This does not mean that there are no single-minded individuals who pursue a "high-risk" sport, fine arts production, or some social organization to the exclusion of almost all else. Nor does it mean that there are no significant differences in leisure styles, in how people do what they do. Stereotypes may blind us to the balances of ordinary leisure styles. For most of the population, however, stereotypes are blurred by the common core in leisure, as well as by the relative diversity in interests and commitments through the life course.

One fundamental flaw of many leisure typologies is that they presume a segregation of leisure. That is, participation in some set of activities is analyzed as a domain of life separated from everything else. Therefore, participation alone is the subject of the analysis. This is a more serious problem even than ignoring the commonalities of the core. It returns to the old survey method of taking lists of activities as representative of the domain of leisure and assuming that all participation in each is the same. All the dimensions of motivation, satisfaction, aims, and styles are brushed aside to focus on the activity label and frequency. More useful is an inclusive approach that identifies the multiple cultural, class, regional, and even localized factors in "lifestyle enclaves" that incorporate leisure as one aspect of several types (Bellah, Madsen, Sullivan, Swidler and Tipton, 1985).

A narrow approach neglects both the existential and the social dimensions of leisure. The "becoming" or existential element of leisure that combines experience with decision and developmental aims is forfeited in utter concentration on what occurs in the events and episodes. The social dimension of roles and relationships that are a larger context of engagement is also excluded from the analysis. Leisure is reduced to how often individuals do certain specified activities formed into distinguishing sets. The full range of discretionary activity, tied and connected into our networks of relationships and expressing something of what we believe we are now and what we seek to become, is lost to a method that measures one factor in differences. Rather a full set of life conditions is the context for embedded leisure styles. Leisure is not just commodity purchase, intimate relationships, single activity investments, or any other one dimension.

The dialectic proposed at the beginning of this chapter presupposes that leisure is not a part of life separated from all else by some mystical label of *freedom* or *intrinsic motivation*. Rather, it is woven into the reality of what we are as individuals and as social and cultural beings who have learned to be what we are. We do not cease to become parents, spouses, kin, lovers, workers, neighbors, friends, colleagues, rivals, or learners the moment we begin a leisure activity. We do not cease to be aggressive or hesitant, rational or emotional, confident or unsure, initiating or responsive, challenge seeking or security minded because we are not being paid to do something. The developing and the social self go with each of us everywhere, including into leisure. To follow the meanings of leisure requires that, at the very least, we come equipped with the questions and the tools of developmental and social psychology and of sociology, inclusively defined.

One inclusive summary statement may suffice if we take it in the fullness of its ramifications: leisure is ethnic. That is, it is behavior learned in particular cultures and subcultures. It is interpreted in the symbols and language forms of a culture, studied with the methods accepted in salient disciplines, carried out with the forms accepted and provided in a particular social context, and evaluated with the value systems learned in actual social institutions. It is separate from nothing that significantly affects our lives. It is integrated into the full fabric of life, of all that we are and seek to become.

Lifestyle Typologies Stressing Leisure

There are a number of lifestyle typologies that integrate leisure into a comprehensive overall schema. They are mostly developed for market identification purposes and have consumption as a central dimension. Among them are the VALS framework and the census-based Claritas marketing formula. For such typologies, the central metaphor is consumption.

The California-located VALS program claims to be quite effective in locating types of consumers based on values as well as demographics such as income and education. Dimensions of work, family/intimacy, community, leisure, life course period, and values are combined into an inclusive typology. Nine styles are delineated: (a) two are need driven: old and poor "survivors" and marginal "sustainers" who lack discretionary resources; (b) the inner-directed, self-centered and self-preoccupied "I am me" youth and "experiential" younger adults for whom leisure and personal growth are central; (c) the outer-directed, a large cluster of middle-mass conventional "belongers," younger and more ambitious "emulators" who use leisure for status, and a sizable number of "achievers" who are doing well economically, experience some time pressure, and tend to make leisure secondary to work-based status. Finally, they locate a few "integrators" who are relatively autonomous, flexible, mature, and balanced. In this typology, leisure is one dimension of overall styles that result in identities that combine with resources to shape the priorities and investments of life as well as strategies for survival among the disinherited (Mitchell, 1983). The schema is updated regularly, but current statistics are proprietary.

The Claritas scheme is even more specific in employing census data to give a geographical "neighborhood" reference to sets of consumer styles. Leisure consumption is quite central to the formulation. The aim is to guide entrepreneurs in locating particular types of retail businesses. Styles, then, mean consumption. Updated from the 1990 census, Claritas identifies "lifestyle enclaves" that consume particular styles of cars, electronics, clothing, media, financial investments, and recreation. Neighborhood types include elite suburbs, urban uptown, country elite, affluent, inner-city upscale and midscale, country rural, urban core (poor), and urban neighborhood marginal. The largest county suburban to Chicago includes "kids and culs-de-sac" who stress parenting, "pools and patios" with elite tastes, "executive suites" into high culture pursuits, and "upward bound" younger residents who do aerobics and buy new electronics in a self-centered lifestyle. Wealth and status are elements in upscale consumerism with leisure purchases significant. An urban fringe community is equally divided among city-connected elites with estates, the younger upward bound, boomtown singles, new homesteaders, and the kids and cul-de-sac clusters. What is distinctive about this schema is its geographical analysis and that leisure is integrated into a consumption-driven framework (Reardon, 1995).

Other consumption styles have been developed in marketing circles to provide investment and planning information for media directors, advertisers, and retailers. Most are available only by subscription and involve complex methodologies and budgets far in excess of anything available to academic research. Some of the dimensions that they highlight are:

- Shopping itself is a major leisure activity. This is true not only for the affluent, but also for the middle mass who frequent discount retailers, shopping "clubs," and specialty stores to fill their nonwork time. Consumption is leisure in the sense of chosen activity.
- The media are central to the whole marketing enterprise as all and especially television portray consuming lifestyles that emphasize leisure in various forms. The images of the "good life" stress both material possessions and purchased experiences with closed environments. Television, the dominant time consumer, is combined with market participation as a leisure lifestyle promoted by investment coalitions that now recognize leisure as a major market segment.
- Some of the experiences promoted are social and in special environments. Most, however, contribute to the evident "privatization" of leisure with electronic entertainment in the home, travel in the private automobile, and focus on the immediate household in ways tied to the life course.
- Small participation bases may be quite adequate for the formation of business enterprises that respond to and create markets. Scuba diving, heliskiing, and surfing may engage less than one half of one percent of the adult population, but a well-located business can be quite successful.

There are dangers to this approach, however. The major one is that of "totalizing" typologies based on selected elements. For example, many consumer-oriented typologies omit entirely the social dimension central to considerable leisure. For the most part, we still value most highly those things we do with other persons whom we enjoy and who are important to us. Total focus on consumption is only one possible approach to leisure styles. Further, totalizing claims are usually based on sales figures rather than inclusive household studies. Any time a study is designed to achieve a certain client-oriented outcome, it will be biased toward particular uses.

Further, there are other style factors that have been given relatively little attention. They include gender and sexual orientation, situated ethnicity, the passages or transitions of the life course, and symbolic meanings:

- Gender is, of course, now receiving more adequate attention. For the study of leisure styles, the most significant change is the emergence of women scholars who are designing research based on women's life patterns and listening to women's voices (see Henderson and Bialeschki, chapter 11, and Shaw, chapter 16 in this volume). The same advance is beginning to develop in relation to sexual orientation. Such issues as the meanings of "social interaction" as leisure will be reformulated by such research. Further, the dimension of differential power and discrimination on an "ordinary life" level will be opened to study and interpretation.

- Ethnicity has been studied primarily in terms of labels that are increasingly meaningless in a more and more diverse society. The complexities of race and ethnicity have been reduced to arbitrary census designations and categories. Again, the meanings of ethnic identification in day-to-day ordinary life situations are only beginning to be explored. Ethnographic studies go far beyond activity participation surveys in understanding the multiple dimensions of lifestyle.

- The life course is dynamic and varied. It is now clear that at any given time, about as many persons are experiencing some significant change or transition in at least one domain of life as are firmly in an identifiable period. A more dynamic framework of the life course is going to be necessary to find how leisure is part of change as well as of stability, of challenge and threat as well as security. Further, it is now clear that the life course is one framework for identifying periods of time scarcity as well as those of relative abundance.

- Finally, we know very little about the symbolic meanings of leisure. One line of promising research focuses on the body as a sign of identity, sexuality, acceptability, and even competence as well as style (Irigaray, 1993). Other symbolic meanings need to be brought to the fore in any really comprehensive studies of leisure styles and behaviors. There are many sources of symbolic metaphors that may illuminate various aspects of the multidimensional phenomenon of leisure from feminist to Marxist and cultural studies to postmodernist (Rojek, 1995).

Sources of Leisure Styles

What do we actually know about leisure styles? Is there any coherent and comprehensive picture? One current cliché is that "it's a multivariate world out there." That is surely the case with leisure. Viewed simply from a methodological perspective, narrowing leisure explanation to a few variables that fit neatly into a research method, any method, is deceptive. Truncated designs, no matter how sophisticated the statistical programs

employed or how accepted the instrumentation, cannot encompass the variegated reality of leisure.

The limitations in the number of variables that can be included in a single analysis is matched by the sketchiness of most measures. For example, an estimate of household income is used to represent all the complexities of a household budget. Ranked occupational status is said to index the full history of employment and its meanings. Marital status and family life cycle are purported to measure all the variations of family responsibilities and investments for both mother and father. And one or a few scaled items summarize all that makes up satisfaction with the complex dimensions and domains of life. Further, one-time measures are assumed to give an adequate picture of the process of life, with all its transitions and traumas.

It's not just a matter of a somewhat more inclusive methodology or an improved method of analysis. Rather, every research method only touches on the phenomenon, gives a biased picture, and leaves out more than can be included. That is why we always need "triangulation," not only of measures, but also of designs and strategies. Good research design can never forego skepticism and self-criticism.

Research, however, is only the beginning. All this stylistic construction through the life course takes place in the midst of continual social change. Most national societies are still developing new levels of participation in the world economic and cultural systems. More developed societies are undergoing the demographic changes of aging with the 1950s boom cohort moving into midlife. Gender roles are changing with entry into the paid labor force. Cultural diversity reflects both domestic empowerment and international migration. Social stratification takes on new economic configurations. And economic and temporal resources for leisure, especially that which is consumption-based, are deeply differentiated both within and across societies despite the worldwide diffusion of mass culture. The social context of leisure is in constant flux.

An even more fundamental question is that of leisure as a phenomenon. As already suggested, leisure is multidimensional. It is existential in being developmental, processual, and individual. It is social in being historical, cultural, and contextual. As a consequence, when we attempt to account for leisure behaviors and styles, we select perspectives that focus on some elements to the exclusion of others. Our research-based explanations are always incomplete.

What, then, are the sources of leisure styles and behaviors?

First, we recognize that we are dealing with *how* as well as *what,* with *why* as well as *where* and *when*.

Second, leisure is a phenomenon of the actor. It is action in the sense of being intentioned as well as responsive, directed as well as determined by opportunities and resources. As each individual is always in the process of becoming, the directions of development, as well as the self-images, self-definitions, and social identities of the present, are part of leisure decisions and meanings. There is always a tension between being and becoming, between what we perceive ourselves to be and what we seek to become. In this sense, leisure is action, not in the simple sense of just doing an activity but in the fuller sense of expressing what we are and aiming toward what we might become. The state of consciousness of the immediate experience is central to the meaning that reaches back into the past of personal history and forward into the future of becoming.

Third, leisure is a social phenomenon. The forms and interpretations of leisure are given in a historical context. They have developed in ways that are specific to a culture and its traditions. They are tied to the ecology and the economy, to the polity and religion, to learning in the school and the home. Not only what is done, but also how and why, are thoroughly ethnic, learned in the realities of a cultural time and place. Further, leisure is social not only in involving other people, but also in having orientations that are connected with the values, traditions, symbol systems, and all that are part of our learned evaluative and conceptualizing processes. Leisure is never separate from the social institutions of the social system and the roles that actors play in them. Therefore, those social ties influence the behaviors and styles of leisure. One recent approach to analyzing these ties is through the social networks that combine a specificity of relationships with a structure of webbed roles (Stokowski, 1994).

Life, then, is both complex and connected, both diverse and integrated. Leisure is not different from other identified domains of life in this way. Leisure style is only one dimension of lifestyle. It is one element of ordinary life, distinguished by its focus on the experience itself as well as by relative openness and lack of prespecification of outcome. It is a life space that offers particular opportunity for existential action. However, it is also a dimension that may be found in the work, family, school, church, and other institutional contexts of life. It is a social construct, different but not separate. It may be alienating as well as bonding, coerced in its roles as well as free in its future orientations. It is dialectical, not a fixed set of structured variables (Kelly, 1981). As a consequence, we cannot list any set of factors that determine leisure styles and behaviors, select indices of those factors, and run them through any program of analysis to give the final and complete word of explanation.

Such a perspective is both sobering and challenging. Although there may be no "magic bullet" in our computers that will do it all, there is the challenge of complexity. There is always the task of bringing together dimensions of leisure in different ways, both complicated and parsimonious, that give a new and useful view of the phenomena. Further, the target is always moving. Leisure is constantly changing in a sociocultural context that is in flux. No final word is possible, since we are always dealing with what was in the past rather than the truly contemporaneous.

Such a view leads to limitless agendas for research and theory building. Nothing is settled with finality. Rather, any approach that even begins to be adequate for delimited questions takes something like the following form: first, the theory, model, or metaphor (Kelly, 1987a) on which the attempt at explanation is based is identified and relevant limitations specified (the "standpoint" of the approach is specified [Harding, 1991]); second, previous research and explanation are critically reviewed, not as a listing of references, but as an analysis of what is known and how that knowledge is limited or contains contradictions; third, a research approach is selected and presented in ways that are as clear about what is not done as about what is done; fourth, research is grounded in the specifics of ordinary life rather than abstracted into preconceived models; fifth, the results are offered as a contribution to explanation, rather than as discrete findings with some derivative "implications"; sixth, the building, deconstruction, or revision of the theory metaphor adopted is attempted in the light of what has been discovered.

The field, then, is not ruled by methods or by conventions. It is not closed off to innovation by what is taught or accepted at any level. Accounting for leisure behaviors and styles, then, is not just doing more and doing it better. Finality does not wait for that super measure or supreme statistical package, the single model that will answer all questions in some globalizing metaphor. Rather, real contributions to understanding begin with the complex actions and meanings that are labeled leisure and recreation. Leisure and research are both dialectical, both multidimensional, and both without final resolution. And isn't that what makes the enterprise of leisure research and theory intriguing?

References

Bacon, W. (1975). Leisure and the alienated worker. *Journal of Leisure Research, 7,* 179–190.

Bellah, R. N., Madsen, R., Sullivan, W., Swidler, A., & Tipton, S. (1985). *Habits of the heart.* Berkeley, CA: University of California Press.

Berger, P., & Luckman, T. (1966). *The social construction of reality.* New York, NY: Penguin Books.

Burch, W. R., Jr. (1965). The play world of camping: Research into the social meaning of outdoor recreation. *American Journal of Sociology, 69,* 604–612.

Cheek, N., & Burch, W. R., Jr. (1976). *The social organization of leisure in human society.* New York, NY: Harper and Row.

Clarke, J., & Critcher, C. (1985). *The devil makes work.* Champaign, IL: University of Illinois Press.

Csikszentmihalyi, M. 1981. Leisure and socialization. *Social Forces, 60,* 332–340.

Field, D. R., & O'Leary, J. T. (1973). Social groups as a basis for assessing participation in selected water activities. *Journal of Leisure Research, 5,* 16–25.

Freysinger, V. J. (1995). The dialectics of leisure and development for men and women in midlife: An interpretive study. *Journal of Leisure Research, 27,* 61–84.

Haggard, L. M., & Williams, D. R. (1992). Identify affirmation through leisure activities: Leisure symbols of the self. *Journal of Leisure Research, 24,* 1–18.

Harding, S. (1991). *Whose science? Whose knowledge? Thinking from women's lives.* Ithaca, NY: Cornell University Press.

Hollingshead, A. (1949). *Elmtown's youth.* New York, NY: John Wiley & Sons, Inc.

Irigaray, L. (1993). *Je, tu, nous: Toward a culture of difference* (A. Martin, Trans.) London, UK: Routledge.

Kelly, J. R. (1980). Outdoor recreation participation: A comparative analysis. *Leisure Sciences, 3,* 129–154.

Kelly, J. R. (1981). Leisure interaction and the social dialectic. *Social Forces, 60,* 304–322.

Kelly, J. R. (1983a). *Leisure identities and interactions.* London, UK: George Allen and Unwin.

Kelly, J. R. (1983b). Leisure styles: A hidden core. *Leisure Sciences, 5,* 321–338.

Kelly, J. R. (1986). Commodification of leisure: Trend or tract? *Loisir et Société/Society and Leisure, 10,* 455–476.

Kelly, J. R. (1987a). *Freedom to be: A new sociology of leisure.* New York, NY: Macmillan Publishing.

Kelly, J. R. (1987b). *Recreation trends toward the year 2000.* Champaign, IL: Sagamore Publishing.

Kelly, J. R. (1987c). *Peoria winter: Styles and resources in later life.* Boston, MA: Lexington Books, The Free Press.

Kelly, J. R. (1987d). Parks and people: What do we know? In R. Hermann & T. Bostedt-Craig (Eds.), *Proceedings of the Conference on Science in the National Parks, 1986.* Ft. Collins, CO: U.S. National Park Service and the George Wright Society.

Kelly, J. R. (1996). *Leisure* (3rd ed.). Boston, MA: Allyn & Bacon.

Kelly, J. R., & Kelly, J. R. (1994). Multiple dimensions of meaning in the domains of work, family, and leisure. *Journal of Leisure Research* 250–274.

Kohn, M. L. (1990). Unresolved issues in the relationship between work and personality. In K. Erikson & S. Vallas (Eds.), *The nature of work.* New Haven, CT: Yale University Press.

Kreps, J. (1968). *Lifetime allocation of work and leisure* (Report No. 22). Washington, DC: U.S. Department of Health, Education, and Welfare.

Linder, S. (1970). *The harried leisure class.* New York, NY: Columbia University Press.

Lundberg, G., Komarovsky, M., & McInerny, M. (1934). *Leisure: A suburban study.* New York, NY: Columbia University Press.

Lynd, H., & Lynd, R. (1956). *Middletown.* New York, NY: Harcourt Brace Jovanovich.

Mitchell, A. (1983). *The nine American lifestyles.* New York, NY: Warner Books.

Parker, S. (1971). *The future of work and leisure.* New York, NY: Praeger.

Rapoport, R., & Rapoport, R. N. (1975). *Leisure and the family life cycle.* Boston, MA: Routledge and Kegan Paul.

Reardon, P. T. (1995). The new geography. *Chicago Tribune,* November 5.

Rojek, C. (1995). *Decentring leisure.* Thousand Oaks, CA: Sage Publications, Inc.

Schmitz-Scherzer, R., Rudinger, G., Angleitner, A., & Bierhoff-Alfermann, D. (1974). Notes on a factor analysis comparative study of the structure of leisure activities in four different samples. *Journal of Leisure Research, 6,* 77–83.

Schor, J. B. (1991). *The overworked American.* New York, NY: Basic Books.

Shamir, B. (1992). Some correlates of leisure identity salience: Three exploratory studies. *Journal of Leisure Research, 24,* 301–323.

Shaw, S. M. (1994). Gender, leisure, and constraint: Towards a framework for the analysis of women's leisure. *Journal of Leisure Research, 26,* 8–22.

Smigel, E. (1963). *Work and leisure.* New Haven, CT: College and University Books.

Snepenger, D., & Crompton, J. (1985). A review of leisure participation models based on the level of discourse taxonomy. *Leisure Sciences, 7,* 443–466.

Stebbins, R. (1979). *Amateurs: On the margin between work and leisure.* Beverly Hills, CA: Sage Publications, Inc.

Stokowski, P. A. (1994). *Leisure in society: A network structural perspective.* New York, NY: Mansell Publications.

Torbert, W. (1973). *Being for the most part puppets.* Cambridge, UK: Schenkman Books.

Wearing, B. (1990). Beyond the ideology of motherhood: Leisure as resistance. *Australian and New Zealand Journal of Sociology, 26,* 36–58.

Wilensky, H. (1963). The uneven distribution of leisure: The impact of economic growth on free time. In E. Smigel (Ed.), *Work and leisure.* New Haven, CT: College and University Press.

Zuzanek, J., & Mannell, R. (1983). Work-leisure relationships from a sociological and social-psychological perspective. *Leisure Studies, 2,* 327–344.

Work and Leisure

Roger C. Mannell
University of Waterloo

Donald G. Reid
University of Guelph

Introduction

People in many jurisdictions are being confronted with major social transformations fuelled by the globalization of the economy and radical technological developments that are changing the way they work and the role of leisure in their lives. There are many different views about how changes in modern technology and the emergence of a global economy are affecting the types of work people do, where they work, when they work, how much they work, and even if they will be able to work at all. Additionally, the lifestyles and leisure styles people lead are caught up in these forces of change, and like views of work, there are competing perspectives about how economic and technological changes are shaping people's nonwork lives and the relationships between work and leisure (see Best, 1988; Reid, 1995; Schor, 1991). This relationship continues to raise highly significant questions both for individuals as they attempt to create meaningful lives

for themselves and for the societies in which they live that are faced with developing policies and providing institutional support in this time of change.

In this chapter, the nature of work and leisure relationships is examined as an aspect of individual behavior and lifestyle arrangements and within the broader context of social and economic change. We start by examining different views of how work and leisure are related in the daily life and experience of the individual. At this social-psychological level of analysis, competing hypotheses have been proposed concerning the influence of people's job-related behavior on their leisure behavior and experience. The assumption is that certain work and leisure relationships are more prevalent. These approaches have typically been based on the assumption that what people do in their leisure is driven by the nature of their work and that to understand leisure we must understand work. As we will see, this assumption of the primacy of work has also influenced views of what life and lifestyles in the future will be like.

As an alternative to this work-primacy model, some researchers have proposed that the ways in which work and leisure are related in people's lives differ among individuals as a function of their social circumstances and even their personalities. There is also growing research interest in how a person's leisure may actually influence his or her work behavior and experience. The discussion of the psychological dynamics of work-leisure relationships will conclude with a look at research on the potential of leisure activity to act as a substitute for lost work roles and the maintenance of psychological well-being and health. In the final section of the chapter, we move into the speculative realm of work and leisure issues. The focus shifts from the individual, and work and leisure are considered in the broader context of social and economic change. Alternative views of the future of work and leisure and their relatedness are examined, and finally, the question of creating "desirable" futures for leisure and work is explored.

Relationships Between Work and Leisure in the Lives of Individuals

Research aimed at understanding how work and leisure are related in people's lives has a long tradition among social scientists and has taken a number of different forms during the past century. The earliest research involved time-budget studies examining changing allocations of time between work and leisure. Other approaches to understanding the relationship between work and leisure have focussed on work reduction and the implicit trade-off people are willing to make between income and more free time. Organizational and planning approaches have been concerned with the impact of alternative work schedules on leisure participation, and a number of studies have focussed on leisure participation as a function of the individual's socio-occupational status. Social historical analyses have mapped shifts in central life interest from work to leisure, and a number of empirical studies have attempted to measure changes in work ethic orientations or attitudes (see Zuzanek and Mannell, 1983, for a discussion of these approaches). Several of these themes continue to be of interest to researchers today. For example, researchers have shown renewed interest in how people allocate their time between work and leisure, particularly as a consequence of the emergence of dual-earner families and concerns about gender equity.

During the past few decades there has also been some interest shown by researchers in how people's actual behavior and experience on the job may be related to their behavior and experience off the job during free time. Unfortunately, the research has been somewhat sporadic and the findings have not been cumulative. Several good ideas have been in circulation and some quite good studies have been reported, but few systematic research programs have appeared, resulting in findings that do little more than scratch the surface of these ideas about work-leisure relationships. Also, the number of researchers involved has been relatively small compared to the number of ideas to explore. However, this research gives us some indication of how work and leisure coexist and influence each other in the lives of individuals, and provides hints for understanding lifestyle changes that may come about due to changes in the nature of work and the workplace. It is this research to which we now turn.

The Impact of Behavior and Experience During Paid Work on Leisure Behavior and Experience

Researchers have typically treated leisure behavior as the dependent variable, that is, as the area of life that is the least constrained, and consequently, most susceptible to the demands of not only work but also other domains of life, such as school, home, and family. In other words, researchers often assume that leisure is more likely to be influenced by experiences in other areas of life than it is to influence what goes on in those other domains. For example, the social roles of parent and worker, particularly "working mother," have been found to substantially reduce the amount of leisure time available to those women who work and have young children (Zuzanek and Smale, 1992). In these types of studies, it has been found that the demands and obligations in the work and family domains combine to strongly influence and, in many cases, constrain behavior in the leisure domain (Horna, 1989).

Consistent with this view, the *spillover* and *compensation* theories have dominated thinking regarding the nature of work's influence on leisure (Kando and Summers, 1971; Wilensky, 1960). These theories suggest that the nature of people's work directly influences their choice of leisure activities. Based on the former theory, workers are thought to participate in leisure activities that have characteristics similar to their job-related activities and tasks. For example, computer skills learned on the job may help a person take advantage of the Internet for the leisure-related purposes of socializing or pursuing hobbies. Conversely, compensation theory suggests that deprivations experienced at work are made up for during leisure, or that people participate in activities which satisfy needs that they cannot satisfy at work. A job that allows little opportunity for risk taking and challenge may result in a person choosing to be highly involved in outdoor adventure activities during leisure. A third approach, *neutrality*, suggests people compartmentalize their experiences of work and leisure, and that work and leisure are essentially unrelated (Parker, 1971).

Research guided by the compensation and spillover theories, where leisure is typically seen to be dominated by the "long arm of the job" (Meissner, 1971), has primarily focussed on how people's work influences their leisure activity preferences (e.g., Bacon, 1975) and satisfaction (e.g., Chambers, 1986). For example, in an early and frequently cited study, Meissner (1971) found that a lack of opportunity for social interaction on the job "spills over" and is associated with less time spent in sociable leisure activities. However, research testing these theories has provided findings that are generally contradictory and inconclusive, though there has been more support for spillover than compensation. The lack of theoretically grounded ideas about what aspects of work and leisure behavior are related has been a significant problem for researchers. As well, these theories have not been particularly useful in explaining how people organize work and leisure in their lives, how these patterns develop, or the impact of work-leisure relationships on individual functioning and satisfaction (Chick and Hood, 1996; Kabanoff, 1980; Mannell and Iso-Ahola, 1985).

Individual Differences in the Way Work and Leisure Are Related in People's Lives

These limitations have led to several efforts at reconceptualization. Some authors have identified the need to clarify the behavioral and experiential components of work and leisure that are related and to improve the precision of measurement of these (e.g., Chick and Hood, 1996; Kabanoff, 1980). Others have argued that the relationship between work and leisure is not static but may vary from day to day (Iso-Ahola, 1980). It has also been suggested that the ways in which people's work and leisure are related may differ according to social and economic conditions (Bishop and Ikeda, 1970) or as a function of their personality (Kabanoff and O'Brien, 1980).

Bishop and Ikeda (1970) found that whether leisure behavior was compensatory or a result of spillover in workers' lives varied according to their socioeconomic circumstances. More recently, Chick and Hood (1996) have proposed a "patterned socialization model" to explain work-leisure relationships. They suggest that the relationship between what people do in their work and leisure is influenced by their prior socialization into both work and leisure as well as the opportunities and constraints present in the immediate social and physical environment. These researchers found that machinists were more likely to participate in machine-based recreation activities (e.g., motorcycling, powerboating, snowmobiling) than nonmachinists and that the level of leisure satisfaction for machinists increased the more they engaged in this type of recreation. Chick and Hood interpreted their results as support for the idea that individuals are socialized to have an interest in machines generally, and that this socialization is expressed in both their work and leisure.

The findings of other researchers have suggested that the ways in which work and leisure are related in people's lives may be a stable individual difference. Mannell and Reid (1992) found that a group of working adults differed substantially according to the extent to which they met each of 16 psychological needs in their work and leisure. It was possible to classify the respondents into a number of groups on the basis of whether their needs were met predominantly in work, in leisure, or in a balanced way in both work and leisure. Particular work-leisure relationships were also found to be more prevalent among individuals with specific educational and occupational experiences, suggesting that the work-leisure orientation of the individual is, at least in part, a result of a variety of socialization influences and his or her current life circumstances.

Kabanoff and O'Brien (1980) proposed that the personality trait "locus of control" would affect whether an individual's leisure was a result of compensation or spillover in response to a low-quality working environment. There was some limited evidence that "internals," who believed they had a fair amount of control over the events in their lives, were more likely to actively compensate in their leisure, and that "externals," who believed they had little control, were more likely to show spillover.

In a study of Israeli female elementary school teachers (Meir and Melamed, 1986), and engineers, physicians, and lawyers (Melamed, Meir and Samson, 1995), researchers looked at the degree of correspondence between the workers' personality-based needs and the opportunities available to satisfy these needs in both their work and their leisure. They found that the opportunity to meet important needs in both work and leisure contributed to job and life satisfaction. When participants were unable to meet their needs at work, engaging in leisure that was congruent with their needs appeared to *compensate* these unmet needs and contribute to job and life satisfaction. The findings suggest that it may be fruitful to explore these individual differences in work and leisure relationships as an important integrative element of lifestyle orientation and satisfaction.

These types of findings suggest that people do differ according to the ways in which work and leisure are related and organized in their lives. There does not seem to be one dominant relationship between work and leisure, but rather a variety of possibilities that differ depending on immediate social and economic circumstances, and important individual differences in needs, attitudes, and personality that are likely the result of socialization influences.

Leisure's Impact on Work

Little research has been reported on the influence of leisure on work. As noted earlier, since leisure is freely chosen, it is often viewed as being at the mercy of other more constrained—and what some observers feel are more important—domains of life. Work rather than leisure is often viewed as a central life interest and critical for self-development and well-being (see Stebbins, chapter 5 in this volume). However, some theories and research have emerged that entertain the idea that people's leisure choices and involvements can influence their work behavior and experience. Early classical theories of play and recreation suggested that leisure is an important element in determining work behavior and satisfaction. The recreation and relaxation theories of play were based on the belief that most work is boring and monotonous and that engagement in play and sports has restorative qualities (see Ellis, 1973). Play and leisure, in this respect, were seen to enhance the quality of work by revitalizing people, so that they would be able to return to the job to work hard day after day.

Ideas like these provided the rationale for work organizations to support recreation programs for employees. In partial response to the demands of the labor movement and concern about poor working conditions for employees, though in large part to encourage the employee to work harder, work organizations began to provide leisure activities to promote employee loyalty, fellowship, and physical and intellectual development. The emerging recognition that employee health and well-being are important for company suc-cess led to the beginning of the wellness movement in the 1970s, with the implementation of leisure and wellness programs to help deal with employee psychological and physical health on the job (Ellis and Richardson, 1991).

Though research into the effectiveness of organizational recreation programs is lacking and generally poorly designed (Ellis and Richardson, 1991), research on the factors affecting job satisfaction provides some evidence that what people do in their leisure can influence work. Job satisfaction research has primarily concentrated on the influence of job-related variables and the influence of job-related factors such as working conditions, pay and promotions, and adequacy of workplace resources (Steers and Porter, 1991). Little attention has been paid to leisure variables, though there have been suggestions that workers' involvement in a variety of activities external to the job can influence satisfaction with paid work (e.g., Near, Rice and Hunt, 1978); leisure appears to be one such nonwork variable.

For example, the more satisfied university staff workers were with the amount of leisure time they had available, the less likely they were to leave their jobs and search for another one (Lounsbury, Gordon, Bergermaier and Francesco, 1982). Kirchmeyer (1993) studied experienced managers and assessed their perceptions of the impact of their nonwork involvements on their work. Both the men and women in her study perceived nonwork involvements, including what they did during their leisure, as supporting and enhancing the quality of their work experiences. Hildebrand and Mannell (1996) found that school teachers perceived their leisure contributed to their job satisfaction by providing for relaxation, relieving stress, providing a positive frame of mind, maintaining self-esteem, and influencing teaching ideas. They also found that a greater frequency of participation in leisure activities by the teachers was associated with higher levels of need satisfaction in leisure, and that these higher levels of leisure satisfaction contributed to higher levels of job satisfaction.

Surprisingly, one type of leisure influence on satisfaction with work that has been neglected is that of vacations. Generally, vacations are viewed as a time for such positive outcomes as escape, tension release, personal improvements, and an expanded opportunity to engage in satisfying activities which should increase life satisfaction and have carry-over effects into the job setting (Klausner, 1968; Rubenstein, 1980). Klausner (1968) found that 25% of the steel workers he studied felt that their "work efficiency" had increased and 16% felt that their jobs were "more interesting" after their vacations.

In a study that directly examined the impact of taking a vacation on job satisfaction, Lounsbury and Hoopes (1986) measured job satisfaction one week before and one week after a vacation. The influence of taking the vacation on job satisfaction differed depending on how satisfying the vacation was judged to be by the individual worker. For those workers who experienced their vacations as highly satisfying, their level of job satisfaction was higher after their vacations than before. Job satisfaction actually decreased for those workers who experienced their vacations as less satisfactory.

It has also been suggested that leisure involvements can be a form of resistance against role constraints that may lead to changes in other areas of life including work. This idea of leisure as resistance has been applied primarily to understanding the role that leisure can play in helping women resist and challenge gender stereotypes that limit opportunities (Freysinger and Flannery, 1992). For example, participation by women in certain types of physical recreation (Bialeschki, 1990) and highly competitive sports (Griffiths, 1988) challenges, and may lead to changes in, dominant views in society about what women can and should do. The phenomenon of leisure as resistance is based on the idea that leisure is a domain of life where people are relatively free to step out of constraining social roles and define and express who they are. However, the effects of leisure on other areas of life, including work, can also be negative. For example, leisure involvements can constrain women's and men's behavior in a variety of life domains if they reinforce traditional views of "femininity" and "masculinity" (Shaw, 1994).

There are likely other ways in which leisure can influence work that have yet to be explored. Some people likely make choices about the type and location of the work they will engage in to accommodate leisure needs. For example, a person may choose to work at a ski resort so as to have access to the slopes; change his or her workweek schedules (e.g., flex time) so as to regularly have long weekends; and intentionally take part-time employment in order to have more time to pursue certain interests in his or her leisure.

Leisure as a Replacement for Work

Another area of research of relevance to work and leisure relationships that has implications for how people respond to changes in the availability of work is the role of leisure in coping with work role loss or work reduction. The loss of a job, whether through retire-

ment or unemployment, can involve the same types of problems—loss of income, social isolation (e.g., loss of contact with friends and coworkers), and psychological losses (e.g., feelings of no longer contributing to society, loss of opportunity to develop and exercise skills and abilities). Of course, loss of a job and the resulting unemployment before the age of retirement is likely to be a more traumatic change due to the lack of a "retirement" income, lack of opportunity to plan for the change, and the social stigma associated with it. Retirement is socially accepted today and is usually seen as a reward after many years of work. Many factors have been proposed to affect successful coping with both retirement and unemployment. Leisure is one of these factors and its impact on psychological well-being when people are dealing with job loss is another important aspect of work and leisure relationships.

The study of reactions to retirement has generated a large body of literature (see Calasanti, 1993; McPherson, 1991). Much of this work has been based on the assumption that being retired is a traumatic event, and that many elderly people, particularly men, do not adjust well. The onset of retirement represents a major transition point that has the potential to alter lifestyle. However, evidence has accumulated that a large portion of retired men have few problems in adjusting to retirement, though there is still substantial variation in the degree of adjustment and the subsequent quality of life experienced (McPherson, 1991). Research has shown that those people who use their free time to continue to participate in similar types of social activity at about the same level as they did prior to retirement, and who have positive attitudes toward leisure, adjust better and are more satisfied with their lives (see Mannell and Dupuis, 1996). However, it has been argued that some types of activity and involvement are better than others. Stebbins (1992; see also chapter 5 in this volume) suggests that serious leisure (pursuits that require the development of skills and a long-term careerlike commitment) can be important to the quality of older retired adults' lives by providing worklike activity, offering a link with friends and relatives, expanding one's social circle, fostering responsibility, and creating the opportunity to feel needed by other people.

A study reported by Chiriboga and Pierce (1993) demonstrates how leisure behavior may play a role in successful retirement and psychological well-being. These researchers examined older adults who were part of a larger longitudinal life span study and who had retired at least five years before the end of the study. The respondents' participation in solitary activities, sports, social activities, and contemplative activities was measured early in retirement and about five years later. Also, measures of the stressful life events they had experienced during the previous year, psychological distress symptoms, happiness, and self-reported health were collected.

Participation levels in the various leisure activities were not related to self-concept at or soon after retirement. After five years, however, the situation had changed. Activity involvement was significantly related to self-concept. Specifically, those retired individuals who engaged more frequently in outdoor and social activities, and participated less in solitary and passive activities, felt more positive about themselves.

Recently there has been increased attention given to the role that leisure can play in helping people contend with unplanned and unwanted job loss and unemployment (e.g., Pesavento Raymond and Kelly, 1991; Reid and Smit, 1986; Spigner and Havitz, 1992–1993). Several theories have been proposed to explain the significance of employment and unemployment, and why unemployment would be expected to result in threats to psychological well-being. Warr (1983) identified nine potentially negative features of unemployment—financial anxiety, less variety in life due to reduced income and more time spent at home, fewer goals or aims in life, reduced opportunity for making important decisions, reduced opportunities to exercise skills or expertise, increase in psychologically threatening activities such as unsuccessful job searches, insecurity about the future, fewer social contacts, and reduced social status.

However, in spite of all these potentially negative consequences of unemployment, not all unemployed people report being worse off in terms of psychological health. In a study of nearly a thousand unemployed men, Warr and Jackson (1984) found that, although 20% reported a decline in health, 8% actually reported an improvement. Consequently, researchers have been interested in discovering the possible moderating factors that may explain the considerable individual variation in response to unemployment. In addition to factors such as attitudes toward paid employment (the more positive, the more psychological distress experienced), age (middle-aged men compared to younger and older men experienced more stress because of greater family responsibilities), length of unemployment (decline in psychological health particularly in middle-aged men during the first few months before it stabilizes), availability of social support (more support, less stress), and local unemployment levels (higher levels, less stress because people are more likely to see their unemployment as due to economic and social conditions beyond their control rather than as a failing on their part), access to constructive and stimulating leisure activity has been found to be important.

Though leisure participation and satisfaction often decrease with unemployment (e.g., Pesavento Raymond and Kelly, 1991; Reid and Smit, 1986), the way in which unemployed people use their free time and leisure can reduce the negative effects to some extent. In a study of unemployed university graduates, Feather and Bond (1983) found that the structured and purposeful use of free time was positively correlated with self-esteem and negatively correlated with depressive symptoms. Other studies have also shown that unemployed people who cope best are engaged in purposeful activity and maintain regular contact with people outside the nuclear family (McKenna and Fryer, 1984; Warr and Jackson, 1984). Much of this "purposeful" activity is what Stebbins (1992) has called serious leisure.

Haworth and Ducker (1991) found that young unemployed adults who were engaged in more challenging and active leisure pursuits also had higher levels of psychological well-being. In a study of unemployed African-American and Hispanic youth in the United States, Pesavento Raymond and Kelly (1991) concluded that leisure appeared to help reduce the negative effects of unemployment. Kilpatrick and Trew (1985) showed that the mental health of a group of unemployed men was affected by how they spent their "free" time. They identified four groups among the people they studied. Members of the passive group spent most of their time watching television or doing nothing. They showed the poorest psychological well-being. Members of the domestic group also spent most of their time at home, but unlike the first, assisted with household tasks. They showed only slightly better mental health than the first group. Members of a third social group spent much of their time with people outside their immediate family. They exhibited superior mental health to the first two groups. Finally, members of a fourth group, the active group, not only spent more time on work-related activities like volunteering, but also engaged more frequently in active leisure pursuits outside the home. They were psychologically affected least by unemployment.

Active involvement in leisure did not completely prevent the unemployed participants in a British study reported by Roberts, Lamb, Dench, and Brodie (1989) from experiencing some health problems. However, among people who were unemployed, those who participated frequently in a wide range of leisure activities were physically healthier.

Winefield, Tiggemann, Winefield, and Goldney (1993) reported the results of a longitudinal study of employment among a group of young people in Australia. They assessed the study participants' psychological well-being by measuring their self-esteem, level of depression, moods, and leisure activity levels at various points in time—for the unemployed young adults this meant early in the period of their unemployment and approximately four years later. The main factors that were found to moderate the effects of unemployment were age, length of unemployment, financial security, social support, and leisure. With respect to leisure, unemployed people whose leisure was characterized as "doing nothing" and "watching television" developed lower self-esteem during the period of unemployment. Those who were engaged in more challenging activities, both social (e.g., sport, dancing) and solitary (e.g., hobbies, reading, cooking) had higher levels of self-esteem. These relationships became much stronger as time passed, and the nature of the individual's leisure became more critical for well-being.

Work and Leisure in the Lives of Individuals: Conclusions

What is experienced in the work domain of people's lives is clearly connected to their experience of the leisure domain. Also, though the influence of work can extend into a person's leisure, it is overly simplistic to assume that work solely determines what goes on in other areas of life, including leisure. Not only can activity and experience in each domain influence the other, but also the social circumstances of people's lives as well as their attitudes, needs, and personality influence how work and leisure are organized and experienced. These work and leisure relationships have implications for well-being and adaptation to the changing conditions of work and leisure.

It is certainly possible to picture social and economic conditions in which work activity and experience may dominate every aspect of a person's life, at least for a period of time. However, both work and leisure may contribute in a balanced way to quality of life, and under some conditions leisure may enhance work experience and even compensate for the lack of work opportunities. Of course, what people do in their work and their leisure does not occur in a social vacuum. The roles that work and leisure play and how they are related in an individual's life are heavily dependent on the social and economic conditions and opportunities that exist in society. It is to a consideration of these broader social and economic conditions that we now turn.

Work and Leisure in the Twenty-First Century: Responding to Social and Economic Changes

Issues concerning the relationship between work and leisure in people's lives have entered the public consciousness. Today people in most developed nations are bombarded from all sides with suggestions for the best way to juggle and balance the various aspects of their lives and lifestyles. Newspapers feature lifestyle sections, weekly television series spotlight different and unique ways of living, and numerous self-help books on lifestyle appear on bookstore shelves. If the number of newspaper articles and popular books written is any indication (e.g., Crosby, 1991), juggling and balancing the work and nonwork aspects of life have become a major preoccupation and challenge.

However, the ways in which people organize and experience their work and leisure are not just a matter of personal taste. Prevailing economic, political, and social conditions shape and structure what is possible and desirable. For example, social critics in the nineteenth century were concerned with the negative impact of industrial work and its associated social and economic conditions on the lifestyles and leisure styles of workers. These social issues spawned the compensatory, spillover, and neutrality work-leisure relationship hypotheses. While sociological and political analyses of work and leisure and their relationship have continued, the past few decades have witnessed a substantial amount of empirical research focussed primarily on the individual, as discussed in earlier sections of this chapter. There have been criticisms that social scientific research on these leisure-related issues has, in fact, been *too* psychological, too myopically focussed on the individual. Many of the factors that influence attitudes, needs and personality, as well as the social situations people encounter during daily life, are themselves influenced by broader social, economic, and technological forces (see Rojek, 1989; Zuzanek, 1991). To fully understand work and leisure and their relationship in people's lives, there is also a need to understand these broader sets of conditions and how they are changing.

There is no shortage of views about the nature of contemporary work and leisure, and the future of work. In fact, social commentators who spend their time peering into the future differ substantially in what they believe will happen with work, though they are typically mute on the issue of the future of leisure. There are major differences of opinion about how much leisure people actually have today, whether it is increasing or decreasing, and if it can play a positive or negative role in people's lives as the opportunities for work change (Robinson and Godbey, 1997; Schor, 1991). For many people there is a distinct possibility of a further growth in nonwork time, though it may be unevenly distributed, with some people actually working longer hours and others becoming underemployed or chronically unemployed. In developed nations, there are currently tremendous differences among people in their work and leisure lifestyle arrangements. On the one hand, unemployment and part-time work have grown at the same time that the number of people working well beyond a 40-hour week has increased (see de Jouvenel, 1993; Reid, 1995). Some of these latter individuals are doing so unwillingly, but to keep their jobs they have little choice as employers continue to downsize and streamline their operations. The pressures of work result in some people taking their "vacation" in hours and afternoons rather than as an extended period away from the office. In other words, on both a short- and long-term basis, people who are experiencing increasing pressures at work are making new choices about how, when, and if to fit leisure into their lives. Some people appear to be thriving on more work; yet, for others, work seems to be a form of addiction or workaholism, driven by problems in other areas of their lives (Killinger, 1991). On the other hand, for children, retirees, the underemployed and unemployed, leisure may account for up to two-thirds or more of their time and activity. Policy discussions have been initiated by governments, employers, and employee groups dealing with the value and feasibility of job sharing and shorter workweeks in an attempt to distribute the work that is available to more people (e.g., Advisory Group on Working Time and the Distribution of Work, 1994). Early retirement policies are also a way of distributing the available work. These policies could result in more free time and possibly more leisure for many people and, at the very least, will influence the relationship between work and leisure in people's lives.

Globalization and Technological Change: Effects on Work and Leisure

The rapid and constant change in our economic structures, fuelled in part by technological change, has been and will continue to be a preoccupation well into the new millennium. For example, the impact in Canada and North America as a whole of the recession that occurred during the early 1990s has dramatically re-shaped business, financial, educational, and government institutions (including leisure services). The economic recessions in the 1980s and 1990s followed the most lengthy period of economic expansion experienced since the Second World War. North American economies were predicted to improve following these economic slumps but they have left their mark on business and industry and, in turn, on the structure of many jobs. The more visible of these changes includes the "migration" of manufacturing jobs to areas where cheaper labor and less stringent environmental laws are found, and the "de-layering" of the middle management levels of many companies and firms.

Developments around the globe are also impacting on the nature of work and leisure. A North American free-trade zone has been developed by Canada, the United States, and Mexico. The European Union has become the largest single-market system in the world. Despite serious fiscal problems, the Japanese-led Pacific Rim countries are continuing to experience rapid economic growth, and many previous communist Eastern European countries, as well as China, are experimenting with some form of free-market system.

These worldwide changes occurring in economic affairs with their concomitant pressures on our social and political institutions raise many fundamental questions. Are well-established monetary policies still workable? What social and economic theories still apply? Who is to benefit from the changes brought about by free trade and the globalization of the economy? Is the apparent turmoil in economic affairs simply cyclical and of short duration (cf., Daly and Cobb, 1989). Are we facing major structural changes in our economic arrangements that will eventually result in radical changes to the way we work, the use of our nonwork time and the role of leisure in our lives (Reid, 1995)?

Alternative Views of the Future

There is no shortage of visions or predictions of the future. In fact, "futures studies" has become a field in its own right (Coyle, 1997). There is a bewildering array of "futures" that have been proposed during the past few decades which have different implications for work and leisure lifestyle arrangements. Government publications are regularly released projecting trends in the economy, work, and jobs of the future. There has been a relentless flood of monographs and books pouring forth from private individuals and organizations that have proclaimed to map the future of work. However, there are substantial difficulties for those who wish to understand work and leisure issues on the basis of these prognostications:

1. most forecasts present only one view of the future—a view that is in competition with other visions;
2. forecasts have proven inaccurate, especially those extrapolating farther into the future than five to ten years;
3. forecasters typically examine only the work domain of life in the future and ignore potential changes in total lifestyle and, in particular, the nonwork and leisure domain; and
4. there is also an underlying assumption of "work determinism," the belief that changes in work will drive changes in the nonwork and leisure aspects of life; little thought or credence is given to the possibility that noneconomic, nonwork and leisure values will and "should" influence future directions.

Many of the predicted futures that have originated since the Second World War can be classified according to the extent to which work will be available and central to people's lives, and how benign the new work and nonwork arrangements will be. Some scenarios describe a future where work is not required, the results of highly automated industrial productivity are evenly distributed, and unlimited leisure is available for everyone. For example, predictions made during the 1950s were based on the belief that technology would reduce the length of the workweek to less than 20 hours by 1990, and yet an increased standard of living would result. In this case, the relationship between work and leisure would not be an issue, because essentially there would be little or no paid work.

Pessimists see this "little or no-work" future and its leisure as potentially highly materialistic, consumer-oriented, and aimless, making human society inhospitable to human development and fulfillment. Optimists, on the other hand, see this "little or no-work" future as an ideal setting for the continued evolution of society, where individual development and control are optimized. This "postmaterialistic society" would stress human and community development, based in leisure and citizenship, rather than economic growth with its emphasis on work: "Instead of individuals serving the economic imperative, the economic system is viewed as a support to individual and social development" (Reid, 1995, p. 52).

Other futures have been forecast which describe developed societies that provide the opportunity for neither mindless consumerism and diversion nor personal development through leisure. These futures are the visions of forecasters who predict economic and social deterioration with rising unemployment and an ever-increasing division between the rich and poor. The most pessimistic see ecological and economic collapse in the future.

Numerous competing shorter term future scenarios have also been suggested during the past several decades (Slaughter, 1993). These views tend to focus primarily on the future of work and say very little about leisure or lifestyle changes in general. While there are different ways to classify these visions, three major short-term futurist themes can be identified. We will label these the Dramatic Change—High-Tech Optimistic Perspective; the Gradual Change—Cautiously Optimistic Perspective; and the Negative Change—Pessimistic Perspective.

Dramatic Change— The High-Tech Optimistic View

This view of the future sees a workplace changing rapidly and full of high technology and wonderful new occupations (e.g., Cetron, 1983; Cetron and Davies, 1991; Cornish, 1985; Naisbitt, 1994; Naisbitt and Aburdene, 1988; Toffler, 1970). It is a fast-paced future with an advanced technology, a computer-driven work force, and a highly automated workplace. Naisbitt, for example, has argued that we are shifting from the Postindustrial Age to an Information Age. A period of rapid job change and new occupations is forecast. Robots and computer-directed automation in the workplace, particularly manufacturing, are expected to replace workers who currently do boring, repetitive, dirty, and dangerous work. Jobs in this sector will require highly skilled generalists who can troubleshoot and solve problems. Outmoded jobs will be compensated for by new jobs in high-technology industries, such as robotics, and an expanding service industry. Jobs based on computer technology, ranging from video-dating services to genetic-engineering firms, are expected to replace traditional manufacturing and resource jobs. Predictions suggest that in the near future a significant majority of people in the work force will be information workers involved in the operation, management, and design of information systems, or in teaching and doing research associated with information systems. The new jobs will be well-paid, exciting, and challenging.

The implications seem to be that this will be a relatively high employment future where most jobs are meaningful and rewarding, and the primary focus of the individual's creativity and effort. This economy of the future is seen to benefit everyone except those who do not want to work. Workfare will replace welfare, which will compel everyone to work if they are to be supported by social assistance. Leisure's function would seem to be diversion and entertainment, and perhaps periodic escape and recuperation from the satisfying rigors of work. This future vision embraces globalization and free enterprise, and leisure is the time which is left over after the more serious matters of life are attended to. Leisure is of only secondary importance, except when it contributes to the economy. For example, tourism is more important than community recreation to commerce because tourists increase the wealth of an area through their spending on goods and services. In other words, leisure itself is turned into an industry.

Gradual Change— The Cautiously Optimistic View

This view is based largely on publications and research from government agencies which monitor job employment trends (e.g., Economic Council of Canada, Statistics Canada, U.S. Bureau of Labor Statistics), as well as the writings of analysts such as Goldstein and Fraser (1985) and Levitan (1987). This type of future perspective is based on a more cautious and critical analysis of postindustrial trends (Slaughter, 1993). The future is visualized as not dramatically different from the present, and jobs—rather than disappearing because they quickly become outmoded—will change and adapt gradually. The majority of new jobs will be in the service industry and not require extensive training. There will be fast growth in the high-technology areas but few new jobs in these areas. Changes in the workplace will still leave occupations looking a great deal like they are at present. The need for advanced computer skills is highly overstated and the availability of clerical work is unlikely to decrease. Finally, changes in the workplace will still leave openings for people from all educational backgrounds as long as they have good basic skills. A workless society where machines have supplanted human workers is not envisioned. However, automation is likely to lead to increased benefits, more time off, and a marginally higher standard of living. Some see an expansion of individual choice in work, the elimination of unpleasant or undesirable work, and the growth of concern for developing work environments to better help workers fulfill self-development needs. In this future, leisure would likely not change much either. As in the first scenario, leisure

would likely continue to become more commercialized and consumption-oriented. In the service of work, leisure would still function as rest, recuperation and a form of periodic escape. However, leisure is more likely to be valued as a legitimate source of personal development and meaningful involvement, and seen as an important contributor to the quality of life.

Negative Change— The Pessimistic View

The pessimistic view of the future of work emphasizes the decline of well-paying jobs, the downscaling of the skills required to do jobs, and high unemployment rates (e.g., Bluestone and Harrison, 1982; Lerner, 1994). Forecasters suggest that there will continue to be a shift away from manufacturing. Automation will result in a downscaling of jobs in terms of wages, full-time workers becoming part-time employees, and the level of challenge and job security decreasing. Some analysts predict that a large portion of the work force could end up working on a limited contract basis. It is expected that many companies will maintain fewer permanent employees and hire these "contingent workers" to work on specific projects as they are needed. Companies can then avoid high benefit costs and easily expand and contract their work force to meet the changing demands of the marketplace. Job opportunities for university graduates are expected to decline, particularly in the professional areas. High unemployment is expected to continue and the middle class to decrease in size with a polarization of the class structure. The future looks bleak for many workers. They can expect to be unemployed or underemployed for extended periods of time. Most of the new jobs created will be "bad jobs," that is, low-skilled, part-time, and low-paying jobs in the private service sector (Economic Council of Canada, 1990). This is a dark vision of the future for the growing number of people whose jobs are predicted to be "deskilled" or "downgraded" in a work force that will become polarized or two-tiered. Leisure itself could become highly stratified, at least in terms of the commercialized leisure goods and services available to individuals. Leisure may also grow in importance as a vehicle for developing work opportunities and skills. It may provide opportunities through volunteer work and serious leisure to develop marketable skills and experience that will appeal to employers. With high rates of unemployment, underemployment, and "poor" jobs, many individuals may have to turn to leisure to provide what meaning and satisfaction will be available in this future.

The Future of Work and Leisure: Work Determinism and an Inevitable Future

Most short- to medium-range future scenarios are based on the assumption that future lifestyle and leisure arrangements will be strongly dependent on work arrangements, that is, they are work-driven predictions. This "work-centered" perspective is strongly associated with beliefs that work is what gives meaning to human life and that meaningful leisure without work is not possible (Reid and Mannell, 1994; see also Stebbins, chapter 5, and Sylvester, chapter 2 in this volume). These futures are typically mute on what leisure will look like and its role in the quality of life. Much of the theory and research on work and leisure reviewed earlier in this chapter are based on attempts to understand how work and leisure are related in people's lives today, and there are clearly a variety of ways in which work and leisure are interconnected. The importance and relevance of this research is dependent on continuation of the opportunity for people both to work and to have choices in their leisure. Predictions that are consistent with the Dramatic Change—High-Tech Optimistic Perspective and the Gradual Change—Cautiously Optimistic Perspective futures assume a continuation of both work and leisure opportunities. However, if the nature and/or availability of either work or leisure were to change dramatically, either through some type of catastrophic economic collapse or through the application of technology and the implementation of social policies that distributed goods and services equitably, work and leisure relationships would likely become irrelevant, at least in the way they are conceptualized at present.

A vision which seems to prevail at the moment, and the one which will undoubtedly dominate for the immediate future, is the *globalized economic and corporatist system model* (Reid, 1995; Saul, 1995) which stresses effectiveness and efficiency, and which demands that people be subordinate to the economy rather than the economy functioning to serve them. Liberalized trade and economic policy gives advantage to those who control financial resources or capital, including transnational corporations which are currently setting the political and economic agenda. The organization of work, therefore, is essentially the prerogative of the employer. Consistent with the third scenario, we are already seeing more contract work, higher real unemployment rates (as opposed to officially announced rates), a large increase in the numbers of the working poor, underemployment, and continued corporate downsizing of the labor force which affects large numbers of people, particularly the young.

How likely are these work-centered futures? Futurology is a form of normative theory, that is, the setting out of what *should* or *could* happen. What is sometimes forgotten is that these "theories" are based on certain assumptions and values. There is also a sense of inevitability about these future trends, as if people and their social organizations had no choice or control over these processes. However, it can be argued that not only should people be interested in how work and leisure are related but also how they "should be" related. The future need not be seen as some predetermined set of conditions towards which humanity is steadily marching, but one which is constantly being created and re-created by the participants in the system (Reid, 1995).

As the millennium is approached, it is legitimate to ask not only what role leisure will play in this new and changing society and in the lives of individuals, but also what role *can* it play. If a structuralist-functionalist view of social processes is taken, leisure can be seen simply as a reflection of the underlying social order and the status quo (Clarke and Critcher, 1985). However, some analysts (e.g., Neulinger, 1990; Reid, 1995; Wachtel, 1989) argue that leisure can be an instrument for social action, a force in opposition to the dominant work-centered paradigm of the future, and a method of social and individual emancipation. In other words, leisure may have a role to play in helping to shape society rather than being shaped by it.

Believing that developed nations are entering a new era of postcapitalism (Drucker, 1993), it has been argued that the analysis "of the relationship between work and leisure within capitalism is, like other features of industrial society, redundant, and should gracefully bow out in favor of new analyses" (Clarke and Critcher, 1985, p. 185). It has also been argued that the economic and technologically driven social changes which are occurring demand more serious consideration by leisure planners and providers, and that this will become increasingly urgent if the full-employment rhetoric of politicians does not materialize. In fact, the "work and jobs for all" ideology does not seem to be a likely outcome. Employment for many people today is not meaningful and rewarding, and satisfactions from other spheres of life are likely to become even more important in the continuing quest for a sense of self-worth and dignity. New thinking on this issue becomes increasingly important as technology continues to replace human labor in the production process at a faster and faster rate (Gorz, 1982).

Viewed in this light, leisure could possibly act as both an agent of reform and the product of a reformation. As an agent of reform, leisure is used as a tool for personal and social development by people who take charge of their lives and communities (Reid and van Dreunen, 1996). Given the changing conditions of work, more and more people may tend to rely on leisure to become psychologically and socially engaged in their everyday lives.

There are many obstacles to changing or increasing the role of leisure in society if, in fact, that is a worthy goal for the twenty-first century. The primary impediment to continued development is that leisure is not perceived to have value beyond being a diversion or an escape from the real world. Even leisure researchers may be part of this problem as they attempt to demonstrate the benefits of leisure to work, communities and the economy (Driver, Brown and Peterson, 1991; Reid and FitzGibbon, 1991). While these efforts may provide short-term legitimation, such strategies can detract from considering leisure an alternative form of social development. It is difficult to alter fundamental perceptions, attitudes and behaviors, and the effort for legitimation may make it even more difficult (Wachtel, 1989, p. 173).

Some researchers (e.g., Burman, 1988; Jahoda, 1982) have concluded that leisure cannot replace work as the central focus of life. They view work as an inherent condition of humanity. This conclusion, however, is derived from the current political, social, and economic reality, as are many assumptions found in research on work-leisure relationships. How can one judge whether leisure can fulfill fundamental psychological needs without having lived in a social system which supports this type of lifestyle? As discussed earlier in this chapter, leisure can assist in the adjustment to changes in life circumstances, including loss of work roles. These possibilities exist even in a hostile social environment which labels the unemployed person on social assistance a social deviant.

Eric Fromm (1989) postulates that human beings have a basic fear of freedom. He argues that people do not want to take complete charge of their lives but desire this function be performed by an external organizing agent. Fromm identified the church as the historical agent at least, since the advent of the medieval period. Today, however, it is the corporation and work which gives direction to the day. Until individuals are willing to create and control daily activity, this motivation will continue to form a significant barrier to balancing leisure with work in everyday life, let alone to considering more significant departures from a work-centered society.

References

Advisory Group on Working Time and the Distribution of Work. (1994). *Report of the advisory group on working time and the distribution of work.* Ottawa, Ontario: Minister of Supply and Services Canada.

Bacon, A. W. (1975). Leisure and the alienated worker: A critical reassessment of three radical theories of work and leisure. *Journal of Leisure Research, 7,* 179–190.

Best, F. (1988). *Reducing workweeks to prevent layoffs: The economic and social impacts of unemployment insurance.* Philadelphia, PA: Temple University Press.

Bialeschki, M. D. (1990). The feminist movement and women's participation in physical recreation. *Journal of Physical Education, Recreation and Dance, 61,* 44–47.

Bishop, D. W., & Ikeda, M. (1970). Status and role factors in the leisure behavior of different occupations. *Sociology and Social Research, 54,* 190–208.

Bluestone, B., & Harrison, B. (1982). *The deindustrialization of America: Plant closings, community abandonment, and the dismantling of basic industry.* New York, NY: Basic Books.

Burman, P. (1988). *Killing time, losing ground.* Toronto, Ontario: Wall & Thompson.

Calasanti, T. M. (1993). Bringing in diversity: Toward an inclusive theory of retirement. *Journal of Aging Studies, 7,* 133–150.

Cetron, M. J. (1983). Getting ready for the jobs of the future. *The Futurist, 17,* 15–22.

Cetron, M., & Davies, O. (1991). Trends shaping the world. *The Futurist, 25,* 11–21.

Chambers, D. A. (1986). The constraints of work and domestic schedules on women's leisure. *Leisure Studies, 5,* 309–325.

Chick, G., & Hood, R. D. (1996). Working and recreating with machines: Outdoor recreation choices among machine-tool workers in western Pennsylvania. *Leisure Sciences, 18,* 333–354.

Chiriboga, D. A., & Pierce, R. C. (1993). Changing contexts of activity. In J. R. Kelly (Ed.), *Activity and aging* (pp. 42–59). Thousand Oaks, CA: Sage Publications, Inc.

Clarke, J., & Critcher, C. (1985). *The devil makes work: Leisure in capitalist Britain.* London, UK: Macmillan Publishing.

Cornish, E. (Ed.). (1985). *The computerized society: Living and working in an electronic age.* Bethesda, MD: World Future Society.

Coyle, G. (1997). The nature and value of futures studies or do futures have a future? *Futures, 29,* 77–93.

Crosby, F. J. (1991). *Juggling: The unexpected advantages of balancing career and home for women and their families.* New York, NY: The Free Press.

Daly, H. E., & Cobb, J. B. (1989). *For the common good.* Boston, MA: Beacon Press.

De Jouvenel, H. (Ed.). (1993). Working time [Special issue]. *Futures, 25,* 491–605.

Driver, B., Brown, P., & Peterson, G. L. (Eds.). (1991). *Benefits of leisure.* State College, PA: Venture Publishing, Inc.

Drucker, P. F. (1993). *Post capitalist society.* New York, NY: Harper.

Economic Council of Canada (1990). *Good jobs, bad jobs: Employment in the service economy.* Ottawa, Ontario: Canadian Government Publishing Centre.

Ellis, M. J. (1973). *Why people play.* Englewood Cliffs, NJ: Prentice-Hall.

Ellis, T., & Richardson, G. (1991). Organizational wellness. In B. L. Driver, P. J. Brown & G. L. Peterson (Eds.), *Benefits of leisure* (pp. 303–329). State College, PA: Venture Publishing, Inc.

Feather, N. T., & Bond, M. J. (1983). Time structure and purposeful activity among employed and unemployed university graduates. *Journal of Occupational Psychology, 56,* 241–254.

Freysinger, V. J., & Flannery, D. (1992). Women's leisure: Affiliation, self-determination, empowerment and resistance? *Loisir et Société/Society and Leisure, 15,* 303–322.

Fromm, E. (1989). *The fear of freedom.* London, UK: Routledge & Kegan Paul.

Goldstein, H., & Fraser, B. (1985). Computer training and the workplace: A little goes a long way. *Occupational Outlook Quarterly, 29,* 24–29.

Gorz, A., (1982). *Farewell to the working class.* Boston, MA: South End.

Griffiths, V. (1988). From playing out to dossing out: Young women and leisure. In E. Wimbush & M. Talbot (Eds.), *Relative freedoms: Women and leisure* (pp. 48–59). Milton Keynes, UK: Open University Press.

Haworth, J. T., & Ducker, J. (1991). Psychological well-being and access to categories of experience in unemployed young adults. *Leisure Studies, 10,* 265–274.

Hildebrand, M., & Mannell, R. C. (1996). Leisure and the job satisfaction of teachers. In P. Stokowski & J. Hultsman (Eds.), *Abstracts of presentations, 1996 Leisure Research Symposium.* Arlington, VA: National Recreation and Parks Association.

Horna, J. L. A. (1989). The dual asymmetry in the married couples' life: The gender-differentiated work, family, and leisure domains. *International Journal of Sociology of the Family, 19,* 113–130.

Iso-Ahola, S. E. (1980). *The social psychology of leisure and recreation.* Dubuque, IA: Wm. C. Brown Publishers.

Jahoda, M. (1982). *Employment and unemployment: A sociological analysis.* Cambridge, UK: Cambridge University Press.

Kabanoff, B. (1980). Work and nonwork: A review of models, methods and findings. *Psychological Bulletin, 88,* 60–77.

Kabanoff, B., & O'Brien, G. E. (1980). Work and leisure: A task attributes analysis. *Journal of Applied Psychology, 65,* 596–609.

Kando, T. M., & Summers, W. C. (1971, July). The impact of work on leisure: Toward a paradigm and research strategy. *Pacific Sociological Review, 310–327.*

Killinger, B. (1991). *Workaholics: The respectable addicts.* Toronto, Ontario: Key Porter Books.

Kilpatrick, R., & Trew, K. (1985). Lifestyles and psychological well-being among unemployed men in Northern Ireland. *Journal of Occupational Psychology, 58,* 207–216.

Kirchmeyer, C. (1993). Nonwork-to-work spillover: A more balanced view of the experiences and coping of professional women and men. *Sex Roles, 28,* 531–552.

Klausner, W. J. (1968). An experiment in leisure. *Science Journal, 4,* 81–85.

Lerner, S. (1994). The future of work in North America: Good jobs, bad jobs, beyond jobs. *Futures, 26,* 185–196.

Levitan, S. A. (1987). Beyond "trendy forecasts." *The Futurist, 21,* 28–33.

Lounsbury, J. W., Gordon, S. R., Bergermaier, R. L., & Francesco, A. M. (1982). Work and nonwork sources of satisfaction in relation to employee intention to turnover. *Journal of Leisure Research, 14,* 285–294.

Lounsbury, J. W., & Hoopes, L. L. (1986). A vacation from work: Changes in work and nonwork outcomes. *Journal of Applied Psychology, 71,* 392–401.

Mannell, R. C., & Dupuis, S. (1996). Life satisfaction. In G. Birren (Ed.), *Encyclopedia of Gerontology* (Vol. 2, pp. 59–64). New York, NY: Academic Press.

Mannell, R. C., & Iso-Ahola, S. E. (1985). Work constraints on leisure: A social-psychological analysis. In M. G. Wade (Ed.), *Constraints on leisure* (pp. 155–187). Springfield, IL: Charles C. Thomas, Publisher.

Mannell, R. C., & Reid, D. G. (1992). Treating the work-leisure relationship as a personality variable and lifestyle indicator. In *Proceedings of the NRPA Leisure Research Symposium* (Cincinnati, Ohio, October 15–18). Arlington, VA: National Recreation and Park Association.

McKenna, S. P., & Fryer, D. M. (1984). Perceived health during layoff and early unemployment. *Occupational Health, 36,* 201–206.

McPherson, B. D. (1991). *Aging as a social process.* Toronto, Ontario: Butterworth.

Meir, E. I., & Melamed, S. (1986). The accumulation of person-environment congruences and well-being. *Journal of Occupational Behavior, 7,* 315–323.

Meissner, M. (1971). The long arm of the job: A study of work and leisure. *Industrial Relations, 10,* 239–260.

Melamed, S., Meir, E. I., & Samson, A. (1995). The benefits of personality-leisure congruence: Evidence and implications. *Journal of Leisure Research, 27,* 25–40.

Naisbitt, J. (1994). *Global paradox.* New York, NY: William Morrow and Company.

Naisbitt, J., & Aburdene, P. (1988). *Megatrends 2000.* New York, NY: Avon.

Near, J., Rice, R., & Hunt, R. (1978). Work and extra-work correlates of life and job satisfaction. *Academy of Management Journal, 21,* 248–264.

Neulinger, J. (1990). *Eden after all: A human metamorphosis.* Culemborg, Netherlands: Giordano Bruno.

Parker, S. R. (1971). *The future of work and leisure.* New York, NY: Praeger.

Pesavento Raymond, L. C., & Kelly, J. R. (1991). Leisure and life satisfaction of unemployed North American urban minority youth. *Loisir et Société/Society and Leisure, 14,* 497–511.

Reid, D. G. (1995). *Work and leisure in the 21st century: From production to citizenship.* Toronto, Ontario: Wall and Emerson.

Reid, D. G., & FitzGibbon, J. E. (1991). An economic evaluation of municipal expenditures: A preliminary report. *Journal of Applied Recreation Research, 16,* 224–255.

Reid, D. G., & Mannell, R. C. (1994). The globalization of the economy and potential new roles for work and leisure. *Loisir et Société/Society and Leisure, 17,* 251–266.

Reid, D. G., & Smit, P. (1986). Recreation participation patterns of the unemployed: A preliminary perspective. *Recreation Research Review, 1,* 43–49.

Reid, D. G., & van Dreunen, E. (1996). Leisure as a social transformation mechanism in community development practice. *Journal of Applied Recreation Research, 21,* 45–65.

Roberts, K., Lamb, K. L., Dench, S., & Brodie, D. A. (1989). Leisure patterns, health status and employment status. *Leisure Studies, 8,* 229–235.

Robinson, J. P., & Godbey, G. (1997). *Time for life: The surprising ways Americans use their time.* University Park, PA: Penn State Press.

Rojek, C. (1989). Leisure and recreation theory. In E. L. Jackson & T. L. Burton (Eds.), *Understanding leisure and recreation: Mapping the past, charting the future* (pp. 69–88). State College, PA: Venture Publishing, Inc.

Rubenstein, C. (1980). Vacations: Expectations, satisfactions, frustrations, fantasies. *Psychology Today, 14,* 62–66, 71–76.

Saul, J. R. (1995). *The unconscious civilization.* Concord, Ontario: House of Anansi.

Schor, J. B. (1991). *The overworked American: The unexpected decline of leisure.* New York, NY: Basic Books.

Shaw, S. M. (1994). Gender, leisure, and constraint: Toward a framework for the analysis of women's leisure. *Journal of Leisure Research, 26,* 8–22.

Slaughter, R. A. (1993). Looking for the real "megatrends." *Futures, 25,* 827–849.

Spigner, C., & Havitz, M. E. (1992–1993). Health, recreation, and the unemployed: An interactive model. *International Quarterly of Community Health Education, 13,* 31–45.

Stebbins, R. A. (1992). *Amateur, professional, and serious leisure.* London, UK: McGill-Queen's University Press.

Steers, R. M., & Porter, L. W. (1991). *Motivation and work behavior.* New York, NY: McGraw-Hill.

Toffler, A. (1970). *Future shock.* New York, NY: Random House, Inc.

Wachtel, P. L. (1989). *The poverty of affluence: A psychological portrait of the American way of life.* New York, NY: Free Press.

Warr, P. B. (1983). Work, jobs, and unemployment. *Bulletin of the British Psychological Society, 36,* 305–311.

Warr, P. B., & Jackson, P. R. (1984). Men without jobs: Some correlates of age and length of unemployment. *Journal of Occupational Psychology, 57,* 77–85.

Wilensky, H. L. (1960). Work, careers, and social integration. *International Social Science Journal, 4,* 543–560.

Winefield, A. H., Tiggemann, M., Winefield, H. R., & Goldney, R. D. (1993). *Growing up with unemployment: A longitudinal study of its psychological impact.* London, UK: Routledge.

Zuzanek, J. (1991). Leisure research in North America: A critical retrospective. *Loisir et Société/Society and Leisure, 14,* 587–596.

Zuzanek, J., & Mannell, R. C. (1983). Work-leisure relationships from a sociological and social-psychological perspective. *Leisure Studies, 2,* 327–344.

Zuzanek, J., & Smale, B. J. A. (1992). Life-cycle variations in across-the-week allocation of time to selected daily activities. *Loisir et Société/Society and Leisure, 15,* 559–586.

Makers of Meanings: Feminist Perspectives on Leisure Research

Karla A. Henderson and M. Deborah Bialeschki
University of North Carolina at Chapel Hill

QUESTIONING STUDENT: What's all this fuss about feminism? Women have it just as good as men; why do we need to examine females different from males?

PATIENT TEACHER: Do girls have the same opportunities as boys for leisure activities? Do women and men share equally in the household and childcare responsibilities in heterosexual marriages? Do we see women and men portrayed similarly in sports and other shows on television?

QUESTIONING STUDENT: Women are getting more attention than men. Why do we see so many articles on women's leisure but nothing about men's leisure?

PATIENT TEACHER: The study of leisure or any academic area traditionally has been the study of men. When women haven't been the same as men, they have been perceived to be inferior.

QUESTIONING STUDENT: Don't feminists hate men and won't they do almost anything to make women look better?

PATIENT TEACHER: The value of feminism lies in making the lives of women visible and in discerning ways that both men and women can make responsible choices in their lives leading to positive social change. That's the contribution that feminism and feminist research can make.

Feminist perspectives are misunderstood, as the preceding conversation suggests, but they also have provided some of the most productive recent ways with which to extend our understanding of human behavior and the meanings of leisure. Feminist researchers have focused attention on leisure and recreation issues for women and have provided ways to challenge the predominantly androcentric perspectives of leisure research prior to the mid 1980s (e.g., Bella, 1989; Glancy, 1991; Henderson, 1990). In this chapter we will concentrate on how feminist perspectives have aided in the critique, correction, integration, and transformation of leisure research. We will provide examples of how feminist perspectives have been useful in reviewing former understandings of leisure and relationships, as well as how feminist perspectives and research on women have given new insights to an understanding of leisure meanings and constraints for both women and men. We will show how old assumptions about the experiences of women along with the methodological pluralism that feminists have used have opened the way for asking new questions. Finally, we will show how the use of feminist perspectives has opened the door in leisure research for social change by providing examples of emerging trends in the field.

Assumptions

In describing feminism and leisure research, it should be recognized that many perspectives on feminism exist. Ever since the term *feminism* was coined near the end of the nineteenth century, those people attached to it, as well as those opposed, have struggled to define it (Sapiro, 1994). Some say that feminism as a philosophy is too broad and others suggest that it is too narrow. Not only is feminism a way of thinking about the world but also a way of acting (Sapiro, 1994). Disagreements over the meanings of feminism are disagreements about how people should think and act. Many views of feminism are possible, just as there are many ways of being a feminist.

Several authors (e.g., Henderson, Bialeschki, Shaw and Freysinger, 1996; Tong, 1989; Yule, 1992) have provided lengthy descriptions of the various kinds of feminism (e.g., liberal, socialist, radical). For example, liberal feminism, as one of the oldest forms of feminist thought, focuses on gender justice by working to address social and legal barriers to women's and men's equal opportunity. Marxist feminists believe women's oppression began with the institution of private property that led to a class system with contemporary outcomes of capitalism and imperialism. Radical feminists analyze and critique the social constructions that serve to ensure male domination; they believe that men's domination of women is the most fundamental form of oppression. Postmodern feminists recognize no one central voice of authority and no central source of power that designates some people (i.e., males) to be part of a dominant culture and everyone else (i.e., females) to be "other" in relation to that dominant culture. An additional example is the ecofeminist perspective that recognizes the importance of healing divisions between nature and culture. The dominance

of men over women and man over nature have parallels to be addressed. Ecofeminists also include a continuum of constructions from liberal to radical perspectives. In all these examples, the particular perspective taken influences how research is conducted and the implications of the results.

We make the assumption in this chapter that a subtle difference exists between research on women (see Shaw, chapter 16 in this volume) and feminist research. They are related but have slightly different foci. Research on women makes the lives of women visible but it is feminist perspectives that demand social change. As Henderson (1994b) suggested, research on gender differences as descriptions of distinctions or oppression has done little directly to change women's lives. In contrast, research on women's lived experiences and the issues of gender from feminist perspectives addressing equality, liberation, and integrity has provided the foundation for social change, not only for women but also for men. In addition, according to Fonow and Cook (1991), the experience of oppression can create a unique type of insight for researchers who have experienced it personally.

Finally, we make the assumption that feminism has the potential to change our understanding of women's leisure and leisure in broader perspectives because it challenges the research process. Dustin (1992), for example, questioned the wisdom of the patriarchal view underlying social science. He challenged the world-view, the separation of humankind from nature, and the objectivity in science that feminists have had as a basis for many of their critiques. Dustin suggested how feminist thinking can contribute to the development of a more caring and connected social science. Further, systems of knowledge are never complete (Collins, 1990) and feminism has paved the way for asking more encompassing questions about leisure.

As in the past 15 years, feminism continues to provide ways to understand leisure more completely. Feminist thoughts show us that what we take for granted about women—language, views of morality, sexuality, spiritual practices, communities, ways of knowing, and ideas about work and play—are all based in fundamental ways on the experience of White men that need to be challenged (Hill, 1990). Feminism is also contributing to methodological-epistemological research approaches and has changed some views on how to understand the world (see Samdahl, chapter 8 in this volume). Epistemology is the study of assumptions about how to know meanings. Methodology concerns actual techniques and practices used in the research process. Feminist perspectives have the possibilities for redefining some of the questions leisure researchers are asking to include women. Whether women should be central to leisure research is not the key as much as not leaving the experiences of women or any other traditionally marginalized group out of the picture. The value of the contributions of feminist perspectives lies in a critique and reevaluation of existing theories, discovery of new ideas and analysis, interdisciplinary linkages, and creation of a new paradigm in our field.

A Critique and Reevaluation of Existing Theories

Feminist researchers doing research by, for, and about women have found a critique of our existing understanding of leisure to be fundamental for moving forward. Science of any kind is an ongoing critique of theory and a refinement of methods, but feminist perspectives have challenged a number of previously held beliefs epistemologically and methodologically.

Individuals who are doing feminist research are mainly women. The field of leisure research, however, has not been a field typically dominated by women. For example, a cursory review of the two leading research journals in North America, the *Journal of Leisure Research* and *Leisure Sciences* from 1986–1995 revealed that three times as many men as women were lead authors. Therefore, women have been "outsiders" to the leisure research process in general. Several Black feminists (Collins, 1990; hooks, 1984) have suggested that being the "outsider within" has the advantages of greater objectivity, the ability to see patterns that insiders are too immersed to see, and the latent advantages of invisibility. Thus, women doing feminist research have been able to see some of the issues that leisure research raises in a way that may not be apparent to some men.

The strategies and methods that feminists have used have also been useful in critiquing and evaluating existing theories. As Fox (1992) suggested, feminism requires a rethinking of epistemology and current knowledge content. Although some feminist researchers in the social sciences have found interpretive research and qualitative data to be most useful in understanding women's lives, unique feminist methods do not exist (Reinharz, 1992). Feminism is not defined by a method but by a way of thinking and acting. Fonow and Cook (1991), for example, described themes that run throughout much of the feminist research: reflexivity or the tendency of feminists to re-

flect upon, examine critically, and explore analytically the nature of the research process; action orientation that is implied in the purpose of the research, topic selection, choice of method, and definition of the researcher's role; affective components, such as restoring emotionality to current rationality; and the use of the situation at hand by exploring the everyday life world of people. Feminist perspectives have also led to greater social responsibility when the "so what?" of research is asked.

Therefore, although no unique feminist methods exist, feminist researchers have expanded the epistemological and methodological possibilities for research. Feminist perspectives applied to leisure studies have encouraged people to become receptive to the idea that interpretive research and qualitative data may be the most appropriate choices in some research situations. Because this view has been articulated (e.g., Fox, 1994; Henderson and Bialeschki, 1992), a greater openness to expanded methods opportunities in leisure research now seems to exist.

In addition to expanded methods, feminist researchers may also have enhanced the ways in which researchers think about and interpret quantitative data. Not only have the possible limitations of such data been exposed, as well as the inherent assumptions that led to those limitations being ignored, but the interpretations of quantitative data also have been improved. To find gender differences means very little without exploring what those differences mean. For example, Jackson and Henderson (1995) examined constraints to leisure according to both between-gender differences and within-gender differences. They found that differences between men and women emerged related to the intensity and nature of the leisure constraints, leading to the conclusion that women met with more constraints in their leisure than men. Their data, however, also demonstrated that the experience of leisure constraints was characterized by as many within-gender differences as between gender differences. Individuals responsible for childcare—who were more likely to be women than men—were more constrained in their leisure. Jackson and Henderson concluded that the cultural interpretation of gender and the function of gender roles was more of a constraint than was actual biological sex. More differences were found among groups of women or men than between them based on societal expectations and roles. In summary, the initial value of feminism has been the critique of traditional methods and ways of thinking about research. Feminism has opened the door to deconstructing and reconstructing researchers' views about leisure sciences and human behavior. These changes, however, are occurring slowly.

Most researchers and students are aware of the need to avoid sexist research. In 1978 Freize and her associates identified a number of errors that result in sexist research, such as studying only an area of life in which men are familiar, formulating hypotheses without considering sex-role stereotypes, theory building that ignores one sex, ignoring the effects of researcher-participant interaction, interpreting gender differences as absolutes, ignoring personal experience in research, and considering feminist interpretations as biases (Freize, Parson, Johnson, Ruble and Zellman, 1978). Some of these errors persist, but many leisure researchers have countered these problems and incorporated their avoidance into what constitutes "good" research. Although critiquing sexist research is only one aspect, the articulation of some previously unchallenged assumptions not only about gender, but also about other traditionally invisible groups in our society, has also emerged because of feminist research.

Confusion still surrounds understanding feminist theory and gender. A useful distinction is between gender as a variable and gender as a symbol of power. As a variable, gender has been important in helping to document differences, such as between the social conditions of women and men. As a pervasive symbol of power, gender provides insight into the construction of gendered institutions as well as the way that women and men experience gender in their lives (Denzin, 1992; Scott, 1986). Theories of gender emphasize that women simply cannot be added to existing formal theories; on the other hand, gender theories that are silent about women are fundamentally flawed. Feminist researchers have also suggested that if we want to fully understand the dimensions of leisure then we must examine gender constructs (Henderson, 1994a, 1994b; Squire, 1994). Squire, for example, suggested that the voices of many "ordinary" tourists are seldom heard because the voices of women tourists have been ignored. Henderson (1994a) focused on the gendered meanings of leisure by suggesting that a number of dimensions must be considered to really understand leisure meanings: values/entitlement, benefits/outcomes, containers/opportunities, negotiated constraints, and life situations.

Feminist researchers have also critiqued some of the dominant traditions in our society. For example, Duquin (1991) challenged the traditional ethic of justice or the rationalistic ethic in the ethic of care that grounds female moral behavior in nurturance, emotional sensitivity, and the importance of relationships. She suggested that sport devalues the ethic of care by how it is structured for girls and women. Devaluation relates to the way the body is used and manipulated and the distancing of people from each other so there

is no empathic response. She implied in her work that changing sports for women will also result in changes for some men that may improve participation for everyone.

An extensive critique has been leveled about definitions and meanings of leisure in recent years, particularly regarding whether leisure is always a positive experience (e.g., Bolla, Dawson and Harrington, 1991; Hunter and Whitson, 1992). For example, Bolla and her colleagues examined the subjective experience of and constraints to enjoyment among women living in Ontario. They found that "leisure as activity" was a weak definition. The positive dimension of leisure involved feeling happy, free, and peaceful and the negative experience of leisure involved feeling passive, selfish, and irritable. Thus, leisure was not automatically a positive activity. Other researchers such as Shaw (1994) and Hunter and Whitson (1992) have also echoed how leisure can be a negative experience, a topic often ignored in mainstream leisure literature. Hunter and Whitson (1992) found that the constraining effects of ideology, particularly related to familism and patriarchy, made leisure difficult for women. For example, common knowledge today shows that women's responsibility for the family's leisure results in them having less time for themselves. Hunter and Whitson (1992) point to leisure as a means to the enjoyment of valued relationships and contend that it is not the activity, but with whom one participates, that makes something leisure. They also found that most women's lives have been constrained in ways that men do not experience. Even those women who were happy with their lives wanted more time for themselves and more opportunities to develop their interests.

Similarly, feminist researchers have helped to re-evaluate existing theory by pointing out the diversity and the contradictions inherent in understanding leisure. Shaw (1994) identified three approaches to an analysis of women's leisure: leisure as constrained, leisure as constraining, and leisure as resistance. She suggested that not only is women's leisure constrained but also women's leisure can be a form of resistance that leads to a struggle against institutionalized power. She contended that acts of resistance occur in leisure settings, such as when girls and women participate in vigorous sports. Leisure viewed as resistance, as well as oppression, was a contradiction also examined by Freysinger and Flannery (1992). Further, the discussion of constraints negotiation (see Jackson and Scott, chapter 18 in this volume) may be, according to Shaw (1994), a starting place for an analysis of resistance.

From a macroperspective, feminist researchers have also critiqued the traditional understandings of leisure. Scraton (1994) suggested that feminist leisure studies conducted in the 1980s made a great empirical contribution because we learned to problematize the definitions of leisure, to recognize that we needed to situate women's leisure holistically, to see how women's lives are constrained, and to articulate how women resist and struggle to define their own leisure spaces and experiences. She concluded that many of the debates centralized in postmodern theory are ones in which feminists have been engaging for some time. Debates around differences, the problems and inadequacy of grand theory, and the rejection of dichotomies are common postmodern themes that feminists have been addressing for a period of time. Whether postmodern theory is or is not applicable to leisure research, she suggested that feminists have been in that foray for years through their critique of what currently exists.

Discovery of New Concepts and Analysis

Although different feminists have other agendas, the purpose of most feminist research in leisure studies has not been to negate all contemporary research, but to enhance our interpretations of leisure behavior. Where appropriate, the discovery of new ideas and analyses may make old interpretations obsolete. Those new interpretations, however, should have implications for broader, not narrower, theory. Any feminist analysis is incomplete without going on to the next step of discovering new concepts and analysis or correcting past misconceptions. If leisure theory of any type is to be useful today we cannot lose sight of the economic, social, political, and physical reality of women. Simply to critique does little good in extending knowledge unless we are ready to incorporate additional ideas and ways of knowing.

Deem (1992) suggested that examining feminism has led to rethinking related to paid work, unpaid work, family, and leisure. She believes that moving the knowledge base forward depends on addressing the structural relationships of power as well as agency and meanings. These analyses should result in trying to address policy issues. Yule (1992) has argued that an urgent need exists for theoretically informed empirical research on leisure policy, gender, and power. We must not return to old theories of oppression with difference only theorized between the categories of women and men. New discoveries, for example, suggest that some women are more oppressed than others; feminist perspectives are helping to uncover those issues.

Using feminist perspectives has resulted in the development of new ideas about the meanings of diversity in leisure research. In using feminism as a corrective device, researchers have challenged the universalizing tendencies in the writing of both White, middle-class feminists (hooks, 1989) as well as White men. Just as we have been critical of the patriarchy for not acknowledging the contributions of women, feminists can also be critical of how women studying women sometimes have ignored diversity. Race is an obvious omission, as are class differences. Lesbians point out heterosexual assumptions in research and practice, and women with disabilities suggest that normative models do not always work (Fine and Asch, 1988). More recent trends in feminist theorizing about difference are grounded in actual differences among women; we are challenged to reconsider theories of *the* woman and replace them with theories of multiplicity (Mascia-Lees, Sharpe and Cohen, 1989). Acknowledging the need for understanding diversity, however, does not compensate for exclusion in writing or research.

Gender analyses have been a useful way for feminist researchers to address new ideas about diversity. For example, in Jackson and Henderson's (1995) examination of constraints to leisure, they found gender differences. As described previously, however, they found variables such as age, income, and family structure were mediating factors that altered, reinforced, or alleviated constraints for women, depending on the nature of the context and the type of constraint. Rather than looking at conclusions about constraints or about biological gender differences between women and men, Jackson and Henderson pointed to the need to think in diversities and pluralisms rather than dualisms and universals.

Although the researchers Shinew, Floyd, McGuire, and Noe (1995) did not identify themselves as coming from a feminist perspective, their research has confirmed some of the emerging conclusions about leisure, gender, and diversity. They found that leisure preferences were different for poor working-class Black women compared to White men and women and middle-class Black men. This research pointed to the need to examine gender related to race and social class as the primary sources of stratification in the United States. Freysinger (1995), in her in-depth interviews with 54 middle-aged working- and middle-class White women and men, found that gender distinctions in adult leisure were modified and, perhaps, even superseded by social class and parental and marital status.

Other researchers have also concluded that women are not one homogeneous, socially undifferentiated class. The British researchers Mowl and Towner (1995) conducted research from the premise that only through developing a deeper understanding of the way individuals and groups perceive different places, through complex mosaics of gender and class relations, can a contextual representation of women's leisure emerge. Mowl and Towner discovered how some women created their own private spaces for leisure that became centers of meanings that are often overlooked by researchers. They suggested that a more humanistic way to study women's leisure would be to develop an understanding of the way individual women perceive and experience their environment and establish how these aspects affected their use of space. Bialeschki and Michener (1994) further provided an expanded view of leisure by their analysis of "full circle" leisure related to how mothers changed the focus of their leisure over their life spans. Wearing (1991) also described the relationship between leisure experiences and the construction of gender identity in different stages of the life cycle and the changes in leisure behavior that may resist traditional areas.

A broader understanding of leisure has also resulted from analyzing some of the issues that have been particularly salient for women and leisure. Feminist research has challenged leisure researchers to examine whether participation and enjoyment are synonymous. For example, Frederick and Shaw (1995) found that the perception of body image did not affect participation in leisure activities but did affect enjoyment. Body image was a major motivator for participating but not necessarily a typical constraint to prevent participation. Whyte and Shaw (1994) explored the effects of fear of violence on women's leisure choices and enjoyment. They found that because of fear women altered their involvement including when, with whom, and where involvement occurred. These modifications resulted in lower levels of enjoyment.

Studies that have examined the context of the lives of particular groups of women have provided new pieces of information for a bigger picture for understanding the leisure of half the population as well as providing new insights into understanding the broader phenomena and implications of leisure. Sheldon and Caldwell (1994) described how therapeutic recreation specialists can help individual women take charge of their lives and recreational activities. Henderson, Bedini, and Hecht (1994) noted how all leisure choices were not disability-determined, but the context of the disability coupled with the self-identity of a woman related to perceptions of herself and her ability to enjoy leisure. Stumbo and Little (1991) examined the leisure needs and characteristics of female offenders who were more often punished than rehabilitated.

As illustrated in the preceding examples, the most useful way that feminist research has informed leisure

theory relates to how feminists have focused on understanding leisure in the context of everyday life along with its social structures. By adopting feminist perspectives in the research process, the often invisible or subtle expectations of most women's lives are acknowledged.

Interdisciplinary Linkages and Collaboration

Another aspect of how feminist perspectives have contributed to leisure research is the way that feminists have further perpetuated the use of collaborative work and the advocacy of expanded methods of research. Collaborative research across disciplines is a trademark of leisure studies, but feminists have further enhanced this value through the incorporation of work done in women's studies, cultural studies, and traditional disciplines. Feminist researchers in leisure studies have acknowledged the inability to explain social phenomena without drawing together the breadth of knowledge available from multiple voices and viewpoints.

The work of feminists has attempted to expand the dialogue about leisure to a wider audience. When anyone feels excluded from a dialogue, they tend to dismiss it. Many feminist researchers have looked for better ways to talk to other leisure researchers about the meanings of gender, to address "mainstream" women, and to discuss gender as it pertains to men and masculinity. As Belenky, Clinchy, Goldberger, and Tarule (1986) suggested, connectedness rather than separation is an essential component of the knowledge validation process.

Several examples of the linking to fields other than women's studies are in the feminist leisure literature. Karsten's (1995) work on a model of leisure, caring, and labor types as they pertained to women's leisure gave insight into contemporary women and men. She identified the traditional family type, modern family type, and individualistic types of leisure. In this research she showed how the latter two are related to women's growing participation in the labor market. She further suggested that modern family type will be difficult for some women because it continues to address the unequal gender relations in labor, caring, and leisure domains. She also highlighted the growing divergence among women and the idea of leisure as time and the quality of leisure based upon either working or not working. Also related to interdisciplinary work on family is the suggestion by Hunter and Whitson (1991) that familism leisure ignores the work the women do to make leisure happen for their families; leisure as free time was not relevant to women with care-giving responsibilities.

Most feminist leisure researchers have tried to go beyond examining leisure as merely free time or activity to scrutinize the connections that exist in women's lives. These linkages also exist for many men, or at least males often are affected by them. Thus, the contribution that feminist researchers have highlighted is the inability for leisure researchers to examine anything in a social vacuum if we are to truly understand it.

Creation of a New Paradigm in Our Field

If feminist perspectives are to contribute to social change then we must examine how feminist researchers and other researchers examining leisure can further our understanding of leisure behavior. Adopting a feminist perspective may help overcome the limitations of cultural traditions by allowing the research to be situated within a political interactionism where the personal is political. For the personal to become political, the experiences and views of others must be shared and considered. For the transformation of personal to political to occur, a study of everyday life is a central priority, and a feminist interpretation of symbolic meaning should be undertaken (Denzin, 1992). Feminist perspectives are subtly changing the ways that leisure researchers, educators, and practitioners view leisure's meanings, not only for women, but also for other previously invisible or marginalized groups, such as people of color, lesbian and gay people, and people with disabilities. A new paradigm has not been created yet, but the potential pieces of that new paradigm are beginning to coalesce and change, albeit slowly, the nature of leisure research.

First, leisure researchers are beginning to integrate critical analyses with personal experience. A focus on self-reflexivity as has been the process of many feminists has been important and useful (e.g., Henderson, 1994b; Orenstein, 1994). If our research does not challenge our own knowledge and psyche, then how can we expect to challenge or change anyone else? Glancy (1993) described a subjective view of leisure that can help us understand ourselves and others in a broader context. Orenstein (1994) talked about her research on schoolgirls and how it helped her confront her own conflict as a young woman regarding the lessons of silence she learned as an adolescent. She acknowledged that at times the pain was so acute, she had to turn away or simply discontinue her research for a short time. Self-reflexivity, as we can see in these examples, allows us to see the contradictions that exist in understanding women's leisure and how it relates to our own lives. This reflexivity that feminist researchers have embraced, has allowed leisure researchers to move beyond trying to find *the* answer, to explaining a range of possibilities that may work for different people.

Second, feminist research "screams" that most research is of little relevance unless ultimately it leads to social change and policy development. Rowe and Brown (1994) suggested that few attempts have been made to link theory and practice through cultural policy interventions. Until that occurs, as Duquin (1991) and Frederick and Shaw (1995) also recommended specifically related to their critiques and analysis, leisure research will not result in wide-sweeping social change. Many feminists believe that researchers need to struggle with not getting caught up in university scholarship that places privilege and power over responsibility. If we believe that the purpose of our research is to create social change for people in society, then we have a responsibility to see that these changes occur. As suggested by hooks (1994), feminist research must emerge from active struggle and engagement with political practice. Although "complex and uncomfortable to speak from a position that is neither inside nor outside, it is this position that necessitates that we merge our scholarship with a clear politics to work against the forces of oppression" (Mascia-Lees et al., 1989, p. 33). Scraton (1994) argued eloquently for the need for feminist analyses that will effect change. She suggested that this change can occur by examining the everyday experience of women and men to recognize shared experiences as well as differences. Further, Scraton noted that the work of feminists and leisure researchers should focus on "shared political intent, the dynamism of theory and the changing world in which we live" (p. 257). Old theories of oppression with the differences theorized between categories of women and men have not moved the social change agenda forward in a way that is necessary if leisure is to be an entitlement for all people.

Third, empowerment is beginning to emerge as an important theme that all leisure researchers may benefit from using. We are not suggesting that empowerment through leisure has not been an assumption of leisure research over the years. The issue of empowerment, however, has been taken for granted rather than articulated in a way that could create social change not only for women, but also for all people. Research on women's leisure has moved beyond identifying theories of oppression to examining what that oppression means not only for women but also for all groups. More specifically, issues of empowerment have led to questions about how to negotiate leisure constraints on an individual as well as a societal level. For example, Samuel (1992) found that seeking personal leisure even through the family leads women toward independence and autonomy and presents the possibility for the creation of new social relationships and values. Shaw (1992) noted that the papers presented in a special issue of *Loisir et Société/Society and Leisure* as a whole emphasized both the constrained exploited nature of women's leisure as well as the possibilities for change. The potential of leisure to function as a challenge to traditional roles serves as a part of empowerment and transformative change.

Fourth, feminist perspectives on women's leisure offer a way to expand the methodological paradigm in which leisure research occurs. Feminist researchers have shown the need for a variety of approaches and methods to understand leisure. Fox (1992) said that properly designed quantitative research need not distort women's experiences and Henderson (1990) suggested that quantitative approaches are useful when the interpretations are grounded in theory and efforts are made to uncover the meanings of the results. As a feminist researcher, Gloor (1992) argued, however, that certain gender differences remain "hidden" if reliance is placed primarily on quantitative data. Although interpretive research is not the domain only of feminists, it has offered a useful way to understand the social construction of women's lives (Henderson and Bialeschki, 1992; Reinharz, 1992). The acknowledgment that many methods are useful, regardless of whether we collect qualitative or quantitative data, has provided new techniques for research in other areas of leisure studies and has expanded ways of knowing about both women and men. The inclusion of a variety of perspectives including what Fox (1994) suggested about contextualist, structurally pluralistic, theory-in-process, inclusivist views of leisure are contributions that feminism has made.

If feminist perspectives are to inform leisure research then we must examine practical strategies coming largely from feminist perspectives that can help us understand leisure behavior and the need for concomitant policy change. A focus on methods alone will not change the paradigm or the way that we understand leisure behavior, although epistemological ideas have shifted the thinking of many leisure researchers. Jayaratne and Stewart (1991) offered several possibilities to consider about the impact of feminist research. For example, when developing any topic, researchers ought to ask what potential the research has for helping women or any other marginalized groups. Feminist researchers also have underlined the importance of doing quality work; because feminist research is sometimes suspect for being biased, this focus on acknowledging that the perspectives taken for any research study suggest a type of bias, has helped to elevate the quality of research in general. All researchers are reminded that bias is inherent in research and there is no such thing as apolitical research. Further, research should be conducted so that implications for policy change are evident and the outcomes of the research are apparent to wider audiences.

Conclusions

If feminist perspectives are to continue to transform ways of viewing leisure research and methods for conducting this research, then we must avoid ghettoizing feminist research and research on women. This research needs to be mainstreamed along with everything else that is being done in the area of leisure studies. Further, we must focus not only on what feminist research tells us about girls and women but also what it tells us about the social constructions of society. The value of feminist perspectives in leisure research is that they have laid the groundwork for examining other groups, methods, and perspectives that previously have been marginalized. The acknowledgment of how diversity of any kind whether related to gender, race, class, disability, or other characteristics must be considered and may provide a basis for broader conceptualizations of leisure behavior.

Feminist perspectives are only beginning to change the paradigm for understanding leisure through the inclusion of diversity, the pluralism of methods, and the implications for social change in people's lives. With these changes will come the realization that women are no longer only bearers of leisure meanings, but they have become makers of meanings.

References

Belenky, M. F., Clinchy, B. M., Goldberger, N. R., & Tarule, J. M. (1986). *Women's ways of knowing*. New York, NY: Basic Book, Inc.

Bella, L. (1989). Women and leisure: Beyond androcentrism. In E. Jackson & T. Burton (Eds.), *Understanding leisure and recreation: Mapping the past, charting the future* (pp. 151–180). State College, PA: Venture Publishing, Inc.

Bialeschki, M. D., & Michener, S. (1994). Reentering leisure: Transition within the role of motherhood. *Journal of Leisure Research, 26,* 57–74.

Bolla, P., Dawson, D., & Harrington, M. (1991). The leisure experience of women in Ontario. *Journal of Applied Recreation Research, 16*(4), 322–348.

Collins, P. H. (1990). *Black feminist thought*. New York, NY: Routledge.

Deem, R. (1992). The sociology of gender and leisure in Britain: Past progress and future prospects. *Loisir et Société/Society and Leisure, 15*(1), 21–38.

Denzin, N. (1992). *Symbolic interactionsim and cultural studies: The politics of interpretation*. Cambridge, MA: Blackwell Publishers.

Duquin, M. E., (1991). Sport, women and the ethic of care. *Journal of Applied Recreation Research, 16*(4), 262–280.

Dustin, D. L. (1992). The dance of the dispossessed: On patriarchy, feminism and the practice of leisure sciences. *Journal of Leisure Research, 24,* 324–332.

Fine, M., & Asch, A. (Eds.). (1988). *Women with disabilities. Essays in psychology, culture and politics*. Philadelphia, PA: Temple University Press.

Fonow, M. M., & Cook, J. A. (1991). Back to the future: A look at the second wave of feminist epistemology and methodology. In M. Fonow & J. Cook (Eds.), *Beyond methodology* (pp. 1–15). Bloomington, IN: Indiana Press.

Fox, K. M. (1992). Choreographing differences in the dance of leisure: The potential of feminist thought. *Journal of Leisure Research, 24,* 333–347.

Fox, K. M. (1994). Negotiating in a world of change: Ecofeminist guideposts for leisure scholarship. *Journal of Leisure Research, 26,* 39–58.

Frederick, C. J., & Shaw, S. M. (1995). Body image as a leisure constraint: Examining the experience of aerobic exercise classes for young women. *Leisure Sciences, 17,* 57–73.

Freize, I., Parson, J., Johnson, P., Ruble, D., & Zellman, G. (1978). *Women and sex roles*. New York, NY: W.W. Norton and Co.

Freysinger, V. J. (1995). The dialectics of leisure and development for women and men in midlife: An interpretive study. *Journal of Leisure Research, 27,* 61–84.

Freysinger, V. J., & Flannery, D. (1992). Women's leisure: Affiliation, self-determination, empowerment, and resistance? *Loisir et Société/Society and Leisure, 15*(1), 303–322.

Glancy, M. (1991). The androcentricism complex. In T. Goodale & P. Witt (Eds.), *Recreation and leisure: Issues in a era of change* (3rd ed., pp. 413–428). State College, PA: Venture Publishing, Inc.

Glancy, M. (1993). Achieving intersubjectivity: The process of becoming the subject in leisure research. *Leisure Studies, 12,* 45–59.

Gloor, D. (1992). Women versus men? The hidden differences in leisure activities. *Loisir et Société/Society and Leisure, 15*(1), 39–62.

Henderson, K. A. (1990). Anatomy is not destiny: A feminist analysis of the scholarship on women's leisure. *Leisure Sciences, 12,* 229–239.

Henderson, K. A. (1994a). Broadening an understanding of women, gender, and leisure. *Journal of Leisure Research, 26,* 1–7.

Henderson, K. A. (1994b). Perspectives on analyzing gender, women, and leisure. *Journal of Leisure Research, 25,* 119–137.

Henderson, K. A., Bedini, L. A., & Hecht, L. (1994). "Not just a wheelchair, not just a woman": Self-identity and leisure. *Therapeutic Recreation Journal, 28*(2), 73–86.

Henderson, K. A., & Bialeschki, M. D. (1992). Leisure research and the social structure of feminism. *Loisir et Société/Society & Leisure, 15*(1), 63–77.

Henderson, K. A., Bialeschki, M. D., Shaw, S. M., & Freysinger, V. J. (1996). *Both gains and gaps: Feminist perspectives on women's leisure*. State College, PA: Venture Publishing, Inc.

Hill, M. (1990). On creating a theory of feminist therapy. *Women & Therapy, 9*(3), 53–65.

hooks, b. (1984). *Feminist theory: From margin to center*. Boston, MA: South End Press.

hooks, b. (1989). *Talking back*. Boston, MA: South End Press.

hooks, b. (1994). *Outlaw culture: Resisting representations*. New York, NY: Routledge.

Hunter, P. L., & Whitson, D. J. (1991). Women, leisure and familism: Relationships and isolation in small town Canada. *Leisure Studies, 10,* 219–233.

Hunter, P. L., & Whitson, D. J. (1992). Women's leisure in a resource industry town: Problems and issues. *Loisir et Société/Society and Leisure, 15*(1), 223–244.

Jackson, E. L., & Henderson, K. A. (1995). Gender-based analysis of leisure constraints. *Leisure Sciences, 17,* 31–51.

Jayaratne, T. E., & Stewart, A. J. (1991). Quantitative and qualitative methods in the social sciences:

Current feminist issues and practical strategies. In M. Fonow & J. Cook (Eds.), *Beyond methodology* (pp. 85–106). Bloomington, IN: Indiana Press.

Karsten, L. (1995). Women's leisure: Divergence, reconceptualization and change—the case of the Netherlands. *Leisure Studies, 14,* 186–201.

Mascia-Lees, F. E., Sharpe, P., & Cohen, C. B. (1989). The postmodernist turn in anthropology: Cautions from a feminist perspective. *Signs, 15,* 7–33.

Mowl, G., & Towner, J. (1995). Women, gender, leisure and place: Towards a more "humanistic" geography of women's leisure. *Leisure Studies, 14,* 102–116.

Orenstein, P. (1994). *Schoolgirls.* New York, NY: Doubleday.

Reinharz, S. (1992). *Feminist methods in social research.* New York, NY: Oxford University Press.

Rowe, D., & Brown, P. (1994). Promoting women's sport: Theory, policy, and practice. *Leisure Studies, 13,* 97–110.

Samuel, N. (1992). Women's aspirations for autonomy: Family leisure and personal leisure [English abstract]. *Loisir et Société/Society and Leisure, 15*(1), 354.

Sapiro, V. (1994). *Women in American society.* Mountain View, CA: Mayfield Publishing Company.

Scott, J. W. (1986). Gender: A useful category of historical analysis. *American Historical Review, 91,* 1053–1075.

Scraton, S. (1994). The changing world of women and leisure: Feminism, "postfeminism," and leisure. *Leisure Studies, 13,* 249–261.

Shaw, S. M. (1992). Introduction. *Loisir et Société/Society and Leisure, 15*(1), 11–20.

Shaw, S. M. (1994). Constraints to women's leisure. *Journal of Leisure Research, 25,* 8–22.

Sheldon, K., & Caldwell, L. (1994). Urinary incontinence in women: Implications for therapeutic recreation. *Therapeutic Recreation Journal, 28*(4), 203–212.

Shinew, K. J., Floyd, M. F., McGuire, F. A., & Noe, F. P. (1995). Gender, race, and subjective social class and their association with leisure preferences. *Leisure Studies, 17,* 75–89.

Squire, S. J. (1994). Gender and tourist experiences: Assessing women's shared meanings for Beatrix Potter. *Leisure Studies, 13,* 195–209.

Stumbo, N. J., & Little, S. L. (1991). Implications for leisure services with incarcerated women. *Therapeutic Recreation Journal, 25*(2), 49–62.

Tong, R. (1989). *Feminist thought.* Boulder, CO: Westview Press, Inc.

Wearing, B. (1991). Leisure and women's identity: Conformity or individuality? *Loisir et Société/Society and Leisure, 14*(2), 575–586.

Whyte, L. B., & Shaw, S. M. (1994). Women's leisure: An exploratory study of fear of violence as a leisure constraint. *Journal of Applied Recreation Research, 19*(1), 5–21.

Yule, J. (1992). Gender and leisure policy. *Leisure Studies, 11,* 157–173.

Spatial Analysis of Leisure and Recreation

Bryan J. A. Smale
University of Waterloo

> Being in one place rather than another makes a difference, as does being near rather than far. (Sack, 1993, p. 326)

Place and space are central aspects of human behavior. Geographers explore the way in which people respond to place and how space is shaped by human behavior. This has been a basic tenet of geographic inquiry, but there has been a lack of consideration of the spatial context in leisure research, despite the critical role it plays in everything that we do.

Numerous writers have described the meaning of place and the extent to which it both affects our lives and, in turn, is affected by our lives in its structure and organization (Gallagher, 1993; Hiss, 1990; Tuan, 1974, 1977; Walmsley, 1988). Place transcends everything that we do and we have come to think of space and place as defining elements in our homes, neighborhoods, and communities. Tuan (1977) has been perhaps the most eloquent writer in describing *place* as something defined by our experiences and endowed

with our values and beliefs. We assign meaning to places, and places bring to mind emotions, feelings, and attitudes connected with the experiences and perceptions we associate with them. The meaning we attach to places is influenced by at least three factors (Walmsley, 1988):

1. the knowledge and familiarity we possess about each place, including its physical attributes and its distance away;
2. how emotionally attached we are to each place, its symbols, and its expected utility in meeting our needs; and
3. the types of behavior we associate with each place.

Such factors are likely to vary from person to person, and to change over time as places evolve, thereby complicating our ability to examine, describe, and analyze places and the spatial variations in these factors. Nevertheless, place and space are integral components of our behavior, and they represent unique conceptual and methodological challenges.

Surprisingly, considerations of place and space are notably absent in the leisure literature. This is especially ironic because leisure researchers increasingly have been stressing the importance of *context* in understanding the experience of leisure in everyday life (e.g., Henderson, Bialeschki, Shaw and Freysinger, 1996). Contextual factors, such as gender, family role and responsibilities, stage in the life course, ethnicity, and social group, all play an important role in defining the nature of our leisure and how we experience it (Horna, 1994; Kelly, 1996). Consequently, our *spatial context*—where we live, our physical place in the community, our spatial relationship to others, and the location, distance, and distribution of recreation opportunities—all exert similar influences. Indeed, we typically define places such as neighborhoods according to the social groups and the characteristics that comprise them (Herbert and Johnson, 1976; Jones and Eyles, 1977; Pacione, 1984), thereby inextricably linking the social and spatial contexts together. In human geography, the spatial context is generally regarded as lying at the root of the choices, preferences, and ultimately, the behavioral patterns expressed by individuals (Golledge and Rushton, 1984).

The purpose of this chapter is to present leisure researchers with some of the dominant concepts and methods of spatial analysis in an effort to encourage the inclusion of a spatial context in our research. An overview of the major tenets of behavioral geography, with which spatial analysis has been most closely identified, is also provided to point out some of the disciplinary links in the social sciences. In addition, selected examples of studies drawn from the leisure literature that incorporate a spatial context are described, along with some suggestions on the possibilities for research in the future.

The Geographic Perspective

A dominant approach to the study of spatial phenomena in human geography is known as *locational analysis,* and its methods and techniques are the realm of *spatial analysis.* Spatial analysis is based on several deterministic assumptions about human behavior, originally borrowing from economic principles regarding the expected decision making and behavior of individuals. A fundamental tenet of these assumptions is that people are rational and seek to optimize their spatial behavior by, for example, minimizing the distance traveled in pursuit of any activity. As a result,

numerous models and methods were developed in spatial analysis that drew heavily on geometry as a means of describing and ultimately explaining spatial form (see Haggett, Cliff and Frey, 1977a, 1977b).

In its early years, locational analysis focused primarily on the spatial form of the landscape—the locations and surfaces that reflected the spatial organization of society. Regularity in societal patterns was expected to produce similarities from place to place as people organized locations to satisfy the "nearness principle" (Morrill, 1970), that is, to minimize the distances between locations and activities in order to reduce costs, maximize satisfaction, and optimize interactions among places. These perspectives gave rise to a belief in highly integrated and interrelated systems of spatial behavior and locational patterns and linkages (Coffey, 1981). The dynamics of these systems are reflected in notions of *spatial behavior* which focuses on the activities and decisions governing behavior, and *behavior in space* which focuses on the structural contexts of, and by inference the constraints to, behavior (Aitken, 1991).

Increasingly, the deterministic nature of locational analysis was challenged by human geographers who argued that cognitive and decision-making variables played an important role in mediating the relationships between location and behavior (Cox, 1995). Out of these discussions arose *behavioral geography,* which introduced psychology and social psychology to the study of spatial behavior. Pointing to the irregular patterns of behavior for various activities, behavioral geographers relaxed some of the assumptions to which locational theorists had adhered and increasingly incorporated cognitive measures in their models of spatial analysis. The evolution of behavioral geography has been discussed in detail by several authors, but Golledge and Timmermans (1990) have provided this concise summary of its development and dominant ingredients:

1. the search for models of society and behavior that provide alternatives to the economically and spatially rational models reflective of early locational theory;

2. the search for means to define and describe environments that are not based solely in an objective physical reality, but reflected the cognitive domain within which decision making and behavior takes place;

3. the emphasis on *processual* rather than *structural* explanations of human activity and its relationship to the physical environment;

4. an increased interest in exploring the spatial dimensions of social, psychological, and social-psychological theories and propositions, especially as they related to decision making and behavior;

5. a shift in emphasis away from examining aggregate populations to the disaggregate scale where the concern was the spatial behavior of individuals and small groups;

6. an increased desire to compile new data sources at the disaggregate level of analysis;

7. the search for alternative methods to complement the highly mathematical and statistical procedures developed in spatial analysis, and which were sensitive to all levels of measurement; and

8. an increased desire to blend geographic inquiry with research in other disciplines to advance theory building and problem solving.

Ultimately, research in behavioral geography converged into two general themes: the role of cognition in spatial behavior; and the spatial context of decision making, choice, preference, and movement behavior (see Golledge and Timmermans, 1990, and Timmermans and Golledge, 1990, for detailed overviews). Cognitive models of spatial behavior focus on individuals' perceptions and knowledge of the environment, and how these factors result in unique spatial patterns and processes of human preference and activity. Gould and White's (1986) seminal work on *mental maps* provides an exemplary source for illustrating how perceptions and environmental learning affect people's behavior. Research on preferences and choice behavior in a spatial context has produced an array of operational models that "explicitly relate choice behavior to the environment through consideration of perceptions, preference formation and decision making" (Timmermans and Golledge, 1990, p. 312). The two dominant areas of inquiry in this theme arguably are based in *spatial choice models* and *spatial interaction modeling*.

Methods of spatial analysis have remained the principal means by which behavioral geographers have attempted to describe and explain spatial behavior and spatial structure, but now, the techniques reflect the evolution in thinking. Increasingly, cognitive measures such as perceptions and preferences are centerpieces in the applications and derivation of models. As new technologies, such as geographic information systems (GIS), enhance the ability to store, analyze, and display spatial data, there has been renewed interest in exploring the synergistic relationships between behav-

ior and the influence of spatial structure, and the way in which patterns of behavior shape spatial structure (Rushton, 1993).

Geographers have long recognized recreation and leisure as important places and activities occurring on the landscape. Recreation geography developed more fully during the 1960s and early 1970s, especially with the appearance of seminal works by Wolfe and Mercer. In his paper for *The Geographical Review*, Wolfe (1964) proposed a comprehensive model of outdoor recreation research that focused on the mobility of individuals between their homes and recreation sites. Mercer (1970) argued that the geographic study of recreation could be divided into two distinct conceptual approaches—those focusing on the *supply* of recreation resources and those focusing on the *demand* for those resources and the factors that affect that demand. Taking their views together, geographic interest in recreation and leisure has subsequently organized along two main themes: the resources devoted to recreation, especially those in natural areas such as parks and other outdoor environments (Cosgrove and Jackson, 1972; Patmore, 1983), and tourism and travel behavior which lent itself to studies of movement. Indeed, interest in the *movement* of people over space, especially issues pertaining to effects of distance and accessibility to recreation resources, has been a dominant theme in the geography of recreation (Smith, 1983). While geographic interest has been primarily limited to these areas, leisure researchers, too, have shown only some interest in embracing a spatial perspective in their explorations of a variety of leisure phenomena. In order to provide leisure researchers with a sense of the spatial perspective, a review of the basic geographic building blocks of spatial analysis is presented next.

Basic Geographic Concepts

There are two fundamental geographic concepts used extensively in spatial analysis: *location* and *distance*. Location can be thought of in terms of *points* representing specific locations in space; *lines* representing routes, pathways, and edges, which collectively form networks; *areas* representing distinct regions; and *surfaces* representing variations in the topography of the landscape. Each aspect of location can be described in terms of selected attributes that may be measured in a variety of ways using the same levels of measurement as in basic statistical procedures—nominal, ordinal, and interval/ratio. Along with location, distance is the most fundamental of concepts associated with geography. The spatial separation between locations, whether it be between physical sites or between recreation participants and the facilities they use, has important implications for behavior. Maps are the vehicles through which we can graphically represent locations and measure distances between them (Campbell, 1993).

Location

Points represent the simplest way in which we can specify the location of objects in space. The dot map can illustrate the spatial distribution of any set of features on the landscape, such as recreation facilities, parks, or other points of interest. In addition, each point in a distribution can be further differentiated by assigning values at some higher level of measure for a selected attribute. The display of information in this manner clearly indicates any distinct spatial patterns in the nature of the distribution (Figure 12.1).

The simplest way in which to measure the location of each point is through a system of Cartesian coordinates, which is a rectangular grid of regular intervals along an *x*-axis (called an *easting*) and a *y*-axis (called a *northing*) covering the entire distribution of points and anchored by an origin or zero point (Goodchild, 1984). Therefore, each point in the distribution, like a bivariate plot, has an *x* and *y* coordinate specifying its location in space relative to all other points in the same space (Figure 12.2A). These coordinates also facilitate the measurement of distance between any pair of points in the distribution.

Lines most often are used in two ways: (1) to represent the boundaries between areas in space where transitions occur, and (2) to represent the routes along which people travel and to connect points of interest. In the latter case, the combination of routes results in networks, the most obvious example of which is the

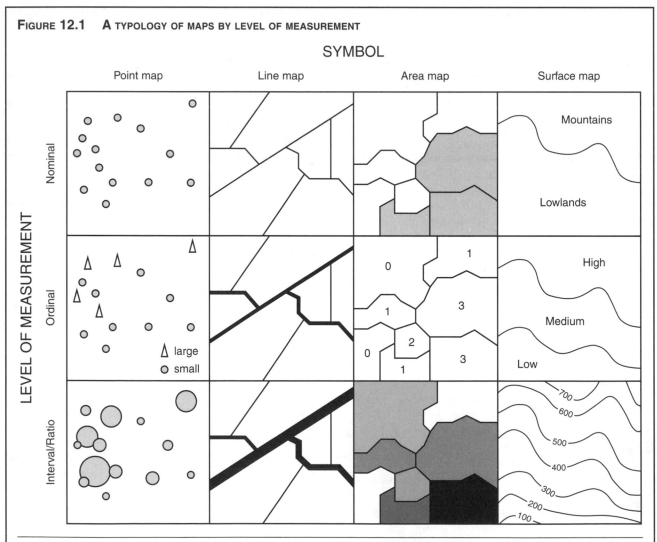

FIGURE 12.1 A TYPOLOGY OF MAPS BY LEVEL OF MEASUREMENT

SOURCE: *Introductory Spatial Analysis* (p. 25), by D. Unwin, 1981, London, UK: Methuen. Copyright 1981 by D. Unwin. Adapted with permission of the author.

road map. The mapping of networks of lines may be based on already established routes, such as roads or pathways, or may be created networks based on the patterns of movement of people in open areas. An example of the latter is Klein's (1993) study of the circulation patterns of visitors to museums in Germany. He illustrated the revealed preferences of visitors for selected exhibits by mapping the percentage of individuals following particular paths in each location. Patterns of lines and networks can be described and compared in the same fashion as points, but lines also introduce the additional elements of *direction* and *connectivity*.

Areas represent perhaps the most familiar spatial units upon which much of our knowledge is based. When we think of the landscape, especially with respect to the built environment, we envision areas as defined by political or perceived boundaries representing neighborhoods, communities, or counties. Two additional elements in the consideration of areas are their *contiguity* and *shape,* both of which present unique measurement challenges. Variations in the qualities possessed by areas can be illustrated using *choropleth maps,* which distinguish areas by classifying and shading each according to some attribute (for

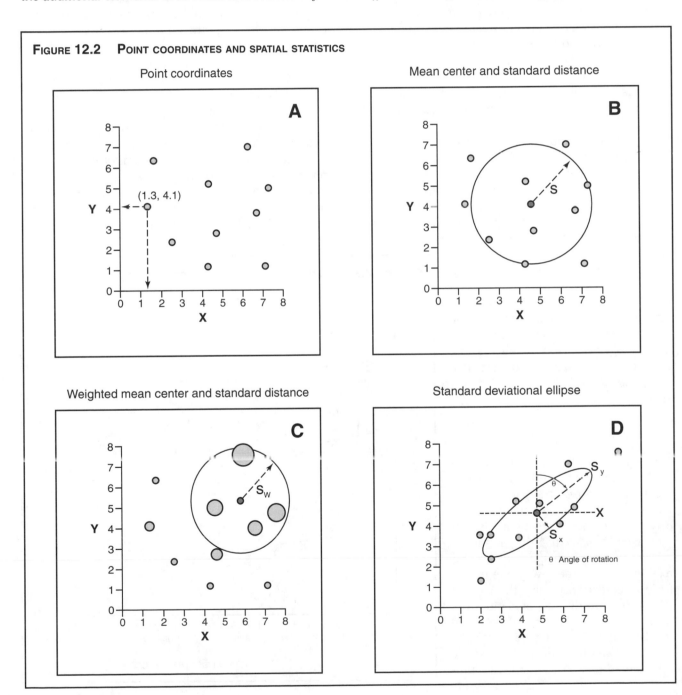

FIGURE 12.2   POINT COORDINATES AND SPATIAL STATISTICS

Point coordinates

Mean center and standard distance

Weighted mean center and standard distance

Standard deviational ellipse

θ Angle of rotation

example, see the area map measured at the interval/ratio level in Figure 12.1, page 180). Area maps are the most useful means of showing distributional patterns of people rather than things because people can be aggregated into meaningful areal units like neighborhoods or census tracts. These areas may also be represented by points on a map by selecting a representative point within the area such as the geographic center or "locational midpoint," or be constructed based on contiguous groupings of logically related points, such as households comprising a neighborhood. With such data structures, however, there are the inevitable concerns about aggregation, scale, sample representativeness, and interpretation (see Goodchild, 1984, for a brief overview of some of these).

Surfaces differ from points, lines, and areas in that they go beyond the discrete nature of these features to portray spatial properties as being continuous across the landscape. The most common type of surface map is the topographic or *contour* map, which illustrates transitions in elevations with the use of *isolines* that connect imaginary points of equal elevation set at value z. Hence, each point on the surface can be represented by its coordinate location (x, y) and its attribute value (z). While traditional surface maps in geography have tended to show variations in the physical landscape, for human geographers—and for leisure researchers—surface maps have the potential to illustrate spatial variations in any quality that can be measured at different points. We could create surface maps that illustrate how the intensity of opinion within a community changes as one moves across the surface, or how frequency of participation in leisure activities changes over space.

Distance

The importance of distance in influencing behavior is reflected in what some regard as the closest thing to a law that exists in human geography—*distance decay*. Distance decay maintains that increases in distance bring about decreases in most forms of behavior; for example, the further away one moves from a recreation facility, the smaller the proportion of the population that uses it.

Different sites have varying abilities to draw participants to them, so the effect of distance on behavior ulti-

mately depends on the characteristics of the sites as well as the participants. Figure 12.3 illustrates how distance might affect rates of participation for different types of recreation sites. In this example, a neighborhood pool might attract large numbers of users from nearby, but its appeal drops off dramatically with each unit increase in distance, in part because it is local, but also because of other nearby opportunities. In contrast, a major sports stadium may be able to draw users from much greater distances, but its appeal may be more specialized, thereby drawing a smaller proportion of the local population. Such a view of the effect of distance has had tremendous implications for facility location decisions and the notion of *efficiency*, which is concerned with the optimal number and distribution of like facilities within a defined region like a community (McAllister, 1976). Other factors such as the participants' origin, length of trip, and type of activity also moderate the distance function (Duffield, 1975).

Distance is a more complex concept to measure than might be expected (Gatrell, 1983). Representing distance as the straight-line separation between two points is the most common means of measurement; that is, physical distances measured in meters, kilometers, or some other similar metric. However, distance can also be measured as an economic cost, as

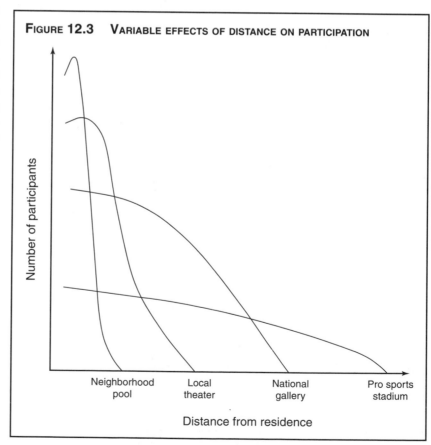

FIGURE 12.3   VARIABLE EFFECTS OF DISTANCE ON PARTICIPATION

Number of participants (vertical axis)

Distance from residence (horizontal axis)

Neighborhood pool   Local theater   National gallery   Pro sports stadium time, or even as social distance, and in all these cases, a distinction can also be made between the physical measure and the perception of distance. Arguably, if the distance to a recreation site is perceived to be less or greater than its actual physical distance, the perception may be more influential on potential use than the objective "reality." Nevertheless, comparisons among different measures of distance have shown that no one measure of distance is necessarily better than another in explaining variations in human behavior for different locations nor different activities (Säisä, Svensson-Gärling, Gärling and Lindberg, 1986). Indeed, the way in which distance is perceived within the context of the behavior is likely indicative of its influence on that behavior.

Methods of Spatial Analysis

Descriptive Methods of Analysis

A variety of strategies have been developed to describe and compare the spatial properties of point and area distribution patterns, networks, and surfaces. Some of the more frequently used methods are described here to illustrate how spatial analysis is, in its most basic form, undertaken. At its core, spatial analysis relies upon descriptive statistics for distributions of locations that are the spatial equivalents of simple descriptive statistics (Smith, 1975). These descriptive measures allow us to examine spatial distributions in the same way that we examine univariate distributions.

Spatial statistics provide researchers with the means to describe various aspects of location. Variously referred to as centrographic measures, or geostatistics, spatial statistics have received little attention by geographers and statisticians alike, despite their fundamental application to the study of spatial phenomena (Ebdon, 1977). Not surprisingly, then, spatial statistics have seen even less consideration in leisure research.

The equivalent to the mean in spatial statistics is the *mean center,* which describes the average location for a distribution of points. Even though the mean center is usually plotted on a map, it does not represent a "real" point in space, but rather is a summary descriptive measure of the distribution in the same tradition as the univariate mean. To determine the mean center, the means of the x and y coordinates of each point in the distribution of interest are calculated separately.

A measure of the variability or dispersion in a distribution, the standard deviation, also has a spatial equivalent in the *standard distance.* The standard distance describes how widely dispersed the points in a spatial distribution are around the mean center. Its calculation is handled much the same way as the standard deviation, except that points are measured in terms of their Euclidean distance from the mean center rather than univariate distance along a single metric. Like the standard deviation, the larger the standard distance, the greater the dispersion of the points around the mean center. Further, one standard distance from the mean center encompasses approximately 68% of the points in the distribution (Figure 12.2B, page 181).

The mean center treats each point in the distribution equally; in other words, each point is given equal weight. In many instances, however, we may wish to distinguish between the locations according to some measurable characteristic, such as size, capacity, or usage. In these cases, we calculate the *weighted* mean center, which introduces the attribute into the determination of the mean center. The important distinction, then, is that the mean center describes the spatial distribution of a set of *locations,* whereas the weighted mean center describes the spatial distribution of some *attribute* associated with those locations. The weighted mean center has its counterpart in the *weighted standard distance* which describes how widely dispersed the weight (i.e., the locations' attribute) is around the weighted mean center (Figure 12.2C, page 181).

Comparisons of mean centers and standard distances for different distributions of locations can answer questions about the underlying similarities or differences in their spatial character. For example, if public recreation facilities are intended to be equally available across a community, should we expect to find the mean center and standard distance of public swimming pools to be essentially the same as public recreation centers? Just as with simple descriptive statistics, differences in the location of the mean centers and standard distances may provide insights into the processes underlying the different distributional patterns of recreation resources and other leisure phenomena.

Another measure of dispersion that adds more description to the nature of spatial distributions is the *standard deviational ellipse.* Like the standard distance, the standard deviational ellipse indicates the amount of dispersion of the points around the mean center, but has the additional capability of describing the *orientation* of the distribution. As its name implies, the elliptical nature of the measure reflects whether or not the distribution is oriented more so in a specific direction rather than evenly dispersed around the mean center in all directions. The calculation of the standard deviational ellipse involves the determination of the distribution's major axis, minor axis, and the rotation of the major axis to position it along the dominant orientation of the distribution (Figure 12.2D, page 181). To measure how strongly biased a distribution is along its major axis, the *coefficient of circularity* is calculated by taking the ratio of the length of the major to the minor axis with a value of 1.0 representing a circle, and therefore, a uniform distribution around the mean center. The smaller the value of the coefficient, the more elliptical the orientation of the distribution (a detailed description of the calculation of the standard deviational ellipse is given in both Ebdon, 1977, and Smith, 1975). If we were to assume that a standard deviational ellipse with a coefficient approximating 1.0 represented, for example, equity in the spatial distribution of community recreation centers (all else being equal), then departures from that expectation would reveal other factors that may have oriented the distribution in specific directions in the community.

These spatial statistics provide the researcher with the basic measures needed for the description and analysis of any distribution of points. Just like their "ordinary" statistical counterparts, spatial statistics allow us to take a sample of observations and examine it according to its central tendencies and dispersion along any of the attributes for which we have information. By identifying subgroups within that sample and calculating the measures for each of them, we can make comparisons and answer questions about the similarities and differences in the spatial patterns of those groups, which then may lead to insights concerning the factors that underlie the processes responsible for the observable patterns.

In addition to spatial statistics, a number of other measures have been devised in geography to describe and distinguish point and areal patterns, types and characteristics of networks of lines, and the nature and gradient of surfaces (Hammond and McCullagh, 1978; Smith, 1975; Unwin, 1981). Point patterns and area measures garner the most attention among spatial analysts, and they also are among the most easily determined and directly related to statistical theory and interpretation. With such indicators, the relationships between patterns of different types can be assessed as well as changes in the patterns and relationships over time.

Points

Perhaps the most frequently used methods are based in a family of techniques called *point pattern analyses*. The analysis of point patterns involves the assessment of a distribution of points according to the expecta-

tion of a random pattern; that is, no recognizable, regular pattern is hypothesized and departures from that expectation are evaluated according to the indicator calculated. One method—*nearest neighbor analysis*—measures the distances between every point in the distribution and its nearest neighbor and evaluates the overall mean distance to the expected mean distance of a random distribution given the number of points and the size of the area in which they are located. A value of 1.0 results if the point pattern matches the expected random pattern. When the value of the statistic approaches zero, the point pattern is increasingly clustered, and when the statistic exceeds a value of 1.0, the point pattern is increasingly dispersed. A maximum value of 2.149 represents a completely uniform pattern. Another method—*quadrat analysis*—uses a similar assumption about the expected random distribution of points within a defined study area, but the statistic is based on a comparison of the mean number of points falling within each cell of a uniform grid overlain on the study area and the expected mean. Both strategies generate summary statistics that allow not only for the description of unique patterns of locations, but also permit the comparisons of different point patterns within the same study area or changes in the same point patterns over time. Empirical examples of both these types of comparisons are provided later in the chapter in Smith's (1985) analysis of the locational patterns of different types of restaurants in cities across Ontario, and in Wall, Dudycha, and Hutchinson's (1985) description of the changing patterns of hotel locations in the city of Toronto from 1950 to 1979.

Area

Fewer specific measures of the patterns reflected in areas or regions have been developed. Differentiating between regions within a study area using choropleth maps on the basis of any behavioral or perceptual attribute may reveal striking spatial patterns, reflecting varying qualities of people living in different parts of a community and may suggest previously unforeseen relationships. However, one especially useful indicator is the *location quotient*. Although it takes on a variety of configurations, a highly generalizable form of the location quotient is defined by the following equation:

$$LQ_i = \frac{a_i / (\sum_{i=1}^{n} a_i / n)}{p_i / (\sum_{i=1}^{n} p_i / n)}$$

where *LQ* is the location quotient for region *i*, *a* is an attribute of region *i*, *p* is the population of region *i*, and *n* is the number of regions comprising the study area. Essentially, the location quotient assesses the extent to which the distribution of the attribute in each region departs from the overall average for the entire study area. Location quotients have been used principally by economic geographers to describe variations across regions in the proportions of individuals in selected labor sectors. However, they are highly adaptable in reflecting variations in study regions for any number of logically related subgroups—such as the proportion of the population that participates in certain leisure activities—and overall population measures. They also have the advantage of resulting in measures that reflect deviations from the normative average of 1.0 (i.e., the region shares the same proportion of the attribute as the study area as a whole). For example, the proportion of youth participants in public recreation programs from each neighborhood relative to the proportion of the total youth population in each neighborhood could be examined for locational patterns. Values of the location quotient below 1.0 would indicate neighborhoods where participation is less than expected given the youth population, and values greater than 1.0 would indicate neighborhoods where participation is higher than expected. These indicators could then be evaluated against other descriptive measures of the neighborhoods to assess underlying factors influencing these revealed patterns of participation.

Units of analysis for areas or regions such as neighborhoods, census tracts, or whole communities also lend themselves to several measures such as *size, density,* and *shape.* The size of an area is an important building block for other indicators such as the point pattern measures, but it also represents an influential factor itself in potentially explaining variations in perceptions and behavior. In fact, size has been a frequently employed surrogate measure of the attractivity of destinations such as parks or resort areas.

Density measures, which are derived from size measures, reflect variations across regions according to selected attributes. For example, a popular planning device is to compare communities, or perhaps neighborhoods within communities, for differences in levels of opportunity for open space by calculating the density of total park land to total community size. As a factor either reflecting or influencing human behavior, a measure of density may be positive or negative. High densities of recreation opportunities within neighborhoods may be seen as a positive influence on behavior, whereas high densities of population may in fact reduce participation due to the possible perception of crowding.

The shape of each of the regions making up an entire area is highly reflective of the spatial structure of that area, and hence, its influence on and from human behavior. The extent to which regions of certain shapes are more or less likely to be associated with some types and intensities of behavior may reveal how we respond to the spatial structure of our communities or neighborhoods. A large number of indicators are available that measure shape, but perhaps the most frequently used measure is the Boyce and Clark (1964) shape index. It is calculated by selecting a point near the center of the region, then measuring the length of a series of regularly spaced radials, usually 16, from the center to the edge of the region. Then, using a circle as the normative value because all the radials would be of equal length, an index is calculated that produces a result ranging from zero for a perfectly circular shape to 200 indicating a straight line. Values of the index rarely exceed 60, which indicates a highly elongated shape for the region.

Many of these measures could be easily incorporated as variables in leisure research to introduce a sense of the influence of space and location on the behavior and perceptions of individuals. For example, levels of use at a number of different urban parks may be associated with their size or shape. In fact, as early as 1961, Jacobs suggested that people were much more likely to make use of *linear* open spaces than the traditional rectangular park areas because their behavior implied a preference for moving along the edges of those spaces. The inclusion of a measure of shape in park use studies may reveal such a preference among recreationists.

Distance

A dominant area of research in geography focusing on the consideration of distance and its influence on human behavior is *spatial interaction modeling.* Spatial interaction is concerned with understanding the movement of people, goods, and ideas between places (Haynes and Fotheringham, 1984). At its core, spatial interaction modeling involves three basic components:

1. the *origin* and its potential to generate the flow of objects,
2. the *destination* and its ability to attract the flow of objects, and
3. the *distance* between origins and destinations, and its affect on constraining movement between them.

The most basic mathematical form of a spatial interaction model is the gravity model, which is specified in this way:

$$I_{ij} = k \, O_i^{\lambda} D_j^{\alpha} d_{ij}^{\beta}$$

where I_{ij} is the interaction between origin i and destination j; O_i is some measure of the generating power or *emissivity* of origin i; D_j is some measure of the drawing power or *attractivity* of destination j; and d_{ij} is some measure of the friction of distance between origin i and destination j. The parameters k, λ, α, and β are estimated in the calibration of the model, typically through regression analysis, and they represent the effect each component has on the interactions. Many new forms of this basic model have evolved over the years as each component and its influences have become better understood (see Pooler, 1994, for an overview). Despite its lack of a strong theoretical foundation, the calibration of the model has nevertheless resulted in reasonably good estimates of flows between the origins and destinations of, for example, consumers, migratory workers, and recreational travelers (Smith, 1995). Estimating the number of travelers to specific destinations, as well as specifying the factors most influential in their travel behavior, was typical of early leisure research using the gravity model (e.g., Baxter and Ewing, 1986; Freund and Wilson, 1974; Malamud, 1973; McAllister and Klett, 1976). In most instances, the effect of distance—regardless of how it was specified—appeared to be the most influential factor in determining numbers of arrivals.

Spatial interaction models are of particular interest to tourism researchers, especially those concerned with predicting visitor flows between tourist origins and host destinations. However, from a practical standpoint, the primary obstacle to wider use of these models is that they are data intensive. Information on the numbers and characteristics of all individuals moving between all pairs of origins (e.g., tourists' home regions) and destinations (e.g., resort areas), as well as some cost function, such as the physical distance between every pair, is necessary before the model can be calibrated. Consequently, attention has shifted either to describing the spatial patterns of tourist movements as a means of revealing travel preferences (e.g., Forer and Pearce, 1984; Mings and McHugh, 1992), or to examining each of the model's components separately. Although truly spatial in nature, descriptive studies of travel patterns have generally ignored unique aspects of the tourists' origins and of the destinations as prescribed in the model. Ironically, studies of the model's individual components have become *aspatial;*

in other words, movements over space are not the focus, but rather, the characteristics of the travelers and of their destinations especially from a marketing perspective as much of the tourism literature now takes on an industry, economic emphasis. Studies of origins are generally concerned with the demographics, preferences, motivations, constraints, and satisfactions of the tourists themselves in an effort to establish meaningful market segments for particular types of travel experiences (e.g., Andereck and Caldwell, 1994; Dodd and Bigotte, 1997; Mansfeld, 1992; Qu and Li, 1997; Tian, Crompton and Witt, 1996). Destination studies attempt to understand what aspects of selected destinations distinguish them from competitors in the travel decision-making process, and recent interest has focused particularly on destination *image*—its meaning, measurement, and influence on destination choices and loyalties (e.g., Baloglu and Brinberg, 1997; Echtner and Ritchie, 1991, 1993; Walmsley and Young, 1998). Finally, studies of the distance component have become more concerned with identifying and examining alternative indicators of the friction of distance to travel. Two types of studies stand out: (1) those that consider *cognitive* distance, with the perception of distance or the perceived cost of overcoming distance the primary issue (e.g., Ankomah, Crompton and Baker, 1995; Walmsley and Jenkins, 1992), and (2) those that focus on the financial *cost* of travel, such as expenditures, prices, and willingness to pay (e.g., Smith, 1995; Yoon and Shafer, 1996). In the latter case, economic demand models have replaced the spatial interaction model as the principal vehicle for explaining and predicting travel behavior.

Recent Developments in Spatial Science

Undoubtedly, the most significant development in recent years that has facilitated research in many areas of geographic inquiry is the field of *geographic information systems* (GIS). Geographic information systems typically involve the development and application of computerized tools for the organization, processing, and analysis of spatial data. Goodchild (1991) has described several distinct areas of spatial science that have become the focus of GIS applications:

1. data collection and management,
2. spatial statistics,
3. data modeling,
4. data structures and indices,
5. algorithms and processes,
6. display of spatial data,

7. analytic tools, and
8. reasoning and cognition.

Basically, GIS is a geographic database management system (Martin, 1996). It is grounded in maps, which comprise the primary form of data input and output, and in the spatial sciences associated with them; hence, GIS extends the potential of basic geographic concepts by making spatial measures and analyses more accessible. In this respect, GIS may then be thought of as both a set of tools that facilitate the display and description of patterns of phenomena in a spatial context (i.e., computer-based cartography), as well as a science facilitating spatial analysis and explanation of the spatial processes that underlie the patterns (Wright, Goodchild and Proctor, 1997). Ultimately, the true nature and power of GIS rests in its potential as science, but it also has lead to a renewed interest in furthering the applications of spatial statistics and descriptions of spatial patterns (Gaile, 1990). Both the natural and social sciences have embraced applications of GIS, although the dynamic nature and the rapid temporal changes of social processes have presented quite unique challenges (Marble, 1990; Martin, 1996.)

Geographic information systems have organized themselves along two major traditions. The first is based in the *raster* approach which takes a study area, overlays a fine, uniform grid of rectangular cells, and then describes selected characteristics of each cell and the relationships among them. The analyses of such relationships lead to an understanding of how a variety of features on and across the landscape may be related to one another (i.e., *spatial autocorrelation*), and thence, correspondingly transform over space. The second tradition is based in the *vector* approach, which identifies discrete objects within the study area (such as points, lines, and/or areas), defines them with a system of coordinates, and then describes their locations. Both approaches create databases defined by the spatial units of analysis that then lend themselves to subsequent analyses, including those techniques described here. With the advent of more powerful and affordable microcomputer systems, GIS applications are increasingly becoming available to spatial analysts with many different interests, including leisure and recreation, although examples of the latter are exceedingly rare. Leisure-related research that has used GIS applications has tended to focus on examining the supply side of recreation (i.e., recreation facilities and open space) and selected demographic characteristics of the population, in large part because the data, especially census data, have been more readily available in existing municipal GIS databases.

Wicks, Backman, Allen, and Van Blaircom (1993) produced maps of the census tracts for the city of Greenville, South Carolina, displaying the distributions of park resources, of the population according to age and income, and finally, of the relative need resulting from the integration of these two factors. Based on the social indicators they selected, their results indicated in which areas of the city the need for park resources may be greatest or at least should be monitored as the character of the local population evolves. Although Wicks et al. (1993) overstated the necessity of having GIS technology available to undertake this descriptive study, they did illustrate how such an integrated database may be used to provide insights into the spatial relationships between recreation resources and the population they are intended to serve.

Two more recent studies using GIS applications in leisure studies focused on equity in the distribution of community recreation resources. Both studies examined alternative measures of accessibility in describing the degree of equity that existed in the distribution of urban parks in Pueblo, Colorado (Talen, 1998), and of playgrounds in Tulsa, Oklahoma (Talen and Anselin, 1998). They further analyzed how these access measures were related to a selection of socioeconomic factors relevant to the resource. For example, in the case of Tulsa, Talen and Anselin (1998) examined the relationship between the proportion of children in each census tract of the city and their access to the available playgrounds. In both papers, GIS was used to display the distribution of the parks and playgrounds as well as segments of the population to allow a visual assessment of the spatial equity in their distributions. More importantly, however, GIS provided the means to assess statistically the spatial relationships between the access measures and the selected socioeconomic factors, using in these cases Moran's *I* statistic, a global measure of spatial autocorrelation. Their findings indicated that, depending on which measure of accessibility is used, quite different relationships between the distribution of resources and the target population are detected—relationships apparent only when spatial analysis is used. For leisure researchers, the results of both studies have important implications for the way in which we think about accessibility issues and ultimately evaluate the distribution of leisure services.

Applications in Leisure Research

Geographic interest in and contributions to leisure and recreation research may be regarded as quite extensive if one were to include all aspects of location, place, space, distance, mobility, and similar basic geographic concepts. Coppock's (1982) overview of the principal geographic themes in the leisure-related literature up to the 1980s is still largely relevant today, although it only hints at the important part that behavioral and perceptual considerations have to understanding leisure phenomena. The books by Cosgrove and Jackson (1972), Smith (1983), and Patmore (1983) on "recreation geography" also provide exemplary overviews, although they, too, focus primarily on the description of recreation resources and travel patterns, and give less attention to the analysis of the spatial aspects of leisure behavior and of the underlying social processes that may explain that behavior.

Certainly, there are many studies that have:

1. focused on specific locations for their unique qualities and, by inference, their influence on recreation;
2. considered differences between sites or communities in the provision of services and programs; and
3. examined the effect that distance or accessibility has on recreational use of different sites.

However, if we confine our discussion to spatial analysis, the leisure literature has been sporadic, with only a few examples appearing in the mid 1970s then again in the mid 1980s, and fragmented, with little connection among studies and little building of knowledge. As a result, most of the exemplary studies based in the leisure literature come from these two periods.

In general, studies using spatial analytic techniques fall into three broad categories. First, and most common, are the studies focusing on recreation resources and opportunities—facilities, parks and open space, and commercial sector services. These may be regarded as opportunity-based or supply-side research. Second, there are the studies that have examined recreation behavior from the human side, whether it be variations in the demographics of people or their recreational participation based on a breakdown by spatial units, such as counties, neighborhoods, or communities. These are the behaviorally based or demand-side research studies. Finally, there are those rarer studies that blend opportunity and behavioral-based perspectives into one spatial analysis in an attempt to understand the interplay of provision and use on the leisure landscape. This three-category breakdown is not dissimilar from the three major areas that Aitken (1991) argued provide internally consistent bodies of theory related to the relationship between people and the environment in behavioral geography.

Opportunity-Based Studies

Most geographic interest in recreation and leisure has been focused on the supply-side and spatial choice models. Essentially, recreation sites are set as the units of analysis and then spatial patterns are described and analyzed. Patmore (1983), for example, devotes considerable time to examining the spatial distributions of several types of recreation facilities and sites in different regions of England and Wales, arguing that the patterns reveal much about the nature of the activities themselves. Characteristics of the sites that may explain variations in their spatial patterns are typically included in these studies, and behavioral indicators associated with each site, such as participation or perceptions, are treated as variables that may explain differences in their use.

A pair of studies by Mitchell (1968, 1973) represents two of the earliest examples of this approach. In these studies, Mitchell examined the effect of, first, the attributes of playgrounds, and second, distances from playgrounds, in generating participation. In each case, these locational factors appeared to have an important role in influencing participation. Supply-side effects on participation also were examined by Beaman, Kim, and Smith (1979) in their study of skiing, hunting, and fishing in 62 different regions across Canada. After first controlling for socioeconomic variations in participation, they were able to empirically derive supply effects specific to each region.

Typical examples of the examination of locational differences in the provision of recreation opportunities are found in the work of Haley (1979, 1985) and Mitchell and Lovingood (1976). Haley (1979) calculated the land area and expenditures devoted to parks and recreation in 76 municipalities in the United States to determine which ones had met traditionally held recreation planning standards. In his 1985 follow-up study, Haley found that the differences between city centers and the suburbs had narrowed, with suburban areas showing significant improvement from previous years. In a study by Mitchell and Lovingood (1976), spatial relationships between park density and selected demographic variables measured at the census tract level in Columbia, South Carolina, provided the focus. They found a general relationship between park density and lower socioeconomic areas within the city, which appeared to contradict earlier beliefs about provision of public open space as outlined by Godbey and Dunn (1978) in their criticism of the study. In their response,

Mitchell and Lovingood's (1978) discussion is reflective of two fundamental issues that later emerge in debates around spatial analysis—level of aggregation of spatial units and the relationship between spatial structure and spatial behavior.

After devising an empirically based strategy for classifying public and private recreation facilities, Lovingood and Mitchell (1978) used nearest neighbor analysis to contrast the two recreation sectors and to speculate on their complementary roles. They found the provision of public recreation facilities to be somewhat more clustered in space than private recreation facilities, and suggested that their purposes and structures helped to explain their complementarity. Smith (1985) used a variety of spatial analysis techniques, including nearest neighbor analysis, in his study of urban restaurants in order to identify factors contributing to their success. In studies of this nature, the spatial structure of the facilities under study revealed important aspects not previously recognized in studies of recreation provision.

Wall et al. (1985) examined change over time in their study of the spatial distribution of hotels and motels in Toronto, Ontario. In their study, they used several point pattern analysis techniques on locations of hotels, in both unweighted form and weighted by room numbers, for five selected years between 1950 and 1979 to illustrate the way in which accommodations had grown in size and become increasingly concentrated in the downtown area of the city. One of the very earliest and still one of the most imaginative applications of point pattern analysis is Rolfe's (1965) analysis of the changing park distribution in Lansing, Michigan, over time. His study was unlike many of the more recent efforts in two respects. First, he examined changes in the distributions of parks over time to determine whether their development had matched changes in population density, and second, he evaluated the results of his nearest neighbor analyses against a hypothesized distribution based on a principle of serving all neighborhoods in the community. This normative approach to the study, where a theoretical evaluative criterion is established at the outset, is not frequently matched by more recent descriptive studies of spatial distributions.

Behaviorally Based Studies

When the units of analysis are selected to represent the origins of the individuals and their characteristics, behavior, and perceptions, the nature of the studies may be regarded as behaviorally based. The fundamental interest for these studies is to identify spatial variations in the leisure behavior of individuals whether or not the behavior is tied to a specific recreation site. Spatial variations in leisure behavior may then reveal other factors that underlie any of these differences.

Information on the origins of individuals is less readily available, and consequently, there are fewer examples of these types of studies. One area that has seen a relative abundance of work has been *sports geography,* which has concerned itself with the spatial patterns of athletes' origins and teams' locations for a variety of sports, both professional and amateur (Bale, 1982, 1989; Rooney, 1974). The concentration by region of the participation in sports, the numbers of teams in various leagues, and per capita production of college and professional athletes is typical of studies in sports geography. In each case, point and discrete areal maps are used to identify spatial patterns and reveal underlying processes that may be contributing to the variations across regions.

On a more local level, studies of spatial patterns of leisure behavior and perceptions are rarer still in the leisure literature. Mitchell and Lovingood (1976) illustrated spatial variations in the demographic characteristics of the population according to census tracts in their study of Columbia, South Carolina, but they did not generate similar maps for recreation behavior. Nevertheless, their maps were highly suggestive of the potential influences that such socioeconomic factors may have on behavior. I used location quotients to describe the census tracts in London, Ontario, according to the membership at a major recreation center, then correlated those indicators with selected demographic characteristics and a distance measure (Smale, 1985). I found that membership was higher than expected in the more affluent areas of the city with larger families and that increased distance from the center did reduce expected membership levels. However, there were variations in the importance of these factors depending on the membership category being considered.

In another study, two sets of location quotients were calculated for 66 regions across Canada to compare their ability to generate and to receive tourists (Smale and Butler, 1985). Our results pointed to regions that had higher than expected abilities to generate domestic travelers given the originating region's population, and regions that received higher than expected proportions of travelers into them. We then compiled the regional indicators according to province and took the ratio of generating to receiving location quotients to determine which provinces were net beneficiaries of domestic tourism. We used a similar approach in our analysis of festivals and special events in the counties of eastern Ontario (Butler and Smale, 1991).

A variation on the behaviorally based studies described here are those studies that included cognitive information on individuals, such as their perceptions of recreation opportunities located in their regions or communities. Although not usually mapped, studies of perceptions typically revealed spatial variations in:

1. the extent of individuals' knowledge of and familiarity with available opportunities (Aldskogius, 1977; Smale, 1983a; Spotts and Stynes, 1984, 1985);

2. the levels of awareness and resultant use of leisure opportunity (Elson, 1976; Hayward and Weitzer, 1984; Perdue, 1987); and

3. the relationship between perceived distance and the use of recreation opportunities (Elson, 1976; Spotts and Stynes, 1984).

The examination of the spatial variations in leisure-related perceptions remains a largely untapped area of research, yet one, which holds considerable promise.

Blended Studies

Difficulty in collecting detailed data plays a large part in limiting the number of examples of blended studies. Information is needed both on the characteristics of the individuals and on the attributes of the recreation sites making up the study area, as well as locational measures on both, such as point coordinates and/or areal classification.

All spatial interaction modeling related to recreation travel and tourism for which there are numerous examples fall in this category because measures of both the participants and the recreation sites are typically included in the derivation of the models. At the community level, Dee and Liebman (1970) and McAllister (1977) are examples of variations on the spatial interaction theme. In both of these cases, a modified gravity model was proposed to explain variations in the recreational use of playgrounds and recreation centers. In both studies, distance from the recreation site was the most important factor in explaining participation, and site characteristics such as size and number of amenities were next most important. Minimizing travel distance was also the underlying assumption in Goodchild and Booth's (1980) study of public swimming pool use, yet their maps of the actual service areas of the pools revealed many instances that violated this assumption. Clearly, distance and the *response* to distance were quite different and pointed to other spatial factors that influenced the decision to participate.

I used a variation of Rolfe's study of change over time in the provision of urban parks, but extended his analysis by including a measure of the population (Smale, 1983b). I calculated the mean centers and standard deviational ellipses for both the distribution of parks and the distribution of the population in the city of London, Ontario, for five separate study years between 1956 and 1976. I theorized that if the parks were equitably provided in the city, the spatial statistics describing their distribution should coincide with those of the population; in other words, the mean centers should fall at the same point and the standard deviational ellipses should show similar orientations. The results of this study showed that over the years, the spatial statistics increasingly converged, suggesting a growing degree of equity in park provision.

In a series of studies using a derivative function of the gravity model called *potential,* I have been able to show how a spatial perspective on both the resources dedicated to recreational use and the individuals who may use those resources can be integrated into a single spatial system reflecting their mutual influence (Smale, 1990, 1994, 1995). I argued that the recreational resources in a community could be regarded as a continuous surface of leisure potential reflecting the relative supply of opportunity. Similarly, the residents' demand for recreation could also be seen as a continuous surface reflecting variations in the relative demand for opportunity. By calculating the potential for each of these surfaces based on a variety of indicators, then taking the ratio of the measures of these two systems at the same points in the community surface, a contour map could be drawn to reflect the spatial variations in recreation demand relative to the available supply. The resultant maps from the 1994 study for the town of Oakville, Ontario, are shown in Figures 12.4, Figure 12.5, and Figure 12.6 (page 192). The first two maps reflect variations across the town in the supply of and demand for public recreation opportunities. The third map (Figure 12.6, page 192), which shows the ratio of the values of the first two maps, reflects disparities in the community surface; that is, departures from equitable provision. Surface values of 1.0 on the map indicate points where demand and supply are in balance, while values below 1.0 indicate points where the demand exceeds supply and values above 1.0 indicate points where supply exceeds demand.

By overlaying maps showing the spatial distributions of recreation behavior and selected demographic characteristics, I was able to identify factors contributing to the revealed departures from the theorized balance under conditions of equity. For example, neighborhoods in which estimated demand exceeded the

FIGURE 12.4   **RECREATION SUPPLY SYSTEM SURFACE**

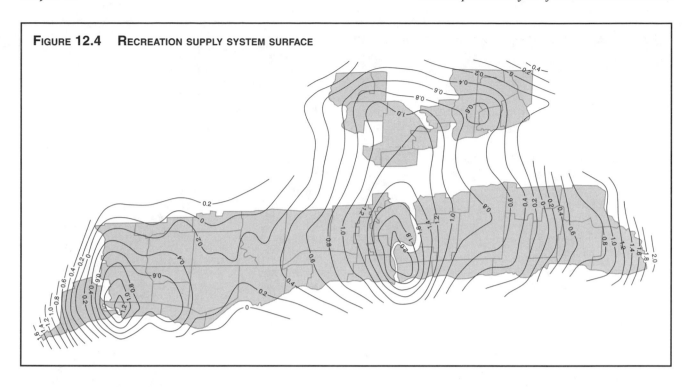

available supply were often characterized either by lower densities of higher income families or by higher densities of young, lower income families. The obvious contrast in these social groups undoubtedly reveals a basic difference in the *need* for public recreation opportunities, with the more affluent residents having exhibited less reliance on public facilities. Such a finding would not have been revealed had some measure of income simply been correlated with the

equity index. In contrast, those areas of the community in which the levels of recreation opportunity exceeded demand were typically characterized by large, multipurpose parks clustered along waterways and the lake, and also by areas where sports fields and facilities were concentrated. Ironically, these recreation areas, which were the most frequently used in the community, were not only meeting expressed levels of demand, but also exceeding them. This finding appears

FIGURE 12.5   **RECREATION DEMAND SYSTEM SURFACE**

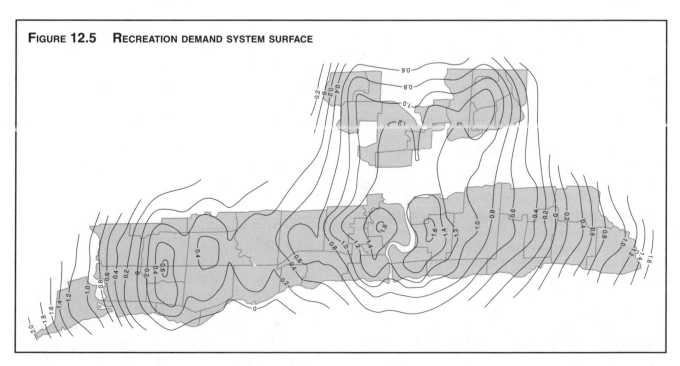

FIGURE 12.6   RECREATION PROVISION EQUITY SYSTEM SURFACE

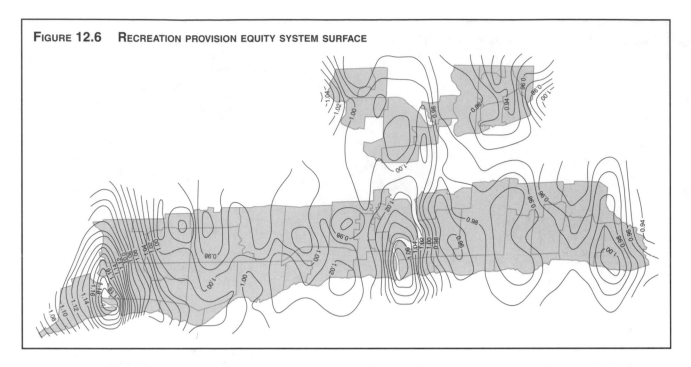

to dispute a typical planning response that increases in opportunity are needed in areas where expressed demand is highest.

Directions for the Future

An important goal for the future is the greater use of a spatial perspective in leisure research to complement the interest in contextual aspects of leisure and recreation. The simple process of including spatial variables in the data gathered as part of our routine collection strategies would be an important first step. For example, in population surveys, a locational variable could be created by assigning Cartesian coordinates to each individual based on his or her household, neighborhood, or spatial reference points for postal or zip codes. By including the coordinates for the recreation opportunities within the study area in the data set, measures of physical distance, accessibility, and relative proximity could be determined, furthering the potential to evaluate the role of the spatial context in explaining leisure behavior, perceptions, and preferences.

Hence, a further objective for spatial analysis in leisure research would be to extend geographic inquiry from purely resource-based to include human-based analyses. People, their behavior, perceptions and preferences can just as easily be regarded within a spatial context as static, physical locations of resources dedicated to recreational use. For example, the research on constraints to leisure may be extended through a spatial perspective, such as in the study by Madge (1997). In her study of public parks in Leicester, En-

gland, Madge showed how fear constrained park use by various social groups (i.e., women, the elderly) and how that fear manifested itself in distinct spatial behavior by each group. Further, microlevel studies of people's locations in specific sites, such as parks, museums, or beaches, would reveal where various social groups and their activities tend to be concentrated or dispersed. Examining these patterns over an extended period of time also may reveal spatial-temporal shifts in their revealed preferences.

Optimally, a blending of the consideration for both people and resources in spatial analysis would yield the greatest benefits. A conceptual starting point for leisure researchers may be found in the components that define spatial interaction models—the people, their characteristics, and their leisure behavior; the places where leisure occurs and the factors that define them; and some reflection of the spatial context that separates the people from the places, whether it be distance, proximity, or perhaps perceived accessibility. However, rather than relying on the traditional linear formulation of the gravity model, alternative theoretical models could be developed building on the existing work in leisure studies. For example, with the advent of structural equation modeling and its theory-driven rather than data-driven intent, the more complex relationships among factors of continuing interest to leisure researchers can be postulated and explored. Certainly, this process can be facilitated by geographic information systems, especially with the advancements in strategies for handling social data and further developments in computer technology.

Gathering, organizing, and analyzing data at this level of detail clearly would benefit from the integration of the perspectives of geographers and other behavioral scientists; in other words, greater multidisciplinary efforts in leisure research.

Another area that has tremendous potential is space-time research. While leisure researchers have shown considerable interest in studies of the allocation of time to various activities, they have not included detailed measures of where these activities have taken place nor attempted to analyze the relationship between place and time. Researchers working within *time-geography* have regarded notions of time and space as basic constraints that individuals must overcome to undertake their activities; yet, they have generally not considered leisure activity in their analyses. However, the unique work by Janelle and Goodchild, in particular, demonstrates the possibilities that exist for understanding behavior in both space and time. Using data from the Halifax time-budget survey—which included activity specific locational measures—they were able to identify the underlying urban ecological structure of the city and travel patterns for different social groups at different times during the day (Goodchild and Janelle, 1984; Goodchild, Klinkenberg and Janelle, 1993; Janelle and Goodchild, 1983; Janelle, Goodchild and Klinkenberg, 1988). For leisure researchers, gathering information in time-budget or experience sampling method studies on the specific location of the respondents for each episode would open the door to a variety of possibilities. For example, the amount of time spent in and of the sequencing of activities, as well as how we experience them, are necessarily tied to *where* the activities are undertaken. Consequently, including locational factors in such studies would enhance our understanding of the *timing of space* (i.e., how much time is spent where, doing what) and the *spacing of time* (i.e., how time is organized around spatial structures and how spatial structure affects the time spent in different places). Through a better understanding the spatial-temporal context of leisure behavior and leisure places, we would create a new window through which to look directly into other aspects of leisure experiences.

Finally, the debate over the utility of spatial analysis in developing theory and a clearer understanding of human behavior continues in geography and should not be ignored by leisure researchers. Much of the criticism has focused on the deterministic view that the spatial analysis procedures, based in a positivist paradigm, have traditionally assumed. Several authors are now reflecting on a postpositivist era in geography and especially locational analysis, where more qualitative approaches associated with humanistic geography are embraced (Cloke, Philo and Sadler, 1991; Shields, 1997). Indeed, the work of feminist geographers in Britain has resulted in some of the most innovative, interpretivist approaches to understanding gendered spatial behavior and structure (Massey, 1994; Women and Geography Study Group, 1997). Thus, even though very little work has been done in leisure studies using a spatial analytic perspective, even less work involving a spatial context has been done using more interpretive methods. We could learn much from individuals by exploring their experiences and symbolic meanings of place and space especially as they relate to the role of leisure in their lives.

References

Aitken, S. C. (1991). Person-environment theories in contemporary perceptual and behavioral geography I: Personality, attitudinal, and spatial choice theories. *Progress in Human Geography, 15*(2), 179–193.

Aldskogius, H. (1977). A conceptual framework and a Swedish case study of recreational behavior and environmental cognition. *Economic Geography, 53*(2), 163–183.

Andereck, K. L., & Caldwell, L. L. (1994). Variable selection in tourism market segmentation models. *Journal of Travel Research, 33*(2), 40–46.

Ankomah, P. K., Crompton, J. L., & Baker, D. A. (1995). A study of pleasure travelers' cognitive distance assessments. *Journal of Travel Research, 34*(2), 12–18.

Bale, J. (1982). *Sport and place: A geography of sport in England, Scotland and Wales.* London, UK: C. Hurst & Co.

Bale, J. (1989). *Sports geography.* London, UK: E & FN Spon.

Baloglu, S., & Brinberg, D. (1997). Affective images of tourism destinations. *Journal of Travel Research, 35*(4), 11–15.

Baxter, M. J., & Ewing, G .O. (1986). A framework for the exploratory development of spatial interaction models: A recreation travel example. *Journal of Leisure Research, 18*(4), 320–336.

Beaman, J., Kim, Y., & Smith, S. L. J. (1979). The effect of recreation supply on participation. *Leisure Sciences, 2*(1), 71–87.

Boyce, R., & Clark, W. (1964). The concept of shape in geography. *Geographical Review, 54,* 561–572.

Butler, R. W., & Smale, B. J. A. (1991). Geographic perspectives on festivals in Ontario. *Journal of Applied Recreation Research, 16*(1), 1–23.

Campbell, J. (1993). *Map use and analysis* (2nd ed.). Dubuque, IA: Wm. C. Brown Publishers.

Cloke, P., Philo, C., & Sadler, D. (1991). *Approaching human geography: An introduction to contemporary theoretical debates.* London, UK: The Guildford Press.

Coffey, W. J. (1981). *Geography: Towards a general spatial systems approach.* London, UK: Methuen.

Coppock, J. T. (1982). Geographical contributions to the study of leisure. *Leisure Studies, 1*(1), 1–27.

Cosgrove, I., & Jackson, R. (1972). *The geography of recreation and leisure.* London, UK: Hutchinson & Co.

Cox, K. R. (1995). Concepts of space, understanding in human geography, and spatial analysis. *Urban Geography, 16*(4), 304–326.

Dee, N., & Liebman, J. C. (1970). A statistical study of attendance at urban playgrounds. *Journal of Leisure Research, 2*(3), 145–159.

Dodd, T., & Bigotte, V. (1997). Perceptual differences among visitor groups to wineries. *Journal of Travel Research, 35*(3), 46–51.

Duffield, B. S. (1975). The nature of recreational travel space. In G. A. C. Searle (Ed.), *Recreational economics and analysis* (pp. 15–35). New York, NY: Longman.

Ebdon, D. (1977). *Statistics in geography.* London, UK: Oxford University Press.

Echtner, C. M., & Ritchie, J. R. B. (1991). The meaning and measurement of destination image. *Journal of Tourism Studies, 2*(2), 2–12.

Echtner, C. M., & Ritchie, J. R. B. (1993). The measurement of destination image: An empirical assessment. *Journal of Travel Research, 31*(4), 3–13.

Elson, M. J. (1976). Activity spaces and recreation spatial behavior. *Town Planning Review, 47*(3), 241–255.

Freund, R. J., & Wilson, R. R. (1974). An example of a gravity model to estimate recreation travel. *Journal of Leisure Research, 6,* 241–256.

Forer, P. C., & Pearce, D. G. (1984). Spatial patterns of package tourism in New Zealand. *New Zealand Geographer, 40*(1), 34–42.

Gaile, G. L. (1990). Whither spatial statistics? *Professional Geographer, 42*(1), 95–100.

Gallagher, W. (1993). *The power of place: How our surroundings shape our thoughts, emotions, and actions.* New York, NY: Poseidon Press.

Gatrell, A. (1983). *Distance and space: A geographical perspective.* Oxford, UK: Clarendon Press.

Godbey, G., & Dunn, D. R. (1978). A critique of "Public urban recreation: An investigation of spatial relationships." *Journal of Leisure Research, 10*(1), 61–67.

Golledge, R. G., & Rushton, G. (1984). A review of analytic behavioral research in geography. In D. T. Herbert & R. J. Johnson (Eds.), *Geography and the urban environment: Progress in research and applications* (Vol. VI, pp. 1–43). New York, NY: John Wiley & Sons, Inc.

Golledge, R. G., & Timmermans, H. (1990). Applications of behavioral research on spatial problems I: Cognition. *Progress in Human Geography, 14*(1), 57–99.

Goodchild, M. F. (1984). Geocoding and geosampling. In G. L. Gaile & C. J. Willmott (Eds.), *Spatial statistics and models* (pp. 33–53). Dordrecht, Netherlands: D. Reidel Publishing.

Goodchild, M. F. (1991). Geographic information systems. *Progress in Human Geography, 15*(2), 194–200.

Goodchild, M. F., & Booth, P. J. (1980). Location and allocation of recreation facilities: Public swimming pools in London, Ontario. *Ontario Geography, 15,* 35–51.

Goodchild, M. F., & Janelle, D. G. (1984). The city around the clock: Space-time patterns of urban ecological structure. *Environment and Planning A, 16*(5), 807–820.

Goodchild, M. F., Klinkenberg, B., & Janelle, D. G. (1993). A factorial model of aggregate spatiotemporal behavior: Application to the diurnal cycle. *Geographical Analysis, 25*(4), 277–294.

Gould, P., & White, R. (1986). *Mental maps* (2nd ed.). Boston, MA: Allen & Unwin.

Haggett, P., Cliff, A. D., & Frey, A. (1977a). *Locational analysis in human geography 1: Locational methods.* London, UK: Edward Arnold.

Haggett, P., Cliff, A. D., & Frey, A. (1977b). *Locational analysis in human geography 2: Locational models.* London, UK: Edward Arnold.

Haley, A. J. (1979). Municipal recreation and park standards in the United States: Central cities and suburbs. *Leisure Sciences, 2*(3/4), 277–289.

Haley, A. J. (1985). Municipal recreation and park standards in the United States: Central cities and suburbs, 1975–1980. *Leisure Sciences, 7*(2), 175–188.

Hammond, R., & McCullagh, P. S. (1978). *Quantitative techniques in geography: An introduction* (2nd ed.). Oxford, UK: Clarendon Press.

Haynes, K. E., & Fotheringham, A. S. (1984). *Gravity and spatial interaction models.* London, UK: Sage Publications, Ltd.

Hayward, D. G., & Weitzer, W. H. (1984). The public's image of urban parks: Past amenity, present ambivalence, uncertain future. *Urban Ecology, 8*(3), 243–268.

Henderson, K. A., Bialeschki, M. D., Shaw, S. M., & Freysinger, V. J. (1996). *Both gains and gaps: Feminist perspectives on women's leisure.* State College, PA: Venture Publishing, Inc.

Herbert, D. T., & Johnson, R. J. (Eds.). (1976). *Social areas in cities: Vol. 2. Spatial perspectives on problems and policies.* London, UK: John Wiley & Sons, Ltd.

Hiss, T. (1990). *The experience of place.* New York, NY: Knopf.

Horna, J. (1994). *The study of leisure.* Toronto, Ontario. Oxford University Press.

Jacobs, J. (1961). *The death and life of great American cities.* New York, NY: Vintage Books.

Janelle, D. G., & Goodchild, M. F. (1983). Diurnal patterns of social group distributions in a Canadian city. *Economic Geography, 59*(4), 403–425.

Janelle, D. G., Goodchild, M. F., & Klinkenberg, B. (1988). Space-time diaries and travel characteristics for different levels of respondent aggregation. *Environment and Planning A, 20*(7), 891–906.

Jones, E., & Eyles, J. (1977). *An introduction to social geography.* Oxford, UK: Oxford University Press.

Kelly, J. R. (1996). *Leisure* (3rd ed.). Boston, MA: Allyn & Bacon.

Klein, H. J. (1993). Tracking visitor circulation in museum settings. *Environment and Behavior, 25*(6), 782–800.

Lovingood, P. E., & Mitchell, L. S. (1978). The structure of public and private recreational systems: Columbia, South Carolina. *Journal of Leisure Research, 10*(1), 21–36.

Madge, C. (1997). Public parks and the geography of fear. *Tijdschrift voor Economische en Sociale Geografie, 88*(3), 237–250.

Malamud, B. (1973). Gravity model calibration of tourist travel to Las Vegas. *Journal of Leisure Research, 5*(4), 23–33.

Mansfeld, Y. (1992). From motivation to actual travel. *Annals of Tourism Research, 19*(3), 399–419.

Marble, D. F. (1990). The potential methodological impact of geographic information systems on the social sciences. In K. M. S. Allen, S. W. Green & E. B. W. Zubrow (Eds.), *Interpreting space: GIS and archaeology* (pp. 9–21). London, UK: Taylor and Francis.

Martin, D. (1996). *Geographic information systems: Socioeconomic applications* (2nd ed.). London, UK: Routledge.

Massey. D. (1994). *Space, place, and gender.* Minneapolis, MN: University of Minnesota Press.

McAllister, D. M. (1976). Equity and efficiency in public facility location. *Geographical Analysis, 8*(1), 47–63.

McAllister, D. M. (1977). An empirical analysis of the spatial behavior of urban public recreation activity. *Geographical Analysis, 9*(2), 174–181.

McAllister, D. M., & Klett, F. R. (1976). A modified gravity model of regional recreation activity with an application to ski trips. *Journal of Leisure Research, 8*(1), 21–34.

Mercer, D. C. (1970). The geography of leisure—A contemporary growth point. *Geography, 55,* 261–273.

Mings, R. C., & McHugh, K. E. (1992). The spatial configuration of travel to Yellowstone National Park. *Journal of Travel Research, 30*(4), 38–46.

Mitchell, L. S. (1968). The facility index as a measure of attendance at recreation sites. *Professional Geographer, 20*(4), 276–278.

Mitchell, L. S. (1973). An analysis of the range and spatial gradient of urban recreation hinterlands. *Professional Geographer, 25*(3), 261–266.

Mitchell, L. S., & Lovingood, P. E. (1976). Public urban recreation: An investigation of spatial relationships. *Journal of Leisure Research, 8*(1), 6–20.

Mitchell, L. S., & Lovingood, P. E. (1978). A response to the critique of "Public urban recreation: An investigation of spatial relationships." *Journal of Leisure Research, 10*(1), 68–72.

Morrill, R. L. (1970). *The spatial organization of society.* Belmont, CA: Wadsworth.

Pacione, M. (1984). Local areas in cities. In D. T. Herbert & R. J. Johnson (Eds.), *Geography and the urban environment: Progress in research and applications* (Vol. VI, pp. 349–392). New York, NY: John Wiley & Sons, Inc.

Patmore, J. A. (1983). *Recreation and resources: Leisure patterns and leisure places.* London, UK: Basil Blackwell.

Perdue, R. R. (1987). The influence of awareness on spatial behavior in recreational boating. *Leisure Sciences, 9*(1), 15–25.

Pooler, J. (1994). An extended family of spatial interaction models. *Progress in Human Geography, 18*(1), 17–39.

Qu, H., & Li, L. (1997). The characteristics and satisfaction of mainland Chinese visitors to Hong Kong. *Journal of Travel Research, 35*(4), 37–41.

Rolfe, E. (1965). Analysis of the spatial distribution of neighborhood parks in Lansing: 1920–1960. *Papers of the Michigan Academy of Science, Arts and Letters, 50,* 479–491.

Rooney, J. (1974). *A geography of American sport.* Reading, MA: Addison-Wesley.

Rushton, G. (1993). Human behavior in spatial analysis. *Urban Geography, 14*(5), 447–456.

Sack, D. (1993). The power of place and space. *Geographical Review, 83*(3), 326–329.

Säisä, J., Svensson-Gärling, A., Gärling, T., & Lindberg, E. (1986). Intraurban cognitive distances: The relationship between judgments of straight-line distances, travel distances, and travel times. *Geographical Analysis, 18*(2), 167–174.

Shields, R. (1997). Spatial stress and resistance: Social meanings of spatialization. In G. Benko & U. Strohmayer (Eds.), *Space and social theory: Interpreting modernity and postmodernity* (pp. 186–202). Oxford, UK: Blackwell.

Smale, B. J. A. (1983a). *Actual and perceived distributions of urban open space.* Sixth Annual Applied Geography Conference, Toronto, Ontario.

Smale, B. J. A. (1983b). Identifying disparities in the provision of urban recreation opportunities. *Recreation Research Review, 10*(4), 24–32.

Smale, B. J. A. (1985). A method for describing spatial variations in recreation participation. *Loisir et Société/Society and Leisure, 8*(2), 735–750.

Smale, B. J. A. (1990). *Spatial equity in the provision of urban recreation opportunities.* Sixth Canadian Congress on Leisure Research, University of Waterloo, Waterloo, Ontario.

Smale, B. J. A. (1994). *The spatial context of leisure behavior: An alternative perspective.* Symposium on Leisure Research, National Recreation and Parks Association, 1994 Congress for Recreation and Parks, Minneapolis, Minnesota.

Smale, B. J. A. (1995). *Spatially derived estimates of neighborhood emissivity and park attractivity in explaining leisure behavior in an urban context.* Symposium on Leisure Research, National Recreation and Parks Association, 1995 Congress for Recreation and Parks, San Antonio, Texas.

Smale, B. J. A., & Butler, R. W. (1985). Domestic tourism in Canada: Regional and provincial patterns. *Ontario Geography, 26,* 37–56.

Smith, D. M. (1975). *Patterns in human geography.* London, UK: Penguin.

Smith, S. L. J. (1983). *Recreation geography.* London, UK: Longman.

Smith, S. L. J. (1985). Location patterns of urban restaurants. *Annals of Tourism Research, 12*(4), 581–602.

Smith, S. L. J. (1995). *Tourism analysis: A handbook* (2nd ed.). Essex, UK: Longman.

Spotts, D. M., & Stynes D. J. (1984). Public awareness and knowledge of urban parks: A case study. *Journal of Park and Recreation Administration, 2*(4), 1–12.

Spotts D. M., & Stynes, D. J. (1985). Measuring the public's familiarity with recreation areas. *Journal of Leisure Research, 17*(4), 253–265.

Talen, E. (1998). Visualizing fairness: Equity maps for planners. *Journal of the American Planning Association, 64*(1), 22–38.

Talen, E., & Anselin, L. (1998). Assessing spatial equity: An evaluation of measures of accessibility to public playgrounds. *Environment and Planning A, 30,* 595–613.

Tian, S., Crompton, J. L., & Witt, P. A. (1996). Integrating constraints and benefits to identify responsive target markets for museum attractions. *Journal of Travel Research, 35*(2), 34–45.

Timmermans, H., & Golledge, R. G. (1990). Applications of behavioral research on spatial problems II: Preference and choice. *Progress in Human Geography, 14*(3), 311–354.

Tuan, Y.-F. (1974). *Topophilia: A study of environmental perception, attitudes, and values.* Englewood Cliffs, NJ: Prentice-Hall.

Tuan, Y.-F. (1977). *Space and place: The perspective of experience.* London, UK: Edward Arnold.

Unwin, D. (1981). *Introductory spatial analysis.* London, UK: Methuen.

Wall, G., Dudycha, D., & Hutchinson, J. (1985). Point pattern analyses of accommodation in Toronto. *Annals of Tourism Research, 12*(4), 603–618.

Walmsley, D. J. (1988). *Urban living: The individual in the city.* Essex, UK: Longman.

Walmsley, D. J., & Jenkins, J. M. (1992). Cognitive distance: A neglected issue in travel behavior. *Journal of Travel Research, 31*(1), 24–29.

Walmsley, D. J., & Young, M. (1998). Evaluative images and tourism: The use of personal constructs to describe the structure of destination images. *Journal of Travel Research, 36*(3), 65–69.

Wicks, B. E., Backman, K. F., Allen, J., & Van Blaricom, D. (1993). Geographic information systems (GIS): A tool for marketing, managing, and planning municipal park systems. *Journal of Park and Recreation Administration, 11*(1), 9–23.

Wolfe, R. I. (1964). Perspective on outdoor recreation: A bibliographical survey. *The Geographic Review, 54,* 203–238.

Women and Geography Study Group (1997). *Feminist geographies: Explorations in diversity and difference.* Essex, UK: Addison Wesley Longman.

Wright, D. J., Goodchild, M. F., & Proctor, J. D. (1997). Demystifying the persistent ambiguity of GIS as "tool" versus "science." *Annals of the Association of American Geographers, 87*(2), 346–362.

Yoon, J., & Shafer, E. L. (1996). Models of U.S. travel demand patterns for the Bahamas. *Journal of Travel Research, 35*(1), 50–56.

Recreation and Conservation: Issues and Prospects

Guy S. Swinnerton
University of Alberta

Introduction

The growth in active outdoor recreation and world tourism has fuelled global concern about the ensuing pressures on the environment and specifically the vulnerability and integrity of national parks and other protected areas. As a result, the possibility of achieving an acceptable balance between heritage conservation and outdoor recreation continues to be a recurring theme in the academic literature and the field of practice. Considerable debate surrounds the question of the extent and significance of the environmental impact of leisure and the appropriateness of policy priorities and management strategies intended to address these and related problems. Whereas skepticism remains as to the level of coexistence that may ultimately be achieved between conservation and recreation use, there is a growing commitment to finding communally developed solutions to many of the problems (see Stankey, McCool, Clark and Brown, chapter 26 in this volume). However, this trend has to be seen within the context of escalating anxiety about the earth's biodiversity and a growing demand for an increasingly diverse range of outdoor recreation and tourism opportunities. At the same time, the importance of ensuring the social and economic sustainability of local populations requires that balancing recreation and conservation interests must be examined within a much wider conceptual and operational context. The purpose of this chapter, therefore, is to examine some of the changing dimensions of research and practice that focus on recreation-conservation issues, particularly within the context of protected areas, and the prospects that exist for achieving a more symbiotic relationship between sustainable use and environmental protection.

Even a cursory examination of the continuously expanding literature on the relationship between recreation and conservation confirms that the use-versus-protection dilemma is now a global phenomenon.

The intensity of this debate has grown as participation in an increasingly wide variety of outdoor recreation, sporting, and tourism activities has resulted in additional pressures being placed on the environment in general and protected areas in particular. Several selected examples from around the world illustrate this concern. Cachay (1993), for example, has commented on the destructive effects of rapidly growing "natural" sports, such as kayaking, mountain hiking and climbing, and skiing, that are representative of the growing tension between sports and the environment in Germany. In Britain the Secretary of State for Employment established a task force to examine the effects of tourism on the environment (Tourism and Environment Task Force, 1991). More recently, concern over the apparent impact of leisure activities on the environment resulted in the House of Commons Environment Committee examining the scope and significance of the problem in the countryside in general and, specifically, in the national parks (House of Commons Environment Committee, 1995).

In Canada, the impact of human use and development on the country's most visited national park, Banff, has been the focus of particular attention. Concern that the ecological integrity of the Park could be permanently damaged resulted in the Minister of Canadian Heritage initiating the Banff–Bow Valley Study in March 1994. The purpose of the study was to "assess the cumulative environmental effects of development and use in the entire Bow River watershed inside the Park" (Banff–Bow Valley Task Force, 1996, p. 1). There is a substantive legacy of visitor impact studies in the United States (Kuss, Graefe and Vaske, 1990) and there has been particular concern over the repercussions of congestion and crowding at many of the units within the national park system (Lime, 1996; see also Manning, chapter 19, and Ewert, Dieser and Voight, chapter 20 in this volume). Rettie (1995, p. 116) has observed that, "many people see the development-versus-nondevelopment dichotomy as *the* principal policy dilemma in the national park system." In response to increased political involvement and commercialization within the national parks, Frome (1992) has called for a "regreening" of national parks and their reinstatement as models of ecological harmony (see also Lowry, 1994; Sellars, 1997). The growth and subsequent impacts of outdoor recreation and inbound tourism in Australia on sensitive environments, such as alpine ecosystems (Good and Grenier, 1994) and coastal fringes (Koloff, 1993), illustrate two areas of concern in the southern hemisphere. Similar issues occur in New Zealand, as is evidenced in the studies cited in a bibliography of outdoor recreation undertaken in that country (Peebles, 1995). In addition, many developing countries attest to the impact of indigenous tourism on both the cultural and environmental integrity of areas that have become the destination points for increasing numbers of international visitors (Butler and Hinch, 1996; Nelson, Butler and Wall, 1993; see also Butler, chapter 7 in this volume).

This apparent conflict between outdoor recreation and the environment is unlikely to diminish. Trends in outdoor recreation and resource-based tourism suggest that, although participation rates are not uniformly increasing, some of the fastest growing outdoor activities are those which require environments in which the attributes of the natural setting are important components of the overall recreation experience. For example, the results of the *U.S. 1994–95 National Survey on Recreation and the Environment* revealed that, although participation in selected consumptive activities, such as hunting and fishing, had declined since the early 1980s, the 10 fastest growing activities over the same period included bird-watching, hiking, backpacking and primitive camping (Cordell, Lewis and McDonald, 1995). According to Hunt (1995), tourists in the twenty-first century will seek more back-to-nature experiences and, as a consequence, conflict resolution involving resource use and sustainability will become a paramount issue. The anticipated growth in ecotourism and adventure tourism was acknowledged in the Banff–Bow Valley Study (Banff–Bow Valley Task Force, 1996), and similar trends are expected in Europe, with particular pressure being put on the countryside, the mountains, and protected areas (Shipp, 1993). In Britain, Vaughan (1996) has drawn attention to the seemingly inevitable conflict between the emergence of new sports and recreation pursuits as components of preventative healthcare and the increasingly conservation-focussed role of the countryside in the post-Rio era and the implementation of Agenda 21 (see Department of the Environment and Ministry of Agriculture, Fisheries and Food, 1995; Johnson, 1993). Despite these and similar studies, Cordell (1995), in a review of outdoor recreation research, noted that significant knowledge gaps remain concerning the impact of recreation on specific components of the natural environment, the application of effective techniques for monitoring and assessment, and the fundamental issue of how much of the environment should be preserved. Pigram (1993), in similar vein, has drawn attention to the need for more proactive policies for dealing with the repercussions of tourism on the rural environment.

Recreation and Conservation: Underlying Themes and Concepts

In the text *Understanding Leisure and Recreation: Mapping the Past, Charting the Future,* I provided an overview of the historical context and evolving relationship between recreation and conservation (Swinnerton, 1989). That chapter also discussed the underlying themes and concepts to the recreation-conservation debate. Although still relevant, it would be redundant to reiterate much of that material in the same level of detail. Consequently, a more selective treatment is adopted in this current chapter. The emphasis is placed on selected themes that have received particular attention over the last decade and are likely to remain central to the recreation-conservation debate.

Many of these themes are symptomatic of the constantly shifting relationship between people and their surroundings and, specifically, how the general public, specific interest groups, and resource agencies assign value and meaning to the environment in general and natural resources in particular. Stankey et al. (see chapter 26 in this volume) comment on the increasing range of demands placed upon natural resources. Williams and Patterson (1996, p. 507) have observed that "American land management agencies are increasingly challenged to address a broader range of meanings and values in natural resource management." They point to not only a "greater ecological consciousness," but also to the new paradigm shifts that focus on the spiritual benefits or deep values associated with natural resources (see Driver, Dustin, Baltic, Elsner and Peterson, 1996) and the "broader context or unit of analysis in natural resource management" (p. 508). This broader context applies not only to expanding the spatial scale of analysis to include ecosystems and landscape regions (see Council of Europe, UNEP and European Center for Nature Conservation, 1996; Forman, 1995; Noss and Cooperrider, 1994) but also consideration of the human dimension as reflected in the concept of place and cultural history (Melnick, 1996; United States Department of Agriculture [USDA] Forest Service, 1996; Wang, Anderson and Jakes, 1996; Williams and Carr, 1993; Williams and Stewart, 1998). Williams and Patterson (1996) discuss these developments in the context of environmental psychology, and specifically three research paradigms proposed by Saegert and Winkel (1990). These three paradigms are the adaptive; the opportunity structure or goal directed; and the sociocultural paradigm. Williams and Patterson (1996) summarize the importance of the sociocultural paradigm by stating that its main strength is "the recognition that environmental meaning extends well beyond biological imperatives and individual goal-oriented constructions, to include the ways in which meaning is socially structured" (p. 513). As a result, it is important to examine the relationship between the natural and social sciences in understanding the recreation-conservation debate and the associated research methods that are being used.

Disciplinary Perspectives and Research Paradigms

An understanding of and potential solution to the recreation-conservation dilemma requires cooperation and convergence from a number of disciplinary perspectives involving both the natural and social sciences. Heberlein (1988) made the case for improving interdisciplinary research 10 years ago in the initial issue of *Society and Natural Resources.* However, this intended integration has not always been fully realized (see, for example, Benton, 1994; Cronon, 1996). The importance of the social sciences in understanding and explaining the phenomenon of leisure and recreation involvement is self-evident, and is clearly illustrated by many of the other chapters in this volume (see, for example, Iso-Ahola, chapter 3; Kelly, chapter 4; Smale, chapter 12; Sylvester, chapter 2). Likewise, it has already been noted that there has been growing recognition of the importance of human dimension research in the area of natural resource management (Ewert, 1996; Force and Machlis, 1997; Machlis, Force and Burch, 1997). In demonstrating the contribution of the social sciences to biodiversity research and management, Machlis (1992, p. 161) has observed that, "biologists, ecologists and conservationists have increasingly grasped a harsh disciplinary reality: solutions to biological problems lie in social, cultural and economic systems." Models that attempt to examine and forecast loss of biodiversity demonstrate not only the importance of an interdisciplinary approach, but the necessity of data sets that apply to both environmental and human systems (Machlis and Forester, 1996). In the related area of ecosystem management, Cortner, Shannon, Wallace, Burke, and Moote (1996) have stressed that, if ecosystem management is to succeed, institutional issues involving legislation, policies and programs have to be addressed.

However, at a more conceptual and philosophical level, considerable controversy revolves around the respective roles of the natural and the social sciences and humanities in describing, analyzing, and interpreting *nature* itself and deciding what is natural within the context of many environmental issues. That outdoor recreation and visitor facilities often put stress on the environment (see Banff–Bow Valley Task Force, 1996; Liddle, 1997; Parks Canada, 1998b) raises the issue as to what constitutes a risk to nature and natural systems if such areas are not entirely natural in the first place. Likewise, if one of the primary purposes of preservation is to protect natural systems through the establishment of designated areas such as national parks or wilderness areas, then one of the inevitable questions is the determination of ecological integrity (see Lemons, 1995; Westra, 1995). A related issue concerns the place of humans in nature and the extent to which they should be considered natural agents of biological change and diversity (Hunter, 1996; Shrader-Frechette and McCoy, 1995). This debate has implications for the acceptability or otherwise of indigenous and aboriginal peoples remaining within protected areas and continuing traditional means of livelihood and land use practices (see Kemf, 1993; McNeely, 1993; Pimbert and Pretty, 1995; Stevens, 1997; West and Brechin, 1991).

Jenseth and Lotto (1996, p. v) state that "nature is more than a biological organism or a physical location . . . nature [is] a cultural and social construction or concept." This social construction of nature is not new (see Evernden, 1992). However, traditional or conventional approaches to studying and understanding nature and the environment in general have relied predominantly on the natural sciences with their emphasis on positivism, quantification and mechanism (Davis, 1996; Funtowicz and Ravetz, 1995; Lemons and Brown, 1995a; Pimbert and Pretty, 1995). Pimbert and Pretty (1995) argue that positivism, as the prevailing scientific method, with its absolutist position, tends to exclude other possibilities of addressing environmental and resource management issues. For example, they contend that the positivist paradigm for conservation has been partly responsible for "a virtually uniform model for protected areas and natural parks" (p. 12) and the frequent exclusion of indigenous peoples from these areas. They also point to the associated neglect of indigenous knowledge and management systems as well as the suppression of local institutions and social organization. In order to overcome these shortcomings, Pimbert and Pretty (1995) suggest that, although there will continue to be an important role for the positivist paradigm for conservation, alternative approaches need to be explored.

To this end, Pretty (cited in Pimbert and Pretty, 1995, p. 19) has suggested five principles that outline the crucial differences between these emerging paradigms and positivist science:

> First, that any belief that sustainability can be precisely defined is flawed. It is a contested concept, and so represents neither a fixed set of practices or technologies, nor a model to describe or impose on the world. . . . Sustainable development is, therefore, not so much a specific strategy as an approach.
>
> Second, problems are always open to interpretation. All actors have uniquely different perspectives on what a problem is, and what constitutes improvement. . . . Thus it is essential to seek multiple perspectives on a problem situation by ensuring the wide involvement of different actors and groups.
>
> Third, the resolution of one problem inevitably leads to the production of another "problem situation," as problems are endemic. . . . in a changing world, there will always be uncertainties.
>
> Fourth, the key feature now becomes the capacity of all actors continually to learn about these changing conditions. . . . They should make uncertainties explicit and encourage rather than obstruct wider public debate. . . . The world is open to multiple interpretations, each valid in its limited context but not necessarily true in absolute terms.
>
> Fifth, systems of learning and interaction are needed to gain an understanding of the multiple perspectives of the various interested parties and encourage their greater involvement.

Several of these principles are particularly relevant to examining the recreation-conservation relationship. The issue of sustainability will be examined in the next section of this chapter that specifically examines the conservation theme and related concepts.

Recognition of the need to involve different stakeholders and interest groups together with scientists in addressing problems of recreation development within protected areas is becoming increasingly common. Factors behind this trend, according to McDonald and Bengston (1995), include the increasing distrust of experts and the neutrality of scientists in dealing with policy questions. In order to address these perceived shortcomings, various mechanisms and processes have been developed to facilitate meaningful public and interest group involvement (see Stankey et al., chapter 26 in this volume). Illustrative of such an approach is the Round Table adopted in the Banff–Bow Valley Study (Banff–Bow Valley Task Force, 1996; Page, 1997). The Round Table consisted of 14 interest sectors, including government representatives; commercial interests; environmental interests; culture and social, health, and educational sectors; and the Task Force that was comprised of scientists from the natural and social sciences.

Decision making associated with environmental issues has become increasingly complex, and Wilkerson and Edgell (1993) have adopted Rittel and Webber's term of "wicked problems" to refer to those problems that are tricky and where potential solutions "invariably produce a new set of problems" (p. 53). An inherent characteristic of many of these types of problems is the need to deal with uncertainty. According to Costanza (1994), the lay public often does not appreciate the fact that "the progress of science has, in general, uncovered *more* uncertainty rather than leading to the absolute precision" that they come to expect (p. 398). Acknowledgment of uncertainty is an integral component of futures modeling, particularly when dealing with situations as complex as the futures outlook of the Banff–Bow Valley, for example (Cornwall and Costanza, 1996). At a policymaking level, the existence of true uncertainty in issues dealing with environmental protection is often addressed through the adoption of the precautionary principle (Costanza, 1994; see also Lemons, 1996).

Examples of the need to be responsive to the dynamics of the real world and to recognize the contributions that the different participants can play is discussed in greater detail by Stankey et al. (see chapter 26 in this volume). They suggest that planning in the future will become increasingly integrative, interactive and adaptive, and in so doing reflect a social learning process.

Much of the current debate over environmental problems and approaches to the ecological crisis stems from the application of a postmodern philosophy view of science (see Gare, 1995; Oelschlaeger, 1995). In contrasting the conventional approach to science with the postmodern view, Davis (1996) notes that with reference to the latter, "what we consider real is partly a function of paradigms, language, conceptual frameworks, culture, class and gender" (p. 420; see also Maser, 1997). The corollary to this perspective is that conventional science is not the sole determinant of reality. Consequently, alternative approaches to inquiry are required that are often qualitative in nature (Davis, 1996; Henderson, 1991). Acknowledgment of these different interpretations of the environment has encouraged the need to accommodate multicultural responses to recreation resource management issues (Dustin, Knopf and Fox, 1993) as well as particular perspectives, such as those represented by feminist views of nature (Henderson, 1996; Jackson, 1994).

Not surprisingly, excessive reliance on a postmodern perspective has not gone unchallenged (see Cronon, 1996; Soulé and Lease, 1995). According to Soulé (1995), deconstruction, as a style of postmodernism, critiques nature at two levels. He is critical of the fact that at one level deconstruction questions the existence of nature and the accuracy of any descriptions of it, and that at a second level, it implies that nature is no longer natural because of the human manipulation of all natural systems. Part of Soulé's (1995) anxiety is over the type of outcomes that might be expected if policies relating to the environment and wildland protection are determined largely by postmodern humanism rather than by conservation biology.

In an attempt to reconcile some of these divergent views, Spirn (1996), while recognizing that landscapes are neither wholly natural nor cultural, acknowledges that "failure to appreciate the dynamic autonomous role of nonhuman features and phenomena promotes the illusion that humans can construct and control everything" (p. 112). She concludes by observing that (p. 113): "All landscapes are constructed. . . . They are phenomena of nature *and* products of culture" (see also Greider and Garkovich, 1994; Melnick, 1996). There have been others who have recognized the need to acknowledge the respective merits of both the conventional and the postmodern approaches to understanding nature and the environmental crisis. Benton and Redclift (1994) in summarizing the former's assessment of the debate (Benton, 1994) make the following observation:

> . . . whilst technocratic *and* many "Deep green" approaches do not give sufficient attention to social, economic and political aspects, many of the most influential social scientific approaches tend to go to the opposite extreme, barely acknowledging the independent reality of "nature" and the "environment" at all. It might seem that a middle way, recognizing the independent reality of both society *and* nature, then studying their interconnection, would resolve the issue. (p. 18)

The relevance of a postmodernism perspective to the recreation-conservation issue is not restricted to the debate over nature and natural landscapes. Recent studies in the political and social theory literature have drawn attention to how society perceives, constructs and relates to places (see Marsden, Murdoch, Lowe, Munton and Flynn, 1993; Urry, 1995). These places include everyday living environments as well as destinations for recreation and tourism (Wilson, 1991). According to Cloke (1993), the political climate associated with privatization and deregulation has resulted in a new commodification of the rural environment. As a result, the countryside experience is packaged, promoted and presented to consumers as a commodity. Cloke has pointed to the explosion in the number of theme parks, rural folk museums, farm parks and tourist and recreation centers as exemplifying this trend. Although Cloke is specifically referring to trends in the British countryside, his observations on "pay-as-you-enter countryside experiences" are becoming increasingly common elsewhere. In the case of North America, Bunce (1994, p. 134) has commented on the "peddling of rural nostalgia" in the Amish region of southern Pennsylvania.

Urry (1995) has used the term "tourist gaze" to refer to the visual consumption of places. Of particular relevance to all types of protected areas is the extent to which even visual consumption requires an increasingly complex infrastructure to support the visitor (see Draper, 1997) and where, ultimately, the original significance of a place is often depleted and compromised (Urry, 1995). For this very reason, Frome (1992) has warned against the dangers of the increasing tendency to treat parks as commodities. He argues that "history demonstrates that whenever a park is treated like a commodity rather than a sanctuary, degradation of the park always follows" (p. 231). Central to Frome's (1992) observation is the fact that national parks and many other types of protected areas have been assigned the dual purpose of conservation and providing opportunities for public enjoyment (see Shultis, 1995; Swinnerton, 1989). Although Runte (1997, p. xxi) has suggested that "no institution is more symbolic of the conservation movement in the United States than the national parks," the concept and practice of conservation has evolved over time. Likewise, the relative importance attached to the two mandates, conservation and recreation, has vacillated over time. These dynamics are not exclusive to national parks in the United States (Frome, 1992; Lowry, 1994; Sellars, 1997), but are characteristic of many park systems throughout the world (Cherry and Rogers, 1996; Dearden and Rollins, 1993; Howard, 1997; Swinnerton, 1989, 1993, 1995a). In addition, there are a variety of other ideologies and approaches to resource management and environmental stewardship that illustrate varying levels of similarity with the fundamental concept of conservation but which in turn demonstrate their own difficulties of interpretation and application. These include sustainable development, ecosystem management, ecological integrity, and restoration ecology. All of these approaches and their respective interpretation have relevance as to how the recreation-conservation debate is considered and addressed.

Conservation and Related Concepts

A central issue in most discussions of the role of parks and protected areas, and specifically the balance between recreation and heritage resource protection, is the concept of conservation. At its most fundamental level, conservation is synonymous with the optimum use of resources over time. I have discussed elsewhere (Swinnerton, 1989) the relationship between conservation and preservation, and more recent examinations of the topic have reiterated many of the same issues (Grumbine, 1996; Klyza, 1996; Philipsen, 1995; Wildes, 1995). All of these authors draw the distinction between an anthropocentric and a biocentric approach to resource management. The former is represented by the *wise use movement* and technocratic utilitarianism. Both Grumbine (1996) and Wildes (1995) observe that the current interest in sustainable development is, in part, a manifestation of this philosophy. In the context of protected areas, the anthropocentric justification for parks and related areas is based on society's self-interest and utility, and on the instrumental conception that, ultimately, the protection of natural areas is a means to an end rather than an end in itself. As a result, the recreation, tourism and commercial functions of these areas are acknowledged, assigned priority and are actively promoted.

In contrast, the biocentric or ecocentric perspective is founded on an ethical orientation that recognizes the inherent and intrinsic value of nature. Biocentrism is one of the fundamental principles of *deep ecology* and as such is seen as the main solution to rectifying the environmental problems caused by the anthropocentric perspective (Jacob, 1994). A biocentric philosophy acknowledges the legitimacy of adopting a nonuse perspective and a preservationist approach. This position emphasizes the protection of biodiversity and the safeguarding of the ecological integrity of national parks and related areas.

Acceptance of the distinction between the concepts of the utilitarian conservationism and preservation is widely recognized as being not simply a philosophical issue or a matter of semantics (Swinnerton, 1989). Reaching an acceptable compromise between recreation use and conservation is initially and fundamentally a matter of policy, which in itself involves making decisions which can never be entirely separated from values, matters of judgment, and ethics (see Lemons, 1995; Norton and Roper-Lindsay, 1992). Consequently, the position taken on the conceptual dualism of an anthropocentric or biocentric approach to conservation has a pervasive influence on how benefits and values are perceived and, indeed, which ones are worthy of consideration, as well as, ultimately, their relative importance and significance.

Reference has already been made to the concept of sustainable development as being illustrative of the wise use approach. A detailed examination of the concept of sustainability is beyond the scope of this chapter (for a more comprehensive review see, for example, Bryant and Marois, 1995; Lemons and Brown, 1995b; Jansson, Hammer, Folke and Costanza, 1994). However, some reference to sustainable development is necessary because of the extensive application of the concept to heritage conservation and protected area management (Aitchison, 1995; Munasinghe and McNeely, 1994; Nelson and Woodley, 1989), tourism development (Countryside Commission, Department of National Heritage, Rural Development Commission and English Tourist Board, 1995; McCool and Watson, 1995; Nelson et al., 1993), the management of sport and outdoor recreation in the countryside (Aitchison and Jones, 1994; Countryside Commission, 1996; Sports Council, 1992), and the conservation and enhancement of the countryside (Countryside Commission, 1993; Wood, 1994).

Contemporary use of the term *sustainable development* can be traced back to the *World Conservation Strategy: Living Resource Conservation for Sustainable Development* (International Union for Conservation of Nature and Natural Resources [IUCN], 1980). The concept received wider public exposure through the work of the World Commission on Environment and Development (frequently referred to as the Brundtland Commission) and its report (1987), *Our Common Future*. In that document, sustainable development is defined as "development that meets the needs of the present without compromising the ability of future generations to meet their own needs" (p. 43). Whereas the initial *World Conservation Strategy* focussed on physical resource conservation, the Brundtland Commission report and the subsequent *Caring for the Earth: A Strategy for Sustainable Living* (IUCN, 1991) were broader in scope and attached more concern to people and a sustainable society (Green, Simmons and Woltjer, 1996).

Despite the frequent application of the idea of sustainable development to issues that require the balancing of use and protection, the concept is ambiguous and difficult to define. McCool (1995, p. 3) has stated that, "sustainability contains the appeal of an attractive model for action but is difficult to implement practically or operationally." Stankey (1995) suggests that the situation will only be rectified if it is acknowledged that sustainability is fundamentally a philosophical construct, that there is meaningful dialogue between citizens and scientists, and that there is major institutional reform. Likewise, Gale and Cordray (1994) contend that progress will only be made in the application of the concept of sustainability if the issue of what should be sustained is more rigorously defined. To this end they present four defining questions: what is sustained, why sustain it, how is sustainability measured, and what are the politics? The resultant nine types of sustainability range from human benefits to ecosystem benefits.

Although the work of Gale and Cordray (1994) demonstrates progress toward clarifying what sustainability is, the outcome does not resolve the fundamental issue as to which type of sustainability should be given priority when two or more types of sustainability are potentially in conflict. For example, the Countryside Commission (1990), in considering sustainability within the national parks of England and Wales, acknowledges the need to consider ecological, economic, cultural and social sustainability. In part to address this dilemma, the Countryside Commission in conjunction with English Nature, English Heritage and the Environment Agency commissioned a study that applies the notion of *environmental capital* to addressing this and related issues. The approach clarifies what attribute(s) or services about a place or object matter for sustainability, and how they would need to be managed to improve or at least not compromise sustainability (CAG Consultants and Land Use Consultants, 1997). Nevertheless, in those situations where choices have to be made, the final decision essentially involves value judgment (see Lemons, 1995; McCool, 1995). Despite these and other advances in clarifying the concept of sustainable development, Grumbine (1996, p. 241) is of the opinion that "sustainable development focuses exclusively on human development" and, as a result, "will not solve the biodiversity crisis or allay the tensions that result from environmental deterioration and rising social inequity." A comparable observation has been made by Callicott and Mumford (1997), who argue that the concept of sustainable development is of limited value to nonanthropocentric and ecologically informed conservation.

Another concept that falls under the broad remit of resource conservation is ecosystem management. Ecosystem management also exhibits problems of definition and application (Gerlach and Bengston, 1994;

Grumbine, 1994, 1996; Woodley and Forbes, 1995). Sellars (1997) notes that, although the concept of ecosystem management has been used by biologists within the U.S. National Park Service since at least the 1960s, it continues to be loosely defined and "remains more of a concept than a reality" (p. 275). Despite Sellars's observation, considerable attention has been focussed on ecosystem management within the last decade, both in terms of its application to forest management (see Bengston, 1994; Gerlach and Bengston, 1994; Leak, Yamasaki, Kittredge, Lamson and Smith, 1997) and the management of national parks and related protected areas (see Agee and Johnson, 1988; Canadian Parks Service, 1993; Woodley, 1997).

In the context of forest management, ecosystem management has been defined as a broad approach that "provides for and considers an array of resource values, plants and animal species, and natural processes at both the landscape and property or landowner level" (Leak et al., p. 1). In contrast to traditional forest management, ecosystem management is seen as being a more holistic approach whereby the traditional economic and utilitarian values of timber are complemented by recognition of the importance of biological diversity and ecological processes at both the ecosystem and landscape levels. In addition, the human dimension, including the wider community interests and the protection of aesthetics, recreational, and spiritual values, is acknowledged and accommodated (Bengston, 1994; Williams and Stewart, 1998). Notwithstanding the adoption of the ecosystem management approach by the USDA Forest Service in the United States (Gerlach and Bengston, 1994), and similar trends in Canada (Alberta Environmental Protection, n.d.; Natural Resources Canada, 1997), there remains at issue the extent to which the new resource management paradigm is really being implemented (Klyza, 1996). For example, Bengston and Xu (1995) have suggested that the relative low level of concern expressed by professional foresters for noninstrumental values, such as aesthetic and moral or spiritual values, helps to explain the continuing conflict with environmentalists over the management of the national forests in the United States. Part of the problem derives from the fact that ecosystem management requires not only new and increased knowledge about the science of ecological systems and biodiversity but also new insights into the social, economic, political and institutional environments within which implementation has to occur (Cortner et al., 1996; Gerlach and Bengston, 1994; Grumbine, 1996; Slocombe, 1993; Woodley and Forbes, 1995).

In the case of national parks and other protected areas, the intended outcome of ecosystem manage-

ment is normally the maintenance of ecological integrity (Canadian Parks Service, 1993, Parks Canada, 1994a, 1998b; Woodley, 1993, 1997). This perspective is also one that is shared by many academic conservation biologists and policy analysts (see Grumbine, 1996). Recent park management plans prepared for national parks within the Canadian park system reflect the adoption of an ecosystem approach. For example, the management plan for Elk Island National Park stresses that ecosystem-based management provides the strategic direction for the park. The management plan also cites Parks Canada's definition of ecosystem-based management as "the integrated management of natural landscapes, ecological processes, physical and biotic components, and human activities, to maintain or enhance the integrity of an ecosystem" (Parks Canada, 1996, p. 16).

The issue of ecological integrity was a key one addressed by the Banff–Bow Valley Task Force (1996). The Task Force, while recognizing the importance of the concept, acknowledged that it was "difficult to operationalize and measure" (p. 94). Despite acceptance of the problem in finding a widely accepted definition of ecological integrity (see Lemons, 1995; Westra and Lemons, 1995; Woodley, 1993), Parks Canada (1998b, p. 23) has suggested that:

> ecological integrity is the condition of an ecosystem where:
>
> - the structure and function of the ecosystem are unimpaired by stresses induced by human activity, and
> - the ecosystem's biological diversity and supporting processes are likely to persist.

This definition is contained in Parks Canada's (1994a) *Guiding Principles and Operational Policies*. In 1996 Parks Canada developed a system for monitoring ecological integrity that involves an assessment framework based on the broad indicators of biodiversity, ecosystem functions and stressors (Parks Canada, 1998b). The necessity of having such a framework is particularly important, as the 1988 amendments to the *National Parks Act* require that maintaining ecological integrity is the first priority when developing park management plans, and that Parks Canada has to report on the state of ecological integrity within the individual national parks (Parks Canada, 1998b; see Lemons, 1995, for a discussion of ecological integrity as it applies to the U.S. national park system).

With reference to the relationship between recreation and conservation within Canada's national parks, the legislation and accompanying policy implies that conservation, as defined in terms of maintaining ecological integrity, takes precedence over the mandate to provide for public enjoyment and recreation. In addition, monitoring of the ecological state of the parks has shown that human activities, and specifically the provision of visitor and tourism facilities, are the source of serious stresses on the ecological integrity of the parks. In the most recent report, 26 out of the 36 national parks which completed the survey indicated that visitor and tourism facilities had significant ecological impacts on the park's ecological integrity. These were the most frequently reported sources of ecological impacts from stresses originating from either within or outside the parks (Parks Canada, 1998b).

Although this discussion of integrity has focussed on the concept of ecological integrity, cultural integrity and the retention of commemorative integrity is becoming an increasingly important dimension of heritage resource management (for example see Parks Canada, 1994a, 1998a). To this end, Parks Canada also monitors the commemorative integrity and level of impairment of its national historic sites (Parks Canada, 1998b).

Another concept that has relevance to conservation is that of restoration. The idea of ecological restoration is not new (Wyant, Meganck and Ham, 1995), and the acknowledged importance of protecting ecological integrity within national parks and related areas has resulted in a growing application of this aspect of conservation (see Baldwin, De Luce and Pletsch, 1994; McNeely, 1993). The task of restoration, however, is not only a challenge for the science of ecology. In many ways, the more difficult issue is the need to contend with the value-laden concept of ecological integrity, the issue of traditional cultural practices and whether or not the intention is to try and restore the area to those conditions that prevailed prior to any human disturbance of the ecosystem (see Higgs et al., 1998; Lemons, 1995). Parks Canada recognizes that ecological integrity must be restored when human use has impaired an ecosystem and restoration is not taking place through natural processes (Parks Canada, 1998b). In Britain, Sheail, Treweek, and Mountford (1997) have discussed restoration and habitat enhancement in terms of the increased importance of "creative conservation" within both protected areas and the working landscapes of the wider countryside.

Broadening the Scope of Protected Areas: Implications for Recreation and Conservation

An understanding of the relationship and level of potential conflict between recreation and conservation is not only influenced by different interpretations of conservation and related concepts. Equally important is the land use planning and resource management context within which outdoor recreation and conservation occur. Consideration of the complete range of situations is beyond the scope of this chapter. Attention is therefore restricted to protected areas and specifically the implications of some of the important changes in the roles and functions of these areas.

Over the past decade a number of the traditional tenets associated with the planning and management of protected areas have become increasingly questioned and critically examined (see Bishop, Phillips and Warren, 1995; Phillips, 1997, 1998; McNeely, 1993; Pimbert and Pretty, 1995). Bishop et al. (1995) in a "deliberately provocative analysis" (p. 293), raised the following criticisms of protected areas:

- Protected areas negate the holistic approach.
- Protected areas encourage the view that conservation is a sector or a land use.
- Protected area boundaries are arbitrary lines on maps.
- Protected areas create a "boundary effect."
- Environmental problems do not stop at protected area boundaries.
- Biological phenomena ignore protected area boundaries.
- Protected area systems are getting too complex.
- There is a growing problem of diminishing returns.
- Some new ecological thinking questions the value of protected areas.
- Physical changes could make protected areas obsolete.
- Protected areas are an inflexible concept.
- Protected areas are too defensive a concept.
- Protected areas are bound to be too weak and small. (p. 294)

Consequently, it has become increasingly evident that, even in the case of protected areas, the recreation-conservation debate cannot be isolated and detached from the broader issues of regional land use planning and community development. Moreover, failure to recognize the different categories of protected areas and their respective management functions seriously undermines any meaningful discussion on the roles and priorities of protected areas and specifically the relationship between recreation and conservation.

Enhancing the Effectiveness of Protected Areas

The shortcomings and dangers associated with perceiving parks and protected areas as "islands" and closed systems are acknowledged both in the context of protecting biodiversity and people-park relationships (see Garratt, 1984; Lucas, 1992; McNeely, 1995; Munro and Willison, 1998; Noss and Cooperrider, 1994; Parks Canada, 1994a; Pimbert and Pretty, 1995; IUCN World Commission on Protected Areas [WCPA], 1997; Zube, 1995). Protected areas have a crucial role to play in biodiversity conservation (see IUCN WCPA, 1997; McNeely, 1993; World Commission on Environment and Development, 1987; World Resources Institute, IUCN and United Nations Environment Program, 1992). However, it is now widely recognized that these core areas have to be complemented and buffered by zones of cooperation as well as corridors and functional connectivity to create interlinked networks of protected areas rather than "islands" of protection (see Hudson, 1991; McNeely, 1993; Noss, 1995; Noss and Cooperrider, 1994). In addition, the conservation role of protected areas has to be complemented by a more sustainable approach to the management of all landscapes and natural resources (see IUCN, 1980, 1991; World Commission on Environment and Development, 1987). The Greater Yellowstone Ecosystem (see Goldstein, 1992; Rasker, 1993; Reading, Clark and Kellert, 1994) and the Yellowstone to Yukon mountain corridor (see Locke, 1997, 1998) are just two examples of a more regional approach to protecting biodiversity (see also Saunier and Meganck, 1995). The development of the European Ecological Network (EECONET) recognizes that conserving the integrity of natural systems requires "a shift in conservation policy—from species to habitats, from sites to ecosystems, and from national to international measures" (IUCN Commission on National Parks and Protected Areas, 1994a, pp. 44–45; see also Council of Europe et al., 1996). In addition, the Caracas Action Plan (McNeely, 1993) recommended that national protected area system plans

and the conservation of biodiversity should not only consider designated protected areas but also the role of private landowners and local communities (see IUCN WCPA, 1997). Recognition of buffer zones, corridors and regional perspectives requires consideration of interagency relationships (Buechner, Schonewald-Cox, Sauvajot and Wilcox, 1992; Grumbine, 1991) and understanding a range of participants in the decision-making process (Primm and Clark, 1996) that result from having to contend with a land mosaic involving a diversity of public land agencies, private sector and commercial interests. These areas frequently involve working landscapes, where the primary concern of most of the stakeholders is neither protecting biodiversity nor providing opportunities for outdoor recreation (see Goldstein, 1992; Munro and Willison, 1998). Moreover, in these situations, stresses on the ecological integrity of the environment are frequently more likely to result from agriculture, commercial forestry, mining, commercial fishing, residential and infrastructure development than from recreation and tourism. The buffer zones and particularly the transition zones of biosphere reserves illustrate many of these symptoms (see Varangu, 1997).

The broadening scope of protected areas is not only an outcome of the need for zones of cooperation, corridors and a bioregional perspective. Equally important is a broadening of the traditional concept of protected areas themselves.

Protected Areas and Alternative Management Objectives

Yellowstone's designation as the world's first national park in 1872 was to some extent an archetype for protected areas that was followed in many countries of the world (see Shultis, 1995). As a result, the prevailing approach to the establishment and management of protected areas was a "conservation philosophy and practice [that] was for many years driven primarily by concern for the protection of wilderness and pristine nature" (Phillips, 1997, p. 31). Scenic protection and the tourism role of national parks were tolerated on the basis of the need for public support and the belief that these uses were preferable to more utilitarian conservation interests involving timber development, mining, and reservoirs (Runte, 1997; Sellars, 1997; Shultis, 1995). However, as the park movement spread, countries did not simply copy the Yellowstone experience (Phillips, 1997). In order to succeed, the establishment of protected areas had to be sensitive to the environmental, administrative, and socioeconomic conditions prevailing in individual countries. This was particularly the case for the establishment of protected areas in those countries, such as Britain and others in Europe, where parks had to be superimposed on a landscape substantially modified as a result of centuries of intensive human activity and existing complex administrative and land use planning structures (IUCN Commission on National Parks and Protected Areas, 1994b; Swinnerton, 1995a). In addition, and over time, the role and function of protected areas together with their attendant values and benefits have become increasingly diversified (see for example Dearden, 1995; de Groot, 1994; Dixon and Sherman, 1990; Government of Alberta, 1992; McNeely, 1993; Munasinghe and McNeely, 1994; White, 1993).

By the beginning of this decade approximately 4 % of the world's total land area had protected status and, globally, more than 140 terms were being applied to identify protected areas of various types (IUCN, 1994a). At a global level, the World Conservation Union [IUCN] (1994a) has developed a definition of a protected area as well as a categorization of protected areas based on different management objectives. The definition of a protected area that has been adopted by the World Conservation Union [IUCN] is as follows:

> An area of land and/or sea especially dedicated to the protection and maintenance of biological diversity, and of natural and associated cultural resources, and managed through legal or other effective means. (1994a, p. 7)

Within this broad parameter, guidelines for protected area management recognize that national parks and protected areas fulfill a variety of goals that extend from strict preservation to those areas that allow for different levels of human use and associated alteration of the natural environment. At the international level, and through its Commission on National Parks and Protected Areas (CNPPA), the World Conservation Union [IUCN] (1994a) uses different primary management objectives as the basis for recognizing six protected area management categories which signify a gradation of human intervention.

The World Conservation Union has identified the following main purposes of protected area management:

- scientific research;
- wilderness protection;
- preservation of species and genetic diversity;
- maintenance of environmental services;

- protection of specific natural and cultural features;
- tourism and recreation;
- education;
- sustainable use of resources from natural ecosystems; and
- maintenance of cultural and traditional attributes.

When these different management objective priorities are applied, six distinct categories of protected areas are recognized and provide the basis for a global inventory of national parks and protected areas (IUCN Commission on National Parks and Protected Areas, 1994a). These are:

- Category I, Strict Nature Reserve/Wilderness Area: protected area managed mainly for science or wilderness protection.
- Category II, National Park: protected area managed mainly for ecosystem protection.
- Category III, Natural Monument: protected area managed mainly for conservation of specific natural features.
- Category IV, Habitat/Species Management Area: protected area managed mainly for conservation through management intervention.
- Category V, Protected Landscape/Seascape: protected area managed mainly for landscape/seascape conservation and recreation.
- Category VI, Managed Resource Protected Area: protected area managed mainly for the sustainable use of natural ecosystems.

Reference to the relative priority of the different management objectives for these six protected area management categories clearly demonstrates the importance of discussing the recreation-conservation balance within the context of a particular management category (see IUCN Commission on National Parks and Protected Areas, 1994a). For example, whereas preservation of species and genetic diversity is a primary objective in Strict Nature Reserves (Category I), National Parks (Category II), Natural Monuments (Category III) and Habitat/Species Management Areas (Category IV), tourism and recreation are primary objectives in National Parks (Category II), Natural Monuments (Category III), and Protected Landscapes (Category V). Balancing recreation and conservation is obviously problematic where these two objectives are of primary importance, as is the case for national parks and natural monuments.

One of the recommendations that came from the IVth World Congress on National Parks and Protected Areas in Caracas in 1992 included the statement that, notwithstanding the intrinsic worth of nature, "increasingly, the resources that justify the establishment of protected areas include cultural landscapes and adapted natural systems created by long-established human activity" (McNeely, 1993, p. 35). Expanding on this perspective, the IUCN Commission on National Parks and Protected Areas (1994b, p. 15) stated that:

> [there] has emerged an approach which puts protected areas at the center of strategies for sustainable development, concentrates on the linkages between protected areas and the areas around, and focuses on the economic benefits that such areas can bring.

A similar perspective has been envisioned as the future role for biosphere reserves. That vision for the twenty-first century includes increased emphasis on the human dimension and on sustainable development together with greater attention being shown toward developing partnerships with local communities (United Nations Educational Scientific and Cultural Organization [UNESCO], 1996). Although these trends have caused concern (see Barborak, 1995), they do signify recognition of the growing importance of Category V, Protected Landscape/Seascape (see Lucas, 1992; Phillips, 1997,1998) and the more recently adopted, Category VI, Managed Resource Protected Areas, of the IUCN's categories of protected areas.

Category V, Protected Landscape/Seascape, is a protected area managed mainly for landscape and seascape conservation and recreation, and is defined by the IUCN Commission on National Parks and Protected Areas (1994a) as an:

> area of land, with coast and sea as appropriate, where the interaction of people and nature over time has produced an area of distinct character with significant aesthetic, ecological and/or cultural value, and is often with high biological diversity. Safeguarding the integrity of this traditional interaction is vital to the protection, maintenance and evolution of such an area. (p. 22)

A distinguishing feature of protected landscapes is that the areas in them are "likely to comprise a mosaic of private and public ownerships operating a variety of management regimes" (IUCN Commission on National Parks and Protected Areas, 1994a, p. 22). The management objectives for such areas are multifaceted. They encompass not only the maintenance of the harmonious interaction of nature and culture through the continuation of traditional land uses but also the provision of opportunities for appropriate forms of recreation and tourism. In addition, the long-term welfare of resident populations within these areas is addressed through fostering the local economy based on natural products, such as agriculture, forestry, fisheries, and sustainable tourism.

Regarded very much as a European concept, Category V, Protected Landscapes/Seascapes, were initially considered, particularly in North America, as being subordinate to the more highly protected areas such as Category II, National Parks. However, with the realization that protected areas have an important role to play in sustainable development and meeting the needs of local populations, the relevance of protected landscapes is being increasingly recognized worldwide (see Countryside Commission and the Council of Europe, 1987; Lucas, 1992; Phillips, 1997, 1998). Category V, Protected Landscape/Seascape, areas comprise 15.2% of the world's protected area in the IUCN's management categories I–V (Category VI was not included in the 1993 list). In Europe, Category V areas account for approximately two-thirds (66.8%) of the protected area (see IUCN Commission on National Parks and Protected Areas, 1994b; World Conservation Monitoring Center and IUCN Commission on National Parks and Protected Areas, 1994).

The national parks of England and Wales are considered by the IUCN to be Category V, Protected Landscapes/Seascapes, and as such illustrate particularly clearly many of the issues associated with balancing conservation and recreation within working landscapes (see Edwards, 1991; MacEwen and MacEwen, 1982; Stedman, 1993; Swinnerton, 1995a, 1995b, 1995c). An estimated 76 million visitor days were made to the national parks in 1994 (Coalter, MacGregor and Denman, 1996). However, although there are specific areas where visitors over the years have caused very significant impacts on the parks' environments (see Countryside Working Group, 1991; Edwards, 1991; Statham, 1993), land uses other than outdoor recreation, such as agriculture and forestry, have had a much more pervasive and extensive impact on the landscape character of the national parks (see Council for National Parks, 1990; Edwards, 1991; Stedman, 1993; Swinnerton, 1995a). The Countryside Commission (1995) has stated that, in relation to the environmental impact of leisure activities on the English countryside, including the national parks, "any damage to the countryside by recreation activity is heavily exceeded by industrialization, farming and urbanization and other forms of economic exploitation" (p. i).

The national parks in England and Wales also illustrate the concern that should be afforded to local populations in the management of protected areas. The original purposes of the national parks, as set out in the *National Parks and Access to the Countryside Act 1949*, were to: (1) preserve and enhance the natural beauty of the areas; and (2) promote their enjoyment by the public (Edwards, 1991). Under the *Countryside Act 1968*, the national park authorities were also to have due regard for the social and economic interests of the people living within the parks and the needs of agriculture and forestry (Edwards, 1991). The *Report of the National Parks Review Panel* (Edwards, 1991, p. 9) noted that "the economic and social well-being of the park community is important for the effective conservation and enjoyment of the parks." To this end, the most recent legislation dealing with the management of national parks, the *Environment Act 1995, Part III National Parks*, acknowledges that "there is no incompatibility between conserving the National Parks and their remaining as living and working communities" (Department of the Environment, 1996, p. 5). Although this statement is an oversimplification of the complex range of circumstances and controversies that arise within the national parks (see Bissix and Bissix, 1995; Council for National Parks, 1990; Edwards, 1991; MacEwen and MacEwen, 1982; Swinnerton, 1995a, 1995c), appropriate management strategies can help to protect natural heritage and wildlife values within working and cultural landscapes while at the same time providing opportunities for outdoor recreation and sustainable tourism (see Countryside Commission, 1997; Aitchison and Beresford, 1992; Sidaway, 1995).

The national parks of England and Wales are just one example of landscapes that have evolved as the result of the interaction between people and nature (see McNeely, 1993; Phillips, 1998). The IUCN Commission on Environmental Strategy and Planning (CESP) defines landscape as "a particular configuration of topography, vegetation cover, land use and settlement pattern which delimits some coherence of natural and cultural processes and activities" (Green et al., 1996, p. 1). Such areas comprise environments that not only demonstrate scenic beauty and historical interest but they may also play an important role in maintaining biodiversity. At the international level, cultural landscapes are being actively considered under the World Heritage Convention (see Buggey, 1994; Phillips, 1997), but there are various initiatives within many individual countries. In England, the Countryside Commission together with English Nature and English Heritage has undertaken the Countryside Character

Programme. The outputs of the program include a map which depicts the natural and cultural dimensions of the English landscape and landscape conservation strategies (Countryside Commission, 1994; Phillips, 1998).

Marsh (1994) has reviewed some of the initiatives in the United States, such as the National Heritage Areas recognized by the U.S. National Park Service, as a basis for considering similar programs in Canada (see also Stokes, Watson, Keller and Keller, 1989). Parks Canada (1994a) defines cultural landscapes as "any geographical area that has been modified, influenced, or given special cultural meaning by people" (p. 119). Indicative of this growing commitment to cultural landscapes was the declaration of the Grand-Pré area in Nova Scotia as Canada's first rural historic district by the Historic Sites and Monuments Board of Canada in 1995 (see Doull, 1995). At the provincial level, the inclusion of a "heritage rangeland" category of protected area within the proposed new *Natural Heritage Act* for Alberta recognizes the role that ranching has played in the management of native grasslands (Alberta Environmental Protection, 1998). Although the primary purpose of this designation is to ensure the preservation of the ecological integrity and biological diversity of the grasslands, there is a cultural landscape dimension that has been created and is being sustained by the ranching industry. A number of the biosphere reserves in Canada, such as the Niagara Escarpment and Charlevoix, contain cultural landscape components within their respective areas (see Borodczak, 1995; Bridgewater, Phillips, Green and Amos, 1996; Varangu, 1997). Following the adoption of the *Seville Strategy* in 1995 (UNESCO, 1996), and its direction for biosphere reserves to extend their transition areas and adopt a more regional perspective, the inclusion of working and cultural landscapes is likely to become increasingly evident within that program (see Burak and Swinnerton, 1998; Jamieson, 1998). At the same time, the attraction of working and cultural landscapes as a basis for sustainable tourism is being increasingly realized and promoted (see Bruns and Stokowski, 1996; Bunce, 1994; Butler, Hall and Jenkins, 1998; Crouch, 1994; Fennell and Weaver, 1997; Fladmark, 1994; Lane, 1994; Pigram, 1993; Swinnerton and Hinch, 1994).

Consideration of cultural landscapes as an extension of simply protecting individual historic buildings or cultural sites in many ways parallels protecting biodiversity at the ecosystem or landscape levels as opposed to solely focussing concern at the species level (see Iacobelli and Kavanagh, 1995). In both instances, working at a broader geographic or spatial scale invariably requires consideration of a more complex range of factors and stakeholders, including resident communities, as well as recreation and conservation interests and alternative land use planning and administrative structures (see Aitchison, 1995; Etchell, 1994, 1996; IUCN Commission on National Parks and Protected Areas, 1994b; Marsden et al., 1993; Nelson and Serafin, 1996; Pierce, 1996).

Balancing Recreation and Conservation: Issues and Prospects

The evidence presented so far in this chapter has demonstrated that protected areas may serve a variety of functions that provide environmental, social, and economic benefits. Many of the functions are not mutually exclusive and may, in some instances, result in synergistic relationships that protect biodiversity while enhancing the range of benefits available for both the visitor and resident populations. In other circumstances, the accommodation of particular functions can seriously jeopardize the ecological integrity of protected areas. In addition, with the broadening scope of protected areas, the balancing of conservation and recreation has become increasingly complicated.

The Continuing Need for Protected Areas

Notwithstanding the shortcomings that have been recognized in the designation, planning and management of protected areas, there is considerable evidence from the scientific literature and the field of practice that there is a continuing need for protected areas. Moreover, the management of these areas has to pay particular attention to safeguarding their ecological integrity in order that they can continue to play their critical role in conserving the world's biodiversity. The following section elaborates on this position and identifies some of the problems that national parks and related areas face in meeting their protection role.

One of the foremost reasons for establishing additional protected areas with the primary function of protecting natural ecosystems is that most jurisdictions continue to fall well below the general guideline for an adequate designated land base to protect biodiversity. The World Commission on Environment and Development (1987) implied that 12% of the earth's land area should be managed explicitly to conserve species and ecosystems. Subsequently, a number of countries adopted the 12% guideline as their long-term goal for protected area designation. However, "less than 5% of the planet's surface is afforded protection under IUCN categories" (McNeely, 1993, p. 47).

At the global level there has been continued expansion of the total area that is protected, but the rate of this expansion has not been consistent on either a temporal or spatial basis (McNeely, Harrison and Dingwall, 1994; World Conservation Monitoring Center and the IUCN Commission on National Parks and Protected Area, 1994). For example, figures for the growth of the world coverage of protected areas compiled on a five-year time frame show that after the major advances made during the first quinquennium of the 1970s, the area designated has been consistently declining and the number of sites has been falling since the early 1980s. However, the growth rates do remain significantly above those achieved prior to 1970. In Canada, the endangered spaces annual progress report card prepared by World Wildlife Fund Canada for the provinces, territories and the federal government shows considerable variation in the level of commitment and progress in putting protected area systems in place (World Wildlife Fund Canada, 1998).

The total amount of protected area within a country or region is only one dimension of assessing the progress being made toward protecting biodiversity. Of equal or even greater significance is the need to establish protected areas that represent biodiversity at a global and regional level (see Iacobelli and Kavanagh, 1994; Noss, 1995; Noss and Cooperrider, 1994). A workshop at the IVth World Congress on National Parks and Protected Areas noted that, "there is a major imbalance in attention given to the various biogeographical regions, including key habitats and ecosystems" (McNeely, 1993, p. 150–151). As result, the workshop recommended that "the global network of protected areas should cover at least 10% of each biome by the year 2000" (p. 151).

In Canada, approximately 8% of the total land area is protected and 51 of its 217 terrestrial ecoregions have over 12% of their respective areas designated within a protected area category that is recognized by the IUCN (Government of Canada, 1996). This regional disparity is also evident from the annual reports prepared by World Wildlife Fund Canada (1998), and from the imbalance that prevails within individual provinces (see Swinnerton, 1993, 1997). Similar problems have been noted in the level of representation of the different bioregions in Europe (see IUCN Commission on National Parks and Protected Areas, 1994b). If attention is directed toward the conservation and level of representation of marine ecosystems, both globally and within individual countries, the gaps and deficiencies are even more evident (see Shackell and Willison, 1995; McNeely, 1993; Munro and Willison, 1998; Parks Canada, 1998b).

Both the *World Conservation Strategy* (IUCN, 1980) and the Brundtland Report (World Commission on Environment and Development, 1987) stated that safeguarding biodiversity was essential to society's existence and development process. In addition, both reports acknowledged that, although biodiversity conservation must encompass more than concern for protected areas (see also Edwards and Abivardi, 1998), parks and related areas had a central role to play in protecting biological diversity (see also Ledec and Goodland, 1988). Not surprisingly, therefore, the recommendation from the IVth World Congress on National Parks and Protected Areas was that the protection of biological diversity must be a "fundamental principle for the identification, establishment, management, and public enjoyment of national parks and other protected areas" (McNeely, 1993, p. 30). Without effective systems of protected areas, there can be no long-term in situ conservation of biological diversity. More specifically, without core areas concern for buffer zones and corridors of connectivity becomes redundant (see Barborak, 1995). Furthermore, conservation measures taken outside protected areas, while complementary to the role of protected areas, can never be more than a partial substitute.

Another critical issue is the size and configuration of individual protected areas (see Iacobelli and Kavanagh, 1994; Noss, 1995, Noss and Cooperrider, 1994). Shafer (1995), for example, has discussed the value and limitations of small reserves, and Noss (1995, p. 53) has argued that "the most sensible approach is to focus on the species of the region of interest that have the most demanding requirement." For the most part, larger protected areas not only have the ability to contain core reserve areas of appropriate size with the increased likelihood of safeguarding ecological integrity (Noss, 1995), but they provide the flexibility to accommodate a range of supporting uses in a mosaic or buffer zone configuration which can have direct human benefits through recreation and tourism (see Government of Alberta, 1992). However, the designation of large protected areas is becoming increasingly problematic because of the concern expressed by the resource sector that important resources will be sterilized for potential future development (see Swinnerton, 1998). Furthermore, the basis for designating protected areas is frequently more dependent on minimizing the loss to natural resource commercial interests than on optimizing the protection of those areas with high ecological integrity and biodiversity values (see Bissix, Anderson and Miles, 1998; Francis, 1998a; Runte, 1997; Swinnerton, 1997). The evidence suggests that Runte's (1997) "worthless lands" thesis continues to apply in many instances.

An argument in favor of putting a strong emphasis on protecting the natural features and processes within protected areas is that the various functions and benefits provided by protected areas are ultimately dependent on the successful continuation of their regulation function that involves the continued proper operation of ecological processes and life support systems (see de Groot, 1994). The case put forward by de Groot also refutes the argument that preservation of natural areas signifies "nonuse" with the corollary that no benefits are being realized for society. However, because the benefits of the regulation function of natural systems is more difficult to evaluate in economic terms, there is a tendency to understate its importance (see McNeely, 1988).

This situation has been compounded by the fact that the onus of proof has often rested with those trying to protect biodiversity and protected areas rather than those who wish to introduce development. Consequently, in the absence of economic data that could demonstrate the benefits of preservation, those advocating protection have been at a distinct disadvantage. Although considerable progress has been made in developing techniques for placing monetary values on a more complete range of protected area benefits, through the use of surrogate market prices, survey-based approaches such as contingent valuation and cost-based approaches (see Munasinghe and McNeely, 1994), the robustness and validity of the derived economic values have often been questioned by pro-development interests. In addition, "quantification of the socioeconomic benefits of natural areas and wildlife in monetary units must be seen as an addition to, and not a replacement of, their many intrinsic and intangible values" (de Groot, 1994, p. 160).

Lemons (1995) has also commented on this problem of the burden of proof in the context of protecting the ecological integrity of national parks. He observes that "those advocating the enhanced protection of parks' resources must demonstrate with reasonable certainty that there is a scientific need for protection" (p. 179). His conclusion is that, in the absence of adequate scientific data, agencies tend to take a middle-of-the-road approach in an attempt to deal with proposed developments and to mitigate against the threats of high levels of visitor use. As a result of this more permissive position, increasing stress is frequently placed on the ecological integrity of parks and other protected areas (see also Frome, 1992). Likewise, Nilsson and Grelsson (1995) have warned against the dangers of taking no action to protect biotic diversity and natural resources on the grounds that there is insufficient knowledge. They cite Soulé's position that "the risks of nonaction may be greater than the risk of inappropriate action" (p. 688).

The *World Conservation Strategy* (IUCN, 1980) suggested that sustainability depended on the inseparable relationship between conservation and economic development. This perspective has often been used as the basis for arguing that even with national parks and other protected areas there should be a balance between use and protection. This assertion has been made despite the longstanding recognition that parks and protected areas around the world have been under increasing pressure from stresses originating both from within and outside their boundaries (see Machlis and Tichnell, 1985; Parks Canada, 1998b). Dearden (1995) has argued that there are increasingly fewer natural areas outside the national parks that are able to support the ecological role of protected areas. In contrast he points to the fact that "the factory role, as a place to work and generate income, dominates the rest of the landscape" (p. 1656). He consequently recommends that, "if compromises between the roles have to be made within national parks, they should be to restrict the role of tourism so that the other roles can be realized" (p. 1656). A similar position has been taken by Rolston (1994) in his discussion of the protection of wilderness areas in the United States. He warns that "some values do not compromise without devaluing them, even destroying them" (p. 27). He suggests that compromise is not balance when the situation is quite unbalanced already, and observes that in such circumstances "a seeming compromise only further skews the imbalance" (p. 27).

Another reason why conservation interests are skeptical about balancing social, economic, and environmental priorities in protected areas is the past record of many park agencies. During the postwar expansion of recreation and tourism in the parks, park authorities responded to market demand. More specifically, they frequently failed to distinguish intrinsic forms of recreation, which were compatible and supportive of the park ethic, from those which were extrinsic in character and which would ultimately detract the park visitor from understanding and appreciating parks as special places (see Swinnerton, 1989). In many ways developments during the 1950s and the early 1960s were forerunners of contemporary commodification of the parks. Dilsaver (1992) has observed that park agencies have tended to be reactionary rather than proactive in attempting to address the conflict of purpose within parks as a result of the "volatile mix of anthropocentrism, autonomy and the automobile" (p. 252). Moreover, park agencies often attempted to alleviate such problems as the overuse of the parks with technical solutions rather than mean-

ingful changes in policy (see Swinnerton, 1989). Dustin and McAvoy (1982) have commented on the adaptability of visitors to adjust to extrinsic recreation environments and have cautioned recreation planners and park managers against responding to the needs of those recreationists to the exclusion of those who continue to seek intrinsic settings and experiences (see also Frome, 1992; Sax, 1980).

Paradoxes of Protected Areas and Their Recreation Use

An examination of the evolution and current status of protected areas results in what may be considered to be a series of paradoxes with reference to the relationship between recreation and conservation within protected areas. Acknowledgment of these paradoxes further demonstrates the dangers inherent in making broad generalizations about this relationship.

An initial paradox is that, despite the emphasis being placed on protecting ecological integrity in park policy and legislation, the trend toward privatization and a business plan approach that focuses on greater financial self-reliance at the park level (see Barborak, 1995; Borbey, 1997) could, in practice, work against the stronger protection mandate. With reference to Canada's national parks, Payne (1997, p. 93) has suggested that "neither ecological nor commemorative integrity can be easily reconciled with a business agenda; both find their meanings in noneconomic terms." Budget reductions at the provincial level have similarly required the development of a business approach to protected area planning and management that has often resulted in significant cutbacks in staff and program areas as well as extending the scope of private sector involvement (see Duffin, 1997; Richards, 1997). Although provincial agencies contend that "natural and cultural heritage has been and remain of paramount importance" (Richards, 1997, p. 69), skepticism exists as to whether or not this commitment can be realized. McNamee (1997) has observed that parks agencies have not yet demonstrated how under a business approach they will address three important mandates—"the completion of protected area networks, their management for ecological integrity, and the provision of key educational services to the public" (p. 88). Morgan (1996) has drawn attention to the policy dilemma involving protection and the demands for increased revenue at the state park level in the United States, and similar concerns have been expressed in the context of America's national parks (Frome, 1992; Lowry, 1994).

A second paradox focuses on the fact that, whereas there is a growing sense of cooperation, partnership, and consensus building between diverse interest groups and stakeholders in the establishment and management of protected areas (see Belland and Zinkan, 1998; Bishop, 1995; Cassady and Cornell, 1992; Etchell, 1996; McNeely, 1995; Parks Canada, 1994a; Swinnerton, 1995a, 1995b, 1995c), there are many instances of major conflicts and adversarial debate between local communities, environmentalists, recreation and tourism interests, and the resource sector (see Alberta Environmental Network, 1998; Bissix et al., 1998; Francis, 1998b; Murray, 1998). In the case of the *Special Places 2000*, an initiative that was launched in 1995 to complete a network of protected areas in Alberta, all but one of the environmental groups have resigned from the multistakeholder provincial coordinating committee that was assigned the overall responsibility for directing the program. Reasons for the resignations include the inadequate rate of progress in designating sites and the fact that the Alberta government will honor existing dispositions and leases, including those for mining, oil and gas exploration, and commercial logging, within proposed protected areas (see Francis, 1998a; Kennett, 1998; Swinnerton, 1997, 1998). In the Banff National Park situation, several of the recommendations made by the Banff–Bow Valley Task Force (1996) to protect and restore the ecological integrity of the area were considered by some commercial and tourism stakeholders to be too restrictive on existing land use patterns and practices and resulted in litigation (see Sillars, 1996).

A third paradox involves the application of a more rigorous scientific approach to protected area designation, planning and management (see Herman, Bondrup-Nielsen, Willison and Munro, 1995; Pigram and Sundell, 1997), while at the same time there is an increasing trend to accommodate local involvement and input from the public (see Francis, 1998a; Kennett, 1998; McNeely, 1993, 1995; Pimbert and Pretty, 1995; Schelhas and Shaw, 1995; Swinnerton, 1997, 1998; see also Stankey et al., chapter 26 in this volume). The need for increased applied research and systematic monitoring in the management of national parks in England and Wales were amongst the recommendations of the *Report of the National Parks Review Panel* (Edwards, 1991, see also Briggs, Tantram and Scott, 1996). Although the U.S. National Park Service has been criticized for its low level of commitment to and support for science-based management (see Frome, 1992; Lowry, 1994; Rettie, 1995; Sellars, 1997), current practices involving both the natural and social sciences (see Machlis, Forester and McKendry, 1994; Wellman, Bunch and Wise, 1995) do contrast with the focus in the early years on *facade management*. That approach involved "protecting and enhancing the scenic facade of nature for the public's enjoyment, but with scant scientific knowledge and little concern for biological consequences" (Sellars, 1997, p. 4–5). In Canada, the corollary to the increased emphasis being placed on protecting ecological integrity within national parks and other protected areas has been the need for scientifically based park designation, monitoring, and assessment (Herman et al., 1995; Parks Canada, 1998b; Ramsay and Whitelaw, 1998; Woodley, 1993, 1997; Woodley and Forbes, 1995). There are numerous examples where there has been successful involvement of local people in environmental monitoring and protected area management with benefits for both protected area agencies and the communities themselves (see McNeely, 1995; Pimbert and Pretty, 1995; Stadel and Nelson, 1995). However, involvement of local communities in the process of designating protected areas and their ongoing management is not without difficulties that often involve finding the appropriate balance between local, regional, and national interests as well as science and indigenous knowledge (see McNeely, 1995; Pimbert and Pretty, 1995; Swinnerton, 1997, 1998). In such instances, political agendas and imperatives are often seen as taking precedence over science (see Francis, 1998a; Kennett, 1998). The process is also complicated by the extension of land management considerations to include intangible, cultural, and spiritual values (see Driver et al., 1996). In assessing the place of science in the designation and management of protected areas, Barbee (1997) has suggested that "science may not be sufficient, but it is always necessary, if a manager is going to justify and then successfully implement any ecosystem-based program" (p. 43).

A final paradox results from the dual mandate that national parks have to accommodate visitors as well as the other management objectives that they and other protected areas are supposed to achieve. The dilemma was recently reiterated by Sheila Copps, Minister of Canadian Heritage, in her foreword to the new management plan for Banff National Park (Parks Canada, 1997):

> This Plan makes it very clear that Banff National Park is, first and foremost, **a place for nature.** Ecological integrity is the cornerstone of Banff National Park and the key to the future. It also recognizes that the park is **a place for people** and **a place for heritage tourism.** Tourism gave birth to this park, and it will always be a place to visit, to experience, and to learn.

Both the Banff–Bow Valley Task Force (1996) and Parks Canada (1997) acknowledge that the quality of the natural environment is fundamental to the tourist and visitor experience within Banff National Park. At the same time, they both recognize that human use and development associated with meeting the needs of the visitor have had negative impacts on the park's ecosystem. The Task Force concluded that continued growth in visitor numbers and related development could cause serious and irreversible harm to the ecological integrity of the park.

A substantive literature exists that documents the environmental impact of outdoor recreation and tourism on the environment (see for example Booth and Cullen, 1995; Cole, 1994; Cole and Landres, 1995; Kuss et al., 1990; Liddle, 1997; Sidaway, 1994; Speight, 1973; Wall, 1989). However, attempting to balance the dual mandate of national parks and protected areas requires progression from consideration of objective measurement or a physical concept to one where the significance of the impact is considered. For example, park visitor perceptions of user impacts and the tolerance of these impacts vary widely (see Noe, Hammitt and Bixler, 1997). As a result, the exercise becomes subjective and value-laden and is extensively discussed in the literature in terms of carrying capacity (see Shelby and Heberlein, 1986) and the Limits of Acceptable Change (LAC) (see McCool and Cole, 1997; Stankey et al., chapter 26 in this volume). Manning's examination (see chapter 19 in this volume) of the relationship between visitor use and crowding as a normative concept is illustrative of this distinction. With reference to national parks, values and difference of opinion are clearly present in the respective positions taken by Hummel (1987) and Frome (1992) regarding the level of development and visitor pressure within national parks in the United States. In Britain, the concern expressed by many national park authorities over the growth in tourism and outdoor recreation and the threat that this would entail for the character of the national parks (see Council for National Parks, 1990; Edwards, 1991; Swinnerton, 1995c) may be contrasted with those who contend that this excessive concern for the repercussions of leisure and sport on national parks and the countryside in general has been largely unfounded on the basis of objective research (see Curry, 1994). The Sports Council (1992) in England and its counterpart in Wales (Sports Council for Wales, 1991), for example, implied that the recommendations of the *National Parks Review Panel* (Edwards, 1991) were overly cautious with regard to recreation within the national parks, and instead argued for a more responsive approach to accommodating the growing demand for a variety of sport and recreation activities. Support for this more accommodating position was based, in part, on the contention that any potential negative impacts resulting from sports and recreation activities could be prevented, or at least contained, to an acceptable level by more positive management.

Finding an acceptable balance between recreational use and resource protection within national parks and protected areas is particularly problematic since the issue of values is involved in both assessing the significance of visitor impacts and determining ecological integrity. With reference to ecological integrity and national parks, Lemons (1995, p. 180) has observed that "there is no a priori scientific definition of ecological integrity, and therefore the concept encompasses perspectives or ways of viewing the world that inevitable reflect value-laden judgments." Nevertheless, both the Banff–Bow Valley Task Force (1996) and Sellars (1997) issue an important word of caution concerning most visitors' impressions of the ecological integrity of the parks. Scenery is an important attraction for most park visitors (see Banff–Bow Valley Task Force, 1996; Coalter et al., 1996; Sellars, 1997), but the visual quality of the landscape provides only very limited insight into an area's ecological health. Sellars (1997, p. 287) summarizes the situation as follows:

> For many, spectacular scenery may create an impression of biological health and provide such satisfaction that little consideration is given to the parks as segments of great ecological complexes under stress. . . . The loss of ecological integrity may have little effect on the aesthetics or the general appearance of an area.

Prospects for Reconciling the Tension Between Recreation and Conservation

While recognizing that tension and conflicts do exist between recreation and conservation, particularly within national parks and protected areas, the evidence provided through the more recent academic and professional literature suggests that there are opportunities for resolving many of these problems (see for example Banff–Bow Valley Task Force, 1996; Cassady and Cornell, 1992; House of Commons Environment Committee, 1995; Knight and Gutzwiller, 1995; Parks Canada, 1997; Tourism and Environment Task Force, 1991). Parks Canada (1997), for example, has stated with reference to the stresses affecting Banff National

Park, that "although there is substantial concern, there is reason for optimism. Remedial measures, mitigation and management can restore and sustain ecological integrity in and adjacent to Banff National Park" (p. 13).

An extensive literature exists on specific techniques for protecting the integrity of parks and wilderness areas while maintaining the quality of the visitor experience that involves both human use management and adaptive resource management (see Banff–Bow Valley Study Task Force, 1996; Brown, McCool and Manfredo, 1987; Cole, 1994; Cole, Peterson and Lucas, 1987; Graefe, Kuss and Vaske, 1990; McArthur, 1994; McCool and Cole, 1997; Nilsen and Tayler, 1998; Swinnerton, 1989). Recent comparative studies and assessments of many of the planning and management frameworks—such as the Recreation Opportunity Spectrum (ROS), the Limits of Acceptable Change (LAC) framework, the Visitor Experience and Resource Protection (VERP) framework, the Process for Visitor Impact Management (VIM), and the Visitor Activities Management Process (VAMP)—reveal both positive outcomes as well as limitations (see McCool and Cole, 1997; Nilsen and Tayler, 1998). Butler (1997), for example, has expressed concern that several of these approaches tend to accommodate incremental development that, over time, favors the visitor and is more tolerant of higher levels of use. In Australia, difficulties with the application of LAC and VIM have largely centered around establishing sufficient stakeholder support and endorsement (see McArthur, 1997). An alternative approach that has been developed in Australia is the Tourism Optimization Management Model (TOMM) that is similar to LAC but can operate at a regional level and can accommodate a multitude of interests, including both public and private land tenures (McArthur, 1997). The recent application of TOMM in Canada confirms its potential for addressing the planning issues encountered in developing tourism opportunities in sensitive and protected areas (McVetty and Wight, 1998). Other mechanisms and techniques that are being increasingly used in an attempt to prevent recreation and conservation conflicts both within protected areas and the wider countryside include the development of criteria for determining what are appropriate activities (see Banff–Bow Valley Task Force, 1996; Parks Canada, 1994b, 1997), and establishing guides for good practice for individual sporting and recreational activities (see Aitchison and Jones, 1994; Sidaway, 1991, 1993). The latter approach is based on the premise that many of the conflicts that occur between sport, recreation and nature conservation may be reduced by making participants more aware of the

environmental impacts that specific activities cause and the means by which conflicts may be prevented. Critical to developing guides for good practice is participatory management that is both proactive and anticipatory in nature (see Aitchison and Jones, 1994).

Irrespective of the effectiveness of individual techniques and mechanisms, no one approach is a panacea for dealing with growing visitor numbers and potentially unacceptable impacts on protected areas and the countryside as a whole. Moreover, these techniques will not be successful unless they are complemented by, and given direction within, appropriate policy frameworks, broader strategies, and the adoption of working principles that purposively attempt to find solutions that are communally acceptable (see Simpson, 1995).

One of the factors that has contributed to the occurrence of conflicts between recreation and conservation within protected areas is lack of clarity and consistency in determining the primary purposes of different types of protected areas. Reference has already been made to the fact that protected areas serve a variety of primary purposes that are reflected in the six distinct categories adopted by the IUCN (IUCN Commission on National Parks and Protected Areas, 1994a). These guidelines are, of necessity, quite broad in order for them to accommodate the range of conditions encountered within protected areas at a global scale. However, the IUCN recognizes that the main initiatives for establishing a network of protected areas have to occur at the level of individual countries (IUCN World Commission on Protected Areas, 1997). Consequently, it is essential that, within individual countries, and where appropriate at lower levels of jurisdiction, such as at the state or provincial levels, a systems planning perspective is adopted. According to the IUCN, there are at least five key characteristics of a system of protected areas (IUCN World Commission on Protected Areas, 1997):

1. representativeness, comprehensiveness and balance;
2. adequacy;
3. coherence and complementarity;
4. consistency; and
5. cost effectiveness, efficiency and equity.

Of particular relevance to the current discussion is the characteristic of consistency. This characteristic acknowledges that "the purpose of each unit is clear to all and so as to maximize the chance that management and use do actually support the objectives" (p. 11). Although many park agencies have adopted park classification systems that recognize the different functions of the various units within the system and specifically their relative priorities in meeting conservation or recreation objectives, there is often a lack of clarity in defining the respective classes and inconsistency in their application (see Alberta Environment Protection, 1998; Swinnerton, 1991, 1993). In addition, the public is often either unaware of the different types of protected areas or confused as to their specific roles. Consequently, the implementation of a clearly defined systems approach to protected areas that is communicated to the public would help to direct potential users to the most appropriate category of protected area and, in so doing, help to lessen user and resource conflicts.

Closely associated with the previous point is the role of marketing in helping to alleviate some of the problems associated with recreation and tourism within protected areas. Groff (1996) has discussed the role of demarketing in reducing the demand and, therefore, problems of crowding and overuse in national and state parks. This approach is in marked contrast to the more traditional concept of marketing as attracting customers and stimulating demand. Park agencies have generally been hesitant to become too closely involved in promoting parks as tourist destinations for this very reason (Swinnerton, 1995c). However, this lack of involvement can create an alternative problem that is clearly illustrated by the circumstances faced by the national park authorities in England and Wales.

In the absence of the national park authorities becoming involved in promoting the public enjoyment and tourism values of the parks, the marketing of these opportunities was almost exclusively undertaken by the public and private sectors of the tourism industry. One of the outcomes of this situation was that the conservation mandate of the national parks was given considerably lower visibility relative to recreation attractions and tourism development within the parks (Swinnerton, 1995c). A survey undertaken for the Countryside Commission (Fielder Green Associates, 1992) revealed that, although most of the tourism business operators were aware of the dual mandate of national parks, the conservation role was very rarely conveyed in promotional material. A recommendation from the study was that the national park authorities should become more proactive by cooperating with the various components of the tourism industry to ensure that the special character of the national parks and their conservation function is conveyed to potential visitors (see Fielder Green Associates, 1992).

A *Heads of Agreement on Tourism in National Parks* was initially concluded in 1978 and reconfirmed in 1989 (see Swinnerton, 1995c), but it has been during the 1990s that significant advances have been made in improving the level of cooperation between the national parks and the tourism industry. Indicative of the trend has been the acceptance of a set of principles for tourism in national parks (English Tourist Board, Rural Development Commission and the Countryside Commission, 1993). These principles address conservation, enjoyment, rural economy, development, design and marketing. At a more applied level the same agencies have cooperated in producing a document titled *Tourism in National Parks: A Guide to Good Practice* (English Tourist Board, Wales Tourist Board, Rural Development Commission, Countryside Council for Wales and the Countryside Commission, 1992). An examination of the more recent management plans prepared by the respective national park authorities reveals a cautious but more positive attitude to sustainable tourism and the development of collaborative partnerships with the various stakeholders in the tourism industry (see Swinnerton, 1995c). At the same time, the tourism industry has become more responsive to the unique qualities of the national parks and the need to protect the character of these areas (see Countryside Commission et al., 1995). A particularly good example of the advantages to be gained from collaborative partnerships in helping reconcile conflict between recreation and tourism within a protected area is afforded by Dartmoor National Park in England (see Swinnerton, 1995c). The Dartmoor Area Tourism Initiative (DATI) illustrates the importance of adopting a proactive and positive approach to addressing conflict that included a multistakeholder steering committee and a strategy that had a regional as opposed to a national park perspective. A central purpose of DATI was to increase the awareness of environmental issues and to promote recreation and tourism opportunities beyond the national park boundary. As a result, the increased pressure of tourism within the park could be reduced, while at the same time appropriate forms of rural tourism would be encouraged to locate where they could contribute to the wider rural economy (see Countryside Commission et al., 1995; Dartmoor Area Tourism Initiative, 1994; Greenwood, 1994; Swinnerton, 1995c).

The Dartmoor situation is just one example of partnerships being a vital component of landscape conservation and the provision of outdoor recreation and tourism opportunities in the national parks and the wider countryside in Britain (see Swinnerton, 1995a, 1995c). In the case of the national parks, O'Riordan (1993, p. 261) has suggested that the need for partnerships has largely arisen because of the national park authorities being "politically fragmented, financially weak, and legally fettered." Another factor is that most of the land within the national parks is in private ownership. Similar circumstances are now being encountered by park and recreation agencies in many countries as a result of privatization, downsizing, and budget reductions in the public sector (see Selin, 1998; Slack, chapter 24 in this volume). In addition, with the broadening scope of protected areas and the need for buffer zones and corridors, the role of partnerships has become increasingly evident. The interest in collaborative partnerships has also been an outcome of the increased demand for democratization in the planning and management of park and recreation resources (LaPage, Vaske and Donnelly, 1995; Selin and Chavez, 1995; see also Stankey et al., chapter 26 in this volume).

Concomitant with the development of partnerships is the adoption of more meaningful dialogue between park agencies, other stakeholders and the general public that results in collaborative decision making as opposed to solely directive or consultative decisions (see McMillan and Murgatroyd, 1994). There is now international recognition that finding solutions to national park and protected area problems, and particularly those involving conflicts between protection and development, will increasingly have to rely on consensus-building strategies involving negotiation and mediation (see Bishop, 1996; Cassady and Cornell, 1992; Cormick, Dale, Emond, Sigurdson and Stuart, 1996; Etchell, 1996; Lewis, 1996; Murray, 1998; Norton and Roper-Lindsay, 1992; Swinnerton, 1997, 1998). Negotiation requires an initial acknowledgment of the different values that are held by conservationists and developers and a process that will ultimately lead to shared attitudes and ideas (see Bruns and Stokowski, 1996; Norton and Roper-Lindsay, 1992). Selected examples from Canada (Banff–Bow Valley Task Force, 1996; McVetty and Wight, 1998; Page, 1997), the United States (Bruns and Stokowski, 1996), and Britain (Rose and Dixon, 1996) reveal that a common element in reaching consensus is a process that involves the development of a communally held vision on an issue or problem (see also Stankey et al., chapter 26 in this volume). The attainment of such a vision is a prerequisite to the successful implementation of more specific visitor and resource management strategies and techniques.

Conclusion

This chapter has attempted to illustrate the complexity and diversity of issues associated with the constantly changing relationship between recreation and conservation. Of necessity, the focus has been primarily confined to issues associated with the apparent conflict between recreation and conservation within protected areas. A review of the relevant academic literature and examples from the field of practice demonstrated that alternative disciplinary perspectives and research paradigms have important implications for how the concept of conservation is interpreted and applied. Equally relevant is the fact that any attempt to reconcile the conflict between recreation and conservation requires information on the human dimension of parks and protected areas and their use as well as the natural science dimension of park environments. An interdisciplinary perspective is obviously required.

The potential for further conflict between recreation and conservation within protected areas in particular seems inevitable with the growth in demand for recreation and tourism opportunities that favor natural settings. This situation is compounded by the concern over the state of the earth's biodiversity and the special role that protected areas have to play in addressing this problem. At the same time, the broadening scope of protected areas means that recreation and conservation problems cannot be isolated from the broader issues of regional land use planning and the concern for the social and economic well-being of communities both within and outside protected areas. Even the optimists who contend that the level of conflict is exaggerated and that many of the problems can be reconciled through proactive planning concede that there is no room for complacency. Finally, and notwithstanding the importance of dialogue and consensus building which can accommodate different value systems, it is critical to remember that protected areas are special places and that they will become increasingly unique as core areas for protecting biodiversity and for providing opportunities for intrinsic forms of outdoor recreation and sustainable tourism which are harmonious with natural features and processes.

References

Aitchison, J. (1995). Rural sustainability and protected landscapes. In C. R. Bryant & C. Marois (Eds.), *The sustainability of rural systems* (pp. 248–259). Montreal, Quebec: Université de Montréal, Départment de Géographie.

Aitchison, J., & Beresford, M. (1992). Sustainable tourism in protected areas: Towards principles and guidelines. In P. Jones (Collator), *Sustainable tourism in protected areas; Proceedings of a workshop held by the Brecon Beacons National Park, Wales* (pp. 2–16). Brecon, UK: Brecon Beacons National Park/International Center for Protected Landscapes.

Aitchison, J., & Jones, P. L. (1994). *A sporting chance for the countryside: Sport and recreation in the Welsh countryside—Case studies of good practice* (Report prepared for the Sports Council for Wales and the Countryside Council for Wales). Aberystwyth, UK: University of Wales, Aberystwyth, Rural Survey Research Unit.

Agee, J. K., & Johnson, D. R. (Eds.). (1988). *Ecosystem management for parks and wilderness.* Seattle. WA: University of Washington Press.

Alberta Environmental Network. (1998). Scientists call for protection instead of Cheviot Mine. *Wild Lands Advocate, 6*(3), 3.

Alberta Environmental Protection. (n.d.). *The Alberta forest legacy: Implementation framework for sustainable forest management.* Edmonton, Alberta: Author.

Alberta Environmental Protection. (1998). *Proposed policy foundation for the Natural Heritage Act: Summary report.* Edmonton, Alberta: Author.

Baldwin, A. D., Jr., De Luce, J., & Pletsch, C. (Eds.). (1994). *Beyond preservation: Restoring and inventing landscapes.* Minneapolis, MN: University of Minnesota Press.

Banff–Bow Valley Task Force. (1996). *Banff–Bow Valley: At the crossroads* (Technical report). Ottawa, Ontario: Minister of Supply and Services Canada.

Barbee, R. D. (1997). No place is an island—The Yellowstone experience. In J. J. Pigram & R. C. Sundell (Eds.), *National parks and protected areas: Selection, delimitation, and management* (pp. 37–43). Armidale, Australia: University of New England, Center for Water Policy Research.

Barborak, J. R. (1995). Institutional options for managing protected areas. In J. A. McNeely (Ed.), *Expanding partnerships in conservation* (pp. 30–38). Washington, DC: Island Press.

Belland, G., & Zinkan, C. (1998). Heritage tourism in Canada's Rocky Mountain Parks: A case study in education and partnership. In N. W. P. Munro & J. H. M. Willison (Eds.), *Linking protected areas with working landscapes conserving biodiversity* (pp. 616–625). Wolfville, Nova Scotia: Science and Management of Protected Areas Association.

Bengston, D. N. (1994). Changing forest values and ecosystem management. *Society and Natural Resources, 7*(6), 515–533.

Bengston, D. N., & Xu, Z. (1995). Changing national forest values: a content analysis (North Central Experiment Station Experiment Station, Research Paper NC-323). St. Paul, MN: USDA Forest Service.

Benton, T. (1994). Biology and social theory in the environmental debate. In M. Redclift & T. Benton (Eds.), *Social theory and the global environment* (pp. 28–50). London, UK: Routledge.

Benton, T., & Redclift. M. (1994). Introduction. In M. Redclift & T. Benton (Eds.), *Social theory and the global environment* (pp. 1–27). London, UK: Routledge.

Bishop, J. (1996). Consensus in the countryside: An overview. In C. Etchell (Ed.), *Consensus in the countryside: Reaching shared agreement in policy, planning and management* (pp. 5–14). Cardiff, UK: University of Wales College of Cardiff, Department of City and Regional Planning, Countryside Recreation Network.

Bishop, S. G. (1995). Partnerships for ecosystem management and sustainable development: Some biosphere reserve models. In R. M. Linn (Ed.), *Sustainable society and protected areas: Contributed papers of the 8th conference on research and resource management in parks and on public lands* (pp. 5–8). Hancock, MI: The George Wright Society.

Bishop, K., Phillips, A., & Warren, L. (1995). Protected forever? Factors shaping the future of protected areas policy. *Land Use Policy, 12*(4), 291–305.

Bissix, G., Anderson, C., & Miles, K. (1998). "Parklocked?"—Sustainable rural development in the northern Cape Breton greater ecosystem. In N. W. P. Munro & J. H. M. Willison (Eds.), *Linking protected areas with working landscapes conserving biodiversity* (pp. 885–892). Wolfville, Nova Scotia: Science and Management of Protected Areas Association.

Bissix, G., & Bissix, S. (1995). Dartmoor (U.K.) National Park's landscape management: Lessons for North America's eastern seaboard. In T. B. Herman, S. Bondrup-Nielsen, J. H. M. Willison & N. W. P. Munro (Eds.), *Ecosystem monitoring and protected areas* (pp. 563–571). Wolfville, Nova Scotia: Science and Management of Protected Areas Association.

Booth, K., & Cullen, R. (1995). Recreation impacts. In P. J. Devlin, R. A. Corbett & C. J. Peebles (Eds.), *Outdoor recreation in New Zealand: Vol. 1, A review and synthesis of the research literature* (pp. 99–135). Wellington, New Zealand: Department of Conservation and Lincoln University.

Borbey, P. (1997). The Parks Canada business plan. In N. Munro (Ed.), *Protected areas in our modern world: Proceedings of a workshop held as part of the IUCN World Conservation Congress, Montreal, October 1996* (pp. 47–53). Halifax, Nova Scotia: Parks Canada.

Borodczak, N. (1995). Ontario's Niagara Escarpment—Implementing the biosphere reserve concept in a highly developed region. *Biosphere Reserves in Canada—Newsletter, 7,* 6.

Bridgewater, P., Phillips, A., Green, M., & Amos, B. (1996). *Biosphere reserves and the IUCN system of protected area management categories.* Canberra, Australia: Australian Nature Conservation Agency/IUCN/UNESCO.

Briggs, D. J., Tantram, D. A. S., & Scott, P. G. (1996). *Improving information for management and decision making in national parks* (Final report to the Countryside Commission). Northampton, UK: Nene College of Higher Education, Nene Center for Research.

Brown, P. J., McCool, S. F., & Manfredo, M. J. (1987). Evolving concepts and tools for recreation user management in wilderness: A state-of-art knowledge review. In R. C. Lucas (Compiler), *Proceedings: National Wilderness Research Conference: Issues, State-of-Knowledge, Future Directions* (Intermountain Research Station General Technical Report INT-220, pp. 320–346). Ogden, UT: USDA Forest Service.

Bruns, D., & Stokowski, P. (1996). Sustaining opportunities to experience early American landscapes. In B. L. Driver, D. Dustin, T. Baltic, G. Elsner & G. Peterson (Eds.), *Nature and the human spirit: Toward an expanded land management ethic* (pp. 321–338). State College, PA: Venture Publishing, Inc.

Bryant, C. R., & Marois, C. (Eds.). (1995). The sustainability of rural systems. *Proceedings, First meeting of the IGU Study Group on the sustainability of rural systems, 1993.* Montreal, Quebec: Université de Montréal, Département de Géographie.

Buechner, M., Schonewald-Cox, C., Sauvajot, R., & Wilcox, B. A. (1992). Cross-boundary issues for national parks. What works "on the ground." *Environmental Management, 16*(6), 799–809.

Buggey, S. (1994). Landscape planning: An international and national perspective. In J. G. Nelson, N. D. Pollock-Ellwand & T. Stroud (Eds.), *Landscape planning: Implications of the proposed new Ontario Heritage Act* (Occasional Paper #25, pp. 19–24). Waterloo, Ontario: University of Waterloo, Heritage Resources Center.

Bunce, M. (1994). *The countryside ideal: Anglo-American images of landscape.* London, UK: Routledge.

Burak, P., & Swinnerton, G. S. (1998). The Beaver Hills: An exploratory application of the biosphere reserve concept in the Aspen Parkland of Alberta. In N.

W. P. Munro & J. H. M. Willison (Eds.), *Linking protected areas with working landscapes conserving biodiversity* (pp. 577–583). Wolfville, Nova Scotia: Science and Management of Protected Areas Association.

Butler, R. W. (1997). The concept of carrying capacity for tourism destinations: Dead or merely buried? In C. Cooper & S. J. Wanhill (Eds.), *Tourism development: Environmental and community issues* (pp. 11–21). Chichester, UK: John Wiley & Sons, Ltd.

Butler, R., Hall, C. M., & Jenkins, J. (Eds.). (1998). *Tourism and recreation in rural areas.* Chichester, UK: John Wiley & Sons, Ltd.

Butler, R., & Hinch, T. (Eds.). (1996). *Tourism and indigenous peoples.* Toronto, Ontario: International Thomson Business Press.

Cachay, K. (1993). Sports and environment, Sports for everyone—Room for everyone? *International Review for the Sociology of Sport, 28*(2/3), 311–323.

CAG Consultants & Land Use Consultants (1997). *What matters and why: Environmental capital: A new approach* (A provisional guide). A report prepared for the Countryside Commission, English Heritage, English Nature, Environment Agency. Cheltenham, UK: Countryside Commission.

Callicott, J. B., & Mumford, K. (1997). Ecological sustainability as a conservation concept. *Conservation Biology, 11*(1), 32–40.

Canadian Parks Service. (1993). *Ecosystem management for managers. Canadian Parks Service national workshop.* Waterloo, Ontario: University of Waterloo, Heritage Resource Center.

Cassady, J., & Cornell, M. R. (1992). Managing and resolving conflict in national parks. *Resolve, 25,* 1, 3–8.

Cherry, G., & Rogers, A. (1996). *Rural change and planning: England and Wales in the twentieth century.* London, UK: E & FN Spon.

Cloke, P. (1993). The countryside as commodity: New rural spaces for leisure. In S. Glyptis (Ed.)., *Leisure and the environment: Essays in honor of Professor J. A. Patmore* (pp. 53–67). London, UK: Belhaven Press.

Coalter, F., MacGregor, C., & Denman, R. (1996). *Visitors to national parks: Summary of the 1994 survey findings* (CCP 503). Cheltenham, UK: Countryside Commission.

Cole, D. N. (1994). Backcountry impact management: Lessons from research. *Trends, 35*(3), 10–14.

Cole, D. N., & Landres, P. B. (1995). Indirect effects of recreationists on wildlife. In R. L. Knight & K. J. Gutzwiller (Eds.), *Wildlife and recreationists: Coexistence through management and research* (pp. 183–202). Washington, DC: Island Press.

Cole, D. N., Petersen, M. E., & Lucas, R. C. (1987). *Managing wilderness recreation use: Common problems and potential solutions* (Intermountain Research Station, General Technical Report INT-230). Ogden, UT: USDA Forest Service.

Cordell, H. K. (1995). Outdoor recreation: resource planning and management. In L. A. Barnett (Ed.), *Research about leisure: Past, present, and future* (2nd ed., pp. 193–214). Champaign, IL: Sagamore Publishing.

Cordell, H. K., Lewis, B., & McDonald, B. L. (1995). Long-term outdoor recreation participation trends. In J. L. Thompson, D. W. Lime, B. Gartner & W. M. Sames (Compilers), *Proceedings of the Fourth International Outdoor Recreation and Tourism Trends Symposium and the 1995 National Recreation Resource Planning Conference* (pp. 35–38). St. Paul, MN: University of Minnesota, College of Natural Resources and Minnesota Extension Service.

Cormick, G., Dale, N., Emond, P., Sigurdson, S. G., & Stuart, B. D. (1996). *Building consensus for a sustainable future: Putting principles into practice.* Ottawa, Ontario: National Round Table on the Environment and the Economy.

Cornwell, L., & Costanza, R. (1996). Futures outlook of the Banff–Bow Valley: A modeling approach to ecological, economic and social issues. In J. Green, C. Pacas, L. Cornwell, & S. Bayley (Eds.), *Ecological outlooks project—A cumulative effects assessment and futures outlook of the Banff–Bow Valley* (Prepared for the Banff–Bow Valley Study, pp. 10-I-10.A-9). Ottawa, Ontario: Department of Canadian Heritage.

Cortner, H. J., Shannon, M. A., Wallace, M. G., Burke, S., & Moote, M. A. (1996). *Institutional barriers and incentives for ecosystem management: A problem analysis* (General Technical Report PNW-GTR-354). Portland, OR: USDA Forest Service.

Costanza, R. (1994). Three general policies to achieve sustainability. In A. M. Jansson, M. Hammer, C. Folke, & R. Costanza (Eds.), *Investing in natural capital: The ecological economics approach to sustainability* (pp. 392–407). Washington, DC: Island Press.

Council of Europe, UNEP & European Center for Nature Conservation. (1996). *The pan-European biological and landscape diversity strategy: A vision for Europe's natural heritage.* Strasbourg, France: Council of Europe.

Council for National Parks. (1990). *A vision for national parks 1990—Evidence to the National Parks Review Panel.* London, UK: Author.

Countryside Commission. (1990). *A study of good practice: Sustainable development: A challenge and opportunity for the national parks of England and Wales* (CCP 286). Cheltenham, UK: Author.

Countryside Commission. (1993). *Position statement: Sustainability and the English countryside* (CCP 432). Cheltenham, UK: Author.

Countryside Commission. (1994). *Countryside character program* [Brochure] (CCP 472). Cheltenham, UK: Author.

Countryside Commission. (1995). *The environmental impact of leisure activities on the English countryside: Countryside Commission evidence to the House of Commons Environment Committee.* Cheltenham, UK: Author.

Countryside Commission. (1996). *A living countryside: Our strategy for the next ten years* (CCP 492). Cheltenham, UK: Author.

Countryside Commission. (1997). *National park management plans guidance* (CCP 525). Cheltenham, UK: Author.

Countryside Commission & the Council of Europe. (1987). *The lake district declaration.* Cheltenham, UK: Countryside Commission.

Countryside Commission, Department of National Heritage, Rural Development Commission, & English Tourist Board. (1995). *Sustainable rural tourism: Opportunities for local action* (CCP 483). Cheltenham, UK: Countryside Commission.

Countryside Working Group. (1991). *Tourism and the environment: Maintaining the balance—Final report to the tourism and environment task force.* London, UK: English Tourist Board & The Employment Department Group.

Cronon, W. (1996). Foreword to the paperback edition. In W. Cronon (Ed.), *Uncommon ground: Rethinking the human place in nature* (pp. 19–22). New York, NY: W.W. Norton & Company.

Crouch, D. (1994). Home, escape and identity: Rural cultures and sustainable tourism. *Journal of Sustainable Tourism, 2*(1&2), 93–101.

Curry, N. (1994). *Countryside recreation, access and land use planning.* London, UK: E & FN Spon.

Dartmoor Area Tourism Initiative. (1994). *Dartmoor area tourism initiative: Final report.* Bovey Tracey, UK: Author.

Davis, J. (1996). An integrated approach to the scientific study of the human spirit. In B. L. Driver, D. Dustin, T. Baltic, G. Elsner & G. Peterson (Eds.), *Nature and the human spirit: Toward an expanded land management ethic* (pp. 417–429). State College, PA: Venture Publishing, Inc.

Dearden, P. (1995). Park literacy and conservation. *Conservation Biology, 9*(6), 1654–1656.

Dearden, P., & Rollins, R. (Eds.). (1993). *Parks and protected areas in Canada: Planning and management.* Toronto, Ontario: Oxford University Press.

De Groot, R. S. (1994). Functions and values of protected areas: A comprehensive framework for assessing the benefits of protected areas to human society. In M. Munasinghe & J. McNeely (Eds.), *Protected* area economic policy: Linking conservation and sustainable development (pp. 159–169). Washington, DC: World Bank and IUCN.

Department of the Environment. (1996). Environment Act 1995, Part III National Parks (Circular 12/96). London, UK: HMSO.

Department of the Environment & the Ministry of Agriculture, Fisheries and Food. (1995). Rural England: A nation committed to a living countryside. London, UK: HMSO.

Dilsaver, L. M. (1992). Stemming the flow: The evolution of controls on visitor numbers and impacts in national parks. In L. M. Dilsaver & C. E. Colton (Eds.), The American environment: Interpretations of past geographies (pp. 235–255). Lanham, MD: Rowan & Littlefield Publishers.

Dixon, J. A., & Sherman, P. B. (1990). Economics of protected areas. A new look at benefits and costs. Washington, DC: Island Press.

Doull, I. (1995). Rural historic districts and the historic sites and monuments board of Canada. ICOMOS Canada Bulletin, 4(2), 7–10.

Draper, D. (1997). Touristic development and water sustainability in Banff and Canmore, Alberta, Canada. Journal of Sustainable Tourism, 5(3), 183–212.

Driver, B. L., Dustin, D., Baltic, T., Elsner, G., & Peterson, G. (Eds.). (1996). Nature and the human spirit: Toward an expanded land management ethic. State College, PA: Venture Publishing, Inc.

Duffin, B. (1997). Developing a business approach to protected areas management: Clarifying and focussing on the mandate. In N. Munro (Ed.), Protected areas in our modern world: Proceedings of a workshop held as part of the IUCN World Conservation Congress, Montreal, October 1996 (pp. 54–60). Halifax, Nova Scotia: Parks Canada.

Dustin, D. L., Knopf, R. C., & Fox, K. M. (1993). Building multicultural responsiveness into outdoor recreation management. In A. W. Ewert, D. J. Chavez & A. W. Magill (Eds.), Culture, conflict, and communication in the wildland-urban interface (pp. 259–265). Boulder, CO: Westview Press.

Dustin, D. L., & McAvoy, L. H. (1982). The decline and fall of quality recreation opportunities and environments? Environmental Ethics, 4, 49–57.

Edwards, P. J., & Abivardi, C. (1998). The value of biodiversity: Where ecology and economy blend. Biological Conservation, 83(3), 239–246.

Edwards, R. (Chairman). (1991). Fit for the future: Report of the national parks review panel. Cheltenham, UK: Countryside Commission.

English Tourist Board, Rural Development Commission & the Countryside Commission. (1993). Principles for tourism in national parks (CCP 431). Cheltenham, UK: Countryside Commission.

English Tourist Board, Wales Tourist Board, Rural Development Commission, Countryside Council for Wales & the Countryside Commission. (1992). Tourism in national parks: A guide to good practice. London, UK: English Tourist Board.

Etchell, C. (Ed.). (1994). Communities in their countryside: Helping communities to help themselves and others enjoy local countryside opportunities. Proceedings of the 1994 National Countryside Recreation Conference. Cardiff, UK: University of Wales, College of Cardiff, Department of City & Regional Planning, Countryside Recreation Network.

Etchell, C. (Ed.). (1996). Consensus in the countryside. Proceedings of a workshop held at Devon County Council, Exeter. Cardiff, UK: University of Wales, College of Cardiff, Department of City & Regional Planning, Countryside Recreation Network.

Evernden, N. (1992). The social creation of nature. Baltimore, MD: Johns Hopkins University Press.

Ewert, A. W. (1996). Natural resource management: The human dimension. Boulder, CO: Westview Press.

Fennell, D. A., & Weaver, D. B. (1997). Vacation farms and ecotourism in Saskatchewan, Canada. Journal of Rural Studies, 13(4), 467–475.

Fielder Green Associates. (1992). National parks marketing and conservation survey (CCP 354). Cheltenham, UK: Countryside Commission.

Fladmark, J. M. (Ed.). (1994). Cultural tourism. Papers presented at the Robert Gordon University Heritage Convention 1994. London, UK: Donhead Publishing, Ltd.

Force, J. E., & Machlis, G. E. (1997). The human ecosystem, Part II: Social indicators in ecosystem management. Society & Natural Resources, 10(4), 369–382.

Forman, R. T. T. (1995). Land mosaics: The ecology of landscapes and regions. Cambridge, UK: Cambridge University Press.

Francis, W. (1998a). Alberta's special places program: A triumph of politics over science. In N. Munro & J. H. M. Willison (Eds.), Linking protected areas with working landscapes conserving biodiversity (pp. 919–926). Wolfville, Nova Scotia: Science and Management of Protected Areas Association.

Francis, W. (1998b). Kananaskis: Why isn't it a park? Wild Lands Advocate, 6(6), 4.

Frome, M. (1992). Regreening the national parks. Tucson, AZ: University of Arizona Press.

Funtowicz, S. O., & Ravetz, J. R. (1995). Science for the postnormal age. In L. Westra & J. Lemons (Eds.), Perspectives on ecological integrity (pp. 146–161). Boston, MA: Kluwer Academic Publishers.

Gale, R. P., & Cordray, S. M. (1994). Making sense of sustainability: Nine answers to what should be sustained? *Rural Sociology, 59*(2), 311–332.

Gare, A. E. (1995). *Postmodernism and the environmental crisis.* London, UK: Routledge.

Garratt, K. (1984). Relationship between adjacent lands and protected areas: Issues of concern for the protected area manager. In J. A. McNeely & K. R. Miller (Eds.), *National parks, conservation, and development: The role of protected areas in sustaining society* (pp. 65–71). Washington, DC: Smithsonian Institution Press.

Gerlach, P. G., & Bengston, D. N. (1994). If ecosystem management is the solution, what's the problem? *Journal of Forestry, 92*(8), 18–21.

Goldstein, B. E. (1992). Can ecosystem management turn an administrative patchwork into a Greater Yellowstone Ecosystem? *The Northwest Environmental Journal, 8,* 285–324.

Good, R., & Grenier, P. (1994). Some environmental impacts of recreation in the Australian Alps. *Australian Parks & Recreation, 30*(4), 20–26.

Government of Alberta. (1992). *Special places 2000: Alberta's natural heritage* [Draft]. Edmonton, Alberta: Author.

Government of Canada. (1996). *The state of Canada's environment—1996.* Ottawa, Ontario: Minister of Public Works and Government Services.

Graefe, A. R., Kuss, F. R., & Vaske, J. J. (1990). *Visitor impact management: The planning framework.* Washington, DC: National Parks and Conservation Association.

Green, B. H., Simmons, E. A., & Woltjer, I. (1996). Landscape conservation: Some steps towards developing a new conservation dimension. *A report of the IUCN-CESP Landscape Conservation Working Group.* Wye, UK: University of London, Wye College, Department of Agriculture, Horticulture and the Environment.

Greenwood, J. (1994). Dartmoor area tourism initiative—A case study of visitor management in and around a national park. In A. V. Seaton (Ed.), *Tourism: The state of the art* (pp. 682–690). Chichester, UK: John Wiley & Sons, Ltd.

Greider, T., & Garkovich, L. (1994). Landscapes: The social construction of nature and the environment. *Rural Sociology, 59*(1), 1–24.

Groff, C. (1996). Demarketing in park and recreation management. In W. F. Kuentzel (Ed.), *Proceedings of the 1996 Northeastern Recreation Research Symposium* (General Technical Report-NE-232, pp. 173–177). Radnor, PA: USDA Forest Service.

Grumbine, R. E. (1991). Cooperation or conflict? Interagency relationships and the future of biodiversity for U.S. parks and forests. *Environmental Management, 15*(1), 27–37.

Grumbine, R. E. (1994). What is ecosystem management? *Conservation Biology, 8*(1), 27–38.

Grumbine, R. E. (1996). Beyond conservation and preservation in American environmental values. In B. L. Driver, D. Dustin, T. Baltic, G. Elsner & G. Peterson (Eds.), *Nature and the human spirit: Toward an expanded land management ethic* (pp. 237–245). State College, PA: Venture Publishing, Inc.

Heberlein, T. A. (1988). Improving interdisciplinary research: Integrating the social and natural sciences. *Society & Natural Resources, 1*(1), 5–16.

Henderson, K. A. (1991). *Dimensions of choice: A qualitative approach to recreation, parks and leisure research.* State College, PA: Venture Publishing, Inc.

Henderson, K. A. (1996). Feminist perspectives, female ways of being, and nature. In B. L. Driver, D. Dustin, T. Baltic, G. Elsner & G. Peterson (Eds.), *Nature and the human spirit: Toward an expanded land management ethic* (pp. 153–162). State College, PA: Venture Publishing, Inc.

Herman, T. B., Bondrup-Nielsen, S., Willison, J. H., & Munro, N. W. P. (Eds.). (1995). Ecosystem monitoring and protected areas. *Proceedings of the Second International Conference on Science and the Management of Protected Areas.* Wolfville, Nova Scotia: Science and Management of Protected Areas Association.

Higgs, E. S., Murray, C., Norton, M., Rhemtulla, J., Anderson, J., & Galbraith, P. (1998). Whose nature is it? Setting goals for ecological restoration in Jasper National Park. In N. W. P. Munro & J. H. M. Willison (Eds.), *Linking protected areas with working landscapes conserving biodiversity* (pp. 781–789). Wolfville, Nova Scotia: Science and Management of Protected Areas Association.

House of Commons Environment Committee. (1995). *The environmental impact of leisure activities* (Vol. 1). London, UK: HMSO.

Howard, H. (1997). Conservation reserve boundaries and management implications in New South Wales. In J. J. Pigram & R. C. Sundell (Eds.), *National parks and protected areas: Selection, delimitation, and management* (pp. 387–401). Armidale, Australia: University of New England, Center for Water Policy Research.

Hudson, W. E. (Ed.). (1991). *Landscape linkages and biodiversity: Defenders of wildlife.* Washington, DC: Island Press.

Hummel, D. (1987). *Stealing the national parks: The destruction of concessions and public access.* Bellevue, WA: The Free Enterprise Press.

Hunt, J. D. (1995). Tourism in the 21st century: From a global to a community perspective. In J. L. Thompson, D. W. Lime, B. Gartner & W. M. Sames (Compilers), *Proceedings of the Fourth International*

Outdoor Recreation and Tourism Trends Symposium and the 1995 National Recreation Resource Planning Conference (pp. 19–23). St. Paul, MN: University of Minnesota, College of Natural Resources and Minnesota Extension Service.

Hunter, M., Jr. (1996). Benchmarks for managing ecosystems: Are human activities natural? *Conservation Biology, 10*(3), 695–697.

Iacobelli, T., & Kavanagh, K. (1995). *A protected areas gap analysis methodology: Planning for the conservation of biodiversity.* Toronto, Ontario: World Wildlife Fund Canada.

International Union for Conservation of Nature and Natural Resources. (1980). *World conservation strategy: Living resource conservation for sustainable development.* Gland, Switzerland: Author.

International Union for Conservation of Nature and Natural Resources World Conservation Union. (1991). *Caring for the earth: A strategy for sustainable living.* Gland, Switzerland: Author.

International Union for Conservation of Nature and Natural Resources Commission on National Parks and Protected Areas (1994a). *Guidelines for protected area management categories.* Gland, Switzerland: IUCN.

International Union for Conservation of Nature and Natural Resources Commission on National Parks and Protected Areas. (1994b). *Parks for life: Action for protected areas in Europe.* Gland, Switzerland: IUCN.

International Union for Conservation of Nature and Natural Resources World Commission on Protected Areas. (1997). *Draft guidelines for national system planning for protected areas* [Draft 4]. Gland, Switzerland: IUCN.

Jackson, C. (1994). Gender analysis and environmentalism. In M. Redclift & T. Benton (Eds.), *Social theory and the global environment* (pp. 113–149). London, UK: Routledge.

Jacob, M. (1994). Sustainable development and deep ecology: An analysis of competing traditions. *Environmental Management, 18*(4), 477–488.

Jamieson, G. S. (1998). A proposal for the Mount Arrowsmith World Biosphere Reserve. In S. Carty, R. Murzon, S. Powell & D. Ramsay (Eds.), *The edge & the Point Niagara Escarpment & Long Point World Biosphere Reserves: Leading Edge '97 Conference Proceedings* (pp. 289–292). Georgetown, Ontario: Niagara Escarpment Commission.

Jansson, A. M., Hammer, M., Folke, C., & Costanza, R. (Eds.). (1994). *Investing in natural capital: The ecological economics approach to sustainability.* Washington, DC: Island Press.

Jenseth, R., & Lotto, E. E. (Eds.). (1996). *Constructing nature: Readings from the American experience.* Upper Saddle River, NJ: Prentice-Hall.

Johnson, S. P. (1993). *The earth summit: The United Nations conference on environment and development (UNCED).* London, UK: Graham & Trotman/Martinus Nijhoff.

Kemf, E. (Ed.). (1993). *The law of the mother: Protecting indigenous peoples in protected areas.* San Francisco, CA: Sierra Club Books.

Kennett, S. A. (1998). Special places 2000: Lessons from the Whaleback and the Castle. *Resources: The Newsletter of the Canadian Institute of Resources Law, 63,* 1–8.

Klyza, C. M. (1996). *Who controls public lands? Mining, forestry, and grazing policies, 1870–1990.* Chapel Hill, NC: University of North Carolina Press.

Knight, R. L., & Gutzwiller, K. J. (Eds.). (1995). *Wildlife and recreationists: Coexistence through management and research.* Washington, DC: Island Press.

Koloff, M. L. (1993). Conflict surrounding tourism development. In A. J. Veal, P. Johnson, & G. Cushman (Eds.), Leisure and tourism: Social and environmental change. *Papers from the World Leisure and Recreation Association Congress, Sydney, Australia, July 1991* (pp. 603–608). Sydney, Australia: University of Technology, Center for Leisure and Tourism Studies.

Kuss, F. R., Graefe, A. R., & Vaske, J. J. (1990). *Visitor impact management: A review of research.* Washington, DC: National Parks and Conservation Association.

Lane, B. (1994). Sustainable rural tourism strategies: A tool for development and conservation. *Journal of Sustainable Tourism, 2*(1&2), 102–111.

LaPage, W. F., Vaske, J. J., & Donnelly, M. P. (1995). Case studies of partnerships in action. *Journal of Park and Recreation Administration, 13*(4), 61–74.

Leak, W. B., Yamasaki, M. Y., Kittredge, D. B., Jr., Lamson, N. I., & Smith, M. L. (1997). *Applied ecosystem management for nonindustrial forest land* (Northern Forest Experiment Station General Technical Report NE-239). Radnor, PA: USDA Forest Service.

Ledec, G., & Goodland, R. (1988). *Wildlands: Their protection and management in economic development.* Washington, DC: The World Bank.

Lemons, J. (1995). Ecological integrity and national parks. In L. Westra & J. Lemons (Eds.), *Perspectives on ecological integrity* (pp. 177–201). Boston, MA: Kluwer Academic Publishers.

Lemons, J. (Ed.). (1996). *Scientific uncertainty and environmental problem solving.* Cambridge, MA: Blackwell Science Inc.

Lemons, J., & Brown, D. A. (Eds.). (1995a). *Sustainable development: Science, ethics, and public policy.* Boston, MA: Kluwer Academic Publishers.

Lemons, J., & Brown, D. A. (1995b). The role of science in sustainable development and environmental protection decision making. In J. Lemons & D. A.

Brown (Eds.), *Sustainable development: Science, ethics, and public policy* (pp. 11–38). Boston, MA: Kluwer Academic Publishers.

Lewis, C. (Ed.). (1996). *Managing conflicts in protected areas.* Gland, Switzerland: IUCN.

Liddle, M. (1997). *Recreation ecology: The ecological impact of outdoor recreation and ecotourism.* London, UK: Chapman and Hall.

Lime, D. W. (Ed.). (1996). *Congestion and crowding in the national park system* (Minnesota Agricultural Experiment Station Miscellaneous Publication 86–1996). St. Paul, MN: University of Minnesota.

Locke, H. (1997). The role of Banff National Park as a protected area in the Yellowstone to Yukon mountain corridor of western North America. In J. G. Nelson & R. Serafin (Eds.), *National parks and protected areas: Keystones to conservation and sustainable development* (pp. 117–124). New York, NY: Springer-Verlag.

Locke, H. (1998). Yellowstone to Yukon conservation initiative. In N. W. P. Munro & J. H. M. Willison (Eds.), *Linking protected areas with working landscapes conserving biodiversity* (pp. 255–259). Wolfville, Nova Scotia: Science and Management of Protected Areas Association.

Lowry, W. R. (1994). *The capacity for wonder: Preserving national parks.* Washington, DC: The Brookings Institution.

Lucas, P. H. C. (1992). *Protected landscapes: A guide for policymakers and planners.* London, UK: Chapman & Hall.

MacEwen, A., & MacEwen, M. (1982). *National parks: Conservation or cosmetics?* London, UK: Allen & Unwin.

Machlis, G. E. (1992). The contribution of sociology to biodiversity research and management. *Biological Conservation, 62*(3), 161–170.

Machlis, G. E., Force, J. E., & Burch, W. R., Jr. (1997). The human ecosystem, Part I: The human ecosystem as an organizing concept in ecosystem management. *Society & Natural Resources, 10*(4), 347–367.

Machlis, G. E., & Forester, D. J. (1996). The relationship between socioeconomic factors and the loss of biodiversity: First efforts at theoretical and quantitative models. In R. C. Szaro & D. W. Johnston (Eds.), *Biodiversity on managed landscapes: Theory and practice* (pp. 121–146). New York, NY: Oxford University Press.

Machlis, G. E., Forester, D. J., & McKendry, J. E. (1994). Gap analysis and national parks: Adding the socioeconomic dimension. *Park Science, 14*(1), 6–10.

Machlis, G. E., & Tichnell, D. L. (1985). *The state of the world's parks: An international assessment for resource management, policy, and research.* Boulder, CO: Westview Press.

Marsden, T., Murdoch, J., Lowe, P., Munton, R., & Flynn, A. (1993). *Constructing the countryside.* London, UK: UCL Press, Ltd.

Marsh, J. (1994). Heritage areas: A perspective from the United States. In J. G. Nelson, N. D. Pollock-Ellwand & T. Stroud (Eds.), *Landscape planning: Implications of the proposed new Ontario Heritage Act* (Occasional Paper #25, pp. 25–29). Waterloo, Ontario: University of Waterloo, Heritage Resources Center.

Maser, C. (1997). Cultural values versus science. *Journal of Sustainable Forestry, 4*(3/4), 45–52.

McArthur, S. (1994). Acknowledging a symbiotic relationship—Better heritage management via better visitor management. *Australian Parks & Recreation, 30*(3), 12–17.

McArthur, S. (1997). Beyond the limits of acceptable change—Introducing TOMM. In *Conference Papers for Tread Lightly on the World Annual Conference.* Brisbane, Australia: Tread Lightly.

McCool, S. F. (1995). Linking tourism, the environment, and concepts of sustainability: Setting the stage. In S. F. McCool & A. E. Watson (Compilers), *Linking tourism, the environment, and sustainability* (General Technical Report INT-GTR-323, pp. 3–7). Ogden, UT: USDA Forest Service.

McCool, S. F., & Cole, D. N. (Compilers). (1997). *Proceedings—Limits of acceptable change and related planning processes: Progress and future directions* (General Technical Report INT-GTR-371). Ogden, UT: USDA Forest Service.

McCool, S. F., & Watson, A. E. (Compilers). (1995). *Linking tourism, the environment, and sustainability* (General Technical Report INT-GTR-323). Ogden, UT: USDA Forest Service.

McDonald, B., & Bengston, D. (1995). Changing social and environmental values. In *Trend trackers. Fourth International Outdoor Recreation & Tourism Trends Symposium and the 1995 National Recreation Resource Planning Conference* (p. 20). St. Paul, MN: University of Minnesota.

McMillan, B., & Murgatroyd, S. (1994). *Opening the door: Improving decisions through public consultation.* Edmonton, Alberta: Dark Horse Books.

McNamee, K. (1997). Who will be left standing: The beggars or the bears? In N. Munro (Ed.), *Protected areas in our modern world: Proceedings of a workshop held as part of the IUCN World Conservation Congress, Montreal, October 1996* (pp. 86–88). Halifax, Nova Scotia: Parks Canada.

McNeely, J. A. (1988). *Economics and biological diversity: Developing and using economic incentives to conserve biological resources.* Gland, Switzerland: IUCN.

McNeely, J. A. (Ed.). (1993). *Parks for life: Report of the IVth World Congress on national parks and protected areas.* Gland, Switzerland: IUCN.

McNeely, J. A. (Ed.). (1995). *Expanding partnerships in conservation.* Washington, DC: Island Press.

McNeely, J. A., Harrison, J., & Dingwall, P. (Eds.). (1994). *Protecting nature: Regional reviews of protected areas.* Gland, Switzerland: IUCN.

McVetty, D., & Wight, P. (1998, October). *Integrated planning to optimize the outcomes of tourism development: The case of Aklavik National Park and Banks Island, NWT.* Paper presented at the Travel and Tourism Research Association (Canada Chapter) 1998 Annual Conference, Toronto, Ontario.

Melnick, R. Z. (1996). Moving toward the middle in a world of extremes: Nature and culture in historic landscapes. *The George Wright Forum, 13*(1), 27–41.

Morgan, J. M. (1996). Resources, recreationists and revenues: A policy dilemma for today's state park systems. *Environmental Ethics, 18*(3), 279–290.

Munasinghe, M., & McNeely, J. (Eds.). (1994). *Protected area economics and policy: Linking conservation and sustainable development.* Washington, DC: The World Bank.

Munro, N. W. P., & Willison, J. H. M. (Eds.). (1998). Linking protected areas with working landscapes conserving biodiversity. *Proceedings of the Third International Conference on Science and Management of Protected Areas, May 1997.* Wolfville, Nova Scotia: Science and Management of Protected Areas Association.

Murray, C. (1998). And then we got reliable science and they thew it out of the door! Mediating environmental conflict in Jasper National Park. In N. W. P. Munro & J. H. M. Willison (Eds.), *Linking protected areas with working landscapes conserving biodiversity* (pp. 584–590). Wolfville, Nova Scotia: Science and Management of Protected Areas.

Natural Resources Canada. (1997). *The state of Canada's forests: Learning from history.* Ottawa, Ontario: Natural Resources Canada, Canadian Forest Service.

Nelson, J. G., Butler, R., & Wall, G. (Eds.). (1993). *Tourism and sustainable development: Monitoring, planning, managing.* Waterloo, Ontario: University of Waterloo, Department of Geography.

Nelson, J. G., & Serafin, R. (1996). Environmental and resource planning and decision making in Canada: A human ecological and a civics approach. In R. Vogeslang (Ed.), *Canada in transition: Results of environmental and human geographical research* (pp. 1–25). Bochum, Germany: Universitatsverlag Dr. N. Brockmeyer.

Nelson, J. G., & Woodley, S. (Eds.). (1989). *Heritage conservation and sustainable development.* Water-loo, Ontario: University of Waterloo, Heritage Resources Center.

Nilsen, P., & Tayler, G. (1998). A comparative analysis of human use planning and management frameworks. In N. W. P. Munro & J. H. M. Willison (Eds.), *Linking protected areas with working landscapes conserving biodiversity* (pp. 861–874). Wolfville, Nova Scotia: Science and Management of Protected Areas Association.

Nilsson, C., & Grelsson, G. (1995). The fragility of ecosystems: A review. *Journal of Applied Ecology, 32*(4), 677–692.

Noe, F. P., Hammitt, W. E., & Bixler, R. D. (1997). Park user perceptions of resource and use impacts under varied situations in three national parks. *Journal of Environmental Management, 49*(3), 323–336.

Norton, D. A., & Roper-Lindsay, J. (1992). Conservation, tourism, and commercial recreation: Conflict or cooperation?—A New Zealand perspective. *Natural Areas Journal, 12*(1), 20–25.

Noss, R. F. (1995). *Maintaining ecological integrity in representative reserve networks.* Toronto, Ontario: World Wildlife Fund Canada.

Noss, R. F., & Cooperrider, A. Y. (1994). *Saving nature's legacy: Protecting and restoring biodiversity.* Washington, DC: Island Press.

Oelschlaeger, M. (Ed.). (1995). *Postmodern environmental ethics.* Albany, NY: State University of New York Press.

O'Riordan, T. (1993). An insider's view of managing the Broads. In S. Glyptis (Ed.), *Leisure and the environment: Essays in honor of Professor J. A. Patmore* (pp. 253–265). London, UK: Belhaven Press.

Page, R. (1997). The process of the Banff–Bow Valley study: Managing controversy. In N. Munro (Ed.), *Protected areas in our modern world: Proceedings of a workshop held as part of the IUCN World Conservation Congress, Montreal, October, 1996* (pp. 119–124). Halifax, Nova Scotia: Parks Canada.

Parks Canada. (1994a). *Guiding principles and operational policies.* Ottawa, Ontario: Minister of Supply and Services Canada.

Parks Canada. (1994b). *A proposed framework for assessing the appropriateness of recreation activities in protected heritage areas.* Ottawa, Ontario: Canadian Heritage, Parks Canada.

Parks Canada. (1996). *Elk Island National Park management plan: 1996.* Ottawa, Ontario: Canadian Heritage, Parks Canada.

Parks Canada. (1997). *Banff National Park: Management plan.* Ottawa, Ontario: Minister of Public Works and Government Services Canada.

Parks Canada. (1998a). *Banff National Park cultural resource management plan*. Banff, Alberta: Canadian Heritage, Parks Canada.

Parks Canada. (1998b). *State of the parks: 1997 report*. Ottawa, Ontario : Minister of Public Works and Government Services Canada.

Payne, R. J. (1997). The new alchemy: Values, benefits and business in protected areas management. In N. Munro (Ed.), *Protected areas in our modern world: Proceedings of a workshop held as part of the IUCN World Conservation Congress, Montreal, October 1996* (pp. 89–94). Halifax, Nova Scotia: Parks Canada.

Peebles, C. J. (1995). *Outdoor recreation in New Zealand: Vol. 2, A bibliography*. Wellington, New Zealand: New Zealand Department of Conservation & Lincoln University.

Philipsen, J. (1995). Nature-based tourism and recreation: Environmental change, perception, ideology and practices. In G. J. Ashworth & A. G. J. Dietvorst (Eds.), *Tourism and spatial transformations* (pp. 183–203). Wallingford, UK: CAB International.

Phillips, A. (1997). Landscape approaches to national parks and protected areas. In J. G. Nelson & R. Serafin (Eds.), *National parks and protected areas: Keystones to conservation and sustainable development* (pp. 31–42). New York, NY: Springer-Verlag.

Phillips, A. (1998). Working landscapes and protected areas: The agenda for the 21st century. In N. W. P. Munro & J. H. M. Willison (Eds.), *Linking protected areas with working landscapes conserving biodiversity* (pp. 3–17). Wolfville, Nova Scotia: Science and Management of Protected Areas Association.

Pierce, J. T. (1996). The conservation challenge in sustaining rural environments. *Journal of Rural Studies, 12*(3), 215–229.

Pigram, J. J. (1993). Planning for tourism in rural areas: Bridging the policy implementation gap. In D. G. Pierce & R. W. Butler (Eds.), *Tourism research: Critiques and challenges* (pp. 156–174). London, UK: Routledge.

Pigram, J. J., & Sundell, R. C. (Eds.). (1997). *National parks and protected areas: Selection, delimitation, and management*. Armidale, Australia: University of New England, Center for Water Policy Research.

Pimbert, M. P., & Pretty, J. N. (1995). *Parks, people and professionals: Putting "participation" into protected area management* (Discussion paper 57). Geneva, Switzerland: United Nations Research Institute for Social Development.

Primm, S. A., & Clark, T. W. (1996). Making sense of the policy process for carnivore conservation. *Conservation Biology, 10*(4), 1036–1045.

Ramsay, D., & Whitelaw, G. (1998). Biosphere reserves and ecological monitoring as part of working landscapes: The Niagara Escarpment Biosphere Reserve experience. In N. W. P. Munro & J. H. M. Willison (Eds.), *Linking protected areas with working landscapes conserving biodiversity* (pp. 295–307). Wolfville, Nova Scotia: Science and Management of Protected Areas Association.

Rasker, R. (1993). Rural development, conservation, and public policy in the Greater Yellowstone Ecosystem. *Society & Natural Resources, 6,* 109–126.

Reading, R. P., Clark, T. W., & Kellert, S. R. (1994). Attitudes and knowledge of people living in the Greater Yellowstone Ecosystem. *Society & Natural Resources, 7,* 349–365.

Rettie, D. F. (1995). *Our national park system: Caring for America's greatest natural and historic treasures.* Urbana, IL: University of Illinois Press.

Richards, N. (1997). The new agenda: Ontario parks and natural heritage protection. In N. Munro (Ed.), *Protected areas in our modern world: Proceedings of a workshop held as part of the IUCN World Conservation Congress, Montreal, October 1996* (pp. 66–71). Halifax, Nova Scotia: Parks Canada.

Rolston, H., III. (1994). *Conserving natural value.* New York, NY: Columbia University Press.

Rose, J., & Dixon, D. (1996). Blackdown Hills AONB management plan community involvement initiative. In C. Etchell (Ed.), *Consensus in the countryside: Reaching shared agreement in policy, planning and management* (pp. 15–20). Cardiff, UK: University of Wales College of Cardiff, Department of City and Regional Planning, Countryside Recreation Network.

Runte, A. (1997). *National parks: The American experience* (3rd ed.). Lincoln, NE: University of Nebraska Press.

Saegert, S., & Winkel, G. H. (1990). Environmental psychology. *Annual Review of Psychology, 41,* 441–477.

Saunier, R. E., & Meganck, R. A. (Eds.). (1995). *Conservation of biodiversity and the new regional planning.* Washington, DC: Organization of American States/IUCN.

Sax, J. L. (1980). *Mountains without handrails: Reflections on the national parks.* Ann Arbor, MI: University of Michigan Press.

Schelhas, J., & Shaw, W. W. (1995). Partnerships between rural people and protected areas: Understanding land use and natural resource decisions. In J. A. McNeely (Ed.), *Expanding partnerships in conservation* (pp. 206–214). Washington, DC: Island Press.

Selin, S. (1998). The promise and pitfalls of collaborating. *Trends, 35*(1), 9–13.

Selin, S., & Chavez, D. (1995). Developing a collaborative model for environmental planning and management. *Environmental Management, 19*(2), 189–195.

Sellars, R. W. (1997). *Preserving nature in the national parks; A history.* New Haven, CT: Yale University Press.

Shackell, N. L., & Willison, M. J. H. (Eds.). (1995). *Marine protected areas and sustainable fisheries.* Wolfville, Nova Scotia: Science and Management of Protected Areas Association.

Shafer, C. L. (1995). Values and shortcomings of small reserves. *BioScience, 45*(2), 80–88.

Sheail, J., Treweek, J. R., & Mountford, J. O. (1997). The U.K. transition from nature preservation to "creative conservation." *Environmental Conservation, 24*(3), 224–235.

Shelby, B., & Heberlein, T. A. (1986). *Carrying capacity in recreation settings.* Corvallis, OR: Oregon State University Press.

Shipp, D. (Ed.). (1993). *Loving them to death? Sustainable tourism in Europe's nature and national parks.* Grafenau, Germany: Federation of Nature and National Parks of Europe.

Shrader-Frechette, K. S., & McCoy, E. D. (1995). Natural landscapes, natural communities and natural ecosystems. *Forest & Conservation History, 39*(3), 138–142.

Shultis, J. (1995). Improving the wilderness: Common factors in creating national parks and equivalent reserves during the nineteenth century. *Forest & Conservation History, 39*(3), 121–129.

Sidaway, R. (1991). *Sport, recreation and nature conservation* (Study 37). London, UK: The Sports Council.

Sidaway, R. (1993). Sport, recreation and nature conservation: Developing good conservation practice. In S. Glyptis (Ed.), *Leisure and the environment: Essays in honor of Professor J. A. Patmore* (pp. 163–173). London, UK: Belhaven Press.

Sidaway, R. (1994). *Recreation and the natural heritage: A research review* (Scottish Natural Heritage Review, No. 25). Edinburgh, UK: Scottish Natural Heritage.

Sidaway, R. (1995). Managing the impacts of recreation by agreeing the limits of acceptable change. In G. J. Ashworth & A. G. J. Dietvorst (Eds.), *Tourism and spatial transformations* (pp. 303–316). Wallingford, UK: CAB International.

Sillars, L (1996). Are parks preserved for—Or from—Ordinary mortals? *Alberta Report, October 28,* 16–18.

Simpson, R. (1995). Towards sustainable tourism for Europe's protected areas—Policies and practice. In A. W. Gilg, R. S. Dilley, O. Furuseth, P. Lowe, G. McDonald & J. Murdoch (Eds.), *Progress in rural policy and planning* (Vol. 5, pp. 125–138). Chichester, UK: John Wiley & Sons, Ltd.

Slocombe, D. S. (1993). Implementing ecosystem-based management: Development of theory, practice, and research for planning and managing a region. *BioScience, 43*(9), 612–622.

Soulé, M. E. (1995). The social siege of nature. In M. E. Soulé & G. Lease (Eds.), *Reinventing nature? Responses to postmodern deconstruction* (pp. 137–170). Washington, DC: Island Press.

Soulé, M. E., & Lease, G. (Eds.). (1995). *Reinventing nature? Responses to postmodern deconstruction.* Washington, DC: Island Press.

Speight, M. C. D. (1973). *Outdoor recreation and its ecological effects: A bibliography and review.* London, UK: University College.

Spirn, A. W. (1996). Constructing nature: The legacy of Frederick Law Olmsted. In W. Cronon (Ed.), *Uncommon ground: Rethinking the human place in nature* (pp. 91–113). New York, NY: W.W. Norton & Company.

Sports Council. (1992). *A countryside for sport: A policy for sport and recreation.* London, UK: Author.

Sports Council for Wales. (1991). *Fit for whom? A fair deal for recreation in national parks* (Sports Update 13). Cardiff, UK: Author.

Stadel, A. V., & Nelson, J. G. (1995). The role of citizen participation in ecosystem monitoring. In T. B. Herman, S. Bondrup-Nielsen, J. H. M. Willison & N. W. P. Munro (Eds.), *Ecosystem monitoring and protected areas* (pp. 409–415). Wolfville, Nova Scotia: Science and Management of Protected Areas Association.

Stankey, G. H. (1995). The pursuit of sustainability: Joining science and public choice. *The George Wright Forum, 12*(3), 11–18.

Statham, D. (1993). Managing the wilder countryside. In S. Glyptis (Ed.), *Leisure and the environment: Essays in honor of Professor J. A. Patmore* (pp. 236–252). London, UK: Belhaven Press.

Stedman, N. (1993). Conservation in national parks. In F. B. Goldsmith & A. Warren (Eds.), *Conservation in progress* (pp. 209–239). Chichester, UK: John Wiley & Sons, Ltd.

Stevens, S. (Ed.). (1997). *Conservation through cultural survival: Indigenous peoples and protected areas.* Washington, DC: Island Press.

Stokes, S. N., Watson, A. E., Keller, G. P., & Keller, J. T. (1989). *Saving America's countryside: A guide to rural conservation.* Baltimore, MD: Johns Hopkins University Press.

Swinnerton, G. S. (1989). Recreation and conservation. In E. L. Jackson & T. L. Burton (Eds.), *Understanding leisure and recreation: Mapping the past, charting the future* (pp. 517–565). State College, PA: Venture Publishing, Inc.

Swinnerton, G. S. (1991). *People, parks, and preservation: Sustaining opportunities.* Edmonton, Alberta: Environment Council of Alberta.

Swinnerton, G. S. (1993). The Alberta park system: Policy and planning. In P. Dearden & R. Rollins (Eds.), *Parks and protected areas in Canada: Planning and management* (pp. 111–136). Toronto, Ontario: Oxford University Press.

Swinnerton, G. S. (1995a). Conservation through partnership: Landscape management within national parks in England and Wales. *Journal of Park and Recreation Administration, 13*(4), 47–60.

Swinnerton, G. S. (1995b). Nature conservation in national parks in England and Wales. In T. B. Herman, S. Bondrup-Nielsen, J. H. M. Willison & N. W. P. Munro (Eds.), *Ecosystem monitoring and protected areas* (pp. 148–153). Wolfville, Nova Scotia: Science and Management of Protected Areas Association.

Swinnerton, G. S. (1995c). Sustainable tourism and protected areas: Partnership trends in Britain's National Parks. In J. L. Thompson, D. W. Lime, B. Gartner & W. M. Sames (Compilers), *Proceedings of the Fourth International Outdoor Recreation and Tourism Trends Symposium and the National Recreation Resources Planning Conference* (pp. 214–218). St. Paul, MN: University of Minnesota, College of Natural Resources and Minnesota Extension Service.

Swinnerton, G. S. (1997). Combining science and public participation in establishing a network of protected areas: The case of Alberta, Canada. In N. Munro (Ed.), *Protected areas in our modern world: Proceedings of a workshop held as part of the IUCN World Conservation Congress, Montreal, October 1996* (pp. 125–134). Halifax, Nova Scotia: Parks Canada.

Swinnerton, G. S. (1998). Special places 2000: Alberta's approach to protecting biodiversity through science and public participation. In N. W. P. Munro & J. H. M. Willison (Eds.), *Linking protected areas with working landscapes conserving biodiversity* (pp. 911–918). Wolfville, Nova Scotia: Science and Management of Protected Areas Association.

Swinnerton, G. S., & Hinch, T. D. (1994). Sustainable rural tourism: Principles and practice. *Trends, 31*(1), 4–8, 48.

Tourism and Environment Task Force. (1991). *Tourism and the environment: Maintaining the balance.* London, UK: English Tourist Board & the Employment Department Group.

United Nations Educational, Scientific and Cultural Organization. (1996). *Biosphere reserves: The Seville Strategy and the statutory framework of the world network.* Paris: Author.

United States Department of Agriculture Forest Service. (1996). Status of the Interior Columbia Basin: Summary of scientific findings (General Technical Report PNW-GTR-385). Portland, OR: USDA Forest Service, Pacific Northwest Research Station.

Urry, J. (1995). *Consuming places.* London, UK: Routledge.

Varangu, A. (1997). A clash of values: Planning to protect the Niagara Escarpment in Ontario, Canada. In J. G. Nelson & R. Serafin (Eds.), *National parks and protected areas: Keystones to conservation and sustainable development* (pp. 65–79). New York, NY: Springer-Verlag.

Vaughan, J. (1996). Sport and recreation in the countryside—A cultural challenge in a post-Rio environment. *Ecos, 17*(3/4). 3–9.

Wall, G. (1989). Perspectives on recreation and the environment. In E. L. Jackson & T. L. Burton (Eds.), *Understanding leisure and recreation: Mapping the past, charting the future* (pp. 453–479). State College, PA: Venture Publishing, Inc.

Wang, G. A., Anderson, D. H., & Jakes, P. J. (1996). Legislating the past: Cultural resource management in the U.S. Forest Service. *Society & Natural Resources, 9*(1), 3–18.

Wellman, B., Bunch, F., & Wise, J. (1995). Five steps to strategic resource management: The Great Sand Dunes ecosystem. In R. M. Linn (Ed.), *Sustainable society and protected areas: Contributed papers of the 8th Conference on Research and Resource Management in Parks and on Public Lands.* Hancock, MI: The George Wright Society.

West, P. C., & Brechin, S. R. (Eds.). (1991). *Resident peoples and national parks: Social dilemmas and strategies in international conservation.* Tucson, AZ: University of Arizona Press.

Westra, L. (1995). Ecosystem integrity and sustainability: The foundation value of the wild. In L. Westra & J. Lemons (Eds.), *Perspectives on integrity* (pp. 12–33). Boston, MA: Kluwer Academic Publishers.

Westra, L., & Lemons, J. (Eds.). (1995). *Perspectives on ecological integrity.* Boston, MA: Kluwer Academic Publishers.

White, A. (1993). *The economic benefits of conserving Canada's endangered spaces.* Toronto, Ontario: World Wildlife Fund Canada.

Wildes, F. T. (1995). Recent themes in conservation philosophy and policy in the United States. *Environmental Conservation, 22*(2), 143–150.

Wilkerson, O. L, & Edgell, M. C. R. (1993). The role and limitations of paradigm research in environmental management. In H. R. Foster (Ed.), *Advances in resource management: Tribute to W. R. Derrick Sewell* (pp. 53–82). London, UK: Belhaven Press.

Williams, D. R., & Carr, D. S. (1993). The sociocultural meanings of outdoor recreation places. In A.

Ewert, D. Chavez & A. Magill (Eds.), *Culture, conflict and communication in the wildland-urban interface* (pp. 209–219). Boulder, CO: Westview Press.

Williams, D. R., & Patterson, M. E. (1996). Environmental meaning and ecosystem management: Perspectives from environmental psychology and human geography. *Society & Natural Resources, 9*(5), 507–521.

Williams, D. R., & Stewart, S. I. (1998). Sense of place. An elusive concept that is finding a home in ecosystem management. *Journal of Forestry, 96*(5), 18–23.

Wilson, A. (1991). *The culture of nature: North American landscape from Disney to the Exxon Valdez.* Toronto, Ontario: Between the Lines.

Wood, R. (Ed.). (1994). Environmental economics, sustainable management and the countryside. *Proceedings of a Workshop held at the Water Services Association, London.* Cardiff, UK: Countryside Recreation Network.

Woodley, S. (1993). Monitoring and measuring ecosystem integrity in Canadian National Parks. In S. Woodley, J. Kay & G. Francis (Eds.), *Ecological integrity and the management of ecosystems* (pp. 155–176). Delray Beach, FL: St. Lucie Press.

Woodley, S. (1997). Science and protected area management: An ecosystem-based perspective. In J. G. Nelson & R. Serafin (Eds.), *National parks and protected areas: Keystones to conservation and sustainable development* (pp. 11–21). New York, NY: Springer-Verlag.

Woodley, S., & Forbes, G. (1995). Ecosystem management and protected areas: Principles, problems and practicalities. In T. B. Herman, S. Bondrup-Nielsen, J. H. M. Willison & N. W. P. Munro (Eds.), *Ecosystem monitoring and protected areas* (pp. 50–58). Wolfville, Nova Scotia: Science and Management of Protected Areas Association.

World Commission on Environment and Development. (1987). *Our common future.* Oxford, UK: Oxford University Press.

World Conservation Monitoring Center & the International Union for Conservation of Nature and Natural Resources Commission on National Parks and Protected Areas. (1994). *1993 United Nations list of national parks and protected areas.* Gland, Switzerland: IUCN.

World Resources Institute, International Union for Conservation of Nature and Natural Resources & United Nations Environment Program. (1992). *Global biodiversity strategy: Policymakers' guide.* Washington, DC: World Resources Institute.

World Wildlife Fund Canada. (1998). *Endangered spaces: Progress report 1997–98.* Toronto, Ontario: Author.

Wyant, J. G., Meganck, R. A., & Ham, S. H. (1995). A planning and decision-making framework for ecological restoration. *Environmental Management, 19*(6), 789–796.

Zube, E. H. (1995). No park is an island. In J. A. McNeely (Ed.), *Expanding partnerships in conservation* (pp. 169–177). Washington, DC: Island Press.

Experiencing Leisure

Leisure Experience
and Satisfaction

Roger C. Mannell
University of Waterloo

A key premise of much of the social-psychological research on leisure is that leisure must be understood from the subjective perspective of the participant—a perspective that is based on the belief that researchers and practitioners not only need to examine what people do in their leisure but how they construe, experience, and appraise what they do. Three research approaches in the study of leisure have emerged that focus on these three processes. These approaches are similar in that leisure is viewed to be best understood from the subjective perspective of the participant, yet they differ in how they treat or conceptualize this subjectivity (Mannell, 1986; Mannell and Iso-Ahola, 1987). The *definitional approach* has involved researchers identifying the attributes and meanings that people must perceive as being associated with an activity or setting for it to be construed or defined as leisure. In other words, what are the criteria used by participants to judge an activity, setting or experience to be leisure, and how can these criteria be observed and mea-

sured? The *immediate conscious experience approach* has been concerned with monitoring the on-site, real-time quality and properties of experiences that accompany leisure participation. That is, what is the actual nature of the experience that accompanies participation? What are participants feeling and thinking during an episode and how can the texture and quality of their experiences be assessed? The *post hoc satisfaction approach* has involved the retrospective study of the satisfactions derived from leisure participation and experience. Researchers have asked what satisfactions are derived from leisure activities, settings, and experiences, and to what extent are leisure involvements satisfying.

This chapter will begin with an overview of the definitional and immediate conscious experience approaches to understanding the subjective nature of leisure, followed by a more extensive review and analysis of theory and research on leisure satisfaction.

The Definitional Approach: Leisure in the Eye of the Beholder

The definitional approach to the study of leisure involves theory and research which attempt to identify the attributes or properties that lead people to construe an activity, setting, or experience as leisure and not something else. Researchers attempting to identify personal definitions of leisure have used a number of social science research methods. The most straightforward approach has been to interview people (e.g., Fine, 1987; Gunter, 1987; Henderson, 1990; Henderson and Rannells, 1988). For example, Gunter (1987) asked various groups of people to describe in writing their most memorable and enjoyable leisure experiences. He then analyzed these "stories" to discover if the leisure experiences that stood out in their minds shared similar characteristics. Feelings of enjoyment, intense involvement, and separation or escape from people's everyday routines were commonly associated with experiences more likely to be construed as leisure.

In an interview following the completion of time diaries, Shaw (1984) had her research participants classify all the activities that they had listed in their diaries as either "work," "leisure," "a mixture of work and leisure," or "neither work nor leisure." She found that some activities, such as cooking, home chores, shopping, childcare, and travel were more frequently defined as leisure by males than by females and that some respondents defined the same activity differently at different times. For example, of those people who reported engaging in cooking more than once during the study, 69% of the time they defined it as leisure on one occasion and as work on another. Additionally, she had her subjects explain their choices. Activities labeled *leisure* were characterized by the perception that they had been freely chosen and intrinsically motivated. She also found that enjoyment, relaxation, and a lack of evaluation by other people seemed to accompany those activities her respondents felt were leisure.

Henderson (1990) carried out life-history interviews with older farm women to develop an understanding of the types of activities and the social and physical settings that were seen by this group of women as leisure. She found that these women, who had worked hard all their lives, typically experienced leisure in their work and family obligations. Opportunities to experience freedom of choice and enjoyment occurred in a variety of activities, social settings, and physical locations—what Henderson called "containers for leisure." Many family obligations and community activities with other women had elements of leisure for the women even though they involved worklike activities.

In two early studies, Iso-Ahola (1979a, 1979b) used several quasi-experiments to test more directly the importance of properties such as perceived freedom and intrinsic motivation for an activity to be construed as leisure. He had his subjects imagine themselves in a variety of recreational situations that varied systematically according to the amount of freedom the individuals had in choosing an activity, the extent to which their participation was intrinsically or extrinsically motivated, and a variety of other factors. Iso-Ahola found perceived freedom and intrinsic motivation were critical criteria for what becomes leisure in people's minds and what does not.

Research techniques such as the Experiential Sampling Method (ESM) developed by Csikszentmihalyi and his colleagues (see Larson and Csikszentmihalyi, 1983) have also been used to examine the experiential properties of leisure. Samdahl (1988) had a group of women and men carry electronic pagers with them during their daily activities. She arranged for them to be randomly signaled throughout the day for a period of one week. Each time the pager emitted a signal (an audible beep), the respondents took out a booklet of brief questionnaires and completed a series of open- and close-ended items indicating their current activity, the social and physical context of their activity, and their psychological state. Samdahl also included several items that followed Iso-Ahola's procedure of asking the study's participants to rate the extent to which what they were involved in was leisure for them. When the respondents perceived that they had chosen to participate in an activity independently of the expectations of other people, that is, low role constraint, and felt that they were expressing their true selves, high self-expression, they were more likely to construe and rate the activity or situation as "leisure."

Samdahl and Jekubovich (1993) combined the ESM and a semistructured qualitative interview to achieve a more comprehensive understanding of what constituted leisure in the mind of the participant. In a study of adults, they not only identified when, where, and in what settings their respondents construed their activities as leisure, but the qualitative interviews provided insights into how these people actively organized their lives to make room for what they actually construed as leisure. Leisure was not a passive occurrence that emerged after other activities were done. Some of the ways the people in this study made room for leisure included getting up before family members, going to a motel with a partner in their home town, arranging family dinners, and altering work schedules.

Based on this type of research, a number of leisure attributes with a variety of labels have been proposed. The most central and commonly agreed upon set of properties is associated with freedom or a lack of constraint. This lack of constraint is a quality typically attributed to situations or settings; the setting is free of requirements that people do anything. Lack of constraint has been called by many names (e.g., freedom of choice, freedom from constraints, the freedom to do something, self-determination, lack of role constraints, low work-relation, and "final" goal-orientation).

There is a second set of attributes commonly identified as being important. Activities, settings, and experiences construed as leisure are likely to be perceived as providing opportunities for the development of competence, self-expression, self-development, or self-realization. When people engage in activities and settings that provide these opportunities, they are said to be intrinsically motivated.

A third major set of properties that have been identified is based on the nature and quality of experiences derived from participation. When an engagement is experienced as enjoyable, fun, or pleasurable, it is more likely to be construed as leisure. The feeling of relaxation as well as its antithesis, intense involvement, have also been suggested as properties of leisure experiences, as have feelings of separation or escape from the everyday routine world, a sense of adventure, spontaneity, and loss of the sense of time. Additionally, experiences with cognitions involving fantasy and creative imagination have been suggested as properties leading to perceptions of leisure.

Of what utility is this type of research? How often do people in the course of their daily lives agonize over whether what they have done is leisure or not? Probably not very often! Usually their thoughts focus on not having enough, having too much, what to do with their free time, how to get more of it, or how to afford leisure. However, this type of research allows researchers to test whether their views of the nature of leisure are consistent with those of the people they are studying. Knowing how people personally define leisure, rather than relying on researcher-imposed judgments, provides a more effective approach to measuring the quantity and quality of leisure experienced and establishing the relationship between leisure and other phenomena.

The Immediate Conscious Experience Approach: The Anatomy of Leisure Experience

A second line of research on the subjective nature of leisure has been concerned with measuring the quality or texture of what people experience during leisure, and examining the impact of the physical and social setting as well as personality factors on this experience. By monitoring leisure experiences, those features of situations, activities, and persons that inhibit or enhance these experiential outcomes can be discovered.

Researchers interested in this type of question have usually gone on-site, into the recreation setting itself, to study leisure experiences—their quality, duration, intensity, and memorability. For example, moods have been monitored in the course of a day trip to a park by having visitors fill out surveys when they entered and then again when they left (More and Payne, 1978) and in leisure breaks (walking and sitting in four different environments) by having students fill out self-administered questionnaires at various times during the experience (Hull, Michael, Walker and Roggenbuck, 1996). Csikszentmihalyi (1975) did extensive interviews with rock climbers, recreational dancers, and chess players. He identified the characteristics of those experiences which his respondents reported to be their best leisure. Episodes that provided intensely absorbing experiences, were challenging, and in which the participants lost track of the time and their awareness of themselves were best remembered and most rewarding. Csikszentmihalyi called these types of experiences *flow*.

A variety of social setting and personality factors that affect how absorbed people become in activities have been studied during free-time periods built into laboratory experiments (e.g., Mannell and Bradley, 1986). In these studies the researchers have been able to examine the impact of various factors (e.g., the amount of freedom of choice participants had, the level of competition in the setting, and the rewards available) on how involved people became in their leisure and the quality of their experiences. In one experiment, Mannell and Bradley (1986) found that not everyone experiences greater leisure as a consequence of higher levels of freedom of choice. People who characteristically believe that they have less control in their lives actually found higher levels of freedom threatening. They were only able to achieve higher quality experiences in more structured and restricted settings.

The development of the Experiential Sampling Method (ESM) has contributed substantially to uncovering regularities in perceptions and feelings of happiness, self-awareness, concentration, and other features of conscious experience in leisure activities and settings. Studies have examined the feelings of intrinsic satisfaction experienced in recreational compared to nonrecreational activities (Graef, Csikszentmihalyi and Gianinno, 1983), the meaning and quality of experiences derived from the leisure activities engaged in by adolescents (Kleiber, Caldwell and Shaw, 1993), moods in different types of social leisure (Larson, Mannell and Zuzanek, 1986), and the experiential outcomes of conditions predicted to foster optimal leisure states (Mannell, Zuzanek and Larson, 1988; Samdahl, 1988).

For example, in a study of the leisure experiences of adolescents (Kleiber, Larson and Csikszentmihalyi, 1986), ESM data were collected and allowed the authors to identify those leisure activities and settings in which adolescents experienced their most positive moods and became most psychologically involved. When the researchers examined the different types of leisure activities in which the adolescents were engaged, they found evidence for two categories of leisure experience. Relaxed leisure was found in the activities of socializing, watching television, reading, and listening to music, as well as the maintenance activities of eating and resting. The authors suggest that this type of leisure provides pleasure without high levels of involvement. The second set of activities included sports, games, artwork, and hobbies. These activities were experienced as freely chosen, intrinsically motivated, and very positive, yet also as challenging and demanding of effort and concentration. The authors argued that participation in these transitional leisure activities offers adolescents a bridge between childhood and adulthood by demonstrating that the enjoyment found in the activities of childhood can also be found in the more demanding activities required of them as they move into adulthood.

This research demonstrates that actual real-time experiences accompanying leisure involvements can be studied directly with a variety of research strategies. It has begun to provide insights into the factors that affect the nature and quality of leisure experiences, factors important to understand for those who wish to improve the quality of their own leisure or that of others. It is to be hoped that research will continue to be undertaken to help better understand the personality and social situational factors that not only affect the quality of experience but also the links between the objective recreation environment and the way leisure is construed and perceived by individual participants.

The Post Hoc Satisfaction Approach

The Satisfaction Construct

Assessing leisure satisfaction is another approach to getting inside the heads of people and seeing leisure from their perspectives. Rather than a concern with what people construe as leisure or the actual experience while engaged in leisure, the satisfaction construct is an "after-the-fact" assessment or experiential consequence of an earlier involvement or set of involvements.

The term *satisfaction* has had a variety of meanings and applications in the study of leisure and leisure services. These differences have their roots in the different conceptual and theoretical treatments of satisfaction found in the social science literature. Conceptualizations of leisure satisfaction differ on two dimensions—source of satisfaction and level of specificity—and can be roughly classified on the basis of these two dimensions. Consider the typology presented in Figure 14.1. It suggests four basic approaches that researchers have taken to defining and studying leisure satisfaction: component and global appraisal-satisfaction, and component and global need-satisfaction. Leisure satisfaction can be motivation- or evaluation-based (source of satisfaction dimension). Researchers differ according to whether they conceptualize the leisure satisfaction construct as being closely tied to the idea of leisure motivation. If they do, leisure satisfaction is seen to result when people meet or "satisfy" corresponding leisure needs or motives through their participation. Leisure needs and satisfactions, then, are two sides of the same coin and are inextricably linked. This form of satisfaction is often called need-satisfaction. In contrast, if leisure satisfaction is conceptualized as being unconnected to needs and motives and is treated as an evaluation of the quality of leisure, we will label it appraisal-satisfaction. This approach views satisfaction as a form of cognitive appraisal or evaluation of the extent to which an individual's leisure style or some aspect of it meets with current expectations.

Leisure satisfaction research can also be distinguished on the basis of level of specificity. Some leisure researchers have been interested in the specific needs and satisfactions that are associated with specific recreational activities or some aspect of them—what we might call a molecular level of analysis. Others have focused on how well people meet all of their needs in leisure and how satisfied they are with the total leisure domain of their lifestyle or their leisure style, a more molar level of analysis. Consequently, the level of specificity in a particular study can be distinguished on the basis of the range of the behavior being considered (specific activity or some component of it versus the whole leisure domain of a person's life) or the need with which the satisfaction is associated (specific need versus sets of leisure needs).

Appraisal-Satisfaction

General Construct

Measures of leisure appraisal-satisfaction are used to assess the quality of people's leisure as they evaluate it. Leisure satisfaction is an alternative to measuring the frequency of leisure participation as an indicator of the quality of leisure styles. Respondents are asked to rate their satisfaction with their total leisure style or some aspect of it on various types

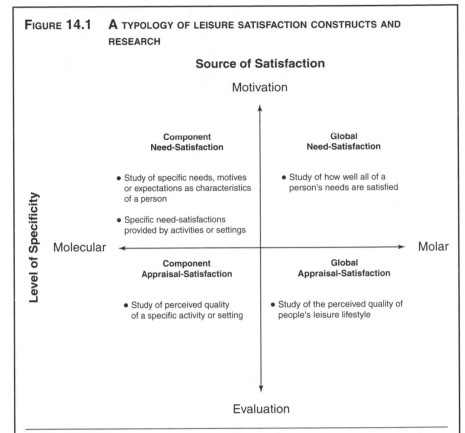

Figure 14.1 A typology of leisure satisfaction constructs and research

Source: "Leisure Satisfaction" by R. C. Mannell in *Understanding Leisure and Recreation: Mapping the Past, Charting the Future* (p. 282), by E. L. Jackson and T. L. Burton (Eds.), 1989, State College, PA: Venture Publishing, Inc. Copyright 1989 by Venture Publishing, Inc. Adapted with permission.

of rating scales. This evaluation approach to conceptualizing and measuring leisure satisfaction has emerged from the extensive research undertaken over the past several decades on the quality of life and subjective well-being of working-aged and elderly retired adults (Mannell and Dupuis, 1996). Initially, these types of studies focused on mental health problems and how well people coped with difficult life events (e.g., Gurin, Veroff and Feld, 1960), but later the issue became subjective well-being (Bradburn, 1969) or the quality of life as a whole (Campbell, Converse and Rodgers, 1976).

The approach reflects a concerted effort to assess the quality of contemporary life other than with the use of objective measures. For example, economists have equated well-being with the gross national income, public health researchers with decreases in high-risk health behaviors, ecologists with the quality of the natural environment, and sociologists with levels of crime, suicide, public violence, and family disintegration. However, it has been argued that "we cannot

understand the psychological quality of a person's life simply from a knowledge of the circumstances in which that person lives" (Campbell, 1980, p. 1), or gain more than a partial explanation of why some people find their lives enjoyable and satisfying and some do not. Well-being or quality of life, then, is treated "as a strictly internal construct, independent of the exterior conditions of a person's life" (Larson, 1978, p. 110). It is generally assumed that people "are able to describe the quality of their own lives, not as precisely as one might like, but with a kind of direct validity that more objective measures do not have" (Campbell, 1980, p. 12).

A major task for researchers has been to achieve consensus on the definition and measurement of well-being or quality of life (Campbell, 1980; Larson, 1978; Ryff and Keyes, 1995; Stock, Okun and Benin, 1986). Three constructs—happiness, satisfaction, and morale—have typically been used to conceptualize well-being. Happiness is considered to reflect the more temporary affective feelings of the present moment. Morale is considered to be a more future-oriented optimism or pessimism with life. Different from happiness and morale, satisfaction "implies an act of judgment, a comparison of what people have to what they think they deserve, expect, or may reasonably aspire to. If the discrepancy is small, the result is satisfaction; if it is large, there is dissatisfaction" (Campbell, 1980, p. 22). The expectations or standards of comparison on which these judgments or appraisals are made are usually left unspecified. Satisfaction has a past orientation—an appraisal of how things have gone up until the present. Whereas happiness and morale reflect the more changeable aspects of well-being, level of satisfaction is considered to be quite stable over time (Campbell, 1980; Stock et al., 1986).

The level of specificity of the behavior or domain of life experience being appraised has been considered an important factor. Sometimes overall measures of how satisfied people are with their lives are collected. Also, a more detailed picture of quality of life has been obtained by examining satisfaction with the major divisions of life, often called "domains." Because of the centrality of work to North American life, work or job satisfaction has been the focus of extensive research and theoretical efforts (Steers and Porter, 1991). Interest in satisfaction with leisure has been increasing.

Component Appraisal-Satisfaction

In the leisure research that has used the appraisal approach, satisfaction has been conceptualized and measured at various levels of specificity. Researchers with more molecular concerns have examined satisfaction with particular components or domains of leisure behavior or experience. Components examined have included specific activities, such as satisfaction with provincial park campgrounds (Foster and Jackson, 1979), tourist destinations (Pearce, 1980), outdoor recreation activity during a day trip (Vaske, Donnelly, Heberlein and Shelby, 1982), attendance at festivals (Mohr, Backman, Gahan and Backman, 1993), and sporting events (Madrigal, 1995). A number of studies have examined a variety of factors that affect satisfaction with outdoor activities, such as hunting (e.g., Hazel, Langenau and Levine, 1990) and boating (e.g., Robertson and Regula, 1994). Standardized measurement scales have been developed to measure satisfaction with participation in specific recreation activities, such as racket sports (Aguilar and Petrakis, 1989).

Research has been reported that takes the level of specification even further. Pizam, Neumann, and Reichel (1978) found that eight components (e.g., beach opportunities, cost, hospitality, commercialization) described tourist satisfaction with a well-known seaside destination. Graefe and Fedler (1986) exam-

ined satisfaction with a chartered recreation fishing outing. They not only measured overall satisfaction with the trip, but satisfaction with various components of the experience (e.g., enjoyment of the outdoors, types and number of fish caught, challenge). Noe (1987) surveyed spectators at a raft-race event. He measured overall satisfaction with the event, as well as satisfaction with 24 specific aspects of the event (e.g., the rafters, food facilities, parking signs, music).

This type of leisure satisfaction research has not been theoretically driven. Researchers have been interested in assessing the quality of a leisure event or activity and those aspects of it that contribute or detract from its quality. For example, Geva and Goldman (1991) used measures of satisfaction to assess the quality of 15 guided tours from Israel to Europe and the United States. By measuring the participants' satisfaction with various aspects of both the tour company's services (e.g., hotels, entertainment, scheduling) and the tour guide (e.g., conduct, expertise), they were able to suggest strategies to increase the likelihood that the tour company would get its fair share of the credit for a successful tour and that participants would choose the company in the future or recommend the company to other travelers. This use of the satisfaction construct has much in common with the notion of service quality used in understanding consumer behavior in leisure contexts (e.g., Colenutt and McCarville, 1994; see also McCarville, chapter 25 in this volume).

Global Appraisal-Satisfaction

At the other end of the specificity continuum—at the molar level of analysis—we find a number of studies that are concerned with satisfaction with the whole leisure domain of life or leisure style. Single-item measures are frequently used, and the domain of behavior to be assessed has been identified in different ways. People have been asked to rate satisfaction with their "present level of leisure participation" (Guin, 1980, p. 200), "amount of spare time" (Lounsbury, Gordon, Bergermaier and Francesco, 1982, p. 290), and "leisure in general" (Iso-Ahola and Weissinger, 1987, p. 360).

The research reported using global appraisal-satisfaction has had several different purposes. One of these has been to examine the factors that affect how satisfied or dissatisfied people are with their leisure styles. To do this, researchers have examined the relationship between leisure satisfaction and other leisure phenomena, such as participation, attitudes, awareness, and boredom. For example, Beard and Ragheb (1980) and Ragheb and Tate (1993) found that leisure participation and attitudes were positively related to leisure satisfaction. Francken and van Raaij (1981) reported leisure satisfaction to be higher for people who are older, have an optimistic outlook, and perceive themselves as having the personal interests and capacity for leisure activity participation. Iso-Ahola and Weissinger (1987) found that the greater people's "boredom in leisure," the less their satisfaction with leisure. The impact on leisure satisfaction of other factors, such as retirement (e.g., Dorfman, Heckert and Hill, 1988), stress (e.g., Cunningham and Bartuska, 1989), and the amount of freedom in leisure people experience (Ellis and Witt, 1994) has been examined.

Leisure satisfaction has also been used as an outcome measure to determine the impact of various kinds of counseling and therapeutic interventions used to improve the quality of people's leisure (e.g., Backman and Mannell, 1986; Zoerink and Lauener, 1991). For example, in a field experiment, Backman and Mannell (1986) found that the leisure satisfaction of institutionalized older adults increased and remained higher after participation in a leisure education and counseling program.

Some research has emerged that examines the relationship between satisfaction with the leisure domain and other domains of life. In an early study by Lounsbury et al. (1982), it was reported that the more satisfaction workers had with their jobs, the higher was their level of leisure satisfaction and the less likely was their intention to leave their jobs. A study of Israeli female elementary school teachers (Meir and Melamed, 1986) and engineers, physicians, and lawyers (Melamed, Meir and Samson, 1995), found that the satisfaction of important needs in both work and leisure contributed to job satisfaction. While Freysinger (1994) found some evidence that frequency of participation in family leisure was associated with higher levels of parental satisfaction, little research has been reported examining leisure and satisfaction with family life.

A second use of the global leisure appraisal-satisfaction approach has been to examine the contributions of leisure to the overall quality of life or life satisfaction. Generally, small but significant positive relationships have been found between frequency of leisure participation and life satisfaction (e.g., Brown, Frankel and Fennell, 1991; Kelly, Steinkamp and Kelly, 1987). However, measures of leisure satisfaction have been found to be better predictors of life satisfaction than have leisure participation measures—the higher leisure satisfaction, the higher life satisfaction (e.g., Brown et al., 1991; Ragheb and Griffith, 1982; Russell, 1987). This relationship between leisure satisfaction and life satisfaction may be moderated by occupation (Willmott, 1971), gender (Brown and Frankel, 1993),

age and ethnicity (Allison, 1991; Allison and Smith, 1990), and marital and employment status (Haavio-Mannila, 1971). For example, in a widely cited study, London, Crandall, and Seals (1977) found that leisure satisfaction was a better predictor of life satisfaction than job satisfaction. However, the pattern was more pronounced for some people than others. Neither leisure nor work satisfaction was important to the quality of life of relatively disadvantaged groups, and leisure satisfaction was more important for individuals with lifestyles not dominated by work activity. Regardless of how satisfying people experience their leisure, their leisure may not strongly influence life satisfaction if they are at a stage in their lives where leisure is overshadowed in importance by other concerns. Yet, there are likely times in people's lives when being satisfied with leisure is highly salient and important to them.

In summary, evidence has been found that what goes on in the leisure domain can influence how people feel about their lives as a whole. There is also a clear indication that life satisfaction is not directly dependent on leisure participation and is influenced more by how satisfied people feel about what they do. However, no simple relationships or links have been found. In fact, the picture is quite complex. The leisure-life satisfaction link appears to vary as a function of a wide range of social experiences as reflected by differences in age, ethnicity, gender, occupation, and social status.

Issues and Problems with Appraisal-Satisfaction

When attempting to understand relationships between what people do in their leisure and other aspects of their behavior and experience, measures that tap satisfaction are often more informative than documenting what they do. There are, however, limitations of the use of the appraisal-satisfaction approach. Foremost is the assumption that people know how satisfied they are. Even Campbell (1980), who used the method extensively, expressed some doubt about this assumption. He found that people change their ratings of satisfaction very little over time, suggesting, perhaps, that they adapt their level of expectation to prevailing circumstances. Consequently, measures of leisure satisfaction may fail to reflect meaningful changes in leisure participation and styles. Also, the ability to discover or establish the antecedents and consequences of leisure using satisfaction-appraisal measures may be limited by this problem.

Second, few standardized measures of leisure satisfaction have been developed, and the comparative advantages of multiple-item versus single-item scales have yet to be demonstrated. Existing scales also seem limited in their ability to penetrate respondents' feelings, particularly when the meaning of satisfaction is left to respondents and a single assessment at one point in time is used. Although respondents are asked to describe their leisure "these days" or "in general," they may be influenced by recent events or swings in mood.

Third, the very strength claimed for the appraisal-satisfaction construct seems to be a limitation as well. Subjectively based variables seem to be better predictors of leisure satisfaction than more objectively based variables (Iso-Ahola and Weissinger, 1987). However, if the objective circumstances in which people find themselves cannot be used to predict satisfaction, of what use is a measure of satisfaction in assessing the adequacy of the actual leisure opportunities, choices, and services available to them? The attempt to find relationships between the objective features of leisure settings, activities and services on the one hand, and satisfaction with these on the other, has been relatively unsuccessful and neglected. For example, one area that has received considerable attention using the appraisal-satisfaction approach is social carrying capacity. Yet, researchers have had difficulty establishing stable and consistent relationships between measures of the objective number of participants in a recreation setting and their satisfaction (Manning, 1985; Tarrant and English, 1996). Dissatisfaction with the satisfaction construct has emerged in the study of other domains of human behavior, as well. For example, researchers have been frustrated by the problems of finding factors in the work environment that consistently affect job satisfaction and by their inability to predict job performance levels and turnover rates from a knowledge of job satisfaction (Steers and Porter, 1991).

Leisure satisfaction is typically measured only at one point in time. Researchers need to monitor changes in satisfaction over time and assess corresponding changes in factors theorized to affect these shifts in satisfaction. More elaborate experimental and quasi-experimental procedures could also be implemented. For example, Backman and Mannell (1986) examined the leisure satisfaction of a group of institutionalized older adults who participated in one of several counseling and noncounseling programs. Leisure satisfaction was measured before, during, and immediately after the programs, and during a follow-up interview six weeks later. Not only were changes in leisure satisfaction related to differences among the programs in which people participated, but also to changes in recreation behavior and leisure attitudes, which were monitored. Stewart and Hull (1992) measured the satisfaction of day hikers several times during an actual hike in the White River National Forest

in Colorado and compared on-site satisfaction with the post hoc satisfaction experienced by the hikers when they recalled the event some time later. On-site and post hoc differences in satisfaction were found and attributed to differences in the effects of the setting. When on-site and involved in the leisure activity or setting, what is happening at the moment may dominate feelings of satisfaction. When rating satisfaction with the episode later (post hoc satisfaction), memories of other past experiences are more likely to surface and become standards of comparison for better or for worse.

Need-Satisfaction

General Construct

Need-satisfaction and various terms including preferences, psychological outcomes and benefits, and experience expectations have been popular motivational constructs in leisure research. Leisure motivation and motivation-based satisfaction constructs continue to be used to explain a wide range of leisure behavior, including activity loyalty (Backman and Crompton, 1991), sport participation among people with and without disabilities (Brasile, Kleiber and Harnisch, 1991), volunteering as recreation (Caldwell and Andereck, 1994), recreational running (Clough, Shepherd and Maughan, 1989), gambling as leisure (Coyle and Kinney, 1990), outdoor recreation (Ewert, 1993), participation in ecotourism (Eagles, 1992), and leisure travel (Fodness, 1994).

Explanations of leisure behavior based on the need-satisfaction construct have both personal and situational components. First, researchers using motivation-based explanations are primarily concerned with what arouses, energizes, or activates leisure behavior, that is, the forces within people that push them to engage in certain behaviors. Second, there is an interest in the characteristics of leisure activities and settings that pull people to select certain activities rather than others. Different leisure activities, settings and experiences are believed to have different need-satisfying properties that result in differences in the attractiveness of the activity and how well participation satisfies needs. The link between leisure needs, activities and settings, and satisfactions is considered to be consistent and stable over time. The assumption is that people have a history of participation in various recreation engagements, have undergone some sort of socialization process, and have learned that when certain needs are aroused, specific recreation engagements will lead to the satisfaction of these needs. Leisure researchers have been trying to identify differences in the packages of satisfactions that different types of leisure activities or settings can provide for participants.

In addition to "needs," a number of other terms have been used to label these internal activating factors, including drive, motive, desire, and expectation. *Drives* are usually restricted to describing biologically based physiological or what are often called survival needs. The term *need* has been used to refer to both physiological and socially learned motives. Also, some motivational theories do not use any of these terms. Instead of motives and needs, the motivational force underlying leisure behavior has been conceptualized as *expectations* (Manfredo, Driver and Brown, 1983). The assumption is that the recreationist is goal-directed, is knowledgeable, thinks rationally, and selects leisure activities that are suitable to fulfill expected and desired outcomes or goals. The source of these "desires" or "expectations" has not been a major issue for expectancy theorists, though the types of expectancies found to be common and important to people are similar to the motives and needs identified by need theorists.

The basic components of a general model of motivation are:

1. needs or preferences;
2. behavior or activity;
3. goals, satisfactions, or psychological benefits; and
4. feedback (see Figure 14.2).

Basically, this model suggests that people possess a multitude of needs, motives, desires, or expectations. First, the emergence of a need creates a state of disequilibrium within people (lack of something, desire for something, awareness of a potential satisfaction in a future situation) which they will try to reduce; hence, the energetic component of motivation. Second, the presence of such needs is generally associated with a belief or expectation that certain actions will lead to the reduction of this disequilibrium; hence, the goal-orientation or direction component of motivation.

Theoretically, then, the following is assumed to be the chain of events. On the basis of some combination of this desire to reduce the internal state of disequilibrium and the belief that certain actions can serve this purpose, people act or behave in a manner that they believe will lead to the desired goal or satisfaction. If the behavior or participation in an activity results in the fulfillment of the need, the experience of satisfaction provides positive feedback that the behavior or activity is appropriate. If the behavior does not result in satisfaction of the need, this negative feedback may result in people modifying or stopping their behavior or activity.

Implicit in the preceding description of the motivational process is a distinction between motivational dispositions and aroused motives (Hilgard, 1962). The motives that are generally important to people are called motivational dispositions and the assumption is that this set of motives differs from one person to another. Motivational dispositions are similar to the idea of personality traits. For example, a person may be generally more achievement-oriented and have a higher need for adventure than his or her best friend. However, not all important motives are likely to operate and influence our behavior at the same time. When our needs are active they are called aroused motives.

There is evidence for the existence of leisure motivation dispositions and consequently the fact that people regularly seek out a consistent set of leisure satisfactions. In a study of students in an outdoor leadership program, Williams, Ellis, Nickerson and Shafer (1988) found that motives for participation in outdoor pursuits (achievement, leadership, nature, escape from social pressure, and escape from physical pressure) varied substantially among the students. Lounsbury and Hoopes (1988), in their study of 139 residents of a community, found that not only did their respondents differ in terms of which leisure motives and satisfactions were important to them, but these differences persisted over a five-year period.

While most behavior is considered to be the result, to varying degrees, of biological, learned, and cognitive motivational needs, there is little consensus as to what constitutes a complete set of human needs, or to what extent they are learned or inherited. There are, however, theorists who have attempted to identify the full range of human needs that form the basis of human behavior, regardless of whether they have their roots in tissue deficits, the central nervous system, cognition, learning, or all of these. These approaches postulate a relatively manageable list of basic needs.

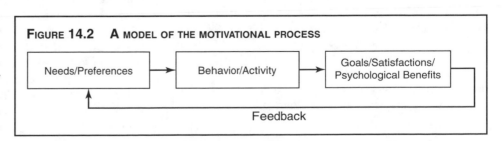

FIGURE 14.2   A MODEL OF THE MOTIVATIONAL PROCESS

Needs/Preferences → Behavior/Activity → Goals/Satisfactions/Psychological Benefits

Feedback

For example, Murray (1938) proposed a list of 28 needs, including the need for achievement, affiliation, dominance, order, understanding, play, autonomy, aggression, and sex. Maslow (1968) theorized that there are just a few basic needs and that there is a hierarchical arrangement of the needs common to all humans, with basic survival needs at the bottom and the uniquely human psychological growth needs at the top. Both theories have been used to guide researchers in the selection of leisure needs and satisfactions. No needs and satisfactions have been discovered that are unique to leisure. Leisure is seen as one of a number of domains of behavior that have the potential to provide for the satisfaction of a wide range of human needs. There seems to be a belief that leisure may be the best domain for this purpose. The individual is freer to choose engagements and so can more easily match current needs with activities known to provide the appropriate satisfactions.

Component Need-Satisfaction

Researchers studying leisure need-satisfaction or comparable approaches have had a theoretical basis for "molecularizing" satisfaction—that is, the need structure of the individual. The general assumption underlying most of the theory and research from this perspective is that leisure provides involvements which can satisfy a number of human needs and provide corresponding leisure satisfactions. The research methods and measurements used have had respondents provide retrospective accounts of the needs that typically motivate their participation or of the satisfactions they usually receive from this participation.

To uncover these leisure needs and the packages of satisfactions available in leisure activities and settings, researchers have had people complete paper-and-pencil scales or inventories. People respond to statements about themselves and rate on scales how important various needs or satisfactions are to them when participating in specific leisure activities or settings. These inventories are often designed specifically for a particular study (e.g., Iso-Ahola and Allen, 1982; Ulrich and Addoms, 1981). Efforts have also been made to develop standardized pencil-and-paper inventories (Beard and Ragheb, 1980; Lounsbury and Hoopes, 1988; Manfredo, Driver and Tarrant, 1996). These standardized inventories have the advantage of allowing easier comparison across studies and different populations. A few researchers have observed and interviewed participants during leisure activities and have drawn conclusions about their leisure satisfactions on the basis of their behavior and the meaning attributed

to this behavior by the participants (e.g., Fine, 1987; Stebbins, 1992).

Well-known and tested inventories are the *recreation experience preference* (REP) scales developed by Driver and his colleagues and the *paragraphs about leisure* (PAL) developed by Tinsley and his associates (see Driver, Tinsley and Manfredo, 1991, for discussion of the development of these two inventories). The leisure needs and satisfactions measured by these instruments were selected on the basis of the experience and observations of the researchers, leisure theory, and psychological need theories such as Murray's (1938). The REP scales were developed primarily to aid managers of parks and other natural areas in identifying the kinds of needs people visiting outdoor recreation sites are seeking to satisfy. Thousands of visitors to outdoor areas have completed these scales. The instrument measures the extent to which specific satisfactions are desired and expected from leisure activities and settings (e.g., enjoy nature, reduce tension, share similar values, independence, creativity, nostalgia, achievement). Each scale of the PAL consists of a single paragraph which describes the satisfaction of a particular psychological need. People are instructed to indicate the extent to which each paragraph is an accurate statement about the satisfactions they receive from a specific leisure activity.

A need inventory developed by Beard and Ragheb (1983) has also been used frequently by researchers, and inventories that focus on specific types of leisure behavior have been developed. For example, travel needs were measured by Crompton (1979). These needs included escape, exploration, self-discovery, relaxation, prestige, regression, family bonding, and social interaction.

A few leisure researchers have focused on single leisure needs. Cheron and Ritchie (1982), Ewert and Hollenhorst (1989), and Robinson (1992) analyzed risk-taking needs, and Crandall (1979) and Glancy and Little (1995) have examined the satisfactions associated with social interaction. Iso-Ahola (1980) and Weissinger and Bandalos (1995) have stressed the need for variety and change, and intrinsic motivation. However, many researchers have attempted to identify a wide range of needs satisfied through leisure that fit into classifications ranging from over thirty to just two basic categories (see Driver et al., 1991; Knopf, 1983; Manning, 1985). In this latter case, Dunn Ross and Iso-Ahola (1991) provided evidence that the motives for participating in a guided tour and subsequent satisfactions received from this participation could be reduced to the dimensions of seeking and escaping. Participants were seeking the satisfactions associated with gaining knowledge and social interaction, and temporary escape from their work and responsibilities.

With the component need-satisfaction approach, researchers have asked people what satisfactions they receive from specific recreation activities or from their participation in selected recreation settings. Tinsley and Johnson (1984) demonstrated that various types of activities produce unique packages of satisfactions. A taxonomy of nine activity types was suggested based on the activities' need-satisfying properties. For example, activities such as doing crossword puzzles, watching television, going to the movies, and reading fiction were found similar in providing satisfactions labeled intellectual aestheticism and solitude, but contributed very little to the satisfactions of companionship, security, service, or self-expression. In contrast, respondents reported that activities such as picnicking and visiting friends and relatives provided high levels of satisfaction of the needs for companionship, service, and security, and little satisfaction of the needs for solitude or power.

Williams and Schreyer (1981) compared the motives of recreational visitors to two distinct wilderness settings, an alpine area and a desert/canyon area. Visitors to the latter environment saw it as providing higher satisfactions for tension release, competence testing, escape, and family togetherness. Stewart and Carpenter (1989) found that the greater the need for solitude among hikers in the Grand Canyon, the more likely they were to engage in their recreation in low-use zones. In another study by Manfredo et al. (1983), wilderness users were found to be seeking different packages of satisfactions which in turn were related to their preferences for activities and environmental settings. For example, users who were attempting to satisfy their needs for risk and achievement showed a preference for areas with rough or undeveloped access, rugged terrain at destination sites, high naturalness, and low probability of meeting other people. Wilderness users who were looking to satisfy the need for solitude, but were low on the needs for achievement, challenge, and risk preferred areas with moderate accessibility, little or no development, low probability of social encounters, and natural surroundings devoid of dangerous situations. A third group preferred more accessible, secure, and managed settings where the likelihood of meeting other people was higher.

These types of findings have been applied to the development and management of physical recreation resources and park areas. By surveying people in outdoor settings, researchers have developed various classification or zoning systems for natural recreation areas based on the leisure need-satisfactions (packages of satisfactions) typically experienced by users in these settings (Driver, Brown, Stankey and Gregoire, 1987). The U.S. Forestry Service has been using the Recreation Opportunity Spectrum (ROS) (see Manning, 1985). Managers inventory and catalogue the various types of settings in their parks (e.g., primitive, semiprimitive motorized, rustic, modern urbanized). These different settings are thought to have distinct need-satisfying properties, and consequently, to provide different packages of satisfactions to visitors.

Global Need-Satisfaction

Assessment of the extent to which all of an individual's needs are met through leisure, global need-satisfaction, has been less frequent. Those studies reported have asked research questions similar to those asked by researchers using the global appraisal-satisfaction construct discussed earlier.

Ragheb and Griffith (1982) reported that the higher the level of leisure participation, the higher the level of global leisure need-satisfaction, which in turn, was positively related to life satisfaction. Russell (1987) also found support for this relationship between leisure need-satisfaction and life satisfaction. Cutler Riddick (1986) found no age-based differences in leisure satisfaction among 18- to 65-year-olds, and knowledge of leisure resources and positive leisure values were strong predispositions for high leisure need-satisfaction. Few attempts have been made to examine differences in how well different types of needs are satisfied or to examine differences in the need-satisfaction profiles of the people studied.

Issues and Problems of
Leisure Need-Satisfaction

Leisure service practitioners have found leisure need-satisfaction constructs useful in helping them think about and plan the types of support, programs, and services that the people they work with want and need. The provision of quality services is seen to be dependent on identifying people's leisure needs, understanding the types of opportunities that can satisfy these needs, and developing the appropriate services (Howe and Qui, 1988; Ragheb, 1988). For example, advocates of this approach have suggested that the provision of leisure counseling (Tinsley, 1984), the management of outdoor recreation resources (Driver et al., 1987), and the development of tourism products and opportunities (Mansfeld, 1992) benefit from this approach.

There are, however, limitations to these constructs. The measurement of need-satisfaction turns out to be as much a problem as the measurement of appraisal-satisfaction. The main access to need and satisfaction states is through the questionable avenue of self-reports. The ability of people to assess their cognitive processes has been severely questioned (Nisbett and Wilson, 1977). When asked what satisfactions they receive from participation, the answers people usually give are often stereotypic, and it "remains to be determined when the expressed leisure needs are accurate indicators of underlying leisure motivation and when they simply mirror cultural explanations" (Iso-Ahola, 1980, p. 248). Also, inconsistencies have been found in responses when measurement occurs at different times. For example, Manfredo (1984) found differences in the reported satisfaction of escaping physical stress among fishermen, when measured both on-site and four months later.

Though the motivational process model on which need-satisfaction approaches are based appears fairly simple and straightforward, and it is a useful tool for sensitizing researchers and practitioners to individual differences in what people are seeking in leisure, in actual fact, motivational processes are dynamic and quite complex. Any individual at any given time usually has a host of needs, desires, and expectations. Not only do these change but they may be in conflict with one another. Thus, given the changing nature of an individual's particular set of motives and given their often conflicting nature, it is exceedingly difficult to observe and measure them. Consequently, more research is needed on the motivational process and, in turn, the link between needs and satisfactions. For example, Iso-Ahola and Allen (1982) measured the needs of participants in an intramural basketball game before and after the engagement. Need-satisfaction was defined by the difference in pregame and postgame need scores. The authors were able to demonstrate that the satisfaction derived from this activity was systematically related to individual differences among the participants, and to the outcome of the game. Using the experiential sampling method to monitor flow experiences while engaged in leisure and nonleisure activities, Mannell, Zuzanek, and Larson (1988) found that, under some conditions, activities chosen for extrinsic reasons produce more intrinsic satisfaction than those intrinsically motivated. Certain activities were implicated more than others in this unexpected finding. The links among the activity, the motives for engaging in it, and the resulting satisfaction are often complex and a result of individual differences and situational factors.

Another difficulty with the need-satisfaction approach is that people may seek a variety of satisfactions by participation in any single leisure activity, and conversely, similar satisfactions may be experienced in different activities. In other words, the need-satisfying properties of activities and settings exist to a large extent in the mind of the participant and not in the activity itself (Driver and Brown, 1984). The same activity can provide different satisfactions depending on the social and/or physical setting in which it occurs and some satisfactions can be achieved in a wide variety of activities and settings while other satisfactions are highly setting and activity specific (e.g., Virden and Knopf, 1989; Yuan and McEwen, 1989).

Different levels of experience in a leisure activity or setting, personality differences, companions, and success in the activity have been found to influence the links between the activity and setting and the satisfactions that people perceive to be available (e.g., Ewert, 1993; Williams et al., 1988; Williams, Schreyer and Knopf, 1990). London, Crandall, and Fitzgibbons (1977) found that some of the individuals they studied perceived that they could satisfy their need for enjoyment and fun in sports activities, yet others saw sports activities as high in the ability to meet social needs. Yuan and McDonald (1990) found that, although people from different cultures engaged in pleasure travel to satisfy similar needs, they preferred different destinations with different characteristics to do so.

Obviously, these activity-satisfaction links are strongly influenced by learning. Knopf (1983, p. 229) has suggested that researchers need to answer such questions as, How do people get to know recreation environments? and How do they learn where to gratify their needs? In other words, research is needed to understand better the socialization process by which people come to believe that participation in certain types of activities and settings will satisfy specific needs. In particular, studies such as Stebbins's (1992) qualitative analyses of the longitudinal changes in the motivations and satisfactions that amateurs experienced in serious leisure should be emulated. The theories that are emerging and being tested to better understand gender, cultural, and ethnic differences in leisure participation may eventually contribute to this knowledge (e.g., Falk, 1995; Floyd, McGuire, Shinew and Noe, 1994; Jackson and Henderson, 1995).

A Final Note

Today there is a great deal of interest in establishing the relationship between leisure and other aspects of people's lives, such as mental health, the quality of life, work, successful retirement, and so on. Policymakers and service providers want to know how equitably the opportunities for leisure are distributed among the members of society, what the barriers are to equitable distribution, and what constraints people feel to participation in meaningful leisure (see Jackson and Scott, chapter 18 in this volume). Any attempt to assess the impact of leisure on the quality of life will to be more successful if we are able to observe and measure the actual amount of leisure experienced, that is subjective leisure, as opposed to just the amount of externally or objectively defined leisure in which people engage.

The definitional, immediate conscious experience, and post hoc satisfaction approaches have been used successfully by researchers in an attempt to gain access to the subjective nature of leisure. The leisure satisfaction construct in particular has attracted the interest of researchers because of its potential as an indicator of important psychological outcomes of leisure behavior, and because of its potential for leisure service applications. However, significant problems of measurement pervade both the appraisal and need-satisfaction approaches. Closely associated with these problems of measurement is the difficulty researchers have had in finding links between satisfaction and the objective world of behavior. It would seem profitable to concentrate on methods of measurement and data collection other than retrospective, pencil-and-paper inventories—methods that involve on-site monitoring and observation.

Finally, it is worth noting that we cannot structure, engineer, or provide experiences directly. Practitioners can foster, encourage, and facilitate meaningful leisure experiences only through the management of the recreation environment and setting, and the provision of concrete opportunities. What the research on the subjective nature of leisure tells us is that there is a need to look for and be sensitive to the links between the objective environment and the way it is perceived by the individual participant.

References

Aguilar, T. E., & Petrakis, E. (1989). Development and initial validation of perceived competence and satisfaction measures for racket sports. *Journal of Leisure Research, 21,* 77–91.

Allison, M. T. (1991). Leisure, sport and quality of life: Those on the fringes. In *Sport for all* (pp. 45–55). New York, NY: Elsevier Science Publishers.

Allison, M. T., & Smith, S. (1990). Leisure and the quality of life: Issues facing racial and ethnic minority elderly. *Therapeutic Recreation Journal, 24,* 50–63.

Backman, S. J., & Crompton, J. L. (1991). The usefulness of selected variables for predicting activity loyalty. *Leisure Sciences, 13,* 205–220.

Backman, S. J., & Mannell, R. C. (1986). Removing attitudinal barriers to leisure behavior and satisfaction: A field experiment among the institutionalized elderly. *Therapeutic Recreation Journal, 20,* 46–53.

Beard, J. G., & Ragheb, M. G. (1980). Measuring leisure satisfaction. *Journal of Leisure Research, 12,* 20–33.

Beard, J. G., & Ragheb, M. G. (1983). Measuring leisure motivation. *Journal of Leisure Research, 15,* 219–228.

Bradburn, N. M. (1969). *The structure of psychological well-being.* Chicago, IL: Aldine Publishing.

Brasile, F. M., Kleiber, D. A., & Harnisch, D. (1991). Analysis of participation incentives among athletes with and without disabilities. *Therapeutic Recreation Journal, 25,* 18–33.

Brown, B. A., & Frankel, B. G. (1993). Activity through the years: Leisure, leisure satisfaction, and life satisfaction. *Sociology of Sport Journal, 10,* 1–17.

Brown, B. A., Frankel, B. G., & Fennell, M. (1991). Happiness through leisure: The impact of type of leisure activity, age, gender and leisure satisfaction on psychological well-being. *Journal of Applied Recreation Research, 16,* 368–392.

Caldwell, L. L., & Andereck K. L. (1994). Motives for initiating and continuing membership in a recreation related voluntary association. *Leisure Sciences, 16,* 33–44.

Campbell, A. (1980). *The sense of well-being in America.* New York, NY: McGraw-Hill.

Campbell, A., Converse, P., & Rodgers, W. (1976). *The quality of American life.* New York, NY: Russell Sage Foundation.

Cheron, E. J., & Ritchie, J. R. B. (1982). Leisure activities and perceived risk. *Journal of Leisure Research, 14,* 139–154.

Clough, P., Shepherd, J., & Maughan, R. (1989). Motives for participation in recreational running. *Journal of Leisure Research, 21,* 297–309.

Colenutt, C. E., & McCarville, R. E. (1994). The client as problem solver: A new look at service recovery. *Journal of Hospitality and Leisure Marketing, 2,* 23–35.

Coyle, C. P., & Kinney, W. B. (1990). A comparison of leisure and gambling motives of compulsive gamblers. *Therapeutic Recreation Journal, 24,* 32–39.

Crandall, R. (1979). Social interaction, affect and leisure. *Journal of Leisure Research, 11,* 165–181.

Crompton, J. L. (1979). Motivations for pleasure vacations. *Annals of Tourism Research, 6,* 408–424.

Csikszentmihalyi, M. (1975). *Beyond boredom and anxiety: The experience of play in work and games.* San Francisco, CA: Jossey-Bass, Inc.

Cunningham, P. H., & Bartuska, T. (1989). The relationship between stress and leisure satisfaction among therapeutic recreation personnel. *Therapeutic Recreation Journal, 23,* 65–70.

Cutler Riddick, C. (1986). Leisure satisfaction precursors. *Journal of Leisure Research, 18,* 259–265.

Dorfman, L. T., Heckert, D. A., & Hill, E. A. (1988). Retirement satisfaction in rural husbands and wives. *Rural Sociology, 53,* 25–39.

Driver, B. L., & Brown, P. J. (1984). Contributions of behavioral scientists to recreation resource management. In I. Altman & J. F. Wohlwill (Eds.), *Behavior and the natural environment* (pp. 307–339). New York, NY: Plenum Press.

Driver, B. L., Brown, P. J., Stankey, G. H., & Gregoire, T. G. (1987). The ROS planning system: Evolution, basic concepts, and research needed. *Leisure Sciences, 9,* 201–212.

Driver, B. L., Tinsley, H. E. A., & Manfredo, M. J. (1991). The paragraphs about leisure and recreation experience preference scales: Results from two inventories designed to assess the breadth of the perceived psychological benefits of leisure. In B. L. Driver, P. J. Brown & G. L. Peterson (Eds.), *Benefits of leisure* (pp. 263–286). State College, PA: Venture Publishing, Inc.

Dunn Ross, E. L., & Iso-Ahola, S. E. (1991). Sightseeing tourists' motivation and satisfaction. *Annals of Tourism Research, 18,* 226–237.

Eagles, P. F. J. (1992). The travel motivations of Canadian ecotourists. *Journal of Travel Research, 31,* 3–7.

Ellis, G. D., & Witt, P. A. (1994). Perceived freedom in leisure and satisfaction: Exploring the factor structure of the perceived freedom components of the leisure diagnostic battery. *Leisure Sciences, 16,* 259–270.

Ewert, A. (1993). Differences in the level of motive importance based on trip outcome, experience level and group type. *Journal of Leisure Research, 25,* 335–349.

Ewert, A., & Hollenhorst, S. (1989). Testing the adventure model: Empirical support for a model of risk recreation participation. *Journal of Leisure Research, 21,* 124–139.

Falk, J. H. (1995). Factors influencing African American leisure time utilization of museums. *Journal of Leisure Research, 27,* 41–60.

Fine, G. A. (1987). *With the boys.* Chicago, IL: The University of Chicago Press.

Floyd, M. F., McGuire, F. A., Shinew, K. J., & Noe, F. P. (1994). Race, class, and leisure activity preferences: Marginality and ethnicity revisited. *Journal of Leisure Research, 26,* 158–173.

Fodness, D. (1994). Measuring tourist motivation. *Annals of Tourism Research, 21,* 555–581.

Foster, R. J., & Jackson, E. L. (1979). Factors associated with camping satisfaction in Alberta provincial park campgrounds. *Journal of Leisure Research, 11,* 292–306.

Francken, D. A., & van Raaij, W. F. (1981). Satisfaction with leisure time activities. *Journal of Leisure Research, 13,* 337–352.

Freysinger, V. (1994). Leisure with children and parental satisfaction: Further evidence of a sex difference in the experience of adult roles and leisure. *Journal of Leisure Research, 26,* 212–226.

Geva, A., & Goldman, A. (1991). Satisfaction measurements in guided tours. *Annals of Tourism Research, 18,* 177–185.

Glancy, M., & Little, S. L. (1995). Studying the social aspects of leisure: Development of the multiple-method field investigation model (MMFI). *Journal of Leisure Research, 27,* 305–325.

Graef, R., Csikszentmihalyi, M., & Gianinno, S. M. (1983). Measuring intrinsic motivation in everyday life. *Leisure Studies, 2,* 155–168.

Graefe, A. R., & Fedler, A. J. (1986). Situational and subjective determinants of satisfaction in marine recreational fishing. *Leisure Sciences, 8,* 275–295.

Guin, R. (1980). Early recreational vehicle tourists: Life satisfaction correlates of leisure satisfaction. *Journal of Leisure Research, 12,* 198–204.

Gunter, B. G. (1987). The leisure experience: Selected properties. *Journal of Leisure Research, 19,* 115–130.

Gurin, G., Veroff, J., & Feld, S. (1960). *Americans view their mental health.* New York, NY: Basic Books.

Haavio-Mannila, E. (1971). Satisfaction with family, work, leisure, and life among men and women. *Human Relations, 24,* 585–601.

Hazel, K. L., Langenau, E. E., Jr., & Levine, R. L. (1990). Dimensions of hunting satisfaction: Multiple-

satisfactions of wild turkey hunting. *Leisure Sciences, 12,* 383–393.

Henderson, K. A. (1990). An oral life history perspective on the containers in which American farm women experienced leisure. *Leisure Studies, 9,* 121–133.

Henderson, K. A., & Rannells, J. S. (1988). Farm women and the meaning of work and leisure: An oral history perspective. *Leisure Sciences, 10,* 41–50.

Hilgard, E. R. (1962). *Introduction to psychology.* New York, NY: Harcourt, Brace and World, Inc.

Howe, C. Z., & Qui, Y. (1988). The programming process revisited: Assumptions underlying the needs-based models. *Journal of Park and Recreation Administration, 6,* 14–27.

Hull, R. B., Michael, S. E., Walker, G. J., & Roggenbuck, J. W. (1996). Ebb and flow of brief leisure experiences. *Leisure Sciences, 18,* 299–314.

Iso-Ahola, S. E. (1979a). Basic dimensions of definitions of leisure. *Journal of Leisure Research, 11,* 28–39.

Iso-Ahola, S. E. (1979b). Some social-psychological determinants of perceptions of leisure: Preliminary evidence. *Leisure Sciences, 2,* 305–314.

Iso-Ahola, S. E. (1980). *The social psychology of leisure and recreation.* Dubuque, IA: Wm. C. Brown Publishers.

Iso-Ahola, S. E., & Allen, J. R. (1982). The dynamics of leisure motivation: The effects of outcome on leisure needs. *Research Quarterly for Exercise and Sport, 53,* 141–149.

Iso-Ahola, S. E., & Weissinger, E. (1987). Leisure and boredom. *Journal of Social and Clinical Psychology, 5,* 356–364.

Jackson, E. L., & Henderson, K. A. (1995). Gender-based analysis of leisure constraints. *Leisure Sciences, 17,* 31–51.

Kelly, J. R., Steinkamp, M. W., & Kelly, J. R. (1987). Later-life satisfaction: Does leisure contribute? *Leisure Sciences, 9,* 189–200.

Kleiber, D. A., Caldwell, L. L., & Shaw, S. M. (1993). Leisure meanings in adolescence. *Loisir et Société/Society and Leisure, 16,* 99–114.

Kleiber, D. A., Larson, R. W., & Csikszentmihalyi, M. (1986). The experience of leisure in adolescence. *Journal of Leisure Research, 18,* 169–176.

Knopf, R. C. (1983). Recreational needs and behavior in natural settings. In I. Altman, & J. F. Wohlwill (Eds.), *Behavior and the natural environment* (pp. 205–240). New York, NY: Plenum Press.

Larson, R. W. (1978). Thirty years of research on the subjective well-being of older Americans. *Journal of Gerontology, 33,* 109–125.

Larson, R. W., & Csikszentmihalyi, M. (1983). The experience sampling method. In H. T. Reis (Ed.), *Naturalistic approaches to studying social interaction* (pp. 41–56). San Francisco, CA: Jossey-Bass, Inc.

Larson, R. W., Mannell, R. C., & Zuzanek, J. (1986). Daily well-being of older adults with friends and family. *Journal of Psychology and Aging, 1,* 117–126.

London, M., Crandall, R., & Fitzgibbons, D. (1977). The psychological structure of leisure: Activities, needs, people. *Journal of Leisure Research, 9,* 252–263.

London, M., Crandall, R., & Seals, G. W. (1977). The contribution of job and leisure satisfaction to quality of life. *Journal of Applied Psychology, 62,* 328–334.

Lounsbury, J. W., Gordon, S. R., Bergermaier, R. L., & Francesco, A. M. (1982). Work and nonwork sources of satisfaction in relation to employee intention to turnover. *Journal of Leisure Research, 14,* 285–294.

Lounsbury, J. W., & Hoopes, L. L. (1988). Five-year stability of leisure activity and motivation factors. *Journal of Leisure Research, 20,* 118–134.

Madrigal, R. (1995). Cognitive and affective determinants of fan satisfaction with sporting event attendance. *Journal of Leisure Research, 27,* 205–227.

Manfredo, M. J. (1984). The comparability of onsite and off-site measures of recreation needs. *Journal of Leisure Research, 16,* 245–249.

Manfredo, M. J., Driver, B. L., & Brown, P. J. (1983). A test of concepts inherent in experience-based setting management for outdoor recreation areas. *Journal of Leisure Research, 15,* 263–283.

Manfredo, M. J., Driver, B. L., & Tarrant, M. A. (1996). Measuring leisure motivation: A meta-analysis of the recreation experience preference scales. *Journal of Leisure Research, 28,* 188–213.

Mannell, R. C. (1986). Problems, progress and usefulness of theory and research on leisure. In *Abstracts from the 1986 symposium on leisure research*. Alexandria, VA: National Recreation and Park Association.

Mannell, R. C., & Bradley, W. (1986). Does greater freedom always lead to greater leisure? Testing a person X environment model of freedom and leisure. *Journal of Leisure Research, 18,* 215–230.

Mannell, R. C., & Dupuis, S. (1996). Life satisfaction. In G. Birren (Ed.), *Encyclopedia of gerontology* (Vol. 2, pp. 59–64). New York, NY: Academic Press.

Mannell, R. C., & Iso-Ahola, S. E. (1987). Psychological nature of leisure and tourism experience. *Annals of Tourism Research, 14,* 314–331.

Mannell, R. C., Zuzanek, J., & Larson, R. W. (1988). Leisure states and "flow" experiences: Testing perceived freedom and intrinsic motivation hypotheses. *Journal of Leisure Research, 20,* 289–304.

Manning, R. E. (1985). *Studies in outdoor recreation: A review and synthesis of the social science literature in outdoor recreation*. Corvallis, OR: Oregon State University Press.

Mansfeld, Y. (1992). From motivation to actual travel. *Annals of Tourism Research, 19,* 399–419.

Maslow, A. (1968). *Toward a psychology of being*. Toronto, Ontario: Van Nos Reinhold.

Meir, E. I., & Melamed, S. (1986). The accumulation of person-environment congruences and well-being. *Journal of Occupational Behavior, 7,* 315–323.

Melamed, S., Meir, E. I., & Samson, A. (1995). The benefits of personality-leisure congruence: Evidence and implications. *Journal of Leisure Research, 27,* 25–40.

Mohr, K., Backman, K. F., Gahan, L. W., & Backman, S. J. (1993). An investigation of festival motivations and event satisfaction by visitor type. *Festival Management and Event Tourism, An International Journal, 3,* 89–97.

More, T. A., & Payne, B. R. (1978). Affective responses to natural areas near cities. *Journal of Leisure Research, 10,* 7–12.

Murray, H. A. (1938). *Explorations and personality*. New York, NY: Oxford.

Nisbett, R. E., & Wilson, T. D. (1977). Psychological review. *Telling More Than We Can Know: Verbal Reports on Mental Processes, 84,* 231–259.

Noe, F. P. (1987). Measurement specification and leisure satisfaction. *Leisure Sciences, 9,* 163–172.

Pearce, P. L. (1980). A favorability-satisfaction model of tourists' evaluations. *Journal of Travel Research, Summer,* 13–17.

Pizam, A., Neumann, Y., & Reichel, A. (1978). Dimensions of tourist satisfaction with a destination area. *Annals of Tourism Research, 5,* 314–322.

Ragheb, M. G. (1988). Leisure and recreation needs or motivations as a basis for program planning. *Journal of Park and Recreation Administration, 6,* 28–40.

Ragheb, M. G., & Griffith, C. A. (1982). The contribution of leisure participation and leisure satisfaction to life satisfaction of older persons. *Journal of Leisure Research, 14,* 295–306.

Ragheb, M. G., & Tate, R. L. (1993). A behavioral model of leisure participation, based on leisure attitude, motivation and satisfaction. *Leisure Studies, 12,* 61–70.

Robertson, R. A., & Regula, J. A. (1994). Recreational displacement and overall satisfaction: A study of central Iowa's licensed boaters. *Journal of Leisure Research, 26,* 174–181.

Robinson, D. W. (1992). A descriptive model of enduring risk recreation involvement. *Journal of Leisure Research, 24,* 52–63.

Russell, R. V. (1987). The importance of recreation satisfaction and activity participation to the life satisfaction of age-segregated retirees. *Journal of Leisure Research, 19,* 273–283.

Ryff, C. D., & Keyes, C. L. M. (1995). The structure of psychological well-being revisited. *Journal of Personality and Social Psychology, 69,* 719–727.

Samdahl, D. M. (1988). A symbolic interactionist model of leisure: Theory and empirical support. *Leisure Sciences, 10,* 27–39.

Samdahl, D. M., & Jekubovich, N. J. (1993). Patterns and characteristics of adult daily leisure. *Loisir et Société/Society and Leisure, 16,* 129–149.

Shaw, S. M. (1984). The measurement of leisure: A quality of life issue. *Loisir et Société/Society and Leisure, 7,* 91–107.

Stebbins, R. A. (1992). *Amateurs, professional, and serious leisure.* London, UK: McGill-Queen's University Press.

Steers, R. M., & Porter, L. W. (1991). *Motivation and work behavior.* New York, NY: McGraw-Hill.

Stewart, W. P., & Carpenter, E. H. (1989). Solitude at Grand Canyon: An application of expectancy theory. *Journal of Leisure Research, 21,* 4–17.

Stewart, W. P., & Hull, B. R. (1992). Satisfaction of what? Post hoc versus real-time construct validity. *Leisure Sciences, 14,* 195–209.

Stock, W. A., Okun, M. A., & Benin, M. H. (1986). Structure of subjective well-being among the elderly. *Psychology and Aging, 1,* 91–102.

Tarrant, M. A., & English, D. B. K. (1996). A crowding-based model of social carrying capacity applications for whitewater boating use. *Journal of Leisure Research, 28,* 155–168.

Tinsley, H. E. A. (1984). The psychological benefits of leisure counseling. *Loisir et Société/Society and Leisure, 7,* 125–140.

Tinsley, H. E. A., & Johnson, T. L. (1984). A preliminary taxonomy of leisure activities. *Journal of Leisure Research, 16,* 234–244.

Ulrich, R. S., & Addoms, D. L. (1981). Psychological and recreational benefits of a residential park. *Journal of Leisure Research, 13,* 43–65.

Vaske, J. J., Donnelly, M. P., Heberlein, T. A., & Shelby, B. (1982). Differences in reported satisfaction ratings by consumptive and nonconsumptive recreationists. *Journal of Leisure Research, 14,* 195–206.

Virden, R. J., & Knopf, R. C. (1989). Activities, experiences, and environmental settings: A case study of recreation opportunity spectrum relationships. *Leisure Sciences, 11,* 159–176.

Weissinger, E., & Bandalos, D. L. (1995). Development, reliability and validity of a scale to measure intrinsic motivation in leisure. Journal of Leisure Research, 27, 379–400.

Williams, D. R., Ellis, G. D., Nickerson, N. P., & Shafer, C. S. (1988). Contributions of time, format, and subject to variation in recreation experience preference measurement. *Journal of Leisure Research, 20,* 57–68.

Williams, D. R., & Schreyer, R. (1981). Characterizing the person-environment interaction for recreation resources planning. In *Proceedings of Applied Geography Conference.* Tempe, AZ: Association of Applied Geographers.

Williams, D. R., Schreyer, R., & Knopf, R. C. (1990). The effect of the experience use history on the multidimensional structure of motivations to participate in leisure activities. *Journal of Leisure Research, 22,* 36–54.

Willmott, P. (1971). Family, work and leisure conflicts among male employees. *Human Relations, 24,* 575–584.

Yuan, M. S., & McEwen, D. (1989). Test for campers' experience preference differences among three ROS setting classes. *Leisure Sciences, 11,* 177–185.

Yuan, S., & McDonald, C. (1990). Motivational determinates of international pleasure time. *Journal of Travel Research, 29,* 42–44.

Zoerink, D. A., & Lauener, K. (1991). Effects of a leisure education program on adults with traumatic brain injury. *Therapeutic Recreation Journal, 25,* 19–28.

Life Span and Life Course Perspectives on Leisure

Valeria J. Freysinger
Miami University

Life span and life course perspectives on continuity and change in human behavior offer useful frameworks for understanding leisure behaviors, motivations, and meanings. In this chapter these perspectives are examined in relation to leisure theory, research, and practice. Both what is known, and questions and challenges with which we are faced when life span or life course perspectives become the framework for understanding leisure, are presented.

The chapter begins with a discussion of the meaning of age and its articulation with other social constructs such as gender, race, and social class. Next, the assumptions of dominant models of development or aging across the life span are discussed. This is followed by a presentation of facts and beliefs about the relationships between leisure and age, and continuity and change in leisure, across the course of life. Both

how leisure is shaped by age and development and how aging and development are shaped by leisure are considered throughout these discussions. Understanding the basic tenets of life span and life course frameworks and what we currently know about leisure across the course of life leads to a number of questions and challenges for leisure researchers and practitioners. These include:

1. Why are longitudinal studies needed? What exactly should longitudinal data sets include? How should they be used and interpreted?
2. Is there an "ageless" definition of leisure? Does age change the meaning of leisure? Why or why not?
3. How does an understanding of the social construction of age impact recreation and leisure service provision?

The author would like to acknowledge the contributions of Mark Searle to the original conceptualization and organization of this chapter.

Discussion of these challenges and questions concludes the chapter.

It is important to remind the reader that this chapter discusses leisure from childhood through old age. It is not focussed solely on childhood and youth nor later adulthood. As a result, the chapter considers and integrates diverse, and often competing, perspectives. First, developmental theorists (e.g., Erikson, 1963; Haan, 1977; Loevinger, 1976) address the life span, but little research has focussed on following individuals through various life stages to assess the relative validity of the assertions contained in developmental theories. Nonetheless, developmental theory is widely believed to represent an important part of our understanding of changes associated with aging. Second, structural theories, or theories which address the social and cultural environments of individuals' lives (e.g., Lawton, 1983; Riley, Johnson and Foner, 1972), have focussed more on the adult part of the life span than on younger ages. Structural theories also suffer from a paucity of longitudinal studies and hence the validity of such theory is lacking. Third, behaviorists (e.g., Baltes and Baltes, 1990; Costa, McCrae and Arenberg, 1983) study all phases or ages of the life span and much longitudinal research has been conducted by these researchers. However, there have only recently been some attempts to integrate this large volume of research. Fourth, little life span and life course research has included those on the margins of society. Persons with disabilities, persons of color, persons with sexual orientations other than heterosexual, the poor, and until recently women (among others), have largely been excluded in our scholarship. Fifth and finally, the body of knowledge surrounding leisure across the course of life has suffered from all of these problems. Most certainly it is a case of too few researchers examining life span issues from too many perspectives resulting in a relatively small body of knowledge. Nonetheless, what has emerged has sometimes been linked to life span scholarship and, as a result, adds significantly to our understanding of the process of aging and leisure across the course of life. The reader is advised to keep these challenges in mind as the various work that has been done is presented. While evidence generated to date allows for many conclusions to be drawn, it also raises many questions that need to be addressed. A goal in this chapter is to consider both what is known and what needs to be examined. Through this process how to best advance our knowledge of leisure across the course of life will be identified.

What Is the Meaning of Age?

To begin to think about how and why age shapes and is shaped by leisure activity motivations and participation, it is useful to think about the meaning of age and how the process of aging is conceptualized. On a simple level, age is an indication of years since birth (chronological age). But while seemingly simple, this quantitative measure of age has multiple meanings. For one, an individual's chronological age is seen as an indication of maturation and experience and hence, her capacity to act or ability to function physically, cognitively, socially, and emotionally. To illustrate, it is likely that we expect someone who is 35 years of age to have more emotional self-control than someone who is 5 years of age. Many of us also are likely to expect a 20-year-old individual to have the capacity for participation in physically demanding outdoor recreation but might be surprised if our 75-year-old parent or grandparent had such capacity—or interest.

Chronological age is also used to assign responsibilities and social roles, as well as rights and privileges to an individual. For example, in North America the grandparent role is often associated with individuals in the fifth decade of life and later. When a child is 16 years old he or she would be expected to have the abilities needed for driving and thus granted the right to seek a driver's license. While some have questioned whether age is as important today as it once was to society's expectations of individuals and individuals' sense of themselves (e.g., Giele, 1980), recent research on adulthood has suggested that it is (Atchley, 1994; Settersten, 1996; Settersten and Hagestad, 1996a, 1996b).

However, chronological age is not only an indicator of years since birth, maturation and experience, roles and responsibilities, and rights and privileges, but also the historical moment in which someone is born and the events that he or she experienced at a particular age as a consequence. A group of individuals who share the same year of birth and subsequent events at the same point in the life span is known as a birth cohort. The concept of a birth cohort is an acknowledgment of the dynamic and historical meaning that age holds. Research has shown that each birth cohort ages in a potentially unique way because of experiencing certain life events at a particular age. Numerous examples of the importance of birth cohort can be cited. For example, the work of Elder, Modell, and Parke (1993) has revealed how older cohorts of youth were differently affected by the Great Depression in the United States than younger cohorts of youth because of the age at which they experienced the Depression. In Canada, prior to the early 1980s, individuals 65 years of age and older were not required to retire while today's generations of older adults are because of the passage of mandatory retirement legislation. Hence, cohorts of older adults prior to and after 1982 have experienced different opportunities and expectations for life in old age. Research might also show that while Title IX affected all girls' and women's opportunities for sport in the United States, its effect was different for females who were just entering or still in school after 1972 (the year of the passage of this legislation) than for those who were already out of school and had had few or no opportunities for participation in intramural or interscholastic sport. Further, for individuals of Asian ancestry who were living in the United States when the Asiatic Exclusion Act of 1924 was in effect, opportunities for development and productive aging would have been strongly shaped by limited opportunities for education, employment, and so on (Jackson, Antonucci and Gibson, 1990).

Finally, and as just suggested, chronological age interacts with other dimensions of personal identity that have social meaning, such as gender, race, ethnicity, and social class, in shaping individuals' experiences of life. For example, research suggests that early physical maturity in girls and boys is viewed differently by adults. While early physical maturity in boys is viewed positively and rewarded, early physical maturity in girls is often viewed with concern. One explanation for this is that boys who are physically mature can participate in sports and the athlete role is one that is valued for boys in North America (Kelly, 1996). On the other hand, early-maturing girls are seen as problematic by adults because of the consequences of sexual activity for girls (i.e., pregnancy). Some scholars further contend that the more negative feelings that North American culture has about early physical maturity in girls is also indicative of a sexual double standard and a devaluing and fear of female sexuality and maturity (Steiner-Adair, 1990; Sugar, 1979).

Another example of the interaction of age and gender can be seen in the consequences of healthcare and retirement policies that do not take gender into account. Women are not only likely to live longer but to experience more chronic (as opposed to acute) illnesses and conditions in later life than men. Because public policy in the United States was not and is not formulated on the lives of women, women are more likely than men to be poor and economically disadvantaged in late life (Rodeheaver, 1987). Older women's health and economic status has conse-

quences for their involvement in leisure. Limited educational opportunities and economic resources have adverse effects on life chances and leisure across age. Working-class young adults, for example, have been found to be more likely to experience unemployment after the completion of compulsory education and deprived leisure patterns with lasting effects are a consequence (Furlong, Campbell and Roberts, 1990). But while such youth might be expected to find employment, older adults may be prohibited from doing so without loss of retirement benefits.

Race and ethnicity also interact with age in significant ways. For example, the cultures of racial and ethnic minority groups provide many rich and unique resources and opportunities for growth and development—and leisure (Allen and Chin-Sang, 1990; Allison and Geiger, 1993; Jackson et al., 1990). At the same time, due to racism, African Americans and some groups of Hispanic Americans (both males and females), are more likely than European Americans to die before reaching the age when full retirement benefits are available. That is, even if public or private retirement benefits are earned, they are less likely to be used for retirement because of death before the age at which retirement with full benefits is possible. The sex ratio (i.e., number of females versus males) in many racial and ethnic minority groups is also larger, earlier than that of dominant groups. One reason for this is that in most (but not all) racial and ethnic groups, the life expectancy of females is greater than that of males, and in some racial and ethnic minority groups, this gap widens earlier. Hence, for women who are interested in marriage, opportunities are few, and the experiences of aging—and leisure—are affected (Gibson, 1994; Jackson et al., 1990).

Hence, age should not be studied independently but should be examined in relation to the multiple ways it changes over time and interacts with other constructs of personal and social identities.

How Is the Process of Aging Conceptualized?

The process of aging has been conceptualized in several different ways. Early models of age-related change were based in psychological research that focussed on the development or maturation of children. It was not until the midtwentieth century that scholars in North America began thinking about development or aging as a lifelong process and began questioning the applicability of existing developmental models and theory for adults (Featherman, 1983). Because of increased life expectancy, a growing population of older adults, and the availability of longitudinal studies which documented that growth or change did not end in adolescence, scholars turned their attention to the second half of life.

Developmental or aging theories emanate from at least three primary models of the process of aging or age-related change. These are the organismic, mechanistic, and contextualistic models (Cavanaugh, 1990). The models differ in their assumptions about the locus and process of change, and the degree to which it is age related. Briefly, the organismic model conceives of aging or development as primarily an internal process; that is, one that is initiated or stimulated by a predetermined readiness within the individual that is directly related to chronological age. While cultures and societies put greater and lesser emphases on the different stages, and influence the rate of development, they do not alter the basic content of development. In other words, as human beings we develop or age as we do because of a genetic predisposition to do so. In this sense, the individual is an active agent in his or her development. Further, development occurs in a series of stages or phases that are age related and there is an end point to development. Finally, development involves structural transformation (i.e., the epigenetic principle). That is, we do not just become "more" of something, but evolve or mature into a qualitatively different being as we age.

In contrast, the mechanistic model maintains that development or aging is primarily an external process. An individual changes in response to external stimuli; that is, humans are passive. Further, the change that is development is not necessarily age related. Rather, change or development can be achieved with the proper stimulus (reward and/or punishment). Hence, there is no end point to development. In addition, change is quantitative. That is, as humans we are like machines and no more than the sum of our parts.

A third model, contextualism, contends that humans develop or change because of both internal and external factors and processes. However, *life span* research, which is based in psychology, emphasizes the individual, while *life course* research, grounded in sociology, emphasizes the environment. In the contextualist model humans are seen as interactive; that is, they actively engage with and shape, as well as respond to, their environment. Development from this perspective occurs from conception to death in the interaction of the biological and psychological individual with his or her social and cultural environment across time. What we are at any point in time is a mix of what we have been as well as what we are to be. History is very important in this model and develop-

ment or aging cannot be separated from it. In addition, change is both qualitative and quantitative. Three types of time are typically taken into account: chronological age, cohort (or history), and time of measurement (or period effects) (Schaie, 1983). The significance of chronological age and cohort to human aging has already been discussed. Time of measurement is a third type of time important to consider, as it refers to what is happening in the environment of the individual at the time he or she is being observed or measured that may be shaping his or her experience of aging. For example, computers and access to the World Wide Web are a part of individuals' lives in many societies today that are radically reshaping the "free-time" activities of those individuals regardless of age or cohort.

Models of aging and development cannot be proven. Rather, their value lies in their usefulness. Each of these models serves as a metaphor, trying to make more concrete (or paint a picture of) a process that is abstract. They suggest to us the questions we might ask and what we might study in order to understand how and why leisure changes across the course of life, and how and why leisure shapes the process of aging or development.

Change and Continuity in Leisure Across the Course of Life

The relationship between leisure and age has been examined in relation to change and continuity in type and frequency of activity participation and leisure motivations. Several conclusions can be made and are discussed in the following way: change and continuity in types of activity, change and continuity in frequency of activity participation, and change and continuity in leisure motivations. Throughout these sections, age-based explanations of the continuity and change in leisure that have been observed are presented.

Change and Continuity in Types of Activity

Research suggests more continuity than change in the types of activities in which individuals participate across the life span, and that continuity of activity participation increases with age. That is, individuals participating in an activity at any given age are more likely than not to have participated in that activity previously (Cheek and Burch, 1976; Knox, 1977; Searle, Mactavish and Brayley, 1993; Yoesting and Burkhead, 1973; Yoesting and Christiansen, 1978). Or to put it another way, while previous participation in an activity does not guarantee continued participation, it makes it much more likely. For example, in a longitudinal study examining interscholastic sport participation between fifth/sixth (Time 1) and ninth/tenth (Time 2) grades, Anderson, Lorenz, and Pease (1986) found that participation at Time 1 was the strongest predictor of adolescents' sport participation at Time 2. Scott and Willits (1989) studied the relationship between adolescent and adult leisure patterns and found "the greater the involvement in a specific type of activity during adolescence, the more frequent the participation in the same type of activity at midlife" (p. 323). They also reported that this positive relationship was stronger for women than for men in the areas of creative and/or artistic and sport activities. Similarly, Freysinger and Ray (1994), in a longitudinal study examining predictors of activity participation in young and middle adulthood, found that participation in free-time activity in young adulthood was a significant predictor of women's, but not men's, participation in free-time activities in middle adulthood. And examining a much shorter span of time, Crawford, Godbey, and Crouter (1986) found relative stability in leisure preferences during the first two years of marriage among childless couples.

Looking at this issue in a slightly different way, Raymore, Barber, Eccles, and Godbey (1995) studied continuity in leisure behavior patterns between adolescence and young adulthood. In this longitudinal study, four clusters of activity patterns were found: Risky, Active (positive, formal, and informal), Diffused, and Home-Based (females only). Stability in activity patterns between adolescence and young adulthood was reported overall for both females and males. At the same time, the Risky pattern was the most common pattern for males in both adolescence and young adulthood while the Positive Active pattern and the Home-Based pattern were the most common patterns for the females during adolescence and young adulthood, respectively.

Yet research also suggests that there is both a "core" and "balance" in leisure activities across the life span (Iso-Ahola, 1980; Kelly, 1974; Kelly, Steinkamp and Kelly, 1986). That is, while participation in some types of activities remain stable across age, activities are dropped and added as well. A number of recent studies have examined the phenomena of starting, ceasing, and replacing activities across the life span (see also Jackson and Scott, chapter 18 in this volume). This and other research has found that at most stages of life (i.e., adolescence through adulthood) individuals start, cease, and replace, as well as continue activities. For example, while older adults are more likely to

drop or not start physically demanding and outside-the-home activities (Gordon, Gaitz and Scott, 1976; Iso-Ahola, Jackson and Dunn, 1994; Kelly et al., 1986; McGuire, O'Leary, Yeh and Dottavio, 1989), a significant increase over the life cycle in the number of people participating in or starting hobbies and home-based activities has also been found (Iso-Ahola et al., 1994; Kelly et al., 1986; Smale and Dupuis, 1993).

Several explanations for continuity and change in types of activity participation have been offered. Kelly et al. (1986) maintain that some activities (core) are stable because they are relatively inexpensive, easily accessible or convenient, take little effort, and/or are enjoyable or important to people. Core activities include reading, talking with family and/or friends, and watching television. Other activities (balance) change in response to the interaction among changing roles, responsibilities, time, resources, opportunities, abilities, norms, and interests. For example, research has shown that adults who are parents of children living at home are more likely to participate in physical activity and sport than nonparents (Unkel, 1981). Being a parent provides both expectations and opportunities for involvement in children's activities and children are more likely to be involved in physical recreation and sport than are adults. At the same time, research has also shown that being a parent reduces parents' time for independent or personal leisure and that the impact of the parental role on parents' leisure is gendered. In heterosexual couples, the personal leisure of mothers is likely to decrease more than that of fathers. At the same time, fathers are more likely to express greater dissatisfaction with the constraints parenting places on their leisure than are mothers (Bernard, 1984; Crawford and Huston, 1993; Dempsey, 1989; Horna, 1989; Wearing and McArthur, 1988).

According to Atchley (1993), continuity in activity is more likely than discontinuity because external or social continuity (i.e., continuity in activities, relationships, roles, and physical environments) contributes to internal continuity (i.e., continuity of identity, self-concept, self-esteem). Individuals are motivated toward internal continuity because it provides them with a sense of security and integrity. So while consistency in the types of activities in which one participates may be interpreted as being "stuck in one's ways" or inflexibility, Atchley contends that continuity of activity is likely to be:

1. a sign of knowing oneself;
2. a means of adapting to changing ability which allows one to maintain a sense of competence (see also, Baltes and Baltes, 1990);

3. a response to the expectations of others; and/or

4. a basis for effective decision making and self-esteem (see Lee, Dattilo, Kleiber and Caldwell, 1996; Pedlar, Dupuis and Gilbert, 1996, for evidence of these in leisure contexts).

Continuity may be a gendered issue. For example, some research suggests that because of notions or constructions of gender, women show greater flexibility (i.e., greater change) in their leisure activity participation than men (Henderson, Bialeschki, Shaw and Freysinger, 1996; Maas and Kuypers, 1975; Seltzer, 1979). Women's lives, specifically the lives of women who are mothers, are constructed such that they are deprived of the opportunity for extended time commitments outside of the maternal or parenting role (Sales, 1977). A cross-sectional study of leisure barriers in adulthood by Witt and Goodale (1981) concluded that the stress that constrains women's leisure across the life cycle appears to be more related to family concerns than for men. The ethic of care which girls and women demonstrate for a variety of reasons, constructs a reality where the needs and interests of others are often put before the needs and interests of self.[1]

Continuity has also been found to vary by pattern of activity participation. In a study of "expanders" (i.e., those adding activities) and "contracters" (i.e., those dropping activities) in outdoor recreation, McGuire, Dottavio, and O'Leary (1987) found that contracters were much more likely than expanders to report that they started current activities before the age of 18; that is, were much more likely to report continuity in their outdoor recreation involvement across the life span. Examining the topic of continuity in another way, McCormick and McGuire (1996) examined leisure's impact on continuity in the social structures of older adults who were lifelong and in-migrant residents of a rural community in the southeastern United States.

---

[1] The gendered experience of agency (independent, autonomous orientation) and affiliation (relationality and an ethic of care) has been attributed to psychodynamic processes (Chodorow, 1978; Huyck, 1994), socialization (Chodorow, 1978; Eagly, 1987), and relations of power (Hare-Mustin and Maracek, 1986). Research suggests that there is a "sex-role crossover" in the agentic orientation of males and the affiliative orientation of females in late midlife when the "parental imperative" no longer dominates (Gilligan, 1982a; Gutmann, 1987). Specifically, while affiliation is maintained, an agentic orientation tends to come to the fore among women whose responsibility for caring for dependent children has decreased. Men, on the other hand, report an increase in affiliation and decrease in agency (Cooper and Gutmann, 1987; Gutmann, 1987).

They found that in-migrant residents used leisure to create and maintain social communities whereas lifelong residents experienced discontinuity in their leisure interactions and social structures. All of this research suggests at least two things: (1) that findings of continuity vary depending on how it is defined and examined; and (2) the contexts of individuals' lives may or may not support continuity which is particularly important if continuity is central to a sense of personal integrity and security as has been suggested (Atchley, 1993).

Continuity and Change in Frequency of Activity Participation

Continuity and change in *frequency* of activity participation across age have also been examined. In general, research has indicated that frequency of activity participation declines with age (Gordon et al., 1976; Kelly et al., 1986). However, decline in frequency of activity participation varies by type of activity. In a cross-sectional analysis of a study which examined participation in six leisure activities and psychological well-being among individuals age 11 years and older, for example, involvement in hobbies and crafts and walking for exercise increased, participation in swimming decreased, while visiting friends, television viewing, and participation in social clubs and organizations showed no significant change with age (Smale and Dupuis, 1993). In another cross-sectional study of individuals age 18 years and older, Jackson (1990) found that with increasing age, desire to begin a new activity declined significantly. At the same time, very few of the *very* active older adults reported a *lack* of desire to begin a new activity. Jackson concluded that "the *lack of desire* for a new activity was reported most frequently among the age groups *already characterized by a narrow range of current activities,* and least frequently among the groups characterized by a wide range of current activities" (p. 64). Further, "older people who have maintained an active and diverse leisure lifestyle may be among the *least* constrained subgroups of the population" (p. 67).

Change and continuity in frequency of activity participation across age has also been found to vary by gender and health. A longitudinal study of adults 50 years of age and older examined the impact of age, sex, and functional health on frequency of participation in nine categories of activity over a 16-year period (Stanley, Freysinger and Horn, 1996). Participation in six of the nine activity categories (participatory sports, hobbies, civic and fraternal organizations, social activities, spectator activities, and traveling) declined over the 16-year period, participation in church and television/radio showed no significant change, and participation in reading increased. Subsequent analysis revealed that sex and functional health mediated change in activity participation. While results were not linear or consistent, in general the older one was and the poorer one's functional health, the greater was the decline reported in activity participation across age. At the same time, women's participation was less likely than men's to decline significantly, even though women reported lower levels of functional health. Stanley et al. concluded that, while gross measures of activity participation and health may be responsible for their results, the pattern of results suggests that in later life, gender differentiates the experience of health and leisure (see also Freysinger, Alessio and Mehdizadeh, 1993; Lawton, 1985).

One might believe that in future cohorts gender will be less important in distinguishing the activity participation of adults, especially in physical activity and sport, because of changing sex roles and opportunities. However, recent research suggests otherwise. A trend analysis (1985–1990) of a national study examining health behaviors of individuals 18 years of age and older in the United States found that:

1. women at all ages reported lower levels of participation than men in most fitness activities (e.g., individual sport, team sports, exercise, physical activity);
2. that between 1985 and 1990 the fitness participation of women in all age groups decreased slightly relative to men; and
3. that younger women showed just as great a decline in fitness participation as their elders.

Further, race was also found to be important in predicting participation in physical recreation. African-American women reported lower levels of participation and Asian-American women slightly higher participation than White women (Robinson and Godbey, 1993). Because of the typically negative relationship between racial and ethnic minority membership and health, education, income, and occupation in the United States, as well as the cultural resources and opportunities different racial and ethnic groups have available (Jackson et al., 1990), it can be expected that race and ethnicity strongly shape leisure participation patterns across the life course. However, the research in this area is quite limited.

Change and Continuity in Leisure Motivations

Several explanations exist for the age-related changes in types and frequency of leisure activity participation that have been observed. Most of these explanations relate to changing motivations for leisure across the life span. Psychosocial theories of development and sociological theories of age often undergird discussions of changing leisure motivations. Consistent with a contextualist model, there are some leisure scholars who have attempted to integrate psychosocial and sociological notions of development and age in seeking to understand leisure across the course of life (see, for example, Kleiber and Kelly, 1980; Osgood and Howe, 1984; Rapoport and Rapoport, 1975). However, the historical component of a contextualist model and the politics of development and aging are rarely taken into account (Griffin, 1981). What we do know about how and why leisure motivations change with age is presented here.

A motive has been defined as "an internal factor that arouses and directs human behavior" (Iso-Ahola, 1989, p. 248) or "the reason(s) which underlie(s) why an individual behaves as he or she does" (Osgood and Howe, 1984, p. 179). *Optimal arousal,* or a balance between too much and too little stimulation, has been purported to be a basic psychological need or motive (Berlyne, 1960; Csikszentmihalyi, 1975). To experience optimal arousal individuals seek a balance of familiarity and novelty. Based on developmental theory (i.e., biopsychosocial theory), the need for stimulation (and hence, familiarity and novelty) has been hypothesized to vary with age (Gordon et al., 1976; Iso-Ahola, 1980, 1989; Kleiber, 1985). Iso-Ahola (1980) suggested that the need for novelty would be highest in middle childhood through middle adulthood, while infants, young children, and older adults would show a greater propensity for familiarity. Kleiber (1985) proposed that emergent motivation, or the motive for novelty, would peak around 40 years of age and then gradually decline while continuing motivation, or the motive for familiarity, would gradually increase after age 40. There has been little research conducted explicitly to investigate these assertions.

In a cross-sectional study of individuals 20 years of age and older, Gordon et al. (1976) found that participation in high-intensity (i.e., highly stimulating) activities was different (i.e., lower) in the older as compared to younger age groups. However, a study which was designed to test Iso-Ahola's hypothesis did not support it. A fairly linear difference across age in those seeking novelty and familiarity, such that each older age group was more likely to report continuation of activities (familiarity) and less likely to report starting new activities (novelty) than each younger age group, was reported (McGuire et al., 1989). However, both of these studies were cross-sectional in design and McGuire et al. examined participation in outdoor recreational activities only, hence, limiting any firm conclusions.

Intrinsic and extrinsic motivation, another defining dimension of leisure (see Iso-Ahola, chapter 3 in this volume), has also been found to vary by age. Specifically, intrinsic motivation, or doing an activity for the sake or enjoyment of the activity itself, has shown a U-shaped relationship with age. For example, as children progress through school, motivation becomes increasingly extrinsic (Harter, 1981; Maehr, 1983). Younger and single adults have reported more extrinsically motivated experiences in daily life than older, family-oriented adults (Graef, Csikszentmihalyi and Giannino, 1983). These changes in intrinsic motivation have been attributed to both external factors or the contexts of individuals' lives, and psychosocial preoccupations.

In middle childhood and adolescence, as well as young adulthood, extrinsic motivations dominate (e.g., grades in school, winning in games and sport, getting a job and making more money). An emphasis on, or the application of, extrinsic rewards has been found to undermine intrinsic motivation (Graef et al., 1983; Iso-Ahola, 1989).[2] The social roles of the late childhood, adolescent, and young adult years emphasize extrinsic rewards. In addition, the psychosocial preoccupations of these ages include concerns about being competent, developing a positive identity or sense of self, establishing oneself in an intimate relationship and occupation, and gaining social recognition (Erikson, 1963), so extrinsic sanctions or motivators are difficult to ignore. However, Kleiber (1985) is one who contends that the achievement motivation of late childhood, adolescence, and young adulthood—which emphasizes competitiveness, internality, and a future orientation—must be abandoned in middle and later adulthood in order to successfully negotiate the psychosocial crises of generativity versus stagnation in middle adulthood, and integrity versus despair in later adulthood (Erikson, 1963), and to realize interiority in both (Neugarten, 1977). Further, Kleiber hypothesizes that leisure, to the extent that it is disengagement from everyday concerns and reengagement in more personally meaningful activity, is one means of adapting to the changes in achievement motivation that midlife

and later adulthood require. While leisure is not inherently valuable to development (Kleiber, 1985, p. 47; see also Kleiber and Ray, 1993):

> in emphasizing the individualistic nature of leisure that is reflected in the idea of disengagement, we allow for a greater potential for the realization of self-determination and integrity; and in emphasizing the personal investment reflected in the idea of engagement we do not preclude the possibility that that experiencing may be shared, cooperative, intimate and community building.

Osgood and Howe (1984) reviewed the scholarship on adult development and developmental theories and identified the changing psychological tasks, social roles, and biological milestones of adulthood. They proposed that leisure motivations change across adulthood because of the interaction of these changing tasks, roles, and milestones and that gender distinguishes leisure in adulthood just as it does adult development. They then hypothesized that the leisure experiences of young adults would be characterized by intimate other, work, and family-related leisure; instrumental, expressive, and sensate activities; role-related experiences; social leisure; sensual transcendence; and goal directedness. Because of the psychological, biological, and social changes experienced in midlife, the leisure of adults at this stage was predicted to involve primarily new experiences, flexible emotional investments, intellectual pursuits, sex-free social interactions, reappraisal of self, and identity consolidation and/or exploration. A reemergence of intimate other related leisure, social reintegration, enrichment and extension of mental and spiritual activities, more time for leisure, and relaxation and solitude was expected in later life (pp. 182–183).

The psychological tasks, social roles, and physical and biological maturational changes of childhood, adolescence, and youth have also been identified (Bronfenbrenner, 1977; Erikson, 1963; Gilligan, Lyons and Hanmer, 1990; Haan, 1977; Havighurst, 1973, 1982; Kohlberg, 1976; Loevinger, 1976).[3] While

---

[2]While the negative relationship between extrinsic rewards and intrinsic motivation is generally true, see Iso-Ahola (1989) for a discussion of the complexity of this relationship.

[3]An in-depth or complete discussion of human development and developmental theory is beyond the scope of this chapter. The reader is referred to the references in the text for further information. The following sources provide additional discussion of human development in the context of leisure specifically: Carnegie Council on Adolescent Development, 1992; Csikszentmihalyi and Larson, 1984; Freysinger, 1995; Gordon et al., 1976; Hendry, Shucksmith, Love and Glendinning, 1993; Iso-Ahola, 1980; Kleiber and Kelly, 1980; Rapoport and Rapoport, 1975; Raymore, 1995; Riley et al., 1972.

research specifically exploring the relationships between leisure and age-related psychological tasks, social roles, and biological milestones of childhood, adolescence, and adulthood is limited, that which has been conducted offers both support for and contradiction of the predictions of Osgood and Howe (1984) and others (e.g., Kleiber and Kelly, 1980).

For example, in middle childhood it is believed that individuals are motivated to gain a sense of competence and social recognition for abilities. Erikson (1963) conceptualized this as the psychosocial crisis of industry versus inferiority. Children's play and games are contexts within which children potentially develop a sense of industry or competence. Further, the play and games of children and youth have been found to be important contexts for the development (or not) of moral reasoning (Weiss and Bredemeier, 1990), as well as creativity and other cognitive, emotional, and social abilities (Barnett and Kleiber, 1982; Fromberg and Bergen, 1998).

Adolescence is defined by the psychosocial crisis of identity versus role diffusion. Identity development is believed to require the development of a separate or individuated sense of self (Erikson, 1963). However, research indicates that this process varies by both race (Ward, 1990) and gender (Gilligan, 1982b). African-American teens specifically must develop a positive sense of racial identity in order to develop a positive personal identity. According to Ward (1990), this process requires African-American teens to reject the oppressive and exploitative images of African Americans that permeate a racist United States at the same time they accept and assert their race. Ward contends that parents are central to racial minority teens' ability to develop positive racial and personal identities and that boys experience this process somewhat differently than girls. Further, her research suggests that recreation agencies, as well as extracurricular activities in schools, play an important role in the identity development of these teens.

Turning to the issue of gender, research has shown that in the preteen and early adolescent years, girls in North America are confronted with a culture that devalues their "voices" and demeans and fears their development (Gilligan et al., 1990; Orenstein, 1994). Involvement in physically active play and recreation has been purported to be one way girls may resist negative cultural images and messages and develop a positive sense of self (Barnett and Kleiber, 1982; Kleiber and Kane, 1984). Similarly, research suggests that leisure is a way for gay, lesbian, and bisexual youth to develop both a sense of community and positive sense of self in a heterosexual culture (Kivel, 1994; Kivel and Kleiber, 1996). Research on the role of recreation and leisure

in the development of identity and a positive sense of self has shown that its impact varies by type of activity and gender (Shaw, 1991; Shaw, Kleiber and Caldwell, 1995; Shaw and Smale, 1994; Smith, Caldwell, Shaw and Kleiber, 1994). Further, while leisure may be a site of resistance to prevailing and oppressive social norms (Freysinger and Flannery, 1992; Henderson and Bialeschki, 1991; Wearing, 1990), stepping outside social expectations may require a strong sense of self, because of the negative sanctions or punishments that such behavior brings (Kleiber and Kane, 1984).

In young adulthood, many individuals are preoccupied with establishing themselves and becoming competent in an intimate relationship, family, and work. The leisure of young adulthood reflects these preoccupations in that: (1) single young adults use leisure as a context for meeting others (Bernard, 1984); and (2) married young adults, especially those with dependent children and especially women, often report limited time and energy for leisure and/or an increase in family leisure (Bernard, 1984; Crawford and Huston, 1993; Wearing and McArthur, 1988). Studies also suggest that the "establishment" concerns of young adulthood make free time not only less available, but also free-time activity relatively less important than family and work (Freysinger and Ray, 1994). Again, the experiences of work, leisure, and family in young adulthood have been found to be powerfully shaped by gender and social class (Bernard, 1984; Freysinger, 1994; Harrington and Dawson, 1995; Kay, 1996; Rapoport and Rapoport, 1975; Rubin, 1976).

Research on midlife adults has found that leisure is an expression of both affiliation and agency (Freysinger, 1995), and that issues which characterize adulthood are gendered and are in flux in midlife (Cooper and Gutmann, 1987; Gilligan, 1982a; Gutmann, 1987). Leisure in young adulthood and midlife also is shaped by the social roles taken on, and social role changes experienced by individuals during this time. Leisure may be used to fulfill, cope with, enhance, and/or escape the responsibilities associated with being a parent (Bialeschki and Michener, 1994; Freysinger, 1994, 1995; Horna, 1989; Wearing and McArthur, 1988) and a spouse or partner (Bialeschki and Pearce, 1997; Freysinger, 1995; Horna, 1993; Orthner and Mancini, 1991)—as well as a means of resisting, challenging, and transforming gendered notions of these social roles (Freysinger and Flannery, 1992; Henderson and Bialeschki, 1991; Wearing, 1990).

In later life, individuals continue to be motivated by needs for a sense of mastery and self-determination (agency) as well as a sense of connection with others (affiliation). Leisure for some is a way to enhance a sense of self-determination or independence in later life (Searle, Mahon, Iso-Ahola, Sdrolias and van Dyck, 1995).[4] Older adults report that leisure helps them cope with the changes that old age brings by providing a context for the establishment and maintenance of relationships with others, by filling time and providing an escape from boredom, and by allowing them to gain a sense of competence and mastery (Kelly et al., 1986). Despite stereotypes of inevitable biological decline, dependency, and constricted activity patterns, research has shown that it is not age per se, but health that is crucial to activity involvement in later life (Kelly et al., 1986; Stanley et al., 1996). And conversely, leisure involvement has been found to contribute to increased physical and mental functioning and health in old age (Riddick, 1993; Riddick and Daniels, 1994).

The psychosocial crisis of later life, integrity versus despair, brings to the fore for older adults the issue of gaining a sense of wholeness and completeness through (Eisenhandler, 1989; Erikson, 1963):

1. acceptance of all that one's life has, and has not, been;
2. acknowledgment of the inevitability of death; and
3. the creation of a meaningful existence.

Much research has been conducted on the relationship between leisure (activity participation or satisfaction) and various measures of psychological well-being (e.g., life satisfaction, morale, happiness) in old age, and this research has generally reported a positive relationship.[5]

---

[4]It should be noted that not all researchers see an emphasis on independence in later life as positive. Rodeheaver (1987) contended that older adults' lives—and indeed all humans' lives—are defined by interdependence. Circumstances of dependence have been created for older adults, however, by social policy. At the same time, U.S. culture denigrates dependence and values independence. Hence, the marginalization of older adults, and older women in particular, is constructed and reproduced in the formulation of social policy (Henderson et al., 1996). See Riley, Kahn and Foner (1995) for a further discussion of how social policy constructs the experience of age.

[5]While positive relationships between leisure activity participation or satisfaction and various measures of well-being have been reported and heralded for years (Riddick, 1993; Freysinger et al., 1993; Larson, 1978), it is uncertain to what extent leisure per se actually changes or increases life satisfaction, happiness, morale, and so forth. Generally leisure accounts for very little of the variance in psychological well-being, and well-being appears to be relatively stable across the later years despite changes in leisure or health, suggesting that psychological well-being is a fairly stable or consistent aspect of personality (a trait) and not a state (Freysinger et al., 1993).

However, it would be inaccurate to equate these conceptualizations of well-being with the Eriksonian concept of integrity. No research has examined leisure in relation to the issues of integrity and despair. However, Atchley (1993) has hypothesized that continuity (i.e., consistency but not sameness) in activities, social relationships, and roles contributes to integrity. Hence, it seems that this is an area ripe for exploration.

Summary

In summary, the research on change and continuity in type and frequency of leisure activity participation across the life span reveals some age-related patterns. However, the research also indicates that there is great heterogeneity in patterns of activity participation across the life span (Cutler and Hendricks, 1990; Iso-Ahola et al., 1994; Kelly et al., 1986; Stanley and Freysinger, 1995; Stanley et al., 1996). Social roles, health, race and ethnicity, sexual orientation, and gender are just some of the factors that distinguish the experience of age and leisure. Further, continuity and change in leisure activity involvement varies by form of the activity (Freysinger and Ray, 1994; Stanley and Freysinger, 1995; Stanley et al., 1996). At the same time, research suggests that, at all ages, some individuals are more likely to seek new experiences, some more likely to continue with familiar activities, and others to withdraw (Jackson and Dunn, 1988; McGuire et al., 1987).

However, caution must be used in drawing conclusions about the impact of age on leisure, because the contexts of our lives are constantly changing (i.e., cohort and period effects), which has led some to assert that intra-individual age-related patterns of change and continuity (or development) are not predictable, only probable (Riegel, 1976). In addition, there is a dearth of leisure research on diverse groups of people. The tremendous heterogeneity that exists *within* any given cohort because of social class, gender, race, ethnicity, sexual orientation, as well as able-bodiedness and personality, has been little explored; hence, our understanding is limited. Finally, it is difficult to compare or integrate the research that does exist examining the relationship between age and leisure activity participation because of:

1. the different designs that are used (e.g., cross-sectional versus panel versus trend);
2. the different age ranges that are examined (e.g., childhood to adolescence, young-old to old-old, or young to middle adulthood); and

3. the different ways that leisure activity participation is measured and analyzed (e.g., if and how activities are categorized, if activities are analyzed individually, as categories, or overall).

Critical Questions and Issues

The research and scholarship presented in this chapter suggest a number of critical questions and issues that need to be addressed in order to advance our understanding of the dialectical relationships between leisure and age. Three of those questions or issues are reiterated here.

Why are longitudinal studies needed? What exactly should longitudinal data sets include? How should they be used and interpreted?

Several scholars have discussed research designs in the context of life span and life course development (e.g., Baltes, 1968; Schaie, 1965). While the language and labels they use vary, there is much similarity in their basic assertions. Because K. W. Schaie is the scholar who initiated discussion of this topic in North America, his perspective is presented here.[6]

According to Schaie (1965), to understand the significance of age to behavior or to understand age-related change one must be able to discern among three types of time: chronological age, birth cohort, and time of measurement. Various research designs (i.e., cross-sectional or one of the longitudinal or sequential designs) operationalize one type or some combination of these types of time. None of the designs, however, allows for the analysis of all three types of time. The specific design one uses, while certainly influenced by pragmatic considerations such as time, cost, urgency of need for information, and so on, should also be influenced by the research question. If one is interested in development and leisure or how and why age shapes leisure, then a longitudinal (panel) design is better than a cross-sectional design. This is because in a cross-sectional study two or more cohorts are measured at one point in time. Hence, if a difference in the leisure participation of 20-year-olds and 60-year-olds is found, it is unclear if that difference is due to age or cohort. For example, a popular belief in North

America is that participation in physical activity and sport decreases with age. However, it may not be age itself (i.e., its biological, psychological, and sociocultural meaning) that is responsible for lower involvement in physical activity and sport, but when one was born. Current generations of older women in particular had few or no opportunities to develop competence or interest in physical activity and sport and, in fact, may have adopted the culture's view that to be female meant to be disinterested in such activity (Henderson et al., 1996). With the passage of Title IX in the United States and changing notions of what it means to be female and male, young and old, attitudes toward, opportunities for, and participation in physical activity and sport in later life may well change in future generations.

A panel design measures the same individual or birth cohort at two or more measurement times. With this type of design, if a difference in leisure participation is found between 20-year-olds and 60-year-olds the researcher may feel more confident that this difference is due to age, though why or how age influences change in leisure participation would still have to be examined based on the variables or issues that were assessed in the study. However, with a panel design the researcher still does not know if the age-related change she found would be found in other cohorts studied across the same span of years. That is, cohort specificity is a problem with panel designs (see Schaie, 1983, for a discussion of other limitations, as well as other advantages, of panel designs).

If one thinks that history (or cohort) would have an effect on the phenomena of interest, then a cohort-sequential design is probably best. This design measures two or more cohorts at two or more measurement times across the same time period or years. Essentially, it is a sequence of panel studies. With this type of design, age and cohort are both varied and, hence, can be separated. For example, if a researcher were interested in changes in leisure satisfaction between middle and later adulthood and thought that both age and history might influence the leisure satisfaction of adults, then he or she would want to use a cohort-sequential design so that he or she could examine both age changes and cohort differences.

As mentioned previously, pragmatic considerations often dictate research design. What then becomes important is the interpretation of the results. If a cross-sectional study, for example, is used because of time and money constraints, then what must be made clear in reporting the results and formulating implications is that age differences and not necessarily age changes were what were measured. Similarly, when a panel design is used, the findings must be set

---

[6]For critical discussions of Schaie's notions of research designs and their use, see Adams, 1978; Botwinick and Arenberg, 1976; Buss, 1973, 1979–80. For a response to some of these criticisms, see Schaie and Baltes, 1975.

within the historical context of the cohort studied and the other limitations that this design carries. There is no perfect design and, hence, what one has and has not found must be made explicit if our research is to contribute to practice, theory, and future research.

Is there an "ageless" definition of leisure? Does age change the meaning of leisure? Why or why not?

This issue can be discussed in at least two ways: (1) in relation to the research that has examined continuity and change in leisure activity, motivations, and meanings; and (2) in relation to the scholarship on the sociocultural meaning and individual experience of age. Focusing on the former suggests that while the "containers," or the social, temporal, and physical contexts of leisure may well vary by age as well as other sociodemographic factors, the meaning of leisure is fairly consistent across individuals (Havighurst, 1957; Henderson et al., 1996). At the same time, some have argued that, when leisure is conceptualized as a relational practice, the leisure of adults and play of children are dramatically different and cannot even be compared (Rojek, 1985). This is because the self is a construct of socialization. That is, the self is produced in interactions with both specific and generalized others at a given time in history. Specific others included one's mother, father, siblings, and friends; generalized others include social institutions such as schools and work. Because children are selves in the making, their play is characterized by selflessness. Openness, volatility, and unpredictability are what characterize the "leisure" or play of children. Adult "play" or leisure, however, is highly monitored or controlled and totally self-conscious or self-constructed. It is organized "to exclude the distinctive features of the child's play world (formlessness, frankness, lack of seriousness, and irrationality) or, instead, to tolerate them only in their mimetic form" (Rojek, 1985, p. 174; see also Elias and Dunning, 1969, for a discussion of mimetic leisure). The answer to the question, is there an "ageless" definition of leisure, from this perspective, then, is no.

Thinking about this question from the perspective of the research on the sociocultural meaning and individuals' experiences of age provides additional insight into these contentions. According to some (e.g., Giele, 1980), chronological age is increasingly irrelevant to how people live out their lives. Giele attributes this to increased societal complexity and technological advancements. Research on identity in later life from both psychological and sociological perspectives does suggest that individuals have an "ageless" sense of self (Atchley, 1993; Kauffman, 1986). In fact, in her re-

search with older adults Kauffman found that: "This [feelings of being old or thoughts about one's age] is always variable, and in my experience, it is never emphasized. Being old per se is not a central feature of the self, nor is it a source of meaning" (1993, p. 17). However, others contend that age is both more and less important than it has been in the past (Neugarten and Hagestad, 1976). Indeed, while perhaps not a central determinant of one's sense of self, in age-stratified societies, actual and perceived chronological age is a basis of norms and expectations and, thus, of the allocation of rights, privileges, and responsibilities; that is, age shapes the distribution of power in age-stratified societies (Featherstone and Wernick, 1995; Kertzer and Schaie, 1989; Riley, Kahn and Foner, 1994). Further, structural and cultural lag (Riley et al., 1994) create a tension between individuals (of all ages) who are transforming the meaning of age and their societal and cultural contexts which are not responding to or prepared for this transformation. Two examples from the documentary video *Acting Our Age* (Aviad, 1987), illustrate this schism between the individual and an age-stratified society. In the video, which focuses on the lives of six diverse older women in the United States, one of the women talks about an experience she had soon after her husband died after a long illness. In an apparent attempt to offer comfort, a family friend told her that "now you can live for your grandchildren." "Like hell I will! To go from somebody's wife and somebody's mother to Tommy's grandmother? I won't do it!" was her response, not because she did not appreciate having grandchildren but because after years of being in her words "a waiter"—that is, someone who waited for her husband and children to come home and bring the outside world to her and then someone who waited while her husband died—she wanted an identity, a name, a life separate from family. In other words, while social norms may still suggest that older women should look to grandmotherhood for meaning and identity in old age, individuals are creating other options for themselves. Another woman in the video talks about being made aware of the images associated with her age when she called a senior center for information on Social Security. The person who answered her phone call provided her with the information she wanted and then asked, "Now do you understand all of this, dear?" Being addressed as "dear" and the assumption of being "stupid" was perceived as condescending and infantilizing, something the women talked about as a common part of their everyday experiences as older women.

Not only is there a schism between the aging individual and both societal structures and cultural norms and images, but as the years of healthy, functional living are extended for some, there may also be a tension between the psychological and corporeal self. Again, an example from *Acting Our Age* illustrates. One of the women talks about an experience she had when getting out of the shower. She reports that she stepped out of the shower, singing and feeling good, and as she was drying herself and putting lotion on her legs she happened to catch a glimpse of herself in the mirror. For a very brief moment she did not recognize herself. In her words, "who I saw in the mirror did not match how I was feeling inside." Physical selves, in terms of appearance and functioning, certainly do change with age, though there is tremendous variability in the onset, rate, and interrelationship of such changes. More importantly, the significance of such changes is culturally determined, not "naturally" mandated.

The idea that the body is physical capital (Bordieu, 1986; Shilling, 1993) provides interesting insights into the meaning of age and leisure, though this notion has received little attention in discussions of leisure and recreation in North America (cf., Freysinger, 1996). As explained by Bordieu (1986), when society places value on certain types of physical form, activity, and performance (e.g., through its valuing of certain types of work or leisure; through its promotion of certain types of bodies as attractive and its implicit or explicit denigration of other types of bodies as unattractive or problematic), it creates forms of physical capital. At the same time, what is valued is not static but changes over time. Yet, "[a]s people age, their capacity to produce and convert physical capital into other resources tends to decline" (Shilling, 1993, p. 139). Still, some individuals have more opportunity to convert physical capital into new and valued forms. However, according to Shilling (1993), all aging bodies are ultimately problematic for the individual because of "the ultimate resistance of the flesh to the reflexive constructions and demands of body projects" (p. 196).

It seems that age is both more and less important to individuals, society, and culture (Neugarten and Hagestad, 1976). The same could probably be said for its relationship to leisure. That is, as life expectancy continues to be extended (for some), as the years of "disease-free" life increase (for some), as economic and demographic changes—and the demands of individuals—alter social roles across the life course, and as cultural norms regarding age change, age will be less important to individuals' lives and leisure. At the same time, however, as long as age distinguishes individual and human maturation it will be given meaning. In North American and many other societies, that meaning structures social relations, institutions, and policy, and permeates cultural practices and power, including leisure.

How does an understanding of the social construction of age impact recreation and leisure service provision?

According to Maddox (1987), rather than being conceived and studied as an independent variable, age should be thought of as a dependent variable. That is, "the social meaning of age which is relevant to our understanding of the life course is not solely determined by biological processes indexed by chronological age" (p. 561). In fact, based on his review of the research on aging in later life, Maddox concluded that social status factors, such as occupation, income, and education—that is, those societal resources that we do or do not have access to across the course of life—shape both mental and physical health, cognitive functioning, patterns of social and leisure activity involvement, and retirement options and decisions in later life and, thus, the meaning and experience of being old. Further, social status factors are influenced by gender, ethnicity, race, and able-bodiedness, as well as age.

Such contentions do not deny the biological processes of aging. Rather, they highlight three things:

1. the modifiability of biological processes;
2. the arbitrary and ever-changing meanings and significance that are attached to those processes by society and culture across history; and
3. the inequities that exist in access to the societal resources that alter development and aging across the life course.

Considering these issues suggests that recreation and leisure programs and services can either serve to reproduce or perpetuate outmoded and often oppressive notions of age; or they can assist in educating about, challenging, and transforming these images and notions, as well as people's lived experiences. This does not mean ignoring the changes that age may bring. Rather it means thinking about who is advantaged and who disadvantaged by the meaning society gives to those changes. It means shifting our perspective and reframing the problems that we see. Social change and improvement of the quality of individuals' lives are purported to have been a part of the philosophy underlying the North America play and recreation movements from their inception. Just as we should think critically about how those goals were pursued and affected different groups of people and for what ends then, so, too, today we should continue to take time for critical reflection on, and discussion of, what it is those of us in recreation and leisure do and who is advantaged and disadvantaged by that. Rethinking popular notions of age and leisure is one place to begin.

References

Adams, J. (1978). Sequential strategies and the separation of age, cohort, and time of measurement contributions to developmental data. *Psychological Bulletin, 85,* 1309–1360.

Allen, K., & Chin-Sang, V. (1990). A lifetime of work: The context and meanings of leisure for aging black women. *The Gerontologist, 30,* 734–740.

Allison, M. T., & Geiger, C. W. (1993). Nature of leisure activities among the Chinese-American elderly. *Leisure Sciences, 15,* 309–319.

Anderson, D. F., Lorenz, F. O., & Pease, D. G. (1986). Prediction of present participation from children's gender, past participation, and attitudes: A longitudinal analysis. *Sociology of Sport Journal, 3,* 101–111.

Atchley, R. C. (1994, November). *Is there life between life course transitions? Applying life-stage concepts in gerontological research.* Presented at the Annual Scientific Meeting of the Gerontological Society of America, Atlanta, GA.

Atchley, R. C. (1993). Continuity theory and the evolution of activity in later life. In J. R. Kelly (Ed.), *Activity and aging* (pp. 5–16). Thousand Oaks, CA: Sage Publications, Inc.

Aviad, M. (Director). (1987). *Acting our age* [video]. (Available from Direct Cinema Limited, P.O. Box 69799, Los Angeles, CA 90069)

Baltes, P. B. (1968). Longitudinal and cross-sectional sequences in the study of age and generation effects. *Human Development, 11,* 145–171.

Baltes, P. B., & Baltes, M. M. (1990). Selective optimization with compensation. In P. B. Baltes & M. M. Baltes (Eds.), *Successful aging: Perspectives from the behavioral sciences* (pp. 1–34). New York, NY: Cambridge University Press.

Barnett, L. A., & Kleiber, D. A. (1982). Concomitants of playfulness in early childhood: Cognitive abilities and gender. *The Journal of Genetic Psychology, 141,* 115–127.

Berlyne, D. E. (1960). *Conflict, arousal and curiosity.* New York, NY: McGraw-Hill.

Bernard, M. (1984). Leisure rich and leisure poor: The leisure patterns of young adults. *Leisure Studies, 3,* 343–361.

Bialeschki, M. D., & Michener, S. (1994). Reentering leisure: Transition within the role of motherhood. *Journal of Leisure Research, 26,* 57–74.

Bialeschki, M. D., & Pearce, K. D. (1997). "I don't want a lifestyle—I want a life": The effect of role negotiations on the leisure of lesbian mothers. *Journal of Leisure Research, 29,* 113–131.

Bordieu, P. (1986). The forms of capital. In J. Richardson (Ed.), *Handbook of theory and research for the sociology of education* (pp. 241–260). New York, NY: Greenwood Press.

Botwinick, J., & Arenberg, D. (1976). Disparate time spans in sequential studies of aging. *Experimental Aging Research, 2,* 55–61.

Bronfenbrenner, U. (1977). Toward an experimental ecology of human development. *American Psychologist, 32,* 513–531.

Buss, A. R. (1973). An extension of developmental models that separate ontogenetic changes and cohort differences. *Psychological Bulletin, 80,* 466–479.

Buss, A. R. (1979–80). Methodological issues in life span developmental psychology from a dialectical perspective. *International Journal of Aging and Human Development, 10,* 121–164.

Carnegie Council on Adolescent Development. (1992). *A matter of time: Risk and opportunity in the nonschool hours.* New York, NY: Carnegie Corporation.

Cavanaugh, J. C. (1990). *Adult development and aging.* Belmont, CA: Wadsworth.

Cheek, N. H., & Burch, W. R. (1976). *The social organization of leisure in human society.* New York, NY: Harper and Row.

Chodorow, N. (1978). *The reproduction of mothering: A psychoanalysis and the sociology of gender.* Berkeley, CA: University of California Press.

Cooper, K. L., & Gutmann, D. L. (1987). Gender identity and ego mastery style in middle-aged, pre- and post-empty-nest women. *The Gerontologist, 27,* 347–352.

Costa, P., McCrae, R., & Arenberg, D. (1983). Recent longitudinal research on personality and aging. In K. W. Schaie (Ed.), *Longitudinal studies of adult psychological development* (pp. 222–265). New York, NY: Guilford Press.

Crawford, D. W., Godbey, G., & Crouter, A. C. (1986). The stability of leisure preferences. *Journal of Leisure Research, 18,* 96–115.

Crawford, D. W., & Huston, T. W. (1993). The impact of the transition to parenthood marital leisure. *Personality and Social Psychology Bulletin, 19*(1), 39–46.

Csikszentmihalyi, M. (1975). *Beyond boredom and anxiety.* San Francisco, CA: Jossey-Bass, Inc.

Csikszentmihalyi, M., & Larson, R. (1984). *Being adolescent: Conflict and growth in the teenage years.* New York, NY: Basic Books.

Cutler, S., & Hendricks, J. (1990). Leisure and time use across the life course. In R. Binstock & L. George (Eds.), *Handbook of aging and the social sciences* (pp. 169–185). New York, NY: Academic Press.

Dempsey, K. (1989). Women's leisure, men's leisure: A study in subordination and exploitation. *Australian and New Zealand Journal of Sociology, 25,* 27–45.

Eagly, A. H. (1987). *Sex differences in social behavior: A social-role interpretation.* Hillsdale, NJ: Erlbaum.

Eisenhandler, S. A. (1989). More than counting years: Social aspects of time and the identity of elders. In L. E. Thomas (Ed.), *Research on adulthood and aging* (pp. 163–181). Albany, NY: State University of New York Press.

Elder, G. H., Modell, J., & Parke, R. D. (1993). *Children in time and place: Developmental and historical insights.* New York, NY: Cambridge University Press.

Elias, N., & Dunning, E. (1969). The quest for excitement in leisure. *Loisir et Société/Society and Leisure, 2,* 50–85.

Erikson, E. H. (1963). *Childhood and society.* New York, NY: Norton.

Featherman, D. (1983). The life span perspective and social science research. In P. O. Baltes & O. G. Brim (Eds.), *Life span development and behavior* (pp. 237–251). New York, NY: Academic Press.

Featherstone, M., & Wernick, A. (Eds.). (1995). *Images of aging: Cultural representations of later life.* London, UK: Routledge.

Freysinger, V. J. (1994). Leisure with children and parental satisfaction: Further evidence of a sex difference in the experience of adult roles and leisure. *Journal of Leisure Research, 26,* 212–226.

Freysinger, V. J. (1995). The dialectics of leisure and development for women and men in midlife: An interpretive study. *Journal of Leisure Research, 27,* 61–84.

Freysinger, V. J. (1996, May). *Studying gender and leisure in later life: Current issues and future directions.* Presented at the University of Georgia International Conference on Women and Leisure, Athens, GA.

Freysinger, V. J., Alessio, H., & Mehdizadeh, S. (1993). Reexamining the morale–physical health–activity relationship: A longitudinal study of time changes and gender differences. *Activities, Adaptation, and Aging, 17*(4), 25–41.

Freysinger, V. J., & Flannery, D. (1992). Women's leisure: Affiliation, self-determination, empowerment and resistance? *Loisir et Société/Society and Leisure, 15,* 303–322.

Freysinger, V. J., & Ray, R. O. (1994). The activity involvement of women and men in young and middle adulthood: A panel study. *Leisure Sciences, 16,* 193–217.

Fromberg, D. P., & Bergen, D. (Eds.). (1998). *Play from birth to twelve: Contexts, perspectives, and meanings.* New York, NY: Van Nostrand Reinhold.

Furlong, A., Campbell, R., & Roberts, K. (1990). The effects of post-16 experiences and social class on the leisure patterns of young adults. *Leisure Studies, 9,* 213–224.

Gibson, R. (1994). Reconceptualizing retirement for black Americans. In E. P. Stoller & R. C. Gibson (Eds.), *Worlds of difference: Inequality in the aging experience* (pp. 120–127). Thousand Oaks, CA: Pine Forge Press.

Giele, J. Z. (1980). Adulthood as transcendence of age and sex. In J. Smelser & E. Erikson (Eds.), *Themes of work and love in adulthood* (pp. 151–173). Cambridge, MA: Harvard University Press.

Gilligan, C. (1982a). Adult development and women's development: Arrangements for a marriage. In J. Z. Giele (Ed.), *Women in the middle years* (pp. 89–114). New York, NY: John Wiley & Sons, Inc.

Gilligan, C. (1982b). *In a different voice.* Cambridge, MA: Harvard University Press.

Gilligan, C., Lyons, N. P., & Hanmer, T. J. (Eds.). (1990). *Making connections: The relational world of adolescent girls at the Emma Willard School.* Cambridge, MA: Harvard University Press.

Gordon, C., Gaitz, C. M., & Scott, J. (1976). Leisure and lives: Personal expressivity across the life span. In R. H. Binstock & E. Shanas (Eds.), *Handbook of aging and the social sciences* (pp. 310–341). New York, NY: Van Nostrand Reinhold Co.

Graef, R., Csikszentmihalyi, M., & Giannino, S. (1983). Measuring intrinsic motivation in everyday life. *Leisure Studies, 2,* 155–168.

Griffin, C. (1981). Young women and leisure: The transition from school to work. In A. Tomlinson (Ed.), *Leisure and social control* (pp. 113–122). Brighton, UK: Brighton Polytechnic.

Gutmann, D. L. (1987). *Reclaimed powers: Toward a new psychology of men and women in later life.* New York, NY: Basic Books.

Haan, N. (1977). *Coping and defending: Processes of self-environment organization.* New York, NY: Atherton Press.

Hare-Mustin, R. T. & Maracek, J. (Eds.). (1986). *Making a difference: Psychology and the construction of gender.* New Haven, CT: Yale University Press.

Harrington, M., & Dawson, D. (1995). Who has it best? Women's labor force participation, perceptions of leisure and constraints to enjoyment of leisure. *Journal of Leisure Research, 27,* 4–24.

Harter, S. (1981). The development of competence motivation in the mastery of cognitive and physical skills: Is there still a place for joy? In G. Roberts & D. Landers (Eds.), *Psychology of motor behavior and sport* (pp. 3–29). Champaign, IL: Human Kinetics.

Havighurst, R. J. (1957). The leisure activities of the middle-aged. *American Journal of Sociology, 63,* 152–162.

Havighurst, R. J. (1973). Social roles, work, leisure and education. In C. Eisdorfer & M. P. Lawton (Eds.), *The psychology of adult development and aging* (pp. 598–619). Washington, DC: APA Press.

Havighurst, R. J. (1982). Life style and leisure patterns: Their evolution through the life cycle. *Proceedings of the International Course in Social Gerontology, 3,* 35–48.

Henderson, K. A., & Bialeschki, M. D. (1991). A sense of entitlement to leisure as constraint and empowerment for women. *Leisure Sciences, 12,* 51–65.

Henderson, K. A., Bialeschki, M. D., Shaw, S., & Freysinger, V. J. (1996). *Both gains and gaps: Feminist perspectives on women's leisure.* State College, PA: Venture Publishing, Inc.

Hendry, L. B., Shucksmith, J., Love, J. G., & Glendinning, A. (1993). *Young people's leisure and lifestyles.* New York, NY: Routledge.

Horna, J. (1989). The leisure component of the parental role. *Journal of Leisure Research, 21,* 228–241.

Horna, J. (1993). Married life and leisure: A multidimensional study of couples. *World Leisure and Recreation, 35*(3), 17–21.

Huyck, M. H. (1994). The relevance of psychodynamic theories for understanding gender among older women. In B. F. Turner & L. E. Troll (Eds.), *Women growing older: Psychological perspectives* (pp. 202–238). Thousand Oaks, CA: Sage Publications, Inc.

Iso-Ahola, S. E. (1980). *The social psychology of leisure and recreation.* Dubuque, IA: Wm. C. Brown Publishers.

Iso-Ahola, S. E. (1989). Motivation for leisure. In E. L. Jackson & T. L. Burton (Eds.), *Understanding leisure and recreation: Mapping the past, charting the future* (pp. 247–279). State College, PA: Venture Publishing, Inc.

Iso-Ahola, S. E., Jackson, E., & Dunn, E. (1994). Starting, ceasing, and replacing leisure activities over the life span. *Journal of Leisure Research, 26,* 227–249.

Jackson, E. L. (1990). Variations in the desire to begin a new leisure activity: Evidence of antecedent constraints? *Journal of Leisure Research, 22,* 55–70.

Jackson, E. L., & Dunn, E. (1988). Integrating ceasing participation with other aspects of leisure behavior. *Journal of Leisure Research, 20,* 31–45.

Jackson, J. S., Antonucci, T. C., & Gibson, R. C. (1990). Cultural, racial, and ethnic minority influences on aging. In J. E. Birren & K. W. Schaie (Eds.), *Handbook of the psychology of aging* (3rd ed., pp. 103–123). New York, NY: Academic Press.

Kauffman, S. R. (1986). *The ageless self: Sources of meaning in later life.* Madison, WI: University of Wisconsin Press.

Kauffman, S. R. (1993). Values as sources of the ageless self. In J. R. Kelly (Ed.), *Activity and aging* (pp. 17–24). Thousand Oaks, CA: Sage Publications, Inc.

Kay, T. (1996). Women's work and women's worth: The leisure implications of women's changing employment patterns. *Leisure Studies, 15,* 49–64.

Kelly, J. R. (1974). Socialization toward leisure: A developmental perspective. *Journal of Leisure Research, 6,* 181–193.

Kelly, J. R. (1996). *Leisure.* Boston, MA: Allyn & Bacon.

Kelly, J. R., Steinkamp, M. W., & Kelly, J. R. (1986). Later life leisure: How they play in Peoria. *The Gerontologist, 6,* 531–537.

Kertzer, D. I., & Schaie, K. W. (1989). *Age structuring in comparative perspective.* Hillsdale, NJ: Lawrence Erlbaum Associates.

Kivel, B. (1994, October). *The paradox of coming out: Lesbian and gay youth and leisure.* Paper presented at the Leisure Research Symposium, Minneapolis, MN.

Kivel, B., & Kleiber, D. A. (1996, October). *A qualitative exploration of lesbian/gay/bisexual youth, identity, and leisure contexts.* Paper presented at the Leisure Research Symposium, Kansas City, MO.

Kleiber, D. A. (1985). Motivational reorientation in adulthood and the resource of leisure. In D. A. Kleiber & M. Maehr (Eds.), *Advances in motivation and achievement: Motivation and adulthood* (pp. 217–250). Greenwich, CT: JAI Press.

Kleiber, D. A., & Kane, M. J. (1984). Sex differences and the use of leisure as adaptive potentiation. *Loisir et Société/Society and Leisure, 7,* 165–173.

Kleiber, D. A., & Kelly, J. R. (1980). Leisure, socialization, and the life cycle. In S. E. Iso-Ahola (Ed.), *Social-psychological perspectives on leisure and recreation* (pp. 91–137). Springfield, IL: Charles C. Thomas.

Kleiber, D. A., & Ray, R. O. (1993). Leisure and generativity. In J. R. Kelly (Ed.), *Activity and aging: Staying involved in later life* (pp. 106–118). Thousand Oaks, CA: Sage Publications, Inc.

Knox, A. B. (1977). *Adult development and learning.* San Francisco, CA: Jossey-Bass, Inc.

Kohlberg, L. (1976). Moral stages and moralization: The cognitive-developmental approach. In T. Lickona (Ed.), *Moral development and behavior: Theory, research, and social issues* (pp. 31–53). New York, NY: Holt, Rinehart & Winston.

Larson, R. (1978). Thirty years of research on the subjective well-being of older adults. *Journal of Gerontology, 16,* 134–143.

Lawton, M. P. (1983). Time, space, and activity. In G. Rowles & R. J. Ohta (Eds.), *Aging and milieu: Environmental perspectives on growing old* (pp. 41–62). New York, NY: Academic Press.

Lawton, M. P. (1985). Activities and leisure. In M. P. Lawton & G. Maddox (Eds.), *Annual review of gerontology and geriatrics* (Vol. 5, pp. 127–164). New York, NY: Springer.

Lee, Y., Dattilo, J., Klieber, D. A., & Caldwell, L. (1996). Exploring the meaning of continuity of recreation activity in the early stages of adjustment for people with spinal cord injury. *Leisure Sciences, 18,* 209–225.

Loevinger, J. (1976). *Ego development: Conceptions and theories.* San Francisco, CA: Jossey-Bass, Inc.

Maas, H. S., & Kuypers, J. A. (1975). *From thirty to seventy.* San Francisco, CA: Jossey-Bass, Inc.

Maddox, G. L. (1987). Aging differently. *The Gerontologist, 27,* 557–564.

Maehr, M. L. (1983). On doing well in science: Why Johnny no longer excels, why Sarah never did. In S. Paris, G. Olson, & H. Stevenson (Eds.), *Learning and motivation in the classroom* (pp. 179–210). Hillsdale, NJ: Erlbaum.

McCormick, B. P., & McGuire, F. (1996). Leisure in community life of older rural residents. *Leisure Sciences, 18,* 77–93.

McGuire, F., Dottavio, F., & O'Leary, J. T. (1987). The relationship of early life experience to later life leisure involvement. *Leisure Sciences, 9,* 251–257.

McGuire, F., O'Leary, J, Yeh, C. K., & Dottavio, F. (1989). Integrating ceasing participation with other aspects of leisure behavior: A replication and extension. *Journal of Leisure Research, 21,* 316–326.

Neugarten, B. L. (1977). Personality and aging. In J. E. Birren & K. W. Schaie (Eds.), *Handbook of the psychology of aging* (pp. 626–649). New York, NY: Academic Press.

Neugarten, B., & Hagestad, G. O. (1976). Age and the life course. In R. H. Binstock & E. Shanas (Eds.), *Handbook of aging and the social sciences* (pp. 35–57). New York, NY: Van Nostrand Reinhold.

Orenstein, P. (1994). *Schoolgirls: Young women, self-esteem, and the confidence gap.* New York, NY: Doubleday.

Orthner, D. K., & Mancini, J. A. (1991). Benefits of leisure for family bonding. In B. L. Driver, P. J. Brown & G. L. Peterson (Eds.), *Benefits of leisure* (pp. 289–302). State College, PA: Venture Publishing, Inc.

Osgood, N. J., & Howe, C. Z. (1984). Psychological aspects of leisure: A life-cycle developmental perspective. *Loisir et Société/Society and Leisure, 7,* 175–195.

Pedlar, A., Dupuis, S., & Gilbert, A. (1996). Resumption of role status through leisure in later life. *Leisure Sciences, 18,* 259–276.

Rapoport, R., & Rapoport, R. N. (1975). *Leisure and the family life cycle.* Boston, MA: Routledge and Kegan Paul.

Raymore, L. (1995). Leisure behavior and the transition from adolescence to young adulthood. *Leisure Studies, 14,* 202–216.

Raymore, L., Barber, B. L., Eccles, J. S., & Godbey, G. (1995, October). *The stability of leisure behavior patterns across the transition from adolescence to young adulthood.* Presented at the Leisure Research Symposium, San Antonio, TX.

Riddick, C. C. (1993). Older women's leisure and the quality of life. In J. R. Kelly (Ed.), *Activity and aging* (pp. 86–98). Thousand Oaks, CA: Sage Publications, Inc.

Riddick, C. C., & Daniels, S. (1984). The relative contribution of leisure activities and other factors to the mental health of older women. *Journal of Leisure Research, 16,* 136–148.

Riegel, K. (1976, October). The dialectics of human development. *American Psychologist,* 689–700.

Riley, M. W., Johnson, M., & Foner, A. (1972). *Aging and society: A sociology of age stratification* (Vol. 3). New York, NY: Russell Sage Foundation.

Riley, M. W., Kahn, R. L., & Foner, A. (1994). *Age and structural lag.* New York, NY: John Wiley & Sons, Inc.

Robinson, J. P., & Godbey, G. (1993). Sport, fitness and the gender gap. *Leisure Sciences, 15,* 291–307.

Rodeheaver, D. (1987). When old age became a social problem, women were left behind. *The Gerontologist, 27,* 741–746.

Rojek, C. (1985). *Capitalism and leisure theory.* London, UK: Tavistock.

Rubin, L. (1976). *Worlds of pain: Life in the working-class family.* New York, NY: Basic Books.

Sales, E. (1977). Women's adult development. In I. Frieze (Ed.), *Women and sex roles: A social-psychological perspective* (pp. 157–190). New York, NY: W. W. Norton & Co., Inc.

Schaie, K. W. (1965). A general model for the study of developmental problems. *Psychological Bulletin, 64,* 92–107.

Schaie, K. W. (1983). *Longitudinal studies of adult psychological development.* New York, NY: Guilford Press.

Schaie, K. W., & Baltes, P. B. (1975). On sequential strategies in developmental research. *Human Development, 18,* 384–390.

Scott, D., & Willits, F. K. (1989). Adolescent leisure and adult leisure patterns: A 37-year follow-up. *Leisure Sciences, 11,* 323–335.

Searle, M. S., Mactavish, J. B., & Brayley, R. E. (1993). Integrating ceasing participation with other aspects of leisure behavior: A replication and extension. *Journal of Leisure Research, 25,* 389–404.

Searle, M. S., Mahon, M. J., Iso-Ahola, S. E., Sdrolias, H. A., & van Dyck, J. (1995). Enhancing a sense of independence and psychological well-being among the elderly: A field experiment. *Journal of Leisure Research, 27,* 107–124.

Seltzer, M. M. (1979). The older woman: Fact, fantasies, and fiction. *Research on Aging, 1,* 139–154.

Settersten, R. A. (1996). Tangled up in time and space. *The Gerontologist, 36,* 551–553.

Settersten, R. A., Jr., & Hagestad, G. O. (1996a). What's the latest? Cultural deadlines for family transition. *The Gerontologist, 36,* 178–188.

Settersten, R. A., Jr., & Hagestad, G. O. (1996b). What's the latest? II: Cultural age deadlines for educational and work transitions. *The Gerontologist, 36,* 602–613.

Shaw, S. M. (1991). Body image among adolescent women: The role of sports and physically active leisure. *Journal of Applied Recreation, 16,* 349–367.

Shaw, S. M., Kleiber, D. A., Caldwell, L. L. (1995). Leisure and identity formation in male and female adolescents. *Journal of Leisure Research, 27,* 245–263.

Shaw, S. M., & Smale, B. J. A. (1994, October). *Adolescent development and the psychosocial benefits of physically active leisure.* Presented at the Leisure Research Symposium, Minneapolis, MN.

Shilling, C. (1993). *The body and social theory.* Thousand Oaks, CA: Sage Publications, Inc.

Smale, B. J., & Dupuis, S. L. (1993). The relationship between leisure activity participation and psychological well-being across the life span. *Journal of Applied Recreation Research, 18,* 281–300.

Smith, E. A., Caldwell, L. L., Shaw, S. M., & Kleiber, D. A. (1994, October). *Development as action in context: Active and reactive leisure orientations among adolescents.* Presented at the Leisure Research Symposium, Minneapolis, MN.

Stanley, D., & Freysinger, V. J. (1995). The impact of age, health, and sex on the frequency of older adults' leisure activity participation: A longitudinal study. *Activities, Adaptation, and Aging, 19*(3), 31–42.

Stanley, D., Freysinger, V. J., & Horn, T. (1996). *Change in, and the impact of age, sex and functional health on, leisure activity participation in later life: A panel study.* Unpublished manuscript, Scripps Gerontology Center, Miami University, Oxford, OH.

Steiner-Adair, C. (1990). The body politic. In C. Gilligan, N. P. Lyons, and T. J. Hanmer (Eds.), *Making connections* (pp. 162–182). Cambridge, MA: Harvard University Press.

Sugar, M. (1979). *Female adolescent development.* New York, NY: Brunner/Mazel, Inc.

Unkel, M. (1981). Physical recreation participation of females and males during the adult life cycle. *Leisure Sciences, 4,* 36–58.

Ward, V. J. (1990). Racial identity formation and transformation. In C. Gilligan, N. P. Lyons, & T. J. Hanmer (Eds.), *Making connections: The relational world of adolescent girls at the Emma Willard School* (pp. 251–232). Cambridge, MA: Harvard University Press.

Wearing, B. (1990). Beyond the ideology of motherhood: Leisure as resistance. *Australian and New Zealand Journal of Sociology, 26,* 36–58.

Wearing, B., & McArthur, L. M. (1988). The family that plays together stays together: Or does it? *Australian Journal of Sex, Marriage and Family, 9,* 150–158.

Weiss, M. R., & Bredemeier, B. J. (1990). Moral development in sport. In K. B. Randolf & J. O. Holloszy (Eds.), *Exercise and sport sciences review* (pp. 331–378). Baltimore, MD: Williams & Wilkins.

Witt, P., & Goodale, T. (1981). The relationship between barriers to leisure enjoyment and family stages. *Leisure Sciences, 4,* 29–49.

Yoesting, D. R., & Burkhead, D. L. (1973). Significance of childhood recreation experience on adult leisure behavior. *Journal of Leisure Research, 5,* 25–36.

Yoesting, D. R., & Christiansen, J. E. (1978). Reexamining the significance of childhood recreation patterns on adult leisure behavior. *Leisure Sciences, 1,* 219–229.

Gender and Leisure

Susan M. Shaw

University of Waterloo

The growth of leisure studies as a field of scholarly inquiry has been paralleled by a similar development of women's studies and feminist research. Recently, men's studies has also emerged as a distinctive and identifiable area (Kimmel and Messner, 1995). This has led to heated debate about whether the focus of study should be women, or gender, or men and women, and it has also led to discussions about the terminology that should be used to identify this diverse range of research (e.g., women's studies, gender studies; see Richardson and Robinson, 1994). Whatever terminology is used, however, it is evident that the study of gender has emerged as an important area of academic interest and analysis.

Initially, the growing areas of gender studies and leisure studies developed quite separately from each other, and through the 1960s and 1970s research on leisure generally paid scant attention to the question of gender. However, starting in the early 1980s, awareness of the need to incorporate gender into leisure re-search began to emerge (e.g., Deem, 1982; Henderson, 1984). At this time, the androcentric nature of earlier research was becoming increasingly evident. For example, leisure activity lists used by researchers tended to focus on "male" activities and to ignore the different life circumstances and leisure experiences of women (Henderson, 1984; Shaw, 1985a). Moreover, work-leisure theories at that time ignored the different relationship that women had to the labor market, and their extensive involvement in family activities and unpaid work in the home (Deem, 1982; Gregory, 1982; Shaw, 1985b).

As a result of the increasing awareness of the importance of gender and the need to understand both women's and men's leisure experiences, a new body of research emerged that examined gender differences in leisure. This research explored gender differences in leisure meanings, leisure participation, leisure time, and leisure interests, as well as in constraints to leisure (e.g., Bialeschki and Henderson, 1986; Jackson and

Henderson, 1995; Shaw, 1985b; Witt and Goodale, 1981). Even in research not focused specifically on differences between men and women, gender was often included as an independent variable in the analyses in recognition that this might be an important factor to take into consideration (e.g., Searle and Jackson, 1985).

Throughout the 1990s, research on gender has progressed from this initial study of differences between women and men to a focus on the influence of societally based gender relations on leisure (see Henderson and Bialeschki, chapter 11 in this volume). This approach is based on the recognition that patriarchal power relations and ideologies about masculinity and femininity do not reside solely at the individual level, but are inextricably linked to broader sociocultural structures. The focus on gender relations means that *gender* is not seen as a fixed or static entity, but that social expectations, ideas about appropriate behaviors, and gender-based power relationships within social institutions are constantly being negotiated and renegotiated. Thus, research within this tradition goes beyond the simple analysis of gender differences to understanding the social context, and the changing social context, of women's and men's lives.

The gender relations approach also incorporates the concept of diversity both among women and among men. The emphasis on diversity arose because of evidence of the wide range of different life experiences among women (and men) from different age groups and social classes, as well as from different ethnic, racial, and cultural backgrounds (Henderson, Bialeschki, Shaw and Freysinger, 1996). At the same time, this approach also recognized certain commonalities among people of the same gender due to overarching societal ideologies and structures.

The gender relations perspective, by emphasizing cultural components of gender, has greatly advanced the study of gender and leisure. It has served to emphasize that neither leisure nor gender can be understood in isolation from other aspects of society, and that both need to be considered within particular cultural and historical contexts. This, in turn, suggests that the relationship between gender and leisure is both complex and dynamic. The relationship is not necessarily unidirectional, and it clearly varies within any one society as well as between different societies and historical periods.

While research on leisure and gender, especially research using a gender relations perspective, is a relatively new and evolving area of study, it is possible to identify three main themes that have emerged over the years. The first theme focuses on activity participation, and includes research on the extent to which activities are gender stereotyped as well as on gender differences in opportunities, experiences, and time for leisure. The second theme revolves around the issue of the gendered nature of leisure constraints, especially constraints relating to societal expectations about appropriate masculine and feminine roles. The third theme explores the gendered outcomes of leisure. Here, emphasis is placed on how leisure and leisure participation may act to reproduce structured gender relations in society through reinforcing (or resisting) dominant cultural attitudes and beliefs about femininity and masculinity. Thus, this third theme examines how leisure affects ideologies and gendered power relations rather than how gender affects leisure.

In this chapter, the contributions of research within each of these three themes to our understanding of the relationship between gender and leisure are examined. I will argue that most of the empirical research, particularly in North America, has focused on the first two themes, and that more attention needs to be directed towards the implications of the third theme. It is also evident that much of the research has focused on women's rather than men's experiences of leisure, and that the gendered nature of men's leisure also deserves greater attention.

The Gendered Basis of Leisure Participation

One approach to understanding the impact of gender on leisure behavior has been to examine gender differences in activity participation or in leisure time. Activity participation studies and time-use surveys have documented the higher participation rates of men in sports and physical activities, and the higher involvement of women in arts and cultural activities. But in many cases these studies have not shown any overall differences between men and women with regard to participation in free-time or recreational activities (e.g., Altergott and McCreedy, 1993; Kinsley and Graves, 1983).

On the other hand, studies which have used different techniques, and particularly studies which have focused on individuals' attitudes and reported subjective experiences, reveal a very different picture. When connotative definitions of leisure are used rather than activity definitions, time-budget analysis shows married women to have significantly less leisure time than married men (Shaw, 1985b). Similarly, studies which ask about time stress, lack of time for leisure, or the feeling of being constantly rushed have consistently shown women to be more likely than men to report experiencing this kind of time crunch (e.g., Firestone and Shelton, 1994; Frederick, 1995; Robinson, 1990).

In addition, life-cycle factors affect both men's and women's time use, and women who are mothers of young children, especially if they are employed, are clearly the group most disadvantaged in terms of time stress and opportunities for leisure for themselves (Frederick, 1995; Zuzanek and Smale, 1995). Qualitative studies exploring women's lives have also revealed the stress experienced because of lack of time, and particularly the difficulties that employed women face in coping with the "second shift" or the double day of paid and unpaid work (Deem, 1986; Hochschild, 1989; Shank, 1986).

Together these studies suggest that activity categorization in traditional time-use and survey research may be problematic because of overestimating women's leisure and failing to take the social context of women's lives into account. For example, a mother taking her young children to the playground or to the swimming pool may well experience this as "work" or "childcare" rather than "leisure." Studies that take account of these subjective experiences and contexts clearly indicate that gender does, in fact, affect not only the availability of time and opportunities for leisure, but also ways in which these are perceived and experienced.

Recognition of the limitations of examining leisure simply by looking at activity participation, combined with a move away from research on gender differences, has led to a greater focus by researchers on the social context of women's (and to a limited extent, men's) lives. The concept of gender relations implies the need to look at how people's lives are gendered and how they are affected by gender-based relations and gender-related ideologies in society as a whole. Thus, specific gender differences represent just one aspect of gender in our society.

Most of the research on the gendered nature of women's lives has focused on women's roles within the family. The holistic nature of many women's lives, and the difficulty of separating work from leisure, has been widely commented on (e.g., Allison and Duncan, 1987; Green, Hebron and Woodward, 1990; Gregory, 1982; Shaw, 1997). For women who are mothers, the ethic of care and responsibility for others often takes precedence over personal leisure needs. This helps to explain why family leisure activities can be experienced as "work" rather than as leisure by many mothers (Shaw, 1992); that is, family-related work includes the emotional work of creating leisure experiences and situations for other family members (Hunter and Whitson, 1992), as well as the more obvious work of household tasks. Thus, paid work, unpaid work, and emotional or interpersonal work can occur at the expense of women's own leisure.

Another approach to understanding the gendered nature of leisure has been through the study of culturally determined expectations and attitudes. This approach focuses on how gender-related ideologies affect the kinds of activities deemed to be appropriate for females or for males during leisure time. There is some research which suggests that individual gender role attitudes are as important as, if not more important than, gender itself in determining leisure behavior (Samdahl, 1992). However, the main focus of this approach has been on the macrolevel societal-ideological context which can also be seen to affect men's and women's leisure participation, rather than on the microlevel context.

Particular attention has been directed towards sports activities, and researchers have investigated the extent to which specific sports are seen to be gendered. In 1967 Methany argued that sports can be clearly dichotomized into those thought to be appropriate for males and those thought to be appropriate for females. According to Methany, "male" sports, such as football, rugby, hockey, wrestling, and boxing, are those that typically involve strength, face-to-face competition, and bodily contact. "Female" sports, on the other hand, such as gymnastics, figure skating, and synchronized swimming, are characterized by their lack of body contact and by their aesthetic nature.

There is evidence of continued gender stereotyping today (Helgeson, 1994), and that this continues to affect views about socially appropriate sports activities for each gender (Holland and Andre, 1994; Kane, 1988; Koivula, 1995). While some girls and women have entered the "male domain" of football, rugby, and hockey, opportunities for females in these sports are greatly limited, as is financial support and public recognition (Theberge, 1994). Some men also participate in "female" sports, such as figure skating, but again, opportunities are limited and social pressure or social stigma can affect participation and interest.

Other leisure activities are stereotyped too, though little research has been directed toward understanding the gendered nature of passive leisure, such as reading books and magazines, watching movies, or participating in hobbies and crafts. For example, while anecdotal evidence about "women's movies" suggests that these products are thought to be gendered, and are sometimes marketed as gendered products, the extent to which participation (i.e., watching movies) is gendered, and why it is gendered, clearly deserves more attention from leisure researchers. Similarly, the division of popular magazines into "men's" and "women's" magazines, affecting the display and marketing of these products as well, is a topic for further research. To what extent is readership actually dichotomized by gender?

Do women have no interest in topics covered in men's magazines and vice versa? Are stereotyped marketing strategies a *response* to different interests, or do they *create* these segmented market needs and interests?

Recently, emphasis on gender relations and on understanding the "postmodern society" has led researchers to look more closely at the issue of diversity. One of the problems of a gender difference approach is that it locates all men in the same category, and similarly fails to differentiate among women. While emphasis at the microlevel social context means that the different experiences of individual women should be taken into consideration, this does not necessarily ensure that diversity is a central construct or issue.

Taking diversity into account means recognizing that individual experiences and contexts vary. However, it also means that there may be identifiable groups who share some commonality of experience, and that shared as well as separate experience may be important in understanding leisure. Thus, cultural background may influence leisure participation, and at the same time gender attitudes within a particular culture may also be a significant factor. Research has shown, for example, that women immigrants from India have different attitudes toward leisure compared to White Anglo-Canadian women, and that their leisure behavior and participation are intimately associated with their attitudes towards gender roles, marriage, parenting, and the family (Tirone and Shaw, 1997). Age and social class also influence leisure behavior and have differential effects on women and men. Again, it is evident that the effect of age and class is due, in part, to different attitudes to such factors as expected family roles of men and women, as well as to attitudes toward paid employment and unpaid work (Freysinger, 1995). In addition, recent research has begun to explore the leisure experiences and participation of women who are lesbians to understand how the social context of their lives as women influences their leisure (Bialeschki, Pearce and Elliott, 1994). Thus, if research is to advance our understanding of gender, it needs to take both differences and commonalities into account.

It is evident from this brief review that understanding the impact of gender on leisure participation is not a simple matter of examining participation, activities, or time use. Instead, there is a need to examine both the microlevel and macrolevel social contexts of people's lives and the gendered nature of these social contexts. It is important to look at how these contexts affect not only activities and time, but also attitudes, experiences, and meanings. Moreover, while there are similarities among women and among men because of the location within the patriarchal order, there is also considerable diversity due to cultural backgrounds and other factors.

Researchers have begun to explore these issues, but a quick perusal of the research completed to date shows that it almost always focuses on women's lives. The gendered nature of men's leisure experiences and leisure participation, and the diversity among men in different social and cultural circumstances, remain largely unexplored territory. Perhaps it is time to explore not only why women's leisure revolves so closely around the family, but why men's is less family-centered. Do variations in gender role attitudes among men affect their leisure and family participation? Are changing attitudes and expectations about fathering affecting men's leisure experiences and choices? Does men's different relationship to the world of paid work affect their leisure differentially? To what extent do men's perceptions, experiences, and meanings of leisure vary, and what accounts for such variations? Moving beyond gender difference research raises more (and more complex) questions, but does not negate the need to explore the interplay between men's and women's lives and the effects of changing power relations on leisure.

Gender as a Constraint on Leisure

Leisure constraints can, in some ways, be seen as the "flip side" of participation or behavior. That is, women's and men's leisure can also be explained in terms of factors that reduce opportunities for leisure. These factors may prevent, reduce, or modify participation, or may adversely affect the quality or enjoyment of the leisure activities. Different types of constraints, for example intrapersonal, interpersonal, and structural constraints (see Jackson and Scott, chapter 18 in this volume), can affect men's and women's behavior in different ways. Most of the empirical research, though, has focused on structural constraints or factors that reduce participation in desired activities (Jackson and Henderson, 1995).

Paralleling research on participation, one approach to constraints research has been to examine gender differences in reported structural constraints. This research has shown, not surprisingly, that women are more constrained than men with regard to household obligations and family commitments (Horna, 1989; Jackson and Henderson, 1995; Searle and Jackson, 1985), and that these constraints are also related to family life cycle (Jackson and Henderson, 1995; Witt and Goodale, 1981). While reported time constraints do not always correlate directly with activity participation (Kay and Jackson, 1991; Shaw, Bonen and McCabe, 1991), the time constraints of employed mothers are evident whatever methodological approach is taken, and time is the most frequently reported *objective* constraint among women (Harrington, Dawson and Bolla, 1992).

Apart from the question of family and household obligations, gender difference research has revealed few significant differences in reported constraints between women and men (Searle and Jackson, 1985). This may be partly because within-gender differences are greater than between-gender differences (Jackson and Henderson, 1995). For example, economic constraints may be related more directly to social class, income, and single parenthood than they are to gender per se. The lack of gender differences in reported constraints may also relate to expectations and/or desire for certain types of activity. Thus, although there is unequal funding and provision of recreation sports opportunities for women and men, and unequal rates of participation (Hall and Richardson, 1982; Robinson and Godbey, 1993; Statistics Canada, 1994), there is little gender difference in reported lack of facilities and opportunities as constraints (Searle and Jackson, 1985; Shaw et al., 1991).

The research that has moved beyond gender comparisons, and has focused instead on the gendered context of peoples' lives, has provided greater insight into leisure constraints, particularly the constraints faced by women in their everyday lives as workers, mothers, and caregivers. Much of the literature on gender and leisure, in fact, can be seen to focus primarily on the way in which women's leisure is constrained, even though such literature does not explicitly incorporate a constraints framework (Shaw, 1994). Where a constraints framework has been used, researchers have not always attempted to categorize constraints as intrapersonal, structural, or interpersonal varieties, perhaps because of the overlap and the difficulty of clearly distinguishing these categories (Henderson and Bialeschki, 1993).

The research on constraints to women's leisure has revealed a number of constraints, not typically included in previous surveys, some of which are unique to women or primarily affect women. One constraint that has been shown to significantly affect the leisure lives of women is the ethic of care. When conceptualized as a constraint, the ethic of care is clearly linked to societal expectations about women's role expectations in the family. But it goes beyond the idea of constraints stemming from the time that women direct to household labor and family responsibilities, to include ways in which such responsibilities are internalized.

Thus the ethic of care comes into play as a constraint when women neglect their own leisure in order to provide for the needs—including physical, social, and emotional needs—of children, spouses, or friends (Henderson and Allen, 1991). According to Harrington et al. (1992), the ethic of care is the major *subjective* constraint that reduces women's enjoyment of leisure.

The ethic of care is linked conceptually and empirically to the concept of lack of sense of entitlement, a constraint which is also thought to disproportionately, if not exclusively, affect women (Henderson and Bialeschki, 1991). Research by Green et al. (1990) has described how some women feel and act as if they do not have a right to leisure for themselves. Moreover, this lack of entitlement is thought to be associated with the ideology of familism, which places emphasis on women's role as family caregiver.

Other constraints on women that have been linked to broader power-based gender relations, as well as ideologies about femininity and appropriate gender roles, are body image and fear of violence. Research has consistently shown women to have high levels of fear of violence (Statistics Canada, 1993), and this fear affects the quality of life that women experience in general, as well as their participation in and enjoyment of leisure (Whyte and Shaw, 1994). Body image, also, is an issue that has concerned many social psychologists and health specialists, because of its impact on young women's health and self-esteem (e.g., Garfinkel, Garner and Goldbloom, 1987). As a constraint on leisure, low body image, along with low self-esteem and lack of confidence, may reduce participation in particular activities, such as swimming or aerobics. It may also reduce enjoyment of these and other activities where the social context of the activity includes an overt emphasis on women's appearance, clothing, weight loss, or body shape (Frederick and Shaw, 1995).

The ethic of care, fear of violence, low body image, and poor self-esteem can all be seen as possible structural constraints (affecting participation) and/or interpersonal constraints (based on interrelationships with other) and/or intrapersonal constraints (reducing the desire to participate in particular activities). Indeed, the gendered nature of leisure constraints has become more evident as the concept of constraints has broadened to encompass interpersonal and intrapersonal as well as structural constraints (see Jackson and Scott, chapter 18 in this volume). Another factor, which has received less attention by researchers, but which may primarily act as an intrapersonal constraint, is that of gender stereotyping of activities. The extent to which leisure participation can be seen as stereotyped was discussed previously, but looking at this idea from a constraints perspective can add to our understanding of this issue.

The stereotyping of leisure activities, with some activities being considered appropriate for males and others considered appropriate for females, will inevitably affect expressed preferences. Even children as young as two years old have shown preference for "appropriate" gender-typed toys (Martin and Little, 1990), and this preference continues throughout childhood (Fisher-Thompson, Sausa and Wright, 1995). Teenagers and adults, too, typically express greater desire for "gender appropriate" activities than those deemed to be inappropriate. This may partly be an issue of skills (for example, women not having learned to play hockey; men not having learned to sew or to figure skate), but it is also manifested as a matter of activity preference. Cultural variation argues against a narrow biological explanation for such gender-based activity preferences. For example, field hockey is considered a male sport in some parts of the world, but is a female sport in North America. Thus, it would seem to be the stereotyping or the culturally determined views about appropriate activities for each gender that limit or constrain leisure options and leisure participation for both men and women. Individual gender role attitudes (Henderson, Stalnaker and Taylor, 1988; Kane, 1990) are also likely to be related to the degree to which stereotyping of activities affects participation or interest.

The idea of gender stereotyping as a constraint has been suggested in the literature (Crawford, Jackson and Godbey, 1991; Jackson, Crawford and Godbey, 1993), but little empirical research has been carried out on this issue. It may be, however, that such stereotyping has a stronger impact on males than on females. This is because of the greater stigma experienced by males if they are seen as "feminine" or "sissy" rather than by females considered to be "tomboys" (Feinman, 1981). Males may also experience higher levels of "constraints into" certain types of participation. For example, males may experience sports as a "compulsory activity," especially when they are young. Organized sports provide a way for boys to "prove their masculinity" to others, and also a way to seek approval from their fathers (Messner, 1994).

The constraints approach, in general, can be seen to provide a different and important perspective that adds to the growing understanding of ways in which gender affects leisure. Like the activity participation perspective, researchers have moved from the study of differences between men and women to studying the broader social context and ways in which gendered life experiences in a patriarchal society influence leisure. Also, like the activity perspective, almost all the research on social context has focused on women's rather than men's lives. With the exception of research on sports from a men's studies perspective (e.g., Messner and Sabo, 1990), little is known about how gender influences men's leisure activities, experiences or constraints.

The Gendered Outcomes of Leisure Practice

Research on leisure participation and leisure constraints examines ways in which gender—being male or female, or living in a gendered society—impacts on leisure. In fact, almost all the empirical research on gender and leisure, especially in North America, takes this approach and focuses on the effect of gender on leisure. However, given that gender is dynamic rather than static, and given that gender ideologies and gender relations are constantly being renegotiated, the relationship between leisure and gender is better conceptualized as bidirectional rather than unidirectional. In other words, leisure can also impact on gender, so that leisure participation can be expected to affect attitudes towards masculinity and femininity. Leisure activities, behaviors, and experiences, then, can function to reproduce or reinforce, or alternately to challenge or resist, patriarchal ideologies and dominant gender relations.

The impact of leisure on gender is both individual and collective. At the individual level, leisure experiences, self-expression, and the development of self-identity though leisure often involve the expression of attitudes and beliefs about femininity and masculinity. This expression leads to attitudinal reinforcement and internalization. In addition, interactions with others during leisure, including interactions with people of the same as well as the opposite gender, also reflect, reinforce, and sometimes challenge ideas about appropriate behaviors for women and men. These microlevel outcomes of leisure, though, also have broader societal implications. This is because individual attitudes and beliefs function collectively in the construction and reconstruction of gender ideologies and gender relations in the broader society.

One example of the reproduction of femininity through leisure is participation in the currently popular pursuit of aerobics. Aerobics classes and the atmosphere generated in these classes often promote the importance of physical appearance and the need for women to fit the societal ideal of the slim body image (Shaw, 1991). Thus, although aerobics participation for women may provide fitness and fun, another outcome of such participation may also be the reinforcement of women's concerns about their body image and the value society places on women's weight, shape, and appearance (Frederick and Shaw, 1995). In these ways, the very act of participation can be seen to be reinforcing traditional ideas about femininity. Of course, aerobics instructors, classes, and the atmosphere within such classes vary, so different classes may have different impacts on participants in terms of attitude reinforcement or change. Without more research looking at the specific ideologies associated with different activities in different settings and different social contexts, it is difficult to determine the gendered outcome of women's participation. However, it is evident that aerobics and other fitness activities are not gender neutral since they do, overtly or covertly, carry messages to participants about appropriate ways of acting.

Similar arguments can be made about the reinforcement or reproduction of masculinity through men's leisure activities, and perhaps especially through men's sports. Messner's (1994) research reveals ways in which organized sports for boys both reflect dominant concepts of masculinity and encourage boys to define themselves in these traditional ways. The rule-bound, competitive, and hierarchical world of organized sports, with its emphasis on conditional self-worth, is described by Messner and Sabo (1990) as a "gendering institution," and one which has a significant impact on both the individual development of masculine identities and the broader gender order.

Aerobics and sports are just two examples of ways in which leisure affects the construction of gender. However, many other leisure activities can be expected to affect ideas about gender as well, including common everyday activities like television watching, and infrequent occasions like celebrations and holidays. Much has been written about the sexism inherent in many television programs and commercials (e.g., Lovdal, 1989; Signorielli, 1989), but less is known about the impact of this leisure activity on individual and collective views of masculinity and femininity. Also, with the exception of Bella's (1992) book, *The Christmas Imperative,* there is a dearth of literature on the gendered nature of holidays and special occasions. Wedding showers and baby showers for women have traditionally focused on and emphasized the role of women as homemakers and caregivers. The male "stag night," on the other hand, promotes the idea of men as sexual predators and marriage as a loss of sexual freedom for men. While many women and men today reject these traditional forms of celebration, such events do continue, and the impact of traditional or nontraditional forms of celebration on participants' views of self or of gender are not known.

A related area worthy of further study is the reproduction of men's and women's sexuality through leisure. The image of men as sexual aggressors and women as sexual objects is frequently reinforced through various leisure outlets, including pornography, movies, and magazines as well as television. Psychologists have examined the impact of pornography on male aggression and violence against women (e.g., Malamuth and Donnerstein, 1984), but there has been less emphasis on the impact of the leisure use of pornography on men's and women's views of masculinity and femininity.

Leisure activities, of course, do not always function to reproduce dominant views. Indeed, because leisure is often freely chosen and self-determined, the potential for resistance to dominant ideologies is probably greater in this area of life compared to work, employment, or household labor. Wearing (1990) has studied ways in which young mothers use leisure to claim their right to independent, freely chosen activities. She has also explored ways in which young women sometimes develop leisure identities that challenge traditional views (Wearing, 1992). Moreover, according to Freysinger and Flannery (1992), self-determined leisure is more likely than affiliative leisure to lead to resistance and women's empowerment.

The distinction between the reproduction of and the resistance to dominant gender relations is sometimes difficult to determine. For example, in a research paper on elite women bodybuilders, Guthrie and Castelnuovo (1992) discuss whether the women involved can be characterized as resisting dominant discourses on feminine beauty, or whether their actions represent compliance. Similarly, male cheerleaders may initially be seen to be challenging dominant views of appropriate masculine behaviors, but a close examination of the activities they perform, such as lifting and throwing, and the distinction drawn between male and female cheerleading moves, suggests that this activity may act to reinforce rather than to challenge traditional conceptualizations (Davis, 1990).

Whether or not the distinction between reproduction and resistance is clear, and whether or not it is appropriate to dichotomize activities in this way, there clearly is a strong argument to be made that leisure does have an effect on gender. That leisure practices can affect both individual and collective conceptualizations of masculinity and femininity is evident, although the nature of this impact and the effects of different kinds of activities in different circumstances and social contexts remain largely an empirical question. The need to explore these gendered outcomes of leisure may be particularly important, given that leisure is less structured than work and that it is characterized by greater degrees of choice and self-expression. Exploring gendered outcomes may also be an important question to pursue at this point in time when gender relations in many parts of the world is currently contested territory.

Conclusion

The study of gender and leisure has shown significant progress over the last 15 to 20 years, but considerable challenges remain ahead. One such challenge is to understand cultural and individual diversity without losing sight of the importance of gender as an organizing principle. Another is to understand ways in which gender relations affect men's leisure lives without diverting attention away from the crucial issue of women's lack of leisure. A third is to explore the effects of leisure practice on the social construction of gender, and to incorporate understanding of the two-directional relationship between gender and leisure into our theorizing.

Addressing these challenges to research and theory also has implications for practice. Focus on diversity should enhance our understanding of the needs of women and men in different life situations. At present we know little about the types of social policies, recreation practices, or individual strategies that might address the needs of women living in poverty, of single parents or noncustodial parents, of First Nations communities, of survivors of sexual abuse, of women or men living with AIDS, or of people from diverse ethnic and cultural backgrounds. We do know that leisure practice is closely tied to the conditions of life and the social location of individuals, but finding practical and effective solutions depends on research aimed at understanding the role of leisure in diverse settings.

Research on men's leisure, too, will not only advance theoretical knowledge, but should point to the kinds of changes that can be made to enhance the leisure lives of both women and men. Men, as well as women, face gender-related constraints, and moving towards gender equity will involve changes in men's lives as well as changes for women.

Perhaps the challenge which will have the most dramatic impact on implications for practice is that of understanding the gendered outcomes of leisure participation. To date, most of the research on gender and leisure has pointed to the need to provide better opportunities for women to enjoy leisure, and to reduce the time stress and other constraints faced by women. While this is clearly an important issue, focusing on leisure outcomes suggests a need to direct attention towards leisure practices themselves. A critical analysis of leisure activities, ranging from high-school proms to basketball tournaments, from video games to pool halls, and from Internet surfing to family vacations, is required. Such analyses need to go beyond the conventional *benefits approach* which focuses narrowly on the positive outcomes of leisure for individuals (see Driver and Bruns, chapter 21 in this volume). Instead, examination of the gendered outcomes of leisure needs to address both negative and positive outcomes, both societal and individual outcomes, and to explore the impact of different types of leisure practice in different social and cultural contexts.

Some of this more critical work on leisure outcomes has already begun among leisure scholars in the United Kingdom and Western Europe. As Coalter (see chapter 31 in this volume) points out, "leisure studies" scholarship in Britain tends to put emphasis on the ideological and cultural context of leisure rather than on individual psychology. Thus, some British sociologists (e.g., Green et al., 1990) have suggested ways in which leisure functions to reproduce unequal gender relations in society. However, more empirical and theoretical research is needed, and such research needs to be applied to North American as well as to other cultural settings. An enhanced understanding of the gendered outcomes of leisure for women and men, for societal meanings of masculinity and femininity, and for the broader gender order in society has a number of implications for practice. These include implications for social action, for societal change, and for professional practice, as well as for individual decision making. Working to change leisure practice could become another way of working towards gender equity in leisure—and a way that complements and enhances existing initiatives.

References

Allison, M., & Duncan, M. (1987). Women, work, and leisure: The days of our lives. *Leisure Sciences, 9,* 43–162.

Altergott, K. C., & McCreedy, C. (1993). Gender and family status across the life course: Constraints of five types of leisure. *Loisir et Société/Society and Leisure, 16,* 151–128.

Bella, L. (1992). *The Christmas imperative.* Halifax, Nova Scotia: Fernwood Publishing.

Bialeschki, M. D., & Henderson, K. A. (1986). Leisure in the common world of women. *Leisure Studies, 5,* 299–308.

Bialeschki, M. D., Pearce, K. D., & Elliot, L. (1994, October). *"I don't want a lifestyle—I want a life": the effect of role negotiations on the leisure of lesbian mothers.* Paper presented at the National Recreation and Parks Association Leisure Research Symposium, Minneapolis, MN.

Crawford, D. W., Jackson, E. L., & Godbey, G. (1991). A hierarchical model of leisure constraints. *Leisure Sciences, 13,* 309–320.

Davis, L. R. (1990). Male cheerleaders and the naturalization of gender. In M. A. Messner & D. F. Sabo (Eds.), *Sport, men and the gender order* (pp. 153–161). Champaign, IL: Human Kinetics.

Deem, R. (1982). Women, leisure and inequality. *Leisure Studies, 1,* 29–46.

Deem, R. (1986). *All work and no play? The sociology of women and leisure.* Milton Keynes, UK: Open University Press.

Feinman, S. (1981). Why is cross-sex behavior more approved for girls than for boys? A status characteristic approach. *Sex Roles, 1,* 289–323.

Firestone, J., & Shelton, B. A. (1994). A comparison of women's and men's leisure time: Subtle effects of the double day. *Leisure Sciences, 16,* 45–60.

Fisher-Thompson, D., Sausa, A. D., & Wright, T. F. (1995). Toy selection for children: Personality and toy request influences. *Sex Roles, 33,* 239–255.

Frederick, C. J., & Shaw, S. M. (1995). Body image as a leisure constraint: Examining the experience of aerobic exercise classes for young women. *Leisure Sciences, 17,* 57–73.

Frederick, J. A. (1995). *As time goes by . . . Time use of Canadians.* Ottawa, Ontario: Statistics Canada.

Freysinger, V. J. (1995, May). *Studying gender and leisure in later life: Current issues and future directions.* Paper presented to the First International Conference on Women and Leisure: Toward a New Understanding, Athens, GA.

Freysinger, V. J., & Flannery, D. (1992). Women's leisure: Affiliation, self-determination, empowerment and resistance? *Loisir et Société/Society and Leisure, 15,* 303–321

Garfinkel, P., Garner, D., & Goldbloom, D. (1987). Eating disorders: Implications for the 1990s. *Canadian Journal of Psychiatry, 32,* 624–630.

Green, D., Hebron, S., & Woodward, D. (1990). *Women's leisure: What leisure?* Basingstoke, UK: Macmillan Publishing.

Gregory, S. (1982). Women among others: Another view. *Leisure Studies, 1,* 47–52.

Guthrie, S. R., & Castelnuovo, S. (1992). Elite women bodybuilders: Models of resistance or compliance? *Play and Culture, 5,* 401–408.

Hall, M. A., & Richardson, D. A. (1982). *Fair ball: Toward sex equality in Canadian sport.* Ottawa, Ontario: Canadian Advisory Council on the Status of Women.

Harrington, M., Dawson, D., & Bolla, P. (1992). Objective and subjective constraints on women's enjoyment of leisure. *Loisir et Société/Society and Leisure, 15,* 203–222.

Helgeson, V. S. (1994). Prototypes and dimensions of masculinity and femininity. *Sex Roles, 31,* 653–682.

Henderson, K. A. (1984, October). *An analysis of sexism in leisure research.* Paper presented to the National Recreation and Park Association Leisure Research Symposium, Orlando, FL.

Henderson, K. A., & Allen, K. R. (1991). The ethic of care: Leisure possibilities and constraints for women. *Loisir et Société/Society and Leisure, 14,* 97–113.

Henderson, K. A., & Bialeschki, M. D. (1991). A sense of entitlement to leisure as constraint and empowerment for women. *Leisure Sciences, 12,* 51–65.

Henderson, K. A., & Bialeschki, M. D. (1993). Exploring an expanded model of women's leisure constraints. *Journal of Applied Recreation Research, 18,* 229–252.

Henderson, K. A., Bialeschki, M. D., Shaw, S. M., & Freysinger, V. J. (1996). *Both gains and gaps: Feminist perspectives on women's leisure.* State College, PA: Venture Publishing, Inc.

Henderson, K. A., Stalnaker, D., & Taylor, G. (1988). The relationship between barriers to recreation and gender-role personality traits for women. *Journal of Leisure Research, 20,* 69–80.

Hochschild, A. (1989). *The second shift.* New York, NY: Avon Books.

Holland, A., & Andre, T. (1994). Athletic participation and the social status of adolescent males and females. *Youth & Society, 25,* 388–407.

Horna, J. L. (1989). The leisure component of the parental role. *Journal of Leisure Research, 21,* 228–241.

Hunter, P. L., & Whitson, D. J. (1992). Women's leisure in a resource industry town: Problems and issues. *Loisir et Société/Society and Leisure, 15*, 223–243.

Jackson, E. L., Crawford, D. W., & Godbey, G. (1993). Negotiation of leisure constraints. *Leisure Sciences, 15*, 1–11.

Jackson, E. L., & Henderson, K. A. (1995). Gender-based analysis of leisure constraints. *Leisure Sciences, 17*, 31–51.

Kane, M. J. (1988). The female athletic role as a status determinant within the social systems of high-school adolescents. *Adolescence, 23*, 253–264.

Kane, M. J. (1990, January). Female involvement in physical recreation—gender role as a constraint. *Journal of Physical Education, Recreation and Dance*, 52–56.

Kay, T., & Jackson, G. (1991). Leisure despite constraint: The impact of leisure constraints on leisure participation. *Journal of Leisure Research, 23*, 301–313.

Kimmel, M. S., & Messner, M. A. (Eds.). (1995). *Men's lives* (3rd ed.). New York, NY: Macmillan Publishing.

Kinsley, B., & Graves, F. (1983). *The time of our lives. Explorations in time use* (Vol. 2). Ottawa, Ontario: Canada Employment and Immigration Commission.

Koivula, N. (1995). Ratings of gender appropriateness of sports participation: Effects of gender-based schematic processing. *Sex Roles, 33*, 543–557.

Lovdal, L. T. (1989). Sex role messages in television commercials: An update. *Sex Roles, 21*, 715–724.

Malamuth, N. M., & Donnerstein, E. (1984). *Pornography and sexual aggression*. Orlando, FL: Academic Press, Inc.

Martin, C. L., & Little, J. K. (1990). The relation of gender understanding to children's sex-typed preferences and gender stereotypes. *Child Development, 61*, 1891–1904.

Messner, M. A. (1994). Boyhood, organized sports and the construction of masculinities. In M. S. Kimmel & M. A. Messner (Eds.), *Men's lives* (3rd ed., pp. 102–114). New York, NY: Macmillan Publishing.

Messner, M., & Sabo, D. (Eds.). (1990). *Sport, men, and the gender order: Critical feminist perspectives*. Champaign, IL: Human Kinetics.

Methany, E. (1967). *Connotations of movement in sport and dance*. Dubuque, IA: Wm. C. Brown Publishers.

Richardson, D., & Robinson, V. (1994). Theorizing women's studies, gender studies and masculinity: The politics of naming. *The European Journal of Women's Studies, 1*, 11–27.

Robinson, J. P. (1990, February). The time squeeze. *American Demographics*, 30–33.

Robinson, J. P., & Godbey, G. (1993). Sport, fairness, and the gender gap. *Leisure Sciences, 15*, 291–307.

Samdahl, D. M. (1992, October). *The effect of gender socialization on labeling experience as "leisure."* Paper presented to the National Recreation and Park Association Leisure Research Symposium, Cincinnati, OH.

Searle, M. S., & Jackson, E. L. (1985). Socioeconomic variations in perceived barriers to recreation participation among would-be participants. *Leisure Sciences, 7*, 227–249.

Shank, J. (1986). An exploration of leisure in the lives of dual-career women. *Journal of Leisure Research, 18*, 300–319.

Shaw, S. M. (1985a). The meaning of leisure in everyday life. *Leisure Sciences, 7*, 1–24.

Shaw, S. M. (1985b). Gender and leisure: Inequality in the distribution of leisure time. *Journal of Leisure Research, 17*, 266–282.

Shaw, S. M. (1991). Body image among adolescent women: The role of sports and physically active leisure. *Journal of Applied Recreation Research, 16*, 349–367.

Shaw, S. M. (1992). Dereifying family leisure: An examination of women's and men's everyday experiences and perceptions of family time. *Leisure Sciences, 14*, 271–286.

Shaw, S. M. (1994). Gender, leisure and constraint: Towards a framework for the analysis of women's leisure. *Journal of Leisure Research, 26*, 8–22.

Shaw, S. M. (1997). Controversies and contradictions in family leisure: An analysis of conflicting paradigms. *Journal of Leisure Research, 29*, 98–112.

Shaw, S. M., Bonen, A., & McCabe, J. F. (1991). Do more constraints mean less leisure? Examining the relationship between constraints and participation. *Journal of Leisure Research, 23*, 286–300.

Signorielli, N. (1989, December). Children, television, and gender roles. *Journal of Adolescent Health Care*, 1–9.

Statistics Canada. (1993). *Changing the landscape: Ending violence—achieving equality. Final report of the Canadian panel on violence again women*. Ottawa, Ontario: Ministry of Supply and Services Canada.

Statistics Canada. (1994). *Sport participation in Canada*. Ottawa, Ontario: Ministry of Supply and Services Canada.

Theberge, N. (1994). Playing with the boys: Manon Rheaume, women's hockey and the struggle for legitimacy. *Canadian Woman Studies, 15*, 37–41.

Tirone, S. C., & Shaw, S. M. (1997). At the center of their lives: Indo Canadian women, their families and leisure. *Journal of Leisure Research, 29*, 225–244.

Wearing, B. M. (1990). Beyond the ideology of motherhood: Leisure as resistance. *Australian and New Zealand Journal of Sociology, 26*, 36–58.

Wearing, B. M. (1992). Leisure and women's identity in late adolescence: Constraints and opportunities. *Loisir et Société/Society and Leisure, 15,* 323–342.

Witt, P., & Goodale, T. (1981). The relationship between barriers to leisure enjoyment and family stages. *Leisure Sciences, 4,* 29–49.

Whyte, L. B., & Shaw, S. M. (1994). Women's leisure: An exploratory study of fear of violence as a leisure constraint. *Journal of Applied Recreation Research, 19,* 5–21.

Zuzanek, J., & Smale, B. J. A. (1995, July). *Uses of time and changing perceptions of time pressure by different life-cycle groups: Recent trends in Canada (1986–1992).* Paper presented to the Thirteenth World Congress of Sociology, Bielefeld, Germany.

Ethnicity, Race, and Leisure

James H. Gramann
Texas A&M University

Maria T. Allison
Arizona State University

In July 1996 the final game of the U.S. Cup soccer tournament was played in the Rose Bowl stadium in Pasadena, California. The contest matched the U.S. and Mexican national teams and featured several stars from both countries. More than 98,000 spectators packed the stadium to watch the match that would decide the winner of the Cup. The demand for tickets was so great that seats which had been held back because they offered poor views of the playing field were released and sold to fans waiting in lines outside the stadium. Stadium workers scrambled to remove tarpaulins covering the bleachers as newly admitted ticket holders flooded into the sections during the game.

Was this incident a testimony to the surging popularity of soccer in a nonsoccer playing country? In part; but that is not all of the story. Most of these fans were cheering for Mexico. Mexican flags and other banners of green, red, and white overwhelmed the red, white, and blue in the stands. Despite the fact that the game was being played on U.S. soil, it was a home game for Mexico. The point is that, in addition to demonstrat-

ing the growing popularity of soccer in the United States, the overwhelming support for the Mexican national team attested even more strongly to the large Hispanic-origin population in southern California. Beyond that, it demonstrated the potential of leisure activities, such as attending spectator sports, to maintain and even strengthen ethnic-group identity in a multicultural society. In this chapter we examine the relationship between leisure and ethnicity, focusing on demographic trends, theoretical and methodological issues, the significance of ethnicity and race as forces shaping leisure behavior, and emerging theoretical and methodological issues that should be considered in the new millennium.

Demographic Trends and Their Significance

The increase in the ethnic diversity of North America is one of the most powerful demographic forces shaping

U.S. and Canadian society today. As the proportion of the population that demographers classify as *White* declines in the new millennium, ethnic and racial diversity and their societal consequences will become even more visible in public policy debates, and have even greater influence on the way we manage and provide leisure services.

The most significant growth of the U.S. population is occurring in its minority groups. Of the 70 million people projected to be added to the U.S. population between 1980 and 2025, 78% will come from increases in its minority populations (Murdock, Backman, Colberg, Hogue and Hamon, 1990). A major force behind the U.S. demographic transformation is the dramatic growth in Hispanic-American populations. Between 1980 and 1990, the number of Hispanic-origin persons living in the United States grew 53.1%, compared to a 9.8% increase in the population as a whole. Currently, Hispanic groups constitute the second largest minority in the United States after African Americans, but are projected to exceed African Americans in numbers by the second decade of the new millennium (U.S. Bureau of the Census, 1994).

Canada is also experiencing increasing ethnic diversity. After persons of English heritage, French Canadians comprise the largest ethnic group in Canada, making up 23% of that nation's total population (Statistics Canada, 1993). However, Canada is also a nation that is being profoundly affected by immigration, particularly in Ontario and British Columbia. Of the total growth in the Canadian population between 1995 and 1996, fully 46% was due to immigration, almost equal to the growth due to natural population increases (Statistics Canada, 1997). Even though, historically, the bulk of immigrants to Canada has come from Europe, immigration into Canada since the 1970s has been dominated by Asian and East Indian groups.

The geographical concentration of ethnic minority groups in the United States and Canada is striking. In U.S. states bordering Mexico, Hispanics (mostly Mexican Americans) substantially surpass African Americans, Asian Americans, and other minority groups in population size. The U.S. Census Bureau (1994) projects that New Mexico will have a Hispanic majority by the year 2020, making it one of two U.S. states—Hawaii being the other—to have a "minority" majority.

Mexican Americans are not the only geographically concentrated ethnic or racial group in the United States. Cuban Americans constitute an important population in south Florida, while Puerto Ricans are prominent in New York and New Jersey. The largest concentration of African Americans is found in the southeast-

ern states and also in the Great Lakes and mid-Atlantic areas. Asian Americans are most concentrated in Hawaii and California.

In Canada, by far the greatest number of French Canadians is in the province of Quebec, while persons of Asian and East Indian origin are found in large numbers in Ontario and British Columbia. These two provinces are also home to Canada's largest population of North American Indians (Statistics Canada, 1997).

The increasing ethnic and racial diversity of North America presents challenges, and thereby opportunities, in virtually every sphere of public policy, including education, job training, nutrition, healthcare, and recreation provision. Issues that exist today can be expected to increase in their scope and magnitude as we move into the new century. Burgeoning ethnic groups, which currently constitute growing consumer markets for some commercial recreation and leisure-travel industries, will become even more important in the twenty-first century. The work forces in these industries and in the public sector will become more racially and culturally diverse, as will the user populations at many public recreation areas. Colleges and universities in the United States and Canada, including programs in recreation and leisure, will continue to grapple with the best ways to adapt to increasing cultural diversity in the classroom, and with how to recruit and retain minority students more effectively.

The nature of this impact will likely vary from region to region within North America, reflecting the pattern of geographical concentration of ethnic groups. A major differentiation may be based on whether a region's ethnic diversity is a product of recent immigration. In parts of the United States, such as the Southwest where immigration is an important demographic force, political battles over English as an official language may be fought with increasing polarization, perhaps approaching the intensity of the language struggle in present-day Quebec. Leisure professionals may find traditional views of service quality increasingly challenged by minority groups who come from quite different cultural backgrounds. For example, customary definitions of a recreation center's or neighborhood park's service area may have to be revised to account for the shorter distances that many members of ethnic and racial minority groups are able to travel for recreation (Gramann, 1996). And as the soccer example at the beginning of this chapter illustrates, the demand for recreation activities that fall outside the Anglo mainstream may increase.

If the current gap between majority-group and minority-group members in access to quality educational and job opportunities persists, then many ethnic differences in the leisure-service sector will be reflected in divisions between administrators and staff, and between professional recreation providers and public users. These divisions will place a premium on the development and practice of effective intercultural communication, and on understanding culturally based differences in the use and meaning of both work and leisure time.

History has taught one lesson well: ethnic and racial divisions are among the most persistent and potentially divisive schisms within any society. Leisure educators and service providers should not expect to be spared the challenges, nor should they ignore the opportunities, that the expanding diversity of the North American population will furnish in the new millennium.

Conceptual and Theoretical Issues in Leisure and Ethnicity

Clearly, the ethnic transformation of North America is a significant issue as we move into the twenty-first century. But it is also an old issue. Differences in the recreation behavior of ethnic and racial groups have been the subject of research for more than three decades. Early studies in the United States (Mueller and Gurin, 1962) documented variation between African Americans and Whites in participation in both rural and urban recreation activities. In general, Blacks were found to have lower participation rates than Whites in most of these activities. Later research has expanded the scope of the early studies to examine differences between a greater number of ethnic groups, including Hispanic, Asian, and Native-American populations. Research on leisure variations within these groups, always a hallmark of recreation studies of White populations, is being extended to ethnic and racial minorities as well. More importantly, social scientists have been trying to understand the causes of ethnic group differences in recreation behavior and are addressing the public policy implications of these causes.

Defining Race and Ethnicity

A recurring criticism of research comparing the recreation patterns of different cultural groups is that researchers interpret racial differences as ethnic differences, thus confounding these two distinct concepts. Definitions of ethnicity focus on country of origin, language, religion, and other cultural traditions (Van den Berghe, 1976). In contrast, definitions of race are based on physical appearance, such as skin color and eye shape. Although many ethnic groups in the United States and Canada are also racially distinct, this is not always the case. The majority of French Canadians belong to the same racial group as most other Canadians. And Hispanic Americans (an ethnic classification) may be White, Black, or Asian. Thus, ethnic distinctions and racial distinctions are not necessarily the same thing.

In the 1990s the U.S. Bureau of the Census employed the following five racial and ethnic groupings in its population estimates and projections: White; Black; Asian and Pacific Islander; American Indian, Eskimo, and Aleut; and Hispanic origin. The first four of these are racial categories, while the last is an ethnic category that includes persons of all racial groups. However, the Census Bureau has been under continual pressure to modify its classification to capture more accurately the demographic character of the nation. One recurring suggestion is to follow the Canadian model and allow persons to specify that they are members of more than one ethnic or racial group. In the 1991 census, almost 29% of Canadians indicated that they were of multiple ethnic or racial origin. Thus, a person could say he or she is *both* Asian and White, *both* Hispanic and Black, or *both* Black and White.

Even though a multiethnic system more accurately reflects reality, if adopted it could have profound implications for social policy and for how the United States views itself as a people and culture. For example, a widely accepted practice in the United States is to classify anyone who is partially of African origin as Black. But what would happen if mixed-race designations became accepted? Would the political influence of African Americans in the United States diminish if a significant percentage of persons currently classified as Black were reclassified as mixed-race? On a more personal level, how would the public's image of mixed-raced celebrities, including Tiger Woods, the "Black" professional golfer, change, if it were emphasized that his racial background is predominantly Asian, with only one African-American relative on his father's side? It is a provocative and yet-unanswered question as to how the cultural world-view of the United States might change if the mixed-race and mixed-ethnic nature of the U.S. population were reflected more accurately in government statistics. Would this become a basis for greater tolerance between people of different racial and cultural backgrounds? Would it become yet another source of the prejudice, bigotry, and discrimination that have plagued the nation since its inception? Or would it have no impact at all?

Theories of Cultural Change

Throughout the history of social science, sociologists have attempted to understand and predict the consequences of ethnic change. Many "modernization" theories of the nineteenth century anticipated the disappearance of important ethnic differences in industrialized nations (Evans and Stephens, 1988). Culturally homogeneous mass societies were predicted to emerge, in part through the assimilation of ethnically distinct immigrant groups into host cultures, and in part due to the advances in communication and transportation that marked the Industrial Revolution.

Many later models of cultural change have also been driven, at least in part, by an assimilationist perspective. In particular, much mainstream sociological research in the United States is heavily influenced by the *Anglo-conformity* and the *melting-pot* ideologies (Gordon, 1964; Yetman, 1985). A basic assumption of Anglo-conformity is that, over time, ethnic minorities in the United States and Canada will be driven to give up their distinctive cultural characteristics and substitute those of the dominant Anglo majority. Conversely, the melting-pot ideology views assimilation as a process in which ethnic differences are shed in the creation of a new culture that is distinct from those that formed it.

A third paradigm exists, which is at odds with the Anglo-conformity and melting-pot models. This *cultural pluralism* ideology (McLemore, 1991) is based on the accommodation of ethnic-group differences within a single sociopolitical system. A variation of the cultural-pluralism paradigm has been labeled *selective acculturation* (Keefe and Padilla, 1987). Keefe and Padilla describe selective acculturation as a process in which certain strategic traits (such as the English language) are adopted quickly by immigrants because they improve economic opportunity, but other traditional cultural values, such as those pertaining to child-rearing practices, family organization, native foods, and music preferences are maintained. While it is argued that selective acculturation appears to characterize many ethnic minorities in the United States, several sociologists believe that it is particularly descriptive of the Mexican-American experience. Mexican Americans have felt pressure to conform to Anglo-American values, but also have maintained a distinctive ethnic identity by maintaining cultural ties to their Mexican heritage (McLemore, 1991; Teske and Nelson, 1976).

A significant criticism of the assimilationist perspective is that it does not apply to the contemporary experience of many ethnic groups which, in contrast to recent immigrants, have a long history in North America. These include Native Americans, French Canadians, Spanish Americans, and African Americans. In fact, rather than assimilating culturally into the dominant society, many members of established subgroups appear to be doing the opposite by emphasizing their ethnic or racial distinctiveness. A form of "ethnic boundary maintenance" (Barth, 1969) seems to occur, in which ethnic groups find ways to build and emphasize cultural differences between themselves and out-group members, while promoting cultural solidarity within their own group. This can be done through language, dress, religious practice, and even through the names that parents choose for their children.

Clearly, classic modernization and assimilation theories are inadequate for explaining the cultural differences that persist between some ethnic groups in values, traditions, mores, norms, and behavior. Rather than disappearing in the new millennium, these differences may become even more pronounced.

Leisure Expressiveness and Ethnic Consciousness

Although the presumption of assimilation that underlies the Anglo-conformity and melting-pot ideologies can be criticized broadly, it may be particularly inappropriate for understanding ethnic influences on leisure behavior. Sociologists (e.g., Kelly, 1987; Samdahl, 1988) argue that leisure has the potential to be both individually and culturally *expressive*. Even though some immigrant groups to North America may quickly adopt those traits of the dominant culture that have adaptive worth, over time leisure can remain an important social space in which traditional cultural values are tolerated by majority-group members, and are expressed and maintained within ethnic subcultures. As such, leisure may play a critical role in the persistence of ethnic-group identity, despite powerful trends towards Anglo conformity in the workplace, at school, and in other arenas of social interaction. From this perspective, the aforementioned soccer game between the United States and Mexico can be seen as an opportunity for Mexican Americans to express pride in their cultural heritage with little fear of social or economic sanction. More evidence for the role of leisure in expressing cultural values is considered later in this chapter.

Research that examines leisure and ethnicity is increasing in its quantity and theoretical sophistication. Before reviewing this literature, we must address several important issues that impinge on the practice of the research itself. The study of leisure and ethnicity is fraught with the potential for disciplinary, ideological, and methodological bias. These issues must be understood in order to evaluate adequately the current state of research on leisure and ethnicity.

Epistemological and Methodological Issues in Leisure and Ethnicity

Historically, race and ethnicity have been emotionally laden concepts. Stanfield (1993a) suggested that racial tension and conflict are continually reified through mass media and the consumptive nature of Western society. Images of race riots, community conflict and the like have become marketable commodities that foster the race-centered nature of today's society. Ongoing debates on discrimination, reverse discrimination, affirmative action, and quotas have become part of the U.S. psyche, and are becoming more overt in Canada. There is every expectation that these patterns will continue into the new millennium.

Only the most removed individuals can be isolated from emotionally charged thoughts and discussions related to race and ethnicity. What, then, is the role of the social scientist in trying to understand ethnic and racial influences on human behavior? How do social scientists deal with the politics of emotion that permeate society as we try systematically to understand the lives and perspectives of African Americans, American and Canadian Indians, persons of Hispanic origin, and other ethnic and racial minority groups? And how do we study the influence of race and ethnicity on leisure behavior within this context? Such concerns, often related to the power and privilege of those in the scientific enterprise, can form the foundation of nonconscious biases in race and ethnicity research. As Stanfield (1993b, p. 17) notes:

> Race saturated everyday language (verbal and nonverbal) reflects and determines how Americans describe themselves and others, especially others with distinctly different phenotypic attributes. Thus the tendency for descriptions of the phenotypically different other to be more socially intense, often negatively so, is the result of historical cultural traditions that encourage citizens to link phenotypic differences with presumptions about moral character, personality, interpersonal behavior, and intelligence. We do not and should not expect social scientists to be any dif-

ferent from other citizens in having been socialized to accept race-laden assumptions about the nature of the world and human nature; social scientists and their disciplines are also products of race-centered society.

If social scientists fail to address these concerns adequately, future efforts at significant and meaningful research will be thwarted.

An *epistemology* is the way in which we come to know those things around us. Our life experiences undergird how we think about things, the nature of the questions we ask, and how we interpret those things that we think about. Regarding race and ethnicity research, there are several epistemological issues that must be considered:

1. whose experiences are we codifying;
2. the oversimplification of the "other"; and
3. moral and ethical concerns.

Whose Experiences Are We Codifying?

An important debate in the social sciences centers on the ability of those who have come from positions of power in the dominant society to meaningfully understand the nature of the life experiences of oppressed or disenfranchised groups, including racial and ethnic populations, women, the poor, and the disabled. Many scholars suggest that science itself is the ongoing creation of intellectual and academic elites who continue to be socialized into positions of privilege and power. These individuals, it is argued, have little grounding in the lives of ethnic and racial minorities. Blauner and Wellman (1973, p. 329) state:

> There are certain aspects of racial phenomena . . . that are difficult, if not im possible, for a member of the oppressing group to grasp empirically and formulate conceptually. These barriers are existential and methodological, as well as political and ethical. We refer here to the nuances of culture and group ethos; to the meaning of oppression and especially psychic relations; to what is called the Black, Mexican-American, the Asian and the Indian experience.

Anderson (1993, p. 41) poses the question in a slightly different way when she asks, "Can dominant groups comprehend the experiences of outsiders and, if so, under what conditions and with which methodological practices?"

A related epistemological concern is that traditional approaches to science, exemplified by logical positivism, are based on the premise of objectivity and value neutrality. At their worst, such approaches foster a sense of detachment from human problems and issues, including those central to race and ethnicity (Oakley, 1981). According to Stanfield (1993a, p. 4):

> The study of racial and ethnic issues in the social sciences has remained deeply grounded in societal folk beliefs. Thus, conceptualizations of research problems and interpretations of collected data in racial and ethnic research often have been preceded by a priori ideological and cultural biases that determine the production of "objective knowledge." For this reason, the gathering and interpretation of statistical and ethnographic data in racial and ethnic research frequently serves to lend a professional gloss to what are in reality nothing more than cultural and social stereotypes and presumptions derived from historically specific folk wisdom.

Assuming the validity of the preceding argument, not only can ideological perspectives influence the nature of the questions asked by social scientists, but they also may affect the interpretation of findings as well. However, Anderson (1993, p. 43) suggests that there are strategies available that can improve the likelihood of meaningful inquiry into racial and ethnic questions:

> White scholars doing research on race and ethnicity should examine self-consciously the influence of institutional racism and the way it shapes the formulation and development of their research, rather than assume a color-blind stance. This is a fundamentally different posture from that advocated by the norms of "unbiased, objective" scientific research, in which one typically denies the influence of one's own status (be it race, gender, class, or other social status) in the shaping of knowledge. It requires that we see ourselves as situated in the action of our research, examining our own social location, not just that of those we study.

Researchers can no more shed their identity and ideological perspectives than can those they study. Yet it is possible to develop an approach to this research that is introspective and moves beyond the taken-for-granted methods and interpretations that have dominated past thinking.

Oversimplification of "Other"

One of the most blatant epistemological assumptions that is made in racial and ethnic studies is that racial categories can be used to infer a multitude of things about groups. What is a "White" person, a "Black" person, or a "Hispanic" individual? In Western society these labels have come to characterize a group's identity without careful analysis of what these concepts mean within the lives of those who are labeled. Survey respondents are asked to check a box that characterizes their ethnicity or race, the responses are aggregated, and a host of characteristics about a group are inferred based on their answers. Stanfield (1993b, p. 21) has referred to this process as the "fallacy of monolithic identity":

> Social researchers have tended to treat race categorization data as unproblematic. While qualitative researchers record subjects' experiences of feeling or being White or Black or of some other racial categorization, quantitative researchers embrace uncritically the statistical categories derived from government documents and survey coding. The vast majority of literature on racially defined populations in the United States is rooted in taken-for-granted objectified conceptions of racial identity.

A second epistemological problem is that racial categories are presumed to characterize an entire group of people. However, ethnic populations are not homogeneous, either in race, ethnicity, or class. Yet categories such as "Black or African American" are used to characterize and reify stereotypical images of one group of people. This overlooks the fact that most minority cultures, just as is true of the "White" culture, are composed of a combination of peoples of different backgrounds. For example, the term *Hispanic* fails to distinguish between individuals of Puerto Rican, Mexican, Spanish, or Cuban heritage, even though each of these groups comes from historically and politically distinct backgrounds. As Stanfield (1993b, p. 34) indicates, "The use of homogeneous and . . . reified terms such as *White* and *Black* buys into and indeed reproduces traditional racial stereotypes more than it facilitates adequate data collection and interpretation." Thus, the uncritical use of race and ethnic categories can lead to oversimplified views of behavior.

The preceding discussion is not to deny the potential utility of social-aggregate analysis. A basic foundation of sociological inquiry is that one's position in society affects one's life chances. All societies are stratified, with race and ethnicity being primary dimensions on which this stratification occurs. To be Black or White in North America has significant sociological meaning, with major implications for access to society's important institutions, including government, education, and the economy. The epistemological problem occurs when social scientists impose their own definition on what it means to be a member of another ethnic group, or when they treat minority groups as culturally homogeneous. The first step in avoiding this pitfall is to be aware that it can occur.

Moral and Ethical Concerns

In the moral and ethical domain, care should be taken to not exploit those who are studied (Dennis, 1993). Often, research has come to mean invading the world of others in the name of academic curiosity, then disappearing. At the very least, researchers should consider meaningful outcomes of their research that might improve the quality of life of those whom they research. As Andersen (1993) and Reinharz (1983) have indicated, the scientific process is an act of self-discovery as well as an attempt to learn about others. Self-reflection regarding one's privilege, motives, and approaches is essential to relevant and meaningful discovery.

Second, care must be taken not to exploit the power differences that eschew from the research-subject relationship. Researchers must be aware that because of their position in society, they have power (real or perceived) over those they study. Concern must be directed toward protecting the rights and integrity of the subjects of research. The human rights of subjects must be seen as more than an institutional exercise within the academic world (Andersen, 1993).

Finally, researchers must analyze carefully the nature of their own values and those of the agencies they work for and with. As Stanfield (1993b, p. 33) notes:

> Researchers who engage in racial and ethnic studies are involved in a highly controversial venture. For decades, much potential sobering knowledge about racial and ethnic issues has been either lost or distorted because researchers have failed to reflect on the implications of their life histories and cultural backgrounds as ideo-

logical intrusions in this emotion-laden field of study.

To do any less is to run the risk of adding to the stereotypes and misrepresentations that exist about ethnic populations, rather than enhancing understanding and discovery.

Although the concerns raised here may make the study of ethnic and racial populations appear daunting, solid qualitative and quantitative research is possible. Key issues to consider include:

1. the need to remain reflective about issues of race and ethnicity within our own life histories;
2. the need to critically question the role and quality of our own research within changing social contexts;
3. the need to increase the use of participatory research that helps subjects enhance the quality of their lives as a result of involvement in the research process;
4. the need to move beyond simplistic social-aggregate models (e.g., "check the box") and utilize multiple-method approaches that enhance insight into the lives of ethnic and racial minority-group members; and
5. the need to design studies that allow subjects to serve as "experts" to inform researchers about their lives, rather than focusing on what the social scientist thinks is relevant.

These issues, if kept foremost in the minds of researchers, may help ensure that the study of leisure and ethnicity is relevant and grounded in the reality of those studied.

Major Themes of Research on Leisure and Ethnicity

A comprehensive understanding of the nature and meaning of leisure in the lives of racial and ethnic populations is still lacking. Research during the 1960s and 1970s focused on recreational differences between African Americans and Whites, while more recent research in the United States has examined the nature of recreation among the fast-growing Hispanic populations. However, there is still little research on Native Americans, Asian Americans, and the large number of new immigrant groups to the United States and Canada.

Racial and Ethnic Differences in Leisure Participation

Most social science research on ethnicity and leisure has focused on differences in outdoor recreation participation between ethnic and racial groups. Early research utilized a social-aggregate approach (Allison, 1988; Kelly, 1980; O'Leary and Benjamin, 1982; Washburne, 1978; Washburne and Wall, 1980), comparing Blacks and Whites on recreational activity patterns and preferences. A growing body of current work focuses on the outdoor recreation behavior of Mexican Americans. In general, results have revealed that racial and ethnic differences exist in outdoor recreation participation patterns. In particular, ethnic minority-group members tend to participate less frequently than Whites in a wide range of outdoor activities. Reasons for these differences continue to be the focus of much of the current research.

Two contrasting explanations have been advanced for differences in recreation participation rates between ethnic groups. The first explanation is termed the "marginality" (or opportunity) thesis. It suggests that ethnic and racial differences are a function of poverty and discrimination against minority groups by the majority group (Washburne, 1978). *Underparticipation* in some activities by minority populations is explained as a function of their marginal position in society (e.g., discrimination, inadequate transportation, underdeveloped programs, lack of facilities) that reduces the opportunity to take part in desired forms of recreation. Differences in participation reflect not only differences in socioeconomic status, but also a history of inequitable treatment in recreation resource allocation and opportunity.

The second explanation for participation differences is termed the *ethnicity* (or subcultural) thesis (Washburne, 1978). This view states that ethnic and racial differences in participation are a function of culturally based value systems, norms, and leisure socialization patterns, rather than being a function of socioeconomic differences. The ethnicity thesis assumes that ethnic groups preserve a distinct subcultural identity and integrity, while at the same time maintaining contact and interaction with the dominant mainstream.

The predominant method of testing the marginality and ethnicity theses has been through the use of social-class indicators. The marginality thesis is tenable if it is found that minority-group underparticipation in certain activities is the result of poverty and other forms of socioeconomic disadvantage and discrimination. However, once these socioeconomic differences are controlled, differences in participation rates should disappear. On the other hand, if the ethnicity thesis is the more viable explanation, cultural differences in participation should persist, with or without differences in socioeconomic patterns. For example, if participation differences are found between African Americans and Whites of the same socioeconomic level, it would be assumed that some other explanation for these differences (e.g., ethnicity) must exist. That is, the differences between groups are a function of cultural tradition, values, mores, norms, and beliefs and are not due to socioeconomic factors affecting the opportunity to participate.

Among the few studies that have tested the marginality-ethnicity framework, most have found support for the ethnicity thesis (Allison, 1988; Dragon, 1986; Dwyer and Hutchison, 1990; Klobus-Edwards, 1981; O'Leary and Benjamin, 1982; Stamps and Stamps, 1985; Washburne, 1978). For example, Dragon (1986) identified distinct cultural differences between Native Americans and White Americans in the meanings each attached to the use of national parks. Kelly (1980), O'Leary and Benjamin (1982) and Washburne (1978) found that African Americans were consistently underrepresented in outdoor recreation pursuits, even when residence and socioeconomic variables that might affect opportunity were controlled. Stamps and Stamps (1985) attempted to identify the degree to which residence in an integrated community would influence the recreational participation of African Americans and Whites. They found that, regardless of social class and living environment, African Americans were more similar to each other in recreational pursuits than they were to Whites. The authors concluded that ethnicity and related cultural values were more powerful than social class and residence in accounting for recreation behavior. Dwyer (1994) compared the participation patterns of Whites, African Americans, Hispanic Americans, and Asian Americans. After controlling for income, age, gender, household size, and location of residence, Dwyer still found significant differences in the participation patterns of some of the groups, providing indirect support for the importance of cultural values in affecting leisure behavior.

Despite this empirical support for the ethnicity thesis, other data confound a straightforward acceptance of one hypothesis over the other. In searching for statistically significant differences, researchers tend to gloss over similarities between groups. For example, in Dwyer's 1994 study it was found that Asian Americans and Whites differed in their participation rates in only three of 24 activities. Hispanic Americans differed from Whites in only four activities. Does this mean that the ethnicity thesis applies to some ethnic groups but not to others? Or are the "similarities" really that? Evidence from qualitative studies of ethnicity and leisure shows that even though two ethnic groups may participate in the same activities, the cultural *meanings* of this participation may differ. Hence, although both Chinese Americans and White Americans may garden, the former group may do it as a way to raise food for traditional Chinese meals, thus maintaining a tie to their native heritage (Allison and Geiger, 1993).

In summary, the marginality and ethnicity hypotheses continue as possible explanations for ethnic and racial differences in recreation behavior. Nevertheless, these two explanations are simplistic versions of actual social processes. Social class does have a powerful influence on behavior. When people, regardless of their race or ethnicity, have limited access, resources, and opportunities to learn and engage in recreational pursuits, their participation will usually be low. Neither can one ignore the powerful influence that one's cultural subgroup has on behavior. Our actions are bounded by values, norms, and expectations that are central to the cultural-transmission process. Cultural identity is not something that is shed when income increases, so it is not surprising that ethnically and racially based differences in recreation participation persist between persons of similar socioeconomic status.

Recent research has proposed new explanations that may also help explain ethnic and racial differences in leisure patterns. Two of these explanations are: (1) the influence of real and perceived discrimination on recreation participation; and (2) recreational pursuits as expressive models of culture.

Perceived Discrimination

Only recently have individual and institutional discrimination been analyzed as factors affecting the leisure behavior of ethnic and racial minorities. The study of discrimination and prejudice is frequently an uncomfortable, value-laden, and difficult undertaking, so researchers tend to avoid it. Despite this, there are a few studies that have focused on the perception of prejudice and how it affects recreation participation. Gobster and Delgado (1992) reported that 10% of the ethnic minority-group users of Chicago's Lincoln Park stated that they had been discriminated against, either by other users or by the police. Reports of discrimination were highest among African Americans (14%), followed by Asian Americans (9%) and Hispanics (7%).

West (1993) speculated that African Americans still fear the potential for discrimination and bigotry in trips through unknown terrain. He reported the reluctance of several African-American youth to travel to Gateway National Recreation Area near New York City be-

cause of the fear of having to cross through unfamiliar "White" territory. He cited other forms of racism as well: "A Black park user in Seattle was racially murdered by a neo-Nazi group; a city park in Chicago had signs posted saying 'Whites only; niggers keep out'" (West, 1993, p. 110). Blahna and Black (1992) and Wallace and Witter (1992) found that Blacks or Hispanics did not visit or camp in particular areas because of perceived discrimination. Again, the most frequently reported sources were either other visitors or the police.

Chavez (1991, 1993) surveyed visitors to a wildland recreation area in southern California. She reported that Hispanics were more likely than Anglos to perceive high levels of discrimination. The primary source was reported to be law enforcement officers, followed by other visitors.

For some groups, the degree of assimilation may affect perceptions of discrimination. Floyd and Gramann (1995) found that Mexican Americans with higher levels of education (socioeconomic assimilation) and who relied more on the English language (an indicator of cultural assimilation) were less likely to report discrimination in recreation settings than their less-assimilated counterparts.

Schreyer and Knopf (1984) argued that people avoid or change their use of certain recreation areas because they believe that the areas have acquired undesirable characteristics. This proposition can be applied to the use of recreation spaces by specific ethnic or racial groups (Gramann, 1996). People may avoid areas where they expect to experience discrimination, or a locale may develop an identity as a site providing the types of experiences desired by a particular group (Williams and Carr, 1993). Members of the "possessing group" lay informal claim to the territory, while other groups learn to stay away from the area. Chavez and colleagues (Chavez, Baas and Winter, 1993; Chavez and Winter, 1993) noted how a recreation area near Los Angeles shifted from a predominantly Anglo-identified area to one that was dominated by Hispanic users. This had significant implications for how the site was managed because the Hispanic users tended to visit in larger groups and stay longer, putting pressure on parking-lot capacity. They also desired a higher level of facility development than did the previous user group.

To date, the study of perceived discrimination has focused almost entirely on user perceptions. Little research has been done to identify how agencies, either implicitly or explicitly, erect institutional barriers that inhibit access to programs. More investigation in the entire area of discrimination and prejudice is essential.

Leisure and the Expression of Culture

One of the criticisms of the marginality thesis is that it is based on an assimilationist paradigm that assumes that if socioeconomic differences between groups disappear, then ethnically based differences in recreation preferences and participation will become less prominent. Although the marginality thesis has provided theoretically interesting and policy-relevant comparisons between groups, it has failed to address the extent to which ethnicity may affect the cultural *meanings* attached to participation in recreation activities. This has obvious implications for surveys that show participation similarities between groups in some activities. Does this mean that the groups really are the same in their use of leisure? Not necessarily.

The cultural pluralism model of ethnic differences implies that leisure, as part of the expressive domain of human interaction, is part of the culture-creation process (Allison, 1988; Kelly, 1983). Because two ethnic groups participate in the same activities does not mean that the activities are perceived in the same way by each group. In fact, similar activities may hold very different meanings for different populations. Allison (1980, 1982) described how Navajo youth transformed their informal game of basketball in a way consistent with the collectivist values of the Navajo culture. The Navajo youth indicated they found their style of play to be much more fun. Similar patterns of cultural expression were found by several other investigators analyzing the nature of play among Native-American groups (Blanchard, 1974; Farrer, 1976; Tindall, 1973) and among African-American youth engaged in pickup basketball (Wyatt, 1976). This pattern is reflected at the international level in the nature of baseball in Japan. Consistent with the Japanese collectivist value orientation, Japanese rules and strategy (e.g., playing for ties) are quite distinct from Anglo-American baseball. Yet the fact that the Japanese adopted American baseball would hardly be proof that they were assimilating into American culture. In general, these data suggest that play and leisure, like other forms of expression, are products of the cultural milieu in which they are found. Thus, leisure patterns are emergent and dynamic and variants that occur between ethnic groups are as dynamic as those that take place within Anglo populations (Allison, 1988).

Another example that reflects the cultural grounding of participation patterns is the family-oriented nature of recreation among many Hispanic groups. Hispanic Americans frequently engage in recreation activities with extended-family members, more so than

do Anglos and African Americans (Carr and Williams, 1993; Hutchison, 1987; Irwin, Gartner and Phelps, 1990). One consequence is that Hispanic-American groups tend to be of larger size. For example, Hutchison (1987) found that Mexican-American groups in Chicago parks averaged 5.7 persons, while Anglo groups averaged only 2.5. Gramann (1996) pointed out that this size differential has created difficulties for managers who typically plan for smaller groups in their areas and often restrict group size by limiting the number of people and vehicles in some types of areas.

Finally, work by Allison and Geiger (1993) among Chinese-American elderly indicated that although many forms of leisure activity participated in by these individuals appeared to be no different from those of Anglo elderly individuals (sewing, walking, gardening, reading, television watching), closer examination revealed that many activities were bound up with Chinese-oriented content and meaning. For example, gardening was perceived as an opportunity to grow Chinese vegetables not readily available in the United States. Sewing provided the means to make traditional and festive clothes. Reading furnished the chance to learn English, but also was a way to keep up with news in China through Chinese newspapers. Thus, despite the fact that many of the Chinese had lived in the United States for 20 years or more, they still utilized much of their recreation activity to express their Chinese heritage. Clearly, similarity in leisure activities between Anglo Americans and Chinese Americans hardly implies complete cultural assimilation by the latter group.

In summary, research shows that much of leisure can be culturally expressive. Although Anglo activities might be adopted by an ethnic group, much of the meaning of the activity may be transformed to fit the distinctive cultural milieu of the participant population.

Leisure and Selective Acculturation

Other research has examined the process of selective acculturation and its relationship to leisure meaning among Hispanic Americans. The hypothesis guiding this research is that, in some cases, ethnic minorities will become more "Anglo-like" in their recreation as their assimilation into Anglo society increases, but that recreation behavior that expresses core cultural values, such as a value on the extended family, will be maintained, despite assimilation pressures. Cultural assimilation is usually measured in these studies by the number of generations a family has lived in the

United States, or by the use of Spanish versus English in everyday settings (Gramann, 1996).

Gramann, Floyd, and Saenz (1993) examined the effect of Hispanic-American acculturation on the importance of family-related and nature-related experiences in outdoor recreation. The investigators found that family experiences were most important to highly acculturated Mexican Americans. They were least important to Anglos and the less-acculturated Mexican Americans. The researchers explained this paradox in terms of selective acculturation and the disrupting effect of immigration on local family ties. The least acculturated respondents were mostly immigrants, and would not be expected to have extensive local family networks. Thus, family experiences in outdoor recreation might be less relevant to this group. However, over time kin networks could be rebuilt in the United States so that the Hispanic-American value of familism could be reexpressed in the recreational styles of subsequent generations. This would explain the greater importance of familism to the most acculturated Mexican Americans. Thus, outdoor recreation appeared to provide an opportunity for certain central values of Hispanic culture to be maintained, despite assimilation on other cultural dimensions, such as language.

In a finding somewhat at odds with that of Gramann et al., Carr and Williams (1993) reported a relationship between the "generational tenure" of Mexican-origin populations and social-group composition. Although Mexican Americans were more likely than Anglos to visit recreation areas with their families, the variation within the Mexican population was substantial. In particular, the proportion who visited with friends increased directly with longer generational tenure in the United States, so that by the second U.S.–born generation the Mexican-American incidence of visiting with friends was more similar to that of Anglos than to less-assimilated Mexicans.

The mixed results from selective-acculturation research indicates that the role of leisure in this process is not well-understood. Although leisure may hold the potential for cultural expression, this potential may not always be realized, or even sought. In fact, it seems reasonable to suggest that in some cases, particularly among young children, leisure may be a critical mechanism of cultural assimilation. In any event, research on selective acculturation does underline an important aspect of ethnicity in North America: ethnic groups are not culturally homogeneous blocs. Cultural variation may occur within a group based on differences in members' level of assimilation into the majority-group society.

Ethnic Boundary Maintenance

A final explanation for the diversity of leisure patterns identified between ethnic groups is that subcultures create boundaries around themselves to highlight differences. Indeed, many definitions of *ethnic group* include the notion that members of the group must be conscious of being at least somewhat different from other groups (Van den Berghe, 1976).

In his analysis of interethnic contact, Barth (1969) suggested that groups find ways through their daily interactions with others to construct and highlight ethnic differences. Ethnic identification (and this can include identification as White or Anglo) becomes an organizing principle which orders social relationships between people into categories and structures. These categories may serve both positive and negative functions. For the group member, the identification may help guide appropriate behavior in particular contexts, and may serve as a reference point that directs the norms, values, and behaviors of its members. On the other hand, group membership may allow for stereotypical behavior to emerge so that members can say (predominantly at an unconscious level) "I am not like that person." Importantly, these organizing concepts and relationships are negotiated from one context to another, and vary individually. Thus, one's ethnicity may not be relevant when one is at a picnic with friends, yet if discrimination is perceived by an individual in a particular setting, ethnic and racial identification becomes extremely relevant. As Kew (1981, p. 4) points out, "the ethnic dimension to identify may be more important to some people than to others and more prominent as an influence in some situations than in other situations." Taft (1977) suggests that, in fact, many individuals develop multicultural or bicultural identities and skills in such areas as language, behavior, and knowledge that allow them to move readily across ethnic boundaries.

This point is illustrated in a series of studies on cultural tourism. In 1989 Evans-Pritchard published a piece entitled, "How 'They' See Us," and Laxon responded in 1991 with an essay titled, "How 'We' See Them." The essence of both of these studies was to identify the nature of images and stereotypes developed by Native Americans of White tourists, and the images that White tourists have of Native Americans. Using qualitative research strategies, both authors found that each group develops stereotypes to help them "deal" with the other. Images of the romanticized "Noble Savage," the "primitive," the "object of culture," and the "social problem" were prevalent among White tourists. Conversely, the tourists were characterized as "greedy," "pushy," and "camera-carrying" by Indians who had to deal with them. Evans-Pritchard describes one exchange between a White tourist and a young Native-American girl named Laureen who was working in a local store (Steiner, 1968, p. 90, as cited in Evans-Pritchard, 1989, p. 97):

> One lady gently touched the young girl's wrist. "Dear, are you a real Indian?" she asked. "I hope you don't mind me asking. But you look so American." There was a stony silence. "I am a buffalo," Laureen said.

Clearly both individuals in this interaction were trying to deal with the dissonance created by the other. This exchange illustrates the delicate and complex nature of ethnic boundaries that emerge as part of intercultural interaction. Unfortunately, little research to date has attempted to document the nature of intercultural and interracial interactions in recreation settings.

Emerging Issues for a New Millennium

Although major strides have been made since the 1960s in understanding the interplay of ethnicity, race, and leisure, there is still much to be learned. Clearly, more qualitative research is needed to better understand the varying perspectives of minority-group members. In the interests of scientific objectivity, social scientists should not impose a rigid disciplinary framework on people who see the world from a fundamentally different viewpoint. Nor should research be confined within a single theoretical tradition. Theories are designed to answer specific questions. The marginality-ethnicity tradition has led social scientists to examine the influence of socioeconomic status on leisure behavior. Although relevant in many respects, this approach fails to consider such equally significant topics as the expression of cultural meaning in leisure and the real and perceived institutional barriers to recreation participation. Even within the marginality-ethnicity tradition, there have been very few studies examining the combined effects of gender and race on leisure. When one considers the disproportionate share of African-American households in the United States that are headed by single females, the policy relevance of this issue becomes very clear.

Beyond these concerns, however, lies an even more basic question: what will it mean to society when "majorities" cease to exist? The day is fast approaching when the phrase "minority group" may lose much of its significance as a social label. If not on a national scale, certainly in such regions as the southwestern United States, White Anglos will no longer constitute a numerical majority by the second or third decade of the new millennium. In fact, White Anglos will not even be the largest *minority* group in this region. Will social and economic disparities be tolerated when the have-nots outnumber the haves? Will Mexican Americans' coming superiority in numbers translate into greater political power, more economic control, better educational opportunities, and enhanced social status? Or will the Anglo minority still rule as a privileged and socially elite "majority class"? If class distinctions along racial and ethnic lines are preserved (or even heightened) in North America, will the United States and Canada follow the path of the Soviet Union, Yugoslavia, Czechoslovakia, and other politically extinct nations and split apart along their ethnic and racial seams? This was almost unthinkable in the United States when Hispanic Americans and African Americans were vastly outnumbered by White Anglo Americans. However, given the strong movement for political independence in Quebec, the possibility of a significant political struggle for Mexican-American nationhood in the Southwest, now barely a ripple, must be acknowledged.

And what will be the role of leisure in this brave new millennium? When the Mexican soccer team plays on U.S. soil will it be a force for greater intercultural understanding, or will it be a symbol of increasing ethnic pluralism and the emergence of nations within nations? To a great extent, we can only speculate on what the new millennium will bring. But this we know already: cultural and racial diversity will be even more visible as a social reality in the twenty-first century. Undeniably, leisure will both shape and be shaped by the fact that North America is fast becoming a disparate polyglot of ethnic and racial groups, none of which will constitute a numerical majority. One of the truly great challenges of the new millennium will lie in our ability to accommodate these unprecedented internal differences in nondivisive and socially beneficial ways. Leisure as a means of cultural expression and as a mechanism for cultural assimilation has the potential both to assist and to hinder in meeting this challenge. Understanding this potential is becoming ever more critical.

References

Allison, M. T. (1980). *A structural analysis of the Navajo basketball system*. Unpublished doctoral dissertation, University of Illinois at Urbana-Champaign, Champaign, IL.

Allison, M. T. (1982). Sport, culture, and socialization. *International Review for the Sociology of Sport, 17,* 11–37.

Allison, M. T. (1988). Breaking boundaries and barriers: Future directions in cross-cultural research. *Leisure Sciences, 10,* 247–259.

Allison, M. T., & Geiger, C. (1993). The nature of leisure activities among the Chinese-American elderly. *Leisure Sciences, 15,* 309–319.

Anderson, M. (1993). Studying across difference: Race, class, and gender in qualitative research. In J. Stanfield & R. Dennis (Eds.), *Race and ethnicity in research methods* (pp. 39–52). Thousand Oaks, CA: Sage Publications, Inc.

Barth, F. (1969). *Ethnic groups and boundaries: The social organization of culture*. London, UK: Allen and Unwin.

Blahna, D., & Black, K. (1992). Racism a concern for recreation managers. In P. H. Gobster (Ed.), *Managing urban and high-use recreation settings* (General Technical Report NC-163, pp. 111–118). St. Paul, MN: USDA Forest Service Northcentral Forest Experiment Station.

Blanchard, K. (1974). Basketball and the culture change process: The Rimrock Navajo case. *Anthropology and Education Quarterly, 5,* 8–13.

Blauner, R., & Wellman, D. (1973). Toward the decolonization of social research. In J. Ladner (Ed.), *The death of white sociology*. New York, NY: Vintage.

Chavez, D. J. (1991). Ethnic and racial group similarities and differences: A tool for resource managers. In C. Sylvester & L. Caldwell (Eds.), *Abstracts from the 1991 symposium on leisure research*. Alexandria, VA: National Recreation and Park Association.

Chavez, D. J. (1993). *Visitor perceptions of crowding and discrimination at two national forests in Southern California* (Research Paper PSW-RP-216). Riverside, CA: USDA Forest Service Pacific Southwest Research Station.

Chavez, D. J., Baas, J., & Winter, P. L. (1993). *Mecca Hills visitor research case study* (Report BLM/CA/ST-93-005-9560). Sacramento, CA: Bureau of Land Management.

Chavez, D. J., & Winter, P. L. (1993). *Report for the Applewhite Picnic Area, Cajon Ranger District, San Bernardino National Forest*. Riverside, CA: USDA Forest Service Pacific Southwest Research Station.

Dennis, R. (1993). Participant observations. In J. Stanfield and R. Dennis (Eds.), *Race and ethnicity in research methods* (pp. 53–74). Thousand Oaks, CA: Sage Publications, Inc.

Dragon, C. (1986). *Native American underrepresentation in national parks: Tests of marginality and ethnicity hypotheses*. Unpublished masters thesis, University of Idaho, Department of Wildland Recreation Management, Moscow, ID.

Dwyer, J. F. (1994). *Customer diversity and the future demand for outdoor recreation* (General Technical Report RM-22). Fort Collins, CO: USDA Forest Service Rocky Mountain Forest and Range Experiment Station.

Dwyer, J. F., & Hutchison, R. (1990). Outdoor recreation participation and preferences by black and white Chicago households. In J. Vining (Ed.), *Social science and natural resource recreation management* (pp. 49–67). Boulder, CO: Westview Press.

Evans, P. B., & Stephens, J. D. (1988). Development and the world economy. In N. J. Smelser (Ed.), *Handbook of sociology* (pp. 739–773). Thousand Oaks, CA: Sage Publications, Inc.

Evans-Pritchard, D. (1989). How "they" see us: Native American images of tourists. *Annals of Tourism Research, 16,* 89–105.

Farrer, C. (1976). Plan and interethnic communication. In D. Lancy & B. Tindall (Eds.), *The anthropological study of play: Problems and prospects*. Champaign, IL: Human Kinetics Press.

Floyd, M. F., & Gramann, J. H. (1995). Perceptions of discrimination in a recreation context. *Journal of Leisure Research, 27,* 192–199.

Gobster, P. H., & Delgado, A. (1992). Ethnicity and recreation use in Chicago's Lincoln Park: In-park user survey findings. In P. H. Gobster (Ed.), *Managing urban parks and high-use recreation settings* (General Technical Report NC-163, pp. 75–81). St. Paul, MN: USDA Forest Service Northcentral Forest Experiment Station.

Gordon, M. (1964). *Assimilation in American life: The role of race, religion, and national origins*. New York, NY: Oxford University Press.

Gramann, J. H. (1996). *Ethnicity, race, and outdoor recreation: A review of trends, policy, and research* (Miscellaneous Paper R-96-1). Vicksburg, MS: U.S. Army Engineer Waterways Experiment Station.

Gramann, J. H., Floyd, M. F., & Saenz, R. (1993). Outdoor recreation and Mexican American ethnicity: A benefits perspective. In A. W. Ewert, D. J. Chavez & A. W. Magill (Eds.), *Culture, conflict, and communication in the wildland-urban interface* (pp. 69–84). Boulder, CO: Westview Press.

Hutchison, R. (1987). Ethnicity and urban recreation: Whites, blacks and Hispanics in Chicago's public parks. *Journal of Leisure Research. 19,* 205–222.

Irwin, P. N., Gartner, W. G., & Phelps, C. C. (1990). Mexican American/Anglo cultural differences as recreation style determinants. *Leisure Sciences, 12,* 335–348.

Keefe, S. E., & Padilla, A. M. (1987). *Chicano ethnicity.* Albuquerque, NM: University of New Mexico Press.

Kelly, J. R. (1980). Outdoor recreation participation: A comparative analysis. *Leisure Sciences, 3,* 129–155.

Kelly, J. R. (1983). *Leisure identities and interactions.* London, UK: Allen and Unwin.

Kelly, J. R. (1987). *Freedom to be: A new sociology of leisure.* New York, NY: Macmillan Publishing.

Kew, S. (1981). *Ethnic groups and leisure.* London, UK: The Sports Council and Social Science Research Center.

Klobus-Edwards, P. K. (1981). Race, residence, and leisure style: Some policy implications. *Leisure Sciences, 4,* 95–112.

Laxon, J. (1991). How "we" see them: Tourism and Native Americans. *Annals of Tourism Research, 18,* 365–391.

McLemore, S. D. (1991). *Racial and ethnic relations in America.* Boston, MA: Allyn & Bacon.

Mueller, E., & Gurin, G. (1962). *Participation in outdoor recreation behavior: Factors affecting demand among American adults* (Outdoor Recreation Resources Review Commission Study Report 20). Washington, DC: U.S. Government Printing Office.

Murdock, S. H., Backman, K., Colberg, E., Hoque, M. R., & Hamm, R. R. (1990). Modeling demographic change and characteristics in the analysis of future demand for leisure services. *Leisure Sciences, 12,* 79–102.

Oakley, A. (1981). Interviewing women. In H. Roberts (Ed.), *Doing feminist research* (pp. 30–61). New York, NY: Routledge & Kegan Paul.

O'Leary, J. T., & Benjamin, P. J. (1982). *Ethnic variation in leisure behavior: The Indiana case* (Indiana Agricultural Experiment Station Bulletin No. 349). West Lafayette, IN: Purdue University.

Reinharz, S. (1983). Experiential analysis: A contribution to feminist research. In G. Bowles & R. Duelli-Klein (Eds.), *Theories of women's studies* (pp. 162–191). New York, NY: Routledge & Kegan Paul.

Samdahl, D. M. (1988). A symbolic interactionist model of leisure: Theory and empirical support. *Leisure Sciences, 10,* 27–39.

Schreyer, R., & Knopf, R. C. (1984). The dynamics of change in outdoor recreation environments—Some equity issues. *Journal of Park and Recreation Administration, 2,* 9–19.

Stamps, S. M., Jr., & Stamps, M. B. (1985). Race, class and leisure activities of urban residents. *Journal of Leisure Research, 17,* 40–56.

Stanfield, J. (1993a). Methodological reflections: An introduction. In J. Stanfield & R. Dennis (Eds.), *Race and ethnicity research methods* (pp. 3–15). Thousand Oaks, CA: Sage Publications, Inc.

Stanfield J. (1993b). Epistemological considerations. In J. Stanfield & R. Dennis (Eds.), *Race and ethnicity in research methods* (pp. 16–36). Thousand Oaks, CA: Sage Publications, Inc.

Statistics Canada. (1993). *Ethnic origin* (Nation series: Data products: 1991 census of population, Catalogue No. 93-315-XPB). Ottawa, Ontario: Author.

Statistics Canada. (1997). CANSIM matrices 5772 to 5778, 6367 to 6379, Components of population growth, Canada, the provinces territories [On-line]. Available: http://www.statcan.ca/english/Pgdb/People/Population/demo33a.htm

Steiner, S. (1968). *The new Indian.* New York, NY: Harper and Row.

Taft, R. (1977). Coping with unfamiliar cultures. In N. Warren (Ed.), *Studies in cross-cultural psychology* (pp. 121–154). New York, NY: Academic Press.

Teske, R. H., Jr., & Nelson, B. (1976). An analysis of differential assimilation rates among middle-class Mexican Americans. *Sociological Quarterly, 17,* 218–235.

Tindall, B. (1973). *Exploration of a "troublesome" agenda based on the sharing of "property-like" information.* Paper presented at the American Anthropological Association meetings, New Orleans, LA.

U.S. Bureau of the Census. (1994). *Projections of the population, by age, sex, race, and Hispanic origin, for the United States: 1993–2050* (Current Population Report Series P25-1104). Washington, DC: U.S. Government Printing Office.

Van den Berghe, P. L. (1976). Ethnic pluralism in industrial societies: A special case? *Ethnicity 3,* 242–255.

Wallace, V. K., & Witter, D. J. (1992). Urban nature centers: What do our constituents want and how can we give it to them? *Legacy 2*(2), 20–24.

Washburne, R. F. (1978). Black underparticipation in wildland recreation: Alternative explanations. *Leisure Sciences, 1,* 175–189.

Washburne, R., & Wall, P. (1980). *Black-white ethnic differences in outdoor recreation* (Research Paper INT-249). Ogden, UT: USDA Forest Service Intermountain Forest and Range Experiment Station.

West, P. C. (1993). The tyranny of metaphor: Interracial relations, minority recreation, and the wildland-urban interface. In A. W. Ewert, D. J. Chavez & A. W. Magill (Eds.), *Culture, conflict, and communication in the wildland-urban interface* (pp. 109–115). Boulder, CO: Westview Press.

Williams, D. R., & Carr, D. S. (1993). The sociocultural meanings of outdoor recreation places. In A. W. Ewert, D. J. Chavez & A. W. Magill (Eds.), *Culture, conflict, and communication in the wildland-urban interface* (pp. 209–219). Boulder, CO: Westview Press.

Wyatt, D. (1976). *Pickup basketball: A case study of clique behavior variation.* Paper presented at the meetings of the American Anthropological Association, Washington, DC.

Yetman, N. R. (1985). *Majority and minority: The dynamics of race and ethnicity in American life* (4th ed.). Boston, MA: Allyn & Bacon.

Constraints to Leisure

Edgar L. Jackson
University of Alberta

David Scott
Texas A&M University

Just imagine the freedom! (Canadian lottery advertising slogan)

DAD: Why don't you go outside and ride your bike?
    NICHOLAS (age 7): I don't have the time.

The key to social science is constraint. (Dahrendorf, 1995)

If one accepts the premise that one of the main goals of leisure research is to understand people's behavior in the leisure domain of their lives, and agrees with the observation that constraints research has become

We wish to thank John Shaw, Monika Stodolska, Val Freysinger, and Sue Shaw for their comments on drafts of this chapter, and Diane Samdahl for an extended e-mail "conversation" as the early ideas for the chapter began to develop.

one of the major themes in leisure studies over the last two decades, then it becomes reasonable to ask, To what extent has leisure constraints research contributed to our understanding of leisure behavior? The purpose of this chapter is to address that question by summarizing accomplishments to date in the field of leisure constraints research, by developing a critique of the field to assess its limitations, and by suggesting potentially fruitful directions for future research. A secondary objective is to direct the reader toward the key sources that ought to be consulted to develop a detailed understanding of the field, and provide researchers with the necessary literature background to embark upon research on leisure constraints. To begin, however, it is useful to outline the emergence of leisure constraints as a distinct focus of investigation in leisure studies, to establish its purposes, and to set some boundaries for the discussion.

Development and Objectives of Leisure Constraints Research

A broad retrospective glance at the last 30 to 40 years of North American research on leisure suggests the existence of a number of short eras, each characterized by certain issues, concepts and theoretical frameworks, methodologies, and disciplinary perspectives (see Kelly, chapter 9 in this volume). The 1950s and 1960s, for example, witnessed a period of almost entirely empirical, quantitative research on recreational activities and leisure participation, focussing primarily on outdoor recreation and its socioeconomic antecedents. Then, reflecting the growing influence of social psychology on leisure studies in the 1970s and 1980s, attention shifted from participation, activity, and time-based conceptions of leisure toward a more subjective or *experiential* definition, emphasizing the meaning and value of leisure as experienced and defined by the participant. Questions about motivations, satisfaction, and the qualitative dimensions of leisure began to take precedence.

Two new topical themes emerged in the 1980s: the benefits of leisure, and constraints on leisure. The focus on benefits (Driver, Brown and Peterson, 1991; Schreyer and Driver, 1989) represented a natural outgrowth of earlier work on leisure motivations and experiences but with much broader conceptual and disciplinary foundations. Benefits research, too, has exhibited a stronger orientation than its predecessors toward practical applications in the areas of policy, planning, and management of leisure services and recreational resources (see Driver and Bruns, chapter 21 in this volume). Still, as in most past leisure and recreation research, the study of benefits began with the "positive" question, Why?—Why do people value leisure and what benefits do they seek? In contrast, leisure constraints research started with the question, Why not?—Why do some people not participate in leisure in general or in particular activities for which they might have the desire? With its initial focus on the "problematic" aspects of initiating leisure participation, constraints research sought to understand factors that impede leisure participation.

As noted elsewhere (Jackson, 1991a, 1991b), research on leisure constraints can fulfill three important functions. First, it enhances our understanding of a phenomenon—the complex ways in which leisure is constrained—that was largely overlooked except for sporadic studies until the early 1980s. Second, insights derived from leisure constraints research have the potential to shed new light on aspects of leisure, such as participation, motivations, and satisfaction, that were previously thought to have been fairly well-understood. Third, the concept of constraints can serve as a device to assist in perceiving new connections among apparently discrete facets of leisure, and therefore as a vehicle to facilitate communication among researchers with diverse disciplinary backgrounds, topical interests, and methodological orientations. It is perhaps this last aspect that best accounts for the virtual explosion of leisure constraints research in recent years.

Not only has the field grown quantitatively but several important qualitative developments have occurred. These are best summarized in important changes in terminology (Jackson, 1991a, 1991b). In the early 1980s the field of interest, had it been recognized as distinct, would have been referred to as "barriers to recreation participation." The conventional terminology is now "constraints to leisure," a change which represents much more than a semantic difference; it is indicative of three fundamental shifts in focus and conceptualization.

First, the more inclusive term *constraints* is now preferred to *barriers,* because the latter fails to capture the entire range of explanations of constrained leisure behavior (Jackson, 1988). Moreover, as Crawford and Godbey (1987) have argued, the word *barrier* tends to direct researchers' attention toward only one type of constraint, that which intervenes between preference and participation. Now, however, a much more comprehensive and complex range of constraints is recognized than was the case when *barriers* was the dominant terminology (Crawford, Jackson and Godbey, 1991; Henderson, Stalnaker and Taylor, 1988; Jackson, 1990a). Second, replacement of the word *recreation* with *leisure* simultaneously represents both broadening the focus of investigation and forging closer links than before with the mainstream of thinking in leisure studies. The third change, dropping the word *participation,* is based on recognition that constraints influence far more than the choice to participate or not, but many other aspects of leisure, including the formation of preferences, the derivation of enjoyment, specialization, and choice of facility, to name but a few. It is also consistent with the evolution of definitions of leisure, away from activity and time-based conceptualizations and toward the meaning of leisure as experienced by the participant rather than as defined by the researcher (e.g., Samdahl, 1991; see also Kelly, chapter 4 in this volume). As a result of these changes, recent research has displayed increasing conceptual and theoretical complexity, while the increasingly sophisticated interpretation of empirical data is beginning to challenge previously held assumptions about leisure constraints.

Despite these generalizations, two main difficulties in summarizing and reviewing the field must be acknowledged. The first problem is that leisure constraints research is evolving rapidly: new papers on constraints continue to be published in nearly every volume of the major North American leisure and recreation research journals and are being presented at the major conferences, such as the National Recreation and Park Association's annual Leisure Research Symposium and the triennial Canadian Congress on Leisure Research. Consequently, not just new empirical findings but new concepts and insights are continually entering and invigorating the field, challenging previous assumptions and thinking, and pointing the way to new directions in research.

Second is the problem of defining precisely what is and what is not "leisure constraints research." As Goodale (1992) has commented:

> Virtually all studies of women and leisure are studies of constraints. . . . Studies of the elderly, of those who have disabilities [and] of various races and ethnic groups are mainly studies of constraints. . . . Constraints research, titles aside, encompasses a very large portion of psychological/social-psychological research on leisure behavior.

Indeed, notwithstanding Dahrendorf's comment quoted at the beginning of this chapter ("the key to social science is constraint"), it is hard to resist an image of leisure constraints research as a sort of giant conceptual Pac-Man, swallowing up everything in leisure studies in its path (Jackson, 1997). For the purposes of this chapter, however, it is desirable to cast a much narrower net than the one implied by Goodale. Instead, the literature to which most reference will be made consists of that which has been defined explicitly as "constraints research" by its authors or can reasonably be described as such by the observer.

What Do We Know About Constraints? The Accomplishments of Leisure Constraints Research

One way to convey the recent importance of leisure constraints research would be to chart growth in the number of refereed articles, book chapters, and papers presented at major conferences over the last 20 years. While it would demonstrate exponential growth in research activity, such a "numerical" account of the growth of leisure constraints research would overlook two key points: that the origins of contemporary leisure constraints research reach much further back than the appearance of the first peer-reviewed academic research articles; and the far more important qualitative developments that have occurred since the mid to late 1980s. To describe leisure constraints research from the latter perspective, it is useful to recognize a number of broadly defined stages. Although five of these are utilized in the following account, it should be noted that, in reality, they have not been absolutely distinct: there has been overlap from one stage to the next. Thus, the organizational framework for what follows has been constructed more for convenience than to represent perfect historical accuracy.

The Origins of Leisure Constraints Research

Although explicit research on leisure constraints is a recent phenomenon in leisure studies, its roots stretch back over a very long period of time. In fact, from one point of view, implicit notions of constraints have been central to practice in the parks and recreation field since its inception, and subsequently to the emergence of leisure studies as a focus of academic investigation. Thus, in establishing a historical context for contemporary leisure constraints research, Goodale and Witt (1989, p. 421) have stated that "the origins of recreation service provision are founded in attempts to overcome the deleterious conditions which precluded or limited recreation participation for one group or another." These authors went on to suggest that "concern about barriers, nonparticipation in recreation activities, and lack of leisure opportunities has always been an important progenitor of park, recreation, and leisure services" (p. 422). Therefore, the first stage of attention to constraints consisted of a long historical period dating back to the nineteenth century; it was an era when supposed barriers to recreation participation and leisure enjoyment were addressed in service delivery, but on the basis of *assumptions* rather than *substantiation in research*. The central assumption was that the main deterrent to leisure participation was the lack of services, and therefore that more widespread and more frequent participation would ensue if such services were to be provided.[1]

Early "Barriers" Studies

Some three to four decades ago, questions about barriers to participation began to be asked explicitly, in particular during the Outdoor Recreation Resources Review Commission (ORRRC) studies (Ferris, 1962; Mueller, Gurin and Wood, 1962), but elsewhere as well (e.g., Tourism and Outdoor Recreation Planning Study [TORPS], 1978). Several points should be noted about this second stage. To begin with, research was carried out largely to provide practical answers to practical questions, rather than to enhance theoretical understanding of leisure and recreation. Second, the emphasis lay on individual specific barriers, such as how a lack of facilities might be responsible for nonparticipation; items were then developed and administered to assess the effects of such barriers. Third—an inevitable outcome of the second point—barriers were typically analyzed on an item-by-item basis in relation to explanatory variables such as socioeconomic and demographic characteristics or recreational activities. There does not appear to have been any notion of a generic concept of barriers or constraints at this stage.

Emergence of a Generic Concept of Constraints

The third stage was characterized by an emerging consciousness of this generic concept of constraints. What effectively happened was that attention shifted away from the second stage focus on questions about specific barriers (e.g., How does a lack of facilities affect participation?), toward the more general question of, What constraints account for nonparticipation? (of which a lack of facilities might be only one of many types). This shift in focus further prompted recognition that constraints were not only *physical* and *external* to the individual (e.g., facility, resource, and service-oriented), but also *internal* (e.g., psychological and economic; cf., Iso-Ahola and Mannell, 1985) and *social* (e.g., marital, family and other interpersonal relations; cf., Crawford and Godbey, 1987; Crawford and Huston, 1993).

Serving both to signify and stimulate this emerging sense of cohesion was the publication of Michael Wade's (1985) edited volume, *Constraints on Leisure,* the title of which symbolized the distinctness of the subfield of investigation within leisure studies and introduced a new language of conceptualization. Moreover, systematic results of empirical research on constraints began to appear in the refereed leisure research journals. Although some papers had been published earlier on issues that subsequently could loosely be interpreted as relating to constraints (e.g., Washburne [1978] on Black underparticipation in outdoor recreation, and McAvoy [1979] and Morgan and Godbey [1978] on leisure-related problems experienced by the elderly), it was not until the early 1980s that research-based articles dealing explicitly with "barriers to leisure" began to be published. A diverse yet subsequently very influential set of four such papers appeared in *Leisure Sciences* and the *Journal of Leisure Research* in 1980 and 1981 (Boothby, Tungatt and Townsend, 1981; Francken and van Raiij, 1981; Romsa and Hoffman, 1980; Witt and Goodale, 1981). These were followed by a scattering of others by the mid 1980s (Godbey, 1985; Howard and Crompton, 1984; Jackson, 1983; Jackson and Searle, 1983, 1985; McGuire, 1982, 1984; McGuire, Dottavio and O'Leary, 1986; Searle and Jackson, 1985a) that to some extent built upon their predecessors.

Looking back from the vantage point of the late 1990s, we can say that the third stage of leisure constraints research displayed two main characteristics. Not surprisingly, these characteristics were closely interrelated, a point which we will elaborate later: most research was essentially quantitative and survey-based, and it focused almost exclusively on the type of constraints that have come to be referred to either as *structural* (Crawford and Godbey, 1987) or *intervening* (Jackson, 1990a; Shaw, Bonen and McCabe, 1991). These constraints are assumed to inhibit participation or some other aspect of leisure engagement *once a preference or desire for an activity has been formed.*

The typical procedure in most of the research reported in this period was the administration of constraints items, usually related to some arbitrarily chosen criterion variable (i.e., domain of constrained leisure, such as the desire but inability to initiate participation in a chosen activity) to survey samples. While there was considerable variation in the number of intervening constraints items included in most such studies, the number typically amounted to between 15 and 25, although some studies used fewer, and others, on

---

[1]A modern counterpart of this assumption is implicit in the Canadian lottery advertising slogan quoted at the beginning of this chapter: "Win a million dollars and your leisure constraints will disappear!"

infrequent occasions, many more. Indeed, a canvass of the literature reveals that several hundred items have been utilized in constraints research over the past couple of decades, although it should be noted that many of these differ more with respect to wording and emphasis than substance. The lists of constraints items usually covered a conventional range of items related to "barriers to participation," such as constraints related to time, costs, facilities, knowledge and awareness of leisure services and resources, lack of partners with whom to participate, and problems with physical skills and abilities. Studies of this kind typically demonstrated that, on average among the adult population, constraints related to time and money dominate people's perceptions of the problems they experience in successful leisure participation, that constraints related to facilities and accessibility are of intermediate importance, and that the lack of physical abilities and social skills are ranked lowest—although this last comment should not be interpreted as denigrating the importance of such constraints among people for whom they are very real, and frequently incapacitating.

It is also worth noting that two basic strategies characterized the approaches researchers took to the measurement and analysis of constraints. In the first type of approach, researchers asked people about the kinds and intensities of constraints they experience with respect to participating in their leisure in general. The other approach was characterized by focussing on specific activities in which people would like to participate, are already participating, or have ceased participating. This approach can further be subdivided into studies that have investigated constraints associated with a single activity (or, on occasion, two activities simultaneously), and those which have examined comparisons of constraints across a broad range of activities. With respect to the first category, specific activities that have received attention include pool (Chick and Roberts, 1989; Chick, Roberts and Romney, 1991), golf and tennis (Backman, 1991; Backman and Crompton, 1989, 1990), trail use (Bialeschki and Henderson, 1988), camping (Dunn, 1990), bridge (Scott, 1991), hunting (Backman and Wright, 1993; Wright and Goodale, 1991), physical exercise (Shaw et al., 1991), and sport fishing (Aas, 1995; Ritter, Ditton and Riechers, 1992).

As far as activity-based comparisons are concerned, examples include Jackson (1983, 1994a) and McCarville and Smale (1993), who examined similarities and differences across a wide range of activity types with which constraints are associated, and Jackson (1994b), who compared constraints to participation in resource-based outdoor recreation with constraints that inhibit participation in other forms of leisure and recreation. What this small body of research has demonstrated is that there are indeed activity-based variations in constraints, but that such variations are typically ones more of intensity or strength than of kind. In other words, people appear to experience a basic core of constraints regardless of their activity preferences. On the other hand, activity-based variations in the strength of constraints, and the occasional ones of kind, warn us against overgeneralizing the findings derived from research on one type of activity to other types without empirical support. They remind practitioners, too, that efforts to alleviate constraints must be based on thorough empirical knowledge of target groups, preferences, and activities.

The Search for Underlying Patterns and Explanations

In retrospect, most early empirical investigations of constraints tended to be based on the assumptions of individual researchers, especially concerning who among the public is most constrained with regard to their access to leisure. They represented little more than the administration of what Godbey (1990) has called "laundry lists" of a few barriers items to samples of the public, without much thought given to their comprehensiveness or to the subjective meaning of the items to survey respondents. Analysis was typically conducted at a rudimentary level, in terms of the assessment of relationships (usually on an item-by-item basis) between measures of constrained leisure (e.g., Howard and Crompton, 1984; Searle and Jackson, 1985a) and demographic variables. Nor were clear distinctions made among the diverse aspects of leisure that might be subject to constraints. Still less attention was paid to the range and complexity of the constraints concept, or the ways in which barriers and perceptions of barriers enter, both overtly and covertly, into the decision-making processes of individuals at all stages of leisure engagement. In short, third stage research on leisure constraints was rarely theory driven, except at the most deep-seated level (see Rojek, 1989; Stockdale, 1989).

In contrast, the fourth stage of leisure constraints research was characterized by increasingly sophisticated efforts to measure leisure constraints and interpret their impact on leisure choices. These developments can largely be seen as efforts to address some fundamental limitations of the kind of research which had preceded them. For example, longer, more complex, and more comprehensive scales of constraints items began to be developed, based on recognition that the short lists of items included in much previous research were superficial and failed to tap the entire array of constraints that impact upon people's leisure behavior. Equally important, and possibly more so, this stage was characterized by three additional developments:

1. recognition that the interpretation and understanding of patterns of constraints would be enhanced by utilizing dimensions or categories of items;
2. broadening of the range of criterion variables against which to measure the impact of constraints; and
3. analysis of some of the factors thought to explain within-population variations in constraints.

A brief discussion of each now follows.

Classification of Constraints and the Recognition of Dimensions

Item-by-item analysis of constraints suffers from a number of limitations, not the least of which is the large amount of data that are produced, reported, and interpreted. Moreover, the results from single items can be strongly affected by subtleties in wording or by the temporal, social, and geographic conditions under which a scale is administered. Therefore, many researchers turned to alternative forms of data analysis and interpretation, based on conceptual and empirical classification methods to identify dimensions or constellations of constraints. This search for regularity has been tackled in a number of ways, ranging from "subjective" groupings utilized purely for the purpose of discussing the results of item-by-item analysis, through conceptual methods of classification, to rigorous computer-based quantitative methods, such as factor analysis, cluster analysis, and multidimensional scaling.

As far as the results of factor analysis are concerned, there has been perhaps as much divergence as similarity in the factor structures, partly due to variations in the number, content, and wording of items, as well as to differences in the samples to which the constraints scales were administered. On the other hand, several common dimensions have emerged in many of these studies (Backman, 1991; Backman and Crompton, 1990; Blazey, 1989; Henderson et al., 1988; Jackson and Dunn, 1987; Jackson and Henderson, 1995; McGuire, 1984; Wright and Goodale, 1991). These include time commitments, costs, facilities and opportunities, skills and abilities, and transportation and access. This degree of commonality in results suggests that there is a stable and meaningful core of leisure constraints regardless of the specific circumstances of a particular study or the nature of the sample.

Despite its analytical advantages, factor analysis, by definition, separates items into discrete groups with high intrafactor correlations but low or negligible interfactor correlations. Therefore, each dimension must be analyzed separately. Moreover, while factor analysis can be used to identify similar types of constraints, it does not necessarily follow that it groups similar people who share common perceptions and experiences of constraints. As a result, factor analysis tends to encourage a fragmented view of how constraints enter into people's recreational decisions, in that it forecloses investigation of the combinations of barriers that individual people experience, and which therefore differentiate among groups of people. Cluster analysis (Jackson, 1993) and multidimensional scaling (Hultsman, 1995) represent attempts to overcome these problems of factor analysis. The emphasis is still on the detection of patterns derived from reducing a multi-item scale to a higher level of generality, but in techniques such as cluster analysis the emphasis shifts away from classifying *items* (constraints), and on to searching for groupings of *people* who share similar attributes expressed in their responses (numerical scores) to questions about constraints items. The major advantage of this alternative approach is that it facilitates the investigation of *combinations* of barriers and constraints that cut across groupings derived from other methods. Thus, its use may ultimately lead to new insights about the operation of constraints, i.e., how people perceive and experience them.

While classification of constraints items data is pragmatically desirable for the purpose of promoting ease of analysis and interpretation of what are frequently large and complex data sets, its use is far more important from the perspective of theory and enhancement of our understanding of the roles of leisure constraints in people's lives. Thus, the trend away from item-by-item analysis and toward classification is symptomatic of how scholars have increasingly sought to improve their understanding of leisure constraints by searching for regularities, or patterns, of perceived barriers among people whose leisure is somehow constrained. The ensuing results, based on the analysis of *dimensions* or *domains* of constraints, have enhanced the ability to detect similarities and differences between studies, and thereby to establish consistencies and generalizations about the impacts of constraints on leisure behavior, and about variables that are associated, statistically and conceptually, with such patterns.

Broadening the Range of Criterion Variables: The "Heterogeneity" Issue

Because most empirical constraints research to the late 1980s addressed intervening constraints, it is not surprising that the body of research typically emphasized nonparticipation and the desire to participate in leisure in general or in a specific activity as the main criterion variable against which to investigate the operation of constraints (e.g., Jackson, 1990a; Jackson and Dunn, 1991; Jackson and Searle, 1983; Searle and Jackson, 1985a). Since then a variety of other criterion variables have been used against which to measure the impact of constraints. These include the inability to maintain participation at or increase it to desired levels (McGuire et al., 1986; Shaw et al., 1991), ceasing participation in former activities (Backman and Crompton, 1989, 1990; Boothby et al., 1981; Dunn, 1990; Jackson and Dunn, 1988; McGuire, O'Leary, Yeh and Dottavio, 1989), the nonuse of public leisure services (Godbey, 1985; Howard and Crompton, 1984; Scott and Jackson, 1996; Scott and Munson, 1994), and insufficient enjoyment of current activities (Francken and van Raiij, 1981; Witt and Goodale, 1981).

Given the wide range of criterion variables, some researchers have questioned whether the arrays of constraints associated with different criterion variables are similar or different. Do work commitments, for example, impact people's desire to participate in leisure activities at the same intensity as people's desire to continue participating? Researchers have, thus, sought to determine the extent to which constrained leisure is an internally *homogeneous* or *heterogeneous* concept (Hultsman, 1993a; Jackson and Dunn, 1991; Jackson and Rucks, 1993; Searle and Brayley, 1992). The results of comparative studies of this kind have been similar to those previously summarized for activity-specific studies. While there is a common core of constraints that tends to emerge regardless of the criterion variable chosen, the relative strength and importance of items and dimensions vary sufficiently among criterion variables to warrant caution in assuming that, say, barriers to participation in leisure in general or in a specific activity are the same as the reasons why people cease participating or are unable to devote more time to leisure. This finding implies that academic researchers must be very careful when designing research and choosing the criterion variable against which to measure the impact of constraints, and preferably should select two or more such variables for inclusion in a single study. Practitioners, too, need to clearly articulate which problematic aspects of leisure they wish to tackle when modifying the delivery of services to alleviate constraints.

Analysis of Demographic Variations in Leisure Constraints

As in most quantitative and survey-based research on leisure behavior, researchers have not simply reported aggregate results for samples as a whole but have also analyzed subsample variations in constraints, usually using various demographic factors as independent variables. From a theoretical point of view, the main purpose of this analytical approach has been to enhance understanding of how and why people experience and perceive constraints on their leisure. From a practical perspective, pinpointing subgroups of the population who are more or less constrained, and in what ways, is thought to enhance the opportunities for target marketing and the development of purposive strategies to alleviate or remove constraints (McGuire and O'Leary, 1992; Scott and Jackson, 1996; Searle and Jackson, 1985b).

Two main directions in the analysis of the influence of demographic variables have been adopted. In the first, the researcher has focussed on a single subgroup, such as women (Bialeschki and Michener, 1994; Bolla, Dawson and Harrington, 1991; Chambers, 1986; Harrington, 1991; Harrington and Dawson, 1995; Harrington, Dawson and Bolla, 1992; Henderson et al., 1988; Jackson and Henderson, 1995; Rublee and Shaw, 1990; Shank, 1986), adolescents[2] (Bernard, 1988; Hultsman, 1992, 1993b; Jackson and Rucks, 1995; McMeeking and Purkayastha, 1995; Raymore, Godbey and Crawford, 1994; Raymore, Godbey, Crawford and von Eye, 1993; Willits and Willits, 1986), or older adults (Blazey, 1987; Buchanan and Allen, 1985; Mannell and Zuzanek, 1991; McGuire, 1982, 1984). In the second, these factors have been used as independent variables to explore cross-sample variations by variables such as gender, age, and income.

As far as the first type of approach is concerned, studies of single subgroups of the population have often provided a richness and depth of data that have been missing from the broader based, *general survey* method characteristic of the latter approach. In addition, focussed research of this kind—especially that of

---

[2]It is interesting to note that most age-based leisure research uses adolescence as the starting point, with relatively little attention to children (see Barnett and Kane, 1985a, 1985b, for exceptions). However, if the conversation with a seven-year-old quoted at the beginning of this chapter is indicative of the general experience of children, at least in middle-class North America, then constraints to leisure can be both experienced and perceived well before adolescence.

a qualitative rather than a quantitative nature—has frequently uncovered constraints that have tended to be excluded from cross-sectional surveys for one reason or another. Thus, for example, Henderson and her colleagues have drawn attention in their studies of women to constraints such as ethic of care and lack of a sense of entitlement to leisure (e.g., Henderson and Allen, 1991; Henderson and Bialeschki, 1991), while Shaw and her colleagues have examined the influence of body image (Frederick and Shaw, 1995) and fear of violence (Whyte and Shaw, 1994). In the area of adolescence studies, constraints such as peer-group pressure, interaction with leaders, and boredom have received more attention than would have occurred in adult-oriented studies, but which nevertheless may be important, both to adolescents and adults (Hultsman, 1992, 1993b).

For the most part, research of the latter kind has indicated that there are indeed statistically significant and frequently striking variations in the perception and experience of constraints. On the whole, for example, women have consistently been shown as more constrained in their leisure than men, while the experience of most types of constraints—time commitments excepted—declines substantially with increasing income. Probably the strongest differences in intervening constraints, however, occur over the life cycle (see Freysinger, chapter 15 in this volume), although patterns of variation tend to differ markedly depending upon the type of constraint: time commitments, for example, typically exhibit an inverted U-shaped relationship, which means that they increase from youth to middle age but decline thereafter, while an opposite pattern usually emerges for constraints related to social relationships, in particular the difficulty of finding partners with whom to participate. Cost-related constraints usually decline with age while lack of skills and abilities increases, but problems with facilities and access do not appear to vary by age.

Most demographic analysis on intervening constraints has tended to analyze each variable discretely; with some exceptions, results of variations in constraints by two or more variables simultaneously have not been reported. However, there are two important reasons why multivariate analysis is useful. First, it acts as a kind of "internal replication" device, demonstrating that patterns of variation in constraints for one socioeconomic variable (e.g., income) remain stable while controlling for the influence of other variables (e.g., gender or age). In a study reported by Scott and Munson (1994), for example, income was the single best predictor of perceived constraints to park visitation. This was true even when controlling for the effects of sex, age, race, and level of education. Second,

and perhaps more importantly, it demonstrates that there are multiple situational factors related to the experience of constraints. For example, Jackson and Henderson (1995) showed that women's experience of most categories of constraints, and time commitments in particular, was exacerbated or alleviated depending on a combination of other circumstances, such as age and stage in the family cycle. Based on these results, Jackson and Henderson also argued that constraints research in particular and leisure studies in general would benefit by adopting a pluralistic approach to demographic variables (see also Freysinger, chapter 15, on age; Henderson and Bialeschki, chapter 11, on women; and Gramann and Allison, chapter 17, on ethnicity, all in this volume). In other words, descriptors such as "male," "female," "young," "elderly," "African American," and so on should not be viewed as monolithic structures characterized by internal consistency and homogeneity; instead, they frequently disguise and divert our attention away from a tremendous amount of within-group variation, which often equals and sometimes exceeds between-group variation.

What, then, have we learned from demographic analysis of variations in constraints to leisure? First, we know that few types of constraints are experienced with equal intensity by all segments of the population; rather, constraints have greater or lesser effects depending on personal and situational circumstances signified by demographic descriptors. Second, no subgroup of the population is entirely free from constraints (although some individuals within each group may be); rather, each group is characterized by its own combination of constraints. Moreover, if we interpret cross-sectional life-cycle data from a developmental perspective, a process of "constraints exchange" appears to occur; in other words, new circumstances—exemplified in this case by age—may lead to the alleviation of some constraints, but they may also create conditions in which new types of constraints begin to emerge. The same is likely true of other variables, such as income and family structure. Finally, as noted previously with respect to multivariate analysis, the experience of constraints within a general demographic category (e.g., age) is modified by and filtered through other circumstances associated with an individual or subgroup (e.g., the presence or absence of children).

Recent and Ongoing Developments

Recent developments reflect the realization among researchers that the field must move beyond the collection of data and adopt a more theoretical and critical posture. Thus, for example, recent constraints research has begun to be enriched by the incorporation of theoretical frameworks adapted from other themes and issues in leisure studies as well as more generally from other social sciences. Coupled with these theoretical changes, there is now an increasing plurality and complexity of data collection techniques. In addition, recent efforts to synthesize and review previous research (Goodale and Witt, 1989; Jackson, 1988, 1991a, 1991b) have led to the identification both of consistencies and contradictions between empirical studies.

Notwithstanding the importance of these developments, the essence of the most recent stage in the evolution of leisure constraints research has been the emergence of increasingly sophisticated models of constraints and how they enter into and influence people's leisure decision making. Of prime importance here is a set of models proposed by Crawford and Godbey (1987). These were followed by the integration of the models into a single hierarchical or sequential model (Crawford et al., 1991), the refinement of this model to develop a series of propositions about how people might negotiate through constraints to achieve leisure-related goals (Jackson, Crawford and Godbey, 1993), some initial empirical investigation of the "negotiation process," and subsequent revisions to the negotiation model. These developments are important enough to warrant a distinct and more detailed account.

Types and Models of Constraints

Assumptions Underlying Early Constraints Research

The origins of recent developments are rooted in challenges to some initial assumptions that many researchers appear to have made, albeit implicitly, when the field of study first began. Looking back from the perspective of what we know in the late 1990s, we can identify three main assumptions, now generally accepted to be false, that set the foundation for early research on leisure constraints. In a nutshell, the implication of these three distinct but connected assumptions was that there is a negative relationship between the experience of constraints and participation in leisure. The first assumption was that the ability to participate in a desired activity is the only important aspect of people's leisure that is affected by constraints or barriers. The essence of this assumption was that people have developed leisure preferences and are able to articulate them. Constraints, therefore, have histori-

cally been defined as those factors that *intervene* between leisure preferences and leisure participation (Crawford and Godbey, 1987). The second assumption was that constraints are insurmountable obstacles to participation. If a constraint is encountered, the outcome is nonparticipation. The final assumption was that people who participate in an activity are, by definition, unconstrained with respect to that participation. In other words, that people engage in an activity has been interpreted as overt evidence for the absence of constraints—otherwise, they would not have been able to participate!

Broadening the Range of Constraints

Despite its initial domination of the field, research on intervening constraints represents only one of several strands in leisure constraints research. At the same time, and contrary to conventional wisdom until the late 1980s, intervening constraints constitute only one of several types of constraints on people's leisure behavior. Thus as far as the first assumption is concerned, we now know that constraints can and do affect many facets of people's leisure, and not solely the ability to participate in a desired activity. This possibility was first raised by Crawford and Godbey (1987), in their theoretical paper on barriers to family leisure. Two distinct but interrelated themes summarize the essence of Crawford and Godbey's contribution. First, they argued that the operation of constraints can only be understood within the broad context of the preference-participation relationship. Second, they proposed that barriers enter this relationship not solely by intervening between a preference for an activity and participation in that activity ("structural" barriers), but also in two other important ways: (a) by influencing preferences; and (b) in terms of their affecting preferences and participation simultaneously.

Crawford and Godbey's (1987) models posited three distinct types of constraints or barriers: structural, intrapersonal, and interpersonal. *Structural constraints* were conceived as those factors that intervene between leisure preference and participation. According to Crawford and Godbey, "structural barriers represent constraints as they are commonly conceptualized" (p. 123). *Intrapersonal constraints* were defined by Crawford and Godbey "as individual psychological states and attributes which interact with leisure preferences rather than intervening between preferences and participation" (p. 322). Intrapersonal constraints exist when, as a result of abilities, personality needs, prior socialization, and perceived reference group attitudes, individuals fail to develop leisure preferences. According to Scott (1991), intrapersonal constraints predispose people to define leisure objects (activities, locales, or services) as appropriate or inappropriate, interesting or uninteresting, available or unavailable, and so on. Finally, *interpersonal constraints* are those barriers that arise out of social interaction with friends, family and others. In a family context, for example, interpersonal constraints may occur when spouses differ in terms of their respective leisure preferences. As noted by Crawford and Godbey, these differences may impact both spouses' leisure preferences and leisure participation.

The Hierarchical Model

Despite the important advancements in thinking represented by Crawford and Godbey's paper, the three models they proposed were discrete and conceptually disconnected. The purpose of a subsequent article by Crawford et al. (1991), therefore, was to suggest that the models could be integrated into a single, hierarchical, structure (Figure 18.1). The essence of this model was summarized as follows:

> As far as leisure participation/nonparticipation is concerned, we propose that constraints are encountered hierarchically, first at the intrapersonal level. Leisure preferences are formed . . . when intrapersonal constraints . . . are absent or their effects have been confronted through some combination of privilege and exercise of the human will. Next, depending on the type of activity, the individual may encounter

constraints at the interpersonal level: this could happen in all activities requiring at least one partner or coparticipant but would likely be less relevant in the case of solitary leisure activities. It is only when this type of constraint has been overcome (if appropriate to the activity) that structural constraints begin to be encountered. Participation will result from the absence of or negotiation through structural constraints. If structural constraints are sufficiently strong, however, the outcome will be nonparticipation.

Elaboration of the ideas contained in and implied by the model led to the development of three propositions. One of these, summarizing a notion of a hierarchy of social privilege in the experience and negotiation of constraints has not, in retrospect, added much to insights arising from the model or to subsequent debate and conceptualization. The other two, however, have had a substantial impact on subsequent research and debate.

The first proposition posited that leisure participation is heavily dependent upon negotiating through an alignment of multiple factors, arranged sequentially, which must be overcome in order to maintain an individual's impetus through these systemic levels. The second proposition suggested that the sequential ordering of constraints represents a hierarchy of importance, in that "behavioral inertia" must first be confronted, and negotiated, at the intrapersonal level. In other words, the constraint levels are arranged from most proximal (intrapersonal) to most distal (structural). Thus, Crawford et al. conceptualized intrapersonal

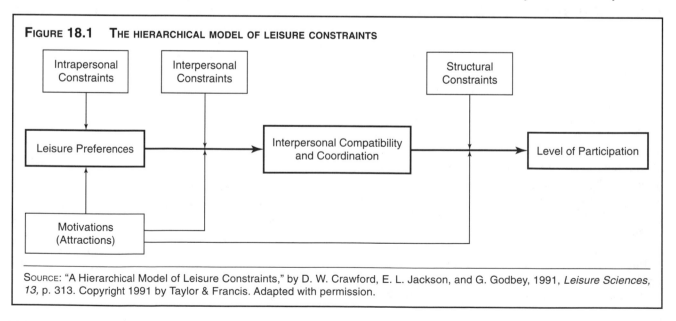

FIGURE 18.1   THE HIERARCHICAL MODEL OF LEISURE CONSTRAINTS

SOURCE: "A Hierarchical Model of Leisure Constraints," by D. W. Crawford, E. L. Jackson, and G. Godbey, 1991, *Leisure Sciences, 13*, p. 313. Copyright 1991 by Taylor & Francis. Adapted with permission.

constraints as being the most powerful, due to the fact that they condition the "will to act," or the "motivation" for participation. The authors concluded that, if the perspective inherent in the hierarchical model was valid, then traditional investigations of leisure constraints have not only emphasized relatively distal behavioral deterrents (intervening constraints), but have neglected those which are arguably more important in the prediction of subsequent behavior.

Crawford et al. recognized that their model was essentially speculative and would require empirical investigation and validation. To some extent, this had already begun to occur by the time the hierarchical model was published. For example, by grouping intrapersonal and interpersonal constraints into the single category of *antecedent* constraints, Henderson et al. (1988) distinguished between antecedent and intervening constraints in their pioneering investigation of constraints to women's leisure. Similarly Jackson (1990a, 1990b) used the concept of antecedent constraints in a pair of papers to speculate about "lack of interest" as an explanation of variations in leisure participation and about activity-related trends over time.

Participation, Constraints, and the Process of Constraints Negotiation

It is not unlikely that this line of research would have continued with little modification had it not been for the publication of a paper by Shaw et al. (1991), which reported no relationship between intervening constraints and participation. Similar results were published by Kay and Jackson (1991). This seemingly puzzling finding—and one which appeared to question the very basis of constraints research—led to two different, but complementary, sets of explanations. First, Shaw et al. (1991) proposed that other types of constraints (antecedent rather than structural) may act as more powerful influences on leisure, an interpretation consistent with Crawford et al.'s second proposition. Alternatively, as Kay and Jackson (1991) suggested, people may participate in leisure "despite constraint." In other words, if participants are equally as constrained as nonparticipants, what sets the two groups apart is not so much differences in the experience of constraints but rather that participants have somehow found the means to address, alleviate, or even overcome their constraints; in short, they have *negotiated* them.

Capitalizing on these findings and interpretations, and elaborating on some assumptions that were implicit in the hierarchical model, Jackson et al. (1993) published a theoretical article that summarized a new perspective on leisure constraints. A key component of this article was a set of six propositions:

1. participation is dependent not on the absence of constraints (although this may be true for some people) but on negotiation through them (such negotiation may modify rather than foreclose participation);
2. variations in the reporting of constraints can be viewed not only as variations in the experience of constraints but also as variations in success in negotiating them;
3. absence of the desire to change current leisure behavior may be partly explained by prior successful negotiation of structural constraints;
4. anticipation of one or more insurmountable interpersonal or structural constraints may suppress the desire for participation;
5. anticipation consists not simply of the anticipation of the presence or intensity of a constraint but also of anticipation of the ability to negotiate it; and
6. both the initiation and outcome of the negotiation process are dependent on the relative strength of, and interactions between, constraints on participating in an activity and motivations for such participation.

In addition to the six propositions, Jackson et al. (1993, p. 8) proposed a three-category typology of people with respect to their responses to constraints, namely:

1. people who do not participate in their desired activity (reactive response);
2. people who, despite experiencing a constraint, do not reduce or otherwise change their participation at all (successful proactive response); and
3. people who participate but in an altered manner (partly successful proactive response).

This conceptual typology, based on speculation, has been empirically supported in a qualitative study of constraints negotiation among women with physical disabilities (Henderson, Bedini, Hecht and Shuler, 1995), in which the three preceding groups were referred to, respectively, as "passive responders," "achievers," and "attempters."

Both preceding and building upon Jackson et al.'s paper, some researchers have identified strategies of both a particular and a general nature with respect to the negotiation of leisure constraints. For example Scott (1991), in his study of participants in contract bridge, identified three main options: acquisition of information about limited opportunities for play; altered scheduling of games to adjust to reduced group membership and individuals' time commitments; and skill development to permit participation in advanced play. Strategies to adjust to time and financial constraints on leisure in general identified by Kay and Jackson (1991) included reducing (but not entirely foregoing) participation, saving money in order to participate, trying to find the cheapest opportunity, making other (non-leisure-related) economies, reducing the amount of time spent on household tasks, and reducing work time. Similarly, Samdahl and Jekubovich (1997a) described how people change work schedules, alter their routines, and select activities which can meet their leisure goals. At a more general level, Jackson and Rucks (1995) distinguished between cognitive and behavioral strategies, the latter being subdivided into modifications of leisure and of nonleisure, and further categorized into modifying the use of time, acquiring skills, changing interpersonal relations, improving finances, physical therapy, and changing leisure aspirations.

Other than identifying these different ways of responding and adapting to constraints, relatively little is known about why some people choose (or are obliged to follow) one set of strategies rather than another. Samdahl and Jekubovich (1997a) have suggested that the desire to share leisure with another person is a profound force that motivates and shapes many patterns of leisure. Hyams (1994) has attempted to pinpoint situational and personal characteristic variables which might encourage people to negotiate constraints. However, much remains to be done in this area of explaining (as opposed to identifying and describing) the negotiation of leisure constraints.

Practical Applications of Constraints Research

To what extent can the results of specific studies and the body of knowledge about leisure constraints assist in enhancing the delivery of leisure and recreation services?[3] It would be facile merely to advocate the provision of more leisure and recreation facilities, better geographically located in relation to centers of latent

[3]For an alternative perspective on practical applications from the one outlined in this chapter, see Henderson (1997).

demand, and at a cheaper cost. Too, there is not as yet much empirical evidence that success in alleviating financial and geographical constraints can be guaranteed; nor would such strategies tackle other influential constraints on leisure, such as time commitments, lack of skills, problems related to interpersonal relations, and, in general, what have been referred to as antecedent constraints. Herein lies one of the main paradoxes of leisure constraints research: despite its avowedly applied thrust (Goodale and Witt, 1989), and the conventional wisdom that more and better research will enhance the development and implementation of practical solutions (e.g., McGuire and O'Leary, 1992; Searle and Jackson, 1985b), there is little indication that practitioners are applying findings from constraints research to improve the planning and marketing of leisure services.

Leisure constraints research cannot impact professional practice until academics develop more potent partnerships with practitioners and leisure service agencies. This is a formidable task. On the one hand, some practitioners may have little interest in incorporating research into their decision-making operations. This may stem from what Crompton (1991) referred to as a "product" orientation to service delivery. That is, park and recreation practitioners have historically regarded their primary task as "providing the facilities, services and programs which they consider to be the most appropriate, as efficiently as they are able, within the resources that they have available" (p. 214). A product orientation (see McCarville, chapter 25 in this volume) is akin to a conception of public recreation which holds that a person's need for leisure is determined by his or her current leisure activity patterns. This concept of recreation need, described by Godbey (1994) as "expressed need," assumes that recreation resources are justly distributed and that people have relatively easy access to them. Agencies and practitioners that maintain a product orientation and the notion of expressed need are unlikely to embrace leisure constraints research because they can generally measure success by way of attendance, profit margin, or simply provide visible proof that a service is being rendered (Goodale, 1991).

On the other hand, there are probably just as many, if not more, practitioners who embrace principles of marketing and other conceptions of recreation need, and are likely to be receptive to leisure constraints research. Unfortunately many of these individuals may find our research dense, esoteric, and lacking in inspiration (Godbey, 1989). In plain truth, we have not done a good enough job at making our research accessible to practitioners. If leisure constraints research is to have practical relevance, we must provide clear and unambiguous implications. As Bannon (1991) so aptly stated, "To bridge the gap between academics and practitioners, we need skilful and tactful interpreters of research" (p. 159).

What specific implications does constraints research have for the delivery of leisure services? First, as noted previously, findings from dozens of studies show that there are significant variations in the nature and intensity of constraints among different subpopulations and types of leisure activity. This suggests that leisure service agencies must individualize their planning and marketing strategies if they are to reach different segments of the population. Alternatively stated, it is important not to generalize broadly based patterns of constraints that occur on average or with respect to an undifferentiated array of activities onto specific subgroups of the population or specific types of leisure and recreation.

Second, practitioners need to consider those constraints that inhibit the development of leisure preferences. In particular, disenfranchised groups in society (the poor, people with disabilities, minority groups, and some women) may not have the same opportunities to develop preferences as others. If leisure service agencies are going to target services to these groups, they will have to understand the *antecedent* constraints impacting these groups' leisure. Moreover, they will need to develop strategies that teach individuals skills and to appreciate different leisure activities and leisure locales. In sum, agencies will have to become advocates for these groups and engage in systematic leisure education.

Research to date, however, has not provided sufficiently clear indications as to what specific strategies, within managers' power and jurisdiction, might potentially alleviate leisure constraints. One exception is a study conducted by Scott and others (Scott and Jackson, 1996; Scott and Munson, 1994) of nonusers and infrequent users of public parks in northeast Ohio. In this case, nonusers and infrequent users of parks were asked whether certain changes in parks operations or programming might result in their using parks more often. A limitation of this study was that behavioral intentions rather than actual behavior were measured. More research is necessary to explore under what conditions people would actually use services offered. To study behavioral change, it may be necessary to use a research approach that incorporates some form of experimental design. Field experiments and single-subject methods may be particularly useful in assessing the impact of change in park delivery on changes on park usage among nonusers.

A Critical Look to the Future of Leisure Constraints Research

The preceding sections of this chapter have painted a fairly optimistic and complimentary picture of leisure constraints research, suggesting that there exists a cohesive body of knowledge, relatively free from contention, that has developed rationally and progressively over the last two to three decades. The conceptual dimensions of the phenomenon have been outlined, theory-based models have been constructed, and there has been some empirical investigation and verification of propositions and hypotheses arising from these models. In particular, recent developments associated with the hierarchical model and the negotiation hypothesis have effectively challenged—but in a positive and constructive way—many of the foundations upon which constraints research first emerged. They also offer the potential for new understandings of the meaning and importance of leisure in individuals' lives, how people make decisions about their leisure, and the influences that shape these decisions, and for new applications of research in the delivery of leisure services. To close at this point, however, would leave the reader with a false impression, failing to acknowledge that this subfield of leisure studies exhibits a number of limitations, and that it has been and continues to be the object of criticism.

Perhaps the most serious challenge has been leveled by Samdahl and Jekubovich (1997a). Among other criticisms, these authors have argued that individuals rarely if ever think explicitly in terms of constraints; thus, given the premise that researchers ought to conceptualize leisure in ways that are more meaningful to the subjects of research than to those who conduct it, the concept of constraints has little if any relevance with respect to understanding leisure. Stated another way, constraint is dismissed as an artificial construct that scholars impose when conceptualizing, conducting, and interpreting their research; the concept has no value for understanding leisure from the perspective of the individual. There is something to be said for this view, not least because it draws attention to the temptation to which some researchers may succumb, namely to artificially abstract, and perhaps overemphasize, aspects of people's lives—such as constraints—that do not receive much overt thought by individuals on a day-to-day basis. On the other hand, the fact that a constraint may not be articulated, let alone perceived, does not necessarily deny its importance as an influence on leisure (Jackson, 1997). Moreover, there can be no doubt that the constraints construct, artificial or not, has been one of the most fruitful sources of new hypotheses and interpretations in leisure studies in the last couple of decades.

For these reasons, in what remains of the chapter, we confine ourselves to several other criticisms, outlining their key components, and using them positively in order to suggest the most desirable avenues and strategies for leisure constraints research in the future. The specific themes include choice of criterion variables; temporal nature of leisure constraints; group-related leisure constraints; development and testing of theory; and methodological changes. At the end of the chapter we will also comment on the interrelatedness of these themes, and what this implies for future directions in research.

Choice of Criterion Variables

Participation and nonparticipation in recreation and leisure activities have dominated as the facets of leisure to which leisure constraints have been assumed to be related, to the neglect of other, and equally important, domains. Indeed, the emphasis on participation and nonparticipation has been one of the major aspects of criticism of leisure constraints research in recent years (see, for example, Leith and Shaw, 1996). It is partly this activity-oriented focus on nonparticipation that explains why intervening constraints have received an undue share of attention, at the expense of intrapersonal and interpersonal constraints—a distinct but associated source of criticism from some observers. However, the argument that constraints research has dwelled *solely* on nonparticipation is not entirely justified because, as we pointed out in an earlier section of this chapter, other criterion variables have been employed in some studies.

Having said this, it must be conceded that the issue has not been attacked at the conceptual level (i.e., by raising the question of the appropriateness of the prevailing nonparticipation, activities, intervening constraints model) but rather by increasing the range of "domains" of leisure with which *intervening* constraints were thought to be associated. Consequently, we know very little about the antecedent constraints that negatively affect the development of leisure preferences, the acquisition of skills, the realization of benefits, the quality of leisure experience, or the use of public park and recreation services, to name but a few. By simultaneously expanding the choice of criterion variables and the range of constraints, we will develop a more comprehensive understanding of constrained leisure.

Arguably, one of the most pressing needs is to better understand those constraints that stymie people's use of public park, recreation, and leisure services, particularly among individuals who have low incomes, and without a doubt investigations in this area would shed light on constraints and leisure decisions in ways that are missing in most current research. Studies have consistently shown that the use of such services tends to be lowest among the poor (Godbey, Graefe and James, 1992; Howard and Crompton, 1984; Scott and Munson, 1994). The question is, how is this finding to be explained, and what are its practical implications? Some would argue that a low income limits the expression of tastes (Howard and Crompton, 1980); thus, price breaks or an increase in income would provide the means by which poor people would be able to act upon their preferences. Others counter that being poor may act more fundamentally to retard the development of leisure preferences (Scott and Munson, 1994). If so, people who are poor may lack the resources to experiment with different leisure styles and have a limited knowledge of what leisure services, activities, and locales are available. These arguments are both speculative and premature, however. Future research is necessary to determine exactly how people with low incomes experience constraints to public park and recreation services within the broader context of the leisure decision-making process.

Temporal Nature of Leisure Constraints

Until recently, most researchers assumed that leisure constraints are monolithic in terms of their impact on people. This assumption has had two implications for how researchers conceive leisure constraints. First, leisure constraints have been generally thought to be insurmountable. As already noted, Jackson et al. (1993) challenged this idea by arguing that participation is dependent not on the absence of constraints but on negotiation through them. Second, constraints are often thought to be stable across time. This idea was challenged by Iso-Ahola and Mannell (1985), who argued that some constraints may be permanent while others may be temporary. A study by Mannell and Zuzanek (1991) confirmed that many constraints are, in fact, temporary and ephemeral in their impact. Using the experience sampling method, they found that constraints to participation in physical activity varied in intensity by time of day. Findings from this study suggest that future research must be more sensitive to the temporal nature of leisure constraints.

Group-Related Leisure Constraints

Leisure constraints research (as with most North American leisure research in general) has been dominated by what Blumer (1969) referred to as variable analysis: aspects of constrained leisure are operationalized in such a way as to facilitate the testing of relationships among variables. Such an approach tends to frame leisure constraints in terms of how various social and especially psychological factors limit individual participation. By focusing exclusively on individual patterns of leisure constraints, we have tended to ignore the interconnectedness of human activity (Meyersohn, 1969). In the context of leisure constraints research, this means that we know very little about how constraints arise in group contexts where individuals are mutually influencing one another.

The importance of this alternative perspective is illustrated by an ethnographic study of bridge players reported by Scott (1991). What was distinctive about this study was its focus of analysis on the group and the broader social world system rather than the individual. This approach provided insight into how group processes (e.g., gate-keeping mechanisms, the coordination of schedules, and group disbandment) made bridge involvement problematic for both newcomers and longtime participants. Similarly, Scott showed how diminished interest in bridge among younger people had led to a number of constraints among older players. An examination of group-related constraints may be particularly useful in helping us better understand the nature of interpersonal constraints, as well as how the experience of such constraints may encourage the adoption of novel negotiation strategies. As noted by Scott, "The fact that bridge requires joint coordination of activity underscores an important difference between solo leisure and group leisure: sustained involvement is highly dependent on other people's action" (Scott, 1991, p. 330).

This comment on the emphasis on the individual in leisure studies in general and constraints research in particular can be taken a step further. Given that empirical research and theoretical development have focussed almost exclusively on individual people, the constraints they perceive and experience, and the negotiation strategies they adopt, the approach has been one of agency, to the general if not uniform neglect of structure (Rojek, 1989). As a result, we have very little empirical evidence of how social structure and social problems translate into constraints for individuals and groups, although some is emerging in the feminist literature (see, for example, Henderson, 1991, and Shaw,

1994). We know still less about how social, political, and economic change influence the emergence or alleviation of constraints and how such changes translate into modifications to leisure. These areas are ripe for investigation, but cannot be tackled without modifications to prevailing methods. Indeed, they may demand a fundamental rethinking of constraints-related concepts and the adoption of alternative philosophical frameworks and methodological strategies from those that currently prevail in the field.

Development and Testing of Theory

Until very recently, most leisure constraints research was highly empirical and guided by few theoretical premises. Even today studies are still being published that include little more than an item-by-item description and analysis of perceived constraints. Our understanding of leisure constraints will continue to mature only if theory is used to guide research. Thus, recent efforts at theory building—the hierarchical model of leisure constraints (Crawford et al., 1991), a theory of ceasing participation (Searle, 1991), and a theory of leisure negotiation (Jackson et al., 1993)—are extremely important as they provide a wealth of propositions and lines of inquiry that can direct research. However, despite the contributions of these theories, they remain largely untested. For example, the only direct and purposive examination of the hierarchical model published to date came in a master's degree study conducted on adolescents' leisure by Raymore in 1992. Results from this study—which were published in Raymore et al. (1993, 1994)—empirically verified the existence of structural, interpersonal, and intrapersonal constraints as distinct categories affecting distinct aspects of leisure decisions. Clearly, much more needs to be done in the way of empirically testing theoretical propositions.

Our understanding of leisure constraints can be furthered by the extension of theories from other disciplines and other areas of leisure studies as well. To some extent this is already occurring, although the full implications of these efforts have yet to be realized. By applying feminist theory to leisure, for example, several researchers have shown how women's leisure is made problematic by an ethic of care and lack of a sense of entitlement to leisure (Henderson, Bialeschki, Shaw, and Freysinger, 1989, 1996). Likewise, Dattilo (1994) applied the theory of learned helplessness to explain why barriers to leisure exist among people with disabilities. The interpretation, by McGuire et al. (1989) and subsequently Iso-Ahola, Jackson, and Dunn (1994) of patterns of ceasing participation in former leisure activities and starting new ones through the life cycle in the context of Iso-Ahola's (1980) model of age-based changes in the relative roles of stability and novelty is another excellent example. So, too, are Backman and Crompton's (1990) incorporation of marketing concepts in their study of active and passive discontinuers from leisure activities, and the use of the approach-avoidance concept by Chick and his colleagues (Chick and Roberts, 1989; Chick et al., 1991) in research on pool players. Scott (1993) explained how time scarcity results in people making adjustments in how they use leisure time. By identifying conceptual connections between serious leisure and the negotiation of leisure constraints, McQuarrie and Jackson (1996) have provided a theoretical framework for thinking about how constraints are experienced and negotiated at important transitional points in people's lives. Feagin and Feagin's (1986) theory of institutional discrimination may provide a useful framework for explaining leisure constraints among minority groups. One premise of that theory is that seemingly neutral organizational and institutional practices in the present systematically reflect or perpetuate the effects of preferential treatment or intentional discrimination in the past. This and other theories may yet be effectual in helping to explain different facets of constrained leisure.

Methodological Changes

Notwithstanding the importance of the preceding suggestions for enhancing the quality of leisure constraints research, in our judgment the most pressing need is for diversification of research approaches. To some extent, this has already begun to occur in constraints research (e.g., Frederick and Shaw, 1995; Henderson et al., 1995; Mannell and Zuzanek, 1991; McCormick, 1991; Scott, 1991; Whyte and Shaw, 1994), but most data have been collected in questionnaire surveys, which have been cross-sectional and almost entirely quantitative and correlative. We contend that knowledge of how constraints enter into people's daily lives can only arise if survey-based data are complemented with other kinds of methodologies, including the experience sampling method, quasi-experimental and single-subject designs, and above all ethnographic-qualitative methods. Survey methods may be particularly well-suited to the collection and analysis of information about intervening constraints, but their use may be limited when it comes to understanding the mechanisms underlying intrapersonal and interpersonal constraints, or even to identifying what these constraints are.

In contrast, qualitative methods of various kinds (e.g., participant observation and in-depth interviewing) offer alternative opportunities to identify and evaluate the impact of these latter kinds of constraints. Indeed, it is precisely *because* qualitative methods have been used that some researchers have discovered constraints such as sense of entitlement, ethic of care, and body image as constraints to leisure (most notably among women)—constraints which likely would have been overlooked in the absence of naturalistic approaches.

Equally important, it has been partly through the use of qualitative methods that some researchers have been able to criticize existing models and suggest innovative interpretations. A key case in point is work conducted by Henderson and Bialeschki (1993), who established a series of propositions about constraints that took issue with the linear nature of the hierarchical model of constraints and negotiation proposed by Crawford et al. (1991) and Jackson et al. (1993). Henderson and Bialeschki's propositions are important contributions because they highlight the complexity of constraints-related concepts, the difficulties researchers encounter in disentangling these concepts and phenomena, and the interwoven relationships that exist among preferences, participation, negotiation, and various categories of constraints. As Henderson and Bialeschki (1993, p. 247) concluded, "constraints are not sequential and hierarchical, but dynamic and integrated." How easy it will be to translate this alternative conceptualization into empirical research has yet to be explored; the important point here, however, is that a potentially important alternative perspective on the very nature of constraints and their influence in people's lives would be unlikely to have emerged if survey-based quantitative methods had remained the sole means by which information about leisure constraints is collected.

The preceding comments should not be interpreted as meaning that we are calling for the abandonment of quantitative surveys of leisure constraints. On the contrary, we strongly advocate their continuation, but with two main modifications. First, future studies must include measures of constraints that have been overlooked in previous survey research, but which have been uncovered in qualitative studies, and for which quantitative items might easily be developed. Second, researchers should strive to build longitudinal designs into their studies. Longitudinal data have been almost entirely absent in leisure constraints research (see Jackson and Witt, 1994, for an exception), but would help to determine whether the experience of leisure constraints is transitory or continuous over time. The extent to which leisure constraints experienced at one stage of life are related to different outcomes at later stages of life, including amount and intensity of leisure involvement, leisure motivations and satisfaction, and the ability to negotiate leisure constraints (see Freysinger, chapter 15 this volume) could also be determined more accurately in longitudinal research. And finally, assessing the impacts of social, economic, and political change on leisure could be enhanced by building questions about constraints into longitudinal research designs.

Where Do We Go From Here?

It was necessary, when developing the preceding critique, to identify a number of specific and discrete criticisms, if only for the sake of clarity and a systematic treatment. Yet it is also important to recognize that the limitations of constraints research as it currently exists are best viewed as being interrelated. Thus, the emphasis on intervening constraints in most past research can be partly explained by the dominance of surveys and quantitative methods and the prevailing influence of social psychology. In other words, the focus on a type of constraint that is easiest to measure using standardized items in quantitative questionnaire surveys is in part a side effect of a preference for certain kinds of methods. Simultaneously the influence of social psychology has encouraged us to ask questions about individual agency to the neglect of broader and perhaps more fundamental social structural "forces," which in turn translate into antecedent constraints.

More fundamentally, the limitations of constraints research stem, to a greater or lesser extent, from the methodologies most commonly adopted by the researchers who have been most influential in the field.[4] In turn, the choice of methods and approaches has been influenced by the research paradigm that has characterized leisure research in North America over the last two or three decades. In a nutshell, this paradigm can be described as a positivist, quantitative, survey-based approach as the prevailing methodological framework, coupled with the dominance of social psychology as the major disciplinary influence

[4]We might also argue that some of the problems of leisure constraints research arise from the social, economic, and political milieu of much university-based social science, with its emphasis on short-term research and the rapid and voluminous publication of MPUs (minimum publishable units). However, this accusation can also be leveled at leisure studies as a whole, as well as the social sciences in general (Sykes, 1988); therefore, to elaborate upon it would be beyond the scope of this chapter.

(Hemingway, 1995; see also Coalter, chapter 31 in this volume). As a result, the findings and insights of leisure constraints research are best viewed, not as the product of objective social science, but more correctly as a product of the *type* of social science from which they have emerged.

What all this implies is that any future changes in focus, such as more research on antecedent constraints of various kinds, will represent not just a change of topic but will also demand different research methods and the incorporation of concepts and methods from other disciplines. The upshot is that any efforts to broaden the scope of leisure constraints research cannot be successful if they are approached merely as "add-ons" to "business as usual" research. Rather, they will demand a fairly fundamental rethinking of concepts, methods, sources of ideas, and so on. To this end, it would be beneficial if North American researchers in the area of leisure constraints made themselves more aware of alternative approaches to leisure studies as practiced elsewhere, most notably in the United Kingdom and Europe (see Coalter, chapter 31 in this volume), in which sociology, structure, qualitative methods and interpretation have played a far more influential role than psychology, agency, and statistical analysis.

Conclusion

To conclude, there is a growing body of consistent knowledge about leisure constraints and constrained leisure, coupled with a welcome debate about fundamental assumptions, appropriate methods, the meaning of results, and implications for practice. Innovations are occurring rapidly, and close theoretical and conceptual ties are being developed, maintained, and strengthened within leisure studies and with the parent social science disciplines. In this chapter, we have tried to summarize what is known about constraints to leisure and, by reviewing some of the main limitations of the field, to suggest some fruitful ways in which it might develop in the future.

One question that researchers may wish to debate is the long-term desirability of identifying leisure constraints as a distinct focus of investigation in leisure studies.[5] At the beginning of the 1990s, one of the authors of this chapter (Jackson, 1991a, 1991b) saw both advantages and disadvantages of constraints research as a distinct field. On the one hand, he argued,

[5]This issue, among others, is addressed in a recent exchange on leisure constraints research: Samdahl and Jekubovich's (1997a) critique of the field is followed by comments from Henderson (1997) and Jackson (1997), with a rejoinder by the first authors (Samdahl and Jekubovich, 1997b).

the identification of leisure constraints and the complexities of constrained leisure may enhance communication among interested researchers, ultimately encouraging the accumulation of knowledge and the development of theory. This has certainly happened in the period of close to a decade since these words were originally written. On the other hand, there was also a perceived danger that the research, and those who contribute to it, will become inward looking, and thus isolated from the broader field of leisure studies. Perhaps what we can say, in retrospect, is that research will and should continue on leisure constraints, but that its greatest long-term contribution will lie in the ways in which constraints research has informed and enhanced leisure studies as a whole, in that it is now commonplace to ask questions about constraints simply as a component of and interpretation in more widely defined investigations.

References

Aas, Ø. (1995). Constraints on sport fishing and effect of management actions to increase participation rates in fishing. *North American Journal of Fisheries Management, 15,* 631–638.

Backman, S. J. (1991). An investigation of the relationship between activity loyalty and perceived constraints. *Journal of Leisure Research, 23,* 332–344.

Backman, S. J., & Crompton, J. L. (1989). Discriminating between continuers and discontinuers of two public leisure services. *Journal of Park and Recreation Administration, 7,* 56–71.

Backman, S. J., & Crompton, J. L. (1990). Differentiating between active and passive discontinuers of two leisure activities. *Journal of Leisure Research, 22,* 197–212.

Backman, S. J., & Wright, B. A. (1993). An exploratory study of the relationship of attitude and the perception of constraints to hunting. *Journal of Park and Recreation Administration, 11,* 1–16.

Bannon, J. J. (1991). The impact of change on public park and recreation administration. In T. L. Goodale & P. A. Witt (Eds.), *Recreation and leisure: Issues in an era of change* (pp. 149–160). State College, PA: Venture Publishing, Inc.

Barnett, L. A., & Kane, M. J. (1985a). Individual constraints on children's play. In M. G. Wade (Ed.), *Constraints on leisure* (pp. 43–82). Springfield, IL: Charles C. Thomas.

Barnett, L. A., & Kane, M. J. (1985b). Environmental constraints on children's play. In M. G. Wade (Ed.), *Constraints on leisure* (pp. 189–225). Springfield, IL: Charles C. Thomas.

Bernard, M. (1988). Leisure-rich and leisure-poor: leisure lifestyles among young adults. *Leisure Sciences, 10,* 131–149.

Bialeschki, M. D., & Henderson, K. A. (1988). Constraints to trail use. *Journal of Park and Recreation Administration, 6,* 20–28.

Bialeschki, M. D., & Michener, S. (1994). Reentering leisure: Transition within the role of motherhood. *Journal of Leisure Research, 26,* 57–74.

Blazey, M. (1987). The differences between participants and nonparticipants in a senior travel program. *Journal of Travel Research, 26,* 7–12.

Blazey, M. A. (1989). *Factors constraining travel among older adults.* Paper presented at the National Recreation and Parks Association Symposium on Leisure Research, San Antonio, TX.

Blumer, H. (1969). *Symbolic interactionism: Perspective and method.* Englewood Cliffs, NJ: Prentice-Hall.

Bolla, P., Dawson, D., & Harrington, M. (1991). The leisure experience of women in Ontario. *Journal of Applied Recreation Research, 16,* 322–348.

Boothby, J., Tungatt, M. F., & Townsend, A. R. (1981). Ceasing participation in sports activity: Reported reasons and their implications. *Journal of Leisure Research, 13,* 1–14.

Buchanan, T., & Allen, L. (1985). Barriers to recreation participation in later life-cycle stages. *Therapeutic Recreation Journal, 19,* 39–50.

Chambers, D. A. (1986). The constraints of work and domestic schedules on women's leisure. *Leisure Studies, 5,* 309–325.

Chick, G., & Roberts, J. M. (1989). Leisure and antileisure in game play. *Leisure Sciences, 11,* 73–84.

Chick, G., Roberts, J. M., & Romney, A. K. (1991). Conflict and quitting in the Monday Nite Pool League. *Leisure Sciences, 13,* 295–308.

Crawford, D. W., & Godbey, G. (1987). Reconceptualizing barriers to family leisure. *Leisure Sciences, 9,* 119–127.

Crawford, D. W., & Huston, T. L. (1993). The impact of the transition to parenthood on marital leisure. *Personality and Social-Psychology Bulletin, 19,* 39–46.

Crawford, D. W., Jackson, E. L., & Godbey, G. (1991). A hierarchical model of leisure constraints. *Leisure Sciences, 13,* 309–320.

Crompton, J. (1991). Marketing: Neither snake oil nor panacea. In T. L. Goodale & P. A. Witt (Eds.), *Recreation and leisure: Issues in an era of change* (pp. 213–229). State College, PA: Venture Publishing, Inc.

Dahrendorf, R. (1995). The many faces of freedom. *LSE Annual Review, 1995,* 38.

Dattilo, J. (1994). *Inclusive leisure services: Responding to the rights of people with disabilities.* State College, PA: Venture Publishing, Inc.

Driver, B. L., Brown, P. J., & Peterson, G. L. (Eds.). (1991). *Benefits of leisure.* State College, PA: Venture Publishing, Inc.

Dunn, E. (1990). Temporary and permanent constraints on participation in camping. In B. J. A. Smale (Ed.), *Leisure challenges: Bringing people, resources, and policy into play—Proceedings of the Sixth Canadian Congress on Leisure Research* (pp. 360–363). Toronto, Ontario: Ontario Research Council on Leisure.

Feagin, J. R., & Feagin, C. B. (1986). *Discrimination American style: Institutional racism and sexism* (2nd ed.). Malabar, FL: Robert E. Krieger Publishing Company.

Ferris, A. L. (1962). *National recreation survey* (Outdoor Recreation Resources Review Commission, Study Report No. 19). Washington, DC: U.S. Government Printing Office.

Francken, D. A., & van Raiij, M. F. (1981). Satisfaction with leisure time activities. *Journal of Leisure Research, 13,* 337–352.

Frederick, C. J., & Shaw, S. M. (1995). Body image as a leisure constraint: Examining the experience of aerobic exercise classes for young adults. *Leisure Sciences, 17,* 57–89.

Godbey, G. (1985). Nonparticipation in public leisure services: A model. *Journal of Park and Recreation Administration, 3,* 1–13.

Godbey, G. (1989). Implications of recreation and leisure research for professionals. In E. L. Jackson & T. L. Burton (Eds.), *Understanding leisure and recreation: Mapping the past, charting the future* (pp. 613–628). State College, PA: Venture Publishing, Inc.

Godbey, G. (1990). Presentation to the special sessions on leisure constraints research, Sixth Canadian Congress on Leisure Research, University of Waterloo.

Godbey, G. (1994). *Leisure in your life: An exploration* (4th ed.). State College, PA: Venture Publishing, Inc.

Godbey, G., Graefe, A., & James, S. W. (1992). *The benefits of local recreation and park services: A nationwide study of the perceptions of the American public.* Washington, DC: National Recreation and Park Association.

Goodale, T. L. (1991). Of Godots and Goodbars: On waiting and looking for change. In T. L. Goodale & P. A. Witt (Eds.), *Recreation and leisure: Issues in an era of change* (pp. 123–135). State College, PA: Venture Publishing, Inc.

Goodale, T. L. (1992). *Constraints research: Performing without a net next time.* Featured speaker presentation, Psychological/Social-Psychological Aspects of Leisure Behavior, Part I, National Recreation and Parks Association Symposium on Leisure Research, Cincinnati, OH.

Goodale, T. L., & Witt, P. A. (1989). Recreation nonparticipation and barriers to leisure. In E. L. Jackson & T. L. Burton (Eds.), *Understanding leisure and recreation: Mapping the past, charting the future* (pp. 421–449). State College, PA: Venture Publishing, Inc.

Harrington, M. A. (1991). Time after work: Constraints on the leisure of working women. *Loisir et Société/Society and Leisure, 14*(1), 115–132.

Harrington, M., & Dawson, D. (1995). Who has it best? Women's labor force participation, perceptions of leisure and constraints to enjoyment of leisure. *Journal of Leisure Research, 27,* 4–24.

Harrington, M., Dawson, D., & Bolla, P. (1992). Objective and subjective constraints on women's enjoyment of leisure. *Loisir et Société/Society and Leisure, 15,* 203–221.

Hemingway, J. L. (1995). Leisure studies and interpretive social inquiry. *Leisure Studies, 14,* 32–47.

Henderson, K. A. (1991). The contribution of feminism to an understanding of leisure constraints. *Journal of Leisure Research, 23,* 363–377.

Henderson, K. A. (1997). A critique of constraints theory: A response. *Journal of Leisure Research, 29,* 453–457.

Henderson, K. A., & Allen, K. (1991). The ethic of care: Leisure possibilities and constraints for women. *Loisir et Société/Society and Leisure, 14*(1), 97–113.

Henderson, K. A., Bedini, L. A., Hecht, L., & Schuler, R. (1995). Women with physical disabilities and the negotiation of leisure constraints. *Leisure Studies, 14,* 17–31.

Henderson, K. A., & Bialeschki, M. D. (1991). A sense of entitlement to leisure as constraint and empowerment for women. *Leisure Sciences, 13,* 51–65.

Henderson, K. A., & Bialeschki, M. D. (1993). Exploring an expanded model of women's leisure constraints. *Journal of Applied Recreation Research, 18,* 229–252.

Henderson, K. A., Bialeschki, M. D., Shaw, S. M., & Freysinger, V. J. (1989). *A leisure of one's own: A feminist perspective on women's leisure.* State College, PA: Venture Publishing, Inc.

Henderson, K. A., Bialeschki, M. D., Shaw, S. M., & Freysinger, V. J. (1996). *Both gains and gaps: Feminist perspectives on women's leisure.* State College, PA: Venture Publishing, Inc.

Henderson, K. A., Stalnaker, D., & Taylor, G. (1988). The relationship between barriers to recreation and gender-role personality traits for women. *Journal of Leisure Research, 20,* 69–80.

Howard, D. R., & Crompton, J. L. (1980). *Financing, managing and marketing recreation & park resources.* Dubuque, IA: Wm. C. Brown Publishers.

Howard, D. R., & Crompton, J. L. (1984). Who are the consumers of public park and recreation services? An analysis of the users and nonusers of three municipal leisure service organizations. *Journal of Park and Recreation Administration, 2,* 33–48.

Hultsman, W. Z. (1992). Constraints to activity participation in early adolescence. *Journal of Early Adolescence, 12,* 280–299.

Hultsman, W. Z. (1993a). Is constrained leisure an internally homogeneous concept? An extension. *Journal of Leisure Research, 25,* 319–334.

Hultsman, W. Z. (1993b). The influence of others as a barrier to recreation participation among early adolescents. *Journal of Leisure Research, 25,* 150–164.

Hultsman, W. Z. (1995). Recognizing patterns of leisure constraints: An extension of the exploration of dimensionality. *Journal of Leisure Research, 27,* 228–244.

Hyams, A. L. (1994). *The influence of perceived competence, activity importance, and barriers on adolescent leisure participation: Exploring the potential for negotiation.* Unpublished masters thesis, Department of Sport and Leisure Studies, University of Nevada–Las Vegas, Las Vegas, NV.

Iso-Ahola, S. E. (1980). *The social psychology of leisure and recreation.* Dubuque, IA: Wm. C. Brown Publishers.

Iso-Ahola, S. E., Jackson, E. L., & Dunn, E. (1994). Starting, ceasing, and replacing leisure activities over the human life span. *Journal of Leisure Research, 26,* 227–249.

Iso-Ahola, S. E., & Mannell, R. C. (1985). Social and psychological constraints on leisure. In M. G. Wade (Ed.), *Constraints on leisure* (pp. 111–151). Springfield, IL: Charles C. Thomas.

Jackson, E. L. (1983). Activity specific barriers to recreation participation. *Leisure Sciences, 6,* 47–60.

Jackson, E. L. (1988). Leisure constraints: A survey of past research. *Leisure Sciences, 10,* 203–215.

Jackson, E. L. (1990a). Variations in the desire to begin a leisure activity: Evidence of antecedent constraints? *Journal of Leisure Research, 22,* 55–70.

Jackson, E. L. (1990b). Trends in leisure preferences: Alternative constraints-related explanations. *Journal of Applied Recreation Research, 15*(3), 129–145.

Jackson, E. L. (1991a). Leisure constraints/Constrained leisure: Special issue introduction. *Journal of Leisure Research, 23,* 279–285.

Jackson, E. L. (1991b). Leisure constraints/Constrained leisure: Special issue introduction. *Leisure Sciences, 13,* 273–278.

Jackson, E. L. (1993). Recognizing patterns of leisure constraints: Results from alternative analyses. *Journal of Leisure Research, 25,* 129–149.

Jackson, E. L. (1994a). Activity-specific constraints on leisure. *Journal of Park and Recreation Administration, 12,* 33–49.

Jackson, E. L. (1994b). Constraints on participation in resource-based outdoor recreation. *Journal of Applied Recreation Research, 19,* 215–245.

Jackson, E. L. (1997). In the eye of the beholder: A comment on Samdahl & Jekubovich (1997), "A critique of leisure constraints: Comparative analyses and understandings." *Journal of Leisure Research, 29,* 458–468.

Jackson, E. L., Crawford, D. W., & Godbey, G. (1993). Negotiation of leisure constraints. *Leisure Sciences, 15,* 1–11.

Jackson, E. L., & Dunn, E. (1987). *Ceasing participation in recreation activities: An analysis of data from the 1984 public opinion survey on recreation.* Edmonton, Alberta: Alberta Recreation and Parks.

Jackson, E. L., & Dunn, E. (1988). Integrating ceasing participation with other aspects of leisure behavior. *Journal of Leisure Research, 20,* 31–45.

Jackson, E. L., & Dunn, E. (1991). Is constrained leisure an internally homogeneous concept? *Leisure Sciences, 13,* 167–184.

Jackson, E. L., & Henderson, K. A. (1995). Gender-based analysis of leisure constraints. *Leisure Sciences, 17,* 31–51.

Jackson, E. L., & Rucks, V. C. (1993). Reasons for ceasing participation and barriers to participation: Further examination of constrained leisure as an internally homogeneous concept. *Leisure Sciences, 15,* 217–230.

Jackson, E. L., & Rucks, V. C. (1995). Negotiation of leisure constraints by junior-high and high-school students: An exploratory study. *Journal of Leisure Research, 27,* 85–105.

Jackson, E. L., & Searle, M. S. (1983). Recreation nonparticipation: Variables related to the desire for new recreational activities. *Recreation Research Review, 10*(2), 5–12.

Jackson, E. L., & Searle, M. S. (1985). Recreation nonparticipation and barriers to participation: Concepts, and models. *Loisir et Société/Society and Leisure, 8,* 693–707.

Jackson, E. L., & Witt, P. A. (1994). Change and stability in leisure constraints: A comparison of two surveys conducted four years apart. *Journal of Leisure Research, 26,* 322–336.

Kay, T., & Jackson, G. (1991). Leisure despite constraint: The impact of leisure constraints on leisure participation. *Journal of Leisure Research, 23,* 301–313.

Leith, D. A, & Shaw, S. M. (1996). *The physical activity nonparticipant: Looking beyond constraints.* Paper presented at the Eighth Canadian Congress on Leisure Research, University of Ottawa, Ottawa, Ontario.

Mannell, R. C., & Zuzanek, J. (1991). The nature and variability of leisure constraints in daily life: The case of the physically active leisure of older adults. *Leisure Sciences, 13,* 337–351.

McAvoy, L. A. (1979). The leisure preferences, problems, and needs of the elderly. *Journal of Leisure Research, 11,* 40–47.

McCarville, R. E., & Smale, B. J. A. (1993). Perceived constraints to leisure participation within five activity domains. *Journal of Park and Recreation Administration, 11,* 40–59.

McCormick, B. (1991). Self-experience as leisure constraint: The case of Alcoholics Anonymous. *Journal of Leisure Research, 23,* 345–362.

McGuire, F. A. (1982). Constraints on leisure involvement in the later years. *Activities, Adaptation and Aging, 3*(1), 17–24.

McGuire, F. A. (1984). A factor analytic study of leisure constraints in advanced adulthood. *Leisure Sciences, 6,* 313–326.

McGuire, F. A., Dottavio, D., & O'Leary, J. T. (1986). Constraints to participation in outdoor recreation across the life span: A nationwide study of limitors and prohibitors. *The Gerontologist, 26,* 538–544.

McGuire, F. A., & O'Leary, J. T. (1992). The implications of leisure constraint research for the delivery of leisure services. *Journal of Park and Recreation Administration, 10,* 31–40.

McGuire, F. A., O'Leary, J. T., Yeh, C.-K., & Dottavio, F. D. (1989). Integrating ceasing participation with other aspects of leisure behavior: A replication and extension. *Journal of Leisure Research, 21,* 316–326.

McMeeking, D., & Purkayastha, B. (1995). "I can't have my mom running me everywhere": Adolescents, leisure, and accessibility. *Journal of Leisure Research, 27,* 360–378.

McQuarrie, F., & Jackson, E. L. (1996). Connections between negotiation of leisure constraints and serious leisure: An exploratory study of adult amateur ice skaters. *Loisir et Société/Society and Leisure, 19,* 459–483.

Meyersohn, R. K. (1969). The sociology of leisure in the United States: Introduction and bibliography, 1945–1965. *Journal of Leisure Research, 1,* 53–68.

Morgan, A., & Godbey, G. (1978). The effect of entering an age-segregated environment upon the leisure activity patterns of older adults. *Journal of Leisure Research, 10,* 177–190.

Mueller, E., Gurin, G., & Wood, M. (1962). *Participation in outdoor recreation: Factors affecting demand among American adults* (Outdoor Recreation Resources Review Commission, Study Report No. 20). Washington, DC: U.S. Government Printing Office.

Raymore, L. A., Godbey, G. C., & Crawford, D. W. (1994). Self-esteem, gender, and socioeconomic status: Their relation to perceptions of constraint on leisure among adolescents. *Journal of Leisure Research 26,* 99–118.

Raymore, L. A., Godbey, G. C., Crawford, D. W., & von Eye, A. (1993). Nature and process of leisure constraints: An empirical test. *Leisure Sciences, 15,* 99–113.

Ritter, C., Ditton, R. B., & Riechers, R. K. (1992). Constraints to sport fishing: Implications for fisheries management. *Fisheries, 17*(4), 16–19.

Rojek, C. (1989). Leisure and recreation theory. In E. L. Jackson & T. L. Burton (Eds.), *Understanding leisure and recreation: Mapping the past, charting the future* (pp. 69–88). State College, PA: Venture Publishing, Inc.

Romsa, G., & Hoffman, W. (1980). An application of nonparticipation data in recreation research: Testing the opportunity theory. *Journal of Leisure Research, 12,* 321–328.

Rublee, C. B., & Shaw, S. M. (1990). Constraints on the leisure and community participation of immigrant women: Implications for social integration. *Loisir et Société/Society and Leisure, 14*(1), 133–150.

Samdahl, D. M. (1991). Issues in the measurement of leisure: A comparison of theoretical and connotative meanings. *Leisure Sciences, 13,* 33–49.

Samdahl, D., & Jekubovich, N. (1997a). A critique of leisure constraints: Comparative analyses and understandings. *Journal of Leisure Research, 29,* 430–452.

Samdahl, D., & Jekubovich, N. (1997b). A rejoinder to Henderson's and Jackson's commentaries on "A critique of leisure constraints," *Journal of Leisure Research, 29,* 469–471.

Schreyer, R., & Driver, B. L. (1989). The benefits of leisure. In E. L. Jackson & T. L. Burton (Eds.), *Understanding leisure and recreation: Mapping the past, charting the future* (pp. 385–419). State College, PA: Venture Publishing, Inc.

Scott, D. (1991). The problematic nature of participation in contract bridge: A qualitative study of group-related constraints. *Leisure Sciences, 13,* 321–336.

Scott, D. (1993). Time scarcity and its implications for leisure behavior and leisure delivery. *Journal of Park and Recreation Administration, 11,* 51–60.

Scott, D., & Jackson, E. L. (1996). Factors that limit and strategies that might encourage people's use of public parks. *Journal of Park and Recreation Administration, 14,* 1–17.

Scott, D., & Munson, W. (1994). Perceived constraints to park usage among individuals with low incomes. *Journal of Park and Recreation Administration, 12,* 52–69.

Searle, M. S. (1991). Propositions for testing social exchange theory in the context of ceasing leisure participation. *Leisure Sciences, 13,* 279–294.

Searle, M. S., & Brayley, R. E. (1992). *Is constrained leisure an internally homogeneous concept? A further examination.* Paper presented at the National Recreation and Parks Association Symposium on Leisure Research, Cincinnati, OH.

Searle, M. S., & Jackson, E. L. (1985a). Socioeconomic variations in perceived barriers to recreation participation among would-be participants. *Leisure Sciences, 7,* 227–249.

Searle, M. S., & Jackson, E. L. (1985b). Recreation nonparticipation and barriers to participation: Considerations for the management of recreation delivery systems. *Journal of Park and Recreation Administration, 3,* 23–36.

Shank, J. (1986). An exploration of leisure in the lives of dual-career women. *Journal of Leisure Research, 18,* 300–319.

Shaw, S. M. (1994). Gender, leisure, and constraint: Towards a framework for the analysis of women's leisure. *Journal of Leisure Research, 26,* 8–22.

Shaw, S. M., Bonen, A., & McCabe, J. F. (1991). Do more constraints mean less leisure? Examining the relationship between constraints and participation. *Journal of Leisure Research, 23,* 286–300.

Stockdale, J. E. (1989). Concepts and measures of leisure participation and preference. In E. L. Jackson & T. L. Burton (Eds.), *Understanding leisure and recreation: Mapping the past, charting the future* (pp. 113–150). State College, PA: Venture Publishing, Inc.

Sykes, C. J. (1988). *Profscam: Professors and the demise of higher education.* New York, NY: St. Martin's Press.

Tourism and Outdoor Recreation Planning Study. (1978). *Tourism and recreational behavior of Ontario residents—Vol. 5: Preference and constraints.* Toronto, Ontario: Author.

Wade, M. G. (Ed.). (1985). *Constraints on leisure.* Springfield, IL: Charles C. Thomas.

Washburne, R. (1978). Black underparticipation in wildlife recreation: Alternative explanations. *Leisure Sciences, 1,* 175–189.

Whyte, L. B., & Shaw, S. M. (1994). Women's leisure: An exploratory study of fear of violence as a leisure constraint. *Journal of Applied Recreation Research, 19,* 5–21.

Willits, W. L., & Willits, F. K. (1986). Adolescent participation in leisure activities: "The less, the more" or "the more, the more"? *Leisure Sciences, 8,* 189–206.

Witt, P. A., & Goodale, T. L. (1981). The relationship between barriers to leisure enjoyment and family stages. *Leisure Sciences, 4,* 29–49.

Wright, B. A., & Goodale, T. L. (1991). Beyond nonparticipation: Validation of interest and frequency of participation categories in constraints research. *Journal of Leisure Research, 23,* 314–331.

Crowding and Carrying Capacity in Outdoor Recreation: From Normative Standards to Standards of Quality

Robert E. Manning

University of Vermont

Introduction

Nearly everyone who visits parks and related areas returns with a variety of stories to tell to family and friends. And with more of us visiting parks than ever before, an increasing number of these stories concern crowding-related issues in their multiple manifestations. A mid-1990s workshop on the national parks in the United States was instructive. Participants enumerated a litany of crowding-related problems that are becoming increasingly familiar: automobile congestion; full parking lots, campgrounds, and lodges; long lines for services; overtaxed rangers and staff; more stringent rules and regulations; higher fees; mandatory use permits; conflicts among visitors; and degraded park resources (Lime, 1996).

A review of the literature in outdoor recreation suggests that crowding and related concerns are perennial issues. Expressions of such concerns can be found even before the post–World War II boom in outdoor recreation (Adams, 1930; Leopold, 1934). Early scientific studies of outdoor recreation documented concern over crowding in a variety of park and outdoor recreation settings (Lime, 1971; Lucas, 1964a; Outdoor Recreation Resources Review Commission, 1962; Stankey, 1973). This concern has intensified as the use of parks and related areas has continued to grow. Again, the U.S. national parks are instructive. Annual visits to the national parks are now counted in the hundreds of millions. In the decade of the 1970s visitation increased by 30 percent. In the 1980s visits rose another 35 percent. If this trend continues, the national park system can expect more than 300 million visits by the beginning of the next millennium.

Within the professional literature, crowding and carrying capacity are often closely linked. For example, from both a research and a management standpoint, crowding is often incorporated within the conceptual framework of carrying capacity. In its most generic form, carrying capacity can be defined as the amount of visitor use that can be appropriately accommodated within a park or related outdoor recreation area. Carrying capacity is based on the notion that the use of parks and related areas has both resource and social impacts. Moreover, these impacts may ultimately cause unacceptable change to resource and social conditions. Crowding is often viewed as the most direct social impact of outdoor recreation.

Crowding and carrying capacity can be linked even more directly through the application of normative theory and methods. Normative theory was developed in the disciplines of sociology and social psychology, and suggests that people often have standards by which elements of behavior may be judged. The theoretical framework of norms provides for a more comprehensive understanding of crowding in outdoor recreation. Moreover, empirical techniques based on norm-related research provide a means of studying personal and social norms for crowding and related issues. These empirical methods can be used to help formulate standards of quality for outdoor recreation, an approach that is at the heart of contemporary carrying capacity models.

Crowding and carrying capacity are long-standing issues in outdoor recreation and are becoming increasingly important. Moreover, they are conceptually linked on both theoretical and methodological levels. This chapter explores these topics along with emerging theoretical and methodological issues.

Crowding in Outdoor Recreation

As noted, crowding can be best understood as a normative concept. Normative theory makes an important distinction between the amount of visitor use and crowding. The amount of visitor use is a physical concept relating to the number of people per unit of space; as such it is subjectively neutral and has no psychological or experiential meaning. Crowding, on the other hand, has a definitive social-psychological or evaluative meaning; it is a subjective and negative judgment about a given amount of visitor use. Thus, for the individual, visitor use may increase to a point where it is perceived to interfere in some way with a desired experience. At this point, the normative standard for visitor use level is exceeded and some degree of perceived crowding begins.

Numerous studies demonstrate that normative standards for crowding in outdoor recreation are dependent upon a variety of circumstances. These circumstances can be grouped into the following three broad categories:

1. personal characteristics of visitors;
2. characteristics of other visitors encountered; and
3. situational variables.

Personal Characteristics of Visitors

Several studies have found that crowding norms are influenced by the personal and cognitive characteristics of visitors. Visitor motivations have consistently been found to influence normative definitions of crowding. A study of visitors to the Buffalo National River, for example, found wide diversity in perceived crowding among a sample of river floaters (Ditton, Fedler and Graefe, 1983). Visitor motivations were found to be important in explaining why some visitors felt crowded while others did not. Some visitors felt crowded and these respondents reported significantly higher ratings on the motivation "to get away from other people." Some visitors did not report feeling crowded and some reported that their enjoyment of the trip was enhanced by contact with other visitors. This latter group reported significantly higher ratings on the motivations "to be part of a group," "to have thrills and excitement," and "to share what I have learned with others." Similar results were obtained in a study of floaters on the Green and Yampa Rivers in Dinosaur National Monument (Roggenbuck and Schreyer, 1977; Schreyer and Roggenbuck, 1978). Visitor motivations also were found to influence crowding perceptions of backcountry hikers in Yosemite National Park (Absher and Lee, 1981). While the amount of visitor use alone explained little of the variance in perceived crowding, the addition of respondent ratings of seven trip motivations substantially increased the variance explained in perceived crowding.

Visitor expectations and preferences for contacts with other visitors also influence crowding perceptions. A study of river rafters on the Colorado River in Grand Canyon National Park found virtually no relationship between various use level or contact measures and perceived crowding (Shelby, 1981). However, statistically significant correlations were found between perceived crowding and both expectations and preferences for contacts with other visitors. Similarly, only a weak relationship was found between use levels and perceived crowding among campers at Katmai National Monument (Womble and Studebaker, 1981). However, expectations and preferences for use level explained substantially more of the variation in perceived crowding. Likewise, only moderate relationships were found between visitor contacts and perceived crowding among hikers at Mount McKinley National Park (Bultena, Field, Womble and Albrecht, 1981). Stronger relationships were found between perceived crowding and both preferences and expectations for contacts with other visitors.

Visitor experience has also been consistently found to influence perceived crowding. Experience level is thought to affect normative definitions of crowding, either through refinement of tastes (Bryan, 1977; Krutilla, 1967; Munley and Smith, 1976) or by virtue of exposure to lower use levels as a result of earlier participation. The bulk of the empirical evidence supports the notion that more experienced visitors are more sensitive to higher use levels. This appears true regardless of how experience is measured: general experience in the activity, rate of participation, experience on-site, or some other dimension. Two studies of backcountry hikers at Grand Canyon National Park have found that repeat visitors have a stronger desire for solitude (Stewart and Carpenter, 1989; Towler, 1977). Similarly, more experienced hikers on the Appalachian Trail expressed stronger preferences for low-density hiking (Murray, 1974).

Characteristics of Other Visitors Encountered

There is considerable evidence that the characteristics of other visitors encountered also influence crowding norms. It seems only reasonable to think that tolerance for meeting other groups would depend, at least to some extent, on the characteristics of such groups. Several studies support this view empirically, with group characteristics most often defined in terms of mode of travel. Studies in the Boundary Waters Canoe Area Wilderness have found that paddling canoeists sharply distinguish among the three types of area users when asked their reactions to meeting other groups (Lewis, Lime and Anderson, 1996; Lime, 1977; Lucas, 1964a, 1964b; Stankey, 1973). They dislike encountering motorboats, are less resentful of encountering motorized canoes, and are relatively tolerant of encountering at least some other paddled canoes. Motor canoeists make similar distinctions, though not as sharply. Thus, canoeists feel crowded at much lower levels of use where motorboats are present.

Other studies also have found differential crowding effects based on mode of travel. Backcountry visitors to Everglades National Park were found to be substantially more sensitive to meeting other visitors who were traveling by motorboat as compared to canoes (Stewart, Snow and Ivey, 1991). Visitors to three western wilderness areas were found to have lower toler-

ances for encountering groups of horseback riders than backpackers (Stanley, 1973).

It has also been suggested that party size affects crowding norms (Lime, 1972). Considerable support has been found for this notion. For example, a majority of visitors to several U.S. wilderness areas reported they would prefer to see five small parties during the day rather than one large party (Stankey, 1973).

The behavior of other groups also seems to affect crowding norms. A study of hikers in a national forest, for example, found that about one third of respondents were bothered by other visitors (West, 1982). However, probing more deeply, it was found that of this group, the majority were bothered by the *behavior* of others, while only a minority were bothered by the *number* of others encountered. Specific forms of behavior reported as bothering respondents were, in descending order: noise, yelling, and loud behavior; littering and polluting lakes; and noncompliance with rules. Respondents exposed to high perceived density (those reporting 10 or more contacts) and negative behavior felt crowded nearly half the time, while respondents exposed to high perceived density but not negative behavior felt crowded only a small percentage of the time.

A third characteristic of other groups that seems to affect crowding norms is the degree to which groups are perceived as being alike. This factor appears closely related to behavior, but is more difficult to measure and study. A finding common to nearly all studies of park and outdoor visitors is that the vast majority of people visit parks in family and/or friendship groups. This suggests that the notion of solitude so often associated with certain types of outdoor recreation may not mean simple isolation from other people. It also suggests an inward focus on interpersonal relationships within the social group. Both of these notions are ultimately important in the concept of alikeness.

Both theoretical and empirical research confirms that solitude in outdoor recreation may have more to do with interaction among group members free from disruptions than with actual isolation (Hammitt, 1982; Hammitt and Patterson, 1991; Hammitt and Rutlin, 1995; Twight, Smith and Wassigner, 1981). This finding suggests that as long as contacts with other groups are not considered disturbing, they do not engender feelings of crowding or dissatisfaction.

A study of backpackers in Yosemite National Park illustrates the notion of perceptions of alikeness (Lee, 1975, 1977). In this study, no relationship was found between perceived crowding and behavioral measures of satisfaction. This finding is attributed to the idea that most social interaction between groups in park and related settings is conducted with little conscious deliberation. People are therefore largely unaware of such social interaction, and it has little effect on perceptions of crowding. The study concluded that the quality of a visitor experience "appears to be closely linked with the opportunity to take for granted the behavior of other visitors," and that "an essential ingredient for such an experience [is] the assumption that other visitors are very much like oneself, and will, therefore, behave in a similar manner." Thus, to the extent that groups are perceived as alike and require little conscious attention, encounters have limited disruptive effects on intimacy and other dimensions of solitude desired by social groups in parks and related settings.

Situational Variables

Finally, the setting in which contacts between visitor groups occurs apparently influences, to some extent, the ways in which those contacts are perceived and evaluated. It was suggested very early in crowding research that there are inter-area differences in crowding norms (Clawson and Knetsch, 1966). Hypothetical curves relating the effects of level of use to the quality of the visitor experience were seen as taking dramatically different shapes for three types of parks and related areas: wilderness, an unimproved campground, and a highly developed campground. That different use levels are appropriate for different types of parks seems obvious in a conceptual way, though not much is known about the issue in a quantitative sense. Some empirical evidence is offered by a study of use level–crowding relationships among visitors to seashore beaches (McConnell, 1977). Different relationships were found at different types of beaches, ranging from a natural area to a highly developed "singles" beach. Similarly, a study of river recreationists found different patterns of desired use levels among users of six river types, ranging from primitive to urban (Manning and Ciali, 1981).

More focus has been placed on intra-area differences in crowding norms. Visitors to wilderness areas, for example, are more sensitive to crowding at campsites than along trails (Burch and Wenger, 1967; Lime, 1977; Lucas, 1980; Stankey, 1973, 1980). Heightened sensitivity to encounters has also been found in the interior of wilderness as opposed to the periphery (Lime, 1977; Stankey, 1973). Given the choice, most wilderness visitors expressed a preference for encounters to occur within the first few miles of the trailhead rather than in interior zones.

Finally, it also has been suggested that crowding may depend to some extent on the physical, nonhuman environment (Hammitt, 1983). An area might be perceived as crowded, for example, because the amount and configuration of facilities prohibit a visitor from functioning as desired, even when only a small number of visitors are present. This issue has received little research attention, though a study of crowding in a developed campground in Katmai National Monument is suggestive (Womble and Studebaker, 1981). This study found very little relationship between level of use and perceived crowding. However, the study went on to use an open-ended comments section of the questionnaire in an effort to identify other factors which might account for unexplained variance in crowding perceptions. Several factors were identified, the most important of which were close proximity of campsites and insufficient facilities. This suggests that design aspects of the recreation environment may be involved in normative definitions of crowding.

A related consideration is the perceived environmental quality of parks. A study of visitors to the Dolly Sods Wilderness Area, West Virginia, created an index of perceived environmental disturbance (Vaske, Graefe and Dempster, 1982). The index was comprised of six items for which respondents rated perceived conditions as worse than, about the same as, or better than expected. Some respondents rated conditions worse than expected, and this had a substantive effect on perceived crowding. When the perceived environmental disturbance index was added to measures of reported, preferred, and expected contacts, the amount of variance explained in perceived crowding rose substantially. Moreover, the environmental disturbance index had the largest effect on perceived crowding of any of the four independent variables. These findings indicate that perceived crowding is influenced not only by the physical presence of others, but also by the environmental impacts left by previous visitors. These findings are consistent with other studies which indicate that park visitors are often more disturbed by the presence of litter or other environmental degradation than by contacts with other visitor groups (Lee, 1975; Lucas, 1980; Stankey, 1973).

From Crowding to Carrying Capacity

As noted earlier, concern over crowding is often incorporated within the concept of carrying capacity. The underlying concept of carrying capacity has a rich history in the natural resource professions. In particular, it has proven a useful concept in wildlife and range management, where it refers to the number of animals of any one species that can be maintained in a given habitat (Dasmann, 1964). Carrying capacity has obvious parallels and intuitive appeal in the field of park and outdoor recreation management. However, the first rigorous applications of carrying capacity to outdoor recreation did not occur until the 1960s.

These initial, scientific applications of carrying capacity suggested that the concept was more complex in this new management context. At first, as might be expected, the focus was placed on the relationship between visitor use and environmental conditions. The working hypothesis was that increasing visitor use causes greater environmental impact as measured by soil compaction, destruction of vegetation, and related variables. It soon became apparent, however, that there was another dimension of carrying capacity dealing with the social aspects of the visitor experience. An early and important report on the application of carrying capacity to outdoor recreation, for example, reported that the study (Wagar, 1964):

> [W]as initiated with the view that the carrying capacity of recreation lands could be determined primarily in terms of ecology and the deterioration of areas. However, it soon became obvious that the resource-oriented point of view must be augmented by consideration of human values.

The point was that, as more people visit an area, not only can the environmental resources of the area be affected, but so too can the quality of the visitor experience. Again, the working hypothesis was that increasing visitor use causes greater social impacts as measured by crowding and related variables. Thus, as applied to outdoor recreation, carrying capacity has two components: environmental and social.

Social Carrying Capacity

The early scientific work on carrying capacity has blossomed into an extended literature on the social aspects of outdoor recreation and their application to carrying capacity (e.g., Kuss, Graefe and Vaske, 1990; Manning, 1986; Shelby and Heberlein, 1986; Stankey and Lime, 1973). But despite the impressive literature base, efforts to determine and apply social carrying capacity have often resulted in frustration. The principal difficulty lies in determining how much social impact, such as crowding, is too much. Given the substantial demand for outdoor recreation, some decline or change in the quality of the visitor experience (e.g., some perceived crowding) is inevitable. But how much decline or change is appropriate or acceptable? This issue is often referred to as the "limits of acceptable change" and is fundamental to social carrying capacity determination (Frissell and Stankey, 1972; Lime, 1970).

This issue is illustrated graphically in Figure 19.1. In this figure, a hypothetical relationship between visitor use and crowding is shown. It is clear from this line that visitor use level and perceived crowding are related: increasing numbers of visitors cause increasing percentages of visitors to report feeling crowded. However, it is not clear at what point carrying capacity has been reached. The relationship in Figure 19.1 illustrates that some crowding is inevitable given even relatively low levels of visitor use. Thus, some level of crowding must be tolerated if parks and related areas are to remain open for public use. For this relationship, X_1 and X_2 represent alternative levels of visitor use that result in alternative levels of crowding as defined by points Y_1 and Y_2, respectively. But which of these points—Y_1 or Y_2, or some other point along this axis—represents the maximum amount of crowding that is acceptable?

To emphasize and further clarify this issue, some writers have suggested distinguishing between descriptive and prescriptive components of social carrying capacity determination (Shelby and Heberlein, 1986). The descriptive component of social carrying capacity focuses on factual, objective data such as the relationship in Figure 19.1. For example, what is the relationship between the amount of visitor use and visitor perceptions of crowding? The prescriptive component concerns the seemingly more subjective issue of how much impact or change in the recreation experience is acceptable. For example, what level of perceived crowding should be allowed before management intervention is appropriate?

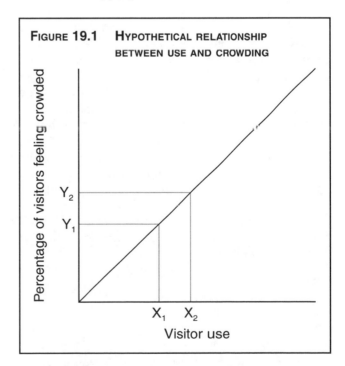

FIGURE 19.1   HYPOTHETICAL RELATIONSHIP BETWEEN USE AND CROWDING

Indicators and Standards of Quality

Recent experience with carrying capacity suggests that answers to these questions can be found through the formulation of indicators and standards of quality (Graefe, Kuss and Vaske, 1990; National Park Service, 1992; Shelby, Stankey and Shindler, 1992; Stankey et al., 1985; Stankey and Manning, 1986). This approach to carrying capacity focuses on defining the type of visitor experience to be provided and then monitoring conditions over time to assess whether or not acceptable conditions have been maintained. Indicators of quality are specific, measurable variables which define the resource and social conditions to be managed within a park or related area. Standards of quality define the minimum acceptable condition of each indicator variable.

A brief example may help illuminate these definitions. An initial description of a park or related area may suggest that social conditions should offer visitors opportunities for solitude. This is a broad, qualitative statement that is helpful in general terms, but is not specific enough to guide management. For example, what constitutes "opportunities for solitude," and how is "solitude" to be measured? Indicators and standards of quality provide answers to these types of questions. It may be determined through a program of research that the number of encounters with other groups along trails is a key measure of opportunities for solitude. Thus, the number of trail encounters with other groups per day may be a good indicator of quality. Moreover, most visitors may report that, once they encounter more than three groups along trails per day, they no longer achieve an acceptable level of solitude. Thus, the standard of quality for the number of trail encounters per day may be appropriately set at three.

By defining indicators and standards of quality, carrying capacity can be determined and managed through a monitoring program. Indicators of quality can be monitored over time and once standards have been violated, carrying capacity has been reached. This approach to carrying capacity is central to contemporary park planning frameworks, including Limits of Acceptable Change (LAC) (Stankey et al., 1985), Visitor Impact Management (VIM) (Graefe et al., 1990) and Visitor Experience and Resource Protection (VERP) (National Park Service, 1993).

A Normative Approach to Standards of Quality

Not surprisingly, one of the most problematic issues in this contemporary approach to carrying capacity has been setting standards of quality. Such standards may be based on a variety of sources, including legal and administrative mandates, agency policy, historic precedent, expert judgment, interest group politics, and public opinion, especially that derived from outdoor recreation visitors. This latter source has special appeal as it involves those people directly interested in and affected by carrying capacity decisions and related management actions.

Research on visitor-based standards of quality has relied heavily on normative theory and related empirical techniques. As applied in outdoor recreation, norms are generally defined as standards that individuals and groups use for evaluating behavior and social and environmental conditions (Donnelly, Vaske and Shelby, 1992; Shelby and Vaske, 1991; Vaske, Graefe, Shelby and Heberlein, 1986). If visitors have normative standards concerning relevant aspects of recreation experiences, then such norms can be studied and used as a basis for formulating standards of quality. In this way, carrying capacity can be determined and managed more effectively.

Application of norms to standards of quality in outdoor recreation is most fully described by Shelby and Heberlein (1986) and Vaske et al. (1986). These applications have relied heavily upon the work of Jackson (1965), who developed a methodology—return potential curves—to measure norms. Using these methods, the personal norms of individuals can be aggregated to test for the existence of social norms or the degree to which norms are shared across groups. Normative research in outdoor recreation has focused largely on the issue of crowding (e.g., Hall and Shelby, 1996; Heberlein, Alfano and Ervin, 1986; Manning, Lime, Freimund and Pitt, 1996; Manning, Lime and Hof, 1996; Manning, Lime, Hof and Freimund, 1995; Patterson and Hammitt, 1990; Shelby, 1981; Shelby and Heberlein, 1986; Vaske et al., 1986; Whittaker and Shelby, 1988; Williams, Roggenbuck and Bange, 1991), but also has been expanded to include other potential indicators of quality, including ecological impacts (Manning et al., 1995; Manning, Lime and Hof, 1996; Shelby, Vaske and Harris, 1988), wildlife management practices (Vaske and Donnelly, 1988), and minimum stream flows (Shelby and Whittaker, 1990).

From Normative Standards to Standards of Quality: Theoretical and Methodological Issues

The concept of norms has attracted considerable attention as an organizing framework in outdoor recreation research and management. In particular, normative theory and methods have special application in understanding crowding in outdoor recreation and setting standards of quality for crowding and other social impacts of increasing outdoor recreation use. Normative theory suggests that outdoor recreation visitors may have standards by which they judge a situation to be crowded or otherwise unacceptable. Moreover, these normative standards can be measured and used as a basis for setting standards of quality by which carrying capacity can be determined and managed.

In these ways, normative theory and methods have enhanced understanding of crowding and the ability to manage crowding and related issues within the context of carrying capacity. However, several theoretical and empirical issues have arisen in the application and development of norms in outdoor recreation. These issues include the application of normative theory to outdoor recreation, the validity of norm-based standards of quality as measured by norm congruence, and norm measurement issues.

Application of Normative Theory to Outdoor Recreation

As described previously, normative theory is an appealing social construct for studying and managing crowding and carrying capacity. However, there are some uncertainties regarding application of the social norms construct in outdoor recreation. As originally developed in sociology, norms usually refer to social rules or standards of behavior. Early social theorists used terms such as customs, mores, and folkways as precursors to the contemporary concept of norms (Cooley, 1914; Sumner, 1940; Tonnies, 1961, 1971). Recent reviews of social norms applied in the recreation context (Heywood, 1996; Noe, 1992; Roggenbuck, Williams, Bange and Dean, 1991) have identified several distinguishing features of norms as traditionally applied. First, actions guided by norms are obligatory and are enforced by sanctions (Homans, 1950; Rossi and Berk, 1985). Second, norms are action-oriented in that they guide behavior (Biddle, 1986; Blake and

Davis, 1964; Cancian, 1975). Third, norms are shared by social groups (Rossi and Berk, 1985). Based on these reviews, it is suggested that recreation researchers may be studying personal norms or preferences rather than social norms. For example, crowding standards of recreationists (e.g., number of river encounters) may not be enforced by any type of social sanction, may not involve modifications of personal behavior, and may not be widely shared.

Other recreation researchers encourage a more expansive interpretation of social norms as they are applied to the context of parks and related areas (Donnelly et al., 1992; Vaske et al., 1986). For example, Shelby and Vaske (1991) suggest that:

1. recreation often involves emerging norms for which strong sanctions and a sense of obligation have yet to fully evolve;
2. recreation-related norms can apply to social and resource conditions as well as behavior because such conditions are often a function of individual behavior (moreover, recreation-related norms often regulate collective rather than individual behavior); and
3. recreation research has documented some degree of consensus regarding a number of recreation-related norms.

It is clear that there are some definitional issues and uncertainties surrounding normative theory and its application to outdoor recreation. Nevertheless, the notion that individuals may have standards about relevant conditions of a recreation experience, and that there may be some consensus about such standards, appears promising as a means to address some of the more difficult, evaluative aspects of crowding and related carrying capacity issues.

Norm Congruence

Recent research attention has focused on the issue of norm congruence. This issue is also referred to as "norm-impact compatibility" (Shelby and Vaske, 1991). Norm congruence is concerned with the extent to which visitors evaluate relevant aspects of their recreation experience in keeping with their normative standards. If visitor norms are to be used in establishing standards of quality, then norm congruence research is important to test the "validity" of visitor norms.

Research findings are generally supportive of norm congruence. Several studies have found that visitors generally respond both cognitively and behaviorally in a way that conforms to their normative standards.

That is, when visitors experience conditions which violate their personal and/or social norms, they tend to report (Lewis, Lime and Anderson, 1996; Manning, Lime and Hof, 1996; Manning, Lime, Freimund and Pitt, 1996; Vaske et al., 1986; Williams et al., 1991):

1. feeling crowded,
2. experiencing a different type of trip than expected,
3. seeing too many people,
4. feeling disturbed by the number of people they saw, and/or
5. taking some action to avoid encounters with other visitors.

Only one study has cast some doubt on norm congruence, and this might be interpreted as an especially strict test (Patterson and Hammitt, 1990). While additional research on this important issue is clearly justified, initial studies lend support to the validity of the normative approach.

Norm Measurement

Several norm measurement approaches and issues have recently emerged in the literature. Traditionally, visitor norms in outdoor recreation have been measured using a numerical approach (Shelby and Heberlein, 1986). That is, respondents are asked to judge the acceptability of alternative levels of social impacts, such as increasing use levels. For example, respondents might be asked to rate the acceptability of a range of encounters with other groups per day along trails. Resulting data are aggregated and graphed to produce a norm curve from which social norms can be derived. This numerical approach is often shortened to reduce respondent burden by simply asking respondents to state the maximum acceptable level of impact. When this shortened version is used, respondents may be given the option of indicating that they cannot state a maximum acceptable level of impact or that the level of impact does not matter.

More recently, visual approaches to measuring visitor norms have been developed (Hof et al., 1994; Manning et al., 1995; Manning, Lime and Hof, 1996; Manning, Lime, Freimund and Pitt, 1996). In this technique, computer software is used to manipulate photographs to depict alternative levels of impact. As with the numerical approach described previously, long and short versions of this measurement technique can be used. The long version asks respondents to evaluate and rate the acceptability of each in a series of photographs. The short version asks respondents to select the photograph that illustrates the highest acceptable level of impact.

A third set of norm measurement and application issues concerns how survey questions are formulated and worded. For example, questions often use the word *acceptability* to probe for respondents' personal norms. But how is this word interpreted by respondents and how should such study findings be applied? Do such questions reveal the preferences of respondents or their absolute tolerance or something in between? Secondly, are personal norms of respondents influenced by knowledge of the management implications of such norms? In other words, if respondents understood more explicitly that their expressed norms would lead to management actions to exclude or otherwise regulate visitors, would they express more tolerance for greater levels of impact? Third, how do personal norms, as conventionally measured in recreation research, relate to norms as externally imposed by others? As noted previously, the sociological literature traditionally suggests that norms involve constraints on individual behavior as imposed by the views of a larger group. Therefore, do respondents feel that their personal norms are similar or dissimilar to the norms of "others"?

The norm measurement approaches and issues described in this chapter are important for at least two reasons. First, some norm measurement techniques may be more appropriate in certain circumstances than others. For example, visual approaches to crowding-related norms may be more relevant to respondents than numerical approaches in high-density situations. Moreover, the long version of norm measurement questions yields richer information on social norms, but is more burdensome to respondents. Furthermore, when measuring norms in high-density situations or with relatively inexperienced visitors, it may be especially important to allow respondents the option of reporting that they cannot state a maximum acceptable level of impact or that the level of impact does not matter. Findings from several studies suggest that visitors to wilderness areas are more likely than visitors to developed areas to have personal crowding norms, and that experienced visitors are more likely than first-time visitors to have personal crowding norms (Roggenbuck et al., 1991; Shelby and Vaske, 1991).

Second, alternative measurement approaches may yield different personal and social norms (Hall and Shelby, 1996; Manning, Valliere and Jacobi, 1997). For example, crowding norms along trails were found to be significantly higher when respondents were explicitly aware of potential management implications than when respondents did not explicitly consider such implications (Manning et al., 1997). This study also found that norms based on the notion of *tolerance* were substantially higher than norms based on the notion of *acceptability*.

Alternative approaches to norm measurement are evolving rapidly, and this has given rise to an increasing number of methodological issues. Innovations in norm measurement approaches will ultimately enhance the ability of researchers and managers to appropriately measure norms in a variety of outdoor recreation contexts. Moreover, continued research will help resolve issues surrounding norm measurement, interpretation, and application.

Conclusion

Crowding and carrying capacity have emerged as central issues in outdoor recreation. As the use of parks and related areas has continued to grow, related social, environmental, and managerial impacts have multiplied: perceived crowding and conflict among visitors has increased, degradation of ecological and cultural resources is more severe and widespread, and managers are forced to implement more restrictive controls on visitor use, including rules and regulations and use limits.

As this chapter demonstrates, crowding and carrying capacity have been the subject of considerable research and management attention. Normative theory and methods have emerged from this body of literature as an important approach to understanding and managing these issues. Normative theory provides a conceptual framework for understanding when and why increasing levels of visitor use may cross a threshold into perceived crowding. Moreover, normative theory has contributed to the concept of standards of quality which form the foundation of contemporary carrying capacity frameworks. Finally, methodological approaches associated with norm measurement have helped make standards of quality more operational. Normative theory and methods have added important insights and empirical techniques that have proven valuable to both researchers and managers. As is often the case, this kind of research has given rise to a number of theoretical and methodological issues. These issues provide an agenda for continued research and experimentation.

References

Absher, J. D., & Lee, R. G. (1981). Density as an incomplete cause of crowding in backcountry settings. *Leisure Sciences, 4*(3), 231–247.

Adams, J. T. (1930). Diminishing returns in modern life. *Harpers, 160,* 529–537.

Biddle, B. J. (1986). Recent developments in role theory. *Annual Review of Sociology, 12,* 67–92.

Blake, J., & Davis, K. (1964). Norms, values, and sanctions. In R. Faris (Ed.), *Handbook of modern sociology.* Chicago, IL: Rand McNally.

Bryan, H. (1977). Leisure value systems and recreational specialization: The case of trout fishermen. *Journal of Leisure Research, 9*(3), 174–187.

Bultena, G. L., Field D. R., Womble, P., & Albrecht, D. (1981). Closing the gates: A study of backcountry use-limitation at Mount McKinley National Park. *Leisure Sciences, 4*(3), 249–267.

Burch, W. R., Jr., & Wenger, W. D, Jr. (1967). *The social characteristics of participants in three styles of family camping* (Research Paper PNW-48). Portland, OR: USDA Forest Service Pacific Northwest Research Station.

Cancian, F. M. (1975). *What are norms? A study of beliefs and actions in a Maya community.* New York, NY: Cambridge University Press.

Clawson, M., & Knetsch, J. L. (1966). *Economics of outdoor recreation.* Baltimore, MD: Johns Hopkins University Press.

Cooley, C. H. (1914). *Social organization.* New York, NY: Charles Scribner's Sons.

Dasmann, R. F. (1964). *Wildlife biology.* New York, NY: John Wiley & Sons, Inc.

Ditton, R. B., Fedler, A. J., & Graefe, A. R. (1983). Factors contributing to perceptions of recreational crowding. *Leisure Sciences, 5*(4), 273–288.

Donnelly, M. P., Vaske, J., & Shelby, B. (1992). Establishing management standards: Selected examples of the normative approach. In B. Shelby, G. Stankey & B. Shindler (Eds.), *Defining wilderness quality: The role of standards in wilderness management—A workshop proceedings* (General Technical Report PNW-305). Portland, OR: USDA Forest Service Pacific Northwest Research Station.

Frissell, S. S., & Stankey, G. H. (1972). *Wilderness environmental quality: Search for social and ecological harmony.* Proceedings of the Society of American Foresters Annual Conference, Washington, DC.

Graefe, A. R., Kuss, F. R., & Vaske, J. J. (1990). *Visitor impact management: The planning framework.* Washington, DC: National Parks and Conservation Association.

Hall, T., & Shelby, B. (1996). Who cares about encounters? Differences between those with and without norms. *Leisure Sciences, 18*(1), 7–22.

Hammitt, W. E. (1982). Cognitive dimensions of wilderness solitude. *Environment and Behavior, 14*(4), 478–493.

Hammitt, W. E. (1983). Toward an ecological approach to perceived crowding in outdoor recreation. *Leisure Sciences, 5*(4), 309–320.

Hammitt, W. E., & Patterson, M. (1991). Coping behavior to avoid visitor encounters: Its relationship to wildland privacy. *Journal of Leisure Research, 23*(3), 225–237.

Hammitt, W. E., & Rutlin, W. (1995). Use encounter standards and curves for achieved privacy in wilderness. *Leisure Sciences, 17,* 245–262.

Heywood, J. (1996). Social regularities in outdoor recreation. *Leisure Sciences, 18*(1), 23–27.

Heberlein, T. A., Alfano, G. E., & Ervin, L. H. (1986). Using a social carrying capacity model to estimate the effects of marina development at the Apostle Islands National Lakeshore. *Leisure Sciences, 8*(3), 257–274.

Hof, M., Hammett, J., Rees, M., Belnap, J., Poe, N., Lime, D., & Manning, R. (1994). Getting a handle on visitor carrying capacity: A pilot project at Arches National Park. *Park Science, 14*(1), 11–13.

Homans, G. C. (1950). *The human group.* New York, NY: Harcourt Brace.

Jackson, J. (1965). Structural characteristics of norms. In I. D. Steiner & M. F. Fishbein (Eds.), *Current studies in social psychology.* New York, NY: Holt, Rinehart, Winston, Inc.

Krutilla, J. V. (1967). Conservation reconsidered. *American Economic Review, 57*(4), 77–786.

Kuss., F. R., Graefe, A. R., & Vaske, J. J. (1990). *Visitor impact management: A review of research.* Washington, DC: National Parks and Conservation Association.

Lee, R. G. (1975). *The management of human components in the Yosemite National Park ecosystem: Final research report.* Berkeley, CA: University of California.

Lee, R. G. (1977). Alone with others: The paradox of privacy in wilderness. *Leisure Sciences, 1*(1), 3–19.

Leopold, A. (1934). Conservation economics. *Journal of Forestry, 32,* 537–554.

Lewis, M. S., Lime, D. W., & Anderson, D. H. (1996). Paddle canoeists' encounter norms in Minnesota's Boundary Waters Canoe Area Wilderness. *Leisure Sciences, 18*(2), 143–160.

Lime, D. W. (1970). Research for determining use capacities of the Boundary Waters canoe area. *Naturalist, 21*(4), 9–13.

Lime, D. W. (1971). *Factors influencing campground use in the Superior National Forest of Minnesota* (Research Paper NC-60). St. Paul, MN: USDA Forest Service Northcentral Forest Experiment Station.

Lime, D. W. (1972). *Large groups in the Boundary Waters Canoe Area—Their numbers, characteristics, and impact* (Research Note NC-142). St. Paul, MN: USDA Forest Service Northcentral Forest Experiment Station.

Lime, D. W. (1977). When the wilderness gets crowded . . . ? *Naturalist, 28*(4), 1–7.

Lime, D. (Ed.). (1996). *Carrying capacity in the national park system* (Minnesota Agricultural Experiment Station Miscellaneous Publication 86–1996). St. Paul, MN: University of Minnesota.

Lucas, R. C. (1964a). *Recreational use of the Quetico-Superior area* (Research Paper LS-8). St. Paul, MN: USDA Forest Service Lake States Forest Experiment Station.

Lucas, R. C. (1964b). *The recreational capacity of Quetico-Superior area* (Research Paper LS-15). St. Paul, MN: USDA Forest Service Lake States Forest Experiment Station.

Lucas, R. C. (1980). Use patterns and visitor characteristics, attitudes, and preferences in nine wilderness and other roadless areas (Research Paper INT-253). Ogden, UT: USDA Forest Service Intermountain Forest and Range Experiment Station.

Manning, R. E. (1986). *Studies in outdoor recreation*. Corvallis, OR: Oregon State University Press.

Manning, R. E., & Ciali, C. P. (1981). Recreation and river types: Social-environmental relationships. *Environmental Management, 5*(2), 109–120.

Manning, R. E., Lime, D., Freimund, W., & Pitt, D. (1996). Crowding norms at frontcountry sites: A visual approach to setting standards of quality. *Leisure Sciences, 18*(1), 39–59.

Manning, R. E., Lime, D., & Hof, M. (1996). Social carrying capacity of natural areas: Theory and application in the national parks. *National Areas Journal, 16*(2), 118–127.

Manning, R. E., Lime, D., Hof, M., & Freimund, W. (1995). The visitor experience and resource protection (VERP) process: The application of carrying capacity to Arches National Park. *The George Wright Forum, 12*(3), 41–55.

Manning, R. E., Valliere, W. A., & Jacobi, C. (1997). Crowding norms for the carriage roads of Acadia National Park. In *Proceedings of the 1996 Northeastern Recreation Research Symposium* (General Technical Report NE-232, pp. 139–145). Radnor, PA: USDA Forest Service Northeastern Forest Experiment Station.

McConnell, K. E. (1977). Congestion and willingness to pay: A study of beach use. *Land Economics, 53*, 185–195.

Munley, V. G., & Smith, V. K. (1976). Learning-by-doing and experience: The case of whitewater recreation. *Land Economics, 52*(4), 545–553.

Murray, J. B. (1974). *Appalachian Trail users in the southern national forests: Their characteristics, attitudes, and management preferences* (Research Paper SE-116). Asheville, NC: USDA Forest Service Southeast Forest Experiment Station.

National Park Service. (1992). *Grand Canyon National Park visitor use management workshop findings and recommendations*. Denver, CO: Denver Service Center.

National Park Service. (1993). *Visitor experience and resource protection process*. Denver, CO: Denver Service Center.

Noe, F. (1992). Further questions about the measurement and conceptualization of backcountry encounter norms. *Journal of Leisure Research, 24*(1), 86–92.

Outdoor Recreation Resources Review Commission. (1962). *Outdoor recreation for America*. Washington, DC: U.S. Government Printing Office.

Patterson, M. E., & Hammitt, W. E. (1990). Backcountry encounter norms, actual reported encounters, and their relationship to wilderness solitude. *Journal of Leisure Research, 22*(3), 259–275.

Roggenbuck, J. W., & Schreyer, R. M. (1977). Relations between river trip motives and perception of crowding, management preference, and experience satisfaction. In *Proceedings of River Recreation Management and Research Symposium* (General Technical Report NC-28, pp. 359–364). St. Paul, MN: USDA Forest Service Northcentral Forest Experiment Station.

Roggenbuck, J. W., Williams, D. R., Bange, S. P., & Dean, D. J. (1991). River float trip encounter norms: Questioning the use of the social norms concept. *Journal of Leisure Research, 23*, 133–153.

Rossi, P. H., & Berk, R. A. (1985). Varieties of normative consensus. *American Sociological Review, 50*, 333–347.

Schreyer, R., & Roggenbuck, J. W. (1978). The influence of experience expectations on crowding perceptions and social-psychological carrying capacities. *Leisure Sciences, 1*(4), 373–394.

Shelby, B. (1981). Crowding models for backcountry recreation. *Land Economics, 56*(1), 43–55.

Shelby, B., & Heberlein, T. A. (1986). *Carrying capacity in recreation settings*. Corvallis, OR: Oregon State University Press.

Shelby, B., Stankey, G., & Shindler, B. (Eds.). (1992). *Defining wilderness quality: The role of standards in wilderness management—A workshop proceedings* (USDA Forest Service General Technical Report PMW-GTR-

305). Portland, OR: USDA Forest Service Pacific Northwest Forest Experiment Station.

Shelby, B., & Vaske, J. J. (1991). Using normative data to develop evaluative standards for resource management: A comment on three recent papers. *Journal of Leisure Research, 23*(2), 173–187.

Shelby, B., Vaske, J. J., & Harris, R. (1988). User standards for ecological impacts at wilderness campsites. *Journal of Leisure Research, 20*(3), 245–256.

Shelby, B., & Whittaker, D. (1990). *Recreation values and instream flow needs on the Delores River.* Paper presented at the Third Conference on Society and Resource Management, College Station, TX.

Stankey, G. H. (1973). *Visitor perception of wilderness recreation carrying capacity* (Research Paper INT-142). Ogden, UT: USDA Forest Service Intermountain Forest and Range Experiment Station.

Stankey, G. H. (1980). *A comparison of carrying capacity perceptions among visitors to two wildernesses* (Research Paper INT-242). Ogden, UT: USDA Forest Service Intermountain Forest and Range Experiment Station.

Stankey, G. H., Cole, D. N., Lucas, R. C., Peterson, M. E., Frissell, S. S., & Washburne, R. F. (1985). *The limits of acceptable change (LAC) system for wilderness planning* (General Technical Report INT-176, pp. 47–57). Ogden, UT: USDA Forest Service Intermountain Forest and Range Experiment Station.

Stankey, G. H., & Lime, D. W. (1973). *Recreational carrying capacity: An annotated bibliography* (General Technical Report INT-3). Ogden, UT: USDA Forest Service Intermountain Forest and Range Experiment Station.

Stankey, G. H., & Manning, R. E. (1986). *Carrying capacity of recreation settings. The President's commission on Americans outdoors: A literature review.* Washington, DC: U.S. Government Printing Office.

Stewart, W. P., & Carpenter, E. H. (1989). Solitude at Grand Canyon: An application of expectancy theory. *Journal of Leisure Research, 21*(1), 4–17.

Stewart, W. P., Snow, R. W., & Ivey, M. I. (1991). Sociological contributions to Everglades backcountry use management plan. *Park Science, 11*(1), 4–5.

Sumner, W. G. (1940). *Folkways: A study of the sociological importance of usages, manners, customs, mores, and morals.* New York, NY: Ginn.

Tonnies, F. (1961). *Custom: An essay on social codes.* Chicago, IL: Heury Regnery.

Tonnies, F. (1971). *On sociology: Pure, applied, and empirical.* Chicago, IL: University of Chicago Press.

Towler, W. L. (1977). Hiker perception of wilderness: A study of the social carrying capacity of Grand Canyon. *Arizona Review, 26*(8–9), 1–10.

Twight, B. W., Smith, W. L., & Wassinger, G. L. (1981). Privacy and camping: Closeness to the self vs. closeness to others. *Leisure Sciences, 4*(4), 427–441.

Vaske, J. J., & Donnelly, M. P. (1988). *Normative evaluations of wildlife management.* Paper presented at the Annual Congress of the National Recreation and Park Association, Indianapolis, IN.

Vaske, J. J., Graefe, A. R., & Dempster, A. (1982). Social and environmental influences on perceived crowding. In *Proceedings of the Wilderness Psychology Group Conference* (pp. 221–227), West Virginia University, Morgantown, WV.

Vaske, J. J., Graefe, A. R., Shelby, B., & Heberlein, T. (1986). Backcountry encounter norms: theory, method, and empirical evidence. *Journal of Leisure Research, 18*(3), 137–153.

Wagar, J. A. (1964). *The carrying capacity of wild lands for recreation* (Forest Science Monograph 7). Washington, DC: Society of American Forests.

West, P. C. (1982). Effects of user behavior on the perception of crowding in backcountry forest recreation. *Forest Science, 28*(1), 95–105.

Whittaker, D., & Shelby, B. (1988). Types of norms for recreation impacts: Extending the social norm concept. *Journal of Leisure Research, 20*(4), 261–273.

Williams, D. R., Roggenbuck, J. W., & Bange, S. P. (1991). The effect of norm-encounter compatibility on crowding perceptions, experience and behavior in river recreation settings. *Journal of Leisure Research, 23,* 154–172.

Womble, P., & Studebaker, S. (1981). Crowding in a national park campground. *Environment and Behavior, 13*(5), 557–573.

Conflict and the Recreational Experience

Alan W. Ewert
University of Indiana

Rodney B. Dieser
University of Northern British Columbia

Alison Voight
Recreation Research, Evaluation and Consulting (Bloomington, Indiana)

Without contraries there is no progression. Attraction, repulsion, reason and energy, love and hate, are necessary to human existence. (William Blake, 1757-1827)

Introduction

In 1997 literally millions of people were testing their mettle by engaging in various recreational activities in the European Alps (Gander and Ingold, 1997). Meanwhile, in North America, many more millions of recreationists were waiting for their chance to run a wild river, visit a national park, or seek out a unique tourism experience. At the end of their trip, most of these recreationists would say they had a high-quality recreation experience—*but not all!* The group who did not have a high-quality experience may have encountered too many people seeking the same type of endeavor, while others spent too much time and energy "battling" the elements. Some of these recreationists may have resented dealing with what they perceived as exceedingly restrictive regulations or uncooperative agency personnel, and others had their recreational experiences impacted by the thoughtless acts of others, some of which were unintentional and others malicious.

What these individuals experienced were different permutations of the many forms of recreational conflict. The purpose of this chapter is to define and explore recreational conflict and its role in the contemporary recreation and leisure scene. While the variables of recreational conflict can occur in any recreation and leisure setting, this chapter will focus on conflict within the framework of outdoor recreation. First, we will discuss the basic premise and definition of conflict research from a recreational and psychological perspective. We will then explore the prevalence as well as the history and theoretical foundations of conflict research in the recreational setting. Following this will be an examination of the major factors influencing recreational conflict, specifically within the context of culture and individual schemata. The chapter will conclude with an overview and discussion of recreation conflict and the implications for management and research strategies.

The Premise and Definition of Recreational Conflict

Premise of Recreational Conflict

Historically, recreational conflict has been characterized as difficulties between different types of uses of the same resource, such as snowmobilers and cross-country skiers being in close proximity. These skiers and snowmobilers represent two different types of users, both seeking a winter recreational experience, but in ways that can often interfere with one another. For example, snowmobiles tend to diminish cross-country skiers' sense of peace and quiet, while the presence of skiers often restricts the sense of freedom and speed that snowmobilers strive for. Past research has typically focused on recreational conflict as a function of activities or behaviors that interfere with each other. This approach by itself, however, does not capture the essence or reveal all the underlying dimensions of recreational conflict. There is more to recreational conflict than a competition for a resource or a perceived infringement of the recreation experience by other groups. We believe there exist two additional factors which are profoundly more influential on the entire spectrum of recreational conflict: culture and the individual thinking process or schema. It is our contention that any contemporary examination of recreational conflict must include a discussion involving culture and individual schemata. Failing to involve these variables by concentrating on the more traditional activity-interference issues would only serve to truncate researchers' understanding of the major forces underlying much of the chronic and pervasive conflicts facing the management of recreation opportunities. In other words, we believe the more challenging and long-term conflicts present in the contemporary recreation setting are increasingly due to cultural issues and individual attributes rather than simple interference of specific activities or goals. For example, conflict could occur when visitors to a day-use recreation area disagree over what constitutes appropriate behavior for that location, or when recreationists participating in the same activity argue about the maximum number of people that should be allowed in a particular site. The importance of culture and individual schemata will be discussed in more detail later in this chapter.

Defining Recreational Conflict

What is recreational conflict and how does it differ from other forms of conflict? Dictionary definitions of conflict include terms such as clash, antagonism, or a situation where one set of demands affects another set of demands (Morehead and Morehead, 1981). From a sociological perspective, conflict can be conceptualized as an overt struggle between individuals or groups within a society, often in response to competition for, and limited access to, scarce resources or opportunities (Jary and Jary, 1991). Depending on the individual belief system, this conflict may be seen as positive evidence of a healthy society, or it may represent evidence suggesting that the institutional framework of society is faulty. It should be further noted that conflict is not restricted to group versus group, or individual versus individual, but can also involve individual-versus-group interests. One example of this would be wildlife poaching, which reflects an activity performed by an individual that has detrimental impacts sustained by a larger population or group. This type of situation is often termed a *social dilemma* (Dawes, 1980; Karp, 1996; Yamagishi, 1994), with the most widely known example being "The Tragedy of the Commons" described by Garrett Hardin (1968).

From an individualistic, or psychological reference point, there has been widespread disagreement as to what the term *conflict* really means (Peterson, 1983). Much of the debate stems from whether there are overt signs of conflict, e.g., hostile action, argument, and so on. Thus, if one doesn't see any conflict, does it actually exist in that situation? Despite this lack of congruence, one prevalent view of conflict is based on the work of Lewin (1948); this view proposes that conflict is present when two people hold incompatible goals, or when one person pursues goals that interfere with the goals of another (Holmes and Murray, 1996; Lewin, 1948).

Within a recreation and leisure context, situations that have the potential to create conflict often include the allocation of resources (e.g., quota systems restricting use), perceptions of goal interference (motorboats versus canoes), differences in motivations (soloists versus large groups), and changes in land or resource use (Driver and Bassett, 1975; Dzurisk, 1983; Gramann and Burdge, 1981; Manning, 1986). Accordingly, we define *recreational conflict* in the following way:

A condition that exists when one person, or group of people, experience or perceive an interference of goals or the likelihood of incompatible goals, as the result of another person's or group's actions, threat of action, or personal/group attributes.

Using this definitional framework, recreational conflict occurs when the goals of one group or person are interfered with by another. Moreover, conflict can also occur when it is perceived that one set of goals is incompatible with another set of goals. It should be noted that, while the development of goals is of fundamental importance within the context of this definition, it is not a static entity. A number of researchers now suggest that goals, and by their proximity, motivations, can be changed within an individual's belief system (Gollwitzer and Moskowitz, 1996). In this case, constructs such as motivations are thought to be antecedents or precursors to the development of goals. People appear to have selective interests and goals that can either be transitory or long term, depending on their recreational experience. For example, someone who had a miserable first attempt at ice climbing may vow never to repeat the experience, thereby changing his or her goal from one of exploring a new activity to one of avoidance. Someone else, however, who experiences a great day of ice climbing, may regard his or her experience as a prelude to continued involvement. From a recreational perspective, there is growing evidence that goals and antecedent motivations can change as a result of factors such as experience level and trip outcome (Bryan, 1979; Ewert, 1993).

Prevalence of Recreational Conflict

It is commonly recognized that outdoor recreation is a popular leisure pursuit throughout the world. For example, in North America, visitation to USDA Forest Service recreation sites has grown from 287 million recreation visitor days in 1992 to 860 million in 1996 (Forest Service Digest, 1997; Zinzer, 1995). Likewise, outdoor recreation is very popular in Canada. For example, in 1989–1990 there were more than 40 million visits to British Columbia forest recreation sites (British Columbia Ministry of Forests, 1991). It would seem reasonable to assume that, with the increased popularity in outdoor recreation, there has also been an increase in potential recreational conflict.

Hendricks (1995) supports the view that recreational conflict is increasing and advocates a resurgence toward understanding recreational conflict:

The recent boom in outdoor recreation technology and continuing evolution of changes in social values has contributed to a renewed interest in recreation conflict. As new user groups such as mountain bikers, snowboarders, and helicopter skiers interact and share natural resources with more traditional backcountry users, land managers and researchers have recognized the need for creative approaches to manage these new interests. (p. 157)

In a similar fashion, Simcox (1996) suggests that natural resource managers need to develop a better management strategy for recreation, particularly as it relates to public land management:

Too many water or downhill skiers make for hazardous skiing. The noise and dust of off-road vehicles disrupts the solitude of others. Too many hunters in one area can create feelings of fear. The visual presence of others can impact one's sense of scenic beauty. Imagine the impact of nude sunbathers on a church group or the conflict created between horseback riders and mountain bikers, cross-country skiers and snowmobilers, water skiers and fishermen, canoeists and power boaters, or even duck hunters and bird watchers. (pp. 356–357)

Not surprisingly, many leisure scholars have predicted that recreational conflict will continue to become more important in the future (Butler, 1993; Edginton, Jordan, DeGraaf and Edginton, 1996; Gibbons and Ruddell, 1995; Jubenville and Twight, 1993; Orams, 1997). In part, understanding recreational conflict is contingent on the quality of our theoretical explanations, both in terms of what they are and how they were developed.

History and Theoretical Foundations of Conflict Research in the Recreational Setting

Not unexpectedly, research on recreational conflict coincided with the dramatic increase in outdoor recreation participation of the 1960s, which included large numbers of visitors to national parks and wilderness areas as access became easier (Williams, 1993). This research typically focused on the impact of one set of recreation activities upon another and the often one-sided or asymmetrical nature of these impacts (i.e., one group's activities having more impact on another group's and vice versa).

A theoretical basis for explaining and describing conflict in a recreation setting was pursued in the 1970s with various explanatory models of recreation conflict emerging. Several predominant theories included goal interference (Jacob and Schreyer, 1980); barriers to recreation goals based on psychological, physical or social constructs (Lindsay, 1980); and incompatibility of activities (Bury, Holland and McEwan, 1983). (See Schneider and Hammitt, 1995a, for a more detailed description of these models.) Of these models, goal interference is the most widely known and describes the interference of an individual's recreation goals by the actions of another. Goal interference is influenced by type of activity, importance of a specific resource, type of recreational experience, and tolerance of different lifestyles. An example of goal interference might be jet skiers who interfere with motor boats, who in turn impact on canoeists, who interfere with people who are fishing.

Jackson and Wong (1982) also suggest that motivations can play an important role in perceived conflicts. In other words, the nature and strength of motivations for participation can increase or lessen the potential for conflict with others. More recently, Schneider and Hammitt (1995a) have added personal locus of control, situational control, values, and belief systems to the list of variables that could influence or intensify conflict situations.

There are other items related to goals, however, that may have implications for understanding recreational conflict. These include goal specificity, type and importance of the needs that the goal satisfies, the effort required to achieve the goal, the number of goals threatened, and the degree to which they are endangered (Paterson and Neufeld, 1989). Goal specificity within a recreational conflict perspective refers to how well-defined an individual's goals are. For example, is the goal of the recreationist merely to have a good time (general specification), or is he interested in pursuing a specific activity at a specific location and for a specific reason? Obviously, the higher the level of specificity the greater the potential for interference and subsequent conflict. (See Locke and Latham, 1990, for a detailed summary of goal specificity.)

The type of need that a particular goal can satisfy often plays an important role in determining the presence and degree of recreational conflict. Deci and Ryan (1991) make the point that "not all needs are created equal." Some needs are construed by the individual

as being more important than others. Consequently, goals that satisfy needs which an individual perceives as very important are often more sensitive to potential interference and, hence, result in a greater likelihood of conflict. In addition, goals that are perceived as being the most important or valuable to an individual often require more effort to achieve (Wright and Brehm, 1989). This finding may help explain why recreational conflict is often intensified with different modes of travel (e.g., motorized versus nonmotorized, stock users versus hikers) and is typically asymmetrical. In other words, one activity impacts more heavily upon another because the user often perceives that he or she is expending more effort than another individual to achieve relatively the same goal (e.g., cross-country skiing versus snowmobiling to visit a secluded and remote site).

In sum, recreational conflict is a complex phenomenon that often contains a number of different yet interacting dimensions, including type of activities (Jackson and Wong, 1982); anticipated or expected consequences or outcomes (Driver, 1975); importance attached to the recreational endeavor (Jacob and Schreyer, 1980); levels of acceptance between users and the ways in which they recreate; and personal attributes, such as levels of experience and specialization (Watson, Niccolucci and Williams, 1994). Moreover, these and other factors often combine in various ways, depending on the specific situation, to create an increased sensitivity leading to conflict (Ramthun, 1995). As a number of researchers have indicated, however, there is often a difference between how people *perceive* a certain situation (i.e., potential-versus-real conflict) and how they actually *behave* or *respond* (Owens, 1985). Thus, conflict is not only a physical event (e.g., seeing too many people along the stream) but is also a psychological and perceptual event, such as "feeling" that an area is too crowded (Roggenbuck, 1992).

Despite the existence of these and other models of recreational conflict, additional work is warranted in developing a better understanding of the extent of conflict in recreation settings, in addition to knowing how conflict actually takes place and where. For a more detailed account of conflict theories within a recreational setting, see Watson and Hendricks (1995).

Major Factors Influencing Recreational Conflict

Vaske, Donnelly, Wittmann, and Laidlaw (1995) have suggested that recreational conflict arises when one group's activities interfere with another's and/or when individuals within a group have differing norms (standards). While new technologies have created the potential for new or intensified conflicts, it should be noted that many of these activities are often esoteric or elitist in nature (e.g., bungee jumping, snowboarding, llama packing) and performed by a relatively minor segment of the population. As such, they will generally affect only a small percentage of recreationists and, in actuality, generate a minimal amount of recreational conflict. Additional issues may have more impact, affect larger numbers of recreationists and create greater overall conflict.

As previously mentioned, many leisure researchers (Bury et al., 1983; Gibbons and Ruddell, 1995; Lindsay, 1980; Ruddell and Gramann, 1994) have attempted to identify the myriad of factors that influence conflict during recreational experiences, including activity style, technology, resource specificity, mode of experience, and lifestyle tolerances (Jacob and Schreyer, 1980). However, there exist two phenomena, in particular, that are often underrepresented in the recreational conflict research literature that may provide additional insight: *culture* and *individual schemata*.

Culture and Recreational Conflict

The assumption made at the beginning of this chapter was that culture is of paramount importance in understanding the concept of recreational conflict. Pedersen (1994) suggests that culture represents a conglomerate of complex and multidimensional variables, including demographics (e.g., age, race, gender), status (e.g., economic, social, educational), and affiliation attributes (e.g., religion, group membership). Because of the complex issues surrounding the concept of culture, it is often difficult to comprise a single, all-encompassing definition. Within the context of this chapter, we believe Pedersen (1994) offers an interesting insight regarding the concept of culture and its pervasiveness. He states:

> the construct of culture broadly defined goes beyond national and ethnic boundaries. Persons from the same ethnic or national group may still experience cultural differences. Not all Blacks have the same experience, nor do all Asians, all American Indians, all Hispanics, all women, all old people, nor all disabled persons. (p. 16)

For the purpose of this chapter, culture is broadly defined as a learned system of beliefs, values, feelings, and rules from which groups of individuals organize their lives (Crapo, 1993). Within this framework, culture directly influences the decision making of the recreationist in terms of types of activities engaged in, location of activity, as well as perception and tolerance level of other recreationists.

Many of the apparent causes of recreational conflict may in fact be related to cultural factors. Ruddell and Gramann (1994) suggest that the violation of "recreation norms," which they define as shared standards of behaviors for specific recreation places and activities, can produce significant levels of recreational conflict. For example, if a group of senior hikers is trying to enjoy the serenity and beauty of a backcountry trail, but instead encounter a group of noisy, raucous teenagers, a recreational conflict seems inevitable. The senior hikers regard the backcountry trail as a place for quiet reflection, appreciation of nature, and physical fitness. The behaviors and recreation norms of the teenagers are perceived as being in violation of the seniors' values and goals. The teenagers feel this is an opportunity to let off steam away from societal rules and regulations. The disdainful looks from the senior hikers violate their rights to pursue recreation as it meets their needs and goals. Culture helps to determine the perceived value individuals assign to a physical place or activity, for which they have developed a psychological attachment and expectation (Adamowicz et al., 1998; Ibrahim, 1993).

To a large extent, attitudes and values are created from the culture that surrounds an individual (Fish, 1996; Pedersen, 1994; Sue and Sue, 1990). Values related to natural environments and resource recreation have been highlighted by many scholars. Jackson (1989) proposed that recreational behaviors such as type of activity preferred, frequency of participation, desired setting, and other recreation-related variables are influenced by values and attitudes. Vaske et al. (1995) found that differences between hunters and nonhunters relative to social values are significant with respect to recreational conflict. Schroeder (1996) argues that values and world-views affect the way people experience natural environments.

Factors that influence recreational conflict, such as norms and violations of norms, personal and group goals, place attachment, judgments, perceptions, and values are all constructed by the individual's culture (Pedersen and Jandt, 1996). Pedersen and Jandt (1996) also argue that all types of conflict can be traced back to culture, and state that, "Culture defines the values and interests that are at the core of conflict, shaping perceptions, shaping alternatives, and defining outcomes as positive and negative" (p. 4). Two specific types of *subcultures,* referred to as collectivistic cultures and individualistic cultures, are important in understanding how culture shapes norms, goals, values, perceptions, and contributes to conflict.

Recreationists can belong to either collectivistic or individualistic cultures. That is to say, the way in which an individual identifies with a particular group is one manifestation of culture. Individualistic cultures give priority to individual goals and define one's identity in terms of personal attributes rather than group identification (Myers, 1993). Not unexpectedly, individualistic culture is at the core of American society (Bellah, Madsen, Sullivan, Swindler and Tipton, 1986; Seligman, 1991). Collectivistic cultures give priority to the goals of the group (Myers, 1993). Interdependence, family involvement, and group identity are important values in collectivistic cultures (Fish, 1996; Ho, 1994). In general, Native-American, Asian-American, African-American, and Mexican-American populations are based upon collectivistic values (Cox, 1993; Jandt and Pedersen, 1994; Pedersen, 1994; Sue and Sue, 1990). On the other hand, members of Western European cultures often tend to value personal initiative, individual rights, and satisfaction of individually determined goals. It should be noted, however, that in actuality, cultures are often composed of a conglomeration of both individual and collective cultural attributes rather than being made of entirely one or the other.

Thus, it is not surprising that recreational conflict can occur when recreation activities and leisure lifestyles, based upon opposing cultures (individualistic versus collectivistic) exist within the same proximity. This has important management implications: for example, should a park manager cater to users desiring a solitary or small group interaction, or, alternatively, provide opportunities for large, extended-family types of recreational opportunities?

Individual Schemata and Recreational Conflict

A second phenomenon, known as *schemata,* is an important variable in recreational conflict and delineates the way an individual forms categories that guide attention, perceptions, and memory (Leahy, 1996). Thoughts, perceptions, and the impressions people form about other people directly influence leisure behaviors (Jordan, 1996; Patrick, 1994). A number of variables which may affect recreation conflict, such as lifestyle tolerance (Jacob and Schreyer, 1980), activity style (Jacob and Schreyer, 1980), and percep-

tions of alikeness (Manning, 1986) are premised upon an individual's schema. Beck, Rush, Shaw and Emery (1979) proposed that schemata lead directly to automatic thought (which can be based upon reality or a distortion of reality), which, in turn, orchestrates how an individual perceives potential conflict. For example, a traditional backpacker may automatically think that heliskiers are rich elitists using their wealth to make it easier to get into the backcountry, when, in fact, they may simply be attempting to experience the same thing as the traditional backpackers (e.g., enjoying nature, solitude or aesthetic scenery). The following are some examples of individual schemata and accompanying thoughts that may ultimately generate recreational conflict:

1. Demanding Standards: "My recreation experiences should be completely satisfying."
2. Control: "I must be in control of my recreation experience all of the time."
3. Entitlement: "I should be able to participate in my recreation endeavor, how and when I want to."
4. Attachment: "No one should be in my recreation spot."
5. Alikeness: "Other recreationists should be like me."
6. Personal Belonging: "Other recreationists should not come here."
7. Self-Reference: "They should do what I want them to do or how I do it."
8. Style: "They should do the activity the way I do it."

A specific, rigidly-held schema can create perceptions of goal interference. A reality-based schema, on the other hand, may help recreationists decrease conflict by creating expectations that match reality and enable them to make appropriate adaptations so they can enjoy the recreation experience. For instance, the entitlement schema (I should be able to participate in my recreation endeavor how and when I want to) suggests that the person's recreation activity and goals should be achievable every time he wishes. This may be unrealistic, as no individual can expect to have a quality recreation experience every time he or she recreates. To expect a quiet, solitary beach experience, despite a holiday weekend, may be an unrealistic entitlement schema.

Management and Research Implications

To this point, we have provided an overview of recreational conflict and have explored the prevalence of recreational conflict, its theoretical foundations, and the tremendous influence culture and schemata play on the development and persistence of recreational conflict (Godbey, 1989). Given the importance that conflict may play in future recreational settings, what are the implications for emerging management and research efforts?

Management Implications

From a management perspective, recreational conflict has typically been couched in terms of interference with the recreation experience by other activities or recreationists. Managers have often attempted to address conflict by changes in site design (Douglass, 1993), conflict resolution strategies (Jordan, 1996), visitor feedback (Schneider and Hammitt, 1995a), and new technology (Ditwiler, 1979). Moreover, Schneider and Hammitt (1995b) suggest that managers can expect visitors to utilize a variety of coping mechanisms in dealing with recreational conflict. These mechanisms include distancing oneself from the source of the conflict, redefining the experience into more positive terms (product shifting, rationalization), and going somewhere else (displacement). Schneider and Hammitt (1995b) also point out that visitors often practice a limited number of coping strategies for dealing with conflict. Managers may also be looking for ways to understand and eventually mitigate conflict on the lands they are responsible for. The following points represent a sample of possible management actions that may provide additional information or partial solutions in dealing with recreational conflict:

- Develop an understanding of the recreation visitor by various demographics: time in country, preferred language, cultural background, and level of experience through surveys, on-site interaction with visitors, interviews, focus groups.
- Understand the attributes associated with a recreational activity. For example, caving not only requires a specific type of natural setting but is also particularly susceptible to problems associated with overcrowding. Thus, managers need to be cognizant of the fact that caving and cavers are especially prone to conflicts related to perceived crowding.
- Cluster or arrange activities that require similar attributes or result in like benefits. This approach will allow the manager more flexibility in terms of possible substitution of activities and distancing of noncompatible uses.
- Appreciate that recreational conflict may be more a response to perceptual differences between individuals or groups than clashes between activities. Likewise, it is a mistake for managers to assume homogeneity within a group (e.g., "all motorcycle riders react in similar ways"). Schneider and Hammitt (1995b) suggest that many recreational conflicts will be emotion focused rather than acting out specific behaviors. That is, visitors will change the way they *think* about a particular issue (e.g., crowding at the local beach) rather than change their *behavior* (Shelby, Bregenzer and Johnson, 1988).

Given the prevalence and importance of issues related to culture, it is becoming increasingly essential for recreation and leisure managers to become aware of cultural components as they relate to recreational conflict. When recreation behaviors, expectations, values, and social system variables have been identified, the leisure manager can better understand how different groups may have similar recreation expectations but varying recreation behaviors. If two recreation groups are able to identify common-ground expectations, such as experiencing nature, feelings of accomplishment, and an optimal experience, even though they have differing behaviors, conflict may be more manageable.

Beyond the impact of culture on recreational conflict is one of perspective. Recreational conflict has existed as long as people have been recreating. But because of the finite nature of desired recreation opportunities and environment, conflict in outdoor recreation settings has become especially visible and often "heated." Despite this, recreation professionals should strive to keep in mind the overall goals and objectives of their management plan, that is, protecting the resource while providing for high-quality recreational opportunities. Succumbing to public pressure and placing greater importance on developing programs for public enjoyment rather than protecting the resources will ultimately lead to diminished natural environments. There will always be a certain level of conflict surrounding highly desirable sites and activities. That conflict, however, does not provide a mandate for the overuse of pristine and fragile natural landscapes. Once these areas are degraded through recreation use, it is unlikely that they will ever return to their original state. Needless to say, managers will come under increasing pressure to provide a variety of recreational opportunities, whether or not these opportunities are congruent with the capacity and characteristics of the natural setting.

Research Implications

Research in recreation conflict has traditionally centered on activities and their associated settings. For example, one group of recreationists is engaged in an activity that interferes in some way with another group of recreationists. Researchers have attempted to understand how this interference takes place, in what ways conflict is created, and how individuals cope with these conflicts. More recently, research efforts have become focused on the measurement of conflict, the association between activities, and the development of new theoretical models and approaches (Watson, 1995).

Given the psychological and sociological contexts of recreational conflict, it is not surprising that there exist a number of additional questions in need of research-generated answers. A sampling of these includes the following:

- What is the potential for conflict surrounding the introduction of new recreational activities, such as mountain biking or jet skiing?
- What is the relationship between outgroup and in-group evaluations? Are there "triggers" or thresholds that precipitate a conflict between groups or individuals?
- Is conflict a cumulative or point-in-time phenomenon? Further, do individuals "habituate" to conflict situations, i.e., do they become less sensitive to the constellation of attributes that initially created the conflict or move to another location (i.e., displacement)?
- What types of physical, social-psychological, and environmental designs can man-

agers incorporate to reduce the likelihood of conflict?
- What educational processes are effective in understanding and reducing recreation conflict, both from a user and management perspective?

Finally, and perhaps of greatest importance, is the realization that people come to a recreation site with differing values. A growing number of researchers have already shifted their efforts to develop a better understanding of the relationship between culture and values held by individuals and groups. We believe that understanding the effects of culture and personal schemata, as well as their consequences to a recreational environment will be the next great research challenge facing the profession. Perhaps Adamowicz et al. (1998) state it most eloquently:

> One of the central premises of these efforts [research] is the recognition that positive interactions between different cultures require the development of a mutual understanding of the cultures involved. Such an effort [research] requires the development of an understanding of value differences between cultures. (p. 52)

Conclusion

As we conclude this chapter, recreational conflict remains a phenomenon that management and scholars have dealt with in the past and will continue to deal with in the future. Research and management must develop a functional partnership if information is to be generated that leads to sound and effective decision making. In the case of recreational conflict, this decision making will necessitate decisions that are sustainable but often not easy to implement. Recognizing the impact that culture and individual schemata have on conflict will aid in the development of strategies which may help mitigate negative situations. And where recreational conflict is inevitable, as it often will be, leisure managers will have the tools to make conflict more manageable, the recreationist's experience more pleasurable, and at the least possible cost to our natural, environmental wonders.

References

Adamowicz, W., Beckley, T., MacDonald, D., Just, L., Luckert, M., Murray, E., & Phillips, W. (1998). In search of forest resource values of indigenous peoples: Are nonmarket valuation techniques applicable? *Society and Natural Resources, 11,* 51–66.

Beck, A. T., Rush, A. J., Shaw, B. F., & Emery, G. (1979). *Cognitive therapy and depression.* New York, NY: Guilford Press.

Bellah, R. N., Madsen, R., Sullivan, W. M., Swindler, A., & Tipton, S. M. (1986). *Habits of the heart: Individualism and commitment in American life.* New York, NY: Harper and Row Publishing.

British Columbia Ministry of Forests. (1991). *Outdoor recreation survey, 1989–90: How British Columbians use and value their public forest land for recreation* (DHHS Publication No. 92–03530). Victoria, British Columbia: Ministry of Forests Printing Office.

Bryan, H. (1979). *Conflict in the great outdoors: Toward understanding and managing for diverse sportsmen preferences* (Sociological Studies 4). Tuscaloosa, AL: Tuscaloosa Bureau of Public Administration, University of Alabama.

Bury, R. L., Holland, S. M., & McEwen, D. E. (1983). Analyzing recreational conflict. *Journal of Soil and Water Conservation,* September–October, 401.

Butler, J. R. (1993). Interpretation as a management tool. In P. Dearden & R. Rollins (Eds.), *Parks and protected areas in Canada: Planning and management* (pp. 211–224). Toronto, Ontario: Oxford University Press.

Cox, T. (1993). *Cultural diversity in organizations.* San Francisco, CA: Berrett-Koehler Publishers.

Crapo, R. H. (1993). *Cultural anthropology: Understanding ourselves and others* (3rd ed.). Guilford, CT: Dushkin Publishing.

Dawes, R. M. (1980). Social dilemmas. *Annual Review of Psychology, 31,* 169–193.

Deci, E. L., & Ryan, R. M. (1991). A motivational approach to self: Integration in personality. In R. Dienstbier (Ed.), *Nebraska symposium on motivation* (Vol. 38, pp. 237–288). Lincoln, NE: University of Nebraska Press.

Ditwiler, C. D. (1979). Can technology decrease natural resource use conflict in recreation. *Search, 10,* 439–441.

Douglass, R. W. (1993). *Forest recreation* (4th ed.). Prospect Heights, IL: Wavelength Press, Inc.

Driver, B. L. (1975). Quantification of outdoor recreationalists' preferences. In B. van der Smissen & J. Meyers (Eds.), *Research: Camping and environmental education* (HPER No. 11, pp. 165–187). University Park, PA: Pennsylvania State University.

Driver, B. L., & Bassett, J. (1975). Defining conflict among river users: A case study Michigan's Au Sable River. *Naturalist, 26,* 19–23.

Dzurisk, A. A. (1983). Multiple-use conflict in a growing economy. *Journal of Urban Planning and Development, 199,* 79–93.

Edginton, C. R., Jordan, D. J., DeGraaf, D. G., & Edginton, S. R. (1996). *Leisure and life satisfaction: Foundational perspectives.* Madison, WI: Brown & Benchmark Publishers.

Ewert, A. W. (1993). Differences in the level of motive importance based on trip outcome, experience level and group type. *Journal of Leisure Research, 25,* 335–349.

Fish, J. (1996). *Culture and therapy: An integrative approach.* Northvale, NJ: Jason Aronson, Inc.

Forest Service News Digest. (1997). December 5, 1997, pp. 1–2.

Gander, H., & P. Ingold. (1997). Reactions of male alpine chamois (*Rupicapra rupicapra*) to hikers, joggers and mountain bikers. *Biological Conservation, 79,* 107–109.

Gibbons, S., & Ruddell, E. J. (1995). The effects of goal orientation and place dependence on select goal interferences among winter backcountry users. *Leisure Sciences, 17,* 171–183.

Godbey, G. (1989). *The future of leisure services: Thriving on change.* State College, PA: Venture Publishing, Inc.

Gollwitzer, P. M., & Moskowitz, G. B. (1996). Goal effect on action and cognition. In E. T. Higgins & A. W. Kruglanski (Eds.), *Social psychology: Handbook of basic principles* (pp. 361–399). New York, NY: Guilford Press.

Gramann, J. H., & Burdge, R. (1981). The effect of recreation goal on conflict perception: The case of water skiers and fishermen. *Journal of Leisure Research, 13,* 15–27.

Hardin, G. (1968). The tragedy of the commons. *Science, 162,* 1243–1248.

Hendricks, W. W. (1995). A resurgence in recreation conflict research: Introduction to the special issue. *Leisure Sciences, 17,* 157–158.

Ho, M. K. (1994). Asian American perspectives. In J. U. Gordeon (Ed.), *Managing multiculturalism in substance abuse services* (pp. 72–98). Thousand Oaks, CA: Sage Publishing, Inc.

Holmes, J. G., & Murray, S. L. (1996). Conflict in close relationships. In E. T. Higgins & A. W. Kruglanski (Eds.), *Social psychology: Handbook of basic principles* (pp. 361–399). New York, NY: Guilford Press.

Ibrahim, F. A. (1993). Existential world-view theory: Transcultural counseling. In J. McFadden (Ed.),

Transcultural counseling: Bilateral and international perspectives (pp. 23–57). Alexandria, VA: American Counseling Association.

Jackson, E. L. (1989). Environmental attitudes, values, and recreation. In E. L. Jackson & T. L. Burton (Eds.), *Understanding leisure and recreation: Mapping the past, charting the future* (pp. 357–383). State College, PA: Venture Publishing, Inc.

Jackson, E. L., & Wong, R. A. (1982). Perceived conflict between urban cross-country skiers and snowmobilers in Alberta. *Journal of Leisure Research, 14,* 47–62.

Jacob, G. R., & Schreyer, R. (1980). Conflict in outdoor recreation: A theoretical perspective. *Journal of Leisure Research, 12,* 368–380.

Jandt, F., & Pedersen, P. (1994). Indigenous meditation strategies in the Asia-Pacific region. *Aspire Newsletter, 4,* 10–11.

Jary, D., & Jary, J. (1991). *The Harper Collins dictionary of sociology.* New York, NY: HarperCollins Publisher.

Jordan, D. J. (1996). *Leadership in leisure services: Making a difference.* State College, PA: Venture Publishing, Inc.

Jubenville, A., & Twight, B. W. (1993). *Outdoor recreation management: Theory and application* (3rd ed.). State College, PA: Venture Publishing, Inc.

Karp, D. G. (1996). Values and their effect on pro-environmental behavior. *Environment and Behavior, 28,* 111–133.

Leahy, R. (1996). *Cognitive therapy: Basic principles and application.* Northvale, NJ: Jason Aronson Inc.

Lewin, K. (1948). The background of conflict in marriage. In G. W. Lewin (Ed.), *Resolving social conflict: Selected papers on group dynamics* (pp. 84–102). New York, NY: Harper.

Lindsay, J. L. (1980). Trends in outdoor recreation activity conflicts. In *Proceedings of the 1980 National Outdoor Recreation Trends Symposium* (Vol. 1, pp. 215–221). Upper Darby, PA: USDA Forest Service.

Locke, E. A., & Latham, G. P. (1990). *A theory of goal setting and task performance.* Englewood Cliffs, NJ: Prentice-Hall.

Manning, R. E. (1986). *Studies in outdoor recreation.* Corvallis, OR: Oregon State University Press.

Morehead, A., & Morehead, L. (1981). *The new American Webster handy college dictionary.* New York, NY: Signet.

Myers, D. G. (1993). *Social psychology* (4th ed.). New York, NY: McGraw Hill, Inc.

Orams, M. B. (1997). Historical accounts of human-dolphin interaction and recent development in wild dolphin-based tourism in Australasia. *Tourism Management, 18,* 317–326.

Owens, P. L. (1985). Conflict as a social interaction process in environment and behavior research: The example of leisure and recreation research. *Journal of Environmental Psychology, 5,* 243–259.

Paterson, R. J., & Neufeld, R. W. (1989). Stress response and parameters of stressful situations. In R. W. Neufeld (Ed.), *Advances in the investigations of psychological stress.* New York, NY: John Wiley & Sons, Inc.

Patrick, G. (1994). The role for leisure in treatment of depression. In D. M. Compton & S. E. Iso-Ahola (Eds.), *Leisure and mental health* (pp. 175–190). Park City, UT: Family Development Resources, Inc.

Pedersen, P. (1994). *A handbook for developing multicultural awareness* (2nd ed.). Alexandria, VA: American Counseling Association.

Pedersen, P., & Jandt, F. E. (1996). Culturally contextual models for creative conflict management. In F. E. Jandt & P. Pedersen (Eds.), *Constructive conflict management: Asian-Pacific cases* (pp. 3–26). Thousand Oaks, CA: Sage Publications, Inc.

Peterson, D. R. (1983). Conflict. In H. H. Kelley, E. Bersheid, A. Christensen, J. H. Harvey, T. L. Huston, G. Levinger, E. McClintock, L. A. Peplan & D. R. Peterson (Eds.), *Close relationships* (pp. 360–396). New York, NY: Freman.

Ramthun, R. (1995). Factors in user group conflict between hikers and mountain bikers. *Leisure Sciences, 17,* 159–169.

Roggenbuck, J. W. (1992). Use of persuasion to reduce resource impacts and visitor conflicts. In M. Manfredo (Ed.), *Influencing human behavior* (pp. 149–208). Champaign, IL: Sagamore Publishing.

Ruddell, E. J., & Gramann, J. H. (1994). Goal orientation, norms, and noise-induced conflict among recreation area users. *Leisure Sciences, 16,* 93–104.

Schneider, I. E., & Hammitt, W. E. (1995a). Visitor response to outdoor recreation conflict: A conceptual approach. *Leisure Sciences, 17,* 223–234.

Schneider, I. E., & Hammitt, W. E. (1995b). Visitor responses to on-site recreation conflict. *Journal of Applied Recreation Research, 20*(4), 249–268.

Schroeder, H. W. (1996). Ecology of the heart: Understanding how people experience natural environments. In A. W. Ewert (Ed.), *Natural resource management: The human dimension* (pp. 13–27). Boulder, CO: Westview Press.

Seligman, M. E. P. (1991). *Learned optimism: How to change your mind and life.* New York, NY: Pocket Books.

Shelby, B., Bregenzer, H., & Johnson, R. (1988). Displacement and product shift: Empirical evidence from two Oregon rivers. *Journal of Leisure Research, 20,* 274–288.

Simcox, D. E. (1996). Outdoor recreation and natural resource lands. In M. J. Leitner & S. F. Leitner (Eds.), *Leisure enhancement* (2nd ed., pp. 337–366). New York, NY: Haworth Press.

Sue, D. W., & Sue, D. (1990). *Counseling the culturally different: Theory and practice* (2nd ed.). New York, NY: John Wiley & Sons, Inc.

Vaske, J. J., Donnelly, M. P., Wittmann, K., & Laidlaw, S. (1995). Interpersonal versus social-value conflict. *Leisure Sciences, 17,* 205–222.

Watson, A. E. (1995). An analysis of recent progress in recreation conflict research and perceptions of future challenges and opportunities. *Leisure Sciences, 17,* 235–238.

Watson, A. E., & Hendricks, W. W. (1995). Recreation conflict research. *Leisure Sciences, 17,* 157–238.

Watson, A. E., Niccolucci, M. J., & Williams, D. R. (1994). The nature of conflict between hikers and recreational stock users in the John Muir Wilderness. *Journal of Leisure Research, 26,* 372–385.

Williams, D. R. (1993). Conflict in the great outdoors. *Parks and Recreation, 28,* 28–34.

Wright, R. A., & Brehm, J. W. (1989) Energization and goal attractiveness. In L. A. Pervin (Ed.), *Goal concepts in personality and social psychology* (pp. 169–210). Hillsdale, NJ: Erlbaum.

Yamagishi, T. (1994). Social dilemmas. In K. S. Cook, G. A. Fine & J. House (Eds.), *Sociological perspectives on social psychology* (pp. 311–334). Boston, MA: Allyn & Bacon.

Zinzer, C. I. (1995). *Outdoor recreation: United States national parks, forests, and public lands.* New York, NY: John Wiley & Sons, Inc.

Delivering Leisure

Concepts and Uses of the Benefits Approach to Leisure

Beverly L. Driver
USDA Forest Service (Retired)

Donald H. Bruns
USDI Bureau of Land Management

Background and Purposes

In the text *Understanding Leisure and Recreation: Mapping the Past, Charting the Future* (Jackson and Burton, 1989), Schreyer and Driver (1989) urged that more attention be given to the benefits, or positive impacts, of leisure. Since that chapter was written, the Benefits Approach to Leisure (BAL) has emerged and attracted parks and recreation practitioners, leisure educators, and leisure scientists in Canada, the United States, and several other countries. This chapter explains why the BAL is needed, its basic concepts, how it is being used, and its advantages over other approaches.[1]

---

[1] Many people have contributed significantly to the development of the Benefits Approach to Leisure. Special acknowledgment is made to Dorothy Anderson, Warren Bacon, Perry Brown, Don Bruns, Geoffrey Godbey, Tom Hoots, Martha Lee, Robert Marans, Joseph Roggenbuck, Daniel Stynes, and Peter Witt.

The BAL was developed and is being used and refined by leisure researchers, educators, policymakers, and managers both to integrate and to direct thinking about the management of leisure and recreation service delivery systems. It is not only a *philosophy* about the roles of leisure in society and how leisure service delivery systems should be managed, but also a *system* for directing leisure research, instruction, policy development, and management. The BAL is recognized as a major and badly needed "paradigm shift" in the way we conceive of and manage recreation resources and programs, and as such, it is more than a management system because it influences how we think about leisure. Specifically, the BAL is an expanded conceptual framework that uses concepts from General Systems Theory to integrate the inputs and physical structure of the leisure and recreation service delivery systems being managed with the outputs of those systems. Under conventional approaches to these delivery systems, attention focuses primarily on the inputs to the system (e.g., investment and maintenance capital, personnel and skills needed, physical resources including facilities, programs, and marketing) and on management of the physical structure of the system (e.g., a swimming pool complex, a campground, or a trail). Too often, if not universally, this supply orientation to management of these inputs and of the structure of the system is viewed as the *ends* of management.

In sharp contrast, the BAL views the management of inputs and of system structure only as *necessary means* to attain the ends of capturing desired outcomes or impacts, and it views the goal of management as one of optimizing net benefits that accrue to individuals, groups of individuals such as family units and local communities, and to the biophysical elements and processes of the physically defined systems being managed. In fact, the BAL requires the writing of clear management objectives for explicitly defined types of *benefit opportunities* that are targeted for provision, and it requires benefits-oriented management prescriptions, guidelines, and standards that will help assure provision of the types and amounts of the benefit opportunities targeted for delivery, both on and off the physical area, site, or facility being managed. By considering both on- and off-site impacts, the BAL requires a comprehensive appraisal of the impacts to on-site users of the services delivered, to local communities, to other stakeholders, and to the biophysical resources. It defines these impacts in terms of beneficial changes that occur, whether desired conditions are maintained, and whether on-site customers have opportunities to realize satisfying recreation experiences.

The fundamental question raised by the BAL is *why* should a particular leisure service be provided. The answer is formulated in terms of clearly defined positive and negative consequences of delivering that service, with the objective being to optimize net benefits—or to add as much value as possible. To do this, leisure policy analysts and managers must understand what values would be added by each leisure service provided, articulate those values, and understand how to capture them.

While the notion of managing recreation resources to realize benefits is not novel, a systematic, conceptually integrated, and operational means of promoting and applying that approach did not exist until the BAL was conceptualized at the 1991 Workshop on Applying Knowledge About the Benefits of Leisure. That workshop was requested by recreation administrators and managers who wanted to know how they could apply the results of research on the benefits of leisure summarized in the state-of-knowledge text *Benefits of Leisure* (Driver, Brown and Peterson, 1991). One half of the 70 participants were managers or administrators of municipal, regional, state, and federal recreation agencies or divisions, and the other half were scientists and educators who had an applied orientation.

After the workshop, several of the participants worked closely to refine the basic concepts of the BAL and to develop guidelines for its implementation. That collaboration has included working with managers of several municipal, state, and federal parks and recreation agencies to pilot test the implementation of the BAL. Evaluations of those pilot tests have led to ongoing modifications of the BAL, and other modifications will be made as the BAL continues to be refined.

When work first started on the BAL in 1991, it was called Benefits-Based Management (BBM) because attention then concentrated on its use to guide management. Now, the BAL is used by leisure scientists, educators, and policymakers as well as by managers. Therefore, the more inclusive concept of the BAL is now used to denote its use beyond management with BBM applied only to that specialized usage.

Why a Benefits Approach to Leisure?

To understand the philosophical and practical dimensions of the BAL, a person must understand the reasons why the BAL was developed.

General Reason for the BAL: Increase Political Parity of Leisure

In most states and provinces, recreation and tourism rank in the top three economic sectors as generators of income and employment. Expenditures on tourism-related international travel generate greater flows of funds between nations than any other economic transaction, including sales of grains, automobiles, or electronic parts and equipment—each of which are big ticket items. Nevertheless, current systems of economic accounting exclude many economic transactions attributable to recreation and tourism (Stynes and Godbey, 1993). If a system of industrial classification were available to accurately include all public and private sectors of the Canadian and U.S. economies that support and provide leisure services, the broadly defined *leisure industrial* sector would certainly lead all others in numbers of employees, expenditures by customers, personal disposable income, and tax revenues generated.

Using another system of accounting, it can be conjectured that leisure services provide more aggregate benefits to society than any other social service, including educational and medical services. This statement might seem startling until one reflects seriously on the broad array of benefits that accrue from the public and private provision and use of leisure services and the pervasiveness of these benefits in all realms of human activity, including work, health, transportation, housing, and education. The scope and magnitude of these benefits can be inferred from Table 21.1 (pages 352–353), which lists many of the benefits that have been attributed to leisure in various publications.[2]

The fact that leisure is big business and probably the most beneficial social service is not fully understood or appreciated by the public and by leisure professionals in the United States and Canada. For example, unlike many countries that have federal departments or ministries responsible for leisure, the arts, and/or tourism, neither the United States nor Canada has federal policies explicitly addressed to leisure. Of course, there is the National Park Service in the United States, the Canadian Parks Service, and recreation management branches or divisions within many other federal agencies in these two countries, but no federal policies exist that broadly recognize, protect, and promote leisure as a significant business and social service. Such policies do exist for agriculture, mining, manufacturing, transportation, health, education, and communications, with several of these sectors represented by federal departmental and ministerial-level status or by special agencies or administrations, which for example in the United States would include the Environmental Protection Agency and the

Food and Drug Administration. The situation is quite similar in Canada.

Obviously there is a paradox: while leisure is the leading economic sector and the most important social service sector, the scope and magnitude of the benefits of leisure are not recognized and appreciated. The following factors have contributed to this relative lack of political parity of leisure:

• Many people in most English-speaking countries still feel some guilt about play and reflect the "work ethic" myth that diminishes the social importance of play (see Sylvester, chapter 2 in this volume).

• Elected officials in the United States and Canada tend to hold the erroneous belief that most or all of the benefits of leisure accrue to the individuals who use leisure services, and that there are few if any spin-off benefits from this use to society in general. This contrasts with their views about the social merits of other social services (e.g., education, health services, police and fire protection, transportation) for which these elected officials acknowledge large benefits to society beyond those that accrue to the direct users of those services. Therefore, these officials have improperly adopted for leisure services the principle of public finance, which dictates that limited public funds should be allocated to a social service that does not promote the general welfare.

• People are generally aware that leisure can renew them physically and mentally and promote their growth and development in many ways, and most individuals are cognizant of some specific benefits they receive. Nevertheless, the public collectively does not understand well the wide scope and tremendous social significance of the benefits of leisure listed in Table 21.1 (pages 352–353).

• People in the leisure professions do not understand well the benefits of leisure and have not articulated sufficiently the scope and magnitude of the benefits they do know about.

• Until quite recently there was no systematic conceptually integrated and easily understood paradigm that leisure professionals widely agreed could be used to promote the social importance of leisure and guide leisure research, education,

---

[2]Sources include the following: the unpublished report of a special team that was appointed by the Outdoor Recreation Resources Review Commission (ORRRC) to study the mental health benefits of recreation (Federal Reporting Company, 1961), Kelly (1981), the section on Recreation Values and Benefits in the *Literature Review* done by the President's Commission on Americans Outdoors (Driver and Peterson, 1986), the *Benefits of Leisure* text (Driver, Brown and Peterson, 1991), *The Benefits of Parks and Recreation: A Catalogue* (Parks and Recreation Federation of Ontario, 1992), *The Benefits of Local Recreation and Park Services: A Nationwide Study of the Perceptions of the American Public* (Godbey, Graefe and James, 1992), the *Benefits of Recreation Research Update* (Sefton and Mummery, 1995), and research publications by Driver (1992, 1994, 1996), Tindall (1995), Stein and Lee (1995), Allen (1996), Bruns (1998), and Lee and Driver (1996). Table 21.1 (pages 352–353) includes known and suggested benefits of leisure to at-risk youth (Schultz, Crompton and Witt, 1995; Witt and Crompton, 1996). See also the Fall 1996 issue of the *Journal of Park and Recreation Administration*, which is devoted to these benefits of leisure programming.

TABLE 21.1   SPECIFIC TYPES AND GENERAL CATEGORIES OF BENEFITS THAT HAVE BEEN ATTRIBUTED TO LEISURE BY RESEARCH

I. Personal Benefits
   A. Psychological
     1. Better mental health and health maintenance
        • Holistic sense of wellness
        • Stress management (prevention, mediation, and restoration)
        • Catharsis
        • Prevention of and reduced depression, anxiety, and anger
        • Positive changes in mood and emotion
     2. Personal development and growth
        • Self-confidence
        • Self-reliance
        • Self-competence
        • Self-assurance
        • Value clarification
        • Improved academic and cognitive performance
        • Independence and autonomy
        • Sense of control over one's life
        • Humility
        • Leadership
        • Aesthetic enhancement
        • Creativity enhancement
        • Spiritual growth
        • Adaptability
        • Cognitive efficiency
        • Problem solving
        • Nature learning
        • Cultural and historic awareness, learning, and appreciation
        • Environmental awareness and understanding
        • Tolerance
        • Balanced competitiveness
        • Balanced living
        • Prevention of problems to at-risk youth
        • Acceptance of one's responsibility
     3. Personal appreciation and satisfaction
        • Sense of freedom
        • Self-actualization
        • Flow and absorption
        • Exhilaration
        • Stimulation
        • Sense of adventure
        • Challenge
        • Nostalgia
        • Quality of life and/or life satisfaction
        • Creative expression
        • Aesthetic appreciation
        • Nature appreciation
        • Spirituality
        • Positive change in mood or emotion

   B. Psychophysiological
     1. Cardiovascular benefits, including prevention of strokes
     2. Reduced or prevented hypertension
     3. Reduced serum cholesterol and triglycerides
     4. Improved control and prevention of diabetes
     5. Prevention of colon cancer
     6. Reduced spinal problems
     7. Decreased body fat and obesity and/or weight control
     8. Improved neuropsychological functioning
     9. Increased bone mass and strength in children
    10. Increased muscle strength and better connective tissue
    11. Respiratory benefits (increased lung capacity, benefits to people with asthma)
    12. Reduced incidence of disease
    13. Improved bladder control of the elderly
    14. Increased life expectancy
    15. Management of menstrual cycles
    16. Management of arthritis
    17. Improved functioning of the immune system
    18. Reduced consumption of alcohol and use of tobacco

II. Social and Cultural Benefits
   A. Community satisfaction
   B. Pride in community and nation (pride in place and patriotism)
   C. Cultural and historical awareness and appreciation
   D. Reduced social alienation
   E. Community and political involvement
   F. Ethnic identity
   G. Social bonding, cohesion, and cooperation
   H. Conflict resolution and harmony
   I. Greater community involvement in environmental decision making
   J. Social support
   K. Support democratic ideal of freedom
   L. Family bonding
   M. Reciprocity and sharing
   N. Social mobility
   O. Community integration
   P. Nurturance of others
   Q. Understanding and tolerance of others
   R. Environmental awareness, sensitivity
   S. Enhanced world view
   T. Socialization and acculturation
   U. Cultural identity
   V. Cultural continuity
   X. Prevention of social problems by at-risk youth

TABLE 21.1   CONTINUED

Y. Developmental benefits of children
III. Economic Benefits
    A. Reduced health costs
    B. Increased productivity
    C. Less work absenteeism
    D. Reduced on-the-job accidents
    E. Decreased job turnover
    F. International balance of payments (from tourism)
    G. Local and regional economic growth
    H. Contributions to net national economic development
IV. Environmental Benefits
    A. Maintenance of physical facilities
    B. Stewardship and preservation of options

C. Husbandry and improved relationships with natural world
D. Understanding of human dependency on the natural world
E. Environmental ethic
F. Public involvement in environmental issues
G. Environmental protection
    1. Ecosystem sustainability
    2. Species diversity
    3. Maintenance of natural scientific laboratories
    4. Preservation of particular natural sites and areas
    5. Preservation of cultural, heritage, and historic sites and areas

SOURCE: Driver (1990a) as updated and not published elsewhere since.

policy development, and management. Such a holistic paradigm now exists with the BAL, and a major reason it was developed was to help increase the political parity of leisure by promoting better understanding of the wide scope and tremendous social significance of the benefits of leisure.

Practical Reasons for the BAL

The concept of managing and using leisure resources for the benefits they provide is not new. It goes back to Aristotle, who viewed the purpose of leisure as promoting contemplation, improved thinking, and excellence of the mind, and thereby, nurturance of people who as better citizens would contribute more to society (Barrett, 1989). Since then, the basic argument underlying the parks and recreation movement in Great Britain, Canada, and the United States in the mid to late 1800s was that recreation and parks contribute greatly to human welfare. Among the well-known civic leaders who articulated these social merits of parks and recreation were Frederick Law Olmsted, who designed some of the best known parks in the United States, including Central Park in New York City (Olmsted and Kimball, 1970), and the Nobel laureate Jane Addams (cf., Addams, 1910).

Somewhere along the way, we in the leisure professions lost sight of our roots and stopped articulating effectively the social merits of leisure. Instead of benefits, we now emphasize administrative efficiency and rely more and more on "bean counting" (e.g., counts of users, revenues generated, numbers of acres of green space and facilities per 1,000 people) to jus-

tify programs. In the process, we have locked into the mentality of providing facilities and marketing programs with too little evaluation of why we were focusing mostly on supply factors (Allen, 1996; Driver, 1994, 1996). Recently, we have returned to our roots and there has been a resurgence of interest in the benefits of leisure for the following practical reasons:

- In these ongoing times of public fiscal stringency, leisure policymakers—at all levels of government—need better information about the benefits of leisure to justify their budget requests. In addition, public policymakers and managers, including those in parks and recreation agencies, are being held more accountable. The public now demands that governmental actions be related to social needs, so public officials must explain more explicitly what goods and services they are providing and be able to articulate clearly the likely desirable and undesirable impacts of the production and use of those goods and services on different segments of society.
- Scientific knowledge about the benefits of leisure has increased considerably during the past decade. This has caused many park and recreation resource managers to reorient their attention away from means alone to both means and ends. As the overwhelming evidence about the economic and social significance (ends) of leisure became better documented, these forward-thinking professionals realized

that their conventional focus on resources, facilities, and programs (means) was necessary but not sufficient. They recognized that sufficiency comes from first questioning why a specific leisure service should or should not be provided. They reasoned that this question should be answered in terms of the desired and obtainable positive values those services would add to the lives of individuals and to society.

- As leisure educators and scientists learned more about the benefits of managing park and recreation resources, they realized that the benefits approach was needed to guide much of their teaching and research. Because they recognized that this approach constituted an important paradigm shift in the way one perceives the delivery of leisure services and leisure behavior, they have supported the development and refinement of the BAL.

The BAL was developed to meet these needs. While its basic logic is grounded in the early roots of the parks and recreation movement, the BAL represents a new philosophical orientation and an easily applied integrated approach to recreation research and instruction, to the development of leisure policies, and to management of leisure services. It offers an operational definition of the benefits of leisure that covers all the benefits. It incorporates the concepts of General Systems Theory and of modern management science and planning. Also it is based on the most recent scientific information about the benefits of leisure. In short, it provides a less intuitive and more objective approach than existed at the time the roots of the BAL were being planted in the late 1800s and early 1900s. These characteristics of the BAL will now be explained.

Definitions and Basic Concepts

Definitions of Recreation Benefits

To make the BAL operational, three types of benefits of leisure have been defined along the following dimensions:

- An *improved condition* (e.g., a gain) of an individual, a group of individuals (e.g., a family, a community, society at large) or another entity such as the physical envi-

ronment (e.g., historic buildings, local amenities, an alpine lake shore, or a species of fauna or flora). Examples of such improved conditions include increased learning about the environment from nature study (Roggenbuck, Loomis and Dagostino, 1990), improved cardiovascular functioning from physical exercise (Paffenbarger, Hyde and Dow, 1991), psychophysiological recovery from the everyday stresses of life (Ulrich, Dimberg and Driver, 1990), closer families from recreating as family units (Orthner and Mancini, 1991), improved skill levels (Easley, 1991), economic benefits (Johnson and Brown, 1991), community stability and development from local physical amenities and tourist expenditures (Allen, 1990), and preservation of germ plasma and maintenance of biodiversity from sustainable ecosystem management (Rolston, 1985, 1991).

- The *prevention of a worse condition* through maintenance of a desired condition. This type of benefit of leisure was added during early applications of the BAL to guide management because we realized that many of the benefits of recreation accrue because of its contribution to the maintenance of a wanted condition. This can happen even though there is no change or gain to create an improved condition. Examples include maintained friendships, health, and community stability; prevention of social problems such as those that can be caused by at-risk youth; and prevention of adverse impacts of tourism, including harm to the physical environment.

- The *realization of a specific satisfying psychological experience*, which we have called psychological outcomes. These types of benefits accrue only to individuals—not to groups or to the physical environment—and include all satisfying psychological outcomes related to leisure. Examples are successfully testing one's skills, enjoying a symphony orchestra, feeling good after physical exertion, experiencing closeness as a family, spiritually being in awe at the sight of sunlight streaming through tall trees, and recovering psychologically from a mental stress.

This third type of benefit of leisure was added to the BAL because, under an outcomes approach, policy analysts and managers must address their customers' preferences for satisfying psychological experiences as well as their desires for the particular improved or maintained conditions covered by the other two types of benefits. Those of us who were developing, applying, and refining the BAL made the judgment that if people derive psychological satisfaction from leisure, they must benefit in some way even though the disbenefits to themselves or to others might be larger than the benefits they realize immediately or over time.

The practical need to expand the BAL's other two types of benefits of leisure became quite apparent after we started pilot testing the BAL to guide the management of several areas. We learned that users' preferences to realize a particular psychological experience frequently denoted specific managerial actions much more clearly than did the improved or maintained conditions that could result from that particular psychological outcome. Assume, for example, that a person realizes the psychological benefit of enhanced aesthetic appreciation from enjoying a scenic vista in a park. It is much easier to write relevant management objectives and prescriptions to manage that vista for scenic enjoyment and to communicate those intentions to the users than to do so for the more abstract benefit of enhancing aesthetic appreciation. The more discrete of these desired psychological outcomes can be measured with reasonable accuracy and validity (Driver, Tinsley and Manfredo, 1991; Manfredo, Driver and Tarrant, 1996). Other outcomes that appear to represent a gestalt of several interacting psychological responses (e.g., nature-based spiritual experiences and attachment to a special place) are more

difficult to define and quantify (Driver, Dustin, Baltic, Elsner and Peterson, 1996).

These three types of benefits of leisure are shown in Figure 21.1, which omits all inputs to management, factors that affect leisure choice and behavior, and all feedback loops. The benefits are created both by managerial actions (as indicated by the bolder lines; e.g., improved local employment opportunities from construction of a facility and maintenance of physical infrastructure) and by the recreationists through participation. Figure 21.1 also shows that disbenefits or negative impacts (e.g., dissatisfying psychological experiences and worse conditions), as well as benefits, can be created by management and by the customers both on and off site.

To avoid the confusion caused in the past, it should be recognized that the concept of benefit adopted by the BAL is not related to how the word *benefit* is used in Benefit-Cost (B-C) analyses, which test the economic efficiency of an investment alternative. In B-C analyses, benefits are defined and measured in terms of some index (e.g., monetary price) of the economic worth of the goods and services that will be provided or protected by the investment being evaluated (Randall, 1984). Results of B-C analyses provide important information to public decision makers, and those data need to be used along with information about the three types of benefits defined by the BAL (Driver and Burch, 1988).

While considering semantics, we will mention that the BAL has adopted the word *customer* to denote the person being served rather than "user," "visitor," or "client." Customer is more accurate because modern

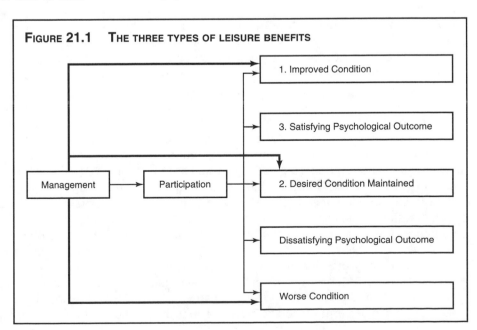

FIGURE 21.1   **THE THREE TYPES OF LEISURE BENEFITS**

1. Improved Condition

3. Satisfying Psychological Outcome

Management → Participation → 2. Desired Condition Maintained

Dissatisfying Psychological Outcome

Worse Condition

dictionaries define that word to include "patron," "client," and "paying guest" and does not limit the word *customer* just to paying guest as some people believe. Also, the concept of customer more inclusively covers impacts to both on- and off-site stakeholders, while the notion of user has historically referred only to the on-site visitor.

Underlying Concepts of the BAL

Delivery of Leisure Services as a Production System

The BAL represents a major shift in how most people view and approach management of any leisure service delivery system, whether delivery of sports-related services or outdoor recreation opportunities. That paradigm shift requires focusing on *why* any leisure service is delivered. To fully understand this new philosophy, one must view management of recreation service delivery systems as management of a production process. This can be done easily within General Systems Theory (Buckley, 1968), under which all systems are conceived as comprising *inputs* that are processed through and interact with the components of the system's *structure* during a *throughput process*, and *outputs* are produced that can be viewed as products, as illustrated here:

Interaction of Inputs

Inputs → Within the → Outputs

System's Structure

An example of such a production system is a farmer who grows corn. The farmer inputs knowledge, labor, seed, fertilizer, and perhaps irrigation water and chemicals to control weeds or corn borers. The physical structure of the system is the corn field and includes the soil as well as sunshine, wind, rain, weed seeds, corn borer larva in the soil, fences, and roads. Through interaction of the rain, soil, temperature, seed, and fertilizer during the throughput process, outputs are produced. Those outputs are corn, corn stalks, and weeds, with the weeds showing that not all outputs are desirable. Similar conceptualizations can be made of other systems, such as a stereo system, the human circulatory system, a car production system, and a leisure service delivery system.

The concept of the recreation production system employed by the BAL has two distinct stages—a first stage and a second stage—as shown in Figure 21.2. That system can be summarized as follows. The recreation manager is usually faced with managing some physically defined entity (analogous to the previously mentioned corn field) such as a park or sports complex to produce specific recreation opportunities and other types of benefits. The first stage inputs (left column of Figure 21.2) comprise the laws and policies that guide the managing agency, capital investments, institutional and cultural values, and mores that influence management (e.g., is nude bathing acceptable or not); managerial knowledge and skills; labor supplied by management including volunteers; the rules, regulations, fees, etc., which need to be imposed; the desires, preferences, expectations, and values of the customers and the things they bring to the site (dogs, radios, equipment); and the values and interests of the off-site customers and stakeholders who are affected by management of the system (e.g., local businesses, tourism agencies, local church groups, environmental groups, and stakeholders who are interested in alternative uses of the site or facility).

The interaction of the first stage inputs with the components of the system's structure during the first throughput process will result in the first stage outputs (products) comprising:

1. social benefits that accrue to local communities directly from the managerial actions (e.g., increased pride in community because of the recreation amenities being managed);
2. economic benefits provided to local communities from the investments made by management;
3. benefits resulting from protection of the physical environment by management;
4. the recreation opportunities produced; and
5. any negative impacts created by managerial action.

The third column of Figure 21.2 lists three types of recreation opportunities as first stage outputs of management. These are activity opportunities, experience opportunities, and other benefit opportunities. The BAL cannot be understood unless one understands the differences among these three types of recreation opportunities. Each is defined here:

- A *recreation activity opportunity* is easy to understand and simply means the opportunity to engage in a particular recreation activity. This could be an opportunity to camp, picnic, play soccer or basketball, hunt, fish, ski, play checkers at a seniors'

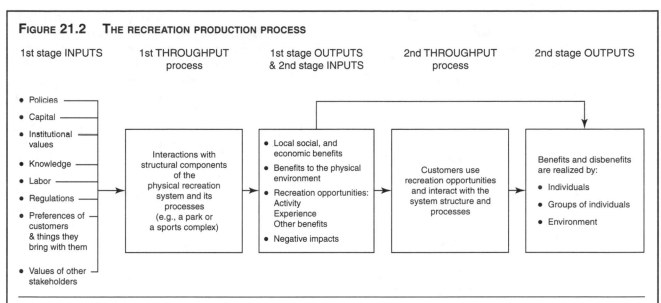

FIGURE 21.2   THE RECREATION PRODUCTION PROCESS

SOURCE: "The Recreation Production Process: The Benefits-Based Approach to Amenity Resource Policy Analysis and Management," by B. L. Driver, 1994, in *Friluftsliv: Effecter og goder, Dn-notat, 1994–7, Direktoratet for Naturforvaltning Tungasletta* [Proceedings, Scandinavian Conference on Recreation: Benefits and Other Positive Effects] (pp. 12–30), Trondheim, Norway: Norwegian Institute of Nature Studies.

center, attend or watch a football game on television, or go to the movies.

- The concept of a *recreation experience opportunity* is more abstract and requires understanding recreation in behavioral terms. Specifically, when one thinks of experience opportunities, one must view recreation not just as the behavior of participating in an activity, but also as an intrinsically rewarding psychological state that is realized from voluntary engagement in selected recreational activities during nonobligated time (Driver and Tocher, 1970). Within this logic, a specific recreation experience is defined as the psychological outcome realized from engaging in a specific recreation activity in a particular recreation setting. Research has shown that recreationists realize a "package" of several discrete desired and satisfying psychological outcomes from such an engagement, with several of them usually contributing more to satisfaction than others (Driver, Tinsley and Manfredo, 1991). Examples include feeling relaxed, introspecting on personal values, experiencing privacy and tranquility, sharing with friends, enjoying one's family, applying and testing skills, enjoying the scenery, being inspired by nature or the arts, and many types of learning (e.g., about a

country, a subculture, or nature). All these psychological outcomes are by definition experienced in the heads and hearts of the recreationists, but that does not mean they cannot be expressed or quantified in a manner useful to managers (Driver, Tinsley and Manfredo, 1991; Manfredo, Driver and Brown, 1983). However, some types of multidimensional psychological experience gestalts (spiritual experiences and psychological attachments to special places) exist that are less discrete and therefore more difficult to quantify (Driver et al., 1996). It should also be emphasized that some psychological outcomes cause dissatisfaction.

From a managerial perspective, the two most important tasks are to understand: (1) which psychological outcomes are perceived to be most satisfying by particular types of recreationists who are engaging in desired activities within preferred settings; and (2) what specific determinative attributes of those settings that influence the realization of satisfying and dissatisfying experiences are under managerial control.

When thinking of recreation experience opportunities, the reader should remember that the third type of benefit of leisure defined previously was the realization of a satisfying psychological outcome. Therefore, any recreation experience opportunity that is used and creates a satisfying psychological outcome for the user has by definition created a benefit.

- The third type of recreation opportunity shown in Figure 21.2 is called an *other benefit opportunity,* and covers *all* the benefits of leisure *other than* the just described benefits of realizing a satisfying psychological outcome, which explains the term *other benefit opportunity.*

Some people find this concept of other benefit opportunities to be confusing. This confusion is probably caused by our previously described need to preserve the option to write management objectives and prescriptions that target specific psychological outcomes for which opportunities will be provided. Remember this need emerged as our pilot tests of the BAL required us to define as a third type of benefit of leisure the realization of a satisfying psychological outcome, because the improved and maintained conditions types of benefits did not always provide clear management direction. If realizing a desired psychological outcome is a benefit, then managers must be able to provide opportunities to do so, which in Figure 21.2 (page 357) is called an "experience opportunity" because the phonetics are better than a "psychological outcome opportunity." Thus, satisfying experience opportunities are one of three general types of benefit opportunity, with opportunities for individuals, groups of individuals, and the physical environment to realize any improved condition or to maintain any desired condition being the other two types. Thus, an "other benefit opportunity" includes all benefit opportunities (i.e., any improved or maintained condition) other than the opportunities to realize satisfying psychological outcomes.

During the second throughput process of the recreation production system, the recreationists use the first stage output of recreation activity opportunities on site to produce satisfying psychological experiences and other benefits for themselves, which are one type of second stage output. The other second stage outputs include any other type of benefit to individuals,

groups of individuals (including local communities), or the physical environment that results immediately or subsequently from management and from use of the recreation opportunities produced.

During the second stage of the recreation production process (Figure 21.2, page 357), the production of satisfying psychological outcomes and other benefits to the users, such as increased learning or physiological recovery from stress is only facilitated by, and not done by, managers. It is done by the recreationists' processing their recreation experiences through their personal psychological and physiological systems. By analogy, medical doctors do not heal their patients; the patients heal themselves because of the "healing opportunities" doctors provide using their professional knowledge about available health service delivery systems. In the same sense, managers of recreation service delivery systems must understand what the ultimate second stage benefits and disbenefits are, just as medical doctors must understand how they impact their patients. Put simply, recreation managers must understand the total production process and not just the first stage of it. This is true whether the BAL is being used to provide an array of many benefit opportunities or whether it targets a single type of benefit, such as preventing or reducing delinquency by a group of at-risk youth.

By adding the second stage, the BAL comprehensively considers all benefits attributable in whole or in part and directly and indirectly to managerial actions. Figure 21.2 (page 357) also shows that disbenefits (undesired impacts) can be produced as first and second stage outputs along with the benefits. A disbenefit may occur as a result of a bad experience, an injury, just disappointment with the activity or with other people who accompany the visitor, or by unwanted impacts of tourist development (Ashworth and Dietvorst, 1995). Or the disbenefit could be user-caused vandalism to a facility, a user-caused forest fire, or one hunter shooting another. Managers need to consider these disbenefits as much as the benefits as they focus on net benefits; they must try to capture and enhance targeted benefits and minimize accompanying disbenefits.

The BAL requires appreciation of the fact that some types of benefits are linked to other types of benefits within the "benefits chain of causality" (Driver, Tinsley and Manfredo, 1991) illustrated by Figure 21.3. That figure gives an example of how one benefit is linked to other subsequent benefits. Figure 21.4 expands this concept and makes it more managerially relevant by showing how the on- and off-site customers and the physical environment benefit in different ways at different times and places. That figure emphasizes again the comprehensiveness of the BAL by showing that

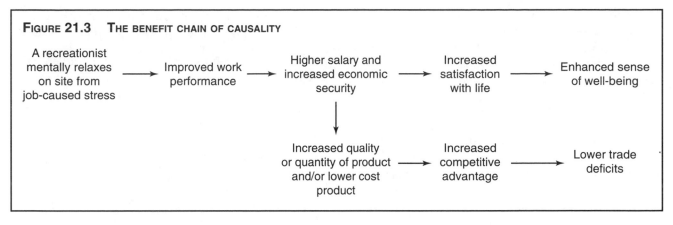

FIGURE 21.3   THE BENEFIT CHAIN OF CAUSALITY

the benefits can be psychological, physiological (an improvement in blood pressure without conscious awareness), economic, social, or environmental. And consistent with the three types of a leisure benefit defined previously, these benefits can reflect an improved condition, maintenance of a desired condition, or the realization of a satisfying psychological experience. They can accrue on site or off site, so they include benefits realized by appreciative users who never go on site yet benefit from articles in magazines and books or from pictures in a coffee-table book. Many of these off-site customers receive sizable satisfaction and benefit just from knowing that resources are being maintained and preserved.

The BAL is silent with respect to where in the benefit chain policymakers, managers, scientists, or educators should concentrate their attention. It does require understanding that the chain exists and appreciation of the fact that different recipients receive different benefits at different times and places, as shown in Figure 21.4. The current state of knowledge about the benefits of leisure now facilitates considerable understanding of these linkages. Additional research will advance that knowledge.

Contrasts With Conventional Approaches

Under the conventional approach to leisure, which has been called *activity-based management* (Driver, 1994), managerial treatment of the recreation production process stops with the production of the first stage outputs and excludes the concept of experience and other ben-

efit opportunities as first stage outputs. Therefore, under the activity-based approach, the outputs of the recreation production system would be the recreation activity opportunities provided, any protection of the physical resources accomplished, and any economic or social benefits realized from the actions of management. In contrast, the BAL includes all these first stage outputs plus the experience opportunities and other benefit opportunities, and it requires managers to address the entirely new second stage of the process. Specifically, under the BAL, the recreation activity, experience, and other benefit opportunities which were created as first stage outputs during the first stage process become inputs to the second stage of that process, and it is during that second stage that most of the benefits of leisure accrue to different recipients at different places and times, as reflected in the benefit chain of causality (Figures 21.3 and 21.4). By ignoring

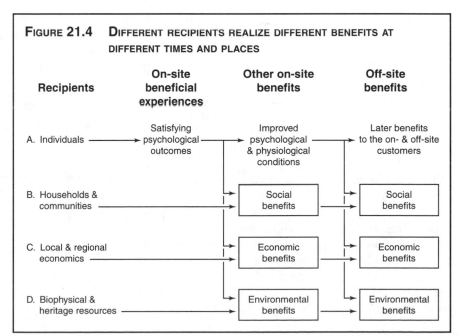

FIGURE 21.4   DIFFERENT RECIPIENTS REALIZE DIFFERENT BENEFITS AT DIFFERENT TIMES AND PLACES

this second stage, the conventional approach is oriented to inputs, not outcomes.

This perspective on the leisure service delivery system is instructive for two reasons. First, it facilitates a clear understanding of how conception of the recreation process under the BAL differs from the conventional activity approach. Second and related, it explains what shift in thinking is necessary to implement the BAL; it makes explicit the need for the planner, manager, administrator, scientist, and educator to understand more specifically what it is that is being produced where, when, and for whom that is either beneficial or detrimental to individuals, groups of individuals, or the physical environment.

Some leisure professionals have suggested that use of the words *benefits approach* is misleading and that the words *outcomes approach* should be used instead. They believe correctly that the focus of leisure policy analysis, management, education, and research should be on *all* the impacts or outcomes of leisure, both desired and undesired—beneficial and disbeneficial. Nevertheless, we maintained the benefits orientation strategically to help public policymakers, leisure professionals, and the public better understand and more accurately articulate the benefits of leisure. As explained previously, this understanding is necessary before leisure will be given its deserved parity with other social services. If a person is more comfortable with the concept of an outcomes approach, those words can be substituted for the benefits approach.

Continuing on semantics, we should mention that some recreation professionals have difficulty with the idea that recreation managers "produce" something, while they do not have trouble with the concept that these same people "provide" opportunities for people to recreate, to learn, or to maintain their health. The position of the BAL is that if recreation opportunities are provided, they must be produced—just as good parents produce opportunities for their children to be reared in safe, stimulating, and healthy environments and as teachers produce learning opportunities. This is not a trivial semantic issue because the problem with the concept of provision is that it does not explicitly denote the responsibility the professional "provider" has for understanding what is being produced, which is a fundamental requirement of the BAL. For example, most park and recreation managers still see themselves as operating within the first stage of the production process and view themselves as resource managers and program *providers,* not as *producers* of benefit opportunities. "Providing" does not denote an outcomes orientation to management of recreation resources, but "production" does so explicitly.

Summary of the Conceptual Orientation of the BAL

The BAL is viewed as a major mental paradigm shift by many leisure professionals. As a review of the basic logic of the BAL, the requirements of that shift are outlined here:

- Leisure service delivery systems must be viewed in systems terms as a production process that focuses attention not only on inputs, programs, and throughput processes but also on all positive and negative impacts to on- and off-site customers and to the physical environment.
- Not only must leisure scientists, educators, policymakers, and managers understand the outcomes focus of the BAL, but their actions also must reflect that understanding. They must "put their money [outcomes-oriented actions] where their mouths [minds] are." Understanding the BAL is not enough; there must be a shift in behaviors and operations.
- The planning for, actual delivery of, and monitoring of the delivery of leisure services must be collaborative efforts involving all stakeholders who affect, are affected by, or just have an interest in the leisure services being delivered. Such involvement, in an ongoing manner, is necessary to assure comprehensive consideration of all beneficial and disbeneficial outcomes.

Uses of the Benefits Approach to Leisure

The BAL is being used to guide leisure research, instruction, policy development, and management. The previously described basic concepts of the BAL apply for all of these uses. Because the focus of this chapter is on the two applied uses of the BAL—to guide the development of leisure policies and to guide management—each of these uses will be elaborated. Each requires that the agency position or reposition itself to focus on the outcomes or impacts of its actions and that it also articulates to its stakeholders and to the general public how the leisure services it provides add great value to the lives of individuals and to society (Crompton, 1993).

The BAL as a Guide for Policy Analysis

Given that the fundamental reason that any action is taken in the public sector is to promote and maintain the welfare of members of a society, all policy analyses—whether for leisure or any other purpose—should be benefits driven. Thus, a benefits-based approach to leisure policy analysis exists when the policies are designed to maximize net benefits. To do this, the policies must be developed using the best information available about the comparative advantages and disadvantages of a leisure-related action versus a non-leisure-related action or of one type of leisure-related action versus another leisure-related action. This requires that the policy analysts and decision makers understand the benefits of leisure, be able to justify allocations of public resources to leisure in terms of these benefits, and be accountable for those allocations in those terms.

In the past, policy decisions regarding leisure were guided mostly by informed intuition, rather than by objective data, about the benefits of leisure. Informed judgment and intuition are certainly important inputs to the development of leisure policies, because elected policymakers are chosen in part to represent the generally highly subjective values of their constituents. Therefore, objective data on the benefits of leisure should not be expected to totally replace informed judgment and intuition in public policymaking. Nevertheless, such data need to be used much more than they have been. Use of the BAL to guide policy development will assure greater use of such objective data because the BAL is science driven and requires that policymakers and managers keep informed about the latest scientific findings about the benefits of leisure.

The BAL as a Guide for Management

As mentioned earlier, when the BAL was first conceptualized, it was called *Benefits-Based Management* because interest then was primarily in using a benefits approach to guide the management of park and recreation resources. Because the term *Benefits-Based Management* is too limiting and does not apply to the other uses of the BAL, it is now used only to refer to the use of the BAL to guide management.

There are two distinct ways in which Benefits-Based Management (BBM) is being applied to guide the management of park and recreation programs and resources. One is where BBM is used to optimize an array of benefit opportunities and is called the *optimize benefit opportunities* approach. The other application of BBM is when leisure services and programs are strategically programmed as a social intervention to help prevent, resolve, or reduce the adverse impacts of a specific social problem or alternatively to capture a targeted benefit. This is called the *create a specific benefit* approach.

Optimize Benefit Opportunities

This use of BBM is to optimize the benefit choice options of the customers served. It is based on the fundamental tenet of all representative systems of government that each citizen is reasonably sovereign and as such should have an array of options from which to choose when making personal choices, such as voting for political representatives, buying an automobile, or deciding which type of recreation opportunity to choose. This logic applies when BBM is used to provide an optimal array of recreation activity, experience, and other benefit opportunities among which choices can be made to meet different individuals' (and groups of individuals') preferences and needs. One of the appeals of BBM is that it has proven to be quite effective in defining what this array should be and how it should be provided.

Create a Specific Benefit

With increasing concern about youth gangs and latch-key children, much attention has been given, especially by municipal park and recreation agencies, to recreation programs for helping prevent specific social problems. Special attention is being given to how structured leisure programs can help prevent at-risk youth from causing problems for themselves and for society. Some of these types of risky behaviors have been identified as proneness to join gangs, delinquency, lack of respect for people in positions of authority, low self-esteem, lack of particular social skills, being a member of a dysfunctional family, teen pregnancy, lack of positive role models, poor performance in school, absenteeism from school, lack of commitment to becoming educated, underachievement in sports, participation in negative leisure activity, and no constructive leisure activity (Schultz et al., 1995). The fall 1996 issue of the *Journal of Park and Recreation Administration* describes this use of BBM and includes results of several case studies.

In contrast to use of leisure programs to avoid a negative social condition, the create a specific benefit approach can also be more positively oriented toward capturing a specific benefit. Examples include leisure programs strategically oriented toward the use of nature-based recreation areas to promote greater environmental understanding and more ecologically sound behaviors such as recycling; promotion of physical activity to improve and maintain physical and mental health; enhancement of family kinship and cohesion; provision of opportunities for the elderly to improve their systems of social interaction and networking; promotion of learning about and increased pride in the history of a local area or of the nation; maintenance and enhancement of the ethnic identity of a particular subculture; and maintenance or improvement of the economic conditions of local communities.

These two distinct applications of BBM are not always clear in practice. Under the optimize benefit opportunities approach, a specific type of benefit (e.g., physical fitness or environmental education) can be emphasized among the several types of benefit opportunities that are being provided. When this happens, the focus is usually not on a particular subset of the customers being served, as under the create a specific benefit approach, but instead the targeted benefit opportunity is offered for any customer who wishes to benefit in that particular way. Nevertheless, an optimize benefit opportunities application could target a particular group, such as a particular local community that needs economic help from expenditures of tourist dollars.

Implications of Applying BBM

Because BBM is by far the major application of the BAL, it deserves special consideration here. While a discussion of how to implement BBM is beyond the scope of this chapter, we will provide an overview of the implications of implementing BBM and the major requirements for doing so. Other existing sources, and papers in progress, provide guidelines for implementing BBM (cf., Alberta Parks and Recreation Association, 1996; Allen, 1996; Driver, 1996; and a guideline being prepared by the National Recreation and Parks Association). Adoption of BBM has the following requirements and ramifications:

- BBM focuses management on adding or maintaining value through the provision of benefits. It does this by reorienting the managerial perspective away from activity-based programs that concentrate only on the first stage of the recreation production system to the perspective that attends to both the first and second stages.
- BBM recognizes that the delivery and use of recreation opportunities is accompa-

nied by disbenefits as well as benefits and that all recreation is not inherently good. The managers must therefore focus on net benefits and target those types of benefits which are desired by the on- and off-site customers.

- Managerial attention shifts from concentrating mostly on on-site customers to concentrating equally on on- and off-site customers so that all relevant benefits that accrue to individuals, to groups of individuals, and to the physical environment will be considered.
- Attention to all the customers requires the building and ongoing maintenance of collaborative partnerships with all affected and affecting stakeholders. BBM recognizes that the parks and recreation agency is not a sole-source provider (Bruns, 1998), so it must work collaboratively with the other providers (e.g., other public agencies, local private enterprises, and local community organizations) that affect the type, amount, and quality of recreation opportunities provided.
- Plan implementation requires the collaborative development of outcomes-directed management objectives, prescriptions, and guidelines and standards that will be supported at the policy level and implemented on the ground using the concept of total quality management. Managerial objectives define and target the type of benefit opportunities that will be provided at designated places and times, both on and off site. Management prescriptions define the managerial actions that will be taken to assure the delivery of the targeted benefit opportunities. The guidelines and standards are used during monitoring as objective measures of the degree to which the types, quantity, and quality of targeted benefit opportunities are actually being delivered. A narrower set of objectives, prescriptions, and standards will be required when BBM is used to create a specific benefit opportunity than when it is used to optimize an array of many benefit opportunities.
- Managers must accurately market the benefit opportunities provided so that both on- and off-site customers can more easily satisfy their benefit preferences and so particular benefit opportunities can be

promoted if the agency has the social mandate or consensus to do so.

- Managers must give more attention than in the past to long-term monitoring, including systematic measurement and documentation, of the degree to which management actions are both helping and hindering actual benefit achievement.
- The BBM system of management should be integrated with the other management systems being used. For example, BBM complements and supplements the other amenity resource management systems of which we are aware. For example, the USDA Forest Service is making good progress in integrating its other amenity resource management systems with BBM. Those other systems include Meaningful Measures for Quality Recreation Management (Jaten and Driver, 1998), which is a site- and project-level management system being implemented to assure the efficient, responsive, and accountable provision of high-quality recreation opportunities; the Scenery Management system (USDA Forest Service, 1995), which is used to protect and maintain visual scenic resources; and the Recreation Opportunity Spectrum system (Driver, 1990b; Driver, Brown, Gregoire and Stankey, 1987; USDA Forest Service, 1982), which helps managers identify and manage recreation settings appropriate for a wide spectrum of recreation activity and experience opportunities that should be provided where, when, and for whom. The recreation management systems that have been adopted by other agencies are compatible with BBM and should be integrated with it. These systems include the Limits of Acceptable Change (LAC) (Stankey et al., 1985), the Visitor Activity Management Process (VAMP) used by the Canadian Parks Service (Nilsen, 1995), the Visitor Experience and Resource Protection (VERP) (Manning, Lime and Hof, 1996) and Visitor Impact Management (VIM) (Graefe, Kuss and Vaske, 1990) systems used by several national parks in the United States.

In a nutshell, full application of BBM requires that certain criteria be met. BBM has been implemented when:

- A paradigm shift has occurred in the minds of the managers that causes them to focus on both the first and second stages of the recreation production system.
- Collaborative partnerships have been established with all customers, other affected and affecting providers, and other stakeholders so their demands will be considered.
- Management objectives, prescriptions, standards, and guidelines are developed and implemented that define the types, amounts, locations, and time of delivery of the benefit opportunities that are targeted for provision.
- A clear means of communicating (i.e., marketing) targeted benefits to the beneficiaries is being used.
- A comprehensive outcomes-oriented monitoring and evaluation process is in place.

Advantages of the Benefits Approach to Leisure

We will close this chapter by summarizing the reasons why the BAL is of growing interest to leisure professionals. The following advantages of the BAL accrue because it:

- *Promotes greater public understanding and appreciation of the social significance of leisure.* This chapter opened with the description of the paradox that while leisure is one of the most important economic sectors and the most beneficial social service, it is not publicly recognized as such. We suggested that one reason for this paradox is that professionals in all the subdisciplines of leisure have not successfully or effectively articulated the social importance of leisure. One of the purposes of the BAL is to provide a framework for promoting more widespread understanding of the important contributions of leisure to improving human welfare. That knowledge helps shift the too frequent perception that leisure is a residual to recognition of the real contributions of leisure to human productivity and happiness. Widespread understanding of the benefits of leisure will increase public support for leisure, and such support is necessary to any profession that delivers a social service that is highly dependent on public funding. In addition, this increased public understanding will facilitate more effective working relationships not only between the public and leisure professionals but also between leisure and other professionals.

- *Justifies allocations of public funds to leisure in the policy arena.* Policymakers need to compare the benefits and costs of alternative uses of public resources. These comparisons, which include but go beyond economic measures of benefit, have grown in importance as demands on public resources have increased and broadened in the face of increasingly stringent agency budgets. As a consequence, public officials, including those in parks and recreation agencies, are being held more accountable. They must explain more explicitly how the public goods and services they provide relate to specific social needs, why those goods and services are being provided, and articulate clearly the likely desirable and undesirable impacts of production and use of those goods and services. The BAL objectively defines those social needs and orients delivery of leisure services explicitly to them. As such, it makes policy decisions less subjective and public policymakers more responsive and accountable.

- *Helps planners and managers develop clearer management objectives.* Once public policy decisions have allocated public resources to a particular type of recreational use, information on benefits improves the ability of recreation planners and managers to define clear management objectives and prescriptions and then to establish more explicit standards and guidelines for meeting those objectives. Provision of exercise trails, opportunities for self-testing, quiet places, sites for socialization of many types (such as enhancing family kinship), and options to be free from specific everyday pressures are examples of discrete management actions that can help assure options to realize specific types of benefits. These clearer management objectives are facilitated by the better understanding of the

outputs of the leisure service delivery system. The BAL requires such understanding and facilitates it by adding the second stage to the recreation production system.

- *Facilitates social interventions.* Increasingly parks and recreation agencies are being given social mandates to promote particular benefits (e.g., environmental learning, increased physical fitness, and the many benefits associated with use of leisure programs to help prevent a specific social problem, such as reduction in crime or substance abuse through programs such as night basketball). While the BAL, itself, is silent with regard to such *social engineering,* it provides guidance on how to meet these social agendas.

- *Facilitates more meaningful recreation demand analyses.* By focusing on ends rather than means, the BAL makes explicit the ultimate recreation products (i.e., benefit opportunities) demanded by different customers. Thus, under the BAL, the on- and off-site customers served are better able to communicate their recreation-related needs to managers than they are when attention is devoted only to demands for activity opportunities.

- *Facilitates a collaborative style of management.* More and more public parks and recreation agencies are adopting a collaborative or participative style of planning and management that actively involves a wide array of partners and stakeholders in the planning and delivery of leisure services. The BAL rejects the common idea that a recreation agency is a sole provider, and it requires a collaborative style of decision making that necessitates forming collaborative partnerships with the other providers who affect provision of the recreation opportunities and with all other affecting, affected, or just interested stakeholders. The BAL provides a useful and effective framework for facilitating such a style of management.

- *Provides flexibility to managers.* Practitioners appreciate the flexibility the BAL affords them. It can be implemented incrementally, and it can be practiced at different degrees of comprehensiveness. For example, one agency and its collaborating partners might decide to focus on only one benefit (e.g., promote physical fitness) or a selected group of most significant and widespread benefits, while another agency and its partners might decide to look more in-depth and more comprehensively at a wider number of benefits (i.e., optimize an array of benefit opportunities).

- *Better identifies conflicts and substitutes.* Conflicts among customers are mostly caused by different individuals and organizations desiring different types of benefits. Thus, by definition, the BAL makes conflicting demands more explicit. It also facilitates better identification of complementary, or noncompetitive, demands and therefore affords better understanding of which recreation activities and settings are and are not substitutes for one another.

- *Enhances the customers' choice processes and their consumer sovereignty.* The BAL assumes that the individual generally knows best what does and does not improve his or her personal welfare. Much of this knowing is derived from experiential learning by trial and error. Certainly, each individual's personal knowledge is highly subjective and is mediated by social norms, mores, personal values, beliefs, and conditioning. Nevertheless, a considerable amount of each individual's personal knowledge comes from factual sources of information that are outside the individual. Examples include research-derived information on the probable effects on an individual's personal welfare of use of seat belts and avoidance of excessive low-density lipid cholesterol in one's bloodstream, hypertension, overexposure to the sun, substance (including tobacco and alcohol) abuse, failure to manage stress, physical inactivity, and poor nutrition. In a similar vein, the information on the likely beneficial (and detrimental) consequences of specific leisure activities required by the BAL helps enhance the choices of leisure opportunities by citizens. In this way, human welfare is promoted, and the role of leisure opportunities in doing so is better understood and appreciated.

- *Facilitates marketing.* Because the BAL makes the products of parks and recreation management explicit, the manag-

ing agencies can use this information to develop more explicit information packages and recreation opportunity availability guides oriented to the specified types of activity, experience, and other benefit opportunities that are being made available where, when, in what amount, and of what relative quality. The BAL also facilitates promotion of specific benefit opportunities if the agency has the social mandate or consensus to do so.

- *Enhances the rationality of recreation fee programs.* Most, if not all, public recreation agencies are having to consider increasing the entrance and use fees they charge. This is an emotion-laden issue in which the double-edged sword of equity cuts in both directions (Driver and Baltic, 1990). One side says don't constrain access by fees, and the other says it is unfair for the nonuser to pay the costs of provision and maintenance of recreation opportunities for users. Some people argue that the users should pay their fair share of these costs, while other people expand this reasoning and say the beneficiaries—and not just the users—should pay. Their logic is that since recreation is known to be a "merit good" that provides spin-off benefits from users to nonusers, it is only fair that those who receive these social benefits (e.g., enhanced local physical amenities) help pay the costs of providing those benefits. The BAL helps implement this "beneficiaries should pay" rationale because it requires identification—and to the extent it is possible, quantification—of all benefits to all beneficiaries. Therefore, the BAL helps identify those beneficiaries to which the costs can be apportioned either as user fees or as tax levies.

- *Advances knowledge.* The scientific community is interested in knowledge about the benefits of leisure, because scientists and educators want to understand better what leisure is and its contributions to human welfare. The BAL helps scientists and educators attain this understanding. That understanding helps advance basic knowledge about recreation and thereby promotes better professional practice.

- *Facilitates additional research.* Given that research is a building process, an understanding of the impacts of leisure behavior nurtures additional hypotheses and research about the benefits of parks and recreation.

- *Promotes better education.* Better understanding of the benefits of leisure facilitates better formal training of students and on-the-job training of practitioners because of that improved knowledge base.

- *Increases pride in the profession.* Lastly, and of subtle but vital importance, the previously cited advantages serve to increase the pride of leisure professionals in their choice of a career. This helps make leisure professionals less defensive and take more pride in their socially important tasks. It also encourages more highly talented people to enter the leisure professions, a trend that has clearly been apparent during the past 20 years as the systematic body of knowledge about leisure behavior has increased.

The BAL, especially BBM, is being applied widely in the provinces of Ontario and Alberta in Canada, and in the United States. The public policymakers and managers who have applied the BAL have found it easy to understand. They like it and think it is the way that recreation policies and managerial directions should be developed and implemented. This sentiment is shared by a growing number of leisure educators and scientists.

Over time the BAL has become easier for practitioners to implement because the procedures used in the past by different federal, state or provincial, and municipal agencies have now become more standardized. This has simplified and expedited the process of implementing the BAL. Several users' guides that are being prepared describe those procedures and will facilitate wider and more consistent use of the BAL.

References

Addams, J. (1910). *Twenty years at Hull House*. New York, NY: Macmillan Publishing.

Alberta Recreation and Park Association. (1996). *Benefits-based management: Awareness into action*. Edmonton, Alberta: Author.

Allen, L. (1990). Benefits of leisure attributes to community satisfaction. *Journal of Leisure Research, 22*(2), 183–196.

Allen, L. (1996). A primer: Benefits-based management of recreation services. *Parks and Recreation, March,* 64–76.

Ashworth, G., & Dietvorst, A. (Eds.). (1995). *Tourism and spatial transformations: Implications for policy and planning*. Tucson, AZ: CAB International.

Barrett, C. (1989). The concept of leisure: Idea and ideal. In T. Winnifrith & C. Barrett (Eds.), *The philosophy of leisure*. London, UK: Macmillan Publishing.

Bruns, D. (1998). Benefits-based recreation-tourism paradigm shifts. In M. Johnson, G. Twynam & W. Haider (Eds.), *Shaping tomorrow's north: The role of tourism and recreation* (pp. 228–256). Thunderbay, Ontario: Lakehead Center for Northern Studies.

Buckley, W. (1968). *Modern systems research for the behavioral scientist*. Chicago, IL: Aldine Publishing Company.

Crompton, J. (1993). Repositioning recreation and park services: An overview. *Trends, 30*(4), 2–5. Washington, DC: Park Practice Program, National Park Service.

Driver, B. (1990a). The North American experience in measuring the benefits of leisure. In E. Hamilton-Smith (Ed.), *Proceedings, National Workshop on Measurement of Recreation Benefits* (pp. 1–57). Bandoora, Australia: Phillip Institute of Technology.

Driver, B. (1990b). Recreation opportunity spectrum: Basic concepts and use in land management planning. In R. Graham & R. Lawrence (Eds.), *Toward serving visitors and managing our resources, Proceedings of a North American Workshop on Visitor Management on Parks and Protected Areas* (pp. 159–183). Waterloo, Ontario: Tourism Research and Education Center, University of Waterloo.

Driver, B. (1992). The benefits of leisure. *Parks and Recreation, 27*(11), 16, 17, 20–25.

Driver, B. (1994). The recreation production process: The benefits-based approach to amenity resource policy analysis and management. In *Friluftsliv: Effekter og goder, Dn-notat, 1994–7, Direktoratet for Naturforvaltning Tungasletta* [Proceedings, Scandinavian Conference on Recreation: Benefits and Other Positive Effects] (pp. 12–30). Trondheim, Norway: Norwegian Institute of Nature Studies.

Driver, B. (1996). Benefits-driven management of natural areas. *Natural Area Journal, 16*(2), 94–99.

Driver, B., & Baltic, T. (1990). Equity in public resource allocations. *Journal of Physical Education, Recreation, and Dance, 61*(8), 53–56.

Driver, B., Brown, P., Gregoire, T., & Stankey, G. (1987). The ROS planning system: Evolution, basic concepts, and research needed. *Leisure Sciences, 9*(3), 203–214.

Driver, B., Brown, P., & Peterson, G. (Eds.). (1991). *Benefits of leisure*. State College, PA: Venture Publishing, Inc.

Driver, B., & Burch, W., Jr. (1988). A framework for more comprehensive valuations of public amenity goods and services. In G. Peterson, B. Driver & R. Gregory (Eds.), *Amenity resource valuation: Integrating economics with other disciplines* (pp. 31–45). State College, PA: Venture Publishing, Inc.

Driver, B., Dustin, D., Baltic, T., Elsner, G., & Peterson, G. (Eds.). (1996). *Nature and the human spirit: Toward an expanded land management ethic*. State College, PA: Venture Publishing, Inc.

Driver, B., & Peterson, G. (Compilers). (1986). Values section (comprised of 11 papers). In *A Literature Review. President's Commission on Americans Outdoors*. Washington, DC: U.S. Government Printing Office.

Driver, B., Tinsley, H., & Manfredo, M. (1991). The paragraphs about leisure and recreation experience preference scales: Results from two inventories designed to access the breadth of the perceived psychological benefits of leisure. In B. Driver, P. Brown & G. Peterson (Eds.), *Benefits of leisure* (pp. 263–286). State College, PA: Venture Publishing, Inc.

Driver, B., & Tocher, R. S. (1970). Toward a behavioral interpretation of recreation with implications for planning. In B. Driver (Ed.), *Elements of outdoor recreation planning* (pp. 9–31). Ann Arbor, MI: The University of Michigan Press.

Easley, A. (1991). Programmed, nonclinical skill development benefits of leisure activities. In B. Driver, P. Brown & G. Peterson (Eds.), *Benefits of leisure* (pp. 145–160). State College, PA: Venture Publishing, Inc.

Federal Reporting Company. (1961). *Transcript of proceedings of outdoor recreation resources review commission's conference on leisure, outdoor recreation, and mental health, June 1, 1961*. Washington, DC: Author.

Godbey, G., Graefe, A., & James, S. (1992). *The benefits of local recreation and park services: A nationwide study of the perceptions of the American public*. State

College, PA: School of Hotel, Restaurant and Recreation Management, The Pennsylvania State University.

Graefe, A., Kuss, F., & Vaske, J. (1990). Visitor impact management. In *Volume two of report examining visitor impact management for the national parks and other recreation lands* (pp. 83–96). Washington, DC: National Parks and Conservation Association.

Jackson, E., & Burton, T. (Eds.). (1989). *Understanding leisure and recreation: Mapping the past, charting the future*. State College, PA: Venture Publishing, Inc.

Jaten, A., & Driver, B. (1998). Meaningful measures for quality recreation management. *Journal of Park and Recreation Administration 16*(3), 43–57.

Johnson, R., & Brown, T. (1991). Beneficial economic consequences of leisure and recreation. In B. Driver, P. Brown & G. Peterson (Eds.), *Benefits of leisure* (pp. 385–391). State College, PA: Venture Publishing, Inc.

Kelly, J. (1981). *Social benefits of outdoor recreation*. Urbana-Champaign, IL: Department of Leisure Studies, University of Illinois.

Lee, M., & Driver, B. (1996). Benefits-based management: A new paradigm for managing amenity resources. In W. Burch Jr., J. Aley, B. Conover & D. Field (Eds.), *Survival of the organizationally fit: Ecosystem management as an adaptive strategy for natural resource organizations in the 21st century.* New York, NY: Taylor and Francis Publishers.

Manfredo, M., Driver, B., & Brown, P. (1983). A test of concepts inherent in experience-based setting management of outdoor recreation areas. *Journal of Leisure Research, 15*(3) 263–283.

Manfredo, M., Driver, B., & Tarrant, M. (1996). Measuring leisure motivation: A meta-analysis of the recreation experience preference scales. *Journal of Leisure Research, 28*(3) 188–213.

Manning, R., Lime, D., & Hof, M. (1996). Social carrying capacity of natural areas: Theory and application in the U.S. national parks. *Natural Areas Journal, 16*(2) 118–127.

Nilsen, P. (1995). Best practice in customer research. In *Proceedings, First International Urban Parks and Waterways Best Practice Conference* (pp. A2-3–A2-17). Melbourne, Australia: Melbourne Parks and Waterways Authority.

Olmsted, F., Jr., & Kimball, T. (Eds.). (1970). *Frederick Law Olmsted, landscape architect, 1822–1903.* New York, NY: Benjamin Bloom, Inc.

Orthner, D., & Mancini, J. (1991). Benefits of leisure family bonding. In B. Driver, P. Brown & G. Peterson (Eds.), *Benefits of Leisure* (pp. 289–301). State College, PA: Venture Publishing, Inc.

Paffenbarger, R., Jr., Hyde, R., & Dow, A. (1991). Health benefits of physical activity. In B. Driver, P. Brown & G. Peterson (Eds.), *Benefits of Leisure* (pp. 49–58). State College, PA: Venture Publishing, Inc.

Parks and Recreation Federation of Ontario. (1992). *The benefits of parks and recreation: A catalogue.* Ottawa, Ontario: Author.

Randall, A. (1984). Benefit-cost analysis as an information system. In G. Peterson & A. Randall (Eds.), *Valuation of wildland resource benefits* (pp. 65–75). Boulder, CO: Westview Press.

Roggenbuck, J., Loomis, J., & Dagostino, J. (1990). The learning benefits of leisure. *Journal of Leisure Research, 22*(2) 112–124.

Rolston, H., III. (1985). Valuing wildlands. *Environmental Ethics, 7,* 23–48.

Rolston, H., III. (1991). Creation and recreation: Environmental benefits and human leisure. In B. Driver, P. Brown & G. Peterson (Eds.), *Benefits of leisure* (pp. 393–406). State College, PA: Venture Publishing, Inc.

Schreyer, R., & Driver, B. (1989). The benefits of leisure. In E. Jackson & T. Burton (Eds.), *Understanding leisure and recreation: Mapping the past, charting the future* (pp. 385–419). State College, PA: Venture Publishing, Inc.

Schultz, L., Crompton, J., & Witt, P. (1995). A national profile of the status of public recreation services for at-risk children and youth. *Journal of Park and Recreation Administration, 13*(3) 1–25.

Sefton, J., & Mummery, W. (1995). *Benefits of recreation research update.* State College, PA: Venture Publishing, Inc.

Stankey, G., Cole, D., Lucas, R., Peterson, M., Frissell, S., & Washburne, R. (1985). *The limits of acceptable (LAC) system for wilderness planning* (General Technical Report INT-176). Ogden, UT: USDA Forest Service Intermountain Forest and Range Experiment Station.

Stein, T., & Lee, M. (1995). Managing recreation resources for positive outcomes: An application of benefits-based management. *Journal of Parks and Recreation Administration, 13*(3) 52–70.

Stynes, D., & Godbey, G. (1993). *Leisure: The new center of the economy* [on line]. Available: http://www.geog.ualberta.ca/als/alswp3.html

Tindall, B. (1995). Beyond fun and games. *Parks and Recreation, March,* 87–93.

Ulrich, R., Dimberg, U., & Driver, B. (1990). Psychophysiological indicators of leisure consequences. *Journal of Leisure Research, 22*(2) 154–166.

USDA Forest Service. (1982). *ROS users' guide.* Washington, DC: U.S. Government Printing Office.

USDA Forest Service. (1995). *Landscape aesthetics: A handbook for scenery management* (Agriculture Handbook 701 System). Washington, DC: U.S. Government Printing Office.

Witt, P., & Crompton, J. (Eds.). (1996). *Recreation programs that work for at-risk youth: The challenge of shaping the future.* State College, PA: Venture Publishing, Inc.

Back to the Future: Leisure Services and the Reemergence of the Enabling Authority of the State

Thomas L. Burton
University of Alberta

Troy D. Glover
University of Waterloo

Drucker (1989) has proposed a model whereby Western societies have passed through several great divides, or watersheds, in their history, during which new ideas took hold and social and political landscapes were changed dramatically. He noted that the medieval world was dominated by the idea of *salvation by faith* (or religion) and that this was ultimately destroyed by the Renaissance and the Reformation. The Renaissance then gave birth to the idea of *salvation by science*—although Drucker does not use this particular term. He does note, however, that, in due course, the ideas of the Renaissance gave way to those of such writers as Adam Smith and Thomas Paine, leading to an emphasis upon the rights of the individual, and what we have called *salvation by industry.* Finally, this itself gave way to ideas of socialism, with their emphasis on *salvation by society* (or government). This last divide occurred sometime during the 1870s and set the political agenda for the century that followed, which saw the establishment of the welfare state—slowly at first and, then, with great rapidity in the years immedi-

ately following the Second World War. The postwar era saw the introduction in many Western countries of such initiatives as unemployment insurance and universal healthcare, together with a vast growth in social expenditures by governments throughout the industrialized world. This growth in direct government involvement in the production and delivery of social goods and services was justified by many as a necessary means of rectifying the imperfections of the market economy, since it was assumed that governments would act in the best interests of their citizens, whereas the market would act according to the dictates of profit.

Drucker (1989) further contends that somewhere between the years 1968 and 1973, Western societies passed through yet another great divide. The doctrines of the welfare state were increasingly questioned as people began to lose faith in salvation by society. In particular, there was a turning away from the idea of social action as a means to the creation of a perfect society. The rise to power of Margaret Thatcher in Britain in 1979 gave practical impetus to these ideas, and is generally considered to mark the beginning of a movement emphasizing limited government intervention in the social and economic lives of citizens. Thatcher condemned the perceived excesses of the *nanny state,* preferring a government role which emphasized problem solving rather than the pursuit of social panaceas. Thatcher and others like her (Reagan in the United States, Douglas in New Zealand, Klein and Harris in Canada) are not antigovernment but, rather, view government in limited terms, concentrating on government's ability to find specific remedies for specific problems. What will work is what motivates action. Furthermore, what will work depends to a very great extent on the fiscal and human resources available to government. The *golden age* of the welfare state (1945–1980 in Canada) was accompanied by vast increases in deficit spending by governments, which later became a factor working to support a changed philosophy.

By the early 1980s the model of direct public production and delivery of social goods and services was becoming increasingly challenged by concerned taxpayers. Severe fiscal imbalance, deficit funding, and accumulated debt at all levels of government led to increased questioning of many of the tenets of the welfare state. There were growing calls for greater fiscal responsibility and accountability on the part of governments. The golden age of the welfare state, in which public opinion was generally supportive of the redistribution among the wider citizenry of the wealth generated from a strong economy, was coming to an end. The stagnation of the economy during the late 1970s brought with it increasingly frequent and popular calls for reduced social spending (Pierson, 1991). As a result, by the mid 1980s, political parties that failed to support welfare reforms and restrictions on social spending received diminished voter support.

In addition to dwindling public support for much of the activity of the welfare state, there was a resurgence of academic, professional, and political support for reduced government intervention in the workings of the market economy. Indeed, a countermovement against the interventionist state was apparent as proponents of the *New Right* voiced concerns about the viability of social spending. The welfare state was increasingly perceived to be uneconomic, unproductive, inefficient, oppressive, and a blatant denial of freedom (Pierson, 1991). Also, public choice theorists voiced their concerns regarding the self-interest inherent in the political process and identified it as a failure of the organization of government. Political actors were viewed as "*rational egoists* who pursue their private interests in both economic and political life" (Self, 1993, p. 4). Put simply, it was argued that the liberal

democratic conditions which the welfare state developed encouraged politicians and bureaucrats to be irresponsible. The institutional framework of government was increasingly portrayed as ineffective and wasteful because it supported the integration of the political and managerial levels of service delivery (Osborne and Gaebler, 1992). Collective choice via state action was believed to yield outcomes that were less efficient or desirable than outcomes determined by private choice through markets.

As a result, a search began for alternatives to direct government production and delivery of social goods and services. Privatization, initially defined as the sale of a government service to the private sector, has been one of the most controversial. There has been considerable debate about privatization, focusing upon such things as greater efficiency in service delivery, on the one side, and a perceived reduction in quality of service, on the other. It is our contention that this debate, at least in the political domain, has created a great deal of heat but little illumination. This is due in great measure to the fact that the concept of privatization itself is poorly understood. As well, it reflects a lack of knowledge of the different roles that government has played historically in the delivery of social goods and services.

Leisure Services and the Enabling Authority of the State

In Canada and the United States, the years from the mid 1950s through the early 1980s saw a significant expansion of municipal leisure services produced and delivered directly by governments to their citizens, in keeping with the tenets of the welfare state. Moreover, while the form of municipal government involvement in leisure has been increasingly questioned during the past decade or so, there has been little attempt to reduce its scale, and only on rare occasions has its legitimacy been questioned. It seems that while a great deal of effort has gone into seeking new and different ways of delivering leisure opportunities in cities and towns— especially where this will lead to significant cost reductions—there is little enthusiasm for those who would have civic (and, indeed, provincial, state, and federal) governments withdraw entirely from the field. Contrary to the general thrust toward a reduced welfare state, it seems that what we have seen over the past decade or so is a rethinking of the ways in which governments have gone about delivering leisure opportunities for their citizens, not a rejection of the validity of their doing so.

This rethinking has been closely aligned with the notion of the *enabling authority of the state*. The fundamental principle embodied in this notion is that a clear distinction should be made between *arranging* a service and *producing* it. In its minimalist version, the argument for the enabling state rests upon the idea that the principal role of the state is to define standards, monitor performance, and ensure redress for unfairness, not to produce services: "In theory, at least, the state need not employ anybody, contracting out all its functions" (Walsh, 1997, p. 39). The distinction between delivering a service—or, more accurately, arranging for its production—and producing that service is a profound one, with enormous consequences for *how* leisure opportunities (and other social goods and services) are actually made available to citizens.

Savas (1987) has distinguished three basic groups involved in the delivery of public services: the *consumer or citizen*, the *service arranger or provider*, and the *service producer*. The consumer or citizen is the individual, household, or group (e.g., people with special needs, youth, the elderly) that obtains or receives a public service. A person who enrolls in swimming classes at a municipal swimming pool is such a consumer. The service arranger or provider is typically the unit of government that "assigns the producer to the consumer, or vice versa, or selects the producer that will serve the consumer" (Savas, 1987, p. 60). A municipal parks and recreation department, for example, arranges that swimming classes will be offered to consumers and determines who will produce them. The service producer is the agency which actually delivers the service, in this case swimming lessons. This agency could be the parks and recreation department itself, or a commercial firm, not-for-profit organization, or voluntary association of citizens contracted by the department.

The second of these groups, the service arranger or provider, exercises what is called the *enabling authority of the state*, since it ensures that a particular service is delivered to consumers. In the previous example, the parks and recreation department ensures that swimming lessons will be made available to consumers. Barnett (1997) suggests that the enabling authority of the state encompasses two key roles for governments. The first requires that governments act to facilitate the production of services for the public by commercial firms and not-for-profit or voluntary organizations. In essence, governments empower such groups to produce leisure opportunities for the community. The second role sees governments offering commercial firms and not-for-profit organizations opportunities to compete for the right to produce those services that the government itself wishes to arrange.

The principal rationale for the adoption of the enabling role of the state is economic:

> Essentially, the primary objective of enabling government is to achieve cost efficiency in the production of government services. Its application requires that a clear distinction be made between the role of government per se, which is related to policy or goal setting, and the production of services necessary to achieve policy objectives. Service production is not seen as necessarily a government function. (Barnett, 1997, p. 68)

For most of the half century that followed the end of the Second World War, it was assumed that the service arranger or provider and the service producer should, of necessity, be one and the same: that government departments and agencies should not only *arrange* for leisure services to be provided, but should also *produce* them, through the activities of government employees. Historically, however, the delivery of public leisure services has been much more diverse than this. Many different kinds of combinations between arrangers-providers and producers have been evident.

The Roles of Government in Public Leisure Service Delivery

Burton (1982) outlined a model incorporating five roles that governments play in the delivery of public leisure services in advanced industrial nations. The first is that of a *direct provider of public leisure services*. This describes the situation in which a government department or agency develops and maintains leisure facilities, operates programs, and delivers services using public funds and public employees. It is the pattern which became dominant in North American cities, towns, and counties in the years from the mid 1950s through the early 1980s. Moreover, it is the model with which most citizens in North America today are most familiar. Direct delivery is exemplified through city-operated swimming pools that are typically built, maintained, and operated by the city's parks and recreation department.

The second role is that of an *arm's length provider of services*. This requires the creation of a publicly owned special-purpose agency which operates outside the regular apparatus of government. Typically, such an agency is funded by a government and has a board of directors appointed by that government. However, the agency is independent of the government in organizing its everyday activities, being required only to report to it on a regular (usually annual) basis. Arm's length agencies are rarely found at the municipal level today, except, perhaps, in the arts and culture domain. But, as we shall see, they were the dominant form of management of urban parks in Canada in the late nineteenth and early twentieth centuries.

Government's third role is as an *enabler and coordinator of services*. In this role, a government department would identify organizations and agencies which produce leisure services for the public and help coordinate their efforts, resources, and activities. This is done most frequently through leadership training schemes of various kinds and by way of government-supported consultation services. Often, municipal parks and recreation departments will assist nongovernmental organizations in identifying needed leisure services and in developing programs.

The fourth role requires that a government act as a *supporter and patron* of nongovernmental leisure service organizations. In this situation, a government recognizes that existing organizations already produce valuable public leisure services and can be encouraged to continue to do so through specialized support, especially (though not exclusively) through grants of capital and operating funds. Those supported are most often not-for-profit organizations, but some commercial groups (e.g., chambers of commerce tourist bureaus) may also receive support.

The final role of government is as a *legislator and regulator* of public leisure activities and organizations. Using their authority to create laws and bylaws, governments exercise control over organizations and individuals engaged in the delivery of public leisure services. They also regulate personal behavior in leisure environments such as local parks, bars, and theaters.

At the time that Burton's study was conducted in 1982, the role of direct provider was one of major significance for municipal governments in Canada. The roles of enabler-coordinator and supporter-patron were less significant, although still important. The roles of arm's length provider and legislator-regulator were of minor significance to municipal governments. In contrast, the enabler-coordinator and supporter-patron roles were major ones for the provincial and federal governments. The legislator-regulator role was also a major one for provincial governments. The roles of direct provider and arm's length provider were relatively minor for both senior levels of government, except in particular sectors. Direct delivery was very important in the parks domain—in national and provincial parks,

forests, and wilderness areas. Arm's length provision was important in broadcasting and in the cultural arts (Burton, 1982). All roles, however, have been evident historically among Canadian governments.

A similar (though clearly not identical) pattern holds true in the United States, where federal and state governments have played very strong roles as direct providers of national and state parks, wilderness areas, and forest recreation areas, but have tended to stay out of the direct delivery of other kinds of recreation facilities, areas, and services. County and city governments, on the other hand, have been significant direct providers of municipal parks, stadiums and swimming pools, playgrounds and sports fields, recreation programs, and so on.

While the various roles that have been discussed here pertain to all levels of government, the principal interest in this chapter is with the activities of municipal governments in urban communities.

Government as Legislator and Regulator: Civic Boosterism and Urban Reform

At the time of Confederation in 1867, Canadian cities and towns were under few pressures to produce and deliver public recreation services. But this situation changed markedly within a relatively short time. As Canadian cities began to grow in size and population, special interest groups, focusing on urban reform and civic boosterism, pushed for urban improvements and properly planned development to enhance living conditions and to promote beautification of their cities (Markham, 1988). Urban reformers focused on such causes as social welfare, public health, urban planning, and government infrastructure. In essence, they were interested in furthering social justice by extending the concept of citizenship to include a wider set of basic goods and services of society than currently was the case. In contrast, civic boosterism centered entirely upon the promotion of the community, with the intent to develop it into a superior place in which to live. Boosters supported initiatives that were expected to enhance the everyday lives of the residents of their communities.

Although both groups remained mutually exclusive, the causes and efforts favored by urban reformers and civic boosters coincided at several points. In particular, the development of urban parks was championed by both groups. Urban reformers believed that parks enhanced the physical, mental, and moral health of all residents by creating a healthy environment (Markham, 1988). They also pressed for civic beautification and town planning to improve the urban environment for residents. In contrast, civic boosters viewed parks as ways of attracting new residents who would bring investment, growth, and prosperity to the community. As a result, some urban reform issues, which also happened to favor booster interests, were viewed positively by boosters. But, invariably, it depended on the immediate situation. For example, boosters discouraged the pursuit of social justice, the search for a healthy environment, and the demand for town planning when they believed the benefits were too costly or when the benefits were expected to profit people other than themselves and their cities (Markham, 1988). Nonetheless, urban reformers and civic boosters combined to create an influential presence in their respective cities and subsequently forced provincial and local governments to respond to their proposals for change. This led directly to legislation aimed at the improvement of opportunities for public leisure through the creation of urban parks. Some examples are:

- In 1883 the *Public Parks Act of Ontario* was passed to facilitate the development of municipal parks throughout Ontario (Wright, 1984).
- In 1892 the *Manitoba Public Parks Act* enabled cities with populations of 25,000 or more to acquire 600 acres of land for public parks; towns could acquire 100 acres (McFarland, 1970).
- In 1912 the *Saskatoon Public Parks Act* gave that city the power to select, acquire, maintain, and operate lands for park purposes (McFarland, 1970).

Each initiative illustrates government's role as a legislator and regulator of public recreation. By using its authority to create laws and establish regulations, government began to exercise control over agencies and individuals engaged in the delivery of leisure services.

The story was similar in the United States, although the particular actors involved were different. The earliest urban parks, developed by Olmstead and others, represented an attempt to beautify cities and to re-create "the rural countryside in the middle of the city" (Goodale and Godbey, 1988, p. 115). They came about through the efforts of affluent individuals and community groups seeking to create oases of beauty and quiet amidst the bustle of the teeming cities. At the same time, social reform movements blossomed. The Settlement House Movement was particularly impor-

tant to the development of *wholesome* recreation opportunities for city dwellers. Goodale and Godbey (1988) note that virtually all of the social reform efforts in leisure emerged from a philosophy that saw organized recreation as a means of furthering the moral development of city dwellers. They note also that these efforts typically evolved from a voluntary base to increased involvement of government. Initially, the latter came in the form of legislation and government regulation of the activities of individuals and the various community and reform groups involved.

Government as Patron and Arm's Length Provider: The Playground Movement

The demands of urban reformers in Canada combined with the efforts of various community groups to extend government's role in the delivery of public leisure services. The National Council of Women (NCW) was formed in 1893 and almost immediately drew attention to the issue of recreation for children and youth. The NCW became the driving force behind the Playground Movement in Canada by arranging for the establishment of supervised summer playgrounds throughout the country (McFarland, 1970). Several civic groups affiliated with the NCW developed playgrounds for children in cities in Nova Scotia, New Brunswick, Quebec, Ontario, Manitoba, and Saskatchewan (McFarland, 1970). Local government supported the NCW's initiatives by becoming patrons of leisure service organizations. They recognized that the NCW and other not-for-profit organizations provided a valuable leisure service and could be encouraged to continue to do so through specialized support, especially (though not exclusively) through monetary grants.

As patrons of leisure services, municipal governments worked with community groups and service clubs to establish other kinds of recreational opportunities for people across Canada, particularly in the West (McFarland, 1970). In 1917 the first Community League was established in Jasper Place, a suburb of Edmonton, signaling the emergence of organized recreation in the city (McFarland, 1970). It brought together various athletic groups, ratepayers associations, and parent-teacher bodies to form a community action group. Jasper Place was the first Community League to receive a block of land from the city to be used for recreation purposes, which was initially developed as a playground. As more community leagues were established, recreation grounds were reserved in almost every area of

Edmonton. Residents of Edmonton also benefited from the work of the Gyro Club, which responded to the city's need for supervised playgrounds. The club raised sufficient funds to open three playgrounds in the city. Similarly, in Saskatoon, the Kinsmen Club opened two playgrounds during the 1920s, while, in Regina, the YMCA played an active role in organizing and operating the city's first playgrounds (Markham, 1988).

In the United States, as early as 1855, a sand pile for children's play was provided in Boston by the Massachusetts Emergency and Hygiene Association. By the end of the century, Boston City Council was providing an annual sum of $3,000 to support the costs of this and other play areas in the city (Butler, 1959). Then, at the turn of the century, the emphasis on playgrounds became intermingled with the interest in the development of urban parks. During the first quarter of the twentieth century, children's needs became an important focus of parks planning. Playgrounds became a standard feature of many city parks, as social reformers like Joseph Lee, supported by organizations such as the National Recreation Association and the Young Women's Christian Association, articulated the need for play spaces for the children of the rapidly growing industrial cities. Like their Canadian counterparts, the leaders of the American Playground Movement were concerned with children's health and behavior in cities. Unlike the early urban parks of the Olmstead era, however, the reform parks with their attendant playgrounds were "not a substitute for the countryside, but for the street" (Goodale and Godbey, 1988, p. 116). They reflected the concerns of social reformers, for whom recreation was part of a wider concern for improved social conditions: recreation was simply "one important factor in life which also had to be integrated with the educational, political, social, religious, and economic realities of neighborhoods and cities" (Duncan, 1985, p. 412).

The Playground Movement in Canada led ultimately to the adoption by government of the role of an arm's length provider of leisure services. This required the creation of publicly owned special-purpose agencies that operated outside the regular apparatus of government. An arm's length organization was funded by government and typically had a government-appointed board of directors. Several illustrations of arm's length provision can be found in Canada's early recorded history, as legislation led to the creation of several parks boards across the country. Under the Ontario *Public Parks Act* of 1883, Port Arthur, Ottawa, Kitchener, Hamilton, Brantford, Sault Sainte Marie, and London were among the first Ontario towns and cities to adopt such a board. In 1893 the Winnipeg Parks Board was appointed in Manitoba. In 1910 Calgary established a parks board that had exclusive control of all parks, cemeteries, and boulevards. However, Vancouver, in British Columbia, was the first city to have a directly elected parks board, established in 1888. Although all boards were established with the responsibility for overseeing the development and operation of parks and playgrounds, each relied heavily on the voluntary contributions of service clubs and community groups, especially as citizens came to demand more services.

The creation of arm's length parks and recreation boards at the municipal level was not a general feature of the development of parks and playgrounds in the United States. Instead, local governments tended to restrict themselves to the role of patron in the early years, providing financial and other support to private, community, and not-for-profit organizations which delivered leisure services directly to citizens. Over time, local governments moved from this role to that of direct provider, as private and community provision gave way to public sector production and delivery. But, they rarely adopted the arm's length approach.

Government as Coordinator: The Community Center Movement

As parks and playgrounds surfaced across Canada, service groups began to focus their attention and efforts on building other recreational facilities, leading to the growth of the Community Center Movement (McFarland, 1970). Government delivered much needed assistance in helping these groups achieve their aims. In 1920 the Ontario government enacted the *Community Halls Act,* which provided financial assistance to rural communities. The act gave the provincial government authority to provide 25% of the construction costs of a community hall or athletic field built by rural municipalities. In 1917 the Vancouver Parks Board cooperated with local community associations in the planning and financing of new community structures. In 1946 the Calgary Community Recreation Association was formed to build and extend several community facilities with the assistance of the City of Calgary. Also in 1946 several facilities were built in Winnipeg after ratepayers passed a bylaw which set aside $500,000 to construct community center buildings and playgrounds. Upon completion, each community center was turned over to an elected local executive for supervision, operation, and maintenance.

The emergence of supervised playgrounds and community centers increased the need for trained leisure professionals. In 1934 the government of British Columbia established a youth-training program in recreation and physical education. In 1936 and 1937 it provided enough funding to run classes for more than 10,000 people. In 1938 and 1939 Alberta and Saskatchewan offered similar programs, with the aid of members of the staff from British Columbia and with financial assistance from the federal government. The federal *Youth Training Act* in 1939 was "designed to promote and assist in the training of unemployed young people between the ages of 16 and 30" (McFarland, 1970). The passage of the act led other provinces, such as Manitoba and New Brunswick, to create youth-training programs. Unfortunately, the outbreak of World War II hindered the development of many of these programs. Nevertheless, the creation of youth-training programs and its related legislation represented government's emerging role as a coordinator of services. That is, governments identified agencies that produced leisure services and encouraged and helped them to coordinate their efforts, resources and activities. This was initially achieved through leadership training, but was later expanded to include government-supported consultation services.

In the United States cooperation between local governments and community groups was not so clearly linked to state and federal leadership programs. During what Cranz (1982) has called the *Recreation Facility Era* in the development of urban parks, local governments often planned recreation programs in conjunction with community recreation groups whose interests were often singular, "such as photography, dog training, or archery" (Goodale and Godbey, 1988, p. 116). In doing this, city and county governments became involved in the whole range of public park delivery: from the development of master plans through the creation of open space standards to the provision of facilities and equipment and the training of recreation leaders, some of whom worked directly for civic governments, others of whom were employed by community groups. But, government programs, particularly at the federal and state levels, tended to reflect a greater interest in direct delivery than was evident in Canada. This was especially noticeable in the public works programs during the Depression years, which included the development of many new parks, not only in the rural countryside, but also in cities (Goodale and Godbey, 1988).

Exercising the Enabling Authority of the State

As legislators and regulators, supporters and patrons, arm's length providers, and coordinators of recreation services, municipal (and other) governments made leisure opportunities available to Canadians and Americans without necessarily producing them directly. In doing this, they exercised the enabling authority of the state. They facilitated opportunities for private philanthropic groups and not-for-profit organizations to produce recreation services directly for consumers. In essence, partnerships based on interdependency were formed, whereby each party remained independent but depended upon the other for particular resources (physical, financial, managerial, and operational). In Canada municipal governments depended upon private groups and not-for-profit organizations to provide facilities and to manage and operate programs, while these groups and organizations depended upon municipal, provincial (and, occasionally, federal) governments to provide grants, leadership training, and appropriate legislation to facilitate the delivery of their services. Essentially, the dominant form of government involvement in the delivery of public leisure services in Canada up to the beginning of the Second World War was by way of its enabling authority. Municipal governments were sometimes direct providers, but were predominantly enablers: even the urban parks that they owned were typically managed by arm's length parks boards. They simply relied on organizations in the not-for-profit sector to produce leisure services for their communities. In the United States civic governments were more frequently involved in direct delivery, but there was still a considerable amount of cooperative activity with community and volunteer groups which reflected the exercise of the enabling authority of the state.

Government as Direct Provider: The Emergence of the Welfare State

Although during the initial development of public recreation in Canada, the not-for-profit sector played a dominant role through the enabling authority of the state, this changed markedly after the Second World War. Governments increasingly became direct providers of leisure services. During the postwar era, initiatives such as the introduction of social insurance, the extension of education and health programs, and the rapid growth of social expenditures characterized the development of the welfare state in Canada (Pierson, 1991). The end result was the large-scale direct production and delivery of a wide range of social goods and services by the public sector. And, even in the United States, where the development of the welfare state was less pronounced, governments became much more involved in the direct production and delivery of social goods and services than they had been heretofore.

In the late 1930s and early 1940s municipal governments in Canada had begun to get involved in the direct delivery of public recreation after social elites acting through community associations pressured local governments to take direct responsibility for park and recreation activities (Andrew, Harvey and Dawson, 1994). These social elites viewed recreational activities as an important means by which the lower social classes could be better integrated into society and, thereby, more easily controlled. Essentially, there was a desire to equalize social conditions and to use the power of the state to offer services more equal in character than those that would be available by market forces alone. Expanded municipal or local activity was considered to be necessary because market forces could not achieve the desired distribution of recreational opportunities.

Thus, as direct local government delivery of recreation increased, the concept of social welfare served to influence municipal objectives in the field. During the 1930s and 1940s, social welfare professionals viewed recreation as a "crucial area for intervention in order to reduce juvenile delinquency" (Andrew et al., 1994, p. 7), echoing the sentiments expressed by the National Council of Women some 40 years earlier. In other words, it was believed to be in the state's best interests to support public recreation as a means of decreasing juvenile delinquency. However, this perspective lost its appeal when the links between delinquency and social conditions, rather than leisure opportunities, were identified by social welfare advocates (Andrew et al., 1994). The social welfare view of recreational activities became less important in the postwar period, when the basic model became one of delivering universal services to a rapidly expanding population. Citizens were seen as having a right to recreation services, and local governments tried to deliver them on an equal basis. Recreation was less likely to be seen as a means of avoiding social problems, and more likely to be regarded simply as one among several legitimate areas of public service. Thereafter, the management of recreation became an increasingly professional field directed at the delivery of services through government-owned and -operated facilities and programs.

The pattern was similar, if less universal, in the United States. In commenting on the Boston sand pile case, Goodale and Godbey observed that the process:

> mirrored other recreation initiatives started by concerned citizens in that it began as a private project and was taken over by government; they were first financed through private philanthropy and later from public monies; the operations moved gradually from private to public property; the recreation activities initially under the supervision of volunteer leaders or matrons were gradually taken over by trained leaders. (Goodale and Godbey, 1988, p. 114)

This pattern paralleled a shift in the rationale for public recreation: from a welfare viewpoint stressing the value of recreation programs for enhanced fitness, strengthened families, and the prevention of juvenile delinquency to an emphasis upon access to recreation and leisure opportunities as individual and community rights. This, in turn, reflected the general philosophy of the welfare state outlined earlier: the idea that public production and delivery is necessary to avoid or rectify imperfections in the marketplace, since market production would leave many city dwellers with little or no access to leisure opportunities. And, as in Canada, this was accompanied by a rapid growth in the numbers of recreation professionals, who "became removed from consideration of philosophical questions concerning recreation and leisure, or answered any question raised by responding that, since the public wanted such services, they were automatically worthwhile" (Goodale and Godbey, 1988, pp. 117–118; see also Dustin and Goodale, chapter 29 in this volume). The argument, in effect, was that leisure services were a good thing and should, therefore, be made available and delivered directly by the public sector as a civic right.

Reemergence of the Enabling Authority of Government

As noted earlier, by the early 1980s the model of direct public delivery of social goods and services was becoming increasingly challenged by concerned taxpayers. There was growing support for market-oriented approaches to the delivery of public services, which led to substantial efforts to restructure government in both Canada and the United States. Political leaders sought to reduce the size of the public service, to assert political control over the bureaucracy, to revamp the machinery of administration, to change patterns of service delivery, and to introduce a new managerial philosophy of resource efficiency and expenditure control (Self, 1993). In addition, governments attempted to adopt many commercial sector concepts of efficient management, such as comprehensive accounting systems, performance contracts, economic incentives (e.g., merit pay), marketing (see McCarville, chapter 25 in this volume), and decentralized management. In particular, they sought to implement alternative forms of public service delivery in many fields, including leisure and recreation. A result was the development of a wide array of alternative methods of delivering public leisure services. Many of these encompassed a return to the enabling roles that had been the dominant forms of government involvement during the early evolution of public leisure services.

Today, leisure services are still considered to be merit goods, but not necessarily an essential service. As a result, the commercial and not-for-profit sectors have taken on larger roles in the delivery of public leisure services. But the role of the state has not simply diminished; it has merely changed back to that of an enabler, whereby governments ensure that services are available by arranging for their delivery without producing them. It is important to note, however, that "when governments push ownership and control into the community, their responsibilities do not end" (Osborne and Gaebler, 1992, p. 73). They may no longer produce particular leisure services, but they retain responsibility for ensuring that many leisure needs are met. In other words, governments have shifted the *delivery* of services, without shifting their *responsibility* for arranging them. Taxpayers expect governments to remain fiscally responsible while also maintaining standards of service delivery. This challenge has led many local governments to consider carefully how they deliver public leisure services.

Alternative Forms of Public Leisure Services Delivery

Glover and Burton (1998) have suggested that municipal governments must consider three factors when choosing among alternative methods for delivering public leisure services: the level of competitive forces; the nature of the good; and the amount of government control. *Level of competitive forces* refers to the level of competition involved in delivering a public service. For example, Compulsory Competitive Tendering (CCT) in Britain involves a mandatory tendering process whereby public, commercial, and not-for-profit organizations are encouraged to bid for a contract to produce public leisure services (Henry, 1993). The bidding involved in obtaining a contract and the attempt to renew it after its expiration encourage suppliers to fulfill the expectations of clients. In principle, competition motivates suppliers to produce quality services. In contrast, competition is absent from public services that are produced directly by municipal governments because they monopolize delivery. Competitive forces are conceptualized along a continuum whereby competition is *high* at one end and *low* at the other. Many degrees of competition are possible on the continuum.

The second variable, *nature of the good,* permits differentiation between social and private goods. A social good is a product that the community determines ought to be available for all. The notion of equality is implicit in the production of the service, as the producer does not control its consumption. For example, outdoor hiking trails in Edmonton, Alberta, are considered a social good that ought to be available for everyone to use at no direct cost to the user. Conversely, a private good is market driven: that is, it is available to those consumers who can afford to pay for it. A theatrical performance is a private good because spectators who wish to watch it are required to pay a stated price to attend the performance. People who cannot afford to pay, or are unwilling to pay the stated price, cannot attend.

Finally, the third variable, *amount of government control,* provides a continuum along which the degree of government regulation is measured. At one end of the continuum is total control; at the other, minimal control. Total control implies complete regulation of a given service. For instance, direct public delivery is completely regulated such that a public sector agency plans, implements, and manages a service. In contrast, minimal control describes a situation in which services are produced outside the public sector and are subjected only to the overall control that government exercises over all commercial activities (for example, taxation). A small private business that offers guided trips in wilderness environments is virtually independent of government control. It is expected to adhere to the laws and regulations set out for small businesses and those pertaining to the use of wilderness environments, but beyond this expectation, it has no connection with the public sector. Together, the level of competitive forces, the nature of the good, and the amount of government control are deemed important factors to consider when deciding on a particular method of delivering public services.

Glover and Burton (1998) went on to identify four specific categories of public leisure services delivery: *governmental arrangements,* which have been the dominant form of delivering public leisure services in many Western countries for several decades; *cross-sector alliances,* involving contractual relationships between public sector departments and agencies and not-for-profit or commercial organizations; *regulated monopolies,* where, by agreement, a nonpublic agency is granted a monopoly to produce public services; and *divestiture,* where public services, lands, or facilities are sold or leased to not-for-profit or commercial organizations. These are depicted, together with the previously defined variables, in the model shown in Figure 22.1. The model has four quadrants corresponding to the four categories of service delivery.

In the first quadrant, *governmental arrangements* reflect social goods characterized by a low level of competition and maximum government control. Direct provision, arm's length provision, intragovernmental partnerships, and intergovernmental partnerships fall into this group. They are similar because the nature of each good is social. However, the level of competitive forces and the amount of government control differs for each kind of governmental arrangement, affecting its position within the quadrant. Direct provision gives the lowest possible level of competition, followed by arm's length provision, intragovernmental partnerships, and intergovernmental partnerships in that order. In the same order, direct provision gives the highest degree of government control, followed by arm's length provision, intragovernmental partnerships, and intergovernmental partnerships respectively. The position of each arrangement within the quadrant must be considered in order to identify differences among and between the four.

In the second quadrant, *cross-sector alliances* are employed to produce social goods characterized by a high level of competition and a moderate level of government control. Public-private partnerships and contracts (or outsourcing) are both intended to ensure the production of social goods, but the competitive forces are somewhat higher for a partnership than for a contractual relationship.[1] Furthermore, private-public partnerships involve less government control than contracts. In general, government control over cross-sector

alliances is less than that involved in governmental arrangements.

In the third quadrant, *regulated monopolies* such as franchises are employed to produce goods characterized by a low level of competition and a moderate level of government control. Like cross-sector alliances, regulated monopolies involve less government control than governmental arrangements.

Finally, in the fourth quadrant, *divestiture* is used to produce private goods characterized by a high level of competition and a minimum level of government control. Lease and sale are similar in that both are employed as a means of producing private goods and involve equally high levels of competition. However, a lease involves more government control than sale, since the arrangement will normally be turned back to the public sector at the termination of the lease. Divestiture involves greater competition and less government control than cross-sector alliances, regulated monopolies, and intergovernmental arrangements.

We contend that the forms of service delivery found in the latter three quadrants all involve some degree of privatization of public services. Traditionally, privatization has been equated exclusively with the sale of public assets to commercial firms or not-for-profit organizations. However, this explanation excludes several modes of public service delivery that involve commercial and voluntary organizations, but which retain a significant level of government involvement. For instance, when a municipal government contracts a commercial firm to manage an ice arena or a swimming pool, essentially it is privatizing that facility, since it is no longer operated by public employees. Again, if a government enlists the aid of the Boys and Girls Club, a not-for-profit organization, to deliver after-school recreation programs for disadvantaged children, thereby acting as a patron of leisure services, this, too, is perceived as privatization because direct service delivery is offered by a nongovernmental organization, despite receiving subsidy from the public sector. In this regard, the authors concur with the definition of Savas (1987), who viewed privatization as "a wide range of alternatives to the direct provision of public service(s) by governments using their own employees." This assertion also corresponds with Walker's view, which claims that privatization "covers all situations where control is passed to the private sector whether it had ever resided there or not" (Walker, 1980, p. xvii). In other words, that which is not a governmental arrangement is considered a form of privatization.

---

[1]While the terms *contract* and *contracting out* have gained general acceptance in public administration and much of the technical literature, a more accurate descriptor is *outsourcing,* since several of the other alternatives in the model (e.g., partnerships) also involve contracts of one kind or another. We have employed the word *contract* here, in deference to popular usage, but caution the reader that it applies to a particular kind of contractual arrangement.

Back to the Future—With a Twist

What, perhaps, is more important than simply defining whether a particular form of public leisure services delivery is, in fact, privatized is the realization that these various alternatives for delivering public leisure services reflect and reinforce the reemergence of the enabling role of the state. This likely explains, at least in part, why various types of enabling roles have been adopted by governments of all political hues in both Canada and the United States, from the left to the right (Liberals, New Democrats, and Progressive Conservatives in Canada; both Democrats and Republicans in the United States). Recognition that this is a historic role helps considerably in reconciling it with ideological party positions! In deciding to opt for partnerships, contracts, and franchises, governments adopt an enabling stance, arranging for services to be produced by commercial firms and not-for-profit organizations entirely, or in partnership with one or both of these. In each of these scenarios, governments retain significant functions as developers of policies and strategies, and monitors of performance. In choosing these forms of delivery, governments are returning to the enabling roles that they performed in earlier periods of Canadian and American history, but in circumstances that require them to be more conscious and deliberate in their choices of what is to be produced. For, whereas in the early years of public recreation they adopted enabling roles in reaction to initiatives begun by private philanthropists and community groups, today they are taking a proactive approach, deciding for themselves which public leisure services will be arranged through their enabling authority.

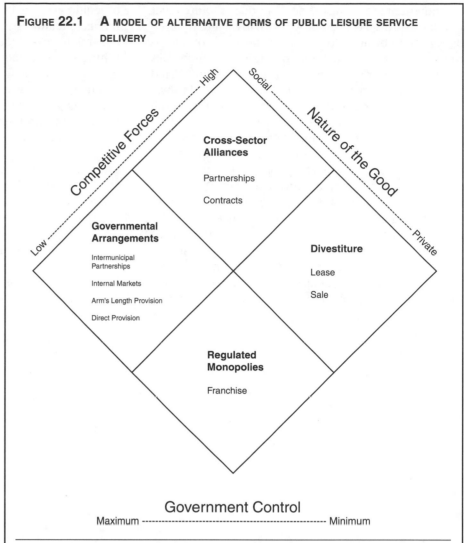

FIGURE 22.1   A MODEL OF ALTERNATIVE FORMS OF PUBLIC LEISURE SERVICE DELIVERY

SOURCE: "A Model of Alternative Forms of Public Leisure Services Delivery" by T. D. Glover and T. L. Burton in *Leisure Management: Issues and Applications* (p. 152), by M. F. Collins and I. S. Cooper (Eds.), 1998, Wallingford, UK: CAB International. Copyright 1998 CAB International. Reprinted with permission.

The return to an enhanced enabling role for municipal governments in the delivery of public leisure services has important ramifications for service delivery. For, although it clearly reflects a return to a form of governmental delivery that was previously dominant and has long existed, the conditions that prevailed before the Second World War when this form of delivery was prevalent in both Canada and the United States and those that prevail now are very different. For one thing, there is a large body of professional public servants that exists in the public leisure services field; and even though many will leave (willingly or otherwise), many will be required to remain, but in dramatically changed roles. The increased use of contractual arrangements to deliver leisure services requires that public leisure service employees be involved in developing, monitoring, and enforcing standards of performance. Contracts must also be audited, which calls for different kinds of accounting systems than existed with direct delivery. And, as noted, public officials will also find that they must concentrate on policy development rather than service delivery. All of these things call for public sector leisure professionals with differing skills from those required in a system emphasizing direct delivery of services by public employees.

The renewed emphasis on the enabling role of the state in the delivery of public leisure services shows that nothing is entirely new in delivering leisure. But it also demonstrates that a great deal is new, because circumstances and conditions have changed significantly. The value in recognizing that the enabling role is a historic and well-established one is that it can serve to move public debate away from the sterile question of legitimacy—whether or not it is right for governments to relinquish direct delivery, that is, to privatize in some form—to focus upon more central questions. Which services does a government wish to arrange through its enabling authority and which through direct delivery? How are public sector professional staff to be educated and trained for the new roles that flow from a predominantly enabling mode of delivery? What characteristics should be sought in the commercial firms and not-for-profit organizations that we wish to engage in the enabling approach? How will public sector agencies determine the specific standards of service quality and performance that must be attained, and maintained, by commercial firms and not-for-profit organizations operating under the enabling authority of government? Most importantly, how can we ensure that communities receive the best quality of public leisure services that can reasonably be afforded by municipal governments?

References

Andrew, C., Harvey, J., & Dawson, D. (1994). Evolution of local state activity: Recreation policy in Toronto. *Leisure Studies, 13,* 1–16.

Barnett, R. R. (1997). Subsidiarity, enabling government and local governance. In P. A. R. Hobson & F. St.-Hilaire (Eds.), *Urban governance and finance: A question of who does what.* Ottawa, Ontario: Reneuf Publishing.

Burton, T. L. (1982). The roles of government in the leisure services delivery system. *Recreation, 4,* 131–150.

Butler, G. (1959). *Introduction to community recreation.* New York, NY: McGraw-Hill.

Cranz, G. (1982). *The politics of park design: A history of urban parks in America.* Cambridge, MA: MIT Press.

Drucker, P. F. (1989). *The new realities.* New York, NY: Harper & Row.

Duncan, M. (1985). Back to our radical roots. In T. L. Goodale & P. A. Witt (Eds.), *Recreation and leisure: Issues in an era of change.* State College, PA: Venture Publishing, Inc.

Glover, T. D., & Burton, T. L. (1998). A model of alternative forms of public leisure services delivery. In M. F. Collins & I. S. Cooper (Eds.), *Leisure management: Issues and applications.* Wallingford, UK: CAB International.

Goodale, T. L., & Godbey, G. C. (1988). *The evolution of leisure: Historical and philosophical perspectives.* State College, PA: Venture Publishing, Inc.

Henry, I. P. (1993). *The politics of leisure policy.* London, UK: Macmillan Publishing.

Markham, S. (1988). *Parks and playgrounds in prairie cities: 1880–1930.* Unpublished doctoral dissertation, University of Alberta, Edmonton, Alberta.

McFarland, E. M. (1970). *The development of public recreation in Canada.* Ottawa, Ontario: Canadian Parks/Recreation Association.

Osborne, D., & Gaebler, T. (1992). *Reinventing government: How the entrepreneurial spirit is transforming the public sector.* New York, NY: Addison-Wesley.

Pierson, C. (1991). *Beyond the welfare state? The new political economy of welfare.* London, UK: Polity.

Savas, E. S. (1987). *Privatization: The key to better government.* Chatham, NJ: Chatham House.

Self, P. (1993). *Government by the market? The politics of public choice.* London, UK: Macmillan Publishing.

Walker, M. A. (1980). Foreword. In T. M. Ohashi & T. P. Roth (Eds.), *Privatization theory and practice: Distributing shares in private and public enterprises.* Vancouver, British Columbia: The Fraser Institute.

Walsh, K. (1997). Markets and the public service. In D. Lorrain & G. Stoker (Eds.), *The privatization of urban services in Europe.* London, UK: Pinter.

Wright, J. R. (1984). *Urban parks in Ontario, Part II: 1860–1914.* Toronto, Ontario: Ministry of Tourism & Recreation.

Forecasting Leisure
and Recreation

A. J. Veal
University of Technology, Sydney

Introduction

Careful consideration and anticipation of possible futures facing society is surely one of the key responsibilities of good government and wise management. One feature of such possible futures is the changing quality and quantity of leisure. The forecasting of leisure and recreation demand is, in historical terms, a recent development. Rapid economic growth in the Western world in the period following the Second World War, together with substantial population increases and growth in leisure time and in the availability of personal transportation had, by the 1960s, led to rapid increases in the demand for leisure and recreation, particularly in the outdoors. Leisure was one of the features of the "affluent society." The resultant increasing pressures on limited resources of land and water prompted governments, at national, state, and local levels, to address the need to plan for future demands: the phenomenon of *mass leisure* (Larrabee and Meyersohn, 1958) was seen as a prob-

lem (Smigel, 1963) and a *challenge* for society (Brightbill, 1960; Dower, 1965).

However, the slowing, and even reversal, of change in a number of economic, demographic, and mobility factors in the 1980s and 1990s has led to a corresponding reduction in the rate of growth in leisure activity and a consequent decline in the urgency with which politicians and policymakers have addressed leisure demand forecasting issues. Other changes have led to a transformation in the way that forecasting is undertaken and its role in policymaking and planning. This chapter provides an introduction to developments in *future-gazing* in the field of leisure and recreation. It is divided into three main sections: the first reviews the origins and changing nature of leisure and recreation demand forecasting over recent decades; the second considers the social change factors which forecasters must take into account when considering the future; and the third reviews and evaluates the range of techniques available to forecasters, and their role and use in the contemporary forecasting environment.

Origins and Changing Context

The origins of modern leisure and recreation forecasting lie in the early 1960s work of the Outdoor Recreation Resources Review Commission (ORRRC, 1962). Through the work of researchers such as Cicchetti (1973), data from the extensive research program of the ORRRC were used to develop a quantitative modeling approach to recreation demand forecasting. This approach used multiple regression equations which related levels of demand to a range of *independent* demographic and socioeconomic variables, such as age, income, and level of education. Estimates of future values of these independent variables were then used to predict future levels of demand for recreation. This modeling approach was extensively applied in the later U.S. Statewide Outdoor Recreation Planning process and also in Europe. In the 1980s and 1990s, however, the approach fell out of favor with planners and policymakers for a number of reasons. First, there were technical reasons for its abandonment. Kelly (1989), for example, claimed that the models had never been successful in their own statistical terms and Brown and Hutson (1979) demonstrated the inaccuracy of some of the early U.S. forecasts. In Britain researchers produced models which were statistically quite satisfactory (e.g., Coppock and Duffield, 1975; Settle, 1977; Veal, 1987, pp. 146–154), but their life span as the basis of planning and policy was, nevertheless, even more short lived than in the United States. It is possible that, with more research, the technical limitations of the quantitative modeling experiment might have been overcome, but other forces were at work.

The second reason for the marginalization of the quantitative modeling approach to forecasting was the slowing of the rate of change in demographic, economic, and mobility factors, as noted previously; so addressing future growth in demand in quantitative terms became less urgent. Third, it was found that the recreation planning and policymaking process was not susceptible to being driven only, or even primarily, by quantified forecasts of demand. Regardless of the accuracy of available forecasts, the role of demand forecasting in the planning and policymaking of government bodies seems less clear than it was thought to be in the past. Fourth, partly in response to these developments, models of planning and policymaking, in recreation and other fields, have changed. These changes in the policy and planning arena are discussed in turn here.

Forecasting and the Policy Process

The relationship between demand forecasts and policy responses in leisure and recreation is less clear than in many other areas. For example, in the case of school-age education, a prediction of a certain level of school-age population at a particular future point in time indicates a clear demand for school places which, society generally agrees, must be met. The consequence of not anticipating and making provision for this demand would be children with no schools to go to. In the case of transport planning, failure to anticipate demand and to cater for it by providing roads or public transport capacity results in traffic congestion. In the area of leisure and recreation, however, the level of demand is more difficult to predict, the consequences of not "getting it right" are uncertain, and the public policy response to any predicted level of demand is ambivalent.

Predicting leisure demand is difficult because it is such a fluid phenomenon. People are adaptable, so that a wide range of alternative future leisure behavior patterns is possible. For example, if the public realizes that local recreation areas are overcrowded on weekends or at holiday times (because demand has not been anticipated and provided for), many may choose to stay at home and enjoy a barbecue in the backyard; or if provision has not been made for live performing arts in a community, people are simply likely to stay at home and watch more television. Thus the consequences of not anticipating and providing for potential demand can appear, on the face of it, not to be serious.

Failure to make appropriate provision *may* have serious social consequences, but the relationship is little understood. Failure to provide for some groups in the community, such as children, youth or older citizens, is often recognized as potentially serious, in terms of personal development, potential criminal behavior, and mental and physical well-being. While governments generally have a broad concern for such groups and their needs, they are not committed to providing facilities for everyone who wishes to, say, play football, go to a park, or attend a concert. Demand forecasts which suggest widespread potential unmet demand can even be seen as a hindrance rather than a help in the policymaking process in situations where financial resources are limited and the general intention is to reduce government outlays.

A further factor which has confounded the relationship between demand and supply, particularly in relation to outdoor recreation, is the changing social attitude toward the environment. While there has been no diminution in the public's interest in and desire to recreate in the outdoor environment, the "greening" of politics has meant that *development,* for recreation as much as for other activities, has become more difficult. The existence of demand is therefore no longer seen as a sufficient argument for development.

Changing Approaches to Planning

Approaches to planning and policymaking in the public sector have changed over the last two decades. In general they have moved away from a *rational-comprehensive* model toward models which are more closely related to "disjointed incrementalism" and "mixed scanning" (Burton, 1989; Van Lier, 1993, p. 6; Veal, 1994).

Given that public resources are always scarce, public bodies can rarely achieve all they—or their clients—would wish, in terms of service delivery. In the 1980s and 1990s politicians have often been given more credit for saving money and reducing taxes than for delivering services. The notion that public bodies could adopt a comprehensive approach to determining and meeting community needs and demands was rejected as unrealistic. Choices had to be made; a less than comprehensive approach had to be adopted. In such an environment services such as leisure and recreation have tended to be accorded a low priority compared with other services that are considered to be more essential, such as education or transport. In addition, within leisure and recreation, planners have been required to choose priorities from among a wide range of desirable projects. Thus, identifying, researching, and evaluating a comprehensive range of services hardly seemed to be wise use of resources when it was known that the majority could not be implemented.

Recreation planning and policymaking no longer cast national, state and local governments as comprehensive providers of leisure facilities and services to the community. Rather than adopting a *comprehensive* approach to planning and provision, as in the past, there is a tendency to adopt an *issues* approach, involving identification of key needs as a result of community consultation and scanning exercises, such as SWOT (strengths-weaknesses-opportunities-threats) analyses. Quantitative demand forecasts may or may not feature in such an approach; generally they do not. Rather, the planning process focuses on *key issues,* such as the problems of youth or of the elderly or a particular environmental problem. The decision to address an issue in a plan can therefore be seen as being as much a matter of political expediency as of demonstrated de-

mand. Political lobbying by pressure groups, even from minority interests which are already well-served with recreation facilities, can be more influential with politicians than technically based demand forecasts.

Further, public bodies have, in recent years, adopted a less interventionist stance in many areas: they are seen as *enablers* and *facilitators,* with services increasingly devolved to community groups or contracted out to the private sector. In such situations, there is a tendency to be less concerned with comprehensive approaches to demand for, and consequently supply of, services: public agencies become more like private sector organizations, less concerned with the total picture, focusing attention on the success of their own limited range of operations. Rather than seeking a demand forecast which translates directly into facility and service requirements, indicators of trends are sought, as a background against which policymaking and planning will take place. The two approaches are represented diagrammatically, and in simplified form, in Figure 23.1. In the old model, a plan was seen as being based primarily on demand forecasts, in a simple, linear, fashion. The new model is more complex: the demand forecast is just one input into the planning process, and its input is indirect, contributing initially to an identification of issues, upon which the plan is based.

The increasing importance of the private sector in areas of recreation formerly dominated by the public sector adds to the complexity of the situation. The activities of the private sector in relation to forecasting are, for understandable commercial reasons, not widely exposed to public scrutiny. Commercial organizations

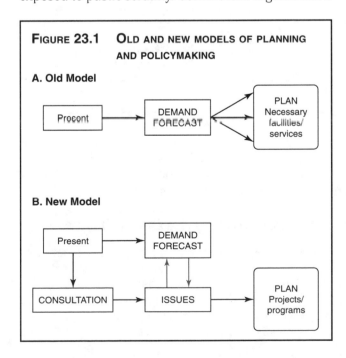

FIGURE 23.1   **OLD AND NEW MODELS OF PLANNING AND POLICYMAKING**

A. Old Model

Present → DEMAND FORECAST ⇄ PLAN Necessary facilities/ services

B. New Model

Present → DEMAND FORECAST

Present → CONSULTATION → ISSUES → PLAN Projects/ programs

DEMAND FORECAST ↕ ISSUES

involved in leisure service provision are generally interested in broad demand forecasts as an environmental input to their planning; they are interested in *trends:* they like to be forewarned about changing tastes and demographic and economic shifts that will affect the market in which they are involved. They are interested in the growth or decline in markets for activities which can be profitably provided for and in indications of their own likely *market share*. In contrast, in the past, it was implicit in the recreation planning model that the public sector provider should seek to estimate and meet all demand.

The Future of Forecasting

In these circumstances, what is the future of forecasting? Clearly its role is changing, particularly in the public sector. In the 1960s and 1970s it was assumed to play a *central* role: demand forecasts would be made and planning would ensure that the predicted levels of demand were provided for. In the 1980s and 1990s the role has changed. In the new millennium the role of forecasting will be *supportive* rather than central. It will be just one input to the planning process along with other, more political and less technical, inputs. In such circumstances, traditional, quantified, comprehensive predictions of recreation demand will still play a role from time to time, but will generally be seen as useful background, rather than foreground. Other types of input will be required, involving general context or scenario setting, more qualitative inputs and more activity-specific or facility-specific trend data. It is in this context that the following discussion of change factors and forecasting techniques is presented.

Change Factors

Changing economic, social, and political environments have caused forecasters to examine a wide and diverse range of factors which impact upon patterns of leisure and recreation demand. A number of the most important of these are discussed here, namely the amount of leisure time, technological change, demographic change, the idea of the product life cycle, changing tastes, and the activities of providers.

The Amount of Leisure Time

Considerable changes in patterns of leisure behavior can and do take place in situations of static or declining leisure time, but an increase or decrease in the amount of leisure time available to the individual is often seen as one of the most important influences on changing leisure behavior. Since at least the beginning of the Industrial Revolution it has been widely believed that technology would deliver more leisure time to the masses: machines would do the work, thus releasing humans for leisure. To some extent this has indeed happened: at the turn of the century the standard working year for a full-time employee in the Western world was around 2,500 hours, and at the height of the Industrial Revolution it was over 3,000 hours[1]—currently the paid working year for such individuals is less than 2,000 hours. But the steady twentieth-century march toward increased leisure time appears to have faltered in recent years. This has been particularly the case in the United States (Schor, 1991). In other parts of the economically developed world, the picture is less clear. For example, in Western Europe it is claimed that working hours fell between 1983 and 1991 (Botsman, 1993). In Japan governments have been legislating to reduce working hours and have been actively encouraging workers to take advantage of their holiday entitlements (Harada, 1996).

Nevertheless, across the developed world, there is a widespread feeling that those in paid work are working longer hours, while millions are unemployed. The industrial system appears to have failed in the task of sharing the available work—and leisure—equitably. It is debatable as to whether this represents a permanent reversal of the long-term trend toward more leisure and less work, a short-term reversal in the trend, or a cyclical phenomenon related to the business cycle—or a combination of each of these factors. Schor (1991) and others, such as Rifkin (1995), have no doubt about the permanent reversal thesis. A temporary reversal thesis is, however, equally plausible; in fact, in the mid 1990s in the United States, millions of new jobs were created and the unemployment trend appears to have been reversed, as also appears to have happened in Britain.

---

[1] The question of working hours *before* the Industrial Revolution is a matter for speculation. Such evidence as there is suggests that workers in preindustrial societies had—and have—far more leisure time than their counterparts in industrial societies. However, the evidence consists largely of records of paid workers, rather than peasants, and information on the number of religious holidays enjoyed during preindustrial times in Europe. The record is necessarily limited on weekly and annual hours worked by members of peasant households, and tends to ignore work which would have continued even on religious holidays, including much of the domestic work done largely by women, the work of servants and the care of animals. Limited education and retirement periods within the life span and a shorter overall life span also complicate comparisons. A considerable amount of evidence on the issue has been assembled by Schor (1991, p. 45).

It is clear that the Western world has been undergoing a major economic adjustment in the face of the challenge of first Japan, and then the Asian "tiger" economies. These countries have experienced or are experiencing a classic industrialization process, similar to that which occurred in Western Europe and North America in the nineteenth century—but they are experiencing it in a dramatically shorter time period. Characteristic of such a process is the ability to draw on an expanding, low-cost labor force, which is required to work long hours. As the West seeks to maintain its competitiveness, it must contain its labor costs: since actually reducing wages would be unacceptable to the labor force, one way of reducing real labor costs is to require employees, formally or informally, to work longer hours. The effect of this can be quite dramatic. For example, an employee working 40 hours a week, taking four weeks holiday a year, eight days of public holiday and, say, five days of "optional" sick leave a year (that is, days off for minor ailments which, when one's job is on the line, one does *not* take off), works a total of 1,816 hours a year. However, an employee who works 50 hours a week, takes only two weeks holiday a year, takes only six public holidays off and no "optional" sick leave, works a total of 2,440 hours a year— an increase of 34%. For those employees who are paid a fixed salary, without overtime payments, this is equivalent to a cut in their rate of pay of 34% per hour. Thus, by working longer hours, as well as making smarter use of technology and drawing on greater reserves of social capital like fully developed educational systems, the West "buys time" to make the necessary adjustments to its economic infrastructure to enable it to survive in the new global economic environment.

The optimistic scenario would see the West emerging from this process as, primarily, the *postindustrial* sector of the world economy, while the Newly Industrialized Countries (NICs) form the *industrial* sector. It is also the case that wage rates and other costs in the NICs are rapidly overhauling those of the West, so they begin to face the same problems as the West, as newer tiger economies and the sleeping giants of India and China come up behind. The pessimistic scenario sees a West which does not adjust quickly enough and goes into relative, and even absolute, economic decline. Both scenarios, however, leave unanswered the question of what will actually happen to work and leisure hours in the future. Both the optimistic and the pessimistic scenarios could see working hours either staying high or returning to a pattern of slow decline. The leisure forecaster cannot, therefore, make simplistic assumptions about what is likely to happen to leisure time in future, but must carefully monitor trends (Robinson and Godbey, 1997; Zuzanek, 1996) and introduce alternative time-use scenarios into any forecasts produced.

Technological Change

Despite the prominence given to leisure time in discussions of the future, it is often not *the* key variable. Technology and the wealth to use it allow people to experience leisure activities which, in the past, required *time*. Thus, for example, when the British aristocracy undertook the Grand Tour of Europe in the nineteenth century the trip took months, whereas the modern version is completed in as little as a few days, through the use of jet aircraft and freeways.

Technological change is driven by the huge sums of money being spent on research and development in industry, government, and universities throughout the world. While relatively little of this effort is explicitly aimed at leisure, its effects invariably have an impact on leisure. Thus, such developments as transistors and computers, plastics, the internal combustion and jet engines and satellites—often developed for defense and industrial purposes—have become the basis of significant leisure industries. Technological forecasting is an art in itself (Martino, 1978), the skill being to predict which items of technology will translate into products or services which people will want, and at a price they will be prepared to pay, and, in the case of leisure, how this will affect patterns of behavior.

The major technological changes of the moment, which are relevant to leisure, would appear to be various multimedia developments and the Internet. The task for the leisure forecaster is to ignore the "hype" and consider the likely impact of these technologies on leisure behavior. While the Internet and broadband cabling may offer a huge range of alternative entertainment "products" to the consumer, and while consumers may pay more for these products than they have paid for free-to-air and cable services in the past, there is no evidence that people will actually spend more time looking at cathode-ray tubes during their leisure time. As with so many technological developments, what is being offered is the opportunity for a wider range of choice and a more *intensive* use of leisure time. There may be microsocial effects, with, for example, different members of the family spending more time apart, "doing their own thing." But such trends, and their effects, can be exaggerated. Human beings are social animals and will always find ways of doing things together, even if it involves apparently antisocial technology: the phenomenon of teenagers gathering in each others' homes or discotheques to socialize against a background of ear-splitting rock music is evidence of this. The family, though changed, has survived repeated waves of technology, including radio, the cinema, television, and the personal stereo. Chances are that it will survive the new technologies also.

As with planning generally, the idea of a linear process feeding into more and more sophisticated consumer goods may change in the future. Technology is seen to have negative as well as positive consequences. Worldwide commitments to reductions in emission of greenhouse gases are likely to result in technological developments being devoted to "greener" products, rather than products which are cheaper, bigger, or faster.

In the nineteenth century, the advent of the railway transformed people's leisure lives in the Western world. In the first half of the twentieth century the spread of electricity and the development of radio and film can be seen as the key technological influences. In the last half-century, the automobile, television, and the jet airliner have revolutionized leisure. Other changes, such as the advent of plastics and computers, have been important but not seminal. Few forecasters of 50, 100 or 150 years ago would have foreseen the effects of these technologies on everyday lives. While the twenty-first century is being examined by far more future-gazers than previous eras, it is highly likely that we will be equally surprised at the extent and sources of the changes that will take place in the next 50 years.

Demographic Change

In the introduction to this chapter, the effects of rapid population growth on leisure and recreation demand in the 1960s and 1970s were noted: more people meant more recreationists demanding more recreational space, placing more pressure on limited resources. The subsequent fading of this factor as a major concern to policymakers in the 1980s and 1990s was also noted. In the economically developed world, with few exceptions, population growth has slowed dramatically in recent decades: in Western Europe absolute *declines* in population have been experienced in some countries (United Nations, 1995). However, while overall populations may not be increasing rapidly, significant change is taking place *within* the population—in particular the people, on average, are getting *older*. This is illustrated in Figure 23.2, which shows that, over the next 10 years in Australia, while the under-50-years age groups show quite small changes, even an absolute decline in one case, rapid growth can be expected in the age groups aged 50 and over, with the biggest relative change being in those aged 80 and over. This sort of change has clear implications for future leisure

and recreation demand, with activities favored by older age groups being in high demand. This type of shift within the population is approached in forecasting terms by the *cross-sectional* method which will be discussed here.

The Product Life Cycle

The product life cycle is a marketing term referring to the way products are taken up by innovative consumers, achieve a period of sales growth, and then go into decline. Persuading consumers that they should replace technologically based goods for newer, superior products has become routine, as any owner of a personal computer will know! From a leisure behavior point of view, however, the pattern of product sales does not necessarily reflect the pattern of participation in the associated leisure activity. For example, in the case of television set manufacturing in the economically developed economies, the rapid growth phase, as sets were purchased by households for the first time, took place in the 1950s and 1960s; the product was then given a second lease on life by the increased availability and popularity of color television in the early 1970s. But once virtually all households were equipped with color television sets, sales fell because only replacement sets and the slow growth of two-set households produced sales. But television *watching* did not experience the same subsequent decline. A similar pattern would have been seen with videocassette recorders more recently: the sale of equipment goes into decline

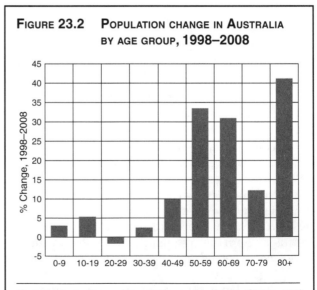

FIGURE 23.2   POPULATION CHANGE IN AUSTRALIA BY AGE GROUP, 1998–2008

Source: Projections of Populations of Australia, States, and Territories, 1995–2051 (p. 128) by Australian Bureau of Statistics, 1996, Canberra, Australia, Author. Copyright 1996 Australian Bureau of Statistics.

once saturation ownership is achieved, but the leisure activity and any services associated with it, such as television show production or video rental, continues.

Statistics related to product life cycle can be deceptive. In the early period of adoption, huge growth rates in sales and ownership are often seen, but from a small base. Later, apparently slower, growth rates can, however, be more significant. For example, if a million households own a product, a growth rate of 100% in a year implies an additional million households becoming owners. If 20 million households own the product, however, a growth rate of only 10% produces an additional 2 million owners.

Once again, the role of the leisure forecaster in relation to new products and services and their life cycles can be seen as countering the "hype" that often appears in mass media accounts, often promoted by interests involved in manufacturing or selling the product, and distinguishing between their industrial effects and their impacts on leisure behavior.

Changing Tastes

Changing tastes are the most difficult of all factors to predict. Some taste changes appear to be long term or permanent, for example, the decline of beer drinking in favor of wine drinking, or the trend in participation away from traditional team sports to more individualistic sports. Others can be short term. For example, in the fashion and popular music industries changing taste is institutionalized: designs are changed each season and new fashions or recordings are released and intensively "plugged." These industries highlight the issues associated with the phenomenon of changing tastes. Just how consumer taste arises and changes is a matter of some sociological debate (Featherstone, 1991; Tomlinson, 1990). While some products and designs may be foisted onto a gullible public, it can be argued that successful products and designs are those which strike a chord with the public, reflect the mood of the buying public, and meet their needs. Since fads, fashions, and crazes are, by definition, fickle, it is almost impossible to predict them, although they also tend to have *product life cycles* like consumer goods, often extending over a number of years.

Again, the role of the leisure forecaster is to monitor trends, seeking to alert policymakers to those trends which are likely to be long term and those which are likely to be ephemeral.

The Activities of Providers

The future is not only determined by demand; it is partly determined by the activities of producers of goods and services. Producers must decide where to research, to invest, to develop, to produce and to market and, in the public sector, to subsidize. It has long been held by some commentators that producers are in the driving seat, determining what is to be made available to the public based entirely on the consideration of production costs and profitability (Adorno and Horkheimer, 1944; Clarke and Critcher, 1985, pp. 100–121; Galbraith, 1958, pp. 133–135). These deterministic analyses tend to ignore, or underestimate, the power of the consumer to choose—and reject—what is on offer. The process is two-way: both producers and consumers play a part in determining what will be produced and consumed.

Thus, for example, theme parks were devised and developed by the Disney Corporation and others and have been extensively developed over the last 40 years. The use of some of the leisure time of the millions of people who choose to visit theme parks each year has therefore been determined by the activities of Disney and other large corporations. In Britain, thousands of indoor sports and leisure centers, built by local municipalities over the last 25 years, now collectively accommodate millions of visits a year. The activities of providers in these cases have been influential in determining the development of the patterns of leisure participation in the United States and Britain during recent decades. However, people do not *have* to visit theme parks or sports and leisure centers, so the producers were only able to *influence* the future by providing something that people wanted.

The investment activities of private and public sector providers of leisure facilities are therefore a factor to be taken into account in leisure and recreation demand forecasting. Recent political and economic trends suggest that the key investment decisions of the near future will be made by private sector organizations rather than public bodies. It follows, therefore, that only investments which can be operated profitably on a *user-pays* basis will be realized. Major public sector investment programs, such as the British indoor sport and leisure center building program referred to previously, will likely not be repeated.

Forecasting Techniques

Forecasting, as a process, needs to change and adapt in the context of the changing environments of planning, policymaking, and social development discussed previously. This process of change and adaptation has been underway for some years, through developments in the range of techniques deployed by forecasters.

One change has been the growing significance of qualitative methods. As recently as 1983, Stynes and his colleagues were promoting a range of quantitative models for outdoor recreation forecasting, with no indication that their usefulness was being questioned. Their review did include, however, an introduction to the qualitative *Delphi* method, indicating an emerging interest in approaches other than the traditional quantitative approaches (Stynes, 1983). In reviews of methods in the late 1980s, the limitations of exclusive reliance on quantitative methods were made clear and they were listed along with a range of formal and informal qualitative and composite methods (Burton, 1989; Veal, 1987; Zalatan, 1994).

Some of the factors reviewed previously remain resistant to systematic forecasting techniques, but they must nevertheless be taken into account in any forecasting exercise, however informally. There are, however, many influences on the future of leisure which can be addressed in a more or less systematic manner, and the techniques available for such a task are outlined here. These techniques have been reviewed on a number of occasions before (Burton, 1989; Veal, 1987, 1994), so are summarized only briefly here. They fall into nine groups:

1. informed speculation;
2. asking the public;
3. asking the experts (the Delphi technique);
4. scenario writing;
5. time-series analysis;
6. spatial models;
7. cross-sectional analysis;
8. comparative analysis; and
9. composite methods.

Informed Speculation

Informed speculation consists of the thoughts and impressions of an author, often included as the final chapter of a book. It is not generally based on any specific techniques or data analysis. Its value arises from the wisdom and experience of the writer. Often the results are not specific forecasts or predictions as such, but the opening up of issues for thought and discussion. Often such discussions are highly personal and prescriptive rather than predictive. Examples of the use of the technique in leisure and recreation include Burton (1970), Kelly and Godbey (1992, pp. 479–512), and Robinson and Godbey (1997, p. 287–302). Speculation on potential futures and possible roles for leisure in such futures is not confined to the leisure literature. Such well-known figures as Bertrand Russell (1935), John Maynard Keynes (1931/1972), and Isaac Asimov (1976) have also offered their visions of a more

leisured future (see Veal, 1987, pp. 22–45). It is notable that, while earlier speculative pieces were concerned with the anticipated, technologically and economically driven growth of leisure time and the increasing range of activities likely to be available, more recent contributions have been more concerned with values and processes and consideration of the potential role of leisure in the evolution of social values and practices.

Asking the Public

Asking leisure and recreation survey respondents what they would like to do or are planning to do in the future is one way of tapping into potential futures. Responses cannot be relied upon as accurate indicators of future demand, since they often simply reflect "wishful thinking." The results can, however, be seen as indicators of sentiment, indicating what activities people may be drawn to do in the future in favorable circumstances. The technique is frequently used in short-term economic and business forecasting, where changes in *consumer sentiment* or *investor confidence* can be important lead indicators of future changes in consumer spending or business investment. An early example of the explicit use of this technique in leisure and tourism was that undertaken by Coppock and Duffield (1975, p. 84) in Scotland, but more recently the technique has tended to be subsumed under the various community consultation methods used at local levels by municipalities, which combine public participation and recreation needs surveys in their planning activity.

Asking the Experts:
The Delphi Technique

Delphi refers to the Delphic oracle who foretold people's fortunes in classical Greece. The modern Delphi technique involves asking a panel of experts about their view of the future in their area of expertise. The panel can range in size from as few as a dozen to several hundred. Experts may be asked a specific question on the major changes they expect to see in their field of expertise over the next, say, 5 or 20 years, or they may be asked to indicate the probability of a number of possible future events taking place. Responses from Round 1 are summarized and fed back to the panel of experts for Round 2 questioning. Round 2, and possibly Round 3, information is collated to provide forecasts. The technique can be useful in addressing the technology and product life-cycle issues discussed previously, since people closely involved in an industry should be able to base their predictions on their knowledge of product development going on in the industry and the time likely to elapse before a product reaches and is adopted within the marketplace. Such a model, of course, fits particularly well with science or technology-based products. Outputs of the exercise can be qualitative or quantitative.

The quality of the forecasts depends very much on the quality of the panel membership. Examples of the use of the Delphi technique in leisure and tourism settings are: Shafer, Moeller and Russell (1977); Chai (1977); and Ng, Brown and Knott (1983). Shafer and Moeller's exercise is of particular interest because of the range of events predicted to happen by the year 2000. These included an average retirement age of 50 years; electric-powered vehicles replace internal combustion engines in recreational vehicles; and holidays on other continents become as common as those inside North America for middle-class Americans.

Despite its high profile, there is little recent literature on the use of the Delphi technique in the leisure area. As with a number of other techniques, tourism researchers appear to be more active users in recent years (cf., Green, Hunter and Moore, 1990).

Scenario Writing

Scenario writing involves devising alternative pictures of the future as characterized by values of key variables and relationships among them. For example, alternative future political scenarios for a country could involve right-wing conservative government or left-wing government. Economically, there could be high or low unemployment. These two dimensions offer four alternative scenarios, as shown in Figure 23.3. Each scenario would have different implications for leisure and recreation: for example, under a conservative government comparatively low expenditure on public leisure facilities would be envisaged, with emphasis being placed on private enterprise provision; a high unemployment scenario would imply large numbers of people with time on their hands, but little money, whereas a low unemployment scenario would imply the reverse.

Alternative scenarios provide a context for other techniques to be employed, whether quantitative or qualitative; as such, scenario writing might be seen as a component of a number of forecasting techniques rather than a technique in its own right. The approach embodies one of the key responses of forecasting to the changed environment, in that it offers the policymaker not a *single* prediction, but a *number* of possibilities. Examples of the use of the technique can be found in Miles, Cole, and Gershuny (1978); Balmer (1979); Martin and Mason (1981); Henry (1988), and Henderson, Bialeschki, Shaw, and Freysinger (1996, pp. 279–283).

Time-Series Analysis

Time-series analysis predicts the future on the basis of past and current trends in the phenomenon being studied, as illustrated in Figure 23.4 (page 394). A prerequisite of the technique is available data extending over a substantial time period. This is not the case for many forms of leisure activity, but it is available for international tourism. The technique is therefore most well-developed in the area of international tourism because information on international tourist arrivals and departures is available extending back over many years.

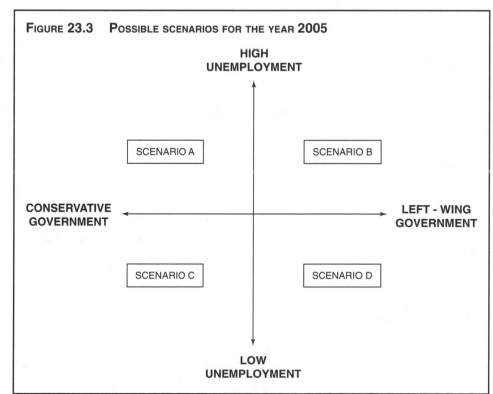

FIGURE 23.3   **POSSIBLE SCENARIOS FOR THE YEAR 2005**

The example in Figure 23.4 shows a simple straight-line trend, but few time series are as simple as this. Complex statistical techniques are available to take account of a variety of trend patterns, including such complexities as seasonal variation. Further complexity can be introduced by relating the demand trend not just to time, but to one or more underlying variables. For example, recreational or tourist trips might be related to levels of income, and international travel might be related to exchange rates or the cost of airfares. When such variables are added to the picture, a model of demand is implied: a structure in which demand is deemed to be determined by causal variables. Such models are termed *structural models*. The technique is further discussed by Stynes (1983) and, in relation to tourism, by Frechtling (1996).

Spatial Models

Spatial techniques rely on the observed fact that people's patterns of demand for certain types of leisure activity are influenced by the locations of available facilities: generally, the further people live from a facility, the less likely they are to visit it (see Smale, chapter 12 in this volume). Visitation tends to fall with increased distance, largely because of the increasing cost, time, and effort involved in traveling longer distances. In the hypothetical catchment area for a recreation facility shown in Figure 23.5, for example, the level of visits per head of population can generally be expected to fall as we move from area A, through B and C to D. This pattern of relationships between distance and level of use can be ascertained from surveys and other user data and can be used to predict the effect of providing new facilities. Using simple gravity models or more complex simulation models of the sort developed by transport planners, the pattern of trips from a network of population centers to a net-

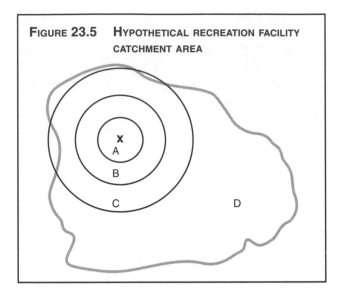

FIGURE 23.5   HYPOTHETICAL RECREATION FACILITY CATCHMENT AREA

work of recreation facilities can be modeled and the effects of changes in the supply of facilities, in the distribution of population or in the transport network can be predicted (Coppock and Duffield, 1975; Ewing, 1983; Smith, 1995, pp. 131–143). Using the Clawson or travel cost method (Clawson and Knetsch, 1962; Smith, 1995, p. 260; Veal, 1994, pp. 148–153), data on demand and distance traveled can be used to derive an economic demand curve which can be used to predict the effects of price changes and to produce cost-benefit evaluations of the recreation facility.

In its most elaborate form, this approach is technically the most sophisticated of the forecasting techniques reviewed, but has generally not been used in recent years, partly because of the general problems with quantitative models, but also because of the costs and effort required to collect sufficient data to establish the model. Simple versions of the model, however, can be a useful aid in planning.

Comparative Method

Dumazedier (1974) argued that a given society might consider futures for itself by examining the experiences of more advanced societies, particularly more economically advanced societies. In particular societies approaching the *postindustrial* phase of development could examine its impact and the ways of coping with it as experienced by the most economically and technologically advanced countries, particularly the United States. Such an approach to considering the future has certain similarities to scenario writing, with the scenarios being provided by other countries rather than having to be devised theoretically. The method was not fully developed in detail by Dumazedier and such factors as cultural and climatic conditions would seem

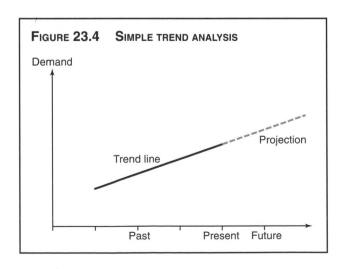

FIGURE 23.4   SIMPLE TREND ANALYSIS

Demand

Projection

Trend line

Past   Present   Future

to raise considerable problems in its application. The approach is used informally by forecasters and may offer potential for developing countries wishing to consider alternative models of development. Naisbitt (1982; Naisbitt and Aburdene, 1990) uses this method to predict changes in American lifestyles, based on interstate rather than international comparisons, with *bellwether* states being identified as the harbingers of the future.

Cross-Sectional Analysis

The cross-sectional technique is based on analysis of variations in leisure participation within or across the community. Participation in most activities is known to vary according to certain factors, such as age, occupation, and income, and this can be quantified. As the structure of the population changes with regard to these underlying variables so, it might be expected, will leisure participation. Thus, for example, since older people participate in sports less frequently than young people, a predicted increase in the proportion of elderly people in the population and a decline in the proportion of young people will lead to a reduction in the overall rate of participation in sports. Whether this results in an absolute decline in participation in sport would depend on the actual figures in a particular situation. Thus information on recreation participation rates from surveys, together with information on future demographic change, can be used to predict future recreation demand. Demographic change is one of the more reliable forms of forecasting, and predictions are readily available from national census organizations. When variables other than age are included, reliable predictions are less readily available. In the case of income levels, it is possible to combine the approach with a scenarios approach, using alternative future levels of income and providing alternative estimates of demand as a result.

The technique can be implemented in two ways. The *cohort* method bases forecasts on projections of future numbers in various sociodemographic groups, for example in five-year age groups. The regression-model approach conducts a model, along the lines of an economic demand model, in which levels of participation are related to a range of independent sociodemographic variables using multiple regression. Once an acceptable equation is established from existing data, the demand forecast is achieved by plugging future values of the independent variables into the equation. This was the main technique used by the early quantitative modelers, discussed previously.

The cross-sectional technique has the limitation of being based entirely on the predicted change in the underlying variable, not on predictions of leisure participation rates per se. Thus, it assumes that old people or young people or poor or prosperous people will continue to participate at the level they do now; all that changes is the numbers in those groups.

Examples of the use of the method are Coppock and Duffield (1975), Lynch and Veal (1996, p. 355), Veal (1987, p. 154), and Young and Willmott (1973, p. 365–375).

Composite Approaches

Many leisure forecasters tend, in practice, to utilize a combination of techniques rather than rely on any one. One method can be used to complement or to overcome the weaknesses of another. Thus the mechanical nature of some of the more quantitative techniques can be modified by results of Delphi exercises, and the broad-brush results of national forecasts can be combined with spatial analysis for application at the local level. Martin and Mason (1981), also known as Leisure Consultants (1990), use a combination of time-series, cross-sectional, and scenario-writing techniques in their forecasting of U.K. leisure patterns. Kelly's (1987) study of recreation trends in the United States utilized cross-sectional cohort methods, time-series analysis, and consideration of qualitative trends in lifestyles and leisure styles. In a study of Australian leisure futures, a basic cohort-based cross-sectional analysis was complemented by consideration of such factors as product life cycles and the effects of changing household composition (Veal, 1991).

Conclusion

In the recent period of economic stagnation and zero population growth in many of the economically developed countries, leisure demand forecasting has not attracted the level of attention of academics that it did in the 1960s and 1970s. But, as the work of Leisure Consultants (1990) and the Henley Centre for Forecasting demonstrates, there is still interest in, and a market for, demand forecasts from the commercial sector. It is notable that, while interest in forecasting community-based leisure and recreation demand is muted, there is considerable interest in tourism forecasting (Frechtling, 1996).

In the public sector, individual municipalities which might be faced with particularly rapid change in their population or in the local economy are forced to consider the medium- to long-term future, including implications for leisure demand, but for the most part, political horizons are limited. This is perhaps understandable when reduced budgets make it difficult to meet today's demands, let alone think about tomorrow. The danger in such a situation is that leisure and recreation will fall foul of the Abilene Paradox (Harvey, 1988), in which one ends up in a location to which no one intended to travel. From time to time it is advisable for organizations and societies as a whole to consider the direction in which they wish to go in the medium to long term. In the case of leisure and recreation, key questions arise over such issues as: the future role of the public and private sectors in leisure provision; the future of traditionally subsidized activities, such as sport and the arts, and the impact of "user pays"; the effects of increasing population and increasing mobility on the environment; the effects of economic restructuring on working hours and lifestyles; the impacts of changing demographic profiles, particularly the aging of the population; and the role of leisure and recreation activity in physical and mental health. None of these issues is new, but they will present new challenges in the changing environment of the twenty-first century.

There is therefore a role for academics and others involved professionally in the leisure field to continue to develop the skills and demonstrate the value of a future-orientated perspective on leisure and recreation demand. Forecasting has traditionally been seen as a purely technical process. But, drawing on the full range of available quantitative and qualitative techniques and linked to new approaches to planning and policy-making, it can also be participatory, it can present alternative possibilities for debate, and it can be educational, democratic, and empowering.

References

Adorno, T. W., & Horkheimer, M. (1944). *The dialectics of enlightenment.* London, UK: Verso.

Asimov, I. (1976). Future fun. In *Today and tomorrow and. . .* (pp. 199–209). London, UK: Scientific Book Club.

Australian Bureau of Statistics. (1996). *Projections of Populations of Australia, states and territories, 1995–2051* (Cat. No. 3222.0). Canberra: Author.

Balmer, K. (1979). *The Elora prescription: A future for recreation.* Toronto, Ontario: Ministry of Culture and Recreation.

Botsman, P. (1993). *Creating jobs in Europe: Strategies and lessons for Australia.* Sydney, Australia: Evatt Foundation.

Brightbill, C. (1960). *The challenge of leisure.* Englewood Cliffs, NJ: Prentice-Hall.

Brown, T. L., & Hutson, D. L. (1979). Evaluation of the ORRRC projections. In *Heritage, conservation and recreation service third nationwide recreation plan: Appendix 2* (Survey Technical Report 4, pp. 259–276). Washington DC: U.S. Government Printing Office.

Burton, T. L. (1970). The shape of things to come. In T. L. Burton (Ed.), *Recreation research and planning* (pp. 242–268). London, UK: Allen & Unwin.

Burton, T. L. (1989). Leisure forecasting, policymaking and planning. In E. L. Jackson & T. L. Burton (Eds.), *Understanding leisure and recreation: Mapping the past, charting the future* (pp. 211–246). State College, PA: Venture Publishing, Inc.

Chai, D. A. (1977). Future of leisure: A Delphi application. *Research Quarterly, 48*(3), 518–524.

Cicchetti, C. J. (1973). *Forecasting recreation in the United States.* Lexington, MA: Lexington Books.

Clarke, J., & Critcher, C. (1985). *The devil makes work: Leisure in capitalist Britain.* London, UK: Macmillan Publishing.

Clawson, M., & Knetsch, J. L. (1962). *Economics of outdoor recreation.* Baltimore, MD: Johns Hopkins Press.

Coppock, J. T., & Duffield, B. S. (1975). *Recreation in the countryside: A spatial analysis.* London, UK: Macmillan Publishing.

Dower, M. (1965). *The fourth wave: The challenge of leisure.* London, UK: Civic Trust.

Dumazedier, J. (1974). *The sociology of leisure.* The Hague, Netherlands: Elsevier.

Ewing, G. O. (1983). Forecasting recreation trip distribution behavior. In S. R. Lieber & D. R. Fesenmaier (Eds.), *Recreation planning and management* (pp. 120–140). London, UK: E & FN Spon.

Featherstone, M. (1991). *Consumer culture and postmodernism.* London, UK: Sage Publications, Ltd.

Frechtling, D. C. (1996). *Practical tourism forecasting.* Oxford, UK: Butterworth-Heinemann.

Galbraith, J. K. (1958). *The affluent society.* Harmondsworth, UK: Penguin.

Green, H., Hunter, C., & Moore, B. (1990). Assessing the environmental impact of tourism development: Use of the Delphi technique. *Tourism Management, 11,* 111–120.

Harada, M. (1996). Japan. In G. Cushman, A. J. Veal & J. Zuzanek (Eds.), *World leisure participation: Free time in the global village* (pp. 153–164). Wallingford, UK: CAB International.

Harvey, J. B. (1988). *The Abilene paradox.* Lexington, MA: Lexington Books.

Henderson, K., Bialeschki, M. D., Shaw, S. M., & Freysinger, V. J. (1996). *Both gains and gaps: Feminist perspectives on women's leisure.* State College, PA: Venture Publishing, Inc.

Henry, I. (1988). Alternative futures for the public leisure service. In J. Bennington & J. White (Eds.), *The future of leisure services* (pp. 207–244). Harlow, UK: Longman.

Kelly, J. R. (1987). *Recreation trends: Toward the year 2000.* Champaign, IL: Management Learning Laboratories.

Kelly, J. R. (1989). Leisure and quality: Beyond the quantitative barrier in research. In T. L. Goodale & P. A. Witt (Eds.), *Recreation and leisure: Issues in an era of change* (pp. 300–314). State College, PA: Venture Publishing, Inc.

Kelly, J. R., & Godbey, G. (1992). *The sociology of leisure.* State College, PA: Venture Publishing, Inc.

Keynes, J. M. (1931/1972). Economic possibilities for our grandchildren. In *The collected writings of John Maynard Keynes, Vol. 9, Essays in persuasion* (pp. 321–332). London, UK: Macmillan Publishing.

Larrabee, E., & Meyersohn, R. (Eds.). (1958). *Mass leisure.* Glencoe, IL: Free Press.

Leisure Consultants. (1990). *UK leisure forecasts.* Sudbury, UK: Author.

Lynch, R., & Veal, A. J. (1996). *Australian leisure.* Melbourne, Australia: Longman.

Martin, W. H., & Mason, S. (1981). *Leisure and work: The choices for 1991 and 2001.* Sudbury, UK: Leisure Consultants.

Martino, J. P. (1978). Technological forecasting. In J. Fowles (Ed.), *Handbook of futures research* (pp. 369–396). Westport, CT: Greenwood.

Miles, I., Cole, S., & Gershuny, J. (1978). Images of the future. In C. Freeman & M. Jahoda (Eds.), *World futures: The great debate* (pp. 279–342). London, UK: Martin Robertson.

Naisbitt, J. (1982). *Megatrends: Ten new directions transforming our lives.* New York, NY: Warner Books.

Naisbitt, J., & Aburdene, P. (1990). *Megatrends 2000.* London, UK: Pan Books.

Ng, D., Brown, B., & Knott, W. (1983). Qualified leisure services manpower requirements: A future perspective. *Recreation Research Review, 10*(1), 13–19.

Outdoor Recreation Resources Review Commission. (1962). *Outdoor recreation for America.* Washington, DC: Author.

Rifkin, J. (1995). *The end of work: The decline of the global labor force and the dawn of the postmarket era.* New York, NY: G. P. Putnams Sons.

Robinson, J. P., & Godbey, G. (1997). *Time for life: The surprising ways Americans use their time.* University Park, PA: Penn State Press.

Russell, B. (1935). *In praise of idleness and other essays.* London, UK: Allen & Unwin.

Schor, J. B. (1991). *The overworked American: The unexpected decline of leisure.* New York, NY: Basic Books.

Settle, J. G. (1977). *Leisure in the north west: A tool for forecasting* (Study No. 11). London, UK: Sports Council.

Shafer, E. L., Moeller, G. H., & Russell, E. G. (1977). Future leisure environments. *Ekistics, 40*(236), 68–72.

Smigel, E. O. (Ed.). (1963). *Work and leisure: A contemporary social problem.* New Haven, CT: College and University Press.

Smith, S. L. J. (1995). *Tourism analysis* (2nd ed.). Harlow, UK: Longman.

Stynes, D. J. (1983). Outdoor recreation forecasting methods. In S. R. Lieber & D. R. Fesenmaier (Eds.), *Recreation planning and management* (pp. 87–188). State College, PA: Venture Publishing, Inc.

Tomlinson, A. (Ed.). (1990). *Consumption, identity, and style: Marketing, meanings and the packaging of pleasure.* London, UK: Routledge.

United Nations. (1995). *World population prospects, the 1994 revision.* New York, NY: Author.

Van Lier, H. N. (1993). New challenges in recreation and tourism planning. In H. N. Van Lier & P. D. Taylor (Eds.), *New challenges in recreation and tourism planning* (pp. 5–16). Amsterdam, Netherlands: Elsevier.

Veal, A. J. (1987). *Leisure and the future.* London, UK: Allen & Unwin.

Veal, A. J. (1991). *Australian leisure futures.* Sydney, Australia: Centre for Leisure and Tourism Studies, University of Technology, Sydney.

Veal, A. J. (1994). *Leisure policy and planning.* Harlow, UK: Longman.

Young, M., & Willmott, P. (1973). *The symmetrical family.* London, UK: Routledge.

Zalatan, A. (1994). *Forecasting methods in sports and recreation.* Toronto, Ontario: Thompson Educational Publishing.

Zuzanek, J. (1996). Canada. In G. Cushman, A. J. Veal & J. Zuzanek (Eds.), *World leisure participation: Free time in the global village* (pp. 35–76). Wallingford, UK: CAB International.

Changing Boundaries and New Management Implications for Leisure Organizations

Trevor Slack

De Montfort University

In the industrialized countries of the world the provision of leisure products and leisure services takes place through a variety of public, private, and voluntary sector organizations. Each of these sectors has had a relatively discrete role in the provision of these products and services. Public sector organizations have traditionally become involved in leisure as a result of the perceived need to regulate popular recreation, as a part of the growth of the welfare state, or as a consequence of the belief that the market will fail to produce an appropriate mix of such goods and services. Private sector agencies are, not surprisingly, involved in the provision of leisure to make a profit; the financial returns of companies like Nike and Disney are testament to the success of this involvement. The functions of voluntary sector organizations involved in leisure range from those that are instrumental (i.e., designed to serve some societal good) to others that are more expressive in nature and serve to satisfy the needs of their membership. Voluntary organizations designed to pro-

tect wilderness areas would be an example of the former, a community bridge club the latter.

The organizations that make up each of these sectors have, for the most part, exhibited an institutionally specific set of structural arrangements, operating procedures, and cultural underpinnings. However, since the early 1980s, contextual pressures from a variety of sources have brought about considerable change in the nature of the organizations in each of these sectors. The traditional boundaries which have demarcated public, voluntary, and private sector agencies have become blurred. Public sector providers of leisure opportunities have been increasingly pressured to forge stronger links with corporate partners (cf., Howard and Crompton, 1995) or to adopt market mechanisms as a means of delivering services (Clarke, 1994; Henry, 1993). Voluntary organizations, which have traditionally been the basis of the community leisure system, are being required to replace their informal operating procedures and loosely coupled structures with a more professional and bureaucratic organizational design

(Kikulis, Slack and Hinings, 1992; Searle and Brayley, 1993), one that is seen as providing a more "business-like" approach to service provision. Leisure organizations in the private sector which have traditionally competed with rival companies for market share are now discovering that it is cooperation not competition that is often the key to company success (see Gorman and Calhoun, 1994, and Yoshino and Rangan, 1995, for examples). As a result, we are starting to see a variety of strategic alliances, joint ventures, licensing agreements, and equity investments occurring which involve companies in the leisure industry.

While there have been some attempts to look at factors precipitating these changes (Coalter, 1995; Gunn, 1990; Henry, 1993), there has been little if any consideration of the organizational and managerial ramifications of such shifts. Given that these types of changes are likely to become more common as we move into the next millennium, this is an important issue for both practicing leisure managers and for academics interested in the structure and operations of leisure organizations. Consequently, in this chapter I will look in more detail at the types of transformations that are occurring in the public, voluntary, and private sector organizations that deliver leisure products and services. I will show that the traditional lines between these three sectors are no longer as clearly demarcated as they have been in the past and that the resultant forms of organization require new operating methods and innovative managerial skills. This chapter focuses, first, on the types of changes that have occurred in public sector leisure organizations. It then examines the changes that are occurring in voluntary sector organizations, and concludes by looking at the new approaches to product and service provision that are being used in the private sector organizations involved in the leisure industry.

The Changing Nature of Public Sector Leisure Organizations

Since the mid 1950s the most basic argument for public sector involvement in the production of goods and services has been the expectation that in certain situations the market fails and state provision is the more effective means of delivery. State intervention in various aspects of leisure has been justified on the basis of the *public good* nature of certain leisure products and services and by the positive externalities that are seen to emanate from this involvement. Occupying potential deviant youth subcultures, creating national pride through sporting success, developing and maintaining a healthy population, increasing awareness of environmental issues, and preserving a nation's cultural heritage are all examples of the types of benefits that have been attributed to state intervention in leisure. As a result of a belief in the success of these interventions, public sector involvement in leisure in countries like Britain, the United States, Canada, and many parts of Western Europe has, over the years, grown considerably. Government agencies at different levels have developed policy documents to guide their involvement in such fields as the arts, culture, sport, and parks; some have even appointed politicians with specific responsibilities for these areas. Large bureaucracies were created to administer government involvement and there was considerable public sector investment in various types of leisure facilities.

In the early 1980s a transformation in the way the public service was managed started to take place. Within the leisure literature there has been a tendency to see the roots of this transformation as paralleling the rise to power of *New Right* politicians such as Margaret Thatcher and Ronald Reagan. Henry (1993, p. 95), for example, points out that in Britain the changes in the delivery of leisure services in the 1980s were precipitated, in large part, by the Conservative government's return to power in 1979 and its policy agenda which "was dominated by new right concerns to impose monetarist prescriptions on public spending and to introduce market discipline in areas of work traditionally seen as public sector dominated." In the United States a similar ideological stance, developed during the Reagan years, resulted in a transformation in the way parks and recreation agencies operated (cf., Schultz, McAvoy and Dustin, 1988).

However, as Walsh (1995, p. 56) points out, these type of changes cannot be solely attributed to "politicians influenced by liberal economic thinking." Indeed a number of countries with left-leaning governments adopted similar reforms. Jung (1993), for example, discusses the reduction of state funding and the move to a market economy for leisure which took place under the Solidarity government in Poland. In addition, factors such as fiscal pressure, the failure of existing systems, and the imitation of one government's actions by another all contributed to the changes that have occurred (Walsh, 1995). The essential nature of the changes that took place involved the introduction of market principles and market mechanisms into the management of public sector leisure facilities and programs (Henry and Bramham, 1993). As Sessoms and Henderson (1994, p. 60) point out, "the public sector became more businesslike, developing programs and services that were self-supporting or which assured the agency some recovery costs."

The foundation for this move to a more market-driven approach to leisure provision has been a change in the way the public sector is structured and the adoption of such mechanisms as user charges, contracts, and the creation of internal markets. In terms of the restructuring of the public sector, this has occurred primarily through a process of downsizing and devolved control. The downsizing of the public sector has been a trend which has not only been seen as acceptable because it has brought about economic savings (albeit maybe short term), but also because it has been a move that parallels the private sector.

The most visible reductions in regard to leisure provision have been in the size and funding of bodies responsible for areas such as sport and the arts. In Britain, for example, in 1988 the Sports Council's board was cut from 32 to 14 members and there was a streamlining of the Council's management structure (Houlihan, 1991). In Canada in 1993 the position of Minister of State for Fitness and Amateur Sport was eliminated by Conservative Prime Minister Kim Campbell, and the size of the Sport Canada bureaucracy was significantly reduced. In 1979 when the Conservative government took power in England, the size of the Arts Council's grant was cut by some £1.1 million despite preelection promises that this would not happen. Similar trends are apparent in the Netherlands where during the 1980s the national-level budget for outdoor recreation was halved (van de Poel, 1993); in Germany where Nahrstedt (1993) comments on the lack of government investment in leisure opportunities during the 1980s; and in the United States where Schultz et al. (1988) talk about dwindling tax support and rising costs being precursors of the adoption of private sector strategies in public parks and recreation agencies.

Increased Links with the Corporate Sector

In many countries this reduction in the size and funding of public sector organizations responsible for leisure opportunities has been accompanied by a push for agencies to make stronger links with the corporate sector. The reorganization of the Sports Council in Britain was, according to the Minister, initiated in part because the Council "needs an input . . . from the private sector to act as a catalyst for generating more income for the elite athletes and programs at the grass roots level" (*Guardian,* 1988, as cited in Houlihan, 1991, p. 92). In Canada the push to look to the private sector for funds was initiated in 1985, when the Nielsen Re-

port suggested that the government should "phase down its funding of Sport Canada over a 10–15 year period in order to give the high-performance athlete development system some time to seek and establish sufficient viability both organizationally and financially to operate relatively independent of government" (Government of Canada, 1985, pp. 258–259, 268); that is to say, to seek private sector funding. The creation of the Institute for Sport Sponsorship and the Arts Council marketing grants in Britain and the now defunct Canadian Sport and Fitness Marketing Incorporated are examples of initiatives designed to facilitate this shift to greater ties with private corporations and to bring about less public sector involvement in the running of these activities. There are similar trends in the Netherlands: van de Poel (1993, p. 57) notes that "terms like sponsorship and privatization have been introduced into the vocabulary of arts policymakers." In the United States public sector agencies have linked with corporate groups in providing tennis courts (Mills, 1994), golf courses (Cook, 1996), and parks (Grass, 1997). And in Britain the Minister of Sport indicated to the Chair of the Sport Council that the government was considering placing responsibility for the funding of elite sport in the hands of commercial sponsors (Henry and Bramham, 1993). The move to create stronger ties with the private sector and thus increase marketlike competition can also be seen in the Canadian government's decision to initiate what is termed a core sport concept. This initiative is also being considered in Britain. The idea behind this move is that, with declining financial resources, the public sector will only fund certain sports and that those not funded must generate their own resources from the private sector. The Canadian experience is that those sports that are being funded are the most visible and successful, while those not being given public sector support are the less visible and less successful sports (i.e., those that are least likely to gain corporate monies).

Devolved Control of Leisure Service Provision and the Adoption of Market Mechanisms

Governments adopting a more market-driven approach to leisure provision have not only sought to reduce the size and funding of the major public sector leisure organizations, but they have also devolved control of service provision. This has occurred most markedly at the regional and local levels. Here, public sector service providers are ostensibly allowed to operate as independent units which control their own budgets and compete for clients. Moves of this nature are evident in such countries as Britain, Canada, and France. Local public sector providers of leisure operate as somewhat independent units that have increasingly assumed the characteristics of private sector organizations by employing market mechanisms such as user charges, contracts, and the creation of internal markets.

In many countries the increase in the use of pricing and charging for public services has been considerable, with charges being brought closer to those that might apply in a free market. McCarville and Smale (1991), for instance, report that in a study of municipal leisure service agencies in Ontario, Canada, almost half of the recreation directors reported that their departments employed a user fee on some of their programs. In Edmonton, Alberta, the cost recovery on the rental of hockey rinks (i.e., the amount users pay) has over the last few years increased from 50% to 70% of the total cost (Kim Sanderson, personal communication, May, 1994). Similar cost-recovery programs are being used to fund the operation of swimming pools, ice rinks, fields, and indoor playing facilities in other Canadian cities (Dockendorf, 1987; Larson, 1996; Robinson, 1994). In Britain, Gratton and Taylor (1991) report that between 1980 and 1991 the percentage cost recovery by local authorities for swimming pools rose from 12% to 36%, for sport centers from 27% to 44%, for outdoor fields from 19% to 22%, and for golf courses from 68% to 109%. In the United States, Crompton and McGregor (1994) found that from 1982–83 to 1987–88 local parks and recreation departments increased their income by an average of $125 million per year from self-generated revenues such as user fees.

In addition to user fees, another common market mechanism that is increasingly being employed in the public sector is the use of contracts. Contracts entail a move from the traditional hierarchical form of public service delivery to a more market-based arm's length method of provision. The public sector agency acts as a client or purchaser who contracts with a provider, either from the private or voluntary sector, (or even another public agency) to provide a good or service. The purchasing agency decides on the good or service needed, lets the contract, and monitors performance; the organization winning the contract is responsible for the provision of the good or service (Walsh, 1995). Although starting to be employed by local government providers of leisure goods and services in a number of countries of the world, the use of contracts as means of reforming public sector provision of leisure has been most pronounced in Britain through the use of the program known as Compulsory Competitive Tendering (CCT).

Originally introduced under the 1980 Local Government Planning and Land Act, the concept of CCT had by the late 1980s been extended to include a wide variety of services, one of which was the operation of leisure facilities and their attendant programs. Facilities such as golf courses, leisure centers, swimming pools, and so on were all affected, and in England by January 1993 all had become subject to the tendering process (Henry, 1993). The basic premise of CCT is that organizational tasks such as grounds maintenance, security of premises, taking bookings, supervising and instruction of activities, were all put up for bid either to private contractors or by the local authority itself. As Henry (1993, p. 99) notes, "the way in which this initiative [was] to be implemented meant that the local authority [who ran the leisure facility] in effect became the clients of contractors who managed their services." The facility managers could of course bid to win their own contracts and so continue to run their own facilities, but the nature of this type of public sector operation was inherently changed under this new scheme. The local authority who put out the tender would control the nature of the contract and the quality of service provided. Initial data provided by Henry (1993, pp. 100–101), however, suggests that in its initial years the CCT process has not seen large numbers of commercial operators get into the provision of public sector leisure. More importantly, what has happened has been the commercialization of existing management interests in the field.

The development of internal markets provides a third approach to the provision of leisure goods and services that is being used by the reformed public sector. Intended to apply market principles to the operation of the public sector, internal markets exhibit three defining features: "the creation of explicit and separate roles for the purchasing and supply of services; the establishment of internal quasi-contracts and trading agreements between these separate roles; and the development of charging and accounting systems" (Walsh, 1995, p. 139). As applied to the provision of leisure services, what we see occurring is that leisure facility managers are being required to contract with the maintenance department within their own municipality for the upkeep of their buildings; cleaning may be similarly contracted, and if the building requires computer support for tasks such as booking playing areas and maintaining accounts, or legal help for liability issues, this is likewise purchased from an internally located central provider. The arguments for this type of system are that it leads to a clear definition of responsibilities, ensures that each aspect of service provision is adequately developed, and creates pressures for efficiencies (Walsh, 1995).

Structural and Operational Changes in Public Sector Leisure Organizations

The composite result of the type of changes outlined here is the transformation of the public sector from a bureaucratic hierarchically structured form of organization to a more differentiated network of independent or quasi-autonomous internal units operating with devolved control (Walsh, 1995). This new model of the public sector and the market mechanisms that underpin it bring with them a number of structural and operational ramifications for the delivery of leisure goods and services.

User fees, for example, are frequently being used to help alleviate financial cutbacks. However, setting appropriate fees for leisure service users is extremely difficult. As Crompton (1984, p. 71) notes, "pricing is one of the most technically difficult and politically sensitive areas in which recreation and parks managers have to make decisions" (see also Berrett, Slack and Whitson, 1993, and McCarville, chapter 25 in this volume). Traditionally, public sector organizations have not been required to generate the type of information necessary to set prices that reflect market conditions. There has, for instance, been little data collected on patterns of facility use or information generated about the reasons why and when people use public sector leisure services. There has been even less information on the impact that pricing changes would have on their use. Fixed costs, variable costs, the socioeconomic characteristics and motivations of users, variations in usage, a demand function for the facility, external benefits that flow to society, and the administrative costs of collecting user fees are all issues which Becker (1975) suggests must be considered before any pricing decision can be made. If, for example, the marginal costs in running a site such as a park are low, then introducing user fees may lead to decreased use and make little difference to net costs. If fixed investment costs are high, such as may be the case in a large multipurpose leisure facility, but marginal variable costs are low, it may be necessary to calculate charges by using a standard charge for the fixed costs and a unit cost to cover what is actually used (Walsh, 1995). This type of situation makes accurate pricing difficult because the required information is simply not available to most public sector providers. Thus, any move to a mechanism such as user fees, if it is to be accurate, requires the public sector to introduce detailed management accounting systems into their operations. This in turn requires a large capital outlay, the hiring of professional staff to operate such a system, and greater levels of communication among the units involved. In turn, these require modifications to the structure and operations of the organizational infrastructure and demand new skills in leisure managers.

Public sector officials involved in leisure provision will also have to take account of the fact that increasing user costs may create additional expenditures for other branches of the public service for which they may be relatively unaccountable. Increasing fees may, for example, reduce usage of leisure facilities and (if we are to believe those who subscribe to the social control benefits of leisure) this may contribute to greater levels of delinquency (see Driver and Bruns, chapter 21 in this volume). This, in turn, will increase costs in policing, another branch of the public service. Traditionally, public sector officials have not been asked to think in these terms.

The use of contracts in the provision of leisure services has the potential to bring about changes in the structure and operation of public sector leisure organizations. The most dramatic of these for public service officials may be a reduction in their numbers and a deterioration in pay and working conditions for those that remain. For those that are still employed, there will be a greater emphasis on monitoring and controlling the quality of service provided by the private contractor than there was when the service was provided in-house. The problems of contract monitoring are vast and will bring about different modes of operation for public sector officials. Public service leisure providers, as purchasers of contracted services, can, for example, require sanctions such as performance bonds, guarantees, or quality assurance systems to ensure that contracts are fulfilled. They can also attempt to ensure that the company being contracted has similar values to their own, thus helping ensure commitment, or they can write contracts which contain mechanisms such as holdbacks or termination agreements. These can be invoked if work is not performed to standard. All of these types of initiatives can present difficulties to public sector employees, who have traditionally not been required to draw up and let contracts or monitor and control their implementation. Developing contracts may require the use of legal or paralegal personnel, performance measures have to be developed for companies winning contracts, and, since contracts are rarely complete in that not all areas can be covered, arbitration mechanisms may have to be built in. All of these shifts have the net effect of bringing about changes in the structure and operations of the public sector organizations providing leisure services and this, in turn, places new demands on their managers.

The use of contracts also has policy implications for leisure managers. If contractors are to be held accountable, increased emphasis will also be placed on public sector officials to create leisure policy. As Henry (1993, p. 102) notes, "for those that fail to specify policy in contractual terms the power to dictate policy direction may well fall to the contractors by default." Given that these contractors may represent private concerns, the possible implications of their setting leisure policy are significant. Their emphasis will likely be on the economic gains they can derive from leisure provision rather than on its social regenerative benefits.

Like user fees and contracts, the creation of internal markets also has the net effect of changing the structure and operation of those organizations providing leisure services and, as such, poses new challenges for leisure managers. Separating out purchaser and provider roles inside a local authority creates a more differentiated organization, and the linkages that are created mean a less hierarchical and more network-based structural form. There are greater internal management costs as specifications of agreements have to be developed, monitoring costs incorporated into agreements, and methods of invoicing and payment developed. There will be greater pressures for formality, although relationships may have to be based on trust. This in turn raises a concern about how conflicts are resolved, because "the internal market operates with quasi-contracts, rather than real ones, since an organization cannot have a contract with itself and the normal legal mechanisms for dealing with contract incompleteness, imprecision and dispute are not available" (Walsh, 1995, p. 160).

These structural and operational changes do not occur in isolation but tend to be linked to one another. To be successful they also need to be paralleled by appropriate cultural change. Traditionally, a culture of professionalism was emphasized within the public sector, but this is gradually being replaced by a philosophy based on managerialism (Clarke, 1994). However, it is not a managerialism grounded in the traditions of hierarchy and bureaucratic control but the type of managerialism that will be required in order to operate in a network form of organization. Here trust, flexibility, increased complexity, decentralized control, and coordination become paramount, and, as the public sector increasingly takes on the attributes of the private sector, it is these issues that public sector leisure managers will have to address.

Changes in Voluntary Leisure Organizations

The changes that have occurred in public sector organizations concerned with the delivery of leisure goods and services have contributed to related changes in the voluntary leisure organizations which the public sector has traditionally supported and, at least in part, funded. The push for public sector organizations to create stronger ties with the private sector and to make use of market mechanisms in the delivery of their programs has resulted in strong institutional pressures for voluntary leisure organizations to become more businesslike in their operations. Also, the reduction of public sector funding to voluntary organizations has meant that many of these organizations have had to turn to the corporate sector for support. In demanding accountability for the money they provide, corporations have required voluntary organizations to become more efficient and effective in their operations.

Traditionally, most voluntary leisure organizations have operated with a set of structural arrangements that Kikulis et al. (1992), writing about sport, term a *kitchen table design*. This refers to the fact that many of these organizations literally operated off the kitchen table of their volunteer president. They had few formalized policies and procedures, and decisions were made informally by the volunteer board. The linkages these organizations maintained were primarily with their counterparts at different regional levels or with local voluntary groups with similar missions to their own. Operating funds came primarily from membership fees and, at times, some small fund-raising ventures. Rarely did any of these organizations hire professional staff, and for the few that did it was usually little more than secretarial help.

Shifts in the Funding Sources for Voluntary Leisure Organizations

Since the 1970s several trends have caused voluntary leisure organizations to abandon much of this traditional mode of operation and adopt a more professional and bureaucratically structured form of organization. Primary among these has been shifts in the funding sources available to voluntary leisure organizations. Specifically, increased government funding throughout the 1970s and much of the 1980s allowed these organizations to increase their program offerings, and many hired professional staff to help operate these programs. More recently, funding from the public sector has been reduced as a culture of fiscal efficiency and entre-preneurism has pervaded government organizations. As a result, voluntary leisure organizations which wished to retain the program offerings that they developed through the 1970s and 1980s have been forced to look to the commercial sector for sponsorships or other forms of support and to be more entrepreneurial in self-generating funds. As Henry (1993, p. 39) notes about arts organizations in Britain, "increased emphasis has been put on reducing [dependence on] state funding and complementing, or in some cases replacing, it with other sources (such as business sponsorship)." These linkages with government and the corporate sector have had the combined effect of increasing the complexity of the environment in which voluntary organizations operate. No longer are links restricted to their counterparts at different geographic levels or other similarly oriented organizations, but may now include government departments, regulatory agencies, corporate groups, television companies, lottery agencies, philanthropic organizations, and public relations bodies, to name but a few. All of these changes have had an impact on the structure of those organizations in the voluntary sector which are concerned with the provision of various leisure activities.

Governments in many countries have, for example, at different times given funds to assist the operation of various voluntary leisure organizations. However, throughout the 1970s and much of the 1980s, this type of support became more systematized and ongoing. Sport in particular has been one of the major recipients of government largesse as politicians in many countries have come to realize the political capital that can be gained from international sporting success. However, increased government financial support has not been restricted to sport, as organizations concerned with the arts, countryside, youth, and culture have all had increased opportunities to apply for government funds. In a number of cases the receipt of these funds has been contingent on the voluntary organization in question exhibiting a more businesslike approach to its operations. Requirements for the development of strategic plans, increased financial accountability, the generation of matching funds, and formally trained staff are but a few of the demands that public sector agencies at different levels have placed on voluntary leisure organizations in receipt of government funds. The effect of these demands and the increased state funding that has been available to voluntary providers has been a shift away from their traditional structure and operating procedures to the type of organizational design that Mintzberg (1979) terms a *professional bureaucracy*. The transition to this type of organizational form involves an increase in the extent to which the policies and operating procedures of these organizations are formalized, an increase in the number of professional staff employed, and—in those organizations that have made the complete transition—the decentralization of operating decisions away from the volunteer board to the level of the professional staff. There has also been a greater demand for specialized roles to manage the increasingly complex environment which these organizations now face.

When, in the early 1990s, many government agencies had to reduce the amount of funding they provided to the voluntary sector, not-for-profit providers of leisure opportunities were forced to turn to the commercial sector for support. As with government agencies, the latter also demanded that in order to be considered for corporate support, in one of its variant forms, the voluntary agencies providing leisure opportunities display the same type of businesslike operations that the government had demanded. This shift also brought about an implicit attempt to "upgrade" the boards of these organizations. That is to say there has been a conscientious attempt by many of these organizations to recruit board members who have professional or managerial qualifications. While, at one point, free time and enthusiasm were all that were required to be a board member of a voluntary leisure organization, the increasing pressures to make these organizations more businesslike has led to planned campaigns to recruit people with the credentials to influence government funding agencies and/or open corporate doors. Macintosh and Whitson (1990), for example, describe the efforts of staff in Canadian sport organizations to recruit board members with "corporate credentials." In Sweden, Olson (1993) talks about businessmen (sic) and bank directors being asked to sit on the boards of sports clubs and associations to help gain private sector investment and sponsorships. The shift to trying to obtain corporate funding has also meant that both staff and membership of voluntary leisure organizations have had to think more strategically in order to position their programs and events as desirable to companies looking for sponsorship opportunities. So, while there has been a shift in the sources of funding for a number of voluntary leisure organizations in recent years, the pressures to operate in a businesslike fashion have been consistent. As a result of the pressures many of these voluntary leisure organizations have experienced, their members and professional staff now face several new structural and operational issues.

Structural and Operational Issues in Voluntary Leisure Organizations

The first and in many ways the most significant of these structural and operational issues involves the nature of the authority structure within this new organizational form. Traditionally, voluntary leisure organizations have operated informally, with decisions being made by the volunteer board. The move to the more businesslike structure of the professional bureaucracy means that the volunteer board gives up the day-to-day operational decisions of the organization to professional staff. The board should operate much like a corporate board, setting policy and the general direction for the organization. For some volunteers this transition has been difficult to make. In fact, Slack and Hinings (1992), in their work on Canadian sport organizations, have shown that, while it has been relatively easy for these organizations to add new staff and formalize operating procedure, attempts to change their authority structure have frequently met with resistance.

In part, resistance to the change stems from the traditional culture of these organizations. As Kimberly (1987) has shown, the history of an organization can have a strong impact on its ability to change. Historically, these voluntary leisure organizations have built up a culture that favors principles of self-help, autonomy from government, loose operating systems, informality, and volunteer control of decision making. The move to a more businesslike organization demands that many of these cultural norms be given up and replaced with a set of values which favor more rational operating methods. While a number of national and regional leisure organizations can be seen to have made this cultural transition, others have made the structural changes necessary for the move to the professional bureaucracy but their values are still rooted in the voluntary culture with which these organizations have traditionally operated. As such, they remain in what Hinings and Greenwood (1988) refer to as a schizoid state—a situation in which structure and process reflect the tension between contradictory sets of ideas and values.

A further change that is required of these voluntary leisure organizations as they move to a more professional and bureaucratic structure involves the relationship between professionals and volunteers. The reason for hiring professional staff to work in voluntary leisure organizations is because these people bring a level of expertise to the organization that it is felt is needed. They also work full time for the organization, thus enabling them to establish a powerful position in its operations. This combination of expertise and centrality often generates resentment among volunteers, who may see themselves (quite rightly in a number of cases) as more knowledgeable than the professionals who have been hired. Amis, Slack, and Berrett (1995) for example, demonstrate this type of situation in Canadian sport organizations as they have become more professional in their operation. This type of tension and the resultant conflict between professionals and volunteers are direct results of the transition to the more businesslike structure and require different management skills than have traditionally been the norm in these organizations.

The increased demands to obtain corporate support also bring with them a requirement for new managerial skills and operating structures. Many of the voluntary leisure organizations seeking this type of support have had to prepare detailed proposals. This has required new and different skills from those previously employed in these organizations. For those that have been successful in securing corporate support there have been a whole new set of demands as companies have, depending on the program or event being sponsored, required hospitality opportunities, television coverage, advertising privileges, marketing rights, and merchandising and licensing opportunities. Again these place considerable demands on volunteers, who have not traditionally had to deal with these issues. The agreements that are created between a sponsoring company and a voluntary organization may come in a number of forms, all of which require different management skills from those that have previously been employed. Issues such as trust, common values, complementary cultures, and monitoring mechanisms all become essential in these arrangements, attributes that in the past were not deemed particularly important in the operation of voluntary leisure organizations.

The potential for conflict between volunteers and professionals, the resistance that is shown to changing the culture of voluntary leisure organizations, the struggles over authority structures, the consistent demands to obtain new sources of funding, and the voluntary leisure organization's ability to manage relationships with funding bodies all raise questions about the permanency of the transitions that have occurred in these organizations. The halcyon years of the late 1970s and early 1980s are over, and the potential loss of funds which is being brought about as a result of the fiscal cutbacks of the 1990s raises questions about the ability of these organizations to maintain the move to a more businesslike form. The change dynamic that results from these different pressures creates a transition process that is uneven and may show reversals in direction (Kikulis, Slack and Hinings, 1995). Managing this process raises further managerial issues for these organizations.

A final concern which emanates from the transition to a more businesslike voluntary organization concerns the possible marginalization of certain types of volunteers. As voluntary leisure organizations have adopted more systematic operating procedures and hired more professional staff, those volunteers who by virtue of their paid employment do not have managerial skills have become somewhat disenfranchised as fully functioning members of the organization. Retaining these people as active and fully participating members is obviously important, but may become increasingly difficult if existing organizational trends occur.

Changes in the Private Sector: The Emergence of Strategic Alliances

Although not as directly linked as the changes that have occurred in the public and voluntary sectors, privately operated leisure organizations have also experienced considerable change over the last decade. With these changes have come new forms of organization and new managerial requirements. The most significant of the changes that have taken place in the private sector is the emergence of strategic alliances as a central means of doing business (others would include such strategies as downsizing and the introduction of initiatives such as Total Quality Management). Very simply, a strategic alliance is "a particular mode of inter-organizational relationship in which the partners make substantial investments in developing a long-term collaborative effort and common orientation" (Mattsson, 1988). Alliances stress cooperation rather than competition between firms. Although there is some debate in the literature over the exact nature of alliances, it is generally accepted that they involve agreements such as joint ventures, equity investments, licensing agreements, joint manufacturing, shared service provision, long-term sourcing agreements, and so on. The globalization of world markets has played a major role in the development of alliances. Motivations behind alliances may range from reducing resource dependence to spreading financial risk to bringing a product to market faster.

Alliances in the Leisure Industry

Within the leisure industry alliances are found in a variety of different types of organizations. At the level of the major corporation, companies such as Coca Cola, IBM, Benetton, and Eastman Kodak, which some may argue are peripheral to the industry but nevertheless play a major role in many leisure activities, are extensively involved in a variety of strategic alliances (cf., Yoshino and Rangan, 1995). Others which are more directly involved in leisure, such as McDonald's, Fox Broadcasting, Disney, the National Football League, and Nike also exhibit considerable involvement in this form of organization. However, alliances are not just limited to the major multinationals; we also find a variety of different types of alliances occurring between smaller scale organizations (cf., Elvin, 1990; Hadwen, 1994). For example, at the local level we may find a group of sporting goods stores establishing some sort of consortium to support minor sport, local merchants working with a community theatre group to promote a dramatic festival, outdoor outfitters cooperating with environmentalists on wilderness preservation projects, or franchise restaurants promoting sporting events. We also see alliances across traditional boundaries. For example, private providers of sports like tennis or squash may link with city recreation departments or schools to ensure maximum facility usage or public providers of leisure services may join with voluntary groups to cooperatively maintain walking trails.

In considering the influence of alliances in the leisure industry, it is important to remember that the arrangements made may involve non-leisure-related organizations. Nike, for example, the world's largest manufacturer of shoes for sporting and recreational activities, has used alliances to its considerable benefit. Even before the term *strategic alliance* became popular, Phil Knight, the CEO of Nike, "based his vision of a successful company on leveraging other firm's resources" (Yoshino and Rangan, 1995, p. 90). For example, in 1973 when Knight ran into sourcing problems for his shoes, he entered into an agreement with Nissho, a Japanese trading company. Nissho helped Knight find sources of supply in the Far East and, with their skills in ocean transportation, dealing with customs, and financing, they looked after the export of the shoes to the United States in return for a commission. However, Knight was careful not to become overreliant on Nissho and he developed a network of alliances in other Asian countries. As well as developing alliances with its manufacturing sources, Nike has also developed links with an extensive network of leisure goods retailers to distribute its footwear and leisure products. These links operate through what is termed a future sales program, in which retailers who order goods five to six months in advance get a 5% to 7% discount and guaranteed delivery within a two-week target date.

In addition to commodity-producing companies like Nike, the use of strategic alliances has also become commonplace in professional sport organizations. The political, cultural, and economic environment of North American professional sport leagues has changed considerably over the last 20 years. The globalization of world markets, the deregulation of television, a recessionary economy, and the growing popularity of professional sport have each contributed to this changing environment (Cousens and Slack, 1996). In order to manage these environmental shifts, the four major professional sport leagues have entered into a series of alliances with their key bargaining partners. The National Football League, for instance, has entered into a joint venture with Rupert Murdoch's News Corporation in order to penetrate European markets. The venture involves the World League of American Football. For Murdoch's News Corporation, the strategic advantages of the alliance are that it can use the popularity of American football and the legitimacy of the NFL to penetrate new European markets. It can also use the NFL to help promote Murdoch's developing North American division of Fox Broadcasting. The NFL benefits from the money News Corporation puts into its coffers and the increased television exposure it gains both in North America and Europe, something which in turn facilitates the increased sales of NFL licensed merchandise.

In addition to their linkages with television broadcast companies, the relationships which a number of professional sport leagues have with corporate sponsors have also changed, as each partner seeks an alliance that will leverage its involvement with the other to gain value-added benefits. Again the NFL, for example, has joined with McDonald's to offer community-based children's programs in order to expand its fan base, enhance its legitimacy, and promote its products. McDonald's accesses the NFL logo and gains from the popularity of football. The NFL gets access to McDonald's marketing expertise and is well-positioned in its retail outlets. Professional sport leagues have also established various types of agreements with merchandising companies to sell licensed products such as T-shirts, videos, and equipment. As a result of these relationships the leagues were able to expand their revenues to over $6.6 billion in 1992, a fivefold increase since 1987. There have also been linkages between municipalities and sport team owners to construct sport and entertainment complexes in many major U.S. cities. Howard and Crompton (1995) suggest that in these situations a complementary situation exists where the municipality involved is able to bring assets such as a substantial land bank, low-cost capital, tax saving, and control over zoning and permits to the bargaining table. The private sector company in turn is able to provide access to capital, specialized management expertise, reduced liability risks, and reduced labor costs. The success of this type of arrangement is evidenced by the plethora of such facilities that are now being constructed (cf., Howard and Crompton, 1995).

Organizations in other sectors of the leisure industry have also employed strategic alliances as a part of their operating procedures. Gunn (1990), for example, calls for closer links between tourist and recreation organizations, suggesting that "there is sufficient overlap to foster cooperation and even alliance" (p. 1). He suggests that development and management in recreation and tourism require similar considerations of design and planning and that both are influenced by similar market preferences, promotional emphases, and resource foundations. Poon (1993, p. 278) supports this general argument and suggests that strategic alliances "abound in the travel and tourism industry." As examples, she notes that over 80% of the top regional airlines in the United States have code-sharing agreements with the major airline companies. She also points out that hotel chains such as Sandals and SuperClub have established alliances with U.S. travel agents, that car rental companies link with airlines with frequent flier programs, and that hotels often join together to gain economies of scale and scope from joint marketing programs.

What these examples demonstrate is that at many levels and in many of the organizations that make up the leisure industry strategic alliances are becoming an accepted way of operating. Although the majority of these links are between private sector organizations, alliances between private groups and public sector agencies can be found, as can agreements between privately operated companies and voluntary sector organizations and between different public agencies. Andereck (1997), for example, discusses how public sector agencies at both the state and federal level came together to form a partnership to facilitate tourism in the state of Arizona. Glover (1997) describes how municipalities in western Canada established a cost-sharing alliance to spread the financial burden associated with the provision of recreation, library, and cultural programs, and Swinnerton (1995) explains how national park authorities in England and Wales have developed partnerships with individual farmers and landowners in order to pursue their conservation mandate (see also LaPage, Vaske and Donnelly, 1995, for more examples of alliances in various areas of leisure).

Issues in Managing Strategic Alliances

Each of these alliances creates a new form of organization (e.g., a joint venture, or a new method of operating, a sourcing agreement, shared service provision) and each requires new managerial skills. The remainder of this section looks briefly at some of the organizational and managerial issues that arise when alliances are formed. It is difficult, if not impossible, to generalize across all alliances situations at every different level. Consequently the focus is primarily on those concerns faced by larger companies, as this is where the largest and most visible alliances are made. However, many of the principles outlined can also be applied to the less grandiose linkages that occur at other levels and between other types of leisure organizations.

In many ways the single most important function in managing alliances is what Yoshino and Rangan (1995) call "establishing the right tone." Essentially, these authors argue that, because an alliance brings two different organizations together, the issue of trust between a firm and its partner is vital to success. In the absence of trust the expectations of the alliance partner may well go unfulfilled, exacerbating suspicion and disappointment and leading to a vicious cycle of decline (Yoshino and Rangan, 1995). Faulkner adopts a similar line of argument and suggests that "positive partner attitudes" that foster mutual trust, commitment, and cultural sensitivity are vital to successful alliances. Mutual trust has been found to have a stabilizing effect on alliances: it helps avoid conflicts and facilitates tolerance of each partner's operating idiosyncrasies. Commitment to an alliance is essential at all levels but particularly between senior managers: Faulkner (1995) suggests that if top management shows commitment to an agreement it is likely to be effective; if they do not, the alliance is more likely to fail. Likewise cultural sensitivity is also a key to alliance success. All organizations operate with different cultures and these differences are quite likely to be accentuated when the organizations operate in different sectors—for example, a municipal leisure department and a voluntary provider of leisure services. Yoshino and Rangan (1995) suggest three aspects of culture that need attention in any alliance. First is the need to avoid the us-versus-them attitude that may prevail in these types of arrangements. The second is to avoid the "not invented here" syndrome, i.e., the suggestion that because the initiative was someone else's idea there is no need to buy into it. Third is a need to strike a balance between cooperating with a partner and competing with that same organization. Glover (1997) draws attention to a slight variant of this latter point in his study of alliances between municipalities: while the agencies concerned saw the benefits of cooperation, they also feared a loss of control over their programs to the municipalities with which they were in partnership.

In addition to these attitudinal changes, which the managers of leisure organizations will have to accept and work towards as their organizations become involved in more cooperative ventures, changes to certain organizational arrangements will also need to be made. A number of areas can be identified from the literature as important for attention. First, the appropriate type of alliance must be established. As noted earlier, alliances can be created in a variety of forms. Joint ventures such as those created when major cultural or sporting events are held involve the development of a new organization with its own board and governance mechanism. Such arrangements have entirely different implications and managerial requirements than the joint use agreements that may be established between schools and local municipalities about facility usage. Leisure managers need to understand and take account of these structural differences in establishing alliances. Second, authority for the alliance must be clearly identified, otherwise excessive time can be wasted in meetings about operational procedures. Dispute mechanisms must be put into place and there is a need for a congruency between the goals of the partners. This latter point requires careful monitoring, because goals which were originally congruent may diverge over time. Writers on alliances also argue that the most comfortable situations are those where there is a clearly established termination procedure in place.

Ultimately, the success of an alliance will depend upon each partner's willingness to meet its obligations. Thus, monitoring a partner's contribution is another managerial requirement of successful alliances. The monitoring that does take place will need to take account of the evolving nature of the alliance relationship and each partner's relative commitment to the agreement. Managers need to understand clearly what aspects of the alliance need to be monitored, break this down into identifiable elements, and track and measure changes in these elements. Strategic alliances also involve the flow, exchange, and processing of information between partners. Managers will need to pay particular attention to this as for obvious reasons it will influence the success of the venture. Free-flowing information can also create opportunities for organizational learning, and managers need to realize and exploit this aspect of the alliance relationship.

While there has been little attempt in the research on leisure organizations to monitor the dynamics of alliance management and operation, the few brief examples presented in this chapter serve to illustrate the fact that this form of organization is becoming more common within the leisure industry. As organizations in general continue to move from hierarchical-based to more network-based structures, the strategic alliance in all its variant forms will become a more popular structural design for the provision of leisure opportunities.

Conclusions

Traditional forms of leisure organization are changing and being replaced by new and sometimes hybrid forms. These changes are such that the lines of demarcation among the sectors are no longer as clear as they once were. Public sector organizations responsible for the delivery of leisure are forging stronger links with the corporate sector and are increasingly using market mechanisms for the provision of services. Voluntary leisure organizations are having to become more businesslike in their operations, and private sector companies in the leisure industry are making increased use of strategic alliances as a means of gaining competitive advantage.

These new forms of organization mean that managers in the leisure industry require new skills to handle these transitions. Such shifts also have ramifications for the training of leisure managers. Traditionally, this training was centered around acquiring the necessary skills to operate a particular facility or provide a particular service (Bacon, 1988). Many managers received what training they had on the job. More recently, the burgeoning of *leisure management* degree programs has led to the incorporation of management discourses into the academic preparation and professional practice of the leisure manager. However, the way in which these programs are taught is such that the courses offered often present only a cursory and uncritical introduction to topics that in the broader field are subject to sustained and critical analysis. As Whitson and Slack (1989, p. 28) point out, the teaching of leisure management cannot be reduced to a set of technical skills but must "be combined with an understanding of the social context of leisure, and the social issues that surround both market and public sector approaches to leisure service delivery."

As such, given the changes I have described and the concern that such shifts to emphasizing effectiveness and efficiency in service provision may erode the social benefits of leisure services (Clarke, 1994; Stormann, 1993), those individuals who teach leisure management must ensure that students are aware of the social, historical, and political context in which leisure is delivered, together with the impact this has on the type and availability of goods and services on offer. They must also ensure that students are challenged to think critically about the management practices in which they will be involved in these new forms of organization. This will require an engagement with the more critical debates over such practices as accounting (Richardson, 1987), human resources management (Townley, 1994), strategy (Whittington, 1993), and organizational studies (Alvesson and Willmott, 1996). Incorporating these type of approaches into our teaching will mean we move away from the courses and curricula which Cushman (1989, p. 252) describes as involving "tightly prescribed and highly prescriptive educational approaches" to ones which present a broader view of leisure as a phenomenon which shapes and is shaped by people's lived experience.

If the trends that I have identified in this chapter are correct, faculty teaching in leisure management programs will also have to change from their traditional focus on leisure provision as a service that is provided by government agencies (and to a lesser extent voluntary organizations) using traditional modes of public sector or voluntary sector provision. The emphasis on this narrowly defined approach is problematic, given the increased involvement of private sector organizations in leisure and the increasing adoption of private sector, market-driven delivery mechanisms by public and voluntary leisure organizations. There is, however, only a small body of research literature on these organizations and approaches from which course instructors can draw. Like our teaching efforts, the research initiatives of leisure management scholars have been primarily limited to the public sector (and to a lesser extent voluntary service providers). Companies like Disney, MGM, Thomas Cook, First Leisure and other major commercial providers of leisure services have received scant attention; so, too, have companies like Nike, Brunswick, Huffy, and Coleman, which provide leisure goods as opposed to services. Similar arguments could be made about research on the structure and operations of leisure organizations being likewise primarily confined to public and voluntary bodies. Since such traditional modes of delivery and the attendant structural and operational arrangements are being increasingly displaced, a continued focus on these topics in leisure management programs will, given the shifts I have described, be highly problematic for the training of future leisure managers. Leisure organizations in all sectors are becoming increasingly complex, and if leisure managers in the next millennium are going to manage these types of changes, then the content of leisure management courses must reflect the nature of the transitions that have been outlined in this chapter.

References

Alvesson, M., & Willmott, H. (1996). *Making sense of management: A critical introduction.* London, UK: Sage Publications, Ltd.

Amis, J., Slack, T., & Berrett, T. (1995). The structural antecedents of conflict in voluntary sport organizations. *Leisure Studies, 14,* 1–17.

Andereck, K. L. (1997). Case study of a multiagency partnership: Effectiveness and constraints. *Journal of Park and Recreation Administration, 15*(2), 44–60.

Bacon, W. (1988). *The professionalization of leisure management.* A paper presented at the Leisure Studies Association 2nd International Congress, Brighton, UK.

Becker, B. (1975). The pricing of educational-recreational facilities: An administrative dilemma. *Journal of Leisure Research, 7,* 86–94.

Berrett, T., Slack, T., & Whitson, D. (1993). Economics and the pricing of sport and leisure. *Journal of Sport Management, 7,* 199–215.

Clarke, A. (1994). Leisure and the new managerialism. In J. Clarke, A. Cochrane & E. McLaughlin (Eds.), *Managing social policy* (pp. 163–181). London, UK: Sage Publications, Ltd.

Coalter, F. (1995). Compulsory competitive tendering for sport and leisure: A lost opportunity. *Managing Leisure, 1,* 3–15.

Cook, L. (1996). An alternative approach to municipal golf course management: The private not-for-profit corporation. *Parks & Recreation, 31*(4), 74–81.

Cousens, L., & Slack, T. (1996). Emerging patterns of interorganizational relations: A network perspective of North American professional sport leagues. *European Journal for Sport Management, 3,* 48–69.

Crompton, J. L. (1984). Treating equals equally: Common abuses in pricing public services. *Parks & Recreation,* September, 67–71.

Crompton, J. L., & McGregor, B. P. (1994). Trends in the financing and staffing of local government parks and recreation services, 1964–65 and 1990–91. *Journal of Park and Recreation Administration, 12*(3), 19–37.

Cushman, G. (1989). Managing the New Zealand leisure and tourism boom: Implications for recreation management education. *Loisir et Société/Society and Leisure, 12,* 247–257.

Dockendorf, N. (1987). Sports fields—Pay and play. *Recreation Canada, 45*(1), 13–16.

Elvin, I. T. (1990). *Sport and physical recreation.* London, UK: Longman.

Faulkner, D. (1995). *International strategic alliances.* London, UK: McGraw-Hill.

Glover, T. D. (1997). *Forming an intermunicipal partnership to deliver public recreation: An embedded single case design.* Unpublished master's thesis, University of Alberta, Edmonton, Alberta.

Gorman, J., & Calhoun, K. (1994). *The name of the game.* New York, NY: John Wiley & Sons, Inc.

Government of Canada. (1985). *Improved program delivery: Health and sports. A study team report to the task force on program review.* Ottawa, Canada: Ministry of Supply and Services.

Grass, J. (1997). Indiana park combines past and future. *Parks & Recreation, 32*(1), 47–53.

Gratton, P., & Taylor, P. (1991). *Economics of leisure services.* London, UK: Longman.

Gunn, C. A. (1990). The new recreation-tourism alliance. *Journal of Park and Recreation Administration, 8*(1), 1–8.

Hadwen, H. (1994). The whole is greater . . . Partnerships in parks and recreation. *Recreation Canada, 52*(4), 23–24.

Henry, I. (1993). *The politics of leisure policy.* Houndmills, UK: Macmillan Publishing.

Henry, I., & Bramham, P. (1993). Leisure policy in Britain. In P. Bramham, I. Henry, H. Mommaas & H. van de Poel (Eds.), *Leisure policy in Europe* (pp. 101–128). Wallingford, UK: CAB International.

Houlihan, B. (1991). *The government and politics of sport.* London, UK: Routledge.

Howard, D. R., & Crompton, J. L. (1995). *Financing sport.* Morgantown, WV: Fitness Information Technology, Inc.

Hinings, C. R., & Greenwood, R. (1988). *The dynamics of strategic change.* Oxford, UK: Basil Blackwell.

Jung, B. (1993). Elements of leisure policy in postwar Poland. In P. Bramham, I. Henry, H. Mommaas & H. van de Poel (Eds.), *Leisure policy in Europe* (pp. 189–210). Wallingford, UK: CAB International.

Kikulis, L., Slack, T., & Hinings, C. R. (1992). Institutionally specific design archetypes: A framework for understanding change in national sport organizations. *International Review for the Sociology of Sport, 27,* 343–370.

Kikulis, L., Slack, T., & Hinings, C. R. (1995). Sector specific patterns of organizational design change. *Journal of Management Studies, 32,* 67–100.

Kimberly, J. (1987). The study of organizations: Towards a biographical perspective. In J. W. Lorsch (Ed.), *Handbook of organizational behavior.* Englewood Cliffs, NJ: Prentice-Hall.

LaPage, W. F., Vaske, J. J., & Donnelly, M. P. (1995). Case studies of partnerships in action. *Journal of Park and Recreation Administration, 13*(4), 61–74.

Larson, P. (1996, March 23). Privatization isn't a panacea. *Edmonton Journal,* p. F8.

Macintosh, D., & Whitson, D. (1990). *The game planners: Transforming Canada's sport system.* Montreal, Quebec: McGill-Queen's University Press.

Mattsson, L. G. (1988). Interaction strategies: A network approach. Working paper cited in D. Faulkner (1995), *International strategic alliances.* London, UK: McGraw-Hill.

McCarville, R. E., & Smale, B. J. A. (1991). Involvement in pricing by municipal recreation agencies. *Journal of Applied Recreation Research, 16,* 200–219.

Mills, J. R. (1994). Partnerships providing service. *Parks & Recreation, 29*(5), 32–34.

Mintzberg, H. (1979). *The structuring of organizations.* Englewood Cliffs, NJ: Prentice-Hall.

Nahrstedt, W. (1993). Leisure policy in Germany. In P. Bramham, I. Henry, H. Mommaas & H. van de Poel (Eds.), *Leisure policy in Europe* (pp. 129–148). Wallingford, UK: CAB International.

Olson, H.-E. (1993). Leisure policy in Sweden. In P. Bramham, I. Henry, H. Mommaas & H. van de Poel (Eds.), *Leisure policy in Europe* (pp. 71–100). Wallingford, UK: CAB International.

Poon, A. (1993). *Tourism, technology and competitive strategies.* Wallingford, UK: CAB International.

Richardson, A. (1987). Accounting as a legitimating institution. *Accounting, Organizations, and Society, 8,* 341–356.

Robinson, A. (1994, April 4). Ball groups to run fields. *Saskatoon Star Phoenix,* p. A3.

Schultz, J. H., McAvoy, L. H., & Dustin, D. L. (1988). What are we in business for? *Parks & Recreation, 23*(1), 52–54.

Searle, M. S., & Brayley, R. E. (1993). *Leisure services in Canada.* State College, PA: Venture Publishing, Inc.

Sessoms, H. D., & Henderson, K. A. (1994). *Introduction to leisure services* (7th ed.). State College, PA: Venture Publishing, Inc.

Slack, T., & Hinings, C. R. (1992). Understanding change in national sport organizations: An integration of theoretical perspectives. *Journal of Sport Management, 6,* 114–132

Stormann, W. F. (1993). The recreation profession, capital, and democracy. *Leisure Sciences, 15,* 49–66.

Swinnerton, G. S. (1995). Conservation through partnership: Landscape management within national parks in England and Wales. *Journal of Park and Recreation Administration, 13*(4), 47–60.

Townley, B. (1994). *Reframing human resources management: Power, ethics, and the subject at work.* London, UK: Sage Publications, Ltd.

Van de Poel, H. (1993). Leisure policy in the Netherlands. In P. Bramham, I. Henry, H. Mommaas & H. van de Poel (Eds.), *Leisure policy in Europe* (pp. 41–70). Wallingford, UK: CAB International.

Walsh, K. (1995). *Public service and market mechanisms.* Houndmills, UK: Macmillan Publishing.

Whitson, D. J., & Slack, T. (1989). Deconstructing the discourse of leisure management. *Loisir et Société/Society and Leisure, 12,* 19–34.

Whittington, R. (1993). *What is strategy and does it matter?* London, UK: Routledge.

Yoshino, M. Y., & Rangan, U. S. (1995). *Strategic alliances: An entrepreneurial approach to globalization.* Boston, MA: Harvard Business School Press.

Marketing Public Leisure Services

Ron McCarville
University of Waterloo

Marketing. Rarely does one word generate such debate among leisure professionals and academics. Advocates tout marketing as a remedy for many of the ills that face providers and participants alike, while opponents denounce it as a calamity for public leisure delivery systems. I suggest in this chapter that such ambivalence arises from general confusion over the nature and function of marketing effort. This chapter seeks to reduce this confusion by defining and reviewing the marketing process. It characterizes marketing as a series of interrelated activities that focus on the client. The ultimate goal of this process is to discover an optimal fit between client preferences and agency capabilities, then to mobilize resources accordingly.

In an early definition, Kotler (1975) suggested that marketing is the "design, implementation, and control of programs seeking to increase the acceptability of a[n] . . . idea or practice in a target group(s)" (p. 79). The private sector was the first to embrace the notion of marketing but the public, private, and not-for-profit sectors have come to recognize the potential of mar-

keting efforts. All three sectors now use selected marketing techniques to enhance service delivery.

This discussion, however, displays a distinct public sector bias. Though the source material often originates with private sector sources, the focus here is on public sector issues and concerns. I have taken this approach because the marketing concept has proven most problematic for public sector leisure providers. For example, the public sector marketing literature is still in its relative infancy. As a result, confusion often dominates discussions and applications of public sector marketing. Although many public sector practitioners report involvement in marketing activity, basic marketing principles are often absent from current programming efforts in North America (Havitz and Spigner, 1993). Further, public sector marketers are faced with many problems unique to that sector. For example, notions of equity, which dominate public sector decision making, complicate the marketing process (Crompton and Lamb, 1986). This public sector bias notwithstanding, the insights offered here should be useful to marketers in all three sectors.

The Role of Marketing

Proponents have long been advocating the application of marketing principles to the delivery of leisure services (Crompton and Lamb, 1986). They suggest that failure to implement marketing principles may impair leisure agencies' ability to serve their communities. As Howard and Crompton (1980) suggest in their early text:

> A recreation and park agency's failure often can be traced to its neglect of the basic wants and desires of its potential consumers. Indeed, it may be argued that the "tax revolt" of the late 1970s indicated that government had failed to implement the marketing concept. (p. 309)

Given marketing's private sector roots, however, there is often considerable ambivalence regarding its application in the public and not-for-profit sectors (Mintz, 1989). Several commentators have condemned marketing and other private sector ideas as practices best ignored by the public sector (Johnson and McLean, 1996). Much of this condemnation seems to arise from the assumption that private sector methods subvert the traditional role of the public sector. Even terminology used by the private sector may be regarded as suspect. In a 1996 address, author and social critic John Ralston Saul suggested that the first necessary step "to regaining free speech is for people to protest whenever bureaucrats use business words such as clients or customer services in referring to citizens" (Simone, 1996, p. A3). Jacobs (1994) discouraged public sector acceptance of private sector methods, believing they are inconsistent with the public good. Schultz, McAvoy, and Dustin (1988) agree with this assessment, asking, as public sector decision makers adopt private sector–based marketing principles, "Who will look out for the interests of racial and ethnic minorities, single-parent families, immigrants, and the urban and rural poor? . . . Who will sustain the fight for the rights of society's underprivileged" (p. 53).

Though marketing seems to represent an easy target for skepticism, is it deserving of this enmity? Is it indeed an adversary to those who hope to serve the community? Havitz (1988) suggests that criticism of marketing may result from confusion between marketing and the more problematic notion of commercialism. Commercialism has been labeled a process of exploitation because it seeks to expropriate the means through which leisure is provided (Butsch, 1990). Butsch suggested that, once a provider controls these means, that same provider also controls the experience. Through commercialization, "that part of our lived experience supposed to be free of domination is transformed through capitalist development" (Butsch, 1990, p. 8) to such an extent that participants may lose control over their own leisure experiences. The prospect of such loss is troubling for public sector leisure providers (Schultz et al., 1988).

Is marketing synonymous with commercialism? Does marketing effort represent value systems that are inconsistent with those of the public sector caregiver? Like Havitz (1988) and others (Crompton, 1985; Crompton and Lamb, 1986), I make a clear distinction between commercialism and marketing effort. I characterize marketing as little more than a process for mobilizing resources. Indeed, it differs little in intent from many traditional planning and programming processes (Bannon, 1976). As such, marketing tools seem appropriate for use within the public and not-for-profit sectors. I suggest that marketing's contribution is one of strategic flexibility. Its tenets focus on mobilizing resources to meet the demands of specific groups within the community. As a result, marketing effort may be used to serve the larger community. It might best be considered as another stage in the natural evolution of traditional planning and programming effort. To ignore or revile the advantages offered by the marketing process is perhaps to throw the proverbial baby out the with the equally proverbial bath water.

Review of Basic Marketing Concepts

Five tenets guide modern marketing effort. They are:

1. an evolving marketing philosophy;
2. a circular planning process which begins and ends with the client;
3. an emphasis on client retention;
4. segmentation; and
5. the marketing mix.

These elements are now being used to enhance a variety of public sector initiatives including social policy and planning, social marketing (Kotler and Roberto, 1989), and health education (Lefebvre, 1992), as well as leisure programming (Crompton and Lamb, 1986). Each tenet is discussed here in terms of its contribution to the delivery of leisure services.

Parenthetically, and with deference to opposition to terminology arising from business, I often use the terms *client* or the more general *consumer* when referring to those to whom leisure providers direct their attentions. Both these terms originate in the world of business and may be rendered suspect as a result. In defense of the term *client, Webster's Collegiate Dictionary* refers to a client as one who is "under the protection of another." This same source suggests that a consumer is one who uses, who absorbs. Like marketing itself, these terms seem entirely appropriate in the context of public sector leisure services and, like the notion of marketing, might be accepted into the lexicon of public and not-for-profit sector marketers.

Marketing Philosophy

Marketing is comprised of a set of tools or activities applied within a coherent procedural framework (Lefebvre, 1992). As discussed later in this chapter, these tools include price, product development, promotion, and distribution (Kotler, 1975). Like all tools and procedures, however, the marketing process must be applied using an overriding philosophy. This philosophy offers a way of thinking about and acting toward the client (Crompton and Lamb, 1986).

The philosophy behind marketing activity has proven problematic over the years. In its earliest stages, marketing focused on the needs of the producer. This general approach is typically referred to as a product orientation. The preferences of the client were largely considered as secondary to those of the marketer. This period is probably best exemplified by a statement attributed to Henry Ford. He was once asked about the selection of colors in which he planned to offer his Model T automobile. He is said to have stated, "My customers can have any color they like, as long as it's black." Apparently, black paint dried more quickly than did other colors, thereby accelerating the production process. In deference to that process, black was adopted regardless of the wishes of the potential buyer. This comment has been widely interpreted to mean that Mr. Ford, an icon of modern business, placed the needs of production over the wishes of the client. This emphasis on production dominated marketing thought early in the twentieth century.

Marketing philosophy began to change during the 1920s, when supply began to exceed demand (Crompton and Lamb, 1986). Producers recognized the need to stimulate demand. For the first time resources were devoted to promotional and sales efforts. This trend was exacerbated by conditions following the Second World War. At war's end, industries that had been expanded to fulfill the wartime demand were converted to peacetime production. Though demand soared as soldiers returned home, supply soon began to exceed demand. It became evident that industry was able to provide more products than consumers were willing to purchase. As a result, marketing effort entered a new phase. It developed a *selling orientation*. This new focus was simply a variant of the old product orientation which had served industry so well. Marketers knew their products, they believed in their products, and they were determined to convince potential consumers to purchase these products. The role of the advertiser was paramount during this period.

This era was often characterized by questionable practice. Corporate advertisers maintained a steady stream of messages designed to cajole client groups into purchasing their products. Schor (1991) reports that women received particular attention during this period:

> Businesses subjected women to a barrage of advertising and social pressure, in order to sell more products. . . . They helped spread the word that a woman who did not purchase the growing array of consumer goods was jeopardizing her family, and missing out on the best life had to offer. (p. 97)

In *The Image Makers,* William Meyers reported that advertisers often:

> played fast and loose with the public. They put marbles in a bowl of soup so the few vegetables it contained would float to the top . . . it's no wonder that by the 1970s advertising executives regularly appeared at the bottom of the public's "most respected profession" list—below insurance salesmen and pawnshop proprietors. (Meyers, 1984, pp. 12–13)

Considerable residue from this period remains today, to such an extent that many fear that a growing acceptance of marketing principles will lead to the victimization of client groups (Jacobs, 1994; Schultz et al., 1988).

Fortunately, widespread dissatisfaction with this *selling* approach led marketers to adopt a more client-centered orientation. In his classic article, "Marketing Myopia," Levitt (1988) made a clear distinction between a selling and a more contemporary marketing perspective. He indicated that:

> selling focuses on the needs of the seller, [whereas] marketing [focuses] on the needs of the buyer. Selling is preoccupied with the seller's needs to convert his

product into cash; marketing with the idea of satisfying the needs of the customer. (p. 10)

Levitt rejected a focus on selling, contending that such efforts are more concerned with tricks and techniques than with marketing.

Like Levitt, Kotler (1983) viewed marketing as a client-centered activity. He believed that the marketer's philosophy must be one of client satisfaction. "Marketing . . . activity is directed at satisfying needs and wants through exchange processes" (Kotler, 1983, p. 6). Drucker (1974) agreed, suggesting that the goal of marketing is to make selling superfluous. Drucker went on to state that the notions of selling and marketing are antithetical. These views represent a client orientation, suggesting that marketing initiatives be assessed in terms of their focus as well as their results. The key question becomes, What has been the focus of this effort? If emphasis has been placed on developing a product in isolation of client preferences, then a product orientation has dominated. If the emphasis has been placed on convincing clients of the merits of a product without first discovering their desires, then a selling approach has been used. Current thinking holds suspect any efforts in which client preferences have been relegated to subordinate status (Lefebvre, 1992).

Philosophy alone is of little importance when considered in isolation. Subsequent planning processes must also focus on the client. Marketing has responded to this requirement by offering a series of planning steps. Although there is considerable debate over the number of steps which comprise market planning, there is general agreement that marketing is a circular set of activities which begin and end with the client (Novelli, 1984).

Market Planning

Marketing effort demands coordination and planning. The first challenge is that of establishing a *strategic context* (Payne, 1993). This context is largely a product of the provider's mission and corporate goals. Private sector goals typically focus on the need to generate adequate profits, while the not-for-profit and public sectors are more concerned with service and resource allocation.

There seems to be growing interest in operationalizing mission and goal statements in terms of *guiding principles*. These principles typically reflect the nature and quality of services the provider hopes to offer. As Wyckoff (1992) suggests, these principles should suggest "how good" the provider plans to become as well as how the provider plans to go about fulfilling that

mandate. For example, Disney's theme parks are guided by about a dozen principles, including safety, courtesy, show, efficiency, management support, cleanliness, assertive friendliness (anticipation of clients' requests), product knowledge (interpreted as mission of agency), and training. Note how these principles outline those things the corporation values as well as how it plans to go about addressing these priorities. All programs, policies, procedures, and responsibility assignments are based on these principles. Though all private and public sector organizations need not adopt the Disney model, the notion of guiding principles provides a useful strategic tool for any service provider. Principles that might be adopted in a leisure context might include convenience, value, safety, opportunity, choice, and satisfaction. These principles can then be used to guide subsequent decision making.

The next stage is one of deciding how best to meet client demands. This stage is known by many other names, ranging from the opportunity assessment to the analysis stage (Novelli, 1984). Payne (1993) labels this the *situation review*. Regardless of its label, this step typically focuses on potential clients while considering provider capabilities within the context offered by the general marketplace or community setting. It requires that the agency assess its own capability to offer relevant products or benefit packages to relevant client groups. It may assess its own current program offerings and review past successes and failures during this stage. It should establish the position of the provider within the context offered by competitors and partners and public preference. The situation review demands that the provider search for competitors (those promoting competing ideas or products), potential partners, and other relevant conditions that exist outside the control of the agency. Key external bodies include regulatory bodies or even special interest groups that might oppose or support various programming initiatives.

This process helps the provider discover product offerings that best appeal to specific client groups while building on the provider's own strengths. It should identify products that are defensible against competitive or counterproductive forces and the effects of foreseeable occurrences or social conditions. For example, there is now considerable interest in providing outreach leisure programs for "at-risk" youth groups (Witt and Crompton, 1996). These programs are designed primarily to reduce potentially destructive behavior among group members. Program planners must address the issues of appeal (understand the desires of the client group), and competitive social forces (antecedent and contextual variables that influence behavior patterns) (Allen, Stevens and Harwell, 1996). A situation review assesses the nature and extent of these forces. Once this review has been completed, marketing strategy can be established.

The next step is one of *strategy formulation* (Payne, 1993). This step is comprised of objective-setting activities and the development of alternative options. The challenge is one of thinking in terms of solutions rather than programs for the target market (Lovelock, 1996). Novelli (1984) suggests that, during this stage, a "blueprint for action" is developed. Each alternative is evaluated in terms of a larger management framework. This framework is concerned with administrative issues like scheduling, financial analyses, and conformance issues (conformance refers to the provider's ability to offer the option given projected resource levels). The blueprint helps the marketer make resource allocation decisions throughout the duration of the process (Novelli, 1984). Optimal strategies must balance provider capabilities with client preferences and product characteristics.

When provider resources are limited, this step may be characterized by exploration of new partnerships. For example, in an effort to "reinvent municipal recreation programming," the Waco, Texas, Leisure Services Department sought partners within the larger community to extend and improve its own capabilities. Having identified several key partners (e.g., citizens, school authorities) during its strategy discussions, it began to foster more formal relationships with those partners. The media was one such partner, so it began to "incorporate media representatives on all program boards" (Gavlik, 1995, p. 115). It also identified the community at large as a potential partner, so it arranged and designed new initiatives accordingly. Resulting adopt-a-trail programs promoted community involvement in facility design and maintenance. Authorities then focused on cooperative arrangements with the local school board. Each of these strategic arrangements was designed to extend the limited resource levels available to the agency.

The next stage focuses on *resource allocation and monitoring*. Kotler and Roberto (1989) have referred to this stage as one of defense. The marketing process is dynamic, so there is a need for ongoing strategic modification. Modification requires evaluation, so this stage may be characterized by extensive information gathering. Long-standing program evaluation literature suggests that client reaction is typically monitored by consulting the client, staff members who interact with the client (Schneider, 1988), confederates like *phantom shoppers* (Kuenzli, 1991), and other service providers (Sewell and Brown, 1990).

Each group offers its own distinct contribution to program evaluation. For example, clients are perhaps the best source for information on the success of programs or their component parts (Parasuraman, 1986). Their ideas may be collected through any variety of surveys, focus groups, or any other vehicle that gathers their views on actual or potential product offerings. Staff members are also an important source of information. Schneider (1988) suggests that employees may be even more important to evaluation than clients. "Each employee has information from *hundreds* of consumers while each consumer has only his or her experiences. . . . My point is that employees are a potential *marvelous* source of critical information" (p. 357). Phantom shoppers also aid in the evaluation process by identifying gaps in service delivery. Typically, these shoppers are used to evaluate staff performance in terms of existing service standards (Kuenzli, 1991). They anonymously consume selected services while evaluating staff response to their requests. They might visit programs or facilities, requesting assistance in one instance, taking part in another, requesting a refund in another. During each encounter they measure staff response against standards established by the organization. This technique is now used widely by retail organizations and may be useful in public and not-for-profit settings.

Finally, agency staff might use other providers to help evaluate their own service offerings. This process, known as benchmarking, dictates that industry leaders' procedures be used as standards against which a comparable agency's own services are compared. Sewell and Brown (1990) remind us that benchmarking efforts need not rely on leaders in a single industry for insight. "Leaders" need only face the same service conditions as those of the benchmarker. To facilitate the selection of leaders from diverse service industries, Lovelock (1996) suggests that service providers might be classified, not by sector, but by variables like the level of service customization possible, the type of relationship that exists between the provider and the client (membership versus other), degree of client or staff contact, and so on. Once this classification has been carried out, a leisure agency may discover that it can gather as much insight from a retail chain or theme park as from another leisure agency.

This monitoring function establishes the circular nature of the marketing process. Marketing begins and ends with efforts to understand the demands of the client as well as that client's reaction to provider initiatives. The evaluative process assists marketers both in understanding the target group and the relative success of product offerings. "Constant tinkering" should result from the monitoring process (Kotler and Roberto, 1989).

Client Retention or Loyalty

The ultimate goal of market planning is that of customer retention or loyalty. As Levitt (1983) suggested, "In marketing . . . the object is to get and keep a customer" (p. 130). In an early paper on loyalty, Buchanan (1985) suggested that loyalty is bound up in notions of commitment, dedication, devotion, and attachment. Each of these notions implies a consistent willingness to embrace one activity (and/or provider) over alternative options. Though traditional indicators had typically relied on behavioral evidence when defining loyalty, Buchanan (1985) conceptualized commitment as a function of:

1. consistent behavior,
2. affective attachment, and
3. involvement in related activities.

Subsequent research has largely supported Buchanan's assumptions. For example, participation alone represents an insufficient indicator of interest in, or support for, a program or provider (Selin, Howard, Udd and Cable, 1988). Backman and Crompton (1991) report that program participants may frequent a given program without attaching any emotional commitment to that program. They termed this as *spurious loyalty,* suggesting that these participants are easily dislodged from such programming initiatives.

All service providers are distressed over *lost* clients: those individuals who once participated in program offerings but have since discontinued that participation (Backman and Crompton, 1991). For the private sector, lost clients represent lost profit. Reichheld (1996) estimates that such loss (which he calls disloyalty) stunts corporate performance by 25% to 50%. He suggests, for example, that loyal clients reduce acquisition costs because fewer clients need to be enticed into programs. Further, loyalty increases base profits because loyal clients tend to increase involvement over time. Finally, positive word-of-mouth communications seem to increase with loyalty. Consequently, loyal clients are more likely to attract fledgling program participants.

Each of these benefits applies to some extent to both the not-for-profit and public sectors. Though they are not as concerned with profit as are their private sector counterparts, they too benefit from loyal clients (Backman and Crompton, 1991). For both sectors, client loss or displacement represents failure to provide for the wants expressed by user groups. Both seek retention because it ensures that participants will continue to benefit from their involvement in leisure activities. Clearly, all service providers prefer loyal clients.

Unfortunately, Backman and Crompton (1991) note impending problems with client retention in the public sector if programs are not changed to better serve various client groups. One important service issue seems that of service failures. Hart, Heskett, and Sasser (1990) suggested that retention often suffers when clients are dissatisfied with some aspect of a service encounter. Known as service failures, such encounters may result in increased complaint behavior, lost goodwill, and reduced customer loyalty (Bearden and Oliver, 1985). Conversely, failures that are resolved to the satisfaction of the client may result in client loyalty and positive word-of-mouth communication (Goodwin and Ross, 1992). Indeed, "'secondary satisfaction' arising from complaint handling may build even stronger loyalties than satisfaction with the initial service" (Goodwin and Ross, 1992, p. 150). The service literature suggests that recovery efforts must include an apology, prompt problem resolution, and "symbolic atonement" (discounts, coupons, upgrades, etc.) as a tangible sign of provider contrition (Colenutt and McCarville, 1994; Goodwin and Ross, 1992).

Segmentation

Discussions of behavioral and emotional variation imply that there is no one group that might be designated as "the public." Within any group, there exist many subgroups. Members of each subgroup display unique interests, talents, and behavior patterns. As a result, marketing eschews the whole in favor of unique groups or *target markets* (Levitt, 1988). Segmentation, the classification of clients with different characteristics or behaviors, represents a cornerstone of marketing effort (Kotler, McDougall and Armstrong, 1988). It recognizes that not all clients are interested in a given product or initiative and that agency resources to seek out potential participants are limited. As a result, segmentation divides or partitions potential clients into identifiable groups whose members share similar characteristics and exhibit common behaviors (Weinstein, 1987). In this way, agency efforts can be directed to the distinct preferences of relevant target groups.

Within the private sector, selection is typically guided by three criteria. The first is responsiveness: will the segment's members respond to the marketer's initiatives? The second is accessibility: can the segment's members be separated from the general population? The last criterion is substantiality: is the segment of sufficient size? Though group size naturally differs from one segment to the next, adequate numbers seem a prerequisite for all programming efforts (Payne, 1993). Typically only those segments that fulfill the conditions imposed by these criteria are targeted.

The public sector marketer may be faced with a segmentation issue not encountered by the traditional private sector marketer. Segments targeted by the public sector marketer often fail the test of responsiveness (Bloom and Novelli, 1981). Whereas those believed most responsive generally receive preferential treatment from the private sector marketer, clients targeted by the public sector may be profoundly unresponsive. Efforts to encourage voting among nonvoters or to encourage physical activity among sedentary subgroups are typical of public sector efforts to appeal to nonresponsive client groups.

Much of the existing leisure research highlights the diversity among the many potential user groups within the community. Such diversity may be described in geographic, cultural, sociodemographic, behavioral, and/or psychographic terms. The nature of most of these descriptors is self-evident. Geographic, cultural, socioeconomic, and behavioral variables describe potential clients in terms of easily measurable life conditions like location, race, gender, age, income, social class, or participation patterns (Floyd and Gramann, 1993; Floyd, Shinew, McGuire and Noe, 1994; Raymore, Godbey and Crawford, 1994).

These descriptors are useful to the leisure marketer. Descriptors like age or gender may act as surrogates for a variety of important life conditions which influence leisure participation (Henderson, 1994). For example, age may influence activity preferences. In some cases, younger participants prefer more active programming opportunities (Donnelly, Vaske, DeRuiter and King, 1996). Gender expectations may also be a factor in determining activity patterns (Henderson, 1994). Raymore et al. (1994) found that female high-school students may report lower self-esteem and more constraints than do their male counterparts. This pattern seems to extend into adulthood. McCarville and Smale (1993) found that the number of reported constraints to leisure were related to gender (women reported more constraints than did men). They also reported that constraints were negatively related to income. In other words, the greater the individual's income, the fewer the number of reported leisure constraints. Such descriptors speak to the various difficulties faced by different target groups as they pursue leisure opportunities (see Jackson and Scott, chapter 18 in this volume). All can be used by the marketer to ameliorate these difficulties.

Although sociodemographic descriptors offer some insight to marketers, they may fail to capture the specific needs and perceptions of these many subgroups.

They might best be used in conjunction with other, perhaps more profound, indicators (Howard and Sheth, 1988). The consumer behavior literature has long held that psychographic indicators like participants' motives and preferences (Howard and Sheth, 1988) will enhance segmentation efforts. Fortunately, leisure researchers have traditionally been interested in these issues. They have segmented client groups in terms of motives and experience (Hollenhorst, Schuett, Olson and Chavez, 1995), constraint patterns (Jackson, 1993), preferences (Sylvia, Sallee and Berry, 1995), involvement profiles (Havitz, Dimanche and Bogle, 1994), their propensity to adopt or discontinue activities over the life course (Jackson and Dunn, 1988; Searle, Mactavish and Brayley, 1993), and benefits sought through participation (Backman, 1994). For example, Backman (1994) reports that the types of benefits sought helped determine eventual site selection of beachgoers in Texas.

This work offers considerable insight to the leisure marketer. It suggests that leisure participants pursue complex, shifting, benefit structures. These benefit structures will vary from one group to the next, and from one point in time to the next (Donnelly et al., 1996). As a result, the marketer must continually discover group members' preferences, behaviors surrounding key consumption decisions, and any other information that might assist with subsequent programming efforts. Programming success is largely a function of the accuracy with which these preferences can be determined.

The Marketing Mix

Marketing efforts focus on the marketing mix. The marketing mix represents the strategic and tactical application of basic marketing principles. The mix, which forms the basis of most activity called marketing, is remarkable both for its simplicity and its robust nature. It offers a basic framework to aid planners in mobilizing agency resources. The marketing mix was originally made up of twelve elements, ranging from personal selling to packaging (Borden, 1969). Since its inception however, it has typically been reduced to four elements known as the four Ps:

1. product;
2. price;
3. promotion; and
4. place or distribution.

Each element is reviewed briefly here. This discussion is intended only to introduce the concept of the mix and its relevance to the marketing process. More complete discussion of the mix is provided later in this chapter.

According to Kotler et al. (1988, p. 208), *product* is generally defined as "anything that can be offered to a market for attention, acquisition, use or consumption that might satisfy a want or a need." These authors suggested that a product possesses three distinct levels. The first is the core product: it represents that which the client seeks from the leisure experience. Though the nature of this search is beyond the scope of this chapter, the literature suggests generally that motivation to participate in leisure is tied to a remarkable array of individual and collective goals (see Iso-Ahola, chapter 3, and Mannell, chapter 14 in this volume). The next product level is the actual product: it represents that which the marketer provides the client. The actual product may take the form of information, programming efforts, or other forms of client assistance.

Inevitably, gaps exist between the product sought by the adopter and that which is provided by the marketer. For example, Scott (1993) suggested that many traditional product characteristics actually inhibit participation. Traditional programs require a commitment of time and energy that client groups may be unable to devote to leisure activity. Participation levels are diminished as a result, so a third product level, called the augmented product, may prove a critical indicator of program success. It represents any additional services and benefits designed to help the client overcome the constraints posed by many traditional programs. Augmentations are intended to aid the client both to consume and to enjoy the actual product.

Consider a golf course program. It offers an obvious blend of core, actual, and augmented products. In terms of a core product, like any leisure activity, golf offers a context for personal expression. It may be used by the participant to pursue a wide variety of personally relevant goals, ranging from enhanced life satisfaction to increased physical and emotional well-being. The actual product is little more than a green space equipped with small flags, sand pits, and water holes. It is the strategic application of the product augmentation which brings a golf course to life for the typical user. Instructions are made available for the neophyte, golf carts for the sedentary, concessions for the hungry, and so on.

Though the role of product augmentations has received little attention in the leisure programming literature, they offer considerable potential for leisure marketers. Augmentations enable clients to virtually customize each leisure encounter to their own specifications. Participants may choose among available augmentations so that individual wants and concerns

might be addressed. Further, augmentations offer a pricing option for public sector marketers. In order to maintain their service ethic, public sector providers may continue to offer basic programs at little or no cost. However, they may charge varying rates for many of these augmentations. Those unable or unwilling to pay related fees may continue to enjoy the basic program at traditional fee levels. Those who wish to enjoy more personalized service levels can pay for that option (thereby helping subsidize more price-sensitive participants).

A *price* is any cost an individual must forego in order to enjoy a product (McCloskey, 1982). Each sector uses price in a way that best meets its particular objectives. In the private sector, prices are used to gauge demand and to meet the cost of fulfilling this demand. Its price levels are generally a function of (Nylen, 1990):

1. cost of service provision,
2. value to the participant, and
3. competitive forces.

The reader might reflect on the difficulty in determining notions of value or of quantifying the notion of "competitive forces." Not surprisingly, several authors have commented on the almost "alchemical" process that generates eventual price levels.

In the public sector, prices have traditionally been used to pursue social goals like income redistribution (Lineberry, 1977). Given the service mandate which dominates the public sector, public pricing initiatives may reflect nonmonetary goals (resource redistribution) as well as those of increasing efficiency or altering demand patterns, and generating revenue (Rosenthal, Loomis and Peterson, 1984). Consequently, public sector price levels may prove even more difficult to establish than their private sector counterparts.

The issue of fees has proven particularly divisive in the public sector. Some commentators have expressed concern that the exclusionary nature of fees is inconsistent with the service ethic which dominates public sector programming (Goodale, 1985; Manning, Callinan, Echelberger, Koenemann and McEwan, 1984). Others are equally certain that fees are an essential component of any program which hopes to serve the community. Ellerbrock (1982) suggested that fees be charged and resulting revenues could be used to subsidize and protect the underprivileged. In a relatively early statement he warned that, "If we have the goal of providing free recreation to all citizens, then we are destined for failure and frustration" (p. 59). He then offered pricing as a means to better serve those with financial need. He reported that "charging those who can afford recreation allows subsidization of a greater number of people who cannot. Striving to subsidize everyone hinders the opportunities for those who are poor" (p. 59).

Promotion is one of the most important elements of the marketing mix. Promotional efforts are intended to convey the client through the stages of the decision-making process. These stages include awareness, interest, evaluation, and trial (Assael, 1984). Promotion is therefore intended to make consumers aware of a product leading to positive attitudes, knowledge, attention, and finally to behavior. As such, promotion deals largely with persuasive communication (Havitz and Crompton, 1990). The promotional challenge is often characterized as one of communicating benefit. The importance of benefit "is characterized by Leo McGinneva's famous clarification about why people buy quarter-inch drill bits: 'they don't want quarter-inch bits. They want quarter-inch holes'" (Levitt, 1983, p. 128).

However, the communication of benefit seems to address only half the problem confronting the potential client. Levitt (1983) suggested that selection from among choices is often an exercise in risk reduction as much as it is a search for benefit. Indeed, fear of mispurchase may act as a primary motivator in many consumption decisions (Assael, 1984). Messages that offer benefits while suggesting reduced risks represent a potent combination for many clients. As a result, the solutions offered by enhanced benefits and reduced risks form the basis for effective promotional campaigns.

The final *P* refers to *place* or distribution. Distribution, the process of presenting products to clients (Kotler et al., 1988), is the least studied of the elements within the marketing mix (Ritchie, 1996). Relatively few distribution-based studies are reported in the marketing, tourism, or leisure literatures. However, a few observations are possible. The traditional marketing literature views distribution as a web that emanates from the producer's shop floor. This literature suggests that, like all webs, this structure demands uniformity of purpose and precise execution if it is to succeed (Deming, 1986). The public sector often responds to these demands by adopting the role of facilitator or assuming primary responsibility for the provision of leisure services to its citizens. Resulting distribution decisions have been based on traditional questions of cooperative arrangements, interagency responsibility, distribution intensity, facility or outlet allocation, and timing (Crompton and Lamb, 1986). However, growing fiscal constraints have stimulated interest in moving beyond the traditional model, by enlarging the role of potential partners in the delivery of leisure services (Pedlar, Dupuis and Gilbert, 1996).

This trend is evident in federal agencies like the USDA Forest Service (Selin and Chavez, 1993) as well as in municipal government agencies (Weissinger and Murphy, 1993).

More recently, those who plan the distribution of services have focused on the act of presenting the service to the client. This act, often called the *moment of truth,* demands that service providers "manage the evidence" in the physical environment. These factors, discussed in more detail later in the chapter, may be *ambient* (like noise or cleanliness), *design related* (like layout and comfort), and *social* (arising from other clients and from staff) (Berry and Parasuraman, 1991). Together they form the *container* in which leisure is more or less likely to occur.

Public Sector Response to Marketing

The application of private sector marketing principles to the pursuit of social concerns has often created an uneasy union (Mintz, 1989). Confusion and even hostility continue to surround the issue of marketing in the public sector. As a result, many public sector decision makers may treat marketing techniques with considerable misgiving. Marketing principles may be rejected as a result of the values they represent. For example, Hemingway (1996) views the process through which leisure might be "marketed and sold as any other commodity" (p. 34) as inherently detrimental to the leisure experience and, ultimately, to the participant. The choice of the words *sold* and *commodity* suggests that, in this instance, marketing is again being confused with commercialism. The notion of marketing is rejected as a result. Jacobs (1994) was even more critical of the application of marketing by public sector decision makers. She suggested that the public sector is inevitably corrupted when it adopts principles used by the private sector. In justifying this assessment, Jacobs divided the world into two basic moral systems. These systems are adopted by those she terms *merchants* and *guardians*. Public agencies like municipal park and recreation departments fall under the guardian designation. She suggested that both groups are corrupted when they adopt the moral codes and values of the other. As a result, public sector agencies that undertake marketing activities risk losing touch with the values unique to caregivers. By way of example, Jacobs referred to hypothetical police officers who might be tempted to assign various fines because of the resources they help accumulate. In such a case, the purposes of the police officers are subverted. Their goal becomes one of revenue generation rather than the maintenance of social order. Jacobs went to considerable length to establish the inevitability of this corruption. In her view, participants in either system must be wary of the moral codes used by the other and adopt them only at their peril.

Antipathy is also generated by widespread misapplication of marketing tools. Over a decade age, Crompton (1985) warned that early marketing efforts were likely to suffer from confusion and inexperienced implementation. Events have largely supported this assumption. It seems that many agencies may be selectively introducing market-based initiatives (like fee programs) without applying other necessary marketing principles. For example, in a regional survey in Canada, McCarville and Smale (1991) found that many public leisure providers, while reporting they were using marketing techniques in their day-to-day operation, failed to apply even rudimentary marketing principles. Few providers adapted programs or fee initiatives in order to respond to the needs of different user groups. In a national study in the United States, Havitz and Spigner (1993) found public agencies rarely segmented their communities according to relevant criteria like income, nor did these agencies offer price discounts to low-income residents or coordinate efforts with official unemployment agencies. These initiatives both confuse and mitigate the role and nature of marketing effort. As a result, even those public sector agencies that have embraced the marketing process may be contributing to its unpopularity.

The issue of segmentation is particularly problematic for many public sector practitioners (Lineberry, 1977). Several authors (Bloom and Novelli, 1981; Havitz and Spigner, 1992; Lefebvre and Flora, 1988) allude to the tendency to resist segmentation in public sector marketing efforts. Tradition suggests that residents should receive equal treatment from the public leisure provider. Focusing on one client group over another suggests that those denied service not only fail to receive their perceived "fair" share but also suffer from the stigma that arises from this condition (Lineberry, 1977). As a result, pressure may exist to ignore segmentation efforts and to "treat everyone the same." Clearly, considerable confusion continues to exist in the application of basic marketing principles.

Research and the Marketing Mix

The Product

There has been some discussion as to whether many public sector marketing efforts actually offer a prod-

uct. One author has suggested, for example, that public information campaigns (made up primarily of promotional initiatives) lack a "product" of any kind (Sarner, 1984). This interpretation is problematic, however. It seems clear that even promotional efforts can have no focus without a basic product to promote. In this chapter I adopt a more traditional view, namely that the product forms the basis of all marketing effort. It is a bundle of benefits produced for the client. According to Kotler and Roberto (1989), a product may be an idea, a social practice, or a specific good or service. All marketing effort must focus on that benefit package, what Lovelock (1996) refers to as the "solution" for each client. Initiatives like information campaigns may lack tangibility, but they offer products and solutions nonetheless.

The literature offers several insights which aid in product development. Any product possesses several characteristics or features (Juran, 1992). These features help the client (Zeithaml, 1991):

1. search for and select from among alternative services,
2. experience the service, and
3. assess that service once it has been consumed.

Product features might include level of complexity, program duration, meeting time, or price.

Clients may consider seemingly inconsequential variables when assessing product features. For example, they may use the appearance of maintenance staff or the skills displayed by fellow patrons to evaluate the quality of a swim at a public pool. This occurs because services are notoriously difficult for clients to evaluate before, during, or following consumption. Consider the difficulty encountered by a typical user evaluating services received from lifeguards at a public pool. Barring an emergency, the user sees only a figure clad in a bathing suit sitting in an elevated tower. Quality assessments of competence, judgment, or skill levels are difficult. Given this difficulty, participants may lack meaningful criteria upon which to evaluate that service. As a result, users may look to seemingly irrelevant but more readily available features, like the appearance of staff or the cleanliness of facilities (Berry and Parasuraman, 1991). This suggests that no product feature should escape the notice of program planners. Juran (1992) suggests that all such features must match the ultimate client's own knowledge and interest.

Though each product feature will help determine the success or acceptability of any programming effort, an emerging literature suggests that product names may represent one of the most important product features. Names are likely to be the first piece of program information gathered by a prospective client (Jacoby, Szybillo and Busata-Schach, 1977). As a result, they play a key role in helping potential participants evaluate a program prior to consumption. For example, McCarville and Garrow (1993) offered students a series of names for a hypothetical fitness program. They found that name selection altered subjects' price expectations by as much as 46% and willingness to pay levels by as much as 47%. Again, the issue of benefit to the client seemed critical to successful communication. A name focusing on benefits generated the highest price expectations and willingness to pay levels. The authors concluded that relevant cues like names are used to assess new product offerings.

Price

Price, the cost a client accepts in order to "consume" a product, receives perhaps the most attention within the marketing mix. Two overlapping themes have emerged in the study of pricing. The first focuses on the role of pricing in leisure service delivery. The second considers the effect of costs on potential participants. In terms of the first theme, early discussions often debated the suitability of fees for public services. Issues of "double billing" (charging once through taxes and again through fees), equity, and displacement often dominated these discussions (Crompton and Lamb, 1986; Harris and Driver, 1987). For many decision makers pricing seems inconsistent with the service principles which guide public sector decision making.

However, views among public decision makers now seem more concerned with "how much to price" than with "to price or not to price." After surveying National Park and Recreation Association members in the Great Lakes region, Brademas and Readnour (1989) predicted that "community recreation agencies in the . . . region will enter the 1990s with a strong reliance on fees and charges" (p. 42). More recent research offers support for their prediction. In a study of 60 small-town municipal recreation departments in the United States, Weissinger and Murphy (1993) found that, in response to increasing fiscal restraint, "the most commonly employed strategy was to implement an increase in an already existing fee structure" (p. 70). McCarville and Smale (1991) reported similar patterns in a regional study in Canada.

Pricing structures follow a number of formats. These formats generally recognize the initial importance of delivery costs (Howard and Selin, 1987) but tend to reflect a variety of priorities like equitable and efficient service delivery (Bamford, Manning, Forcier and Koenemann, 1988; Crompton and Lamb, 1986;

Stevenson, 1989). For example, differential fee structures are often used to smooth demand. These structures alter fee levels based on criteria like time, participant group, product, or place. They may be used to manage demand in overutilized resource settings or to gather resources from one group in order to subsidize another. Peak load pricing (charging different prices for the same services at different points in time) may also be used to alter demand and to generate revenue (Stevenson, 1989). Such pricing techniques offer decision makers and clients meaningful price alternatives for a variety of services. Recent increases in agency revenues have been attributed largely to the implementation of these and other fee programs. However, the potential of fees to generate additional revenue seems limited (Crompton and MacGregor, 1994).

The second theme in the pricing literature considers the effect of costs on potential participants. It recognizes that such costs may be psychic, opportunity, monetary, and convenience-based. Costs may emerge either from within the individual or may be imposed by external forces or conditions. For example, Scott and Jackson (1996) found that costs of participation among older women included "safety issues, lack of companionship, and poor health" (p. 1). This finding also suggests that costs may influence participation, either by diminishing the desire to participate or by removing the perceived opportunity to do so (even though the desire still exists).

Though many costs must be borne by the participant (Scott and Jackson, 1996), much of the pricing literature has been concerned with monetary costs. Several patterns are emerging within this literature. Consumers are keenly interested in monetary price. It is likely to be one of the first pieces of information they seek regarding a product (Jacoby, Chestnut, Weigl and Fisher, 1976). Further, potential participants may use price as a guide in making leisure choices. For example, Reiling, Cheng, and Trott (1992) found that campers at state parks in Maine planned to reduce their camping activity if prices were increased.

Traditional efforts have focused on sociodemographic indicators when explaining reaction to fees (Manning et al., 1984). These variables typically include age, income, level of education, race, and work and family status. Such indicators are intuitively appealing. It is reasonable to expect, for example, that the impact of fees is not consistent across client groups (Reiling et al., 1992; Walsh, Peterson and McKean, 1989). Their relative influence likely ebbs and flows as social, personal, or activity-based conditions change (Hultsman, 1995). For example, Reiling et al. (1992) found that low-income campers were more likely than high-income campers to be displaced by fees using the same facilities. The pricing research is replete with studies which lend further support to this assumption.

However, recent research suggests that such indicators fail to explain much of the variation evident in public response to fees. Participants' idiosyncratic preferences and motivations may confound reaction to price. This reaction may be influenced by past experiences (Kerr and Manfredo, 1991), level of involvement with (Havitz and Dimanche, 1990), or commitment to, the product (Buchanan, 1985), individual price tolerances (Howard and Selin, 1987; Lichtenstein, Bloch and Black, 1988), or notions of value (More and Dustin, 1996).

The variable of past experience has been particularly useful in predicting response to price. In a study of New Zealand backcountry hut users, Kerr and Manfredo (1991) found that past paying behavior influenced future paying intentions. They reported that payment experience was sometimes more influential than was the actual price being charged. Those with previous payment experience were relatively untroubled by projected fees at the test sites. Those unaccustomed to paying fees did not intend to pay proposed fees at those same sites. McCarville, Reiling, and White (1996) reported comparable results at U.S. Army Corps of Engineers' day-use areas in the United States. It seems that the context offered by experience aids many participants in evaluating subsequent price information. However, the salience of this experience may be prone to recency effects (McCarville, 1996): if payment experience is irregular or if considerable time has passed since last payment, the importance of price last paid may be diminished.

The challenge of pricing is one of finding a balance between the requirements of the agency and those of the client. The key to this challenge seems to lie in the introduction of various fee structures combined with the imaginative use of various checks and balances. For example, the availability of discount opportunities seems a viable option as fees continue to be introduced. Further, the negative impact of fees may be tempered by negotiated subsidies and flexible payment options. Emmett, Havitz, and McCarville (1996) reported a case study in which several stages of assistance were offered to disadvantaged clients. The most basic assistance option focused on existing choices already available to the client. Particular attention was devoted to ongoing discount programs. The second level of assistance focused on easing the payment of fees. For example, staff were able to arrange payment schedules which best suited the personal needs of the client. The final level of the assistance program was the negotiated subsidy. This subsidy might take the form of a voucher, an activity pass, or simply free access to existing programs. It was found that these measures were able to mitigate the potentially exclusionary effects of fees.

Promotion

Promotion is concerned with those variables needed to bring the product to the attention of the client group. Although traditional promotional techniques include advertising, publicity, sales promotions, and even personal selling (Goddard, 1994), the public sector has generally restricted its promotional efforts to regular mass mailings which outline program offerings. Public sector leisure providers seem hesitant to use promotional techniques that may appear ostentatious to the general public or to policymakers.

Whatever the promotional technique, however, all promotions are largely concerned with persuasion. Persuasive efforts may follow one of two approaches. First, messages may appeal to the nondeliberative or passive route to persuasion. Nondeliberative messages typically rely on affective or emotional appeal in order to persuade the client (Reis and Trout, 1986). It seems that persuasive effects enjoyed by emotional appeals may result more from cues generated by the message (e.g., mood) than from any elaboration of the actual message content (Batra, 1986). In other words, once an individual has a positive feeling toward a given leisure program, he or she may be more likely to attend. Further, the individual is more likely to respond in a positive manner to subsequent messages or cues related to that program. In this way, cognitive processes and assessments may be facilitated by preexisting affective dispositions (Batra, 1986).

The second approach is more cognitive in its appeal. This approach provides specific bits of information designed to convince the reader of the merits of a product. This approach follows the deliberative or active route to persuasion. Though deliberative messages are more likely to generate counterarguments (thereby compromising their effectiveness) they offer many advantages over their nondeliberative counterparts. Clients are more likely to reflect on the merits of the message (and the target product). As a result, such communication is more likely to influence product attitude (Munch, Boller and Swasy, 1993) and this influence is less likely to decay over time. As a result, the impact of deliberative messages can be much more lasting than their effect-based counterparts (Assael, 1984). Indeed, these messages may influence attitudes long after the content of the original message is forgotten (Chattopadhyay and Nedungadi, 1992).

Leisure research on promotional effort has typically focused on understanding client information search patterns. For example, Uysal, McDonald, and Reid (1990) examined the information sources used by selected international visitors in their decision to visit national parks in the United States. Though they found considerable variation in the importance of various information sources, professional and personal sources of advice tended to dominate information search. A few visitors also relied heavily on print-based messages gathered through books, pamphlets, and brochures.

Schuett (1993) conducted a similar study while focusing on whitewater kayakers in the United States. He considered the importance of different information sources among kayakers in various sociodemographic and behavioral subgroups. Again, professional and personal sources of information dominated search patterns. Search patterns also varied with gender, skill, and experience. For example, males placed greater emphasis on friends when planning trips, while females were more likely to look to clubs for information. More experienced group members relied less on professional advice than on that provided by friends: "[A]s frequency of participation increased, the information from [professional sources like] professional outfitters, outdoor stores, newspapers and brochures became less important" (p. 72).

This reliance on friends and family seems to be based largely on credibility. The social interaction that often characterizes elevated levels of participation offers participants ready and reliable sources of personal information (Manfredo and Bright, 1991). As a result, they may abandon more formal information sources as experience grows. For example, Manfredo and Bright (1991) considered the effectiveness of brochures on wilderness users. Their study was concerned with persuasive communications and behavior change. They considered the role of message elaboration (number of thoughts generated, acquisition of new beliefs, and changes in old beliefs) on subsequent behavior patterns. Like Schuett (1993), they reported that prior knowledge and source credibility directly influenced the persuasion process.

Place or Distribution

I suggested earlier that the service encounter forms the very basis of leisure delivery systems. MacKay and Crompton (1990) considered it essential that public sector providers better understand the service encounter, suggesting that, "given the centrality of service quality to the mission of recreation agencies, [such] research . . . should be a prime concern" (p. 54). They recommended that this research be based generally

on the pioneering work conducted by Zeithaml, Parasuraman, and Berry (1990).

Zeithaml et al. (1990) suggested that, when evaluating the service encounter, clients typically look to five categories of "quality determinants." These determinants are:

1. tangibles (appearance of facilities, staff and other participants),
2. reliability (consistent delivery of the promised service),
3. assurance (competent, knowledgeable staff),
4. empathy (caring, individualized attention), and
5. responsiveness (willingness to provide prompt attention).

Zeithaml et al. (1990) developed a SERVQUAL instrument to facilitate the measurement of clients' perceptions of these factors during a service encounter. MacKay and Crompton (1990) found that, although they originated in the private sector, these categories generally applied to public sector leisure settings. They concluded that the five determinants "described the basic structure of service quality" (p. 54) and recommended that they be used to monitor and evaluate leisure service efforts within the public sector. Wright, Duray, and Goodale (1992) later used an adapted version of the Zeithaml et al. (1990) SERVQUAL scale to determine clients' assessments of service quality at several county recreation centers. They, too, concluded that the determinants, as developed by Zeithaml et al. (1990), could be applied within the context of public leisure services.

Once these determinants of service quality have been established, the next issue is one of application. How can programming efforts be regulated so that the demands of the client are addressed during each service encounter? The service literature suggests that such control is best achieved by dividing the encounter into its various frontstage and backstage components. The frontstage service encounter has been compared to a performance (Grove and Fisk, 1996). Like any performance, the encounter is influenced by interaction between the client and the setting. For example, it is influenced by the presence and appearance of staff and audience members, their interpersonal competence and so on. It is further influenced by the physical setting made up of background features beneath and within the client's immediate awareness (Berry and Parasuraman, 1991; Grove and Fisk, 1996). The relative importance of these features may differ from one setting to the next (MacKay and Crompton, 1990).

The client may occasionally be asked to aid in the provision of frontstage operations. Under extraordinary circumstances clients may even be asked to solve problems created by organizational deficiencies. This issue is particularly germane in the case of service failures. Two conditions conspire against service providers in their efforts to recover from service failures. Such efforts tend to be labor intensive (Berry and Parasuraman, 1991) and are more likely to occur when existing resource levels are already strained to capacity (Lovelock, 1992). Consequently, staff may be unable to devote the extra time needed to accomplish service recovery. Under these conditions, the service provider might consider enlisting the aid of the client when establishing the service blueprint. Colenutt and McCarville (1994) pursued this idea in an experiment which monitored hotel guests' response to three hypothetical scenarios. Each scenario suggested that a service failure had occurred. Guests asked to undertake this self-help solution seemed willing to do so, but only when they were offered a discount in return for their inconvenience. It seems that service providers can, under certain circumstances, involve their clients in service delivery and recovery efforts.

Backstage operations are those systems or infrastructures that support the production of customer service (Davidow and Uttal, 1989). Though they may include complex networks of people, physical facilities, or information systems, they are typically invisible to the ultimate consumer. Backstage operations can be physical (e.g., facility design, equipment, materials and supplies), human (e.g., scheduling or training), or information-based (e.g., quality-control processes) in nature.

The coordination of backstage effort has proven problematic over the years. Those who act behind the scenes are, by necessity, removed from actual service encounters. Consequently, they may fail to appreciate the needs of front-line staff during those encounters. Resulting policies and procedures may be inadequate, thereby creating gaps in service (Zeithaml et al., 1990). Increasingly, service providers are turning to the process of blueprinting to overcome these concerns (Zeithaml et al., 1990). Blueprinting "considers every activity needed to create and deliver a service, as well as specifying the linkages between these activities" (Lovelock, 1991, p. 230).

The hospitality industry has been particularly successful in this regard, where blueprinting is used to guide employee training and internal processes (Meyer and Westerbarkey, 1996). Successful blueprinting efforts tend to include specific time dimensions, means

of identifying and addressing errors or fail points, and the extent to which standardized procedures can vary in order to address these errors (Lovelock, 1991). Consider the example of a leisure agency blueprinting backstage activities surrounding a typical registration. Time-based standards might be established concerning waiting in line to register, the amount of time it takes to process a single application, the time it takes to process a refund, and so on. Errors or problems might be flagged if time targets are violated or when complaints about the process are registered. Staff might then be empowered to break with standard operating procedure when these errors occur.

Conclusions

Leisure providers continue to struggle with the pernicious issue of participation or, more accurately, nonparticipation. It seems that current programming efforts often fail to interest a diverse and seemingly unresponsive marketplace. Several authors now suggest that interest in traditional leisure programming (and especially those programs offered through municipal agencies) is flagging (Howard, 1992; Warnick and Howard, 1986). The weekly work load of an average family seems to be increasing with the passage of time (Schor, 1991; Schwartz-Cowan, 1983). Leisure activity seems to be suffering as a result. In *The Overworked American,* Schor (1991) contends that modern Western society has generally failed to integrate meaningful leisure or physical activity into the everyday lives of its members. Several indicators seem to support this assertion. Shaw (1990) and others (Harper, Neider, Godbey and Lamont, 1996) report that the pace of daily living seems to be accelerating, both at the workplace and in the home.

The relentless pace of contemporary life seems to originate with what Borgmann (1984) called the *technological imperative.* He argued that production must be fuelled by consumption so while the work ethic encourages production it must also encourage consumerism. Suggesting that production and consumption each reinforce the other in an upward spiral, Borgmann believed that meaningful leisure opportunities are limited by the process. Schor (1991) labeled the phenomenon the *erosion of leisure.* Scitovsky (1992), relying on a variety of indicators, suggested that with the erosion of leisure people are becoming less satisfied with their lives. These conditions suggest a compelling role for the marketing of leisure services. Marketing action represents a coherent, coordinated effort designed to influence behavior, to facilitate participation. If potential participants are constrained by reduced interest or opportunity, if constraint resolution requires negotiation, if constraints fall more heavily on some than on others, then marketing effort may ameliorate their potentially debilitating effects (see Jackson and Scott, 1996; see also chapter 18 in this volume). Marketing tools may be used to considerable effect in countering this erosion of leisure.

My description of marketing effort suggests that it is not unlike traditional planning processes. Indeed, I have characterized marketing as a natural step in the evolution of programming effort. It represents the strategic application of resources to serve the client. As such, marketing processes seem entirely appropriate for all, regardless of the sector in which they operate. However, marketing effort is limited by the skill of the practitioner. Mere acceptance of the concept of marketing does not ensure the adoption of marketing principles. Effective application requires both knowledge and skill. Unfortunately, there seems to be considerable confusion in the application of these basic principles. It seems appropriate that steps be taken to reduce confusion and the misapplication of marketing principles. An emerging leisure marketing literature (complemented by the broader services marketing and consumer behavior literatures) now offers considerable conceptual and practical insight for the marketer and the researcher. Such insight should be made available to all students undertaking leisure studies at the college, undergraduate, or graduate levels.

Another solution to such confusion lies in the continued dissemination of practical information to leisure providers. Decision makers must be informed of successful initiatives. This information is often relegated to the so-called *gray literature,* made up largely of in-house manuals and policy statements. Means must be found to share these initiatives with wider audiences than is now the case. The compilation of case study materials like Crompton's (1987) *Doing More With Less* or Havitz's (1995) more recent *Models of Change,* which offer the combined wisdom of many marketing leaders, should be encouraged. Agencies might also benefit from benchmarking activities wherein they compare their own policies to those of industry leaders (Lovelock, 1988). These insights should also be shared with as wide an audience as is practical.

Further, there is a need for research to facilitate improved decision making in the field. Programmers need ready access to relevant data. Clearly, a need for coordination exists around both the collection and dissemination of data. Much of the existing research effort is reported primarily in the academic literature and often fails to reach the practitioner. A mechanism could be sought which collects, organizes, and makes accessible marketing-related information. Its goal might be one of linking science to practice, ensuring that those responsible for marketing, programming, and policy are kept abreast of emerging developments. The rapidly evolving Internet would seem an ideal venue for such an effort.

From a more tactical perspective, an individual agency's marketing efforts may benefit from coordination of effort afforded through selective centralization. For example, the Colgate organization has developed the concept of the *bundle book* in order to deal with uncertainty and confusion over marketing objectives and practices (Kindel, 1996). The bundle book, which is created centrally, provides front-line managers with "all they need to know about the brand, down to the smallest detail; includ[ing] product attributes, market research, pricing objectives, even advertising, public relations, and point-of-sale materials" (p. 27). Leisure marketing efforts might benefit from this approach. Agency staff might develop a coherent, focused marketing strategy, then use the book concept to communicate the strategy with other staff members. Such efforts can direct and guide practitioners, thereby ensuring consistency, maximizing resource allocation, and focusing the attention of staff members. Marketing efforts and the ultimate client will benefit from such initiatives.

References

Allen, L., Stevens, B., & Harwell, R. (1996). Benefits-based management activity planning model for youth in at-risk environments. *Journal of Park and Recreation Administration, 14*(3), 10–19.

Assael, H. (1984). *Consumer behavior and marketing action.* Boston, MA: Kent.

Backman, S. (1994). Using a person-situation approach to market segmentation. *Journal of Park and Recreation Administration, 12*(1), 1–16.

Backman, S., & Crompton, J. (1991). Differentiating between high, spurious, latent, and low loyalty participants in two leisure activities. *Journal of Park and Recreation Administration, 9*(2), 1–17.

Bamford, T., Manning, R., Forcier, L., & Koenemann, E. (1988). Differential campsite pricing: An experiment. *Journal of Leisure Research, 20*(4), 324–342.

Bannon, J. (1976). *Leisure resources: Its comprehensive planning.* Englewood Cliffs, NJ: Prentice-Hall.

Batra, R. (1986). Affective advertising: Role, processes, and measurement. In R. Peterson, W. Hoyer & W. Wilson (Eds.), *The role of affect in consumer behavior* (pp. 53–118). Toronto, Ontario: Lexington Books.

Bearden, W., & Oliver, R. (1985). The role of public and private complaining in satisfaction with problem resolution. *The Journal of Consumer Affairs, 19*(2), 222–240.

Berry, L., & Parasuraman, A. (1991). *Marketing services: Competing through quality.* New York, NY: The Free Press.

Bloom, P., & Novelli, W. (1981). Problems and challenges in social marketing. *Journal of Marketing, 45,* 79–88.

Borden, N. (1969). The concept of the marketing mix. In B. Enis & K. Cox (Eds.), *Marketing classics: A selection of influential articles* (pp. 429–437). Toronto, Ontario: Allyn & Bacon.

Borgmann, A. (1984). *Technology and the character of contemporary life: A philosophical inquiry.* Chicago, IL: University of Chicago Press.

Brademas, D., & Readnour, J. (1989). Status of fees and charges in public leisure service agencies. *Journal of Park and Recreation Administration, 7*(4), 42–55.

Buchanan, T. (1985). Commitment and leisure behavior: A theoretical perspective. *Leisure Sciences, 7*(4), 401–420.

Butsch, R. (1990). Leisure and hegemony in America. In R. Butsch (Ed.), *For fun and profit: The transformation of leisure into consumption* (pp. 3–27). Philadelphia, PA: Temple University Press.

Chattopadhyay, A., & Nedungadi, P. (1992). Does attitude toward the ad endure? The moderating effects of attention and delay. *Journal of Consumer Research, 19,* 26–33.

Colenutt, C., & McCarville, R. (1994). The client as problem solver: A new look at service recovery. *Journal of Hospitality & Leisure Marketing, 2*(3), 23–35.

Crompton, J. (1985). Marketing: Neither snake oil nor panacea. In T. Goodale & P. Witt (Eds.), *Recreation and leisure: Issues in an era of change* (pp. 175–194). State College, PA: Venture Publishing, Inc.

Crompton, J. (1987). *Doing more with less in parks and recreation services.* State College, PA: Venture Publishing, Inc.

Crompton, J., & Lamb, C. (1986). *Marketing government and social services.* New York, NY: John Wiley & Sons, Inc.

Crompton, J., & McGregor, B. (1994). Trends in financing and staffing of local government park and recreation services, 1964–65 and 1990–91. *Journal of Park and Recreation Administration, 12*(3), 19–37.

Davidow, W., & Uttal, B. (1989). *Total customer service.* New York, NY: Harper & Row.

Deming, E. (1986). *Out of the crisis* (2nd ed.). Cambridge, MA: Massachusetts Institute of Technology Center for Advanced Engineering Study.

Donnelly, M., Vaske, J., DeRuiter, D., & King, T. (1996). Person-occasion segmentation of state park visitors. *Journal of Park and Recreation Administration, 14*(2), 96–106.

Drucker, P. (1974) *Management: Tasks, responsibilities, practices.* New York, NY: Harper & Row.

Ellerbrock, M. (1982, January). Some straight talk on user fees. *Parks and Recreation,* 59–62.

Emmett, J., Havitz, M., & McCarville, R. (1996). A price subsidy policy for socioeconomically disadvantaged recreation participants. *Journal of Park and Recreation Administration, 14*(1), 63–80.

Floyd, M., & Gramann, J. (1993). Effects of acculturation and structural assimilation in resource-based recreation: The case of Mexican Americans. *Journal of Leisure Research, 25*(1), 6–21.

Floyd, M., Shinew, K., McGuire, F., & Noe, F. (1994). Race, class, and leisure activity preferences: Marginality and ethnicity. *Journal of Leisure Research, 26*(2), 158–173.

Gavlik, S. (1995). Reinventing recreation programming: Waco leisure services department. In M. Havitz (Ed.), *Models of change in municipal parks and recreation: A book of innovative case studies* (pp. 109–120). State College, PA: Venture Publishing, Inc.

Goddard, E. (1994). Untitled opening address. In *Proceedings of the NEC-63 Conference on promotion in the marketing mix: What works, where and why* (pp. 8–13). Guelph, Ontario: University of Guelph.

Goodale, T. (1985). Prevailing winds and bending mandates. In T. Goodale & P. Witt (Eds.), *Recreation and leisure: Issues in an era of change* (pp. 195–207). State College, PA.: Venture Publishing, Inc.

Goodwin, C., & Ross, I. (1992). Consumer responses to service failures: Influence of procedural and interactional fairness perceptions. *Journal of Business Research, 25,* 149–163.

Grove, S., & Fisk, R. (1996). The dramaturgy of services exchange. In C. Lovelock (Ed.), *Services marketing* (3rd ed., pp. 97–105). Toronto, Ontario: Prentice-Hall.

Harper, J., Neider, D., Godbey, G., & Lamont, D. (1996). *The use and benefits of local government recreation and park services: A Canadian perspective.* Winnipeg, Manitoba: Health, Leisure & Human Performance Research Institute.

Harris, C., & Driver, B. (1987, May). User fees: Pros and cons. *Journal of Forestry,* 25–29.

Hart, C., Heskett, J., & Sasser, E. (1990, July–August). The profitable art of service recovery. *Harvard Business Review,* 148–156.

Havitz, M. (1988, May). Marketing is not synonymous with commercialism. *Parks and Recreation,* 34–36.

Havitz, M. (1995). *Models of change in municipal parks and recreation: A book of innovative case studies.* State College, PA: Venture Publishing, Inc.

Havitz, M., & Crompton, J. (1990). The influence of persuasive messages on propensity to purchase selected recreational services from public or commercial suppliers. *Journal of Leisure Research, 22*(1), 71–88.

Havitz, M., & Dimanche, F. (1990). Propositions for testing the involvement construct in recreational and tourism contexts. *Leisure Sciences, 12,* 179–195.

Havitz, M., Dimanche, F., & Bogle, T. (1994). Segmenting the adults fitness market using involvement profiles. *Journal of Park and Recreation Administration, 12*(3), 38–56.

Havitz, M., & Spigner, C. (1993) The role of park and recreation services. *Trends, 30*(4), 31–48.

Hemingway, J. (1996). Emancipating leisure: The recovery of freedom in leisure. *Journal of Leisure Research, 28*(1), 27–43.

Henderson, K. (1994). Perspective on analyzing gender, women, and leisure. *Journal of Leisure Research, 26*(3), 119–137.

Hollenhorst, S., Schuett, M., Olson, D., & Chavez, D. (1995). An examination of the characteristics, preferences, and attitudes of mountain bike users of the national forests. *Journal of Park and Recreation Administration, 13*(3), 41–51.

Howard, D. (1992). Participation rates in selected sport and fitness activities. *Journal of Sport Management, 6,* 191–205.

Howard, D., & Crompton, J. (1980). *Financing, managing, and marketing recreation & park resources.* Dubuque, IA: Wm. C. Brown Publishers.

Howard, D., & Selin, S. (1987). A method for establishing consumer price tolerance levels for public recreation services. *Journal of Park & Recreation Administration, 5*(3), 48–59.

Howard, J., & Sheth, J. (1988). A theory of buying behavior. In B. Enis & K. Cox (Eds.), *Marketing classics: A selection of influential articles* (pp. 105–123). Toronto, Ontario: Allyn & Bacon.

Hultsman, W. (1995), Recognizing patterns of leisure constraints: An extension of the exploration of dimensionality. *Journal of Leisure Research, 27*(3), 228–244.

Jackson, E. (1993). Recognizing patterns of leisure constraints: Results from alternative analyses. *Journal of Leisure Research, 25*(2), 129–149.

Jackson, E., & Dunn, E. (1988). Integrating ceasing participation with other aspects of leisure behavior. *Journal of Leisure Research, 20,* 31–45.

Jacobs, J. (1994). *Systems of survival.* New York, NY: Vintage Books.

Jacoby, J., Chestnut, R., Weigl, K., & Fisher, W. (1976). Prepurchase information acquisition: Description of a process methodology. In B. Anderson (Ed.), *Advances in consumer research* (pp. 306–314). Cincinnati, OH: Association for Consumer Research.

Jacoby, J., Szybillo, G., & Busata-Schach, J. (1977). Information acquisition in brand choice situations. *Journal of Consumer Research, 2,* 209–216.

Johnson, R., & McLean, D. (1996, May-June). Public sector marketing: Improving services or compromising values? *Parks & Recreation Canada,* 21–24.

Juran, J. (1992). *Juran on quality by design.* Toronto, Ontario: Maxwell Macmillan Canada.

Kerr, G., & Manfredo, M. (1991). An attitudinal-based model of pricing for recreation services. *Journal of Leisure Research, 23*(1), 37–50.

Kindel, S. (1996, September). A brush with success: Colgate-Palmolive company. *Hemispheres,* 27–30.

Kotler, P. (1975). *Marketing for nonprofit organizations.* Englewood Cliffs, NJ: Prentice-Hall.

Kotler, P. (1983). *Principles of marketing* (2nd ed.). Englewood Cliffs, NJ: Prentice-Hall.

Kotler, P., McDougall, G., & Armstrong, G. (1988). *Marketing* (Canadian ed.). Englewood Cliffs, NJ: Prentice-Hall.

Kotler, P., & Roberto, E. (1989). *Social marketing: Strategies for changing public behavior.* Englewood Cliffs, NJ: Prentice-Hall.

Kuenzli, G. (1991, June). *How to "phantom shop" your YMCA*. Los Angeles, CA: Management Resource Center, YMCAs of Southern California.

Lefebvre, R. (1992). The social marketing imbroglio in health promotion. *Health Promotion International, 7,* 61–64.

Lefebvre, R., & Flora, J. (1988). Social marketing and public health intervention. *Health Education Quarterly, 15,* 299–315.

Levitt, T. (1983). *The marketing imagination.* New York, NY: The Free Press.

Levitt, T. (1988). Marketing myopia. In B. Enis & K. Cox (Eds.), *Marketing classics: A selection of influential articles* (pp. 3–21). Toronto, Ontario: Allyn & Bacon.

Lichtenstein, D., Bloch, P., & Black, W. (1988). Correlates of price acceptability. *Journal of Consumer Research, 15,* 243–252.

Lineberry, R. (1977). *Equality and urban policy.* Beverly Hills, CA: Sage Publications, Inc.

Lovelock, C. (1988). Classifying services to gain strategic marketing insights. In C. Lovelock (Ed.), *Managing services: Marketing, operations, and human resources* (1st ed., pp. 44–57). Toronto, Ontario: Prentice-Hall.

Lovelock, C. (1991). Creating and delivering services. In C. Lovelock (Ed.), *Services marketing* (2nd ed., pp. 223–235). Toronto, Ontario: Prentice-Hall.

Lovelock, C. (1992). Are services really different? In C. Lovelock (Ed.), *Managing services: Marketing, operations, and human resources* (2nd ed., pp. 1–8). Toronto, Ontario: Prentice-Hall.

Lovelock, C. (1996). Developing and managing the customer-service function. In C. Lovelock (Ed.), *Services marketing* (2nd ed., pp. 490–507). Toronto, Ontario: Prentice-Hall.

MacKay, K., & Crompton, J. (1990). Measuring the quality of recreation services. *Journal of Park and Recreation Administration, 11*(1), 47–56.

Manfredo, M., & Bright, A. (1991). A model for assessing the effects of communications on recreationists. *Journal of Leisure Research 23*(1), 1–20.

Manning, R., Callinan, E., Echelberger, E., Koenemann, E., & McEwan, D. (1984). Differential Fees: Raising revenue, distributing demand. *Journal of Park and Recreation Administration, 2*(1), 20–38.

McCarville, R. (1996). The importance of price last paid in developing price expectations for a public leisure service. *Journal of Park and Recreation Administration, 14*(4), 52–64.

McCarville, R., & Garrow, G. (1993). Name selection and response to a hypothetical recreation program. *Journal of Park and Recreation Administration, 11*(2), 1–15.

McCarville, R. Reiling, S., & White, C. (1996). The role of fairness in users' assessments of first-time fees for a public recreation service. *Leisure Sciences, 18*(1), 61–76.

McCarville, R., & Smale, B. (1991). Involvement in pricing by municipal recreation agencies. *Journal of Applied Recreation Research, 16*(3), 200–219.

McCarville, R., & Smale, B. (1993). Perceived constraints to leisure participation within five activity domains. *Journal of Park and Recreation Administration, 11*(2), 1–15.

McClosky, D. (1982). *The applied theory of price.* New York, NY: Macmillan Publishing.

Meyer, A., & Westerbarkey, P. (1996). Measuring and managing hotel guest satisfaction. In M. Olsen, R. Teare & E. Gummesson (Eds.), *Service quality in hospitality organizations* (pp. 185–203). New York, NY: Cassell.

Meyers, W. (1984) *The image makers.* Toronto, Ontario: Times Books.

Mintz, J. (1989). Social marketing: New weapon in an old struggle. *Health Promotion, 27,* 6–12.

More, T. A., & Dustin, D. L. (1996). Behavioral consequences of campground user fees. *Journal of Park and Recreation Administration, 14*(1), 81–93.

Munch, J. M., Boller, G. W., & Swasy, J. L. (1993). The effects of argument structure and affective tagging on product attitude formation. *Journal of Consumer Research, 20*(September), 294–302.

Novelli, W. (1984). Applying social marketing to health promotion and disease prevention. In K. Glanz, F. Lewis & B. Rimer (Eds.), *Health behavior and health education* (pp. 342–369). San Francisco, CA: Jossey-Bass, Inc.

Nylen, D. (1990) *Marketing decision-making handbook.* Toronto, Ontario: Prentice-Hall.

Parasuraman, A. (1986). *Marketing research.* Don Mills, Ontario: Addison-Wesley.

Payne, A. (1993). *The essence of services marketing.* Toronto, Ontario: Prentice-Hall.

Pedlar, A., Dupuis, C., & Gilbert, A. (1996). Resumption of role status through leisure in later life. *Leisure Sciences 18*(3), 259–276.

Raymore, L., Godbey, G., & Crawford, D. (1994). Self-esteem, gender, and socioeconomics status: Their relation to perceptions of constraint on leisure among adolescents. *Journal of Leisure Research, 26*(2), 99–118.

Reichheld, F. (1996). *The loyalty effect.* Boston, MA: Harvard Business School Press.

Reiling, S., Cheng, H., & Trott, C. (1992). Measuring the discriminatory impact associated with higher recreational fees. *Leisure Sciences, 14*(2), 121–138.

Reis, A., & Trout, J. (1986). *Positioning: The battle for your mind.* New York, NY: Warner Books.

Ritchie, K. (1996). Beacons of light in an expanding universe: An assessment of the state-of-the-art in tourism marketing/marketing research. *Journal of Travel & Tourism Research, 5*(4), 49–84.

Rosenthal, D., Loomis, J., & Peterson, G. (1984). Pricing for efficiency and revenue in public recreation areas. *Journal of Leisure Research, 16*(3), 195–208.

Sarner, M. (1984). Marketing health to Canadians. *Health Education, 23,* 2–9.

Schneider, B. (1988). Notes on climate and culture. In C. Lovelock (Ed.), *Managing services: Marketing, operations, and human resources* (pp. 352–358). Toronto, Ontario: Prentice-Hall.

Schor, J. (1991). *The overworked American.* New York, NY: Basic Books.

Schuett, M. (1993). Information sources and risk recreation: The case of whitewater kayakers. *Journal of Park and Recreation Administration, 11*(1), 67–78.

Schultz, J., McAvoy, L., & Dustin, D. (1988). What are we in business for? *Parks and Recreation, 23*(1), 52–54.

Schwartz-Cowan, R. (1983). *More work for mother.* New York, NY: Basic Books.

Scitovsky, T. (1992). *The joyless economy.* Toronto, Ontario: Oxford University Press.

Scott, D. (1993). Time scarcity and its implications for leisure behavior and leisure delivery. *Journal of Park and Recreation Administration, 11*(3), 51–61.

Scott, D., & Jackson, E. (1996). Factors that limit and strategies that might encourage people's use of public parks. *Journal of Park and Recreation Administration, 14*(1), 1–17.

Searle, M., Mactavish, K., & Brayley, R. (1993). Integrating ceasing participation with other aspects of leisure behavior: A replication and extension. *Journal of Leisure Research, 25*(4), 389–404.

Selin, S., & Chavez, D. (1993). Recreation partnerships and the USDA forest service: Managers' perception of the impact of the national recreation strategy. *Journal of Park and Recreation Administration, 11*(1), 1–11.

Selin, S., Howard, D., Udd, E., & Cable, T. (1988). An analysis of consumer loyalty to municipal recreation programs. *Leisure Sciences, 10,* 217–223.

Sewell, C., & Brown, P. (1990). *Customers for life.* Toronto, Ontario: Pocket Books.

Shaw, S. (1990). Where has all the leisure gone: The distribution and redistribution of leisure. In B. Smale (Ed.), *Proceedings: Sixth Canadian Congress on Leisure Research* (pp. 1–4). Waterloo, Ontario: Ontario Research Council on Leisure.

Simone, R. (1996, November 21). Free speech at risk, author says. *The Record,* pp. A1, A3.

Stevenson, S. (1989). A test of peak-load pricing on senior citizen recreationists: A case study of Steamboat Lake State Park. *Journal of Park and Recreation Administration, 7*(1), 58–68.

Sylvia, G., Sallee, C., & Berry, H. (1995). Determining leisure program formats based on participant preferences. *Journal of Park and Recreation Administration, 13*(2), 55–73.

Uysal, M., McDonald, C., & Reid, L. (1990). Sources of information used by international visitors to U.S. parks and natural areas. *Journal of Park and Recreation Administration, 8*(1), 51–59.

Walsh, R., Peterson, G., & McKean, J. (1989). Distribution and efficiency effects of alternative recreation funding models. *Journal of Leisure Research, 21*(4), 327–347.

Warnick, R., & Howard, D. (1986). Market share analysis of selected leisure services from 1979 to 1982. *Journal of Park and Recreation Administration, 4*(3), 64–76.

Weinstein, A. (1987). *Market segmentation.* Chicago, IL: Probus Publishing.

Weissinger, E., & Murphy, W. (1993). A survey of fiscal conditions in small-town public recreation departments from 1987 to 1991. *Journal of Park and Recreation Administration, 11*(3), 61–72.

Witt, P., & Crompton, J. (1996). The at-risk youth recreation project. *Journal of Park and Recreation Administration, 14*(3), 1–9.

Wright, B., Duray, N., & Goodale, T. (1992). Assessing perceptions of recreation center quality: An application of recent advancements in service quality research. *Journal of Park and Recreation Administration, 10*(3), 33–48.

Wyckoff, D. (1992). New tools for achieving service quality. In C. Lovelock (Ed.), *Managing services* (2nd ed., pp. 236–249). Toronto, Ontario: Prentice-Hall.

Zeithaml, V. (1991). How consumer evaluation processes differ between goods and services. In C. Lovelock (Ed.), *Services marketing* (2nd ed., pp. 39–47). Toronto, Ontario: Prentice-Hall.

Zeithaml, V., Parasuraman, A., & Berry, L. (1990). *Delivering quality service.* New York, NY: The Free Press.

Institutional and Organizational Challenges to Managing Natural Resources for Recreation: A Social Learning Model

CHAPTER

26

George H. Stankey
Pacific Northwest Research Station, Corvallis, Oregon

Stephen F. McCool
University of Montana

Roger N. Clark
Pacific Northwest Research, Seattle, Washington

Perry J. Brown
University of Montana

Introduction

An extensive and varied natural resource base has long provided a suite of values for human society. These include commodity values, such as timber and range; ecological values, such as biodiversity; and environmental quality values, such as air and water quality (Stankey and Clark, 1992). It also includes public use values, such as outdoor recreation and tourism. Camping, hiking, fishing, and many other activities are dependent upon, or owe much of their enjoyment to, the natural resource setting—forests, rivers, mountains, and plains—in which they take place. The importance of these natural resource settings to the provision and enjoyment of outdoor recreation has been reaffirmed numerous times (Outdoor Recreation Resources Review Commission, 1962; President's Commission on Americans Outdoors, 1986).

While the importance of natural resource settings to outdoor recreation is clear and widely accepted, their management is both complex and contentious. Two major factors underlie this. First, these settings are important for the production of a range of other goods and services: from commodity outputs such as timber or services as diverse as water to drive hydroelectric generators or to satisfy the needs of agriculture and industry, to their role in the provision of conservation values such as biodiversity. Although opportunities for compatible management and the joint production of different goods and services are available, there are also cases where incompatibilities and conflicts exist. Second, management of natural resources for one set of purposes (e.g., timber production) leads to changes that have consequences (positive and negative) for outdoor recreation; conversely, management of the same natural resources for outdoor recreation leads to changes and consequences for other uses. Such interdependencies and interrelationships are sufficient to confound the task of managing natural resources, but they are further exacerbated by the traditional functional structure of many natural resource management organizations (e.g., along timber, wildlife, or recreation lines) and budgeting processes that contribute to isolation and noncoordination in planning and management.

At the close of the twentieth century, we face increasing contentiousness about natural resource management. In part, this reflects the growing level and range of demands placed upon the natural resource base: more people demanding greater amounts of a wider range of goods and services. However, it also is a manifestation of the very nature of natural resources; they are human constructs whose meaning and importance change in response to a variety of factors. Hays (1988), for instance, has described the evolving conception of the "environmental forest" as a resource. Forests, once valued primarily for their commodity outputs, are now increasingly valued for a host of other goods and services—environmental, aesthetic, conservation—whose production is inconsistent with, or at least adversely affected by, the production of traditional commodity values. However, the extent to which natural resource management institutions—planning protocols, policies, laws, organizations—are responsive and sensitive to these changing public perceptions is arguable. Wilkinson (1992, p. 17) describes such institutions as the "Lords of Yesterday": ideas, policies, programs, and statutes "that arose under wholly different social and economic conditions but . . . remain in effect due to inertia, powerful lobbying forces, and lack of public awareness." And as Westley (1995) warns, the long-term survival of institutions which fail to be responsive to a changing environment is problematic.

The management of natural resources for outdoor recreation exemplifies many of the conflicts confronting natural resource management today. However, debates about outdoor recreation versus other uses are only one part of this conflict. Even given a decision to manage natural resources for outdoor recreation, difficult questions remain about what types of outdoor recreation opportunities to provide, how much, where, and by whom. There is also a complex set of questions regarding the distribution of benefits from recreation resource management, including the equity of access to these resources. Finally, the use of natural resources for recreational purposes leads to impacts upon those resources; such an allocation also imposes opportunity costs upon those who seek to use them for other purposes. How can such decisions be made systematically, logically, and defensibly?

In this chapter, we discuss our experience in the development of planning and management frameworks designed to deal with such kinds of questions. First, we outline two planning frameworks with which

we have been involved in both the development and application stages. These are the Recreation Opportunity Spectrum (ROS), an approach for providing a diverse range of recreational opportunities, and the Limits of Acceptable Change (LAC), a framework for dealing with managing impact and change in recreation settings (many of our comments with regard to these two particular planning frameworks are also applicable to other systems; e.g., see Driver and Bruns, chapter 21 in this volume). We then turn to a discussion of the limitations of the traditional, synoptic planning approaches upon which natural resource management institutions largely depend today. We present a framework that links the decision-making environment, including knowledge of causation as well as societal goals and objectives, with appropriate institutional and decision-making structures. Using the LAC framework as an example, we conclude with a discussion of how a social learning model can be adapted to be more responsive to public concerns and, at the same time, integrate technical and scientific understanding.

Developing Frameworks for Linking Outdoor Recreation and Natural Resources

Whether intended or not, almost all natural resource management activities affect outdoor recreation opportunities. These effects are not necessarily negative; for example, changes in the level or character of road systems in an area to serve timber management might provide needed recreation settings that meet current demand. In the final analysis, an assessment as to whether such changes are negative or positive is dependent upon recreationists' requirements, preferences, and expectations. Also, such activities involve a mixture of benefits and costs; using the transportation example, those interested in road-based recreation opportunities will find improved access a benefit, while those using the area because of the lack of developed transportation likely will evaluate the change negatively. Effective and informative multiresource management must afford managers, planners, and users an understanding of these interactions and interrelationships occurring within the natural resource system. There is a need, then, for frameworks within which the following kinds of questions might be addressed:

- What are the setting attributes and characteristics that people require and/or prefer?
- What are the positive and negative effects on, and of, recreation use in areas where other resource uses occur?
- How important are these effects upon the uses and experiences of visitors?
- How do we promote management decisions and actions that are consistent with the management objectives for areas?
- What management tools might be used to mitigate adverse effects and enhance positive effects associated with other resource uses?
- How do we integrate more effectively outdoor recreation management and other resource uses in such a way as to minimize conflict and maximize complementarity?

Providing Diversity in Recreation Settings: The Recreation Opportunity Spectrum

The need for a framework to address such questions played a major role in development of the Recreation Opportunity Spectrum (ROS). The background to development of the ROS has been described elsewhere (Driver, Brown, Stankey and Gregoire, 1987), but several features of the framework should be noted. First, the ROS was an effort to respond to the need for *diversity* in recreation settings. Given the pluralism in tastes for settings arrayed along a continuum "from the paved to the primeval" (Nash, 1982, p. 425), the framework sought to facilitate the systematic provision of a spectrum of conditions. Second, because many outdoor recreation opportunities occur in natural resource settings where other management activities are present, it was important that the system facilitate assessment and evaluation of the reciprocal effects between recreation and these other activities. Third, the ROS brought a behavioral foundation to the concept of outdoor recreation, as opposed to the traditional emphasis on activities; it also assigned importance to the concept of "consumer sovereignty," i.e., that the preferences of visitors were crucial to the identification of recreation settings and essential to understanding their behavior. Thus, it initiated utilization of a consumer-oriented paradigm to guide recreation planning and management (Driver et al., 1987).

Development of the ROS planning approach arose from parallel work undertaken by Driver and Brown (1978) and Clark and Stankey (1979). The concept of a *recreational opportunity setting,* defined as the combination of biological, physical, social, and managerial conditions that give value to a place, was integral in both approaches, resting on a similar premise: recreationists seek a variety of recreational opportunity settings, and through their participation in different activities in these settings, derive a variety of experiences and benefits.

The specific linkage between the ROS and other natural resource management activities also drew explicit attention in both formulations. For example, the physical component of a recreational opportunity setting included relatively permanent human structures, such as roads, dams, and timber harvest units. Clark and Stankey (1979) and Stankey and Brown (1981) stressed the importance of nonrecreation resource uses. Such activities met the criteria for defining relevant setting factors (such factors should be observable and measurable; directly under management control; related to the choice behavior of recreationists; and characterized by a range of condition, e.g., from pervasive to absent). Also, attention to activities such as grazing, mining, and logging helped define the extent to which they were compatible with various outdoor recreation opportunities. Of course, such judgments of compatibility would differ among different people and also according to the form and scale of the activity. Timber harvesting, for instance, might be compatible with some forms of outdoor recreation if it did not involve an extensive scale or if the specific prescription used (e.g., selective harvesting) did not exceed public judgments of acceptability and appropriateness (Clark, Koch, Hogans, Christensen and Hendee, 1984).

Because the recreation resource is a composite of social, biological, and physical resources, coupled with their management, recreation managers face complex challenges. Given the typically functional nature of most natural resource management organizations, in which specific resources are the responsibility of different departments or divisions, integrated planning and management is problematic. One result of this division of responsibility is that adverse impacts on resource systems that have existing or potential recreation value can occur easily, unfolding before anyone is aware of those effects. Thus, it seemed important in the development of the ROS that a language be adopted that different functional specialists could share and understand. The focus on recreation opportunities sought to define such settings in terms that held meaning for different specialists, be they silviculturalists, wildlife biologists, or engineers, and that were also relevant to how such settings were managed from a recreation perspective.[1]

The ROS typically has been applied at a regional scale (Driver et al., 1987). As a result, published guidelines for its application provide only general direction; its utility, for example, in developing specific criteria and standards for site management is limited in that planners must develop specific guidelines for individual areas. Examples of this exist, but it is a time-consuming, complex task. Thus, a derivative effort stemming from the ROS has focused attention on the management at the microsite attribute level, i.e., site-specific features that include many of the elements discussed here under the physical, social, and managerial setting labels. These features give sites recreational significance in terms of experience opportunities provided and affect the nature of possible activities. They also identify management actions most likely to affect recreation use in either positive or negative ways (Clark and Stankey, 1986).

Attributes are features that define an area or site as a recreational resource. Knowing what these attributes are, their relative importance to recreationists participating in different activities or seeking different experiences, and the sensitivity of the attributes to change are essential inputs to integrated resource management. Alterations to settings induced by nonrecreational resource uses can greatly change the type of recreational opportunities available. Conversely, maintaining the essential attributes of a recreational opportunity setting might represent a significant constraint on other uses.

A knowledge of specific attributes and conditions that limit recreation use at sites can be valuable. For example, if an otherwise viable campsite on the coast of southeast Alaska is limited by an excessive bathoslope (secure anchoring is not possible because of an excessively steep underwater slope), it might be possible to overcome this constraint through construction of an artificial mooring. A decision as to whether this should be done would be affected by information about alternative sites within the immediate area, the appropriateness of the facility in light of area management objectives, and anticipated demand for the newly created opportunity, as well as costs.

---

[1]For example, concepts such as home range, travel corridor, territory, and hiding cover describe behavioral phenomena associated with both wildlife and recreation, and the use of such terms can facilitate discussion and understanding of these concepts among people interested in wildlife or recreation, or in silvicultural treatments to enhance habitat for either (see Clark, 1987, 1988; Thomas, 1979).

When conflicts between recreation sites and nonrecreation resource uses such as timber harvesting appear likely, a variety of techniques might be adopted to mitigate undesirable effects. For example, the timing, spacing, and/or design of the proposed harvest can be modified. Design of the transportation network could be altered so as to either facilitate access or limit it. In southeast Alaska, for instance, there is limited automobile access on many islands; roads developed primarily to accommodate timber harvests could be designed so as to increase opportunities for motor-access recreation. Conversely, access could be limited, by design, regulation, or a combination of the two.

Work on management of site attributes could address some of the debate over the role of logging in certain areas. Studies in the Pacific Northwest demonstrate there are important recreation values in multiple-use forests, even where timber harvesting occurs. However, as Clark et al. (1984) note:

> the observations and findings from this research should not be construed as an excuse to log previously unlogged areas. Rather, the results of our work indicate that when a decision is made to harvest timber for commodity values, it may also be possible to provide some quality recreation opportunities in such areas. There may also be situations, however, where silvicultural alternatives should be considered expressly for recreation, rather than production of commodities. Management objectives guide such decisions.

To make such an approach work requires that critical recreation sites and their attributes be identified and measured early in the planning process. In this regard, recreation is little different from fish and wildlife management; knowledge of critical habitat and of the consequences likely to occur under differing management regimes is fundamental to good decision making. However, with such information in hand, it should be possible to test alternative timing, spacing, and design options for their ability to protect key recreation opportunities in areas where intensive management for other resource values is planned. However, in addition to a planning framework within which such issues are assessed, there is also a need for a forum in which alternative interests, values, and perspectives, including those of recreationists, local residents, managers, and various technical specialists can be presented. In efforts to apply the ROS, the extent to which such forums have been successfully developed is arguable. As a result, successful application of the ROS has often been stymied by the lack of adequate functional integration, by conflicting interests, or by application in a mechanistic, uncritical manner. As we shall discuss later, new approaches to applying the ROS are needed.

Limits of Acceptable Change: The Carrying Capacity Problem Redefined

There has long been concern among recreation managers, researchers, and users regarding the impacts of recreation use on both resources and visitor experiences. Although such concerns arose as early as the 1930s, they gained particular salience following the end of World War II, as the postwar boom led to increasing levels of recreation use in America's forests and parks. The associated impacts on resources—vegetation, soil, water quality—led to the search for a framework within which such impacts could be evaluated and upon which decisions about the management of recreation use might be based.

The concept of carrying capacity, drawn from wildlife and range management, held a powerful, intuitive appeal as basis for such a framework. At its simplest, it suggested that the sites upon which recreation use occurred had a definable limit to the use they could tolerate; once that limit was reached, significant, perhaps irreversible, damage to the resource base would occur. In this calculus, it was obvious that if such a level could be determined through scientific research, then subsequent management decisions to limit use would have a sound, objective basis.

However, the search for a measure of site carrying capacity proved largely futile (Stankey and McCool, 1984). Beginning in the 1980s much of the research in this area began to redirect its attention from a question of "how much is too much" to the question of defining what resource conditions (e.g., vegetation, soils, water quality) and social conditions (e.g., level and type of use, location of use) are desired and then undertaking the management actions necessary to ensure those conditions.

From this work emerged the concept of the *Limits of Acceptable Change* or LAC (Stankey, Cole, Lucas, Petersen and Frissell, 1985). The LAC process rests on several fundamental premises. First, it accepts that change in resource conditions is inevitable; natural systems are dynamic and will change irrespective of human actions. Second, the LAC recognizes that recreation use leads to change; this human-induced change might or might not be appropriate for an area, depending upon the specific objectives for it. Third, in managing such change, a variety of actions are possible; limiting use (which had been the principal focus in carrying capacity studies) is only one action that might be taken to control impacts that are judged to be unacceptable. Fourth, the identification of a condition as unacceptable is fundamentally a value judgment; hence, its determination is a function not only of biological knowledge but also of social choices as well.

The LAC incorporates many of the ROS concepts into a framework within which decisions about appropriate and acceptable levels of impact upon recreation settings and experiences can be made. As such, it is not a mechanistic blueprint, but a process that requires conscious, deliberate reflection. It is composed of four major components:

1. the specification of acceptable and achievable resource conditions, as defined by a measurable set of indicators (e.g., level of vegetation loss at campsites, level of encounters while traveling along trails);
2. an analysis of the relationship between existing conditions and those judged acceptable;
3. identification of management actions necessary to ensure that desired conditions are achieved or maintained; and
4. a program of monitoring and evaluation to assess management effectiveness.

The LAC was first applied in the Bob Marshall, Great Bear, and Scapegoat Wildernesses, which lie along the Continental Divide in western Montana. This 680,000 hectare wilderness "complex" provided an opportunity for development, refinement, and experimentation in how the LAC concept might be applied in an "on the ground" application. Working with area managers, commercial outfitters, environmentalists, and local citizens, we were able simultaneously to fashion the LAC concept, to apply it, and, based upon feedback, to modify and revise the system as appropriate.

It has been a decade since the LAC first was implemented in the Bob Marshall Wilderness complex. Since implementation, it has provided the overall framework for decision making with respect to campsite rehabilitation and management, law enforcement and ranger patrols, and visitor education programs. Following the initial application, the LAC was adopted by managers of other wildernesses (McCoy et al., 1995), and adapted to deal with national park *carrying capacity* mandates (National Park Service, 1993; Hof et al., 1994) as well as nature-based tourism developments (McCool, 1994). As compared to applications of the ROS, the LAC—especially with regard to its use in the Bob Marshall Wilderness complex—has proved remarkably effective. Given its close link to the ROS, one might ask why the LAC has achieved a higher level of effective implementation. As we shall describe, the answer seems to lie in how the LAC was applied, not only as a technical planning system, but also as a framework for the exercise of social choice and learning.

Decision Strategies and Organizations

At their core, both the ROS and LAC frameworks represent examples of the social reform tradition of planning. More specifically, they are rational-comprehensive or synoptic models: they involve the formulation of *goals and objectives;* they identify *alternatives,* describe *consequences* and *evaluate* them; and they lead to *decisions* that are *implemented* and later *assessed* (Friedmann, 1987). Such planning typically has been conducted by subject matter "experts" who are generally isolated (purposefully) from the sociopolitical context in order to ensure "objective" decisions. The ROS and LAC frameworks certainly do not have to be cast in this framework, but generally they have been, consistent with the theory of social reform planning that this is the ideal way to make and implement policy regarding technically complex issues.

Yet, implementation of such a planning model is under increasing criticism today. Successful implementation of natural resource plans based on this "expert-driven," rational-comprehensive model is increasingly problematic. Such plans, including those focused on recreation, frequently are the object of formal administrative appeals, citizen protests, and litigation. Rational-comprehensive plans implicitly assume that all that is needed for implementation is a planning process that rests upon a sound, objective, and competent technical foundation. However, in reality, such plans, by definition, affect the flow and allocation of values—be they commodity, aesthetic, scientific, or other forms—to people. Because planning leads to decisions that affect values, it is inevitably a political undertaking. Moreover, when stakeholders hold veto power over the decision process (through their capacity to file appeals or to challenge those decisions legally), successful implementation becomes problematic.

Such considerations unfold in many recreation planning decisions. For example, a primary purpose of the ROS system is to provide diversity in recreational opportunities as well as an assessment of the conse-

quences of other management decisions on the provision of such opportunities. These are fundamentally allocation choices, with implications for what is (and is not) provided, for whom, where, when, and how. The decision to provide a particular type of recreation opportunity (featuring high levels of infrastructure and development) is a de facto decision not to provide a dispersed, undeveloped setting. Similarly, decisions to permit nonrecreation activities, such as timber harvesting, have direct implications for the type of recreation setting provided and thus, who will be served (and who will not be served) by virtue of that decision.

The application of the LAC even more directly affects allocation of values. Because it is especially concerned with decisions regarding the nature of impact, either social or resource, it inevitably confronts questions that involve limiting public access to, and use of, resources. Again, this is ultimately a political and value judgment, whose resolution purely through technical analyses is not possible.

Thus, as we became involved in implementation of these planning frameworks, it became increasingly apparent that we needed to rethink how the processes through which the frameworks were applied needed to be modified so as to, on the one hand, take advantage of the strengths of the rational-comprehensive model, and on the other, to avoid its limitations. We turn now to a discussion of some concepts for identifying the requisite qualities of such a modified model.

When Causation and Preference Differ

In a paper published four decades ago, Thompson and Tuden (1987) outlined a framework for considering the decision-making behavior of organizations. Their framework was grounded in four basic presumptions:

1. there are several types of decisions to be made in, and on behalf of, organizations;
2. each type of decision calls for a different strategy;
3. there are several structures that facilitate these decisions; and
4. the resulting organizational behavior defines variations in decision processes.

Thompson and Tuden argued that decisions involve two key elements. First, there is a question of causation; this concerns explanation of past, present, and/ or future events. Such questions are fundamentally concerned with the extent of certainty surrounding some question, or conversely, what level of uncertainty surrounds our understanding of apparent causation. To resolve uncertainty, we turn to an examination of evidence, with such inquiry typically based upon science (Forester, 1993). Such questions fundamentally involve the issue of means because they demand an understanding of the differential consequences of alternatives.

Second, decisions involve an element related to ends, with *preferences for certain outcomes*. Because of the pluralism of values, there will be conflicting judgments about preferred outcomes; here, we are confronted with the twin problems of ambiguity and conflict, rather than uncertainty. In some cases, clear differences in preferred outcomes exist; e.g., wilderness versus timber production or one type of recreation opportunity versus another. In other cases, there exists no pattern of preference at all; the question as to what goals should be pursued is highly ambiguous. As Forester (1993, p. 89) writes, "Faced with uncertainty we wonder if a particular strategy will work; faced with ambiguity we wonder what we should take as the standard of what works in the first place."

Given a simple two-by-two matrix that describes the extent to which agreement or disagreement exists on causation and on preferred outcomes, we can identify four different decision issues and the associated institutional structure best adapted to resolving such a type of decision (Figure 26.1). For example, when there is agreement on both causation and preference (Cell A), decisions are computational; that is, they are largely technical and mechanical, and implementing them is most efficiently achieved through bureaucratic structures. Because agreement on causation and preference exists, rational-comprehensive planning processes work well. However, when agreement exists on preference but not on causation (Cell B), a small, collegial forum, involving expert judgment and a "triangulation" approach to decision making, leads to a decision process based upon majority rules. Because in this case, the nature of causation is disputed, experimentation might be especially important; some views of adaptive management would fit here as examples of where an improved understanding of the relationship between cause and effect is sought as a means of improving decisions (Lee, 1993).

When there is agreement on causation, but not preference (Cell C), neither computation nor collective judgment are appropriate. Given the pluralism of interests, the decision structure must ensure representation of the range of interests that hold a stake in the outcome, and decisions will often involve some form of compromise among various competing interests. Resolution of differences necessarily involves negotiation and bargaining among competing interests. However, when examining Cell D of this matrix, we confront an especially difficult situation. Here, there is agreement on neither causation nor preference: both uncertainty and ambiguity are high. This is the realm of the "wicked problem" (Allen and Gould, 1986), and when it comes to describing either the decision processes through which we answer such questions or the appropriate institutional structures we employ to implement such decisions, we have little other than "inspiration" to go on (Thompson and Tuden, 1987).

Another feature of responding to problems within this realm is the need to accommodate their technical complexity as well as to respond in a way that accommodates democratic principles. This twofold dimension reflects "the quandary": "how can the democratic ideal of public control be made consistent with the realities of a society dominated by technically complex policy questions" (Pierce and Lovrich, 1983, p. 1). Processes to respond effectively to this quandary are needed that both inform the decision-making process and facilitate participation.

FIGURE 26.1 RELATIONSHIP AMONG CAUSATION BELIEF, OUTCOME PREFERENCE, AND INSTITUTIONAL STRUCTURES

Preferences about possible outcomes

	Agreement	**Disagreement**
	A	**C**
Agreement	Computation (Bureaucracy)	Compromise (Representative structure)
Beliefs about causation	**B**	**D**
Disagreement	Judgment (Collegial structure)	Inspiration (????)

SOURCE: "Strategies, Structures, and Processes of Organizational Decision" by J. D. Thompson and A. Tuden in *Comparative Studies in Administration: Management and Technology* (pp. 195–217), by J. D. Thompson, P. B. Hammond, R. W. Hawkes, B. H. Junker and A. Tuden (Eds.), 1987, New York, NY: Garland Publishing. Copyright 1987 Garland Publishing. Adapted with permission.

Another way of conceiving of the situation characterizing Cell D is that it represents a "zone of turbulence" (Lawrence and Lorsch, 1969); that is, the environment within which an organization must work (and to which any planning framework must be sensitive) can be described along intersecting continua of certainty/uncertainty and stability/change (Figure 26.2). The combination of high uncertainty, rapid change, and, at least implicitly, high ambiguity, strains the capacity of conventional organizational structures and processes. As Friedmann (1987) notes, organizations operating under these conditions have a need for adaptability, a high level of response capacity, and rapid feedback in response to their actions. Paehlke and Torgerson (1990) elaborate further, suggesting that organizations need to be characterized by being noncompartmentalized, open, decentralized, flexible, and antitechnocratic. To this we add that organizations operating successfully in a turbulent environment must know "who they are" in the sense that they possess a clear mission and institutional (self-) concept. Those institutions characterized by such security respond and adapt, while those whose identity is unclear or in flux can be blown off course and flounder in the winds of change.

In this zone of turbulence, organizations operate in an environment they cannot fully predict or directly control; thus, organizational survival is dependent upon continuing contact with that environment so as to obtain feedback and modify behavior accordingly (Michael, 1973). However, organizations typically are able to incorporate stimuli from the environment only so long *as that information does not challenge the paradigms upon which the planning processes are based* (emphasis added; Westley, 1995, p. 39,). As Sabatier and Jenkins-Smith note, (1993, p. 19) "members of various coalitions seek to better understand the world in order to further their policy objectives. [However] they will resist information suggesting their basic beliefs may be invalid or unattainable." In extreme cases, the lack of a learning or responsive capacity can prove fatal to long-term survival. Conversely, organizations that demonstrate an ability to be adaptive can survive even dramatic changes in the environment within which they exist (see Clarke and McCool, 1985, pp. 13–33, for a discussion of this issue as applied to the U.S. Army Corps of Engineers).

Failure to accurately interpret the changing environment within which the organization exists can also lead to a misinterpretation as to the fundamental nature of the problems confronting that organization, which, in turn, can lead to inappropriate and ineffective solutions. For example, Caldwell (1990) has proposed three *levels of comprehension* regarding the causes, explanations, and likely remedies of environ-

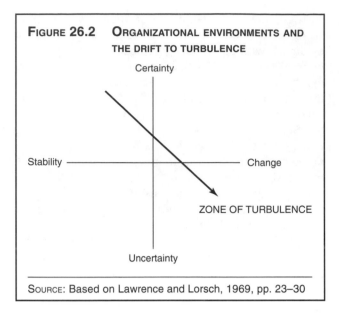

FIGURE 26.2 ORGANIZATIONAL ENVIRONMENTS AND THE DRIFT TO TURBULENCE

SOURCE: Based on Lawrence and Lorsch, 1969, pp. 23–30

mental impairment. At level one, problems are seen as incidental, the result of errors, accidents, or ignorance. Such problems are resolved through education and exhortations "to do better." Addressing the problem of littering through such programs as Keep America Beautiful would be an example. Level two problems result from operational errors in policy planning and execution, due to ineffective management, inadequate data, and poor operating procedures. They can be resolved through laws and regulations, improved technological assessment, impact statements, and more thorough review. Environmental Impact Statements are a response to problems at this level. At level three, however, systemic problems are deeply imbedded in the underlying systems and paradigms. They are an inherent by-product of prevailing socioeconomic and technological systems. As a consequence, their resolution demands fundamental changes in these underlying technological and behavioral systems, including a restructuring of institutions.

While there is an increasing sense that many natural resource problems facing us are systemic, rather than incidental or operational, there is little agreement as to what the appropriate solution or most effective institutional structure might be. Typically, we treat systemic problems as though they were operational; we seek more data or impose new regulations. Yet, such responses are ill-suited to contend with the underlying problems and can, in fact, become problems themselves. Again, this is consistent with the discussion regarding Cell D in Figure 26.1 (page 441).

In light of this discussion, we begin to see why the successful application of the ROS and LAC frameworks to resolve issues of high complexity, ambiguity, and uncertainty has proved problematic. The dominance of the expert-based rational-comprehensive paradigm, grounded in a belief in rationality, scientific management, efficiency, and objectivity, has been described and critiqued extensively by others (e.g., Hays, 1959; Wondolleck, 1988). While suited to the solution of well-defined, narrowly framed questions, the paradigm has proved unable to deal with questions and issues of a prescriptive nature, in which value judgments are not only present but inevitable and dominant (Wondolleck, 1988) on both the supply and demand side of the planning equation. Although the model remains remarkably persistent and enduring, it is at the risk of hindering an organization's capacity to respond to a rapidly changing political environment that is increasingly pluralistic, distrustful, and politically aware and active.

A Social Learning Model Approach: Applying the Limits of Acceptable Change

As we confronted the challenge of applying the LAC in a manner that accommodated both the technical complexity of the underlying issues as well as provided a forum within which a wide range of stakeholders, including visitors, interested citizens, managers, and scientists could participate, we turned to the social learning literature.

Social learning is a broad, encompassing tradition in planning, stemming from the philosophical pragmatism of John Dewey. However, the core feature of social learning is a focus on *action*: "purposeful activity taken by an actor, individual or collective, within the actor's environment" (Friedmann, 1987, p. 183). Social learning approaches are characterized by:

1. Providing opportunities for interaction and deliberation.
2. Being inherently political, in that they involve questions of the nature and distribution of values.
3. Representing all interests who ultimately hold veto power in the discussions and decisions. The intent here is to create a microcosm of the "political marketplace" (Caulfield, 1975).
4. Integrating perspectives, knowledge, and interests.
5. Honoring a wide conception of relevant knowledge, admitting both the formal knowledge of science as well as the experiential or personal knowledge held by citizens.
6. Centering on a task-oriented action group—a dynamic, interactive group focused on an issue.
7. Involving a decision that feeds back into the learning process. Indeed, the fundamental purpose is to build learning among group participants in a way that facilitates action.

In the initial application of the LAC in the Bob Marshall Wilderness Complex (BMWC), a social learning approach was taken (McCool and Stankey, 1986; Stokes, 1990). The approach was based on Friedmann's (1973) theory of transactive planning. In this situation, agency planners and managers were brought together with scientists and various publics as a task force (see point 6) in order to create opportunities for *dialogue*, which then could lead to *learning*, culminating in *societal guidance* (creation of a plan that could be implemented). Within the task force, all forms of knowledge were considered legitimate (point 5) and, while legal proscriptions prohibited the direct involvement of citizens in making decisions, the decisions were made in real time in front of all participants.

Joining Social Learning and the Limits of Acceptable Change

A plan of management for the Bob Marshall Wilderness had been prepared in the early 1970s. It included a statement of objectives, a discussion of conditions and issues, proposed management actions, and so forth. However, in the judgment of both area managers and wilderness visitors, the plan had little bearing on day-to-day management; did little to help resolve complex, difficult questions; omitted ownership of ideas and actions by stakeholders; and failed to lead to responsive management.

The Bob Marshall Wilderness, the core of the complex, has been described as the crown jewel of the National Wilderness Preservation System (NWPS) and deserved much better planning. Named after Bob Marshall, the dynamic director of the USDA Forest Service's Division of Recreation in the late 1930s, the area provides a diverse range of biophysical conditions, from alpine meadows to lush valleys, and is home to the grizzly bear, wolf, and a host of other species.

The area had a number of severe and escalating management problems. Heavy recreational horse use had left some trails muddy wallows, stretching over long distances. Conflicts between horseback riders and backpackers occurred, administrative structures were scattered throughout the area, and primitive airstrips were present. Concerns existed about the effects of recreational use, both backpacker and stock use, on endangered species. Growing concerns about efforts to restore historical fire regimes and the effects of such a program on both wildlife and recreation use were expressed.

Because of these and other issues, area managers were interested in developing a new management plan. Concurrent with this interest, efforts within the Intermountain Research Station's Wilderness Management Research program to develop an alternative approach to the "carrying capacity" issue were underway. Finally, the recreation staff officer on the Flathead National Forest who, as a doctoral student (Stokes, 1982), had applied Friedmann's (1973) theory of transactive planning to river management planning, helped complete the necessary linkage of events, circumstances, and individuals. A new management plan was to be developed, but it was to be guided by an alternative paradigmatic framework, grounded in social learning.

The social learning model and its specific application utilizing the transactive planning framework was comprised of several specific characteristics, each of which was designed to satisfy either the general requirements of social learning theory and/or the institutional requirements of operating in highly ambiguous, uncertain, and politically unsettled environments. These specific characteristics include the following.

Recognize the Pluralism in Values and Interests

All values, interests, and/or concerns with regard to the BMWC were to be represented in discussions. It was important these values, interests, and concerns be represented in both a horizontal sense (e.g., embracing the diverse views among recreationists) as well as vertically (cognizant of concerns at the local, regional, and national levels). This reflected explicit recognition of the pluralism known to exist with regard to values and interests. It also acknowledged that the area was significant not only at the state and regional levels, but also at the national, and likely international, levels as well. Thus it was important that the discussions that occurred with regard to the area's future management be sensitive and responsive to values and concerns held across the country and over a wide range of interests.

The inclusive perspective was also justified on the grounds that veto power was held by many interests over any potential decision. That is, the purposeful or inadvertent exclusion of interests could place future decisions at risk because of the failure to take into account such interests or to create a sense of ownership on their part in those decisions. One practical implication is that in developing the task force, we did not select who would (or would not) participate. Participation was self-selected and an open door policy was practiced throughout the process.

Recognize the Legitimacy of Many Forms of Knowledge

A second fundamental characteristic of the social learning model is that it honors alternative forms of knowledge. Thus, not only was the formal, scientific knowledge held by agency and university scientists taken into account, but the experiential or personal knowledge held by visitors, local residents, and others also was actively sought and utilized. This resulted in two important benefits.

First, it acknowledged that the knowledge needed to solve the complex problems confronting the group was held by many people (Lang, 1990). Formal science was an obvious source of such understanding; however, in many cases, it was incomplete or had to be interpolated from studies conducted elsewhere. Thus, it was necessary to interpret such knowledge within a new context and the extent to which that knowledge could be confidently applied was often problematic. Here, the juxtaposition of formal knowledge vis-à-vis the experiential knowledge of citizens proved beneficial, contributing important insight as to its applicability. Experiential knowledge also contributed important historical understanding, as revealed by stories, photos, and the like that had been passed down from families and friends.

Second, a broad inclusive view of relevant knowledge promoted an increased perception of legitimization among participants. As individuals became increasingly aware and appreciative of the knowledge that others had to contribute, there was a consequent rise in their appreciation of the legitimacy of other's views and concerns. Such sharing of knowledge, experiences, and perspectives helped provoke a shift from purely self-interest to common interest. As Weick (1979, p. 92) has observed:

> Once the members [of a group] converge on interlocked behavior as the means to pursue diverse ends, there occurs a subtle shift away from diverse to *common ends*. The diverse ends remain, but they become subordinated to an emerging set of shared

ends. This shift is one of the most striking that occurs in group life and is exceedingly complex.

A Science That Informs Rather Than Dictates Discussion

As suggested earlier, the BMWC task force faced a number of complex technical questions: the relationship of use to impact, the likely response of different environmental settings to differing levels and types of use, and so on. Such questions demanded that the process have access to good, sound scientific knowledge. However, as Paehlke and Torgerson (1990) have noted, expertise, almost by definition, is specialized and insufficient by itself for handling many types of environmental problems. Moreover, the complexity and multifaceted nature of many issues leads to legitimate disputes about cause and effect; experts often disagree with one another as to causal factors and/or likely responses (Schwarz and Thompson, 1990). Thus, the role of science in the task force was explicitly designed to facilitate an understanding of this complexity, to serve as a source of state-of-the-art knowledge, and to create a sense of understanding as to the probabilistic nature of the knowledge.

The consequences of this precept were interesting. Initially, many of the technical subject specialists were uneasy with the situation. Some saw the planning exercise as one that denigrated the importance of scientific knowledge; in its most extreme form, there was a view that the process abdicated science in favor of some kind of "majority-rules" view. However, as time passed, this view diminished, in large part due to the influence of the second characteristic of social learning: honor a wide range of knowledge. As the inherent complexity of many issues became apparent, citizens increasingly turned to specialists for their insight. Ironically, rather than denigrating or downplaying the importance of scientific expertise, the process actually enhanced its appreciation. However, it also led to an increasing appreciation on the part of the technical specialists for the insight and perceptive observations of citizen members. For example, citizens often were able to contribute observations that filled in site-specific knowledge to the predictions and theoretical discussion offered by specialists. Additionally, public scrutiny likely led to an increased technical competency; the questioning of subject matter experts by citizens motivated by a deep, personal concern with the area, coupled with their capacity to link personal knowledge with technical and theoretical understanding, were powerful complementary forces. The result was that both groups increasingly honored and respected the knowledge held by the other; moreover, it likely resulted in an increased, rather than diminished, role for formal science.

One specific measure as to how this kind of process contributes to a more informed decision-making process is revealed in an assessment by McCoy et al. (1995). In a review of over 20 LAC-based planning efforts, they found that when a citizen task force was involved, similar to that used in the BMWC, the ability of agency planners to specify physical, social, and managerial attributes to guide decisions was much improved than when done by the agency alone. In the BMWC, citizen involvement in formulating a complex set of area indicators and standards against which decisions about acceptable levels of impact would be made, was substantive, informed, and critical.

Active Engagement and Learn by Doing

The process assigned high priority to learning through active engagement of participants in real problems, real data, and real management decisions. For example, field trips proved useful in discussing problems, alternative management options, and as a means of testing proposed indicators and standards against reality. Group members were active in data collection; some campsite inventory data, for example, were provided by citizens and management action priorities were clearly a result of dialogue among task force members. This demonstrated the potential value of *joint fact-finding* as a means of facilitating meaningful and satisfying participation (Wondolleck, 1988). It also acted to *democratize* access to data, preventing a situation from developing in which a single group, such as resource managers, controlled the information required to make a decision.

Such active engagement with real-world problems helped create an enhanced appreciation for the complexity of issues facing resource managers. Choices about management decisions that might have seemed obvious, given one's particular interest, became increasingly problematic as knowledge of the issue grew (including an increasing recognition of the legitimacy of alternative perspectives).

The importance of this active, real-world engagement is heightened because learning typically is more likely in active, rather than passive, situations (Daniels and Walker, 1996). Again, this dovetails with the earlier discussion about the importance of recognizing the breadth of relevant knowledge; the social learning model used here required all participants to serve as active resources to discussions rather than either simply presenters or listeners.

Decision Making
Through Consensus

Any group process requires a means through which it reaches decisions and takes action; for example, groups might rely upon a majority-rules voting process. However, following the theory of transactive planning, the BMWC task force adopted consensus as the basis upon which decisions were made. Although consensus has been criticized as "the lowest common denominator of . . . democracies" (Beer, 1975, as cited in Friedmann, 1987, p. 141), others see it as the principal means through which societal guidance takes place. However, if consensus is to work, there must be both equal access to the knowledge needed to inform pending decisions as well as equal ability to understand that knowledge (it also implies no conscious deception, such as falsifying data or not fully reporting it).

Thus, we see again the value of the precept of mutual learning which underlaid the task force. Consensus flowed out of a process in which information was shared, interpreted, and discussed in an open manner. It was available to all and was subject to critical analysis and questioning. Having said that, there were numerous occasions when sharp conflicts over information and its implications occurred. However, the principle of consensus required that *all* members support any decision before moving on. From such a "decision rule," the task force evolved a working definition of consensus as *grudging agreement;* that is, there had to be at least minimal concurrence on the part of all individuals with a decision before it was taken as the sentiment of the task force. Often, this resulted in negotiations between interests within the task force who sought quid pro quo arrangements with others. Thus, the process of compromise, coming to a resolution by addressing issues rather than stating positions, was critical to development of such grudging agreement. As noted earlier, the task force was intended to constitute a "microcosm of the political marketplace" (Caulfield, 1975), and the negotiation among interests was integral to this process.

Ongoing Monitoring Is Essential
to the Learning Process

The task force strongly endorsed the need for ongoing monitoring following adoption of a recommended management program. Through the learning engendered by the process, participants became increasingly aware of the limits of knowledge and understanding. Thus, the resulting plan rests upon a recognition of the importance of flexibility and adaptation. Over time, as conditions change and new knowledge emerges,

changes in indicators, standards, and/or management actions are likely. Because of their participation in the process, it is likely that changes recommended by the USDA Forest Service in the future will be better understood; the task force process helped engender a recognition of the provisional nature of the knowledge base upon which the plan was based and the likely need to revise as that knowledge base changes.

Linking People, Place and Process

A final aspect of the BMWC planning exercise that merits attention is that it provided a forum in which three key elements of planning were integrated. This includes *people,* embracing an array of concepts that reveal how they understand and value the world around them as well as to how they are organized (from individual to large-scale populations); *places,* representing both physical space as well as the symbolic meanings assigned to them; and *processes,* involving both basic biophysical processes as well as the sociocultural processes that influence the relationship among people and between people and their environment (Stankey and Clark, 1992).

These three elements can be thought of as interlinking realms. As the Venn diagram in Figure 26.3 suggests, attention can focus on any individual sector, such as a study of recreationists or of the ecological processes. Often, study focuses on an area of overlap; we study recreationists in a particular place. However, a particular strength of the LAC project in the Bob Marshall Wilderness Complex is found in the way in which it focused attention on the overlap of all three elements. It involved how people value and use a place and facilitated an understanding of social, ecological, and planning processes as a means of making decisions. As we reflect upon the experience in applying the ROS, we can observe that frequently our attention

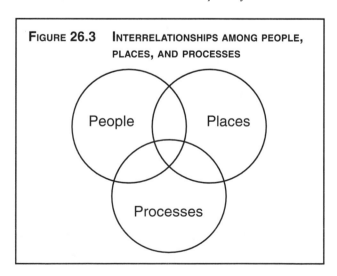

FIGURE 26.3   INTERRELATIONSHIPS AMONG PEOPLE, PLACES, AND PROCESSES

only addressed one or two of the elements. However, in the Bob Marshall exercise, the "grounding" of the effort in place helped achieve a heretofore unprecedented level of integration and interaction among citizens, managers, and scientists. The attachment of individuals to this place could have been either functional (e.g., recreationists) or symbolic (e.g., meaning) or both, but in the final analysis, the linkage of place to people and processes facilitated by the social learning approach to applying the LAC appears to have played a major role in achieving a successful outcome. Although the notion of success, even in this context, is multidimensional, in the case of the BMWC, it can loosely be defined as the achievement of consensus and ownership by the public in the plan.

The New Millennium: What Does It Hold?

We have noted the strength of the ROS and LAC planning frameworks in addressing the challenges of providing recreation in multiple-use situations and in an era of rapid social change. We have argued that these systems, if executed primarily as expert-based, rational-comprehensive planning processes, will be difficult to implement where there is disagreement about cause-effect relationships and ambiguity or conflict over goals. In these situations, combining the strengths of rational-comprehensive planning processes with social learning is more likely to lead to plans that can be implemented. However, there are a number of trends suggesting the increased importance of social learning–based planning processes regardless of the situation. We offer a short description of these trends and suggest implications for the design of recreation planning.

First, there will be continuing and even an increased demand for access to, and influence upon, decisions that affect values of concern to citizens; the capacity to influence decision making processes will also grow. Implied is a continuing wariness by citizens of experts and government. It also implies increased pressures for public scrutiny of decisions and an unwillingness to accept decisions unquestioningly. Because of the broad range of values and interests within society, it will lead to an increased sense of a proliferation of values which command and demand attention by policymakers.

Second, contrary to the view that the land allocation issue has been resolved in the United States, we will see increased efforts to revisit such allocation decisions. This includes allocations for various types of withdrawals (e.g., national parks and wilderness), allocations for particular land uses (e.g., timber harvest, water with-

drawals), and allocations made through law as well as administrative procedures.

Third, there will be continuing concern as to the adequacy of the various institutional apparatus to adapt to, respond to, and cope with the value changes stemming from a dynamic society, coupled with improved understanding of natural systems. For example, despite rising interest in the concept of ecosystem management, critics (e.g., Grumbine, 1994, Slocumbe, 1993) point to institutional inadequacy (e.g., an inability to work across organizational boundaries) as the most severe constraint on its implementation.

Fourth, continued demographic changes in society (e.g., age and ethnic composition, spatial distribution) will challenge traditional ways in which decisions are made as well as the nature of the problems which must be confronted, and, as noted in the third point earlier, the capacity of institutions to respond. This has major implications for discussions and decisions relative to what recreation opportunities are provided, where, in what relative amounts, by whom, and so on.

Finally, there will be a continued, perhaps growing, awareness of the limits of science in resolving crucial social questions. The complex, diverse range of demands of a society that increasingly asserts its right of access to, and influence upon, decisions, coupled with an increasing appreciation of the complexity of the biophysical, social, and economic systems within which we exist, will call for new approaches to scientific inquiry (e.g., as evidenced by the growing interest in adaptive management; see Lee, 1993; Gunderson, Holling and Light, 1995) as well as for the relationship between science and public choice.

Many other factors could be added to this list. However, in our judgment, we see these as key to a consideration of how we approach resolving the kinds of questions associated with Cell D in Figure 26.1 (page 441): questions of both great ambiguity as well as uncertainty. As we have noted, the capacity of rational-comprehensive models to deal adequately with such issues is problematic. ROS and LAC are, at their core, representative of rational-comprehensive planning processes. The strength and effectiveness of such processes is based on their capacity to provoke a systematic search for means to achieve designated goals and explicitness in evaluation of alternatives. Yet, in order to succeed fully, these strengths must be augmented by taking a social learning approach. Such an approach would indicate that recreation planning in the new millennium will be characterized by being *integrative, interactive,* and *adaptive.*

Integrative planning means that recreation is viewed within the context of multiple values of natural resources or ecosystems, and incorporates not only expert-based knowledge but experiential knowledge as well. Integration in this sense requires a mutually agreed upon definition of issues and a holistic approach, and involves application of different disciplines to commonly defined problems. Because knowledge is widely dispersed and provisional, effective action requires involvement of different disciplines in resolving planning issues.

Interactive planning is fundamental to learning. Interactive planning depends on dialogue that leads to mutual learning among participants. Interaction provides the opportunity for participants to "work through" (Yankelovich, 1991) the complex issues of providing recreation opportunities on wildlands and results in broadened appreciation and application of relevant knowledge.

Adaptive planning is needed simply because we are not very good at predicting the future. Uncertainty characterizes almost all decisions; surprises, rather than unexpected, should be viewed as the norm (Lee, 1993). Treating management as an experiment leads to greater knowledge about the effects of actions and provides information needed to refine our models of the real world.

Social learning approaches, therefore, use the structure of rational-comprehensive processes to provide the framework for learning. Rational-comprehensive processes suggest what questions need to be asked and in what sequence; they indicate the information needed by whom and when; and they challenge participants to proceed through planning in such a way that decisions can be traced. Social learning enhances the capability of an organization and its clients to apply all relevant knowledge; it provides the context within which all types of knowledge are considered appropriate and can be shared; and eventually leads to more informed planners and clients.

References

Allen, G. M., & Gould, E. M., Jr. (1986). Complexity, wickedness, and public forests. *Journal of Forestry, 84*(4), 20–23.

Caldwell, L. K. (1990). *Between two worlds: Science, the environmental movement, and policy choice.* New York, NY: Cambridge University Press.

Caulfield, H. P., Jr. (1975). Politics of multiple objective planning. In *Proceedings of the Multiple Objective Planning and Decision-Making Conference.* Moscow, ID: Idaho Research Foundation.

Clark, R. N. (1987). Recreation management: A question of integration. *Western Wildlands, 13*(1), 20–23.

Clark, R. N. (1988). Enhancing recreation opportunities in silvicultural planning. In W. C. Schmidt (Ed.), *Proceedings—Future Forests of the Mountain West: A Stand Culture Symposium* (General Technical Report INT-243, pp. 61–69). Ogden, UT: USDA Forest Service Intermountain Research Station.

Clark, R. N., Koch, R. W., Hogans, M. L., Christensen, H. H., & Hendee, J. C. (1984). *The value of roaded, multiple-use areas as recreation sites in three national forests of the Pacific Northwest* (Research Paper PNW 319). Portland, OR: USDA Forest Service Pacific Northwest Research Station.

Clark, R. N., & Stanley, G. H. (1979). *The recreation opportunity spectrum: A framework for planning, management, and research* (General Technical Report PNW-98). Portland, OR: USDA Forest Service Pacific Northwest Research Station.

Clark, R. N., & Stanley, G. H. (1986). Site attributes—A key to managing wilderness and dispersed recreation. In Robert C. Lucas (Compiler), *Proceedings—National Wilderness Research Conference: Current Research* (General Technical Report INT-212, pp. 509–515). Ogden, UT: USDA Forest Service Intermountain Research Station.

Clarke, J. N., & McCool, D. (1985). *Staking out the terrain: Power differentials among natural resource management agencies.* Albany, NY: State University of New York.

Daniels, S. E., & Walker, G. B. (1996). Collaborative learning: Improving public deliberation in ecosystem-based management. *Environmental Impact Assessment Review, 16,* 71–102.

Driver, B. L., & Brown, P. J. (1978). The opportunity spectrum concept and behavior information in outdoor recreation resource supply inventories: A rationale. In G. H. Lund, V. J. LaBau, P. F. Pfolliott & D. W. Robinson (Eds.), *Integrated inventories of renewable natural resources: Proceedings of the workshop* (General Technical Report RM-55, pp. 24–31). Fort Collins, CO: USDA Forest Service Rocky Mountain Forest and Range Experiment Station.

Driver, B. L., Brown, P. J., Stanley, G. H., & Gregoire, T. G. (1987). The ROS planning system: Evolution, basic concepts, and research needed. *Leisure Sciences, 9,* 201–212.

Forester, J. (1993). *Critical theory, public policy, and planning practice: Toward a critical pragmatism.* Albany, NY: State University of New York.

Friedmann, J. (1973). *Retracking America.* Emmaus, PA: Rodale Press.

Friedmann, J. (1987). *Planning in the public domain: From knowledge to action.* Princeton, NJ: Princeton University Press.

Grumbine, R. E. (1994). What is ecosystem management? *Conservation Biology, 8,* 27–38.

Gunderson, L. H., Holling, C. S., Light, S. S. (Eds.). (1995). *Barriers & bridges to the renewal of ecosystems and institutions.* New York, NY: Columbia University Press.

Hays, S. P. (1988). The new environmental forest. *University of Colorado Law Review, 59,* 517–550.

Hof, M., Hammett, J., Rees, M., Belnap, J., Poe, N., Lime, D., & Manning, B. (1994). Getting a handle on visitor carrying capacity—A pilot project at Arches National Park. *Park Science, 14*(1), 11–13.

Lang, R. (1990). Achieving integration in resource planning. In R. Lang (Ed.), *Integrated approaches to resource planning and management* (pp. 27–50). Calgary, Alberta: University of Calgary Press.

Lawrence, P. R., & Lorsch, J. W. (1969). *Developing organizations: Diagnosis and action.* Reading, MA: Addison-Wesley.

Lee, K. N. (1993). *Compass and gyroscope: Integrating science and politics for the environment.* Washington, DC: Island Press.

McCool, S. F. (1994). Planning for sustainable nature-dependent tourism development: The limits of acceptable change system. *Tourism Recreation Research, 19*(2), 51–55.

McCool, S. F., & Stanley, G. H. (1986). Planning and social change: Responding to the revolution in recreation demand. In *Proceedings, Division 6, International Union of Forest Research Organizations* (pp. 67–77). Ljubljana, Slovenia: IUFRO Secretariat.

McCoy, K. L., Krumpe, E. E., & Allen, S. (1995). Limits of acceptable change planning—Evaluating implementation by the U.S. forest service. *International Journal of Wilderness, 1*(2), 18–22.

Michael, D. N. (1973). *On learning to plan—And planning to learn.* San Francisco, CA: Jossey-Bass, Inc.

Nash, R. (1982). *Wilderness and the American mind* (3rd ed.). New Haven, CT: Yale University Press.

National Park Service. (1993). *VERP: A process for addressing visitor carrying capacity in the national park system*. Denver, CO: Denver Service Center, National Park Service.

Outdoor Recreation Resources Review Commission. (1962). *Outdoor recreation for America*. Washington, DC: U.S. Government Printing Office.

Paehlke, R., & Torgerson, D. (1990). Environmental politics and the administrative state. In R. Paehlke & D. Torgerson (Eds.), *Managing Leviathan: Environmental politics and the administrative state* (pp. 285–301). Peterborough, Ontario: Broadview Press.

Pierce, J. C., & Lovrich, N. P. (1983). Trust in the technical information provided by interest groups: The views of legislators, activists, experts, and the general public. *Policy Studies Journal, 11*, 626–639.

President's Commission on Americans Outdoors. (1986). *A literature review*. Washington, DC: U.S. Government Printing Office.

Sabatier, P., & Jenkins-Smith, H. (1993). *Policy change and learning: An advocacy coalition approach*. Boulder, CO: Westview Press.

Schwarz, M., & Thompson, M. (1990). *Divided we stand: Redefining politics, technology, and social choice*. Philadelphia, PA: University of Pennsylvania Press.

Slocumbe, D. S. (1993). Implementing ecosystem-based management. *Bioscience, 43*(9), 612–623.

Stankey, G. H., & Brown, P. J. (1981). A technique for recreation planning and management in tomorrow's forests. In *Proceedings of XVII IUFRO World Congress, Division 6, Kyoto, Japan*, 63–74.

Stankey, G. H., & Clark, R. N. (1992). *Social aspects of new perspectives in forestry: A problem analysis*. Milford, PA: Grey Towers Press.

Stankey, G. H., Cole, D. N., Lucas, R. C., Petersen, M. E., & Frissell, S. S. (1985). *The limits of acceptable change (LAC) system for wilderness planning* (General Technical Report INT-176). Ogden, UT: USDA Forest Service Intermountain Forest and Range Experiment Station.

Stankey, G. H., & McCool, S. F. (1984). Carrying capacity in recreational settings: Evolution, appraisal, and application. *Leisure Sciences, 6*(4), 453–474.

Stokes, G. L. (1982). *Conservation of the Blackfoot River Corridor—An application of transactive planning theory*. Unpublished doctoral dissertation, Colorado State University, Fort Collins, CO.

Stokes, G. L. (1990). The evolution of wilderness management: The Bob Marshall Wilderness complex. *Journal of Forestry, 88*(10), 15–20.

Thomas, J. W. (Ed.). (1979). *Wildlife habitats in managed forests* (USDA Forest Service Agricultural Handbook 533). Washington, DC: U.S. Government Printing Office.

Thompson, J. D., & Tuden, A. (1987). Strategies, structures, and processes of organizational decision. In J. D. Thompson, P. B. Hammond, R. W. Hawkes, B. H. Junker & A. Tuden (Eds.), *Comparative studies in administration: Management and technology* (pp. 195–217). New York, NY: Garland Publishing, Inc.

Weick, K. W. (1979). *The social psychology of organizing*. Reading, PA: Addison-Wesley.

Westley, F. (1995). Governing design: The management of social systems and ecosystems management. In L. H. Gunderson, C. S. Holling, & S. S. Light (Eds.), *Barriers & bridges to the renewal of ecosystems and institutions* (pp. 391–427). New York, NY: Columbia University Press.

Wilkinson, C. F. (1992). *Crossing the next meridian: Land, water, and the future of the west*. Washington, DC: Island Press.

Wondolleck, J. M. (1988). *Public lands conflict and resolution: Managing national forest disputes*. New York, NY: Plenum Publishing Co.

Yankelovich, D. (1991). *Coming to public judgment: Making democracy work in a complex world*. Syracuse, NY: Syracuse University Press.

Inclusion and Leisure Service Delivery

John Dattilo and Richard Williams

University of Georgia

Introduction

The primary goal of many leisure service professionals is to facilitate leisure experiences for their participants. While debate continues as to the definition of leisure, it can be said, with some degree of confidence, that self-determination plays an important role in leisure involvement (Dattilo and Kleiber, 1993). Self-determination involves acting as the primary causal agent in one's life and making choices and decisions regarding one's life free from external influence or interference (Wehmeyer, 1996). Also, it is widely held that self-determination includes the perception of freedom to make choices and the ability to initiate chosen leisure activities (see Iso-Ahola, chapter 3 in this volume). As such, self-determination is an important consideration in facilitating inclusive leisure for people with disabilities (Dattilo, 1995; Dattilo and St. Peter, 1991). Wall and Dattilo (1995) suggested that by creating environments that are option-rich, responsive, and informative, participants will increase the likelihood

of becoming self-determined. In short, the condition of self-determination occurs when people take control of their freedom.

Unfortunately, within the context of leisure services, many of the 43 million Americans and 4.2 million Canadians with disabilities (*Statistical Abstract of the United States,* 1992; *Canada Year Book,* 1997) are neither encouraged to be self-determined nor feel intrinsically motivated (Dattilo, 1995). This occurs, in part, because many people continue to be prohibited from leisure services on the basis of disability (Schleien, Germ and McAvoy, 1996). This prohibition, which results from programs that are not inclusive, violates the rights of people with disabilities and increases the likelihood that they will not experience meaningful leisure participation.

According to Dattilo (1994), the premise of inclusive leisure services is to create an environment in which all people feel they are welcome and can access supports needed for leisure participation. Although specific to educational settings, the discussion of

Tomlinson et al. (1997) about the benefits of inclusion pertain to leisure settings as well. They stated that inclusion can facilitate "the creation of communities of learning in which a variety of learners engage in a broad mix of educational experiences designed to maximize the contribution of each learner to self and to the whole" (Tomlinson et al., 1997, p. 270). Hunt and Goetz (1997) concluded that students with disabilities can achieve academic and learning success as they experience acceptance, interactions, and friendships in inclusive settings, while students without disabilities experience positive outcomes when students with disabilities are their classmates. It is the challenge for recreation professionals to achieve similar success that some teachers in inclusive classrooms have experienced.

Although research has documented successful inclusive services, especially for individuals with disabilities (e.g., Baker, Wang and Walberg, 1995; Logan et al., 1995), many professionals resist mandates to provide services for a wide range of learners (Behar and George, 1994). For example, Stainback and Stainback (1996, p. 383) listed arguments people have made against inclusion:

> Regular education is not prepared; integration is a plot to reduce funds to students with disabilities; there is a need for further analysis and study; we need to maintain a continuum of services; students with disabilities need special treatments and interventions.

Similar sentiments have been expressed by leisure service providers. In addition, Turnbull and Ruef (1997) reported that even though the body of research and policy supporting inclusion of people with disabilities into educational and community experiences is expanding (e.g., Hasazi, Johnston, Liggett and Schattman, 1994; Osborne and Dimatta, 1994), families, schools, and communities continue to experience substantial barriers to achieving successful inclusion (e.g., Horner, Diemer and Brazeau, 1992).

Despite the controversy over inclusion and the associated barriers to providing inclusive services, it is our position that many leisure services can be more inclusive of people with disabilities, and that inclusion is clearly the ethical path for leisure services. Not only are inclusive leisure services ethical, *all* participants can benefit from such services. The belief that all people can learn, participate in, and benefit from shared educational experiences is at the foundation of inclusion (Grenot-Scheyer, Schwartz and Meyer, 1997). Such a belief encourages the provision of appropriate support and modifications for participation and learning.

Since the "move toward inclusive recreation opportunities is challenging park and recreation agencies to develop better ways to deliver quality services to all of their consumers" (Broida, 1995, p. 55), rather than providing segregated services outside typical community contexts, professionals must work within the ongoing activities to provide support which facilitates participation and independence (Grenot-Scheyer et al., 1997). What follows is a discussion of ways that increase the likelihood that leisure services can be more inclusive of people with disabilities. One way to begin a discussion of inclusion begins with attitudes toward people with disabilities and the ways in which these attitudes can be influenced.

Understanding Attitude Development

Because attitudes play such an important role in the way people perceive one another, it can be helpful for leisure service professionals to understand the way attitudes develop. Fishbein and Ajzen (1975) described attitude development and expression as proceeding in the following stages: antecedents to beliefs, beliefs, attitudes, intentions, and behaviors. Unfounded, negative, ignorant, or fearful beliefs about people with disabilities can result in negative attitudes and subsequent unequal behaviors toward people with disabilities. An important first step in developing inclusive leisure services is for leisure service providers to examine both their own attitudes and the attitudes of others toward people with disabilities.

Societal attitudes can play an important role in the lives of people with disabilities. For instance, when people are perceived as being different from the arbitrary norm of the society in which they live, typically they are stigmatized and labeled as *deviant* (see Rojek, chapter 6 in this volume). A *stigma* is an undesired difference that separates a person from society (Goffman, 1963), even to the degree that the person is perceived as not quite human (Goffman, 1974). Similarly, a *deviant* is a person who has been labeled as significantly different from societal norms (Wolfensberger, 1972). A person's disability is not the origin of a stigma or a deviancy; rather, society assigns stigma and deviant labels to people with undesirable differences. For instance, people with disabling conditions that result in nothing other than an appearance that is different than most people's appearance (e.g., people who have had facial burns) are frequently stigmatized by other members of society.

Additional concepts that can be considered when understanding attitude development are stereotypes and prejudice. Ottati and Lee (1995, pp. 30–31) stated that:

> Although no single definition of "stereotype" is unanimously accepted, most researchers agree that stereotypes involve ascribing characteristics to social groups or segments of society. These characteristics may include traits (e.g., industrious), physical attributes, societal roles (e.g., occupation), or even specific behaviors.

Regardless of differences in definition of the word *stereotype,* there is considerable agreement that stereotypes constitute people's beliefs about groups, beliefs that may be positive or negative, accurate or inaccurate (Jussim, McCauley and Lee, 1995). Although a stereotype is not necessarily negative or inaccurate, some stereotypes are systematically biased in that stereotypes about in-groups (e.g., people without disabilities) will be more positive than stereotypes ascribed to out-groups (e.g., people without disabilities) (Stangor, 1995). In addition to inaccurate and negative stereotypes concerning gender, social class, and race, these types of stereotypes exist about people with disabilities. For example, it is a negative and inaccurate stereotype that people receiving psychiatric counseling typically physically harm themselves and others.

Prejudice involves the development of a judgment in disregard of a person's rights, resulting in that individual being injured or damaged in some way. For example, some people mistakenly believe that adults with cognitive disabilities are childlike and should be treated like children. Such a prejudice often results in adults with cognitive disabilities being denied the opportunity to participate in adult-oriented activities, hold jobs, or develop intimate relationships.

Negative attitudes frequently lead to negative behaviors. Two of the common behavioral manifestations of negative attitudes are segregation and discrimination (Dattilo, 1994). *Segregation* requires the separation or isolation of a group or individual in a restricted area by discriminatory means. Such segregation results in members of the group, or an individual, receiving treatment that is different from other people. In the recent past, the practice of separating people with disabilities from other members of society was largely accepted. According to Stainback, Stainback, and Stefanich (1996, p. 19), this separation "communicates the message that either we do not want to accept everyone or that some people are not worth the effort to make the accommodations necessary to keep them included." For example, some recreation programs offer only a limited number of "special" programs that are meant solely for people with disabilities. In such programs, people with disabilities are encouraged to participate in the special programs and are discouraged from participating in general recreation programs.

Discrimination involves a person making a distinction categorically rather than individually about another person, then acting toward that person differently than they would toward another person. While people discriminate all the time (say for instance between chocolate and vanilla ice cream), it is often considered distasteful and unfair to discriminate against someone on the basis of a disability. Almost always, a disability is no basis for discrimination.

When people without disabilities hold negative attitudes toward people with disabilities, there are three common reactions: the self-fulfilling prophecy, the spread phenomenon, and the overexaggeration assumption. The self-fulfilling prophecy occurs when one person's expectations become an accurate prediction of another person's behavior (Rosenthal and Jacobson, 1968). A person labeled as deviant is expected to behave consistently as a deviant (Algozzine, Mercer and Countermine, 1977), and this expectation can be quite powerful. For instance, if a recreation professional were to mistakenly believe that all people with cognitive disabilities act silly all the time, then the people with cognitive disabilities in this professional's programs are more likely to act silly than they might otherwise be. Similarly, by holding the expectation that people with disabilities do not want to participate in general recreation programs, recreation professionals might influence the beliefs and behaviors of participants with disabilities.

The spread phenomenon is the association of additional imperfections to a person on the basis of another disabling condition (Tripp and Sherrill, 1991). For example, people may assume that a person with mental retardation lacks physical skills. However, mental disabilities are not necessarily associated with physical disabilities. Both people with and without disabilities have different physical skills and abilities.

The overexaggeration assumption is the common assumption that people with disabilities think primarily about their disabilities and want to discuss little else. An overexaggeration assumption limits the degree to which people without disabilities can develop relationships with people with disabilities because it stifles natural conversation and interaction. Many people with disabilities have full and interesting lives and rarely want to dwell on their disability any more than they want to dwell on any other element of their lives.

Negative attitudes are important to consider because they can have such a profound effect on the lives of others. Unfortunately, negative attitudes can arise when people come in contact with people with disabilities. Negative attitudes toward people with disabilities can result in such things as stigmatization, negative labeling (e.g., deviant), discrimination, stereotyping, segregation, exclusion, and devaluation.

Improving Attitudes

Fortunately, negative attitudes can be changed, and leisure service professionals can do much to improve the attitudes of others toward people with disabilities. Additionally, since the attitudes of leisure service professionals impact the leisure opportunities and lifestyles of individuals with disabilities, it is important for leisure service professionals to examine their own attitudes.

Leisure service professionals' perceived ability to work with people with disabilities is related to attitudes (Rizzo and Wright, 1987). Thus it is not surprising that the quality of interaction between leisure service professionals and people with disabilities seems to be more important than merely the quantity of interaction in forming favorable attitudes (Rizzo and Vispoel, 1991). The more competent leisure service professionals perceive themselves to be, the better their attitudes toward people with disabilities tend to be.

There are many ways in which professionals can enhance their perceived competence in working with individuals with disabilities. For instance, there are a number of college courses in which professionals can enroll to familiarize themselves with different types of disabilities. Also, there are many conferences, presentations, and discussions that focus on people with disabilities. Attending such events might help professionals feel more competent. Experiencing simulations of a disability, such as spending an afternoon in a wheelchair, can increase a professional's understanding of what it is like to have a disability.[1] Most importantly, direct contact with people with disabilities helps professionals gain confidence in their ability to work with people with disabilities.

Other strategies can be employed to help the leisure service provider improve the attitudes of others toward people with disabilities. Leisure service professionals can lead by example, by adopting inclusive beliefs that help to improve everyone's attitudes. There are a number of important beliefs about inclusion that professionals might communicate to participants. For instance, many proponents of inclusion focus on similarities between people while acknowledging and accepting that there are differences between people. Bogdan and Taylor (1982) suggested that inclusion entails viewing all people as part of humanity. Hutchison and McGill (1992) advocated taking a person-centered approach to developing services.

Holding and communicating such beliefs can produce positive results. When leisure service professionals focus on similarities, they help people discover things they have in common as a basis for a positive relationship (Yuker, 1988). Viewing all people as part of humanity encourages people without disabilities to define people with disabilities as being "like us" despite their significant behavioral and/or physical differences (Bogdan and Taylor, 1982). For example, a person with a disability in an art class is viewed by classmates as they view each other (as another aspiring artist, as an accomplished artist, as a person who is fun to sit next to), not simply as a person with a disability. A person-centered approach involves viewing everyone as unique, complete, and having unknown potential for growth and development (Hutchison and McGill, 1992). It is both unfair and counterproductive to presume someone's limitations.

Leisure service professionals can take many actions to change negative perceptions of people with disabilities. For example, programs that are structured to promote positive interactions among participants with and without disabilities tend to promote the development of positive attitudes (Donaldson, 1980). Promoting extensive personal contact in a casual setting between people with and without disabilities can develop more accepting attitudes (Hamilton and Anderson, 1991; Patrick, 1987). In addition, facilitating equal status between people with and without disabilities contributes to positive attitudes (Levy, Jessop, Rimmerman and Levy, 1992). Participating in cooperative activities, rather than competitive ones, tends to promote positive interaction and good attitudes (Johnson and Johnson, 1984). Promoting effective communication can reduce the strain often associated with interaction (Jones et al., 1984). One particularly effective way in which communication can be promoted is through the sharing of expectations (Makas, 1988). Finally, encouraging age-appropriate activities for people with disabilities may reduce the stigmatizing effects of a disability.

Using Sensitive Terminology

The use of sensitive terminology in reference to people with disabilities is a matter of courtesy and accuracy

---

[1] While simulations are useful, readers are strongly encouraged to consult guidelines for conducting a simulation, such as those presented by Curtis and Shaver (1987), Dattilo (1994), and Perlman (1987).

and helps promote the notion that people with and without disabilities are equally entitled to the same things. What follows is a set of guidelines that may be useful in determining the most appropriate terminology to use.

Since everyone has essentially the same basic needs, it is sensible to focus on similarities rather than differences. An indication that people with disabilities are being treated differently than other people is the use of labels such as *special population* and *special child*. When a group affiliation is relevant, it is helpful to consider the person first. Putting the person before the disability (e.g., "a person with mental retardation" rather than "the mentally retarded person") reflects that a person has attributes other than a disability. People with mental retardation (or any other disability) need not be defined by a single attribute. In addition, by avoiding grouping people by medical diagnosis (e.g., the blind or the retarded), focus is placed on individuals.

Specific words can be used which support individuals rather than demean them. Saying, "a woman who uses a wheelchair" is more dignified and specific than saying, "a woman who is confined to a wheelchair" or "a woman who is wheelchair-bound." When someone uses a form of transportation other than walking (e.g., a bicycle), the person is not identified as being bound to that mode of transportation (e.g., bicycle-bound).

Language can be used to communicate dignity and respect for individuals with disabilities. Referring to adults with disabilities as childlike and discussions of mental age compromise the dignity of adults with disabilities. Many words used to describe people with disabilities, such as *deaf-mute, feeble-minded,* or *lunatic,* are no longer acceptable because of their association with negative traits such as helplessness, deviancy, and dependency and have since been replaced with, currently, more sensitive phrases, such as *people with hearing and speech disorders, a person with a developmental disability,* and *someone who has impaired mental health.* When needing to identify people who are or are not disabled, referring to these groups as *people without disabilities* is currently more sensitive than using the word *normal,* which implies that the presence or absence of a disability is the single trait that separates people into one of two categories, normal or abnormal. Once again, such a label can be demeaning and is inaccurate.

It is helpful to use terms consistently and accurately, such as *impairment, disability,* and *handicap.* An impairment is a permanent or temporary diminishment in strength (Gunn, 1975). A disability is a reduction in a skill or power. A handicap is a limitation that varies from one situation to another because the handicap occurs as a result of interaction between environmental conditions and the individual. For example, an eye injury can result in a person having a visual impairment. As a result of the visual impairment, he or she may be visually disabled. Although this person may be handicapped in a movie theater, he or she will not be handicapped listening to the radio.

While the use of sensitive terminology has been the source of some confusion and derision in recent years, it is the responsibility of leisure service professionals to keep up-to-date on the most recent usage guidelines. What is most sensitive and accepted today may be offensive to some individuals in the future. By using sensitive terminology, professionals can act more effectively as advocates for the rights of people with disabilities. The best rule of thumb when deciding how to refer to individuals in the most sensitive manner is to ask the individuals what they prefer.

Overcoming Barriers to Leisure

Consistently, people with disabilities report that negative attitudes represent the most devastating barrier they experience. People with disabilities perceive these negative attitudes and respond accordingly. Among the counterproductive ways people with disabilities respond to negative attitudes are psychological reactance (Brehm, 1977) and learned helplessness (Seligman, 1975).

According to Brehm (1977), psychological reactance occurs when an option that had been available becomes unavailable. Suddenly, the now-unavailable option becomes more attractive than it had been. For instance, if a man were offered a choice among swimming, hiking, or boating and later boating were removed as an option, then boating may become a more attractive option to him than it had been. Initially, a person typically tries to exert more control over the situation by petitioning for the reinstatement of the removed option. If attempts at reestablishing control fail, people will often relinquish freedom altogether and adopt a helpless identity.

Learned helplessness occurs when people experience systematic and sustained lack of control over their environments (Seligman, 1975). When people have limited knowledge and skills and few opportunities for choice, they will begin to believe that their environments are not responsive to their actions. As a result, they will learn to be helpless and stop any attempts at exploration. By stopping attempts at exploration, knowledge, skills, and opportunities for choice are slowly eroded. Sometimes with the best of intentions, others (e.g., family members, recreation professionals, teachers) make almost all choices for people with disabilities. Without intending to, many people teach people with disabilities to be helpless by denying them opportunities for choice. In addition, some people learn to be helpless when a person's skills and knowledge do not match the objectives of a program or activity (Stainback, Stainback and Stefanich, 1996).

Theories like reactance and learned helplessness help clarify the difficulty some people face in becoming self-determined. Choice and control, both elements of self-determination, are of central importance to leisure. Thus it becomes clear that reactance and learned helplessness are important considerations for leisure service professionals.

Facilitating Self-Determination

The ways in which leisure service professionals deliver services have an impact on people with disabilities. The fundamental goal of many recreation programs is to "set the stage" for people to enjoy themselves (Dattilo and Light, 1993; Dattilo and O'Keefe, 1992). Because self-determination contributes to enjoyment (Dattilo and Kleiber, 1993), it is important for leisure service professionals to provide services to people with disabilities that foster self-determination.

Ward (1988) defined self-determination as both the attitudes and abilities that lead individuals to identify their goals and the ability to initiate action to achieve those goals. All services for people with disabilities can expand "the individual's capacity for self-determination, decision making, and exercising choice" (Kaplan, 1995, p. 327). To encourage self-determination, Wehmeyer and Schwartz (1997) suggested that professionals provide: (1) activities that optimally challenge the person and promote autonomy by supporting initiation of activities; and (2) opportunities to express preferences, make choices, and experience outcomes based on those choices.

There are many strategies that leisure service professionals can use to enhance self-determination in the people who attend their programs. Strategies that utilize inclusive leisure services may be especially useful in achieving a sense of self-determination for people with disabilities (Baker-Roth, McLaughlin, Weitzenkamp and Womeldorff, 1995).

Although "opportunities to express preferences and make choices based on those preferences pervade virtually every aspect of daily life" (Faw, Davis and Peck, 1996, p. 173), leisure activities for many people with disabilities are often determined by service providers (Bannerman, Sheldon, Sherman and Harchik, 1990). The lack of self-initiated leisure activities continues to be a barrier to the fulfillment of self-determined behavior for many people with disabilities (Dattilo and Schleien, 1994; Mahon, 1994).

Providing opportunities for choice and respecting the choices made by program participants are important. As Searle, Mahon, Iso-Ahola, Sdrolias and van Dyck (1995, p. 120) noted, "The strength of a leisure education intervention may lie in its addressing the issue of choice." For example, Devine, Malley, Sheldon, Dattilo, and Gast (1997) demonstrated that people with disabilities can be taught to make meaningful choices during free time and initiate chosen leisure activities. By choosing, participants demonstrated enhanced self-determination and reduced learned helplessness.

Choices can be provided by having a variety of inclusive programs. Additionally, within specific programs there are many opportunities for encouraging choices. For example, within a single crafts session, participants can choose between projects, materials with which to work, colors of paint, design patterns, and so forth. With a little effort, almost any program can be adapted to include many choices for participants. Since expressing preferences and making choices are important self-determination skills for people with disabilities to learn (Bannerman et al., 1990; Foxx, Faw, Taylor, Davis and Fulia, 1993), attempts at improving their quality of life should include increased opportunities to learn these skills (Faw et al., 1996).

Communication is important to self-determination in that effective communication facilitates involvement with others. Very few (if any) people choose to pursue only solitary leisure. Many people with disabilities do not initiate conversations as often as people without disabilities and frequently assume the subordinate role of respondent (Dattilo and Camarata, 1991; Dattilo and O'Keefe, 1992). Leisure service professionals should encourage people with disabilities to initiate communication by providing a supportive environment. There are several techniques leisure service professionals can use to foster supportive environments. These include simply approaching a person and paying attention to what he or she has to say (Dattilo and Light, 1993). Since some people with disabilities have impaired communication skills, it is important to give people plenty of time to react to questions and requests (Dattilo and Light, 1993).

Although active participation by people with disabilities is one goal of inclusive programs, sometimes people with disabilities do not have the skills to participate fully. Rather than excluding people who currently do not posses all the skills needed for full participation, partial participation is encouraged (Brown et al., 1979). Partial participation involves the use of adaptations (e.g., rule changes, adaptive devices) and provides assistance needed to facilitate leisure participation. Further, partial participation allows for people's skills to be used (Krebs and Block, 1992), while providing the opportunity to experience the exhilaration and satisfaction associated with the challenge inherent in a particular activity (Dattilo and Murphy, 1987). For example, while some people with physical disabilities may not have all of the skills needed for bowling, they can experience the fun, social interaction, and challenge of bowling with some assistance of recreation personnel or adaptive equipment. With bowling there are many simple adaptations, such as ramps used by some people with physical disabilities, and guide rails used by some people with visual impairments.

By expanding leisure repertoires and increasing competence, people with disabilities have more activities to choose from when they have free time. Thus, people who have large leisure repertoires and who perceive they are competent are in a better situation to experience leisure than those who do not. Additionally, according to Iso-Ahola (1980), increased competence in an activity can lead to feelings of personal control. Having a variety of activities in which a person feels confident to choose can enhance self-determination. Self-determination allows people to have primary choice and control in the decisions and actions taken in their lives (Brotherson, Cook, Cunconan-Lahr and Wehmeyer, 1995; Cunconan-Lahr and Brotherson, 1996).

Developing Comprehensive Leisure Education

Wade and Hoover (1985) identified a lack of education and training for people with disabilities as a major constraint to developing a sense of control during leisure participation. Leisure education programs have been developed to help overcome the lack of knowledge in many people with disabilities. O'Dell and Taylor (1996) encouraged leisure service professionals to educate people for leisure because the more informed people are the better their experience. Dattilo and Hoge (1999) extended previous research by Bedini, Bullock and Driscoll (1993); their findings suggested that youth with disabilities involved in a leisure education program conducted in the public schools and the com-

munity enjoyed themselves as they acquired socially valid leisure knowledge and skills.

Dattilo and colleagues (Dattilo and Murphy, 1991; Dattilo and St. Peter, 1991) developed a comprehensive leisure education program to address the needs of people with disabilities who were making the transition to adulthood. Studies have been conducted using this approach to leisure education with older adults living in nursing homes (Lovell, Dattilo and Jekubovich, 1996), older adults who are home-centered (Dunn and Wilhite, 1997), people with chemical dependencies (Jekubovich and Dattilo, 1998), adults with mental retardation (Williams and Dattilo, 1998), and youth with mental retardation (Dattilo and Hoge, 1999). A comprehensive leisure education program can consist of four components that work together to facilitate independent community leisure participation. The four components include:

1. a leisure education course,
2. leisure coaching,
3. family and friend support, and
4. follow-up services.

Hemmeter, Ault, Collins, and Meyer (1996) stated that the success of programs designed to promote inclusion of people with disabilities depends on instructional strategies implemented in the classroom. A leisure education course can include many different elements, including instruction on awareness of self in leisure, leisure appreciation, self-determination, decision-making skills, knowledge and utilization of resources, social interaction skills, and recreation activity skills. Dattilo and colleagues encouraged leisure service professionals to develop leisure education courses that are tailored to meet the needs of participants and promote awareness, knowledge, and application. For example, the TRAIL Leisure Education Program was implemented in several special education high-school classrooms (Dattilo and Hoge, 1999).

After assessing attitudes of community recreation participants, Sparrow, Shinkfield, and Karnilowicz (1993) concluded that gaining entry into a recreation program may not be sufficient to promote peer acceptance of people with disabilities; supports (e.g., a leisure coach) are needed to facilitate success. When investigating inclusion of people with disabilities, researchers reported that positive attitudes are enhanced in the presence of sufficient resource support (Minke, Baer, Deemer and Griffin, 1996). For leisure education to enhance perceived leisure control, opportunities must exist for participants' involvement in chosen activities with support (e.g., a leisure coach) (Searle et al., 1995).

A leisure coach provides systematic community-based leisure instruction and support. Instead of leisure coaches conducting activities, typically they are intended to help facilitate participation in existing inclusive community recreation programs. As participants gain independence in accessing community recreation, leisure coaches withdraw their support. For example, a leisure coach could help a person with a disability explore an interest in music through participation in a community choir. The leisure coach might make initial contacts with the choir director and supply transportation to the first few choir practices. Once the person with a disability becomes established in an activity, it is likely that the roles of the leisure coach will be assumed either by the person with the disability or by other people associated with the activity. Heikinaro-Johansson, Sherrill, French, and Huuhka (1995) documented the effectiveness of professionals (such as leisure coaches) acting as consultants to other professionals (such as leisure service providers) to help integrate people with disabilities into inclusive environments.

Based on compelling evidence that sociocultural factors outside the classroom influence development and inclusion of individuals with disabilities, Sontag (1996) stated that family functioning and community context are critical issues for professionals. All people have needs for companionship and emotional support that are best met through contact with a person's peers and family (Romer, White and Haring, 1996). Although leisure services focus on the person's needs, Mactavish (1997, p. 71) recommended a strategy "that acknowledges the importance of families in facilitating the recreation experiences of individuals with disabilities." Therefore, a leisure education program that obtains support of the family and friends of the individual with disabilities through the use of workshops and meetings can help participants generalize and monitor skills learned in the classroom and through community-based instruction. Family members and friends can help support, encourage, and facilitate the recreation activities of a person with a disability.

Follow-up services are designed to help participants maintain leisure skills (Anderson and Allen, 1985). If, for instance, a person with a disability were to quit an activity that had been facilitated through the leisure education program, a leisure coach might help the person reengage in the activity or find another activity in which to participate. Sometimes people choose to discontinue participation in an activity for a variety of legitimate reasons, and leisure service providers should respect participants' decisions. However, if a participant does not appear to have freely chosen to discontinue participation, recreation professionals have the responsibility to help facilitate reengagement in the activity.

Comprehensive leisure education programs are designed with the ultimate purpose of having people with disabilities experience meaningful leisure within their homes and communities. Leisure service providers are encouraged to develop such programs in order to meet the needs of people with disabilities.

Making Reasonable Adaptations and Accommodations

When various aspects of programs are adapted for people with disabilities, these individuals are better accommodated so that they can be included in leisure services. Many adaptations are easy to perform, take little time to do, and cost little or no money. Before making adaptations and accommodations, there are several issues to consider. It is helpful to place emphasis on the person first by individualizing adaptations to the needs of each participant, focussing on abilities, and attempting to make the challenges of the program compatible with the skills of the participants. To encourage the autonomy of participants, leisure service professionals can make adaptations that facilitate independence (rather than dependence), check to determine if the adaptation is necessary, and view any adaptation as transitional. That is to say, as a participant's skills increase, adaptations can decrease so that the challenge is enhanced and meets the skill level of the participant.

Involving participants in the adaptation process by discussing adaptations with them is a useful practice. By involving participants in the adaptation process, leisure service professionals can gain insight into the feasibility and safety of proposed adaptations. Once adaptations are in place, continuous evaluation can detect any problems that may exist, and if problems are found with adaptations, they can be adjusted accordingly. Although adaptations can facilitate participation, each adaptation makes the program less like the original activity. If a program becomes too unlike the original task, the ability of the participants to engage in that activity in other environments is less likely. For instance, if the extent of adaptations in a rehabilitation hospital consists of expensive and cumbersome equipment, it will likely be difficult for participants to find such equipment in inclusive settings in their communities. Having only learned an activity with the use of the hospital's equipment, a participant would be unlikely to have the skills necessary to participate without the equipment. It is important for recreation professionals to consider adaptations that generalize to different settings.

Many aspects of programs can be adapted, such as materials, activities, environment, participants, and instructional strategies. When large jigsaw puzzle pieces are used or a pinball machine is leveled to slow the ball down, the materials used in an activity are being altered so that they match the skills of participants. Similarly, materials can be altered in terms of weight (e.g., substituting foam balls), stabilization (e.g., using clamps), durability (e.g., laminating game boards), and safety (e.g., removing sharp edges).

Another way to adapt programs is to alter activities so that people with different skills can participate. For instance, in a game of Old Maid, the physical requirements of the game can be changed by reducing the length of the game. Reducing the number of cards changes the cognitive requirements of the game, and reducing the number of people required to participate alters the social conditions of the game. Likewise, the environment where programs take place can be altered. For example, for someone with a hearing impairment, it might be helpful to alter a program in terms of sensory factors by reducing the amount of noise during the program. Also, a program's environment can be adapted by altering the participation area. For instance, some participants may find that extending boundaries in a soccer game helps facilitate their participation.

Participants themselves can be altered so that they are better able to participate in programs. Positioning participants closer together in a volleyball game may be helpful. One or more prostheses can be used. Sometimes a prosthetic alteration is as simple as building up the handle of a paintbrush. Sensory aids (such as corrective lenses), different modes of communication (such as augmentative and alternative communication systems), and different methods of mobility (such as using a wheelchair) might facilitate a person's participation in a program. Some participants might need lessons until their skills improve to the point where they can participate.

Another area of adaptation requires that leisure service professionals examine their methods of instruc-

tion (Stainback, Stainback and Stefanich, 1996). For instance, it is important that instructors establish objectives for their lessons. Having objectives helps the instructor determine whether material is being learned. Additionally, it is helpful for instructors to develop instructional steps. Taking steps to achieve a task can encourage participants to learn in a logical and progressive manner, and it allows for achieving small goals in the course of learning. In addition, having instructional prompts helps instructors facilitate learning. As participants learn new skills, instructors can allow plenty of time for practice. Finally, instructors can be very aware of their interactions with participants. Although sometimes forgotten by an instructor, both encouraging and discouraging comments are often remembered for a long time by participants.

Leisure service professionals have both a legal and a moral imperative to make reasonable adaptations to include into recreation programs people with disabilities. The principles and strategies for making adaptations mentioned in this section should help practitioners to meet the varying needs and abilities of people who attend recreation programs. Often with little effort, programs can be adapted so that active leisure participation for persons with disabilities can be facilitated.

Conclusion

We hope that this chapter has given the reader the inspiration to take action on at least some of the ideas presented. By some estimates, people with disabilities are members of the largest minority group in the world, and it is a minority that anyone might join at any time. The people who make up this minority can be our mothers and fathers, our sisters and brothers, our spouses, our children, and our neighbors, and they deserve our kindness, dignity, and respect. There is little justification for continuing to exclude people with disabilities from the mainstream of society, and particularly from leisure services. Rather than waiting for a change in society to precipitate a change in leisure services, leisure service professionals are encouraged to lead the way by promoting inclusion.

References

Algozzine, B., Mercer, C. D., & Countermine, T. (1977). The effects of labels and behavior on teacher expectations. *Exceptional Children, 44*(2), 131–132.

Anderson, S. C., & Allen, L. R. (1985). Effects of a leisure education program on activity involvement and social interactions of mentally retarded persons. *Adapted Physical Activity Quarterly, 2*(2), 107–116.

Baker, E., Wang, M., & Walberg, H. (1995). The effects of inclusion on learning. *Educational Leadership, 52*(4), 33–35.

Baker-Roth, S., McLaughlin, E., Weitzenkamp, D., & Womeldorff, L. (1995). The impact of therapeutic recreation community liaison on successful reintegration of individuals with traumatic brain injury. *Therapeutic Recreation Journal, 29*(4), 316–326.

Bannerman, D. J., Sheldon, J. B., Sherman, J. A., & Harchik, A. E. (1990). Balancing the right to habilitation with the right to personal liberties: The rights of people with developmental disabilities to eat too many doughnuts and take a nap. *Journal of Applied Behavior Analysis, 23,* 79–89.

Bedini, L. A., Bullock, C. C., & Driscoll, L. B. (1993). The effects of leisure education to the successful transition of students with mental retardation from school to adult life. *Therapeutic Recreation Journal, 26*(2), 70–82.

Behar, L., & George, P. (1994). Teachers as change agents: Implications for how teachers use curriculum knowledge. *Professions Education Researcher Quarterly, 16*(1), 8–11.

Bogdan, R., & Taylor, S. J. (1982). *Inside out: The social meaning of mental retardation.* Toronto, Ontario: University of Toronto Press.

Brehm, J. (1977). *A theory of psychological reactance.* New York, NY: Academic Press.

Broida, J. K. (1995). Community options for all individuals. *Parks and Recreation, 30*(5), 55–59.

Brotherson, M. J., Cook, S., Cunconan-Lahr, R., & Wehmeyer, M. I. (1995). Policy supporting self-determination in the environments of children with disabilities. *Education and Training in Mental Retardation and Developmental Disabilities, 30*(1), 3–14.

Brown, L., Branston-McClean, M. B., Baumgart, D. Vincent, L., Falvey, M., & Schroeder, J. (1979). Using the characteristics of current and subsequent least restrictive environments in the development of curricular content for severely handicapped students. *AAESPH Review, 4,* 407–424.

Canada Year Book. (1997). Ottawa, Ontario: Statistics Canada.

Cunconan-Lahr, R., & Brotherson, M. J. (1996). Advocacy in disability policy: Parents and consumers as advocates. *Mental Retardation, 34,* 352–358.

Curtis, C. K., & Shaver, J. P. (1987). Modifying attitudes toward persons with disabilities: A review of reviews. *International Journal of Special Education, 2,* 103–129.

Dattilo, J. (1994). *Inclusive leisure services: Responding to the rights of people with disabilities.* State College, PA: Venture Publishing, Inc.

Dattilo, J. (1995). Instruction for preference and generalization. In S. Schleien, L. Meyer, L. Heyne & B. Brandt. *Lifelong leisure skills and lifestyles for persons with developmental disabilities* (pp. 133–145). Baltimore, MD: Paul H. Brookes.

Dattilo, J., & Camarata, S. (1991). Facilitating conversation through self-initiated augmentative communication treatment. *Journal of Applied Behavior Analysis, 24*(2), 369–378.

Dattilo, J., & Hoge, G. (1999). Effects of a leisure education program on youth with mental retardation. *Education and Training in Mental Retardation and Developmental Disabilities, 34*(1), 20–34.

Dattilo, J., Kleiber, D. A. (1993). Psychological perspectives for therapeutic recreation research. In M. Malkin & C. Z. Howe (Eds.), *Research in therapeutic recreation: Concepts and methods.* State College, PA: Venture Publishing, Inc.

Dattilo, J., & Light, J. (1993). Setting the stage for leisure: Encouraging reciprocal communication for people using augmentative and alternative communication systems through facilitator instruction. *Therapeutic Recreation Journal, 27*(3), 156–171.

Dattilo, J., & Murphy, W. D. (1987). The challenge of adventure recreation for individuals with disabilities. *Therapeutic Recreation Journal, 21*(3), 14–21.

Dattilo, J., & Murphy, W. D. (1991). *Leisure education program planning: A systematic approach.* State College, PA: Venture Publishing, Inc.

Dattilo, J., & O'Keefe, B. M. (1992). Setting the stage for leisure: Encouraging adults with mental retardation who use augmentative and alternative communication systems to share conversations. *Therapeutic Recreation Journal, 26*(1), 27–37.

Dattilo, J., & Schleien, S. J. 1994). Understanding leisure services for individuals with mental retardation. *Mental Retardation, 32*(1), 53–59.

Dattilo, J., & St. Peter, S. (1991). A model for including leisure education in transition services for young adults with mental retardation. *Education and Training in Mental Retardation, 26*(4), 420–432.

Devine, M., Malley, S., Sheldon, K., Dattilo, J., & Gast, D. (1977). Promoting self-initiated community leisure participation for adults with mental retardation.

Education and Training in Mental Retardation and Developmental Disabilities, 32(3), 241–254.

Donaldson, J. (1980). Changing attitudes toward handicapped persons: A review of analysis and research. *Exceptional Children, 46,* 504–515.

Dunn, N. J., & Wilhite, B. (1997). The effects of a leisure education program on leisure participation and psychosocial well-being of two older women who are home-centered. *Therapeutic Recreation Journal, 31*(1), 53–71.

Faw, G. D., Davis, P. K., Peck, C. (1996). Increasing self-determination: Teaching people with mental retardation to evaluate residential options. *Journal of Applied Behavior Analysis, 29*(2), 173–188.

Fishbein, M., & Ajzen, I. (1975). *Belief, attitude, intention and behavior: An introduction to theory and research.* Reading, MA: Addison-Wesley.

Foxx, R. M., Faw, G. D., Taylor, S., Davis, P. K., & Fulia, R. (1993). "Would I be able to . . . ?" Teaching clients to assess the availability of their community living life style preferences. *American Journal on Mental Retardation, 98*(2), 235–248.

Goffman, E. (1963). *Stigma: Notes on the management of spoiled identity.* Englewood Cliffs, NJ: Prentice-Hall.

Goffman, E. (1974). *Stigma.* New York, NY: Jason Aronson.

Grenot-Scheyer, M., Schwartz, I. S., & Meyer, L. H. (1997). Blending best practices for young children: Inclusive early childhood programs. *TASH Newsletter, 23*(4), 8–10.

Gunn, S. L. (1975). *Basic terminology for therapeutic recreation and other action therapies.* Champaign, IL: Stipes.

Hamilton, E. J., & Anderson, S. (1991). Effects of leisure activities on attitudes toward people with disabilities. *Therapeutic Recreation Journal, 17*(3), 50–57.

Hasazi, S. B., Johnston, A. P., Liggett, A., & Schattman, R. (1994). A qualitative policy study of the least restrictive environment provision of the Individuals with Disabilities Education Act. *Exceptional Children, 60,* 491–507.

Heikinaro-Johansson, P., Sherrill, C., French, R., & Huuhka, H. (1995). Adapted physical education consultant service model to facilitate integration. *Adapted Physical Activity Quarterly, 12,* 12–33.

Hemmeter, M. L., Ault, M. J., Collins, B. C., & Meyer, S. (1996). *Education and Training in Mental Retardation and Developmental Disabilities, 31,* 203–212.

Horner, R. H., Diemer, S., & Brazeau, K. (1992). Educational support for students with severe problem behaviors in Oregon: A descriptive analysis from the 1987–1988 school year. *The Journal of the Association for Persons with Severe Handicaps, 17*(3), 154–169.

Hunt, P., & Goetz, L. (1997). Research on inclusive educational programs, practices, and outcomes for students with severe disabilities. *The Journal of Special Education, 31*(1), 3–29.

Hutchison, P., & McGill, J. (1992). *Leisure, integration and community.* Concord, Ontario: Leisurability Publications, Inc.

Iso-Ahola, S. E. (1980). *The social psychology of leisure and recreation.* Dubuque, IA: Wm. C. Brown Publishers.

Jekubovich, N., & Dattilo, J. (1998). *The effects of a leisure education program on adults with chemical dependencies.* Manuscript submitted for publication.

Johnson, D. W., & Johnson, R. T. (1984). *Cooperation in the classroom.* Edina, MN: Interaction Book Co.

Jones, E. E., Farina, A., Hastorf, A. H., Markus, H., Miller, D. T., & Scott, R. A. (1984). *Social stigma: The psychology of marked relationships.* New York, NY: Freeman.

Jussim, L. J., McCauley, C. R., & Lee, Y.-T. (1995). Why study stereotype accuracy and inaccuracy? In Y.-T. Lee, L. J. Jussim, & C. R. McCauley (Eds.), *Stereotype accuracy: Toward appreciating group differences* (pp. 3–27). Washington, DC: American Psychological Association.

Kaplan, C. (1995). Enhancing the consumer-family-staff relationship in adult services. *Mental Retardation, 31*(5), 326–331.

Krebs, P. L., & Block, M. E. (1992). Transition of students with disabilities into community recreation: The role of the adapted physical educator. *Adapted Physical Activity Quarterly, 9*(4), 305–315.

Levy, J. M., Jessop, D. J., Rimmerman, A., & Levy, P. H. (1992). Attitudes of Fortune 500 corporate executives toward the employability of persons with severe disabilities: A national study. *Mental Retardation, 30*(2), 67–75.

Logan, K., Diaz, E., Piperno, M., Rankin, D., MacFarland, A., & Bargamian, K. (1995). How inclusion built a community of learners. *Educational Leadership, 52*(4), 42–44.

Lovell, T., Dattilo, J., & Jekubovich, N. (1996). Effects of leisure education on individuals aging with disabilities. *Activities, Adaptations and Aging, 21*(2), 37–58.

Mactavish, J. B. (1997). Building bridges between families and providers of community leisure services. In S. J. Schleien, M. T. Ray & F. P. Green (Eds.), *Community recreation and people with disabilities: Strategies for inclusion* (2nd ed., pp. 71–84). Baltimore, MD: Brookes.

Mahon, M. J. (1994). The use of self-control techniques to facilitate self-determination skills during leisure in adolescents and young adults with mild and moderate mental retardation. *Therapeutic Recreation Journal, 28*(2), 58–72.

Makas, E. (1988). Positive attitudes toward disabled people: Disabled and nondisabled person's perspectives. *Journal of Social Sciences, 44*(1), 49–61.

Minke, K. M., Baer, G. G., Deemer, S. A., & Griffin, S. M. (1996). Teachers' experiences with inclusive classrooms: Implications for special education reform. *The Journal of Special Education, 30*(2), 152–186.

O'Dell, I., & Taylor, G. A. (1996). The role of leisure education in parks and recreation. *Parks and Recreation, 31*(5), 14–20.

Osborne, A. G., & Dimatta, P. (1994). The IDEA's least restrictive environment mandate: Legal implications. *Exceptional Children, 61*(1), 6–14.

Ottati, V., & Lee, Y.-T. (1995). Accuracy: A neglected component of stereotype research. In Y.-T. Lee, L. J. Jussim, & C. R. McCauley (Eds.), *Stereotype accuracy: Toward appreciating group differences* (pp. 29–59). Washington, DC: American Psychological Association.

Patrick, G. D. (1987). Improving attitudes toward disabled persons. *Adapted Physical Activity Quarterly, 4*(4), 316–325.

Perlman, I. (1987, March). To help the handicapped, talk to them. *Glamour,* p. 64.

Rizzo, T. L., & Vispoel, W. P. (1991). Physical educators' attributes and attitudes toward teaching students with handicaps. *Adapted Physical Activity Quarterly, 8,* 4–11.

Rizzo, T. L., & Wright, R. G. (1987). Secondary school physical educators' attitudes toward teaching students with handicaps. *American Corrective Therapy Journal, 41*(2), 52–55.

Romer, L. T., White, J., & Haring, N. G. (1996). The effect of peer mediated social competency training on the type and frequency of social contacts with students with deaf-blindness. *Education and Training in Mental Retardation and Developmental Disabilities, 31,* 324–338.

Rosenthal, R., & Jacobson, L. (1968). *Pygmalion in the classroom.* New York, NY: Holt, Rinehart, & Winston.

Schleien, S. J., Germ, P. A., & McAvoy, L. H. (1996). Inclusive community leisure services: Recommended professional practices and barriers encountered. *Therapeutic Recreation Journal, 30*(4), 260–273.

Searle, M. S., Mahon, M. J., Iso-Ahola, S. E., Sdrolias, H. A., & van Dyck, J. (1995). Enhancing a sense of independence and psychological well-being among the elderly: A field experiment. *Journal of Leisure Research, 27*(2), 107–124.

Seligman, M. (1975). *Helplessness: On depression, development, and death.* San Francisco, CA: W. H. Freeman.

Sontag, J. C. (1996). Toward a comprehensive theoretical framework for disability research: Bronfenbrenner revisited. *The Journal of Special Education, 30*(3), 319–344.

Sparrow, W. A., Shinkfield, A. J., Karnilowicz, W. (1993). Constraints on the participation of individuals with mental retardation in mainstream recreation. *Mental Retardation, 31*(6), 403–411.

Stainback, S., & Stainback, W. (Eds.). (1996). *Inclusion: A guide for educators.* Baltimore, MD: P.H. Brookes Publishing.

Stainback, W., Stainback, S., & Stefanich, G. (1996). Learning together in inclusive classrooms: What about curriculum? *Exceptional Children,* 14–19.

Stangor, C. (1995). Content and application inaccuracy in social stereotyping. In Y.-T. Lee, L. J. Jussim, & C. R. McCauley (Eds.), *Stereotype accuracy: Toward appreciating group differences* (pp. 275–312). Washington, DC: American Psychological Association.

Statistical Abstract of the United States. (1992). Washington, DC: U.S. Government Printing Office.

Tomlinson, C. A., Callahan, C. M., Tomchin, E. M., Eiss, N., Imbeau, M., & Landrum, M. (1997). Becoming architects of communities of learning: Addressing academic diversity in contemporary classrooms. *Exceptional Children, 63*(2), 269–282.

Tripp, A., & Sherrill, C. (1991). Attitude theories of relevance to adapted physical education. *Adapted Physical Activity Quarterly, 8,* 12–27.

Turnbull, A. P., & Ruef, M. (1997). Family perspectives on inclusive lifestyle issues for people with problem behavior. *Exceptional Children, 63*(2), 211–227.

Wade, M. G., & Hoover, J. H. (1985). Mental retardation as a constraint on leisure. In M. G. Wade (Ed.), *Constraints on leisure* (pp. 83–110). Springfield, IL: Charles C. Thomas.

Wall, M. E., & Dattilo, J. (1995). Creating option-rich learning environments: Facilitating self-determination. *Journal of Special Education, 29*(3), 276–294.

Ward, M. J. (1988). The many facets of self-determination. *National Information Center for Children and Youth With Disabilities: Transition Summary, 5,* 2–3.

Wehmeyer, M. L. (1996). Student self-report measure of self-determination for students with cognitive disabilities. *Education and Training in Mental Retardation and Developmental Disabilities, 31,* 282–293.

Wehmeyer, M. L., & Schwarz, M. (1997). Self-determination and positive adult outcomes: A follow-up study of youth with mental retardation or learning disabilities. *Exceptional Children, 6*(2), 245–255.

Williams, R., & Dattilo, J. (1998). *Effects of a leisure education on self-determination, social interaction, and positive affect of young adults with mental retardation.* Manuscript submitted for publication.

Wolfensberger, W. (1972). *Normalization: The principle of normalization in human services*. Toronto, Ontario: National Institute on Mental Retardation.

Yuker, H. E. (1988). *Attitudes toward people with disabilities*. New York, NY: Springer Publishing Company.

Debating Leisure

Leisure Theory in the Information Age

Wes Cooper
University of Alberta

Introduction

The Information Age is upon us, as we are frequently reminded by such authors as Jeremy Rifkin (1995) in *The End of Work*. Hoping to complement his analysis, I want to explore the implications of an idea I will call *Alpha*, or the *Symbolic Construct Hypothesis:* "We and our environments are increasingly becoming symbolic constructs." A symbol is something that has a meaning, in virtue of which it represents. A book is essentially a symbolic thing, a rock is not. To say that we and our environments are becoming increasingly symbolically constructed is, therefore, to say that we are becoming more like books and less like rocks. There is more *representation* in our environments from television, computing, photography, newspapers and magazines, and so forth, and relatively less attention paid to what is represented, the world without representation. Our work and leisure more and more take the form of symbol manipulation rather than manipulation of the physical environment, and because our

personal identity is forged in significant measure by our work and leisure activities, it follows that we and our environments are increasingly becoming symbolic constructs.

It is important to emphasize that this is not an altogether new phenomenon. We didn't need the Information Age to have chinwaggers on the telephone or couch potatoes in front of the television set. For that matter, we have been gradually "disappearing" from the physical world ever since *Homo sapiens* became a language user. Long before the Information Age, significant steps toward our "vanishing" were taken by the invention of writing and the printing press, and of systems of representation from calculus to art, and indeed by the construction of social reality generally. A lawyer is considerably less "visible" than a tree because the legal culture that surrounds him and defines him is a thick but invisible system of rules that attains its reality through our acceptance rather than by brute physical powers, such as a tree's capacity to irradiate our retinas or block a path. Still, the onset of the Information Age is a significant step in our becoming "disembodied," significant especially because the *worlds* of work and leisure are becoming more symbolic. It is easy to spot a trend toward greater degrees of systematicity and completeness as we *extend* these symbolic worlds in which we work and play. (Writers like William Gibson [1984] have built careers around imagining the future of this trend.)

Gathering these implications of Alpha into two general categories—normative implications for work and leisure, and methodological implications for the study of it—I will defend two further hypotheses. The first is *Beta,* or the *Trial-and-Error Hypothesis:* "A piecemeal, trial-and-error approach should be adopted toward the increasing symbol-construction aspect of work and leisure." In particular, we should avoid the science-fiction and Luddite extremes of either welcoming or deploring the trend that Alpha states. Historical trends are not inevitabilities, and they need not be accepted or rejected as a "package deal." For instance, someone might reasonably welcome increasingly symbolic work while resisting it in his or her leisure, or vice versa. Much depends on individual temperament and the set of opportunities one has to choose from. A writer or a programmer could happily embrace a career that immerses him or her in a symbolic workplace, while judging that free time goes best on ski slopes or nature trails, where the symbolic aspect is relatively minimal. A farmer or a truck driver, conversely, might opt for leisure activities such as reading or television-viewing or computer-gaming, where the symbolic aspect is relatively great. All sorts of permutations are possible here, both at the microlevel of individual choice and the macrolevel of social policy. At the macrolevel, for instance, it might be sound social policy, perhaps on the grounds of economic efficiency and environmental concern, to encourage the "wired" workplace, telecommuting, and the like, whereas leisure might be directed, perhaps on the grounds of public health, toward various sorts of physical activity. The present point is not to endorse any particular social policy or individual choice, but rather to recommend an open-minded approach to work and leisure that allows us to experiment with the "right" mix of the symbolic and nonsymbolic.

Third, and finally, I will be discussing *Gamma,* or the *Symbolic Utility Hypothesis:* "It is sound methodology to attend to the symbolic dimension of work and leisure in a scientific manner, and to inquire into the role of symbolic utility in making our lives go best." What I want to suggest with Gamma is that the symbolic dimension of our lives can be studied scientifically, and that "scientific" need not mean avoiding cultural meanings in favor of regularities or laws of

the sort that the natural sciences seek. Once it is accepted that human beings are symbol-creating beings and that they live within largely symbolic worlds (their cultures), the theory of work and leisure must make the study of meanings basic, and relegate inquiry into statistical or lawlike regularities to a subordinate level. As it takes this "symbolic turn," it must find ways of becoming critical of the meanings that can be described in a society's work and leisure; a culture's shared understandings as they exist at any given time are not necessarily for the best.

Alpha: The Symbolic Construction Hypothesis

To highlight the meaning of Alpha, consider one important way in which it may be denied:

> Human beings are bodies of a certain biological sort, and they have certain desires and beliefs. Working at such-and-such is all about marshalling body, belief, and desire such that one's bodily movements are instrumental toward such-and-such. And taking one's leisure in such-and-such is just marshalling the same trio for its own sake, not the further ends at which work aims (e.g., a paycheck). Alpha's talk about symbolic environments and human beings as symbolic constructions is irrelevant.

This alternative position, however, makes three linked mistakes: a mistake about the *object* of work or leisure; a mistake about the *instrumentalities* involved in either; and a mistake about the *contents* of one's beliefs and desires. The object of work or leisure is not simply a bodily movement or a motion of matter external to one's body, but it is rather the farmer's work of planting the crop or the golfer's leisure of playing nine holes, and so forth. These activities are saturated with particular meanings related to farming and golf, and they are precisely *not* bare abstractions such as "such-and-such," nor symbol-free concreta such as "matter in motion." The instrumental activities involved with them are by the same token neither abstractions nor concreta. And, similarly, the contents of one's desires and belief have meanings, such as "I want to plant the crop in order to reap the harvest" and "I want to play nine holes, just because," and these are quite different from wanting to move one's body this way in order to make matter move in that way later on, or simply wanting to move one's body in such a way as to put a round object in a hole.

The impact of symbolic invention has meant that, increasingly, the object of what we do is symbolic. Playing a video game of golfing, say, has not only a social meaning among us, but it is a leisure activity aimed, not at a real (physical) golf ball (which has a thick social meaning of its own) but at a virtual (purely symbolic) one. We work and take leisure with symbolic representations, as well as doing so within a densely symbolic milieu.

A second aspect of the impact of symbols on work and leisure, not entirely separate from the first, has to do with our recent discovery of how to use symbols to animate the inanimate, giving intelligence to the silicon in our computers and craftsmanship to the steel in our factory robots, changing the workplace forever, whether it be a white-collar office or a blue-collar factory, and in so doing changing the environment of leisure, too, partly because the objects used in work, notably the computer, are coming to be the same objects used in leisure. Smart machines may eventually reveal the hollowness of the call for "full employment," and the need to begin thinking about other ways of dealing with systemic unemployment, such as Rifkin's proposal for state-supported volunteer work, or perhaps a guaranteed income and greater equity in access to the wealth created by symbol-enhanced silicon and metal. Such proposals could improve the work and leisure landscape for countless people who would otherwise live bleak lives, affording them meaningful work and a measure of freedom to do what they want to do for its own sake—the most ancient and truest notion of leisure—instead of negotiating the obstacles to survival our societies are creating for the poor and jobless.

So the symbolically constructive aspect of ourselves and our environments is pervasive and familiar. But Alpha does more than remind us of this, for it gestures toward future possibilities, such as the increasing importance of virtual spaces in our lives. The virtual geographies of computer networks, commonly known collectively as *the Net,* are becoming a genuine alternative to the geographies of the office and home as venues for work and leisure, creating a *Third Place* that is purely symbolic. The worker who relates to his or her coworkers electronically—through e-mail, faxes, videoconferencing, and so forth—is just as much a denizen of this Third Place as the *computerjugen* that puzzle Slouka:

> What are we to make of this large-scale tinkering with the human mind and its time-tested orbit? What should those of us in RL [real life] make of the dizzying proliferation (and ever-increasing sophis-

tication) of cyberspace communities—the so-called MUDs and MOOs and MUSHes?[1] Or of the fact that an entire generation of *computerjugen* is now spending its leisure time in electronically generated space, experiencing what cyberspace theorists like to call "lucid dreaming in an awake state"? Or that cyberization—the movement to animate everyday objects in order to make them more responsive to our needs—is making rapid progress? In a word, how seriously should we be taking all this? (Slouka, 1995, p. 8)

The increasing importance of virtual space can best be explained by a comparison of virtual environments to our minds—that is, to our subjective consciousness. In *The Origin of Consciousness in the Breakdown of the Bicameral Mind,* Julian Jaynes (1976) presented the provocative hypothesis that consciousness is a relatively new phenomenon for the human race, perhaps only 3,000 years old. Arguing from analysis of ancient texts such as the *Iliad* ("There is in general no consciousness in the *Iliad*"), Jaynes proposed that human beings had "bicameral minds," one half given over to automatism (as we are familiar with it from "driving without awareness" over long stretches of boring highway), the other half given over to hallucinatory voices telling us what to do, the voices of "gods":

> The characters of the *Iliad* do not sit down and think out what to do. They have no conscious minds such as we say we have, and certainly no introspections. It is impossible for us with our subjectivity to appreciate what it was like. When

---

[1] A MUD is a Multi-User Dungeon. MUDs began appearing on the Net in the eighties, as young hackers learned how to make single-user computer games like Adventure, Zork, and the like accessible to many people at the same time, allowing them to interact, talk to teach other, and so forth in a "virtual reality." A MOO (MUD, Object-Oriented) is a species of MUD favored by educators who use them as teaching aids. The proliferation of educational MOOs illustrates the point of *Beta*'s look-and-see approach to the artifacts of the Information Age, for even if Slouka were fully justified in his condemnation of adventuring MUDs and social MUDs as constituting a "high-tech assault on reality" (I don't think he is), the condemnation wouldn't extend to uses of MUD technology to complement students' classroom experience and increase the educational value of their courses. (I must, however, confess an interest here: I am the chief administrator for an educational MOO that I use in philosophy courses. [It can be accessed at the telnet address "eva.humn.arts.ualberta.ca" on port 8888.])

Agamemnon, king of men, robs Achilles of his mistress, it is a god that grasps Achilles by his yellow hair and warns him not to strike Agamemnon. It is a god who then rises out of the gray sea and consoles him in his tears of wrath on the beach by his black ships, a god who whispers low to Helen to sweep her heart with homesick longing, a god who hides Paris in a mist in front of the attacking Menelaus, a god who tells Glaucus to take bronze for gold, a god who leads the armies into battle, who speaks to each soldier at the turning points, who debates and teaches Hector what he must do, who urges the soldiers on or defeats them by casting them in spells or drawing mists over their visual fields. It is the gods who start quarrels among men that really cause the war, and then plan its strategy. It is one god who makes Achilles promise not to go into battle, another who urges him to go, and another who then clothes him in a golden fire reaching up to heaven and screams through his throat across the bloodied trench at the Trojans, rousing in them ungovernable panic. In fact, the gods take the place of consciousness. (Jaynes, 1976, p. 74)

These gods, "organizations of the central nervous system and . . . personae in the sense of poignant consistencies through time, amalgams of parental or admonitory images," were lost to humanity early on in the first millennium B.C., according to Jaynes's account, and subjective consciousness took their place.

My interest in the story is to compare the emergence of consciousness, that "subjective space," with the emergence of "virtual space" that is beginning in our lifetimes. Just as subjective consciousness has become essential to our personal identity, may we expect our presence in virtual space to become equally so? Both spaces involve the systematic use of metaphors drawn from physical space. Both render the subject less transparent to those in their physical environment. But whereas subjective space is essentially private, virtual space is not. On the contrary, one is put in contact with personae, not the personae of gods, but of people who have chosen to share your virtual space. It is sometimes said that we are currently enduring a fourth great shock to the human ego. The first, administered by the likes of Copernicus, dislodged us from the center of the universe. The second, delivered by Darwin, told us that we are continuous with the rest of the animal kingdom. The third, Freud's,

challenged our self-knowledge and rationality. And the fourth, associated with the computer revolution, is challenging our sense of a discontinuity between us and machines. If I am right about the importance of virtual space, the most important continuity between man and machine will be this: some machines, specifically computers, are enabling the creation of more and more elaborate, extensive, useful, enjoyable, and sociable virtual spaces, which will become second nature to us in the same way that subjective consciousness has become so—a Third Place in which we will create radically new educational institutions, radically new forms of work, and radically new forms of leisure.

Alpha is a promise or a warning (depending on your point of view) about the increasing symbolic-to-non-symbolic ratio in our lives and environments. Although leisure and work are causal processes in a real physical world, they inevitably have a symbolic dimension, because human beings are, uniquely, creatures of culture. Especially over the last few millennia, as the phenomenon of human culture has come to dominate human life, what we do is preponderantly determined by shared understandings handed down from generation to generation in a society's cultural life. Not only is the cultural aspect of our identities becoming ever thicker, but it is changing ever faster, and the changes are momentous. This is particularly true of open societies in the past few centuries, where processes of creation and dissemination of new ideas, especially ones in which new technologies have figured in direct or subtle ways, have been occurring at an unprecedented pace. Think of the myriad direct ways in which the technological spin-offs of science have changed our societies over the past three centuries, or the subtle ways in which recent technologies are making the physically weak less prey to, or dependent upon, the physically strong, changing forever, in ways unparalleled in the rest of the animal kingdom, the relationship between the sexes—an important datum for a feminist theory of work and leisure. And, more generally, theorists of work and leisure must be students of the myriad of ways in which culture is changing us. Perhaps no cultural change has affected us so quickly and profoundly as the current transition to an Information Age.

For other animals, there isn't much to be said about the satisfaction of hunger, for instance, beyond the physical processes involved, whereas among human beings these are the foundation for a towering symbolic structure, or rather many structures of meaning, both at individual and cultural levels. Eating is expressive of these meanings as well as instrumental to further ends, such as pleasant sensations, nutrition, and survival, and all of this complicates enormously the study of eating as a leisure activity. By the same token our work and leisure activities have cultural meanings that help define who we are. These cultural meanings, which in large measure are conceptions of our agency and character, are an important source of motivation; we want to *do* and *be* certain things, in addition to our behavior's "payoff" in income or psychic benefits. As I will be trying to illustrate in this chapter, work and leisure have meaning (symbolic utility) in virtue of a culture's shared understandings, as well as expected utility in terms of causal outcomes. Theory about work and leisure must understand the workings of symbolic utility in order to heal methodological rifts, advocate enlightened public policy, and track important cultural trends.

Beta: The Trial-and-Error Hypothesis

Beta, the Trial-and-Error Hypothesis, aims to steer a course between two extremes. One is the fatalistic position expressed in the statement that the changes being wrought by the computer and related technologies have such momentum that they will roll along whatever we may think or do. As in some writings of John Perry Barlow and Kevin Kelly, this fatalism is often coupled with enthusiasm for the new world of the future and an admonition to get in step with it. An opposite, or Luddite, view argues that we can and must roll back the new technologies in order get back in touch with reality. This view has more respectable sources than the Unabomber, among them Mark Slouka's (1995) declaration of war against "cyberspace and the high-tech assault on reality."

Slouka is typical of both enthusiasts for and detractors of the information revolution, in associating it with a postmodern interest in artifice and the idea of a plurality of realities. Most of the people who are caught up in the debate seem to identify reality with objective, tangible, unsullied-by-technology reality, and this causes confusion, leading one side to think that respect for reality depends on a life lived close to the natural world, in the spirit of Rousseau's Noble Savage, and leading the other side to exult in leaving the physical world behind, destroying the "myth" of reality in favor of a chaos of many narratives—the conceit of the postmodernists. It seems more reasonable to assume that we all live in one world, a fundamentally physical world but one which we are constantly transforming with our technologies, sometimes to good effect and sometimes to bad. Our symbolic activity, as in our construction of social reality, presupposes this physical world, including our biological bodies, and

this is ultimately a reason, elaborated by John Searle (1995a, 1995b) and others, to be skeptical about dreams in the artificial-intelligence community that our minds might be programs, and therefore separable from the "wetware" of our bodies in the way that software is separable from the hardware it runs on. But it is *not* a reason, according to Beta, to free ourselves from symbolization. That would turn us into beasts. There is no magic line separating good "low" technology from bad "high" technology, even assuming we had an unproblematic definition of the difference between low- and high-tech, so that anything on the wrong side of that line would be "spawned by the computer world" and constitutes "an attack on reality as human beings have always known it" (Slouka, 1995, p. 4). Rather, we have to judge these new technologies by their fruits, which may be quite different from case to case. Beta's middle-ground approach is called for.

The piecemeal approach advocated by Beta rejects the false dichotomy between abandoning reality in a postmodern chaos of many worlds, on the one hand, and on the other hand a return to a golden age of freedom from high technology. It assumes that we, as individuals and societies, can experiment with the new technologies on a pragmatic trial-and-error basis. It may be inevitable that some of the new technologies will pass the test of this pragmatic approach, but that is very different from the fatalistic attitude that the changes of the Information Age defy selectivity and choice. Beta requires some confidence in the capacity of human beings to cope with a changing world. That is what we are good at, the evolutionary trick that separates us from most other living things.[2]

Change calls for monitoring for unexpected consequences, but it is excessive (and on a par with such

---

[2]It is not unreasonable to hypothesize that those who follow us will increasingly be selected for their capacity to flourish in the complex life world implied by our immersion in symbolic worlds and their ability to make the counterbalancing adjustments needed in the (nonsymbolic) physical world. (This is certainly true if one is thinking of selection at a cultural level, and perhaps true at the level of natural selection as well.) Human beings excel at adapting to new environments, especially by the use of technology, and part of the adaptation is learning how to deal with new stresses and other problems. Our capacity for adaptation mitigates my worry about our ability to respond to the complexities of a counterbalance strategy. The employment of such strategies may even allow an indirect return to a more natural environment: not the direct return of neo-Luddite renunciation of modern technology, but rather a process requiring mobilization of information about the environment that only computers can provide, and the use of them to create prosperity without the side effects that industrialization has made us familiar with.

attitudes as "If human beings were meant to fly, God would have given them wings") to suppose that our new ability to immerse ourselves in virtual environments is going to cause us to lose contact with physical reality and actual community. Simply put, we are capable enough of incorporating symbolic environments into lives that include full contact with reality as well. There are exceptions to this rule who will be harmed by the newest changes, but that has always been true of change. The plasticity of human nature has served us well for millennia of cultural shocks, and it will continue to do so as we judiciously absorb the changes of the Information Age.

Although the information revolution is fundamentally changing reality, it is a mistake to conflate the virtual dimension it adds to reality with the fakery that critics of consumer society deplore (plastic trees, Disneyland, etc.). For instance, a virtual university is, or can be, a real university, not a fake one. Its being real is a function of its being accredited to educate students in certain areas, and so forth. The fact that it does this through the Internet, say, and not via a physical campus is irrelevant to its being real rather than fake. (Of course a virtual university can be a scam, but so can one with a geographical base. A trial-and-error approach is required to determine what works, and the answer is not likely to be a simple blanket rejection or endorsement of geographical rather than virtual, or the converse.) The new virtual dimension of experience is no more deserving of this conflation than is the numerical dimension introduced by the invention of numbers thousands of years ago. Recognition that numbers have profoundly affected reality doesn't mean, for instance, that one has to devote a lot of attention to mathematical formulas for the creation of devices of mass destruction or the construction of fakery. There is more to reality than the tangibly physical, as both numbers and virtual reality, and indeed our very minds, reveal.

Gamma: The Symbolic Utility Hypothesis

Continuing the Aristotelian "middle way" approach that Beta began by avoiding the technophile and technophobe extremes, Gamma, the Symbolic Utility Hypothesis, tries to find a methodological *via media* for the study of work and leisure, a way that will be responsive to their increasingly socially constructed dimension while retaining scientific rigor and predictive power. Gamma hypothesizes that *Rational Choice Theory* (RCT) can occupy the important middle ground that will separate theory about work and leisure both

from prescientific journalism and from scientistic aping of the natural sciences. Furthermore, recent developments in RCT, in which the orthodox utility-maximizing model of rationality is augmented by the weight that symbolic considerations have for us, promise ways of spanning the gap between *quantitative* and *qualitative* approaches to leisure theory. The basic idea is that the qualitative approach provides concrete symbolic structures that the quantitative approach needs in order to avoid an excessively abstract and *economic* conception of human agency.

Work and leisure theory is particularly vulnerable to a schism between students of the subject with an erudite and utopian bent and those who favor a realistic and practical approach. At one extreme—Josef Pieper comes to mind—there are seraphic visions of the good life and the meaning of leisure, with little or no insight into how they are to be grafted onto the causal-cum-social processes of the real world. A critic might ask: How could a rationally self-interested individual implement Pieper's vision (Pieper, 1952) in a utility-maximizing life plan? At the other extreme—gravity models of leisure trip distribution might be cited, or perhaps Nielsen ratings of television viewing—there is information with marketplace value but little that it can tell people about the deeper significance of what those trips and viewings mean, or whether those activities contribute to their living well.

Is there a mediation between these extremes? Can the schism be overcome? Gamma is a mediating posture toward a methodological issue about the Great Divide within each of the social sciences, not exclusive of leisure studies, between those who espouse a "hard," quantitative, law-seeking vision of the discipline and those who prefer a "soft," qualitative, interpretive idea of it. Recent work in Rational Choice Theory, by introducing the idea of "symbolic utility," suggests ways of narrowing the Divide. Briefly, what brings about the narrowing is the following line of reasoning: both the tough-minded and the tender-minded (to give them William James' labels) must acknowledge the rationality of their subject matter: people at work and leisure. The nomic generalizations of the former as well as the local knowledge of the latter are laced with presumptions about the rationality of people. (Nothing is comparable in the natural sciences, of course, since they don't deal with rational agents.) But the tough-minded have traditionally opted for a *thin* theory of rationality, that of the utility-maximizing egoist in welfare economics. In contrast, the tender-minded have insisted on a *thick* theory of rationality, one imbued with the local colorings of particular cultures and almost certainly at odds with the abstract prescriptions of egoistic utility maximization. But a recent *decision-value* conception of rational choice, which introduces symbolic utility into calculations about what maximizes utility, promises to blend the rigor of decision theory with sensitivity to the importance of a culture's common meanings and shared understandings.

It will be instructive to explain Gamma's conception of decision value and symbolic utility by showing how it allays a certain concern about Alpha, namely that the trend toward an increased ratio of the symbolic to the nonsymbolic in our lives and environments would be taken to unacceptable extremes by a decision-value account of rational choice that maximizes symbolic utility. It would lead to just the sort of disregard for the natural world, our biological bodies, and real-life physical communities that Slouka worries about. This position misconstrues decision value, for two reasons. First, decision value (DV) is like the orthodox conception of rational choice as maximizing expected utility (EU), except that it *attaches weight* to symbolic utility (SU). It aims at finding a balance between maximizing *outcomes* or *payoffs* and maximizing what has positive meaning for an agent. For instance, it might counsel returning found money to its owner because of the symbolic utility of doing the right thing, whereas maximizing EU without weighing SU might counsel keeping the money. Being moral has symbolic utility for us, and this may make it rational to do the right thing even when it doesn't maximize expected utility.[3] Maximizing decision value is maximizing the weighted sum of expected utility and symbolic utility, and consequently it does not imply that it simply maximizes considerations of symbolic utility.

Second, what has symbolic utility for us need not involve increasing the ratio of symbolic to nonsymbolic in our lives and environments. On the contrary, a person might attach high symbolic utility to leading a back-to-the-land life, or devoting himself or herself to a sport with a low symbolic-to-non-symbolic ratio, and so forth. So although Alpha and DV both are sensitive to the symbolic dimension of our lives, DV does not automatically sanction every step in the direction that Alpha hypothesizes. On the contrary, if Beta's case-by-case, person-by-person, technology-by-technology, society-by-society approach is correct, DV will make a myriad of recommendations with widely differing symbolic-to-non-symbolic ratios. This will be disappointing to those who think there is a single ideal of human life, located in a science-fiction future or a past golden age, but to the rest of us, Beta's approach will express what Bertrand Russell once phrased as "a robust sense of reality."

Conclusion: A Critical Theory of Work and Leisure

The foregoing account of decision value and symbolic utility represents, not a fiat about how leisure theorists and other social scientists should pursue their inquiries, but rather a sketch of the in-principle methodological unity of these disparate inquiries. The progress of the discipline depends on the genius of the individual, and attempts to force it into a mold, as opposed to categorizing ex post facto the directions that inquiry tends to take, are likely to be useless and ignored, if not inhibiting and resented. But it can be helpful, as an aid to collegiality and perhaps as a spur to some integrative scholarship, for there to be a perspective from which diverse methodologies ultimately contribute to a complex but harmonious unity.

Decision value is one such unity. It need not be the only one, and the perspective that it takes to be fundamental—the perspective of rational agency—need not always be in the foreground of inquiry. For one thing, a large and central question for any social science is: How does individual rational agency aggregate in social settings? Many people choosing independently from one another can create stunningly unexpected and unforeseen consequences, and social scientists are rightly concerned to describe and monitor such patterns. But it is significant that rational agency is in the background of these inquiries. Even if an algorithm borrowed from a natural science nicely describes some social regularity, we know that the mechanism of this regularity involves the choices of individuals with certain desires and beliefs, within an action-guiding thick cultural context of common meanings. These contexts, desires, and beliefs can change

---

[3]The general outlines of the DV solution to the famous Prisoners' Dilemma should be obvious. The rationality of suboptimal choices in the Prisoner's Dilemma (PD) depends on thinking of rationality as maximizing expected utility. Given this assumption and certain others (for instance, that it's a one-shot PD, such that the two players can't adopt a tit-for-tat strategy of conditional cooperation), it is rational for each prisoner to confess (defect), even though the optimal outcome is for both to keep quiet (cooperate). But DV challenges the conventional wisdom. The rational choice takes into account the weight of symbolic utility, and in the prisoners' case that could be the utility of conceiving oneself as a cooperative person, and the importance of that conception of oneself may have sufficient weight that the rational choice becomes the optimal one. (See Nozick, 1993, for further details of this and other aspects of the decision value model of rationality.)

in such a way as to upset the regularity, and this signifies a ground-floor difference between the social regularity and the natural regularity from which the hypothetical algorithm is borrowed; namely, we can change our behavior, and thereby its aggregate effects, in ways that atoms, molecules, and biological organs cannot. We are human beings, indeed, but not mere physical things subject only to causal laws. At the same time we are not autonomous and solitary angels either. The influence of embodiment on decision making (captured by EU in the DV formula) and the influence of culture (captured by SU) is pervasive and profound. The aegis of decision value helps to keep us correctly situated between organism and angel.

It has always been a part of the self-understanding of leisure theory that it was concerned with characterizing and enabling good lives for people. As information mounts exponentially and as scientific and mathematical technique becomes more sophisticated, there should be concern that this self-understanding remain intact and flourishing. Gamma proposes that orientation toward decision value can help keep us focused on this ideal. A good life for you is one that it is rational for you to lead, and DV gives us an account of what that rationality consists in, an account moreover that is sensitive to the symbolic dimension of our lives and responsive to values that have important meanings for us, over and above their payoff in expected utility.

One straightforward way in which theory can help people lead good lives is by way of informing people of options available to them and relieving them of false belief. This has been recognized, on the Gown side of leisure theory's Town & Gown dual nature, by de Grazia's (1964) warning about what the Industrial Revolution, the assembly line, and the clock have been doing to our sense of time and our relationship toward nature; and on the Town side by informing leisure consumers of the products and services available, often indirectly through students who have graduated from our programs to take up managerial positions in which part of the job description involves public relations and public information services. This educational function of theory is implicit in DV, since utility is calculated on the basis of *considered* preferences, and considered preference surely involves being well-informed about one's opportunities. Belief can be taken as given, which may be useful for some predictive (and manipulative) purposes, but normally a *critical* theory of work and

leisure, as I shall call it, will adopt a normative stance toward accepted belief, enabling a what-they-are-doing-is-wrong critique: "If these agents were fully informed, they wouldn't be working or taking their leisure in the ways they do." Clearly, leisure theory's legacy of concern with the good life insists that it should regularly adopt this normative posture.

Another responsibility for a critical theory of work and leisure arises because a culture's meanings, largely determining individuals' symbolic utility profiles, may be *sick*. Let a sick culture be one in which there is often a great disparity between expected utility and symbolic utility: the values a culture teaches to live by are making their lives "economically" worse—that is, worse in terms of EU, or conversely something with low SU tends to have high EU. An example of the former: human sacrifices in a religious ritual, tending to have relatively low EU in their outcome (in this case pain and death), without many positives to be noted in the sacrifices' further consequences. An example of the latter: eating forbidden foods might stave off starvation.

I would like to attach to the Gamma hypothesis, then, the idea that work and leisure theory should be concerned to seek out and study such disparities and recommend courses of action that remove them. Critique of the influence of religion on culture was crucial to the Reformation. Critique of cultural values regarding race and gender was required in order to overcome slavery and the disenfranchisement of women; female genital mutilation, blood sports, prevention of full participation in civil society by minorities, and so forth, are examples of problems at the level of culture rather than the individual. And looking to the future, is the high symbolic utility we assign to work, so high that for many it is necessary to self-respect, becoming dysfunctional as we empower the machines of the Information Age to do more and more of the necessary labor? Are we confronting a clash between high SU of work and low EU? If so, should we change cultural values so that people's self-respect is less reliant on their contribution to the work force? How would we go about doing that? Or should we dismantle the new machines? And how would we go about doing that?

I would like to see work and leisure theory take on a diagnostic and corrective function with regard to cultural malaise, and Gamma's orientation toward decision value could help to center theory on this critical task.

References

De Grazia, S. (1964). *Of time, work, and leisure.* Garden City, NY: Anchor Books.

Gibson, W. (1984). *Neuromancer.* New York, NY: Ace Books.

Jaynes, J. (1976). *The origin of consciousness in the breakdown of the bicameral mind.* Boston, MA: Houghton Mifflin Company.

Nozick, R. (1993). *The nature of rationality.* Princeton, NJ: Princeton University Press.

Pieper, J. (1952). *Leisure, the basis of culture* (A. Dru, Trans.). London, UK: Faber & Faber.

Rifkin, J. (1995). *The end of work.* New York, NY: G.P. Putnam's Sons.

Searle, J. (1995). *The rediscovery of the mind.* Cambridge, MA: MIT Press.

Searle, J. (1995). *The construction of social reality.* New York, NY: Free Press.

Slouka, M. (1995). *War of the worlds.* New York, NY: Basic Books.

Reflections on Recreation, Park, and Leisure Studies

Daniel L. Dustin

Florida International University

Thomas L. Goodale

George Mason University

It is difficult to talk about where recreation, park, and leisure studies are or ought to be going in the new millennium without first talking about its origins. In the absence of some reference point, we are ill-equipped to evaluate whether it is on course, whether it needs to regain its bearings, or whether it is irrevocably lost at sea. To establish that reference point, we begin this chapter by discussing the philosophical moorings of recreation, park, and leisure studies in higher education. Then we describe the changing tides that are affecting not only the course of these curricula, but also the course of colleges and universities themselves. Finally, we discuss a unifying principle for guiding this important area of human inquiry on its voyage into the twenty-first century.

But we do so only with numerous caveats and disclaimers, and we do so "up front" rather than interject bit by bit, paragraph after paragraph. Our focus is the United States. Because Canada and the United States share a 3,000-mile border, because most Canadians live within 100 miles of that border, and because

people, goods, and ideas have crossed that border thousands of times a day for hundreds of years, some of what characterizes the United States characterizes Canada as well. Thus, playgrounds emerged in Halifax, Nova Scotia, at about the time they emerged in Boston, Massachusetts. Community centers emerged in Winnipeg, Manitoba, at about the time they emerged in Chicago, Illinois. It was the same with the emergence and evolution of degree programs in parks, recreation, and leisure studies in colleges and universities.

Differences remain, however. Canada's government mirrors England's. One-third of her people speak French as a "first" language and identify with a distinctly French culture. Her provinces have more powers than do states in the United States. Higher education is a bit different too, the differences more of degree than of kind. With its land grant colleges, community colleges, guaranteed places for high-school graduates, and open admissions, the United States has gone further than has Canada to accommodate everyone with high-school or equivalent diplomas and train all comers for jobs, occupations, or careers. This is found but to a lesser extent in higher education in Canada, which still retains some of its British and European heritage: more selective admissions, for example, and appreciation of the liberal arts, the classics, and the past.

What differentiates higher education in Canada from that in the United States differentiates the United States even more from programs in England and other English-speaking countries, particularly Australia and New Zealand. Programs in the European continent and other countries are similarly, indeed perhaps more, different. Programs in the Netherlands are more visible in North America than are programs in other nations, if only because of North Americans' participation in its Center of Excellence, which the World Leisure and Recreation Association (headed by Canadian professors for many years) helped launch. Most university programs outside Canada and the United States have strong tourism, hospitality, and economic development components. They have emerged mainly in the European continent and English-speaking nations, and mainly in the past decade, though many have older roots to be sure. Just as the United States has national associations organized around recreation, parks, and leisure education and research, there is an Australia and New Zealand Association for Leisure Studies (ANZALS) and a European Association for Tourism and Leisure Education (ATLAS). There is a Canadian Association for Leisure Studies (CALS) and a triannual Canadian Congress on Leisure Research (CCLR) comparable to the annual Symposium on Leisure Research in the United States. International communication and collaboration has increased significantly in the past decade, and research and scholarly publications remain healthy despite the appearance in recent years of a number of additional and more narrowly focused journals.

There is much of importance and value in these academic and scholarly developments. All, we hope, have bright futures. It is not easy, on the other hand, to be sanguine about developments in the United States (perhaps excepting tourism and hospitality), and that is the principal reason for the U.S. focus in what follows. In addition, there are more programs and students of parks and recreation and/or leisure studies in the United States than in all other countries combined. Admittedly, there is a dearth of accurate and comparable data, but guides to college and university degree programs in the United States list several hundred, more or fewer depending on how broadly or narrowly the field is defined. Does one, for example, include therapeutic recreation? In many of those hundreds of programs there are hundreds of undergraduate majors. To a large degree, emphases such as therapeutic

recreation do not appear on the big screen of international leisure studies and research, which has other foci. Similarly, much research and scholarly activity is based in graduate-level degree programs. While there may be more programs and students in graduate degree programs now than in previous years, undergraduates outnumber them by some large multiple, more than ten to one as a guess. And undergraduates do not appear on the big screen of international level leisure studies and research either. In fact undergraduates are all but forgotten in many of our discussions.

But they are there, several thousand of them, studying in parks, recreation, and/or leisure studies curricula. And less and less do they share a university experience if that is understood as being a member of a community of masters and scholars for a few years. Of course some students, undergraduate as well as graduate, are full-time, in-residence students whose classes are small and whose outside obligations are limited. Unfortunately these circumstances characterize a shrinking minority of our students, and the forces at work seem certain to shrink their number even more. That seems to be the mainstream and the future, and thus the concern and the focus of what follows.

Philosophical Moorings

The first undergraduate program in parks and recreation was established at the University of Minnesota in 1937. The need for such a program was evident as a consequence of both the First World War and the Great Depression. In both instances, large numbers of people with time on their hands could have benefited from professionals in recreation planning, programming, and leadership. Moreover, many of President Franklin Roosevelt's New Deal projects involved recreation area and facility development, and they demonstrated a need for natural resource-based professionals as well. The emergence of undergraduate programs in parks and recreation at Minnesota and elsewhere was, then, at its core, a response to social needs. Initially, these curricula were guided by a public service ethic. Many of the job opportunities were in the public and quasi-public sectors, and graduates of these programs saw themselves, by and large, as public servants. Whether the setting was a municipal park and recreation department, a Boy's or Girl's Club; a camp for Scouts or Guides; a YMCA, YWCA or a "J" Y; a hospital; or a morale, welfare, and recreation unit of the armed forces, the professional mission was governed by a concern for providing leisure services that contributed to a better quality of life for individuals in community. Youth services, therapeutic recreation, and outdoor education and camping were the foci of most programs.

Following the Second World War, there was an upsurge of interest in parks and recreation. The demand for outdoor recreation opportunities grew dramatically as the general public, equipped with more money, mobility, free time, and education about available opportunities, began to exercise en masse their right to visit their recreational properties. It was time to enjoy the fruits of peace and prosperity brought about by the great victory over the Axis powers. The '50s and '60s were characterized by tremendous growth in demand for leisure services and by the construction of areas and facilities to accommodate that demand. Public funds were available to support the expansion of services, and tax dollars were plentiful to underwrite the delivery of programs and services. These were good times for the field. Curricula proliferated and students energized with a missionary zeal flocked to them. In 1965, at the height of this period of growth and development, several professional organizations that were involved independently in the provision of leisure services united to form the National Recreation and Park Association (NRPA), an organization that remains the principal mouthpiece for the professional and lay community in the United States.

It was during this period that leisure studies emerged as an adjunct to the professional preparation of students to work in the field. While the professional preparation programs were geared specifically to educating students for careers in parks and recreation, leisure studies was devoted to understanding the phenomenon of leisure and its significance in contemporary life. Most notably at universities with graduate degree programs, social scientists began to study leisure and leisure-related issues and to employ the results of that inquiry in planning leisure services for the future. Initially based on the descriptive studies of community sociology, leisure studies gradually became the province of analytical social psychology and of individual perception and behavior. The emergence of leisure studies also accompanied a growing interest in the environment and a concomitant concern for the impacts of recreational uses of the environment. It was at this point that leisure came to be talked about as a "problem," not, as earlier, by the custodians of morality but by the stewards of the environment. The success of leisure service provision was being challenged by burgeoning demand for leisure service opportunities at a time when limits to growth and development were starting to be felt. The concepts of *constraints, recreational carrying capacity,* and *substitutability* appeared in the literature.

If the '50s, '60s, and early '70s were the heyday for leisure services and leisure studies, the late 1970s ushered in an era of limits. Highlighting this period was California's tax revolt, culminating in Proposition 13, which limited the amount of property tax that could be levied on homeowners to 1 % of the assessed value of a property at the time of its purchase. Since public parks and recreation were subsidized by property taxes, Proposition 13 effectively undercut the funding source for the delivery of leisure services. If California, a bellwether state, was drastically reducing the public subsidy of parks and recreation, it was only a matter of time before the rest of the country would follow suit. The repercussions were bound to be felt in Canada, too. Provincial as well as municipal governments continue coping with gaps between tax support on one hand and growing demands and needs on the other (see Burton & Glover, chapter 22 in this volume). The field of parks and recreation, and its professional preparation programs in higher education, adapted accordingly. So did leisure studies. The emphasis shifted from public recreation to private or commercial recreation, and then to tourism; from public funding to private funding; from public sector practices to private sector practices. The field's ethic of public service suffered as a result. If the general populace no longer supported the provision of parks and recreation as public goods, then the field would offer them, and study them, as merit, or even, private goods.

At the end of the twentieth century the profession is a segmented and sometimes disjointed community that is reflected in a highly segmented and disjointed collection of curricula in colleges and universities throughout North America. Attempts at unification currently revolve around the "benefits are endless" campaign, around the association of recreation with health, and around demonstrating the utility of parks and recreation as a medium for working with at-risk youth. There is also in the United States, as elsewhere, an emphasis on tourism and hospitality, primarily as a source of economic development and revenue generation. These emphases reinforce both the preventive and restorative functions of recreation while also strengthening, via economic benefits, managerial and political aspects of park and recreation services. Health and well-being, conceived broadly, may be a unifying theme for a disparate field, since we can speak comfortably not merely of individual health but also the health of families, communities, and the natural environment which sustains all life. Admirable as they are, however, it is not clear whether these efforts will unify the field. Moreover, what will become of recreation, park, and leisure studies in higher education is likely to be a function of what will become of higher education itself. For that reason, we now turn to that larger context within which these highly segmented and disjointed programs must find their way.

The Changing Tides of Higher Education

The vast majority of recreation, park, and leisure studies programs are housed in public colleges and universities. But the word *public* seems less and less descriptive of their nature. At receptions where college and university administrators congregate, one is likely to hear that their schools were once state supported, then state assisted, and now are merely state located. In this and many other ways, public colleges and universities are beginning to resemble private institutions which more and more resemble private enterprises. Caps on tuition and fees, coupled with greatly reduced state and federal support, have had a number of far-ranging consequences. Chief among them has been an increasing concern for economic efficiency. When it comes to fund-raising, public universities are out there "pitching" with their private counterparts, and campaigning not merely for several hundred million dollars but, in a few cases, a billion dollars or more (Bruker, 1998, p. C1). College and university presidents do little but lobby and fund-raise. This is increasingly true of deans, and even department chairpersons in recreation, park, and leisure studies. One such department chairperson launched, for his department, a $1 million campaign (Vessell, 1998).

The privatization of public colleges and universities is felt in many other ways besides monopolizing the time and energy of administrators: larger and larger classes to realize "seat count" efficiencies; "writing across the curriculum" requirements in an effort to compensate for earlier failures in the public schools, and lower division course enrollments often numbering in the hundreds and for which there are, understandably, no writing assignments; professors who must generate their own dollars for teaching and research assistants, travel, manuscript preparation and the like; and thus intrapreneurial and entrepreneurial competition which, in effect, privatizes an institution founded as a community of masters and scholars. Faculty and students are summoned once a year to the survey research phone bank to employ their telemarketing skills to raise money from alumni. Everyone, students included, becomes a salesperson, and hyperbole becomes standard English. Large gifts for specific purposes also influence directions and priorities. Administrators spend more and more time with those who have given or could give large sums of money (Bruker, 1998, p. C2). There are also more and more imitations of Orwell's grim headmistress, whose three categories of students included those to be treated generously, those to be treated adequately, and those who may be ill-treated to some extent, depending on their parents' ability to pay (Orwell, 1935). We have no measures of what students may be learning from all this, though we know that much learning takes place outside the classroom.

Confusion Over the Purpose of Higher Education

We are also not really sure what we want students to learn and then, as a result, to become. We contrast education for work with education for leisure, education for careers with education for citizenship. Since Plato we have thought education prepared one to govern or be governed, and in the final analysis to be self-governed. Our more recent and homegrown tradition has been education for citizenship in a democracy. That was Jefferson's notion and also that of our best education philosophers and leaders ever since. This is not inconsistent with the fact that the first universities, dating to the twelfth century, prepared students for the professions: medicine, law, translation, the priesthood, and government (civil) service. The purpose of all these professions was to serve the community and the state.

In 1912, despite their differences, Theodore Roosevelt and Woodrow Wilson agreed that:

> economic and political institutions should be assessed for their tendency to promote or erode the moral qualities that self-government requires. Like Jefferson before them, they worried about the sort of citizens that the economic arrangements of their day were likely to produce. They argued, in different ways, for a political economy of citizenship. (Sandel, 1996, p. 62)

"By the 1960s," Sandel argued, "the political economy of citizenship was replaced by economic growth and its distribution." The development of citizens was replaced by the development of consumers, whose primary functions were to get and spend money. So while, in February 1998, most leaders in the United States bemoaned the very poor math and science test scores of its twelfth grade students compared to those of students from 20 other countries, one widely read economist, Robert J. Samuelson, asked, "If our students are so bad, why is the economy so good?" (Samuelson, 1998, p. A15). His answer was that people do not learn only in school. Does that mean that schools no longer matter, or that ever-increasing consumption is the only thing that does?

Probably everyone who teaches in programs with an internship component has heard students say the internship was the best part of their program. Perhaps today's university has become, as Alfred North Whitehead suggested 70 years ago, a mere ghost of itself and should be given up. Faculty research and conveying information to students are functions that can be:

> performed at a cheaper rate outside these very expensive institutions. Books are cheap, and the system of apprenticeship is well-understood. So far as the mere imparting of information is concerned, no university has had any justification for existence since the popularization of printing in the fifteenth century. (Whitehead, 1929, p. 97)

The Atomization of Inquiry

The root of the problem, Whitehead said, was over-specialization into too many narrow professions, the result of which was passive absorption of lifeless techniques taught in too many courses in too many programs which become, consequently, too disjointed. The ivy-covered tower has become the Tower of Babel. Courses, and even programs, in risk recreation, eco-tourism, sports merchandising, and event management have parallels across the university. The proliferation of narrow career specializations reflects the job and work orientations not just of students and parents but of the culture as a whole. If education is to set you free, it is to do so not through knowing the truth but by helping you get a well-paying job. The ideals of education have been reduced to learning current practices in some career field. Devoid of real knowledge, much less wisdom, stagnation sets in (Whitehead, 1929, p. 40). Today, with so much emphasis on "the real world" and on practical experience, internships, practicums, teams and cohorts, shadowing people in the field, case studies and problem solving, and with teachers and courses evaluated on how immediately practical application of the material can be made, it seems we are building an apprentice system, a very inefficient one.

The problem of career specialization is exacerbated as would-be professions increasingly impose their wishes on career-oriented programs. It is true, of course, that the traditional professions have always set the requirements for entry into their respective fields,

particularly medicine, law, and engineering. Yet even with these professions, law and medicine especially, the public has grown disillusioned. The assurance of competent service the professions give in exchange for self-governance too often appears to be self-serving rather than serving the community. Meanwhile, the career field of recreation, parks, and leisure services, seeking the status of a profession and the attendant recognition, has set in place systems to accredit college and university curricula and to certify professionals for the field.

As in other fields, the rationale for recreation and park accreditation and certification programs has always been that such programs assure the public, whose safety, health, and welfare are at stake, that park, recreation, and leisure service professionals are highly trained in their specialties and thus highly competent. In today's business jargon, this is quality assurance. Witt (1991), however, noted that assurance of quality was only one side of what seems to be, inevitably, a two-sided coin. The other side, he pointed out, was the self-interest of the profession's practitioners. One of the purposes of accreditation and certification is to keep others out. That is clear in the efforts to get employers to make certification a requirement for employment. This side of the coin is not discussed in polite company and is not usually committed to paper, at least not by the proponents of accreditation and certification. But in a discussion published in the field's annual on higher education, *Schole,* separate critiques by Ellis (1991) and Sylvester (1991), were rebutted by Jamieson (1991) and van der Smissen (1991) on the basis that accreditation and certification were useful to those accredited and certified, that is, to the profession rather than the community.

Similarly, after years of concern that the designation Certified Leisure Professional garnered as much derision as deference, the desire to change the title of the certificate was voiced by leaders of the many branches, sections, and districts of NRPA at a "Town Hall" meeting in Washington, DC, in February, 1998. Subsequently, in an e-mail message to a few thousand Listserv subscribers, NRPA's president wrote, in a refreshingly candid way:

> In a two-way dialogue between the attendees and NRPA's top leadership, it was agreed that the primary reason for having a certification program was to market our profession among those outside our organization. If the term "leisure" is getting in the way of our being taken seriously by those we most desperately want to impress, then the designation should

be changed. (C. Jarvi, personal communication, 1998)

The Education Business

It is not only the content of higher education that needs rethinking, it is the way the content is increasingly being delivered as well. Psychologists tell us that human beings are proximal by nature, that we are social beings. We enjoy one another's company and interacting in ways that are proximate and convivial. Are advances in teaching technology bringing students and professors closer together? Or are they merely reflecting the power of economic efficiency as the paramount planning principle?

In response to one of the current laments about "The next university: Drive-Thru U," as described in an article in *The New Yorker* by James Traub (1997), College of William and Mary President, Dr. Tim Sullivan wrote:

> Traub's observation about a class he visited says it all: "What was a little hard to get used to . . . was the lack of intellectual, as opposed to professional, curiosity. Ideas had value only insofar as they could be put to use—if they could do something for you." In fact, the university's founder asserts that an idea can "do something for you" only if you can "apply what you've learned the next day at work." The next university appeals to those who understand that "higher education is a passport to a better life," but who "don't want to buy something they're not using." It gives its customers nothing less than what they want—and, sadly, nothing more. (Sullivan, 1998, p. 1)

What Traub described and Sullivan lamented, "the next university," is already well underway. It can be found wherever there is a highway interchange, a building with rentable space, and convenient parking. Courses geared to on-the-job skills are taught by part-time instructors at convenient hours: no labs, no libraries, no student unions, no cultural activities, no intramurals or intercollegiate sports, and, as Sullivan disconsolately noted, no homecoming. There is no place to come home to, no *there* there. While the Universities of Phoenix and of Ottawa, Kansas, may be further along than most, many universities, old and new, are scrambling—as entrepreneurs they must—to capture new markets by making courses, mainly career-oriented, as convenient as they can.

The ultimate expression of this is distance learning, correspondence courses and degree programs in electronic form. Students take courses at home or at the office or wherever they can log on, often asynchronously (i.e., free of any schedule except their own). Perhaps the epitome of Electronic or Internet or On-Line U is Western Governors' University, a consortium of several western states collaborating to offer, electronically, scores of degree and certificate programs. No traditional universities and no programs within them are untouched by this. Master's degrees in recreation, park, and leisure studies can be completed on weekends, and courses long available in various distance learning formats are moving from print, video tape, and interactive television to synchronous and asynchronous World Wide Web formats. Not since the printing press has technology had such an impact on learning and the dissemination of information.

The education business is a, perhaps even the, force driving universities. The University of Phoenix is the principal subsidiary of the Apollo Group which trades on the NASDAQ exchange (a share worth $2 in 1994 was worth $35 in 1997, adjusted for stock splits). Many Arizona State University professors got in early (Bruker, 1998). This is called covering your bets. There is much discussion of "total quality education" (Bonser, 1992), and awards are given to various campus program and service units for "quality customer service." Success means the stakeholders, if not also the stockholders, are happy, and the sovereign consumer has replaced the student as well as the citizen. We speak of the recreation business and leisure industry (Kelly, 1985; Dustin, McAvoy & Schultz, 1987; Schultz, McAvoy & Dustin, 1988). Catering to business interests is evident in many other ways, most obviously in the growth of business schools. By the early 1990s, about one-fourth of all college graduates completed business degrees. In recreation, parks, and leisure service fields, more and more students were drawn to private and commercial recreation, tourism, resort recreation and the like. What was a decidedly public service orientation to the field in its formative years has shifted. This may be due in large part to the perception that downsizing governments at all levels means no jobs in public parks and recreation. The mission and tradition of public service dating to the 1100s for colleges and universities and the 1940s and 1950s for recreation and parks degree programs continue to fade as private interests ascend.

Privatization takes many forms. Universities become, necessarily, privatized as funds from public coffers shrink. Privatization means outsourcing products and services once provided in-house. But there is also the privatization of experience. The most compelling example is that of television, far and away the most time-consuming leisure activity of all time. It is experienced passively and in isolation, except when sports fans gather to watch and party. Putnam's arguments in "Bowling Alone" (1995) and "The Strange Disappearance of Civic America" (1996) are compelling. We have lost civic capital due to privatizing our experiences, and television is a leading cause. Computers, used mainly for entertainment, magnify the problem. They only give the illusion of enhancing proximity (see Cooper, chapter 28 in this volume).

The university experience has become increasingly privatized, too. Full-time resident students are a shrinking minority. Traub (1997) estimated they make up only about 16% of the students now enrolled in college and university courses. Increasingly, students commute to class, and then commute to work, home, or elsewhere. Increasing numbers telecommute, to school as well as to work. The community of masters and scholars so characteristic of earlier times, and thought by so many to be an essential part of higher education, is an experience fewer and fewer students share. There is no community at Drive-Thru U, and Electronic, Internet, or On-Line U privatize even more. Privatization means the lack of interaction with people, face-to-face, and on a regular basis in spaces which belong to all. The give and take of dialogue and argument is less and less a feature of daily life, even among students. And so the foundations of an education for citizenship in a democracy have been weakened (Hemingway, 1996; Stormann, 1995). Degrees and certificates have become commodities one buys because, like a car, they can get you somewhere and, like a suit, they make you presentable.

Whither Higher Education?

The rising tide in higher education that is carrying recreation, park, and leisure studies along with it is thus characterized by economic efficiency, increasing specialization, accreditation of curricula, technological distancing, certification of professionals, and privatization of services. Where that rising tide will ultimately take these curricula is unclear, but it does appear that the direction is farther and farther away from their philosophical moorings. For a field that has long prided itself on public service and the community-building properties of its programs and practices, the climate within which its future scholars and practitioners are being educated is anything but communal. If this trend continues, the philosophical underpinnings of recre-

ation, park, and leisure studies are destined to become less communal as well.

At issue is the significance of higher education to our democratic way of life. The twentieth century has seen the rise of academic professionalism and the emergence of colleges and universities as its principal institutional expressions (Albert, 1980). The Jeffersonian ideal of educating citizens for responsible citizenship has been replaced by training professionals for highly specialized careers. Broad and highly integrative thinking is sacrificed for narrow and highly technical thinking, and curricular offerings are shaped by market forces more so than by any particular quest for truth or understanding. The measure of a successful college education is in the starting pay, and college as preparation for public life has been replaced by a preoccupation with self and a corresponding withdrawal from the civic arena (Havel, 1986). In the end, the diploma is seen largely as a "ticket" to something bigger and better in the way of consumer purchasing power. Should recreation, park, and leisure studies educators be alarmed by this trend? Should they be trying to counter these forces within their spheres of influence? Should they be professing something more enduring, something more ennobling? We think so.

Creating Citizens

The educational philosopher, Eugene Debs, said "intelligent discontent is the mainspring of civilization." We agree:

> At a minimum, we should reexamine our curricula to assure students know at what their nation succeeds and at what it fails, and give them some sense that what they do with their lives makes a difference—inevitably—for better or worse. We should not accredit any program that does not teach these things, or certify as a professional anyone who does not know, and feel, these things. (Goodale, 1998, p. 2)

Almost every educator of any note has said that is what education is all about:

> It is not enough to teach a man a specialty. Through it he may become a kind of useful machine but not a harmoniously developed personality. It is essential that the student acquire an understanding of and a lively feeling for values. He must acquire a vivid sense of the beautiful and

of the morally good. Otherwise he—with his specialized knowledge—more closely resembles a well-trained dog than a harmoniously developed person. He must learn to understand the motives of human beings, their illusions, and their sufferings in order to acquire a proper relationship to individual fellow men and to the community. (Einstein, 1954/1982, pp. 66–67)

How do recreation, park, and leisure studies measure up to this description of a worthwhile education? That depends on what the field stands for, what its mission is, how that mission is reflected in the way its future professionals are educated, and what lessons, skills, values, and ethics are vital to that mission. It also depends on the extent to which recreation, park, and leisure studies are preparing students for a career and the extent to which they are preparing students to participate actively and responsibly in their communities.

Without widespread agreement about these matters, the field is rudderless. There is nothing to guide or steer it toward a preferred future. Indeed, there is little sense of a preferred future other than wanting to do whatever it takes to stay afloat. It is akin to treading water. Surely, there must be a higher purpose for the profession and its associated curricula. Surely, there must be something greater to strive for. To that end, we conclude this chapter with a brief discussion of what we perceive to be the heart of the matter. What kind of graduates should programs in recreation, park, and leisure studies be turning out into the world?

A Unifying Principle

Regardless of one's philosophical orientation to recreation, park, and leisure studies, a unifying principle we toilers in the field ought to be able to rally around is the cultivation of socially responsible college graduates. By socially responsible, we mean graduates who are committed to understanding the nature of the relationship between their actions and the consequences of those actions, and then conducting their lives as best they can in light of that understanding. Education is, above all else, illumination, the bringing to light of connections between actions and consequences. Education can be especially powerful if it demonstrates that the locus of action, the locus of control, is within the students themselves, and, therefore, that the roots of responsibility are within them as well. Education can be empowering. As students recognize more connections, as they become more educated, they become not only more aware of the world around them, but

they become more responsible for the welfare of that world. In our judgment, that is to the good.

Armed with such a college education, our students will then be better positioned to look after the health and well-being of the community of life (Schweitzer, 1965). In that regard, we toilers ought to be able to agree that the earth is the source that sustains us (Rolston, 1996), and that the welfare of the community of life is ultimately dependent on the welfare of this planet (Leopold, 1949). Furthermore, we ought to be able to agree that humankind occupies a privileged position in the Great Chain of Being (Peterson, 1996; Schumacher, 1977), and that we have a corresponding moral responsibility to be good stewards of the earth (Dustin, McAvoy and Schultz, 1995). The actions, stances, and educational foundations of those purporting to represent the field should be based squarely on a fundamental appreciation of that reality.

Moreover, toilers in the field ought to champion the interconnectedness that defines the relationship between recreation, park, and leisure studies, the natural world, and the ideal of democratic citizenship. In a thoughtful essay, "Liberal Democracy and the Fate of the Earth," J. Ronald Engel (1992, pp. 64–65) reminded us that to the extent the natural world is jeopardized by the actions of humankind, it is a failure of "we the people" to take moral responsibility for our world. And that failure, in turn, can only be explained by our failure to truly understand ourselves as citizens of a larger community of life. For whatever reason, we have twisted the meaning of a liberal democracy such that we see it only as "a philosophy for the pursuit of private happiness, not for public citizenship" (Engel, 1992, p. 70). We mistake opportunity for freedom. We mistake consumption for growth. We mistake self-aggrandizement for self-fulfillment. Our failure rests in our inadequate conception of citizenship, of what it means to be a socially responsible member of the larger world.

Our notion of a good citizen is "one who obeys the laws, pays taxes, votes ritualistically for preselected candidates, and 'minds his or her own business'" (Bookchin, 1987, p. 9). There is little transcendent quality to our lives, little evidence that we feel connected in any significant way to anything larger than ourselves. All too many of us enjoy the privileges of being born into a liberal democracy without fully understanding its corresponding obligations. We champion the ideal of individual human rights without understanding that such rights are desirable only to the extent they complement the welfare of the larger community of life. We little understand the meaning of interdependence, cooperation, and symbiosis. We little understand the meaning of ecology (Dustin, 1996).

Fortunately, there are other views, ecological views, of what it means to be a contributing member of a liberal democracy. Thoreau, for example, wrote, "I will sift the sunbeams for the public good. I know of no riches I would keep back. I have no private good, unless it be my peculiar ability to serve the public" (Thoreau, 1962, p. 106). And John Muir spoke of the futility of trying to examine any one thing when it is, in fact, connected to everything else in the universe. The view of a liberal democracy that emanates from these nature-based insights, Engel contends, is "rooted in the principle of individuals in community, which is the principle of citizenship, which is the principle of ecology" (Engel, 1992, p. 72).

The challenge Engel leaves us with is how to go about cultivating citizens who properly understand their place in, and responsibility for, the natural world. "Create citizens," said the French philosopher Rousseau (1913, p. 251), "and you will have everything you need." This is the work we toilers ought to be doing in recreation, park, and leisure studies, work that is central to the health and well-being not only of ourselves and the community of life but also of our democratic way of life. Democracy is a vehicle for personal and social growth that should have as its ultimate goals harmonious reciprocity among people and between people and the Earth. Our curricula should nurture the necessary abilities and dispositions to make these goals attainable. Our mandate, as Barry Lopez so eloquently expressed it, is to help people:

> discover the continent again. We need to
> see the land with a less acquisitive frame

of mind. We need to sojourn in it again, to discover the lineaments of cooperation with it. We need to discover the difference between the kind of independence that is a desire to be responsible to no one but the self—the independence of the adolescent—and the independence that means the assumption of responsibility in society, the independence of people who no longer need to be supervised. (Lopez, 1992, p. 49)

On the eve of the twenty-first century, the educational challenges before us are daunting. They are made even more so by what has been described as a crisis of culture, a crisis of character in North America. Feelings of anomie and alienation abound. People do not think they can make a difference. They retreat to the privacy of their own homes with little regard for the larger world that is, in the end, home to us all. But these problems only serve to highlight once more the centrality of recreation, park, and leisure studies in combating the erosion of the meaning of democratic citizenship. Through the work we do we can equip people with the necessary education to make a difference in their day-to-day lives. When we do our best work we lift people up and out of their self-absorption to reveal the beauty, complexity, and mystery of the larger world. We nurture that transcendent quality that is so sorely missing from so many lives. What better role for recreation, park, and leisure studies to play as we voyage into the new millennium?

References

Albert, R. (1980). Professionalism and educational reform. *The Journal of Higher Education, 51*(5), 497–518.

Bonser, C. (1992). Total quality education. *Public Administration Review,* September/October, 504– 512.

Bookchin, M. (1987). *The rise of urbanization and the decline of citizenship.* San Francisco, CA: Sierra Club Books.

Bruker, N. (1998). BMOC: Big money on campus. *Washington Post,* February 22, pp. C1, 12.

Dustin, D. (1996). Citizenship in an ecological age. In P. Allison (Ed.), *Proceedings of the 1993 and 1995 Bradford Institute on Americans Outdoors,* Vol. VI, pp. 6–16.

Dustin, D., McAvoy, L., & Schultz, J. (1987). Beware of the merchant mentality. *Trends, 24*(3), 44–47.

Dustin, D., McAvoy, L., & Schultz, J. (1995). *Stewards of access/Custodians of choice: A philosophical foundation for the park and recreation profession.* Champaign, IL: Sagamore Publishing.

Einstein, A. (1954/1982). *Ideas and opinions* (C. Seelig, Ed.). New York, NY: Crown Publishers.

Ellis, G. (1991). The training of competent technocrats. *Schole: A Journal of Leisure Studies and Recreation Education, 6,* 105–111.

Engel, J. (1992). Liberal democracy and the fate of the earth. In S. Rockefeller & J. Elder (Eds.), *Spirit and nature* (pp. 59–81). Boston, MA: Beacon Press.

Goodale, T. (1998). President's message. *SPRE Newsletter, 22*(1), 1–2.

Havel, V. (1986). *Living the truth.* Boston, MA: Faber & Faber.

Hemingway, J. (1996). Emancipating leisure: The recovery of freedom in leisure. *Journal of Leisure Research, 28,* 27–43.

Jamieson, L. (1991). Why certification? *Schole: A Journal of Leisure Studies and Recreation Education, 6,* 101–104.

Kelly, J. (1985). *Recreation business.* New York, NY: John Wiley & Sons, Inc.

Leopold, A. (1949). *A Sand County almanac.* New York, NY: Oxford University Press.

Lopez, B. (1992). *The rediscovery of North America.* New York, NY: Vintage Books.

Orwell, G. (1935). *A clergyman's daughter.* New York, NY: Harcourt Brace.

Peterson, G. (1996). Four corners of human ecology: Different paradigms of human relationships with the earth. In B. Driver, D. Dustin, T. Baltic, G. Elsner, & G. Peterson (Eds.), *Nature and the human spirit: Toward an expanded land management ethic* (pp. 25–38). State College, PA: Venture Publishing, Inc.

Putnam, R. (1995). Bowling alone: America's declining social capital. *Journal of Democracy, 6,* 65–78.

Putnam, R. (1996). The strange disappearance of civic America. *American Prospect, 24,* 34–38.

Rolston, H. (1996). Nature, spirit, and landscape management. In B. Driver, D. Dustin, T. Baltic, G. Elsner, & G. Peterson (Eds.), *Nature and the human spirit: Toward an expanded land management ethic* (pp. 17–24). State College, PA: Venture Publishing, Inc.

Rousseau, J. (1913). *A discourse on political economy. Social contract and discourse.* London, UK: Dent.

Samuelson, R. (1998). Stupid students, smart economy. *Washington Post,* March 12, p. A15.

Sandel, M. (1996, March). America's search for a new philosophy. *Atlantic, 280*(3), 57–74.

Schultz, J., McAvoy, L., & Dustin, D. (1988). What are we in business for? *Parks & Recreation, 23*(1), 52–54.

Schumacher, E. (1977). *A guide for the perplexed.* New York, NY: Harper & Row.

Schweitzer, A. (1965). *The teaching of reverence for life.* New York, NY: Holt, Rinehart & Winston.

Stormann, W. (1995). The recreation profession, capitalism and democracy. *Leisure Sciences, 15,* 49–66.

Sullivan, T. (1997, November). In a letter to "Friends of William and Mary," Cited in T. Goodale, President's message, *SPRE Newsletter, 22*(3), 1–3.

Sylvester, C. (1991). A critical commentary on credentialing in leisure services. *Schole: A Journal of Leisure Studies and Recreation Education, 6,* 112–123.

Thoreau, H. (1962). *Journal of Henry D. Thoreau* (Vol. 1). New York, NY: Dover Publications.

Traub, J. (1997). The next university: Drive thru U. *The New Yorker,* October 20 & 27, pp. 114–124.

Van der Smissen, B. (1991). Credentialing: A management tool and a professional vehicle. *Schole: A Journal of Leisure Studies and Recreation Education, 6,* 94–100.

Vessell, R. (1998). Presentation at a meeting of recreation and park department chairs in Phoenix, AZ, February 27.

Whitehead, A. (1929). *The aims of education.* New York, NY: New American Library.

Witt, P. (1991). Gaining professional status: Who benefits? In T. Goodale & P. Witt (Eds.), *Recreation and leisure: Issues in an era of change* (3rd ed., pp. 263–274). State College, PA: Venture Publishing, Inc.

Critique and Emancipation: Toward a Critical Theory of Leisure

John L. Hemingway
University of North Carolina at Chapel Hill

The charge for this chapter was to explore the relevance to leisure studies of developments in contemporary philosophy. I have interpreted this to mean developments in contemporary social and political theory, specifically the various models of social inquiry being debated. Given the lack of theory-oriented discussion in leisure studies, and given the importance of adequate theoretic frameworks in any emerging field of inquiry, it will be useful to consider approaches to theory that have occupied the attention of our colleagues elsewhere in the social sciences, and to ask whether any of the alternatives currently on the table can be of particular use in leisure studies.

Beginning, then, with some introductory comments on the nature of theory itself, the discussion turns to the underdeveloped state of theory in leisure studies. This raises the issue of paradigms for theory, of which there are four that, at least as broadly characterized here, appear to be the main antagonists in current discussion: positivism, postpositivism, constructivism, and critical theory. If the considerations to be advanced here have any merit, it is the last which has the most to offer leisure studies. Following summary discussions of the other three paradigms, the chapter therefore provides a more extended treatment of critical theory and several of its defining themes. These raise complex but unavoidable issues in any adequate review of critical theory's applicability to the study of leisure. By its very nature, critical theory is political in the broad sense, and thus introduces political elements into social inquiry; how this contributes to a politics of leisure is taken up next. The final section illustrates the possible application of critical theory to leisure studies by offering a set of theses for the critical analysis of leisure. The discussion as a whole suggests new and broadened directions for leisure inquiry, in part because a critical theoretic approach

My father passed away during the writing of this chapter. He taught me a great deal about freedom and critical thinking; I would therefore like to dedicate this chapter to his memory.

reveals an expanded conception of leisure. To demonstrate the value of this approach, and the expanded conception of leisure it provides, is the underlying purpose of this chapter.

In advance of this, however, several preparatory comments are in order. It is important to emphasize the theoretic pluralism in contemporary social science. Unlike the decades of the "behavioral revolution," when derivatives of positivism held sway and drove other conceptions of inquiry from the field, the current existence of at least four rival positions necessarily raises the question of which is the most appropriate for the study of leisure. How one answers this question depends in part on how one conceptualizes leisure. Here I want to offer several propositions that will be taken as given for present purposes. First, any field of inquiry must be structured in such a way that it adequately addresses the phenomena it investigates. Second, leisure is a multidimensional phenomenon, that is, leisure cuts across many aspects of our social and individual being. Leisure is not a simple phenomenon, easily isolated. It occurs in many forms, at many times and places. It follows, third, that the study of leisure must therefore necessarily be multidimensional. There is no single epistemology or methodology, and certainly no single discipline, that meets the test of the first two propositions, i.e., that adequately reflects in itself leisure's multidimensionality. This being so, the study of leisure must become *transdisciplinary* if it is adequately to address leisure's multidimensional nature.

Leisure studies has often been thought of in this way, as transdisciplinary, and as the chapters in this volume illustrate, there are multiple perspectives present within the field. This is no guarantee of transdisciplinarity, however. The field may in fact be better characterized as *multi*disciplinary rather than *trans*disciplinary. The multiple perspectives in the field are not often in communication with one another. They tend, instead, to be oriented toward what may be called the *home disciplines* or to be withdrawn into themselves. This tendency works against the creation of research programs that move not only across several perspectives in the field, but also across several disciplines. Given the persistence of the "tyranny of the disciplines," at least within North American academia, this is neither surprising nor unique to leisure studies. It is distressing, nonetheless, because it runs counter to leisure's multidimensionality and thus inhibits theoretical work adequate to the phenomenon of leisure.

The mere presence of multiple perspectives in the field does not suffice as grounds for transdisciplinarity. The means to the necessary conversations are lacking. To establish these requires a substantial reorientation in how leisure researchers are educated and leisure studies curricula organized (a requirement again not unique to leisure studies). Ultimately, transdisciplinarity exists in the individual scholar, in familiarity with several fields of inquiry at once, conceptually and substantively, epistemologically and methodologically. Such an admittedly high standard might well represent a lifetime's effort, one perhaps not many of us will be able to achieve. But this is a topic for another time. Of immediate concern is the question of how theory may serve as a guide to the transdisciplinary study of leisure. Theory may be the link joining the several perspectives operating within leisure studies, a way past the isolating tendencies of disciplinarity and specialization. It should be clear that this is *not* to say these perspectives and their supporting research programs should be melded into one. This would contradict leisure's multidimensionality. It is more reasonable to ask how theory may raise questions cutting across perspectives and joining researchers together even where they hold differing views on epistemology and methodology. The possibility of such theory would represent a tentative step toward transdisciplinarity. Taking this step, however, requires a better understanding of the nature of theory and of the alternative paradigms for theory in play within the social sciences.

Paradigms for Inquiry

Discussion of these issues in leisure studies, while scarce, has not been altogether lacking. Even where attention has been given to them, however, the limitations of the prevailing conceptions of theory in leisure studies have been revealed. In her useful analysis of the lack of theoretically informed research in the field, Stockdale (1989) argues it is necessary to rise above the "information gathering" focus of much contemporary leisure research, and that to do this the development of theory is necessary. But Stockdale, as do most leisure researchers, proceeds with a limited view of what constitutes theory, remaining squarely within what will shortly be labeled the postpositivist paradigm by naming the "explanation and prediction" of leisure behavior as the "ultimate end" of leisure research. This is, however, only one among several conceptions of theory.

Discussions of theory in leisure studies have generally proceeded as Stockdale does, with the assumption that only one paradigm of theory has relevance to the field (e.g., Weissinger, 1995). Where, for example, Stockdale offers social representation theory as a possible exit from leisure studies' theoretic muddle, this may also be understood as simply the a priori affirmation of a specific *paradigm* for theory. Calls for "more theory" in the field are, in fact, usually calls for more of one particular paradigm of theory. There is no doubt that some conception of positivist-inspired theory has long been dominant in the social sciences, but there is equally no doubt that the debate on paradigms of theory has continued and perhaps intensified in recent years (see Bernstein, 1978, 1983, for lucid discussions of this). This debate has been slow to emerge in leisure studies, and then mostly outside North America, so the field has yet fully to consider the existence of several alternatives to positivist-based theory. Until this expanded debate occurs, the field will, given the prevalence of the postpositivist paradigm, find its research being funneled into a narrow range of research questions and methodologies unable in themselves to attain the transdisciplinarity necessary for the multidimensional investigation of leisure.

As a first step, it is necessary to recognize the complexity of theory. Theory always involves propositions about the structure of what is taken to be social "reality," so that theory itself is part of the construction of the very social world we wish to investigate.[1] In Calhoun's (1995) words, theory constitutes "our very access to the social world, including the facts about which we theorize and the practical actions through which we test propositions and understanding" (p. 7). Theory is an intervention in that social world and so necessarily makes crucial assumptions about that world's structure. These assumptions are the coordinates along which theory-based inquiry orients itself, the beginning point and road map. But these coordinates arise from within the theory, and not from the social world, on which they are imposed. It should be no surprise that theory, at least as conventionally conceived, is reflected in the social world and empirical findings about it. Finding regularities in behavior, as for example in leisure preferences and satisfactions, is not remarkable when the expectation of them is built into the epistemological and methodological doctrines that pass for theory in much of social science. After all, these expectations contribute to the construction of the social world being investigated.

This has significance for the social function of theory. Theorizing is every bit a social phenomenon as any we investigate. There is a reciprocal relation between (1) theorizing as the construction of the so-

cial world we ask questions about and (2) the function of theorizing in that social world. The assumptions made in theory about the social world contribute to whether theorizing becomes one aspect of the reproduction of that world, and thus plays a conserving role; or whether theorizing becomes a self-reflective enterprise intended to reveal contradictions in social practices that limit human development, and thus plays a radical role. I will argue in what follows that critical theory falls into the radical camp; it will be clear from earlier essays (Hemingway, 1995, 1996) that I regard more traditionally conceived empirical theory to play a largely conserving role. But for the moment this point can be better illustrated through a brief summary of the assumptions made about the social world by the leading alternative paradigms in social research.[2]

The term *paradigm* is at best imprecise, but can be understood as indicating a model of propositions and beliefs, explicit and implicit, held by a community of researchers about the conduct of their work, the structure of what they study, the nature of their findings, how these findings are to be fitted together, and the social meaning(s) of the resulting statements. Benhabib's (1996) "nontechnical" definition is perhaps as clear as any. She characterizes a paradigm as "a coherent set of assumptions, some articulated and some not, which guide, influence, structure, or help 'format' a vision of theory and politics" (p. 27). In any event, three components of such a model are generally identified: the ontological, addressing the presumed nature of reality; the epistemological, addressing the manner in which this reality may be known; and the methodological, addressing the means by which this knowledge may be gained. To these I would add a fourth component, the valuational, addressing the underlying historically conditioned values attached to inquiry and those who carry it out. The four paradigms named earlier—positivism, postpositivism, constructivism, and critical theory—may be contrasted with each other using the four components just named.[3]

---

[1] I have dealt with this issue at some length on another occasion (Hemingway, 1995). Since theory is always in evolution, not all I say in this chapter will be in agreement with my earlier writing. Conversations with Don McLean helped clarify some issues that were troublesome in my earlier statement. I want also to acknowledge here the helpful comments and encouragement of Charlie Sylvester and Ben Hunnicutt, who are of course absolved of responsibility for any weaknesses remaining in this chapter.

[2] I owe my initial familiarity with this formulation of the issue to Keith Hollinshead, whose invitation to participate in a symposium on alternative paradigms sponsored by the International Sociological Association's research committee on international tourism was the impetus to considering the question more broadly.

[3] Its substantive shortcomings and occasional superficiality aside, the collection edited by E. Guba under the title *The Paradigm Dialog* (1990) is a useful introduction to the issues raised here. Although my general description of the alternative paradigms follows to some extent Guba's introductory essay to this volume, "The Alternative Paradigm Dialog" (pp. 17–27), my conclusions, particularly regarding critical theory and constructivism, are sharply different from his.

Positivism and Postpositivism

Positivism is perhaps the most familiar paradigm for theory. Ontologically, it holds that there is a discoverable external reality describable in statements of increasing generality until these take nomological form, that is, the form of natural laws specifying causal (rather than only correlational) relationships among phenomena. Such statements are taken to be universalizable, that is, independent of temporal and cultural factors. Epistemologically, positivism holds that the knower and the known must be separated. Explanation and prediction, based on measurement, are the forms in which knowledge is to be stated if it is to count as such. A proposition's truth content rests on the type of data that support it and the means by which these data are collected and analyzed. Epistemological statements can be measured against what is known ontologically, that is, what is known about the presumed external world. Methodologically, positivism insists on "value-free" inquiry, with propositions drawn from existing, preferably more general, statements; these propositions are stated in advance and tested under specified and controlled conditions, with mathematically rigorous methods valued over others.

Postpositivism developed in response to the general discrediting of the claims made by its predecessor. It consists generally of tempering the absolutism of positivism by the recognition that although the aims of positivism are laudatory, the imperfections of methods and the complexity of the phenomena make achieving them highly unlikely. Ontologically, then, postpositivism holds that although there is an external reality describable by lawlike statements, these will always be only approximate because external reality will never be understood in its totality. Epistemologically, postpositivism maintains the separation of knower and known while acknowledging this can never be complete. Nonetheless, it aims at something like statements of cause and effect, but understands these will always be only partial and perhaps expressed correlationally. Given incomplete knowledge of the external world, new propositions cannot be measured against it satisfactorily. They must, as Guba (1990, p. 21) points out, be evaluated by the "critical community," i.e., the community of scholars working in the relevant specialty, whose views find their expression in journals, research meetings, and so on. A scholarly "consensus" determines which propositions will be accepted, and which not. Value-freedom remains the ideal and the critical community its protector. Methodologically, postpositivism grudgingly abandons the positivist claim that experimentally gained knowledge alone counts, and accepts less rigorously derived statements, particularly when several nonexperimental techniques have been brought to bear on the phenomena in question. Inductive statements, sometimes called grounded theory, are accepted as sources of testable propositions.

The ontological, epistemological, and methodological differences between positivism and postpositivism are those of degree, not of kind. Valuationally they are hardly different at all. There is a belief in the fallibility of human judgment, particularly as it is corrupted by self-interest. There is also a conviction that true knowledge can therefore be only that of which we ourselves are not part, that is, the knower and the known must be kept steadfastly separated. This requires a withdrawal from that which is studied, a dispassionate objectivity, leading ultimately to varying degrees of determinism. Though human beings may take themselves to be acting in a world governed in part, at least, by their own wills and volitions, in the end this is only a delusion. Human beings are part of an immensely complex social reality, but it is not one they themselves make.

Constructivism

Positivism and postpositivism have shaped much of modern inquiry, in the social as well as the natural sciences. They are also the paradigms against which contemporary social inquiry has begun to react in the forms of constructivism and critical theory. Constructivism has emerged with particular force over the past two decades. It is not dissimilar to, and in fact is partly derived from, what is called *postmodernism,* which has flourished in some areas of the humanities and may be regarded as rejecting what Toulmin (1990, p. 11) terms modernity's "quest for certainty."[4]

Such a loosely defined body of thought is difficult to summarize, but constructivism may be said to rest on the claim that human beings are far more constitutive of their world than positivism and postpositivism acknowledge. At the extreme end are those who, like Guba (1990, p. 27), claim that the "world" exists only "in the minds of its constructors," a nonsensical statement when taken as literally as Guba and others seem to mean it. Ontologically, then, constructivism adopts a relativist approach, emphasizing the local over the universal, and asserting the existence of multiple realities, as opposed to a single external reality. These multiple realities are grounded in the individual experiences out of which the specific identities of the knowers

---

[4]It will hardly show in the brief discussion that follows, but my understanding of postmodernism has been influenced by an earlier project undertaken with Karla Henderson.

emerge. Epistemology and ontology melt into one another in constructivism, for its epistemology simply repeats its ontological claim in a different way by maintaining that knowledge is subjective rather than objective. The knower and the known are linked together in the knower's experience of the known; knowledge is the product of this experience and is inseparable from it. In this spirit, constructivist methodology emphasizes the individual and the unique. Its resistance to "totalizing" accounts is reflected in Lyotard's (in)famous statement that postmodernism is "incredulity toward metanarratives" (1984, p. xxiv). Individual reports of experience must be credited as authentic. At most, they can be explicated to reveal hidden meanings and compared to other reports similarly explicated with the hope that something like generalizations will appear. These, however, do not take precedence over the localized reports of experience on which they are based, and cannot be taken as stand-ins for lawlike statements from which testable propositions may be generated.

Valuationally, constructivism advances individual human experience to the foreground. In direct opposition to positivism and postpositivism, it elevates the individual, specific, and local above the totality, the general, and the universal. Constructivism is unconcerned with issues of the fallibility of human judgment. Self-interest and incompleteness are simply parts of the world built by individual experience. In the end, this experience itself becomes sanctified. Any challenge from the outside is rejected as an attempt to subordinate individual experience to unwarranted claims of authority. The relativism inherent in constructivism is profoundly suspicious of threats to individual autonomy, to the imposition of standards of "true and false," "right and wrong," "good and bad" alien to a specific individual's experience of the world. Ultimately, constructivism descends into a chaos of individual identities, each grounded in its own unique interpretation of its individual experience.

The Critical Theory Enterprise

So much for three of the competing paradigms for theory. We turn now to the fourth, critical theory, advanced here as the alternative of most value in the study of leisure. Simply stated, critical theory aims to steer a course between the reification of human action (that is, treating human action as a thing or object) in positivism and postpositivism, and the relativism inherent in constructivism, all the while seeking contact between theory and practice aimed at the emancipation of hu-

man capacities.[5] How critical theory does this can be illustrated by examining three themes within it: (a) historical specificity and the nature of critique; (b) difference, defined as plurivocity and polyphony; and (c) the emancipation of human capacities, which receives particular emphasis in the following discussion. In this discussion, the four elements of a paradigm identified earlier (ontology, epistemology, methodology, and values) are integrated rather than separated as earlier, allowing a more detailed presentation of critical theory. The reader may wish to review the summary at the end of this section, where these four elements are again treated separately, to enable more ready comparison of critical theory with the three other paradigms.

Historical Specificity and the Nature of Critique

Social inquiry has not generally acknowledged the *historicity* of social phenomena. It has frequently failed to understand that social phenomena are "historically conditioned" and not aspects of an atemporal social "brute reality" or "given" (Bernstein, 1978, p. 106). Critical theory, however, is specifically historical, making explicit the historicity of social action against a normative horizon (discussed here as emancipation, defined provisionally as the release of human potential). Social action occurs in specific historical contexts and takes specific historical forms. These contexts and forms often have dimensions unrecognized either at the time or by the actors. Critical theory strives to make apparent the specific historical context in which social action is situated, particularly those elements which have become so much a part of that action (e.g., in daily experience) that the actors themselves no longer see them either as the results of previous action or of historical context. In their apparent immediacy these elements have become part of the "given," accepted as the "natural" context in which human beings act. Critical theory explores the historical process of reification by which social practices and conditions

---

[5]Reasonably accessible accounts of critical theory and its history may be found in the following: for its philosophical foundations, see Benhabib (1986) and Hoy and McCarthy (1994); for its history, particularly its association with the Institute of Social Research, see Jay (1996); for a richly detailed history that includes many of the minor as well as the major figures in critical theory's development, see Wiggershaus (1994); for a survey of the contributions of the major thinkers, see Held (1980); for useful selections from the writings of influential critical theorists, see Arato and Gebhardt (1993) and Bronner and Kellner (1989).

created by human action come to be regarded as "quasi-natural" and to "dominate over the apparently more contingent quality of human life" (Calhoun, 1995, p. 15). Building on Marx's analysis (1990, chapter 1) of the commodity relationship as the foundation of capitalism, and inspired by Lukács's important essay on reification (1922/1971), critical theorists have explored how the artifacts of human activity come to appear independent from, and even determinative of, human action.

Historicity of Human Activity

Critical theory proceeds by developing an "empirically rich" basis for its analysis, an analysis that acknowledges two related features of human action: first, that such action is irreducibly historical; second, that such action takes its substance from a particular cultural context (Calhoun, 1995, pp. 89–90). These points are joined with the proposition that, in their current state, human beings are always less than they could be (Horkheimer, 1937/1972, pp. 209–10; this is a seminal essay in the development of critical theory). In this current state, human beings are confronted with the contradiction between historical actuality on the one hand and human potential on the other. In Horkheimer's words, "the critical theory of society . . . has for its object men as producers of their historical way of life in its totality" but it does not take this totality as an absolute "given," for critical theory "is not concerned with goals imposed by existent ways of life, but with men and all their potentialities" (pp. 244, 245). The historically specific conditions in which human action occurs are the bases of critical theory's empirical analysis of social roles, practices, and institutions; the concept of emancipation is the normative horizon for their critique. It is any contradiction between these—social roles, practices, and institutions on the one hand; and emancipation on the other—that critical theory challenges.

Self-Reflexivity in Critical Theory

Critique has so far been characterized as the historically specific explication of social roles, practices, and institutions (hereafter also referred to as *social specifics* to avoid repetition) with reference to their effects on human potential. A further component is self-reflexivity. Critique is the effort, in Marx's words (1977, p. 38), to obtain a "self-understanding" by the participants of the principles that structure social specifics. Social inquiry is a form (albeit too often highly formalized and opaque to the uninitiated) of reflection about

these and their surrounding social and material conditions, carried on by individuals who are participants in them if for no other reason than that they have chosen to examine them. From the critical point of view there is no such thing as a pure or detached observer. This is more than a matter of "value freedom" or "value neutrality." The researcher shares in the web of historically developed understandings about which social phenomena are relevant to and appropriate for social inquiry, about the proper manner in which inquiry is to be conducted, and about expectations for the use of its results. Where "traditional theory" (essentially equivalent to positivism and postpositivism) regards "the social genesis of a problem" as "external to itself" (Horkheimer, 1937/1972, p. 244), critical theory argues that because there is no means to escape the "social genesis" of the problems it investigates, this must itself become a subject for inquiry.

Thematizing the historical embeddedness both of what it investigates and the investigation itself is the source of critical theory's self-reflexivity. Where positivism and postpositivism separate the researcher from what is researched, and where constructivism fractures this relationship into multiple sites among which any critical judgment is difficult if not impossible, critical theory makes its own enterprise a conscious focus of critical attention. The questions critical theory addresses are understood to have form, content, and importance shaped by historically specific human values and action predicated on them. Critical theory explicitly queries why *these* questions have arisen and been selected for attention in a specific set of historical circumstances (e.g., workers' leisure in the 1920s and 1930s, gender and racial differences in the 1980s and 1990s). How are they analyzed? What is treated as natural, as part of a social "given," and what as manifestations of human historical action? What is the interaction between inquiry and inquirer? What elements in society are interested in their resolution (e.g., in the appeal to IQ in social policy planning or in the effects of ethnicity on learning)? These are not trivial issues; the function of inquiry in society at large depends on their resolution.

Social Function of Inquiry

The social function of inquiry ranges from conservative to radical. Conventionally ("traditionally" in Horkheimer's phrase), inquiry examines the mechanisms by which society is reproduced, attempting to account for them in their continuity or discontinuity under the cloak of a neutrality supposedly ensured by the separation of researcher from the object of research. In fact, this approach contributes itself to the reproduction of society. The separation of researcher from the "researched" lends to the phenomena concerned with the misleading appearance of being social "givens" rather than the product of historical human action. Such inquiry plays a conservative role in society (cf., Horkheimer, 1937/1972, pp. 196, 208), regarding any practical intervention in society as beyond its scope and reflected in the conventional binary oppositions between "research and values," "knowledge and action," or "theory and practice." Conventional inquiry achieves its self-conception by failing to recognize itself as a historically grounded social practice. Failing to do so, conventional inquiry tends to replicate existing social practices and conditions by regarding the phenomena it analyses as part of a social "given" from which it is separated. Is it merely coincidence, for example, that there has been a burst of interest in the economic aspects of leisure in a time when "the market" has assumed mystical qualities as the natural arrangement of human transactions? Does such economic analysis of leisure reinforce or challenge existing presuppositions about human interaction? It is neither a coincidence, I think, nor is such analysis sufficiently reflective about its social function.

Critical theory, on the other hand, by virtue of its self-reflexivity, aims not only to explicate existing social roles, practices, and institutions, but to *change* them as well. It thus has an at least potentially radical social function. Applying a range of analytic techniques, among them methods from conventional social analysis, critical theory assists social action "by helping [to] see beyond the immediacy of what *is* at any given moment to conceptualize something that could be" (Calhoun, 1995, p. 9). Critical theory aims not just to identify contradictions in social practices and conditions limiting the release of human capacities, but also to provide the foundations for practical action to remove these contradictions.[6] Failure to thematize its own historicity would contribute to the replication of the very social conditions and practices critical theory challenges. It takes the "real situations" of human beings regarded as producers of "their own historical way of life in its totality" as its "starting point," but not merely as "data to be verified and predicted according to the laws of probability" (Horkheimer, p. 244). It takes them instead in relation to historically grounded conceptions of human potentialities (p. 245) with "the conviction that men have other possibilities than to lose themselves in the status quo" (p. 248). Critical theory is thus always a political basis for carrying theory over into practice, for intervention in the social world. This intervention is the drive for emancipation, the release and development of human capacities, to which our discussion turns after exploring the need for critical theory to attend to the concept of difference.

Difference: Plurivocity and Polyphony

Early critical theory was strongly influenced by the universalism in the philosophies of Kant, Hegel, Marx, and (more distantly) Aristotle. This is evident in the work of critical theory's most prominent early practitioners, Max Horkheimer and Theodor Adorno (e.g., 1944/1972), who sharply attacked the "culture industry's" role in the degradation of "high culture"; it remains evident today in the work of critical theory's most active contemporary thinker, Jürgen Habermas (e.g., in his analysis of discourse ethics and communicative action). Among the more telling criticisms of critical theory is, therefore, that it betrays its own principle of historical specificity by failing to confront adequately questions raised by difference (see, e.g., Fraser, 1989, specifically the essay "What's Critical About Critical Theory?").

Critical theory's error was to forget that historical and cultural contingencies render the identity of each person opaque, for each person's identity is grounded in the particularities of his or her historical situation. No universal self-justifying principles can be applied equally across all such individuals (cf., Benhabib, 1992, p. 4). There has historically been a general failure in social science to recognize this, reflected in inattention to issues of gender, race, ethnicity, age, and physical and mental condition. This error, in which early critical theory is implicated, has a contemporary parallel in "identity politics," particularly the insistence that individuals are determined by one among these many previously unacknowledged factors. Both errors are due in significant part to the unspoken and false assumption that individuals may for purposes of social inquiry be placed in a single social world whose features are defined in advance by the purposes of inquiry. Culture, however, and the individual identities developed within it, is a plurivocal and polyphonic enterprise, that is, culture is multivoiced and multithemed (cf., Taylor, 1985, pp. 248–292). Human beings live in multiple social worlds all at the same time and find themselves necessarily adjusting among the multiple social roles they therefore occupy. The individual is in many ways the intersection of these social worlds, and the

---

[6]For discussions of how critical theory informs practice, see Forester (1985) and, particularly for a more radical view, Leonard (1990). It is important to note that by its very nature, social and political action grounded in critical theory appears in nontraditional settings and forms, e.g., the "new social movements," environmental action, "lifestyle"-based movements.

individual's integration of them is a defining characteristic of his or her personality (cf., Calhoun, 1995, p. xv).

In the light of this, the reformulation of critical theory Benhabib (1992) suggests has some importance for the development of a critical analysis of leisure. Benhabib wishes to develop a "communicative universalism" that moves the theoretical issue *from* noncontradiction of a universal maxim (which forces argument toward one-dimensionality, as in the question What is true leisure? which can be answered only trivially or so generally as to be of little use in studying historically existing leisure) *to* a question of action among individuals in historically specific conditions (who address grounded questions like What is leisure now? with the prerequisite conditions for effective engagement in such action treated as universal principles). Benhabib's proposal to reformulate critical theory on a principle of communicative universalism directs us away from the hitherto dominant convention in social science of treating individuals as if they live in a single social world, while avoiding constructivist relativism. Instead, critical social inquiry examines the intersubjective cultural process out of which there emerges some social understanding of the multiple forms of, and sites for, leisure in a particular society. Following Benhabib, critical social inquiry is open to any number of voices arguing along any number of themes as they develop an understanding of what leisure is in their intersubjectively defined historical situation. This means taking people as they are placed in their multiple social roles and as they understand those roles, rather than imposing preconceived universal and one-dimensional conceptions on them.

Benhabib structures communicative universalism to incorporate, for example, the feminist challenge to separating artificially the public and the private (1992, p. 12), which has rendered women's leisure (among other activities) invisible. By insisting on attention to the many voices hitherto often excluded from social analysis, and by recognizing that these voices are grounded in varying historical situations, the full complexity of social phenomena, leisure included, may become more visible. To continue speaking about human identity as though all identities are universally shaped in the same ways by the same social and material forces or as though they are organized along a single dimension (e.g., race, gender) is in both cases dangerously misleading. There is no single social role a person always fills and from which he or she always

engages the social world, nor is there any absolute distinction between public and private social roles, a point which assumes more significance in examining the political implications of leisure. For the present, Taylor's (1979, p. 52) observation that "we are aware of a world through a 'we' before we are through an 'I'" is telling, for our conception of who we are tends to emerge before any possible reflection on what it is to be a person, and what kind of person in what specific historical circumstances. Who we are, and the standpoint(s) from which we regard our world, is thus very much a historical social product. Any reflection on what we are becoming must occur within the constraints of our own personal history, the constraints of historically available conceptions of personhood, and the determinate resources available to us.

From the interplay among these—our socially emergent identities, our social and material conditions, and our expanding reflections on them—the sense might grow that who we are does not exhaust the possibilities of who we might become. If critical social analysis is as Benhabib (1992) defines it, "the critical uncovering of premises and arguments which are implicit not only in contemporary cultural and intellectual debates but in the institutions and social practices of our lives as well" (p. 7), then the normative thrust of our awareness of constraints on who we might become is toward overcoming these constraints. If we understand critical theory as examining the conditions under which critical dialog may occur, then the joining of many voices in this dialog might result in a conversation that eventually alters the horizon against which we see both ourselves and our historical situation.

Emancipation

This critical conversation, which is necessarily polyphonic and plurivocal; that is, multithemed and multivoiced, both within and among individuals, lies at the heart of emancipation, the valuational focus of critical theory. It requires that some social space be opened in which the complex features of human identity may be given force, their content explored and expanded. The disappearance of such a space, and the consequent impoverishment of social roles in a dominant capitalist culture, was a theme contributing to early critical theory's pessimism. In Jürgen Habermas's work, however, an optimism surfaces that suggests at least the possibility of establishing the necessary social space for the formation and expression of human identity, but that also requires radical reformation of existing social specifics.[7]

Rationalization and the Closing of Social Space

For our purposes, the most important concept in Habermas's early work is that of the "public sphere," which may be defined as that social space occupied by individuals in their public roles as members of groups, secondary associations, and extended social relations, but excluding strictly occupational or governmental roles. Benhabib (1992, p. 12) briefly describes the public sphere as "the crucial domain of interaction which mediates between the macropolitical institutions of a democratic polity and the private sphere," the latter consisting of primary social relations. This public sphere contributed to the development of an articulate public by providing social space for critical conversation, and through this to the expansion of ideas about rights and liberties (see particularly Habermas, 1962/1989). Leisure practices were significant in defining the public sphere and activity within it, for example in the provision of sites for discussion and interaction among members of a community in such institutions as coffee houses, taverns, lodges, and fraternal organizations.

In this and his more recent work (especially Habermas, 1984, 1987; these are lucidly summarized in Kissling, 1990), Habermas has analyzed the subsequent fundamental restructuring of the public sphere in Western society, and with it changes in historically available social roles. This restructuring was accelerated by the process of industrialization, one result of which was the narrowing of social roles through what Habermas terms *rationalization,* a concept he borrows from Max Weber (e.g., 1947, pp. 184–85). If we think of rationality as the constitutive and regulatory rules by which social roles, practices, and institutions are created and structured (see Hemingway, 1995, pp. 38–39), then changes in the underlying rationality entail changes in these social specifics as well (with the caveats that there may be a significant lag between his-

torical changes in rationality and subsequent social changes, and that these changes may well be indirect and subterranean). Habermas contends that the process of rationalization tends toward subsuming social roles, practices, and institutions under one set of rules, that is, under one form of rationality. The dynamics of industrialization are grounded in an instrumental, means-ends-oriented rationality. Instrumental rationality, originally dominant in the economic and governmental spheres, has increasingly driven other forms of rationality (what Habermas terms the expressive, normative, and communicative) more and more from their former places in the private and public spheres. The eclipse of other forms of rationality by the increasingly dominant instrumental form (that is, the increasing presence of means-ends calculations throughout society) is in Habermas's view the chief source of the shrinking of social roles as industrialization proceeded, and which persists now in what has been called postindustrial society. The result is the diminution of the social space within which these now reduced social roles, practices, and institutions might have served as the basis for the exploration of human identities.

Rights and the Opening of Social Space

In analyzing the requirements for a democratic society, Habermas (1992) argues for the recovery of this social space. It has its basis in communicative action (though this does not, or at least should not—Habermas is not altogether clear on this point—exclude action grounded in other noninstrumental rationalities). The nature of this social space is both the subject and the result of an ongoing conversation among equal individuals, whose aims are to arrive at some mutually agreed upon definition of their common situation (and thus also of where they differ) and to understand its implications for themselves individually and collectively. This conversation entails the reciprocal offer of and critical response to reasons, and should be independent of mere weight of numbers or instrumentally grounded power (e.g., wealth, social position). Its focus is not instrumental, to persuade others to one's point of view for the purpose of achieving one's individually defined goals, but rather to establish together the social space in which one's possibilities can be discovered and pursued.

The communicative equality of the participants in this conversation is vital to its success. Merely formal equality, or equality without the means to act equally, is empty. This therefore requires attention to the social conditions of the participants. As Habermas argues, economic and social advantages should not pervert

---

[7]See McCarthy (1978) for an extensive bibliography of Habermas's work to that date. Habermas continues to publish important work; for major expansions of his theory, see particularly, 1984, 1987, and 1992. A translation of this latter work was published in 1996 as *Between Facts and Norms: Contributions to a Discourse Theory of Law and Democracy* (W. Rehg, trans.), Cambridge, MA: MIT Press. I do not want to suggest Habermas is definitive of contemporary critical theory. This is most definitely *not* the case. Significant differences exist within critical theory, and generalizations across its various representatives should be treated carefully.

communicative action into instrumental action. Put another way, each participant should be so situated to permit equal access to the social space in which this conversation is conducted. This issue is both structural (i.e., creating a social space accessible to all who wish to enter it) and procedural (i.e., enabling the communicative participation of all those who wish to contribute). It raises the question of *rights* as fundamental to the establishment and protection of equality. The "original meaning" of rights, according to Habermas (1992, p. 494), is to secure the private and public autonomy of individuals both as the premise of communicatively grounded action and as one of its aims, namely, to further the expansion and refinement of rights themselves. Rights therefore include not only the familiar political and civil ones, but also rights to conditions enabling participation in the ongoing conversation among equal individuals. These include fundamental rights to "work, security, health, a home, nutrition, education, leisure, and fundamental life necessities" (p. 490); they emerge from the concerns people must address in their daily lives (p. 495), and are by extension among the dimensions along which human identities are established. Our individual attempts to address any one of these concerns interact with how we address others. They also affect and are affected by the similar attempts of other people and by the material conditions of our historically specific situation. The achievement of identity is therefore private and public, complex (i.e., plurivocal and polyphonic), and historically situated. It requires commonly defined and achieved social space in which each person's communicative equality is made more effective by an extended system of rights protecting the communicative equality of all.

Rights Grounded in Human Capacities

Autonomy and equality are, as we have just seen, grounded in a system of rights. These rights are themselves in turn grounded in human capacities; they are aimed at the identification, protection, development, and expansion of these capacities. Bypassing philosophical complexities, human beings have certain abilities by virtue of what they are. Not only can these abilities be developed, amplified, expanded, and integrated, but human beings enjoy and appear to seek out opportunities for such activity. Abilities become particularly relevant for social and political theory as human *capacities,* that is, when human abilities are interpreted within a specific social framework with specific conceptions of human activity. Abilities become capacities in historically specific contexts.

If this holds, then what human capacities are and should be must be an integral part of the critical conversation introduced earlier. Capacities are not given, but are created by the interaction of human abilities and historically situated social contexts. They become the focus of intense debate because they define what it is to be a fully human being within this social context. They fill out the picture of what fully human activity consists. They are the basis for claims to support, recognition, and protection, as well as claims to opposition, denial, and repression. Most importantly, we can reason from existing capacities and their actually existing development (as opposed to ideologically grounded claims about this) to the potential existence of additional capacities and their development, to greater degrees of development for existing capacities, and to the expansion of existing capacities across the members of a specific society. The contrast between these potentialities and the actually existing development of present capacities provides a basis for critical analysis and action in society. It is at the elucidation of this contrast between potentiality and actuality, and its practical implications, that critical theory aims.

Recalling earlier discussion, critical theory takes human beings as bearers of multiple socially grounded capacities recognized within specific historical conditions, requiring for their development a defined social space attuned to the complexity of human identity. Prevailing social practices, roles, and institutions are regarded as inadequate both to the development and expansion of human capacities, and to the expression of complex human identities. This can be stated as the analytic difference between the emancipatory *potential* of social practices, roles, and institutions, on the one hand, and their actual emancipatory *content* on the other. Emancipatory content is assessed by the relative presence or absence of conditions fostering emancipatory activity, i.e., the development and expansion of human capacities. Any critical analysis must necessarily open itself to the critique of existing social specifics from the standpoint of identifying historically existing conditions restricting emancipatory activity with the further intention of finding the means for the release of emancipatory potential.

Two Conceptions of Human Activity: Acquisitive and Developmental

This intention cannot be given adequate theoretical or practical expression, however, without an analysis of the nature of human activity necessary for the task of emancipation. As noted earlier, theory may perform either a conservative or a radical social function. And as Habermas makes clear, the rationalities underlying human activity play central roles in determining the emancipatory content and potential of that activity. Thus theory's social function is, in part, determined by the presumed structure of human activity. As Euben (1996, p. 73) comments, "A theory that adopts the same notion of rationality as the structure it studies helps that structure operate rather than effects a theoretical distance from it." To the degree that the study of social phenomena, leisure included, accepts uncritically currently dominant notions of human activity, to that degree it reinforces them, and so performs a conservative social function. If the emancipatory social space at which critical theory aims is, in fact, to be achieved either theoretically or practically, critical theory must first explicate the dominant conception of human activity in actually existing historical conditions and then provide an alternative that might form the basis for practical action. This, it should be noted, is an exercise in which leisure studies has yet to engage, an omission seriously retarding much of leisure research's emancipatory value.

Not all such conceptions of human activity have the same implications for the expansion and development of human capacities lying at the heart of emancipation. Recognizing the risks in creating binary oppositions, it is nonetheless useful to identify two broad conceptions of human activity that have been historically influential and which draw on different rationalities. These are the acquisitive and the developmental. The former has played a major role in structuring European and particularly Anglo-American society.[8] Despite differences in emphasis, the acquisitive conception remains current within a wide variety of social inquiry, though it emerged into prominence several centuries ago. In this conception, human beings are regarded as bundles of unending appetites and desires (Hobbes); the rationality of human activity consists in mastering ways to satisfy them that secure life and liberty while allowing accumulation of goods (Locke). The satisfaction of individual appetites and desires then becomes the basis of a utilitarian common good defined as the greatest accumulation by the greatest number (Bentham, James Mill). From these origins, the acquisitive conception has gone on to shape Western free market economic theory and "realist" theories of democracy.

In the acquisitive view, human identity rests at bottom on how and to what degree individuals' appetites and desires have been satisfied, that is, on what they have acquired. These acquisitions might be categorized using the four forms of capital Pierre Bourdieu identifies (1987, pp. 3–4): economic, cultural, social, and symbolic.[9] These capitals represent, as Hobbes already notes in *Leviathan,* forms of power, and it is for these forms of acquisitively grounded power that people are said to strive as the very core of their social beings. Not to have it is to be consigned to social insignificance and impotence. The idea of human beings as blank slates, lying at the center of Locke's psychology and (when mixed with various religious motifs) determinative of much Anglo-American culture, has been extended to the individual's social identity as well. The individual is a composite of those attributes he or she has acquired, pursuing the satisfaction of common human appetites and desires to create himself or herself as a distinct identity. The burden here falls entirely on the individual, not only to acquire but to recognize those attributes that are desirable given existing historical conceptions of what it is to be a human being. The development of society then consists of uncounted numbers of transactions among individuals as they pursue the acquisitive creation of their social identities. Success or failure rides on the individual's

---

[9]Bourdieu's comments are worth quoting at some length to clarify discussion in the text:

> The social world can be conceived as a multidimensional space that can be constructed empirically by discovering the main factors of differentiation which account for the differences observed in a given social universe, or, in other words, by discovering the powers or forms of *capital* which are or can become efficient, like aces in a game of cards, in this particular universe, that is, in the struggle (or competition) for the appropriation of scarce goods of which this universe is the site. It follows that the structure of this space is given by the distribution of the various forms of capital . . . those properties capable of conferring strength, power and consequently profit on their holder. . . . These fundamental social powers are . . . firstly *economic* capital, in its various kinds; secondly *cultural* capital or better, informational capital, again in its different kinds; and thirdly two forms of capital that are very strongly correlated, *social* capital, which consists of resources based in connections and group membership, and *symbolic* capital, which is the form different kinds of capital take once they are perceived and recognized as legitimate.

---

[8]For incisive discussions of the historical emergence of the acquisitive conception of human activity, see Hirschman (1977), Macpherson (1962), and Polanyi (1944). Some components of the acquisitive conception and their relation to contemporary leisure are discussed in Hemingway (1991).

ability to recognize and to acquire the appropriate forms of capital. One's social identity, who one is or is not, rests on acquisitive success or failure.

The second historically significant conception, with a heritage extending back to Aristotle, is the developmental. In it, human beings are conceived as bundles of abilities rising from such human characteristics as reason and language, abilities that become *capacities* when defined socially and historically. In this conception, it is the nature of human beings to seek development of their capacities as far as they are able. Unlike the abstract individualism inherent in the acquisitive conception, the development of human capacities requires a historically specific social context. Capacities, however, should not be confused with social roles. They are instead the "building blocks" out of which social roles are constructed. Different roles demand different mixes of capacities. To the degree these are regarded as "higher" capacities, and to the degree a social role requires their fuller development, the social role is itself regarded as "higher" in content and human significance. The developmental conception has yielded strikingly different social theories, from those at best aristocratic and hierarchical (e.g., Aristotle, Hegel) through those moderating the effects of acquisition but with acquisitive content (e.g., Green, Rawls) to radical egalitarianism (e.g., Marx). Central to the moderate and radical theories is the idea that society itself has an interest in the fullest possible development of human capacities, both in range and degree, and that these capacities therefore represent rights to be protected and expanded by social and political arrangements fostering cooperation among people pursuing their own capacities. Human beings as active in society are in a sense born as already social creatures with abilities that are socially interpreted and developed as capacities. These are the basis of mutual expectations among individuals and within society: on the one hand, that these capacities will be recognized as the basis of rights to conditions for their development; on the other, that they will in fact be developed as the basis for a strengthened and enriched society.

Social roles will look different depending on which conception of human activity is adopted. Thinking unhistorically results in submerging in the "given" the fact that a historically effective choice was made for the dominant acquisitive conception that has shaped so much of our Western thinking about what it is to be a human being (see the sources cited in footnote 8). To say this choice has had important social consequences is hardly sufficient. As even neoconservative commentary has suggested, the "ontological individualism" resulting from the acquisitive conception has led to a fragmented social order composed of indi-

viduals in competition with themselves for something they cannot quite identify (Bellah, Madsen, Sullivan, Swidler and Tipton, 1985, which is representative of, but more eloquent than, most of this literature). This affects the entire range of social roles, not least in leisure. The traditional association of leisure and freedom loses its force if that freedom is (and it is) shaped by unacknowledged historical factors, such as the acquisitive conception of human activity and the social roles and practices resulting from it. Rojek (1995) has gone so far as to question whether the association of freedom and contemporary leisure remains appropriate: "what we understand by the term [leisure] is socially conditioned, which makes conventional associations of 'freedom,' 'choice' and 'self-determination' with leisure unsupportable" (p. 1). In a social context shaped by the acquisitive conception, and in which instrumentalism has colonized a large range of social roles, these roles can only duplicate each other and are thus unlikely to be but temporarily satisfying. Again Rojek: "Our leisure is a restless quest for choice, freedom and self-determination in the heart of modern culture which is objectively unable to deliver these experiences except as momentary diversions" (p. 110). It is remarkable that in a field which has seen constraints and barriers to "leisure satisfaction" become among its dominant themes, the arguably greatest constraint—the historically operative acquisitive conception of human activity—has remained largely unthematized through an unspoken ahistorical assumption that this conception is in fact natural and "given," rather than historically evolved through human activity.

Human activity is, of course, not the sole force at work shaping social practices, roles, and institutions. It is not independent of external circumstances, which impose multiple limitations (cf., Horkheimer, 1937/1972, p. 210). What does remain open to human activity is the spirit of the social world human beings evolve in response to these external circumstances. Critical theory insists that we not mistake reified human activity, whether in material forms such as machines and computer programs or in social forms such as government and the corporation, as part of what is extrinsic to human activity. To confuse what they themselves have shaped and formed for something "given" external to them is perhaps the most basic form of human alienation. The acquisitive conception of human activity, by its projection of human identity into the things people acquire, contributes significantly to the alienation of human activity into a supposedly "given" social world. Nor is any recovery from this alienation available within the acquisitive conception.

The alternative is to rethink the dominant acquisitive conception from the perspective of the emancipation of human capacities, that is, to reflect on the content and structure of social roles and practices from the developmental conception of human activity. Something like this is the sense of Horkheimer's distinction between critical and traditional theory, as discussed earlier. Horkheimer insists that, although critical theory must begin with the "real situations" (1944/ 1972, p. 244) in which human beings find themselves, these situations must not be taken as defining human beings. They are, in fact, the opposite: they constrain human beings within a dominant if often subterranean conception of their activity, thereby narrowing the range of what it is to be human (p. 248). Horkheimer, and with him all subsequent critical theory, insists that to be human includes having and experiencing possibilities extending beyond such narrowly conceived "real situations." The analysis of human activity must acknowledge these "potentialities" just as much, perhaps more, than it does what is taken to be "real" (p. 245). Such analysis must include not only what human beings are, but what they have it in them to become, given the rejection of the constraining acquisitive conception of their activity and, with this, of the social roles and practices based on it. To include possibility in the analysis of human activity is necessarily to turn toward a developmental conception of that activity, one that clears a space not only for the theoretic explication of social roles and practices, but also for practical intervention in them: "The issue is not simply the theory of emancipation; it is its practice as well" (p. 233).

Summary

This section has traversed difficult territory. It will therefore perhaps be useful to summarize it using the paradigm schema introduced earlier. This will serve both to sum up the preceding extended discussion of critical theory and to facilitate its comparison to the brief sketches of positivism, postpositivism, and constructivism presented previously.

It will be remembered that there are four components to a theoretic paradigm: ontology, epistemology, methodology, and values. Ontologically, as we have seen, critical theory accepts the existence of an external social reality, but does not regard it as immutably given. Instead, critical theory understands this reality to be the product of human interactions under historically specific material and social conditions (e.g., late capitalist Western liberal democracy with its attendant maldistributed abundance, as in the United States, Canada, and Western Europe). Critical theory therefore introduces a temporal dimension (specifically

omitted in positivism and postpositivism) reflected in its epistemology. If the world in which human beings act is constituted out of their interactions within (presumably) identifiable material and social conditions, then all knowledge claims are historically specific, that is, conditioned by the historically existing material and social conditions in which such claims emerge. The knower and the known are joined together by their historical specificity and the results of social inquiry are not universalizable. General statements must be carefully delimited by specification of the historical conditions under which they apply. Nonetheless, as we saw in Benhabib's concept of communicative universalism, critical theory is willing to entertain certain forms of universalism focusing on the prerequisite conditions for human activity, in contrast to constructivism, which even in its mild forms has difficulty overcoming its particularism and escaping relativism. Methodologically, critical theory proceeds as its name suggests, through a process of critical evaluation of knowledge claims. This process is best described as dialectical and hermeneutical, identifying the relationships between the knower and the known while teasing out the often hidden meanings of social practices. Both epistemologically and methodologically, critical theory is exceptionally careful to examine the degree to which any social inquiry reinforces rather than critiques existing social practices, roles, and institutions.

It will be clear from the preceding discussion that a chief component of critical theory is its valuational dimension, resting on the concept of emancipation. Critical theory takes human beings to be, at their best, autonomous agents possessing a range of capacities realized to a greater or lesser extent in a given historical situation and in given social practices, roles, and institutions. The application of empirical social scientific methods is aimed at uncovering the actual extent to which capacities are realized; normative critique is intended to identify manifest and latent barriers to their fuller realization, as well as the degree to which social inquiry itself serves to reinforce or to challenge such barriers. It is this valuational element that propels critical social inquiry into the realm of the political, to which I now turn.

Toward a Politics of Leisure

Critical theory is unavoidably politically charged. Its fundamental task is to query the difference between the emancipatory content of existing social roles, practices, and institutions—measured by their contribution to the fuller development and expression of human capacities—and their emancipatory potential. It remains grounded in an empirically rich analysis of the present projected against a horizon of normative possibilities. In this way it escapes the conservatism of positivist inspired research, with its emphasis on the social "given" and rejection of "value-laden" questions, and the relativism (some would say nihilism) of constructivism, with its inability to make critical comparative statements. Critical theory is more than simply joining empirical and normative research strategies. The critical fruitfulness of bringing together different epistemologies and methodologies results only from their focus on a common theme: the emancipation of human capacities. It is this focus that both encourages, in fact demands, transdisciplinary inquiry and introduces a political element into it. By further understanding itself to be part of its own inquiry, critical theory also raises the question of the political role of scholars and scholarship.

Radical Democracy: Expanding the Political

To adopt a critical theoretic perspective is therefore necessarily to acknowledge the political contents and meanings of leisure. Perhaps this is only fitting, given the symbolic meaning the leisure studies field attaches to leisure's classical heritage (see Sylvester, chapter 2 in this volume), which of course includes a political element in the importance of leisure for active citizenship. It is also to ask whether existing conceptions of the political are adequate for critical inquiry generally and into leisure specifically. Those conceptions of the political prevailing in the United States, and perhaps increasingly elsewhere among the Western democracies, are too narrow either to support critical inquiry or to explicate the political elements in leisure.[10] They revolve around interest-based competition for decision-making influence and its spoils among tightly defined groups, especially those working within the economic and governmental hierarchies. Underlying these narrow conceptions of the political is the acquisitive conception of human activity, with its fundamental instrumentalism and presumption of an adversarial stance toward others. The basic political acts arising out of this combination, other than the perfunctory "duty" of voting, are the instrumental calculation of interest and the manipulative persuasion of others.

These conceptions of the political fail to provide an adequate basis for a critically inspired politics of leisure.[11] Failing to challenge them relegates leisure to a conservative social function, in which, for example, the commodification of leisure or the rational calculation of benefits (see, e.g., Schreyer and Driver, 1989) contribute to the replication of acquisitively grounded social roles and practices. The developmental conception of human activity, on the other hand, understands the political as an arena for the emancipation of human capacities. To establish this arena there is politically only one possibility: radical democracy, and with it radically expanded conceptions of human capacities. Rather than defining politics as irredeemably adversarial, radical democracy conceives the political as a process through which people work out together what capacities they wish to recognize and to develop. Radical democratic politics, as Lummis (1996, p. 90) defines them, are "the activity by which human beings choose and build their life together."

Such politics are at once critical and radical, at least in their potential. They are critical because they address a historically existing state of affairs from the standpoint of an ideal that is always evolving, namely, democracy. Democracy extends beyond representative institutions and rights embodied in legal codes, though these are obviously necessary. It is instead a *process* that is always changing and (one hopes) growing, part of this growth being an expanding understanding of what social conditions and human capacities are necessary to sustain its momentum. Thus, if radical democratic politics are in this fashion always critical, they are also always radical because the very process of democratic critique points beyond any existing state of affairs toward greater democratization. Radical democracy requires all forms of power to justify themselves, power being here provisionally defined, following Bourdieu, as having economic, social, cultural, and symbolic forms. Such power is manifested in leisure no less than elsewhere in society, and perhaps more so to the degree it remains invisible and unthematized. As Habermas (1992) argues pointedly, forms of power migrate, so that, for example, economic power becomes social power, which can in turn become cultural and symbolic power, all the while sustaining the interests of the original economic power. Such migration is visible in leisure, as for example in its commodification or in its instrumentalization as a

---

[10]For classic statements of the conceptions referred to here, see Schumpeter (1942) and Downs (1957). For a powerful critical response, and argument for a participatory form of democracy, see Barber (1984); see also Davis's (1964) criticism of "realist" conceptions of democracy.

[11]The availability of free time as a political resource within the conventional understanding of the political should not be overlooked, however, even where its significance has decreased in the face of the expanded importance of money as a means of participation (see Verba, Schlozman, and Brady, 1995).

means of social control. The radical democratic conception of politics denies the legitimacy of such migration in favor of ongoing reflection on the distribution of power in society, and its manifestations in social roles, practices, and institutions. Radical democratic politics are therefore at least in part a self-reflective process aimed at recognizing human capacities, including those obscured in the myth of the social "given," and at creating conditions under which these capacities may be at least somewhat more fully developed. Like theory, then, conceptions of the political (democratic conceptions very much included) can be assessed by testing whether they tend to conserve an existing state of affairs, and the distribution of power within it; or tend to change this state, and with it the range of human capacities recognized and developed.

Radical democratic politics are concerned with choices, choices people may make freely and effectively. They are at least in part the process of, first, uncovering historical choices that have been submerged in the social "given"; second, opening again choices on matters previously thought to have been closed as a part of the "given"; and, third, bringing this to bear on opening new choices directed at expanding the range of human capacities. This process has as one of its chief aims steadily increasing the capacity of individuals to take part in it. There are any number of conditions necessary for this to be possible, emancipated leisure among them. Radical democratic politics therefore work toward establishing these conditions to avoid reducing the range of actually available choices to merely abstract and formal availability (recall Habermas's list of experientially grounded rights, 1992, p. 490; see also Gould, 1988, for a useful if not fully radical survey of this topic). As Aristotle pointed out long enough ago that the lesson should have been learned, leisure is among the first principles of human social existence (1948, p. 1337b), for on it depends access to such fundamental human activities as education, reflection, and politics as defined previously, choosing and building in common the lives people will live together. These interconnected activities all require committed participation, which in turn expands the capacities necessary for further and more effective participation in them and other activities. This, as has been said, is precisely the aim of radical democratic politics: the expression and development of human capacities to transform the emancipatory *potential* in social roles, practices, and institutions into emancipatory *content*.

Leisure as Political

Leisure has a central place in this expanded conception of the political. Regarded as a "bridge phenomenon," leisure connects the private and the public spheres. As a major arena in which multiple social roles are enacted, it contributes to the creation of the social space necessary for radical democracy. Indeed, radical democracy *requires* a radicalized conception of leisure, one focusing on the actualization of leisure's emancipatory potential. Transcending the narrow range to which the acquisitive conception of human activity consigns the political, developmentally focused radical democratic politics demands attention to the social bases of human activity, to the interconnections among social roles, practices, institutions, and forms of power; and to the forms and content of private and public activity. There are, from this perspective, at least three ways in which leisure is directly political.

It is political, first, because political activity of all kinds is carried on within leisure contexts, whether in more private forms of information gathering, in the increasingly public discussion and analysis of issues, or in fully public participation in political events and activities. Leisure is at least to some degree a prerequisite for all this (see Verba et al., 1995, for a discussion of leisure as among the resources necessary for political participation). There has been little interest, however, in the role leisure has in shaping modern citizenship, despite the fact that the availability of meaningful leisure would seem to be a significant filter through which those who would take an interest and be active in political action must necessarily pass.

Leisure is political, second, because it is a social phenomenon, and all social phenomena necessarily reflect their historical situatedness in a specific society under specific conditions. This includes the social roles, practices, and institutions present in that society, who occupies them, and the distribution of resources throughout that society. A central issue is the possible discrepancies between ideological defenses of those roles, practices, institutions, and distributions, on the one hand, and the actualities of each, on the other. Such discrepancies are significant because they reveal the gaps between the possibly emancipatory potentials of these roles and institutions, and their actual emancipatory content, along with their general accessibility and the resources available to enable this access. Social phenomena reflect the existing distributions of power in a specific historical society. To repeat again Bourdieu's forms of capital and hence of power, these distributions take economic, cultural, social, and symbolic forms. Leisure's contents and forms reflect the actual distributions of these forms of power. Studying leisure *non*critically reinforces these distributions and enhances their ideological justification. There is, in this sense, no politically neutral leisure or leisure studies.

Leisure is political, third, because it offers a potential arena for challenging dominant conceptions of human activity and for overturning dominant patterns of power in a given society. Here coupling Bourdieu's forms of capital and Habermas's forms of rationality opens the way for the critical analysis of leisure's emancipatory content. Given the prevalence of the acquisitive conception of human activity, the intrusion in leisure of instrumentally grounded activity represents the colonization of leisure by an at least presumptively "foreign" rationality and, with it, the migration of different forms of power into an arena of at least presumptively free activity. Both colonization and migration reinforce in leisure existing patterns of social dominance, whatever the ideological representation of freedom in leisure might be. It is surely clear that the patterns and content of leisure have undergone significant changes since the beginnings of industrialization, and that these changes have political importance in the broad sense of the political introduced earlier. But any arena in which such colonization and migration can be exposed is also an arena in which they can be resisted. The recovery in leisure of noninstrumental rationalities (e.g., what Habermas calls communicative, expressive, and normative rationalities) and the rejection of ideologically justified distributions of power are, at least potentially, two forms of resistance to existing patterns of social dominance, and with this, the clearing of social space for the expansion of human capacities. It may be that in a society in which work has become a principal and perhaps primary focus of energy and which controls the creation of social identities (see, e.g., Hochschild, 1997), leisure is the only arena in which people have opportunity to encounter others, whether in the private or the public spheres, on something other than the instrumental grounds characterizing work relationships. Noninstrumental relationships certainly occur in work, and there will perhaps always be some instrumental elements in leisure. Nonetheless, leisure

might provide the preeminent arena in which noninstrumentally and developmentally oriented activity may emerge. Such an emancipatory leisure arena might then provide the social space in which the development and expansion of human capacities could become a dominant theme.[12]

Leisure studies has too often neglected the political element in leisure, thereby failing to confront one of leisure's more important connections to society as a whole (but see Rojek, 1985, 1996; and Wilson, 1988). It is a virtue of critical theory that it recalls this to our attention. Only a theoretic framework open to the political in the broad sense adequately addresses the emancipatory content and potential of leisure. Such a politically open framework is also necessary to unfold a radical democratic society based on the developmental conception of human activity. Leisure plays, or can play, a central role in the emergence of such a society; critical theory is better suited to illuminate how this is the case than are the other paradigms of theory.

---

[12]Leisure's political content as an arena for emancipatory activity can be illustrated by two examples. The first is the "new social movements," which encompass a wide and diverse range of issue-oriented activity, addressing such concerns as women's issues, ethnic and racial identity, the recovery of community solidarity, environmental and ecological threats, and participatory democracy (Boggs, 1986, p. 9). These movements work in the public sphere. By contesting the artificial barrier between private and public, and by challenging the notion that social issues must be addressed through existing administrative and representative institutions, these new social movements bring together people from disparate backgrounds who encounter each other in at least potentially noninstrumentally and developmentally oriented activity (cf., Cohen, 1985; Offe, 1987, pp. 65, 68–69). The second example of leisure as an emancipatory arena is the development of democratic attitudes. In his excellent analysis of democratic reform in contemporary Italy, Putnam (1993a) found a strong association between support for democracy and participation in secondary associations, the most common of which were sports and leisure clubs, as well as civic, charitable, artistic, and religious groups (p. 92). A sense of civic engagement and competence grows out of such memberships, which are an education in democratic values and procedures (Putnam, 1993b). Bonds of civic trust, identity, and virtue were all higher in those regions of Italy where patterns of leisure-based associational membership were well-established. This creates what Putnam terms *social capital,* a capital that increases the more it is used, since it was in those regions where this capital was richest that its history ran deepest.

Theses for a Critical Analysis of Leisure

With this reminder, it is important at the conclusion of this chapter to return to the question of theory's role in fostering transdisciplinary study of leisure. What has been under discussion here is one *paradigm* for theory, namely, critical theory. As a paradigm for theory, critical theory is characterized by a number of general propositions about the nature of human activity and its analysis, on which most of its practitioners would substantially agree. Among these are the insistence on the historical specificity of all social phenomena, the complexity of social phenomena, the importance of attending to difference in understanding them, and the focus on the emancipation of human capacities. Two other propositions are conceptually linked to the foregoing: the developmental conception of human activity; and the political content of leisure as a social phenomenon. But if there would be some broad agreement on these propositions as a critical paradigm for theory, this does *not* mean there is one and only one substantive critical theory.

A paradigm shapes and guides the theory-building enterprise, but does not supply its specific content. Given leisure's multidimensionality, there could be no one substantive theory adequate to the whole of it. To bring together the resources necessary for the transdisciplinary study of leisure requires room for a considerable number of alternative research frameworks which might not always be completely epistemologically or methodologically congruent. What would unite them is some sense of agreement beyond the trivial on the general propositions indicated previously. An empirically rich critical analysis of leisure, which might differ on issues of epistemology and method, must in any event include a shared normative commitment to the emancipation of human capacities and thus to the idea that present historical conditions do not exhaust human possibilities.

This aspect of the critical theory paradigm is important for the critical study of leisure. As noted earlier, leisure studies can be more accurately characterized as *multi*disciplinary rather than *trans*disciplinary. This comes about because many of the approaches within the field take their reference points from within their home disciplines or, in other words, outside lei-

sure studies.[13] The critical theory paradigm does not sever so much as transcend these connections by drawing on much of what already goes forward in the study of leisure, in the home disciplines, and in other fields not frequently represented in our literature. By reaching out to these various other enterprises in the name both of the study of historically specific leisure practices and of the emancipatory potential to be found in leisure, the presuppositions of critical theory provide a basis for bringing together a variety of means to probe a broad array of social roles, processes, and institutions (as well as their natural and material circumstances) that bear on the emancipatory content and potential of leisure. Clearly the concepts of emancipation and development of human capacities are not limited to one or a few fields of inquiry, but instead provide links to any number of them to the degree traditional disciplinary barriers may be dissolved. It is good to remember that failure to dissolve these barriers is in a sense to reinforce them, and thus works directly against what critically inspired scholarship intends, that is, the challenge of any historically existing distribution of social power in the name of emancipatorily and developmentally conceived human action.

Having said this much, it is appropriate in closing to suggest some possible themes to which a critically motivated theory of leisure might initially turn its attention. I prefer to label these themes as preliminary

---

[13]It is perhaps worth speculating whether this will necessarily continue in any event. There has been a great deal of discussion about the need for leisure studies to train its own doctoral students, who will move into the field's teaching and research corps, rather than either sending them elsewhere in the university for doctoral preparation or looking to students with interests in leisure but prepared in other fields. The ability to supply its own doctoral students seems to some to be an indicator of the field's maturation. There are serious questions whether this is intellectually desirable for a transdisciplinary field of inquiry. Leisure studies, already small enough, is too likely to become entirely inbred and stagnant without a steady infusion of scholars from outside the field and the ideas they bring with them. Neither disciplinary fragmentation nor disciplinary monolithism are desirable; to substitute the latter as a cure for the former simply substitutes a new set of intellectual problems for the old. A truly transdisciplinary field of inquiry, guided by common theoretical commitments and drawing on the work of scholars from a number of fields, is far more attractive, if also perhaps more difficult to achieve.

theses for a critical analysis of leisure, which if unfolded in their implications might begin to provide the empirical richness and conceptual refinement necessary for a critical theory of leisure. At least in spirit, they are intended to draw together a number of fields of inquiry in order to illuminate specific aspects of leisure's contents and meanings.

First, a critical analysis of leisure examines the empirical content of leisure practices against an articulated historical horizon; this is the requirement of historical specificity.

Second, a critical analysis of leisure identifies and explores the contradictions between the content of leisure practices and the emancipatory potential of leisure.

Third, a critical analysis of leisure recognizes that all social phenomena are complex, that is, plurivocal and polyphonic, and respects this complexity in its inquiry.

Fourth, a critical analysis of leisure is sensitive to the different forms of power and to their migration within society. It therefore interrogates leisure practices to determine the degree to which they are shaped by nonemancipatory forms of power.

Fifth, a critical analysis of leisure recognizes that commodification and consumption-oriented practices reflect an instrumental rationality foreign to leisure's emancipatory potential.

Sixth, a critical analysis of leisure remains connected to practice, and enables action based on an extended theoretic framework intended to increase the emancipatory content of leisure practices (e.g., in the administration of leisure services, the distribution of leisure and other emancipatory resources in society, and in the avoidance of replicating existing patterns of social domination).

Seventh, a critical analysis of leisure acknowledges leisure's political content in the broad sense of the political, and explores the connections between emancipatory leisure practices and the enablement of radical democratic citizenship.

Eighth, a critical analysis of leisure is not misled by issues of "free time," but addresses instead the content of leisure practices and their social and political meanings. The amount of "free time" available in any society is irrelevant if it is tied to nonemancipatory conditions and practices, if in fact activities during that "free time" emulate or reinforce nonemancipatory conditions and practices. To the degree that leisure reflects

and is tied to work, as for example in dependency on the ability to consume or acquire, to that degree leisure's emancipatory content is questionable. It is the content, and not the amount, of "free time" that is of primary concern in the critical analysis of leisure.

Ninth, a critical analysis of leisure rejects any suggestion that human capacities are fixed, looking always to the expansion and development of these capacities as the core of a radical democratic society and as the measure of the degree of emancipation in leisure as well as other social practices.

Tenth, a critical analysis of leisure recognizes that leisure cannot be emancipating unless this critical analysis is itself emancipated from alien rationalities and forms of power, which entails recognizing the conservative or radical implications of the manners in which leisure is studied.

Finally, it is worth turning to a famous thesis 11 that succinctly captures the ethical and practical intentions of critical theory. "The philosophers have only *interpreted* the world," Marx wrote in his *Theses on Feuerbach* (1845/1968); "the point, however, is to *change* it."

If we amend *philosophers* to *scholars,* we have a fair statement of the spirit animating critical social inquiry, the critical analysis of leisure included. To separate oneself from that which one studies, to maintain the "givenness" of the social world and the fixity of human capacities, or to deny not just the possibility but the very need for critical analysis of forms and distributions of power in social roles, practices, and institutions are all to contribute to the replication of existing patterns of social domination with their underlying forms and distributions of power. To deny that these exist, or that they have relevance to one's inquiry, is to allow them to go unchallenged and to contribute to their enduring presence in society. Scholarship is not an activity apart from what goes on in society; it is rather very much entangled in it. Inquiry and reflection have the capacity, however, to pry open the social "given" and to point the way beyond it. This is the intention of critical social inquiry. The theses offered here, based on the preceding discussion, are intended to contribute to a critical analysis of leisure that opens itself to the multidimensional nature of leisure and sees it in its full social complexity, but recognizes in this complexity the arena for the emancipation in leisure of human capacities otherwise limited and stunted. This would be a fine theme around which to gather the transdisciplinary study of leisure.

References

Arato, A., & Gebhardt, E. (1993). *The essential Frankfurt School reader*. New York, NY: Continuum.

Aristotle. (1948). *Politics* (corrected edition, E. Barker, Trans.). Oxford, UK: Clarendon Press.

Barber, R. (1984). *Strong democracy: Participatory politics for a new age*. Berkeley, CA: University of California Press.

Bellah, R., Madsen, R., Sullivan, W., Swidler, A., & Tipton, S. (1985). *Habits of the heart: Individualism and commitment in American life*. Berkeley, CA: University of California Press.

Benhabib, S. (1986). *Critique, norm, and utopia: A study of the foundations of critical theory*. New York, NY: Columbia University Press.

Benhabib, S. (1992). *Situating the self: Gender, community, and postmodernism in contemporary ethics*. New York, NY: Routledge.

Benhabib, S. (1996). From identity politics to social feminism: A plea for the nineties. In D. Trend (Ed.), *Radical democracy: Identity, citizenship, and the state* (pp. 27–41). New York, NY: Routledge.

Bernstein, R. (1978). *The restructuring of social and political theory*. Philadelphia, PA: University of Pennsylvania Press.

Bernstein, R. (1983). *Beyond objectivism and relativism: Science, hermeneutics, and praxis*. Philadelphia, PA: University of Pennsylvania Press.

Boggs, C. (1986). *Social movements and political power: Emerging forms of radicalism in the West*. Philadelphia, PA: Temple University Press.

Bourdieu, P. (1987). What makes a social class? On the theoretical and practical existence of groups. *Berkeley Journal of Sociology, 32*, 1–18.

Bronner, S., & Kellner, D. (1989). *Critical theory and society: A reader*. New York, NY: Routledge.

Calhoun, C. (1995). *Critical social theory: Culture, history, and the challenge of difference*. Oxford, UK: Basil Blackwell, Ltd.

Cohen, J. (1985). Strategy or identity: New theoretical paradigms and contemporary social movements. *Social Research, 52*, 663–716.

Davis, L. (1964). The cost of the new realism. *Western Political Quarterly, 17*, 37–46.

Downs, A. (1957). *An economic theory of democracy*. New York, NY: Harper & Row.

Euben, J. (1996). Taking it to the streets: Radical democracy, radicalizing theory. In D. Trend (Ed.), *Radical democracy: Identity, citizenship, and the state* (pp. 62–77). New York, NY: Routledge.

Forester, J. (Ed.). (1985). *Critical theory and public life*. Cambridge, MA: MIT Press.

Fraser, N. (1989). *Unruly practices: Power, discourse, and gender in contemporary social theory*. Minneapolis, MN: University of Minnesota Press.

Gould, C. (1988). *Rethinking democracy: Freedom and social cooperation in politics, economy, and society*. Cambridge, UK: Cambridge University Press.

Guba, E. (Ed.). (1990). *The paradigm dialog*. Thousand Oaks, CA: Sage Publications, Inc.

Habermas, J. (1984). *The theory of communicative action, Vol. 1: Reason and the rationalization of society* (T. McCarthy, Trans.). Cambridge, MA: MIT Press.

Habermas, J. (1987). *The theory of communicative action, Vol. 2: Lifeworld and system: A critique of functionalist reason* (T. McCarthy, Trans.). Cambridge, MA: MIT Press.

Habermas, J. (1962/1989). *The structural transformation of the public sphere: An inquiry into a category of bourgeois society* (T. McCarthy, Trans.). Cambridge, MA: MIT Press.

Habermas, J. (1992). *Faktizität und geltung: Beiträge zur diskurstheorie des rechts und des demokratischen rechtstaats*. Frankfurt am Main, Germany: Suhrkamp.

Held, D. (1980). *Introduction to critical theory: Horkeimer to Habermas*. Berkeley, CA: University of California Press.

Hemingway, J. (1991). Leisure and democracy: Incompatible ideals? In G. Fain (Ed.), *Leisure and ethics: Reflections on the philosophy of leisure* (pp. 59–81). Reston, VA: American Association for Leisure and Recreation.

Hemingway, J. (1995). Leisure studies and interpretive social inquiry. *Leisure Studies, 14*, 32–47.

Hemingway, J. (1996). Emancipating leisure. The recovery of freedom in leisure. *Journal of Leisure Research, 28*, 27–43.

Hirschman, A. (1977). *The passions and the interests: Political arguments for capitalism before its triumph*. Princeton, NJ: Princeton University Press.

Hochschild, A. (1997). *The time bind: When work becomes home and home becomes work*. New York, NY: Metropolitan Books/Henry Holt.

Horkheimer, M. (1937/1972). Traditional and critical theory. In *Critical theory: Selected essays* (M. O'Connell, Trans., pp. 188–225). New York, NY: Continuum.

Horkheimer, M., & Adorno, T. (1972). *Dialectic of enlightenment*. New York, NY: Herder and Herder.

Hoy, D., & McCarthy, T. (1994). *Critical theory*. Oxford, UK: Basil Blackwell, Ltd.

Jay, M. (1996). *The dialectical imagination: A history of the Frankfurt School and the Institute of Social Research*. Berkeley, CA: University of California Press.

Kissling, C. (1990). Die theorie des kommuni-kativen handelns in diskussion. *Freiburger Zeitschrift für Philosophie und Theologie, 37,* 233–252.

Leonard, S. (1990). *Critical theory in political practice.* Princeton, NJ: Princeton University Press.

Lukács, G. (1971). Reification and the consciousness of the proletariat. In *History and class consciousness: Studies in Marxist dialectics* (R. Livingstone, Trans., pp. 83– 222). Cambridge, MA: MIT Press.

Lummis, C. (1996). *Radical democracy.* Ithaca, NY: Cornell University Press.

Lyotard, J.-F. (1984). *The postmodern condition: A report on knowledge* (G. Bennington & B. Massumi, Trans.). Minneapolis, MN: University of Minnesota Press.

Macpherson, C. (1962). *The political theory of possessive individualism, Hobbes to Locke.* Oxford, UK: Oxford University Press.

Marx, K. (1977). *Selected writings* (D. McLellan, Ed.). New York, NY: Oxford University Press.

Marx, K. (1945/1968). Theses on Feuerbach. In K. Marx & F. Engels (Eds.), *Selected writings* (Vol. 1, pp. 11–15). Moscow, Russia: Progress Publishers.

Marx, K. (1990). Capital: A critique of political economy, Vol 1 (B. Fowkes, Trans.). Harmondsworth, UK: Penquin Classics.

McCarthy, T. (1978). *The critical theory of Jürgen Habermas.* Cambridge, MA: MIT Press.

Offe, C. (1987). Challenging the boundaries of institutional politics: Social movements since the 1960s. In C. Maier (Ed.), *Changing boundaries of the political: Essays on the evolving balance between the state and society, public and private in Europe* (pp. 63–106). Cambridge, UK: Cambridge University Press.

Polanyi, K. (1944). *The great transformation: The economic and political origins of our time.* Boston, MA: Beacon Press.

Putnam, R. (1993a). *Making democracy work: Civic traditions in modern Italy.* Princeton, NJ: Princeton University Press.

Putnam, R. (1993b). The prosperous community: Social capital and public life. *The American Prospect, 13*(Spring), 35–42.

Rojek, C. (1985). *Capitalism and leisure theory.* London, UK: Tavistock.

Rojek, C. (1995). *Decentring leisure: Rethinking leisure theory.* Thousand Oaks, CA: Sage Publications, Inc.

Schreyer, R., & Driver, B. (1989). The benefits of leisure. In E. Jackson & T. Burton (Eds.), *Understanding leisure and recreation: Mapping the past, charting the future* (pp. 385–419). State College, PA: Venture Publishing, Inc.

Schumpeter, J. (1942). *Capitalism, socialism, and democracy.* New York, NY: Harper & Row.

Stockdale, J. (1989). Concepts and measures of leisure participation and preference. In E. Jackson & T. Burton (Eds.), *Understanding leisure and recreation: Mapping the past, charting the future* (pp. 113–150). State College, PA: Venture Publishing, Inc.

Taylor, C. (1979). Interpretation and the sciences of man. In P. Rabinow & W. Sullivan (Eds.), *Interpretive social science: A reader* (pp. 25–71). Berkeley, CA: University of California Press.

Taylor, C. (1985). *Philosophical papers, Vol. 1: Human agency and language.* Cambridge, UK: Cambridge University Press.

Toulmin, S. (1990). *Cosmopolis: The hidden agenda of modernity.* New York, NY: Free Press.

Verba, S., Schlozman, K., & Brady, H. (1995). *Voice and equality: Civic voluntarism and American politics.* Cambridge, MA: Harvard University Press.

Weber, M. (1947). *Theory of social and economic organization* (T. Parsons, Ed.). New York, NY: Free Press.

Weissinger, E. (1995). Judging the relevance of deductive inquiry: The central role of theory. *Leisure Sciences, 17,* 141–145.

Wiggershaus, R. (1994). *The Frankfurt School: Its history, theory, and political significance.* Cambridge, MA: MIT Press.

Wilson, J. (1988). *Politics and leisure.* Boston, MA: Unwin Hyman.

Leisure Sciences and Leisure Studies: The Challenge of Meaning

Fred Coalter

Centre for Leisure Research, University of Edinburgh

Leisure Sciences and Leisure Studies: A Continuum or Different Paradigms?

Unlike most of the contributions to this book, this chapter is not concerned with providing a "state-of-the-art" analysis of research into a specific aspect of leisure. Instead, its purpose is to compare and contrast North American *leisure sciences* (the subject of much of this volume) and British *leisure studies* and to suggest that, despite substantial epistemological and methodological differences, both are confronting similar dilemmas concerning limitations to their understanding of the societal and social meanings of leisure. Clearly, such comparisons entail the dual risks of imposing false

An earlier version of this chapter was published in *Leisure Sciences*, Vol. 19, No. 4, 1997.

homogeneities and false dichotomies (Burton, 1996). For example, this volume illustrates a diversity of perspectives within the broad field of North American leisure sciences. Further, Kelly (see chapter 4 in this volume) illustrates the historical existence of a number of "common wisdoms" within North American leisure sciences and suggests that, despite the current dominance of a positivist paradigm, change and development are inevitable. In the case of British leisure studies, Roberts (1987) has argued that it is not possible to identify anything as coherent as "British leisure theory."

Moreover, the relationship between North American leisure sciences and British leisure studies could be regarded as a continuum, with a number of writers nominally within the North American leisure sciences community adopting perspectives closely allied to aspects of British leisure studies (see Kelly, chapter 4; Hemingway, chapter 30; and Stebbins, chapter 5 in this volume). This is especially the case among feminist writers such as Henderson and Bialeschki and Shaw (see chapters 11 and 16 in this volume). At the other end of the continuum there are a few members of the British leisure studies community who adopt the positivistic approaches characteristic of much of leisure sciences (for a rare example, see Stockdale, 1987). Nevertheless, it is possible to identify broad predominant (if not exclusive) domain assumptions which characterize and distinguish between North American leisure sciences and British leisure studies, and which can be regarded as having different epistemological, methodological, and theoretical perspectives. These are outlined schematically in Table 31.1.

Leisure Sciences and Leisure Studies: The Need For New Agendas?

The predominant perspectives in North American leisure sciences and British leisure studies can usefully be regarded as being underpinned by differing theoretical orientations. Craib (1984) suggests that social theory combines three different dimensions, which are present in all theorizing, but are given varying emphases by different theorists and academic communities. The *cognitive* element of theory is concerned with establishing knowledge about certain aspects of the social world, the *affective* dimension embodies the experience and the feelings of the theorist, and the *normative* dimension makes assumptions about how the world ought to be. Although, as we have already noted, certain writers within the leisure sciences community adopt perspectives closely allied to aspects of leisure studies, it is nevertheless possible to argue that cognitive theory is the predominant orientation in *leisure sciences,* with normative theorizing being the predominant characteristic of *leisure studies.*

Within leisure sciences, the preeminent position held by positivist epistemology and empiricist research methods means that a high premium is placed on the validity of methods and the strength of statistical correlations. In this regard, Hemingway (1995, p. 36) suggests that a major characteristic of "empiricist research methods" in leisure sciences is to "reduce enquiry to technique." Conversely, the predominant concerns within leisure studies relate to the normative citizenship paradigm (Coalter, 1988), with emphasis placed on the strategic social policy (or theoretical) implications of the work, with no regard for statistically significant evidence. Further, it can be argued that the affective components of both leisure sciences and leisure studies relate to broader sociopolitical components—the liberal individualism of North America and the British concern with collectivism and social hierarchies.

TABLE 31.1	DOMAIN ASSUMPTIONS IN NORTH AMERICAN LEISURE SCIENCES AND BRITISH LEISURE STUDIES
Leisure Sciences	**Leisure Studies**
Cognitive theory	Normative theory
What is leisure?	Leisure as "not leisure"
Liberal individualism	Collectivist welfarism
Freedom and choice	Social and cultural reproduction
Social psychology of leisure	Sociology of leisure
Leisure without society	Society *in* leisure
Satisfactions and benefits	The ideology of leisure
Difference	Reproduction

Despite the differences outlined in Table 31.1, it would seem that both North American leisure sciences and British leisure studies have arrived at a similar "crossroads"—a recognition of an underdeveloped understanding of the sociocultural and contextual meaning of leisure and leisure satisfactions (see Kelly, chapter 4; Mannell, chapter 14; Henderson and Bialeschki, chapter 11; and Shaw, chapter 16 in this volume). It could also be argued that this situation partly reflects the rather narrow areas of research which have characterized both leisure sciences and leisure studies. Rojek (see chapter 6 in this volume) contends that the ideology of leisure, by emphasizing personal enhancement and social health, has led to a failure to understand the importance of "the dark side of free-time activity." More broadly, both leisure sciences (under the influence of the National Recreation and Parks Association [NRPA]: see Chick, 1997; Veal, 1989) and leisure studies (with its concerns with public policy, public leisure provision, and citizenship) have largely neglected the study of commercial forms of leisure and consumption (a failure acknowledged in the British Leisure Studies Association's 1997 annual conference, "Leisure, Culture and Commerce"—although many of the papers adopted leisure studies' historically critical approach to commercial leisure).

This relative neglect in part underlies the current dilemmas posed for British leisure studies by external social and cultural changes. Its close relationship to sociology and social policy and concerns with issues of citizenship and inequality have meant that theories of the "postmodern condition" have presented a challenge to its collectivist, welfarist, and liberationist analyses of leisure (in which issues of social and cultural reproduction have been given precedence over consumption). In contrast, the current dilemmas facing North American leisure sciences (outlined in several of the chapters in this volume) seem to reflect internal forces. There is an increased questioning of the limitations of positivist methodologies and analyses which present "leisure without society," failing to address the social or societal meanings of leisure (critics within the leisure sciences tradition include Burton, 1996; Hemingway, 1990, 1995; Henderson, 1991; and Jackson and Burton, 1989; see also Hemingway, chapter 30, and Henderson and Bialeschki, chapter 11 in this volume). Goodale (1990, p. 296), expressing the concerns of many critics of the predominant paradigm in leisure sciences, argues that "leisure research has become increasingly positivist, operationalist, and reductionist, passing from social and political bases to psychological." More generally, Hemingway (see chapter 30 in this volume) regrets the lack of theory-oriented discussion in leisure sciences.

In North American leisure sciences the depth of questioning may be indicated by the fact that Kelly, a preeminent scholar within the leisure sciences community, has argued for a suspension of "the ideologies of freedom and openness in favor of research that is truly situated in the actual contexts of leisure interaction" (Kelly, 1994, p. 87). Even more radically, he has suggested that "the idea that leisure has a unique set of meanings . . . or that it is the sole proprietor of freedom and intrinsic meaning is a dangerous oversimplification" (Kelly and Kelly, 1994, p. 273). Clearly there is a questioning about the future agendas for both leisure sciences and leisure studies.

British Leisure Studies: Leisure as "Not Leisure"

British leisure studies is a smaller and less specialized area of study than North American leisure sciences. Further, there is an absence of a predominant methodological paradigm of the sort which characterizes leisure sciences. In part this is because many so-called leisure scholars in Britain have just one foot in the field (Roberts, 1987). Few of the mainstream leisure studies writers are "leisure-centered," confining their analyses simply to the study of leisure. Analysis and interpretation have tended to take place within broader areas of study (such as cultural studies, sociology, economics,

feminist studies, policy analysis) and have reflected the structural, conceptual, and theoretical concerns of these fields. Interestingly, Hemingway (see chapter 30 in this volume) regrets the "tyranny of the disciplines" in North American academia, suggesting that the various perspectives in leisure sciences rarely communicate, being oriented toward their core disciplines.

One effect of this in British leisure studies has been a tendency to view leisure largely in terms of a product of economic, social, cultural, and political factors which are "not leisure" (Clarke and Critcher, 1985, p. xiii). As a consequence the leisure studies' orientation has been to view leisure as a "site" where broader social, political, and cultural relations and conflicts are visible. The main commitment is usually to investigate divisions and inequalities based on class, gender, and (less so) ethnicity. This reflects a more general concern with the differential distribution of power and structural determinants of inequalities of opportunities (Murdock, 1994; Scraton and Talbot, 1989), the changing nature of citizenship (Coalter, 1998; Ravenscroft, 1995), the impact of industrialization, the role of the state and, latterly, the postmodern condition as evidenced in leisure (Rojek, 1993). In this regard, Henry (1995, p. 49) argues that "much of the research effort in the field of leisure studies in the late 1980s and early 1990s has been dominated by a concern to trace and/or explain the cultural implications of the fragmentation of social structure."

Consequently, the concern has been less with producing the definitive definition of leisure and its properties than with the possibilities of the *concept* of leisure for the exploration of broader social, cultural, and political issues. For example, Clarke and Critcher (1985, p. xiii) state that "our interest . . . is not really in 'leisure' itself, it is in what leisure can tell us about the development, structure and organization of the whole society." Although Clarke and Critcher's analyses and interpretations have many critics within British leisure studies, their fundamental commitment to a "holistic approach" remains a predominant concern. As a result of this approach, the *individual* freedoms, choices, and satisfactions supposedly inherent in leisure are more often viewed in ideological and cultural terms, rather than the psychological categories widely used in leisure sciences (see Iso-Ahola, chapter 3 in this volume; see also Mannell, chapter 14 in this volume, for an admission of the limitations of some of these approaches).

Within British leisure studies, leisure generally has not been conceptualized in terms of individual consumption, self-expression, and fulfillment. Rather, it is viewed as a site for the *reproduction* (or at least reflection) of wider economic, social, and cultural inequalities. Under the influence of certain forms of historiography (Bailey, 1989), neo-Marxism (Clarke and Critcher, 1985), cultural studies (Tomlinson, 1989), and a range of feminisms (Wimbush and Talbot, 1988), leisure has been analyzed as a site of inequality, struggle, cultural contestation, negotiation, and resistance. Rather than simply a *leisure in society* approach, we have a *society in leisure* approach. Instead of attempts to develop a specialist leisure sociology (or psychology), we have had a number of *sociologies of leisure*. As the issues in leisure are viewed simply as the classic questions of sociology (Coalter and Parry, 1984; Tomlinson, 1989), there is little need for specialized sociologies. In fact the search for such coherence is deemed "an irrelevancy" (Clarke and Critcher, 1985, p. xiii).

Rather than a concern with individuals, individual psychologies, benefits, and satisfactions, the leisure studies orientation has been toward broader social aggregates and issues of inequality of power, hegemonic processes, collective identities, access, and provision of opportunities and social citizenship. With a *society in leisure* approach, analysis and interpretation tend to draw on structural forms of explanation. Categories of class and gender are predominant in the literature and are linked to "reproductionist" theories concerning the nature of capitalism and processes of exploitation, hegemony, patriarchy, and so on. In parallel with these sociologies of leisure, predominant (if often implicit) themes in British leisure policy analysis are the relationships between public leisure provision and rights of citizenship and the role of the state as guarantor of such rights (Coalter, 1998). The predominant concern is not with analyzing and celebrating individual or group *difference* (Scraton, 1994), but with addressing issues of *inequality* of power and opportunity, within a collectivist welfare perspective (rather than the liberal individualism implicit in much North American leisure sciences).

North American leisure sciences is much more leisure-centered than leisure studies. Predominant concerns have been to define leisure (largely in sociopsychological terms), and to illustrate motivations, satisfactions, and benefits, and to explore constraints (Goodale and Witt, 1989; see also Jackson and Scott, chapter 18 in this volume). Certainly the work in leisure sciences on benefits has contributed to a level of understanding of certain motivations and experiences associated with participation in a range of leisure (or recreational) activities which does not exist in the leisure studies literature (see Driver, Brown and Peterson, 1991; see also Mannell, chapter 14 in this volume). However, critics within leisure sciences have suggested that this concentration on individual satisfactions and

benefits presents us with *leisure without society,* and recent debates identify a need for broader analyses based on a conception of *leisure in society* (Jackson and Burton, 1989; Kelly and Kelly, 1994; see also Kelly, chapter 4 in this volume).

Conversely, theoretical approaches in British leisure studies which concentrate on processes of social and cultural *reproduction* are often accompanied by a skepticism about subjectivities and leisure "benefits" and "satisfactions." Underlying most leisure studies' sociological analyses are unresolved dilemmas about the "ideology of leisure" and the extent to which "perceived freedom" and notions of "choice" are more socially circumscribed than is recognized, or even are mere ideological constructs, through which hegemonic processes are at work. However, a more mainstream sociological concern is that an overemphasis on psychological constructs, such as "leisure as a state of mind" (Neulinger, 1981), "perceived freedom," maximum arousal (Iso-Ahola, 1980), or "flow" (Csikszentmihalyi, 1982), are in danger of confusing the sociological concept of *leisure* with the psychological experience of *pleasure*. Hemingway (1995) suggests that this approach reflects the epistemological assumptions of the dominant empiricist mode of investigation within leisure sciences. The emphasis on a positivist methodology means that leisure is "operationalized" in terms of measurable logical and psychological categories. This results in an ignoring of the socially and culturally specific "constitutive rules" (Hemingway, 1995, p. 38) through which the individual and socially shared meanings as to what constitutes leisure are constructed and sustained (for similar arguments see Henderson and Bialeschki, chapter 11; Kelly, chapter 4; and Shaw, chapter 16 in this volume).

The issue of "constitutive rules" is also raised by theories of postmodernism which, according to Rojek (1995, p. 1), insist that:

> What we understand about the term [leisure] is socially conditioned, which makes conventional associations of "freedom," "choice" and "self-determination" with leisure insupportable. Leisure studies is about . . . what freedom, choice, flexibility and satisfaction mean in relation to determinate social formations. . . . [O]ne cannot separate leisure from the rest of life and claim that it has unique laws. . . . [T]he object of leisure is subsumed by the subject of culture.

Postmodernism and Leisure Studies

The arguments that the nature and meaning of freedom, choice, and flexibility are socially determined, that the object of leisure is subsumed by the subject of culture, and that leisure cannot be regarded as a separate charmed realm of self-fulfillment, seem to present greater challenges to the liberal individualism of leisure sciences than to leisure studies. For example, Kelly (chapter 4 in this volume), although not directly addressing the issues of postmodernism, argues that leisure is always *of* culture; it is ethnic. He challenges many of the existing orientations within leisure sciences and outlines a new agenda which encompasses most of these issues. Further, we have already noted Kelly and Kelly's (1994) contention that leisure cannot be regarded as the sole proprietor of freedom and intrinsic meaning. The postmodernist challenge has had a much greater impact in British leisure studies, with its stronger sociological orientation and its emphasis on structural and collectivist forms of analysis. According to one British theorist (Rojek, 1993), postmodernism has produced a crisis in British leisure studies' collectivist theorizing and has undermined the ability of most leisure studies scholars to sustain their commitment to emancipatory politics.

Arguments about a "postmodern condition" suggest that rapid economic and social change—the emergence of post-Fordist forms of organization, the growth of the service sector and service class, the fracturing of traditional collectivist cultures, and the domination of much of life by electronic media—has produced fundamental social, cultural, economic, and political dislocation. Old collective identities and common interests (class, gender, race, community, and even nation) have become fragmented and diffuse. It is asserted that status now depends less on one's place in production systems than on one's accomplishments in the sphere of consumption, one's access to, and manipulation of, cultural codes and signs. Consumption is seen as central to the construction of a wide variety of personal and social identities, indicated and fuelled by the decline of mass consumption and the proliferation of niche markets (Rojek, 1993). Such analyses raise particularly important questions for British leisure studies, with its emphasis on collectivities and shared identities (usually founded in shared material and/or ideological circumstances).

However, postmodern arguments are not simply about the empirical fact of diversity and fragmentation. The fundamental challenge relates to the *meaning* of these activities, and it is here that leisure studies

(and leisure sciences) seem not yet to have met the challenge. In the supposedly "decentered" conditions of postmodernity it is argued that the relationship between the form of leisure-consumption and material (and collective) realities has been broken. Reality is now seen to reside in the signs, codes, and representation (advertising, fashion, media) which are consumed and used in the individual search for a sense of self. Therefore, the nature and meaning of the leisure-consumption experience have changed. In addition to the individualizing impact of social and cultural fragmentation, arguments about "hyperreality" and "staged authenticity" suggest that everyday life has been emptied of meaning, with spectacle replacing meaning and sensation overpowering value (Rojek, 1993).

In such conditions, the evolutionary liberal-humanist ideology, which views leisure as a site of freedom, choice, self-improvement, and self-development (and an essential component of social citizenship) is regarded as illusory (Rojek, 1995). There are no longer any reliable signposts to point to the direction of self-improvement and self-actualization. The way forward is "to emancipate leisure from the modernist burden of *necessarily* connoting freedom, choice, life-satisfaction and escape" and to "recover what the illusions of modernism have concealed" (Rojek, 1995, p. 192). Such assertions seem to raise fundamental questions about the moral, epistemological, political, and sociological basis of the "leisure studies project," whether it be neo-Marxism, feminism(s), or liberal humanism.

Although issues of postmodernism have not been addressed systematically in the leisure sciences literature, the contention that it is misguided to conceptualize leisure solely in positive terms finds echoes in certain analyses emerging from leisure sciences. For example, although not addressing directly issues of postmodernity, Kelly and Kelly (1994) suggest, as has already been noted, that it is an oversimplification to regard leisure as the sole proprietor of freedom and intrinsic meaning. Further, Shaw (see chapter 16 in this volume) proposes that there is a need to go beyond the conventional benefits approach and examine the possible negative aspects of leisure. However, these critical comments from within leisure sciences seem to derive more from an increasing realization of the limitations of the dominant paradigm, rather than (as in the case of leisure studies) in response to theoretical propositions about changed sociocultural circumstances.

The response of some within British leisure studies has been to argue that the postmodernist desire to describe and celebrate *difference* leads to the ignoring of *inequality* and *disadvantage* (Henry, 1995; Murdock, 1994; Scraton, 1994). Further, its relativism is regarded as undermining the basis for a moral dimension to social theory and policy analysis (Henry, 1995). This has led to an insistence on the continuing relevance of structural analyses and the need to talk about *life chances* rather than *lifestyles* (Murdock, 1994; Scraton, 1994). For example, Murdock (1994, p. 242) quotes Grossberg's (1992, p. 359) contention that, "In an effort to give culture its due, theorists of sign value and the struggles over the meanings of goods too often go overboard, erasing the relations between culture and specific economic and political realities." He suggests that discussions of the postmodern condition are over-dependent for their illustrations on the service classes. Although accurately describing certain sociocultural changes, there is a failure to give a full account of the *uneven nature* of the presumed changes and their sociopolitical consequences. He points to dramatically increased income polarization and the emergence of an expanding underclass. Further, both Murdock (1994) and Scraton (1994) suggest that postmodernist analyses are not only class-biased, they are largely gender-blind, ignoring the changing, and often deteriorating, condition of women in the labor force. Much of the dramatic increase in female employment is accounted for by part-time and low-paid jobs and must be viewed within the context of the restructuring of patriarchal relations and changing connections between domestic life and public life (Scraton, 1994).

Scraton (1994) suggests that the issue of diversity has long been recognized and a subject of debate within feminism—clearly women are differentiated by class, race, and age (see Shaw, chapter 16 in this volume). However, she asserts that there remains a "shared condition" which must be taken as the starting point of analysis. She concludes that there is little evidence that the world is changing to such an extent that we no longer need to center the social debate (or leisure studies' analyses) around inequalities and systems of exploitation and oppression.

Scraton and Bramham (1995, p. 34) quote McLennon (1992) on the:

> [D]angers of moving from the ideals of the Enlightenment and modernity which stressed emancipation and the need to improve people's lives. By focussing on pleasures, fantasies and pastiches, post-modernism neglects many people's lives which remain influenced by their experiences of poverty, gender and racism.

Further, leisure studies critics of postmodernism have suggested that, by concentrating on forms of conspicuous consumption within the new service class,

postmodern analyses largely ignore the ordinary—the situated and negotiated nature of everyday life. For example, Crouch and Tomlinson (1994) suggest that leisure is lived in social networks and communities that are often tightly bounded, and is often self-generated or organized and not dependent on commodities and forms of electronic media. From within leisure sciences, Kelly (see chapter 4 in this volume) contends that most leisure takes place in and around the home, serving to integrate immediate communities and develop primary relationships.

The Challenge of Meaning

Despite the ability to illustrate continuing socioeconomic inequalities (and propose this as a continuing agenda for leisure studies), the issue of the changing meanings and significance of leisure remains. The contentions about the postmodern condition—dislocation, fragmentation, spectacle and hyperreality, depthlessness, the fracturing of the relationship between the real and the sign, the "decenteredness" of everyday life, consumption as the major site for self-actualization—raise propositions about a subject which, perhaps paradoxically, neither leisure studies nor leisure sciences has dealt with successfully: the social and individual *meaning* of leisure diversity and behavior.

The relative absence of such issues from leisure studies and leisure sciences is surprising. Some versions of the postmodern condition read like a restatement of issues recognized, and *celebrated,* by the "founding fathers" of British leisure studies (and clearly implicit in the liberal individualism which underpins much work in leisure sciences). For example, the introduction to one of the first British leisure studies textbooks (Smith, Parker and Smith, 1973, pp. 7–8) acknowledged the "pluralization" of social life and stated that:

> [T]he growth of individualized self-awareness underpins the movement toward ego-conscious symbolism. . . . Status symbols and lifestyles are becoming expressions of individual taste rather than reflections of economic position or social class. . . . There are some things that only money can buy but they are becoming fewer and more people are able to buy them.

In 1974 Burns was suggesting that we need to examine individuals' psychosocial commitment to a range of available statuses in seeking to give expression to positive aspects of their self-image. In France Dumazadier (1974, p. 40) referred to "a new social need for the individual to be his [sic] own master" and asserted that the subjectivity of the individual had become "a value in itself." In the United States in the early 1980s, Kelly (1983) was proposing an existentialist-oriented form of symbolic interactionism in which the concept of "role identity" displaced the simple intrinsic-extrinsic approach to motivation, with analysis concentrating on the enactment potential of the leisure opportunity.

However, such assertions and theoretical propositions have not formed a systematic research agenda for leisure studies or leisure sciences. Within leisure studies the individualizing assumptions of these analyses were often rejected (reinforced by the absence of sociopsychological research), and those influenced by the cultural studies tradition were content to embrace various forms of semiotics and "read" the (usually collective) meanings of activities. In leisure sciences, Kelly (1994, p. 82) suggests that "the study of leisure as an interactional process became marginal . . . as the structural-functional model, with its common employment of survey research, correlational analysis and demographic independent variables became taken-for-granted in most funded research on leisure and recreation" (see Chick, 1997, for an analysis of the role of the NRPA in this process). A recent response within leisure studies to the supposed failures of collectivist theorizing proposed the analytical utility of the concept of *lifestyle* (Veal, 1989). However, British leisure studies critics firmly rejected this on the basis that such market research–oriented statistical aggregates are essentially empiricist and tell us little about "antecedent" (i.e., structural) causes (Critcher, 1989; Scraton and Talbot, 1989). Nevertheless, why leisure choices are made and their situated *meaning* still remain central, and largely unexplored, questions for leisure studies.

Leisure Sciences: The Emergence of a New Agenda?

Although postmodernism has posed a challenge to the *normative* sociological theorizing of leisure studies, its impact on the more cognitive emphases of leisure sciences appears to have been minimal. The failure of postmodernism to create the same "crisis" in leisure sciences may be explained by a number of factors. First, the predominance of social-psychological approaches and the lower salience of *sociological* theorizing has meant that the analysis of *leisure* in *society* or more specifically *society* in *leisure* has not been a major concern (see Kelly, chapter 4; Mannell, chapter 14; and Shaw, chapter 16 in this volume). Second, leisure sciences' emphasis on individuals and individual psychology could be taken to imply that the postmodernist contentions about fragmentation, decline of collectivist identities, and diversity are self-evident. This is reinforced by the apparent lack of utility of traditional sociodemographic variables in explaining (or more accurately, predicting) leisure behavior (Kelly, 1980).

However, there are other, more ideological, factors which may explain the lack of impact of postmodern analyses in leisure sciences. For example, the largely benign and "nonideological" nature of the postmodernist emphasis on difference and diversity fits well with the sociopolitical ideologies in the United States. Hemingway (see chapter 30 in this volume) argues that such sociopolitical ideologies are too narrow to support the explication of the political aspects of leisure. This, in turn, is reflected in an underlying ideology of leisure as "freedom and openness" (Kelly, 1994, p. 87), which articulates much more strongly with the broader sociopolitical culture—liberal individualism, optimism, achievement-orientation, and self-improvement—than in social-democratic Britain, with its much more collectivist views of social citizenship and social hierarchies.

Nevertheless, some scholars within leisure sciences have called into question the theoretical, methodological, and social assumptions of this paradigm. For example, Jackson and Burton (1989) suggest the need for a greater recognition of the relationship between leisure-consumption and social and economic change, and the need to place and interpret research results in a broad societal context. Burton (1996, p. 19) argues that the reification of methodology within the dominant scientific rationalist epistemology (with its concentration on surveys, correlational methods, and model building) produces "an obsession with method that is divorced from substance" and mitigates against the generation of new ideas. Clearly the limitations of the more absolutist claims of positivism have been acknowledged by many researchers (see Mannell, chapter 14, and Samdahl, chapter 8 in this volume) and many are now working within what Hemingway (see chapter 30 in this volume) describes as "postpositivism." However, Hemingway (see chapter 30 in this volume) maintains that the ontological, epistemological, and methodological differences between positivism and postpositivism are those of degree and not of kind. They certainly do not permit researchers to move beyond the presentation of "surface interpretations" and the investigation of "regulative rules" (Hemingway, 1995, p. 41; see also chapter 30 in this volume) to explore the social "constitutive rules" that define and giving meaning to social practices. More fundamentally, certain scholars within North American leisure sciences have emphasized the need for a critical awareness of the epistemological and ontological assumptions which underpin the predominant positivist paradigm and the extent to which these restrict the nature of the issues deemed worthy (or capable) of investigation (Hemingway, 1990, 1995; Henderson, 1990; see also Hemingway, chapter 30; Samdahl, chapter 8; and Shaw, chapter 16 in this volume).

Paralleling the calls for an acknowledgment of the limits of positivist methodology and empiricist methods have been calls for greater efforts to understand *why* people choose particular forms of leisure and the nature of the *meanings* attributed to activity (e.g., Jackson, 1989). Echoing some of the postmodernist arguments, Kelly (1994, p. 87) argues that the way forward for leisure sciences is to suspend "the ideologies of freedom and openness . . . in favor of research that is truly situated in the actual contexts of leisure interaction." Kelly (1994; see also chapters 4 and 9 in this volume) insists that leisure is *in* and *of* particular cultures and, significantly in the light of the postmodernist contentions about dislocation and fragmentation, that leisure may still be the context for expressing and creating community (Kelly, 1989).

More fundamentally, Kelly and Kelly (1994) express a willingness to consider the proposition that "leisure is more a dimension or quality of action than a separate domain" (Kelly and Kelly, 1994, p. 251). Although not as fundamental as Rojek's (1995) assertion that the object of leisure is subsumed by the subject of culture, and that freedom, choice, and self-determination is a realm of fantasy, some leisure sciences scholars seem to be acknowledging the need to investigate the *postmodern condition*, if not to accept the postmodernist interpretation. It would seem that there is an implicit acceptance that issues of ontology (how people construct, understand and either do or do not find meaning in their [leisure] lives) may be more important than issues of epistemology—what Hemingway (1995, p. 36) has referred to as the "tendency to reduce inquiry to technique." The issue of "meaning" appears to be on the agenda of some leisure sciences scholars.

The Feminist Challenge Within Leisure Sciences

Within leisure sciences perhaps the most systematic challenge to the positivist-individualistic paradigm is presented by feminist researchers. From a British leisure studies perspective it is interesting to note that feminist writers appear to be the most consistently *international* in orientation of those working in leisure sciences—stepping outside the positivist, sociopsychological tradition for *theoretical* perspectives to analyze the condition of women, seeking to understand "situated meaning" and the role played by structure and ideology in creating contexts and meaning. For example, Henderson (1991, pp. 367–368) suggests that:

> [P]art of the inability to understand constraints on women's leisure may be due to an inadequate and narrow definition of constraints that has focussed primarily on intervening and structural aspects of constraints. . . . To understand individual constraints on women it is necessary to examine the a priori social context of manifested constraints on leisure. . . . Thus it is the *context* that becomes particularly evident in an analysis of leisure and its concomitant constraints.

From a broader methodological and theoretical perspective, the contribution of feminist researchers has not simply been to "put women on the agenda." Shaw (see chapter 16 in this volume) outlines the progress from an initial concern to illustrate gender differences in opportunities and experiences, via the exploration of the gendered nature of constraints to an exploration of how leisure affects ideologies and gendered power relations. Although there is a variety of feminist perspectives, they are all agreed on the need to move beyond individualizing psychological descriptions of intervening and structural constraints. They emphasize the need for a more thoroughly *sociological* analysis of *antecedent* conditions. As Henderson (1991, p. 373) has argued, "the leftist feminist position seeks to address issues about the values, structures and the interaction of content and process . . . [it begins] to address how constraints research can be applied not only to individuals but also to social institutions." To achieve this there is a need to go beyond "dualistic, totalizing and essentialist views of leisure" in order to "understand meanings in more encompassing ways" (Henderson, 1996, p. 151).

It seems inevitable that, as in other academic areas, feminism will have an increasing influence within leisure sciences. Many of its basic methodological and theoretical issues seem unavoidable. For example, Shaw (see chapter 16 in this volume) suggests that the types of questions that have been addressed regarding women's leisure—the gendered nature of leisure experiences, attitudes, and meanings—should now be extended to include men. Further, she suggests that feminist research has illustrated the need to go beyond simple definitions of constraints and/or satisfactions and to explore the way in which leisure practices serve to reproduce and reinforce all forms of social relations—an agenda closely parallel to that of British leisure studies.

Although not necessarily accepting the liberationist politics of the "feminist project," others within leisure sciences seem to share the feminist concern with the limitations of positivistic research strategies and the need for a more thorough exploration of the "foundation of our science and what it is that informs leisure research" (Henderson, 1990, p. 288; see also Hemingway, chapter 30 in this volume). However, feminist and other nonpositivist researchers within North American leisure sciences seem to face stronger, and more intimately related, epistemological and political obstacles than exist within British leisure studies.

In Britain feminist writers challenged what they saw as a "dominant positivist paradigm" (Stanley, 1980). Such approaches, however, were never as dominant as asserted, often restricted to government-sponsored, planning-oriented survey work undertaken by the first generation of British leisure studies researchers (Veal, 1994). Further, the positivist paradigm was certainly not so closely associated with professional training, *academic* legitimacy, and promotion as appears to be the case in North America (see Chick, 1997, for an analysis of the influence of the NRPA in defining research agendas and appropriate methodologies). In Britain, with looser links to professional organizations, the academic acceptance of the value of qualitative and ethnographic work and its adoption was much easier. Further, feminist researchers within British leisure studies were able to work within a predominantly collectivist welfare and citizenship paradigm, which was centrally concerned with inequalities of power and opportunities (albeit from a gendered perspective). This is not to say that the radical feminist critique of "gendered methodology" was accepted unproblematically (for example, see Hargreaves, 1992, for a critical comment within leisure studies and Hammersley, 1995, for a more general comment on feminist methodology).

Within leisure sciences, sympathetic academics have suggested that the required embracing of qualitative and ethnographic work is simply a matter of illustrating the value of methodological pluralism, of mutual understanding, tolerance, and communication (Burton and Jackson, 1989), or "a greater inclusiveness in leisure theory, methodology and practice" (Henderson, 1990, p. 288). However, such aspirations for a "revised project" (Kelly, 1994, p. 93; see also chapter 4 in this volume) may underestimate the radical nature of the issues raised by feminism and other approaches critical of the positivist paradigm. Burton (1996) hints at the strength of obstacles to change when he notes that increased questioning of positivist, quantitative science "has not led to a serious reexamination of the appropriate place of logic and reason in the social domain, but to a series of squabbles about the appropriate relevance of nonquantitative . . . investigation into social phenomena" (Burton, 1996, p. 18). Further, Shaw (see chapter 16 in this volume), while acknowledging a greater acceptance of methodological pluralism, suggests that a focus on methods alone will not change the paradigm—it is not simply a matter of "adding methods." Clearly, methods are based on both ontological and epistemological assumptions (see Hemingway, chapter 30, and Samdahl, chapter 8 in this volume) and it is these which are being brought into question. For example, with its emphasis on "antecedent conditions," a priori social contexts and structural constraints, feminism seems closer to the political economy of British leisure studies than the cognitive theorizing of North American leisure sciences. Consequently, the development of a revised project may require confrontation, rather than accommodation, with the epistemological, political, academic, and professional power of the dominant paradigm. For example, one response of the dominant paradigm may be to "accommodate" the "revised project" by ghettoizing it—a concern expressed by Henderson and Bialeschki (see chapter 11 in this volume), and also echoed in the theme of the Leisure Studies Association's 1998 conference, "The Big Ghetto: Gender, Sexuality and Leisure."

It is possible that a continuing commitment to "scientific rationalism" by recreation professionals and public agencies, with whom leisure science has historically close links, may be an obstacle to theoretical and academic development. The historic emphasis on "scientificity"—on quantification and correlation—may reflect an understandable status-anxiety of North American leisure sciences and the desire for academic legitimacy and professional relevance. The dilemmas posed by such factors are indicated by Henderson and Bialeschki's (see chapter 11 in this volume) contention that many feminists believe that researchers need to avoid getting caught up in university scholarship that places privilege and power over responsibility. Further, there seem to be broader sociocultural factors supporting and reinforcing the dominance of positivist methodologies and underpinning continuing differences between leisure sciences and leisure studies. In this regard, Gans's (1988) description of middle-American values as being concerned with obtaining personal control over the general environment in order to minimize threat and unwanted surprise seems close to the spirit of positivist methodologies (see Hemingway, chapter 30 in this volume). If this is the case, the postmodern condition presents an even greater theoretical and methodological challenge to leisure sciences than to leisure studies. For example, one commentator has suggested that, whereas the predominant concerns of modernism (and it could be argued, leisure sciences) were essentially epistemological (the exploration of the process of knowledge and interpretation), the concerns of postmodernism are ontological, "involving questions of being and feeling, and incorporating a tendency to disintegration and indiscriminateness . . . and random happenstance instead of elaborate formal patterning" (Smith, 1994, pp. 309–310). Perhaps this is why Burton (1996, p. 29) argues that "leisure studies" (although his target seems to be leisure *sciences*) "could use a lot more lateral thinking."

Conclusion

British leisure studies and North American leisure sciences, by different routes, seem to have arrived at a sort of crossroads. Neither has addressed satisfactorily the situated nature of leisure *meanings* and their relationship to wider sources of meaning and identity. In leisure sciences the recognition of the situated nature of meaning has been accompanied by a skepticism about dualist and essentialist approaches to the study of leisure (Henderson, 1996). This also has been accompanied by the questioning of the "limits of leisure." For example, Kelly and Kelly (1994) suggest that, although the field of "leisure studies" (by which they presumably mean leisure sciences) has considerable investment in the idea that leisure is fundamentally different from the rest of life, it is possible that "all or most of the meanings that people find in leisure are . . . also found in other domains of life" (Kelly and Kelly, 1994, p. 250). Reinforcing this point, Bella (1989, p. 171) contends that:

[T]he significant questions, then, have to do with relationships served through an activity, not whether that activity can be described as "leisure." . . . The meaning of the activity is in the relationships served through that activity, not in the activity itself.

These comments could be interpreted as a shift toward a *leisure in society* approach (if not a *society in leisure* approach). For example Henderson (1996, p. 150) suggests that "leisure [science] researchers are only beginning to uncover the numerous dimensions of . . . gender, class, race, disability, sexuality . . . that can contribute to inclusive theories about leisure behavior" (see also Kelly, 1994, and Mannell, chapter 14 in this volume). Others are proposing more radical solutions via the adoption of "antipositivist" methodologies to explore the "constitutive rules" (Hemingway, 1995) and understand the basis of "intersubjectivity" in leisure (Glancy, 1993). While leisure studies historically has concentrated on these "numerous dimensions," there seems to be an increasing recognition of the need to acknowledge and explore the meaning of the supposed fragmentation and diversity associated with a *postmodern condition* (Giddens, 1990)—even if in so doing some remain reluctant to abandon liberationist agendas (Henry, 1995; Scraton, 1994).

Although postmodernist analyses have been interpreted as a threat to British leisure studies, the fact that they often remain at the level of assertion and lack rigorous empirical exploration of their hypotheses presents an opportunity and a challenge. The challenge for leisure studies and leisure sciences scholars is to explore the lived everyday lives of people (Crouch and Tomlinson, 1994; Kelly, 1994; see also Kelly, chapter 4 in this volume)—the meanings of activities and the relationships supporting activity and given expression through activity. Leisure researchers can explore the extent to which everyday life has been emptied of meaning, the extent to which "spectacle" has replaced meaning and sensation has overpowered value (Rojek, 1993), and the extent to which leisure experiences have the character of "depthlessness." Does reality now reside in the signs, codes, and representations (advertising, fashion, media), and has the relationship between the form of leisure-consumption and material (and collective) reality been broken? How far are people building or sustaining a common culture or communities around leisure in an age of fragmentation, dispersal, and exclusion? What is the role and (perhaps most importantly) what are the limits of leisure in such changed circumstances? Kelly (1989) suggests that in the face of such challenges leisure sciences should adopt a position of "methodological modesty"—understanding issues of ontology may be more important. This also implies questions about the limits of leisure (something which has always been implicit in leisure studies)—the relationship between leisure meanings and other sources of meaning and identity. For example, Kelly and Kelly (1994) question the extent to which there are meanings and satisfactions which are solely the property of leisure, and Roberts (1997, p. 14) has argued that, for young people, leisure does not act "as a crucial base for identity construction and maintenance."

Such questions pose fundamental issues both for British leisure studies' structural and liberationist *society in leisure* analyses and North American leisure sciences' *leisure without society* perspective. They seem to point to the limits of positivism, the need for a weakening of the methodological boundaries of leisure sciences, and the expansion of the already fluid boundaries of leisure studies.

References

Bailey, P. (1989). Leisure, culture and the historian: Reviewing the first generation of leisure historiography in Britain. *Leisure Studies, 8,* 107–128.

Bella, L. (1989). Women and leisure: Beyond androcentrism. In E. Jackson & T. Burton (Eds.), *Understanding leisure and recreation: Mapping the past, charting the future* (p. 151–180). State College, PA: Venture Publishing, Inc.

Burns, T. (1974). Leisure in industrial society. In M. Smith et al. (Eds.), *Leisure and society in Britain.* London, UK: Allen Lane.

Burton, T. L. (1996). Safety nets and security blankets: False dichotomies in leisure studies. *Leisure Studies, 15,* 17–30.

Burton, T. L., & Jackson, E. L. (1989). Charting the future. In E. Jackson & T. Burton (Eds.), *Understanding leisure and recreation: Mapping the past, charting the future* (p. 629–642). State College, PA: Venture Publishing, Inc.

Chick, G. (1997). Crossroads and crises, or much ado about nothing? A comment on Mommaas and Coalter. *Leisure Sciences, 19,* 285–290.

Clarke, J., & Critcher, C. (1985). *The devil makes work.* London, UK: Macmillan Publishing.

Coalter, F. (1998). Leisure studies, leisure policy and social citizenship: The failure of welfare or the limits of welfare? *Leisure Studies, 17,* 21–36.

Coalter, F., & Parry, N. (1984). *Leisure sociology or the sociology of leisure?* (Papers in Leisure Studies, No 4). London, UK: Polytechnic of North London.

Craib, I. (1984). *Modern social theory: From Parsons to Habermas.* Brighton, UK: Harvester Press.

Critcher, C. (1989). A communication in response to "Leisure, lifestyle and status: Pluralist framework for analysis." *Leisure Studies, 13,* 159–160.

Crouch, D., & Tomlinson, A. (1994). Collective self-generated consumption: Leisure, space and cultural identity in late modernity. In I. Henry (Ed.), *Leisure: Modernity, postmodernity and lifestyles* (Leisure Studies Association, Publication No. 48, pp. 309–321). Brighton, UK: Leisure Studies Association.

Csikszentmihalyi, M. (1982). Towards a psychology of optimal experience. In L. Wheeler (Ed.), *Review of personality and social psychology.* Beverly Hills, CA: Sage Publications, Inc.

Driver, B., Brown, P., & Peterson, G. (Eds.). (1991). *Benefits of leisure.* State College, PA: Venture Publishing, Inc.

Dumazadier, J. (1974). *The sociology of leisure.* New York, NY: Elsevier.

Gans, H. J. (1988). *Middle-American individualism: The future of liberal democracy.* New York, NY: Free Press.

Giddens, A. (1990). *The consequences of modernity.* Cambridge, UK: Polity Press.

Glancy, M. (1993). Achieving intersubjectivity: The process of becoming the subject in leisure research. *Leisure Studies, 12,* 45–60.

Goodale, T. L. (1990). Perceived freedom as leisure's antithesis. *Journal of Leisure Research, 22,* 296–302.

Goodale, T. L., & Witt, P. A. (1989). Recreation nonparticipation and barriers to leisure. In E. L. Jackson & T. L. Burton (Eds.), *Understanding leisure and recreation: Mapping the past, charting the future* (pp. 421–449). State College, PA: Venture Publishing, Inc.

Grossberg, L. (1992). *We gotta get out of this place: Popular conservatism and postmodern culture.* London, UK: Routledge.

Hammersley, M. (1995). *The politics of social research.* London, UK: Sage Publications, Ltd.

Hargreaves, J. (1992). Revisiting the hegemony thesis. In J. Sugden & C. Knox (Eds.), *Leisure in the 1990s: Rolling back the welfare state* (Leisure Studies Association, Publication No. 46, pp. 263–280). Brighton, UK: Leisure Studies Association.

Hemingway, J. (1990). Opening windows on an interpretative leisure studies. *Journal of Leisure Research, 22,* 303–308.

Hemingway, J. (1995). Leisure studies and interpretive social inquiry. *Leisure Studies, 14,* 32–47.

Henderson, K. A. (1990). Leisure science, dominant paradigms, and philosophy: An introduction. *Journal of Leisure Research, 22,* 283–289.

Henderson, K. A. (1991). The contribution of feminism to an understanding of leisure constraints. *Journal of Leisure Research, 23,* 363–377.

Henderson, K. A. (1996). One size doesn't fit all: The meanings of women's leisure. *Journal of Leisure Research, 28,* 139–154.

Henry, I. (1995). Leisure and social stratification: The response of the state to social restructuring in Britain. In K. Roberts (Ed.), *Leisure and social stratification* (Leisure Studies Association, Publication No. 53, pp. 49–58). Brighton, UK: Leisure Studies Association.

Iso-Ahola, S. E. (1980). *The social psychology of leisure and recreation.* Dubuque, IA: Wm. C. Brown Publishers.

Jackson, E. L. (1989). Environmental attitudes, values, and recreation. In E. L. Jackson & T. L. Burton (Eds.), *Understanding leisure and recreation: Mapping the past, charting the future* (pp. 357–383). State College, PA: Venture Publishing, Inc.

Jackson, E. L., & Burton, T. L. (1989). Mapping the past. In E. L. Jackson & T. L. Burton (Eds.), *Understanding leisure and recreation: Mapping the past, charting the future* (pp. 3–28). State College, PA: Venture Publishing, Inc.

Kelly, J. R. (1980). Outdoor recreation participation: A comparative analysis. *Leisure Sciences, 3,* 129–154.

Kelly, J. R. (1983). *Leisure identities and interactions.* London, UK: George Allen & Unwin.

Kelly, J. R. (1989). Leisure behaviors and styles: Social, economic and cultural factors. In E. L. Jackson & T. L. Burton (Eds.), *Understanding leisure and recreation: Mapping the past, charting the future* (pp. 89–111). State College, PA: Venture Publishing, Inc.

Kelly, J. R. (1994). The symbolic interaction metaphor and leisure. *Leisure Studies, 13,* 81–96.

Kelly, J. R., & Kelly, J. R. (1994). Multiple dimensions of meaning in the domains of work, family and leisure. *Journal of Leisure Research, 26,* 251–274.

Murdock, G. (1994). New times/Hard times: Leisure, participation and the common good. *Leisure Studies, 13,* 239–248.

Neulinger, J. (1981). *To leisure: An introduction.* Boston, MA: Allyn & Bacon.

Ravenscroft, N. (1995). Leisure, consumerism and active citizenship in the U.K. *Managing Leisure: An International Journal, 1,* 163–174.

Roberts, K. (1987). *Leisure and social change in the 1980s.* Paper presented at the Fifth Canadian Congress on Leisure Research, Dalhousie University, Halifax, Nova Scotia.

Roberts, K. (1997). Same activities, different meanings: British youth cultures in the 1990s. *Leisure Studies, 16,* 1–16.

Rojek, C. (1993). After popular culture: Hyperreality and leisure. *Leisure Studies, 12,* 277–289.

Rojek, C. (1995). *Decentring leisure: Rethinking leisure theory.* London, UK: Sage Publications, Ltd.

Scraton, S. (1994). The changing world of women and leisure: Feminism, "postfeminism" and leisure. *Leisure Studies, 13,* 249–261.

Scraton, S., & Bramham, P. (1995). Leisure and postmodernity. In M. Haralambos (Ed.), *Developments in sociology.* Ormskirk, UK: Causeway Press.

Scraton, S., & Talbot, M. A. (1989). Response to "Leisure, lifestyle and status: A Pluralist framework for analysis." *Leisure Studies, 13,* 155–158.

Smith, A. L. (1994). Is there an American culture? In J. Mitchell and R. Maidment (Eds.), *Culture: The United States in the twentieth century.* Milton Keynes, UK: Hodder and Stoughton/Open University.

Smith, M., Parker, S., & Smith, C. (1973). *Leisure and society in Britain.* London, UK: Allen Lane.

Stanley, L. (1980). *The problem of women and leisure: An ideological construct and a radical feminist alternative.* Paper presented to the Leisure in the '80s Forum sponsored by Capital Radio, September 1980.

Stockdale, J. (1987). *Methodological techniques in leisure research.* London, UK: Sports Council and Economic and Social Research Council.

Tomlinson, A. (1989). Whose side are they on? Leisure studies and cultural studies in Britain. *Leisure Studies, 6,* 97–106.

Veal, A. J. (1989). Leisure, lifestyle and status: A pluralist framework. *Leisure Studies, 8,* 141–154.

Veal, A. J. (1994). Intersubjectivity and the transatlantic divide: A comment on Glancy (and Ragheb and Tate). *Leisure Studies, 12,* 211–216.

Wimbush, E., & Talbot, M. (Eds.). (1988). *Relative freedoms: Women and leisure.* Milton Keynes, UK: Open University Press.

Postscript

Some degree of critical retrospection and reflection is an essential prerequisite for assessing probable and desirable futures. This is as true in leisure studies as it is in any and every other area of life. Thus, while the principal thrust of the chapters in this book is forward-looking rather than backward-glancing, they all contain, in some measure, an element of review and assessment of what has been achieved in the various areas that are addressed. This final chapter by Driver, however, offers a more general and wide-ranging overview of the accomplishments of leisure studies—one which adopts an avowedly retrospective posture. Bev Driver has spent close to 40 very active years in leisure studies, in both academic and government research environments. Although he has recently retired from his research position with the USDA Forest Ser-

vice, Driver continues to be active in both research and publication. More significantly for present purposes, he is also an unabashed and unapologetic promoter of the benefits of leisure and a veritable enthusiast for the more general accomplishments of, and in, our field. Driver's central message in this concluding chapter—that there is a great deal to be proud of and to celebrate in the accomplishments of North American leisure studies during the past four decades—is not just a stark contrast to the sometimes overfrequent self-criticism and breast-beating that is so often the mark of many academic fields (and which appears, we must admit, from time to time in this volume). It also reminds us that we do have a strong foundation on which to build as we, in leisure studies, enter the third millennium.

ELJ/TLB

Recognizing and Celebrating Progress in Leisure Studies

Beverly L. Driver
USDA Forest Service (Retired)

As we approach the twenty-first century, it is a good time to ask: What progress has been made so far in and by leisure studies? Many of the chapters in this text consider that question from a specific perspective, such as progress made by studies on gender differences, on constraints, in social psychology, in tourism, and so on. This chapter addresses our progress from a more general perspective and focuses on the related questions of How much pride can we take in what we have done as a profession? and What are the major challenges facing us as we enter the new millennium?

Several authors herein have referred to the thoughts in 400–300 B.C. of Socrates, Plato, and Aristotle about leisure and its roles in a society. And such philosophical writings have continued until today. In fact, they were instrumental in creating the parks and recreation movements in England, Canada, and the United States in the mid 1800s and early

1900s. So, if we appropriately consider both philosophical and systematic scientific (research) inquiry as leisure *studies,* it is clear that such studies have existed for at least two and one-half millennia. That time span collapses, however, when we look only at leisure *research.* Kelly, for example, in his two chapters in this volume (see chapters 4 and 9), points out that, except for a few studies of leisure within the context of the broader community (e.g., Hollingshead, 1949; Lundberg, Komarovsky and McInerny, 1934; Lynd & Lynd, 1956), there were very few *sociological* studies of leisure before about 1960. I believe the broader statement can be made that there were very few empirical studies of leisure *by any discipline* before 1960. Put simply, the state of our empirically supported knowledge has developed mostly within the past 40 years. For that reason, the temporal period to be considered in this chapter is very short and constitutes only the four decades between 1960 and the present.

The results of past leisure studies have been applied to advance three "states" of leisure concern—

Special appreciation is expressed to Dan Stynes and Don Bruns for helpful comments on early drafts of this chapter.

the state of the arts (what we know about leisure), the state of management practice (the actual delivery of leisure services), and the state of academic education (especially formal education gained in colleges and universities). Just as the state of our arts has advanced rapidly during the past 40 years, so have the states of education and managerial practice. In the remainder of this chapter, I will outline chronologically the progress that I have witnessed in each of these three states during that very short period of time. Despite the pessimistic tone of some authors of chapters in this text regarding the current states of the art, practice, and education, I believe we have come a long way in essentially less than a half-century and have much to be proud of. That is the major point I want to make.

I should emphasize at the outset that, while I try herein to summarize progress made in all areas of leisure inquiry and practice, my perceptions are filtered by my experiences mostly in outdoor recreation. But given that caveat, I believe that the conclusions I reach can be generalized to all subfields of leisure studies.

State of the Arts

Here, I will trace historically improvements in our science-based knowledge. In this discussion of the evolution of the state of the arts, I focus on the role of *scientific* leisure research because those impacts can be tracked better than can those of more philosophical writings. But such an orientation is not meant to depreciate the philosophical contributions to our knowledge, which I judge would have about the same chronology of impact that I offer here for the results of scientific research. And besides, several chapters in this text do an excellent job of tracing the philosophical contributions to the state of our knowledge.

Before 1960

Little systematic research was done in any of the subareas of leisure studies before 1960. There were several sociological studies including the aforementioned ones, a few investigations of the impacts of outdoor recreationists on the biophysical environment, several replications of essentially the same research design to estimate the economic impacts of tourists by calculations of economic multipliers, and a little research on means for estimating recreational use of dispersed recreation areas. This conclusion is supported by Volume 27 of the Outdoor Recreation Resources Review Commission's (1962) *Bibliography and Literature Review,* which lists few empirical studies prior to the time that review was done in the late 1950s. More broadly, the *Journal of Leisure Research* was not published until

the mid 1960s. Therefore, the state of knowledge in 1960 was primarily based on philosophical writings, the experiences of leisure professionals (especially managers), and informed intuition; there were few empirically supported theories of leisure.

1960–1964

Because of rapid increases in recreational use, especially outdoor recreation, following the end of World War II, the U.S. Congress created the Outdoor Recreation Resources Review Commission (ORRRC) in 1958. The *Summary* and 27 other volumes of reports by the ORRRC were published in 1962, and they had a profound effect on the near future of all leisure research. Many of these volumes were research-oriented and represented systematic and in-depth evaluations by nationally known scholars in many disciplines, notably sociology and economics. While the studies focused on outdoor recreation, that concept broadly covered the use of urban parks and open spaces, so the ORRRC did not limit its attention solely to hinterland recreation. For example the Commission found in its *Summary* volume that "Parks and other recreation areas are only part of the answer. The most important recreation of all is the kind that people find in their everyday lives." As such, the ORRRC reports focused national attention on the state of all recreation in the United States.

The ORRRC reports also stimulated Congressional establishment of the Bureau of Outdoor Recreation in 1962 and passage of the Land and Water Conservation Fund Act in 1965. That act allowed federal grants to federal, state, and local (county and municipal) parks and recreation agencies according to needs (demands and supplies) identified by State Comprehensive Outdoor Recreation Plans, or SCORPs. Many, if not most, of those SCORPs were prepared in part or their entirety by consulting leisure scientists associated with universities. Those opportunities stimulated much interest and accelerated the amount of outdoor recreation research being done. More significantly from the macroperspective taken here, the work of leisure scientists on the SCORPs helped stimulate research in other areas of leisure simply because leisure research is an applied area of inquiry that addresses many common problems across its many subspecialities. Therefore, over time the same advancements in theories and methods of the basic disciplines of economics, sociology, psychology, social psychology, geography, and so on, which were sometimes first applied more widely to outdoor recreation, have been applied to other areas such as community recreation programming, therapeutic recreation, and tourism, to name but a few. In turn, theories and methods first applied to other areas have been applied to outdoor recreation. The basic leisure behavior is frequently the same regardless of whether the setting is outdoor or indoor (i.e., whether hiking or playing tennis). So the basic questions regarding motivations, perceived economic and other values, conflicts, gender and ethnic differences, carrying capacities, and needs for efficient financial practices are generally the same regardless of the type of recreation. Thus, the stimulation of outdoor recreation research by the need to make the SCORPs in the mid 1960s had a multiplier effect on most other areas of leisure research, and *vice versa*.

Synergistically, de Grazia's (1962) seminal work, *Of Time, Work and Leisure,* along with other influential texts published in the early 1960s, helped promote wider interest in leisure and in leisure studies. About this time, too, there was tremendous growth in the number of universities and colleges that offered courses and degrees in leisure studies. And it should be repeated that a major causative factor was the rapidly growing rates of participation in recreation activities. In summary, by 1965 not only were the number of leisure studies increasing exponentially, but the scope of inquiry also was expanding rapidly to include new academic disciplines. Therefore, 1960–1964 can be called the period of scientific identification.

1965–1969

During the last half of the 1960s, economic impact and sociological studies expanded in number. More significantly, this period marked the emergence of new disciplines and orientations in leisure research. Economists began more systematic work on estimating the economic worth of so-called "nonmarketed (unpriced) services," such as publicly provided recreation opportunities, resulting in development of the *contingent valuation* and *travel cost* methods of analysis. Scientific studies began evaluating the cardiovascular benefits of physical activity, which at first looked at the physical demands of different types of work. Although attention of the applied research being done was directed at recreation activity opportunities until near the end of this period, interest in the psychological and social-psychological dimensions of leisure expanded rapidly in the late 1960s. This promoted wider inclusion of the concept of "recreation experience opportunities" in the litany and stimulated more studies on the motivations of leisure. Anthropologists and political scientists also developed stronger and wider interests in leisure. Concomitantly, curricula in leisure studies continued to expand. The years 1965–1969 reflect scientific intensification and diversification.

The 1970s

The 1970s reflected a continuation, intensification, and expansion of the trends started in the 1960s. Research in the social sciences was slowly gaining more credence, and the theories and methods of all the social science disciplines were improving considerably: witness the turnaround in the opinions of many sociologists and psychologists in the early to mid 1970s who questioned if research could usefully predict relationships between attitudes and actual behavior. And in experimental recreation economics, rather sophisticated designs were developed and applied successfully. There was literally an explosion of psychological and social-psychological studies addressing many aspects of leisure preference, meaning, motivation, and behavior (with one example being Csikszentmihalyi's concept of flow), which were later refined in the 1980s. Particularly influential was the emergence of applications of the theories and methods of market research to recreation and tourism to provide a better customer orientation. Work on the cardiovascular and other physical health benefits of exercise was expanded and changed public perceptions about these benefits of leisure activity, influencing more people to take up running and jogging. Interest in tourism as a separate area of inquiry grew rapidly, and several new journals for that field were created (see Butler, chapter 7 in this volume). Work expanded considerably in sports psychology, and there were expansions of efforts to define the role of play in child development. Academic programs in leisure studies continued to expand, with more and more educational institutions granting master's and doctoral degrees in those areas. Many of the areas and subareas of research started in the 1970s were continued and expanded in the 1980s. The results of research in several of these areas contributed substantively to the development of the new and improved recreation management systems and tools that were developed and implemented in the 1980s and 1990s—as elaborated in this chapter under the discussion of advancements in the state of management practice. The 1970s can be called the period of rapid expansion of leisure studies. And perhaps I should make more explicit here that the major application of the results of research to advancement of any state of the arts is to further advance that state of the arts by stimulating more research. Such stimulation was expanding not only the state of the arts within the established subspecialties of leisure, but also helping create new areas of specialization, as well as causing scientists from other disciplines to start leisure studies.

The 1980s

The 1980s reflected the same basic trends and patterns of the 1970s, but there were orders of magnitude differences in the numbers of studies conducted in all realms of inquiry. Particularly characteristic of this decade were more specialization and greater confidence and self-assurance of the scientists because of the positive results being found from the application of theoretically sounder research designs and the use of improved methods. Greater specialization was evidenced by attention to:

1. The role of leisure in nurturing and maintaining ethnic and other subcultural values and identities as well as causing cross-cultural differences in patterns of recreation participation.
2. Sense of place and psychological attachment to special places.
3. The concept of flow.
4. Leisure and human spirituality.
5. The topic of recreation and leisure constraints.
6. The focusing of attention on the beneficial consequences of leisure activity.
7. Concern about the handicapped and otherwise disadvantaged or physically challenged people.
8. Growth in the psychophysiological aspects of leisure behavior, especially its contributions to mental as well as physical health, with the latter being documented more thoroughly by research on other than the cardiovascular benefits of exercise.
9. Development of subspecialties within tourism, such as ecotourism.
10. Improved identity by, and better definition of, other areas of inquiry, such as therapeutic recreation.
11. Merging of recreation with related areas of inquiry, such as the human dimensions of wildlife, which addressed not only the recreational aspects of hunting but also of viewing and learning about wildlife of all types.
12. Gender differences.
13. Marketing research that went considerably beyond just the "selling" of leisure services.

This period witnessed the creation of new leisure-related journals and the involvement of new disciplines not previously concerned with leisure. Better theories were being applied and developed, as were improved research methods. More qualitative studies were done to supplement and complement the more quantitative ones. Great contributions were made to the state of knowledge during this decade, which can be called the decade of maturity.

The 1990s

I don't detect as many changes in leisure research in the 1990s as I did during the period 1960–1990. The high quality of research evidenced in the 1980s has continued, as have the specialization and substantive contributions to the state of knowledge. Some notable changes have been greater attention to the spiritual dimension of leisure (cf., Driver, Dustin, Baltic, Elsner & Peterson, 1996), an increased number of studies on sense of place (cf., Roberts, 1996), and a resurgence of economic impact studies. Particularly significant have been changes in the orientations of the leisure scientists, especially those working closely with practitioners. Specifically, there has been greater sensitivity to the need to expand the concept of the recreation customer away from just the on-site visitor or user to include all customers that affect, are affected by, or are just interested in, the services delivered (Driver, 1999). Expanded applications of the theories and methods of market research have greatly enhanced this customer orientation. In addition, there has been continued merging of recreation and tourism, which has enriched the field, in part because tourism needs to take a customer orientation, and some of that has rubbed off on other recreation professionals, who used to have a jaundiced view of tourism. Leisure scientists are also now aware of the fiscal stringency facing all public park and recreation agencies, which explains the increased research devoted to the financial dimensions of service delivery.

Significant, too, has been the widespread orientation of the public toward the qualitative dimensions of their lives, which has enhanced their sensitivity to their personal choices that both promote and deter the realization of desired qualitative aspects of their lives. These "quality of life" choices include those related to exercising, good nutrition, stress management, avoidance of drug abuse, and in general being more sensitive to how life choices impact personal health and well-being, including the impacts of alternative leisure pursuits. Such an introspective public has helped cause park and recreation managers to be more concerned about Total Quality Management, which in turn has stimulated considerable research attention to the question of what constitutes high-quality recreation opportunities.

These and other changes in society have also interacted to cause the public to demand that it be more involved in recreation resource allocation and managerial decisions, the effect of which was to reorient considerable leisure research away from the concept of public involvement that was promoted by the National Environmental Policy Act of 1969 to the concept of collaborative partnerships involving all customers. For example, there is now more research being devoted to leisure-related public policy formation and implementation. In addition, there is greater concern about the efficiency and accountability of public agencies, which has also stimulated new types of research and research approaches. For example, there is greater collaboration between leisure scientists and practitioners in the other social services, as witnessed by the rapid growth of multidisciplinary studies of the role of leisure programming—in concert with actions by the justice, educational, and social welfare agencies—in preventing the social problems caused by at-risk youth (e.g., Witt & Crompton, 1996). Relatedly, there has been more willingness of leisure scientists to get down in the trenches and work with practitioners to get the results of their research applied. And there is more being written about the future directions of industrialized societies and the role of leisure in such (e.g., Godbey, 1995). In sum, leisure research in the 1990s continued to advance rapidly the state of the arts.

Summary

The preceding outline demonstrates rather convincingly that tremendous advances were made in the state of the arts in leisure studies between 1960 and the present. From a scientific perspective, we essentially moved during that short period of time from a state of knowledge that was based primarily on intuition and informed judgment to one that was science-based and quite broad in topical coverage. This is no small accomplishment. Of course, there is much more to learn about the different aspects of leisure, as this text, and the one it updates (Jackson and Burton, 1989), amply document, but much has been achieved since 1960.

State of Management Practice

Before 1960

Although parks and recreation practitioners were dedicated and did a good job of delivering recreation services to meet public demands prior to 1960, most of what they did was guided by informed judgment and

intuition. There was little science-based management simply because, as explained previously, there was very little leisure science before 1960. More significantly, few widely adopted and implemented managerial systems were being applied; each manager followed his or her own interpretation of which types of recreation programs and facilities should be provided to accommodate perceived demands for different recreation activity opportunities. Prior to the mid 1970s, public parks and recreation agencies had no widely accepted systems for inventorying and classifying the recreation potentials of the recreation resources they managed. For example, in the USDA Forest Service, as many as four different systems were being used on the same national forest with each offering different systems of classification, so coordination of efforts was impossible. Lastly, prior to 1960, many of the practitioners did not have formal academic training in leisure studies simply because of the absence of sufficient programs in the universities and colleges.

The 1960s

Because of rapidly increasing use of park and recreation resources and the other factors identified for the 1960s in the preceding chronology on leisure research, greater public attention became focused on managerial practices in the 1960s. Because of these factors, systematic approaches started to emerge to facilitate improved management. This period also witnessed much more involvement of leisure scientists with practitioners, which also helped to promote better management. Lastly, and quite significantly, there was a plethora of environmental legislation in the 1960s at all levels of government which had wide public support. This legislation promoted additional leisure research, especially on the means of delivering leisure services that were more responsive to public demands and better involved the public in policy and managerial decisions. That legislation, for example, was one stimulus for the large amount of research on constraints that is discussed herein by Jackson and Scott (see chapter 18 in this volume).

The 1970s

Because of the outlined influences on management of the 1960s, many practitioners were ready to make considerable changes in their practices. During this decade considerable attention was devoted to upgrading professional skills via various means, such as in-service training. Closer associations were established with applications-oriented leisure professionals in academic and research institutions who were willing to risk working on projects that frequently contributed little to the publish-or-perish reward systems within which they operated. As mentioned previously, the need to do the SCORPs to qualify for federal grants—as well as managerial recognition of the need for better data of many types—encouraged these collaborative efforts. As a result, much more parks and recreation management was based on better data about recreation demand and factors that influenced recreation behavior and satisfaction. Particularly significant were the joint management-research efforts that addressed topics such as recreation area carrying capacity, development of better means to estimate the recreational use of dispersed areas, how to manage to enhance the quality of the recreation experience, what were the constraints on participation among different client groups, and can more systematic and cost-effective recreation resource planning systems be developed? As a result, tremendous changes had been made in managerial practice by the end of the 1970s.

The 1980s

Pressures intensified in the 1980s for practitioners to be more responsive to customer needs and preferences—to consider all their customers and not only the on-site visitors but also members of local communities, local businesses, and other private and public enterprises. Other pressures increased for the administrators and managers to be more accountable for their actions in ways that could be documented. Growing fiscal stringency at all levels of government caused increased concern about cost-effectiveness, not only to be more accountable but to cope with reduced budgets. And improved accountability meant better ability of the practitioners to articulate the relative social benefits and costs of alternative actions. These expectations of public park and recreation administrators and managers required that they have expertise in modern management science, including the philosophy of Total Quality Management. They also needed skills in forming collaborative partnerships with all stakeholders and knowledge about how specific leisure services positively and negatively impacted the various stakeholders (e.g., Wondolleck, 1996). Those managers also needed to know how to use data about the economic values of different types of opportunities and which financial procedures were most applicable. During the 1980s many managers gained and applied these new skills and worked closely with leisure scientists to do so and to get the necessary data to apply these skills effectively and responsibly. Thereby, the simplistic "recreation-is-only-an-activity" approach to management that was followed until about

the mid 1970s was incrementally supplemented by a broader paradigm about what the delivery of leisure services meant and entailed and about what the roles of those services were in a society (Driver, 1994).

In a nutshell, by the end of the 1980s, the state of managerial practice had moved considerably away from being based primarily on informed intuition, and many science-based management systems and tools were being applied widely. This was no small accomplishment, and one that would not have occurred without the support of the results of leisure studies. Many examples can be given of how collaborative efforts between leisure scientists and park and recreation managers helped contribute to these rapid advancements in the state of practice in the 1980s. Examples from outdoor recreation include the development of the Recreation Opportunity Spectrum and Limits of Acceptable Chance systems described by Stankey, McCool, Brown, and Clark (see chapter 26 in this volume), the Visitor Impact Management and Visitor Experience and Resource Protection impact management systems reviewed by Manning herein (see chapter 19 in this volume), and the Meaningful Measures system described elsewhere by Jaten and Driver (1998).[1] Space does not permit elaborating how other research has helped advance the state of managerial practice during the 1980s (and 1990s). Included must be the research on constraints, the role of leisure in maintaining ethnic identities, special needs of the "disadvantaged," which appropriate financial tools to use, gender differences, and effects of different stages in the life cycle—each of which has been considered by one or more authors in this text. While some of these authors despair about the lack of the use of the results of their research, I see a different picture that reflects great impact in all areas of inquiry, albeit generally without reference to the scientist that had the impact.

The 1990s

As for the previously outlined advancements in the state of the arts, the 1990s represented continuation of the advancements in the state of managerial practice. Two major causative factors were increased professionalism of the managers and intensification of the changing public expectations of management outlined at the beginning of the immediately preceding section. In a sense, needed managerial directions continued to

---

[1] Incidentally, the empirical support for many of these new managerial systems came from the type of research on the motivations of leisure that Iso-Ahola said was "futile" (see chapter 3 in this volume).

become clearer, which better defined how leisure scientists could assist the practitioners. The new management systems and technologies developed and applied during the 1980s were refined, and new science-based management tools and concepts were also implemented to further advance the state of managerial practice, such as to better accommodate the spiritual dimensions of leisure. Notable examples were the rapid development, refinement, and broad acceptance in several countries of the concept of Benefits-Based Management, which is described herein by Driver and Bruns (see chapter 21 in this volume), and expansion of applied efforts to address the problems of at-risk youth (e.g., Witt & Crompton, 1996). As a consequence, informed managers continued to modify their concepts of what the delivery of leisure services was about, especially how those services can best be delivered to enhance the lives of individuals and promote the general welfare. Particularly pronounced in the 1990s was greatly increased interest of practitioners in getting the results of leisure research applied and greater willingness to work at the community level with the various stakeholders. In fact, many public park and recreation agencies now have administrative directives that mandate a community-based approach. While market research has continued to have positive effects, a downside has been the growth of a "selling mentality," perhaps explained by growing public fiscal stringency in the 1980s and 1990s.

Summary

In summary, as for advancements of the states of the art, *and strongly associated with it,* there were tremendous advancements made in the state of parks and recreation managerial practice between 1960 and the present. I repeat that these advancements were made during the short span of about 40 years. Of course more progress is needed. We should do a better job of getting the results of leisure studies applied in leisure policy development, administration, planning, and management. Elsewhere (Driver, 1989), I have pointed out some of the major obstacles to more effective technology transfer, as has Godbey (1989). I do not have more to add here other than for some subsequent statements about it taking a "special breed of cat" to do effective applied research (see the following).

State of Academic Education

Because both the states of the arts and of practice had advanced so impressively, little comment seems nec-

essary about the commitment advancements in the state of leisure education; the substantive content of such education in an applied field such as recreation depends on advancements in the states of the art and of management practice. The field has expanded considerably since 1960, and there has been a proliferation of subspecialities, such as commercial recreation, therapeutic recreation and leisure counseling, recreation for the elderly, ecotourism, and wilderness management. Opportunities have emerged to teach more substance than just meanings, which in the past too frequently meant the personal reflections of the instructor. Research methods and the theories being tested have improved and become more sophisticated.

Incrementally—but not sufficiently—leisure has become recognized as a legitimate academic area; witness the growth in curricula and academic departments of leisure studies since 1960 and the greatly increased number of undergraduate and graduate students and professors. Tourism and recreation are slowly becoming appreciated as big business and more worthy of serious concern nationally. Also, awareness has grown recently that, since leisure pervades practically all dimensions of human life (e.g., mental and physical health, learning, spirituality, work, unemployment, retirement, economic stability, self-concept, ethnic identity, development of children, environmental management, transportation, communication, many of the service industries, the justice system and prevention of crime, social networking of everyone), we in the so-called leisure professions must work closely with these other social services and enterprises. Some educational institutions are changing to meet these needs.

I realize that many changes are still needed in leisure education as we enter the twenty-first century, and some of these changes are suggested in chapters in this text, such as the one by Dustin and Goodale (see chapter 29). But I reiterate, we should also recognize the progress that has been made.

Summary on Progress Made

I hope that I have demonstrated that great advancements have been made in the states of the arts, managerial practice, and education since 1960. In fact, few areas of scientific inquiry have realized such advancements in so short a time. The only other two that come to mind are communication science and space engineering.

On a personal note, I will mention that over time I have witnessed greatly increased professional quality of the practitioners, students (especially graduate students) who now enroll in leisure studies, leisure educators, and those who do leisure studies. After I finished my undergraduate degree and began my professional career in 1957, the quality was noticeably lower. Too many of the parks and recreation practitioners were not highly respected then by members of other professions with whom I worked. In the early to mid 1960s, many students I knew transferred to leisure studies because they could not succeed in the curricula in which they originally enrolled. And most of my associates in research and education then did not have much depth in a particular discipline and were weak in research methods. My peers in other disciplines recognized this, as did I. I have seen light years of improvement in the professional and other qualities of practitioners, students, and my professional associates since the early 1960s. Sure, we still have the good ol' boys and girls who have not changed, but each year they become fewer and fewer in number. And we still have challenges facing us, as elaborated in the next section. Nevertheless, we have come a long way in a short time, and I am proud to be a member of our profession.

Some Needed Future Directions

Most of the chapters in this text explicitly state or imply likely future trends or changes, relevant to the specific topics addressed, that will impact the states of the leisure arts, management practice, and education. I will not repeat those arguments or develop a long list of things that will likely impact leisure studies, management practice, and education in the future. Instead, I will consider briefly those things that I perceive will most significantly impact our continued professional growth. They are outlined under the following categories: Applying the Results of Leisure Studies; Professional Images of Leisure; Research; Leisure Education; Moderation in All Things; and Leisure and the Coming Society.

Applying the Results of Leisure Studies

As indicated in the previous section, I believe that a good job is being done of getting the results of leisure studies applied readily to further advance the states of the arts and of education. While great strides have been made in establishing closer working relations between practitioners and leisure professionals in the academic and research institutions, much additional progress is needed in achieving better technology transfer to the actual delivery of leisure services. Of course, information dissemination centers and publishing of special reports written for practitioners have been helpful, but I am convinced that it takes a special breed of cat to both maintain a creditable scientific reputation *and* be able to work effectively with practitioners. Both personal skills are needed for effective technology transfer, because if the research credibility is not possessed or lost, the person will not be effective, at least not for long. Educational institutions having a service mission, as well as teaching and research missions, and research organizations having an applications section are not enough: there must be the right breed of cat, and except on rare occasions, the scientist(s) who developed the technology must be involved directly. Put differently, it is my belief that the best applications work is done by credible scientists, not someone hired to represent them. The problem is that not all scientists have the temperament, personality, or motivation to work with practitioners, so lists of behaviors that will promote technology transfer don't really help those people; they might be able to put some powder on their spots, but most of them cannot change those spots. Maybe, special recruitments should be made for the right breed of cat. Certainly, the reward structures of many research and academic institutions should be modified to encourage applications work by those with the capabilities. But back to "spots," I think it is a waste of scare resources to try to "pressure" the wrong breed of cat to do more applications work; those traits do not change easily. Thus, the answer is in getting more of that breed who have the right spots on line. A respected practitioner who reviewed this chapter suggested I emphasize that it also takes a special-breed-of-cat recreation planner, manager, and administrator to work effectively with leisure scientists to get the results of research applied.

Professional Images

While getting the results of leisure studies applied to the delivery of leisure services is an important needed future direction, a more important challenge is to change the image of leisure in the minds of the public policymakers, other service-providing agencies, and the general public—in short, everyone. These people outside our profession with whom we work and on whom we depend for resources and support simply do not understand the great contributions of leisure to social welfare. As Crompton (1993) and Crompton and Witt (1998) have said, we must "reposition" ourselves as a profession so that those outside it will have proper and positive perceptions about our profession that will appropriately reflect the tremendous progress we have made and the great benefit we provide to society. A major theme of this chapter has been that we in the leisure professions have much to be proud of. But who knows about those accomplishments outside our profession? We must spread the word.

On the same line of thought, we now have good documentation that the benefits of leisure are tremendous—so much so that I now firmly believe that leisure, broadly conceived, provides as much or more total benefits to the citizens of most industrialized countries (i.e., ones in which basic needs for food, shelter, health services, and sanitation have been taken care of reasonably well) than any other social service, including health and educational services (Driver, 1998, 1999). This conclusion about the great social significance of leisure is based in part on the pervasiveness of leisure services to all domains of human endeavor commented on previously and documented by the large volume of literature on the benefits of leisure (see Driver and Bruns, chapter 21 in this volume, for a review of that literature) and in part on the great size of the "leisure economic sector" of many, if not most, countries. The following passages from Driver (1999) about the large magnitude of money spent on leisure and leisure-related expenditures by public agencies, private enterprises, and citizens substantiate this view:

> In the United States, the following statistics on the economic impacts of domestic and international travel document the size of the "leisure industry":
>
> - In 1995 international travelers spent $79.7 billion in the United States, and American travelers spent $60.2 billion outside the United States, creating a trade balance surplus of $19.5 billion. The size of the surplus rose 4% over 1994. The surplus from travel grew for the seventh straight year. Travel is one of the few economic sectors that generates a positive trade balance.
> - During 1995 domestic and international travelers together spent $421.5 billion in the United States, which is a 5.8% increase over 1994. When induced and indirect effects are added to those expenditures, the estimated total expenditures for 1995 were about $1,017 billion. That total translates into about 16.5 million jobs, travel-related payrolls of about $116 billion, and $64 billion in federal, state, and local tax revenues for that year.
> - Pleasure-related travel accounted for 69% of all U.S. domestic or resident travel in 1995. Seventeen percent of domestic business trips in 1995 combined business with pleasure, which represents a 4% increase over 1994. I could find no statistics for the percentage of international travel that is estimated to be pleasure-related, but it is logical to assume it is as high or higher than that for resident travelers.
> - In 1995 travel and the related tourism it stimulated was the third largest retail industry in the United States, after automotive dealers and food stores. The projections for the foreseeable future are for expenditures in that sector to continue to increase as a percentage of total expenditures of the retail sale industries of the United States (The Tourism Works for America 1996, U.S. Travel Data Center 1994, Washington, DC).

While these statistics document that recreation and tourism are very large, they are just portions of the leisure services sector; current systems of accounting systems exclude many components that should be included. A few examples of components that should be included are:

- All entertainment expenditures, such as cassette tapes and compact discs, operas, symphonies, rock groups, all professional sports, the winter and summer Olympics, and all nonbusiness uses of television and radio, including the costs of production, distribution, salaries, travel, capital investments in buildings and other infrastructure, and costs of viewing equipment, gate fees, and travel paid by the spectators, patrons, and viewers.
- The costs of acquiring, maintaining, and using summer homes, boats and yachts, airplanes, guns, fishing rods, cameras, and clothes for leisure.

- The costs of acquiring, maintaining, and using personal vehicles (e.g., sports utility vehicles, vans, pickups) and personal computers that should be allocated to leisure.
- The costs of entertaining guests both inside and outside one's home.
- A leisure-related share of the total costs of public libraries and continuing education courses.

It seems likely that a leisure services sector which includes all its parts would be the biggest economic sector of the U.S. economy in terms of salaries paid, employment generated, and expenditures made by consumers. If reasonably sovereign consumers willingly allocate so much of their resources to support that leisure services sector, the benefits they receive must be reasonably commensurate with the expenditures. Thus, leisure services must be extremely valuable.

But, as said, who knows about this value? To reiterate, it is up to those of us in the leisure professions to spread the word. It is our most important challenge, and we can do it honestly.

Research

Only a few of many possible topics will be addressed here. First, there is the need for better funding of leisure studies so that more longitudinal and replicative studies can be done. A big problem is that those working in leisure studies frequently have to opportunistically chase the funding. This too often means having to change research orientation instead of being able to pursue a particular topic in more depth. One answer might be the formation of more interuniversity consortia or centers that pool the fund-getting resources of several institutions. Another part of the answer is to continue to raise the public's, and public elected officials', understanding of the tremendous contributions that leisure makes to public welfare, the need for which was emphasized previously. Second, given the rapid acceptance of the benefits framework for conceptualizing leisure and for directing the delivery of leisure services, much additional research is needed to relate the inputs of recreation delivery systems to the outputs of those systems (see Driver and Bruns, chapter 21 in this volume, for an elaboration). Third, while we have made great progress in advancing the state of the arts, I and many of my associates

are concerned that the community of leisure scientists is becoming ingrown and not working as much, or as effectively, as we have in the past with professionals in the parent disciplines. We are developing a "homegrown" attitude that we can do anything. As a consequence some of us see too many "copycat" studies and demise of the creativity needed to advance theory. We have probably solved the easy problems, and we need the best help we can get in working on the more difficult ones.

Leisure Education

Despite the progress made in academic leisure education, there are problems. For example, I see an excessive proliferation of different programs that dilute and diffuse scarce resources and frequently create course offerings that have much duplication. Is this proliferation of programs needed, given that the basic theories of leisure apply to most of the various subspecialties? In addition, many of the faculty are counseling and mentoring too many students. And some leisure studies units are too isolated from the rest of the university or college.

Moderation in All Things

This discussion reflects my personal biases which are shared by several of my associates. First, I feel that too many of our colleagues have become rather esoteric and/or utopian. Yes, changes are needed in many societies to more fully incorporate the benefits of leisure, but I doubt if leisure can ever have the role and significance that some associates advocate. I am quite suspect of utopians, find others are too, and believe those writings deter from promoting the positive image of leisure, which I argued earlier is vitally important if the leisure professions are to gain political and public parity with the other social services with whom we compete for scare resources. Let's focus on what we can do. Second, we seem to be beating some dead horses. For example, some years ago—and for several years—there were rather heated and somewhat divisive debates in sessions of the Leisure Research Symposium about the relative merits of quantitative and qualitative research, and some of these "this-or-that" arguments are found in several chapters in this text. To be sure, more qualitative studies are needed, *but* so are more quantitative studies. It is not an either-or situation. The field is big enough for all of us to play, and there is much to be done. Let's stop the divisiveness and get on with it; suit your pleasure and god bless.

Leisure and the Coming Society

We each need to be sensitive to the rapid changes in society and the implications to leisure of such. For an excellent discussion of these interactions, see Godbey (1995). A sampling of the changes discussed by Godbey that will impact leisure includes:

- Rapid increases in the world's population and aging of the populations of many countries.
- Widening of the income gap between the haves and have-nots.
- Creation of a highly integrated world economy.
- International threats of terrorism.
- Continued diversification of the "roles" of women.
- Ethnic diversification of populations.
- Growing numbers of people who feel more rushed.
- Advancements in transportation.
- Continuation of the information and communication revolution.

- Growing percentages of the labor force in the service industries.

Conclusions

I conclude by emphasizing the four themes of this chapter. First, we must recognize that we have come a long way since 1960, and we should take great pride in that progress. Second, we need to recognize more fully and widely within the profession that leisure is as important to social welfare as any other social service and that it is very significant economically. Third, we must each maintain as high professional standards as possible, which means keeping abreast of the changing states of the arts, managerial practice, and education, getting out of the way if you are of the old guard and don't want to keep up, not perpetuating myths, not be too utopian, and not be divisive while still encouraging healthy dissent and debate. Fourth, and most importantly, we must promote a positive image outside our profession by informing everyone about the progress we have made as an applied area of scientific inquiry and the great social benefits of leisure, including but not confined to its tremendous significance economically.

References

Crompton, J. (1993). Repositioning recreation and park services: An overview. *Trends [Justifying Perception and Park Services to Decision Makers], 30*(4), 2–5. Washington, DC: National Park Service, U.S. Department of the Interior.

Crompton, J., & Witt, P. (1998). Repositioning: The key to building community support. *Parks and Recreation,* October, pp. 80–90.

De Grazia, S. (1962). *Of time, work and leisure.* New York, NY: The Twentieth Century Fund.

Driver, B. (1989). Applied leisure research: Benefits to scientists and practitioners and their respective roles. In E. L. Jackson & T. L. Burton (Eds.), *Understanding leisure and recreation: Mapping the past, charting the future* (pp. 597–609). State College, PA: Venture Publishing, Inc.

Driver, B. (1994). The recreation production process: The benefits-based approach to amenity resource policy analysis and management. In *Friluftsliv: Effekter og goder, Dn-notat, 1994–7, Direktoratet for Naturforvaltning Tungasletta* [Proceedings, Scandinavian Conferrce on Recreation: Benefits and Other Positive Effects] (pp. 12–30). Trondheim, Norway: Norwegian Institute of Nature Studies.

Driver, B. (1998). The benefits are endless. . . . But why? *Parks and Recreation,* January, 26–32.

Driver, B. (1999). Management of outdoor recreation and related public amenity resources for the benefits they provide. In H. K. Cornell (Principal Investigator), *Outdoor recreation in American life: A national assessment of demand and supply* (pp. 2–15). Champaign, IL: Sagamore Publishing.

Driver, B., Dustin, D., Baltic, T., Elsner, G., & Peterson, G. (Eds.). (1996). *Nature and the human spirit: Toward an expanded land management ethic.* State College, PA: Venture Publishing, Inc.

Godbey G. (1989). Implications of recreation and leisure research for professionals. In E. L. Jackson & T. L. Burton (Eds.), *Understanding leisure and recreation: Mapping the past, charting the future* (pp. 613–628). State College, PA: Venture Publishing, Inc.

Godbey, G. (1995). Things will never be the same: Prospects for outdoor recreation and tourism in an era of exponential change. In J. Thompson, D. Lime, B. Gardner & W. Sames (Compilers), *Proceedings of the Fourth International Outdoor Recreation & Tourism Trends Conference* (pp. 3–13). St. Paul, MN: The University of Minnesota.

Jackson, E. L., & Burton, T. L. (1989). *Understanding leisure and recreation: Mapping the past, charting the future.* State College, PA: Venture Publishing, Inc.

Jaten, A., & Driver, B. (1998). Meaningful measures for quality recreation management. *Journal of Park and Recreation Administration ,16*(3), 43–57.

Hollingshead, A. (1949). *Elmstown's youth.* New York, NY: John Wiley & Sons, Inc.

Lundberg, G., Komarovsky, M., & McInerny, M. (1934). *Leisure: A suburban study.* New York, NY: Columbia University Press.

Lynd, H., & Lynd, R. (1956). *Middletown.* New York, NY: Harcourt Brace Jovanovich.

Outdoor Recreation Resources Review Commission. (1962). *Bibliography and history* (ORRRC Study Reports, Report Number 27). Washington, DC: U.S. Government Printing Office.

Roberts, E. (1996). Place and spirit in public land management. In B. Driver, D. Dustin, T. Baltic, G. Elsner & G. Peterson (Eds.), *Nature and the human spirit: Toward an expanded land management ethic* (pp. 61–80). State College, PA: Venture Publishing, Inc.

Witt, P., & Crompton, J. (Eds.). (1996). *Recreation programs that work for at-risk youth: The challenge of shaping the future.* State College, PA: Venture Publishing, Inc.

Wondolleck, J. (1996). Incorporating hard-to-define-values into public lands decision making: A conflict management perspective. In B. Driver, D. Dustin, T. Baltic, G. Elsner & G. Peterson (Eds.), *Nature and the human spirit: Toward an expanded land management ethic* (pp. 257–262). State College, PA: Venture Publishing, Inc.

The Editors and Contributors

MARIA T. ALLISON completed both her Bachelor and Master of Science degrees at the University of New Mexico. She received her doctorate from the University of Illinois at Champaign-Urbana with a specialization in sociology of sport. Having been raised in the Southwest, Dr. Allison spent her early professional years teaching high school and working with Navajo, Zuni, and Hispanic youth in New Mexico. This early experience led to her lifelong research interest in ethnicity, intercultural relations, and the nature of cultural differences in play, sport, and leisure. Her current work focuses on the ways in which human service agencies erect institutional barriers to program access for diverse populations. Dr. Allison has had her work published in more than 10 countries. She is the former chair of her department and also served as the President of the International Committee for Sociology of Sport of the International Sociological Association. She is a fellow of the Academy of Leisure Sciences and a former associate editor of *Leisure Sciences*. She regularly teaches a large introductory campus-wide course, "Leisure and the Quality of Life;" graduate seminars on "Research Methods" and "Social Psychological Perspectives on Leisure;" and a new seminar course titled "Leisure, Diversity, and the Community."

M. DEBORAH BIALESCHKI was born to a farm family in the heart of Illinois and grew up with four younger brothers and a sister. They were always outside in their play and work, so she grew up with an appreciation for the environment and all that lives there. She also recognized early on that there were significant differences in what society thought acceptable for boys and girls, especially related to sports and physical activities. When these personal experiences were combined with her formal education, she ended up with a bachelor's degree in education from Eastern Illinois University (focus on physical education and biology), a master's degree from the University of Minnesota (focus on recreation, park, and leisure studies) and a doctorate from the University of Wisconsin–Madison (focus on recreation and women's studies). Added in for good

535

measure was some high-school teaching, working as a seasonal naturalist, and time with the Minnesota Department of Natural Resources as an assistant accessibility coordinator. Dr. Bialeschki's research and teaching interests continue to center on issues related to women's leisure, the outdoors, and social change. Her professional service has ranged from serving in editorial capacities with journals in the field to leadership positions with organizations such as SPRE, ACA, and WLRA.

PERRY J. BROWN is the dean of the School of Forestry at the University of Montana–Missoula. He received his university education at Utah State University and the University of Michigan. A Westerner by birth and experience, he served on the forest science faculty of Utah State University, the recreation resources faculty of Colorado State University, and as department head of forest recreation resources and then as associate dean of the College of Forestry at Oregon State University before joining the Montana faculty as dean in 1994. He is an internationally known scholar in the areas of recreational use of natural resources and natural resource planning. He has authored over 140 papers, book chapters and books, and has mentored over 50 master's and doctoral students. With colleagues in the USDA Forest Service and the USDI Bureau of Land Management he helped develop the Recreation Opportunity Spectrum framework for planning and management and, in collaboration with Beverly L. Driver, laid the foundation for much current research on the benefits of leisure. In addition, he has served in numerous advising and consulting capacities for the USDA Forest Service and the USDI Bureau of Land Management in the areas of recreation, planning, visual resources, and policy. He currently is the deputy coordinator of Division VI of the International Union of Forest Research Organizations and serves on IUFRO's Extended Executive Board. He has lectured and consulted in numerous countries throughout the world. He also is the President-elect (1998–1999, President 2000–2001) of the National Association of Professional Forestry Schools and Colleges in the United States and serves on NAPFSC's Executive Board.

THOMAS L. BURTON took a Bachelor of Science (economics) degree at the University of London in 1963, and a doctoral degree in land economics from the same university in 1967. He has held appointments as assistant lecturer in the Department of Economics at Wye College, University of London, from 1963 to 1966; lecturer in the Center for Urban and Regional Studies at the University of Birmingham from 1966 to 1969; assistant professor in the Department of Parks and Recre-

ation Resources at Michigan State University from 1969 to 1970; associate professor and graduate chairman in the School of Urban and Regional Planning, University of Waterloo, from 1970 to 1973; and consultant to the Ministry of State for Urban Affairs, Government of Canada, from 1973 to 1976. In 1976 he joined the University of Alberta, where he was a professor in the Department of Recreation and Leisure Studies (formerly Recreation Administration) until 1997, serving as department chair from 1979 to 1988, associate dean of the faculty of Physical Education and Recreation from 1991 to 1994, and acting dean in 1997. He has held visiting professorships at the University of British Columbia; the Phillip Institute of Technology (now the Royal Melbourne Institute of Technology) in Melbourne, Australia; and at the Pennsylvania State University. Dr. Burton is the author of seven books in the recreation, resource, planning, and research fields, as well as more than 60 research reports, articles, and papers. He was founding president of the Canadian Association for Leisure Studies from 1981 to 1984, and served a second term as president from 1987 to 1990. He is a life member of the World Leisure and Recreation Association, and a fellow of the Academy of Leisure Sciences. He received the Award of Merit from the Alberta Recreation and Parks Association for distinguished service to the field in 1997. Dr. Burton took early retirement from the University of Alberta in June 1997 to spend more time with his family and to become more involved in volunteer activities, although he continues to teach selected courses and to supervise graduate students in his capacity as professor emeritus. Presently, he volunteers with ChildFind Alberta, the Alberta Recreation and Parks Association, and several other local groups in Edmonton.

RICHARD W. BUTLER is professor of tourism and deputy head of the School of Management Studies for the Service Sector at the University of Surrey, England. Born in Birmingham, England, he was educated at Nottingham University (Bachelor of Arts Honors in geography) and Glasgow University (doctorate in geography) and taught in the geography department at the University of Western Ontario from 1967 to 1997. He served two terms as president of the International Academy for the Study of Tourism (1993–97) and as president of the Canadian Association of Leisure Studies and president of the Ontario Research Council on Leisure. His main research interests are in tourism, particularly in the development cycles of destinations, the social impacts of tourism, the relationship between the media and tourism, and sustainable development concepts applied to tourism. His geographical experience includes Europe, North America, and the South

Pacific, and he has had a lifelong fascination and research interests in small islands and peripheral areas. His recent publications include *Tourism and Recreation in Rural Areas* (with C. M. Hall and J. Jenkins) and *Tourism and Indigenous Peoples* (with T. Hinch). He is currently working on volumes on tourism and national parks and tourism and the media. He is joint editor of the new journal *International Review of Tourism and Hospitality* and is on the editorial boards of several other major tourism journals. He was awarded the Roy Wolfe Award of the Association of American Geographers in 1994, and is a fellow of the Royal Geographical Society.

FRED COALTER is director of the Center for Leisure Research at the University of Edinburgh, a contract research unit which undertakes policy-oriented research for local and national government agencies. Mr. Coalter specializes in policy, planning, and management-oriented research in sport and recreation. He has researched and written widely on issues of pricing, the implication of trends in sports participation, and the impact of changing modes of delivery of public sector leisure services. He is a former chair of the Leisure Studies Association and is a member of the editorial boards of *Leisure Studies* and *Managing Leisure: An International Journal.*

WES COOPER took a Bachelor of Arts (philosophy) degree at Occidental College, Los Angeles, in 1966; a Bachelors of Letters degree at the University of Oxford in 1971; and a doctoral degree in philosophy at the University of Calgary in 1976. He has taught at the University of Alberta as sessional lecturer (1971–72), assistant professor (1972–78), associate professor (1978–90), and professor (since 1990). He has also taught at the University of Maryland (1970–71). Dr. Cooper has published extensively in philosophical journals on topics in the areas of philosophy of mind and social philosophy. In recent years he has written extensively about William James, and also about work and leisure. He is the chief administrator for Golden Compass MOO, an educational virtual reality that supports courses at the University of Alberta and elsewhere in computer ethics and cyberphilosophy.

JOHN DATTILO obtained two bachelor's degrees from the Pennsylvania State University, one in recreation and parks and another in special education; a master's degree from the University of Arizona in recreation; and a doctorate from the University of Illinois in leisure studies. His instructional assignments over the past decade at the University of Nebraska, the Pennsylvania State University and the University of Georgia have

included teaching graduate and undergraduate courses on leisure for people with disabilities, leisure education, and research methods. He has supervised or been a member of 30 doctoral and master's examination committees. Dr. Dattilo has lectured throughout the United States, in the Netherlands, Brazil, and Canada. He is a faculty member of the World Leisure and Recreation Association's International Center of Excellence and was recently inducted into the Tau Chapter of Phi Beta Delta, Honor Society for International Scholars. Dr. Dattilo has written three textbooks: *Leisure Education Program Planning, Behavior Modification in Therapeutic Recreation,* and *Inclusive Leisure Services.* In addition, he has published approximately 80 articles and has made over 130 presentations before learned societies and professional groups. He has served on the editorial boards of three journals with international circulation and has been a reviewer on many occasions for several journals. Over the past 10 years, Dr. Dattilo has developed 15 funded projects totaling over $2 million which have supported research and training in therapeutic recreation. Much of his research has examined the effects of interventions designed to enhance the self-determination of people with disabilities relative to their leisure participation. In recognition for this line of research, he was awarded the G. Lawrence Rarick Research Award by the National Council for Physical Education and Recreation for People with Disabilities.

RODNEY B. DIESER received his Bachelor of Science and Master of Science in parks, recreation, and tourism from the University of Utah. His educational focus while at the University of Utah was therapeutic recreation with a minor in educational psychology. After studying and teaching in the faculty of Natural Resources and Environmental Studies at the University of Northern British Columbia, he began a doctorate at the University of Alberta in the Department of Physical Education and Recreation. His research focus is on how a sweat-lodge ceremony can be used as therapeutic recreation intervention among Native Americans who are in treatment for alcohol and substance dependency. He is also interested in multicultural aspects of leisure theory and services. He is founder of Schole Counseling and Recreation Therapy, a consulting business in the field of therapeutic recreation.

BEVERLY L. DRIVER retired from a research position with the USDA Forest Service in August 1997, but remains active professionally. His latest research interest centers on identifying and quantifying consequences of leisure activities deemed desirable and beneficial by individual participants and by society. His previous research focused upon developing psychometric instruments, such as the Recreation Experience Preference scales, to evaluate the motivational bases of leisure choices. He has devoted much attention to the practical application of research results, and in the process has played either the, or a, lead role in the development of three of the four amenity resource management systems now used by the USDA Forest Service and by many other agencies in the United States and several foreign countries. Dr. Driver served on the faculty of the University of Michigan's School of Natural Resources for six years and as a lecturer in Yale University's School of Forestry and Environmental Studies for 18 months. He has received the National Recreation and Park Association's National Research (Roosevelt) Award, USDA's Superior Service Award, and the USDA Forest Service's Superior and Distinguished Science Awards, among others. He is a past president of the Academy of Leisure Sciences, and has authored over 140 scientific publications.

DANIEL L. DUSTIN is a professor in the Department of Health, Physical Education, and Recreation at Florida International University in Miami. He holds a bachelor's degree in geography and a master's degree in resource planning and conservation from the University of Michigan, and a doctoral degree in education with an emphasis in recreation and park administration from the University of Minnesota. Dr. Dustin's main academic interests center on environmental stewardship and the moral and ethical bases for leisure and recreation activity preferences and behaviors. A past president of both the Society of Park and Recreation Educators and the Academy of Leisure Sciences, he is a recipient of the National Recreation and Park Association's Literary Award, and in 1994 he was made an honorary lifetime member of the California Park Rangers Association for his contributions to the literature of outdoor recreation planning and policy. Among his recent works as a contributing author and editor are: *Wilderness in America: Personal Perspectives; Beyond Promotion and Tenure: On Being a Professor; For the Good of the Order: Administering Academic Programs in Higher Education; Stewards of Access/Custodians of Choice: A Philosophical Foundation for the Park and Recreation Profession; Nature and the Human Spirit: Toward an Expanded Land Management Ethic;* and *The Wilderness Within: Reflections on Leisure and Life.*

ALAN W. EWERT received his doctorate from the University of Oregon in recreation and park management. At the time his chapter was written, he was professor and program chair of Resource Recreation and Tourism in the faculty of Natural Resources and Environmental

Studies at the University of Northern British Columbia in Prince George, British Columbia. Prior to accepting his position as program chair, Dr. Ewert was the branch chief of Recreation, Wilderness and Urban Forestry Research with the USDA Forest Service, based in Washington, DC. His books include *Outdoor Adventure Pursuits: Foundations, Models and Theories; Culture, Conflict and Communication in the Wildland-Urban Interface* (coeditor), and *Natural Resource Management: The Human Dimension* (editor). In addition, he has written over 150 articles related to various aspects of recreation and natural resources and is currently an executive editor of the *Journal of Environmental Education* and the *International Journal of Wilderness.* Dr. Ewert was elected to the Academy of Leisure Sciences in 1993. In September of 1998 he assumed the Patricia and Joel Meier Endowed Chairship at Indiana University.

VALERIA J. FREYSINGER is an associate professor in the Department of Physical Education, Health and Sport Studies at Miami University of Ohio. She went to Miami in 1988 after receiving her master's and doctoral degrees from the University of Wisconsin–Madison, where she was a student in the Department of Continuing and Vocational Education. The focus of Dr. Freysinger's graduate work was gendered experiences of leisure and adult development. She has continued with this focus in her teaching and scholarship at Miami University. Dr. Freysinger has coauthored two books on women, gender, and leisure, as well as an undergraduate text addressing current issues in recreation and leisure. She has presented numerous papers and published a number of book chapters and research articles focusing on age, gender, race, social class, life span development, and leisure. She has served as associate and guest editor and reviewer for several refereed research journals and conferences and has been a visiting professor in the World Leisure and Recreation Association's International Center of Excellence in the Netherlands.

TROY D. GLOVER received his master's degree in recreation and leisure studies at the University of Alberta in the Faculty of Physical Education and Recreation. He is presently a doctoral candidate at the University of Waterloo in the Department of Recreation and Leisure Studies. Mr. Glover's scholarly interests include the financing of urban leisure services, the politics of public leisure policy development, and alternative forms of leisure services delivery and their implications for efficiency, effectiveness, and equity.

GEOFFREY GODBEY is professor of leisure studies at the Pennsylvania State University. He has authored or coauthored several books and over 100 articles dealing with leisure behavior, history and philosophies of leisure, leisure service organizations, and the future of leisure and leisure services. He has been president of SPRE and president of the Academy of Leisure Sciences, and is a member of the board of directors of the World Leisure and Recreation Association. He has won the National Literary Award from National Recreation and Parks Association and the Distinguished Alumnus Award from the State University of New York–Cortland. Dr. Godbey has written for and has been featured in a wide variety of mass-circulation magazines and newspapers and has been featured on network television. Associate editor and editorial board member of numerous periodicals and a founder of Venture Publishing, he has given invited presentations in 15 countries. His most recent books are *Time for Life* and *Leisure and Leisure Services in the 21st Century.*

THOMAS L. GOODALE is professor of health, fitness and recreation at George Mason University, having taught previously at the State University of New York–Cortland, the University of Wisconsin–Green Bay, and the University of Ottawa, where he served a term as chair of its bilingual program in leisure studies. He has served as editor of *Leisure Sciences,* and as associate editor of that journal and other research journals in the field. He is coauthor of *The Evolution of Leisure: Historical and Philosophical Perspectives,* and coeditor of *Recreation and Leisure: Issues in an Era of Change.* He is a distinguished colleague and currently president of the Society of Park and Recreation Educators, a past president of the Academy of Leisure Sciences, a distinguished alumnus of the State University of New York–Cortland, a member of the Advisory Board of TV Free America, and recipient of the National Recreation and Park Association's National Literary Award. His principal professional interest is a liberal studies approach to teaching undergraduates about leisure.

JAMES H. GRAMANN received his bachelor's and master's degrees from the University of Washington and his doctoral degree from the University of Illinois at Urbana-Champaign. His research and teaching centers on the social psychological aspects of leisure, especially outdoor recreation behavior. Dr. Gramann holds joint appointments in recreation, park and tourism sciences and rural sociology at Texas A&M University. He was formerly regional research sociologist for the Southwest and Western regions of the U.S. National Park Service and has served on several advisory groups related to protected area management in the United States. Many of Dr. Gramann's former graduate students are faculty members at major universities in the

United States and overseas. Dr. Gramann is a former member of the editorial board of the *Journal of Leisure Research,* and has been elected to several honor societies, including Phi Beta Delta, Xi Sigma Pi, and Phi Kappa Phi. He has been recognized as a Wakonse Teaching Fellow at Texas A&M University, where he teaches an introductory course on recreation and parks, in addition to an upper-division case-study course on protected area management, and a graduate course dealing with the social science foundations of recreation, parks, and tourism. He serves as associate head for graduate programs and research in the Department of Recreation, Park and Tourism Sciences.

JOHN L. HEMINGWAY is by birth and temperament a native of the Midwestern United States, Dr. Hemingway earned a bachelor's degree at Grinnell College in political science (1971). Following military service, he earned a doctoral degree in political science (1979) and a master's degree in recreation education at the University of Iowa (1983). Having taught seven years at Old Dominion University, in 1990 he moved to St. Cloud State University and in 1991 to Washington State University. In 1998 he joined the Department of Recreation and Leisure Studies at the University of North Carolina at Chapel Hill, where he is currently an associate professor. His research interests are concentrated in the philosophy of inquiry in the study of leisure and in the political and social meanings of leisure. His recent work has explored the application of critical theory, particularly that of Jürgen Habermas, to the study of leisure, specifically the study of freedom in leisure set in a broader historical context. His immediate concern is the analysis of systematic political, social, and economic constraints on freedom in leisure. He has published a number of articles on this theme and is currently at work on a book which analyzes the historical evolution of the interaction between leisure, freedom, and forms of citizenship. He coedited a volume entitled *Philosophy of Therapeutic Recreation: Ideas and Issues* (1987), served as an associate editor of *Leisure Sciences* (1988–1991), and as a co-book review editor of *Leisure Sciences* (1994–1997).

KARLA A. HENDERSON is a white, middle-aged feminist. Although she has lived in North Carolina for the past 12 years, she considers herself a Midwesterner at heart. She earned both a bachelor's degree (in education) and a master's degree (in counseling) at Iowa State University and did her doctoral degree (education-recreation, park, and leisure studies) at the University of Minnesota. Her academic journey has included teaching positions at the University of Wisconsin–Madison and Texas Woman's University. She is currently professor and chair of leisure studies and recreation administration at the University of North Carolina–Chapel Hill. Her research interests include women and leisure, diverse and underserved populations, social psychology of leisure, and research and evaluation methods. She has written textbooks on feminist approaches to leisure and on qualitative research. Dr. Henderson has been actively involved in a number of professional organizations, and most recently received the Distinguished Colleague Award from the Society of Park and Recreation Educators. She is a past president of SPRE, the Academy of Leisure Sciences, and the Research Consortium of AAHPERD. When she isn't working, she enjoys all types of outdoor activities, plays in two local community bands, is owned by two cats, and runs a marathon every now and again.

Seppo E. Iso-Ahola received his bachelor's degree from the University of Jyväskylä, Finland, in 1971; a master's degree from the University of Illinois in 1972; a master's degree from the University of Jyväskylä in 1973; and a doctoral degree from the University of Illinois in 1976. He was assistant and associate professor at the University of Iowa from 1976 to 1981, and associate professor (1981–1984) and professor (since 1984) at the University of Maryland. He has published over 70 research articles in various scientific journals in psychology, kinesiology, and leisure studies, and has authored four books dealing with the social psychology of leisure and sports. He was editor of the *Journal of Leisure Research* between 1983 and 1986 and of *Scandinavian Journal of Medicine and Science in Sport* between 1994 and 1997. He received the Theodore and Franklin Roosevelt Award for Excellence in Recreation and Park Research in 1987, the Charles Brightbill Award in 1987, and the Allen V. Sapora Research Award in 1993.

Edgar L. Jackson is a native of Great Britain and a graduate (in geography) of the London School of Economics and Political Science. Dr. Jackson continued his education in Canada, completing a master's degree in geography at the University of Calgary and a doctorate in geography at the University of Toronto. He began his teaching career at Toronto in 1974 and moved to Alberta in 1975, where he is professor in the Department of Earth and Atmospheric Sciences. His research interests have focused upon a variety of topics related to leisure and recreation, including the relationship between outdoor recreation participation and attitudes to the natural environment, satisfaction in outdoor recreation, and conflict. In recent years he has concentrated largely on constraints to leisure participation and enjoyment, an area in which he has published

numerous journal articles and several contract reports for the Alberta government. He coedited (with Tim Burton) and wrote portions of the 1989 text, *Understanding Leisure and Recreation: Mapping the Past, Charting the Future.* Dr. Jackson was an associate editor of the *Journal of Leisure Research* from 1988 to 1995, Secretary of the Canadian Association for Leisure Studies (CALS) for two three-year terms (1987–1993), and president of CALS from 1996 to 1999. He received the Allen V. Sapora Research Award and the National Recreation and Park Association's Roosevelt Research Award in 1995, and was president of the Academy of Leisure Sciences (ALS) from 1995 to 1996. He also maintains the ALS and CALS World Wide Web sites.

John R. Kelly is professor emeritus in the Department of Leisure Studies at the University of Illinois at Urbana-Champaign, where he was on the faculty from 1975. His doctorate in sociology is from the University of Oregon, and he has received master's degrees from the University of Oregon, Yale, and the University of Southern California. He is the author of several books, including *Leisure* (an introduction to leisure studies), *Leisure Identities and Interactions* (a study of personal development and expression through the life course), *Recreation Business* (an introduction to market-sector leisure provisions), *Freedom to Be: A New Sociology of Leisure* (a critical analysis of theory and research), *Peoria Winter: Styles and Resources in Later Life* (a study of coping with later life changes), and *Recreation Trends Toward the Year 2000* (an analysis of national participation in recreation activities). Dr. Kelly has published many chapters in edited books, nine technical reports for federal agencies and business consultants, and numerous journal articles. He was the founding chair of the Commission on Research of the World Leisure and Recreation Association and is a member of the Academy of Leisure Sciences.

Roger C. Mannell is a social psychologist and professor of recreation and leisure studies. He completed his doctorate in psychology at the University of Windsor in 1977. Dr. Mannell was director of the Center of Leisure Studies at Acadia University in Nova Scotia before joining the University of Waterloo as a faculty member in 1979, where he served as chair of the Department of Recreation and Leisure Studies from 1990 to 1996. He has been a regular contributor to behavioral research on leisure, and in particular has been interested in social and personality factors that influence leisure choices and how these choices affect the quality of life and mental health. His research has also included studies of the impact of the changing relationship between work and leisure on the lifestyles of workers. Dr. Mannell has served as an associate editor for the *Journal of Leisure Research* and *Leisure Sciences*. Elected a fellow of the Academy of Leisure Sciences in 1987, he was also the 1989 recipient of the Allen V. Sapora Research Award and in 1991 was awarded the Theodore and Franklin Roosevelt Research Excellence Award by the National Recreation and Parks Association. He coauthored (with Doug Kleiber) a book titled *A Social Psychology of Leisure*.

ROBERT E. MANNING is professor of natural resources at the University of Vermont, where he chairs the Recreation Management Program. He earned a bachelor's degree in biology from Washington College (Maryland) and master's and doctoral degrees from Michigan State University in the Departments of Park and Recreation Resources and Resource Development, respectively. Following his doctoral program, he worked as a senior planner for the Maryland Department of Natural Resources, then joined the faculty at the University of Vermont in 1976. He teaches courses in the history, philosophy, and management of parks and related areas and in environmental history and philosophy. His research interests include carrying capacity of parks and related areas, park management, and environmental values and ethics. Much of Dr. Manning's research focuses on the U.S. national parks, and he has spent three yearlong sabbaticals with the U.S. National Park Service at Grand Canyon National Park, Yosemite National Park, and the Washington Office. He has published widely in the fields of outdoor recreation and natural resources and is author of *Studies in Outdoor Recreation*. He currently serves as policy review editor for the journal *Society and Natural Resources*.

RON MCCARVILLE received a Bachelor of Science in recreation administration, a Bachelor of Education in elementary education, and a Masters of Recreation degree from Acadia University. He worked as a recreation coordinator in Nova Scotia from 1977 to 1985, then attended Texas A&M University, where he received a doctorate from the Department of Recreation, Park and Tourism Sciences in 1989. Upon graduation Dr. McCarville joined the Department of Recreation and Leisure Studies at the University of Waterloo, where he teaches advanced courses in management, quality assurance, consumer behavior, and marketing. He also teaches a campus-wide introductory course on leisure and lifestyle. His primary research interests are in public sector pricing, sponsorship, persuasive communication, and user satisfaction. Dr. McCarville has worked extensively with community leisure agencies, national volunteer organizations and with federal agencies in both the United States and Canada. In particular, he

has worked with the Canadian Park Service on many initiatives, ranging from policy development to staff training. His work appears in journals such as the *Journal of Leisure Research, Leisure Sciences, Journal of Park and Recreation Administration, Journal of Sport Management,* and *Journal of Hospitality and Leisure Marketing*. He currently serves on the editorial review board of the *Journal of Leisure Research*.

STEPHEN F. MCCOOL received his doctoral and master's degrees from the University of Minnesota, where he was enrolled in the School of Forestry majoring in outdoor recreation management. His bachelor's degree is in forest resources management from the University of Idaho. Currently, he serves as professor of wildland recreation management in the School of Forestry at the University of Montana in Missoula, Montana, where he teaches classes in protected area and recreation planning. Dr. McCool serves on the World Commission on Protected Areas and sits on its Task Force on Tourism and National Parks. His research interests focus on a variety of aspects of protected area planning and management, including applications of the Limits of Acceptable Change process, public participation in planning, the concept of sustainability as it applies to the tourism and protected area interface, and the effectiveness of various approaches to planning for protected areas.

DONALD G. REID's interests are in the effects of globalization and technology in the workplace on work and leisure patterns. He is particularly interested in leisure patterns of marginalized groups in society, such as First Nations Communities and the unemployed. His work also includes examining leisure as an instrument for community development. He is also interested in the impacts of tourism development on communities and culture in the developing world, particularly southern Africa. His present research is located in Kenya.

CHRIS ROJEK is professor of sociology and culture at the Theory, Culture and Society Center, Nottingham Trent University. He is the author of several books on leisure, most notably *Capitalism and Leisure Theory, Ways of Escape: Modern Transformations in Leisure and Travel, Decentring Leisure,* and *Conspicuous Leisure and Its Consequences*. He is a regular contributor to *Leisure Studies* and *Loisir et Société/Society and Leisure*. He has spoken at many international conferences in New Zealand, Australia, North America, and Western Europe.

DIANE M. SAMDAHL received a bachelor's degree in natural resources from the University of Wisconsin–Madison (1976), a master's degree in sociology from the

University of Washington (1979), and a doctoral degree in leisure studies from the University of Illinois (1986). She has held faculty positions at the University of Wisconsin–Madison and the University of Oregon. Currently she is at the University of Georgia, where she is an associate professor in the Department of Recreation and Leisure Studies and an affiliate faculty member in the Women's Studies Program. Dr. Samdahl's early interests addressed social aspects of natural resource management and she worked for several years with the USDA Forest Service in Seattle, Washington. Her more contemporary work examines leisure as an everyday phenomenon, with particular emphasis on women and other marginalized populations. In spite of a strong background in survey research methods and advanced statistics, Dr. Samdahl has been moving towards interpretive research in recent years. She has been an associate editor for the *Journal of Leisure Research* and *Leisure Sciences* and has authored over 40 research-based publications and presentations in leisure studies.

DAVID SCOTT has been an assistant professor and extension specialist in the Department of Recreation, Park and Tourism Sciences at Texas A&M University since the fall of 1994. He holds a bachelor's degree in sociology and political science from Purdue University and master's and doctoral degrees in recreation and parks from the Pennsylvania State University. Between 1991 and 1994 Dr. Scott was employed as manager of research and program evaluation for Cleveland Metroparks in Cleveland, Ohio, where he was responsible for conducting marketing and evaluation studies of various park district facilities and programs, including Cleveland Metroparks Zoo, and household surveys to determine why people did not use parks in northeast Ohio. Dr. Scott's research interests include leisure constraints and nonuse of public park and recreation services, leisure socialization and changing nature of leisure involvement, and leisure social worlds and adult play groups. Articles of his have appeared in a number of scholarly journals, including *Environment and Behavior, Festival Management & Event Tourism, Journal of Leisure Research, Journal of Park and Recreation Administration, Leisure Sciences, Play and Culture,* and *Loisir et Société/Society and Leisure.* Dr. Scott has served as an associate editor for the *Journal of Leisure Research* and *Journal of Park and Recreation Administration.* He was the 1994 recipient of the Willard E. Sutherland Award presented by the American Academy for Park and Recreation Administration for a paper he had published in the *Journal of Park and Recreation Administration.* He was also awarded the 1995–1996 Center for Teaching Excellence Scholar for the College of Agriculture and Life Sciences at Texas A&M University.

SUSAN M. SHAW is a professor in the Department of Recreation and Leisure Studies at the University of Waterloo in Ontario, Canada. She has a doctorate in sociology, and taught at Dalhousie University in Nova Scotia before moving to Waterloo in 1991. Her research interests have included the intersection of work, leisure and the family, as well as perceptions of time and the gendered nature of time use. More recently, her research has concentrated on women's leisure, including ways in which women's leisure is constrained, and ways in which everyday leisure practice constrains women through the reproduction of dominant ideologies and gendered power relations. Dr. Shaw is a fellow of the Academy of Leisure Sciences, an associate editor for *Loisir et Société/Society and Leisure,* and a past president of the Canadian Association for Leisure Studies.

TREVOR SLACK was born in Great Britain and attended Borough Road College of Physical Education. He completed his bachelor's, master's, and doctoral degrees at the University of Alberta. From 1984 until 1996 he was a member of the faculty at the University of Alberta, where he held positions as associate dean (research and graduate programs) in the Faculty of Physical Education and Recreation and adjunct professor in the Faculty of Business. He is currently professor and head of the School of Physical Education, Sport, and Leisure at De Montfort University in England. Dr. Slack has also worked as a visiting fellow at the Center for Corporate Strategy and Change in the University of Warwick's Business School. His primary research interests are in organizational strategy and organizational change. Articles written by Dr. Slack have appeared in such journals as the *Journal of Sport Management, Leisure Studies, Organizational Studies,* and the *Journal of Management Studies.* His latest book, *Understanding Sport Organizations,* was published in 1996 by Human Kinetics. Dr. Slack is the editor of the *Journal of Sport Management* and sits on the editorial boards of several other journals.

BRYAN J. A. SMALE received both his bachelor's and master's degrees in recreation and leisure studies from the University of Waterloo before completing his doctorate in geography at the University of Western Ontario. He is currently associate professor in the Department of Recreation and Leisure Studies at the University of Waterloo, as well as the associate dean for computing and special projects in the Faculty of Applied Health Sciences. His research interests are quite eclectic, and include such areas as urban recreation, recreation geography, spatial perspectives on leisure, quality of community life, leisure and well-being across the life span, statistical applications, and research methods. He has been editor of *Ontario Geography,* and more recently, of the *Journal of Applied Recreation Research.*

GEORGE H. STANKEY received his bachelor's and master's degrees in geography from Oregon State University, and his doctorate, also in geography, from Michigan State University. Following school, he spent much of the next 20 years as a research social scientist with the USDA Forest Service's Intermountain Research Station in the Wilderness Management Research Unit in Missoula, Montana. His work focused on studies of wilderness visitor attitudes, values, and behavior, as well as on a variety of issues dealing with the human and natural resource management interface. He also held faculty affiliate appointments in both the School of Forestry and the Department of Geography at the University of Montana. In the early 1980s and again in the late 1980s, he spent two two-year assignments working in Australia, where he both taught university-level courses in Canberra and Sydney and served on the staff of the New South Wales National Parks and Wildlife Service. He returned to the United States in 1989, as a professor in the Department of Forest Resources at Oregon State University. He returned to the USDA Forest Service as a social scientist assigned to the People and Natural Resources Program of the Pacific Northwest Research Station in 1995. He has published widely in the natural resource and social science field, is a coauthor of the text *Wilderness Management,* and is a member of the World Commission on National Parks and Protected Areas of the World Conservation Union. His current areas of research interest include adaptive management and social learning models, and evolving institutional structures for resource management.

ROBERT A. STEBBINS received his doctorate in 1964 from the University of Minnesota. He is presently professor in, and former head of, the Department of Sociology at the University of Calgary. He has also taught at Memorial University of Newfoundland and the University of Texas at Arlington. He served as president of the Social Science Federation of Canada in 1991–1992, after having served as president of the Canadian Sociology and Anthropology Association in 1988–1989. His research interests include humor, work, leisure, the work and leisure dimensions of deviance, and the leisure basis of Francophone communities outside Quebec. He has published numerous journal articles and book chapters, as well as 21 books. Most of his work in leisure studies has centered on serious leisure (a term he coined in 1982), as expressed in research dating from 1973 on amateurs (actors, magicians, musicians, archaeologists, astronomers, baseball and football players, and stand-up comics), hobbyists (barbershop singers, cultural tourists), and career volunteers (urban Francophones). Work in these areas completed before 1992 was summarized and theoretically elaborated in *Amateurs, Professionals, and Serious Leisure.* Recently, he completed an adult education guide to serious leisure titled *After Work: The Search for an Optimal Leisure Lifestyle.*

GUY S. SWINNERTON was born in Wales and took a bachelor's degree in geography at the London School of Economics and Political Science (1965). He continued his education at the University of British Columbia, where he obtained a master's degree in geography (1969). Between 1967 and 1969 he was a research officer with the Canada Land Inventory Program in Victoria, British Columbia. He then returned to Britain to the Countryside Planning Unit at Wye College, University of London, and earned a doctorate in land use studies (1974). Between 1973 and 1978 he was principal lecturer in land use studies and director of the Natural Resources and Rural Economy Program at Seale-Hayne College in southwest England. In 1978 he joined the Faculty of Physical Education and Recreation at the University of Alberta and is currently professor and coordinator of the Bachelor of Arts Recreation Administration Degree Program. Dr. Swinnerton's research interests focus on the planning and management of national parks and protected areas, landscape conservation involving natural and cultural environments and outdoor recreation, and sustainable tourism in rural areas. He has written extensively on these topics as they relate to Canada and Great Britain. Dr. Swinnerton served as a member of the Scientific Review Committee for the Banff–Bow Valley Study and is currently the academic representative on a provincial committee responsible for designating a system of protected areas for the Province of Alberta.

CHARLES SYLVESTER received his bachelor's and master's degrees from the University of Maryland. He completed his doctorate at the University of Oregon in 1984. He began teaching in 1984 at Western Washington University, where he is professor in the Department of Physical Education, Health, and Recreation. He lives in Bellingham, Washington, with his wife, Kathy, and his dogs, Augie, Winston, and Dewey.

A. J. VEAL is head of the School of Leisure and Tourism Studies at the University of Technology, Sydney, Australia. He has a degree in economics from the University of Bristol, England. Before moving to Australia from the United Kingdom in 1986, he worked in local government and at the Universities of Birmingham and North London. In the United Kingdom he was responsible for numerous research and consultancy projects for national organizations such as the Sports Council and the Countryside Commission, and for a number of local authorities, and was chair of the Leisure Studies Association. In Australia his research has focussed on leisure demand forecasting and local recreation needs and demand studies. He is author of numerous reports and articles on leisure and tourism, and several books, including *Leisure and the Future, Leisure Policy and Planning* and *Research Methods for Leisure and Tourism,* and is joint author of *Australian Leisure* and joint editor of *World Leisure Participation: Free Time in the Global Village.* He has been a member of the editorial advisory board of *Leisure Studies* since 1982, and is currently a member of the board of directors of the World Leisure and Recreation Association and of the board of the Australian and New Zealand Association for Leisure Studies.

ALISON VOIGHT received her bachelor's degree in biology from Oakland University in Michigan. She earned her master's degree in recreation administration in Kentucky, where she also served as director of recreational therapy in psychiatry at the University of Kentucky Medical Center for three years. After her tenure in Kentucky, she completed her doctorate at the University of Oregon in leisure studies and counseling psychology. Dr. Voight has taught therapeutic recreation and related subjects at several institutions, including Western Washington University and the Ohio State University. She has been a sessional instructor at the University of Northern British Columbia, teaching courses in ethnobiology and recreation for special needs. Her research emphases and publications have involved social psychology of leisure and outdoor adventure therapy for special populations. Dr. Voight is currently a consultant with *Recreation Research, Evaluation and Consulting.*

RICHARD WILLIAMS earned two bachelor's degrees, a Bachelor of Arts in English literature from the University of Georgia in 1987 and a Bachelor of Science in therapeutic recreation from Virginia Commonwealth University in 1994. Additionally, he earned a Master of Arts degree in recreation and leisure studies at the University of Georgia in 1996. Currently, he is working on his doctoral degree in recreation and leisure studies at the University of Georgia. Mr. Williams has presented at regional and national conferences, and his research interests include leisure education and therapeutic humor.

Index

Other Books From Venture Publishing

Effective Management in Therapeutic Recreation Service
 by Gerald S. O'Morrow and Marcia Jean Carter
Evaluating Leisure Services: Making Enlightened Decisions
 by Karla A. Henderson with M. Deborah Bialeschki
The Evolution of Leisure: Historical and Philosophical Perspectives (Second Printing)
 by Thomas Goodale and Geoffrey Godbey
Experience Marketing: Strategies for the New Millennium
 by Ellen L. O'Sullivan and Kathy J. Spangler
File o' Fun: A Recreation Planner for Games & Activities—Third Edition
 by Jane Harris Ericson and Diane Ruth Albright
The Game Finder—A Leader's Guide to Great Activities
 by Annette C. Moore
Getting People Involved in Life and Activities: Effective Motivating Techniques
 by Jeanne Adams
Great Special Events and Activities
 by Annie Morton, Angie Prosser and Sue Spangler
Inclusive Leisure Services: Responding to the Rights of People With Disabilities
 by John Dattilo
Internships in Recreation and Leisure Services: A Practical Guide for Students (Second Edition)
 by Edward E. Seagle, Jr., Ralph W. Smith and Lola M. Dalton
Interpretation of Cultural and Natural Resources
 by Douglas M. Knudson, Ted T. Cable and Larry Beck
Introduction to Leisure Services—7th Edition
 by H. Douglas Sessoms and Karla A. Henderson
Leadership and Administration of Outdoor Pursuits, Second Edition
 by Phyllis Ford and James Blanchard
Leadership in Leisure Services: Making a Difference
 by Debra J. Jordan
Leisure and Leisure Services in the 21st Century
 by Geoffrey Godbey
The Leisure Diagnostic Battery: Users Manual and Sample Forms
 by Peter A. Witt and Gary Ellis
Leisure Education: A Manual of Activities and Resources
 by Norma J. Stumbo and Steven R. Thompson
Leisure Education II: More Activities and Resources
 by Norma J. Stumbo
Leisure Education III: More Goal-Oriented Activities
 by Norma J. Stumbo

Leisure Education IV: Activities for Individuals With Substance Addictions
 by Norma J. Stumbo
Leisure Education Program Planning: A Systematic Approach
 by John Dattilo and William D. Murphy
Leisure in Your Life: An Exploration—Fourth Edition
 by Geoffrey Godbey
Leisure Services in Canada: An Introduction
 by Mark S. Searle and Russell E. Brayley
The Lifestory Re-Play Circle: A Manual of Activities and Techniques
 by Rosilyn Wilder
Marketing for Parks, Recreation, and Leisure
 by Ellen L. O'Sullivan
Models of Change in Municipal Parks and Recreation: A Book of Innovative Case Studies
 edited by Mark E. Havitz
More Than a Game: A New Focus on Senior Activity Services
 by Brenda Corbett
Nature and the Human Spirit: Toward an Expanded Land Management Ethic
 edited by B. L. Driver, Daniel Dustin, Tony Baltic, Gary Elsner, and George Peterson
Outdoor Recreation Management: Theory and Application, Third Edition
 by Alan Jubenville and Ben Twight
Planning Parks for People, Second Edition
 by John Hultsman, Richard L. Cottrell and Wendy Z. Hultsman
The Process of Recreation Programming Theory and Technique, Third Edition
 by Patricia Farrell and Herberta M. Lundegren
Programming for Parks, Recreation, and Leisure Services: A Servant Leadership Approach
 By Donald G. DeGraaf, Debra J. Jordan and Kathy H. DeGraaf
Protocols for Recreation Therapy Programs
 edited by Jill Kelland, along with the Recreation Therapy Staff at Alberta Hospital Edmonton
Quality Management: Applications for Therapeutic Recreation
 edited by Bob Riley
A Recovery Workbook: The Road Back From Substance Abuse
 By April K. Neal and Michael J. Taleff
Recreation and Leisure: Issues in an Era of Change, Third Edition
 edited by Thomas Goodale and Peter A. Witt
Recreation Economic Decisions: Comparing Benefits and Costs (Second Edition)
 by John B. Loomis and Richard G. Walsh

Recreation Programming and Activities for Older Adults
 by Jerold E. Elliott and Judith A. Sorg-Elliott
Recreation Programs That Work for At-Risk Youth: The Challenge of Shaping the Future
 by Peter A. Witt and John L. Crompton
Reference Manual for Writing Rehabilitation Therapy Treatment Plans
 by Penny Hogberg and Mary Johnson
Research in Therapeutic Recreation: Concepts and Methods
 edited by Marjorie J. Malkin and Christine Z. Howe
Simple Expressions: Creative and Therapeutic Arts for the Elderly in Long-Term Care Facilities
 by Vicki Parsons
A Social History of Leisure Since 1600
 by Gary Cross
A Social Psychology of Leisure
 by Roger C. Mannell and Douglas A. Kleiber
The Sociology of Leisure
 by John R. Kelly and Geoffrey Godbey

Steps to Successful Programming: A Student Handbook to Accompany Programming for Parks, Recreation, and Leisure Services
 By Donald G. DeGraaf, Debra J. Jordan and Kathy H. DeGraaf
Therapeutic Activity Intervention With the Elderly: Foundations & Practices
 by Barbara A. Hawkins, Marti E. May and Nancy Brattain Rogers
Therapeutic Recreation: Cases and Exercises
 by Barbara C. Wilhite and M. Jean Keller
Therapeutic Recreation in the Nursing Home
 by Linda Buettner and Shelley L. Martin
Therapeutic Recreation Protocol for Treatment of Substance Addictions
 by Rozanne W. Faulkner
Time for Life: The Surprising Ways Americans Use Their Time
 by John P. Robinson and Geoffrey Godbey
A Training Manual for Americans With Disabilities Act Compliance in Parks and Recreation Settings
 by Carol Stensrud

Venture Publishing, Inc.
1999 Cato Avenue
State College, PA 16801
Phone: (814) 234-4561; Fax: (814) 234-1651